THE ENCYCLOPEDIA OF TAOISM

THE ENCYCLOPEDIA

OF TAOISM

I

Edited by

Fabrizio Pregadio

Routledge
Taylor & Francis Group

LONDON AND NEW YORK

First published 2008
by Routledge
2 Park Square, Milton Park, Abingdon, Oxon OX 14 4RN
www.routledge.co.uk

Simultaneously published in the USA and Canada
by Routledge
270 Madison Avenue, New York, NY 10016
www.routledge.com

Routledge is an imprint of the Taylor and Francis Group, an informa business

Typeset in Dante by Birdtrack Press
Printed and bound in Great Britain by
TJ International Ltd, Padstow, Cornwall

British Library Cataloguing in Publication Data
A catalogue record for this title is available

Library of Congress Cataloguing-in-Publication Data
Library of Congress Control Number: 2007937681

ISBN13: 978-0-7007-1200-7

Table of Contents

Volume I

Foreword, by T.H. Barrett   vii

Contributors   xi

Introduction   xiii

Conventions, Format of the Entries, Abbreviations and Symbols   xxi

Synoptic Table of Contents   xxv

List of Illustrations   xliii

List of Tables   xlvii

Taoism: An Overview   1

   List of entries   3

   Entries   5

Entries A through L   197

Volume II

Entries M through Z   729

Appendix: Reference Works for the Study of Taoism   1311

Bibliographies   1333

   Sources in the Daozang *(Taoist Canon)*   1335

   Abbreviations of Serials   1361

   Studies   1362

Periodization of Chinese History   1465

Pinyin to Wade-Giles Conversion Table   1473

Wade-Giles to Pinyin Conversion Table   1477

Index   1481

Foreword

by

T. H. Barrett

Taoism has been for over half a millennium the East Asian religious tradition most consistently despised and rejected in the West, esteemed if at all for the wrong reasons, and seldom enough at that. As early as 1569 the pioneering missionary Friar Gaspar da Cruz, O.P., while at one point conceding the great respect shown by the Chinese to Taoist priests, avers at another that they live "wickedly and filthily." This was perhaps due to a simple misunderstanding that caused him to assume that all Taoist priests were supposed to be celibate. But to the Counter-Reformation sensibilities of later Jesuits like Matteo Ricci and his many successors the very idea of a non-celibate priesthood must have been quite disturbing in any case, so that we subsequently find very little dissent from this first damning indictment. Even in the nineteenth century the Protestant missionaries, who often arrived as married couples, continued to heap scorn upon the Taoists, though now as part of a generally negative assessment of Chinese culture that contrasted with the positive evaluation of some aspects of China espoused by those who followed Ricci's missionary strategy.

It is true that one or two ancient texts associated with the Taoist tradition were in the late nineteenth century clasped firmly to the bosom of Western theosophy, a cultural movement that manifested a great generosity of spirit towards Asian wisdom whilst usually denying any validity to the views of contemporary Asians themselves—the lofty mysticism of a Laozi was held to be something quite beyond the grasp of his latter day heirs, intelligible only to illuminati on the theosophists' own spiritual plane. Whether missionaries or mystics, then, the received opinion in the West would have been that republished as recently as 1990 in *A Confucian Notebook* by Edward Herbert, which first appeared in 1950. In this work we are summarily informed that "Taoism" beyond those favoured early texts is simply "a synonym for superstition and imposture." In such a hostile climate accurate knowledge concerning Taoism was until the very end of the twentieth century remarkably hard to come by. Matters of tone and judgment apart, a handbook such as Samuel Couling's *Encyclopaedia Sinica* of 1917, for example, demonstrates a completely insouciant vagueness on such basic questions as the size of the Taoist canon or the number of texts it contains.

This is all the more regrettable since by the time that Couling's handbook appeared a certain amount of progress had been made in investigating the canon by scholars writing in French. The gradual emergence of the field of Taoist Studies during the twentieth century in fact affected the English-speaking world at a remarkably late point: amongst pioneers we may find Chinese (though not that many, given the anti-religious spirit abroad in the Republican and early Communist eras), Japanese, French, Germans and other Europeans, but with the exception of researchers in the History of Science scarcely a soul from Great Britain, the English-speaking Commonwealth, or the United States. Nor has the rectification of this anomaly seen anything like a smooth progress. Too many engaged in the task of building up and spreading the knowledge originally available only in French were lost to us before their time, from Henri Maspero, who died in Buchenwald in 1945, to Anna Seidel, Michel Strickmann and Isabelle Robinet, whose more recent deaths have dealt successive blows to the field. The first named had scarcely any students, and was only able to exert a posthumous but utterly crucial inspiration through his writings, but we owe a particular debt to the others, whose teaching activities in the late twentieth century (together with those of one or two less unfortunate scholars, such as K. M. Schipper) finally established the small corps of researchers without whom the production of this encyclopedia would not have been remotely possible.

Even so the unprecedented large-scale collaborative effort required, calling on expertise right across the globe, would probably have been expended in vain were it not for the Herculean labours of the editor. When I was first approached to suggest the name of someone who could undertake this task, I realized that only a scholar with broad international contacts and the highest academic standards would be capable of bringing such a project to completion. Little did I realise that persistence, too, would be a quality that Fabrizio Pregadio would have to call upon in full measure, and that an undertaking conceived on one continent and based on the religious traditions of another would after a more than elephantine period of gestation eventually see the light of day in the New World of an entirely different hemisphere. For all the minor shortcomings that may be discovered in this compilation, and for all the scholarship it may contain that may one day appear outdated and in need of revision, he at least should be absolved from any blame and indeed allowed a full measure of self-congratulation, for he has worked as hard and as meticulously as anyone possibly could.

The publishers, too, should surely allow themselves a measure of self-congratulation, and especially those individuals who have helped sustain the project throughout the institutional changes on their side that have been almost as dramatic as those witnessed by the editor in his academic travels. Given that with the notable exception of the work of Joseph Needham and his associates the British academic contribution to the study of Taoism has been more or less nugatory, I am particularly glad that the British publishing industry at least has played its part in rectifying the wrongs of the centuries. But now is no time for us in these small islands to rest upon our laurels. As China once more takes up the leading role amongst nations commensurate with the size of its population and the richness of its cultural heritage, the very insularity that once allowed our forefathers in a fit of imperial absent-mindedness to treat China with an insolence that was not even perceived as such at the time still needs to be broken down and replaced with a more fraternal respect and, crucially, understanding. I sincerely hope that the small contribution to international cultural awareness we have helped—with so many others—to make in uncovering one of the more neglected aspects of China's heritage through this encyclopedia will be by no means the last.

Contributors

Poul ANDERSEN	University of Hawaii at Manoa, USA
ASANO Haruji 浅野春二	Kokugakuin daigaku (Kokugakuin University), Japan
Farzeen BALDRIAN-HUSSEIN	Independent scholar, Germany
T. H. BARRETT	School of Oriental and African Studies (SOAS), England
Catherine BELL	Santa Clara University, USA
Charles D. BENN	Independent scholar, USA
Stephen R. BOKENKAMP	Indiana University, USA
Judith M. BOLTZ	University of Washington, USA
CHEN Yaoting 陳耀庭	Shanghai shehui kexueyuan (Shanghai Academy of Social Sciences), People's Republic of China
Philip CLART	University of Missouri-Columbia, USA
Theodore A. COOK	Stanford University, USA
Mark CSIKSZENTMIHALYI	University of Wisconsin-Madison, USA
Christopher CULLEN	Needham Research Institute, England
Martina DARGA	Independent scholar, Germany
Catherine DESPEUX	Institut National des Langues et Civilisations Orientales (INALCO), France
Ute ENGELHARDT	Ludwig-Maximilians-Universität München, Germany
Grégoire ESPESSET	Independent scholar, France
Monica ESPOSITO	Kyōto daigaku Jinbun kagaku kenkyūjo (Institute for Research in Humanities, Kyoto University), Japan
Vincent GOOSSAERT	Centre National de la Recherche Scientifique (CNRS), France
Caroline GYSS	Centre National de la Recherche Scientifique (CNRS), France

Barend ter HAAR	Universiteit Leiden, Holland
Elisabeth HSU	Oxford University, England
Paul R. KATZ	Academia Sinica, Taiwan, Republic of China
KIM Daeyeol	Institut National des Langues et Civilisations Orientales, France
Russell KIRKLAND	University of Georgia, USA
Terry KLEEMAN	University of Colorado, USA
Livia KOHN	Boston University, USA
MARUYAMA Hiroshi 丸山宏	Tsukuba daigaku (University of Tsukuba), Japan
Amy Lynn MILLER	Independent scholar, USA
MIURA Kunio 三浦國雄	Ōsaka shiritsu daigaku (Osaka City University), Japan
Christine MOLLIER	Centre National de la Recherche Scientifique (CNRS), France
MUGITANI Kunio 麥谷邦夫	Kyōto daigaku Jinbun kagaku kenkyūjo (Institute for Research in Humanities, Kyoto University), Japan
Peter NICKERSON	Duke University, USA
† *Julian PAS*	
Benjamin PENNY	Australian National University, Australia
Fabrizio PREGADIO	Stanford University, USA
Gil RAZ	Dartmouth College, USA
† *Isabelle ROBINET*	
James ROBSON	University of Michigan, USA
SAKADE Yoshinobu 坂出祥伸	Ōsaka shiritsu daigaku (Osaka City University), Japan
Lowell SKAR	University of Colorado, USA
Thomas E. SMITH	Independent scholar, Taiwan, Republic of China
Elena VALUSSI	Independent scholar, USA
YAMADA Toshiaki 山田利明	Tōyō daigaku (Toyo University), Japan
Robin D. S. YATES	McGill University, Canada
YOSHIKAWA Tadao 吉川忠夫	Hanazono daigaku (Hanazono University), Japan

INTRODUCTION

Many readers will view *The Encyclopedia of Taoism* as one of the countless tools that provide, according to the stereotyped formulation, "fast and easy access" to an assortment of facts and data. Undoubtedly, those readers will be correct in reckoning the present book among the growing collection of reference works—encyclopedias, dictionaries, catalogues, indexes, bibliographies, and so forth—that some might view as one of the "signs of the times." Beyond its purpose as a convenient source of information, however, this book intends to illustrate the central principles and historical forms of Taoism, which is among the most misconceived traditions of antiquity that have survived to the present day. Neither the incessant feed of commercial publications on Taoism, nor the attempts to define Taoism in relation to science, medicine, psychology, ethics, and other branches of modern Western learning, have done much to eliminate those misconceptions, and often such efforts have contributed to their formation and dissemination. Readers will have different views on the qualitative aspects of the book, but in this regard *The Encyclopedia of Taoism* should help to dispel at least the most flagrant misinterpretations that surround a form of doctrine and practice whose features often contrast sharply—and sometimes radically—with the modern Western worldview.

The Encyclopedia of Taoism provides an overview of the Taoist tradition through a wide selection of themes, reflects the current state of Taoist scholarship, and aims to contribute to a better understanding of this and related fields of study. It also endeavors to acquaint a wider public with the viewpoints of researchers working in this area, a task made difficult by some of the assumptions predominant within broad sectors of academia and of the so-called general public. On the one hand, scholars working in the field of Taoist studies—an area that has grown beyond all expectations, perhaps even too rapidly, in the last three or four decades, as the present book also attests—are well aware of the richness and complexity of the Taoist tradition. Academic study, however, is not always capable of explicating the nature of Taoist teachings and the reasons for their plurality of forms to a wider audience. Not only are scholars accustomed to writing for other scholars, but the adoption of different standpoints and methodologies within the field results in an elaborate landscape of views and opinions that often contradict one another. Being typically relativist, moreover, scholarship cannot have—and in fact normally does not

claim to have—the final word on many of the most important notions associated with a tradition like Taoism: the continued search for the "new" (new
theories, perspectives, and interpretations periodically replacing each other)
that is vital for scholarship lies at the opposite end of the spectrum from the
pursuit of the "old" (the primordial, original, or unchangeable) that charac-
terizes premodern teachings like Taoism. On the other hand, many people
outside the field of Taoist studies who are attracted by the cryptic sayings of
the *Daode jing* and fascinated by the enigmatic stories of the *Zhuangzi* find it
difficult or even unimportant to consider that Taoism has a proper history.
Recent translations of other texts, addressed to the lay public, do not provide
much help, as even the best among them consist of literal renditions that offer
little or no support to the reader, or contain cursory and superficial "historical
introductions." It is not surprising, therefore, that many people outside the
field of Taoist studies are surprised or confused as they learn that the history
of Taoism does not end with those two major books but is also populated by
gods, demons, saints, immortals, rituals, exorcism, talismans, and elixirs, to
mention just a handful of the main components. Yet, for its masters, priests,
and adepts, this is what Taoism has been for about two and a half millennia.

According to one of several ways to understand it, the bewildering variety of
forms that one observes in Taoism originates in the continuous reformulation of certain basic principles (in which belief, let it be said once, plays no
part), and in the creation or modification of forms of individual and collective
practice. This process of ongoing renewal, initiated by Taoist masters, priests,
adepts, codifiers, commentators, and others, has responded to varying external circumstances and settings—historical events, social milieux, intellectual
trends, and religious cults—and aims to ensure that their tradition (a word
that is etymologically synonymous with "transmission") survives without
major breaks.

  With regard to the principles, this perspective presupposes that change occurs
in the realm of spoken, written, and visual representations of essential notions
that by their own nature are not tied to particular places, times, cultures, or
languages. The many expressions of Taoist practice are ways of framing and
periodically recodifying ritual practices and self-cultivation methods, adapting
them to particular settings according to the characteristics and needs of different
individuals or groups, and to the changing circumstances mentioned above.
One of the unifying features that underlies this variety of forms is the ideal,
but fundamental, view that Taoist doctrines and practices—where "practices"
again refers to both self-cultivation and ritual—ultimately derive from the Dao
itself, usually through the intermediation of deities (seen as "transformations"
of the Dao) or realized beings (anonymous or identified, historical or legendary, but always described as having "attained to the Dao") who have revealed

them to humanity as a whole or to particular circles or groups. Teachings and methods aim to make it possible for various individuals and communities to "return" to the Dao, and at the same time to discourage them from beliefs and practices deemed to be unproductive or even harmful.

This historical process of continuous renovation is strongly influenced by the incorporation of external elements (Buddhism is the most conspicuous example), paralleled by the less frequent but likewise significant reverse phenomenon of "disconnection" of certain components from their doctrinal sources, especially in the domain of practice. Even more widespread and elaborate are the exchanges between Taoism and the Chinese folk religion, which lead not only to the assimilation of religious elements such as local deities and cults into the domain of Taoism, but also to instances of Taoist priests performing, besides Taoist rituals, a variety of additional religious functions, such as exorcism and ritual healing—functions that are also fulfilled by other religious specialists who, on the contrary, are not entitled to officiate the properly Taoist liturgy. Scholars often claim that such phenomena of exchange and reformulation result from competition among different religious groups, and label the incorporation of external elements into Taoism—from Buddhism, the folk religion, or elsewhere—as appropriation. These views may or may not be accurate, but in any case the phenomena under discussion are far from being arbitrary or unjustified: they may occur because of analogy of contents, the intent to connect (or bring back) "loose" forms of practice to doctrinal principles, the ambition to elevate life for individuals and communities, or simply the need to comply with local customs.

As a result, like all major traditions in which the preservation of the inner doctrinal core primarily relies on transmission from master to disciple (or rather on "initiatory chains" that may not even be historical in nature), Taoism also plays a comprehensive social role that involves two overlapping processes: the integration of features of the folk religion that do not intrinsically conflict with that core, and the creation of forms of practice meant to address the needs of wider groups beyond the circles of adepts. These two aspects of Taoism, which in a very general sense pertain to the distinction between "esoteric" and "exoteric," highlight the crucial function of transmission—in both its forms, initiation and ordination—not only as an essential feature of the Taoist tradition, but also as one of the key elements that differentiate it from the native varieties of folk religion in China.

While several scholars would certainly dispute or at least qualify this understanding of Taoism, consideration of these and related points might help to solve the dilemma of whether Taoism is philosophy or religion. These two notions did not exist in premodern China in the sense with which they are meant in the modern Western world, and their use in Taoist scholarship has raised questions that have not yet been answered in a satisfying way. Whereas in earlier times Taoism was deemed by Western scholars to be nothing but philosophy, and any involvement in the domain of religion was either denied or classified as "superstition," in the last few decades Taoist scholarship has shifted to the opposite extreme, sometimes even going so far as to deny any foundational role to a work like the *Daode jing* (the latter opinion has been held only by a few scholars working primarily in the broader field of Chinese religion rather than Taoism). The same quandary surrounds the related issue of *daojia* versus *daojiao*, the two terms to which the first entries in this book are devoted. Even though the origins of these terms may lie in mere biblio-graphic categories, Taoists have sometimes used them interchangeably to denote what we call "Taoism," and sometimes separately to distinguish the teachings of the *Daode jing* (and a few other works including the *Zhuangzi*) from "all the rest." While these terms do not seem to have raised major issues at any time in the history of Taoism, the questions that they have generated in the scholarly realm are largely products of their early flawed translation, or rather interpretation, as "philosophical Taoism" and "religious Taoism," respectively. Based on the way of seeing outlined above, Taoism is not exactly either a philosophy or a religion, but rather a set of consistent doctrinal notions that have taken many forms and given rise to a large variety of individual and collective practices throughout the history of the tradition. Taoist ideas and practices have always been in touch with various philosophical and religious trends, generating an intricate net of intellectual and religious phenomena that on the surface may appear to be unrelated to each other.

Scholars who face this range of phenomena take different approaches according to their individual interests and inclinations. Some emphasize doctrinal content while others stress religious features, some focus on ritual practices and others on self-cultivation methods, and so forth. This variety of approaches, as noted above, has sometimes occasioned the neglect, margin-alization, or even rejection of certain components in favor of others. Taoism itself, however, does not lack examples of comprehensive models of teachings and practices coordinated in a hierarchical arrangement, the most important being the Three Caverns (*sandong*). Whether these models can be reproduced in scholarship is not the point. What is crucial is rather the fact that attention to the central principles allows one to identify the position that individual forms and phenomena associated with Taoism occupy within the tradition as a whole, and to eschew reductive interpretations, including those that view Taoism exclusively as a religion, or as a philosophy.

The Encyclopedia of Taoism aims to provide its readers with a tool to appreciate the complexity of this tradition and its multiple historical sources, representa-tives, and manifestations. It does so by offering a large number of entries—most of which would better be characterized as short essays—on those manifold facets, concerned not only with their specific nature but also with the links or differences that exist among them. An initial list of about 1,800 potential topics drawn up in the earliest stage of this project was later reduced to a more manageable and efficient number. Contributors have played a role in shaping the final table of contents by suggesting that entries be added, deleted, or merged. This lengthy but indispensable process has resulted in the approximately 800 entries that compose the present book.

These entries are divided into two main sections. Although the first section is entitled "Taoism: An Overview," it does not consist of a systematic description of Taoism, which is an impossible task given the lack of "system" that is characteristic of this and all other traditional teachings. Rather, these essays aim to provide a short but fairly comprehensive exposition of themes and issues that cross over the boundaries of individual traditions, texts, or authors. The seventy or so relevant entries appear under the following categories: Definitions; Lineages and Traditions; Scriptures and Texts; Cosmology; Deities and Spirits; Sacred Sites; Views of the Human Being; Views of Society; Religious Organization; Aspects of Religious Practice and Experience; Taoism and Chinese Thought and Religion; Taoism and Chinese Society; Taoism and Chinese Culture; and Taoism outside China.

The second section of the book contains entries arranged in alphabetical order. The essays here are concerned with schools, lineages, and traditions (ca. 30 entries); persons (ca. 150 entries); texts (ca. 200 entries); terms (including ritual and self-cultivation practices, ca. 225 entries); divinities and immortals (ca. 80 entries); temples (ca. 20 entries); and mountains (ca. 20 entries). Needless to say, there is no difference of status between the entries in the first and second sections of the book, but only one of focus, which is broader in the first part and sharper in the second. The alphabetical arrangement makes it easy to locate entries in the second part, but this system will not be helpful to readers who wish to identify all entries related to a comprehensive topic, such as a particular Taoist lineage. For this reason, the Synoptic Table of Contents provides a "reading guide" that users of this book may find convenient to consult.

As should be clear from the earlier part of this introduction, the most difficult task in editing this work, but also the most absorbing one, has been the attempt to mediate between the scholarly outlook of the forty-six contributors and the perspectives of the intended readership. No one, myself included, will be entirely satisfied with the results. Scholars will likely find many features incorporated for the benefit of non-specialist readers to be superfluous, and non-specialist readers will surely deem many details provided for the sake of consistent scholarly style to be redundant.

In principle, the readership of *The Encyclopedia of Taoism* consists of scholars, students, and the elusive "learned public." In addition to Taoist studies, the main fields relevant to its subject matter are Chinese studies, religious studies, and, broadly speaking, the humanistic disciplines. Beyond this convenient formulation, the precise identity of one's readership is the most significant question for those who write a work like this one. The artificial landscapes created by marketing do not help much in drawing an accurate mental map of the actual readers of a book and their different expectations, especially if that book, as does the present one, attempts to cover a vast and largely unfamiliar territory. Nevertheless, I would like to try to clarify briefly what various readers may expect to find in this encyclopedia.

Originally planned as a collection of short essays on a large number of subjects, *The Encyclopedia of Taoism* has preserved this format, without attempting to simplify a subject that is by nature complex. Readers who wish to become acquainted with topics and issues related to Taoism—as well as those who wish to know how Taoism has dealt with topics and issues shared with other traditions—may find here reliable accounts written by specialists in the academic field of Taoist studies (in almost all cases, contributors have written on topics relevant to their own specialization within the field). Throughout the lengthy editorial process, however, the book has also taken on many of the features of a specialized reference work. I deem this to be a positive development and would be pleased if students and scholars find *The Encyclopedia of Taoism* helpful for study, research, and possibly also for teaching. Cross-references, bibliographies, lists of related entries, and other features of the book should enable all readers to use *The Encyclopedia of Taoism* as a starting point for further investigation.

From the beginning of the editorial process, the expectations and requirements of the non-specialist reader have been kept in mind. In particular, care has been taken to provide, whenever possible, consistent translations of Chinese terms, in order to make the continuity among entries dealing with related topics clearer to readers who must depend on the English translations to find their way through the book. I am indebted to all contributors for assenting to this general principle, even though this has often meant they have had to cast aside their preferred translations and replace them with others. Nevertheless, *The Encyclopedia of Taoism* still reflects the current lack of consensus among scholars on how several major terms found in Taoist texts should be rendered into English. Those terms that have retained multiple translations in this work include, for instance, *xin*, variously translated as "mind," "heart," "mind-heart," or "heart-mind"; *wuxing*, translated as "five agents" or "five phases"; *xianren*, translated as "immortal" or "transcendent"; and *zhenren*, translated as "true man," "real man," "authentic man," or "perfected."

The Encyclopedia of Taoism has been in preparation for much longer than most people involved would have wished or imagined when the project began. I apologize for this delay, for which I am ultimately responsible. I have been honored by the trust that so many colleagues have accorded to me, and I hope that they will be among the first to benefit from this book. Beyond this, I am grateful to all contributors for their support and encouragement, and for the patience they have displayed at all stages. All of them have taught me many important things.

I am certain that all the authors of this book join me in remembering two of us who have not seen their contributions published. Julian Pas passed away on June 12, 2000, and Isabelle Robinet on June 23 of the same year. Julian contributed many of the illustrations that appear in this book. Having published his *Historical Dictionary of Taoism* in 1998 (in cooperation with Mam Kam Leung; Lanham, Md., and London: The Scarecrow Press), he responded to my invitation by sending about five dozen original black-and-white photographs, from which I have selected those that match the content of the entries most closely. *The Encyclopedia of Taoism* would have been not only much less attractive but also much less valuable without his help. Isabelle wrote about sixty entries, all of which reflect her profound understanding of the multiple levels of the Taoist discourse. "And with these, it makes almost a book," she wrote to me when she sent her last batch of entries; indeed, her essays might be read as one of several books that an attentive reader can find contained within *the Encyclopedia of Taoism*.

I am grateful to the three production editors who helped begin the project and bring it to completion. Jonathan Price of Curzon Press contacted me in late 1996 with an invitation to take care of this book; his enthusiasm and the genuine interest that he showed in the subject of the encyclopedia are among the factors that persuaded me to accept this task. Since the project moved under Routledge's aegis, Dominic Shryane has displayed an almost unimaginable patience in helping to solve all kinds of major and minor issues. And in the final but decisive stages of the project, Gerard Greenway has made sure that everything moved in the right direction so that the book would, at long last, see the light of day.

George Clonos and Ben Brose, graduate students of the Department of Religious Studies, Stanford University, have closely collaborated with me at various stages; I have enjoyed their help and friendship. Carl Bielefeldt, Bernard Faure, Michael Zimmermann, Michael Loewe, Ed Shaughnessy, Nicola di Cosmo, and Bent Nielsen have offered their advice and contributed to improve certain details of the book. Poul Andersen, Kim Daeyeol, Monica Esposito, and Vincent Goossaert, in addition to writing their own essays, have helped in areas beyond my expertise. Gaynor Sekimori, Joachim Kurtz, Jason

Josephson, and Dominic Steavu have drafted translations of entries originally submitted in Chinese and Japanese. Su Xiaoqin, Yang Zhaohua, Kenneth Koo, and Noreen Khawaja have provided much-needed assistance. I am also grateful to Mitamura Keiko, Tanaka Fumio, and Tsuchiya Masaaki who have coauthored some entries with Yamada Toshiaki.

A special, heartfelt thank goes to Sarah Fremerman Aptilon, who copyedited the book with exceptional dedication and care for detail; her task included making entries that are written by contributors who speak about ten different native languages readable in English. David Goodrich of Birdtrack Press has given a splendid shape to the book, with his expertise in several East Asian writing systems and his readiness to improve even the most minute of details. Kitamura Yoshiko has offered constant support and has helped in more ways than I could ever say. Finally—and everyone will understand that here I am simply reverting the actual order of things—I wish to thank Tim Barrett, and not only for agreeing to write his foreword in addition to several essays. What exactly he did for this book is still somehow unclear to me; he may even have done nothing, of course in the Taoist sense.

Fabrizio Pregadio

CONVENTIONS, FORMAT OF THE ENTRIES, ABBREVIATIONS AND SYMBOLS

Conventions

Systems of transcription. The *pinyin* system of alphabetic transliteration from Chinese is used throughout the book, except in quotations of passages from works that adopt the Wade-Giles system. Conversion tables from and to the *pinyin* and the Wade-Giles systems are found at the end of the book. For the Japanese and the Korean languages, the book adopts the Hepburn and the McCune-Reischauer systems of transcription, respectively.

Personal names. Chinese, Japanese, and Korean personal names are cited following the native convention, with the surname preceding the first name. Persons are typically referred to with their *ming* 名 (given name). The headings of entries devoted to persons indicate, when they are known and when this information is significant, the person's *zi* 字 (variously referred to in English as cognomen, courtesy name, or style) and *hao* 號 (appellation or sobriquet).

Official titles. Official titles are translated according to Charles O. Hucker, *A Dictionary of Official Titles in Imperial China* (Hucker 1985), except where contributors have indicated that they prefer different translations.

Place names. As a rule, place names are followed by the corresponding Chinese characters and the indication of the present-day province. Chinese characters are omitted, however, for the following place names that occur repeatedly throughout the book: Beijing (Peking) 北京, Chengdu 成都, Chang'an 長安, Guangzhou (Canton) 廣州, Fuzhou 福州, Hangzhou 杭州, Kaifeng 開封, Luoyang 洛陽, Nanchang 南昌, Nanjing 南京, Shanghai 上海, Suzhou 蘇州, and Xi'an 西安.

Titles of texts. Titles of texts are typically followed by the corresponding Chinese characters and an English translation. Chinese characters are omitted for texts that have independent entries in the book, for titles of the Standard Histories, and in parenthetical bibliographic references. Titles of works found in the Taoist Canon (*Daozang* 道藏) are often given in abbreviated form; the full titles are found in the bibliography of sources in the Taoist Canon (pp. 1335–60).

Editions. Most of the texts cited in this book are found in the Taoist Canon. References to these texts typically include, at the first occurrence in an entry, the abbreviation CT followed by the number assigned to the text in the catalogue by Kristofer Schipper, *Concordance du Tao-tsang: Titres des ouvrages* (Schipper 1975b). The bibliography of sources in the Taoist Canon (pp. 1335–60) provides the corresponding numbers in two other catalogues, namely *Daozang zimu yinde* 道藏子目引得 (Combined Indices to the Authors and Titles of Books in Two Collections of Taoist Literature; Weng Dujian 1935) and *Daozang tiyao* 道藏提要 (A Conspectus of the Taoist Canon; Ren Jiyu and Zhong Zhaopeng 1991).

   Citations of the *Taiping jing* 太平經 and the *Baopu zi neipian* 抱朴子內 篇 refer to the editions published by Wang Ming 王明 (Wang Ming 1960 and Wang Ming 1985, respectively). All references of the Standard Histories refer to the Zhonghua shuju 中華書局 editions. The editions used for other texts are indicated within the entries.

Dynasties, rulers, and reign periods. The dates of dynasties, rulers, and reign periods, as well as the corresponding Chinese characters, are found in the tables on pp. 1465–66 ("Periodization of Chinese History") and pp. 1467–70 ("Rulers and Reign Periods").

Format of the entries

The *Encyclopedia of Taoism* has been conceived from the beginning to function as a starting point for further study and research. Cross-references, lists of related entries, and bibliographies—in addition to the Synoptic Table of Contents and the final indexes—serve this purpose.

Cross-references. Through the broad use of cross-references, marked by an asterisk (*) at the first relevant occurrence of a term within an entry, virtually all the entries in the book lead the reader to other entries. Cross-references are not supplied, however, for four entries whose subjects are repeatedly mentioned in the book, namely "Dao," "Laozi," "Daode jing," and "Yin and Yang." Cross-references to entries found in the first part of the book ("Taoism: An Overview") are indicated in SMALL CAPITALS; the page numbers of the individual entries in this part of the book are found on pp. 3–4.

Related entries. Most entries conclude with a list of related entries. While the cross-references within the main body of an entry refer to any item that has its own independent entry in the book, the final list of related entries is more focused and indicates other entries closely associated with the main subject of that particular entry—for instance, the author of a text, or the tradition with which a technical term is predominantly associated.

Bibliographies. With few exceptions, all entries include a selected bibliography. Priority has been given to books and articles in Western languages (especially English and French), but the bibliographies also include important studies in Chinese and Japanese. References to the author and year are keyed to the bibliography of secondary literature found on pp. 1362–1464. Reproductions of manuscripts, critical editions, translations, indexes, and concordances are identified as such in parentheses. Studies cited within the main body of an entry, on the other hand, concern specific topics and are not necessarily duplicated in the final list of bibliographic references.

While several standard works in Western languages, Chinese, and Japanese are routinely cited in most relevant entries, other general reference works on Taoism do not appear in the bibliographies. These works, which readers are invited to consult whenever possible, include in particular *Daozang tiyao* 道藏提要 (A Conspectus of the Taoist Canon; Ren Jiyu and Zhong Zhaopeng 1991), *Daoism Handbook* (Kohn 2000b), the recently published *Taoist Canon: A Historical Companion to the Daozang* (Schipper and Verellen 2004), as well as Chinese and Japanese dictionaries and encyclopedias, among which one might mention *Zhonghua daojiao da cidian* 中华道教大辞典 (Great Dictionary of Chinese Taoism; Hu Fuchen 1995), *Daojiao da cidian* 道教大辞典 (Great Dictionary of Taoism; Zhongguo daojiao xiehui and Suzhou daojjiao xiehui 1994), *Dōkyō no dai jiten* 道教の大事典 (Great Encyclopedia of Taoism; Sakade Yoshinobu 1994a), and *Dōkyō jiten* 道教事典 (Encyclopedia of Taoism; Noguchi Tetsurō et al. 1994).

Abbreviations and symbols

BCE	Before Common Era
CE	Common Era
comm.	commentary
crit. ed.	critical edition
CT	*Concordance du Tao-tsang: Titres des ouvrages* (Schipper 1975b)
DMB	*Dictionary of Ming Biography, 1368–1644* (Goodrich and Fang 1976)
ECCP	*Eminent Chinese of the Ch'ing Period* (Hummell 1943–44)
IC	*The Indiana Companion to Traditional Chinese Literature* (Nienhauser 1986)
j.	*juan* 卷 (chapter or other subdivision of a text)
ms., mss.	manuscript, manuscripts

P.	Pelliot collection of Dunhuang manuscripts
part.	partial
S.	Stein collection of Dunhuang manuscripts
SB	*Sung Biographies* (Franke H. 1976)
sec.	section(s)
T.	Taishō Buddhist Canon
trans.	translation; translated by
YJQQ	*Yunji qiqian* 雲笈七籤 (Seven Lots from the Bookbag of the Clouds)
※	Closely related entries
📖	Suggestions for further reading

For abbreviations of titles of serials, see p. 1361.

Synoptic Table of Contents

I. Overview

Definitions

daojia 道家   5   *daojiao* 道教   8

Lineages and Traditions

Lineages   11   Ordination and priesthood   17
Transmission   13   Syncretism   20
Initiation   16

Scriptures and Texts

Revelations and sacred texts   24   *fu* 符   35
Scripture and exegesis   26   *lu* 籙   39
Daozang and subsidiary compilations   28   Hagiography   42
sandong 三洞   33   Epigraphy   44

Cosmogony and Cosmology

Cosmogony   47   Macrocosm and microcosm   56
Cosmology   51   Numerology   59

Deities and Spirits

Deities: The pantheon   61   Otherworldly bureaucracy   67
Demons and spirits   63   Hell   69

Sacred Sites

Taoist sacred sites   72

Views of the Human Being

Taoist views of the human body   75   Death and afterlife   86
Inner deities   80   Rebirth   90
Birth   85   Transcendence and immortality   91

Views of Human Society

Messianism and millenarianism   94   Ethics and morals   99
Apocalyptic eschatology   97

Religious Organization

Monasticism   102   Temples and shrines   106
Monastic code   104   Taoist lay associations   110

Religious Practice and Experience

Asceticism   112   Mysticism   120
Divination, omens, and prophecy   113   Seasonal observances   122
Magic   116   Taoist music   125
Meditation and visualization   118

Taoism and Chinese Religion and Thought

Taoism and Chinese mythology   129   Taoism and Chinese Buddhism   141
Taoism and early Chinese religion   130   Taoism and popular religion   145
Taoism and early Chinese thought   132   Taoism and popular sects   150
Taoism and the apocrypha   135   Taoism and local cults   152
Taoism and Confucianism   137   Taoism and medium cults   156
Taoism and Neo-Confucianism   139   Taoism and ancestor worship   159

Taoism and Chinese Society

Taoism and the state   162   Taoism and secret societies   170
Taoism and the civil service   Women in Taoism   171
   examinations   165   Taoism in the People's Republic of
Taoism and local communities   167   China   174

Taoism and Chinese Culture

Taoism and Chinese literature   176   Taoism and Chinese art   183
Taoism and Chinese theatre   179   Taoism and the military arts   185

Taoism Outside China

Taoism and the Yao people   188   Taoism in Japan   192
Taoism in the Korean peninsula   190

II. The Taoist Universe

1. Doctrinal Notions

bianhua 變化   229   *jing, qi, shen* 精 · 氣 · 神   562
Dao 道   304   *qingjing* 清靜   799
de 德   353   *sanyi* 三一   854
dong and *jing* 動 · 靜   363   *sanyuan* 三元   856
fan 反 (返)   401   *ti* and *yong* 體 · 用   973
gushen 谷神   466   *tianxin* 天心   988
hundun 混沌   523   *wu* and *you* 無 · 有   1042
ji 機   536   *wuji* and *taiji* 無極 · 太極   1057

wuwei 無為	1067	*xuanpin* 玄牝	1138
xiang 象	1086	*yi* [intention] 意	1158
xiantian and *houtian* 先天・後天	1094	*yi* [oneness] 一	1159
xin 心	1100	Yin and Yang 陰陽	1164
xing 形	1102	*yuanqi* 元氣	1192
xing and *ming* 性・命	1103	*zaohua* 造化	1214
xinzhai 心齋	1110	*ziran* 自然	1302
xuan 玄	1126		

2. Transcendence and Immortality

lianxing 鍊形	649	*shijie* 尸解	896
shengren 聖人	879	*xianren* 仙人	1092
shenren 神人	885	*zhenren* 真人	1265

3. Taoist Thought

EARLY TEXTS

Daode jing 道德經	311	*Huainan zi* 淮南子	495
Laozi Heshang gong zhangju 老子 河上公章句	619	*Liezi* 列子	654
		Neiye 內業	771
Laozi Xiang'er zhu 老子想爾注	622	*Zhuangzi* 莊子	1297
Wang Bi 王弼	1005	Cheng Xuanying 成玄英	264
Yan Zun 嚴遵	1146	Guo Xiang 郭象	462

COMMENTARIES TO EARLY TEXTS

Cheng Xuanying 成玄英	264	*Laozi Xiang'er zhu* 老子想爾注	622
Guo Xiang 郭象	462	Wang Bi 王弼	1005
Laozi Heshang gong zhangju 老子河上公章句	619	Yan Zun 嚴遵	1146

LATER TRADITIONS

Chongxuan 重玄	274	Xuanxue 玄學	1141
qingtan 清談	802		

LATER AUTHORS

Chen Tuan 陳摶	257	Shao Yong 邵雍	876
Li Rong 李榮	641	Xi Kang 嵇康	1085

Later Texts

(see also Taoism and Chinese Buddhism: Texts)

Huashu 化書	517	*Xisheng jing* 西昇經	1114
Wenzi 文子	1038	*Xuanzhu xinjing* 玄珠心鏡	1143
Wuneng zi 無能子	1059	*Yuanqi lun* 元氣論	1192

4. Cosmos and Cosmology

COSMOLOGICAL EMBLEMS

bagua	八卦	201	*siling*	四靈	908
beidou	北斗	224	*tianmen* and *dihu*	天門 · 地戶	978
ganzhi	干支	435	*wuxing*	五行	1068
jiugong	九宮	590	*xiu*	宿	1115
sanwu	三五	853	*zi*	子	1301

TEXTS AND CHARTS

Hetu and *Luoshu*	河圖 · 洛書	483	*Yijing*	易經	1161
Taiji tu	太極圖	934			

5. Heaven and Earth

HEAVENS AND CELESTIAL PALACES

Daluo tian	大羅天	299	*sanshi'er tian*	三十二天	847
jiutian	九天	593	*sanshiliu tian*	三十六天	849

SACRED GEOGRAPHY

dongtian and *fudi*	洞天 · 福地	368	Penglai	蓬萊	788
Fengdu	豐都	421	*wuyue*	五嶽	1072
Kunlun	崑崙山	602			

TEXTS

Dongming ji	洞冥記	367	*Wuyue zhenxing tu*	五嶽真形圖	1075
Shizhou ji	十洲記	898			

6. Deities

MAJOR TAOIST DEITIES

Beidi	北帝	222	*Laojun bashiyi hua tu*	老君八十一	
Beidou xingjun	北斗星君	226		化圖	606
Changsheng dadi	長生大帝	247	*Laozi bianhua jing*	老子變化經	617
Dongyue dadi	東嶽大帝	377	*Laozi ming*	老子銘	621
Doumu	斗姆	382	*Youlong zhuan*	猶龍傳	1187
Heisha	黑煞	478	Puhua tianzun	普化天尊	795
Jinque dijun	金闕帝君	581	*sanguan*	三官	833
Jiuku tianzun	救苦天尊	592	*sanhuang*	三皇	836
Laozi and Laojun	老子 · 老君	611	*sanqing*	三清	840
Hunyuan shengji	混元聖紀	525	Taiyi	太一	956
Kaitian jing	開天經	597	Yuhuang	玉皇	1197
			Zhenwu	真武	1266

OTHER DIVINE BEINGS

Baosheng dadi 保生大帝	218	Qingtong 青童	803
Bixia yuanjun 碧霞元君	235	Siming 司命	914
Fengbo 風伯	419	Wang lingguan 王靈官	1013
Hebo 河伯	477	Wen Qiong 溫瓊	1032
Hong'en zhenjun 洪恩真君	485	Wenchang 文昌	1033
Huangdi 黃帝	504	Xiwang mu 西王母	1119
Leishen 雷神	629	Xuannü 玄女	1136
Linshui furen 臨水夫人	682	yunü 玉女	1206
Mazu 媽祖	741	Yushi 雨師	1207

GODS OF POPULAR RELIGION

caishen 財神	243	Tudi gong 土地公	999
Ceshen 廁神	245	wangye 王爺	1026
Chenghuang 城隍	266	wenshen 瘟神	1040
Guan Yu 關羽	454	yaowang 藥王	1153
menshen 門神	744	Zaoshen 灶神	1215

TEXTS

Han Wudi neizhuan 漢武帝內傳	472	Wenchang huashu 文昌化書	1035

7. Immortals and Hagiography

IMMORTALS

Anqi sheng 安期生	199	Rong Cheng 容成	822
baxian 八仙	220	Su Lin 素林	919
Chisong zi 赤松子	271	Su Yuanming 蘇元明	920
Dongfang Shuo 東方朔	366	Wang Xuanfu 王玄甫	1018
Fei Changfang 費長房	416	Wang Yuan 王遠	1019
Gan Ji 干吉	433	Wangzi Qiao 王子喬	1028
Gengsang zi 庚桑子	445	Wei Huacun 魏華存	1031
Guangcheng zi 廣成子	457	Xu Fu 徐福	1121
Guigu zi 鬼谷子	460	Xu Jia 徐甲	1122
Liu Haichan 劉海蟾	686	Xu Xun 許遜	1124
Lü Dongbin 呂洞賓	712	Yin Changsheng 陰長生	1167
Qinyuan chun 沁園春	807	Yin Xi 尹喜	1169
Taiyi jinhua zongzhi 太一金華宗旨	961	Yue Zichang 樂子長	1196
Lüzu quanshu 呂祖全書	726	Zhang Guolao 張果老	1225
Magu 麻姑	731	Zhang Sanfeng 張三丰	1233
Maming sheng 馬鳴生	732	Zhongli Quan 鍾離權	1283
Maojun 茅君	733	Ziyang zhenren 紫陽真人	1303
Pengzu 彭祖	790		

HAGIOGRAPHIES OF LAOZI (LAOJUN)

Hunyuan shengji 混元聖紀	525	*Laozi bianhua jing* 老子變化經	617
Kaitian jing 開天經	597	*Laozi ming* 老子銘	621
Laojun bashiyi hua tu 老君八十一化圖	606	*Youlong zhuan* 猶龍傳	1187

OTHER HAGIOGRAPHIC TEXTS AND COMPILATIONS

Chunyang Lü zhenren wenji　純陽呂
　　真人文集　　　　　　　280
Daoxue zhuan　道學傳　　　333
Dongxian zhuan　洞仙傳　　373
Liexian zhuan　列仙傳　　　653
Lishi zhenxian tidao tongjian　歷世
　　真仙體道通鑑　　　683
Lüzu quanshu　呂祖全書　　726

Nanyue jiu zhenren zhuan　南嶽九真
　　人傳　　　　　　　756
Sandong qunxian lu　三洞群仙錄　831
Shenxian zhuan　神仙傳　　887
Soushen ji　搜神記　　　918
Xianyuan bianzhu　仙苑編珠　1095
Xu xianzhuan　續仙傳　　1123
Xuanpin lu　玄品錄　　　1140
Yongcheng jixian lu　墉城集仙錄　1183

8. The Human Being

INNER LOCI AND COMPONENTS OF THE HUMAN BEING

bajing　八景　　　　　210
dantian　丹田　　　　　302
dumai and *renmai*　督脈・任脈　389
hun and *po*　魂・魄　　　521
jingluo　經絡　　　　　565
mingmen　命門　　　　750

mingtang　明堂　　　　751
niwan　泥丸　　　　　775
qixue　氣血　　　　　812
sanguan　三關　　　　833
wuzang　五臟　　　　1078
xuanguan　玄關　　　1131

CHARTS OF THE INNER BODY

Neijing tu and *Xiuzhen tu*　　內景圖・修真圖　　767

9. Ethics and Morals

NOTIONS AND TERMS

chengfu　承負　　　　　265
jie [precepts]　戒　　　546

TEXTS

Laojun shuo yibai bashi jie　老君說
　　一百八十戒　　　608

Taishang ganying pian　太上感應篇　948
Xiang'er jie　想爾戒　　1088

10. Temples, Abbeys, Shrines

Baiyun guan [Beijing]　白雲觀　207
Chaotian gong [Beijing]　朝天宮　250
Dongxiao gong [Dadi shan]　洞霄宮　374
Dongyue miao [Beijing]　東嶽廟　380
Louguan [Zhouzhi, Shaanxi]　樓觀　708
Pantao gong [Beijing]　蟠桃宮　783
Qingyang gong [Chengdu]　青羊宮　806
Shangqing gong [Longhu shan]　上清宮　867
Taiqing gong [Bozhou, Henan]　太清宮　943

Tongbo guan [Tiantai shan]　桐柏觀　995
Tongdao guan [1. Chang'an;
　　2. Zhongnan shan]　通道觀　997
Xuandu guan [Chang'an]　玄都觀　1129
Xuanmiao guan [Suzhou]　玄妙官　1135
Yongle gong [Ruicheng, Shanxi]
　　永樂宮　　　　　1184
Yulong wanshou gong [Xishan]
　　玉隆萬壽宮　　　1199

RELATED NOTIONS AND TERMS

daoyuan　道院　　　　　337

11. Mountains and Mountain Monographs

MOUNTAINS

Emei shan　峨嵋山	397	Luofu shan　羅浮山	722
Gezao shan　閣皂山	447	Lushan　廬山	725
Heming shan　鶴鳴山	479	Maoshan　茅山	734
Hengshan [Hunan]　衡山	480	*Maoshan zhi*　茅山志	736
Nanyue jiu zhenren zhuan　南嶽九		Nanyue　南嶽	755
真人傳	756	Qingcheng shan　青城山	798
Nanyue xiaolu　南嶽小錄	757	Songshan　嵩山	917
Nanyue zongsheng ji　南嶽總勝集	758	Taishan　泰山	947
Hengshan [Shanxi]　恆山	481	Tiantai shan　天台山	987
Huashan　華山	516	Wangwu shan　王屋山	1025
Huoshan　霍山	533	Wudang shan　武當山	1052
Laoshan　嶗山	610	Wuyi shan　武夷山	1071
Longhu shan　龍虎山	702	Xishan　西山	1111

MOUNTAIN MONOGRAPHS

Maoshan zhi　茅山志	736	*Nanyue xiaolu*　南嶽小錄	757
Nanyue jiu zhenren zhuan　南嶽九		*Nanyue zongsheng ji*　南嶽總勝集	758
真人傳	756		

12. Textual Corpora and Literary Genres

TAOIST CANON

Da Jin Xuandu baozang　大金玄都		*Wanli xu daozang*　萬曆續道藏	1029
寶藏	291	*Xuandu baozang*　玄都寶藏	1128
Da Song Tiangong baozang　大宋天		*Zhenghe Wanshou daozang*　政和萬壽	
宮寶藏	292	道藏	1251
Sandong qionggang　三洞瓊綱	829	*Zhengtong daozang*　正統道藏	1254

OTHER COLLECTANEA

Daozang jinghua　道藏精華	338	*Daozang xubian*　道藏續編	347
Daozang jinghua lu　道藏精華錄	340	*Zangwai daoshu*　藏外道書	1210
Daozang jiyao　道藏輯要	341	*Zhuang-Lin xu daozang*　莊林續道藏	1296

CATALOGUES

Daozang mulu xiangzhu　道藏目錄詳注	345	*Lingbao jingmu*　靈寶經目	672
Daozang quejing mulu　道藏闕經目錄	346	*Sandong jingshu mulu*　三洞經書目錄	828

MANUSCRIPTS

Dunhuang manuscripts	392	Mawangdui manuscripts	738
Guodian manuscripts	464	Yinqueshan manuscripts	1174

LITERARY GENRES

baojuan　寶卷	212	*yulu*　語錄	1200
shanshu　善書	872		

III. History

1. Pre-Han and Han Background

fangji 方技	405	*Taiping jing* 太平經	938
fangshi 方士	406	Yellow Turbans	1156
Huang-Lao 黃老	508	Zhang Liang 張良	1230
Li Hong 李弘	638	*zhongmin* 種民	1285
taiping 太平	937		

2. Tianshi dao

Tianshi dao 天師道	981	Wudoumi dao 五斗米道	1055

HAN-DYNASTY CELESTIAL MASTERS

Zhang Daoling 張道陵	1222	Zhang Lu 張魯	1232
Zhang Heng 張衡	1227		

TEXTS

Chisong zi zhangli 赤松子章曆	272	*Shangqing huangshu guodu yi* 上清	
Han tianshi shijia 漢天師世家	470	黃書過度儀	868
Laozi Xiang'er zhu 老子想爾注	622	*Xuandu lüwen* 玄都律文	1130
Nüqing guilü 女青鬼律	780	*Zhengyi fawen jing* 正一法文經	1260
Santian neijie jing 三天內解經	852	*Zhengyi weiyi jing* 正一威儀經	1261

RELATED NOTIONS AND TERMS

chu 廚	279	*sanhui* 三會	839
heqi 合氣	482	*tianshi* 天師	979
jijiu 祭酒	550	*zhi* [parishes] 治	1274

3. Six Dynasties Communities and Cults

COMMUNITIES AND CULTS

Bojia dao 帛家道	236	Lijia dao 李家道	656
Dacheng 大成	294	Louguan pai 樓觀派	710

PERSONS

Bao Jing 鮑靚	211	Kou Qianzhi 寇謙之	601
Fan Changsheng 范長生	402	*Laojun yinsong jiejing* 老君音誦	
Ge Hong 葛洪	442	誡經	609
Baopu zi 抱朴子	215	Li Xiong 李雄	644
Shenxian zhuan 神仙傳	887	Sun En 孫恩	924
Ge Xuan 葛玄	444	Zheng Yin 鄭隱	1250

TEXTS

Baopu zi 抱朴子	215	*Sanhuang wen* 三皇文	837
Dongyuan shenzhou jing 洞淵神咒經	375	*Wushang biyao* 無上祕要	1062
Laojun yinsong jiejing 老君音誦誡經	609	*Wuyue zhenxing tu* 五嶽真形圖	1075

4. Shangqing

Shangqing　上清　　　　　　858

SAINTS AND IMMORTALS

Maojun　茅君　　　　　　733　　Wei Huacun　魏華存　　　1031
Su Lin　素林　　　　　　　919　　Ziyang zhenren　紫陽真人　1303
Wang Yuan　王遠　　　　　1019

PERSONS

Sun Youyue　孫遊嶽　　　　928　　Dengzhen yinjue　登真隱訣　356
Tao Hongjing　陶弘景　　　968　　Zhenling weiye tu　真靈位業圖　1263
　Zhengao　真誥　　　　　1248　　Yang Xi　楊羲　　　　　　1147

TEXTS

Basu jing　八素經　　　　　219　　Shangqing dao leishi xiang　上清道類
Ciyi jing　雌一經　　　　　286　　　事相　　　　　　　　　866
Dadong zhenjing　大洞真經　295　　Siji mingke jing　四極明科經　907
Dengzhen yinjue　登真隱訣　356　　Suling jing　素靈經　　　　921
Housheng daojun lieji　後聖道君　　Taidan yinshu　太丹隱書　931
　列紀　　　　　　　　　491　　Taixiao langshu　太霄琅書　955
Jiuzhen zhongjing　九真中經　594　　Zhengao　真誥　　　　　1248
Lingshu ziwen　靈書紫文　680　　Zhenling weiye tu　真靈位業圖　1263

RELATED NOTIONS AND TERMS

housheng　後聖　　　　　490

5. Lingbao

Lingbao　靈寶　　　　　　663

PERSONS

Ge Chaofu　葛巢甫　　　　440　　Lingbao jingmu　靈寶經目　672
Lu Xiujing　陸修靜　　　　717　　Lingbao shoudu yi　靈寶授度儀　674
　Daomen kelüe　道門科略　323　　Sandong jingshu mulu　三洞經書目錄　828

TEXTS

Buxu ci　步虛詞　　　　　241　　Lingbao shoudu yi　靈寶授度儀　674
Daomen kelüe　道門科略　323　　Lingbao wufu xu　靈寶五符序　675
Duren jing　度人經　　　　394　　Shengshen jing　生神經　　881
Ershisi sheng tu　二十四生圖　397　　Wupian zhenwen　五篇真文　1060

RELATED NOTIONS AND TERMS

lingbao　靈寶　　　　　　661　　pudu　普度　　　　　　792
dafan yinyu　大梵隱語　　297

6. Sui, Tang, and Five Dynasties

PERSONS

Du Guangting　杜光庭　　　　　385
 Daojiao lingyan ji　道教靈驗記　319
 Lidai chongdao ji　歷代崇道記　652
 Yongcheng jixian lu　墉城集仙錄　1183
He Zhizhang　賀知章　　　　　476
Huang Lingwei　黃靈微　　　　501
Huanzhen xiansheng　幻真先生　515
Li Ao　李翱　　　　　　　　　631
Li Chunfeng　李淳風　　　　　633
Li Hanguang　李含光　　　　　637
Li Quan　李筌　　　　　　　　641
Luo Gongyuan　羅公遠　　　　721
Lüqiu Fangyuan　閭丘方遠　　724
Nie Shidao　聶師道　　　　　773
Pan Shizheng　潘師正　　　　782
Shi Jianwu　施肩吾　　　　　893
Sima Chengzhen　司馬承禎　　911

Fuqi jingyi lun　服氣精義論　431
Zuowang lun　坐忘論　　　　1309
Sun Simiao　孫思邈　　　　　925
 Cunshen lianqi ming　存神錬氣銘　289
 Sheyang zhenzhong fang　攝養枕中方　892
 Taiqing danjing yaojue　太清丹經
  要訣　　　　　　　　　942
Wang Bing　王冰　　　　　　1007
Wang Yuanzhi　王遠知　　　1020
Wu Yun　吳筠　　　　　　　1048
 Shenxian kexue lun　神仙可學論　886
Ye Fashan　葉法善　　　　　1154
Yin Wencao　尹文操　　　　1168
Zhang Wanfu　張萬福　　　　1236
Zhang Zixiang　張子祥　　　1241
Zhao Guizhen　趙歸真　　　1244

TEXTS

Daodian lun　道典論　　　　　315
Daojiao lingyan ji　道教靈驗記　319
Daojiao yishu　道教義樞　　　321
Fengdao kejie　奉道科戒　　　420
Lidai chongdao ji　歷代崇道記　652

Sandong zhunang　三洞珠囊　　832
Shenxian kexue lun　神仙可學論　886
Wudou jing　五斗經　　　　　1053
Xuanmen dayi　玄門大義　　　1134
Yiqie daojing yinyi　一切道經音義　1178

7. Song, Jin, and Yuan Movements, Cults, and Codifications

JINGMING DAO

Jingming dao　淨明道　　　　　567
Jingming zhongxiao quanshu 淨明忠孝全書 571

Liu Yu　劉玉　　　　　　　　692

LEIFA

Lei Shizhong　雷時中　　　　625
leifa　雷法　　　　　　　　　627
Mo Qiyan　莫起炎　　　　　　752

Sa Shoujian　薩守堅　　　　　825
Wang Weiyi　王惟一　　　　　1016

LINGBAO DAFA

Lingbao dafa　靈寶大法　　　　671
Lingbao lingjiao jidu jinshu　靈寶領教
 濟度金書　　　　　　　673
Lingbao wuliang duren shangjing dafa
 靈寶無量度人上經大法　678

Ning Benli　寧本立　　　　　774
Shangqing lingbao dafa [CT 219 and
 1222–23] 上清靈寶大法　870

QINGWEI

Huang Shunshen　黃舜申　　　503
Qingwei　清微　　　　　　　　804

Qingwei xianpu　清微仙譜　　　805

SHANGQING

Liu Hunkang   劉混康   689   Zhu Ziying   朱自英   1295

SHENXIAO

Gaoshang Shenxiao zongshi shoujing shi   Shenxiao   神霄   889
高上神霄宗師受經式   439   Wang Wenqing   王文卿   1017
Lin Lingsu   林靈素   657

TAIYI JIAO

Taiyi jiao   太一教   959   Xiao Fudao   蕭輔道   1096

TIANXIN ZHENGFA

Deng Yougong   鄧有功   354   Tan Zixiao   譚紫霄   963
Rao Dongtian   饒洞天   821   Tianxin zhengfa   天心正法   989
Taishang zhuguo jiumin zongzhen biyao
太上助國救民總真祕要   951

TONGCHU

Tongchu   童初   996

YUTANG DAFA

Lu Shizhong   路時中   715

XUANJIAO

Xuanjiao   玄教   1132

ZHEN DADAO

Liu Deren   劉德仁   685   Zhen dadao   真大道   1247

ZHENGYI

Wu Quanjie   吳全節   1045   Zhang Sicheng   張嗣成   1235
Zhang Jixian   張繼先   1228   Zhang Zongyan   張宗演   1242
Zhang Keda   張可大   1229   Zhengyi   正一   1258
Zhang Liusun   張留孫   1231

OTHER PERSONS

Chen Jingyuan   陳景元   251   Wang Qinruo   王欽若   1014
Dong Sijing   董思靖   365   Yisheng baode zhuan   翊聖保德傳   1180
Du Daojian   杜道堅   383   Xiao Yingsou   蕭應搜   1097
Guo Gangfeng   郭岡鳳   461   Xue Jizhao   薛季昭   1145
Lei Siqi   雷思齊   626

OTHER TEXTS

Daofa huiyuan   道法會元   316   Yunji qiqian   雲笈七籤   1203
Jinsuo liuzhu yin   金鎖流珠引   582   Yushu jing   玉樞經   1208
Yisheng baode zhuan   翊聖保德傳   1180

8. Quanzhen

Quanzhen　全真　　　　　　　　814

PERSONS

Hao Datong　郝大通　　　474
Ji Zhizhen　姬志真　　　537
Li Daoqian　李道謙　　　636
　Qizhen nianpu　七真年譜　813
　Ganshui xianyuan lu　甘水仙源錄　434
Liu Chuxuan　劉處玄　　　684
Ma Yu　馬鈺　　　729
Qiu Chuji　邱處機　　　808
　Changchun zhenren xiyou ji　長春
　真人西游記　　　246
Song Defang　宋德方　　　915

Sun Bu'er　孫不二　　　922
Tan Chuduan　譚處端　　　962
Wang Chuyi　王處一　　　1011
Wang Zhe　王嚞　　　1020
　Chongyang lijiao shiwu lun　重陽
　立教十五論　　　276
　Chongyang Quanzhen ji　重陽全真集　277
Wang Zhijin　王志瑾　　　1024
Yin Zhiping　尹志平　　　1171
Yu Daoxian　于道顯　　　1189

TEXTS

Changchun zhenren xiyou ji　長春
　真人西游記　　　246
Chongyang lijiao shiwu lun　重陽
　立教十五論　　　276
Chongyang Quanzhen ji　重陽全真集　277

Ganshui xianyuan lu　甘水仙源錄　　434
Jinlian zhengzong ji　金蓮正宗記　578
Minghe yuyin　鳴鶴餘音　　　749
Qizhen nianpu　七真年譜　　813
Zhenxian beiji　真仙碑記　　1268

RELATED NOTIONS AND TERMS

huandu　環堵　　　500
zuobo　坐鉢　　　1303

9. Ming and Qing

ZHENGYI

Zhang Guoxiang　張國祥　　1226
Zhang Yuanxu　張元旭　　1238

Zhang Yuchu　張宇初　　1239
　Daomen shigui　道門十規　324
　Zhang Zhengchang　張正常　1240

QUANZHEN

Chen Minggui　陳銘珪　　253
He Daoquan　何道全　　　475

JINGMING DAO

Liu Yuanran　劉淵然　　693
Shao Yizheng　邵以正　　875

Zhu Quan　朱權　　1294
　Tianhuang zhidao Taiqing yuce
　天皇至道太清玉冊　974

OTHER PERSONS

Leng Qian　冷謙　　630
Lin Zhao'en　林兆恩　660
Lou Jinyuan　婁近垣　706

Shao Yuanjie　邵元節　878
Tao Zhongwen　陶仲文　971
Zhao Yizhen　趙宜真　1245

TEXTS

Chuzhen jielü　初真戒律　　　284　*Tianhuang zhidao Taiqing yuce*
Daomen shigui　道門十規　　　324　　天皇至道太清玉冊　　　974
Kaixin fayao　開心法要　　　599

10. Contemporary Taoism

Chen Yingning　陳攖寧　　　261　Zhang Enpu　張恩溥　　　1224
Yi Xinying　易心瑩　　　1160

IV. Forms of Religious Practice and Experience

1. Yangsheng *(Nourishing Life)*

yangsheng　養生　　　1148

PRACTICES

bigu　辟穀　　　233　*liuzi jue*　六字訣　　　698
biqi　閉氣　　　234　*qigong*　氣功　　　796
buqi　布氣　　　240　*taiji quan*　太極拳　　　932
daoyin　導引　　　334　*taixi*　胎息　　　953
fangzhong shu　房中術　　　409　*tiaoqi*　調氣　　　994
fuqi　服氣　　　430　*tuna*　吐納　　　1000
huanjing bunao　還精補腦　　　514　*xingqi*　行氣　　　1108
lianqi　鍊氣　　　648　*zhongxi*　踵息　　　1286

TEXTS

Chifeng sui　赤鳳髓　　　268　*Yangsheng yaoji*　養生要集　　　1151
Taixi jing　胎息經　　　954　*Yangxing yanming lu*　養性延命錄　　　1152
Xinyin jing　心印經　　　1108

RELATED MEDICAL WORKS

Huangdi neijing　黃帝內經　　　506　*Zhubing yuanhou lun*　諸病源候論　　　1300
Ishinpō　醫心方　　　535

2. Meditation

PRACTICES

bugang　步綱　　　237　*neiguan*　內觀　　　766
cun　存　　　287　*shouyi*　守一　　　902
ding　定　　　358　*yuanyou*　遠遊　　　1195
guan　觀　　　452　*zuowang*　坐忘　　　1308
jingzuo　靜坐　　　575

TEXTS

Cunshen lianqi ming 存神錬氣銘	289	*Shangsheng xiuzhen sanyao* 上乘
Dingguan jing 定觀經	359	修真三要	871
Fuqi jingyi lun 服氣精義論	431	*Sheyang zhenzhong fang* 攝養枕中方	892
Huangting jing 黃庭經	511	*Tianyin zi* 天隱子	993
Laozi zhongjing 老子中經	624	*Wuchu jing* 五廚經	1051
Qingjing jing 清靜經	800	*Zuowang lun* 坐忘論	1309

3. Alchemy

jindan 金丹	551	*nüdan* 女丹	778
neidan 內丹	762	*waidan* 外丹	1002

ZHOUYI CANTONG QI AND RELATED TEXTS

Guwen Zhouyi cantong qi 古文周易		*Zhouyi cantong qi* 周易參同契	1289
參同契	466	*Zhouyi cantong qi kaoyi* 周易參同
Longhu jing 龍虎經	701	契考異	1292

TAIQING

Jinye jing 金液經	587	*Taiqing danjing yaojue* 太清丹經要訣	942
Jiudan jing 九丹經	588	*Taiqing jing* 太清經	945
Taiqing 太清	941	*Taiqing shibi ji* 太清石壁記	946

PERSONS RELATED TO WAIDAN

Chen Shaowei 陳少微	256	Li Shaojun 李少君	643
Hugang zi 狐剛子	519	Yuanyang zi 元陽子	1194

OTHER WAIDAN TEXTS

Danfang jianyuan 丹方鑑源	300	*Sanshiliu shuifa* 三十六水法	849
Danfang xuzhi 丹房須知	301	*Shiyao erya* 石藥爾雅	897

ZHENYUAN

Zhenyuan 真元	1269

ZHONG-LÜ

Lingbao bifa 靈寶畢法	669	Zhong-Lü 種呂	1277
Qinyuan chun 沁園春	807	Zhongli Quan 鍾離權	1283
Xishan qunxian huizhen ji 西山群仙		Lü Dongbin 呂洞賓	712
會真記	1112	*Zhong-Lü chuandao ji* 種呂傳道集	1279

NANZONG AND LATER RELATED AUTHORS AND TEXTS

Bai Yuchan 白玉蟾	203	Shi Tai 石泰	894
Chen Nan 陳楠	254	Weng Baoguang 翁葆光	1036
Chen Zhixu 陳致虛	262	*Wuzhen pian* 悟真篇	1081
Jindan dayao 金丹大要	557	*Xiuzhen shishu* 修真十書	1118
Jindan sibai zi 金丹四百字	558	Xue Daoguang 薛道光	1144
Li Daochun 李道純	634	Yu Yan 俞琰	1190
Miao Shanshi 苗善時	745	Zhang Boduan 張伯端	1220
Nanzong 南宗	759	*Zhonghe ji* 中和集	1282
Peng Si 彭耜	786		

WU-LIU PAI

Huiming jing 慧命經	520	Wu Shouyang 伍守陽	1046
Liu Huayang 柳華陽	688	Wu-Liu pai 伍柳派	1049

LONGMEN

Liu Yiming 劉一明	690	Min Yide 閔一得	747
Daoshu shi'er zhong 道書十二種	331	Wang Changyue 王常月	1008
Longmen 龍門	704	*Chuzhen jielü* 初真戒律	284

OTHER PERSONS RELATED TO NEIDAN

Chen Xianwei 陳顯微	260	Peng Dingqiu 彭定求	784
Dong Dening 董德寧	364	Peng Haogu 彭好古	785
Fu Jinquan 傅金銓	425	Peng Xiao 彭曉	787
Li Xiyue 李西月	645	Qiu Zhao'ao 仇兆鰲	811
Liu Zhigu 劉知古	694	Wang Jie 王玠	1012
Lu Xixing 陸西星	719	Zhao Bichen 趙避塵	1243
Fanghu waishi 方壺外史	404		

OTHER NEIDAN TEXTS

Chongbi danjing 沖碧丹經	273	*Ruyao jing* 入藥經	823
Daoshu 道樞	329	*Taiyi jinhua zongzhi* 太一金華宗旨	961
Fanghu waishi 方壺外史	404	*Xingming guizhi* 性命圭旨	1106
Guizhong zhinan 規中指南	461	*Yinfu jing* 陰符經	1173
Jindan dacheng ji 金丹大成集	556		

RELATED NOTIONS AND TERMS

chushen 出神	282	*liuyi ni* 六一泥	697
dianhua 點化	357	*longhu* 龍虎	700
dinglu 鼎爐	360	*muyu* 沐浴	753
fu [crucible] 釜	424	*shengtai* 聖胎	883
huandan 還丹	498	*shuangxiu* 雙修	906
huohou 火候	526	*zhan chilong* 斬赤龍	1219
jinye 金液	586	*zhoutian* 周天	1287
langgan 琅玕	605		

4. Ritual

OFFICIANTS

daoshi 道士	326	*dujiang* 都講	388
daozhang 道長	350		

RITUALS

gongde 功德	449	*tou longjian* 投龍簡	998
huanglu zhai 黃籙齋	510	*tutan zhai* 塗炭齋	1001
jiao 醮	539	*wenjiao* 瘟醮	1038
jinlu zhai 金籙齋	580	*yulu zhai* 玉籙齋	1202
luotian dajiao 羅天大醮	723	*zhai* 齋	1216
pudu 普度	792		

STAGES OF 'JIAO' AND 'GONGDE' RITUALS

baibiao　拜表	206	*kaitong minglu*　開通冥路	598
daochang　道場	310	*muyu*　沐浴	753
fabiao　發表	399	*poyu*　破獄	792
fang shema　放赦馬	403	*suqi*　宿啟	930
fendeng　分燈	418	*tianku*　填庫	977
guoqiao　過橋	465	*wugong*　午供	1056
jintan　禁壇	583	*zhengjiao*　正醮	1253

TEXTS

Chaotian baochan　朝天寶懺	249	*Wushang huanglu dazhai licheng yi*	
Daomen kefan da quanji　道門科範大		無上黃籙大齋立成儀	1066
全集	322	*Zhaijie lu*　齋戒錄	1218
Lingbao yujian　靈寶玉鑑	679		

RELATED NOTIONS AND TERMS

bianshen　變身 / 變神	230	*keyi*　科儀	600
chanhui　懺悔	248	*liandu*　鍊度	646
chushen　出神	282	*mijue (bijue)*　祕訣	746
faqi　法器	411	*ruyi*　入意	824
falu　發爐	400	*sanchao*　三朝	826
fashi　法師	416	*shoujue*　手訣	899
gongcao　功曹	448	*shu*　疏	904
guanfu　冠服	455	*tang-ki*　童乩	964
hongtou and *wutou*　紅頭・烏頭	488	*wuying*　五營	1071
huoju　火居	532	*xianglu*　香爐	1089
jiangshen　降神	538	*xingdao*　行道	1105
kaiguang　開光	596	*zhiqian*　紙錢	1276

V. Taoism and Chinese Buddhism

PERSONS

Fu Yi　傅奕	426	Gu Huan　顧歡	451
Yixia lun　夷夏論	1181	Tanluan　曇鸞	967

TEXTS

Benji jing　本際經	227	*Huahu jing*　化胡經	491
Bianzheng lun　辯正論	232	*Xiaodao lun*　笑道論	1098
Cantong qi　參同契	244	*Xuanzhu lu*　玄珠錄	1142
Dasheng miaolin jing　大乘妙林經	352	*Yebao yinyuan jing*　業報因緣經	1155
Haikong zhizang jing　海空智藏經	469	*Yixia lun*　夷夏論	1181
Hongming ji　弘明記	487	*Zhenzheng lun*　甄正論	1270

VI. Miscellaneous Terms Related to Religious Ideas and Practices

benming 本命	228	*jinji* 禁忌	576
fuji 扶乩	428	*jinxiang* 進香	585
gengshen 庚申	446	*liujia* and *liuding* 六甲 · 六丁	695
gui 鬼	458	*sanshi* and *jiuchong* 三尸 · 九蟲	844
hanshi san 寒食散	473	*santian* and *liutian* 三天 · 六天	851
huoling 火鈴	532	*songjing* 誦經	916
jie [kalpa] 劫	545	*Tianpeng zhou* 天蓬咒	979
jiji ru lüling 急急如律令	549	*yinsi* 淫祀	1176
jing and *jian* 鏡 · 劍	559	*zhi* [excrescences] 芝	1271
jingshi 靜室	573	*zuodao* 左道	1307

VII. Associations

Nippon dōkyō gakkai 日本道教學會	775	Zhongguo daojiao xiehui 中國道教協會	1281

List of Illustrations

1 Zhang Yuanxian, sixty-fourth Celestial Master, reads an ordination text   18

2 A candidate to ordination climbs a ladder of thirty-six swords   18

3 "Primordial graphs" in a revealed text   25

4 Taoist Master Chen Rongsheng writes a talisman (*fu*)   36

5 Talismans (*fu*)   37

6 "Great Register of the Most High Orthodox Unity for Removing Evil"   40

7 Ordination certificate   41

8 The cosmogonic sequence of the Five Greats (*wutai*)   54

9 The Taoist altar as a microcosm   57

10 Human figure surrounded by emblems associated with Yin and Yang and the Five Agents   57

11 An immortal   76

12 The head and the inner body   77

13 The body as a mountain   78

14 Inner deities of the *Authentic Scripture of the Great Cavern*   82–83

15 Taoist novices at the Baiyun guan (Abbey of the White Clouds)   103

16 Pavilion of the Three Clarities and the Four Sovereigns, Baiyun guan (Abbey of the White Clouds)   107

17 Medium during pilgrimage tour   157

18 Talismans for curing illness used by Japanese Shugendō practitioners   194

19 *Chart of the Way of the Elixir in Nine Cycles for the Cultivation of Perfection*   195

20 The eight trigrams   202

21 Entrance arch to the Baiyun guan (Abbey of the White Clouds)   208

22 The Eight Immortals   221

23 The Northern Dipper   225

24 Treading the twenty-eight lunar mansions   238

25 Chenghuang (City God)   267

26 Egress of the Spirit   283

27 Visualization of the Lords of the thirty-nine "gates" of the human body   296

28 *Daoyin* postures in a Mawangdui manuscript   335

29 An alchemical tripod   361

30 Great Emperor of the Eastern Peak   378

31 Control Channel and Function Channel   390

32 Ritual tools   412–13

33 Fei Changfang enters his gourd   417

34 A Taoist master lights a candle during the Division of the Lamps
    ceremony   418

35 Great Emperor of Fengdu   422

36 "Planchette writing" (*fuji*)   429

37 Taoist Master Chen Rongsheng wears a heavy brocaded *daopao*
    ("robe of the Dao")   456

38 *Chart of the Yellow River* and *Writ of the Luo River*   484

39 A "red-head" ritual master   489

40 The Yellow Court   512

41 Opening verses of the *Scripture of the Yellow Court*   513

42 The three *hun* and seven *po*   522

43 *Hundun* (" . . . a cinnabar-red animal shaped like a sack with six legs
    and four wings . . .")   524

44 Diagram of the "fire phases"   527

45 The "fire phases" in the human body   528

46 Taoist Master Chen Rongsheng presides at an Offering ritual   540

47 Sword presented by Sima Chengzhen to Tang Xuanzong   560

48 Emblems inscribed on the reverse side of mirrors   561

49 Primordial pneuma (*yuanqi*) in the *Scripture and Illustration for the
    Mysterious Contemplation of the Mountain of the Bird-Men*   563

50 Floor plan for a "quiet chamber"   574

51 Laozi as the author of the *Daode jing*   612

52 Laozi as a deity   614

53 Talismans of the Five Emperors in the *Prolegomena to the Five Talismans of
    the Numinous Treasure*   676

54 The immortal Liu Haichan   687

55 Dragon and Tiger joining their essences in the alchemical tripod   701

56 An episode from the life of Lü Dongbin   713

57 Fragments of the Mawangdui manuscript of the *Daode jing*   739

58 Entrance to Mazu temple (Tianhou gong) in Lukang, Taiwan   742

59 The alchemical process represented by trigrams of the *Book of Changes*   763

60 *Chart of the Inner Warp*   768

61 *Chart for the Cultivation of Perfection*   769

62 The Nine Palaces of the Mud Pellet   776

63 Qiu Chuji   809

64 The Three Clarities   842

65 The "three corpses" and the "nine worms"   845

66 Generation of the inner Infant   883

67 Taoist Master He Canghai performs a mudrā during a ritual of exorcism   900

68 Mudrā or "instructions for (practices in) the hand" (*shoujue*)   901

69 Taoist Master Chen Rongsheng recites a memorial during an
    Offering ritual   905

70 *Taiji tu* (Diagram of the Great Ultimate) and *Wuji tu* (Diagram of the
    Ultimateless)   935

71 Early representation of the Great One (Taiyi)   957

72 A medium (*tang-ki*) wields a wooden divination chair   965

73 The three main talismans of Tianxin zhengfa (Correct Method of the
    Celestial Heart)   990

74 Wang Changyue   1009

75 Ordination platform, Baiyun guan (Abbey of the White Clouds)   1010

76 A section of the *Perfected Script in Five Tablets*   1061

77 "Production" sequence and "conquest' sequence of the Five Agents   1069

78 The "real forms" of the Five Peaks   1076

79 The five viscera with their deities and animal spirits   1079

80 Worshipper in the Wenchang Palace (Wenchang gong)   1090

81 Early representation of immortals as winged beings   1093

82 The twenty-eight lunar lodges arranged around the Northern Dipper   1116

83 The Mysterious Female as a symbol of the conjunction of Yin and Yang   1139

84 Yin and Yang   1165

85 Pavilion of the Three Clarities, Yongle gong (Palace of Eternal Joy)   1185

86 The Jade Emperor (Yuhuang)   1198

87 Zhang Daoling, first Celestial Master   1223

88 Zhenwu (Perfected Warrior)   1267

89 "Numinous mushrooms" or "excrescences" (*zhi*)   1272

90 Monks in front of the headquarters of the Chinese Taoist Association   1281

List of Tables

1 Yin and Yang entities according to the Mawangdui manuscript *Cheng* (Designations) — 52

2 The eight trigrams and their main associations — 201

3 Contents of the *Daozang xubian* (Sequel to the Taoist Canon) — 348

4 The ten major Grotto-Heavens — 369

5 The thirty-six minor Grotto-Heavens — 370

6 The seventy-two Blissful Lands — 371

7 The ten Celestial Stems and the twelve Earthly Branches — 436

8 The ten Celestial Stems and their associations — 436

9 The twelve Earthly Branches and their associations — 437

10 The sexagesimal cycle of the Celestial Stems and the Earthly Branches — 438

11 Program of a two-day Merit (*gongde*) ritual — 450

12 Published translations of *Huainan zi* chapters into Western languages — 497

13 The twelve "sovereign hexagrams" (*bigua*) and their relation to other duodenary series — 529

14 Program of a three-day Offering (*jiao*) ritual — 541

15 The cosmogonic stages of *Daode jing* sec. 42, and their correspondence with the stages of the *neidan* practice — 555

16 The Lingbao textual corpus — 665–66

17 The Five Patriarchs and the Seven Real Men (or Seven Perfected) of Quanzhen — 815

18 The Three Clarities (*sanqing*) and their associations — 841

19 The Thirty-two Heavens — 848

20 The Thirty-six Heavens — 850

21 The Shangqing textual corpus — 859–60

22 The forty-five Shangqing patriarchs — 861

23 The sixty-four Celestial Masters — 983

24 Contents of the *Wushang biyao* (Supreme Secret Essentials) — 1064–65

25 The five agents (or five phases, *wuxing*) and their main correlations — 1070

26 The twenty-eight lunar lodges (*xiu*) — 1117

27 The twelve divisions of the Taoist Canon — 1257

28 The twenty-four parishes of early Tianshi dao — 1275

Taoism:
An Overview

LIST OF ENTRIES

DEFINITIONS

daojia   5   *daojiao*   8

LINEAGES AND TRADITIONS

Lineages   11   Ordination and priesthood   17
Transmission   13   Syncretism   20
Initiation   16

SCRIPTURES AND TEXTS

Revelations and sacred texts   24   *fu* 符   35
Scripture and exegesis   26   *lu* 籙   39
Daozang and subsidiary compilations   28   Hagiography   42
sandong 三洞   33   Epigraphy   44

COSMOGONY AND COSMOLOGY

Cosmogony   47   Macrocosm and microcosm   56
Cosmology   51   Numerology   59

DEITIES AND SPIRITS

Deities: The pantheon   61   Otherworldly bureaucracy   67
Demons and spirits   63   Hell   69

SACRED SITES

Taoist sacred sites   72

VIEWS OF THE HUMAN BEING

Taoist views of the human body   75   Death and afterlife   86
Inner deities   80   Rebirth   90
Birth   85   Transcendence and immortality   91

VIEWS OF HUMAN SOCIETY

Messianism and millenarianism   94   Ethics and morals   99
Apocalyptic eschatology   97

RELIGIOUS ORGANIZATION

Monasticism   102   Temples and shrines   106
Monastic code   104   Taoist lay associations   110

RELIGIOUS PRACTICE AND EXPERIENCE

Asceticism   112   Mysticism   120
Divination, omens, and prophecy   113   Seasonal observances   122
Magic   116   Taoist music   125
Meditation and visualization   118

TAOISM AND CHINESE THOUGHT AND RELIGION

Taoism and Chinese mythology   129   Taoism and Chinese Buddhism   141
Taoism and early Chinese religion   130   Taoism and popular religion   145
Taoism and early Chinese thought   132   Taoism and popular sects   150
Taoism and the apocrypha   135   Taoism and local cults   152
Taoism and Confucianism   137   Taoism and medium cults   156
Taoism and Neo-Confucianism   139   Taoism and ancestor worship   159

TAOISM AND CHINESE SOCIETY

Taoism and the state   162   Taoism and secret societies   170
Taoism and the civil service   Women in Taoism   171
    examinations   165   Taoism in the People's Republic of
Taoism and local communities   167   China   174

TAOISM AND CHINESE CULTURE

Taoism and Chinese literature   176   Taoism and Chinese art   183
Taoism and Chinese theatre   179   Taoism and the military arts   185

TAOISM OUTSIDE CHINA

Taoism and the Yao people   188   Taoism in Japan   192
Taoism in the Korean peninsula   190

DEFINITIONS

daojia

道家

Taoism; "Lineage(s) of the Way"

The term *daojia* is a topic of debate among scholars, mainly concerning whether early Taoism constituted a "school" or "lineage," as the term *jia* seems to imply, and the distinction between *daojia* and *DAOJIAO, which is often understood to mean the religious forms of Taoism. The term *daojia* itself originated with Han historiographers as a bibliographic label, but has also been applied to texts related to Taoist religion in such modern compilations as the *Sibu beiyao* 四部備要 (Complete Essentials from the Four Sections of Literature) and the *Sibu congkan* 四部叢刊 (Collectanea from the Four Sections of Literature).

According to many modern interpreters, *daojia* began with Laozi and Zhuangzi 莊子. Some scholars suggest that this classification is an *ex post facto* creation, arguing that Laozi and Zhuangzi were independent thinkers and that—at least as far as the first seven, authentic chapters of the *Zhuangzi are concerned—there is no evidence that they influenced each other. Similar circumstances, however, are common to several schools of philosophy and religion both in China and elsewhere. Confucius himself intended only to transmit and restore the lost order of the Zhou kingdom, with no awareness that he was beginning a school of thought. Moreover, the so-called *daojia* is only one of the roots of what came to be Taoism.

The main point, therefore, is not whether the *daojia* was a school—most specialists agree that it was not. Even though the features of *daojia* are found mainly in the *Daode jing* and the *Zhuangzi*, other texts and authors reflect these trends, each with its own emphasis. Some of the main Warring States thinkers and texts belonging to this group are Shen Dao 慎到 (as reported in the *Zhuangzi*, *j*. 33), Yang Zhu 楊朱, Heguan zi 鶡冠子, the *Neiye* (Inner Training) and *Xinshu* 心術 (Arts of the Heart) chapters of the *Guanzi* 管子, and the *Daoyuan* 道原 (Dao, the Origin; trans. Yates 1997, 171–77) scroll of the *Mawangdui manuscripts. Later, Han syncretism, as expressed in the *Huainan zi* and by the *Huang-Lao school, tended to combine the thought of the *Daode jing* and the *Zhuangzi* with a philosophical exploitation of the Yellow Emperor (*Huangdi) and certain features of the legalist school of thought.

From the third century onward, the *Xuanxue (Arcane Learning) thinkers and the *Liezi can be related to the *daojia*. In the Six Dynasties and the Tang periods, Taoist classics like the *Qingjing jing, the *Xisheng jing, the *Yinfu jing, the texts on *neiguan (inner observation) and *zuowang (sitting in oblivion), and the *Chongxuan (Twofold Mystery) trend of thought are much indebted to it. The main points that unite these thinkers and texts are outlined below.

The notion of dao. First, the term *daojia* and its translation as "Taoism" derive from a new significance given to the word *dao* 道 in the *Daode jing*, the *Zhuangzi*, and other texts. The basic meanings of *dao* are "way" and "to say," hence "the way one should walk and that is taught," "guideline," and "method." In these texts the term took on a new meaning of Ultimate Truth, in the sense of the unique way that subsumes all the multiple human ways, and that is primal because nothing was before it and it is the source of everything. According to the *Daode jing* and the *Zhuangzi*, the Dao cannot actually be named and is beyond anything that can be grasped or delimited, but is open to personal experience. Both texts favor an apophatic approach that was entirely absent in the other teachings of their time. Having no form, because it exists before anything has taken form, the Dao can take all forms: it is both formless and multiform, and changes according to circumstances. No one can claim to possess or know it. As the source of everything, it is inexhaustible and endless; its Virtue or Efficacy (*de) is strength and light, and encompasses all life. Both the *Daode jing* and the *Zhuangzi* stress the necessity of following the natural order of the Dao and of Nourishing Life (*yangsheng), maintaining that this is sufficient for one's own well-being.

Return to the Origin. The *Daode jing* and the *Zhuangzi* share the same concern for the origin of things. Unlike any other trend of thought in the Warring States period, these texts emphasize the necessity of "returning" (*fan or *fu* 復) to the Dao, i.e., turning within oneself toward the Origin. This is essential to know and experience the Dao, and to fully understand the particular with regard to the two polar aspects of the Dao: indeterminate totality and receptive unity, on one side, and existence as organic diversity, on the other. Turning within oneself affords the quiescence required to experience the Dao. It consists in concentrating and unifying one's spirit (*shen) and will (*zhi* 志) on this experience, and in being receptive and compliant in order to receive this Dao. Hence the practice of concentration on the One (*yi), seen throughout the history of Taoism. This concentration means freeing oneself from desires, emotions, and prejudices, renouncing the conceptual self, and not getting entangled in knowledge and social concerns. The goal is to return to one's original nature and to pristine simplicity of the authentic state of things, which Taoists sometimes call the "great clod" (*dakuai* 大塊). It is related to an intuitive vision of the world as a unified whole, and a perception of the value and the natural strength (*qi) of life. This is not merely a reflection of the limitations of language, as some have claimed, but an intuitive, personal and sometimes mystical awareness that goes beyond language, conceptual thought, and social or moral practices and doctrines.

Based on this vision, the *Daode jing* and especially the *Zhuangzi* offer an ideal of the human being that has deeply influenced Chinese thought. The Taoist saint (*shengren) is before and beyond appellation and individual existence, and possesses cosmic and nearly divine stature and powers. He is an incarnation of the Dao and its Virtue, and dwells on the border between humanity and the Dao.

Is Taoism philosophical? Another issue in the debate among scholars is whether or not *daojia* is "philosophical." Indeed, Zhuangzi and the Taoist saint are neither pro- nor antiphilosophical. They dwell in a open space where one thinks without being caught up in thought, and sees in a multifaceted "perspectivist" way. In addition, there is a fantastic vein in the *Zhuangzi* that is not philosophical and that was later developed in Taoism, particularly by the *Shangqing school.

Daojia has also been labelled "non-purposive," "non-instrumental," and "contemplative" (e.g., by Creel 1970, 37–48), but these definitions are inadequate for three reasons. First, some trends of *daojiao*, or so-called "religious Taoism," are also non-purposive and contemplative. Second, concentration on the Dao or Oneness, and renunciation of social and personal values and activities, necessarily imply some "purposive" techniques of self-cultivation that the *daojia* texts often allude to. Third, various early *daojia* texts refer to political applications. The main difference between *daojia* and *daojiao* is perhaps that *daojiao* primarily aims at establishing a connection with the sacred, either as a relationship with deities and spirits or as the attainment of personal transcendence. The question of immortality is related to this point.

The *daojia* dimension of Taoism is absent in several Taoist trends and texts, and others appropriated the *Daode jing* without much regard for its many possible meanings. The *Xiang'er commentary exemplifies this attitude. Nevertheless, the philosophical spirit and features embraced by the term *daojia* are apparent throughout most of the history of Taoism, beginning with the *Taiping jing (Scripture of Great Peace), which may be the earliest extant *daojiao* text. With Yin-Yang and *wuxing cosmology, the *daojia* has given Taoism one of its most basic conceptual frameworks, without which no religion can have a structured and coherent worldview.

Isabelle ROBINET

📖 Barrett 2000; Graham 1989, 170–234; Izutsu Toshihiko 1983, 287–486; Kirkland

2000; Li Shen 1995; Robinet 1997b, 1–23; Schwartz 1985, 186–255; Seidel 1997; Tang Junyi 1986, 1: 262–436; Thompson 1993

※ DAOJIAO

daojiao

道教

Taoism; Taoist teaching; "Teaching(s) of the Way"

This term, now denoting the religion which is the topic of this encyclopedia, originally meant no more than "Teaching of the Way"—though even this is misleading, in that inculcation rather than education is implied by "teaching." All early instances of the term, therefore, have a rather vague application: in preimperial times Mohists use it with reference to the classical traditions of the sages, more or less equivalent to Confucianism; from the late Han onward Buddhists use it also as an elegant synonym for *fojiao* 佛教, "The Teachings of the Buddha." Only in the fifth century do we find it used in the sense that it has now acquired; only then did such a term become necessary.

Up to that point various religious groups whose adherents rallied together under the new label had already come into existence, from the Celestial Masters (*Tianshi dao) onward. But although they shared a common belief in the values of empire—authority and order—they remained distinct from one another, as did those individuals who adhered to traditions of ancient occult learning going back to the Han, if not earlier, which had remained outside the Han state's synthesis of learning under the banner of Confucianism. These individuals tended to use the word *DAOJIA, a term first attested in the early second century BCE (*Shiji*, 56.2062), and used thereafter both by doxographers retrospectively describing presumed groups of texts of the preimperial period and as a term for masters of self-cultivation and the pursuit of immortality—we must suppose there was some link between early texts and contemporary masters in the Han mind.

But by the fifth century the implicit unity of all these individuals and groups over against the disparate, "uncontrolled" cults of local religion could now be replaced by a conscious unity across diversity on the model of Buddhism, where many different doctrines were accorded the same status as Buddha's word. Dynasties of the early fifth century in both the north and the south came to the conclusion that organized religion on the Buddhist model was more of a help than a threat, especially after the rebellion of *Sun En and similar incidents underlined just what the results of the corruption of "higher" religion by less agreeable elements might result in. The establishment of an externally verifiable canonical literature; the codification of rituals and priestly standards in general; the beginnings of monastic foundations of the Buddhist type—all these represent the creation of a "religion" out of a much looser assemblage of religious elements, and obviously some sort of unifying name was necessary. The *Yixia lun* (Essay on the Barbarians and the Chinese) of *Gu Huan (420/428–483/491) is usually taken as the scene of its first appearance in this sense, though its presence in the biography of *Kou Qianzhi (365?–448) in the *Weishu* (History of the Wei; trans. Ware 1933, 228–35) may attest a somewhat earlier occurrence, and an essay by Zhou Yong 周顒 to which Gu was responding already implicitly refers to Buddhism and Taoism as contrasting *jiao*.

It was, of course, inevitable that the Buddhists should have attempted to disassemble this construct polemically. Uncertain of their control of physical sacred space in China, where numinous places were already cult sites, they were anxious to deny their newly organized rivals cultural space by imposing a contrast between the otherworldly concerns of Buddhism leading to *nirvāṇa*, and (by analogy with the Indian case of the old Hindu gods) the sublunary status of all other religious phenomena. Laozi was acceptable as a philosopher, but had had no soteriological intent; pursuit of immortality within this world was fine (though success was, of course, dependent on *karma*); even some forms of religious observance might be tolerable—but not the aping of Buddhism's grand conception of the cosmos and the human condition.

This attempt at stifling *daojiao* at birth was frustrated by its clear political appeal as a religion much more in tune with Chinese imperial symbolism than Buddhism. On these grounds it garnered widespread support from dynasties such as the Northern Wei, the Northern Zhou and (most definitively) the Tang. During the Tang epoch the categories of the Three Teachings (of Confucius, Laozi and the Buddha) proved such a convenient way of ordering the intellectual interests of the elite—even though they were far from mutually substitutable equivalents—that at a conceptual level they became an irreducible part of Chinese culture.

The consolidation of Neo-Confucianism under Zhu Xi 朱熹 (1130–1200; SB 282–90) affected discourse on *daojiao* in slightly different ways, as may be seen from his *Recorded Sayings* under this heading (*Zhuzi yulei* 朱子語類, Zhonghua shuju ed., 125.3005–6). He himself generally prefers the Han usage *daojia* to refer to everything from Laozi down to the religion of his contemporaries, and under that term does support the Buddhist charge of plagiarism against Taoism, mainly with a view to recapturing for Confucians elements of the state cult of Heaven which had fallen under Taoist control during the Tang. He evidently treats *daojiao* as a synonym for *daojia*, and uses it in opposition to *rujiao* 儒教, "Confucianism," stating that Confucianism may not be too vigorous, but Taoism has declined the most; another dictum specifies this decline (in *daojia*, in this case) as having taken place in two phases, from Laozi to the pursuit of immortality, and thence to the rituals and prayers which put it on a par with shamanic religion.

This rhetoric of decline, essential to the self-image of the Neo-Confucians as revivers of their Way, imposed a unity on the phenomenon known indifferently as *daojia/daojiao* in a completely ahistorical fashion, but a fashion that was irresistible to Protestant missionaries of the nineteenth century, whose religion was founded upon a somewhat analogous rhetoric with regard to Catholic Christianity. Meanwhile, Japanese scholars, under the greater traditional influence of medieval Buddhist polemics (see *Bianzheng lun*) tended to bifurcate *daojia*, signifying the philosopher Laozi and his peers, from *daojiao*, signifying the religious elements opposed to Buddhism—this, too, clearly appealed to the Protestant element in Western thought. (Fukui Fumimasa 1995, 14, lists the key Japanese contributions to clarifying this issue; Penny 1998 explores some Protestant approaches to Taoism.)

Thus the manipulation of the term *daojiao* by non-Taoists to suit their own agendas has in no small measure created the marked twentieth century confusion as to what Taoism is and was. It has at last been observed in a good discussion of the topic by Stephen R. Bokenkamp (1997, 11), that Taoists were perfectly capable of defining themselves through their own writings. By relying on those writings this encyclopedia seeks to make clear what *daojiao* meant to those who appropriated this term as their own: for a complete definition, the reader is hereby cross-referred to the sum total of other entries in this volume.

T. H. BARRETT

📖 Barrett 2000; Chen Guofu 1963, 259 and 271–74; Fukui Fumimasa 1995; Kirkland 2000; Robinet 1997b, 1–23; Seidel 1997; Thompson 1993

※ DAOJIA

LINEAGES AND TRADITIONS

Lineages

Lineages in Taoism highlighted connections between human beings and the sacred Way. People in China had long seen their society and its traditions as families organized by their reverence for recognized forebears. These organizations created cultural identities when people ritually linked themselves to predecessors, whether biological or imagined. Using ritual to acknowledge those who had passed on and their living heirs helped to strengthen society and to fashion a structure of depersonalized ancestors able to support that society. The genealogical imperative of Chinese civilization was typically patriarchal, focusing on male ancestors and descendants more than their female counterparts. These lineages also provided a rich resource for structuring and strengthening the political, religious, and cultural dimensions of Chinese lives.

Classical thinkers saw some key ideas of China's bronze civilizations of the Central Plains, such as the notion of ancestors and their living representatives, as signs of how a unified *qi distributed itself across social space. Ritual could keep this differentiated qi in good order within a family, whose duties were the source of Chinese ethical responsibility and moral behavior. Han scholars used familial models to structure various political and cultural forms, including that of a common "family" (*jia* 家) binding together the presumed authors of diverse writings. Genealogical presumptions organized both writings and cultural forms, broadening their influence in Chinese culture.

Taoist traditions tapped into these ancestral sociocultural sources for creating identities in China, but gave them a new foundation, the patterned condensations of qi that manifest the sacred Way. Taoism went further, however; from its first movements in the second century CE, it stressed that this cosmic Way also regularly becomes part of human history. The sacred and anthropomorphic incarnations of the sacred Way in human society—as patriarchs, transcendents, and saints—had their counterparts in the human body, composed of qi that could be refined and purified through ritual and meditation, and thus became the means for reuniting with the Way. Since everything in the world partook of qi that was rooted in the singular Way, the various Taoist traditions were so many sets of revealed reminders of the sacred sources of human life, and represented means to ritually and spiritually reconnect human life with these sources. Patriarchs, transcendents, and masters distributed these reminders to worthy human beings.

As was typical in China, heirs to this Way imagined their sacred learning and the spiritual ties to the Way and its human embodiments as "families" (*jia*), "lineages" (*zong* 宗), or "branches" (*pai* 派), whose "patriarchs" or "ancestors" (*zu* 祖) that had emanated from the Way distributed scriptures (see *REVELATIONS AND SACRED TEXTS), talismans (*FU), and ritual systems (*fa* 法) to worthy people. Taoist movements retained the key social value of family responsibility. The focus on the well-being of ancestors and the family reflected in early Taoist texts served as a template for other social values, including those articulated through ritual and scripture. Taoist initiation structured access to levels of understanding and deployed those aspects of the Way that best served human beings. Through moral living and sacred learning, an adept also gained access to larger and more powerful arrays of ritual forebears and living representatives who were charged with ensuring the orderly workings of the Way in the world. Taoist rituals served not only as reminders of proper order manifested in the Way, but also worked to instill that order in them.

Lineages in the history of Taoism. The best-known examples of lineage in Taoism appear in the chains of Celestial Masters (*tianshi) stemming from *Zhang Daoling, the *Shangqing (Highest Clarity) patriarchs *Wei Huacun and *Yang Xi, and sacred lines of Taoist learning, extending all the way down to the eighteenth-century genealogical compilations of the *Longmen (Gate of the Dragon) branch of *Quanzhen (Complete Perfection) teachings. For the great Yuan hagiographer Zhao Daoyi 趙道一 (fl. 1294–1307), humans who "perfected transcendence and embodied the Way" came from all over China and from all social levels. At the same time, Taoist initiates embodied the purest emanations of the Way and replicated their activities in the world, reflecting the basic family values of filiality, brotherly concern, and benevolence. The Taoist initiate worked not only to save self, ancestors, and all living beings, but also to bring order to the natural world.

Over time, lineages that had begun as local traditions become embedded in grander visions of their ties to the Way, including elaborate spiritual genealogies connecting recent human preceptors to the primordial Way. Later traditions often stressed ties to classical Taoist traditions such as *Zhengyi (Orthodox Unity), *Lingbao (Numinous Treasure), Shangqing, and *Jingming dao (Pure and Bright Way). This process gave rise to tensions between innovation and tradition, which may be seen in the *Tianxin zhengfa (Correct Method of the Celestial Heart), *Lingbao dafa (Great Rites of the Numinous Treasure), and *Shenxiao (Divine Empyrean) traditions, as well as in the cults to various local deities credited with issuing new Taoist teachings. Traditions like Quanzhen and *Qingwei (Pure Tenuity) worship their forebears as deities.

As Taoist traditions proliferated, the sacred genealogies that sought to legitimate contemporary belief and practice expanded and extended, showing how previously separate chains were actually part of elaborate webs of spiritual authority originating in the purest emanations of the Way itself. Thus, for example, what began as two separate local traditions, the *Bai Yuchan (1194–1229?) *neidan* tradition and *Wang Zhe's (1113–70) Quanzhen legacy, became known by early Ming times as the Southern and Northern Lineages (Nanbei zong 南北宗; see under *Nanzong), a unity that by the late nineteenth century had become embedded in the larger penta-directional set of traditions that also included *Li Daochun's (fl. 1288–92) Central Branch (Zhongpai 中派), *Lu Xixing's (1520–1601 or 1606) Eastern Branch (Dongpai 東派), and *Li Xiyue's (1806–56) Western Branch (Xipai 西派).

Lowell SKAR

📖 Bokenkamp 1997, 10–20; Keightley 1990

Transmission

The simplest form of transmission in China was pedagogical. A teacher such as Confucius orally passed on his learning to his pupils who recorded his wisdom for later posterity. An erudite might also personally present a text containing his wisdom to a deserving recipient. Another type of transmission appeared in the "weft texts" (*weishu* 緯書; see *TAOISM AND THE APOCRYPHA) that were popular during the reign of Wang Mang (r. 9–23). Those texts were the repositories of myths, and each was associated with one of the Confucian classics. A "dragon-horse" bearing the eight trigrams (*bagua*) of the *Yijing on its back emerged from the Yellow River to convey them to Fu Xi 伏羲 who copied them. A yellow dragon bearing the *Chart of the [Yellow] River (Hetu)* on its back crawled out of the river and presented it to *Huangdi. A giant, black tortoise carrying a talisman in its beak came forth from the water, placed it on an altar before Huangdi and departed. A numinous turtle with the *Writ of the Luo [River] (Luoshu)* imprinted on its cinnabar red shell in azure script emerged from the Luo River and transmitted it to Cangjie 倉頡, a divinity known as the inventor of writing. (On these two charts, see the entry *Hetu and Luoshu.) The trigrams, chart, talismans (*FU), and texts were tokens that confirmed Heaven's conferral of the mandate on the ancient sage kings, and they became essential elements of Taoist rituals and ordinations.

On June 11 of 142, the Most High Lord Lao (Taishang Laojun 太上老君), i.e., Laozi deified (*Laojun), descended to Mount Heming (*Heming shan, Sichuan) and bestowed the Dao of the Covenant with the Powers of Orthodox Unity (*zhengyi mengwei* 正一盟威) on *Zhang Daoling. This tradition, perhaps a later fabrication, was another sort of transmission, a personal revelation to a living human from a deity. What Zhang precisely received on that occasion is not at all clear since various sources supply different titles. Evidence seems to indicate that the works of Zhang or other *Tianshi dao leaders included registers (*LU), talismans, petitions, and codes. Later in the Six Dynasties, the priesthood, Zhang's successors, was responsible for inducting juveniles and young people into the faith. The rites involved transmitting registers.

Scriptural transmission. The *fangshi introduced another form of transmission involving arcane texts, some of which made their way into the alchemical tradition of Taoism. *Ge Hong traced their transmission back to *Zuo Ci (fl. ca. 200) and was one of the recipients of works at an altar (*tan* 壇) in the mountains of what is now northeast Jiangxi. There he received from his master three texts on alchemy under an oath of covenant (*meng* 盟) as well as secret oral instructions (*koujue* 口訣) on their meaning that could not be written down (see *Taiqing). Originally, a deity (*shenren) had bestowed them on Zuo who in turn transmitted them to Ge's uncle, *Ge Xuan, who passed them on Ge's master, *Zheng Yin.

Ge Hong mentions another form of transmission involving the *Sanhuang wen (Script of the Three Sovereigns). Immortals hide copies of it in caves on all of the sacred mountains. When a person qualified to attain the Dao enters one of the mountains and earnestly meditated, its god will open the grotto and permit him to view the text. The process, however, was a little more complicated, as there were two traditions concerning the revelation of the scripture; but in both cases the text appeared spontaneously on the walls of grottoes after the persons stared at it or meditated and fasted. When they were able to discerning the writing, the two left pledges, copied the scriptures and departed.

Transmission and revelations in the Six Dynasties. The oldest reliable accounts of divine transmission to humankind date from the second half of the fourth century. Between 364 and 371, a dozen or so of the Perfected appeared to *Yang Xi in nocturnal visions to bestow upon him more than ten *Shangqing scriptures and hagiographies as well as more than forty scrolls of oral instructions. Of all the Taoist revelations that occurred between 142 and 400, this is the only one that appears to have been the product of true ecstatic experience because Yang and his patrons, the Xus 許, kept detailed transcripts of the epiphanies. The influence of older occult sources is evident in the scriptures; the visions may have been nothing more than instruments for reshaping earlier writs and procedures to conform to Yang's new insights and agenda.

In the fifth century, the *Lingbao order added a new twist to the lore of transmission. They contended that their scriptures had emerged before creation as coagulations of *qi (pneuma). After the gods appeared, the Celestial Worthy of Original Commencement (Yuanshi tianzun 元始天尊; see *sanqing) had the texts cast on gold tablets and stored in his celestial archives. Thereafter, he granted lesser deities access to them if they underwent the proper rituals. Five eons passed before the Celestial Worthy decided it was time transmit the texts to a mortal. At his behest three of the Perfected descended with a cortege of carriages, an escort of cavaliers and a retinue of immortal lads and jade maids in the millions. That host landed on Mount Tiantai (*Tiantai shan, Zhejiang) where the Perfected bestowed the scriptures, one by one, on Ge Hong's uncle who had made himself worthy of receiving them by suffering through innumerable reincarnations and having compassionately vowed to strive for the salvation of all mankind.

Transmission and ordination. These traditions, however fanciful, served a purpose. They established the sanctity of the scriptures as direct gifts from the gods. They also laid the foundations for mundane transmissions of sacred texts. Once the texts found their way into human hands it was the responsibility of the recipients to pass them on to worthy recipients. By the fifth century with the appearance of the first liturgy for ordinations, compiled by *Lu Xiujing, the process of transmission became codified (see *Lingbao shoudu yi*). Taoist investitures were the liturgical confirmation of a master's transmission of texts to his disciple and were overwhelmingly juridical in nature. There were three legal formalities required of ordinands. The first were covenants by which they bound themselves to the gods and promised to venerate the scriptures. The punishment for violating such pacts was condemnation to the dark prisons of eternal night in hell. The second were vows. Ordinands gave their word that they would be temperate, chaste, compassionate, humane, benevolent, tolerant, and filial. The third were oaths. Ordinands swore never to transmit the canon indiscriminately, reveal its contents, violate its admonitions, converse or disparage the scriptures, or bestow the texts for a fee. To guarantee that they would never breach their word, they had to submit pledges in the form of gold, cash and textiles.

Charles D. BENN

📖 Benn 1991, 72–98; Lagerwey 1981b, 105–20, 117–40, and 149–70; Seidel 1983a; Stein R. A. 1968; Stein R. A. 1969a

※ INITIATION; LINEAGES; ORDINATION AND PRIESTHOOD; REVELATIONS AND SACRED TEXTS

Initiation

In Taoism, the problem of how knowledge and skill are transmitted to the next generation (*chuanshou* 傳授) is not dealt with in a systematic or regulated way, but rather as a direct confrontation between master and disciple. This theme will be considered here centering on the treatment given in *Ge Hong's (283–343) *Baopu zi*. Ge Hong repeatedly stresses that if a person earnestly wishes to achieve immortality he should study under a master, and if a good master is not chosen, there can be no success. The entire chapter 14 ("Qinqiu" 勤求, "Seek Diligently") of the *Baopu zi* deals with this theme.

> Although students of the future must make it their duty to seek a master, it is vital that they do so having made very sure of him first. A person of poor and narrow knowledge will be powerless to help them to achieve the Way, because his actions will be shallow, his virtue weak, his accomplishment feeble, and his resources scarce. (14.257–58; see trans. Ware 1966, 237)

Ge Hong calls an excellent teacher an "enlightened master" or *mingshi* 明師, and repeatedly speaks about such a person. He says, for instance:

> If you wish to become a divine immortal (*shenxian* 神仙), you must grasp the essential. The essential consists of treasuring the essence (*baojing* 寶精; see *jing), circulating breath (*xingqi), and ingesting the Great Medicine. In these three, however, there is profundity and shallowness. You cannot learn all about them in a short time unless you meet an enlightened master and go through much hard work. (8.149; see trans. Ware 1966, 138)

Ge Hong's "enlightened master," as depicted in the *Baopu zi*, does not merely imply a wise teacher. As *ming* (enlightened) can mean *sheng* 聖 (saint, or sage) in contrast to *su* 俗 (worldly; Maspero 1933), *mingshi* can be interpreted as a person who is permitted, by means of a pact with the deities, to transmit the Taoist scriptures and techniques (Yoshikawa Tadao 1980). Therefore Ge Hong encourages people to seek an enlightened master, because without one, they cannot be taught the esoteric scriptures and secret teachings. He also says that refining the elixir cannot be easily done without receiving secret teachings from an enlightened master (Ware 1966, 270.)

A master gives this one-to-one transmission, or *shishou* 師受, only to a person in whom he has confidence and who is fit to receive the secret transmission. Ge Hong says that certain alchemical texts and methods must only be transmitted to the wise, even if the master is offered a mountain of gold for their secrets (Ware 1966, 75). The transmission of such texts to someone inferior would bring down heavenly punishment. Fear of the "retribution of

Heaven" is found not only in the *Baopu zi* but also in other Taoist writings from the Six Dynasties. For instance, the **Nüqing guilü* (Demon Statutes of Nüqing; 3.3b) says that Heaven will decrease by 300 the allotment of points that determine the length of life of anyone who shows the scriptures to a lay person or divulges the secret teachings.

MIURA Kunio

📖 Mollier 1990, 117–18; Robinet 1984, 1: 120–21; Robinet 1990a; Seidel 1983a, 327–35 and passim; Stein R. A. 1968; Yoshikawa Tadao 1980; see also bibliography for the entry **TRANSMISSION*

※ LINEAGES; ORDINATION AND PRIESTHOOD; SYNCRETISM; TRANSMISSION

Ordination and priesthood

Taoist ordination developed in the Six Dynasties under the influence of both traditional pledges used for political covenants and membership ceremonies of the Buddhist *saṅgha*. Like the former, it is essentially a rite of cosmic empowerment and change in social status; like the latter, it requires a set number of masters and witnesses, involves the chanting of various ritual incantations, and is formalized through the transference of a new title and a set of religious robes.

The earliest record of a ceremony for the transmission of Taoist scriptures is found in the **Laojun yinsong jiejing* (Scripture on Precepts of Lord Lao, Recited [to the Melody in the Clouds]) of **Kou Qianzhi (365?–448). Here a rite is prescribed that involves the presence of a group of masters and recipients, the formal bowing and performance of obeisances, and the ritual chanting of the precepts (**jie*) as presented in the scripture. The precepts are at the center of the ceremony, and the text explains that they "must always be venerated and treated with great diligence" and should not be transmitted except with the prescribed methods (1a).

Another early glimpse of Taoist ordination is found in the preface to the fourth-century **Laojun shuo yibai bashi jie* (The Hundred and Eighty Precepts Spoken by Lord Lao), recovered from **Dunhuang. The text emphasizes that, in order to receive the precepts, adepts must purify themselves by bathing, abstention from the five pungent vegetables, and changing into fresh clothing. After bowing to their master, they receive the rules by reciting them three times and vowing to observe them. When the transmission is over, adepts obtain the text of the precepts and make one copy so they can venerate the text.

Fig. 1. Zhang Yuanxian 張源先, sixty-fourth Celestial Master (*tianshi), reads an ordination text in Kaohsiung, Taiwan (December 1978). Photograph by Julian Pas.

Fig. 2. As part of the ordination ritual, a candidate must climb a ladder of thirty-six swords and recite texts on top of the ladder. Each blade is "protected" by a paper talisman (*fu). Kaohsiung, Taiwan (December 1978). Photograph by Julian Pas.

More elaborate ordination ceremonies, which more actively integrate Buddhist procedures, appear in Tang-dynasty sources, such as the *Fengdao kejie (Codes and Precepts for Worshipping the Dao) and the Chuanshou sandong jingjie falu lüeshuo 傳授三洞經戒法錄略說 (Synopsis of Transmissions for Scriptures, Precepts, and Liturgical Registers of the Three Caverns; CT 1241; Benn 1991, 148–51), which also specify an integrated ordination or priestly hierarchy. The earliest Taoist ranks known, which became the foundation of the hierarchy, are those of the Way of the Celestial Masters (*Tianshi dao), in which different types and numbers of protective generals are listed in registers and presented to disciples. Ranks here include register disciple (lusheng 錄生), demon trooper (guizu 鬼卒), Dao official (daoguan 道官), and libationer (*jijiu). Anyone holding registers of 150 generals, as described in *Lu Xiujing's *Daomen kelüe (Abridged Codes for the Taoist Community), had to be good, loyal, simple, careful, prudent, diligent, and utterly dedicated to the Dao. They made up the avant-garde of the religion. Another frequently bestowed rank was that of Exalted Mystery (Gaoxuan 高玄), associated with the Daode *jing* and a set of ten precepts, subdivided into three levels, beginning with the status of "disciples of unsullied belief" (*qingxin dizi* 清信弟子; Bokenkamp 1989, 18–20; see also under **jie*).

The integrated ordination system that was dominant throughout the Tang dynasty had eight ranks, which are listed below from lowest to highest:

1. Orthodox Unity (Zhengyi 正一; Celestial Masters)

2. Divine Spells (Shenzhou 神咒)

3. Exalted Mystery (Gaoxuan 高玄)

4. Cavern of Spirit (Dongshen 洞神)

5. Ascension to the Mystery (Shengxuan 昇玄)

6. Cavern of Mystery (Dongxuan 洞玄)

7. Cavern of Perfection (Dongzhen 洞真)

8. Three Caverns (*Sandong 三洞)

As ordinands passed on to higher levels, the requirements became more rigorous, monastic status was essential, and ceremonies grew more intricate. One example of a Cavern of Mystery (i.e., *Lingbao) ceremony is described in great detail in the *Chuanshou sandong jingjie falu lüeshuo* (see Benn 1991), on the occasion of the ordination of the two Tang princesses Gold-Immortal and Jade-Perfected, held in February, 711.

Typically, candidates for ordination were carefully chosen and underwent extended periods of ritual and scriptural training under the guidance of an Ordination Master (*dushi* 度師) with the active support of their families and sponsors from the community. At the time of ordination they would present themselves before three masters—the Ordination Master, the Registration Master (*jishi* 籍師) and the Scripture Master (*jingshi* 經師), five to ten witnesses, a group of officiating priests, and representatives of their families and the community. In various formal rituals, they bid farewell to their fathers and lords, to whom they bowed for the last time; surrendered themselves fully to the Three Treasures of Dao, scriptures, and masters; delivered extensive material pledges to benefit the Taoist community; and vowed to uphold the precepts and faithfully carry out their religious responsibilities.

In return they were equipped with the insignia of their new status: religious names as well as formal titles, vestments (see under **guanfu*), and headdresses. They also received the scriptures and precepts relevant to their new ranks (which they copied within three days of the ceremony, in order to keep one copy with them at all times even to take them to the grave), as well as empowering tokens such as contracts (to identify themselves among the celestial officers), talismans and registers (to control the gods, gain protection, and ensure the correct delivery of memorials; see *FU and *LU), ordinances (to grant free passage on earth and in heaven), and various ritual techniques (spells, incantations, sacred gestures, and so forth).

The fully ordained Taoist was considered a member of the divine rather than the earthly community, and wielded considerable power. No distinction was made in the ranking and empowering of women, whose only special mark was an elaborate headdress, which also gave them the general appellation *nüguan* 女冠 or "female hats."

Livia KOHN

📖 Benn 1991, 72–98; Benn 2000; Despeux 1986; Kohn 2003a; Kohn 2004b; Lagerwey 1987b; Little 2000b, 208–13; Ozaki Masaharu 1986b; Schipper 1978, 376–81; Schipper 1985c; Schipper 1993, 82–88

※ LINEAGES; MONASTIC CODE; MONASTICISM

Syncretism

Taoism took shape through the integration of various trends of thought and religious practice. Unlike Confucians and Buddhists, most Taoists accepted and even asserted this syncretic tendency. This is one of the reasons it is difficult to give Taoism an exact definition. In fact, syncretism enriched Taoism but can also be a source of confusion to its students; some Taoist texts are veritable patchworks resulting from centuries of progressive additions.

Han to Tang. From the Warring States period onward, Taoism inherited not only the texts and thought of the *Daode jing* and the *Zhuangzi*, but also Yin-Yang and *wuxing* cosmology, which provided its conceptual framework. These elements blended with remnants of early myths and with physiological practices dating from the same period. In spite of the scorn shown by the *Daode jing* for Confucian values, some of these too were adopted into Taoist teachings. Legalist features are also apparent in the *Huang-Lao current, which served one of the links between the *Daode jing* and later Taoism.

Taoism inherited a large amount of features from Han religious and intellectual syncretism. Most important among them are the quest for longevity and the variety of related learning and lore, including medicine, alchemy, cosmology, and astrology. The Han "weft texts" (*weishu* 緯書) left traces that still survive in present-day Taoism (see *TAOISM AND THE APOCRYPHA). The *Huainan zi, also a syncretic work, has a strong Taoist flavor. Moreover, the organization of the Han-dynasty Celestial Masters (*Tianshi dao) was modeled on the administration of the empire, and its relation to the gods followed bureaucratic procedures similar to imperial ones. The Celestial Masters adopted the *Daode* *jing* as a book for physical and moral cultivation (see *Xiang'er*), and integrated Confucian virtues into their religion. Their meditation chambers (*jingshi*) replicated the halls used by Confucian literati for reading the classics. In addition, some of the gods of the Celestial Masters originated as popular deities.

During the Six Dynasties, the *Shangqing school harmoniously blended various earlier trends: the legacy of Han cosmology, the Han literary patrimony, some elements borrowed from the Celestial Masters, traces of *Wang Bi's use of the terms *wu and *you* (Non-being and Being). Just as *Ge Hong had done some decades earlier, Shangqing Taoism incorporated the image of the saint (*shengren) found in the *Chuci* 楚辭 (Songs of Chu; trans. Hawkes 1985) and the *Zhuangzi*, along with the *Zhuangzi's* notion of the Dao. The *Lingbao school in turn drew much inspiration from the traditions of Ge Hong, Shangqing, and the Celestial Masters, as well as from certain Confucian traditions. To these it added a real Buddhist influence for the first time in Taoism, especially in its notion of universal salvation (*pudu). The Lingbao cosmology and pantheon were also adapted from Buddhism and earlier Taoism.

The Tang period witnessed close relations among Taoism, Buddhism and Confucianism, and conscious efforts to harmonize the so-called Three Teachings. The Taoist schools of Xiaodao 孝道 (Way of Filiality) and *Jingming dao (Pure and Bright Way) emphasized the Confucian virtues of loyalty and filiality. Taoists, who had already considered the Confucian and Buddhist disciplines as parallel and complementary to their own, began to expand their exchanges with Buddhists. From at least the sixth century onward, some mountains, such as Mount Tai (*Taishan, Shandong), hosted both Taoist and Buddhist communities who lived in harmony with each other. Taoist and Buddhist voices asserted the fundamental identity of their respective goals.

After external religious elements were incorporated from the fifth century onward, cosmological elements coalesced during the Tang period. Taoist texts also began to incorporate Madhyamaka dialectics into a coherent theoretical view of Taoism (see *Chongxuan), and the notion of emptiness evolved in accordance with its Buddhist meaning. A curious combination of Taoism and Buddhism thus developed, which nevertheless remained remarkably true to the Taoist philosophical and religious perspective. The Buddhist theory of the Body of Manifestation (*huashen* 化身, *nirmāṇakāya*) and the Body of Response (*yingshen* 應身, *saṃbhogakāya*) was adopted to explain the multiplicity of teachings, schools, and deities: all teachings are only forms of the formless Ultimate Truth, or the Body of the Law (*fashen* 法身, *dharmakāya*) that cannot be seen or even thought of; all gods are avatars of the Dao or Yuanshi tianzun 元始天尊 (Celestial Worthy of Original Commencement; see *sanqing), taking forms adapted to the circumstances and the capacities of the faithful. Lists of deities were created to synthesize and reorder the pantheon of the Shangqing and Lingbao schools. In spite of these well-intentioned efforts to coordinate different sets of gods, discrepancies appear frequently in both cosmology and the pantheon, and the identities of some divinities are unstable. This, however, did not matter much to the Taoists, as they saw all divinities as only "names" or "traces" and as fundamentally one.

The Song period. During the Song period, with the emergence of Neo-Confucianism—another syncretic movement—Taoist syncretism became deeper and more widespread, mainly in *neidan* and ritual. Most of the Song ritual schools, including the *Shenxiao, *Qingwei, and *Tongchu, assimilated features from the *Zhengyi, Shangqing, and Lingbao schools, the *Daode jing*, and *neidan* and Buddhist Tantric practices. Incorporating earlier doctrines, beliefs, traditions, and ancient masters was in fact a way for these schools to strengthen their authority.

Neidan, which flourished at that time, synthesized Taoist elements (including breathing exercises, *waidan language, and visualizations), Buddhist speculations, Chan didactic methods, and a systematic use of the *Yijing trigrams and hexagrams. *Neidan* sinified the Buddhist dialectic of Non-being and Being, giving it the form of a dialectic between Yin and Yang. Such borrowings were more than conceptual or semantic; *neidan* authors tended to equate the Three Teachings, although at times they emphasized their differences. They claimed that the ultimate goal of the Three Teachings was the same, even though their language and methods differed, on the grounds that Ultimate Truth was beyond all differences and formulations, and that the Three Teachings had the same way to achieve it, namely, through quiescence. Language and images (*xiang) had to be rejected to attain their ultimate meaning, so that the differences among the teachings pertained to the relative truth, not to the ultimate one. The Buddhist system of *panjiao* 判教 (classification of teachings) was applied to explain the differences of meaning carried by a single term; these differences occur within the framework of a didactic procedure that was present in both *neidan* and other teachings. Every teaching is part of the whole unutterable truth. Thus Taoists equated terms pertaining to the Three Teachings, such as Great Ultimate (*taiji), "full awakening" (*yuanjue* 圓覺), Chaos (*hundun), and Golden Elixir (*jindan), or *nirvāṇa* and Dao, in the same way they had done earlier for Taoist alchemical, cosmological and physiological terms. Taoist masters commented on Confucian as well as Buddhist texts for their disciples, and sometimes even explained Confucianism using Buddhist terms. With regard to Neo-Confucian thought, Taoists adopted its new language, referring to such notions as *li* 理 (Principle), or inner nature versus vital force (*xing and *ming). They quoted the traditional Chinese classics and other Confucian or Neo-Confucian texts and authors. Among Buddhist *sūtras*, the *Hṛdaya* (Heart), *Vajracchedikā* (Diamond), *Śūraṃgama* (Heroic Progress), and *Prajñāpāramitā* (Perfection of Wisdom) are the most frequently cited.

Because of the broad use of Buddhist and Confucian notions, the meaning of the terms underwent an evolution. The term *xin (heart-mind and spirit) took on a Buddhist sense. The notion of *xing* as fundamental inner nature lost its original Taoist, Buddhist or Confucian connotations, and was equated with the Dao or with the Mysterious Pass (*xuanguan), which hosts the transcendent and primordial parcel of light (a purely Taoist notion) concealed in all beings.

Isabelle ROBINET

📖 Boltz J. M. 1987a, passim; Liu and Berling 1982; Robinet 1977, 77–95, 117–34, and 191–203; Robinet 1985b; Robinet 1986a; Robinet 1997b, passim; Stein R. A. 1979; Zürcher 1980

※ LINEAGES; TAOISM AND CHINESE BUDDHISM; TAOISM AND CONFUCIANISM; TAOISM AND EARLY CHINESE RELIGION; TAOISM AND EARLY CHINESE THOUGHT; TAOISM AND LOCAL CULTS; TAOISM AND MEDIUM CULTS; TAOISM AND NEO-CONFUCIANISM; TAOISM AND POPULAR RELIGION; TAOISM AND POPULAR SECTS

SCRIPTURES AND TEXTS

Revelations and sacred texts

The status of sacred texts or *jing* 經 (scriptures) in Taoism was theorized and developed in the context of the *Shangqing and *Lingbao revelations. Both schools in turn defined the role of texts according to the *fangshi* lore of Han times and *Ge Hong's tradition in the early Six Dynasties. The function of Taoist scriptures is related to the sacred origin and cosmic value of writing and graphic representation, which is rooted in Chinese antiquity.

The divine nature of Taoist scriptures. In Taoism, sacred texts have a primary meaning and importance, existing prior to the world. They are the condensed form of the Original Pneuma (*yuanqi), spontaneously born from the Void. They are said to have first appeared as rays of light too luminous for the human eye to behold, just as the Ultimate Truth cannot be grasped by thought. Symbolizing the celestial effluvia that come down to earth, they solidified as they descended, congealing into a permanent material form. Thus the scriptures are deemed to be the embodiment and receptacle of the original life force. They first became nebulous "cloud seals" (*yunzhuan* 雲篆) and then were written down in non-human characters of jade on tablets of gold, and stored in celestial palaces or sacred mountains. Their transcription into human writing happened later: over the course of thousands of precosmic eras, they were transmitted only among deities, until at last certain deities revealed them to humanity, or they were discovered in caves.

Although the prototypes of the scriptures remain in Heaven, their human versions are like trails leading to their celestial counterparts. In one of its senses, the word *jing* means "guide" or "way": the scriptures are guides or threads that connect adepts with deities and the Origin of the world. They are auspicious tokens of Heaven's grace, certifying its protection, equivalent in this respect to talismans (*FU) and other symbolic treasures that were owned by ruling families, which attest to Heaven's blessing (see *lingbao).

By unveiling the "real form" (*zhenxing* 真形) or real sound of divine figures and places, the scriptures serve as tools of salvation in two senses. On one hand, they represent a contract with the gods who bestowed them; on the other, they convey the esoteric knowledge of the unseen world, whose hidden form is the real one. The texts embody these "real" forms and sounds, beheld and heard by the highest divinities in their contemplation. In fact, a *jing* often originates as a picture or an invocation. Writing and sound reflect and

Fig. 3. "Primordial graphs" in a revealed text. *Lingbao wuliang duren shangpin miaojing* 靈寶無量度人上品妙經 (Wondrous Scripture of the Upper Chapters of the Numinous Treasure on Limitless Salvation; CT 1), 5.21a.

complement each other: copying a text is a pious act, texts are meant to be present during rituals, and spells must be written down; but texts should also be recited, and their terrestrial recitation is echoed by the deities who chant them in Heaven.

These notions account for the form of the sacred scriptures, which differs not only from the Confucian classics but also from other Taoist writings containing essays or teachings by a known master. The *jing* are either anonymous or ascribed to legendary immortals; they are often cryptic as they contain a secret language, and timeless as they give no indication of historical places or features.

Transmission in the world. Transmission of the sacred scriptures within the human world was subject to specific rules, which the Shangqing school was the first to emphasize. These ritual rules of transmission were later codified in bureaucratic form. The scriptures were to be transmitted from master to disciple after a fast that lasted several days. The two parties swore a covenant (*meng* 盟) after performing a rite inspired by ancient ceremonies of consecration and feudal bonding, in which gods and spirits were invited as witnesses. The disciple gave gifts to his master as tokens of sincerity, called *xin* 信 (pledges). Rings and seals were broken in two parts, and master and disciple each retained one half, thus reproducing the ancient tesserae (*fu*) used in contracts.

Above all, disciples swore never to reveal the scriptures to the uninitiated. A text could be transmitted only to those who were worthy of receiving it, who were predestined to immortality, and whose names were inscribed in the celestial registers. Receiving a text was thus an assurance of one's qualification for immortality. Legitimate possessors of a scripture gained with it divine protection of jade boys and jade women (*yunü) who watched over the book and its holder. The possession of a text also implied duties: adepts paid homage to it and practiced the methods that it contained. On the other hand, improperly obtaining a text amounted to "stealing a treasure from Heaven" and nullified its power.

The sacred text resolved the issue of the relation between innate predestination (adepts must have their name inscribed in the heavens in order to obtain immortality) and practice, and also between what later was called subitaneous (dun 頓) and gradual (jian 漸) awakening. Moreover, in the Shangqing school the sacred text played the same role the master had in earlier Taoist traditions. The real guide was now the scripture, and its increased importance marked the evolution of Taoism from an oral to a written tradition. Even the "oral instructions" (koujue 口訣), originally given only in speech, often were written down in later times. In this context, the master became no more that a guarantor of the legitimacy of the transmission. He did not officiate, and the methods did not bear his name as they had in ancient times. He served as a link in the chain that, through the scriptures, connected a lineage of human beings to Heaven.

Isabelle ROBINET

📖 Bokenkamp 1997, 188–94; Campany 1993, 21–25; Kamitsuka Yoshiko 1999, 361–414; Kohn 1993b, 35–43; Lagerwey 1981b, 104–35; Robinet 1984, 1: 107–23; Robinet 1993: 19–28; Seidel 1989–90, 250–54

※ SCRIPTURE AND EXEGESIS; TRANSMISSION

Scripture and exegesis

"Scripture" is a Western term usually applied to the Bible as revered by the Jews and by Christians (Smith W. C. 1993, x), and must be applied to traditions like Taoism with caution. Laurence Thompson (1985, 204) has argued that the term scripture, when defined as text with religious authority that is "subject to exegesis but not criticism," applies to many but not all texts in the Taoist Canon. Since the *Daode jing*, the exegetical enterprise has been an important feature of Taoism, as commentaries and revision of a continuously expanding core of scripture has been one of the central means by which subtraditions invented and renewed themselves.

The use of the term scripture in the Taoist context requires attention to the differences in canon formation in Western and Asian contexts. In his comparative study of Confucian and Western exegesis, John B. Henderson observes that the Chinese model is perhaps more similar to the Hindu distinction between *śruti* (revealed scripture) and *smṛti* (explanations of saints and prophets). Borrowing Wang Chong's 王充 (27–ca. 100 CE) distinction between the *jing* 經 (classics, or scriptures) of the *shengren (sages) and the commentaries of the *xianren* 賢人 (worthies), Henderson notes that in China the hierarchical distinction between classic and commentary is made "according to their respective sources" (1991, 71).

While the silk manuscript versions interred at *Mawangdui in 168 BCE do not identify the work attributed to Laozi as a *jing*, the bibliographic survey of the *Hanshu* (History of the Former Han; ca. 90 CE) does list several versions of the scripture with different types of exegesis. Among them are two lost works in *jingshuo* 經說 (scripture and explanation) format attributed to a Mister Fu (Fu shi 傅氏) and a Xu Shaoji 徐少季 (30.1729). This and the ascription of supernatural characteristics to Laozi in Han texts like the *Shiji* (Records of the Historian; ca. 100 BCE) show that the text was a "scripture" by the early Han dynasty at the latest. If two chapters of the late Warring States *Han Feizi* 韓非子 (ca. 240 BCE) dedicated to explaining and illustrating the *Daode jing* are authentic (Liao 1939–59, 1: 169–227), then it may have had that status earlier. Soon afterward, the text was used as a religious scripture, chanted for its magical efficacy by the early *Tianshi dao (Way of the Celestial Masters; Kohn 1998h, 145). Several of the earliest commentaries on the text were preserved in the *Dunhuang caves and rediscovered at the start of the twentieth century (Kusuyama Haruki 1992, 3–63), and more than sixty others are preserved in the Taoist Canon.

While many titles in the Canon besides the *Daode jing* are classified as *jing*, many of these "classics" or "scriptures" do not have a history of exegesis. By contrast, some texts not usually labelled *jing* have commentaries in the Canon. Examples of the latter are the commentaries to the Warring States military classic *Sunzi* 孫子 (Book of Master Sun) and the alchemical classic *Zhouyi cantong qi (Token for the Agreement of the Three According to the Book of Changes). Other texts, like the Warring States *Nanhua zhenjing* 南華真經 (Authentic Scripture of Southern Florescence, usually known as the *Zhuangzi) and the composite *Chongxu zhide zhenjing* 沖虛至德真經 (Authentic Scripture on the Ultimate Virtue of Unfathomable Emptiness, usually known as the *Liezi), were made canonical and given the status of *jing* by imperial fiat during the Tang dynasty. Other classics with numerous commentaries in the Canon include the *Yinfu jing (Scripture of the Hidden Accordance), the *Duren jing (Scripture on Salvation), and the *Qingjing jing (Scripture of Clarity and

Quiescence). The combination of pre-Qin works with Song works indicates that there is no single criterion of authorship or period that determines what works are considered either as *jing* or as worthy of commentary.

The nature of Taoist exegesis changed over time, in many ways consistent with changes in the Chinese exegetical tradition as a whole. Taking the *Daode jing* as an example, the readings of various commentators reflect a wide variety of points of view. The Song master Zhao Shi'an 趙實菴 (fl. 1152) distinguished three major concerns against which it had been read: non-action, longevity, and politics. It was also widely commented on by Buddhists and Confucians. This variety of exegesis has led some to distinguish Taoist exegesis from the rest of the exegetical tradition. Isabelle Robinet has observed Taoist texts "took their authority from revelation, which gave them an original stature and released them from dependence on their antecedents. . . . It also explains why [they] could have been commented on by people of such diverse orientations" (1999b, 154–55).

Mark CSIKSZENTMIHALYI

📖 Henderson 1991; Kohn 1992b; Kohn 1998e; Robinet 1984, 1: 107–22 and 193–94; Robinet 1993, 19–28; Robinet 1997b, 125–28; Thompson 1985; Wu Kuang-ming 2000

※ DAOZANG AND SUBSIDIARY COMPILATIONS; REVELATIONS AND SACRED TEXTS; TRANSMISSION

Daozang and subsidiary compilations

What has popularly come to be known as the *Daozang* 道藏 (Taoist Canon) is indisputably the foremost body of texts for research in the field of Taoist studies. The Ming Canon of 1445, or so-called **Zhengtong daozang* (Taoist Canon of the Zhengtong Reign Period), lies at the heart of all modern editions of the Canon. Its origins are closely linked to catalogues of Taoist writings prepared more than a millennium earlier. Canonic collections to which the Ming Canon is heir were produced under Tang, Song, Jurchen, and Mongol rulerships.

To some extent, each successive Canon may be regarded as the result of a working relationship between church and state. Both parties may very well have had particular needs in mind but if there was any motivation uniting them on this mission, it would have been the desire for ritual order. By joining forces to define a Taoist Canon imperial and clerical leaders could exercise their respective powers of regulatory control. Like all such endeavors, the compilation of every Canon in turn allowed the demarcation of textual authority to be established anew.

Later collections of texts derived from the *Zhengtong daozang* obviously narrow its boundaries. Those that stand in supplement to it alternatively offer an expansion of canonic limits. All such anthologies, as well as bibliographic guides to the Canon itself, serve to make the vast textual heritage of Taoist teachings more accessible.

Catalogues and Canons through the Ming. There is as yet no definitive study tracing the history of the *Daozang*. Canonic compilations prior to the Tang are particularly difficult to document, owing to disparate accounts found in a variety of texts ranging from Buddhist polemical writings to historical and topographical works. One of the more frequently cited resources is a stele inscription dating to 1275, but certain portions of this text remain to be verified. A copy of the inscription is appended to the *Daozang quejing mulu* (Index of Scriptures Missing from the Taoist Canon), presumably compiled by the editors of the Ming Canon. The anonymous text is entitled *Daozang zunjing lidai gangmu* 道藏尊經歷代綱目 (Historical Survey of the Revered Scriptures of the Taoist Canon). It will serve here as an anchor for the summary of the early history of the Canon that follows.

The origins of the Ming Canon are commonly traced to the editorial endeavors of *Lu Xiujing (406–77), codifier of the *Lingbao corpus. His preface to the *Lingbao jingmu (Catalogue of Lingbao Scriptures) dates to 437. The catalogue he reportedly submitted to Song Mingdi (r. 465–72) in 471 is assumed to be what is known as the *Sandong jingshu mulu (Index of Scriptures and Writings of the Three Caverns). A collection of texts collated under the supervision of the Director of the Bureau of Evaluation in 471 is said to have been approximately a third of the size of that catalogued by Lu.

The titles of two catalogues are dated to the time of Zhou Wudi (r. 560–78). Buddhist accounts speak of a *Xuandu [guan] jing mu[lu]* 玄都[觀]經目[錄] (Index of the Scriptures of the [Abbey of the] Mysterious Metropolis), produced in 569 at the *Xuandu guan (Abbey of the Mysterious Metropolis) in the capital of Chang'an (Shaanxi). Taoist writings speak of a *[Sandong] zhunang [jingmu]* [三洞]珠囊[經目] ([Catalogue of the Scriptures in] the Pearl Satchel [of the Three Caverns]), produced in 574 at the *Tongdao guan (Abbey of the Pervasive Way) in Chang'an.

By the next century, during the early Tang period, additional catalogues of Taoist texts appear to have been compiled in succession. *Yin Wencao (622–88) is credited with a *Yuwei jingmu* 玉緯經目 (Catalogue of the Scriptures of the Jade Weft Texts). Although there is no apparent trace of this text, the compilation of an *Yiqie daojing mu* 一切道經目 (Catalogue of the Complete Taoist Scriptures) is confirmed by the extant prefaces of the compiler Shi Chongxuan 史崇玄 (or Shi Chong 史崇, ?–713) and Tang Xuanzong (r. 712–56). Another catalogue, also lost, accompanied what came to be known as the *Kaiyuan* *daozang* 開元道藏 (Taoist Canon of the Kaiyuan Reign Period), in reference to the reign period (713–41) during which it was compiled. Entitled *Sandong qionggang (Exquisite Compendium of the Three Caverns), this catalogue is ascribed to a Taoist Master named Zhang Xianting 張仙庭. Neither catalogue nor Canon is thought to have survived the An Lushan 安祿山 and Shi Siming 史思明 uprisings of 755–63. Later efforts to recompile a Canon apparently met a similar fate following the Huang Chao 黃巢 rebellion of 874–84.

Three canonic compilations of significance arose during the Song. A comprehensive search and collation of texts began in the year 990, at the command of Song Taizong (r. 976–97). The catalogue to this initial Canon of the Song bore the title *Sandong sifu jingmu* 三洞四輔經目 (Catalogue of the Scriptures of the Three Caverns and Four Supplements). By 1009, Song Zhenzong (r. 997–1022) had authorized a new recension of the Canon. Seven years later the Minister of Rites *Wang Qinruo (962–1025) presented the emperor with a catalogue entitled *Baowen tonglu* 寶文統錄 (Comprehensive Register of Precious Literature). The Canon of 1016 came to be known as the *Da Song Tiangong baozang* (Precious Canon of the Celestial Palace of the Great Song). The successor to this Canon is the *Zhenghe Wanshou daozang* (Taoist Canon of the Ten-Thousand-Fold Longevity of the Zhenghe Reign Period). Compiled under the aegis of Song Huizong (r. 1100–1125), it is the first Taoist Canon to have been produced in print. Approximately 70,000 blocks were cut for this Canon, a task apparently not completed until 1119 in Fuzhou (Fujian), a major publication center at that time.

The Canon of 1119 served as the foundation for a new compilation undertaken in 1190 by the authority of the Jurchen ruler Zhangzong (r. 1190–1208). Completed in 1192, the *Da Jin Xuandu baozang* (Precious Canon of the Mysterious Metropolis of the Great Jin) provided in turn the backbone for a Canon edited under the direction of the *Quanzhen patriarch *Song Defang (1183–1247). It was replaced in 1244 by the [*Da Yuan*] *Xuandu baozang* (Precious Canon of the Mysterious Metropolis). Although Khubilai khan (r. 1260–94) later ordered the destruction of both texts and printing blocks of this Canon, small components of it have rather miraculously survived.

The so-called *Zhengtong daozang*, or *Da Ming daozang jing* 大明道藏經 (Scriptures of the Taoist Canon of the Great Ming), may be regarded as the culmination of Taoist canonic compilations undertaken within the imperial age of China. The forty-third Celestial Master *Zhang Yuchu (1361–1410) served as the initial editor, by the command of the Yongle Emperor (r. 1403–24). It was only by the grace of his great-grandson the Zhengtong Emperor (r. 1436–49) that publication of the Ming Canon was finally accomplished in 1445. An addendum to the some 1400 titles in this Canon was completed in 1607. This supplemental collection of some fifty titles is given the title *Da Ming xu daozang* *jing* 大明續道藏經 (Scriptures in Supplement to the Taoist Canon of the Great Ming). It is more popularly known as the *Wanli xu daozang (Supplementary Taoist Canon of the Wanli Reign Period), in reference to its compilation by order of the Wanli Emperor (r. 1573–1620). The responsibility for it fell to the fiftieth Celestial Master *Zhang Guoxiang (?–1611).

Modern editions. Access to the Ming Canon remained limited until the Hanfen lou 涵芬樓 branch of the Commercial Press in Shanghai issued a thread-bound edition in 1923–26. The former Minister of Education Fu Zengxiang 傅增湘 (1872–1950) played a major role in the achievement of this landmark in publication. His persuasive endorsement of the academic value of the Canon convinced President Xu Shichang 徐世昌 (1855–1939) to authorize a government subsidy for the project.

The copy of the Ming Canon photolithographically reproduced in 1,120 threadbound fascicles by Hanfen lou came from the *Baiyun guan (Abbey of the White Clouds) in Beijing. Missing portions of it are known to have been replaced in 1845. Reprints of the Hanfen lou edition have made the Ming Canon even more accessible, beginning with the threadbound copy issued in 1962 by the Yiwen 藝文 Publishing House in Taipei. Among the more widely available editions in modern binding is the 60-volume *Zhengtong daozang* produced by the same publishing house in 1977. Another edition, the 36-volume *Daozang*, appeared in 1988 as a joint publication of Wenwu chubanshe 文物出版社 in Beijing, the Shanghai shudian 上海書店, and the Tianjin guji chubanshe 天津古籍出版社. This new edition overcomes a number of defects in earlier editions, replacing missing texts as well as correcting misplacements, but it also retains and introduces new defects.

A reorganized, punctuated edition of the Taoist Canon is now in print. Intermittent reports on this team effort began to appear as early as 1997 in *Zhongguo daojiao* 中國道教 (Chinese Taoism), a publication of the *Zhongguo daojiao xiehui (Chinese Taoist Association) headquartered at the Baiyun guan in Beijing. The final product is the 49-volume *Zhonghua daozang* 中華道藏 (Taoist Canon of China) published by Huaxia chubanshe in 2003.

Indices. Available indices are not in agreement on the total number of titles contained in the Ming Canon. This discrepancy primarily reflects the occasional difficulty in determining where one text ends and the next begins. The earliest annotated table of contents to the Ming Canon, the *Daozang mulu xiangzhu* (Detailed Commentary on the Index of the Taoist Canon) ascribed to Bai Yunji 白雲霽, dates to 1626. It has been superceded by the *Daozang zimu yinde* 道藏子目引得 (Combined Indices to the Authors and Titles of Books in Two Collections of Taoist Literature), compiled in 1935 by Weng Dujian 翁獨健. This volume in the Harvard-Yenching Institute Sinological Index

Series lists altogether 1476 titles in the *Daozang* and indicates which texts are also found in the *Daozang jiyao* (Essentials of the Taoist Canon) of 1906. An additional list of the texts recorded in the *Daozang jiyao* alone is followed by indices to both titles and compilers. The closing index to biographies is keyed to seventy-seven hagiographic resources in the Canon.

An index volume accompanying the 60-volume edition of the *Zhengtong daozang* lists altogether 1487 titles in the Canon. Li Diankui 李殿魁 is responsible for this reedition of the *Concordance du Tao-tsang* compiled under the direction of Kristofer Schipper in 1975. The editors of the *Daozang tiyao* 道藏提要 (A Conspectus of the Taoist Canon), Ren Jiyu 任繼愈 and Zhong Zhaopeng 鍾肇鵬, alternatively list a total of 1473 titles in the Canon. This collection of abstracts for all texts in the Canon also includes a supplement of brief biographical accounts on compilers cited. Another comprehensive guide to the Canon has been under preparation since 1979, with the establishment of the "Projet Tao-tsang" under the auspices of the European Science Foundation. The results of this massive collaborative enterprise, edited by Kristofer Schipper and Franciscus Verellen, have been published in 2004 by the University of Chicago Press under the title *The Taoist Canon: A Historical Companion to the Daozang*.

The recently published *Xinbian daozang mulu* 新編道藏目錄 (A Newly-Compiled Index to the Taoist Canon) compiled by Zhong Zhaopeng (1999) presents a reorganized table of contents to the Canon. This two-volume threadbound publication lists a total of 1527 titles under six major headings and twenty-two subheadings. Recorded under each title are the fascicle number(s) in the Hanfen lou edition and volume number(s) in the 60-volume Yiwen edition. The few editorial notes recorded after this data in some entries offer clarifications of provenance. The appearance of the 1988 edition late in the course of his work on this index led the compiler to add a chart listing the fascicle numbers of the Hanfen lou edition in correspondence with its thirty-six volumes (labelled *Sanjia ben* 三家本). The second volume of this publication contains indices to compilers and titles.

Subsidiary compilations. The *Daozang jiyao* mentioned above is by far the largest of anthologies chiefly derived from the Ming Canon. Other collections of note include the *Daoshu shi'er zhong (Twelve Books on the Dao), the *Daozang jinghua (Essential Splendors of the Taoist Canon), and the *Daozang jinghua lu (Record of the Essential Splendors of the Taoist Canon). Publications that go beyond the Canon include the *Daozang xubian (Sequel to the Taoist Canon), the *Zhuang-Lin xu daozang (Supplementary Taoist Canon of Zhuang[-Chen Dengyun] and Lin [Rumei]), and the *Zangwai daoshu (Taoist Texts Outside the Canon).

Specialized publications not to be overlooked include the collections of texts pertinent to the Taoist heritage that have been recovered from *Dunhuang

(Gansu) as well as from archaeological sites such as *Mawangdui (Hunan) and *Guodian (Hubei). In addition to the *Tonkō dōkyō* 敦煌道經 (Taoist Scriptures from Dunhuang) compiled by Ōfuchi Ninji 大淵忍爾 (Ōfuchi Ninji 1978–79) there is now in print a five-volume *Dunhuang daozang* 敦煌道藏 (Taoist Canon of Dunhuang) edited by Li Defan 李德范 (1999). The study of Taoist institutional history should also be enhanced by the recent publication of a 36-volume *Zhongguo daoguan zhi congkan* 中國道觀志叢刊 (Collectanea of Monographs of Taoist Temples in China), edited by Gao Xiaojian 高小健 (2000). This publication will not only supplement monastic records in the Taoist Canon but also surely offer further supplement to the invaluable yet still largely overlooked *Daojia jinshi lüe* 道家金石略 (A Collection of Taoist Epigraphy) compiled by Chen Yuan 陳垣 (1988). The recent appearance of so many new resources is truly without precedent in the field of Taoist studies.

Judith M. BOLTZ

📖 Bokenkamp 2001; Boltz J. M. 1987a, 247–50; Boltz J. M. 1987c; Boltz J. M. 1993b; Boltz J. M. 1994; Chen Guofu 1963, 106–231; Chen Yuan 1988, 618; Fukui Kōjun 1958, 134–213; Lagerwey 1981b, 222–73; Liu Ts'un-yan 1982; van der Loon 1984, 29–63; Ōfuchi Ninji 1979; Ōfuchi Ninji 1991, 217–58; Ren Jiyu and Zhong Zhaopeng 1991; Schipper 1975b; Schipper and Verellen 2004; Seidel 1989–90, 231–36; Shi Bo'er and Li Diankui 1977; Weng Dujian 1935; Yoshioka Yoshitoyo 1955; Zhong Zhaopeng 1993; Zhong Zhaopeng 1999; Zhu Yueli 1992, 123–72 and 311–60; Zhu Yueli 1996

※ For related entries see the Synoptic Table of Contents, sec. II.12 ("Textual Corpora and Literary Genres")

sandong

三洞

Three Caverns

The term *sandong* refers to the three major components of the Taoist Canon (see table 18): Dongzhen 洞真 (Cavern of Perfection), Dongxuan 洞玄 (Cavern of Mystery), and Dongshen 洞神 (Cavern of Spirit). These three units came to be identified with the scriptural legacies of *Shangqing (Highest Clarity), *Lingbao (Numinous Treasure), and *Sanhuang 三皇 (Three Sovereigns; see *Sanhuang wen*), respectively. Although the designation of the Buddhist Canon as *sanzang* 三藏 (Tripiṭaka), denoting three genres of *sūtra*, *vinaya*, and *abhidharma*, would appear to be its obvious parallel, the term *sandong* in reference to the Taoist Canon has never been applied to separate genres of writing. It corresponds more readily to the Buddhist concept of *sansheng* 三乘 (Three Vehicles), denoting separate schools of teachings. There is as yet no definitive study tracing the history of the concept of *sandong* as an organizing principle behind the compilation of the Taoist Canon. The legacy of this term remains problematic in part owing to variant, sometimes conflicting, accounts contained in both the Taoist and the Buddhist Canon.

The term *sandong* is notably absent from the inventory of *Zheng Yin's (ca. 215–ca. 302) library that his disciple *Ge Hong (283–343) provides in the *Baopu zi* (Book of the Master Who Embraces Simplicity). A passage from the *Sanhuang jing* 三皇經 (Scripture of the Three Sovereigns) recorded in the late sixth-century *Wushang biyao* (Supreme Secret Essentials, 6.5a-b; Lagerwey 1981b, 82) identifies the *sanhuang* trinity as the *zunshen* 尊神 (venerable deities) of *sandong*. The *qi*, or life-force, of *sandong* is defined as the condensed transformation of the *sanyuan* (Three Primes): Tianbao jun 天寶君 (Lord of Celestial Treasure), Lingbao jun 靈寶君 (Lord of Numinous Treasure) and Shenbao jun 神寶君 (Lord of Divine Treasure). The three deities Tianhuang 天皇, Dihuang 地皇, and Renhuang 人皇, in turn, are equated with the life-force of Dadong 大洞 (Great Cavern), Dongxuan, and Dongshen, respectively.

The *Shengshen jing (Scripture of the Life-Giving Spirits; CT 318, 1a-b) names the three lords of the *sanyuan* trinity as the *zunshen* of Dadong, Dongxuan, and Dongshen. No correspondence to *sanhuang* is acknowledged in this central scripture of the Lingbao corpus codified by *Lu Xiujing (406–77). The designation *Sandong dizi* 三洞弟子 (Disciple of the Three Caverns) notably precedes Lu's name, as the author of the *Lingbao jingmu xu* 靈寶經目序 (Preface to a Catalogue of Lingbao Scriptures). It is recorded in the eleventh-century *Yunji qiqian* (Seven Lots from the Bookbag of the Clouds, 4.4a), with a date of Yuanjia 元嘉 14 (437). An entry for this title in one *juan* registered in the inventory of the Song imperial library would seem to indicate that a copy of the catalogue intact with preface survived into the early twelfth century. The extant preface itself makes no reference to *sandong*. Lu does allude to a collective conferral of the *sandong* in the declaration preceding his guide to ordination (*Lingbao shoudu yi, biao* 表, 2a).

Lu Xiujing is widely credited with compiling a *Sandong jingshu mulu (Index of Scriptures and Writings of the Three Caverns). It is remarkable that no Song library catalogue lists this text. The catalogue of scriptures that Lu is said to have submitted in 471, according to pre-Song Buddhist polemical treatises, is generally assumed to have borne this title. The earliest apparent reference to this title in the name of Master Lu 陸先生 occurs in the *Daojiao yishu (Pivot of Meaning of the Taoist Teaching; 2.3b), compiled ca. 700 by Meng Anpai 孟安排. This text echoes the *Shengshen jing* passage on guardians of the Three Caverns, with Dongzhen replacing Dadong as the heading for the Shangqing corpus centering on the *Dadong zhenjing*. Here the heritage of the Three Caverns is presented as a unified, single Great Vehicle (*tongyi dasheng* 同一大乘).

An alternative, hierarchical, perception of the Three Caverns is conveyed in a presumably earlier text, noted for its transcript of an exchange between Tang Tianhuang 唐天皇 (i.e., Gaozong, r. 649–83) and *Pan Shizheng (585–682) at Zhongyue 中嶽, i.e., Mount Song (*Songshan, Henan). In this anonymous compilation, the *Daomen jingfa xiangcheng cixu* 道門經法相承次序 (The Scriptures and Methods of Taoism in Orderly Sequence; CT 1128, 1.1b–2a), Dongzhen, Dongxuan, and Dongshen are designated *dasheng* 大乘 (Great Vehicle), *zhongsheng* 中乘 (Middle Vehicle), and *xiasheng* 下乘 (Lower Vehicle), respectively. Competition from Buddhist schools of teachings could very well have led to abandonment of this stratification of scriptural categories in favor of a unified presentation of disparate teachings. Both views are represented with no apparent conflict in lengthy accounts on the history of *sandong* in the *Yunji qiqian* (3.4a–7b; 6.1a–12a).

Judith M. BOLTZ

📖 Bokenkamp 1997, 190–94; Bokenkamp 2001; Chen Guofu 1963, 1–4, 106–7; Fukui Kōjun 1958, 138–70; Kohn 1993b, 65–71; Lagerwey 1981b, 24–26, 82; van der Loon 1984, 171; Ōfuchi Ninji 1979; Ōfuchi Ninji 1997, 12–72 (= 1964, 217–76); Ozaki Masaharu 1983b, 75–88; Pregadio 2006b, 43–47, 152–55; Qing Xitai 1988–95, 1: 536–52; Robinet 1984, 1: 75–85 and 195–97; Zhu Yueli 1992, 173–80

※ Sanqing; *Sandong jingshu mulu*; COSMOGONY; DAOZANG AND SUBSIDIARY COMPILATIONS

fu

符

talisman, tally, charm

Taoist talismans are diagrams, conceived as a form of celestial writing, that derive their power from the matching celestial counterpart kept by the deities who bestowed them. Known also as *qi* 契 (or 栔) or *quan* 券, tallies were used in pre-Han China to verify written orders of the king and as contracts and signs of authority held by the king's vassals. Authentication was achieved by joining the two split halves of the tally. From this mundane use, the term *fu* came to be applied to omens of divine approbation authenticating a ruler's receipt of the mandate to rule, known as *fuming* 符命. Taoist talismans derive

Fig. 4. Taoist Master Chen Rongsheng 陳榮盛 writes a talisman in his
Tainan, Taiwan, home office (January 1979). Photograph by Julian Pas.

both from this tradition and from the medical use of *fu* to bind demons and
cure disease.

The most influential Taoist account of the origins of *fu*, found in the
*Zhengao, relates them to a primordial form of writing that emerged with the
differentiation of the Dao at the birth of the cosmos, still used by the highest gods and available to humans who have received them through proper
transmission. The earliest script, the Writing of the Three Primes and Eight
Conjunctions (*sanyuan bahui zhi shu* 三元八會之書), later became fragmented
and simplified into various mortal scripts. The second primordial script, the
Cloud-seal Emblems of the Eight Dragons (*balong yunzhuan zhi zhang* 八龍雲
篆之章), remained unchanged and is the form used in *fu*. The name given this
script seems to imply that the odd "graphs" inscribed on Taoist talismans were
fashioned to resemble ancient, supposedly purer, forms of Chinese graphs,
known as "seal script."

Generally written in vermilion or black ink on rectangular pieces of wood,
bamboo, silk, stone, or paper, talismans often do include recognizable symbols
and words, but they are not meant to be read by humans. Legible only to
the gods, they give power over troops of divine protectors, both within and
without the body. The ritual uses of *fu* are many. The early Celestial Masters
healed the sick through submission of confessional petitions and the ingestion
of water into which the ashes of burned talismans had been mixed. In other
cases, they were ingested whole with honey. Talismans were used to mark
sacred space and represent the cycles of sacred time. As protective amulets,

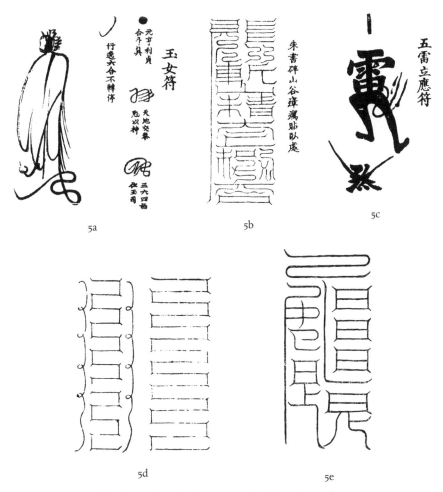

Fig. 5. Examples of talismans (see also figs. 18, 53 and 73).

(a) Talisman of the Jade Women, in *Wushang xuanyuan santian Yutang dafa* 無上玄元三天玉堂大法 (Great Rites of the Jade Hall of the Three Heavens, of the Supreme Mysterious Origin; CT 220), 21.5b.

(b) Talisman for Removing the Miasma of Mountains and Valleys, in *Lingbao wuliang duren shangpin miaojing* 靈寶無量度人上品妙經 (Wondrous Scripture of the Upper Chapters of the Numinous Treasure on Limitless Salvation; CT 1), 45.13b. See comments in Chen Hsiang-ch'un 1942, 47–48.

(c) A "Thunder talisman," in *Fahai yizhu* 法海遺珠 (Uncollected Pearls from the Ocean of Rituals; CT 1166), 23.7b.

(d) Talisman for Expelling the Demons (on the right, a variant of its inner part), in *Huangdi jiuding shendan jingjue* 黃帝九鼎神丹經訣 (Instructions on the Scripture of the Divine Elixirs of the Nine Tripods of the Yellow Emperor; CT 885; see *Jiudan jing*), 5.9a–10a.

(e) Talisman for Entering a Mountain, in *Baopu zi*, j. 17.

they might be ingested or worn on the person when engaging in ritual or prior to encountering danger. They were held to reveal the true forms of deities or to serve as passports that might aid the passage from the earth-prisons of the dead, who received them in spiritual form after ritual burning. As aids in meditation, *fu* might bring the user face to face with a deity or reveal the inner workings of the cosmos. Finally, in ritual, *fu* are not always written, but might be inscribed in the air with sword, staff, or thunderblock, and activated by breath-magic.

Whole scriptures were created with talismans as their centerpiece. Such, for instance, is the case with the *Lingbao wufu xu* (Prolegomena to the Five Talismans of the Numinous Treasure), the *Wupian zhenwen* (Perfected Script in Five Tablets), and the *Wucheng fu* 五稱符 (Five Talismans of Correspondence) of the ancient *Lingbao scriptures, as well as with the *Lingbao suling zhenfu* 靈寶素靈真符 (Authentic Talismans of the Immaculate Numen of the Numinous Treasure) transmitted by *Du Guangting. In these cases, the primordial divine form of the scripture was said to reside in the talismans themselves. The scripture that contains them only recounts their origin and uses. The centrality of these useful divine "texts" can be seen in the fact that the twelve traditional generic subdivisions of each "cavern" (see *SANDONG) of the Taoist Canon listed "Divine Talismans" (*shenfu* 神符) second, right after "Basic Texts" (*benwen* 本文; see table 27). Consequently, all ritual compendia came to contain talismans, as well as directions for their writing and use. The rigor Taoists showed in transmitting and inscribing talismans can be seen in how extremely well examples found in the *Dunhuang manuscripts or archeologically excavated accord with those printed in the Ming canon.

Related forms of divine writing, not always easy to distinguish from *fu*, are known by a variety of names, including "cloud seal-script," "secret language of the Great Brahmā" (*dafan yinyu*) and "registers" (*LU). Various forms of charts (*tu* 圖) also function as talismans, though they are separately listed in Taoist bibliographies.

Stephen R. BOKENKAMP

📖 Campany 2002, 61–69; Chen Hsiang-ch'un 1942; Despeux 2000a; Drexler 1994; Harper 1998, 179–83 and 301; Lagerwey 1981b, 106–10; Lagerwey 1986; Legeza 1975; Little 2000b, 201–7; des Rotours 1952; Seidel 1983a; Strickmann 2002, 123–93 and passim; Wang Yucheng 1996; Wang Yucheng 1999

※ LU

lu

錄

register

In Taoism the term "register" refers to records that identify an individual either in this world or in the otherworld, and to lists of deities and supernatural beings over which an initiate has command. Texts listing demon names have been found in a Shuihudi 睡虎地 (Hubei) tomb dated to 217 BCE (Harper 1985). Their symbolism and meaning anticipates their usage in both Taoist religion and in Chinese tales of the otherworld; in particular, these documents are related to the belief that one can control demons and spirits simply by knowing their names. Later Han dynasty tomb texts also mention registers of life and death (Seidel 1987e), foreshadowing another Taoist *topos*.

During the Han dynasty, registers were also one of many items bestowed by Heaven signaling the mandate to rule. Begun in the Zhou period, religious legitimation was granted with the appearance of special objects and was gradually replaced with written documents and diagrams (see *lingbao*, and *TAOISM AND THE APOCRYPHA*). Wang Mang (r. 9–23) tapped into this tradition, using texts to validate the establishment of his own dynasty and to legitimize his control of the throne. In his *Dongjing fu* 東京賦 (Rhapsody on the Eastern Capital), Zhang Heng 張衡 (78–139; IC 211–12) describes the bestowal of registers and charts on Gaozu (r. 202–195 BCE), the founder of the Han dynasty, at his investiture (Knechtges 1982–96, 1: 245). Both registers and charts were later bestowed on Taoist masters during their ordination rituals.

Registers in Taoist traditions. Registers were the earliest documents of the Celestial Masters (*Tianshi dao). Their maintenance was crucial for the religious and social organization of the church. The Celestial Masters, heading a theocracy in the second century Sichuan area, kept records of all births, deaths, and marriages, using them to determine taxes and corvée labor requirements. As copies of these records were also kept in the otherworld, it behooved the populace to update them periodically. Any mistake might lead to the ineffectiveness of deities to aid the living in healing rituals, or to being summoned to the world of the dead prematurely: during the Six Dynasties, many tales circulated concerning mistaken summons to the otherworld due to errors in the registers of life and death. To update the registers, the Celestial Masters held three

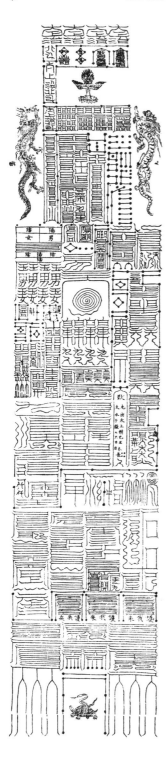

assemblies a year (*sanhui*), during which the otherworldly officials also congregated to correct and collate their copies of these records. Registers were just as important in later Taoist traditions. To become a transcendent in the *Shangqing tradition, one's name had to be inscribed in the celestial registers (Bokenkamp 1997, 355–60); in the *Lingbao tradition, rituals were timed to coincide with these celestial assemblies.

The registers kept in the otherworld also recorded one's misdeeds. The *Taiping jing* (Scripture of Great Peace), a second-century text associated with another religious movement of the Han dynasty, describes registers of misdeeds that adversely affect the length of one's life span. Both the Shangqing and Lingbao traditions inherited the notion of registers of life and death, but the number of gods in charge of monitoring human behavior increased. These registers and the idea that one's actions affect these otherworldly records appear throughout Taoist scriptures and in Six Dynasties *zhiguai* 志怪 tales ("records of the strange").

Beginning with the Celestial Masters tradition, registers also listed protective deities. During the transmission of a scripture, the adept swore a covenant (*meng* 盟), recalling the bond forged between lord and vassal. This use and role of registers was replaced in the Shangqing tradition by the possession, knowledge, and use of revealed

Fig. 6. Great Register of the Most High Orthodox Unity for Removing Evil (*Taishang zhengyi bixie dalu* 太上正一辟邪大籙). *Sanwu zhengyi mengwei lu* 三五正一盟威籙 (Register of the Covenant with the Powers of Orthodox Unity of the Three and Five; CT 1208), 6.10b–13a.

Fig. 7. Ordination certificate bestowed in 1981. Reproduced with
permission of Princeton University Press from Dean 1993, 54.

scriptures. Later, the Shangqing tradition developed its own ordination
registers.

Bestowal of registers in ordination. In later Taoist ordination and investiture rites,
the adept receives registers listing protective deities. As the adept advances, he
is given a longer register with more deities. The register records the names
and attributes of the divine generals and their soldiers whom the adept calls
upon in visualizations and spells to protect the possessor, affect healing, and
convey petitions to the otherworld. In return, the adept agrees to obey certain
precepts. In effect, the adept is entering into a contract with the deities as well
as the master who bestows the register.

    During the first ordination rite held at seven years of age, the adept receives
the Child Register of the Highest One General (*Taishang yi jiangjun tongzi lu* 太
上一將軍童子籙). At the next ordination stage, the adept is given more commandments to obey as well as a register listing ten otherworldly generals under
his power. During adolescence, the adept receives a register of seventy-five
generals. For women, the register is referred to as Upper Numinous (*shangling*
上靈), and for men it is called Upper Transcendent (*shangxian* 上仙). If two
initiates marry, their registers are combined for a total of one hundred fifty
deities, the highest ordination level for a layperson. The next level of ordination, where one receives one hundred eighty deities to summon as well as one
hundred eighty commandments to obey, is limited to masters.

    The Celestial Masters ordination registers, called Registers of the Pneumas
of the Twenty-four Parishes (*ershisi zhi qi lu* 二十四治氣籙), are referred
to as Esoteric Registers (*neilu* 內籙) for the masters and Exoteric Registers

(*wailu* 外籙) for the laity. The Esoteric Registers are in the form of chart-registers (*tulu* 圖籙), which consist of images or maps of the cosmos and the names of transcendents, and thereby act as passes for safe conduct to the otherworld. The talismanic registers (*fulu* 符籙), which are the Exoteric Registers of the laity, are excerpts from the more comprehensive registers of the masters.

Amy Lynn MILLER

📖 Benn 1991, passim; Dean 1993, 53–58; Kroll 1986a, 108–13; Lagerwey 1987c, 157–61 and passim; Ren Jiyu 1990, 340–90; Robinet 1993, 143–51; Robinet 1997b, 57–58; Schipper 1978, 376–81; Schipper 1985c; Schipper 1993, 60–71; Seidel 1979; Seidel 1981, 241–47; Seidel 1983a, 323–32 and passim

※ FU [talisman]; ORDINATION AND PRIESTHOOD; TRANSMISSION

Hagiography

The Taoist biographical tradition primarily celebrates the exploits of immortals, those who have transcended the bounds of a standard life and attained the deathless and supreme state. It records their extraordinary feats and their powers and capabilities that exceed those of normal people. In some instances the biographies recount how these figures attained their exalted condition, for all of them passed from a human existence to a transcendent one, and why such a destiny fell to them and no-one else. Importantly, however, the biographies do not, in general, describe the techniques by which immortality was attained. Discussions of the preparation of elixirs, rules for entering sacred mountains and writing of talismans (*FU) are notable by their scarcity in Taoist hagiography. Rather, the purpose of these biographies appears to be to provide evidence for the existence of immortals and records of models for emulation, rather than to give instructions on the attainment of immortality. For that, keen readers would have to look elsewhere.

Discussions of the purpose of Taoist biographies found in prefaces to collections and the like justify their existence on two major grounds. First, the lives recorded countered the perennial objection that immortality was not possible and that those who claimed to have attained it were simply charlatans. Secondly, the collections were often defined by their position in a debate that resounds through the history of immortality, namely whether the ability to gain this exalted state was dependent on the fate one received at birth (length of life was, and to some extent still is, regarded as fated) or whether immortality was something that anybody could attain given the right information, sufficient study and apparently boundless enthusiasm. The *loci classici* for the two sides of this discussion are *Xi Kang's (223–62) *Yangsheng lun* 養生論 (Essay on Nourishing Life) and *Wu Yun's (?–778) **Shenxian kexue lun* (An Essay on How One May Become a Divine Immortal Through Training) respectively. Other motivations may be inferred from some collections compiled with a specific purpose in mind. Notable among these are the desire to record (or invent) a lineage or line of transmission such as the **Han tianshi shijia* (Lineage of the Han Celestial Master) which records the lives of the Celestial Masters from *Zhang Daoling, who ascended to Heaven in the second century, to the forty-ninth Celestial Master, Zhang Yongxu 張永緒, who lived in the sixteenth century. Another motivation is revealed in *Du Guangting's (lost) *Wangshi shenxian zhuan* 王氏神仙傳 (Biographies of Immortals of the Family Name Wang; Yan Yiping 1974, vol. 1) where a particular family is exalted—in this case the family of the ruler of the state of Shu in which court Du found himself. Similarly, there exist collections with a regional focus which bolster local pride and those associated with specific mountains or other cult sites.

Biographies of Taoist immortals—especially lesser known ones—are often remarkably stable over time. The rewriting of biographies, or the composition of a new one where an older version exists, is generally an indication that the subject of the biography has gained a new importance or a new role.

The earliest collection in the tradition is **Liexian zhuan* (Biographies of Exemplary Immortals) which may indeed, perversely, be said to predate Taoism itself. Traditionally attributed to Liu Xiang 劉向 (77–8 or 6 BCE; IC 583–84), its very existence points to the prevalence of the idea of immortality in early China. Its biographies are short with only the most rudimentary narrative. In the second collection that survives, *Ge Hong's (283–343) **Shenxian zhuan* (Biographies of Divine Immortals), the biographies are much fuller but still are rarely more than a few pages long. Various collections followed Ge's model: **Dongxian zhuan* (Biographies of Cavern Immortals; by Jiansu zi 見素子 who has not been satisfactorily identified, Six Dynasties), **Daoxue zhuan* (Biographies of Those who Studied the Dao; by Ma Shu of the Chen dynasty), **Xu xianzhuan* (Sequel to Biographies of Immortals; by Shen Fen 沈汾 of the Southern Tang dynasty). Du Guangting was a pivotal figure in the history of Taoist hagiography as he was in so many areas of Taoism. Among his works were the aforementioned *Wangshi shenxian zhuan*, the *Xianzhuan shiyi* 仙傳 拾遺 (Uncollected Biographies of Immortals; Yan Yiping 1974, vol. 1), and the **Yongcheng jixian lu* (Records of the Immortals Gathered in the Walled City), which was an important attempt at comprehensive classification. Later, Zhao Daoyi 趙道一 (fl. 1294–1307) completed his monumental **Lishi zhenxian tidao* *tongjian* (Comprehensive Mirror of Perfected Immortals and Those Who Embodied the Dao through the Ages) with over 900 biographies. This collection also broke new ground by including biographies of greater length than previously seen, some taking an entire chapter.

Benjamin PENNY

📖 Bokenkamp 1986c, 143–45; Boltz J. M. 1986c, 156–59; Boltz J. M. 1987a, 54–101; Bumbacher 2000c; Campany 1996, 294–306; Campany 2002; Chen Guofu 1963, 233–51; Giles L. 1948; Kaltenmark 1953; Penny 2000; Sawada Mizuho 1988; Seidel 1989–90, 246–48

※ For related entries see the Synoptic Table of Contents, sec. II.7 ("Immortals and Hagiography")

Epigraphy

Taoist epigraphy mainly consists of inscriptions on stone (stelae) and, to a lesser extent, on bronze or other metals (bells, incense burners, and various liturgical implements). Whereas early studies focused on their artistic quality (e.g., the *Yihe ming* 瘞鶴銘, *Inscription on the Burial of a Crane*, or the many Yuan Taoist stelae from the brush of Zhao Mengfu 趙孟頫, 1254–1322) or their philological value (e.g., the Tang dynasty stele of the *Daode jing* at Yixian 易縣, Hebei), in recent decades scholars have begun to tap their vast potential as resources for social history. As religious archives are unavailable, epigraphic sources yield the richest documentation on the life of Taoist communities in the past. Especially the reverse sides (*beiyin* 碑陰) of the stelae, with their lists of religious personalities, their titles, and the names of their patrons, provide firsthand information on the economic basis and social background of Taoist establishments. Since stelae were often used as a public and reliable records for grants, contracts, or other official acts, they also document the legal status of communities. Moreover, inscriptions are a primary source for the history of cults, and even data on rituals or alchemical practices are available in stelae devoted to such issues.

Taoist inscriptions do not formally differ from other Chinese epigraphic sources. Most of their authors are lay people: sympathetic or, occasionally, critical literati. Their often standardized format and formulaic expressions are the same as those of their counterparts in Confucian, Buddhist, or popular contexts. However, Taoist epigraphy also includes some peculiar genres, however, including calligraphic samples of roaming immortals like *Lü Dongbin, or charts of the human body for use in meditation (see *Neijing tu and *Xiuzhen *tu*). These stelae, along with the alchemical poems frequently carved on stone from the Song onward, attest to the open diffusion and potentially vast audience of seemingly arcane and mystical expressions of the Taoist tradition.

The earliest inscriptions related to Taoism are those of the cults to immortals dating from the Han period. Some of them, like the Tang Gongfang 唐公房 stele (Schipper 1991a; Campany 1996, 187–92), have been known for a long time, while others, like the *Fei Zhi bei* 肥致碑, are still being discovered today (Schipper 1997b; Little 2000b, 150–51). These early stelae bear devices—for instance, holes for offerings—showing that, in accordance with their archaic function, stelae were themselves the objects of rites: the erect stone represented the god. This notion seems to disappear shortly after the Han. During the Six Dynasties, Taoist communities produced iconic stelae (*zaoxiang bei* 造像碑) comparable to better-known Buddhist ones. We have many inscriptions from the Tang period onward devoted to Taoist temples and abbeys, as well as funerary stelae of eminent Taoists (Confucian-style *muzhi ming* 墓誌銘, or, rarely, Buddhist-style *taming* 塔銘). The Yuan dynasty is a Golden Age of Taoist epigraphy, and especially the *Quanzhen order seems to have promoted the systematic erection of stelae in all its communities. An exhaustive count of extant Taoist inscriptions dating from the Jin and Yuan periods yields some 1,100 items, about 500 of which are of Quanzhen provenance. This only includes inscriptions primarily concerned with the activities of the *daoshi, and does not consider the titles of lost inscriptions or inscriptions for shrines of popular cults which were also often staffed by Taoists. A corpus of this size is the best resource with which to gauge the presence of Taoism and its variations in space and time.

Like all Chinese inscriptions, the Taoist ones are scattered among records in old epigraphic treatises, local gazetteers, literary anthologies and recent archeological publications; collections of rubbings in Chinese, Japanese and Western libraries; and the actual stelae when they still exist. Whereas ancient inscriptions are well documented, those of the Ming, Qing, and contemporary periods are rarely published and must be collected through library study and fieldwork. These more recent inscriptions are nevertheless important to chart the history of modern Taoism, since few canonical or historiographical works are available for this period.

Recent fieldwork, for example, has documented fifty-three stelae dating from the Ming onward in the *Baiyun guan (Abbey of the White Clouds; Marsone 1999), and fifty-four of the same period at the *Louguan (Tiered Abbey); Wang Zhongxin 1995). Thousands of smaller sites await similar investigation. For the earlier periods, the situation has much improved since the publication of *Daojia jinshi lüe* 道家金石略 (A Collection of Taoist Epigraphy; Chen Yuan 1988), an anthology compiled by the great scholar Chen Yuan 陳垣 (1880–1971)

in the 1930s as he was working on the history of Quanzhen, and posthumously completed and published. The anthology includes inscriptions from the Han to the Ming, but nearly 900 of its 1,500 texts date from the Jin-Yuan period. Extant Taoist inscriptions number over 10,000 in all, but it will take decades before a comprehensive survey is available.

Vincent GOOSSAERT

📖 Boltz J. M. 1987a, 121–28; Goossaert 1997; Schipper 1991a; Schipper 1997b

※ *Ganshui xianyuan lu*; *Zhenxian beiji*

COSMOGONY AND COSMOLOGY

Cosmogony

1. Overview

In systems of thought based on a once and for all creation of the cosmos by a deity, or at least by a demiurge, the origin of the cosmos is a moment of the utmost significance in which the eternal and the temporal intersect. For quite different reasons, twenty-first century cosmologists pay great attention to elucidating exactly what happened in the first instants after the cosmic explosion known as the Big Bang. Such considerations are largely irrelevant to the understanding of ancient Chinese thought, in which divine creative activity was no longer a part of the intellectual landscape by the time cosmological speculation can be traced in the later Warring States period. Nor was cosmogony a major philosophical issue. Even at times when we seem at first sight to be confronting a cosmogonic discourse, as in the case of Zhou Dunyi's 周敦頤 (1017–73; SB 277–81) *Taiji tu shuo* 太極圖說 (Explanation of the Diagram of the Great Ultimate), it is more likely that reference is being made not so much to a temporal sequence of evolution as to an order of ontological priority.

When cosmogonic writing is found in its true sense of an account of the origin of the present cosmos from some preceding state (which includes the possibility of Non-being; see *wu and you*), two characteristics stand out, apart from the absence of a divine creator. Firstly, there is no element of explicit teleology. The universe is not there as part of some wider purpose, or to exhibit some message. Secondly, the universe is not a chance production, but is the result of the unfolding of an implicit order.

One of the fullest and clearest early cosmogonies was composed by the astronomer, poet, technologist and courtier Zhang Heng 張衡 (78–139; IC 211–12) around 120 CE. It forms part of a text, *Lingxian* 靈憲 (perhaps "The Numinous Structure"), in which he sets out to give a complete account of the large-scale order of heaven and earth.

> Before the Great Plainness (or Great Basis, Taisu 太素) [came to be], there was dark limpidity and mysterious quiescence, dim and dark. No image of it can be formed. Its midst was void; its exterior was non-existence. Things remained thus for long ages; this is called obscurity (*mingxing* 溟涬). It was the root of the Dao.

When the root of the Dao had been established, from the non-existent (*wu*)
there grew existence (*you*). The Great Basis first began to sprout, to sprout
though as yet with no outer sign. The *qi* was all together, and all appeared as
one—an undivided Chaos (*hundun bufen* 渾沌不分). So the *Account of the Dao*
(*Daozhi* 道志, i.e., the *Daode jing*) says "There is a thing confusedly formed, born
before Heaven and Earth." The body of its *qi* could by no means yet be given a
shape. Its stillings and quickenings could by no means yet be given regularity.
Things remained thus for more long ages; this was [the stage called] vast and
floodlike (*panghong* 庬鴻). It was the stem of the Dao.

When the stem of the Dao had been grown, creatures came into being and
shapes were formed. At this stage, the original *qi* split and divided, hard and
soft first divided, pure and turbid took up different positions. Heaven formed
on the outside, and Earth became fixed within. Heaven took its body from
the Yang, so it was round and in motion; Earth took its body from the Yin, so
it was flat and quiescent. Through motion there was action and giving forth;
through quiescence there was conjoining and transformation. Through binding
together there was fertilization, and in time all the kinds of things were brought
to growth. This is called the Great Origin (*Taiyuan* 太元). It was the fruition
of the Dao. (*Hou Hanshu*, *Zhi* 志, 10.3215, commentary)

The presence of accounts of the emergence of the cosmos from non-existence and primal Chaos might prompt the obvious question as to whether
(and if so when) it might revert to non-existence, and if so whether it might
in time reemerge. Such questions do not however seem to have been raised
systematically in ancient China before the coming of Buddhism, and unlike
the case of ancient Greece and later Europe, the question of the eternity or
temporality of the existence of the cosmos does not seem to have been seen
as an important issue.

Christopher CULLEN

📖 Kaltenmark 1959; Le Blanc 1989; Major 1993, 23–28; Mathieu 1992; Schafer
1977a, 21–31

2. Taoist notions

The return to the Origin (*yuan* 元), or to the Dao as the source and foundation
of the world, is one of the main notions running throughout Taoism. Several
facets of this notion must be examined for its importance to be appreciated.
First, Taoist writers often compound the ideas of the absolute Origin and
the beginning of existence. These ideas, however, are not entirely equivalent:
while the Origin is an ever-present foundation in both space and time, the
beginning of existence must be located in an unknown past. Second, both
ideas are equally paradoxical: on the one hand, the absolute Origin cannot
be something determinate, but if it were nothing it would not be the Origin;

on the other hand, a beginning assumes that something already exists and that it has already begun to begin, as shown in *Zhuangzi* 2. A third issue concerns the shift from unity to multiplicity: the notion of the Origin has the paradoxical feature of a limit or a threshold, as it is the moment in which the indeterminate Dao takes form.

The following outline is only concerned with the notions of formation of the cosmos in Taoism, and does not consider the related but different themes of the succession of plural worlds, or the ordering of the world by mythical emperors and other cultural heroes.

Metaphorical time. The first brief hints of cosmogony in Taoism appear in some passages of *Daode jing* 21, 25, and 42, and are frequently quoted in later texts. The theme was further expanded in descriptive, narrative, mythical, or theogonic fashions, which are often blended with each other.

Time, measured in cosmic eras (*kalpas*, **jie*) or in myriad pneumas (**qi*), occurs as a metaphor. The Origin-beginning of the cosmos is set in the remote past, to indicate that it is unlike anything occurring in the phenomenal world. Various cosmogonic stages, however, are described as sequences of generations or transformations to emphasize the continuity between unity and multiplicity. Since in the Origin-beginning there is nothing, the texts rely on images evoking void, silence, desert, obscurity, immobility, or an immense open space. Nevertheless, several terms that connote original Chaos contain the semantic indicator "water" (*shui* 水) or "vegetation" (*cao* 艸), in accordance with the claim that paradoxically there is something in this void—the first signs or sprouts of the world (e.g., *Daode jing* 21).

The Origin-beginning is one: the Dao, the One (**yi*), Original Pneuma (**yuanqi*), or Chaos (**hundun*). This unity harbors the seed of multiplicity and the patterns of the world. It contains three principles merged in one: pneuma (*qi*), form (**xing*), and matter (*zhi* 質), or Yin, Yang, and the Central Harmony (*zhonghe* 中和). The number 3 represents in Taoism the notion of a complex and organized unity (see **NUMEROLOGY*). Numbers, which measure the time of precosmic eras, symbolically express the maturation the three components must attain before they separate from each other.

Threefold and fivefold patterns. Taoism employs two main cosmogonic patterns, one threefold and the other fivefold, which are related to the vertical and horizontal axes of the world. From these patterns arise all other celestial and terrestrial configurations.

The threefold pattern is first seen in the **Shengshen jing* (Scripture of the Life-Giving Spirits; CT 318, 1a-b). This *Lingbao text associates three precosmic eras with the Three Treasures (*sanbao* 三寶), the teaching of Three Caverns (**SANDONG*), and the Three Pneumas (*sanqi* 三氣; see **sanyuan*) named

Mysterious (*xuan* 玄), Original (*yuan* 元), and Inaugural (*shi* 始). First, these triads are blended in unity in the Void, then they generate the highest Heavens, and finally they divide into Heaven and Earth. Since the fifth century, this pattern has been enriched by texts that associate the Three Pneumas with the three highest Heavens, the three corporeal divinities (the Three Primes, *sanyuan), the three qualities of the Dao—said to be invisible (*yi* 夷), inaudible (*xi* 希), and imperceptible (*wei* 微) in *Daode jing* 14—and the three bodies (*sanshen* 三身) or appearances of the Ultimate Truth. This view of a single but threefold Origin gave rise to meditation practices focused on the three corporeal deities and to speculations on the Three Ones (*sanyi); later it also merged with *neidan notions. Another threefold pattern is represented by the *sanhuang, or Three Sovereigns, two of whom are precosmic.

The fivefold pattern first appears in the Han "weft texts" (*weishu* 緯書; see *TAOISM AND THE APOCRYPHA) and in the opening chapter of the *Liezi. This pattern imagines a genesis in five stages called Five Greats (*wutai* 五太; see fig. 8): *taiyi* 太易 (Great Simplicity), *taichu* 太初 (Great Beginning), *taishi* 太始 (Great Commencement), *taisu* 太素 (Great Plainness), and *taiji 太極 (Great Ultimate). The second, third and fourth stages are the origin of pneuma, form, and matter, respectively. They evolve progressively but are in a state of chaotic unity until they transform into the One (the *taiji*), which is the "beginning of form." This pattern was adopted by Taoist texts from the Tang period onward, and was related to the *wuxing. In *neidan*, it was integrated with the view that the cosmos begins with the union of the trigrams *qian* 乾 ☰ (pure Yang) and *kun* 坤 ☷ (pure Yin), which generate the eight trigrams (*bagua); it was also related to fire phasing (*huohou) and the birth of the immortal embryo (*shengtai).

In fact, there are several variations of the main cosmogonic themes outlined above. In the early Lingbao texts, for example, the number of precosmic eras ranges from three to four or five, called Draconic Magnificence (*longhan* 龍漢), Extended Vigor (*yankang* 延康), Vermilion Brilliance (*chiming* 赤明), Opening Luminary (*kaihuang* 開皇), and Higher Luminary (*shanghuang* 上皇). Some of these precosmic eras are represented as former worlds. In addition, a syncretic tendency blended these systems together, creating an extremely complex cosmogonic process. In some instances, Taoist scriptures describe the state that antedates the world in an attempt to prove that they, or the schools which they represent, are anterior and superior to other scriptures or schools, in a "cosmological battle" (Bokenkamp 1997, 190) that generates a *regressus ad infinitum*.

Primordial deities. Taoist cosmogonies are often theogonies, based on the notion of a god as creator and teacher of the world. In this view, a primordial divinity exists in emptiness and takes form progressively. Transforming its name and appearance, it fashions the celestial and human worlds that constitute its own body. This divinity governs and teaches through scriptures, first transmitted in Heaven and later to humans in written form. There was also disagreement about the identity of the primordial deity, who was usually thought to be either Yuanshi tianzun 元始天尊 (Celestial Worthy of Original Commencement; see *sanqing) or *Laojun. In the Lingbao cosmogony, the Tianzun 天尊 (Celestial Worthy) takes the name Yuanshi tianzun in the Vermilion Brilliance era. The notion of gods changing appearances in precosmic eras and throughout the history of humankind appears to be a compromise in the struggle for priority among Taoist schools: all deities are seen as names and apparitions of the one, primordial, and ultimate Truth.

Isabelle ROBINET

📖 Bokenkamp 1997, 188–98, 207–9; Girardot 1976; Girardot 1977; Girardot 1978b; Girardot 1983; Kalinowski 1996; Le Blanc 1989; Mathieu 1992; Mugitani Kunio 1979; Peerenboom 1990; Robinet 1977, 149–203; Robinet 1994b; Robinet 1995c; Robinet 1997a; Robinet 2002; Robinet forthcoming

※ *hundun*; *sanyuan*; *wu* and *you*; *wuji* and *taiji*; *xiantian* and *houtian*; *xing*; *yi* [oneness]; *yuanqi*; COSMOLOGY

Cosmology

1. Overview

By the beginning of the imperial age in China, the dominant patterns of cosmological thinking that had emerged were clearly of the correlative type. This entry briefly introduces the two main patterns, those of Yin and Yang and the *wuxing*. The next entry, "Cosmology: Taoist Notions," describes the application of these and other configurations of emblems in Taoism.

Yin and Yang. Let us consider first the simple binary scheme of Yin and Yang, two terms whose earliest identifiable meanings appear to be "the dark (northern) side of a hill" and "the sunny (southern) side of a hill." The earliest lengthy statement of the Yin-Yang system comes from a text of the late third century BCE found in the 168 BCE tomb at *Mawangdui, entitled *Cheng* 稱 (Designations; trans. Yates 1997, 155–69; see also Graham 1989, 330–31). We are told at the outset: "In sorting things out, use Yin and Yang." There then follows the list reproduced in table 1. It should be quite clear that Yin and Yang are not substances of any kind, nor are they "forces" or "energies": they are simply the names that label the typical partners in a whole series of parallel relationships.

Table 1.

YIN	YANG	YIN	YANG
Earth	Heaven	Child	Father
Autumn	Spring	Younger brother	Elder brother
Winter	Summer	Younger	Older
Night	Day	Base	Noble
Small states	Large states	Narrow-minded	Broad-minded
Unimportant states	Important states	Mourning	Taking a wife, begetting a child
Non-action	Action	Being controlled by others	Controlling others
Contracting	Stretching	Host	Guest
Minister	Ruler	Laborers	Soldiers
Below	Above	Silence	Speech
Woman	Man	Receiving	Giving

Yin and Yang entities according to the *Mawangdui manuscript *Cheng* 稱
(Designations). Based on Yates 1997, 169, and Graham 1989, 330–31.

And clearly nothing is Yin or Yang in itself and outside the context of a relationship: without Yin there is no Yang, and vice versa.

This simple system has a wide range of applications. Thus in Chinese medicine, a function such as digestion is seen as Yang, whereas the physical substrate that enables this function is seen as Yin. Supposing one has a severely malnourished patient, Yin-Yang thinking will draw attention to the need to restore both sides of the digestive partnership together, since a large meal given at once will demand Yang activity that the weakened Yin substrate cannot sustain. Thus initial nourishment should be small, with a gradual increase as function and substrate strengthen one another.

Wuxing. By the early imperial period, another correlative system was also well elaborated—not in competition with Yin-Yang, but in complementary relation with it. This was the so-called *wuxing*, a term which can reasonably be translated as Five Phases or Five Agents. Here the groupings go by fives, not by twos. The headings for this list of fivefold correlations are drawn from important elements in the functioning of the natural world: Wood (*mu* 木), Fire (*huo* 火), Soil (*tu* 土), Metal (*jin* 金), and Water (*shui* 水). The correlations of these five emblems are shown in table 25.

Clearly any pattern that can include numbers, seasons, directions, colors and types of animal is not talking of physical ingredients like the ancient Greek elements, but is correlating systems of relationship. But if Yin-Yang thinking posits an alternation of activity, what happens when we have five phases? In fact two main types of pattern are said to occur (see fig. 77). The so-called "production" sequence (*xiangsheng* 相生) follows the circumference of the circle: thus Wood grows from Water, Wood produced Fire, Fire produces Soil (ashes), Metals grow in the Soil (as was thought), and Water condenses on Metal. In the "conquest' sequence (*xiangke* 相克) shown by the cross-lines, Water puts out Fire, Fire melts Metal, Metal cuts Wood, Wood (as a primitive spade) digs Soil, and Soil dams up Water.

Among other forms of correlative thinking in China was of course the elaborate system of correlations between the eight trigrams (*bagua) and the sixty-four hexagrams of the *Yijing and the whole of the cosmos. The importance attached to such thinking varied from period to period, and of course its suffered a major blow with the popularization of the more mechanical style of modern scientific thinking. But it is certainly still alive and well in the world of Taoist practices, as well as in divination and traditional medicine.

Christopher CULLEN

📖 Graham 1986c; Graham 1989, 318–58; Harper 1999; Henderson 1984; Kalinowski 1991; Le Blanc 1985; Major 1978; Major 1987b; Major 1993; Needham 1956, 216–345; Onozawa Seiichi, Fukunaga Mitsuji, and Yamanoi Yū 1978; Schwartz 1985, 350–82

2. Taoist notions

While Confucianism mainly deals with relations among human beings in society, Taoism focuses on human relations with Nature: unlike Confucians, Taoists maintain that one cannot understand human affairs without knowing how the cosmos functions, because the Dao is the totality of what exists and the whole world is a manifestation of the Dao. Moreover, in Taoism the human being is seen as a microcosm related in an analogical and organic way to the pattern of the world. In order to attain physical and mental health, and to achieve immortality, therefore, one should know and follow the cosmic laws. Cosmology thus plays a basic role in Taoism. That is why around the third century CE, when Confucianism rejected the cosmological speculations it had incorporated during the Han period, Taoism became the main heir of *fangshi lore and Han naturalistic thought, and contributed to their renewal in Neo-Confucianism from the eleventh century onward.

The Taoist view of the cosmos. For the Taoist saint (*shengren), first as depicted in the *Zhuangzi, the cosmological dimension serves as a means to go beyond the self. The world that Taoism deals with is not exactly the same as the world of the cosmologists: Taoist cosmology is based on the common Yin-Yang and

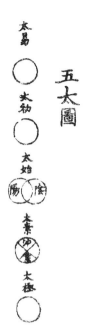

Fig. 8. The cosmogonic sequence of the Five Greats (*wutai* 五太): Great Simplicity, Great Beginning, Great Commencement, Great Plainness, and Great Ultimate. *Daofa huiyuan* (Corpus of Taoist Ritual; CT 1220), 1.9b.

wuxing patterns, but adds a divine dimension to this system. The cosmos is an imaginary world where "spirits are embodied and bodies are spiritualized" (see *xiang*). Even more than deities, cosmology therefore provides the necessary mediation between the Absolute and the human beings. Accordingly, many Taoist practices aim at fashioning a material or ideal microcosm: the ritual altar, the alchemical laboratory, and the human body itself are tools to know the cosmos, stride along it, and finally go beyond it.

Taoist alchemists further state that a parcel of the Original Pneuma (*yuanqi*), a sparkle of light that antedates the formation of the world, lies within each and every thing and being (see *dianhua*). The way Taoists travel in the world thus runs in two directions, unlike the way of the cosmologists: not only from the Dao to multiplicity, following the unfolding of the world (*shun* 順, lit., "continuation"), but also from multiplicity to the Dao, in a reverse order (*ni* 逆, lit., "inversion") that Taoism calls "return" (*fan*).

The foundation and source of the world is the One (*yi*), an aspect of the Dao or the Original Pneuma. The world consequently has internal coherence and adheres to general laws and rhythms. These patterns regulate various systems which, despite their differences, resonate with each other with respect to these laws. Moreover, the world is a continuum: although the human mind perceives divisions and reference points in the world, they only have a conventional and provisional value. Taoists emphasize this point more often and more strongly than the cosmologists. Various means are available to reconcile the unity of the world with the multiplicity of its aspects. One stresses the "fluidity" of the Dao or the Original Pneuma, which can take all forms because it has none; another focuses on the circulation of the Original Pneuma which, like a whirlwind, spins the cosmos around and bestows a specific virtue or character to each of its sectors; while another offers a dynamic view of a constantly changing world, whose mutations happen in a way akin to birth or to a seed that grows into a tree, without any disruption.

But the world cannot appear without taking form, which means that it requires outlines that delineate things and separate them from one another. This occurs through a long process of parturition from the indeterminate

Formless (*wuxing* 無形) to form (*xing*). Then there appears the first and ultimate "line," or limit, the *taiji* (Great Ultimate), which generates the division into two (Yin and Yang, or Heaven and Earth). These two basic principles do not give birth to a dualistic view of the world because they do not apply to the human world, but merely delineate its frame. The human world lies between these two limits, and Taoism is concerned with their mingling and fluctuation.

Numerical and geographical patterns. Unlike the cosmologists, Taoists privilege the number 3 instead of the number 4, which evokes the four seasons and the four major trigrams. As stated in *Daode jing* 42, the number 3 represents the recovered Original Unity that gives birth to the "ten thousand things." Accordingly, the main structures of the world are threefold and fivefold (see *sanwu*). The vertical structure is threefold and is mainly associated with three realms above, below, and in the middle. These are variously called Yin, Yang, and Central Harmony (*zhonghe* 中和, the median pneuma); or Heaven, Earth, and Humanity; or (by the early *Tianshi dao) Heaven, Earth, and Water (see under *sanguan). The horizontal structure is fivefold, with the *wuxing* as the main mark-points.

The combination of the four cardinal directions with above and below constitute the traditional six directions of the world mentioned in Taoists texts. The *Lingbao texts in turn borrow from Buddhism the notion of ten directions, or the eight directions of the compass plus above and below.

The fantastic aspect of the Taoist world can be observed in its view of the underworld, the heavens, and what is above the heavens. North is the land of death and hells, while south is the land of salvation and paradise. The poles of the earth, where Taoists like to roam, are traditionally believed to be dangerous and inhabited by barbarians and monsters, but for the Taoists they abound in propitious pneuma and deities (see *yuanyou).

For the Taoists, finally, the Heaven and Earth that we know and inhabit are not eternal. They have a beginning and will undergo an apocalyptic end, only to be replaced by others.

Isabelle ROBINET

📖 Bokenkamp 1997, 15–20, 165–66, and 234–37; Lagerwey 1981b, 33–38, 40–42, and 80–82; Major 1993; Robinet 1984, 1: 130–40 and 221–27; Robinet 1997b, 7–14, 42–46, 92–94, 158–62, and 234–39; Robinet forthcoming; Schipper and Wang 1986

※ COSMOGONY; DIVINATION, OMENS, AND PROPHECY; MACROCOSM AND MICROCOSM; NUMEROLOGY; TAOIST VIEWS OF THE HUMAN BODY; for other related entries see the Synoptic Table of Contents, sec. II.1 ("Doctrinal Notions") and sec. II.4 ("Cosmos and Cosmology")

Macrocosm and microcosm

Like several other cultures, China has developed the macrocosm-microcosm theory in different forms. Taoism has borrowed some of them and elaborated others. These multiple formulations are not restricted to the universe and the human being, as other components come into play. The first is the state: the human community with its codes, hierarchies, and physical seats of power ideally mirrors the configuration and order of Heaven; reciprocally, Heaven is an administrative system managed through bureaucratic procedures similar to those performed at court and in government offices. The second is the ritual area, whose altars (*tan* 壇) correspond to the cosmos and its temporal and spatial configurations. Other environments and surroundings, including gardens and gourds, are also said to represent a "cosmos in miniature."

Cosmos, human being, society, and ritual area are analogically related to each other, so that an event or an action that occurs within any of these domains can be relevant for the others; this is determined by the principle of "resonance" (*ganying* 感應, lit. "impulse and response"), by which things belonging to the same class or category (*lei* 類) influence each other. Ritual, for instance, reestablishes the original bond between humans and gods, and a Real Man (**zhenren*) or a Saint (**shengren*) benefits the whole human community in which he lives by aligning himself with the forces that rule the cosmos. On the other hand, a ruler who ignores Heaven's omens brings about natural calamities and social disturbances.

In many cases, the conduits linking each domain to the others are the abstract emblems of correlative cosmology, or the gods of the outer and inner pantheons. Emblems and gods are related to each other, as several divinities correspond to cosmological notions. Symbolic numbers (see *NUMEROLOGY) and images (**xiang*) play a central role in establishing these relationships. In Taoism, however, numbers and images also perform an even more important function, as they serve to express both the emanation from Dao to macrocosm, and the reverse process of return to the Dao (**fan*), which is often performed with the support of a microcosmic framework.

Cosmos, gods, and the human body. The macrocosm-microcosm theory lies at the core of correlative cosmology. The pattern of the Five Agents (**wuxing*) in particular forges relations among various sets of entities and phenomena, such as numbers, colors, spatial directions, seasons, planets, musical notes, and so forth. Within these sets, the relation of the five viscera (**wuzang*) to the seasons and directions aligns the human microcosm to the macrocosmic categories of space and time. An example of the adaptation of this theory in Taoism is the

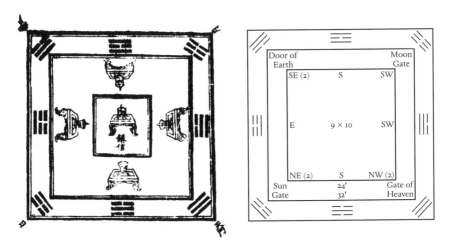

Door of Earth			Moon Gate
SE (2)	S		SW
E	9 × 10		SW
NE (2)	S		NW (2)
Sun Gate	24' 32'		Gate of Heaven

Fig. 9. The Taoist altar as a microcosm. *Wushang biyao* (Supreme Secret Essentials; CT 1138), 52.1a. The diagram on the right is based on Lagerwey 1987c, 36; see his comments ibid., 30–36.

Fig. 10. Human figure surrounded by emblems associated with Yin and Yang and the Five Agents (*wuxing*): Dragon (Yang) and Tiger (Yin); the hare in Moon (Yang within Yin) and the crow in the Sun (Yin within Yang); trigrams of the Book of Changes (*Yijing*); and names of ingredients of the Inner Elixir (*neidan*). *Yunji qiqian* (Seven Lots from the Bookbag of the Clouds; CT 1032), 72.34a.

practice of absorbing the pneumas (*qi) of the five directions (Maspero 1981, 506–13; Eskildsen 1998, 53–56). In other instances, the macrocosm-microcosm theory establishes looser analogies between cosmic phenomena and functions or organs of the human body. Here too, the identification with the cosmos is not only spatial but also temporal. Several Han texts, for example, indicate correspondences between the 360, 365, or 366 days of the year and the identical numbers of joints (*jie* 節) in the body.

The human being, moreover, is home to a host of major and minor gods. The most important among them dwell both in Heaven and within the individual, and therefore play a role in connecting the two realms. The gods who dwell in the three Cinnabar Fields (*dantian) are, according to different texts, the Three Primes (*sanyuan, which represent original, precosmic pneumas) or the Three Ones (*sanyi, which represent the three basic levels of the cosmos). The twenty-four body spirits formed by the three sets of Eight Effulgences (*bajing) are also related to the three Cinnabar Fields; they correspond to the twenty-four *jieqi* 節氣 (energy nodes) of the year, and each set represents Heaven, Earth, and Humanity within the human being. In another formulation, the main inner gods rule over 18,000 other inner deities; when an adept meditates on these deities, Heaven "makes 18,000 more divinities descend to complete the inner body. This makes 36,000 gods altogether, who raise the whole body and let it ascend to Heaven" (*Wushang biyao, 5.12b–14b; see Maspero 1981, 347, and Lagerwey 1981b, 79–80). The inner landscape of divine beings and their palaces is depicted in the *Neijing tu* (Chart of the Inner Warp; see *Neijing tu and Xiuzhen tu, and fig. 19), a representation related to other pictures that portray the body as a mountain, which in itself is a microcosm (Lagerwey 1991, 127–42; Despeux 1994, 194–98).

Macrocosm and microcosm in ritual and alchemy. Taoist ritual represents a complete time cycle, and its arrangement of altars reproduces the spatial structure of the cosmos (Lagerwey 1987c, 25–48; see fig. 9). In a manner reminiscent of the body spirits mentioned above, an altar described in the *Wushang biyao (Supreme Secret Essentials) has each side measuring twenty-four feet, corresponding to the twenty-four periods of the year, and is provided with three tables assigned to the Three Sovereigns (*sanhuang) of Heaven, Earth, and Humanity (49.1a–2a; Lagerwey 1981b, 152–53). Spatial correspondences are also apparent in another altar, which is arranged in such a way as to correspond to the eight trigrams (*bagua) at its four sides and the four corners, and the twelve Earthly Branches (*dizhi* 地支; see *ganzhi) along its periphery (Schipper and Wang 1986, 191, fig. 3). The altar, moreover, is a microcosm not only in relation to the cosmos in its temporal and spatial aspects, but also to the deities who inhabit it. Images of these deities are painted on scrolls and placed in positions (*wei* 位) to which their respective gods descend to take part in the ceremony.

The macrocosm-microcosm theory is also one of the main modes of expression in *waidan and *neidan (see fig. 10). Based on the emblems of correlative cosmology, the elixir represents all the temporal and spatial features of the cosmos. As stated in the *Zhouyi cantong qi (Token for the Agreement of the Three According to the Book of Changes), for instance, the 384 scruples (zhu 銖) that compose one symbolic pound of elixir correspond to the number of lines in the sixty-four hexagrams of the *Yijing. Thus the elixir incorporates the cosmos and all its actual and potential changes. In both waidan and neidan, macrocosmic time sequences are reproduced in the system of fire phasing (*huohou), while in waidan the spatial arrangement of instruments on the alchemical altar is also established according to cosmological principles (Sivin 1980, 279–92).

Fabrizio PREGADIO

📖 Fung Yu-lan 1952–53, 2: 7–132; Girardot 1983; Granet 1934, 342–88; Kominami Ichirō 1989; Lagerwey 1987c, 3–48; Needham 1956, 294–303; Schipper and Wang 1986; Sivin 1980, 221–92; Stein R. A. 1990

※ COSMOGONY; COSMOLOGY; INNER DEITIES; NUMEROLOGY; TAOIST VIEWS OF THE HUMAN BODY

Numerology

In classical Chinese thought, numbers have a meaning germane to natural order. As natural order is a manifestation of the Dao, numbers play a primary role in cosmogony and cosmology. They are said to have appeared along with images (*xiang), before forms (*xing) and names. Heaven, Earth, and the "ten thousand things" (wanwu 萬物) are born, move, and act through numbers that represent the movement and quiescence (*dong and jing) of Yin and Yang, i.e., their rhythm and the laws governing their transformations. Numbers applied to cosmogonic and cosmological cycles, or to alchemical cycles, measure periods of evolution, maturing, and decline, and their exhaustion marks the end of the world. Some numbers are also significant marking points: they ascribe qualities, provide meaning, and serve as tools to correlate different domains—e.g., cosmos and body, Earth and Heaven, temporal and spatial distribution—and make them *commensurable*. For instance, there are three parts in the human body (head, chest, and abdomen) and three heavenly bodies (sun, moon, and stars), just as there are three levels in the world (Heaven, Earth, and the space between them); there are five viscera (*wuzang) in the body and five openings in the human face, as there are five Agents (*wuxing), five planets, and so forth.

Numbers can be cardinal or ordinal. One, in the sense of "unique," is either identified with the Dao or considered as an outcome of the Dao: it engenders the world by its unfolding. In the sense of "first," it is associated with the agent Water. The One splits into the Two to give rise to the fundamental and dynamic bipolarity of the world. The Two in turn generate the Three, which represent Primordial Unity and the joining of the two primordial entities. Five is the matrix of the quinary order based on the four cardinal directions and the center. As such it is the addition of Four plus One; but it also represents the Center, which both separates and links the "generative" (sheng 生) numbers (from 1 to 5) and the "performative" (cheng 成) numbers (from 6 to 9). Six and nine are the extreme numbers of Yin and Yang, the two complementary forces of the world represented by Water (Yin) and Fire (Yang).

Since the world is the unfolding of the One to multiplicity, returning to the Origin (*fan) means going back through time. The left-turning movement of Yang is the normal direction of this unfolding (shun 順, lit., "continuation"), which aims at giving life to other beings (procreation) but ultimately leads toward death. The right-turning movement of Yin is the direction of reversal and decrease (ni 逆, lit., "inversion"), the return to the Origin, the way to give life to the inner immortal embryo (*shengtai, Embryo of Sainthood). Taoists therefore assume a progression of numbers from the One to Multiplicity as well as an inverse progression, the return to the One.

However, numbers are only metaphorical, as *neidan alchemists, who heavily rely on them, often emphasize. Their role is limited by that which cannot be measured, comprehended, or ordered: the infinitely great and the infinitely small subtlety of movement and change.

Isabelle ROBINET

📖 Granet 1934, 149–299; Major 1990; Major 1984; Robinet 1994a; Schipper and Wang 1986

※ *sanwu*; *Hetu* and *Luoshu*; COSMOGONY; COSMOLOGY; MACROCOSM AND MICROCOSM

DEITIES AND SPIRITS

Deities: The pantheon

Defining the Taoist pantheon depends on how one defines Taoism itself. The present entry briefly discusses the pantheon on the basis of selected sources in the Taoist Canon. While these sources give a somewhat different image of the pantheon compared to the deities venerated in present-day Taoism, they help to show how the modern pantheon is the result of historical development.

The Taoist pantheon, in fact, has always been extremely unstable. From earliest times, as new divinities were added, some older ones disappeared, and their ranking changed over time. An important factor in this fluidity has been the Chinese view of religion itself, in which the realm of the deities reflected the structure of the imperial court, centered on the emperor who was considered the representative on earth of the supreme god, Shangdi 上帝 (Highest Emperor). The imperial courts of Shangdi in Heaven and the emperor on earth shared a similar configuration. Thus the earthly emperor conferred titles on a large number of deities, and had the authority to decide which of them were orthodox and which were not. Consequently, the names and rankings of Taoist deities often depended on the imperial court. In later times the pantheon expanded through the incorporation of popular deities. In this sense, a clearly defined Taoist pantheon never existed in the past, any more than it exists in the present day.

Early Taoist deities. The earliest record of a Taoist deity is associated with the worship of Laozi (*Laojun, Lord Lao) within the Way of the Celestial Masters (*Tianshi dao), established by *Zhang Daoling in the mid-second century CE. Laozi was also deified around the same time within the Later Han court (see under *Laozi ming), which may have been influenced by the *Huang-Lao tradition. There is very little evidence on how the veneration of Laozi was carried out by the Celestial Masters, but statues of Laozi as a sage who had attained the Dao certainly reflect a view of this figure that had become widespread by the second century.

No evidence can be found in the received text of the *Taiping jing (Scripture of Great Peace) to link the contemporary Taiping dao 太平道 (Way of Great Peace; see *Yellow Turbans) to the Laozi cult. In the early fourth-century *Baopu zi (Book of the Master Who Embraces Simplicity), *Ge Hong (283–343) describes Laozi as the founder of Taoism and states that certain talismans

(*FU) and secret rites originated with him, but does not mention his cult. By the time the *Shangqing texts appear in the middle of the fourth century, however, titles such as Laojun (Lord Lao) and Daojun 道君 (Lord of the Dao) point to a deification of Laozi and the Dao. One of the main deities then was Huanglao jun 黃老君 (Yellow Old Lord, a name formed by the combination of the names of *Huangdi and Laozi). Meditating upon this deity and making it manifest within one's *niwan (the upper *dantian or Cinnabar Field) was a way to attain immortality. The highest development in the deification of the Dao is Yuanshi tianzun 元始天尊 (Celestial Worthy of Original Commencement; see *sanqing). This deity, who appears in the *Lingbao texts of the fifth century, is the supreme god who is the "beginning of everything," that is, the Dao. By comparison, the Northern Celestial Masters of *Kou Qianzhi (365?–448) considered Laojun (i.e., the deified Laozi) to be the founder of Taoism. There were thus some differences in how the pantheon developed in northern and southern China.

Tao Hongjing's pantheon. It was *Tao Hongjing (456–536) who first constructed a single pantheon synthesizing the various lineages of divinities from a Shangqing viewpoint. This pantheon is contained in the *Zhenling weiye tu (Chart of the Ranks and Functions of the Real Numinous Beings), which served as the basis for later systematizations. In this work, the deities are divided into seven ranks, with Yuanshi tianzun at the summit. Each rank is further divided into three classes, middle, left and right, of which the middle is of the highest standing and the right is of the lowest. Yuanshi tianzun is ranked as the god of the middle class of the first rank and stands at the head of all the deities, residing in the Great Canopy Heaven (*Daluo tian) above the Three Clarities (*sanqing), i.e., the celestial domains of Highest Clarity (shangqing), Jade Clarity (yuqing), and Great Clarity (taiqing).

Special features of the *Zhenling weiye tu* are that Laojun is placed in the fourth rank; that Confucian sages such as Yao 堯, Shun 舜, and Confucius himself are ranked above him; and that emperors and well-known historical persons who have embraced Taoism are listed as deities. The lowest, seventh rank is occupied by deities of the underworld and by "demon-officials" (guiguan 鬼官) who serve the bureaucracy of hell. Placing Laojun in the fourth rank indicates not only the ideological standpoint of the Shangqing school, but also the fact that Taoism was no longer merely a belief in Laozi but had come to embrace a more complex "Dao."

Later developments. The appearance of such works as the *Yebao yinyuan jing (Scripture on the Causes of Karmic Retribution), which mentions the belief in the Celestial Worthy Who Relieves Suffering (*Jiuku tianzun) and its ten manifestations, indicates that Taoism continued to create new deities as new scriptures were composed. Yuanshi tianzun remained the supreme deity until the Song dynasty, when Zhenzong (r. 997–1022) made *Yuhuang, the Jade Sovereign, supreme god by imperial decree, and Huizong (r. 1100–1125) bestowed upon him the title of Haotian Yuhuang shangdi 昊天玉皇上帝 (Jade Sovereign of the Vast Heaven, Highest Emperor). At the same time, divine or semidivine beings originally related to Buddhism and Confucianism were accepted into ranks of Taoist deities, a further demonstration of the ever-changing nature of the Taoist pantheon.

YAMADA Toshiaki

📖 Chan A. K. L. 1990; Ishii Masako 1983a; Kubo Noritada 1986; Lagerwey 1981b, 91–102; Little 2000b, 227–311; Ma Shutian 1996; Maspero 1981, 75–196, 364–72, and 431–41; Robinet 1997b, 18–19, 67–70, and 158–62; Shahar and Weller 1996; Stevens 1997; Stevens 2001; Verellen 1994; Yamada Toshiaki 1995a

※ HELL; OTHERWORLDLY BUREAUCRACY; TAOISM AND CHINESE MYTHOLOGY; for other related entries see the Synoptic Table of Contents, sec. II.6 ("Deities")

Demons and spirits

Chinese demonology and related beliefs and practices became involved with the Taoist religion in at least three ways. Taoism incorporated a number of late Zhou and Han ideas and techniques concerning demons and spirits. The demonization of deities of local, popular cults gave Taoists a way of distinguishing themselves from popular religion. Taoists' reincorporation of those same demons/popular gods allowed Taoism to draw upon the energies of the "shamanic substrate" or "popular complex" of Chinese religion.

Incorporation of early ideas and techniques. Ancient, pre-Taoist ideas about the invisible world did not sharply divide its inhabitants into good and evil ones. The natures of various *guishen* 鬼神, "demons and sundry spirits," ranged from the entirely malevolent to the potentially helpful. The early demonological tradition was devoted to identifying such spirits, figuring out the likelihood of their being harmful or helpful and, thus, whether one should seek to drive them off or obtain their aid (Harper 1985, 459–60 and n. 1).

The vitality of early demonography is attested in legends surrounding the sage king Yu's 禹 nine cauldrons, which, by depicting the "hundred [spirit] creatures" (*baiwu* 白物), allowed the people to know the forms of harmful spirits; extant texts such as the *Shanhai jing* 山海經 (Scripture of Mountains and Seas; see Kiang Chao-yuan 1937); and the numerous lost books on identifying and controlling harmful spectres recorded in the bibliographic treatise of the *Hanshu* (History of the Former Han). Archaeological evidence has been even more fruitful. A book whose title was probably *Rishu* 日書 (Book of Days—much of the book's content is hemerological) was recovered in the mid-1970s from an early third century BCE tomb in Shuihudi 睡虎地 (Hubei). One section called "Spellbinding ("Jie" 詰) begins with a brief prologue, after which virtually all of its seventy entries follow the same sequence: the type of demon is described and named, then appropriate exorcistic measures are prescribed (Harper 1985, esp. 492–94; Harper 1996).

The most notable example of the absorption of this demonographic tradition into Taoism is the ca. 400 CE *Nüqing guilü* (Demon Statutes of Nüqing; some parts of the text may be one or more centuries older). Most of the text is comprised of a roster of demons: "If one knows the name of the demon, it will return to its real form (*zhenxing* 真形) and no longer harass one. . . . The demon that is a tree sprite (*mujing* 木精) is named Qunyao 群夭. . . . The demon that is a tiger sprite is named Jianzhuang zi 健莊子" (2.1a-b). Special attention is given to the spirits of the sixty days of the sexagesimal cycle (see *ganzhi*). They have human forms, but are covered only by red hair; they have ears but no eyes. If one remembers the appropriate demon's name for a given day (and, presumably, calls it out), then one can avoid its depredations (1.4b–7b). The *Nüqing guilü* also prescribes various protective spells and talismans for avoiding demonic harm.

Thus the *Nüqing guilü*, like the "Spellbinding" text written centuries before, places the same emphasis on magical control over demons through various exorcistic measures, but especially through the ability to identify any given spectre by name. Still, given that the *Nüqing guilü* is a Taoist scripture—revealed by the Most High Lord Lao (*Laojun) to the Celestial Master *Zhang Daoling—the nature and function of the demonic is presented in a very different context. The opening of the scripture describes the revelatory situation. In the beginning, people were free from demonic harassment; demonic hordes were loosed upon the world only when the moral behavior of humankind deteriorated (1.1a). Followers of the Dao should have relatively little to fear if their actions remain correct; for them, problems only arise when demons overstep their correct functions (punishing evil). The *Nüqing guilü* thus functioned to aid adherents when they encountered such rebellious demons. Taoist ethics (spelled out in a code of twenty-two items—for humans, not spirits—in *j.* 3 of the *Nüqing guilü*) became conjoined with the demonographic tradition.

Demonization of popular deities. The addition of this moral component was not the only way in which Taoism changed the demonological tradition that had preceded it. While early conceptions of the spirit world had drawn only a vague and unstable line between good and evil supernatural beings, the Celestial Masters and their followers established a much sharper one. According to *Lu Xiujing's *Daomen kelüe (Abridged Codes for the Taoist Community), one of the chief features of the new Taoist regime had been the following: "The spirits (shen 神) do not eat or drink"—i.e., the deities of local, popular cults were no longer to receive sacrificial offerings. Continued worship of such deities was forbidden as "licentious sacrifice" (*yinsi). Indeed, such gods were unmasked by Taoist revelation: they were really demons, "stale pneumas" (guqi 故氣) of the demonic realm of the Six Heavens (see *santian and liutian). Thus the "gods" of the people are caricatured as rapacious exploiters, promising blessings to those who give them cult, but dealing out only impoverishment, disease, and early death (1a-b, trans. Nickerson 1996a, 352; see also *Santian neijie jing, 1.6a-b, trans. Bokenkamp 1997, 216–17).

The cosmology of the administration of the dead, the Six Heavens of *Fengdu, became highly developed in Taoism, for instance in j. 15–16 of the *Zhengao (Declarations of the Perfected). Drawing on Han period accounts of Mount Tai (*Taishan, Shandong), the Zhengao sets out an elaborate bureaucracy for this fabulous mountain in the northeastern seas, positions in which all are filled by dead historical personages. Elsewhere, however, the *Shangqing scriptures name talismans, spells, and texts for, inter alia, "eliminating," "overawing," and even "invoking" the demonic powers of the Six Heavens (Nickerson 1996b, esp. 582–83), again emphasizing the value of placing the powers of the demonic under the control of the adept through use of appropriate techniques, such as talismans, spells, or even the simple act of naming.

From demon to god. Through meritorious service to the Dao, certain demons could move up through the ranks, eventually to the status of transcendent immortal, making the line between the divine and the demonic a highly porous one. According to the Zhengao, most of the demonic officials of the Six Heavens, after specified years of service and advancement through the ranks, can eventually reach transcendent status. Similarly, in the Nüqing guilü the Celestial Master states that he is sending out demon lords of the five directions (wufang guizhu 五方鬼主), each with command over a myriad of demonic troops. If other spectres are found to be "overstepping their bounds"—attacking with disease not only sinners but also good people—Taoists should call out the name of the appropriate demon lord (depending on the illness contracted). The demon lords are to disperse the recalcitrant demons, forcibly if necessary, and bring aid and succor to the worthy. If they do this, then these lords eventually will rise above their demonic status and have their names listed on the Registers of Life (shenglu 生錄; 6.2a-b; see similar language in the fifth century stratum of the *Dongyuan shenzhou jing; 2.6a–7b).

This pattern was to become even more common in ensuing centuries. Zhao Gongming 趙公明 is named in *Tao Hongjing's own notes in the *Zhengao* as a fever demon (10.17b). However, the *Nüqing guilü* names Zhao as one of the demon lords just mentioned—and hence as a spirit capable of rising from demonic to divine status. This was precisely what happened. By Song times, Zhao had become a Taoist spirit-general, one of the Prime Marshals (*yuanshuai* 元帥). His powers, and those of his subordinates, could then be drawn upon by Taoist priests and lay ritual masters (*fashi*). Similar careers—from object of popular cult to a place in the Taoist pantheon—may be traced for other figures who became important in Song and later times, e.g. *Wen Qiong and Ma Sheng 馬勝 (Lagerwey 1987c, 241–52; Cedzich 1995; Davis E. 2001, esp. 278–79 note 14, and 284–87 note 49). However, this is not to say all followers of such deities took cognizance of the Taoist "superscriptions" that turned the gods of the people into Taoist spirit-functionaries (Katz P. R. 1990; Katz P. R. 1995a). Nor was it the case that the tensions between local cults, on the one hand, and Taoism (together with central government authority), on the other, had become completely relaxed. State officials, sometimes themselves trained in Taoist exorcistic techniques, might still come into conflict with local deities and their supporters (Boltz J. M. 1993a).

Although the barriers separating the Taoist/divine from the popular/demonic became even more permeable during Song times, they still continued to exist, and the Song produced its share of "demon statutes": the *Shangqing gusui lingwen guilü* 上清骨髓靈文鬼律 (Devil's Code of the Spinal Numinous Script of the Highest Clarity; CT 461), edited by *Deng Yougong some time before 1116, and several others. However, these new statutes were very different from the medieval *Nüqing guilü*. The Song statutes address demons themselves—such as those that attach themselves to or possess humans—and also members of the lower echelons of the Taoist otherworldly administration, such as spirit generals and their minions (and even Taoist ritual masters), who fail to protect people from demons. Such statutes then go on to specify the punishments to be suffered by the guilty. Hence, disease and misfortune were no longer attributed to the misbehavior of the afflicted, to human sinners, but instead to the demons and other beings that had allowed people to be harmed in the first place (Davis E. 2001, 22–23, 41–42). The medieval link between misfortune and immorality had been severed, and thus the forces of the spirit world were expected only to behave properly and leave people alone (or help them), not to enforce a revealed Taoist moral code.

The three modes of interaction between Taoism and demonology delineated above may appear to represent chronological phases. Contemporary practice, however, evinces the continued prevalence of each of those several modes of interrelationship. For instance, the horoscopic calculations, sometimes carried out by Taoist priests or ritual-masters themselves, that determine which malign astral spirit a client may have "offended" (*fan* 犯) or "bumped into" (*chong* 衝) can be traced back to ancient mantic practices, including those described in the *Rishu*. And today as well, the identification of such malefic spirits leads to subsequent exorcistic rites (Hou Ching-lang 1979).

Peter NICKERSON

☐ Boltz J. M. 1993a; Cedzich 1993; Davis E. 2001; Harper 1985; Harper 1996; Hou Ching-lang 1979; Kiang Chao-yuan 1937; Kamitsuka Yoshiko 1996; Kamitsuka Yoshiko 1999, 211–71; Katz P. R. 1990; Katz P. R. 1995a; Mollier 1997; Nickerson 1996a; Nickerson 1996b; Schipper 1971; Strickmann 2002

※ *gui*; TAOISM AND POPULAR RELIGION

Otherworldly bureaucracy

Taoist texts abound in bureaucratic elements and images, particularly in their view of the otherworld and the relation of Taoist adepts to it. Far from being a Taoist innovation, these bureaucratic features are borrowed from earlier religious practices and ideas. At the time of the Shang dynasty, the otherworld was ruled by hierarchically ranked deceased members of the royal family. The interaction between the living rulers and these otherworldly beings was already marked by bureaucratic elements, such as the importance of written documents, the fulfillment of duties, the use of titles, and the emphasis on hierarchy and order (Keightley 1978b). The Zhou dynasty built on this image, presenting an afterlife ruled by a celestial sovereign surrounded by a court of deceased nobles. Archaeological evidence and tomb texts show that by the second century BCE, when China had already established a centralized system of government, the otherworld was conceived of as a complex bureaucratic administration. Both the pantheon of otherworldly beings, hierarchically arranged into offices with fixed titles and roles, and the manner of interaction through written communiques and even bribes was based on a bureaucratic idiom.

One major function of the otherworldly bureaucracy was record-keeping. Offices and officials in charge of these documents appear in funerary texts as early as the second century BCE. In particular, Mount Tai (*Taishan, Shandong) developed in the early Han dynasty as an administrative and judiciary site responsible for determining the life span of individuals. This concern with techniques for procuring longevity and the view of the otherworld as monitoring human behavior was part of a common ideology, which later reappeared not only in Taoism and Buddhism but also in *zhiguai* 志怪 texts ("records of the strange"; Campany 1996). From these shared religious ideas, Taoism adopted various offices and officials in charge of longevity and the registers of life and death, such as the Director of Destinies (*Siming), and added new ones, such as the Three Offices (*sanguan, of Heaven, Earth, and Water). These deities, who inspected human behavior, could adversely affect one's life span, prevent advancement in the celestial hierarchy, or relegate one to the tortures of the "earth prisons" (*diyu* 地獄) until merit from descendants would set one free.

Entering the otherworldly pantheon. Despite the wholesale adoption of the otherworld as a record-keeping archive in charge of life spans, Taoism focused on transcendence rather than longevity as the primary goal. In the *Baopu zi*, an early-fourth-century work, longevity is subordinated as a means to aid in the acquisition of transcendence (*xian* 仙; see *xianren). In the slightly later *Shangqing tradition, transcendence in turn is relegated to a position inferior to that of a Perfected (*zhenren).

The Shangqing tradition provided a detailed description of the otherworldly realm, which formed the basis of all later Taoist ideas on the otherworld. Below the Heavens of the Three Clarities (*sanqing), the middle of which houses the Perfected and the lowest of which hosts the transcendents, are the Nine Palaces (*jiugong) and the Grotto-Heavens (*dongtian*; see *dongtian and *fudi*), the latter of which are populated by earthly transcendents (*dixian* 地仙). The lowest realm, the Six Heavens (*liutian*; see *santian and *liutian*) and *Fengdu, are the administrative abodes of those who have not attained the rank of Perfected or Transcendent.

Those who do not become Perfected in this life undergo post-mortem refinement, advancing through the ranks of the otherworld in much the same manner as in the secular bureaucracy. This preoccupation with appointment to office and promotion is found in the *Zhengao (Declarations of the Perfected), which reflects the concerns of an elite recently pushed from political office and power.

Control over the otherworldly bureaucracy. In an attempt to differentiate themselves from other religious specialists, the Taoists adopted a role similar to the one played by Han dynasty officials. They borrowed the image of a bureaucratic otherworld, abolished sacrifices to the demons of popular religion (not sanctioned either by Taoism or the state), replaced blood sacrifices with written communiques to the gods, and incorporated popular deities into the Taoist pantheon as minor gods (and Han officials as transcendents).

Taoist priests wield control over the otherworldly bureaucracy through registers (*LU) received during ordination. Adepts interact with this otherworldly bureaucracy both in ritual and in visualization. Since the body is a microcosm of the external world, they journey within themselves to address the deities of the cosmos and to lay documents before celestial officials.

Amy Lynn MILLER

📖 Bokenkamp 1989; Lagerwey 1981b, 87–104; Lévi 1989a; Maspero 1981, 75–195, 263–430; Needham 1974, 93–113; Nickerson 1994; Robinet 1997b, 62–65; Seidel 1978a; Seidel 1987a; Seidel 1987c; Seidel 1987e; Seidel 1989–90, 254–58; Yü Ying-shih 1981

※ DEATH AND AFTERLIFE; DEITIES: THE PANTHEON; HELL; TAOISM AND CHINESE MYTHOLOGY

Hell

In the Western world, hell typically refers to a place of eternal punishment where people are sent as retribution for their sins. In Taoism, the same sort of realm exists as a counterpart to celestial spheres; however, Taoist hell is usually a temporary abode, not necessarily for those who are damned but for those who are not yet part of the celestial hierarchy. The inhabitants can escape from this netherworld, in which they may or may not endure bodily punishments, either by working their way up the ranks of the otherworldly bureaucracy or through the merit of their living descendants.

Early Chinese ideas of the otherworld. Many features of the Taoist hell have their roots in earlier Chinese ideas. During the Shang dynasty, the otherworld was composed of deceased members of the royal family (Keightley 1978b). This royal image continued into the Zhou period, when the heavens were administered by a celestial ruler surrounded by a court of nobles. This paradise was paired with a subterranean realm, usually called the Yellow Springs (*huangquan* 黃 泉), where, one supposes, commoners went to labor on waterworks as they had in this world.

According to Han dynasty tomb texts, by the second century BCE the otherworld was fully bureaucratized and replete with tax offices, tribunals, and prisons, a virtual mirror of the government in this world. As in the Yellow Springs, the dead were locked away with the help of jailors (*yushi* 獄使) beneath the sacred mountains, particularly Mount Tai (*Taishan, Shandong), to keep them from harming the living. A celestial ruler and administration governed these subterranean offices, recalling the Zhou dynasty dichotomy between celestial and subterranean realms. Registers (*LU) recorded one's life span as well as good and bad deeds committed. The use of the term *jie* 解 (to release from culpability) in these documents indicates that the *hun* and *po* souls of the dead were imprisoned for misdeeds, though punishments are not made explicit. The roots of a bureaucratic otherworld where the dead were judged was coalescing.

Taoist views. In addition to inheriting the idea of a celestial bureaucracy and the image of a bureaucratized subterranean world filled with interrogations, judgements, and imprisonment, Taoism also retained the dichotomy between celestial and terrestrial realms and the belief that the dead could physically harm the living.

In the *Taiping jing (Scripture of Great Peace), a text of the second century CE, there are four celestial judicial departments (*cao* 曹) where deeds are monitored and registers kept, reminiscent of the Four Palaces (*sigong* 四宮) or Four Guardians (*sishou* 四守) mentioned in the *Huainan zi (Major 1993, 68, 80, 296). Those who commit evil deeds are afflicted by disease, have their life spans shortened, and after death face torture under interrogation, reflecting Han dynasty penal practices; the Celestial Masters (*Tianshi dao) tradition similarly stressed longevity and often saw disease as a punishment for misdeeds. The Three Offices (*sanguan, of Heaven, Earth, and Water) in the otherworld judge the affairs of the living and send *gui (low-ranking demonic officials) to afflict them with illness, recalling earlier ideas of the dead harming the living. These *gui* dwell in the Six Heavens (*liutian*), an abode for non-initiates, in contrast to Taoists who inhabit the Three Heavens (*santian*; see *santian and *liutian*).

The *Shangqing tradition adopted and elaborated on this administrative structure of the otherworld. In their systematization, the Six Heavens are situated beneath Mount Luofeng 羅酆, also called *Fengdu (the name of the Zhou dynasty capital). This subterranean realm is home to souls who have acquired merit through moral behavior or meditational techniques, but not in sufficient quantity to enter the ranks of the celestial hierarchy. They are interrogated and judged by the Three Offices, which either assign them to minor bureaucratic posts as *gui* or condemn them to corvée labor.

Buddhist influence. In the mid-second century CE, when Buddhist *sūtras* began to be translated into Chinese, the ideas of *karma* and reincarnation found their way into the Taoist conception of the otherworld. Although by this time the Chinese had a well-developed idea of the otherworld as a bureaucratic realm and a prison, conceptualizations focused on administrative procedures and the process of interrogation and torture. The living were often punished with disease; post-mortem punishments were not described in detail. Buddhism introduced a systematic structure of hells and elaborate tortures that led to vivid descriptions of the punishments and sufferings endured in Taoist texts, particularly those of the early *Lingbao tradition (ca. 400 CE).

Among the terms used in the Lingbao corpus to refer to the otherworldly realm for sinners is *diyu* 地獄 ("earth prisons"). Traditionally understood as introduced by Buddhism, this term meshed well with the Chinese image of the otherworld as a subterranean penal institution. While punishments and tortures, based on Han penal codes as well as on Buddhist hells, are elaborately described, Lingbao scriptures focus on saving the inhabitants of hell, and on the numerous rites to do so. Influenced by the Buddhist ideas of universal salvation (*pudu) and the transfer of merit, these rites erase the names of the unfortunate from the registers of the dead, inscribe them in the registers of transcendents, and either cause their transfer to the Heavenly Hall (*tiantang* 天堂) or ensure a propitious rebirth.

In the early tenth century, Buddhist and Chinese ideas on the otherworld coalesced in the appearance of the Buddhist *Shiwang jing* 十王經 (Scripture of the Ten Kings; Teiser 1994). A few centuries later, Taoism responded with similar scriptures on the tribunals of the ten Perfected Lords (*zhenjun* 真君), one with the most complete bureaucracy being the *Difu shiwang badu yi* 地府 十王拔度儀 (Liturgies for Salvation from the Ten Kings of the Earth Administration; CT 215; Teiser 1993, 137). In the twelfth century, *Shenxiao rituals, developing out of Lingbao funerary ceremonies, involved saving the dead from hell through meditation and visualization techniques. In the last several centuries, ideas on hell which developed in Taoist and Buddhist contexts have continued in popular morality books (*shanshu).

Amy Lynn MILLER

📖 Boltz J. M. 1983; Campany 1990; Eberhard 1967, 24–59; Miller A. L. 1995; Nickerson 1997; Robinet 1993, 216–20; Sakamoto Kaname 1990; Sawada Mizuho 1968; Seidel 1987a; Seidel 1987e; Teiser 1993; Teiser 1994; Thompson 1989; Xiao Dengfu 1989; Yü Ying-shih 1981

※ Fengdu; DEATH AND AFTERLIFE; OTHERWORLDLY BUREAUCRACY; REBIRTH

SACRED SITES

Taoist sacred sites

In considering Taoist sacred sites, it might be best to begin by distinguishing between natural sites (caves and mountains) and man-made sanctuaries (temples, monasteries, and shrines). For Taoist practitioners, mountains and caves are sites for the practice of self-cultivation, the goal of which was to attain longevity or immortality. They also constitute places of refuge, liberation, and transcendence. Worship at such natural sites involves a journey that can be either upward or inward, or in some cases both. For mountains, the journey's goal is not to attain the summit, but to locate and enter caves containing Grotto-Heavens (*dongtian). Such a journey is in many ways a rite of passage, involving entry through portals and the crossing of streams. The journey can be fraught with danger, and adepts had to purify themselves and perform rituals before ascending. Mountains are also renowned for containing exotic animals, for example deer and cranes.

Mountains have traditionally been home to all manner of hermits or recluses (yinshi 隱士). Like their Near Eastern counterparts, some remained secluded throughout their religious careers, but others chose to return to the world after completing their regimens or self-cultivation or asceticism in order to advise emperors or provide succor and salvation for the masses (Brown 1982; Eskildsen 1998; Porter 1993). These adepts also studied a mountain's flora, especially medicinal herbs that could be used in preparing alchemical elixirs. They were also interested in the mountain's geomancy (fengshui 風水), including a site's "earth texture" (diwen 地文; Ward 1995). Of particular significance were texts that attempted to guide practitioners through underground passages to the Grotto-Heavens below the mountains, such as the *Wuyue zhenxing tu (Charts of the Real Forms of the Five Peaks), and the Fengdu shan zhenxing tu 酆都山真形圖 (Chart of the Real Form of Mount Fengdu). The Grotto-Heavens on mountains often contained scriptures and treasures (especially swords) hidden in these caves by immortals, and the most fortunate adepts might even encounter an immortal in person. Some Taoist mountains could also be sites for ritual suicide, including ingesting poisonous elixirs or throwing one's body off a cliff (Strickmann 1979, 129–38; Lagerwey 1992, 319–20).

Perhaps the best-known Chinese mountains with clear links to Taoism—and in most cases Buddhism as well—are the Five Peaks (*wuyue): *Taishan (Shandong), *Hengshan 衡山 (Hunan), *Huashan (Shaanxi), *Hengshan 恆山

(Shanxi), and *Songshan (Henan). Taoist masters also produced hierarchical ranking of the ten great and thirty-six lesser Grotto-Heavens and seventy-two Blissful Lands (*fudi). There are also the so-called guardian mountains (*zhenshan* 鎮山), which are said to have been spatially fixed during the Zhou dynasty. Other important mountains have been intimately linked to the history of Taoist movements, including *Longhu shan and the Way of the Celestial Masters (*Tianshi dao) movement; *Maoshan and *Shangqing; Zhongnan shan 終南山 and *Quanzhen, etc. At the same time, however, no mountain was the exclusive property of a particular Taoist movement, and many were home to Buddhist and other non-Taoist practitioners. Taken as a whole, the location of mountains and Grotto-Heavens neatly matches the pattern of Taoism's historical growth.

While mountains and caves can be imposing wonders, on another level they can serve as both macrocosm and microcosm. In China and the West, the grotto has long been a metaphor for the cosmos (Miller 1982; Stein R. A. 1990; Verellen 1995). In China, a grotto can symbolize both the womb that gives life, and a tomb that houses the dead. Cave entrances were literally referred to as "mouths of the mountain" (*shankou* 山口), from which issued the *qi exhaled by the mountain. In some texts, the inside of a mountain is conceived of as a respiratory system.

Records of man-made Taoist sites date back to at least the Han dynasty. Such sites ranged in size from small "quiet chambers" (*jingshi) and thatched huts (*lu* 盧), where adepts could practice self-cultivation, to monasteries and abbeys (*guan* 觀), where Taoist monks and nuns resided and practiced self-cultivation, and large-scale palaces (*gong* 宮) often patronized by the imperial court. The layout of a Taoist sacred site could vary significantly, but in general their sacred space seems to have been arranged in a way that would present the Taoist pantheon and Taoist cosmology to practitioners and local worshippers (Steinhardt 2000). Like mountains, few Taoist temples were exclusively Taoist, but also coexisted with Buddhist and especially local cult sites (Katz P. R. 1999, 41–51; Robson 1995). Temples also preserved examples of Taoist art, and were sites for the performance of Taoist music. Their festivals (*yingshen saihui* 迎神賽會) and temple fairs (*miaohui* 廟會) provided an important occasion for interaction between Taoists, officials, elites, and members of the local community. Of particular significance were the lay associations (*hui* 會) that worked with Taoists to organize these events, which were also occasions for performances of local dramas and intensive economic activities (see *TAOIST LAY ASSOCIATIONS). Taoist temples were also sites for pilgrimages, during which worshippers approached a sacred mountain or temple (*chaoshan* 朝山; *chaosheng* 朝聖) and presented incense to its deity (*jinxiang). (See also the entry *TEMPLES AND SHRINES).

Viewed from a social historical perspective, both natural and man-made Taoist sacred sites featured extensive interaction between Taoists and lay worshippers, who attempted to impose their interpretations and representations on sacred space by means of a wide range of texts, including stele inscriptions, gazetteers, murals, rituals, oral traditions, and dramatic performances. As recent work on the Palace of Eternal Joy (*Yongle gong) and other temples has shown, Taoist sites were diverse and complicated, and represented a multiplicity of meanings to different groups of patrons (Katz P. R. 1999, 16–17 and 50–51; Miller T. G. 2000).

Paul R. KATZ

📖 Ward 1995; Brown 1982; Doub 1979; Hachiya Kunio 1990; Hachiya Kunio 1995; Hahn 1988; Hahn 2000; Little 2000b, 147–61; Miller N. 1982; Munakata Kiyohiko 1991; Nara Yukihiro 1998; Naquin and Yü 1992; Schipper 1960; Schipper 1985a; Stein R. A. 1990, 209–72; see also bibliography for the entry *TEMPLES AND SHRINES

※ TEMPLES AND SHRINES; for other related entries see the Synoptic Table of Contents, sec. II.10 ("Temples, Abbeys, Shrines") and sec. II.11 ("Mountains and Mountain Monographs")

VIEWS OF THE HUMAN BEING

Taoist views of the human body

Three main terms define the traditional Chinese views of the human body. The first, *ti* 體 or "body," designates the physical frame as an ordered whole made of interdependent parts. The second, *xing* 形 or "form," mainly refers to the body as the counterpart and residence of spirit (*shen*; see *lianxing*). The third, *shen* 身 or "person," denotes the whole human being, including its non-material aspects ranging from thinking and feeling to personality and social role. These terms show that the Western notion of "body" as physical structure is inadequate to convey the complexity of the Chinese views. The specifically Taoist views are further enriched by significant varieties among different traditions. In the absence of a single way of seeing the body shared by all Taoist traditions, this entry outlines some of the main themes that emerge from different contexts.

Body and state. The human body and the state are two microcosms related not only to the macrocosm but also to each other (see *MACROCOSM AND MICROCOSM*). The body is often described with bureaucratic metaphors, and governing the state is often likened to self-cultivation. This analogy runs throughout Heshang gong's 河上公 commentary to the *Daode jing* and is restated in later texts. One of Heshang gong's relevant passages reads: "If in governing the body one cherishes one's breath, the body will be complete. If in governing the country one cherishes the people, the country will be peaceful. Governing the body means to inhale and exhale essence and pneuma (*jing* and *qi*) without letting one's ears hear them. Governing the country means to distribute virtue (*de*) and bestow grace (*hui* 惠) without letting the lower ones know it" (*Laozi Heshang gong zhangju* 10; see Erkes 1950, 27). At the center of the bureaucratic metaphor are the five viscera (*wuzang*), described as "offices" (or "officers," *guan* 官) in both Taoist and medical texts including the *Huangdi neijing* (Inner Scripture of the Yellow Emperor; *Suwen* 素問, sec. 3.8).

Body and cosmos. Taoism adds much to the theory of the correspondence between cosmos and human body, beginning with descriptions that focus on *Laojun, the divine aspect of Laozi. According to the *Laozi bianhua jing* (Scripture of the Transformations of Laozi), the *Kaitian jing* (Scripture of the Opening of Heaven), and other texts, Laozi exists at the beginning of the formation of the cosmos and reappears throughout human history, transforming

Fig. 11. An immortal. Painting by Liang Kai 梁楷 (thirteenth century). National Palace Museum, Taipei, Taiwan, Republic of China..

his body each time. In other instances, the cosmos itself is seen as the body of Laozi, a theme that appears to have originated in myths concerning Pan Gu 盤古, the "cosmic man" (Seidel 1969, 93–96; Girardot 1983, 191–97). A text quoted in the Buddhist *Xiaodao lun* (Essays to Ridicule the Dao) describes the cosmic body of Laozi as follows: "Laozi transformed his body. His left eye became the sun; his right eye, the moon; his head, Mount *Kunlun; his beard, the planets and constellations; his bones, the dragons; his flesh, the quadrupeds; his intestine, the snakes; his stomach, the sea; his fingers, the five peaks (*wuyue); his hair, the trees and the herbs; his heart, the Flowery Canopy (*huagai* 華蓋, i.e., Cassiopea in heaven and the lungs in the body); and his kidneys, the Real Father and the Real Mother of humanity" (T. 2103, 9.144b; see Kohn 1995a, 54–55).

Attesting to the continuity among different times and traditions, an echo of this passage is found in an invocation that the Taoist priest pronounces at the beginning of the Offering (*jiao) ritual, when he performs a series of purifications of outer and inner space. With the Great Spell for the Transformation of the Body (*da bianshen zhou* 大變身咒), the priest identifies himself with the cosmos and with some of the divinities who inhabit it (Lagerwey 1987c, 71–72; Andersen 1995, 195; see under *bianshen).

The body as residence of gods and spirits. The spirits of the viscera have a human shape and the texts provide details on their names, heights, garments, and functions. Since the earliest descriptions, found in the *Taiping jing* (Scripture

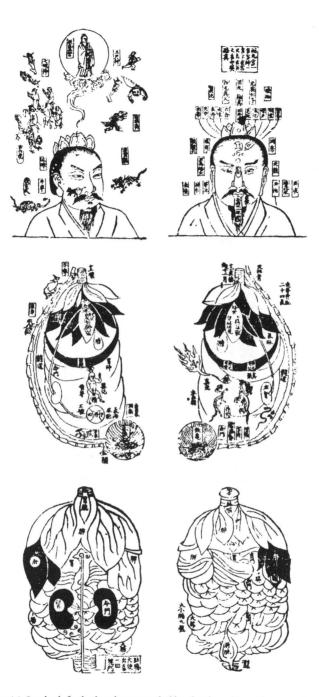

Fig. 12. (a) On the left, the head surrounded by the three *hun, the seven *po, and the four emblematic animals (*siling); on the right, locations of deities and nomenclature of components of the head. (b) Loci of the inner body, viewed from the left side and the right side. (c) The trunk and the five viscera, viewed from the front and the back. Representations attributed to Yanluo zi 煙蘿子 (tenth century?), in *Xiuzhen shishu (Ten Books on the Cultivation of Perfection; CT 263), 18.2a–3b.

Fig. 13. The human body represented as a mountain. Depicted here are the Cinnabar
Fields (*dantian*), the Three Passes (*sanguan*), and the palaces of the inner deities. *Duren
shangpin miaojing neiyi* 度人上品妙經內義 (Inner Meaning of the Wondrous Scripture
of the Upper Chapters on Salvation; CT 90), 8a-b. See Despeux 1994, 38–40.

of Great Peace; Robinet 1993, 64–66), these details are provided as support for
meditation: visualizing the inner gods causes them to remain in their corporeal abodes and perform their functions, while their departure would result
in illness and death. More extended descriptions of the inner deities are found
in the *Huangting jing* (Scripture of the Yellow Court) and especially in the
Laozi zhongjing (Central Scripture of Laozi), and were later developed by the
*Shangqing school. The *Huangting jing* describes the gods of the five viscera
and of the *niwan*, the upper Cinnabar Field (*dantian*) located in the region
of the brain. The *Laozi zhongjing* features a group of deities who dwell in different regions of the human body, all of whom are differerent forms taken

by the Great One (*Taiyi). In both texts, the deities of the viscera perform administrative functions within the body, establishing a link with the views of the medical texts referred to above.

In other instances, the viscera are the seats of impersonal forces. According to the Heshang gong commentary and to medical texts, the *hun "soul" (representing the Yang components of the human being), the *po "soul" (representing the Yin components), the essence (*jing), the spirit (*shen), and the Intention (*yi) respectively reside in the liver, lungs, kidneys, heart, and spleen. Elsewhere, hun and po are represented in a divinized form; in this case, the hun deities are said to number three and the po seven (see fig. 42). They are often mentioned with the "three corpses" and "nine worms" (*sanshi and jiuchong), malevolent spirits who report the faults and sins of the individual in which they dwell to the Director of Destinies (*Siming). Accumulating merit through good actions, abstaining from cereals (*bigu), and performing rites on the *gengshen day (the fifty-seventh of the sexagesimal cycle) were among the methods used to neutralize them.

The body as mountain and landscape. The *Wushang biyao (Supreme Secret Principles, 41.3b; Lagerwey 1981b, 136) associates the Authentic Talismans of the Five Emperors (wudi zhenfu 五帝真符) with the five planets in heaven, the five sacred mountains on earth, and the five viscera in the human body. The body itself is often represented as a mountain (Despeux 1990, 194–98; Lagerwey 1991, 127–42). Liang Kai 梁楷 (thirteenth century) painted a famous scroll that depicts an immortal—possibly meant to be Laozi himself—as a mountain, using the technique normally applied for painting landscapes (fig. 11). Images of the body as a mountain are also found in Taoist texts (for an example, see fig. 13). They illustrate loci in the body that are important for the practices of Nourishing Life (*yangsheng) and inner alchemy (*neidan). Some of these sites are represented as palaces that function as headquarters for the administration of the inner body: here too the metaphor of the government of the country as the government of the body is apparent. In turn, the visual depictions of the body as a mountain are related to the best-known Taoist image of the inner body, the Neijing tu (Chart of the Inner Warp; see *Neijing tu and Xiuzhen tu, and figs. 60 and 61), which maps the body as a landscape whose features (e.g., the watercourse, the mill, the furnace) have symbolic meanings in neidan. (For another example, see fig. 19.)

The body in inner alchemy. The neidan view of the body is complex, and remarkable differences occur among various subtraditions and authors. In general, the main components of the inner elixir (essence, pneuma, and spirit, or *jing, qi, and shen), as well as the tripod and the furnace (*dinglu), are said to be found within the human being. Beyond this basic premise, neidan shares some of the views outlined above and dismisses others. For instance, it inherits from traditional medicine the importance of the Control and Function channels (*dumai* and *renmai*) that play a central role in the circulation of essence (see *zhoutian*); on the other hand, *neidan* practice as it was codified during the Song period does not involve visualizing the inner gods.

Neidan, however, is more than a technique, and the importance it gives to immaterial notions such as inner nature and vital force (*xing* and *ming*), or inner nature and individual qualities (*xing* 性 and *qing* 情), shows that its focus is not the physical body. *Li Daochun (fl. 1288–92) explains that the various notions and practices have multiple "points of application" or "points of operation" (*zuoyong chu* 作用處); they take on different meanings at different levels, from the physical to the spiritual and beyond this distinction (see especially *Zhonghe ji*, 2.15b–17a). An example is the Mysterious Pass (*xuanguan*), which according to different authors is located between the eyebrows, between the kidneys, in the gallbladder, in the navel, or elsewhere, while other say it has no precise location in the body. As Li Daochun remarks: "The Mysterious Pass is the most mysterious and wondrous pivotal pass (*jiguan* 機關). How can it have a fixed position? If you place it in the body (*shen*), this is not correct. If you separate it from the body and search for it outside the body, this is also not correct" (*Zhonghe ji*, 3.3a).

Fabrizio PREGADIO

📖 Andersen 1995; Despeux 1990, 187–219; Despeux 1994; Despeux 1996; Engelhardt 2000, 94–100; Ishida Hidemi 1989; Katō Chie 2002; Kohn 1991b; Lagerwey 1981b, 77–80; Larre 1982; Lévi 1989b; Maspero 1981, 448–59; Robinet 1989b; Rochat de la Vallée n.d.; Sakade Yoshinobu 1983b; Saso 1997; Schipper 1978; Schipper 1993; Sivin 1987, 117–167; Sivin 1995; Yamada Toshiaki 1989a; Yates 1994a

※ *bianshen*; *lianxing*; BIRTH; DEATH AND AFTERLIFE; INNER DEITIES; MACROCOSM AND MICROCOSM; REBIRTH; TRANSCENDENCE AND IMMORTALITY; for other related entries see the Synoptic Table of Contents, sec. II.8 ("The Human Being")

Inner deities

Besides the celestial gods and goddesses who reside in heaven, a veritable pantheon of Taoist deities also exists within the human being. These deities fulfill various related functions: they personify abstract notions such as the Dao, Yin and Yang, or the Five Agents (*wuxing*); they allow the human being to communicate with the major—and in several cases corresponding—gods of the outer pantheon; they act as officers in the bureaucratic system that manages the whole body; they perform healing tasks by supporting the balance of the body's functions; and they are objects of meditation. The basic purpose of visualizing them is to "maintain" them (*cun) in their proper locations, nourish them with one's inner pneumas and essences, and invoke them so that in turn they provide protection and sustenance. This is said to ensure health, longevity, or immortality, and to defend one from calamities caused by demons and other noxious entities.

Gods of the head and viscera. The *Taiping jing* (Scripture of Great Peace) is the earliest text containing references to the gods of the five viscera (*wuzang, i.e., heart, lungs, liver, kidneys, and spleen). Each is represented wearing a single garment the color of the current season, or three layers of clothing related to the pneuma (*qi) of the current season and the next two seasons (Robinet 1993, 64–66). Visualization of the gods of the viscera is also mentioned in a related text, the *Taiping jing shengjun bizhi* 太平經聖君祕旨 (Secret Directions of the Holy Lord on the Scripture of Great Peace; CT 1102, 3a; Kohn 1993b, 196).

Systematic descriptions of the inner gods are first found in the "Inner" ("Nei" 內) version of the *Huangting jing* (Scripture of the Yellow Court). In particular, this source mentions the gods of the head and the inner organs. The deities of the head (sec. 8) reside in the hair, brain, eyes, nose, ears, tongue, and teeth. Their actions are governed by the Muddy Pellet (*niwan, the upper Cinnabar Field or *dantian) which in turn hosts nine more gods, the Nine Real Men (*jiuzhen* 九真), in its nine rooms (see *dantian*).

The gods of the inner organs (sec. 9–14) include those of the five viscera and of the gallbladder (*dan* 膽), an organ that represents all "six receptacles" (*liufu* 六腑; see *wuzang) in the *Huangting jing* and other texts. Each of these organs is called a "department" or a "ministry" (*bu* 部) and is managed by a god who resides in a "palace" (*gong* 宮) within that organ. The various gods are identified by their names and the colors of their garments (for instance, the god of the liver wears "a wrapping gown of green brocade," the god of the spleen "a yellow gown," and so forth, based on the *wuxing* associations); by the function that they supervise in the body (regulating breath, digesting food, etc.); and by the corresponding part of the face on which they rule (eyes, nose, etc.). Other prominent gods mentioned in the *Huangting jing* are the Great One, who resides in the upper *dantian*; Blossomless (Wuying 無英) and White Prime (Baiyuan 白元), in the upper *dantian*; and the Peach Child (Taohai 桃孩, also known as Peach Vigor or Taokang 桃康), in the lower *dantian* (sec. 9, 11, 15, 17, and 20; for illustrations of these gods in the *Dadong zhenjing*, see fig. 14).

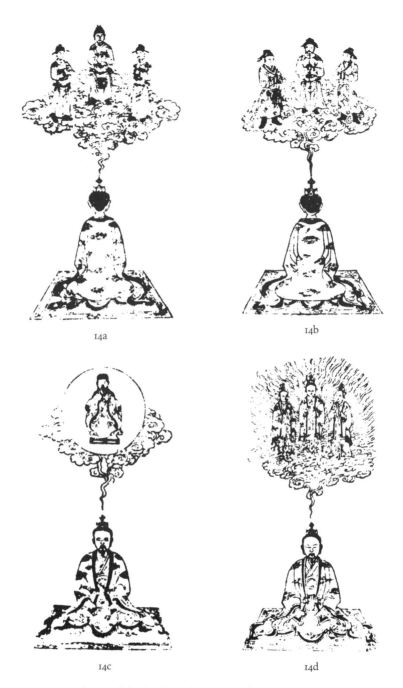

Fig. 14. Inner deities of the *Dadong zhenjing*: (a) Blossomless (Wuying 無英); (b) White Prime (Baiyuan 白元); (c) Director of Destinies (*Siming 司命); (d) Red Child (Chizi 赤子) in the Mud Pellet (*niwan); (e) Peach Vigor (Taokang 桃康), or Peach Child (Taohai 桃孩); (f) Venerable Lord Emperor One (Diyi zunshen 帝一尊神). *Shangqing dadong zhenjing* 上清大洞真經 (Authentic Scripture of the Great Cavern of the Highest Clarity; CT 6).

14e   14e

A related but by no means identical system is reflected in the *Laozi zhongjing* (Central Scripture of Laozi), where the scope of the pantheon is much wider and the nomenclature of the inner gods is, with few exceptions, different. Leaving aside a host of minor spirits mentioned throughout the text, the major gods are those described in the first twelve sections. They are represented as transformations of a single sovereign deity, the Supreme Great One (Shangshang Taiyi 上上太一), who is the Original Pneuma (*yuanqi*) spontaneously issued from the Dao and appears under varying names and forms, including the Lord of the Dao (Daojun 道君) and *Laojun. In several of these appearances, the Great One has as his spouse the Jade Woman of Mysterious Radiance of Great Yin (Taiyin xuanguang yunü 太陰玄光玉女). All these gods are said to reside both in the heavens and in the human being (and sometimes on earth as well); the usual formula that connects these different planes to each other is "human beings also have it" (*ren yi you zhi* 人亦有之), to introduce their placement within the body. The Dao itself resides in the human being as the Supreme Lord of the Central Ultimate (Shangshang zhongji jun 上上中極君; sec. 39); it is the individual "self" (*wu* 吾), also called Zidan 子丹 (Child-Cinnabar) or Red Infant (*chizi* 赤子; sec. 12 and passim).

The One as an inner god. In the *Baopu zi*, one of the two types of meditation defined as Guarding the One (*shouyi*) is also based on visualizing the One as a god residing within the human being (the other type consists in multiplying one's "form," *xing* 形, or in hiding it to escape harm caused by demons).

Drawing from an anonymous text, *Ge Hong provides a short description of the features of the One and his multiple locations. According to this passage (see under *dantian), the One alternately resides in each of the three Cinnabar Fields, and takes different names and vestments at each of these loci.

*Shangqing Taoism later developed this view of the One dwelling at different times in the Cinnabar Fields into the notion of the Three Ones, each of whom permanently resides in its own Field. A well-known Shangqing visualization method based on the Three Ones is described in the *Suling jing (CT 1314, 27a–38b; see under *sanyi).

Later history. Visualization practices such as those described above appear to have fallen into disuse by the Tang period, replaced first by the *neiguan type of meditation, based on inner contemplation and awareness of mind, and then by *neidan practices, focused on the refining of one's inner essence, pneuma, and spirit (*jing, qi, and shen). Neither practice is based on visualization of gods, although the Neiguan jing 內觀經 (Scripture of Inner Observation; CT 641; trans. Kohn 1989b) mentions several major inner deities in its model of the "perfected body."

Visualizing the inner gods continued to play an important role in liturgy, however, where the priest summons his inner gods and dispatches them to submit petitions in Heaven (for details, see under *bianshen, *chushen, and *liandu). This function is attested from medieval times (Bokenkamp 1996c) to the present day (Lagerwey 1987c, 121–23; Schipper 1993, 96–97). Neidan has preserved visible traces of earlier practices in both of its best-known charts of the inner body, the *Neijing tu and Xiuzhen tu. The Neijing tu includes several divine beings in its representation of the "inner landscape," and the Xiuzhen tu explicates its visual map of the inner alchemical process with passages related to the Huangting jing (Despeux 1994, 51–64 and passim).

Fabrizio PREGADIO

📖 Andersen 1979; Boltz J. M. 1983; Despeux 1994; Kakiuchi Tomoyuki 1998; Katō Chie 1996; Katō Chie 2002, 61–73; Kohn 1989a; Kominami Ichirō 1992; Lagerwey 1981b, 79–80; Maspero 1981, 272–86, 346–64, 364–72, and 431–41; Pregadio 2006a; Robinet 1989c; Robinet 1993; Schipper 1979a; Schipper 1993, 108–12; Schipper 1995c; Yamada Toshiaki 1989a

※ MEDITATION AND VISUALIZATION; TAOIST VIEWS OF THE HUMAN BODY

Birth

Most Taoist sources consider *jing or "essence" to be the life germ: when Heaven and Earth "exchange their essences" (jiaojing 交精), Yin and Yang generate the "ten thousand things." A human being similarly "receives life" (shousheng 受生 or bingsheng 稟生) at conception through the exchange of essences between father and mother. Birth is only one step in a person's development, which culminates at the age of sixteen for males and fourteen for females. According to this view, one is "born" as soon as one is conceived, and birth represents only a transition from inner to outer life. From the Song period onward, this event was seen as the transition from the precelestial state (*xiantian) to the postcelestial state (*houtian).

Gestation therefore is an essential period of life. During this time, the various physiological elements are progressively formed, and one receives the different cosmic pneumas (*qi) as well as the spirits and divinities who inhabit the microcosm of one's body. This process, however, also creates blocks that one must overcome during one's lifetime in order to attain immortality (the so-called "mortal knots" in the embryo).

The various Taoist traditions interpret the phases and elements of gestation in different ways, as shown by the following examples.

Physiological development. Several sources, both Taoist and medical, cite with minor variations the classical description of embryonic development first found in *Huainan zi 7 (trans. Schipper 1993, 117). In the first month, a ball of lard (gao 膏) appears; in the second, the preliminary form of the embryo (die 胅); in the third, the full form of the embryo (tai 胎); in the fourth, the muscle tissues (ji 肌); in the fifth, the tendons (jin 筋); in the sixth, the bones (gu 骨); in the seventh, the embryo is complete; in the eighth, it moves; in the ninth, it turns upside down; and in the tenth, it is born.

Inner spirits and divinities. The most frequently cited description of embryonic development is found in the Neiguan jing 內觀經 (Scripture of Inner Observation; CT 641, 1b; trans. Kohn 1989b). In the first month, essence and blood coagulate in the womb; in the second, the preliminary form of the embryo takes shape; in the third, the three *hun appear, and in the fourth, the seven *po; in the fifth, the five viscera (*wuzang) are formed and their divinities take up residence within them; in the sixth, the six receptacles (liufu 六腑; see *wuzang) take shape; in the seventh, the seven orifices are opened; in the eight, the "eight effulgences" (*bajing) descend into the body; in the ninth, the inner residences and palaces are properly arranged; in the tenth, the gestation process is completed and birth occurs.

Celestial pneumas. According to the *Yebao yinyuan jing (19.1b–2a, and YJQQ 29.1b–2b), the embryo is imbued with nine pneumas in the first nine months of gestation. In the third month, the *hun* are formed, and in the fourth, the *po.* In the ninth month, 36,000 deities descend into the body, and birth occurs during the tenth month. A *Lingbao document, the *Shengshen jing (Scripture of the Life-Giving Spirits), explains how the deities are created from different cosmic pneumas, and how the embryo is nourished during gestation by the Three Primes (*sanyuan) and the pneumas of the Nine Heavens (*jiutian). At the time of birth, some divinities descend to the courtyard of the house to protect the newborn child (CT 318, 2a, and YJQQ 29.2b–3a).

The *Jiuzhen zhongjing (Central Scripture of the Nine Real Men; CT 1376, 1.2b–3a, and YJQQ 30.6a) establishes a distinction between the inner spirits, such as the *hun* or the *po*—which are produced by supernatural spirits (*ling* 靈) and the pneumas of the parents—and the outer spirits, who come to reside within the person.

Mortal knots. The *Shangqing views of birth are described in the *Taidan yinshu (Concealed Writ of the Great Cinnabar [Palace]; CT 1330, 38b–39b, and YJQQ 29.4b) and the *Taijing zhongji jing* 胎精中記經 (Scripture of the Central Record of the Essence of the Embryo; CT 1382). After the Yin and Yang pneumas merge, during each month of gestation the embryo receives the pneuma of one of the Nine Heavens. Twelve knots and twelve joints strengthen the embryo, but they also create fetters that adepts must untie during their time on earth to attain immortality (see Robinet 1993, 139–43).

Catherine DESPEUX

📖 Furth 1995; Furth 1999, 94–133; Katō Chie 2000; Katō Chie 2002; Larre 1982, 169–75; Miyazawa Masayori 1984a; Robinet 1993, 139–43; Schipper 1993, 119–29

※ DEATH AND AFTERLIFE; REBIRTH; TAOIST VIEWS OF THE HUMAN BODY

Death and afterlife

Early views. Notions of death and the afterlife in Taoism—and the rites created to deal with them—evolved from two largely distinct strains of thought and practice: those connected with the search for transcendence and immortality, and juridical motifs relating to a bureaucratized afterlife. The former concerned, among other aspects, various methods for the attainment of life everlasting (e.g., *waidan) as well a rich lore concerning immortals and the fantastic lands they inhabited.

The juridical features of the Chinese afterworld, though they may be traced back to Warring States precedents (von Falkenhausen 1994; Harper 1994), are best exemplified by first and second century CE documents placed in tombs, known as grave-securing writs (zhenmu wen 鎮墓文). These set out the orders of a Celestial Monarch (Tiandi 天帝), relayed through his Envoy (shizhe 使者) to an elaborate spirit-bureaucracy of the tomb. The cosmology thereby implied suggests a prototype of later Chinese notions of hells and other underworld domains (see under *HELL). The deceased is placed under the jurisdiction of the Lord of Mount Tai (*Taishan) and subject to a regime that includes population registration, corvée labor, and taxation.

Early Taoism's fusion of the immortality cult with the "religion of the Celestial Monarch" (Seidel 1987e) is evident already in the *Xiang'er commentary. It states that the Great Darkness (Taiyin 太陰) is where advanced Taoists, feigning death, "refine their forms" (*lianxing) in order to be reborn with perfected bodies. Those who are less virtuous are "taken away in service of the Earth Offices" (Rao Zongyi 1956, 22, 46, and 77; Bokenkamp 1997, 102) The text expresses both the alchemical metaphor of refining the body through smelting away the grosser form (thus attaining prolonged life) and the juridical notion of the underworld as a place of incarceration.

Administering the dead. Fourth-century materials collected in the *Zhengao (Declarations of the Perfected) evince how such ideas were expanded upon. The center of the administration of the dead has shifted to the Six Heavens of *Fengdu (on the Six Heavens see *santian and liutian). All the newly dead pass through Fengdu and are judged and sent off to appropriate afterworld destinations depending on the contents of their files, which record their (and their ancestors') merits and demerits. Those who are virtuous—but not virtuous enough to have attained immediate transcendence—may become officials in Fengdu, advancing by steps to immortal realms. Others, such as great generals and dynastic founders, their files having been stained by too much blood, are consigned to demonic office in Fengdu forever. Developing the notion of "release from the corpse" (*shijie) already suggested in the Xiang'er, the Zhengao also provides for the possibility that a person who had accumulated "hidden merit" in his or her family for generations might simply provide a bone from his or her foot to the Three Offices (*sanguan, of Heaven, Earth, and Water) of Fengdu. Then one could eventually—possibly after having been reborn into a different clan—feign death, avoid the land of the shades altogether, and achieve transcendence (Zhengao, j. 15–16).

By the end of the fourth century or early fifth century, a variety of materials attest to increasingly elaborate soteriologies among a number of Taoist groups. Celestial Master (*Tianshi dao) tomb ordinances from the fifth and early sixth centuries, excavated in Hunan and Hubei, address a pantheon of tomb spirits that shares many members with the Han grave-securing writs, but the orders proceed from the deified Laozi. Additionally, the tomb spirits are instructed, not only to forbear from harassing the deceased and the survivors, but also to assist the deceased with her or his ascent to the Three Heavens: "shampooing and bathing, capping and girding him," "sealing and binding up his *hun and po, and opening the way for him."

"Salvation through extinction." A *Lingbao scripture, the Miedu wulian shengshi miaojing 滅度五鍊生尸妙經 (Wondrous Scripture on Salvation through Extinction and the Fivefold Refinement of the Corpse; CT 369), likewise prescribes the use of a set of five tomb ordinances, with the exact content of each varying according to the *wuxing. These Lingbao ordinances are highly consistent both with the Celestial Master ordinances and their Han dynasty predecessors. According to the Lingbao ordinances, the deceased's body is to go to Great Darkness, while the hun is to be released from the underground prison of the hells of the Nine Shades (jiuyou 九幽). This dual transfer is preparatory to the reunification of spirit and body and their rebirth in the human world after a set number of years. These notions are founded on the Lingbao notion of "salvation through extinction" (miedu 滅度). Initially an early Chinese Buddhist term for nirvāṇa, here the phrase refers to successive cycles of death, ascent to heaven, and rebirth, by which the individual eventually could reach the rank of "transcendent king" (Bokenkamp 1989; Bokenkamp 1990; Nickerson 1996b, chapter 3).

Likewise echoing the Xiang'er's conception of Great Darkness, the Lingbao *Duren jing (Scripture on Salvation) claims that those of insufficient merit will have to pass bodily through Darkness. However, recitation of the scripture can release their spirits to the Southern Palace (Nangong 南宮). Then the deceased may, after repeated cycles of rebirth, achieve transcendence (Bokenkamp 1997, 428–89). The connection between alchemical transformation and salvation was deepened through new forms of mortuary rites developed in the Song, in particular that of Salvation through Refinement (*liandu), in which the priest's own inner-alchemical visualizations effected the deliverance of the deceased (Boltz J. M. 1983).

Sepulchral plaints. Notions of death and afterlife in early Taoism relate not only to rites for the newly deceased, but also and especially to the need to settle the spirits of the unquiet dead. Such problems typically took the form of sepulchral plaints (zhongsong 冢訟)—lawsuits filed before the magistracies of the underworld by the aggrieved dead—either directly against the living or against their deceased kin (and still causing illness or death among the living owing to the legal principle of the collective responsibility of relatives; on the early forms of this notion see under *chengfu*). The *Zhengao* details several such cases that affected the Xu 許 family (the patrons of *Yang Xi, who revealed the *Shangqing scriptures), for instance the troubles encountered by Xu Mi 許謐 (303–76) when a man his deceased uncle had murdered filed a complaint before the Water Official of the Three Offices.

The sepulchral plaint became the chief explanation for misfortune in medieval Taoism, and the medieval manual for petitioning celestial officials, *Chisong zi zhangli* (Master Red-Pine's Almanac of Petitions), contains two versions of a "Great Petition for Sepulchral Plaints" ("Da zhongsong zhang" 大塚訟章; trans. Nickerson 1997) that detail the supplicant's difficulties, attribute them to the misdeeds of deceased kin, and call down a panoply of celestial officials to rectify all problems related to the plaint. Such problems include not only those directly concerned with the plaintiff's suit, but in particular those connected with demons of tombs, offended spirits of the earth, and the "prohibitions and taboos" (*jinji*) of astrology and geomancy. Unsurprisingly, the *Chisong zi zhangli* often relates problems with tombs and the dead to problems of soteriology, as where the result of the resolution of a sepulchral plaint and the release of the departed to heaven is his or her inability to cause disease among, or further file complaints against, the living (6.1b–2b). Soteriology is once more linked with juridical/exorcistic concerns.

Death and the afterlife in Taoist ritual. Much of the later history of these issues may be considered under the rubric of *TAOISM AND ANCESTOR WORSHIP. It might simply be noted here that many of the patterns outlined above have persisted to the present. Taoist rites for the dead (the ritual of Merit, *gongde*) still center on the rite of Opening a Road in the Darkness (*kaitong minglu*) so that the deceased may leave the underworld, ascend to the Southern Palace, and be reborn. This ritual is customarily followed by that of Dispatching the Writ of Pardon (*fang shema*), a document received from the Chancellery of the Three Heavens and addressed to the Court of the Nine Shades in Fengdu, which again effects the release of the departed. Typically in the event of early or violent deaths, the priest, wearing a red headcloth signifying the militaristic/exorcistic role of the Red-head (*hongtou* 紅頭) ritual master (see *hongtou and wutou*), may subsequently carry out an Attack on the Fortress (*dacheng* 打城; see *poyu*), a vernacular rite parallel to the preceding classical ones. The release of the deceased is this time effected by palpable theatre. The priest violently destroys a paper edifice—the Fortress of Those Who Have Died Unjustly (*wangsi cheng* 枉死城)—and releases a figurine representing the departed. At least in southern Taiwan, the Attack on the Fortress is even more frequently performed by ritual masters in local temples as an independent rite—to release spirits of dead kin (who have returned to afflict the living with illness and other misfortunes) from sufferings in the underworld.

Peter NICKERSON

📖 Bokenkamp 1989; Bokenkamp 1990; Boltz J. M. 1983; de Bruyn 1999; Campany 1990; Campany 2002, 47–60; Graham 1978; Harper 1994; Loewe 1982; Nickerson 1996b; Robinet 1979b; Seidel 1987a; Seidel 1987c; Seidel 1987e; Yü Ying-shih 1987

※ *shijie*; BIRTH; OTHERWORLDLY BUREAUCRACY; REBIRTH; TRANSCENDENCE AND IMMORTALITY

Rebirth

Rebirth is not an issue in early Taoist texts, where the end of human life is seen as a transformation, either into an ancestor or into other forms of life. It first appears under Buddhist influence in the fifth century, especially in the *Lingbao school, in two forms: on this earth as another human being or animal; and in heaven as an immortal.

The first case is closely linked with the doctrine of *karma* and retribution, according to which one's moral behavior during this life determines one's fate after death. As outlined in the Sui-dynasty *Yebao yinyuan jing* (Scripture on the Causes of Karmic Retribution), high moral stature and numerous good deeds will typically lead to an advantageous rebirth, such as in a noble and prosperous family. Crimes of various sorts, on the other hand, are punished by appropriate levels of suffering, first in a set of eighteen hells, later by rebirth in lowly forms—for example, as a worm living in excrement for "lasciviously violating the holy person of a monk or nun," or as a monkey for stealing holy vessels and the like.

The second form of rebirth involves the ritual petition for the transfer of one's ancestors from the realm of the dead to that of eternal life. They are officially transferred from *Fengdu to the Southern Palace (Nangong 南宮), where they undergo a sort of inner-alchemical refinement. One way to achieve this relocation is through the practice of visualization and ecstatic excursion, during which the adept visits the dignitaries on high and formally petitions for the transfer of both his own and his ancestors' registers.

The other way to achieve celestial rebirth is through rituals performed at the time of burial as specified in the *Mingzhen ke* 明真科 (Code of the Luminous Perfected; CT 1411). To assure a rebirth in the celestial realm, the five tablets of the "Perfect Text in Cinnabar Writing" (see under *Wupian zhenwen*) are set up on five tables placed according to the five directions, together with various offerings of gold and silk as well as a set of cast dragons. The rite ensures that the deceased will be clothed in an appropriate garment during his wait for transformation, while the dragons, cast and pointed in the five directions, carry the message of his impending transfer to all the relevant officers of the otherworld.

Livia KOHN

📖 Bokenkamp 1989; Bokenkamp 1996c; Campany 1990; Harper 1994; Kohn 1998d; Robinet 1984, 1: 170–73

※ *lianxing*; *shijie*; BIRTH; DEATH AND AFTERLIFE; TRANSCENDENCE AND IMMORTALITY

Transcendence and immortality

One of the most difficult issues in the study of Taoism is how to understand the final goal of the Taoist life. The difficulty owes not merely to insufficient research, or even to the murkiness and disparity of the data, but also to the interpretive lenses through which specialists and non-specialists alike have viewed the issue. For generations, many writers maintained, for instance, that what ultimately distinguished the "philosophical Taoists" of antiquity from the "religious Taoists" of imperial times was that the latter were devoted to achieving a "physical immortality." That artificial distinction invited overemphasis on certain elements of Taoism, where practitioners at least discussed the use of material substances and processes (e.g., "elixirs") as supposed means of achieving the spiritual goal. Such elements were indeed present in Taoism, but their importance has often been exaggerated because of their amazing alienity from the modern Enlightenment mentality and from models of religious life known from other traditions.

We must be careful not to mistake the part for the whole, and must carefully consider a wide array of Taoist phenomena, and numerous divergent models, within the minds and lives of Taoists of different periods and different traditions. We must also distinguish the religious models of practicing Taoists from the highly romanticized conceptions of "immortals" that always abounded in Chinese literature, art, and culture. The ultimate distinction is that among Taoists, the goal was never simply to find a means of obviating the death-event, but rather to attain an exalted state of existence through assimilation to higher realities. Among Taoists, such attainment generally assumed a process of personal purification and enhanced awareness of reality, i.e., a

process of moral, spiritual, and cognitive growth (Kirkland 1992b). Once one
has completed such a process, one is assumed to have somehow reached a
state that will not be extinguished when the physical body dies. Beyond these
generalities, concepts varied widely, not only between the classical Taoist texts
and later "religious" practitioners, but among Taoists of every segment of the
tradition.

A common problem involves the term *xian* 仙 or **xianren* 仙人, commonly
translated as "immortal." Both in China and beyond, this term has widely been
regarded as a key feature of "Taoism" as it developed in imperial times. In the
early and mid-twentieth century, leading scholars (e.g., Henri Maspero and H.
G. Creel) argued over whether the ancient writers of *Daode jing* and **Zhuangzi*
envisioned such attainment of a deathless state. Some argued that the classical
Taoists only sought a more spiritualized life and an unworried acceptance of
inevitable death. The **Liezi*, a text originally of the fourth century CE whose
received version borrows much from the *Zhuangzi*, seems to insist upon the
finality of death, with no indication that one can transcend it. Certainly, many
passages of *Daode jing* and *Zhuangzi* suggest that one's goal should be to live a
spiritualized life until death occurs, but others (e.g., *Daode jing* 50) clearly com-
mend learning how to prevent death. The term *xian* occurs in neither the *Daode
jing* nor the **Neiye*, and in *Zhuangzi* it does not appear among its many terms
for the idealized person (**zhenren*, etc.). But in *Zhuangzi* 12, a wise border guard
tells Yao that the "sage" (or "saint," **shengren*) "after a thousand years departs
and ascends as a *xian*," and in *Zhuangzi* 1 a character is ridiculed for doubting
the reality of the invulnerable "spiritual person" (**shenren*) of Mount Gushe
(Gushe zhi shan 姑射之山), who ascends on dragons and extends protection
and blessings to people. These passages are quite consistent with most later
images of the *xian*, and suggest that such a state is both theoretically possible
and a worthy goal.

Writings of Han times (Kaltenmark 1953) mention *xian* as denizens of distant
realms, often winged beings who can fly between earth and higher worlds. In
his *Shiji* (Records of the Historian; 28.1368–69), Sima Qian 司馬遷 mentions
men of Yan 燕 (Shandong) who "shed their mortal forms and melted away,
relying upon matters involving spiritual beings (*guishen* 鬼神)." Though such
images are quite vague, they provided fuel for centuries of religious and literary elaboration, both Taoist and non-Taoist. For instance, in literature from
Han to Tang times, the goddess **Xiwang mu* (Queen Mother of the West)
"controlled access to immortality," but while poets wove bittersweet images of
"immortality" as an unattainable beatitude (Cahill 1993), Taoist writers firmly
believed that one can transcend "the human condition" if one can only learn
the subtle secrets and practice them diligently enough.

The most famous of all such writers was **Ge Hong* (283–343), who attempted to convince "gentlemen" that the pursuit of deathlessness through alchemy was a feasible and honorable goal (Barrett 1987a). Such beliefs did reappear among some leading *Shangqing practitioners, such as *Tao Hongjing, but were subordinated to a pursuit of spiritual elevation that was assumed to require the loss of bodily life (Strickmann 1979). Some depictions of the process of *shijie ("liberation by means of a corpse") intimate that exceptional men and women could undergo a transformation that merely simulated death (Robinet 1979b). But we must read carefully to distinguish metaphors from practical ideals (Bokenkamp 1989). Though many accounts depict leading practitioners as having "ascended to immortality," most Taoist texts actually suggest a "post-mortem immortality" (Seidel 1987c).

Stories of "immortals" who continue to live for hundreds of years are generally products of literary imagination, not Taoist religious practice (Kirkland 1992b). Yet, Taoism was the only Chinese tradition that provided colorful images of a happy personal afterlife. And it is clear that while some Taoists used such images as recruitment devices, luring novices into a process of spiritual self-cultivation, others did occasionally ponder the theoretical possibilities of attaining an idealized state beyond death. For instance, the famed Tang poet and *daoshi *Wu Yun (?–778) is credited with a text entitled *An Essay on How One May Become a Divine Immortal Through Training* (*Shenxian kexue lun). And even the "Fifteen Articles" of the *Quanzhen founder, *Wang Zhe (1113–70), says that the successful reclusive meditator attains the status of *xian* while still alive in the mortal body (*Chongyang lijiao shiwu lun*, article 12). Such ambivalent concepts of transcendence endure among twentieth-century Taoists, for human minds vary in how they conceive spiritual goals.

Russell KIRKLAND

📖 Bokenkamp 1989; Bokenkamp 1990; Cahill 1993; Campany 2002, 75–80; Chen E. M. 1973a; DeWoskin 1990; Kirkland 1992b; Kohn 1990b; Kohn 1993b, 277–363; Kominami Ichirō 1992; Liebenthal 1952; Lagerwey 1981b, 183–221; Little 2000b, 147–61 and 313–35; Loewe 1979; Loewe 1982; Penny 2000; Robinet 1984, 1: 161–80; Robinet 1986b; Robinet 1993, 42–48; Robinet 1997b, 48–50, 82–91, and 128–32; Seidel 1987a; Seidel 1987c; Seidel 1989–90, 246–48; Spiro 1990; Strickmann 1979; Yamada Toshiaki 1983b; Yoshikawa Tadao 1992b; Yü Ying-shih 1964; Yü Ying-shih 1981; Yü Ying-shih 1987

※ *lianxing; shengren; shenren; shijie; xianren; zhenren;* DEATH AND AFTERLIFE; REBIRTH; TAOIST VIEWS OF THE HUMAN BODY

VIEWS OF HUMAN SOCIETY

Messianism and millenarianism

Messianic beliefs played a central role in medieval Taoism and formed, in different ways, the irreducible theological nucleus of every Taoist movement. Millenarian expectations and visions of the end of the world, along with the messianic hopes that usually accompany them, never ceased to be a source of religious fanaticism in China, and acted as a major factor in the emergence of marginal currents of Taoism. They are the roots of a long messianic and millenarian tradition that has spanned the whole of Chinese history.

The origins of Chinese messianism can be traced to the Former Han dynasty. The first attested movement arose in the third year BCE. Its followers worshipped the goddess *Xiwang mu (Queen Mother of the West), transmitted her edict with frenzied enthusiasm, and awaited the arrival of people with vertical eyes. The movement spread throughout northern China, all the way up to the imperial court (Loewe 1979, 98–101). In later times Xiwang mu did not continue to play this charismatic role, but reappeared as various avatars (e.g., Wusheng Laomu 無生老母 or Unborn Venerable Mother) in subsequent millenarian movements, until as late as the Eight Trigrams uprising of 1813 (Naquin 1976).

The Taoist messiah expected in medieval times, especially during the intensive millenarian effervescence of the second to the seventh centuries, was *Li Hong, that is, the deified Laozi or *Laojun. As the supreme divinity of the Taoist pantheon, Laojun was venerated by the first large-scale Taoist movements of the second century. According to the founding legend of the *Tianshi dao theology, Laozi had appeared in the year 142 CE to inaugurate a new moral order called the Way of the Orthodox Unity (*Zhengyi, the alternative appellation of the Tianshi dao organization), and to bestow the title of Celestial Master (*tianshi) on *Zhang Daoling. This epiphany marks the beginning of the Tianshi dao, whose mission was, from generation to generation, to secure religious teaching for the people in order to save the world. The messianic kingdom established by the Celestial Masters in Shu 蜀 (Sichuan) lasted more than twenty years. In 215, its chief, *Zhang Lu, surrendered to General Cao Cao 曹操 (155–220), the virtual founder of the Wei dynasty. The Celestial Master organization was thus scattered throughout the whole state, and eventually came to embody the spiritual power complementary to official ideology. Adorned with the insignia of orthodoxy, the Taoist Church became the representative of moral and religious order, and in turn set itself up against other millenarian sects.

This destiny was not shared by the other main contemporary Taoist millenarian movement, the Taiping dao 太平道 (Way of Great Peace) of the *Yellow Turbans. Active in eastern China, and close to the Celestial Masters in their practices and ideology—emphasizing disease caused by sins, therapy through confessions and talismans, recitation of the *Daode jing*, and so forth—the Yellow Turbans went so far as to threaten the power of the Han dynasty. Their insurrection of the year 184 was violently repressed. The movement thus was not institutionalized, but continued to exist underground. The utopia of the Great Peace (*taiping*) remained a powerful detonator for millenarian uprisings, such as the great rebellion of *Sun En which blew up in southern China in 399. The followers of these movements considered a change of sovereign as a sine qua non condition for the success of the messianic realization, since the emperor was believed to incarnate the cosmic as well as the political order. The advent of the reign of Great Peace necessarily implied the renewal of the Heavenly Mandate (*tianming* 天命).

During the period of partition of the Six Dynasties, while northern China was ruled by non-Chinese peoples, southern China—the guarantor of ancestral cultural and religious traditions—became the location of an unceasing messianic effervescence. Prophets of the rural masses called Li or Li Hong multiplied, stirring up anxieties about the coming end of the world among their followers. Although these self-proclaimed prophets claimed to act under Laojun's authority, they were not only persecuted by officials but also attacked by orthodox Taoism, which condemned them as charlatans and heretics.

The second-century Taoist millenarian movements are known to us essentially through the accounts of the official dynastic histories. The firsthand accounts that have survived, preserved in the Taoist Canon and among the *Dunhuang manuscripts, date to the second and third centuries. But it was mainly during the fourth to sixth centuries in southern China that an abundant messianic literature was produced by both marginal Taoist sects and mainstream, official Taoist movements. In fact, by that time messianic beliefs were not limited to the uneducated masses, but had also become an important concern of the Taoist elite. Their literary apocalypses were said to be transmitted to earth in times of intense cosmic and moral crisis to save the "seed-people" (*zhongmin*). All of these texts predict the advent of the messiah Li Hong and the inauguration of the ideal reign of Great Peace. The main Taoist apocalyptic scripture, entitled *Dongyuan shenzhou jing (Scripture of the Divine Spells of the Cavernous Abyss), was produced at the beginning of the fifth century by a religious community active in the Jiangnan 江南 region. Liturgically organized on the margins of the Celestial Masters, with its own clergy and rituals, this millenarian sect underwent a process of institutionalization, and during the Tang dynasty became one of the clerical orders of the official Taoist priesthood. Other contemporary messianic sects were similarly absorbed into the orthodox establishment. Such was the case with the movement of the Northern Emperor (*Beidi), whose exorcist preachers of the end of the world were transformed, a few centuries later, into official Taoist masters of exorcism (Mollier 1997).

Imperial dynasties adopted messianic beliefs to legitimize their rule. The *Taiping jing (Scripture of Great Peace) in its different versions was used to legitimize the rule of both Han Shundi (r. 125–144) and Han Huandi (r. 146–168); and the name Li was taken both by Wang Mang (r. 9–23) to justify his political usurpation, and by Han Guangwu (r. 25–57) to validate his dynastic restoration. The Han house became intimately linked with the name Li, and so too did the Tang dynasty, which claimed to trace its genealogy back to Laozi. The Sui house similarly established its power according to current messianic beliefs. The impact of Taoist-inspired imperial messianism was thus powerful and long lasting. Motivating peasant revolts, the tradition of Taoist messianism and millenarianism also became, at the opposite end of the Chinese social spectrum, the keystone of the nationalistic ideology of the ruling dynasties.

In medieval Chinese culture and society the power of messianism was so great that Mahāyāna (Great Vehicle) Buddhism, recently established in China, also began to circulate prophecies emphasizing its pantheon of Buddhas and bodhisattvas, and to sound the alarm of the "end of the dharma," echoing Taoist apocalyptic threats. The reciprocal influence of the two religions was considerable. A sixth-century scripture, the Laozi huahu miaojing 老子化胡妙經 (Wondrous Scripture of the Conversion of the Barbarians by Laozi; Seidel 1984), goes as far as to predict the advent of the Taoist messiah, the Perfect Lord Li Hong, accompanied by Maitreya, the messianic Buddha.

Through the centuries other foreign religions—Manicheism, Christianity, Islam—have also enriched Chinese messianism and millenarianism with their own notions and systems. This apparently inextinguishable tradition has persisted to the present day, now addressing the needs of modern societies, but still proclaiming eschatological visions and utopian expectations very close to those of the Taoist beliefs of the first centuries of the Common Era.

Christine MOLLIER

📖 Bokenkamp 1994; Dubs 1942; Goodman 1994; Kaltenmark 1979b; Kohn 1998f; Levy 1956; Mollier 1990; Schipper 1979b; Seidel 1969; Seidel 1969–70; Seidel 1983b; Seidel 1984; Seidel 1997; Shek 1987; Stein R. A. 1963; Sunayama Minoru 1975; Sunayama Minoru 1990, 69–92; Tsukamoto Zenryū 1975

※ Li Hong; housheng; taiping; zhongmin; APOCALYPTIC ESCHATOLOGY

Apocalyptic eschatology

Visions of the end of the world become fully expressed in Taoist literature only between the end of the fourth and the beginning of the fifth centuries CE. This is a rather late appearance if one considers that a millenarian tradition of at least two centuries precedes it. The *Laozi bianhua jing (Scripture of the Transformations of Laozi) and the *Laozi zhongjing (Central Scripture of Laozi), which contain the first written traces of a Taoist messianic and apocalyptic movement, date from the second and third centuries CE. However, these two texts, both predicting *Laojun's Parousia, contain only the embryo of Taoist messianic thought.

A growing body of apocalyptic literature arose during the Six Dynasties at a crucial point in the history of Chinese religion. At that time, Taoism faced the growing challenge of Mahāyāna (Great Vehicle) Buddhism, predominantly in northern China which had been occupied for a century by non-Chinese peoples. Southern Taoism considered itself the guardian of ancestral religious and cultural traditions. Its attitude toward Buddhism was ambivalent: while greatly influenced by the sophisticated concepts of the foreign religion (especially in the realm of eschatology), Taoism rejected it as an imported usurpatory tradition. Forced to compete with Buddhism, Taoists developed the idea of a national religion, and strived to define its identity. In reaction to the proliferation of Mahāyāna *sūtras*, they produced their own holy scriptures, which revealed the words of a personified Dao. These "Taoist *sūtras*" are said to have been born of the primordial energies before the generation of the universe. Stored in heaven, they are transmitted to the human world only during times of crisis to restore order and save the people. The faithful receive them by divine means—that is, through mediumistic techniques—and are entrusted with their transmission to fellow human beings.

The first Taoist accounts of the coming apocalypse appeared in the wave of revealed scriptures produced by this Taoist reaction to Buddhism. Preserved both in the Taoist Canon and among the *Dunhuang manuscripts, the apocalyptic literature consists of about a dozen works, most of which derive from the main institutionalized schools of medieval Taoism. This is the case, specifically, with the Laojun bianhua wuji jing 老君變化無極經 (Scripture of the Endless Transformations of Lord Lao; CT 1195) and the Zhengyi tianshi gao Zhao Sheng koujue 正一天師告趙昇口訣 (Oral Instructions Declared by the Celestial Master of Orthodox Unity to Zhao Sheng; CT 1273), both issued by the *Tianshi dao organization. Two other texts, the *Housheng daojun lieji (Chronicle of the Lord of the Dao, Saint of the Latter Age; CT 442) and the Santian zhengfa jing

三天正法經 (Scripture of the Orthodox Law of the Three Heavens; CT 1203; Ozaki Masaharu 1974), describe the *Shangqing elite's vision of the end of the world. The finest examples of Taoist apocalyptic eschatology, however, were produced by sectarian movements, notably the *Laozi huahu miaojing* 老子化 胡妙經 (Wondrous Scripture of the Conversion of the Barbarians by Laozi; S. 2081; Seidel 1984) associated with a marginal current of *Lingbao (see *Huahu jing*), and the *Dongyuan shenzhou jing* (Scripture of the Divine Spells of the Cavernous Abyss; CT 335), recorded by a sect of devotees active in the region of the southern Yangzi River at the beginning of the fifth century.

Despite their different origins, the extant texts present an identical theology, cosmology, and messianic ideology. They claim that the end of the world will happen in a *jiashen* 甲申 year (the twenty-first of the sexagesimal cycle), and that it will be preceded by calamities: court proceedings, imprisonments, wars, fires, floods, and above all, innumerable diseases. These calamities will be brought about by huge armies of demons, mostly the souls of the dead worshipped by popular cults and by the state religion. The messianic movements understood illness as the outstanding mark of sin, and recommended the recitation of sacred scriptures (see *songjing*), the use of talismans (*FU), the practice of confession, and the performance of rituals as healing techniques. They condemned the heterodox cults (*yinsi) characterized by the slaughter of animals offered to demonic spirits. Emphasis was also placed on explaining the advent of the apocalypse as the result of concurrent causes: cosmologically, the end of time was unavoidable because of the exhaustion of cosmic energies and the impending end of the *kalpa* (*jie); morally, the cosmic end was necessary to purge the whole universe of irreligious, depraved creatures. The texts express hope for a renewed theocratic society led by the divine *Li Hong (Laozi's appellation as the messiah), who would appear on earth in a *renchen* 壬辰 year (the twenty-ninth of the sexagesimal cycle), eight years after the end of the world. This renewed world would be exclusively populated by the "seed-people" (*zhongmin), the elected ones predestined for immortality and salvation.

The divine transmission of sacred scriptures is thus the most obvious confirmation of one's elected status. It allows the initiate and his entire family and lineage to enjoy the bliss of the messianic kingdom. The perfect universe anticipated by Taoist devotees is seen as a return to the Golden Age of early antiquity, and as a regeneration of original purity.

Christine MOLLIER

📖 Bokenkamp 1994; Bokenkamp 1997, 295–99; Kobayashi Masayoshi 1990, 403–81; Mollier 1990; Robinet 1984, 1: 138–40; Seidel 1984

※ *housheng*; *zhongmin*; MESSIANISM AND MILLENARIANISM

Ethics and morals

Taoist ethical thinking developed on the basis of ancient Chinese thought and in conjunction with Buddhism. Its key tenets, which existed by the fifth century, developed in three phases. The first of these is the ancient indigenous view that prevailed from the Zhou through the Han. It focused on the notion of reciprocity (*shu* 恕) both within society and in a broader, supernatural context. If people harmed other beings or natural forces, their deeds were believed to be judged by a celestial administration and to return to cause them suffering. While this placed the responsibility for one's good or bad fortune squarely on one's own actions, there was also the simultaneous belief that people had certain inborn qualities or a "destiny" (*ming* 命) that would direct their lives and the deeds they committed. Human life in ancient China was thus understood as unfolding through a combination of self-induced good and bad fortune and the inborn character or fate one received from Heaven at birth.

This already complex understanding was later expanded by the early Taoists to include three further factors. The first was the belief that fate could be inherited from one's ancestors, expressed especially in the *Taiping jing* (Scripture of Great Peace) in the notion of *chengfu* or "inherited burden." The second was the idea that the celestial administration had supervisory and punishing agents who dwelled deep within the human body. In particular, these were represented by the "three corpses" (*sanshi*; see *sanshi* and *jiuchong*) described first in the *Baopu zi*, entities who worked hard toward the destruction of the human body, and reported to and acted upon orders from the celestial authorities. The third factor was the attachment of numerical values to good and bad deeds, a theory outlined especially in the *Chisong zi zhong jiejing* 赤松子中誡 經 (Central Scripture on Precepts by Master Red-Pine; CT 185), which would result in specific adjustment of the length of a person's life span. All three of these factors served to clarify the individual's position in the universe, both within a supernatural family network and through closer interaction with the cosmic bureaucrats; fate thus became more calculable as deeds and days were counted with greater exactness.

Buddhist influence. Buddhism was the key factor of the third phase of Taoist ethical development. Although vaguely present and exerting some influence from the second century onward, its notions of *karma* and rebirth became an active factor in the Chinese understanding of fate only after major waves of scriptural translation in both north and south China around the year 400 brought access to a better understanding of Buddhist doctrine. At that time four new factors entered the system: (1) the belief in rebirth and the retribution of sins or good deeds accumulated during one's own former lives, added to those committed by oneself in this life and to those of one's ancestors; (2) the vision of long-term supernatural torture chambers known as "earth prisons" (*diyu* 地獄) or hells, as well as punishment through rebirth as an animal or hungry ghost; (3) trust in the efficacy of various forms of ritual, such as rites of repentance (*chanhui) and the making of offerings, to alleviate the karmic burden; and (4) an increasing faith in savior figures, such as bodhisattvas, gods, and Perfected (*zhenren), who would use their limitless power and compassion to raise people from the worldly mire.

*Lingbao Taoists of the fifth century embraced the Buddhist vision with particular enthusiasm. In accordance with the general Chinese tendency, they emphasized lay, bodhisattva-oriented practice, and most of the rules they established governed the devotional activities of the common people, such as the performance of repentance rituals, the giving of charity, and the sponsorship of festivals. These rules were often rather vague in nature and provided general moral guidelines more than specific behavioral instructions.

Still, the new vision was not incorporated into the older tradition entirely without conflict. As Erik Zürcher (1980) points out, there were three areas of particular difficulty. First, the notion of ancestral inheritance was blurred in light of the belief in individual rebirth, raising the question of who really was to blame. Second, the traditional clear division of the afterlife into Heaven and the underworld was now complicated by the possibility of another alternative, rebirth. Third, the general sense of communal unity and collective guilt was disrupted by the strong individualism of Buddhism.

These three stages of the early development of Taoist ethical thought correspond loosely to those outlined for the Western tradition by Paul Ricoeur (1967), who sees an unfolding of ethical thinking from defilement (cosmic) to sin (social) to guilt (individual).

Later developments. From the fifth century onward, Taoist ethics continued to be nurtured under Buddhist influence (especially in the doctrines of *karma* and rebirth; see *Yebao yinyuan jing), and to be cultivated through monastic codes (see *Fengdao kejie) and meditative techniques. In the Song, the Taoist ethical vision broadened, and there was a greater popular concern with deeds and their retribution. The highly popular *Taishang ganying pian* was compiled in the 1150s, and many people began keeping ledgers of merit and demerit (*gongguo ge* 功過格; Brokaw 1991) to take stock of their moral deeds and cosmic standing. This suggested a rather mercantile approach to the problem of ethics, which nevertheless did not significantly deviate from the basic ethical thought that had first developed in the middle ages.

Livia KOHN

📖 Allinson 1994; Eberhard 1967; Hendrischke 1991; Hsü Cho-yun 1975; Kirkland 1995a; Kirkland 2002; Kleeman 1991; Kohn 1993–95; Kohn 1998a; Kohn 2004a; Lagerwey 1981b, 84–87; Maspero 1981, 321–24; Strickmann 1985; Zürcher 1980, 129–41

※ *jie* [precepts]; *shanshu*; for other related entries see the Synoptic Table of Contents, sec. II.9 ("Ethics and Morals")

RELIGIOUS ORGANIZATION

Monasticism

The origins of Taoist monasticism are obscure. The most ancient forms of organized Taoism did not have a monastic tradition; the Celestial Masters (*Tianshi dao) emphasized the importance of marriage and the transmission of their teachings from father to son. In the fourth century, the followers of *Shangqing tended to remain unmarried in order to be able to devote their energies to the Dao, realizing that, as Michel Strickmann (1978a, 471) puts it, "with the Perfected, a far purer union could be achieved than that vulgar coupling of the flesh offered either by secular marriage or by the rites of the Celestial Master." As a result, in their centers of activity (*Maoshan, *Lushan, *Tiantai shan), married and celibate practitioners lived side by side, following a regimen similar to that of Buddhist monastics but based on more traditional Chinese conceptions of religious practice (e.g., abstention from meat to avoid offending the celestials). The appellation *chujia* 出家, "renunciant" or "one who has left the family," was mainly used for those who had resolved to take vows and leave ordinary family life behind, such as girls determined to remain unmarried.

A tendency toward a more formal resignation from family life first appeared in the fifth century, probably due to the increasing number of Buddhist monks and the growing independence of their institutions. *Kou Qianzhi (365?–448) thus became one of the first Taoists to live like a Buddhist monk in a quasi-monastic institution, the Chongxu si 崇虛寺 (Temple for the Veneration of Emptiness). Similarly, in the south, both *Lu Xiujing (406–77) and *Tao Hongjing (456–536) lived either in mountain centers or in the capital but did not have families to distract them from their main endeavors. Still, often their followers were not as dedicated but either remained in their villages or, as in the case of Tao's disciple Zhou Ziliang 周子良 (497–516), brought their families with them to the mountain.

A clear distinction between lay and monastic practitioners and a system of formal ordination procedures only evolved toward the late fifth century: in the south, when followers of *Lingbao created sets of Taoist precepts (*jie) under Buddhist influence; and in the north with the growth and flourishing of the monastic *Louguan (Tiered Abbey) center. Specific rules and imperial sponsorship for monasteries began to flourish only in the Tang, when Taoism was favored at court and many flocked to the religion.

Fig. 15. Taoist novices at the *Baiyun guan (Abbey of the White Clouds), Beijing.
Reproduced from Zhongguo daojiao xiehui 1983.

On the whole, medieval Taoist monasteries resembled closely to their Buddhist counterpart. Still, differences persisted. Official celibacy among Taoists, for example, was not required until the early Song, when monks and nuns had to be properly registered as such. Moreover, the main type of Taoist monastic institution that still survives today belongs to the school of *Quanzhen, which arose only in the thirteenth century, strongly influenced by the Chan monasteries that dominated during the Song.

Livia KOHN

📖 Hackmann 1919–20; Hillery 1992; Kohn 2001; Kohn 2003b; Lagerwey 1987b; Ozaki Masaharu 1986b; Qing Xitai 1988–95, 1: 553–68; Schipper 1984; Yoshioka Yoshitoyo 1979

※ MONASTIC CODE; ORDINATION AND PRIESTHOOD; TEMPLES AND SHRINES

Monastic code

Monasticism appeared within Taoism around the fifth century. At that time it was only one of several possible modes of religious life, and the choice of celibate living (*chujia* 出家), either individual or communal, was not of great consequence to the all-important initiation into priesthood. In monastic codes dating from the Tang, like the *Qianzhen ke* 千真科 (Code of the Thousand Real Men; CT 1410), prescriptions for celibate and married (*zaijia* 在家) practitioners are given together. Communities (*guan* 觀) housed celibate priests, married priests with their families, and married priests living temporarily in celibate groups. This shows that at that time there was no monastic order within Taoism. The first and only monastic order appeared with *Quanzhen, which organized its adepts into purely monastic communities subject to common discipline and rules.

Texts. All Quanzhen adepts are celibate and take the Ten Precepts for Cultivating the Truth (*xiuzhen shijie* 修真十戒), regularly used as celibacy precepts (and in other liturgical contexts) from the Tang period to this day. Quanzhen adepts, however, must also obey the specific rules of their monastery of residence. Unlike precepts, these rules are enforced by this-worldly powers, namely the abbot (*fangzhang* 方丈) and, for major crimes, the secular state. The earliest known monastic code that includes rules is the *Quanzhen qinggui* 全真清規 (Rules of Purity of Quanzhen; CT 1235), dating from the fourteenth century. While no set of rules enforced in all Taoist monasteries seems to have existed at any one time, the *Quanzhen qinggui* and similar works likely were used as models that strongly influenced subsequent compilations. Later sets of codes include excerpts cited in the *Tianhuang zhidao Taiqing yuce (Jade Fascicles of Great Clarity on the Ultimate Way of the Celestial Sovereign), dating from the early fifteenth century, and the *Qinggui xuanmiao* 清規玄妙 (Mysterious Wonder of the Rules of Purity), compiled in the early nineteenth century by the *Longmen master *Min Yide.

The *Quanzhen qinggui* consists of thirteen different short texts of different origin. The first ones describe the ordination ceremony, the program of practice for a novice, and how a novice should conduct himself. They are followed by lyrical texts about Taoist life, which focus on communal practice and especially the group meditation with the bowl (*zuobo). Then comes the set of punishments, which were to be written on a board, or *guibang* 規榜, and hung in the assembly hall, the dining hall, or the travelling monks' reception room so that everyone would know the local rules. A few more general descriptions conclude this short collection. Later codes, especially the *Qinggui xuanmiao*, contain more detailed entries on the Taoists' vestments and belongings, and on the hierarchical organization of the monastery. Nevertheless, these documents are far less detailed than the Buddhist codes—in particular, the *Baizhang qinggui* 百丈清規 (Rules of Purity of Master Baizhang; T. 2025) family of texts that flourished from the Song onward and its rich legacy—and cover fewer aspects of monastic life, especially in the ritual realm. There are also fewer existing editions, and none that were issued with imperial approval; this suggests that Taoism, even in its most official forms, gave less importance to standardization of its practices than did Buddhism.

Rules of conduct. The most salient feature of Taoist monastic codes is the complete independence granted to each monastery in determining its own rules. On the other hand, descriptive texts enjoyed large circulation; the *Qinggui xuanmiao*, for example, was edited on Mount Huagai (Huagai shan 華蓋山, Jiangxi) and found to be still in use in the early twentieth century by Heinrich Hackmann on Mount Lao (*Laoshan, Shandong); it was also rewritten under the title *Xuanmen bidu* 玄門必讀 (Required Reading for the School of Mysteries) and used on the Luofu Mountains (*Luofu shan, Guangdong) in the same period. Such works gave travelling monks a formal common culture, especially with regard to the procedure for taking up temporary residence (*guadan* 掛單) in a monastery or temple, which under the Qing could last for theoretically unlimited periods in "public" (*shifang* 十方) monasteries, and for three days in the "private" (*zisun* 子孫) ones. The highly ritualized ceremony was intended to distinguish real monks and nuns from pretenders, ensuring that only ordained Taoists would gain access to temples or monasteries. Each community, however, decided on its own *guibang* or set of rules and punishments. For instance, on Mount Wudang (*Wudang shan, Hubei), where several communities belonging to different orders coexisted, each maintained its own set of rules. At least fifteen *guibang* dating from the fourteenth to the mid-twentieth centuries are extant, either in mountain gazetteers, or noted down by Japanese or Chinese observers in the twentieth century.

Taken together, these different sets of rules allow a general picture of Taoist monastic discipline to emerge. The most common punishments were kneeling down in prayer for the time it took for an incense stick to burn (*guixiang* 跪香), paying a fine (*fa* 罰), public censure (*gongze* 公責), demotion (*qiandan* 遷丹 or 遷單, *cuidan* 催丹), flogging (*zhang* 杖), expulsion (*gechu* 革出), ignominious expulsion (*zhuchu* 逐出), deferment to civilian justice, and death on a pyre (*huohua* 火化 or *fenxing* 焚形). These punishments may have been subject to different interpretations, were not all used in every monastery, and could also be combined. They strongly suggest, however, that discipline was not taken lightly. The provision for capital punishment, included in at least seven sets of rules, was applied in one notorious instance in 1946, when the last prior of the *Baiyun guan (Abbey of the White Clouds) in Beijing, An Shilin 安世霖, was condemned to death by a council of twelve monks and burned in the great courtyard.

The constraints of Taoist monasticism were as sharp as their ideal was lofty. No more than twenty large monasteries have existed during the modern period; most Taoists monks and nuns lived in small temples or travelled, and came to the larger establishments for training and monastic ordination. Under the Longmen system, which has dominated Taoist monasteries since the mid-seventeenth century, ordinands stay one hundred days (later reduced to fifty-three at the Baiyun guan) at a "public" monastery that hosts an ordination platform, and follow a very intensive and demanding course of preparation under specific rules.

Vincent GOOSSAERT

📖 Goossaert 1997, 259–301; Goossaert 2004; Hackmann 1919–20; Kohn 2001; Kohn 2004a; Kohn 2004b; Tsuzuki Akiko 2002

※ *jie* [precepts]; ETHICS AND MORALS; MONASTICISM; ORDINATION AND PRIESTHOOD

Temples and shrines

To study Taoist temples and shrines is to raise the question of the relationship between Taoism and Chinese religion. This relationship is a topic of scholarly debate; some see Taoism as the written expression of popular cults, while others see it as an elite tradition that formed as a reaction against those very cults. Actually, these views need not contradict each other. Most Chinese temples and shrines devoted to the cults of local deities or saints were never controlled by any established religion, neither Taoist, Buddhist, nor Confucian.

Early communal Taoism—the Way of the Celestial Masters (*Tianshi dao)—was for theological reasons strongly opposed to local cults, which it saw as dangerous and eventually destructive pacts with demons, and thus it actively supported their suppression. The Celestial Masters also permitted, however, limited forms of certain cults (ancestors, domestic gods), which suggests that those who sought to completely reform Chinese religion had to make compromises with prevalent beliefs from very early on. The *Lingbao revelations ushered in a greater acceptance of dealings with the dead (ancestors and local gods all being dead people), thus rescinding the Celestial Masters' precept that the living and the dead should not come into contact with each

Fig. 16. Pavilion of the Three Clarities and the Four Sovereigns (Sanqing Siyu dian 三清四御殿). *Baiyun guan (Abbey of the White Clouds), Beijing. Reproduced from Zhongguo daojiao xiehui 1983.

other. In a further step to close the gap between pure Taoist and non-Taoist devotional practice, Lingbao also laid the foundation for the Taoist adoption of Buddhist-style icons, and from the fifth century onward we witness the spread of statues and iconic stelae (and devotional associations) for the cults of Laozi and various Celestial Worthies (*tianzun* 天尊).

During the Tang, the early Taoist opposition to local cults gradually evolved into cooperation, which came to fruition in the tenth to thirteenth centuries. During that period, many local saints were included in the outer, phenomenal part (*houtian) of the Taoist liturgical pantheon. Some Taoist lineages even formed around local saints (such as *Xu Xun), who became their spiritual ancestors. Taoists (and Buddhists) began to be employed in or even build temples devoted to such saints, and these temples, rather than the more purely Taoist abbeys (*guan* 觀), became the prime venue for Taoist activities throughout China. Yet the Celestial Masters' project was not forgotten, as Taoists always strove to recast the local cults they supported (and which supported them) in a Taoist light.

Taoist institutions. Taoist temples and shrines may therefore be divided into two broad categories: Taoist institutions, and the temples and shrines of local saints that were integrated into a Taoist liturgical and theological framework. In the first category, the earliest attested types are temples of immortals, which appear in the epigraphic records of the later Han. These are indeed among the first well-documented temples of any kind in Chinese history, and predate—and were never part of—the Celestial Masters organization. They were apparently built by groups of devotees who prayed to immortals for protection in general, but also for initiation in immortality techniques. Such temples devoted to miraculous ascetics, men or women, appear frequently throughout Chinese history, and many came to resemble in every respect temples of local saints.

A second type of Taoist institution appears with the Way of the Celestial Masters, which commanded the building of meeting halls for its parishes (*zhi). Also, each priest, as well as many wealthy devotees, had a chapel (*jingshi) for meditation and prayer. Meeting halls and chapels contained no icons or offerings, but merely an incense burner and writing material. Beginning around the fourth century, groups of eremites and disciples gathering around the chapel of a master, or a site where immortals had practiced before leaving this world, slowly formed more or less permanent communities with lodgings, teaching halls, and shrines. These were institutionalized under the name of "abbeys," a process aided by state recognition and financial support. The abbeys came to be considered monasteries just like their Buddhist counterparts.

With the gradual dissolution of the Celestial Masters' parish system, the abbeys became the main type of Taoist institution. They housed married or celibate priests, in permanent residence or for training and ordination. The largest state-sponsored abbeys were centers of learning, with libraries and Taoist scholars compiling erudite works. The largest rituals, sponsored either by the state or by local communities, took place in abbeys. Like Buddhist monasteries, particularly under the Tang, the abbeys were centers for local religious life. They were built in cities, on major mountains, or on sites historically connected to Taoist hagiography (*Louguan, *Taiqing gong, and others). In accordance with Taoist theology, however, the abbeys housed no shrines except those devoted to the purest deities, such as the *sanqing (Three Clarities), Laozi, and the various Celestial Worthies.

The *Quanzhen order, which formed during the late twelfth century, soon came to control most of the preexisting abbeys, and introduced rules calling for stricter cohesion of the clerical community (see under *MONASTIC CODE). A the same time, the general evolution of Chinese society caused the focus of local life to move from monastic institutions (either Buddhist or Taoist) to temples of local saints. In the modern period, some twenty-five Quanzhen monasteries serve as training and ordination centers, while most Quanzhen clerics live in temples of local saints (it should be noted that many institutions named *guan* or "abbey" have actually been converted to private hermitages or temples of saints). Similarly, while *Zhengyi clerics control a few large institutions (e.g., those on *Longhu shan, or the *Xuanmiao guan in Suzhou), the great majority of them work for temples they do not own or control. Taoist clerical institutions active in the modern period are highly prestigious sites because of their long history and the charisma of the clerical community practicing there, but few of them remain. Their architecture and art, while reflecting Taoist themes, are not fundamentally different from those of other religious or secular buildings.

Temples of local saints. The second category of Taoist temples consists of those enshrining local saints, built and managed by lay communities but employing Taoist clerics either as resident priests (*zhuchi* 住持) on a contractual basis, or inviting them to perform rituals during festivals. Such temples (and lay communities) are not strictly Taoist, as is evident from certain non-Taoist practices (such as blood sacrifices) that are carried out in these communities. They are indissolubly linked to Taoism, however, since they absolutely require Taoist ritual for temple consecration and regular renewal of the alliance with the gods (through a *jiao, or Offering, ritual). Taoists legitimize these cults not only by providing liturgical services, but also by helping to incorporate the local god into their pantheon, through Taoist canonization (a process directed in the modern period by the Celestial Masters) and the writing of scriptures and hagiography that cast the god as an incarnation of a Taoist cosmic deity. The Taoist clergy wields no effective control over these temples, as is also the case with the Buddhist clergy and its temples today; yet Taoism continues to deeply influence the cultic life of most Chinese temples and shrines.

Vincent GOOSSAERT

📖 Chen Guofu 1963, 266–68; Dean 1993; Goossaert 2000b; Hachiya Kunio 1995; Kohn 2000a; Naquin 2000; Reiter 1983; Schipper 1991a; Steinhardt 1987; Steinhardt 2000

※ MONASTICISM; TAOISM AND LOCAL CULTS; TAOIST LAY ASSOCIATIONS; TAOIST SACRED SITES; for other related entries see the Synoptic Table of Contents, sec. II.10 ("Temples, Abbeys, Shrines")

Taoist lay associations

Lay associations are a major means by which Taoism interacts with society in modern China. Many types of lay religious associations have flourished throughout Chinese history; the role of clerics in organizing them has varied, and has tended to decrease in premodern and modern times. In any case, there is no Taoist (or Buddhist) clerical establishment that imposes its structure on the laity; rather, self-contained groups serve as independent vehicles to salvation, and relate freely to each other through a system of informal networks.

Many if not most Chinese of the first millennium belonged to the parishes (*zhi) of the *Tianshi dao movement, whose comprehensive liturgical organization of society obviated any need for other religious structures. This framework seems to have gradually disappeared around the beginning of the second millennium. Meanwhile, pious lay associations supported the spread of Buddhism in China; such groups were variously called yi 邑, she 社 or hui 會, and these names continue to be used today. Votive inscriptions, the earliest detailed sources on such organizations, actually also refer to associations of Taoist devotees, composed of people belonging to the *Zhengyi organization but gathering independently to finance merit-making activities, notably cults to icons and rituals for the dead, both practices strongly influenced by *Lingbao formulations.

In the late Tang and especially the Song periods, the growth of local temple cults and later the rise of corporate entities (lineages, guilds, and so forth) made possible the rise of groups with a religious identity, related to the clergy but more independent from it than before. These groups founded temples for which they sought, and sometimes obtained, official recognition, and employed either Buddhist or Taoist clergy to run them. The temple served as the seat for one or more associations, and came to replace the earth altar (she) and clerical institutions as the focus of local religious identity.

In general, the various Chinese lay associations are based on village or neighborhood community, occupation, kinship, or common place of origin for travellers and migrants; they are not denominational. Their leaders, in modern times, usually consider themselves to be Confucian, which is largely a matter of social standing. They provide education, welfare, and moral guidance in accordance with Confucian expectations, and also are at the center of the production and consumption of morality books (*shanshu) and ledgers of merit and demerit (gongguo ge 功過格; Brokaw 1991). Many of them, however, have strong links to Taoist ritual and individual practice. These groups can therefore be dubbed "Taoist lay associations," although they also reflect the ideal of the coexistence of the Three Teachings (Confucianism, Taoism, and Buddhism).

The *Quanzhen order likely played a role in the general trend of guilds, associations, and charities traditionally concerned with Buddhist piety (as documented in the *Dunhuang documents and Fangshan 房山 stelae colophons, for instance) turning to Taoist concerns and cults. The rise of Quanzhen was supported by many local *hui*, and their leaders, the *huishou* 會首, often appear in their inscriptions, as well as in the collected works of the masters, much more frequently than they do in any other part of the Canon. Moreover, lay Quanzhen groups organized around the spirit-writing cult of Lü Dongbin are among the most strictly Taoist of all lay religious associations found in modern China.

Taoist lay associations simultaneously play several roles. They organize festivals centered around the performance of Taoist rituals, a very costly affair. They also support the religious communities, although in the late imperial period they tended to favor shrines rather than abbeys, which were sometimes seen as the preserve of the gentry. Several associations were directly involved in liturgical activities, especially the performance of music and opera. Among the best examples are the well-studied Dongjing hui 洞經會 (associations for the performance of rituals centered around the recitation of the *Wenchang dadong zhenjing* 文昌大洞真經) in Yunnan, but similar groups could be found in every province.

Association members also conduct charitable and devotional activities, such as communicating with the gods through spirit writing (see *fuji*). Members usually engage in self-cultivation practices, for which Taoist masters provided guidance. One of the functions of the Quanzhen associations was to teach *neidan* meditation techniques to the public, but by the late imperial period all religious associations—as well as the sectarian movements, from which they should be distinguished—practiced some form of psycho-physiological practice (*neigong* 內功). The great *qigong* associations of the 1980s and 90s, where religious features are much less apparent, are the direct heirs of those groups.

Many such associations are still active. The historical sources for their study are not easily accessible, as no complete association archives are known to be extant, although some booklets and manuals are available. Most records are carved on stone stelae erected by these groups in their shrines. Pilgrimage associations also often erected stelae at both ends of their journeys and other places of activity.

Vincent GOOSSAERT

📖 Lei Hongan 1989–90; Noguchi Tetsurō 1983; Schipper 1977a; Schipper 1997a

※ TAOISM AND LOCAL COMMUNITIES; TAOISM AND LOCAL CULTS; TEMPLES AND SHRINES

RELIGIOUS PRACTICE AND EXPERIENCE

Asceticism

In the *Encyclopedia of Religion* (Eliade 1987), asceticism is defined as "a voluntary, sustained, and at least partially systematic program of self-discipline and self-denial in which immediate, sensual, or profane gratifications are renounced in order to attain a higher spiritual state or a more thorough absorption in the sacred" (Kaelber 1987, 441). Typically associated with radical self-denial and the suppression of physical desires, asceticism tends to be dominant in religions that propose an eternal, unchanging, and pure soul trapped in a transient and defiled body. In Indian religions, for example, its techniques include long periods of fasting, sexual abstinence, bodily tortures (lying on a bed of nails, hanging upside-down, or exposure to extreme heat, cold, or water, for example), as well as the control of various bodily functions and rules of hygiene. Similarly, in medieval Christianity, devotees practiced self-flagellation, wore hair shirts, and spent many hours kneeling on the stone floors of churches. This form of severe asceticism almost always involves an active hostility toward the body, and a sense of the physical self as sinful, dirty, defiled, and undesirable, a major obstacle to salvation which must be overcome.

In China, there are few known examples of severe asceticism. On the contrary, the dominant mode of Chinese culture is expressly antiascetic. Confucianism declares that the body is a gift every person receives from his or her parents, and that any harm or intrusive change it is subjected to constitutes a violation of filiality. Also, any form of radical hermitism is seen as a rejection of society and family, the mainstays of Chinese life, and cannot be tolerated. Body and family are essential aspects of the individual identity, and one can only realize virtue by cultivating them in a harmonious and beneficent way.

Taoism differs from both of these religious modes, and incorporates a form of "mild" asceticism (with the possible exception of *Quanzhen during the early stages of its development; see Eskildsen 1990). This tendency is evident in the practices of its key forerunners, ancient immortality seekers and Buddhists. These devotees underwent various kinds of discipline, usually associated with hermitism and the simplification of bodily needs, in order to attain spiritual states; but in both cases the body was considered essential for this undertaking. It had to be transformed, and thus removed from society and disciplined, but not tortured. Buddhism in particular prides itself on cultivating the "middle path," which means the rejection of both indulgence and severe asceticism. Also, Buddhist doctrine emphasizes that among all forms of rebirth, the human is the most valuable, because it alone allows the conscious experience of attachment and suffering which will lead to *nirvāṇa* or full liberation.

Taoist asceticism, then, manifests in a variety of practices, such as hermitism, dietary techniques, and methods of sexual control. Hermitism means separation from family and society in favor of a life in the wilderness. Taoist immortals are well known for this rejection of worldly life, and famous for their unkempt appearance and easy communion with nature. These features are documented from the earliest sources (e.g., the *Liexian zhuan*) to the present day, when a hermit Bill Porter encountered in the Zhongnan mountains (Zhongnan shan 終南山, Shaanxi), upon being asked how he had fared under Mao Zedong, widened his eyes and asked: "Mao who?" (Porter 1993).

Dietary techniques range from total fasts, during which the intake of food is replaced by the ingestion of *qi (pneuma; see *fuqi) and the swallowing of saliva, to exchanging ordinary food for concocted drugs or natural foodstuffs. Again, we have documents from the earliest times (Guifu 桂父 or the Persimmon Man in the *Liexian zhuan*; see Kaltenmark 1953, 118–20) to today, as in the case of the hermit lady Porter met who lived only on walnuts. Sexual control (see *fangzhong shu) comes in two forms, either as celibacy or as *coitus interruptus*. Both involve the retention of bodily fluids or vital *qi*, here in the form of *jing (semen) which instead of being ejaculated is redirected "to nourish the brain" (see *huanjing bunao).

While certain adverse reactions may occur in the early stages of the practice and a degree of hardship is to be expected, the practice of asceticism in Taoism is meant to refine and purify the body, which is described as becoming lighter, softer, and younger.

Livia KOHN

📖 Eskildsen 1998; Porter 1993; Vervoorn 1990

Divination, omens, and prophecy

Means of diagnosing the present and predicting the future such as divination, reading omens, and prophecy have a long history in China, and play a role in both popular religion and in Taoism. Prophecy, in particular, played a major role in early Taoist messianic movements (see *MESSIANISM AND MILLENARIANISM) and in later Taoist traditions such as *Shangqing.

Divination was among the traditions that influenced the formation of Taoism in the Han dynasty. The earliest documented instance of such prediction may be dated to the Shang court (ca. 1600–1045 BCE). These "oracle bones"—in reality, inscribed cattle scapula and tortoise plastrons—record inquiries addressed to the ancestors of the royal house of the Shang. The application of heat produced a crack in the bone or shell that was interpreted as a divine communication (see Keightley 1978a). The idea of addressing divinations to assure or request good fortune is one that outlived the Shang. Li Ling reports that the bamboo slips found at Baoshan 包山 (Hubei; burial dated ca. 316 BCE) contain divinations addressed to anthropomorphic deities and celestial officials, as well as spirits of rivers and mountains, doorways, dwellings and directions (2000a, 286–93).

The Zhou period *Yijing consisted of sixty-four hexagrams made up of six solid (—) and broken (--) lines. An elaborate method of casting milfoil stalks determined a hexagram or hexagrams that embodied the natural potential for change of the moment of the divination. Because the milfoil casting was seen as an objective measurement of the situation at the moment of the casting, milfoil divination was in many ways a precursor of the omenological methods of the Han.

The development of methods of reading omens perhaps derived from astronomy and calendrical science, two disciplines of great importance to the legitimation of authority from at least the Zhou period. By the Han, these fields had developed numerous technical subdisciplines based on assumptions seen in the *Huainan zi (ca. 139 BCE) of a relationship of resonance between the heavens and the human world (Le Blanc 1985). One example of such a development is the practice of weather divination, described in the Han or pre-Han manual discovered at *Mawangdui in 1973 (burial dated 168 BCE) called Tianwen qixiang zazhan 天文氣象雜占 (Miscellaneous Prognostications According to Heavenly Patterns and Pneuma Images). This text provides military divinations related to meteorological phenomena influenced by *qi (see Loewe 1994a). In the Han, a specialized office called Watcher of Pneuma (houqi 候氣) was composed of twelve experts who worked under the Grand Astrologer (taishi ling 太史令), alongside the Watchers of the Stars (houxing 候星) and the Watchers of the Wind (houfeng 候風; Bielenstein 1980, 22–23). The move from divination in the strict sense—i.e., practice that assumes a divinity—to omenology during the late Warring States and early imperial period coincided with the development of a more naturalistic conception of Heaven (tian 天) at that time (Csikszentmihalyi 2000, 61–67). During this period, critics of divination like Wang Fu 王符 (78–163 CE) accepted the existence of spirit messengers of Heaven, and argued simply that these messengers did not have time to answer the questions of human beings, a viewpoint that implicitly accepted the cosmological assumptions behind the reading of omens (Qianfu lun 潛夫論, Zhuzi jicheng ed., 25.125–26). Many of these technical disciplines were integrated into later Taoist practices (Xiao Dengfu 1988).

Calendrical and other omens played a role in early Taoist messianic movements. Numerous prophetic texts sprung up in the battle for legitimacy that
ended in the founding of the Later Han in 25 CE (Hendrischke 2000, 135–43),
and this genre became the basis for the genre of apocryphal texts that thrived
from the Later Han up through the Six Dynasties period (Dull 1966; Seidel 1983a;
Yasui Kōzan 1987; see *TAOISM AND THE APOCRYPHA). The *Yellow Turbans
movement in eastern China planned its uprising for the first year of the sexagesimal cycle in 184 CE because of its auspiciousness (*Hou Hanshu*, 71.2299). As
Barbara Hendrischke has shown, movements such as the Yellow Turbans and
the *Wudoumi dao (Way of the Five Pecks of Rice) in the southwest claimed
to be authorized by Heaven. Related works such as the *Taiping jing* detail
messages from Heaven in the form of omens (Hendrischke 1985). This was
the foundational period for Taoist messianism, which recognized the cyclical
reappearance of avatars of *Laojun (Lord Lao) throughout history (Seidel
1969; Schipper 1979b), as seen in such discovered texts as the *Dunhuang *Laozi
bianhua jing* (Scripture of the Transformations of Laozi) and received texts
such as the Six Dynasties *Laojun bianhua wuji jing* 老君變化無極經 (Scripture
of the Endless Transformations of Lord Lao; CT 1195).

Two of the more significant influences of this stress on prophecy were on
Taoist eschatology (see *APOCALYPTIC ESCHATOLOGY) and cosmology. The
Han belief in authority deriving from messages from Heaven, adopted in the
apocryphal texts and adapted by early messianic movements, was developed
in the revelation-based traditions of Shangqing and *Lingbao Taoism. The
messianic figure *Li Hong became a central figure in Taoist eschatology,
evolving from a revolutionary ideal to a messiah that would lead the chosen
into a Heavenly kingdom (Seidel 1969–70). The astronomical emphasis of Han
omenology and its underlying assumption of resonance between the stars and
the human world also undergirds the Taoist emphasis on the understanding
of the thirty-six Shangqing heavens (*sanshiliu tian*), related visualization techniques, and ecstatic journeys through the heavens (*yuanyou*) that are central
to Shangqing meditation practice (Robinet 1993).

Mark CSIKSZENTMIHALYI

📖 Andersen 1994; Csikszentmihalyi 2000; DeWoskin 1983; Harper 1999;
Kalinowski 1989–90; Kalinowski 1991; Keightley 1978a; Keightley 1984; Li
Ling 2000a; Li Ling 2000b; Loewe 1994a; Ngo 1976; Sakade Yoshinobu 2000;
Shaughnessy 1997

※ *fangji*; *Yijing*; APOCALYPTIC ESCHATOLOGY; COSMOLOGY; MESSIANISM AND
MILLENARIANISM; TAOISM AND THE APOCRYPHA

Magic

"Magic" is commonly designated by the word *fashu* 法術 in Chinese and *jujutsu* 咒術 in Japanese (corresponding to Chin. *zhoushu*). In magic, supernormal power is acquired by means of physical and mental techniques, symbolic words and actions, or special implements, with the purpose of controlling natural phenomena or supernatural entities such as spirits (**gui*) and deities, or one's own existence or vital force. Sometimes divination is also included among these techniques.

Before the rise of the Taoist religion, such techniques were widely used in China in the form of "shamanic arts" (or "arts of the spirit-mediums," *wushu* 巫術) and also as "methods and arts" (*fangshu* 方術 or **fangji*) acquired by the **fangshi* (masters of methods). Taoism, calling them *fashu* 法術 (methods and arts) and *daofa* 道法 (ways and methods), absorbed some of these techniques as important ingredients in its own practices, and rejected others. For instance, in the Way of the Five Pecks of Rice (**Wudoumi dao*), one way to treat illness was to have patients drink water containing the ashes of a burned talisman (*fushui* 符水). According to **Baopu zi* 17, which describes various types of magic (*fashu*), practitioners can avoid harm from wild animals or malignant beings if they wear "talismans for entering the mountains" (*rushan fu* 入山符) against their bodies, or if they use mirrors to frighten off mountain spirits. *Baopu zi* 5 gives a detailed description of how spells and the use of the breath can bind an object to do as one desires (see Harper 1998, 173–83). Nevertheless, Taoism also drew a distinction between itself and some forms of magic and divination. For instance, in the **Laojun shuo yibai bashi jie* (The Hundred and Eighty Precepts Spoken by Lord Lao), Taoist masters are forbidden to associate themselves with *fengshui* 風水 ("wind and water," i.e., geomancy), astrology, and other popular divination techniques. In addition, because of the importance it placed on ethics, Taoism did not participate in the practice of so-called "evil" or "perverse arts" (*yaoshu* 妖術, *xieshu* 邪術), or sorcery, to bring down sworn enemies.

In the traditional classification of the Taoist Canon into Three Caverns (**SANDONG*) and Four Supplements (*sifu* 四輔; see **DAOZANG AND SUBSID-IARY COMPILATIONS*) there is no indication of where works on magic are to be found. In the **Zhengtong daozang* of the Ming period, relevant texts are located in the sections called Divine Talismans (*shenfu* 神符), Numinous Charts (*lingtu* 靈圖), and Techniques (*zhongshu* 眾術). In recent years, there have been attempts to replace the traditional classification scheme of the Canon with new ones. Examples are Zhu Yueli's *Daozang fenlei jieti* (Zhu Yueli 1996) and Zhong Zhaopeng's *Xinbian Daozang mulu* (Zhong Zhaopeng 1999). The former scheme contains discrete versions titled Magic (*fashu*) and Arts of the

Numbers (*shushu* 數術, including astrology, choosing lucky days, *fengshui*, and divination tallies) within its first division, Philosophy (*zhexue* 哲學). The latter scheme includes the items Ways and Methods (*daofa*), Talismans (*fujue* 符訣), Divination Arts (*zhanbu shushu* 占卜數術) and Hemerology (*kanyu* 堪輿; on this term see Loewe 1982, 96–97) under the category Ways and Arts (*daoshu* 道術). When the writings of the *Zhengtong daozang* are classified in this way, it is easy to see how thoroughly some forms of magic and divination have been absorbed into Taoism. Several of these forms are briefly described below.

Talismans (*FU). These are strips of paper, cotton, or wood on which diagrams or stylized graphs are written. Some, like the *bochūfu* 墓中符 in Okinawan funerary rites, are written on tiles. They have several functions, including evoking the deities, exorcizing evil, and curing sickness, and the style in which they are written varies according to the purpose. Even today in Beijing's *Baiyun guan (Abbey of the White Clouds), young monks are taught how to write talismans. It is said that when a priest writes a talisman, he blows his own breath into it (see *buqi). Taoist seals and sacred diagrams, like those that appear in the **Wuyue zhenxing tu* (Charts of the Real Forms of the Five Peaks) are basically another type of talismans.

Spells (*zhoufa* 咒法). A technique in which special magical words are uttered as commands to realize one's wishes or to change objects at will. They are also called "charm spells" (*jinzhou*), and often end with the phrase *jiji ru lüling ("Promptly, promptly, in accordance with the statutes and ordinances!"). Many Taoist texts include incantatory spells in verse (*zhouci* 咒辭).

"Practices in the hand" (*shoujue). This is a technique for controlling natural phenomena or regulating pneuma (*qi) within the practitioner's body by forming various shapes with the fingers of one or both hands. These formations are also often used during rituals or in conjunction with talismans and spells.

"Walking along the guideline" (*bugang). A technique for acquiring the power of the Northern Dipper (*beidou) by making a pattern of steps in the shape of that constellation. This has long been used in rituals in combination with the Pace of Yu (*Yubu* 禹步).

Thunder Rites (*leifa). A magical practice to endow oneself with the power of thunder. This was originally a folk practice, but its popularity grew in the late Northern Song dynasty and it was incorporated into Taoism. Combined with the techniques of inner alchemy (*neidan), it was prized as a way to generate a resonance between macrocosm and microcosm. The *Daofa huiyuan includes a variety of magical practices employing the power of thunder.

MIURA Kunio

📖 DeWoskin 1983; van Gulik 1954; Harper 1987a; Harper 1998, 148–83; Harper 1999; Robinet 1993, 29–37; Strickmann 2002

※ *zuodao*

Meditation and visualization

Psychological research on meditation defines it as an effort to focus the mind on a particular object or objects and—following the lead of the Buddhist tradition—distinguishes two fundamental types: concentrative and insight meditation (Samuels and Samuels 1975; Shapiro and Walsh 1984). Concentrative meditation involves focusing the mind on a single object with the goal of attaining one-pointedness; insight meditation is the practice of maintaining an open awareness to all stimuli in an undiscriminating fashion. Typically this training begins with the close control of attention in concentration, and only when one-pointedness has been fully attained, it moves on to the open awareness of insight.

The Taoist tradition incorporates both types of meditation, and also strongly emphasizes visualization, which can be understood as a mixture of the two. Deities or celestial powers are visualized according to painted or textually described icons; then, once their presence has been fully established, meditators engage in interaction with them, opening themselves to their various divine stimuli.

These distinct types of meditation are practiced within particular Taoist traditions. Concentrative meditation, known as *ding ("concentration") or shou 守 ("guarding"; see *shouyi), is closely associated with the Daode jing and its quietistic tendencies, as well as with alchemical and longevity techniques that enhance the physical energies of the practitioner. Insight meditation, known as *guan ("observation"), was introduced through Buddhism and played a role in the integrated tradition after the sixth century; this practice involved merging one's individual consciousness with Emptiness and attaining oneness with the Dao. Visualization, known as *cun ("actualization"), is the backbone of medieval religious practice, and central to both the *Shangqing and *Lingbao schools.

Meditation and Taoist traditions. The first evidence for Taoist meditation dates to the second century CE. The Daode jing commentary by Heshang gong 河上公 (see *Laozi Heshang gong zhangju) proposes a concentrative focus on the breath for harmonization with the Dao; fragments of the *Taiping jing (Scripture of Great Peace) describe the enhancement of body energies through visualizing different colors within the major organs of the body (*Taiping jing shengjun bizhi* 太平經聖君祕旨 or *Secret Directions of the Holy Lord on the Scripture of Great Peace*; CT 1102; trans. Kohn 1993b, 193–97). In the third century, the first formal visualization texts appear, forerunners of Shangqing practices. These mainly consist of the *Laozi zhongjing and the *Huangting jing. In addition, instructions on how to visualize interior deities and how to spiritually multiply one's body with the help of a magical mirror are also contained in *Ge Hong's *Baopu zi of the early fourth century.

The Shangqing scriptures with their manifold forms of visualization emerge in the mid-fourth century. The practices they describe include not only concentration on the *bajing (Eight Effulgences) and visualization of gods in the body, but also active interaction with the gods, ecstatic excursions to the stars and the heavens of the immortals (*yuanyou), and the activation of inner energies in a protoform of inner alchemy (*neidan). The world of meditation in this tradition is incomparably rich and colorful, with gods, immortals, body energies, and cosmic sprouts vying for the adept's attention.

Similar techniques are adopted in the Lingbao and *Tianshi dao traditions in the fifth century. From this time onward an early Buddhist influence is also evident, so that texts like the *Xisheng jing advocate a rudimentary form of insight practice in the dispassionate observation of body, self, and world and the cultivation of an empty state of consciousness called no-mind (wuxin 無心). This tendency is strengthened in the sixth and seventh centuries, when encyclopedic works such as the *Wushang biyao (CT 1138) and the *Daojiao yishu (CT 1129) present a variety of techniques and give sophisticated instructions on the practice of different kinds of guan or "observation," including the observation of Emptiness, partial Emptiness, and Being, along the lines of the Madhyamaka two-truths theory (see *Chongxuan).

The high Tang, in the eighth century, can be considered a heyday of Taoist meditation. Works by masters such as *Sun Simiao (*Cunshen lianqi ming), *Sima Chengzhen (*Zuowang lun, *Tianyin zi), and *Wu Yun (*Shenxian kexue lun) describe in detail the unfolding of a meditative consciousness as the practitioner proceeds through a variety of systematically integrated practices. These lead from concentration exercises through visualizations of body energies and celestial deities to a state of total absorption in the Dao and insight-observation of the world. It is also around this time that texts like the *Qingjing jing—devotional works with strong meditative elements often associated with the divine Laozi—are first compiled, reflecting a trend that gains further momentum toward the end of the dynasty.

Under the Song, the integration of various forms of meditation practice continues, but two new areas of emphasis unfold: inner alchemy (neidan), with its circulation and refinement of inner energies in a rhythm based on the *Yijing; and close engagement with starry deities, such as the Star Lords of the Northern Dipper (*Beidou xingjun) and the Three Terraces (santai 三台, three pairs of stars in Ursa Major), and warrior protectors, such as the Dark Warrior (Xuanwu 玄武; see *Zhenwu) and the Mother of the Dipper (*Doumu). Both practices rely heavily on visualization but also make use of concentration exercises, and aim for an immortal state of mind akin to the no-mind of insight meditation.

Later dynasties see a continuation of this tendency, with the caveat that under the Ming inner alchemical practices are increasingly mixed with Chan

Buddhist practices and that both Taoism and Buddhism are adopted by growing numbers of literati, and thus exert a stronger influence on Confucianism.
Also, in the Qing, the first specialized texts on inner alchemy for women
(*nüdan) are written, and new forms of physical meditation, such as *taiji
quan, are being developed. In the twentieth century, Taoist meditation has
been largely absorbed by the *qigong movement, which—in accordance with
its popular tendencies—mainly employs concentrative exercises but also favors
the circulation of energy in an inner-alchemical mode.

Livia KOHN

📖 Kohn 1989a; Kohn 1989b; Lu K'uan Yü 1964; Maspero 1981, 272–86, 346–64,
364–72, 431–41; Robinet 1976; Robinet 1989c; Robinet 1993; Roth 1991a; Zhang
Zehong 1999c

✳ DEITIES: THE PANTHEON; INNER DEITIES; for other related entries see the
Synoptic Table of Contents, sec. IV.2 ("Meditation")

Mysticism

Mysticism is commonly defined in the West as an experience that is inef-
fable, transient, felt to be true, and impossible to consciously induce. From
an Eastern perspective, it is more fruitful to think of mysticism as a religious
quest, an effort undertaken to attain a certain state, which typically proceeds
in stages known as *purgative* (emptying of old concepts), *illuminative* (gaining
new insights), and *unitive* (attaining oneness or union). This process guides the
adept toward the attainment of a cosmic self. The goal of the practice, then, is
a newly integrated personality, a self more cosmic yet also more human than
the one left behind, free from desires and emotions, fully one with the Dao.
This goal and the steps leading to it are often described in Western theoretical
discussions or works of mystical philosophy, typically in four central points,
just as in the "perennial philosophy" identified in the West: (1) that material
reality is only the visible aspect of some deeper and more real ground of existence; (2) that human beings cannot perceive this ground with their senses but
have the faculty to intuit it; (3) that both human beings and the world consist
of two levels, a deep, real self and a superficial, desire-centered ego; (4) that
the key to real life and truth is the shedding of the ego and recovery of the
deeper ground of existence, both psychologically and in relation to the world
through mystical union (see Happold 1970; Katz S. T. 1983).

In Taoism, mystical realization is traditionally described as the attainment
of immortality, defined both as a transcendent state in paradise, serving as
a celestial bureaucrat in one of the many heavens (see *OTHERWORLDLY

BUREAUCRACY), and as a psychological or mystical state on earth, character-ized by a high degree of mental calm and sagely behavior. In either case, the individual is dissolved as a personalized entity and becomes in mind and body a replica of the universe, part of primordial energy, spirit, and the Dao. As such he or she attains true immortality and can live as long as heaven and earth do. Within this framework, there are two distinct yet interrelated patterns, an *ecstatic* and an *enstatic* mode of immortality. The ecstatic mode emphasizes the psychological aspect of this process, finds expression in much shamanic and flight imagery, and envisions the mystical process as one of becoming lighter and brighter. The enstatic mode is more physically oriented, gives rise to images of fullness, stability, absorption, and stillness, and emphasizes union and oneness, the merging with darkness and the unconscious.

Mysticism and Taoist traditions. Historically three types of Taoist mysticism can be distinguished. First, there is the tradition of the *Daode jing* (with its numerous related texts) and the *Yijing, which favors the enstatic mode and combines quietistic, concentrative practice with a strong emphasis on physi-cal exercises. The aim of this practice is the complete alignment of the body with the rhythm of the universe. The body is understood as a microcosmic replica of the country (see *MACROCOSM AND MICROCOSM), and the ordering of oneself—in a sense that is close to Confucian understanding—is parallel and prerequisite to the ordering of the state and the world. The sage in the *Daode jing* is ideally the ruler, who rests in non-action (*wuwei) and lets the currents of the world flow freely through him. Having attained a purity of cosmic dimension, both sage and world attain a calm and tranquil oneness with the Dao.

Second, there is the more ecstatic mode found in the *Zhuangzi* and its various successors. This style of mysticism focuses more on an intellectual, mind-oriented practice, which is not altogether unlike Buddhist insight medita-tion and merged with Buddhism in the middle ages, also influencing the way Buddhism was received in China. The basic assumption here is that human beings lost their original oneness with the Dao because they developed con-sciousness. Consequently, the "chaotification" or complete reorganization of consciousness is the avowed aim of this tradition. Its main technique is a form of meditation called "sitting in oblivion" (*zuowang), the "fasting of the mind" (*xinzhai), and in later times "observation" (*guan).

Third, there is the practice of visualizations (*cun) and ecstatic excursions (*yuanyou) of the *Shangqing school, which traces its origins back to sha-manic models and has adepts engage in visionary journeys to the far ends of the world and up into the sky, allowing them to perfectly attune themselves to the rhythmical movements of the entire cosmos. After this stage has been perfected, adepts place themselves at the center of the cosmos by becoming one with the axis around which everything revolves. They identify themselves with the Northern Dipper (*beidou), the central controlling agency of the universe. Permanent residence among the stars is thus ensured.

In the heyday of Taoist mysticism, during the Tang dynasty, these three types are merged to form one integrated system. Adepts underwent a set of stages that began with the body—its purification and alignment with the rhythm of the seasons—and then went on to reorganize the conscious mind, in order to eventually transcend the world and take up residence in the heavens. Representative texts of this trend are *Sun Simiao's *Cunshen lianqi ming, and *Sima Chengzhen's *Fuqi jingyi lun, *Zuowang lun and *Tianyin zi.

This integrated model of Taoist mysticism was later taken over by inner alchemy (*neidan), which made it the basis for its own vision of mystical union. In this system, the immortal embryo (*shengtai, Embryo of Sainthood) created through revolutions of ever subtler energies within the body takes on the role of the cosmic self, which can come and go throughout the universe at will in an ecstatic mode, or merge completely with the central power of the world in enstasy. Taoist mysticism has survived in this form since the Song dynasty and is still practiced today, in a more rudimentary and medically reinterpreted form, both in monasteries and among *qigong practitioners.

Livia KOHN

📖 Kohn 1990b; Kohn 1992a; Robinet 1989b; Roth 1995

Seasonal observances

Although the annual schedule of feasts and fasts according to the lunar calendar honored at Taoist abbeys may vary from one to the next, all are united in upholding major seasonal observances. The roots of such observances are closely intertwined with a code of practice ostensibly dating to the Zhou 周 period. Both the "Quli" 曲禮 chapter of the *Liji* 禮記 (Records of Rites; trans. Legge 1885, 1: 61–119) and chapter 25A of the *Hanshu* (History of the Former Han) outline Zhou forms of homage prescribed according to a hierarchy of social status, from the Son of Heaven to the population at large. The account in the latter text adds that each level is established by canonic ritual so as to prohibit "excessive cults" (*yinsi).

The *Daomen kelüe* (Abridged Codes for the Taoist Community; 1b), a manual conveyed in the name of the *Lingbao codifier *Lu Xiujing (406–77), includes a passage remarkably similar to the *Hanshu* account. The restrictions governing the population at large specify not only whom to honor but also when: ancestors on the auspicious days of the five *la* 臘, the God of Soil (*she*

社) in the second month, and the Stove God (*Zaoshen) in the eighth month. A comparable set of instructions appears in an analogous fifth-century text dedicated to reforming contemporary practice, the *Santian neijie jing (Scripture of the Inner Explication of the Three Heavens, 1.6a). Both texts advocate a restoration of ritual standards ascribed to the *Zhengyi covenant of the Celestial Master movement.

The Daomen kelüe also speaks of the Three Assemblies (*sanhui) associated with the establishment of the Celestial Master parishes (*zhi). These meetings were scheduled on the seventh day of the first month, the seventh day of the seventh month, and the fifth day of the tenth month. After household registers were examined and revised, parishioners were given instruction and sent home to teach members of the household. The dates given the three assemblies mark the occasions when the parishes themselves were established, eight at a time, according to a Zhengyi qi zhi tu 正一氣治圖 (Chart of the Parishes of the Life-force of Orthodox Unity), cited in the sixth-century *Wushang biyao (Supreme Secret Essentials, 23.4a–9b; Lagerwey 1981b, 103–4).

The legacy of the Three Assemblies appears to be closely linked to the tradition of paying homage to the Three Offices (*sanguan) on the fifteenth of the first, seventh, and tenth months. These three dates, known collectively as *sanyuan, serve as the anchors of the calendar year for all Taoist communities. An early account documenting the custom of honoring sanyuan is contained in the pre-Tang *Chisong zi zhangli (Master Red-Pine's Almanac of Petitions, 2.4b–5b). According to the late recension of this text in the Taoist Canon, the fifteenth of the first, seventh, and tenth months (shangyuan 上元, zhongyuan 中元, xiayuan 下元) are the days set aside for inspection by the Officers of Heaven, Earth, and the Water (Tianguan 天官, Diguan 地官, Shuiguan 水官), respectively. Readers are advised to pray for good fortune while engaging in a retreat on these three days. The sequence of Three Assemblies subsequently recorded in this text differs slightly from the fifth-century texts cited above in specifying the date of the first assembly on the fifth of the first month.

Precisely when and how increasingly complex annual cycles of feasts and fasts evolved from a fundamentally agrarian custom of marking seasons remains to be determined. Three calendars listing days to be commemorated twelve months of the year are contained in the Taoist Canon. One exemplar is incorporated in the thirteenth-century *Xiuzhen shishu (Ten Books on the Cultivation of Perfection, 25.1a–5b). It is recorded as a list of days on which one observes abstinence (zhuri jieji zhi chen 逐日戒忌之辰), with directives on when to abstain from food, alcoholic beverages, and/or conjugal relations. The introduction to the calendar itself closes with the admonition that failure to observe the taboos is tantamount to committing suicide. Among days to be commemorated is not only the birth date of Xuanyuan daojun 玄元道君 (Lord of the Dao of Mysterious Origin), i.e. Laozi, on the fifteenth of the second month, but also that of the Buddha on the eighth of the fourth month. The equally eclectic nature of such calendars in the modern-day *tongshu* 通 書, or almanac, suggests its heritage may be traced to this early calendar of unknown provenance.

A derivative calendar appears as the opening component of the *Xu zhenjun yuxia ji* 許真君玉匣記 (Record of the Jade Case of Perfected Lord Xu; CT 1480; Kalinowski 1989–90, 102–3), associated with the patriarch of the *Jingming dao (Pure and Bright Way), *Xu Xun (trad. 239–374). It is titled *Zhushen shengdan lingjie riqi* 諸神聖誕令節日期 (Dates of Festivals for the Birthdays of Various Deities). All listings are designated as birthdays, including those marking the conventional dates for paying homage to the Officers of Heaven, Earth, and Water. A number of entries are devoted to various Buddhas and bodhisattvas as well as deities of regional prominence. Although some passages echo the calendar in the *Xiuzhen shishu*, abstinence is not the sole form of observation recommended. Readers are advised in closing to mark birthdays by giving alms to the *saṅgha*, offering paper money, reading scripture, and reciting the name of the Buddha. The quantity of merit thereby accruing is said to be a hundred-thousand-fold beyond that of any ordinary day. An appended segment with an anecdote set in Jinan 濟南 (Shandong) in the year 1455 may perhaps have some bearing on the provenance of the calendar itself.

A far more intricately devised calendar is contained in another text within the 1607 supplement to the Taoist Canon. It appears as the first unit under the heading of "Chaoxiu jichen zhang" 朝修吉辰章 (Section on Auspicious Days for Cultivation of Reverence) in the *Tianhuang zhidao Taiqing yuce* (Jade Fascicles of Great Clarity on the Ultimate Way of the Celestial Sovereign, 7.1a–20b) compiled by *Zhu Quan (1378–1448) in 1444. This calendar marks not only days of birth but also the days of ascent and descent for a vast host of deities. Some occasions are to be observed by holding an assembly, whereas the entry for the fifteenth of the seventh month marking Zhongyuan is notable for specifying a *jiao (Offering) ritual overseen by Taoist masters (*daoshi). In another remarkable contrast to the two other calendars, the eighth of the fourth month here is not identified as the birthday of the Buddha but as the day on which the Most High Lord Lao (Taishang Laojun 太上老君; see *Laozi and Laojun) headed West to "convert the barbarians" (*huahu* 化胡). All three calendars merit collation with contemporary counterparts honored at various Taoist abbeys, as well as with the dates of commemoration recorded in hagiographies such as the sixteenth-century *Soushen ji* (In Search of the Sacred).

Judith M. BOLTZ

📖 Bodde 1975; Bokenkamp 1997, 186–229; de Groot 1886; Lagerwey 1981b, 103–4; Lagerwey 1987c, 18–24; Nakamura Hiroichi 1983; Nickerson 1996a; Schipper 1993, 23–31, 65; Stein R. A. 1979; Thompson 1987b; Yuan Zhihong 1990

Taoist music

If ritual lies at the heart of the complex Taoist heritage of China, then music is its very soul. Extensive studies of the heart and soul of Taoist practice have only recently begun to appear in significant quantity. The fruits of this fairly new field of research in Taoist studies reflect in part a renewed interest in documenting the performance practices of major abbeys throughout the continent of China as well as in the outlying communities of Hong Kong and Taiwan. Historical studies of the musical component of Taoist practice are comparatively few in number. It is an area of research that, like contemporary field work, requires close attention to time and place. The study of music as a component of any form of religious practice is fundamentally a study of who performs what, when, where, and how.

The way in which any school of religious teachings views musical expression inevitably shapes the way in which music may figure within any form of practice. Early schools of Taoist teachings generally sought to reform the cacophonous musical settings characteristic of many community rituals. As increasingly diverse forms of Taoist ritual have evolved, so, too, has the role of music taken on new dimensions in these settings over time. Conservative approaches have in some locales been replaced by a tolerance of musical variety in Taoist ritual that even permits the incorporation of Western instruments such as the electric organ.

The role of the patron in defining the musical component of ritual performance cannot be underestimated, from authority figures of state to local community leaders. An instrumental ensemble often serves as a critical link uniting clergy and the lay community in ritual settings. Who plays what for Taoist ritual staged at any site is clearly determined by the resources available. Associations of professional and amateur instrumentalists have thus time and again been in a position to shape and reshape repertoires of ritual music. Many Taoist masters, moreover, have gained recognition in their own right as outstanding performers of folk as well as ritual music. The fact that the process of ordination itself has long entailed training in music has done much to both nurture and sustain the vitality of musical expression in Taoist ritual.

Early history. Passages in the received version of the **Taiping jing* (Scripture of Great Peace) allude to the therapeutic value of music according to the resonance of the five pitches (*wuyin* 五音) within corresponding organs of the body. Comparable reflections of correlative thought may be found in any number of writings. Statements of concern in such texts regarding the inherent hazards of disharmony find more concrete expression in early writings seeking to reform certain contemporary modes of musical expression. For example, in *j.* 9 of the *Baopu zi* (Book of the Master Who Embraces Simplicity), *Ge Hong (283–343) derides those who beat drums and dance in support of their faith in spectres. Similar behavior is condemned as well in the *Santian neijie jing* (Scripture of the Inner Explication of the Three Heavens), dating a century later.

The more subdued form of ritual practice counselled by these early southern treatises can also be documented in the north. It is epitomized by a body of incantations allegedly conveyed to *Kou Qianzhi (365?–448) by Lord Lao (*Laojun). According to the *Laojun yinsong jiejing* (Scripture on Precepts of Lord Lao, Recited [to the Melody in the Clouds]), the ritual of ordination entailed tonal incantation but those unschooled in that practice were allowed to chant in a monotone style.

Incantation is also the dominant form of musical expression favored in the early teachings ascribed to both the *Shangqing and *Lingbao movements. Reference to the well-known *Buxu ci* (Lyrics for Pacing the Void) can be traced to a Shangqing scripture dating to ca. 364–75. A ten-verse sequence is recorded in the *Yujing shan buxu jing* 玉京山步虛經 (Scripture of the Jade Capitol Mountain on Pacing the Void; CT 1439), a component of the Lingbao corpus codified by *Lu Xiujing (406–77). The incantation itself is meant to accompany circumambulation of the incense burner and may have been devised on the model of the Buddhist form of psalmody known as *fanbai* 梵唄. The limping style of circling the censer, known as Yubu 禹步, or the Pace of Yu, is thought to have evolved from a mediumistic practice common to the Chu 楚 region (approximately corresponding to modern Hubei, Anhui and Hunan). By the Tang, the musical setting for "Pacing the Void" became a fixed component of the category of court entertainment known as *yanyue* 燕樂 (banquet music).

Precisely when instrumental accompaniment came to be integrated into Taoist practice remains to be determined. According to the early eighth-century *Yaoxiu keyi jielü chao* 要修科儀戒律鈔 (Excerpts from the Essential Liturgies and Observances; CT 463), a *Taizhen ke* 太真科 (Code of the Great Perfected) speaks of a suspended bell (*zhong* 鐘) and chime (*qing* 磬). These two percussion instruments are reportedly struck prior to an assembly not only to alert the masses but also to evoke a host of numina. Reed instruments apparently did not come to be incorporated into Taoist ritual performance until the Tang. Plucked and bowed string instruments were added even later. Of all the so-called *faqi* 法器 (ritual instruments), percussion instruments have always held a dominant position.

Like the term *faqi* (lit., "dharma instruments") itself, the use of some instruments can be dated to the introduction of Buddhism into China. A prime example is the hollowed-out block of carved wood known as the *muyu* 木魚 (wooden fish), which is conventionally struck to set the tempo for chanting scripture. Aside from borrowed instruments, it also became common practice during the Tang to retitle tunes from the Buddhist repertoire performed at court according to current Taoist nomenclature. Such is the case for tunes ostensibly composed by Tang Xuanzong (r. 712–56) himself. But for the composition of new music for performance at the shrine in Xi'an (Shaanxi) honoring Laozi as the imperial ancestor, the emperor turned to *Sima Chengzhen (647–735) and other renowned Taoist masters.

From Song to modern times. The role of emperor as composer of liturgical music gained new prominence in the Song during periods of heightened imperial patronage of Taoist institutions. Numerous compositions ascribed to both Song Zhenzong (r. 997–1022) and Song Huizong (r. 1100–1125) are contained in the *Yuyin fashi* 玉音法事 (Jade Tune Ritual; CT 607). First compiled during Huizong's reign, the version of this unusual anthology in the Taoist Canon appears to have been derived from a Southern Song copy of the text. It includes a peculiar form of curved-line notation that calls to mind equally enigmatic Tibetan and Japanese Buddhist notational systems.

Massive anthologies of ritual compiled from the Song to Ming also attest to highly evolved and sometimes conflicting traditions of ritual music. One particularly rich resource setting forth the central musical roles of the high priest, or *gaogong* 高功 (see *daozhang), and chief cantor, or *dujiang, is based on the legacy of Liu Yongguang 留用光 (1134–1206), headquartered at Mount Longhu (*Longhu shan, Jiangxi). Compiled by his disciple Jiang Shuyu 蔣叔輿 (1162–1223), the *Wushang huanglu dazhai licheng yi (Standard Liturgies of the Supreme Great Yellow Register Retreat) draws on ritual codes ranging from Lu Xiujing to *Du Guangting (850–933). It reflects centuries of continuity in the written and oral transmission of Lingbao teachings that inform yet today the ritual musical practices of many Taoist communities.

Another remarkable anthology with musical notation in the Taoist Canon dates to the early Ming. The *Da Ming yuzhi xuanjiao yuezhang* 大明禦製玄教樂章 (Musical Stanzas on Mysterious Teachings Composed under the Imperial Aegis of the Great Ming; CT 981) includes notation according to the so-called *gongche* 工尺 system. Among selections for which pitch is noted in this manner are lyrics in tribute to Xuantian shangdi 玄天上帝 (Highest Emperor of the Dark Heaven). Mount Wudang (*Wudang shan, Hubei), home to this guardian of special significance to the Yongle Emperor (r. 1403–24), is renowned for its tradition of Taoist ritual music.

The musical heritage of Mount Wudang is well-documented in one of the first studies of its kind, the *Zhongguo Wudang shan daojiao yinyue* 中國武當山道教音樂 (Taoist Music at Mount Wudang in China). Prepared under the editorship of Shi Xinmin 史新民, this 1987 publication is an early product of the team of researchers working on a series entitled *Zhongguo minzu minjian qiyue qu jicheng* 中國民族民間器樂曲集成 (Anthology of Ethnic and Folk Instrumental Songs in China). It is in this series of provincially organized monographs under way that appendices on both vocal and instrumental music documented at Buddhist and Taoist sites will be found.

Additional sites where Taoist musical practice has drawn scholarly attention include Mount Lao (*Laoshan, Shandong), Macao, Shanghai, Hong Kong, and Lijiang 麗江 (Yunnan), home to a Naxi Dongjing hui 洞經會 (an association for the performance of music; Rees 2000). Musicologists generally identify various regional forms of practice with either the *Quanzhen lineage of the north or the *Zhengyi (Orthodox Unity) patriarchy of the south. Advocates of the former rely upon the *Quanzhen zhengyun* 全真正韻 (Correct Tunes of Quanzhen), an anthology of uncertain date that includes notation for percussion instruments alone (Ren Zongquan 2000). Whereas the Quanzhen heritage of musical practice is relatively free of folk traditions, the various legacies of Zhengyi practice typically draw on disparate forms of regional vocal and instrumental practice.

The influence of regional musical practice is particularly well-attested in coastal communities of the south. Elements of Taoist ritual performances in Shanghai, for example, recall the operatic tradition of Kunqu 昆曲 as well as the locally popular ensemble practice known as Jiangnan sizhu 江南絲竹 (Silk and Bamboo of Jiangnan). Similarly, the singing of ballads in the tradition known as Nanguan 南管 (Southern Pipes) may be heard in Taoist ritual performances of Fujian communities. The fact that ordained Taoists have long been at home with liturgical and folk musical practice alike has no doubt encouraged flexibility in the ritual music repertoire. Similarly, lay musicians adept at both Buddhist and Taoist liturgical music in addition to diverse popular traditions will also no doubt continue to play a role in stimulating new forms of Taoist musical practice. Its very survival is closely tied to the ease with which it continues to adapt to the changing demands of society.

Judith M. BOLTZ

📖 Cao Benye 1991; Cao Benye and Liu Hong 1996; Chen Guofu 1963, 291–307; Chen Guofu 1981; Chen Zhentao 1991; Gan Shaocheng 1996; Jones 1995, 25–32, 230–31, and 248–56; Kaltenmark 1979b, 21–23, 44; Lagerwey 1987c, 50–51 and 265–90; Lei Hongan 1989–90; Lü Ch'ui-k'uan 1988; Lü Chuikuan 1994; Schipper 1989a; Shi Xinmin 1987; Takimoto Yūzō and Liu Hong 2000; Takimoto Yūzō 1992; Tian Qing 1997, 54–80; Tsao Benyeh and Shi Xinmin 1992; Witzleben 1995, 15–16 and 19–21; Wong Isabel 1987; Zhou Zhenxi and Shi Xinmin 1994

※ TAOISM AND CHINESE THEATRE

TAOISM AND
CHINESE RELIGION AND THOUGHT

Taoism and Chinese mythology

Taoism has a rich mythology that inherits much from Chinese mainstream and Buddhist traditions, as it is both embedded in and separate from them. In particular, it shares the political dimension of Chinese myth in its concern for sage rule, heroic conquest, and perfect social harmony founded in Great Peace (*taiping*). On the other hand, it differs significantly from mainstream patterns in that it focuses less on the interests of the Chinese empire as a whole than on the definition of the Taoists' role within it. Going far beyond the mundane concerns of this world, it provides a vision of the higher and truer realm of the Dao that transcends even the most enlightened sage ruler. In addition, a number of traditional Chinese cosmological views, such as immanence, cyclicity, and disregard of creation (see *COSMOLOGY), are significantly altered in the Taoist universe, which adds elements of transcendence, teleological linearity, and a strong concern with origins.

On the whole Taoist mythology, though diversified by historical and sectarian developments, is more coherent and integrated than its mainstream Chinese counterpart. There have been fewer efforts to rewrite it into ethical and political charters; it has largely kept out of the way of literati scorn; and it found a strong supporting system in the religious vision of Buddhism, both a rival and a source of inspiration. Still, Taoist mythology is no match for Greek or Indian mythology, disjointed as it is because of sectarian schisms and its rather late emergence. Taoist religion was only organized between the second and fifth centuries CE. Furthermore, in China fictional narrative has tended to develop from historiography, giving their narratives more of a spiral than a linear structure. Thus the extensive mythological epics, instead of appearing at the beginning of the tradition, coalesced at its end, in the thirteenth and fourteenth centuries, by which time the tradition in the West had long been significantly transformed.

Several distinct phases and types of Taoist myths can be distinguished. The earliest myths, already known and transmitted under the Han, describe the nature and abodes of the immortals (*xianren*), their mysterious paradises (see *Kunlun, and *Penglai), and the practices and magic of the *fangshi. Next, in the third and fourth centuries, the practices and motifs of outer alchemy (*waidan*) contributed substantially to the growing store of Taoist symbols, which included gourds (Girardot 1983, passim; Stein R. A. 1990, 58–77), mirrors (see under *jing and jian), and talismans (*FU), as well as mica, jade, and other substances. With the emergence of the medieval schools, a formal cosmology and sacred Taoist geography emerge, describing heavens, grotto-heavens (*dongtian), immortals' continents, underworld realms, and divinities dwelling within the body. Later Taoists took a growing interest in hagiography and the inner world, which was explored especially in inner alchemy (*neidan). Tantric influence further expanded the pantheon with colorful and military elements.

Compared to aspects of Taoism, its mythology has hardly been studied at all. This is partly because even mainstream Chinese myth, which as been largely ignored by the traditional upper classes and only brought into the foreground in the revolutionary climate of the 1920s, has never quite been taken seriously by scholars. There are now at least some efforts underway to understand its history, cultural patterns, and inherent structures. For Taoist mythology, however, not even that can be said, and both its history and meaning remain largely unexplored.

Livia KOHN

📖 Birrell 1993; Girardot 1983; Girardot 1987a; Kohn 1998b; Verellen 1994

※ DEITIES: THE PANTHEON; TAOISM AND EARLY CHINESE RELIGION

Taoism and early Chinese religion

Early Chinese religion is an inherently plural phenomenon, because prior to the unification of the Qin in 221 BCE, radically different regional traditions developed in relative isolation from one and other. The unification of the Qin and Han was most notable for the interactions between these previously separate traditions and the many attempts at developing a synthetic structure that would allow their integration. One of the most influential structures, at that time, was that of the transcendent Dao, a universal framework that provided the framework for integrating local practices and customs. Accordingly, the elevation of Dao to its central position in Taoism was a reflection of the attempt to integrate elements from a number of distinct traditions into a synthetic system suitable for a new age.

Among the strains of early Chinese religion were the official systems of state worship, experts in immortality and transcendence from the coastal provinces, Chu 楚 specialists in communication with the spirits, and masters of what Lin Yutang 林語堂 (1895–1976) called the "religion of the li [i.e., ritual]," (1938,

13–17). Elements of each of these strains became part of the Han synthetic structures that were the basis for the religious movements that formed the foundation of Taoism.

The "official religion" of the Shang, Zhou, and the early imperial period was influential not only on the organization of Taoism, but also on elements of its sacred geography such as the bureaucratic structure of the underworld. The connection between rulership and communication with the ancestors in the Shang, and with Heaven (*tian* 天) in the Zhou, are both instances of authority deriving from privileged contact with the supernatural world. In imperial China, the link between the ruler and Heaven was augmented by the emperor's authority over interpreting omens that were messages from Heaven. Anna Seidel has shown how the use of talismans (*FU) in the Six Dynasties period was part of an attempt to recreate the order of the Han dynasty (Seidel 1983a). In a similar way, elements of imperial control such as registers and bureaucratic procedures were projected onto the spirit world and became important element of Taoist liturgy (see *OTHERWORLDLY BUREAUCRACY).

Different traditions of "spirit transcendence" (*shenxian* 神仙) from the eastern areas of Qi 齊 and the southern regions of Huainan 淮南 and Chu were a basis for later Taoist alchemical practices. The masters of methods (*fangshi*) from these areas were patronized by Qin and Han emperors on the basis of their claims to be able to create elixirs of immortality and transmute cinnabar to gold. Qing Xitai has connected "spirit transcendence" practices in Han texts like the lost *Taiyi zazi huangye* 泰壹雜子黃冶 (Great Unity and Various Disciples' Golden Smelting) with later Taoist methods for attaining longevity (1994, 3: 295). Related medical traditions that stressed the maintenance of an equilibrium between the constituents of the body—essence, life energy, and spirit (*jing, qi, shen*)—seen in Han texts like the *Huainan zi* and the *Huangdi neijing*, are embellished in later Taoism alchemical traditions.

Communication with the spirits in the service of healing was associated with both the *wu* 巫 ("shaman") and the *yi* 醫 ("physician") doctors of the early period. Lin Fushi has documented Han sources showing that shamans were able to channel the spirits of the dead, perform exorcisms, and cure illness (1988, 56–67). Zhao Zhongming has linked Taoist notions of immortality such as "ascending to immortality" (*dengxian* 登仙) to early descriptions of shamans (1993, 84–94). It is in the context of healing practices that the category of revealed texts began to develop in the early empire, and this category was central in later Taoist traditions like *Shangqing and *Lingbao (Csikszentmihalyi 2002).

Ritual in early China is most closely associated with the teachings of Confucius, and early Confucians developed a large body of theory that explained the efficacy of ritual in self-cultivation. One school of early Confucianism in particular, associated with Mencius (Mengzi 孟子, ca. 370–ca. 290 BCE), links ritual self-cultivation with the development of *qi* associated with certain virtues. Mark Csikszentmihalyi (1998) has argued for the influence of this Confucian school on Han dynasty *Huang-Lao Taoism. The emphasis on *xiao* 孝 (filiality) in Song and Yuan Taoism may also be seen as a reflection of Confucian values on Taoism.

These examples only begin to demonstrate the way in which particular traditions developed in the decentralized world of early Chinese religion were unified in the synthetic atmosphere of the Han and then integrated into early Taoist movements. More detailed examinations of these dynamics are available in the work of Anna Seidel (1969, 1982, 1987e), Fukui Kōjun (1958), and Xiao Dengfu (1988).

Mark CSIKSZENTMIHALYI

📖 Csikszentmihalyi 2002; von Falkenhausen 1994; Li Ling 2000a; Li Ling 2000b; Seidel 1969; Seidel 1982; Seidel 1987e; Xiao Dengfu 1988

※ TAOISM AND CHINESE MYTHOLOGY

Taoism and early Chinese thought

The relation of Taoism to early Chinese thought must be considered on two levels: 1. the place of the sources of "classical Taoism" (the *Neiye*, *Daode jing*, and *Zhuangzi*) within the context of pre-Qin intellectual history; and 2. the influence of other aspects of early Chinese thought upon the evolution of later Taoism. The former topic has been widely discussed in both Asia and the West; the latter has barely begun to be explored. Accurate interpretation of early Chinese thought requires undoing centuries of reifications of classical "schools" and even of well-known "thinkers," including the fictitious Laozi (Graham 1986b). We must also carefully avoid misunderstandings that have resulted from uncritical acceptance of the biases of late-imperial Confucians.

Classical Taoism apparently sprang from ideas of individuals and groups of southerly Chinese states in late Zhou times, when other intellectual traditions were evolving across the Chinese landscape: the Mohist organization, various Confucian schools, several Legalist theorists, and the murky groups who produced the ideas known as Yin-Yang and *wuxing*.

Confucianism was a humanistic value-system based on the teachings of Kong Qiu 孔丘 (Kongzi 孔子, trad. 551–479 BCE), of the northeastern state of Lu 魯 (in modern Shandong). The gaps between Confucian and Taoist values reflect the fact that the two traditions arose in different regions among members of different social classes, and responded to different sociocultural conditions. The teachers of various Confucian subtraditions idealized the traditional Zhou aristocracy and its values as means of correcting the problems of their age.

Mohism was the only early Chinese value-system actually embodied in a cohesive social organization. Mozi 墨子 (ca. 470–ca. 400 BCE) despised the Zhou aristocracy, and trained his followers as missionaries to recruit a communal society dedicated to carrying out his sociocultural goals. He rationalized his social activism by utilitarian ethics and theistic claims. His organization's authoritarian structure and ideological rigidity gave it coherence, but discouraged many potential participants. Mo's universalistic social vision may have contributed to similar tendencies in post-Han Taoist traditions such as *Tianshi dao and *Lingbao.

Mozi, like Confucius, was apparently from Lu, and Confucians and Mohists shared a fundamental focus—active involvement with societal affairs to reshape the polity, and individual morality, into directions more wholesome than those in which most rulers were leading their lands. These issues were apparently not so compelling to the inhabitants of such southerly lands as Chu 楚 (approximately corresponding to modern Hubei, Anhui and Hunan). Chu, long a separate country with distinct cultural and political traditions, competed with the northern states of the Zhou confederation, until eventually conquered by Qin 秦 in 221 BCE, resulting in China's first unification. Historically, classical Taoism seems to have emerged from Chu and its southerly neighbors. While Sima Qian's 司馬遷 (145?–86? BCE) identification of Laozi in his *Shiji* (Records of the Historian; 63.2139–43; trans. Lau 1982, x-xi) as a native of Chu is historically dubious, recent research has produced a steady stream of evidence linking the *Daode jing* to that non-Zhou state (Kirkland 1996b). The *Neiye*, which influenced the *Daode jing*, shows little trace of the main sociopolitical issues over which the Confucians and Mohists contended, any more than such issues interested Zhuangzi.

Elsewhere, apparently in the far northeast, other minds were evolving the explanatory system known as the Yin-Yang school (*yinyang jia* 陰陽家) No one knows any historical details about its originators. All that we know is that such ideas emerged quite independently of any of the individuals or communities that produced the classical Taoist texts, and had little influence on Taoism before Han times. During the first century of the Han, the thinkers who contributed to the *Huainan zi* began to integrate such ideas into the Taoist worldview, just as Dong Zhongshu 董仲舒 (ca. 195–115 BCE) and later Han Confucians integrated Yin-Yang thought, and later the separate *wuxing* explanatory system, into the Confucian worldview (Kirkland 1995a; Queen 1996). The modern belief that the ideas of Yin and Yang originated within classical Taoism is quite erroneous

The main exponents of Legalist principles were the Qin official Shang Yang 商鞅 (ca. 385–338 BCE), the Han 韓 official Shen Buhai 申不害 (ca. 400–ca. 340 BCE), and the Han scion Han Feizi 韓非子 (ca. 280–ca. 233 BCE). Shen developed the political concept of non-action (*wuwei; Creel 1974), and Han Feizi, though a student of the Confucian thinker Xunzi 荀子 (ca. 335–ca. 238 BCE), adapted Taoist cosmology for political purposes: to him, the ruler should be thought of as a transcendent being, far above all human concerns. Two chapters of Han Feizi's text—the "Jie Lao" 解老 or "Explicating the *Laozi*" (j. 20; Liao 1939–59, 1: 169–206) and the "Yu Lao" 喻老 or "Illustrating the *Laozi*" (j. 21; id., 1: 207–27)—explicate *Daode jing* passages. Other blends of Taoist, Legalist, and *yinyang/wuxing* ideas appear in other texts of late classical and early Han times (Yates 1997; Chang L. S. and Yu Feng 1998; see *Yinqueshan manuscripts and *Mawangdui manuscripts).

Perhaps what most distinguished Taoists from other early Chinese thinkers was Taoists' faith in nonpersonalized spiritual realities, and in the transformative power of the individual who has fully cultivated them. Confucians, like Mohists, accepted the idea of *Tian* 天 (Heaven), but seldom regarded it as vital to personal self-cultivation, and only Mencius (Mengzi 孟子, ca. 370–ca. 290 BCE) advocated cultivation of *qi (life-energy). Generally, the Confucians argued that one should transform society by cultivating moral virtues and urging rulers to do likewise. Early Taoists were more focused on bio-spiritual cultivation, and sometimes suggested that such cultivation by rulers would transform the world. The newly-discovered *Guodian manuscripts of the *Daode jing* have little further sociopolitical program. The notion that Taoism arose as a reaction against Confucianism is erroneous, for those manuscripts lack the condemnation of Confucian ideas found in the received text. Some scholars now believe that the final redactor of the *Daode jing* was responding to the concerns of intellectuals in the Jixia 稷下 academy of Qi 齊 (modern Shandong) when he added to the Taoist message a response to other schools. What they shared with Zhuangzi was cynicism regarding the hope that collective individual/societal effort can effect desirable change (Kirkland 1996b). They did not distrust "human nature," as Mozi and Xunzi did, but they were often aware of the socially constructed nature of cultural and psychological "realities." They insisted that we should rely instead upon natural realities, the subtle salutary forces that humans neither created nor controlled. Thus, the *Neiye* advocated the cultivation of vital essence, life-energy, and spirit (*jing, qi, shen); the *Zhuangzi* advocated reverting to a "Celestial Mechanism" (*tianji* 天機; see *ji) that is independent of psycho-cultural constructs; and the *Daode jing* advocated abandonment of self-concern and a return to the life-force that is the origin and life-matrix of all things. All three suggest that a properly cultivated person can exert a subtle transformative power, acting as a conduit for the natural salutary forces that should guide and empower peoples' lives (Kirkland 2001).

Russell KIRKLAND

📖 Graham 1989; Hsiao Kung-chuan 1979; Kirkland 2001; Schwartz 1985

※ TAOISM AND CONFUCIANISM

Taoism and the apocrypha

Apocrypha (*weishu* 緯書, *chenwei* or *chanwei* 讖緯) are prophecies and mythical interpretations of the classics designed to legitimate a rising new ruler. They develop first around the end of the Former Han dynasty, when the Heavenly Mandate (*tianming* 天命) was obviously failing and a renewal was expected. Wang Mang (r. 9–23), the usurper of the Han throne, made heavy use of them, as did his successor, Han Guangwu (r. 25–57), and several emperors after him.

Origins. As Anna Seidel (1983a) has shown, the idea of legitimating signs from heaven goes far back in Chinese history and is already apparent in the earliest sources. In the beginning such signs were wondrous objects—marvelous stones, precious gems, unusual jades—found within a kingdom and brought to the ruling house as heavenly markers (see **lingbao*). An early example is the *Hetu* 河圖 (Chart of the [Yellow] River; see **Hetu* and *Luoshu*), which is first mentioned in the *Shujing* 書經 (Book of Documents; trans. Legge 1879, 554) and was, as far as we can tell, a precious stone that served as part of the regalia of the Zhou ruling house.

In a second stage of development, the precious stones were also appreciated for their unusual markings, interpreted as charts or maps presented by heaven to the ruler. These divine maps contained the essence of the realm in symbolic form and thus provided the ruler with celestial control over his land. From the diagram stage, the sacred sign unfolded further to include a divine message spelled out in language and thus graduated to being a sacred text or scripture. The text might be there to elucidate the chart or might in itself contain the power of rulership and universal control. In a fourth step, finally, the sacred sign as scripture grew into a whole series of texts, which then constituted the bulk of what we call apocryphal literature.

Around the first century BCE, when sacred signs are first thought to have appeared as actual texts, the Confucian classics were reinterpreted as wondrous indications of heaven's favor and given a highly mythical reading. As a result, the "apocrypha" comprise two different branches, *chen* (or *chan* 讖,

"prophecies") and *wei* (緯, lit., "weft"). The first continues the sacred signs of old and includes newly found wondrous objects, cosmic charts, and revealed texts. The second consists of mythical interpretations of the Confucian classics (*jing* 經, lit., "warp") and the ancient signs of old, including also the *Hetu*. Both were transmitted predominantly by the *fangshi or magical practitioners, people who engaged in spiritual practices and fortune-telling and had an active relationship with the divine. The reinterpretation of the Confucian classics, however, was also undertaken by minor officials and intellectuals of the New Text school (*jinwen jia* 今文家). Being charged with high political sentiment, Han-dynasty apocrypha have for the most part been lost due to repeated proscriptions. Their remaining fragments were collected by Yasui Kōzan and Nakamura Shōhachi (1971–88).

Influence on Taoism. The impact of the apocrypha on Taoism is manifold. Sacred signs from heaven were continued in Taoist *FU (talismans, tallies, and charms), understood to be direct representations of celestial power. Taoist rituals of initiation and ordination paralleled imperial rites of investiture, both consisting of the transfer of royal or religious regalia from one generation to the next. Moreover, the wielding of power with talismans, along with the acquisition of an administrative role in the otherworld and the juridical way of thinking that went with it, are characteristic of Taoist ritual and can be directly linked to ancient forms of imperial authority, its symbols and execution. The same holds true for the typical form of Taoist communication with heaven through petitions: as heaven was thought to communicate with humanity through formal writings, it was only natural that religious practitioners should adopt the same style of correspondence. Some key features of the religion's ritual can therefore be traced not only to imperial forms of authority, but also to their interpretation and application in the apocrypha.

The *Hetu* and other early divine signs—such as the *Luoshu* 洛書 (Writ of the Luo [River]); see *Hetu and Luoshu)—also became key Taoist materials, as talismans and the focus of sacred scriptures, while charts and maps of the universe were central to the acquisition of Taoist power. The *Wuyue zhenxing tu* (Charts of the Real Forms of the Five Peaks), for example, a highly symbolic representation of the five sacred mountains (*wuyue), conveyed spiritual powers to its possessor, granting a divine view of their structure and providing the key to their utmost reality.

Scriptures as revealed directly from heaven, moreover, have been the backbone of Taoist revelations ever since the early middle ages. They have a clear origin in the apocrypha, as in the case of the first version of the *Taiping jing (Scripture of Great Peace) that was presented as a divine sign of the end of the Former Han's mandate by a *fangshi* from Shandong during the reign of Han Chengdi (r. 33–7 BCE). Not only in form, but also in content did the apocrypha influence Taoism, as many features of the heroes of the Confucian *wei* continued in the religion. Thus the divine Laozi takes on the bodily signs of the mythical emperors Yu 禹 and Shun 舜, having three openings in his ears and four pupils in his eyes; he is described as reappearing under different sage names in every dynasty, picking up on a series of sage advisers to mythical rulers spelled out in the apocrypha. Also, the apocrypha contain lists of gods and demons, which may be seen as the precursors of Taoist registers (*LU) and demon-manuals. They even describe certain divinities of the body, a feature essential to later Taoist worldview.

Both in doctrine and practice, Taoism thus inherits an ancient tradition that begins with royal insignia and the ruler's communication with heaven, and is actively continued in the apocrypha and by the *fangshi* of the Han.

Livia KOHN

📖 Bokenkamp 1994; Chen Pan 1993; Dull 1966; Kaltenmark 1947; Kamitsuka Yoshiko 1999, 362–66; Ngo 1976; Robinet 1997b, 44–45; Seidel 1983a; Yasui Kōzan 1979; Yasui Kōzan 1987; Yasui Kōzan and Nakamura Shōhachi 1966; Yasui Kōzan and Nakamura Shōhachi 1971–88

※ *lingbao* [the term]; *Hetu* and *Luoshu*; FU [talisman]; LU; REVELATIONS AND SACRED TEXTS; SYNCRETISM

Taoism and Confucianism

The relationship of early Confucianism and Taoism was more complex than many modern minds imagine. Looking back through 2000 years, with lenses shaped by modern Confucian and Western biases, we have commonly assumed that Taoism arose mainly as a reaction against Confucianism. Indeed, many writers have simplistically presented Confucianism and Taoism in a dualistic caricature. A more accurate appraisal requires careful analysis of the social, cultural and political realities of early China.

Modern assumptions that Confucianism was founded by Confucius (traditional dates 551–479 BCE) and Taoism by Laozi are in error. Confucius, for his part, maintained that his ideals were not his own formulations, but only a restatement of the values bequeathed by the wise and virtuous men of earlier eras. There is some reason to believe that certain behavioral ideals, stressing honor and propriety, had in fact been cherished by members of the ruling clans of the various statelets of Confucius' day. Those patterns of *noblesse oblige* were transformed by Confucius from a social ideal, requiring aristocratic status, into a moral ideal that any conscientious man should develop and practice. Yet all

Confucians considered social responsibility a primary concern. Even the more "cosmic" or "mystical" dimensions of classical Confucianism—e.g., those expounded in the *Zhongyong* 中庸 (Centrality and Commonality)—retain a social focus, insisting that the ultimate reason for a person to cultivate Confucian ideals is to lead a sociopolitical transformation. Despite the disparities between other proponents of classical Confucianism, such as Mencius (Mengzi 孟子, ca. 370–ca. 290 BCE) and Xunzi 荀子 (ca. 335–ca. 238 BCE), their core concerns were resolutely humanistic. Confucians always insisted that their ideals are to be attained in everyday life, through moral cultivation and the fulfillment of one's proper roles in society.

Contrary to modern misconceptions, early Taoists shared much with early Confucians. By the end of the classical period, several thinkers—artificially segregated by later writers into various "schools"—integrated Taoist ideals with Confucian ideals. In fact, both Mencius and Xunzi also did so. To understand such facts, one must consider that the thinkers of pre-Qin China did not classify themselves as "Confucian" or "Taoist," and surely did not assume any contradiction between the two traditions. All such thinkers—including the compilers of the *Neiye*—insisted that it is possible and morally necessary for individuals to develop or transform themselves in ways that most people do not, thereby enhancing personal well-being and the well-being of others around us. No such thinkers gave priority to state concerns, as did the Legalists, or to social activism devoid of self-cultivation, as did Mozi 墨子 (ca. 470–ca. 400 BCE). None saw our lives as being beyond our ability to transform and perfect. They did all generally share a belief that our lives should somehow accord with *tian* 天 (Heaven), but none succumbed to the theistic moralism of Mozi: for the thinkers that we now call Confucian and Taoist, the individual is never to become a slavish follower of any external authority (whether political or supernatural), but rather a thoughtful practitioner of meaningful ideals that any serious mind can understand. Confucians seem to have assumed that such minds were found only in men; Taoists, though mostly male, seem not to have shared that assumption, and some (especially contributors to *Daode jing*) commended seeking sensible lessons in women's life-experiences.

Both Confucians and Taoists, nonetheless, assumed that the world should have a human ruler, and that he should live by, and promote, the ideals propounded by the thinker in question. While *Zhuangzi* may have considered government irrelevant, he did not condemn its existence. So while some Taoists may have been less interested in existing Chinese social and political institutions than Confucians, they did not denounce monarchy or aristocracy, and would have not understood or condoned modern ideals of egalitarianism or radical individualism. To all of them, no one is encouraged to discover or practice any "new" truth.

Where Confucians and Taoists parted ways is that the former viewed the world primarily in terms of inherited sociopolitical norms, while the latter focused on humans' continuities with the invisible dimensions of reality that Confucians were often reluctant to discuss. Some modern interpreters, including scholars, simplistically maintain that Confucians advocated activism while Taoists commended non-action (*wuwei). In reality, Confucius advocated *wuwei* by rulers, as did both the *Daode jing* and such Legalists as Shen Buhai 申不害 (ca. 400–ca. 340 BCE). Modern writers also generally neglect the fact that Mencius saw the cultivation of *qi as part of a gentleman's self-cultivation (see *Neiye*). Such matters deserve attention as we reappraise Chinese traditions.

Russell KIRKLAND

📖 Kirkland 1995a; Kirkland 1996a; Kirkland 2001; Kusuyama Haruki 1983a; Seidel 1989–90, 275–78

※ SYNCRETISM; TAOISM AND EARLY CHINESE THOUGHT; TAOISM AND NEO-CONFUCIANISM

Taoism and Neo-Confucianism

The overall attitude of Neo-Confucians to Taoism has never been studied in the same way as the generally implacable opposition of Cheng-Zhu 程朱 followers to Buddhism, or even the more flexible attitudes of cultural leaders like Su Shi 蘇軾 (Su Dongpo 蘇東坡, 1037–1101; SB 900–968) to the attractions of Chan. This in part no doubt reflects the fact that it was explicitly not considered as anything like as serious an issue as the need to define the Confucian stance over against the foreign religion. Both Chinese traditions, after all, had come to share much in common, from a conventional morality to a metaphysics based on the concept of *qi. Earlier, Han Yu 韓愈 (768–824; IC 397–40) had indeed criticized the "non-action" (*wuwei) of Laozi, in part perhaps as a protest against a dynasty temporarily rendered inert by its problems, and which had been forced to draw heavily on the existing ideological capital it had invested in state Taoism. His attitude is but partially reflected in eleventh-century writers like Ouyang Xiu 歐陽修 (1007–72; SB 808–16), who carps at the Taoist devotions of Tang figures, but himself displays a remarkable competence at composing Taoist prayers when required by the emperor to do so.

Those such as the Cheng brothers (Cheng Hao 程顥, 1032–85, and Cheng Yi 程頤, 1033–1107; SB 169–79) concerned with the establishment of new Confucian methods of self-cultivation likewise criticize the methods used by Tang Taoists like *Sima Chengzhen, but their theoretical pronouncements on

Laozi and his thought fall short even of the ringing but hardly incisive tones of Han Yu. Where we do find an anti-Taoist stance is in situations in which Confucian interests are threatened. Taoist involvement in Tang ideology is retrospectively attributed to imperial failings in the historiography of Fan Zuyu 范祖禹 (1041–98; SB 338–45), while Taoist priests of the Song like *Chen Jingyuan, who in 1091 was appointed to state service for his bibliographical erudition, attracted disparagement. Of Taoism as a communal religion we find hardly a word of criticism; rather, cults such as that of *Magu seem to have been well supported by all but the most hardline Confucian masters.

The increasing trend from *waidan to *neidan alchemy also tended to render opposition from Confucian circles somewhat muted, since it patently did not lead to any cases of alchemical poisoning of the sort that occurred in the late Tang. Eventually we find even the great Southern Song Neo-Confucian Zhu Xi 朱熹 (1130–1200; SB 282–90) taking an interest in the *Zhouyi cantong qi, if not exactly endorsing it (see *Zhouyi cantong qi kaoyi). In certain contexts, it is true, Neo-Confucians do tend to repeat the very old criticism that any pursuit of immortality is unnatural, "stealing from nature," but overall Zhu Xi's account of Taoism (*DAOJIAO) does not amount to a vigorous denunciation, and propagators of his synthesis of the Neo-Confucian legacy such as Chen Chun 陳淳 (1159–1223; SB 95–97) would seem to sustain the same underwhelming verdict: "All they want is to be pure and quiet and to engage themselves in things outside of the mundane world so as to improve their own being. . . . As such, the doctrines of Taoism have not deluded people too much," in the translation of Wing-tsit Chan (1986, 168).

The same pattern continues under later dynasties, but becomes more complex. The historical Hai Rui 海瑞 (1514–87; DMB 474–79) was dismissed from office for protesting Taoist involvement at court, but by his day some Taoists in local society were making even more explicit than in the past their support for Confucian morality, as in the case of the *Jingming dao, while the practice of distributing morality books (*shanshu) allowed Neo-Confucians an expedient excuse for promoting morality through the medium of religion; local pride might likewise excuse supporting the building of religious institutions as well. Apparent deliberate syncretism or hybridism too was in the air in the late Ming, as in the case of and his "Three in One" (sanyi 三一) movement—this, however, might equally be regarded as a stroke of genius by a sectarian leader who, knowing better than meddle with the normal mix of millenarian Buddhism, coopted all three officially tolerated traditions at once to create a cult that could not simply be dismissed as subversive. Interestingly, his teachings—for example those on meditation—show that Neo-Confucianism too had elements of practice to contribute to religious synthesis which could be combined effortlessly with neidan-derived exercises. Even so, the publication of Taoist texts during the Qing suggest that there was a strong market for *neidan* works among ostensible adherents of Neo-Confucianism.

T. H. BARRETT

📖 Barrett 1992; Dean 1998; Liu Ts'un-yan 1971; Seidel 1989–90, 275–78; Sunayama Minoru 1993

※ SYNCRETISM; TAOISM AND CONFUCIANISM

Taoism and Chinese Buddhism

Buddhism in China jostled for cultural space with Taoism from the start, and as a result over the centuries the two religions interacted constantly, affecting each other in a complex pattern of exchanges going far beyond any simple borrowing. Since the foreign religion was obliged to develop a strong polemical and historiographic voice to explain itself to non-Buddhists, East Asian scholarship has tended to take at face value Buddhist pronouncements about Taoist "plagiarism" and as a result references to Taoism as a "pseudo-Buddhist" religion may be found in Western scholarship of a generation ago; we now know that this was not the whole truth.

The earliest material evidence for Chinese Buddhism in the second century CE already places the Buddha in exactly the same milieu that produced the beginnings of organized Taoism, in that archaeological evidence shows the image of the Buddha occupying a place reserved for the lord of the dead—a role occasionally played by Laozi, too. This cannot but have supported the speculation already evident at the same time that Laozi and the Buddha were in fact the same, in that after his departure westward Laozi had merely adopted an expedient guise to pass on a version of his message to an Indian audience. The notion that an attractive novelty from abroad was merely the reintroduction of something from the Chinese past recurs in the early stages of China's more recent encounter with the West, and may explain the categorization in the third century CE of both Buddhism and the old Chinese esoteric lore eventually absorbed into the Taoist legacy under the rubric of *neixue* 內學, "esoteric studies." By the fourth century, we see clear signs of the absorption of Buddhist material into *Shangqing scriptures, in the case of the *Sūtra in Forty-two Sections (Sishi'er zhang jing* 四十二章經), and soon thereafter in the *Lingbao texts a veritable recasting of all available elements of Buddhism into a new Chinese religious form, securely attributed to a primordial epoch at the dawn of the universe we live in, long before the Buddha appeared in India.

By "available" is indicated the fact that Taoism always tended to absorb what elements of Buddhism became common currency in Chinese religion; it is important to note, however, that Buddhism found itself equally under pressure to deal in the common currency too. Thus it has been demonstrated that a Chinese Buddhist apocryphal text, the *Hu shenming jing* 護身命經 (Sūtra on Protecting Life; T. 2866), shows an awareness of the Lingbao reformulation of Buddhism; but a later Buddhist apocryphon on the same theme seems in turn to be reflected in a further generation of Buddhist-inspired Taoist literature of the Tang. That literature, too, despite its quite extensive incorporation of lightly altered Buddhist materials, was also able to inspire Buddhist responses which, as Robert Sharf (2002) has shown, should not be underrated for their religious value.

Nor should the accusations of plagiarism voiced by the Buddhists obscure the fact that this trading in a common currency took place at a number of different levels, of which the interchange of blocs of textual material was perhaps only the most obvious. Sometimes titles were traded, with a partial or complete replacement of content, as with the Chan use of the Taoist alchemical title *Cantong qi* 參同契 (Token for the Agreement of the Three; see *Cantong qi* and *Zhouyi cantong qi*); sometimes terminology was traded, picking up new nuances on the way, as perhaps with the term *chongxuan* (Twofold Mystery) whose philosophical overtones in seventh century Taoism may have been affected by Buddhist use. Indeed, the pioneering work of Kamata Shigeo demonstrates elegantly how a study of this interaction may allow us to separate what was common currency from what was not: the notion of "emptiness" (*kong* 空), for example, was quite clearly intelligible to Taoists, even if in the long run they preferred a metaphysics based on *qi*, while the new Yogācāra philosophy imported in the seventh century was not.

But even where concepts did become common currency, tensions were not thereby eliminated. The notion of *karma*, for example, appeared already in the Buddhist sources for the Lingbao scriptures, and became in time a component of Taoist ethical thinking. Yet from the time of *Lu Xiujing (406–77) until at least the end of the Tang a protracted debate seems to have been carried out between Buddhists and Taoists over whether the notions of causality (*yinyuan* 因緣) could be reconciled with spontaneity (*ziran). Were Taoist gods, and indeed the Taoist universe, in some sense "immoral," in that they appeared at the dawn of time "spontaneously," rather than as the result of the aeons of moral effort needed to perfect Buddhahood?

In part such debates, notably over the notorious *Huahu jing (Scripture of the Conversion of Barbarians), which encapsulated in polemical form the notion that Laozi was a the author of Buddhism, emerge as the result of competition for patronage which was itself the product of the establishment of both religions as partners of the state in the fifth century. The role of the state in the creation of Chinese Buddhism and Taoism was in many ways crucial: the state required, for example, a well-defined canon to ensure against the corruption of subversive ideas; well-defined standards of clerical behavior to ensure the against the corruption of the clergy; and indeed a well-defined clergy, so that their particular privileges should not spread to a wider group. To a large extent Buddhism, with its celibate monks and well-organized canon was therefore taken as the model, though a "closed" canon defined by catalogue was actually unusual in Buddhism, and the essentially non-hierarchical Buddhist clergy to some degree had to accept a more Taoist, hierarchical model in the form of "monk-officials" who acted as overseers; the emergence of the Buddhist novitiate in China as occupying more than a brief, transitional status may also betoken Taoist influence. By contrast, Buddhism never accepted a non-celibate clergy after the pattern of the Taoist Celestial Masters (*Tianshi dao); where non-celibates played the role of Buddhist monks, this was perhaps usually a matter of supply and demand, where the religious needs of an expanding population exceeded the ability of properly ordained monks to provide. This in itself marked a long-term trend toward a Taoist model, where Buddhists moved from genuine monastic self-sufficiency toward an income based on the provision of religious services. The richly detailed vision of the afterlife which Buddhism brought from India gave it some competitive edge in the funeral business, though it is noteworthy that in such popular, non-canonical texts as the *Scripture of the Ten Kings of Hell* (*Diyu shiwang jing* 地獄十王經) investigated by Stephen Teiser (1994) room has been made in this collective kingship for the "Taoist" Lord of Mount Tai (*Taishan), and a more Chinese conception of posthumous bureaucracy is everywhere in evidence. The attempts of the founder of the Ming dynasty to regulate the lives of those providing funerary services, the *yingfu seng* 應赴 僧 or "monks on call," represented no doubt a belated attempt to recognize and control the reality of what the Buddhist clergy eventually became, just as in the tenth century what had been a perennial problem as to how to control the married Celestial Master clergy within a state system predicated on monasticism was solved by subcontracting responsibility for guaranteeing their quality to the Zhang 張 family of Mount Longhu (*Longhu shan).

In short, over time the institutional factors which served to preserve doctrinal distinctions were themselves subject to a certain amount of change. That change might be seen as tending toward syncretism, but before reaching that conclusion, it is worth considering other factors which served to keep Taoism and Buddhism apart, namely the self-images of the traditions maintained by their adherents themselves, independent of state policies, no matter whether the latter sought to create ideological consensus or to divide and rule. These self-images took some time to emerge, for the assumption of underlying unity expressed in the *Huahu jing* was a powerful one. Yet ultimately the Buddhists at least by the early sixth century had begun to articulate a relationship which was not even coordinate or "separate but equal," as in the distinctions between *nei* 內, "esoteric," versus *wai* 外, "exoteric," but clearly involved the subordination of Taoism (with Confucianism) as "worldly," rather than "beyond this world" (*chushi* 出世), in its implications. Thus, as in the case of Zongmi 宗密 (780–841) and other prominent Buddhists of his day like the poet Bai Juyi 白居易 (772–846), a place could be found for Taoism insofar as it was content to be considered a this-worldly teaching, but the assignment of this relative value cannot be said to amount to syncretism.

Little has been done to assess the Taoist perspective on the relative value of Buddhism, but those who have examined for example the use of the *Heart Sūtra* in *Quanzhen Taoism have not thereby concluded that within that movement non-Taoist elements were perceived in a completely coordinate rather than subordinate way. In the long run, perhaps, there were shifts here also: the resolute Chineseness of Chan Buddhism, for example, may have undercut the ethnocentric strain in Taoist anti-Buddhism, while the essentially Indian scholastic distinction between the worldly and the otherworldly may have become muted in Chan rhetoric, with its emphasis on the elimination of all dichotomies. This could explain why, for example, a handbook included in the supplement to the Ming canon, the *Soushen ji* (In Search of the Sacred), includes Buddhist cults as such, in the form popularly practiced, not as recontextualized within Taoist circles. And formerly, where Taoist and Buddhist meditation schemes had always looked similar (whether through contact, or through convergence on universal psychological norms), the eventual language of *neidan* practice, from the start a multivalent kaleidoscope of images as much as a technical system of descriptive language, absorbed Buddhist terminology in such a way as to render late texts like the *Secret of the Golden Flower* (*Taiyi jinhua zongzhi*) at the very least religious hybrids much more challenging than any reformulation of Buddhism within the Lingbao corpus. Once again, however, this last case may involve institutional factors as well: where Buddhist and Taoist notions of self-development had, because of the late Ming rise in a print culture, become very widely available to any literate person without the mediation of religious professionals, the market expected no less than the most exciting that both traditions had to offer in any new publications.

The preceding two or three paragraphs have inevitably been more speculative than is usual in a work of reference. For we have hardly marshalled all the historical evidence necessary to understand the interaction between Buddhism and Taoism, yet any general statement concerning their relationship must move beyond mere recitations of fact to look at the broader patterns that make sense of those facts. But let us sum up what we know. Chinese Buddhism and Taoism grew up together in an environment in which a strong sense of religious identity was probably available only to a minority—to the properly-ordained Chinese Buddhist monk who had absorbed an accurate knowledge of the religion from a foreign master; to the priest or "libationer" (*jijiu*) within a movement which still maintained the reforming zeal and hostility to popular religion of its late Han founders. Yet the fifth century state, in both North and South China, required rigid definitions of identity for its own purposes, if it was to use either religion as some sort of surrogate in ordering society.

The consequences were immediate. Every major persecution of Buddhism—in 446 under the Northern Wei, in 574 under the Northern Zhou and in 845 under the Tang—was at least partly attributable to rivalry with Taoism. When the Buddhists finally gained their chance to fight back, winning the support of the Mongol Khubilai khan in 1281, the counterblow, aimed at Taoist literature through the burning of all texts and woodblocks in the canon save those for the *Daode jing*, caused such losses that reconstructing the history of Taoism has become no easy task. Yet that deadly rivalry throughout stimulated not religious isolation and purism, but constant, mutual interaction. The reconstructive task before us is therefore not a single, but a double one.

T. H. BARRETT

📖 Aoki Takashi 1993; Barrett 1990; Fukui Fumimasa 1983; Kamata Shigeo 1968; Lagerwey 1981b, 21–28; Robinet 2004; Seidel 1984; Seidel 1989–90, 287–96; Sharf 2002; Strickmann 2002; Zürcher 1980

※ SYNCRETISM; TAOISM AND THE STATE; for other related entries see the Synoptic Table of Contents, sec. V ("Taoism and Chinese Buddhism")

Taoism and popular religion

Previous models. Scholars have provided a variety of formulations to account for interactions between Taoism and popular religion. Taoism, along with Buddhism and the state cult, has been defined as "institutionalized" and contrasted with "unorganized and diffuse" popular religion. The two, nonetheless, must then be seen as involved in a constant, dialectical process of mutual borrowing (Stein R. A. 1979). If one places more emphasis on the rhetoric of a number of early Taoist texts, in which popular cults and practices are described as "profane" (*su* 俗) and forbidden to Taoist adherents, the relationship must be seen as antagonistic. Taoists treat their deities—celestial functionaries communicated with by means of written documents—as fundamentally superior to the gods of popular cults, who receive sacrifice and communicate with their devotees through spirit-mediums (Strickmann 1979).

Views based more on modern practice, particularly in southern Taiwan, have emphasized relations among three kinds of religious practitioners: spirit-mediums (*tâng-ki or jitong), Taoist priests (*daoshi), but also "Red-head ritual masters" (hongtou fashi 紅頭法師; see *hongtou and wutou). The ritual masters are seen as occupying a mediating position. The three may form a hierarchy, as defined by the polar opposition of "alienation" (spirit-mediums) and "self-realization" (priests; see Lagerwey 1987c). Alternatively, the contemporary situation may be envisioned according to a substructure / superstructure model. The whole arrangement is founded on the "popular complex" personified by the medium, and also including the ritual master, who similarly is tied to the local temple. On the other hand, Taoist ritual provides a superstructure that legitimizes and organizes the activities of local, popular religion—a superstructure principally provided by the classical liturgies of the Taoist priest, but that again involves the ritual master and his "vernacular Taoist" rites (Schipper 1985e). Proponents of this view see Taoism as drawing energy from the "shamanic substrate" of popular religion, while at the same time reshaping it. This reshaping occurs through textualization—giving popular deities Taoist identities and writing scriptures for them—and through ritual, structuring popular festivals by means of the temporal organization of Taoist liturgy, in particular the *jiao (Dean 1993; but see Katz P. R. 1995a). Attempts have also been made to distinguish "popular Taoism," whose historical roots lie in popular religion, from "organized Taoism," characterized by its reception of state patronage (Sakai Tadao and Fukui Fumimasa 1983).

The problem of the popular. What all such approaches elide, however, is the question of what exactly, in the Chinese context, constitutes "popular religion." Or, even more to the point, how does one determine the ways in which Taoism related and relates to the religion of the people if no attention is given to determining what constitutes the problematic category of "the people" (see Wang Jing 2001)? Most accounts simply deem as popular what Taoists often prohibited, in particular local cults and attendant practices of sacrifice and mediumism. This, however, is to ignore questions of social, economic, and educational stratification that normally have informed the study of popular culture (see, e.g., Bourdieu 1984; Johnson 1985a).

Any attempt to characterize interactions between Taoism and popular religion along a single elite / popular spectrum is fraught with difficulties. The viewpoints summarized above involve a variety of contrasts: official / non-official, elite / common, literate / non-literate, organized / diffuse. These comprise a still non-exhaustive set of binary oppositions any one or more of which may be highly relevant when determining—in a given historical, social, and local context—what comprises the popular. However, since the popular is thus always oppositionally defined (see Bennett 1986), and Taoism frequently straddles both sides of such binarisms, popular religion and its relationship with Taoism cannot be reified. Perhaps the whole question needs to be reformulated: To what degree does it make sense to contrast Taoism, a religion defined in terms of organizational, ritual, and scriptural traditions—i.e., in terms of historical continuity—with popular religion, a sociological category whose principal referents concern class and other social distinctions?

Taoism's beginnings. With these caveats in mind, one may proceed to examine the history of Taoism and its relationships with popular religion (as variously construed). When the Way of the Celestial Masters emerged as the basis and core for the developing Taoist tradition, it drew on pre-Taoist practices that were closely linked with popular religion. The grave-securing writs (*zhenmu wen* 鎮墓文) written on bottles that have been found in tombs of the Later Han dynasty likely were created by "village elders, exorcists and specialists in funerary rites" (Seidel 1989–90). The writs issue the commands of a Celestial Emperor (Tiandi 天帝) that are to be delivered by his Envoy (*shizhe* 使者) and transmitted to a minor spirit-bureaucracy of the tomb (Seidel 1987e). Thus the entire otherworldly documentary/bureaucratic framework of the Celestial Masters—as represented, for instance, by their penitential "handwritten documents of the Three Offices" (*sanguan shoushu* 三官手書; see *sanguan) and the later petitions (*zhang* 章) to "celestial officials" (*tianguan* 天官)—was anticipated by the grave-securing writs, the products of Han-dynasty village religion. Early Taoism also drew extensively on still-older traditions of mortuary exorcism and the recalling of souls, personified by a variety of shaman-exorcists, most notably the so-called *fangxiang* 方相. Both literate and non-literate forms of magico-religious practices, such as various forms of divination and other techniques often associated with "masters of methods" (*fangshi), were similarly integrated into Taoist practice (Nickerson 1994; Nickerson 1996b; Nickerson 1997).

Messianic groups who embraced apocalyptic visions of the future influenced Taoism's origins. In one text from about 185 CE, the *Laozi bianhua jing* (Scripture of the Transformations of Laozi), populist notions are clearly expressed. The people's sufferings are described in detail; the deified Laozi promises to descend to earth, save his followers, and "shake" the ruling Han regime (Seidel 1969–70). While such overt, antistate apocalypticism was renounced by the Celestial Masters after *Zhang Lu's surrender to Cao Cao 曹操, it appears again in Celestial Master texts like the probably early fifth-century *Zhengyi tianshi gao Zhao Sheng koujue* 正一天師告趙昇口訣 (Oral Instructions Declared by the Celestial Master of Orthodox Unity to Zhao Sheng; CT 1273) which specifically calls for the downfall of the Jin dynasty as part of its apocalyptic program.

Early prohibitions on sacrificial and mantic practices. As has been frequently noted (e.g., Stein R. A. 1979), Taoists, precisely because they relied upon traditions of practice they claimed to have superseded, were compelled to try to distinguish themselves from their popular predecessors and competitors. They did so by prohibiting a variety of popular practices. The *Xiang'er* commentary to the *Daode jing* prohibits "sacrifices and food offerings" as means of "commerce with deviant forces" (Bokenkamp 1997, esp. 119–20; Rao Zongyi 1956, 34). The *Laojun shuo yibai bashi jie* (The Hundred and Eighty Precepts Spoken by Lord Lao; CT 786, 2a–20b, and other versions), a list of prohibitions for Taoist libationers (*jijiu*) from the ca. mid-fourth century, likewise enjoins against "giving cult to other spirits" (spirits other than one's own ancestors), as well as several varieties of astrology and geomancy. By the fifth century, such prohibitions were further expanded and codified, as well as placed within a larger context of mytho-historical narrative, in the *Daomen kelüe* (Abridged Codes for the Taoist Community) of *Lu Xiujing (see also the roughly contemporaneous *Santian neijie jing* or *Scripture of the Inner Explication of the Three Heavens*). On a more practical level, Taoist opposition to the local cults of southeastern China meshed with actual state suppression. Such suppression was supported by Taoists rhetorically and, in all likelihood, more tangibly as well: scriptures of the period provide instructions for talismans and other protective measures for "attacking shrines" of local deities (*famiao* 伐廟).

Rapprochement. Nonetheless, already in early medieval times, Taoism was including in its rites a number of prohibited practices, and the popular cults themselves were beginning to employ Taoist priests. The petition texts of the *Chisong zi zhangli* (Master Red-Pine's Almanac of Petitions), a compendium of Celestial Master ritual practice, evince the early development of a relationship of complementarity, even of de facto collaboration, between Taoism and the formerly banned diviners and mediums (most of these petitions can be dated to Six Dynasties or even earlier times). Taoist priests even cast horoscopes themselves. On the other hand, Lu Xiujing's criticisms of the "inferior" Taoist priests of his day suggest that the local cults were beginning to make use of Taoist ritual, willingly provided by peripatetic priests. Finally, one might note the incorporation within the Taoist pantheon of a variety of recipients of popular worship. Such deities were first demonized—often by associating them with the Six Heavens of *Fengdu (on the Six Heavens see *santian* and *liutian*)—and then offered advancement in the Taoist otherworldly administration if they used their powers in service of the Dao and its faithful (Nickerson 1996b, chapter 8). This anticipated the subsequent large-scale adoption of popular deities within the Taoist pantheon. The stage was already set for the emergence of yet more thoroughgoing convergences beginning in the late Tang and the Song.

Transition in the Song. These subsequent developments concern in particular the evolving relationship between Taoism and local cults. Interactions between Taoist priests and popular practitioners were similarly transformed. Especially important is the emergence of new lineages of lay Taoist practitioners (as opposed to formally ordained priests) known as "ritual masters" (**fashi*). The wide diffusion by Southern Song times of such exorcistic and therapeutic lineages—such as the **Tianxin zhengfa* (Correct Method of the Celestial Heart) and the Wu leifa 五雷法 (Five Thunder Rites; see **leifa*)—is attested not only in ritual manuals such as the **Daofa huiyuan* (Corpus of Taoist Ritual) but also in detailed anecdotes collected in Hong Mai's 洪邁 (1123–1202) *Yijian zhi* 夷堅志 (Heard and Written by Yijian). The rituals of these new lineages, performed both by the lay ritual masters themselves and by priests, often involved spirit-mediums, especially to speak on behalf of deceased ancestors (during funerary rites) or aggrieved spirits—in healing/exorcism rituals (Davis E. 2001). With the ritual master as a *tertium quid* between the Taoist priest and the spirit-medium, the forms of cooperation and complementarity that were nascent in the early medieval period became even more fully elaborated.

Taoism and popular religion today. The triad of medium, ritual master, and priest that forms the basis for the notion of "shamanic substructure and Taoist superstructure" in contemporary religion had thus already formed in the Song. Today, that pattern is elaborated in numerous ways. Turning again to southern Taiwanese evidence, we see spirit-mediums acting on their own as diviners, diagnosticians, and healers during séances at temples and spirit-shrines (*shentan* 神壇). However, they also commonly assist Red-head ritual masters in the performance of a variety of rites and ensure the presence of the deities they serve at large-scale temple festivals, including the *jiao* that are overseen by Taoist priests. In turn, the priests may, by a simple change of headgear, themselves perform red-head rituals. Indeed, as further data are collected, in particular in the People's Republic, the situation is likely to appear even more fluid. The relatively well-structured relations characteristic of Taoist and popular practitioners in southern Taiwan may well prove to be very localized phenomena.

Taoism's dependence since its inception upon the energies of popular religion's shamanic substrate ensured the maintenance of close ties between the organized religion and its sometime rivals. Moreover, that dependence has produced a historical trajectory according to which Taoism grew ever closer to the "religion of the people." Indeed, discussions of "Taoism and popular religion" are perhaps most often really about the various ways that Taoist and popular religious adherents have sought, and continue to seek, access to supernatural benefits and authority. These modes of communication can be placed along a spectrum defined by immediate access—as through spirit-possession—and mediated communication, typified by the written petitions and memorials of the priest. However, immediate forms of communication are employed by many others besides spirit-mediums and their devotees, and many practitioners other than priests use texts in their commerce with the divine bureaucracy. The opposition between immediate and mediated access to the supernatural cannot be neatly correlated with any of the elite / popular binarisms described above (with the possible exception of the contrast between oral and written cultures). Instead, the ritual and the social categories once again tend to crosscut one another.

Peter NICKERSON

📖 Bennett 1986; Cohen 1987; Davis E. 2001; Dean 1993; Feuchtwang 1992; Johnson 1985a; Lagerwey 1987c; Lagerwey 1996; Little 2000b, 255–73; Ma Shutian 1997; Nickerson 1996b; Okuzaki Hiroshi 1983; Robinet 1997b, 62–65; Sakai Tadao and Fukui Fumimasa 1983; Schipper 1985e; Seidel 1969–70; Seidel 1987e; Seidel 1989–90, 283–86; Stein R. A. 1969b; Stein R. A. 1979; Zhang Zehong 1999b; Zong Li and Liu Qun 1987

※ *fuji*; *yinsi*; SYNCRETISM; TAOISM AND ANCESTOR WORSHIP; TAOISM AND LOCAL COMMUNITIES; TAOISM AND LOCAL CULTS; TAOISM AND MEDIUM CULTS; TAOISM AND POPULAR SECTS

Taoism and popular sects

Popular sects are voluntary religious associations run and patronized by lay people unaffiliated with the major institutional religions of China. While earlier religious movements, including the early Way of the Celestial Masters (*Tianshi dao), may be loosely classified as popular sectarian, as a technical term "popular sectarianism" is usually applied to a wide variety of lay religious associations flourishing in early modern and contemporary China. The founders of these groups frequently were religious virtuosi who in a syncretic manner fashioned a new, popularized system of doctrine and practice out of the Three Teachings (Confucianism, Taoism, Buddhism). They recorded their teachings in a genre of religious literature called *baojuan* (precious scrolls).

In many (though not all) sects, diverse elements drawn from these sources were rearranged around a shared eschatological vision that focuses on the Unborn Venerable Mother (Wusheng Laomu 無生老母) as the ultimate origin and destination of humankind. Oblivious of their divine origins, humans sadly have become mired in the desires and illusions of the world and are no longer aware of the bliss that awaits them once they return to their Mother. This return has now become an urgent concern, as the world is about to reach a cataclysmic end at the conclusion of the current third epoch of a three-stage cosmic cycle. In this millenarian atmosphere, emissaries of the Mother appear to call upon humans to remember their true nature and make their way back to the Mother's paradise, thereby to survive the imminent end of the world. Elements of this sectarian eschatology can again be traced back to the Three Teachings: the three-stage cosmic cycle is of Buddhist provenance, while in the Unborn Venerable Mother we may see an echo of the Queen Mother of the West (*Xiwang mu), or perhaps more generally of the Dao as the mother of all things, to which all things return (cf *Daode jing* 1). Despite these derivations, as a charter myth and central organizing vision the Mother theme is specifically sectarian in nature and supplies a consistent core structure to which a diverse assortment of other concepts can be attached.

While most sects insist on the validity of all Three Teachings, the nature and composition of their borrowings from them vary from sect to sect. In many groups it is their Buddhist features that are most noticeable, but Taoism also has had a major impact on the popular sectarian tradition. Particularly strong is the influence of *neidan, whose techniques and vocabulary were emulated and popularized for example by the Way of Yellow Heaven (Huangtian dao 黃天道), founded in the middle of the sixteenth century by Li Bin 李賓 (?–1562). For this sect, which repeatedly referred to its way as that of "Complete Perfection" (Quanzhen dao 全真道; see *Quanzhen), the return to the Mother was accomplished through the concoction of a Golden Elixir (*jindan), described in language clearly derived from the *neidan* manuals current at the time. Another group with strong Taoist characteristics is the Way of the Prior Heavenly Realm (Xiantian dao 先天道), whose writings integrate *neidan* terminology with the sectarian Mother mythology. In particular, this sect teaches a form of *neidan* called Mysterious Practice in Nine Stages (*jiujie xuangong* 九節玄功) which will lead its practitioner to "transcend the profane and enter the sacred" (*chaofan rusheng* 超凡入聖). While in some precious scrolls alchemical terminology appears to serve more symbolic than practical purposes, modified forms of *neidan* have played an important role in the religious life of several sects, including the aforementioned Way of the Prior Heavenly Realm and the Teaching of the Three-in-One (Sanyi jiao 三一教) founded by *Lin Zhao'en (1517–98). In the latter group we have clear evidence that the founder's version of *neidan* held and still holds a central place among the religious practices of his followers.

Another area of overlap between Taoist and sectarian practices is spirit writing (see *fuji). By the nineteenth century several popular sects, particularly in the Way of the Prior Heavenly Realm, had come to adopt spirit writing as their preferred mode of communication with the divine realm. The precious scrolls were replaced as the main carriers of sectarian doctrine by spirit-written texts, whose format resembled that of writings produced by Taoist planchette cults. Close contact with the milieu of these planchette cults led to greater sectarian emphasis on certain deities and immortals traditionally associated with spirit writing, chief among them the immortal *Lü Dongbin. His image can be found in the shrines of many modern-day popular sects such as the Way of Pervading Unity (Yiguan dao 一貫道) and the Society of Goodness (Tongshan she 同善社), where he is venerated as an emissary and spokesman of the Venerable Mother. Nowadays, popular sects continue to interact actively with the Taoist tradition, borrowing, adapting and transforming those Taoist elements that promise to assist their followers on their path toward salvation.

Philip CLART

📖 Berling 1980; Dean 1998; Lin Wanchuan 1986; Ma Xisha and Han Bingfang 1992; Overmyer 1976; Overmyer 1999; Topley 1963

※ *baojuan*; MESSIANISM AND MILLENARIANISM; TAOISM AND LOCAL CULTS; TAOISM AND MEDIUM CULTS; TAOISM AND POPULAR RELIGION

Taoism and local cults

Few problems in the study of Chinese religion deserve greater attention than the complex process of interaction between Taoism and local cults. Unfortunately, few problems have also been as controversial. Over the past three decades, research on this topic has tended to focus on two diametrically opposed viewpoints. On one side are scholars who study Taoism, many of whom tend to view it as a "higher" or "elevated" form of Chinese popular religion which could structure cult worship through a Taoist liturgical framework (Dean 1993; Lagerwey 1987c; Schipper 1985d; Schipper 1985e; Schipper 1993). On the other are scholars who study local cults, most of whom downplay or underestimate the important role Taoism could play in the growth of such cults. Some have even argued that lay believers could not worship the deities summoned by *daoshi* in their rituals (Hansen 1990, 26). Each of these views is grounded in an element of truth. Taoists often present their religion as being superior to local cults, and many Taoist deities are seldom worshipped by members of local communities. Yet, both views fail to appreciate the degree whereto Taoism and local cults shaped each other, indeed depended on each other.

The complex relationship between Taoism and local cults may well derive from the fact that Taoism, being a religion indigenous to China, inevitably absorbed yet also modified numerous popular beliefs and practices during its historical development. Matters are further complicated by the fact that the chief rival of Taoism throughout Chinese history was not Buddhism, or even the state; rather, it was the "nameless religion" of the masses (Strickmann 2002, 4). This state of affairs resulted in Taoism and local cults being simultaneously in competition with and yet also highly similar to each other. Even in recent decades, some scholars and most laymen (including government officials) equate the terms "Taoism" and "popular religion." Faced with such a situation, Taoist leaders have consistently made concerted efforts to define their religion as "orthodox" or "correct" (*zheng* 正), while following the state in labelling local cults as *yinsi ("licentious" or "illicit" cults). In doing so, they attempted to portray themselves as being both morally and ritually superior to those same cults they attempted to absorb, reform, or aid the state in suppressing. Despite these efforts, however, Taoism was never fully able to achieve its goal of reforming or even eradicating those local cults it considered to be "heterodox." Far more common are cases of *daoshi* absorbing and attempting to redefine local deities as "orthodox" Taoist gods, sometimes even grudgingly accepting the hated representations of those local cults they had once attempted to destroy.

Incorporation of local cults. The above processes may well have shaped the development of the *Tianshi dao / *Zhengyi dao, established in Sichuan by *Zhang Lu and his followers during the waning years of the Han dynasty. The choice of the latter autonym, which means "Way of the Orthodox Unity," appears to be linked to this movement's efforts to establish its liturgical orthopraxy in a region teeming with numerous local cults supported by both Han and non-Han peoples (Kleeman 1998). Zhang and his successors attempted to absorb local beliefs and practices—including various healing, exorcistic, and mortuary rites, music, ecstatic possession, and so forth—simultaneously identifying themselves as a separate and superior movement which aimed at reforming many popular practices deemed "excessive" or "heterodox." Thus, Taoist leaders promoted a "pure bond" (*qingyue* 清約) between practitioners and the gods, whereby Taoist deities and popular gods who converted to Taoism would forgo "bloody [i.e., meat] offerings" (*xueshi* 血食) in favor of vegetarian ones, while Taoist specialists would not accept payment for ritual services (Bokenkamp 1997, 10–15; Kleeman 1994b; Nickerson 1996a, 348).

This sense of liturgical orthopraxy appears quite clearly in a number of the earliest Tianshi scriptures. For example, the "Dadao jia lingjie" 大道家令戒 (Commands and Admonitions for the Families of the Great Dao; trans. Bokenkamp 1997, 148–85), composed during the middle of the third century, claims that when Laozi appeared in a revelation to the first Celestial Master *Zhang Daoling in 142 CE he stated: "What are demons—the term *gui* 鬼 is also used in Taoist texts to refer to popular deities—that the people should only fear them and not place faith in the Dao?" The text continues to reprimand the contemporary Taoist faithful for consulting spirit mediums (*Zhengyi fawen Tianshi jiaojie kejing* 正一法文天師教戒科經; CT 789, 14a and 17a; Bokenkamp 1997, 171 and 178).

These ideas are developed in greater detail in medieval Taoist scriptures such as the *Santian neijie jing (Scripture of the Inner Explication of the Three Heavens), ascribed to the fifth century. This text claims that Zhang Daoling formed a covenant with the Three Offices (*sanguan, of Haven, Earth, and Water) and the stellar deity Taisui 太歲 (Jupiter) "so that they then entered the orthodox system of the Three Heavens (see *santian and *liutian*) and no longer oppressed the faithful" by requiring bloody offerings or lavish temples (Schipper 1993, 61).

Attempts at reform. The extent whereto Taoism was actually able to reform local cults is another matter entirely. While medieval Taoists frequently attacked *yinsi*, such efforts rarely had any lasting impact, particularly since many Taoist coverts persisted in worshipping local deities with meat offerings, despite the exhortations of their leaders (Stein R. A. 1963; Stein R. A. 1979). Medieval Taoist leaders strongly opposed such practices, formulating agendas expressed in polemical scriptures such as the *Daomen kelüe (Abridged Codes for the Taoist Community), compiled in the fifth century by *Lu Xiujing. According to this text, the world had entered a degenerate age in which people worshipped the souls of the unruly dead, particularly soldiers who had fallen in battle. Lu proposed numerous liturgical and organizational reforms to combat such decay, but the deities included in various registers (*LU) transmitted to ordinary Taoist believers were full of "spirit generals" who seem in many ways little different from the slain soldiers mentioned above (Nickerson 1996a, 348, 352, 356). In addition, the ecstatic and occasionally erotic visions of young *Shangqing Taoists such as *Yang Xi (330–86) and Zhou Ziliang 周子良 (497–516) appear little different from the shamanic rituals Taoist leaders so often derided (Bokenkamp 1996b; Kroll 1996c).

One of the most interesting and widely researched examples of the interaction between Taoism and local cults involves the cult of the plague-fighting deity *Wen Qiong, which was highly popular throughout south China from at least the Song dynasty. The Taoist Canon contains a hagiography about Wen written by the *Shenxiao Taoist, Huang Gongjin 黃公瑾 (fl. 1274), entitled *Diqi shangjiang Wen taibao zhuan* 地祇上將溫太保傳 (Biography of Grand Guardian Wen, Highest General of the Earth Spirits; CT 780). According to this text, Wen was a Tang-dynasty military leader who later worked as a butcher before accepting a position as a spirit-medium in the *Dongyue dadi temple at Mount Tai (*Taishan, Shandong). Wen was later miraculously transformed into a deity, and ended up serving in the temple's chthonic bureaucracy. The bulk of the hagiography is devoted to describing Wen's exploits as a Taoist deity who works to "support the orthodox Way" (*fuchi zhengdao* 扶持正道) by helping Taoist specialists destroy all manner of *yinsi*. Wen is also lauded for refusing popular temples, official titles, and meat offerings, choosing instead to be worshipped in Taoist **jiao* rituals.

Huang Gongjin's hagiography of Wen Qiong clearly expresses Taoist conceptions of liturgical orthopraxy. According to this work, local deities could support Taoism by joining its pantheon while also rejecting popular practices such as official titles and meat offerings. However, these Taoist ideals appear to have had little influence on local cults. This is not to deny the important role that *daoshi* played in the spread of Wen's cult throughout south China by founding or restoring many of his earliest temples (Katz P. R. 1995a, 117–41). Yet, if one examines non-Taoist sources one finds a very different image of Wen Qiong from that contained in Taoist hagiographies. For example, a temple inscription composed in 1355 by the scholar-official Song Lian 宋濂 (1310–81), as well as hagiographies in various Ming-dynasty *soushen* 搜神 ("searching for the sacred") collections, mention Wen's links to Taoism but place greater emphasis on his role as a literatus. Another very different representation of Wen may be found in late imperial fiction and modern folktales, which portray him as someone who defies the Taoist heavenly bureaucracy by preventing **wenshen* (plague spirits) from poisoning local wells (Katz P. R. 1995a, 97–106). Late imperial sources about temples and festivals to Wen also reveal that he usually received meat offerings (Katz P. R. 1995a, 143–74).

Another fascinating example involves the cults of the Wutong 五通, demonic spirits who could make worshippers fabulously wealthy but who often demanded sexual favors in return. Taoists, Buddhists, local elites, and the state all attempted to eradicate or reform these cults, largely without lasting success (Boltz J. M. 1993a; Cedzich 1985; Cedzich 1995; von Glahn 1991).

In considering the relationship between Taoism and local cults, it might be useful to compare Taoist attempts to influence the latter to the early Christian practice of converting popular local deities into saints while transforming their hagiographies (as well as iconographies and rituals) to fit the criteria of Christianity (see for example Brown 1981; Hertz 1983). As the Christian Church tried to absorb ancient European and Near Eastern cults of various nature and tutelary spirits and mold such deities into more acceptable saints, so Taoist movements from the Han dynasty onward strove to convert those local gods whose cults could not be eradicated into deities conforming to Taoist norms. However, the evidence collected to date suggests that Taoism proved less successful than Christianity in this effort. The reasons for this have yet to be fully understood, but appear to be linked to the frequent inability of "institutional religions" in China such as Taoism to effectively influence local society (Yang C. K. 1961, 301–40), and the active "reception" and reinterpretation of Taoist doctrine by non-Taoist worshippers (Katz P. R. 1997).

Paul R. KATZ

📖 Boltz J. M. 1993a; Dean 1993; Hansen 1990; Kanai Noriyuki 1983; Katz P. R. 1995a; Kleeman 1994b; Kleeman 1998; Schipper 1985d; Schipper 1985e; Stein R. A. 1963; Stein R. A. 1979

※ *yinsi*; TAOISM AND LOCAL COMMUNITIES; TAOISM AND POPULAR RELIGION; TAOISM AND POPULAR SECTS; TAOISM AND THE STATE

Taoism and medium cults

The beginnings of Taoism were closely bound up with medium cults, both as sources for or analogues of Taoist practice and as objects of criticism and attack. According to the *Hou Hanshu* (History of the Later Han) and the *Sanguo zhi* (History of the Three Kingdoms), *Zhang Lu was a practitioner of "demonic arts" (*guidao* 鬼道), which he learned from his mother. While the exact nature of *guidao* is difficult to determine, it appears to have involved the evocation of minor deities or spirits, followed by the reception of the spirits' oracles through the speech of spirit-mediums (Stein R. A. 1979, 60–61; but see Cedzich 1987 and Cedzich 1993 on the meaning of *gui* in the early *Tianshi dao* or Way of the Celestial Masters).

Even more intriguing than these outsiders' accounts are references in an early Celestial Master text, the 255 CE "Dadao jia lingjie" 大道家令戒 (Commands and Admonitions for the Families of the Great Dao), to the practice of *jueqi* 決氣: "breaking through," "distinguishing voices coming from," or "comprehending voices in" pneumas (*Zhengyi fawen Tianshi jiaojie kejing* 正一 法文天師教戒科經; CT 789, 12a–9b; Bokenkamp 1997, 151–52). It would appear that, in the early decades of the Way of the Celestial Masters, communications were received from the beyond and transmitted vocally. (These might either be valid, divine transmissions or merely the deceptions of ghosts.) A strong argument may be made that the "Lingjie" was itself a communication from Zhang Lu received via this method (Bokenkamp 1997, 149–85, esp. 151 and 162 n. 11). But some kind of typological distinction between *jueqi* and popular mediumism must have been made. Other features typical of medium cults, such as the provision of sacrificial offerings in order to facilitate communication with the spirits who spoke through mediums, were prohibited in the Celestial Masters' *Xiang'er* commentary to the *Daode jing* (Rao Zongyi 1956, 34).

Fig. 17. Medium during pilgrimage tour to Wuzhi shan
五指山, Hsinchu, Taiwan (November 1994). Photograph
by Julian Pas. See also fig. 72.

A similar ambiguity pervades Taoism's relationship in later times with the mediums and the god-cults in which they officiated. By the fourth and fifth centuries, Taoism had come to define itself in terms of its opposition to the medium cults and their deities. We shall probably never know precisely how *Yang Xi created the late fourth century *Shangqing scriptures during his midnight meetings with the celestial Perfected. We are given to understand from the scriptures themselves that this involved the descent of Yang's immortal informants into his oratory and their revelation to him of scriptural material and other instructions (which it was then Yang's duty to transcribe on the spot). This is certainly reminiscent of mediumistic and other shamanic communications with the divine in China—e.g., as depicted in the *Chuci* 楚辭 (Songs of Chu; trans. Hawkes 1985) and elsewhere (although one might note the absence of an audience; see Rouget 1985). It perhaps resembles even more closely divination with the planchette, a form of automatic writing (see *fuji*).

The Shangqing school's own origins may owe more than a little to a medium cult. In his commentary on the *Zhengao* (11.9b), *Tao Hongjing reports that during his time there existed on Mount Mao (*Maoshan, Jiangsu) a popular cult to the three Mao brothers (see under *Maojun), the transcendent sources of some of the Shangqing revelations, and that there were numerous temples dedicated to the trio. Popular worship of the Mao brothers involved blood sacrifice and spirit-possession; rites at one of the temples on Mount Mao were directed by a female medium or "invocator" (zhu 祝). Tao attempts to deal with this difficulty—the connection of the medium cult with the "pure" religious regime of the Taoism of Mount Mao—by constructing a chronology in which the (Taoist-style) ascent to transcendent immortality of the Mao brothers came prior to the establishment of popular worship (which was instituted in response to the witnessing of that ascent). However, it is quite likely that, out of piety, Tao reversed the order of events, and that the ascription of transcendent status and revelatory capacities to the Mao brothers by the Mount Mao Taoists actually postdated, and perhaps was inspired by, the preexisting medium cult (Schipper 1985e).

Nonetheless, Shangqing Taoism, like other Taoist movements of Southern Dynasties times, fulminated against the "gods of the profane" (sushen 俗神), and Shangqing writings themselves provided instructions for the destruction of popular temples (e.g. *Dengzhen yinjue; 3.21b). The dual tendencies of conflict and assimilation that characterized Taoist/popular religious interactions were nowhere more apparent than in the way Taoists dealt with medium-cults (and, though there is less surviving evidence, in the way the medium cults dealt with the Taoists).

The trend toward the assimilation by Taoism of popular cults, deities, and practices—especially from Song times onward—is dealt with elsewhere in this volume (see *TAOISM AND POPULAR RELIGION, *TAOISM AND LOCAL CULTS, *DEMONS AND SPIRITS), and spirit-medium cults were no exception to, and indeed were a major component of, this trend. This historical tendency continued, as evinced by studies of late imperial Taoist history and scriptural production, as well as by recent ethnographic evidence. Already established popular cults might begin their incorporation within Taoism through the composition of songs of invocation by local ritual masters (though to speak of incorporation is in many cases to speak from the perspective of Taoism alone, not that of the often largely independent cults themselves; see Katz P. R. 1995a). Subsequently, some cult deities might have full-scale Taoist scriptures composed for them, which often gave those gods esoteric identities as astral deities in the Taoist pantheon. Such scriptures could, however, simply be kept among the manuscript collections of local Taoist priests. Cults with promoters having close connections to the imperial government, on the other hand—at least up to the time when the Ming Taoist Canon was compiled—would be represented in the Canon by a full variety of scriptures, not only liturgical texts, but also historical accounts and records of mediums' pronouncements (Dean 1993, esp. 18, 30–32). Today, for instance in southern Taiwan, one may witness *jiao conducted by Taoist priests—even those of some standing—at popular temples established and controlled by charismatic spirit-mediums.

Peter NICKERSON

📖 Cedzich 1993; Cheu Hock Tong 1988; Nickerson 1994; Schipper 1985e; Stein R. A. 1979; Strickmann 1977

※ *fuji*; *tâng-ki*; TAOISM AND POPULAR RELIGION; TAOISM AND POPULAR SECTS

Taoism and ancestor worship

Ancestor worship in China has generally been considered the province either of "diffuse" Chinese religion or, more specifically, Confucianism. Indeed, the archaic ancestral cult as practiced until the Eastern Zhou was codified in Confucian classics such as the *Yili* 儀禮 (Ceremonials) and, in modified form, continues to be practiced among Chinese families and extended kin-groups today. However, by the mid-Eastern Zhou the ancestral temple had lost its role as the center of the ancestral cult (in favor the tomb) and new modes of dealing with and caring for the dead became central concerns (von Falkenhausen 1994). Thus it is not inappropriate to speak of Taoism and the cult of ancestors—in terms of the rites developed within Taoism to ensure the welfare of the deceased, as well as relations between Taoist mortuary rites / rituals of salvation and ancient, Confucianized forms of ancestor "worship."

The early period. The attitude of the early Taoist religion toward the traditional ancestral cult was ambiguous at best. The *Xiang'er* commentary to the *Daode jing* claims that the Dao created sexual intercourse because of the importance of "the continuation of ancestral sacrifice and the survival of the species"; but "heaven and earth lack ancestral shrines" (like transcendent immortals, they do not reproduce). Elsewhere the same text claims that making food offerings to the dead and praying at ancestral shrines is prohibited by the Dao and that violators will be penalized (Bokenkamp 1997, 84 and 119). Other scholars have taken the early Taoist admonition—"the spirits do not drink or eat" (see, e.g., *Daomen kelüe*, 1b)—to include even offerings to ancestors. Therefore early Taoist adherents may have felt negligent and even guilty toward their deceased forebears.

However, concern for ancestors (and for their care and feeding by tradi-tional means) was impossible for the early Taoists to eradicate, even had they wanted to. Instead, a stance of accommodation was adopted. *Lu Xiujing's *Daomen kelüe* (Abridged Codes for the Taoist Community) allows offerings to the family dead, but only five times each year, on the five *la* days (*wula* 五臘, i.e., 1/1, 5/5, 7/7, 1/10, and in the twelfth lunar month—day not specified—in the Chinese calendar; see *Chisong zi zhangli*, 2.17b–18a). At the same time, or even before, the basic rite of the early Taoist Church, that of "petitioning celestial officials" (*zou tianguan* 奏天官) had been turned to soteriological ends, as evinced by the *Chisong zi zhangli* (Master Red-Pine's Almanac of Petitions). This medieval ritual manual includes model documents such as the "Petition for Release From Punishment" ("Jiezhe zhang" 解謫章, 6.1b–2b), in which the descendants of the deceased through the mediation of a Taoist priest seek to "release the departed, that he might leave the paths of darkness [in the underworld] forever, and ascend and be transferred to the Hall of Blessings (*futang* 福堂) [in the heavens]."

Lingbao rites. With the emergence of the *Lingbao scriptures and their codifica-tion by Lu Xiujing, new rituals for the salvation of ancestors were developed. The Yellow Register Retreat (*huanglu zhai) is mentioned as one among twelve Taoist Retreats in one of Lu's writings (*Wugan wen* 五感文; CT 1278). Though the ritual script does not appear in the Taoist Canon as an independent text, the Retreat is described in the *Wushang biyao (Supreme Secret Essentials; Lagerwey 1981b, 163–65). An altar is established surrounded by gates for each of the ten directions, with a large incense burner and a nine foot tall lamp installed in the center. Framed by the "opening" and the "closing" of the in-cense burner, the principal actions include the request by the Master of Rites for transcendent officials "to assist in the ritual for saving the souls of the dead of nine generations of the host [the ritual's sponsor]"; the "Confession to the Ten Directions," in which the Master declares the host's willingness to take refuge with the deities of each such direction; and the presentation of silk and gold to assure the ancestors' release and ascent.

This sequence was to remain the heart of Taoist rites for the dead, as elabo-rated by *Du Guangting (850–933) and further developed during the Song. The changes that are particular to the Song concern various actions designed to convey the Master (or spirits under his direction) to the underworld, then conduct the deceased to the ritual area. This was done to ensure their trans-formation into gods or beneficent ancestors (Davis E. 2001, 227–36). The Song rites for the dead may in turn be traced all the way to the present, for example in the Merit rituals (*gongde) conducted today by Taoist priests in southern Taiwan.

Other features. Two other facets of recent Taoist involvement with the ancestral cult might be briefly mentioned. The rite called Destruction of Hell (*poyu) was one of the Song Taoist innovations alluded to above. In intent and basic format, at least, it is clearly related to the Red-head (*hongtou* 紅頭; see *hong-tou* and *wutou*) ritual master's rite of Attack on the Fortress (*dacheng* 打城; see *Death and the afterlife). It should also be pointed out that, during the Attack, on the altar set up for the deceased are sometimes placed ancestral tablets belonging to the family or families sponsoring the ritual. Also occasion-ally seen are various paraphernalia for conducting the marriages of female relatives who died unmarried (*minghun* 冥婚, or so-called "ghost marriages," which allow women to receive ancestral offerings as part of the agnatic groups of their "husbands"). The ritual masters assist in straightening out lines of descent and alliance within the traditional ancestral cult, allowing wandering souls to take their proper places on family shrines.

Finally, representing a virtually complete fusion of Taoist death ritual and the ancestral cult, reference might be made to a forty-nine day rite carried out after the death of a Taoist master in Gaoxiong, Taiwan and observed by the author of the present entry. The concluding act of the ritual occurred when the high priest (*gaogong* 高功; see *daozhang*), who had been conducting the ritual of Merit during the final days, placed the deceased Taoist master's spirit-tablet on his family's ancestral shrine.

Peter NICKERSON

📖 Davis E. 2001, 171–99; von Falkenhausen 1994; Kleeman 1994b

※ TAOISM AND POPULAR RELIGION

TAOISM AND CHINESE SOCIETY

Taoism and the state

The late-twentieth-century rise in historical research on Taoism has had its most radical impact on our understanding of the relationship between Taoism and the state. While in the past the words would probably have conjured up images of *Zhuangzi refusing to become a bureaucrat, now, thanks to the works of Anna Seidel (1938–91), a strong conceptual link between Taoism as a religious tradition and bureaucracy is accepted as fundamental to our understanding of its role. Specifically, we now know that the rise of bureaucratic state organization in preimperial China soon started to affect conceptions of the unseen world of the spirits, so that by the second century CE, when the imperial bureaucracy began to lose its hold on a troubled and restless society, it was to this unseen empire that intermediaries like the Celestial Masters (*Tianshi dao) started to appeal, using the terminology of bureaucratic written communications. Despite the undoubted presence of an anti-imperial, anarchic strain within the Taoist tradition from preimperial times, the tension between religion and the state at this point, as at many later points, arose not from a radically different vision of society, but from an identical alternative based on the better ordered empire of the gods. Though images of royalty and empire are not uncommon in other religions, Taoism is unique in extending its imagery from the highest levels of rulership to embrace the ranks of officialdom and the culture of scribal administration.

This explains an even greater tension, first noticed by Rolf A. Stein (1979), between Taoism, often as an ally of bureaucracy, and local religion during the Six Dynasties. This tension has been traced into the Tang and even the Song by Judith M. Boltz (1993a) and others, though thereafter it became muted as popular religion itself to a large degree absorbed what has been termed the "imperial metaphor." But the Tang-Song period of alliance against local cults only became possible once official doubts about the priesthood's capacity to supplant them had been allayed. This happened in the early fifth century, when the alternative policy of leaving them alone, either at the risk of seeing their organizations fall prey to religious adventurers (the cause of serious rebellion in South China, 399–411; see *Sun En) or so as to forego their value in the reorganization of an agrarian society already devastated by war (as in the North), was abandoned.

It was this period that saw Taoism emerge as an organized, state-recognized religion with a defined canon and clerical regulations like those of the Buddhist clergy, which though in a sense autonomous had always ceded to kings in India the important role of ensuring the quality of its membership and enforcing its adherence to its own rules. We do not, however, see the institution of formal offices (what might be termed *daoguan* 道官 or "Office for Taoism," though this is a much later usage) to oversee the Taoist clergy in the same way as among the Buddhists at this point. The earliest Taoist known to have exercised such a supervisory function is Meng Jingyi 孟景翼, appointed the greater of two *daozheng* 道正, "Regulators of the Dao," in 503, almost a century later than the appearance of monk officials (*Daoxue zhuan* 7, in the reconstruction of Bumbacher 2000c, 219–223).

This, however, may simply reflect gaps in our sources: certainly in North China *Kou Qianzhi (365?–448) exercised some sort of recognized leadership over Taoism, though he fulfilled no named government function known to us. The Northern Wei and its successor states maintained from the late fifth century onward specific subdepartments of government to oversee the Buddhist clergy, and to judge from the example of Wang Daoyi 王道義 (ca. 470) given in the *Weishu* (History of the Wei; trans. Ware 1933, 241), they also took on responsibility for Taoists. The northern tradition of state intervention in religious affairs was to culminate under the Northern Zhou in 574 in the conversion of the *Xuandu guan monastery into the *Tongdao guan, a state controlled institute used to create the encyclopedic *Wushang biyao (Supreme Secret Essentials), the embodiment of Taoism refashioned in the interests of the state.

Though state ideology swung back to a much greater interest in the use of Buddhism for ideological purposes under the Sui, indicated by the reappearance of a Xuandu guan in their new capital much overshadowed in importance by a new metropolitan chief Buddhist monastery, and though the early Tang exercised great caution in matters of religion, the Northern Zhou had demonstrated the possibilities of a synthetic "state Taoism." Gradually during the seventh century the Tang started to create their own synthesis, making particular use of the supposed descent of the ruling family from Laozi, and after the more Buddhist interlude of the Zhou regime under the Empress Wu returned to this task during the reign of Xuanzong (r. 712–56).

This period, especially the latter part, saw so much state activity in support of Taoism that special commissionerships became necessary for senior Taoists to serve as intermediaries between the regular bureaucracy and the Taoist community. At the same time some bureaucrats became Taoist priests, and some priests were awarded bureaucratic rank, though sporadic occurrences of the latter honor may be found both before and after this point. Taoist examinations, based on the preimperial texts anciently classified as *DAOJIA were instituted, and remained throughout the dynasty (see *TAOISM AND THE CIVIL SERVICE EXAMINATIONS). This period of innovation, however, was followed by rebellions against the dynasty and so by retrenchment and regularization, the only presumed change being the introduction of a new regulatory office, the *daolu si* 道錄司 or "Office for the Registration of Taoists," during the ninth century, though this is an extrapolation from the creation of such an organ for Buddhists.

The shift in Chinese society that took place from the late Tang to early Song affected relations between Taoism and the state in complex ways. The decline of the aristocratic clans with their roots in Six Dynasties culture from which the Tang rulers had sprung made it less necessary for the ruling house to stress its divine origins, while the new bureaucracy which asserted its legitimacy through education in Confucianism proved less susceptible to control through imperial assertions of divine authority. Even so, it would appear that Taoism and Buddhism continued to receive the patronage of that elite, rather than local religion. The world of popular cults, however, had changed as well, attracting the patronage of powerful forces in local society outside the bureaucracy which, together with changes in communications, helped them to spread, sometimes transregionally. Simultaneously the annexation of elements from the "higher" religions to the lower, or alternatively the popularization at the lower level of forms of the higher religions, often blurred the boundaries of former times. The emperor Huizong (r. 1100–1125), in a celebrated episode in 1119–20 which saw Buddhism forced to adopt a Chinese nomenclature, may have been trying to reconcile Buddhism and Taoism so as to promote the latter in a form that could reach into the new local religious environment as a national ideology in times of danger. The subsequent collapse of the Northern Song, however, strengthened the alternative policy of extending state patronage to popular forms of religion which had secured backing powerful enough to assure respectability. Supervision of the Taoist clergy now extended to the prefectural level, each of which had a *daozheng si* 道正司, "Office for the Regulation of Taoists."

The eventual conquest of China by the Mongols brought to the whole empire for the first time a ruling house untouched by Chinese political traditions, which tended to see religious groups not as a problem for bureaucratic control but as potential agents of imperial power within a much looser structure of government. This unparalleled opportunity for patronage, however, excited fierce competition between Buddhists and Taoists, resulting in the famous decision of Khubilai to destroy the Taoist Canon in 1281 (see *Da Jin Xuandu baozang*). Mongol preference for non-Chinese supervision over Chinese subjects, however, ensured that it was Tibetan Buddhists who profited most from this.

Government control came back with a vengeance following the establishment of the Ming dynasty in 1368, especially since the Hongwu Emperor (r. 1368–98), having risen from poverty, had an unusually clear awareness of the power of religion in local society. An incessant reformer, he abolished his first government office for control of Taoism, the Xuanjiao yuan 玄教院 (Institute for the Mysterious Teaching), in 1382 in favor of a system in which a central *daolu si* stood at the apex of a hierarchy of local offices stretching all the way down to the district level, whilst each monastery was obliged to maintain a register of any travelling Taoists who might visit. This proved appealing enough to the now more autocratic state to last to the close of the Chinese empire. It did not, of course, prevent emperors from succumbing to the influence of individual Taoists, and indeed the Ming showed a greater penchant for this than most. Only the Manchus, with their background of shamanism and strong links with Tibeto-Mongol Buddhism, combined with a desire to show themselves masters of Chinese Confucian culture, literally could find little room for Taoism at court, apart from one hall for the worship of Xuantian shangdi 玄天上帝 (Highest Emperor of the Dark Heaven; see *Beidi).

T. H. BARRETT

📖 Barrett 1996; Boltz J. M. 1993a; Hymes 2002, 171–205; Seidel 1983a; Stein R. A. 1979

※ TAOISM AND LOCAL CULTS; TAOISM AND THE CIVIL SERVICE EXAMINATIONS

Taoism and the civil service examinations

In 741, Tang Xuanzong (r. 712–56) established the Examination on Taoism (*daoju* 道舉) and the Chongxuan xue 崇玄學 or School for the Veneration of the Mystery. Ironically Empress Wu (r. 690–705), who was more inclined toward Buddhism, was the first ruler to propose incorporating Taoism into the civil service examinations when she proposed adding a question on the *Daode jing* to them in 675. In 693, she rescinded the regulation, but Xuanzong restored it in 733 as he became more deeply involved in Taoism and more earnest in using it as a dynastic ideology.

By 741, Xuanzong had come to the conclusion that he needed to establish a national school system in Taoist studies to further his political ends. So he founded Chongxuan xue in both of his capitals—Chang'an and Luoyang—and delegated to the governors of the 331 prefectures the task of instituting schools with the same title in their districts. The quota of students for the schools in the capitals was one hundred each, while that for prefectures was a portion of those allocated for all schools (sixty, fifty and forty for large, medium and small prefectures). The curriculum consisted of instruction in four texts: the *Daode jing*, *Zhuangzi*, *Wenzi*, and *Liezi*. In 742, the emperor ordered the addition of a fifth text, the *Gengsang zi*; however, it never became part of the course of study because his scholars demonstrated clearly that it was a forgery. In a decree of 743, he set a limit of three years for Taoist students to graduate, a far more stringent limit than that set for those enrolled in the Directorate of the Sons of State (Guozi jian 國子監) where instruction centered on the classics, histories and other fields and the maximum tenure was nine years. Those in charge of capital schools and prefectural governors sent graduates of the Chongxuan xue to the capital late in the year to compete in the examination on Taoism during the following spring.

Until 754, the subjects for the Examination on Taoism were the same four texts that served as the curriculum of the Chongxuan xue. In that year Xuanzong dropped the *Daode jing* from the examination and replaced it with the **Yijing*. The format of the Examination on Taoism was the same as that for the *mingjing* 明經 examination on Confucian classics. It had four parts. First, candidates had to fill in passages that examiners had deleted from ten quotations taken from each text. Four to five correct answers out of ten was a passing mark. An oral examination followed. Third, the candidates had to answer ten questions on the interpretation of the classics. Six satisfactory answers was a passing mark. Finally, they wrote three essays on contemporary problems. In a decree of 743 the emperor reduced the passing grades in the Examination on Taoism to three or four for fill-ins and five for interpretative questions. Apparently even that act of favor was insufficient to attract the number of students that he desired. So in 748 he granted two further boons to recruit men of Taoist learning. He authorized those with knowledge of the four Taoist classics to recommended themselves, that is they could apply directly to prefectural governors for permission to sit for the examination. Candidates for other civil service examinations had to obtain a recommendation from local notables in their districts before they could apply. Xuanzong also reduced the number of questions that graduates of the Examination on Taoism had to answer on the Placement Examination (*xuan* 選). The Placement Examination was the final ordeal that graduates of all examinations had to undergo before they received appointments to office. It evaluated the candidates' character, eloquence, calligraphy, and judgment. By that act the emperor apparently thought that Taoist studies would become a preferred course for men seeking office.

In 743, Xuanzong changed the name of the Chongxuan xue in the capitals to Chongxuan guan 崇玄館 (Institute for the Veneration of the Mystery) and established posts at each for a Grand Academician (*da xueshi* 大學士). Tang institutes were both schools and bodies of scholars who provided counsel to the throne, executed research, and compiled literary collections. They were the most prestigious educational and scholastic organs of the court. Consequently, it was the custom of emperors to appoint the highest-ranking ministers to the posts of Grand Academician, and Xuanzong was no exception. The most important task the Chongxuan guan performed during his reign was to copy the *Yiqie daojing* 一切道經 (Complete Taoist Scriptures), a large library or repository of Taoist texts in 3,744 scrolls that the emperor had had assembled and personally proofread (see **Yiqie daojing yinyi*). His ultimate objective was to have the copies sent out to the capitals of ten circuits where Envoys of Inquiry (*caifang shi* 採訪使) there would, in turn, have them recopied. The project, commissioned in 749, was unprecedented and testifies to the emperor's intention of propagating Taoism and preserving its scriptures.

In 763, Tang Daizong (r. 762–79) abolished the Examination on Taoism and dispersed the students of the Chongxuan guan. In 768, however, he restored the schools in the capitals and apparently resurrected the examination because two questions for it dating from 802 and 803 have survived.

Charles D. BENN

📕 Barrett 1996, 65–73; Benn 1977, 255–98

※ TAOISM AND THE STATE

Taoism and local communities

The relationship between Taoism and local communities has been extremely varied and complex, marked by different forms of interaction influenced by both socioeconomic and political forces affecting a particular locale, as well as the organizational nature of the Taoist movement which existed at that locale. Despite the importance of this topic in terms of better understanding China's social and religious history, it has yet to be thoroughly and comprehensively researched. Much of the data have been collected by historians studying the origins of Taoism in Sichuan and ethnographers working in southeastern China and Taiwan, and interpretations of these data have often been shaped by agendas involving the assertion of the ritual superiority of Taoism over local cults.

Based on the data currently available, the relationship between Taoism and local communities appears to have been marked by five forms of interaction: 1. Taoist theocracies ruling over local communities; 2. Taoist organizations playing a leading role in controlling the socioreligious activities of local communities; 3. Taoist villages serving the ritual needs of nearby communities; 4. Taoist masters and their disciples living amid local communities and serving the ritual needs of individuals or the community as a whole; 5. eremitic traditions of Taoism which existed apart from local communities.

Modes of interaction. Theocratic states established by members of the *Tianshi dao existed in southwestern China during the second and third centuries CE. This region was divided into twenty-four parishes (*zhi), each of which was led by a libationer (*jijiu). Inside these parishes, local chiefs (zhang 長) organized "charity lodges" (yishe 義舍) to administer individual neighborhoods. Household registration was undertaken, and people were governed according to a legal code, although punishments were relatively lenient. Those who broke the rules in the code were pardoned three times, after which they were forced to perform public works such as repairing local roads. The best-known examples of such a theocracy are the Hanzhong 漢中 community led by *Zhang Lu (Bokenkamp 1997, 34–37) and the Cheng 成 (later Cheng-Han 成 漢) kingdom founded during the early fourth century by Li Te 李特 and his son *Li Xiong (Kleeman 1998; see *Dacheng).

The second mode of interaction, Taoists leading local communities in terms of their socioreligious activities, can be most clearly seen in *Quanzhen Taoism. Numerous scholars have studied this movement, but almost exclusively in terms of its doctrinal and political history. However, Vincent Goossaert (1997, 354–67) has used 487 examples of Quanzhen *EPIGRAPHY to document how Taoist monks and nuns belonging to this movement founded and/or led ritual associations at popular temples which were taken over by the movement. Scholars who research the socioreligious history of late imperial Beijing have also found evidence for Taoists founding and leading ritual organizations at that city's *Dongyue dadi temple (see the papers published in the journal *Sanjiao wenxian* 三教文獻: *Matériaux pour l'étude de la religion chinoise*, I, 1997). Nonetheless, such a situation does not seem to have prevailed at all Taoist sites: for example, ritual associations at the *Yongle gong were led by lay members of the community, although Quanzhen Taoists did participate in their affairs (Katz P. R. 1996).

A fascinating example of the relationship of Taoism with local communities is the case of Taoist villages (daoshi cun 道士村), where Taoism and local community largely overlap. However, we know little about the history of such villages or the ways in which Taoists residing there interact with individuals or communities who hire them to perform rituals. Most of the data on such villages collected so far come from central Zhejiang (Xu Hongtu 1995a), and have only been collected during fieldwork on ritual operas published in the *Minsu quyi congshu* 民俗曲藝叢書 (*Monograph Series of Studies in Chinese Ritual, Theatre and Folklore*). This phenomenon merits further study in the future.

By far the best-known form of interaction between Taoism and local communities involves individual *daoshi, *fashi, and their disciples who live in local communities but do not lead them. These men marry and have children, with their sons frequently becoming their disciples. Such Taoists, usually members of the *Zhengyi, Lüshan 閭山, or Sannai 三奶 traditions, are frequently hired to perform rituals for individuals or the entire community, particularly exorcistic rites and communal Offering (*jiao) and Retreat (*zhai) rituals. However, these Taoists are not in charge of the ritual associations which sponsor such rites. In spite of the large body of scholarship existing on this form of interaction between Taoism and local communities, particularly in Fujian and Taiwan (see for example Dean 1993; Lagerwey 1987c; Schipper 1974; Schipper 1977a; Schipper 1985e), and the additional research undertaken on this topic for the Song dynasty (Boltz J. M. 1993a; Hymes 1996; Hymes 2002; Katz P. R. 1995a; Skar 1996–97), the extent whereto such a relationship existed during other periods of Chinese history, and in which parts of China, is still relatively unknown (see for example Stein R. A. 1979).

Finally, there are examples of eremitic Taoists who chose to live beyond the reach of local communities (see *ASCETICISM). A great deal has been published on those individuals who during their lifetimes were frequently unaffiliated with any particular Taoist movement (see for example Baldrian-Hussein 1996–97; Despeux 1990; Katz P. R. 1996; Strickmann 1994). In addition, the members of two of the most renowned Taoist organizations, the *Shangqing movement of medieval China and the Quanzhen movement, also practiced eremitism, again frequently atop mountains (Eskildsen 1990; Eskildsen 1998; Goossaert 1997, 130–301). However, one must remember that eremitism was rarely a permanent way of life for practicing Taoists, and that after completing a period of eremitic self-cultivation and descending from the mountaintop many Taoist men and women travelled the land, performed rituals, and converted others to Taoism (for a similar analysis of eremitism in the Near East, see Brown 1982). In the case of Shangqing Taoism, it is interesting to note that while this movement has long been studied in terms of its scriptural and ritual achievements, there are relatively little data on its members playing leading roles in local communities. When we turn our attention to Quanzhen Taoism, however, we soon find that the members of this movement could be both hermits and active proselytizers/organizers at different stages of their careers. Some hermits did not even have to leave their mountains to encounter the general public, as many Taoist mountains could also attract large numbers of pilgrims.

Paul R. KATZ

📖 Davis E. 2001; Dean 1993; Goossaert 1997; Hymes 2002; Kleeman 1998; Lagerwey 1987c; Schipper 1974; Schipper 1977a; Schipper 1985e; Schipper 1997a; Seidel 1969; Stein R. A. 1963; Stein R. A. 1979; Strickmann 1994

※ TAOISM AND LOCAL CULTS; TAOISM AND POPULAR RELIGION

Taoism and secret societies

"Secret societies" is a Western term derived from the pejorative nineteenth-century discourse on Freemasonic and Jewish groups, which were ascribed state-undermining intentions. In relation to China, it is mainly used to refer to organizations such as the Triads (Tiandi hui 天地會) and the Gathering of Brothers and Elders (Gelao hui 哥老會), while its application to new religious groups or "sects" is less common. The term was first associated with the Triads by Gustave Schlegel (*Thian ti hwui: The Hung-league, or Heaven-earth-league*, 1866) and was adopted by William Stanton in his book on the Triads in Hong Kong (*The Triad Society*, 1900). It then entered Japanese and Chinese usage as *himitsu kessha* 祕密結社 and *bimi shehui* 祕密社會, respectively, through Hirayama Shū's 平山周 plagiarization of Stanton's book (*Shina Kakumeitō oyobi himitsu kessha* 支那革命党及秘密結社 [The Chinese Revolutionary Party and the secret societies], 1911).

The danger of using this term as an analytical label lies in its undue emphasis on the purported secrecy of rituals and groups or networks. The nature of secrecy in early Triad lore is the same as, for instance, in the Celestial Masters (*Tianshi dao) tradition and various new religious groups—namely, the exclusive transmission of a body of lore by a teacher to selected adepts through a blood covenant (*meng* 盟). This lore is believed to confer power, and therefore its transmission must be carefully regulated. In mature Triad ritual and in the rituals of the groups known since the late nineteenth century as the Gathering of Brothers and Elders, the transfer of esoteric knowledge became less central and initiation focused on the establishment of a collective network. Nonetheless, initiates were not allowed to reveal the Triad lore to outsiders, and only in this sense the qualification "secret" is appropriate.

The Triads worship five former Buddhist monks of the Shaolin 少林 (Small Forest) Monastery (variously located in Gansu or different southern provinces, but not to be confused with the Shaolin Monastery in Dengfeng 登封, Henan) as their founding patriarchs. They are not vegetarian, however, and in the covenant ritual participants drink liquor mixed with human or—more often—cockerel blood to confirm a sacred oath of mutual support and brotherhood. Therefore, the Triads cannot be considered Buddhist in any meaningful way. Some scholars have also suggested that Triad practices are linked to Taoist ritual, since one central implement used in the initiation rite is a bushel with exorcist objects inside. However, this implement is used in many Chinese rituals, not only in Taoist traditions *per se*; in fact, its non-Taoist uses can be traced back to before the Tang period.

The basic structure of the Triad initiation ritual is inspired by the journey of man through the landscape of life and death, a theme also developed by Taoist traditions but by no means their exclusive possession or creation. A second major source of Triad lore is eighteenth-century demonological and messianic traditions, which were neither Taoist or Buddhist. They defined the apocalyptic threat as the advent of violent demons who would cause war, plague, and other disasters, who were to be vanquished by ritual means (such as talismans, *FU), and would be followed by the coming of a prince in the form of divine general (shenjiang 神將) leading divine armies (shenbing 神兵).

Barend ter HAAR

📖 ter Haar 1998b; ter Haar 1993; Murray 1994; Overmyer 1976; Ownby 1996

Women in Taoism

Women appear in several guises in Taoism: as wives of the Celestial Masters, as practicing adepts, as companions for sexual practices (*fangzhong shu), and as divinities. They are called "female masters" (nüshi 女師), "female officers" (nüguan 女官) in the Way of the Celestial Masters (*Tianshi dao), "female Taoist masters" (nü daoshi 女道士) in the Song period, and Maidens of the Dao (daogu 道姑) from the Song onward. Their status in Taoism has reflected their rank in Chinese society, where the rule was submission to men—especially the husband—and the mothers of male children enjoyed the highest respect. Women rarely took part in rituals, and they had limited powers and few possibilities to write. Their ability to communicate with the divine was recognized, however, and they were entrusted with revealed texts.

Women, therefore, essentially appear as divine beings in Taoism, in varying degrees according to the different schools, and have been especially venerated as mothers. Taoism is sometimes said to favor the female principle because of the importance it gives to the Yin principle, but this is not entirely correct. On the one hand, the image of the mother is venerated, but on the other, the image of the woman—like that of the Yin principle—is ambiguous.

Women in Taoist history. The first important phase of the history of women in Taoism is the fourth century, when the *Shangqing school recognized a woman, *Wei Huacun (251–334), as the school's matriarch. The most famous Taoist women were associated with this school, within which they transmitted scriptures and methods, and served as initiators and tutors. The status of women in Taoism reached a peak during the Tang period, particularly in the eighth century, when women formed one third of the clergy. Two daughters of Tang Ruizong (r. 684–90, 710–12) and sisters of Tang Xuanzong (r. 712–56) became Taoist nuns in Chang'an monasteries; their ordination rite was described by *Zhang Wanfu (Despeux 1986; Benn 1991).

Women also played an important role in the *Quanzhen school, which was founded at the end of the twelfth century. The list of its seven founders (*qizhen* 七真; see table 17) includes a woman, *Sun Bu'er (1119–83), whose cult became increasingly important during the Yuan, Ming and Qing periods. This prestige did not last long, however, as references to Taoist women become less frequent in the late Yuan and early Ming periods. The image of women is more complex in Qing sectarianism, which witnessed a revival of the tendency to honor women as matriarchs.

Female divinities and immortals. Cults of female deities developed mainly in the southern and coastal regions of Anhui, Hunan, Jiangxi, Fujian, Guangxi, and Guangdong. Cult sites in these provinces were centers of intense religious activity and pilgrimage sites that attracted both male and female devotees. The growth and reputation of the cults depended on their recognition by official Taoist institutions, learned circles, and the imperial court, which occurred from the eighth century onward.

The most famous female divinity in Taoism is the Queen Mother of the West (*Xiwang mu). Despite her unrivalled beauty, she was originally described as a demon. Her worship peaked during the Tang period, and was later replaced by cults radiated through sectarian movements and small congregations that often practiced spirit writing (see *fuji). In the Ming and Qing periods, the Queen Mother descended to the altar and took the name of Unborn Venerable Mother (Wusheng laomu 無生老母). In this form she is still venerated by women, especially in popular milieux.

Apart from the Queen Mother, Taoism includes several other female divinities. The most famous is Immortal Maiden He (He xiangu 何仙姑), whose name appears in the list of the Eight Immortals (*baxian); her cult was established between the Tang and Song dynasties. The cult of *Mazu, the fishermen's goddess, appeared in Fujian at the end of the tenth century. Chen Jinggu 陳靖姑, known as the Lady of the Water's Edge (*Linshui furen), protected women, children, and mediums in Fujian. Zu Shu 祖舒 (fl. 889–904), who came from Guangxi, was the matriarch of the *Qingwei school, a tradition that emphasized therapy and exorcism. Finally, Cao Wenyi 曹文逸, who was invited to the capital by Song Huizong (r. 1100–1125), wrote a commentary to the *Daode jing* and a long poem on *neidan entitled *Lingyuan dadao ge* 靈源大道歌 (Song of the Great Dao, the Numinous Source; trans. Despeux 1990, 83–93).

Hagiographic collections generally include biographies of both men and women, but two works dealing exclusively with the lives of women were composed in two periods that were important for the history of women in Taoism. The first text is the *Yongcheng jixian lu (Records of the Immortals Gathered in the Walled City; CT 783, and YJQQ 114–16), compiled by *Du Guangting (850–933). The second is the Houji 後集 (Later Compilation; CT 298) portion of Zhao Daoyi's 趙道一 (fl. 1294–1307) *Lishi zhenxian tidao tongjian (Comprehensive Mirror of Perfected Immortals and Those Who Embodied the Dao through the Ages), which contains 120 biographies, including almost all those of the Yongcheng jixian lu and fourteen additional biographies for the Song period.

Practices and texts. Women have played an important role in Taoist sexual practices. In the school of the Celestial Masters, adepts practicing the collective rituals of "merging pneumas" (*heqi) led a religious life ruled by a strict moral code. In the Shangqing school, sexuality was transposed into the realm of the imaginary, and practitioners often joined in meditation with female deities.

A body of literature describing techniques of inner alchemy for women (*nüdan) appeared in the eighteenth and nineteenth centuries. It consists of about thirty documents of unequal length, the earliest dating from 1743 and the most recent from 1892. These texts are generally attributed to male and female divinities and were transmitted through spirit writing. The *Daozang xubian (Sequel to the Taoist Canon), edited in 1834 by *Min Yide, contains the Nü jindan jue 女金丹訣 (Instructions on the Golden Elixir for Women), transmitted by Sun Bu'er and received in 1799 in Wulin 武林 (Zhejiang) by one of Min's disciples, Shen Qiyun 沈契雲 (1708–86); and the Xiwang mu nüxiu zhengtu shize 西王母女修正途十則 (Ten Principles of the Queen Mother of the West on the Correct Path of Female Cultivation; trans. Wile 1992, 193–201), transmitted in 1795 by Li Niwan 李泥丸. Another compilation containing nüdan texts, the Daoshu shiqi zhong 道書十七種 (Seventeen Books on the Dao), was edited by *Fu Jinquan in the early nineteenth century. Most of these texts were republished in He Longxiang's 賀龍驤 Nüdan hebian 女丹合編 (Collected Works on Inner Alchemy for Women), a supplement to the 1906 edition of the *Daozang jiyao. Also worthy of mention are the Nüzi daojiao congshu 女子道教叢書 (Collectanea on Taoism for Women), compiled by *Yi Xinying (1896–1976), and the commentaries to some treatises on female alchemy by *Chen Yingning, who was active in the 1930s.

Catherine DESPEUX

📖 Cahill 1990; Despeux 1986; Despeux 1990; Despeux 2000b; Despeux and Kohn 2003; Little 2000b, 275–89; Overmyer 1991; Zhan Shichuang 1990

※ Huang Lingwei; Sun Bu'er; Wei Huacun; nüdan; Yongcheng jixian lu

Taoism in the People's Republic of China

In the half century since the founding of the People's Republic of China on October 1, 1949, the fate of Taoism, like that of the Chinese state and nation, has taken many twists and turns. Its history may be divided into four main periods. In the first period, from 1949 to 1956, Taoism wavered between life and death. According to the estimations of individuals involved, in 1949 there were almost 10,000 Taoist temples in China, inhabited by approximately 50,000 Taoist priests, with many others living scattered throughout the country. When the People's Republic of China was founded, citizens were guaranteed the right to freedom of religious belief in articles 5 and 53 of the "Common Program of the Chinese People's Political Consultative Conference" (1949). However, under the influence of the Soviet views on religion and "leftist" religious policies, the land on which Taoist temples were built was confiscated, the abbots of some temples were accused and denounced as landlords, and popular belief in Taoism came under pressure from public opinion. During this time it was difficult to preserve Taoism, and Taoist priests suffered many hardships.

In the second period, from 1957 to 1965, the number of Taoist temples and priests decreased dramatically. In 1957, the first nationwide, cross-sectarian Taoist organization in Chinese history, the Chinese Taoist Association (*Zhongguo daojiao xiehui), was established with government approval. Yue Chongdai 嶽崇岱 (1888–1958), the first chairman of the association, was received by the government and the president; on the occasion of national political consultations, his photograph and one of his speeches were printed in the *People's Daily* (*Renmin ribao* 人民日報), the organ of the Chinese Communist Party, on April 4, 1957. Just when Taoism was opening a new page in its history, however, the Chinese "antirightist" campaign began. Yue Chongdai was denounced as a "rightist" and committed suicide. Although the Chinese Taoist Association continued to exist under the direction of his successor, *Chen Yingning, by then only 637 Taoist temples remained in all of China, and the number of Taoist priests living in temples had dwindled to no more than 5,000. The overwhelming majority of the Taoist priests lived outside the temples, and had left the clergy to become laborers or peasants.

In the third period, from 1966 to 1977, during the "Great Cultural Revolution," Taoism, like other religions, was subjected to persecutions: temples were closed, books were burned, monks and nuns were forced to return to secular life, and some Taoist leaders were denounced as "class enemies." On the surface it appeared that Taoism had vanished from the territory of the People's Republic of China.

In the fourth period, from 1978 until today, the People's Republic of China has corrected the "leftist" policies that had thrown the country into disorder. In 1982, the Central Committee of the Chinese Communist Party promulgated the "Basic Viewpoints and Basic Policies toward Religious Questions in China during the Socialist Period," and in that same year the State Council announced that the first twenty-one Taoist temples had been reinstated and reopened. In the past two decades, Taoism in the People's Republic of China has undergone a comprehensive recovery, and finds itself today in the most advantageous period of its development over the last hundred years. By the end of 1997, according to unofficial estimates, 1,557 Taoist temples had been reopened all over China; approximately 26,000 Taoist priests inhabited these temples; and more than 50,000 Taoist priests of the *Zhengyi school were active throughout the country. Eighty-three Taoist organizations on the provincial, municipal and communal levels had been established nationwide, two Taoist academies providing university level education had been founded, three Taoist periodicals (*Zhongguo daojiao* 中國道教, *Shanghai daojiao* 上海道教, and *Sanqin daojiao* 三秦道教) are published for general or private circulation, and after an interlude of more than sixty years the *Quanzhen institution of issuing admonitions (*fangjie* 放戒) and the Zhengyi institution of conferring registers (*shoulu* 授籙) have been reinstated. Moreover, unified national regulations have been established to guide the administration of Taoist temples and the activities of Zhengyi Taoist priests working outside the temples.

Compared with earlier times, Taoism in the People's Republic has already developed a number of new characteristics. In particular, the religious doctrine now stresses compatibility with secular developments and progress, and current social institutions are upheld. On the organizational level, cross-sectarian unity and alliances are now emphasized; in the area of religious activities, the tradition and purity of Taoist religious practice is preserved; and in the education of Taoist followers, new pedagogical methods are used and curricula are employed.

CHEN Yaoting

📖 Chen Yaoting 1988; Dean 1986; Dean 1989b; Dean 1993; Hachiya Kunio 1995; Hahn 1986; Hahn 1989; Jan Yün-hua 1984; Lagerwey 1991; Lai Chi-tim 2003; Li Yangzheng 2000; Lü and Lagerwey 1992; Pas 1989a; Pas 1989b; Qing Xitai 1988–95, 4: 481–520

TAOISM AND CHINESE CULTURE

Taoism and Chinese literature

Taoist collections contain representative samples of nearly every generic form known to Chinese literature. This entry outlines several of the most fully-studied and clearest influences of Taoist narrative on Chinese letters.

Hagiography. As a type of composition whose purpose is to recount an event or series of events, narrative was identified with history in early China. Even narrative passages occurring in the works of philosophers were generally regarded as historical illustration. During the Han, writers increasingly turned their attention to figures on the margins of society, recluses, alchemists, wonder-workers, and paragons of the various *xian* ("immortal" or "transcendent"; see **xianren*) cults. Taoist hagiography grew symbiotically with this genre of literature which came to be known as *zhiguai* 志怪 from *Zhuangzi's citation from an otherwise unknown work that he credited to "one with his intentions set on the strange" (*zhiguai zhe* 志怪者). The earliest Taoist collection of this sort is the *Liexian zhuan (Biographies of Exemplary Immortals), attributed to Liu Xiang 劉向 (77–8 or 6 BCE). Early works devoted to a single figure begin with the accounts of the career of Laozi in the **Laozi bianhua jing* (Scripture of the Transformations of Laozi).

Following the Han, the list of hagiographic collections is extensive. Some works, such as the *Shenxian zhuan of *Ge Hong, are Taoist in orientation, while others, such as Gan Bao's 干寶 (ca. 340) *Soushen ji (In Search of the Sacred) or Hong Mai's 洪邁 (1123–1202) *Yijian zhi* 夷堅志 (Heard and Written by Yijian; Chang Fu-jui 1968), indiscriminately mix accounts of Taoists with those of other wonder-workers, ghosts, oddities, holy places, and the like.

While such works are quite diverse in content, they share a common aim, the documentation of anomalies, spiritual occurrences, and extraordinary people that fell beyond the purview of imperially-sponsored history. Their goal, in short, was to collect evidence of the supernatural in the human world. In this respect, they share the evidential and didactic aims of Taoist hagiography found in scriptural works or in collections. *Zhiguai* and hagiography tended to borrow from or respond to one another, so that, for instance, *Yang Xi's communications from the Perfected amplify on the biographies appearing in the *Shenxian zhuan*, as *Tao Hongjing notes. Gu Kuang 顧況 (ca. 725–814; IC 486–87), even lists Taoist works containing significant hagiographic sections—the *Zhengao and *Zhoushi mingtong ji* 周氏冥通記 (Records of Mr. Zhou's Communications with the Unseen; CT 302; trans. Mugitani Kunio and Yoshikawa Tadao 2003, part. trans. Bokenkamp 1996a)—with other *zhiguai* in his preface to Dai Fu's 戴孚 *Guangyi ji* 廣異記 (Record of Widespread Anomalies). Canonical biographical works, such as the *Lishi zhenxian tidao tongjian, compiled by Zhao Daoyi 趙道一 (fl. 1294–1307), draw heavily on and are indistinguishable from this *zhiguai* tradition. (See also the entry *HAGIOGRAPHY.)

Fantastic travel. Following in the tradition of the *Mu tianzi zhuan* 穆天子傳 (Biography of Mu, Son of Heaven; trans. Mathieu 1978), the *Shanhai jing* 山海 經 (Scripture of Mountains and Seas; trans. Mathieu 1983), and the *Yuanyou* 遠 遊 (Far Roaming) poem of the *Chuci* 楚辭 (Songs of Chu; trans. Kroll 1996b), a number of Taoist scriptures locate the sources of knowledge and spiritual power beyond the borders of the known world. Several scriptures, beginning with those of the *Shangqing and *Lingbao traditions, open with a brief account of the revealing deity's travels in search of the text. Earliest to find imitation in secular works, though, were narratives revealing separate worlds hidden within holy mountains found in texts like the *Lingbao wufu xu (Prolegomena to the Five Talismans of the Numinous Treasure). Tales of this sort began to appear in *zhiguai* collections as well as the writings of literati during the Jin, Tao Yuanming's 陶淵明 (Tao Qian 陶潛, 365–427; IC 766–69) *Taohua yuan ji* 桃花源記 (Record of the Peach Blossom Font; Bokenkamp 1986d) being the most notable early example.

As the earth is associated with Yin and the proper domain of the feminine, goddesses often inhabit cavern paradises while the questing humans are male. The erotic potential of this scenario is often explored in secular works like the anonymous Tang-period *You xianku* 遊仙窟 (A Jaunt into the Grotto of the Transcendents; trans. Levy 1965). Less scandalous, but no less enticing, tales feature Taoist spirit journeys. A *Dunhuang manuscript entitled *Ye Jingneng shi* 葉淨能詩 (Poem on Ye Jingneng) tells of the Taoist Ye guiding Tang Xuanzong on journeys to Chengdu to view the lamps during the moon-festival and even to the palaces of the moon. The work bears a close relationship to the canonical *Tang Ye zhenren zhuan* 唐葉真人傳 (Biography of the Perfected Ye of the Tang Dynasty; CT 779), concerning the historical *Ye Fashan (631–720), but the tale appears in a number of other forms, including the rhapsody.

Another popular, though less than desirable, destination was the underworld. Early secular tales of the hells and those who were able to safely visit them draw specificity from scriptural accounts. Eventually, such tales found Buddhist expression in the indigenously-composed *Fo shuo yulanpen jing* 佛 說盂蘭盆經 (Scripture of the Avalambana Spoken by the Buddha) and the Dunhuang tale of Mulian's 目連 rescue of his mother.

Demonography. Texts like the *Nüqing guilü (Demon Statutes of Nüqing) and the *Dongyuan shenzhou jing (Scripture of the Divine Spells of the Cavernous

Abyss) present both lists of the demons of pestilence and misfortune and the stuff of drama, recording the *dramatis personae* for the many demon-quelling rites found in the Taoist religion. Tales loosely based on ritual scenarios were popular throughout Chinese history. Taoist accounts emphasize the difficulty of recognizing demons in their fiendish disguises since, once identified and named, demons tend to lose their power. This aspect of Taoist demonology features in many a plot even where Taoists themselves do not appear. This is particularly the case with that widespread story-type, tales of delicious but dangerous fox-fairies. Demon-quelling Taoists appear frequently as well. Hong Mai's *Yijian zhi* has drawn scholarly attention for the information it reveals on religion in Song society as well as for its fascinating portrayals of the Taoist war on the forces of disorder. Evidence of this theme in literature ranges from Taoist tales of Wu Meng 吳猛 (?–374?) to such secular works as the *Fengshen yanyi* 封神演義 (Investiture of the Gods; IC 384–86) and the entertaining account of *Zhang Daoling's exploits found in Pu Songling's 蒲松齡 (1640–1715) *Liaozhai zhiyi* 聊齋志異 (Strange Tales from Leisure Studio; IC 563–65).

Morality tales. Another narrative type born of scriptural *exempla* is the morality tale. Even in the early Lingbao scriptures, the ten precepts (Bokenkamp 1989, 18–20) are presented in a scripture meant to be widely circulated which contains a long narrative based on the popular *Vessantara-jātaka* from Kang Senghui's 康僧會 (late third century) *Liudu jijing* 六度集經 (Collection [of Tales] on the Six Pāramitās) as well as an account of the Celestial Worthy's promulgation of the precepts in a former world-system. Such morality tracts eventually developed into a popular literary form. For example, the *Wenchang huashu, an account of the transformations of the god *Wenchang revealed through spirit writing (see *fuji) in 1181, with its poetic introductions and prose core, had a marked influence on the development of the early Chinese novel.

It would be a mistake to view explicitly moralistic literature as the only heritor of the Taoist morality tale. Buddhist and Taoist versions of this form were so widely-imitated that even late imperial pornographic novels frequently end with a moralistic *deus ex machina*, either in the form of a moralizing priest or a death-bed conversion.

The picaresque. Taoist scriptural literature possesses yet another highly influential mode of narrative which might be labelled the "picaresque." Comparable to later morality tales, such works as the *Han Wudi neizhuan (Inner Biography of Emperor Wu of the Han), an account of the Han emperor's unsuccessful attempts to learn the secrets of transcendence from the Queen Mother of the West (*Xiwang mu), focus on the frailty of humans in their quest for the divine. The figure of the "banished Transcendent" (*zhexian* 謫仙), represented in this tale by *Dongfang Shuo (ca. 160–ca. 93 BCE), became highly popular in the tale literature of Tang and later times, leading to such novels as the *Journey to the West* (*Xiyou ji* 西遊記; IC 413–18). One pronounced feature of the banished Transcendent is that he or she is at first unrecognized. This becomes a common *topos* in the "evidentiary tales" (*yan* 驗) collected by *Du Guangting, which detail the workings of the Dao in the lives of women and commoners.

Dialogic literature. While not properly a type of narrative, dialogical treatises (*yulu), commonly associated with Chan Buddhism, appear in great numbers in the Taoist Canon as well. While extended passages of dialogue appear in many early Taoist scriptures (see especially *Ge Xuan), records of a living master's teachings come to prominence in the Song dynasty with two works, the *Baiwen pian* 百問篇 (Folios of the Hundred Questions; in *Daoshu, 5.7a–22a) and the *Zhong-Lü chuandao ji* (Anthology of Zhongli Quan's Transmission of the Dao to Lü Dongbin), both of which purport to transcribe the teachings that *Zhongli Quan bestowed on his disciple *Lü Dongbin. These works continue the tradition begun with the Confucian *Analects* and stand at the headwaters of *Quanzhen Taoism.

Stephen R. BOKENKAMP

📖 Bokenkamp 1986d; Bokenkamp 1991; Boltz J. M. 1987a; Campany 1990; Campany 1996; Campany 2002; Davis E. 2001; Kleeman 1994a; Kohn 1998b; Li Fengmao 1986; Li Fengmao 1996; Liu J. J. Y. 1987; Schafer 1985; Schipper 1965; Verellen 1992; Yūsa Noboru 1983

Taoism and Chinese theatre

The concepts and practice of ritual and theatre are so closely intertwined that it is virtually impossible to speak of one without the other. Research on the interrelationship of Taoist forms of ritual and Chinese theatre itself is a fairly new field of study. Publications on various aspects of this subject that have begun to appear in recent years are largely the results of extensive field work. Textual studies have yet to materialize in any quantity but will no doubt increase as resources become more widely available, especially if preparation of critical editions now under way continues to be pursued. Of special note is the recently published *Minjian jili yu yishi xiju* 民間祭禮与儀式戲劇 (Folk Sacrifice and Ceremony Drama) edited by Hu Tiancheng 胡天成 (1999), rich with photographic and textual documentation of theatrical performance in conjunction with Taoist funeral services.

To speak of the theatrical elements of ritual is also to speak of the ritual elements of theatre. Piet van der Loon's seminal essay on the ritual origins of theatre, published in 1977, has established the foundation for research in this area. He has himself been a moving force behind the recent surge of interest in ritual theatre, preparing critical editions of early marionette (*kuilei* 傀儡) scripts and working with an international team of scholars documenting surviving traditions of the exorcistic performative practice known as Nuoxi 儺戲. Critical editions of scripts as well as research on various forms of ritual theatre will be found in the ongoing series *Minsu quyi* 民俗曲藝 (Folk Operatic Arts).

If Taoist ritual and Chinese theatre may be said fundamentally to share a rich heritage of exorcistic practice, the common ground they occupy extends in many directions. Each in some sense serves to purge demons from the minds of their beholders. Each is staged in some sense as a cathartic experience by which the audience willingly agrees to engage in a suspension of belief. Each is dependent upon the viewer's acceptance of the new identities taken on by a cast of performers. Each in some sense provides a form of therapeutic release by inviting the audience to engage in a visionary journey into the unknown.

Theatrical aspects of Taoist ritual. All forms of Taoist ritual permit consideration as theatrical forms of expression. Those staged as public spectacles are the most obvious exemplars of theatrical ritual. The history of both **jiao* (Offering) and **zhai* (Retreat) rituals is inherently a component of the history of Chinese theatre. As such, the identities of major playwrights may be sought in formulators of the **Lingbao school of teachings. From the early codification of **Lu Xiujing* (406–77) to voluminous anthologies of ritual compiled from the Song to Ming, the Lingbao legacy remains the best documented heritage of ritual performance in the Taoist Canon. Diverse forms of *jiao* and *zhai* appear to have emerged partly in response to competing ritual spectacles staged by Buddhist clergy. Ritual innovations can also be traced to rival schools of Taoist teachings.

Among the best-known examples of highly theatrical forms of Taoist ritual are those associated with the rite of **pudu* (Universal Salvation) commemorating lost souls on the fifteenth of the seventh lunar month. It is on this day, known as *zhongyuan* 中元, that celebrants envision deliverance of the dead from a state of suffering in purgatory. Individual families typically arrange for such rituals when a funeral or commemorative mourning service is in order. Ritual codes vary but a common form of this service documented in Tainan 臺南 (Taiwan) features a virtual attack on a simulacrum of purgatory. What marks this as the climax of the ritual is the participation of spectators who encircle the miniature likeness of purgatory and join in smashing it to release the souls imprisoned within. Such performances traditionally fell to mediums. As witnessed in Taiwan, the scene of destruction entails a lengthy dramatic dialogue culminating in a vision of liberation that often serves as an emotional catharsis for participants. What it effectively aims to achieve is the deliverance of not only incarcerated souls but also anyone among the living perceived to be in their bondage.

A theatrically inspired ritual smashing of purgatory was apparently popular as early as the Southern Song, for it found a critic in Jin Yunzhong 金允中 (fl. 1224–25). As an advocate for restoring the decorum of early Lingbao practice, Jin argued for a discretely, silent approach rather than the public spectacle that many of his contemporaries seemed to favor. The source of Jin's irritation could perhaps have been an increasingly vernacular adaptation of classical forms of ritual. It is this contrast between classical and vernacular forms of speech that in many locales distinguishes the ritual per se from theatrical accretions. Exceptions include symbolic theatrical interludes featured in Taoist rituals of Cantonese communities, with little if any speech rendered in an archaic style known as *xitai guanhua* 戲抬官話 (stage Mandarin). Equally formulaic, highly stylized interludes by operatic troupes of Beiguan 北管 (Northern Pipes) are also characteristic components of Taoist *jiao* in northern Taiwan.

How and when classical forms of ritual gave way to drama in the vernacular remains unclear. Modern-day practice is largely characterized by the saying: *Gongde tou, zuoxi wei* 功德頭, 作戲尾 (Merit first, "play" last). Among the so-called *fashi xi* 法事戲 (liturgical drama) commonly added to the "merit," or ritual proper, are adaptations of the Mulian 目連 cycle. Older generations of Taoist clergy are known to register opposition to such operatic fare on the grounds of its obvious Buddhist origins. The very fact that it has become an integral part of Taoist ritual practice in many regions attests to its widespread audience appeal. The bawdy improvisations that vernacular "play" of this sort inevitably invites would appear to provide above all another form of release, allowing any tears that remain to be overcome by laughter.

Taoist thematic aspects of Chinese theatre. The journey to the underworld central to the Mulian cycle is also a common theme taken up in centuries of Chinese theatrical entertainment. Early examples may be found in the repertoire of Yuan *zaju* 雜劇, or the so-called variety plays. Dramatic works on this theme fall in the category of *shenxian daohua* 神仙道化 (Conversion to the Way by Divine Transcendents), according to the classification scheme established by the Ming prince and playwright *Zhu Quan (1378–1448). Contemporary Chinese scholars generally refer to such operatic fare as *dutuo xi* 度脫戲 (deliverance plays).

A comprehensive study of deliverance plays drawn from Buddhist as well as Taoist lore has yet to be undertaken. Like their anecdotal counterparts, they invite comparison with hagiographic lore on rites of initiation. The importance of reading such scripts in conjunction with pertinent resources in the Taoist Canon is demonstrated by David Hawkes in a noteworthy essay titled "Quanzhen Plays and Quanzhen Masters" (1981). The playwrights and editors of this body of operatic literature have been found to be at home with hagiographic lore as well as *Quanzhen teachings. Most cast the Quanzhen patriarch *Lü Dongbin in the role of savior. The scene of deliverance staged at the close of these plays commonly features an assembly of the *baxian, or Eight Immortals. Allusion to this popular ensemble is conspicuous by its absence in plays featuring the Quanzhen patriarch *Ma Yu (1123–84).

Plays on the theme of deliverance continued to be written and performed for centuries after the Yuan. The Ming prince Zhu Yuodun 朱有燉 (1379–1439; DMB 380–81) composed these plays for performance at birthday celebrations. Of note in *Chinese Theater 1100–1450: A Source Book* by Wilt Idema and Stephen H. West (1982) are translations of a Ming edition of the anonymous Yuan play "Han Zhongli dutuo Lan Caihe" 漢鍾離度脫藍采和 (Zhongli of the Han delivers Lan Caihe) as well as a selection from the "Yaochi hui baxian qing-shou" 瑤池會八仙慶壽 (The Eight Immortals of Turquoise Pond Assembly Celebrate Longevity). The latter evokes any number of regional balladic traditions featuring birthday greetings conveyed by the eight immortals. Both plays, moreover, include a song by Lan Caihe derived from a legacy of chantefable called *daoqing* 道情 (Ono Shihei 1964). The origins of this originally didactic ballad form are commonly traced to this very image of Lan singing and dancing while keeping the beat with clappers. It is a genre that awaits investigation in light of diverse operatic traditions by this name popular in many regions, from Shaanxi to Jiangxi.

Among additional performative practices with close ties to Taoist lore is the rich legacy of marionette theatre in communities of Fujian and Taiwan. Puppeteers are traditionally ordained *fashi, or "ritual masters." As Kristofer Schipper points out in his early study of this theatrical form (1966), the manipulation of puppets is not unlike the collaboration of Taoist master and medium. Such performances are typically introduced by ritual preludes. A recent comparative study of these preludes by Robin Ruizendaal (2000) finds them to be better preserved in smaller villages in the periphery than within the center of marionette practice in Quanzhou 泉州 (Fujian). Further studies are essential if the memory as well as practice is to be preserved of these and all other forms of ritual theatre in danger of losing ground to modernization.

Judith M. BOLTZ

📖 Brandon 1987; Ch'iu K'un-liang 1989; Chu Kun-liang 1991; Dean 1989a; Hawkes 1981; Hu Tiancheng 1999; Idema 1985, 63–93; Idema and West 1982, 300–343; Lagerwey 1987c, 202–37; Liu Zhongyu 2002; Long Bide 1993; van der Loon 1977; Ruizendaal 2000; Schipper 1966; Schipper 1989b; Schipper 1993, 44–55; Tanaka Issei 1981; Tanaka Issei 1985; Tanaka Issei 1989a; Tanaka Issei 1993; Zhan Shichuang 1997a

※ TAOIST MUSIC

Taoism and Chinese art

Does a "Taoist art" exist? We may confidently answer in the affirmative if we restrict this notion to the liturgical art of Taoism. This category includes various forms of poetry, psalmody, songs, hymns, and instrumental music, as well as murals and paintings associated with the Taoist liturgy, priests' embroidered robes, and ritual paraphernalia. Outside the ritual context, however, Taoist art is more difficult to apprehend. In the architecture and sculpture of Taoist temples, for instance, there is no specifically Taoist pattern. Like all large traditional buildings in China, Taoist, Confucian, or Buddhist temples (in fact, even mosques and synagogues) are based on the single model of palace architecture, with decorated halls following one another on a south-north axis, separated by courtyards and gardens. The importance of the halls, which are usually single-storied, is conveyed through the height of their base, the width of their façades, and the decorative richness of their roofs and balustrades. Indeed, Taoist temples are often called *gong* 宮 or "palaces." The best known of these structures, due to its long history and its splendid fourteenth-century murals, is the *Yongle gong or Palace of Eternal Joy in southern Shanxi.

There is also no identifiably Taoist or Buddhist artistic technique or style, for the same artists or craftsmen gathered in workshops, which were sometimes quite large, to build and decorate Taoist and Buddhist temples alike. Chapter 3 of the *Lidai minghua ji* 歷代名畫記 (Records of Famous Painters of Successive Generations), compiled by Zhang Yanyuan 張彥遠 (ca. 815–ca. 875) with a preface dated 847, records numerous temples he visited in the area of Chang'an (Shaanxi) and Luoyang (Henan), shortly before the massive destructions that occurred due to the state persecution of Buddhism. The mural decorations of many of these temples, either Buddhist or Taoist, were credited to Wu Daozi 吳道子 (?–792), the most famous figurative painter in China. Wu has since then been considered a patron saint for all Chinese religious painters.

In Shanxi, with its rich and well-preserved tradition of mural paintings, some workshops achieved a regional and interregional development before modern times. The same lay artists worked on various sites and projects, some as itinerants traveling from one site to the next according to the command. This system, still observed in Taiwan only a few decades ago, may explain the widespread diffusion of iconographic motifs, techniques, and styles throughout China. Thus, in a Six Dynasties votive stele, carved with a frontal triad of deities whose model is typically Buddhist, one may recognize a Taoist origin only from the iconographic forms of the figures: in particular, Laozi represented as a bearded aged man holding a fan in the form of a banana leaf (a form that would prove remarkably durable). In later Taoist sculpture and painting, representations continue to borrow from Buddhist iconographic canons, with only minor features identifying the Taoist gods. For instance, in some hanging scrolls depicting the Taoist triad of the Three Clarities (*sanqing), these deities appear to be seated sometimes on armchairs, and sometimes—in a Buddhist guise—in *dhyāna* (meditation) position on lotus flowers (one such example is kept at the Metropolitan Museum of Art in New York).

Influence on Chinese art. The influence of Taoism on Chinese art, however, has not been confined to the domain of liturgical art. Taoism pervades all Chinese art, not only with particular motifs but also through a specific vision that conceives of space and time as a cyclic continuum. This vision is supported by notions such as Yin and Yang, the Five Phases (*wuxing), and vital energy (*qi). The idea of an ever-changing world in a cyclic time was inherited from the cosmology of the *ru* 儒, the Confucian literati of Han China. Moreover, as the indigenous religion of China, Taoism has transmitted both vestiges of the ancient religion and fragments of local traditions from the former feudal kingdoms.

The art of the sacred area is one of the topics still awaiting closer investigation in the field of Taoist studies. It is in the concept of spatial organization that one can observe the most important Taoist influence. When entering the sacred space of the ritual, Taoist priests claim to "enter the mountain" (*rushan* 入山). This metaphor refers to the mountain as an essential feature of the Chinese worldview; the paradise is conceived not as a closed garden (as it happens to be in Persia and in most of the Near-Eastern traditions) but as mountains inhabited by immortals and wild animals living in untrodden nature. Both written talismans (*FU), giving the names of good or evil spirits, and magic bronze mirror allow adepts to travel safely in the wilderness, by revealing the true form of any spirit one may meet on the mountain paths (see under *jing and *jian*).

The Taoist notion of the "real form" (*zhenxing* 真形; see *xing), the hidden internal configuration of a living organism, is best illustrated in landscape painting and in the art of gardens. In China, these arts reached a level of subtlety and sophistication—in spite of their naturalness—that they never enjoyed in the Western world. As early as the fifth century, Chinese authors formalized criteria of aesthetics that highlight the qualities of spontaneity (*ziran) and emptiness (*xu* 虛 or *kong* 空; see under *wu and *you*), making the artist not an interpreter but a kind of vessel through which the energy of Nature flows onto the silk or sheet of paper, thus giving the painting internal life and dynamism. Many great painters of China are deemed to have been Taoist themselves, such as Gu Kaizhi 顧愷之 (392–467) who is also the author of a treatise on landscape painting filled with Taoist inspiration, and a millennium later, Huang Gongwang 黃公望 (1269–1354) and Fang Congyi 方從義 (1301?–1391), both Taoist priests and landscape painters.

Caroline GYSS

📖 Delahaye 1981; Jin Weinuo 1997; Kamitsuka Yoshiko 1993; Katz P. R. 1993; Legeza 1975; Little 2000a; Little 2000b; Liu Yang 2001a; Liu Yang 2001b; Pontynen 1980; Reiter 1988b; Sakade Yoshinobu 1994c; Schipper forthcoming; Seidel 1989–90, 269–73 and 280–82; Thompson 1987c; Yamada Toshiaki 1995a

Taoism and the military arts

From the very beginning of the written tradition of Taoism, there existed a close relation between it and Chinese military theory and practice. The *Daode jing* contains passages that propounded ideas about the nature of warfare (that weapons are inauspicious implements; desolation follows an army) and the proper way for the ruler to engage in combat (conquer strength by manifesting weakness; do not value victory; do not attempt to dominate the world by force of arms) that were immensely influential in later times. Over the centuries some scholars even interpreted the text as being in essence a military manual. While it is not possible at present to determine whether that text or the canonical *Sunzi bingfa* 孫子兵法 (Master Sun's Art of War) is earlier in date, clear parallels exist between their respective philosophical approaches (Ames 1993; Lau and Ames 1996). Generals were encouraged not to act out of anger; to practice self-cultivation to strengthen their *qi and harmonize it with the cosmos; to unify the army with their own person; to make minute preparations and assessments of their own and the enemy's strengths and weaknesses before embarking on a campaign; to attack only when victory was certain, for the highest type of victory was to win without ever having to actually engage in combat; to be formless (*wuxing* 無形) while forcing the enemy to show his form (*youxing* 有形); to manipulate emptiness (*xu* 虛) and fullness (*shi* 實), the regular (*zheng* 正) and the irregular (*qi* 奇) forces; and to adapt to the ever-changing conditions on the battlefield by seizing the positional advantage (*shi* 勢). Many later Taoist philosophical treatises, such as the *Heguan zi* 鶡冠子 (Book of Master Heguan), the *Huang-Lao texts from *Mawangdui, the *Wenzi, the *Huainan zi, and the *Guigu zi, contain observations on the conduct of warfare, elaborating in different ways on the ideas of the *Daode jing*, and insisting on the importance of harmonizing one's conduct with the Dao to ensure victory.

Talismans, elixirs, and the military arts. Connections between Taoism and the
military were present not just in philosophical and military texts and discourses.
The written tallies used in the military of Warring States, Qin and Han times
to impart authority to military officers and to control access to militarily sensi-
tive areas were adopted and transformed by Taoists into talismans (*FU) that
were powerful apotropaic and exorcistic devices and symbols of a master's
power to command supernatural generals who were capable of controlling
the myriad dangerous spirits that inhabited the cosmos. Joseph Needham has
also shown that Taoist alchemists in the late Tang and Five Dynasties period
were prominent in the discovery of the deflagratory properties of the mixture
of ingredients called gunpowder (*huoyao* 火藥), the chemical compound that
completely revolutionized warfare throughout the world, the first formula of
which is found in the eleventh-century official military encyclopedia *Wujing
zongyao* 武經總要 (Complete Essentials of the Military Canons; Needham
1986, 117–25). In the late Ming, on the other hand, the famous and influential
general Qi Jiguang 戚繼光 incorporated the techniques of *wushu* 武術 (martial arts) for the training of his new army in unarmed combat as well as in
wielding swords, pikes, and wooden staffs.

Divination and the military arts. Another very important connection between
Taoist and military practices was in the realm of divination, of interpreting,
manipulating, and controlling temporal cycles in order to ensure that action
was in accordance with cosmic time. Taoist masters and military men drew
upon the same set of esoteric techniques to ensure success in their activities.
For the Taoists, rituals had to be correctly harmonized with the cosmos as
well internally appropriately timed for them to be efficacious. Military activity
was the subject of inquiry by divination as early as the late Shang dynasty (late
second millennium BCE) and was an important site of ritual performance in the
succeeding Zhou period. Military ritual maintained its importance throughout
the imperial period, being considered as one of the five types of rituals (*wuli*
五禮) essential for the survival of the state. Although some military texts,
such as the late Warring States *Weiliao zi* 尉繚子 (or *Yuliao zi*, one of the seven
military canons established in the Song dynasty as required reading for the
military examinations), objected to the divinatory arts, military prognostication (*bingzhan* 兵占) came to be one of the main genres of military writing
from the Han times onward under the influence of Yin-Yang speculation, appearing in all military encyclopedias starting with the Tang Taoist *Li Quan's
Shenji zhidi Taibai yinjing 神機制敵太白陰經 (The Yin Canon of Venus, the
Spiritual Pivot for Conquering the Enemy; mid-eighth century; Rand 1979),
and an essential tool employed by later generals to achieve victory. The same
techniques were deployed by both Taoists and military experts, such as the
method of the Hidden Stem (*dunjia* 遁甲), the Irregular Gates (*qimen* 奇門),

the *liuren* 六壬 method, and the *Taiyi (Great One) method (Schipper and Wang 1986, 198–201; Kalinowski 1991). Indeed, the great god Taiyi, who first appears in the recently discovered fourth-century BCE *Guodian hoard from the state of Chu in the cosmological text *Taiyi sheng shui* 太一生水 (The Great One Generated Water) associated with fragments later incorporated into the *Daode jing*, came to be worshipped as the God of War in medieval times (Li Ling 1995–96), and other powerful deities in the celestial hierarchy, such as the Thunder Sire (Leigong 雷公) and the Master of Rain (*Yushi), were appealed to and worshipped both by Taoists and military men throughout the imperial period.

Robin D. S. YATES

📖 Jiang Guozhu 1998; Rand 1979; Rand 1979–80

※ Li Quan

TAOISM OUTSIDE CHINA

Taoism and the Yao people

Groups classed as Yao (most commonly written 猺, 瑤, or 傜) make prominent use of Taoist texts, liturgical paintings, and ritual forms, many of which only emerged in China from Song times. The Yao ethnonym includes various ethnolinguistic groups who have interacted with Chinese (and other Southeast Asian) societies and states in the last millennium. The main Yao group speaks a (Sino-Tibetan) language known as Mien or its Mun, Byau Min and Yau Min variants, and share many customs and ways of living with groups speaking forms of Hmong, T'ai/Kadai, and some southeastern Chinese dialects.

Yao "Taoism" took shape amid the interactions of Chinese customs and traditions with Mien village-based and oral practices focused on the worship of ancestors, stemming from their ultimate ancestor Pien Hung 盤王, and various nature deities, gods of the living, and spirits of the dead. Consisting of clusters of ritually-integrated clans, Yao society has never developed enduring political forms beyond the village level. Taoist rites and beliefs, along with Chinese religious language and divine bureaucratic protocols, provided Yao (and other) groups a grander socioreligious structure than their native social and religious forms had. Yao communities crafted a communal form of Taoism to forge an identity across generations and among communities (linking their origins in Pien Hung to exalted spiritual bureaucracies), and to establish a practical ritual means (initiation into transcendent ranks associated with ritualized Yao ancestors) of consolidating and enhancing this loose, but larger, cultural identity.

Taoist religious rites, writings, and symbols added a new dimension to Yao society in addition to other Chinese cultural forms (calendars, funerary rites, naming practices) and native methods of controlling spirits. Spirit mediums and exorcists handled minor problems by appealing to lesser spirits and ancestors for such difficulties as disease, childbirth, accidents, and rain. Funerals aim to return deceased relatives to their spiritual homeland, the Plum Mountain Grottoes (Meishan dong 梅山洞), which many Yao texts also claim as the source of their traditions; this purgatorial voyage culminates in eventual salvation and assembly with other ancestors. Weddings unite both the couple and their "soldiers of the netherworld" (*yin beng* 陰兵, *mien beng* 神兵, *peng ma* 兵馬) into a new household.

Taoism supplemented traditional Mien society by providing it with a supralo-cal sacred organization to better highlight the myths, ancestors, rites, places, and gods that were central to Yao identity. Initiation ceremonies—mostly for young men and strongly reminiscent of both early and popular forms of Taoism—integrated new participants into Yao social networks and spiritual hierarchies. Yao "ancestors" (*tzu tsung* 祖宗) were an adept's ritual forebears who were but part of the fuller array of celestial Branch Offices (*heng fei* 行司) also filled with grand Taoist deities who oversaw the workings of Yao society and the world.

The initial "hanging of the lamp" (*kwa tang* 掛燈) ceremony granted males not just a ritual name (*fa bua* 法名) and control over a squad of "spirit-soldiers," but an authoritative seal (*yen* 印) and an authenticating certificate (*tieh* 牒), permitting them to perform ritual exorcisms by ordering their spirit soldiers about, and to ascend into heaven as transcendents after death. Additional social and spiritual status accrued not just through marriage, producing children, and caring for ancestors, but also through ritually gaining control over new "spirit soldiers" and performing merit-making rituals. These ritual activities culminated in one's rise to the Saving Master (*dou sai* 度師) level, or the less common Supplemental Assignment (*chia tse* 加職) and Honors Section (*pwang ko* 封科) ranks. Today the expense and difficulty of rising beyond the rank of Saving Master means these ranks have become increasingly rare. The most elaborate, lengthy, and important multihousehold thanksgiving ceremony, known as the *zo dan* 歌堂, honors the Lords of the Altars (*miu hung* 廟王) all the way back to their great ancestor Pien Hung, usually as a way of releasing stress after difficulties or a disaster. Lasting up to five days and nights, and involving many priests using their full ritual powers, it honors Pien Hung, and recounts his help to the Yao since their voyage over the sea.

Yao priests use colorful sets of Chinese-style paintings depicting Taoist gods and ritualized Yao ancestors in their larger ceremonies. The core set consists of the general assembly of Yao ancestors, transcendents and Taoist gods (called *tzu tsung* 祖宗 in small or *heng fei* 行司 in full), flanked right and left by the guardian Grand Defender (*tai wai* 太尉), and the ritual initiator, Sea Banner (*hoi fan* 海旛). Full sets can consist of some two dozen paintings. During important ceremonies each officiant will display certain paintings during the appropriate rites.

The sources and significance of Taoism in Yao ritual traditions require further study. Many ritual texts and practices include key features of the new Song ritual traditions, including the *Tianxin zhengfa (Correct Method of the Celestial Heart) and the Thunder Rites (*leifa*), but other aspects rely on popular forms of religion linked to Meishan 梅山, Mount Lü (Lüshan 閭山, Jiangxi), and Yangzhou 揚州, some of which were apparently known to *Bai

Yuchan (1194–1229?) in Fujian and are still popular there today. Guangdong dialects are often used in Yao Taoist ritual chanting.

Lowell SKAR

📖 ter Haar 1998a; Kandre 1976; Kleeman 2002, 32–33; Lemoine 1982; Lemoine 1983; Lemoine and Chiao 1991; Maruyama Hiroshi 1986b; Maspero 1981, 197–247; Pourret 2002; Shiratori Yoshirō 1975; Strickmann 1982

Taoism in the Korean peninsula

Among the areas within the so-called Chinese cultural sphere (defined by the use of writing systems based on Chinese), the Korean peninsula shows more evidence than any other area besides China for the transmission and acceptance of Taoism. To substantiate the presence of Taoism, four conditions should be fulfilled: the introduction of doctrines (specifically, scriptures), the building of edifices (temples), the existence of religious specialists (priests), and the establishment of an organization of believers (a religious association). In Japan's case, while the first can be found, there is as yet, as far as modern scholarship can confirm, no conclusive evidence for the presence of the other three. Though there is no doubt that Taoism was transmitted in some form to Japan, it disappeared as an autonomous entity when it was absorbed into an independent system called Onmyōdō 陰陽道 (Way of Yin and Yang), based on the Chinese theories of Yin and Yang and the Five Agents (*wuxing*). (See *TAOISM IN JAPAN.)

Evidence for "Korean Taoism." Korea's case is different. According to both histories of the Tang dynasty (*Jiu Tangshu* and *Xin Tangshu*) and the Korean *Samguk sagi* 三國史記 (Historical Records of the Three Kingdoms; 1146), Tang Gaozu (r. 618–26) sent Taoist priests and a statue of a Celestial Worthy (*tianzun* 天尊) to the kingdom of Koguryŏ in 624, and had the priests read the *Daode jing* before the Korean king and his court. The first Taoist temple in Korea was built at the beginning of the twelfth century, under the Koryŏ dynasty (918–1392). Named Bokwŏn kung 福源宮 (Palace of the Source of Happiness), it housed statues of the Three Clarities (*sanqing) and was served by more than ten white-robed Korean Taoist priests. The temple met opposition from Confucians in the next reign and was closed down together with other Taoist facilities. The Sogyŏk chŏn 昭格殿 (Pavilion of Brilliant Investigation) continued its functions for a time, but was eventually reduced in scale and renamed Sogyŏk sŏ 昭格署 (Bureau of Brilliant Investigation) before being forced to close completely. Nevertheless, at one point in history, the first three of the above four conditions were met on the Korean peninsula. There is no evidence, on the other hand, that any Taoist organization, such as the *Tianshi dao or *Quanzhen, was ever established there. However, since it cannot be denied that Taoism, in the process of its acceptance in Korea, combined with folk cults and religious movements that possessed organizations, it may be said that indirectly a religious association also existed.

Korean inner alchemy. Prominent among early Taoist (and early Buddhist) rituals were those performed to protect the state on behalf of the court and the royal family. When these state rituals declined with the rise of Neo-Confucianism under the Yi dynasty (1392–1910), the intelligentsia shifted its interests to practices based on Nourishing Life (*yangsheng) and *neidan. Out of these grew a Korean *neidan* school, the Haedong sŏnp'a 海東仙派 (Lineage of Immortality in Korea), around the fifteenth or sixteenth century. Chŏng Ryŏm 鄭磏 (1506–49) is well known as the author of the *Pukch'ang pigyŏl* 北窗祕訣 (Secret Instructions from the Northern Studio), a manual of *neidan* techniques. His younger brother Chŏng Sŏk 鄭碏 participated in the compilation of the *Tong'ŭi pogam* 東醫寶鑑 (Precious Mirror of Eastern Medicine), a comprehensive medical text strongly influenced by *neidan* ideas. According to the *Haedong chŏndo rok* 海東傳道錄 (Account of the Transmission of the Way in Korea), the main representatives of the Haedong sŏnp'a include Kim Kagi 金可紀 (fl. ca. 830), Kim Sisŭp 金時習 (1435–93), and Nam Kungtu 南宮斗 (1526–1620). Another important legacy of Korean *neidan* is represented by several commentaries to the **Zhouyi cantong qi*, the first of which was the *Chuyŏk ch'amt'ong kye chuhae* 周易參同契注解 (Explication of the *Zhouyi cantong qi*; 1639) by Kwŏn Kŭkjung 權克中 (1585–1659).

In present-day South Korea, a group called Kuksŏn to 國仙道 (Way of the National Immortals) follows a *neidan*-type practice centering mainly on breathing techniques. Although members deny any influence from Taoism and assert that their ideas and practices are native to Korea, this group may be seen in some ways as a modern development of the Haedong sŏnp'a.

Korean research on Taoism. After Yi Kyegyŏng's 李圭景 (1788-?) *Oju yŏnmun changsŏn sango* 五洲衍文長箋散稿 (Miscellaneous Essays from the Five Islands), two major studies on Taoism in Korea are Yi Nŭnghwa's *Chosŏn togyosa* (A History of Korean Taoism; 1959) and Ch'a Chuhwan's *Han'guk ŭi togyo sasang* (Taoist Thought in Korea; 1984). The Korean Association for the Study of Taoist Thought (Han'guk togyo sasangsa yŏn'guhoe 韓國道教思想研究會) was formed in 1986. It changed its name to Korean Association of Taoist Culture (Han'guk togyo munhwa hakhoe 韓國道教文化學會) in 1997 and expanded its organization. Research activities are being developed with Korean Taoism as the main area of study, and Chinese Taoism as a secondary theme. By the year 2000, the Association had published more than ten research reports.

MIURA Kunio

📖 Ch'a Chuhwan 1984; Fukunaga Mitsuji 1989; Jung Jae-seo 2000; Qing Xitai 1988–95, 4: 567–78; Seidel 1989–90, 297–99; Ueda Masaaki 1989; To Kwangsun 1983; Yi Nŭnghwa 1959

Taoism in Japan

Opinion is divided among Japanese scholars as to whether Taoism was ever formally transmitted to Japan. Fukunaga Mitsuji asserts that transmission indeed occurred and that Taoism has exerted a remarkable influence in Japan (see, e.g., Fukunaga Mitsuji 1982 and Fukunaga Mitsuji 1986). While this view is accepted by some scholars working in the field of ancient Japanese history, few scholars of Taoism would concur. There were no Taoist priests in ancient Japan, and therefore no temples. Moreover, unlike Korea (see *TAOISM IN THE KOREAN PENINSULA), no Taoist *jiao (Offering) or *zhai (Retreat) rituals were ever held in Japan. It is, therefore, safe to say that Taoism did not reach Japan as an organized religion in any official way.

On the other hand, Taoism did influence Japanese culture. This happened in various ways: (1) as ideas about the immortals; (2) in association with Tang Esoteric Buddhism (*mijiao* 密教, Jap. *mikkyō*); (3) in association with the Sui and Tang legal codes that provided a model for the Japanese *ritsuryō* 律令 and were incorporated into court ritual; (4) in association with the import of Sui and Tang medicine; and (5) intermingled with folk customs brought from the continent, particularly the southeastern regions.

Tales of immortals. Ancient Japan had a great number of folk tales and legends about immortals, including *Hagoromo* 羽衣 (The Feathered Robe; trans. Waley 1922, 177–85) in praise of a female immortal; the story of Urashima Tarō 浦島太郎 who travelled to the realm of the immortals far across the sea (trans. Sieffert 1993, 19–32); and the tale of Tajima Mori 田島間守 who went searching for the *tachibana* 橘 (mandarin orange) fruit in the realm of Tokoyo 常世 (Akima Toshio 1993). Ōe no Masafusa 大江匡房 (1041–IIII) included many tales of immortals in his *Honchō shinsenden* 本朝神仙傳 (Biographies of Immortals in Japan; trans. Kleine and Kohn 1999), e.g., the story of the immortal of Kume 久米 who fell to earth when he saw the white leg of a girl. There is no way, however, to establish how such stories came to Japan.

Taoism and Esoteric Buddhism. Esoteric Buddhism was transmitted to Japan during the eighth century, as shown by sculpture, texts such as the *Darani shūkyō* 陀羅尼集經 (Sūtra of Collected Dhāraṇīs), and the performance of rites for rain based on the *Mahāmegha-sūtra* (Sūtra of the Great Cloud). The formal transmission of Esoteric Buddhism, however, was accomplished by two Japanese priests who studied in China, Saichō 最澄 (767–822) and Kūkai 空海 (774–835). Kūkai already had a good knowledge of Taoism, as can be seen in his *Sankyō shiki* 三教指歸 (Pointers to the Meaning of the Three Teachings). With the formal transmission of Tang Esoteric Buddhism to Japan, the heavily Taoist-influenced elements within it were imported as well. This phenomenon was particularly marked in the use of spells and talismans (*FU). Thus even today the talismans issued by the temples of Mount Kōya (Kōyasan 高野山), the headquarters of Shingon Buddhism, show a clear Taoist influence.

Legal codes and Taoist rituals. During the eighth century, Japan modeled its legal code on Sui and Tang law and institutions. Among the numerous court rituals introduced at that time were some Taoist rites practiced by the Chinese royal houses; and since the Tang rulers, in particular, were fervent followers of Taoism, Taoist rites naturally came to be accepted as components of Japanese court ritual (Yamanaka Yutaka 1972). On New Year's Day, for instance, the emperor ritually purified the four quarters and venerated their governing deities. During the Great Purification (*ooharae* 大祓) rites at the end of the sixth and twelfth lunar months, the Highest Emperor of the August Heaven (Huangtian shangdi 皇天上帝), the Great Lords of the Three Poles (Sanji daijun 三極大君), the Director of Destinies (*Siming), the Director of the Registers (Siji 司籍), the King Lord of the East (Dongwang gong 東王公), the Queen Mother of the West (*Xiwang mu), and the Five Emperors (Wudi 五帝) were invoked to avert calamities. These invocations, like the Chinese ones, ended with the phrase *jiji ru lüling* ("Promptly, promptly, in accordance with the statutes and ordinances!"). Even the term used by the Japanese for their sovereign, *tennō* 天皇 (lit., Celestial Sovereign, Chin. *tianhuang*), was used during the Tang dynasty as a title of the emperor (Tsuda Sōkichi 1996).

Medicine. The *Ishinpō (Methods from the Heart of Medicine), compiled by Tamba no Yasuyori 丹波康賴 in 984, is a summa of the Sui- and Tang-dynasty medical knowledge and prescriptions that had been transmitted to the Japanese court. Once again, however, we do not know how such transmission occurred. Chapters 19 and 20 of this work deal with the application and ingestion of mineral drugs, quoting from a large number of Tang sources. Mineral drugs have a close relation to alchemy, and it is known that Emperor Ninmyō (r. 810–50) was cured of an illness by taking the Elixir of the Golden Liquor (see *jinye). The *Ishinpō* also preserved quotations from lost Chinese works, concerned for instance with meditation practices and sexual techniques. Administratively,

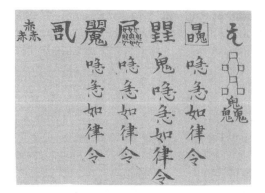

Fig. 18. Talismans for curing illness used by Japanese Shugendō practitioners. Reproduced from Sakade Yoshinobu 1994a, 375.

during the Nara and Heian periods (eighth to twelfth centuries), medicine and medical training were supervised by the Bureau of Medicine (Tenyakuryō 典藥寮), attached to the Ministry of Central Affairs (Nakatsukasashō 中務省). Among the officers in the Bureau, court physicians were ranked as *jugon hakushi* 咒禁博士 (Doctors of Spells and Enchantments) or *jugonshi* 咒禁師 (Masters of Spells and Enchantments). These terms also were modeled on the Tang system, and strongly suggest that Taoist spells were practiced and taught.

Popular practices. The best-known example of a Japanese folk custom associated with Taoism is the cult known as *kōshin* (Chin. **gengshen*). It was customary for people to stay awake and to avoid eating meat during the night on days designated by the cyclical characters *gengshen*. This tradition had taken root by the beginning of the ninth century, and its practice among court ladies is referred to in the *Genji monogatari* 源氏物語 (Tale of Genji; trans. Waley 1926–33). The text most closely associated with the *kōshin* cult in Japan is the *Rōshi shū kōshin kyū chōsei kyō* 老子守庚申求長生經 (Scripture of Laozi on Guarding the *kōshin* Day and Searching for Longevity; Kubo Noritada 1997), but whether this work was compiled in China or by a Buddhist priest in Japan is uncertain. Later various related texts appeared that were instrumental in spreading the cult, which has continued to the present day. Another Japanese customary practice possibly influenced by Taoism is the midsummer *chūgen* 中元 (Chin. *zhongyuan*) celebration that was adopted in the form of the Buddhist *urabon-e* 盂蘭盆會 (Chin. *yulanpen hui*). This is clearly one of the Taoist **sanyuan* (Three Primes) festivals: the *zhongyuan* day (the fifteenth of the seventh lunar month) was the day when the deities of the earth were venerated. Even today the custom of exchanging gifts on this day continues. Furthermore, the belief in talismans to protect the home had its origins in the veneration of the guardian deity of the north, Xuanwu 玄武 (Dark Warrior; see **Zhenwu*), and this custom also continues today in combination with the

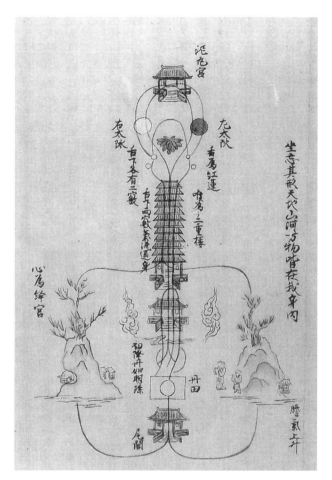

Fig. 19. *Shūshin kyūten tandō zu* 修真九轉丹道圖 (Chart of the Way of the Elixir in Nine Cycles for the Cultivation of Perfection). From top to bottom along the vertical axis: upper Cinnabar Field (Muddy Pellet, *niwan*); eyes; tongue (Red Lotus, *honglian* 紅蓮); trachea (Twelve-storied Pavilion, *shi'er chong lou* 十二重樓); middle Cinnabar Field (Crimson Palace, *jianggong* 絳宮); lower Cinnar Field (*dantian*); Caudal Funnel (*weilü* 尾閭; see *sanguan*). Manuscript in the Yoshida Collection, Tenri Central Library, Tenri University, Japan. Reproduced from Katō Chie 2002, 121.

cult of Myōken 妙見. Taoist elements can also be found within the doctrine and ritual of Ise Shintō 伊勢神道 and Yoshida Shintō 吉田神道.

Taoist influence, therefore, is demonstrably strong within Japanese culture. It should be understood, however, that Taoism did not exert any fundamental influence on the formation of Japanese culture, and that the Japanese people never did consciously accept Taoism as part of their religious beliefs or customs.

SAKADE Yoshinobu

📖 Barrett 1994a; Barrett 2000; Bock 1985; Fukunaga Mitsuji 1982; Fukunaga Mitsuji 1986; Kohn 1995b; Masuo Shin'ichirō 1988; Masuo Shin'ichirō 2000; Nakamura Shōhachi 1983; Noguchi Tetsurō et al. 1996–97; Sakade Yoshinobu 1989a; Seidel 1981; Seidel 1989–90, 299–304; Shimode Sekiyo 1972; Shimode Sekiyo 1975; Shimode Sekiyo 1997; Shinkawa Tokio 1997

Entries

(in alphabetical order)

Anqi Sheng

安期生

Anqi Sheng is a legendary immortal, reputed to have been a thousand years old during the reign of Qin Shi huangdi (r. 221–210 BCE). According to the *Liexian zhuan* (Biographies of Exemplary Immortals; trans. Kaltenmark 1953, 115–18), he was from Langya 琅琊 (Shandong). He sold medicines by the coast, and was known as the Thousand Year-Old Gentleman (Qiansui weng 千歲翁). The same source relates that when Qin Shi huangdi was travelling east, he spoke with Anqi for three days and nights. The emperor gave him a large quantity of jade and gold. Anqi returned the treasure, along with a pair of red jade slippers and a message inviting the emperor to seek him several years later on the island of *Penglai in the eastern sea. The emperor later sent an expedition in search of Anqi, but it was unable to reach Penglai. The *Shiji* (Records of the Historian; trans. Watson 1961, 2: 39) records the Han dynasty alchemist *Li Shaojun's claim to have visited Anqi Sheng during his travels on the eastern sea, where he had seen the legendary immortal eat jujubes as big as melons. Han Wudi (r. 141–87 BCE), like Qin Shi huangdi before him, sent explorers on an unsuccessful mission to find Anqi on Penglai. Anqi Sheng learned his arts, according to the *Gaoshi zhuan* 高士傳 (Biographies of Eminent Gentlemen, compiled by Huangfu Mi 皇甫謐, 215–82), from Heshang zhangren 河上丈人 (Great Man of the River Bank), an ancient master sometimes identified with the author of the *Daode jing* commentary known as *Laozi Heshang gong zhangju*.

Anqi Sheng occupies an important place in the *Taiqing and *Shangqing traditions. He is held to be one of the earliest Taiqing masters, and is said to have transmitted the Method of the Furnace Fire for the Divine Elixir (*shendan luhuo zhi fang* 神丹爐火之方) to Li Shaojun, and to have provided *Maming sheng with the Method of the Elixir of the Golden Liquor (*jinye danfa* 金液丹法). His name appears in Shangqing scriptures as one of the Perfected of the Four Poles (Siji zhenren 四極真人), and he is identified as the Perfected of the Northern Pole (Beiji zhenren 北極真人) in *Tao Hongjing's *Zhenling weiye tu* (Chart of the Ranks and Functions of the Perfected Numinous Beings).

In literary works, Anqi Sheng's name continued to be linked with the island of Penglai, as for example in Mu Hua's 木華 (fl. 290) *Haifu* 海賦 (Rhapsody on the Sea; trans. Knechtges 1982–96, 2: 305–20). Several geographical locations in China are also associated with this famous immortal, including the site near Guangzhou (Canton) where he is said to have lived, and a mica-rich mountain in Shandong that was named after him.

Theodore A. COOK

📖 Campany 2002, 225–27; Giles L. 1948, 34; Kaltenmark 1953, 115–18; Kohn 1993b, 353; Qing Xitai 1994, 3: 72–73; Robinet 1984, 11–19 passim

※ HAGIOGRAPHY

bagua

八卦

eight trigrams

B

The eight trigrams of the *Yijing* are different combinations of three lines (*yao* 爻). The lines have two forms: unbroken (—) representing Yang, and broken (– –) representing Yin. When the trigrams are joined in pairs, one above the other, they form the sixty-four hexagrams.

Tradition attributes the origin of the trigrams to Fu Xi 伏羲 or other mythical figures. Used in divination, the trigrams originally served as images of elements in nature and human society, as described in the *Zuozhuan* 左傳 (Commentary of Zuo), the *Guoyu* 國語 (Discourses of the States), and especially the *Shuogua* 說卦 (Explanation of the Trigrams) appendix to the *Yijing*. Moreover, since ancient times the trigrams had been invested with significance as markers of the combinations and permutations of the forces that generate the world and all beings in it. While the trigrams together symbolize the whole of the cosmos, as stated in the *Xici* 繫辭 (Appended Statements) appendix to the *Yijing*, each represents one of eight categories of beings and objects (for some examples, see table 2).

Arrangements. The graphic arrangements of the eight trigrams express therefore a specific cosmological system and social order. The *Yijing* and its early commentaries describe various arrangements. Among them, two are especially important in Taoism, one representing the precelestial state and the other representing the postcelestial state (*xiantian and houtian; see fig. 20).

Table 2

乾	兌	離	震	巽	坎	艮	坤
qian	*dui*	*li*	*zhen*	*sun*	*kan*	*gen*	*kun*
heaven	lake	fire	thunder	wind	water	mountain	earth
father	youngest daughter	second daughter	eldest son	eldest daughter	second son	youngest son	mother
south	southeast	east	northeast	southwest	west	northwest	north
northwest	west	south	east	southeast	north	northeast	southwest

The eight trigrams and their main associations: elements in nature, family relations, and directions in the cosmological configurations "prior to Heaven" and "posterior to Heaven" (*xiantian and houtian).

201

Fig. 20. Arrangement of the eight trigrams in the cosmological configurations
"prior to Heaven" and "posterior to Heaven" (*xiantian and houtian).

The precelestial arrangement, associated with Fu Xi, is only alluded to in
the *Yijing* but was developed by later scholars and finally formulated by *Shao
Yong (1012–77). This arrangement is characterized by a spatially balanced disposition with four opposed antagonistic pairs. *Qian* 乾 ☰ (Heaven, Yang) and
kun 坤 ☷ (Earth, Yin) form the vertical south-north axis, *li* 離 ☲ (Fire, Yang)
and *kan* 坎 ☵ (Water, Yin) set the horizontal east-west axis. This arrangement
represents the primordial structure of the universe, the eternal and original
nature of the world, and the state before things begin to turn and time starts
to unfold.

The postcelestial arrangement, traditionally associated with King Wen of
the Zhou (Wenwang 文王, r. 1099–1050 BCE), originated from statements in
the *Shuogua* and was adopted as early as Han times. *Zhen* 震 ☳, having a Yang
line under two Yin lines and standing for Thunder and spring, is located in
the east; *li* 離 ☲, having a Yin line between two Yang lines and standing for
Fire and summer, is to the south; *dui* 兌 ☱, having two Yang lines under a Yin
line and standing for Lake and autumn, is to the west; and *kan* 坎 ☵, having a
Yang line between two Yin lines and standing for Water and winter, is to the
north. This arrangement represents the phenomenal world, the state after
change has begun, and the universe in operation.

Uses in Taoism. The trigrams and their arrangements are used in Taoism to
indicate natural forces and cosmological values on the spatiotemporal plane,
and to establish or restore cosmological order. The *Shuogua* had already related
the trigrams to eight parts of the human body. In early Taoist texts such as
the *Lingbao wufu xu (Prologemena to the Five Talismans of the Numinous
Treasure), they are related to the inner spirits (the *bagua shen* 八卦神, or "gods

of the eight trigrams") who protect the adept, or to the temporal divisions on which the adept meditates.

In alchemy, the trigrams symbolize ingredients and elixirs (Pregadio 2000, 182–85). Native cinnabar and native lead respectively correspond to *li* ☲ and *kan* ☵, which represent Yang and Yin in their postcelestial state. They contain Real Mercury and Real Lead which respectively correspond to authentic Yang (the inner Yin line of *li*) and authentic Yin (the inner Yang line of *kan*). When the alchemical process is described through these emblems, it consists in drawing the inner Yin line out of *li* and the inner Yang line of *kan*, exchanging them to restore *qian* ☰ and *kun* ☷, and then joining *qian* and *kun* to recreate the single unbroken line (—) that represents the Primordial One. The final product of the alchemical work is said to represent Pure Yang, the stage before the division of the Primordial One into the two. The trigrams can also be inscribed on alchemical instruments such as the tripod and the furnace (*dinglu).

In ritual, to represent an idealized (or sacred) space to be visited by deities, and to reestablish the order of nature, officiants place the trigrams in their postcelestial arrangement around the altar. By stepping on the trigrams, the priest activates their principles and summons their spirits, following the example of the mythical emperor Yu 禹 (see *bugang). The trigrams are also one of the motifs embroidered on Taoist sacerdotal robes.

KIM Daeyeol

📖 Cammann 1990; Lagerwey 1987c, 10–17; Li Daoping 1994, 541–737; Nielsen 1990; Robinet 1989a; Suzuki Yoshijirō 1974, 134–41, 246–58

※ *Yijing*; COSMOLOGY

Bai Yuchan

白玉蟾

1194–1229?; original name: Ge Changgeng 葛長庚; *hao*: Haiqiong zi 海瓊子 (Master of Haiqiong), Hainan weng 海南翁 (Gentleman of Hainan), Qiongshan daoren 瓊山道人 (The Taoist of Mount Qiong), Bin'an 蠙庵 (Hermitage of the Oyster), Wuyi sanren 武夷散人 (Vagabond of Mount Wuyi), Shenxiao sanli 神霄散吏 (Vagrant Official of the Divine Empyrean)

This key figure in Southern Song Taoism and *neidan was, by most contemporary accounts, the son of the important Ge 葛 clan from Fuzhou (Fujian). Hagiographies relate his Qiongzhou 瓊州 (Hainan) birth to the fact that his grandfather had been posted there as the prefectural superintendent of schools for classical learning. These sources report that, after his father died young, his mother remarried into a Bai 白 family from Leizhou 雷州 (Guangdong), which her son thereafter took as his surname, with Yuchan ("Jade Toad") as his given name. Bai's lack of concern for poetic decorum allegedly led him to abandon his early classical education in favor of spiritual matters, and he had become a disciple of the adept *Chen Nan by 1205. Before Chen passed away in 1213, Bai is said to have received from him both the *neidan* teachings passed down from *Zhang Boduan and the teachings of Celestial Lord Xin (Xin tianjun 辛天君) on the Thunder Rites (*leifa*). This knowledge became the foundation of what Bai taught his disciples and followers.

From 1213 to 1215, Bai apparently lived as an itinerant religious practitioner, traveling up the east coast of China from Leizhou to Zhangzhou 漳州, Quanzhou 泉州, and Fuzhou (all now in Fujian province), distributing texts and performing rituals for various interested elite, before turning inland. He settled in the Wuyi mountains (*Wuyi shan, Fujian) in late 1215, aided by the patronage of the local literatus Zhan Yanfu 詹琰夫 and the retired Zhejiang scholar Su Sen 蘇森. He gained his reputation among the local literati partly, by impressing them with his remarkable calligraphy and painting.

Over the next seven years Bai was very active, teaching alchemy, performing and teaching rituals, and writing literary texts. During this period he frequented religious centers in Fujian, Jiangxi, and Zhejiang, but very little is known of him or his activities after 1222. He evidently took on the role of a self-declared *Shenxiao (Divine Empyrean) ritual practitioner who stressed the Thunder Rites, or a recipient and interpreter of the texts and traditions of *neidan*. He is also credited with a coherent set of hagiographies and essays on the *Jingming dao (Pure and Bright Way) traditions tied to *Xu Xun, the main *Zhengyi (Orthodox Unity) temple on Mount Longhu (*Longhu shan, Jiangxi), and the main Taoist temple in the Wuyi mountains. A few texts bearing Bai's name date to 1227 and 1229, suggesting that he may have been active until about that time, but like many of the texts ascribed to him, the circumstances of his passing are more a matter of commemorative cultic practices than hard historical facts. By the time his two main disciples, *Peng Si (fl. 1217–51) and Liu Yuanchang 留元長 (fl. 1217–37), assembled their master's teachings for publication in 1237, Bai's mortal existence had certainly ended, though he remained a source of revealed wisdom for his devotees for centuries to come.

Besides initiating a score or so disciples between 1215 and 1222, Bai also separately taught other groups of adepts eager to learn about the contemplative alchemy of Zhang Boduan, and the Thunder Rites tied to the Shenxiao legacy of *Wang Wenqing. He seems to have helped to establish the Thunder Ministry (Leibu 雷部) and its role among the other new celestial bureaucracies invoked by Taoist ritual practitioners from the Song period onward. One of Bai's most important contributions was the promotion of the *Yushu jing (Scripture of the Jade Pivot) and its revealing deity, the Celestial Worthy of Universal Transformation (*Puhua tianzun), both associated with Bai and both evolved forms of Shenxiao teachings.

Works. Among the main extant texts that bear witness to Bai's teachings are those found in the Ming Taoist Canon, including the *Haiqiong Bai zhenren yulu* 海瓊白真人語錄 (Recorded Sayings of the Perfected Bai of Haiqiong; CT 1307; Qing Xitai 1994, 2: 219–21), the *Haiqiong wendao ji* 海瓊問道集 (Anthology of Haiqiong's Queries on the Dao; CT 1308), the *Haiqiong chuandao ji* 海瓊傳道集 (Anthology of Haiqiong's Transmission of the Dao; CT 1309), and the *Jingyu xuanwen* 靜餘玄問 (Tranquil Remnants and Queries on the Mystery; CT 1252). Three anthologies in the *Xiuzhen shishu (Ten Books on the Cultivation of Perfection; CT 263)—i.e., the *Yulong ji* 玉隆集 (Anthology of [the Abbey of] Jade Beneficence, j. 31–36), *Shangqing ji* 上清集 (Anthology of [the Abbey of] Highest Clarity, j. 37–44), and *Wuyi ji* 武夷集 (Anthology of [the Abbey of Mount] Wuyi, j. 45–52)—are associated, respectively, with the cult centers of Xu Xun (in the Western Hills or *Xishan, Jiangxi), the Zhengyi order (Mount Longhu, Jiangxi), and the Lords Wu 武 and Yi 夷 (Wuyi mountains, Fujian). A very interesting alchemical text, the *Chongbi danjing (Scripture of the Elixir for Piercing the Jasper Heaven), is atypically rich in both history and doctrine and worth a separate study. There are also numerous shorter texts associated with Bai, such as the annotated *Yushu jing* (CT 99), whose compiler seems to have pieced together parts of Bai's ritual memorials to explain the structures and processes of this key text on the Thunder Ministry. In addition, the *Daofa huiyuan (Corpus of Taoist Ritual) contains many texts on the Thunder Rites that are attributed to Bai or his disciples.

Outside of the Ming Taoist Canon, there is also the distinctive commentary *Daode baozhang* 道德寶章 (Precious Stanzas of the Way and Its Virtue), which is included in the anthology of his teachings compiled by Peng Si and Liu Yuanchang and printed in 1237, with a preface by the official Pan Fang 盤枋 dated 1236. Later extensions, revisions, and editions of Bai's writings include those by the Hongwu emperor Zhu Yuanzhang's 朱元璋 seventeenth son, *Zhu Quan (1378–1448), dated 1442; a work by the Ming scholar Lin Yousheng 林有聲 with a preface by He Jigao 何繼高, dated 1594; one by Peng Zhu 彭耜 dated 1791; another with an 1869 preface by Xu Baoheng 許寶珩; and a recent compilation with a preface by Xiao Tianshi 蕭天石 from 1969 and published in 1976 by a committee headed by Wang Mengyun 王夢雲.

Lowell SKAR

📖 Berling 1993; Boltz J. M. 1987a, 72–73 and 176–79; Davis E. 2001, 76–78 and 129–34; Hymes 2002, 89–90, 174–75; Miyakawa Hisayuki 1978; Qing Xitai 1988–95, 3: 120–28 and 155–67; Yokote Yutaka 1996a

※ *leifa*; *neidan*; *Chongbi danjing*; *Yushu jing*; Nanzong; Shenxiao

baibiao

拜表

Presenting the Memorial

The term *baibiao* is one among several alternative terms that refer to the central act in Taoist ritual, the transmission of a document to heaven. At least since the latter part of the Tang dynasty, it has been used typically with reference to the inner transmission of the document performed by the high priest (*gaogong* 高功; alternating in this respect with the term *baizhang* 拜章, "presenting a petition"), while the most ancient term for the whole process of transmission, *shangzhang* 上章 ("sending up a petition"), has continued to be used in most cases to designate the total process. The most elaborate major ritual in the program of a classical Taoist *jiao (Offering), which includes such a transmission of a document, is referred to in many places (for instance in Shanghai and in southern Taiwan) as *jinbiao* 進表 ("presenting the Memorial"), though in some places, and in many ritual manuscripts, the term *dengtai baibiao* 登臺拜表 ("ascending a platform to present the Memorial") is used (see Saso 1975, 3323–3436). In fact, the *jinbiao* is often performed on a stage outside the closed ritual area, and it not only represents the first major ritual in which the priests step out of this closed area and into the public arena, but in a number of local traditions stands out as the climax and structural core of the whole program. In southern Taiwan it consists of an elaborate ritual play, in which the priests enact an audience with the Jade Sovereign (*Yuhuang, to whom the Memorial is transmitted), and it is accompanied by huge displays of offerings to the Jade Sovereign around the stage (including newly slaughtered whole pigs and sheep).

From the perspective of the priests, however, this ritual represents in a sense only an outer, somewhat more theatrical and thus more "popular" sequel to the transmissions of documents to the supreme Taoist gods, which have already taken place inside the closed ritual area, in the Three Audiences (*sanchao). The sequence of rites that accomplishes the transmission of the concrete paper document comprises the purification of the sacred area, the reading of the document and of a "passport" (*guan* 關) which is given to the messenger spirit called "official of the Memorial" (*biaoguan* 表官), the offering of three cups of wine to this messenger, and the circumambulation of the ritual area by the whole group of priests, one of whom holds the concrete document and takes it to the exit. In the Three Audiences (as performed in the classical tradition of southern Taiwan), this ritual theatre of transmission may be extended with an inner transmission, that is, with the meditative journey to heaven in order to deliver the document to the Most High (Taishang 太上), performed by the high priest as he crouches on the floor of the temple and remains still for some ten minutes.

Poul ANDERSEN

📖 Andersen 1989–90b, 40–47; Andersen 1990; Andersen 1995; Cedzich 1987, 82–102; Lagerwey 1987c, 149–67; Lagerwey 1991, 152–56; Lü and Lagerwey 1992, 39–44; Maruyama Hiroshi 1986a; Matsumoto Kōichi 1983, 220–22; Nickerson 1996b, 278–302; Ōfuchi Ninji 1983, 336–42; Saso 1975, 3323–3436; Schipper 1974; Zhang Enpu 1954

※ *jiao*; *sanchao*; *shu*

Baiyun guan

白雲觀

Abbey of the White Clouds (Beijing)

The Baiyun guan is the most famous Taoist abbey in present-day China. Founded as the Tianchang guan 天長觀 (Abbey of Celestial Perpetuity) in the mid-eighth century, it was one of the state-sponsored abbeys staffed by the official elite Taoist clergy. From 1125 to 1215, under the Jin dynasty, it served as the headquarters of the Taoist administration and played a major role in the imperial cults. After Beijing fell to the Mongols, the abbey, then called Taiji gong 太極宮 (Palace of the Great Ultimate), was damaged but was soon taken over by the *Quanzhen patriarch *Qiu Chuji (1148–1227) and renamed Changchun gong 長春宮 (Palace of Perpetual Spring) after his Taoist name. From that time to the advent of the Ming it was the seat of the Quanzhen patriarchy, known as *tangxia* 堂下.

After Qiu Chuji's death, his successor, *Yin Zhiping (1169–1251), built a memorial shrine over Qiu's grave just east of the Changchun gong, around which a contemplative community was founded under the name of Baiyun guan. The Changchun gong disappeared in the Ming period but the Baiyun guan lived on, supervised by Taoist officials who, in spite of their *Zhengyi

Fig. 21. Entrance arch to the Baiyun guan (Abbey of the White Clouds), Beijing
(February 1985). Photograph by Julian Pas.

observance, maintained the abbey's prestigious tradition of Quanzhen training in asceticism and meditation. In early Qing times, when the Zhengyi monopoly over Taoist administration was questioned and the Quanzhen fortunes
improved, the reformist Quanzhen monk *Wang Changyue (?–1680) gained
control of the place and turned it into the main center of his own *Longmen
lineage, which continues to supervise the whole of Quanzhen's institutional
life to this day. The Baiyun guan hosted a permanent community of monks
(no nuns were admitted before 1978, except during ordinations), numbering
around 200 under the late Qing and the Republic.

The Baiyun guan as it can be visited today is not very different in shape from
late imperial times; only some conventual buildings have been demolished.
However, the names of several halls, and the divinities they house, have changed
since its reopening. The north-south axis passes through the main gates and
the hall of the tutelary god. One then successively enters the Yuhuang dian
玉皇殿 (Pavilion of the Jade Sovereign), the Laolü tang 老律堂 (Hall of the
Discipline of the Elders), the Qiuzu dian 丘祖殿 (Pavilion of Patriarch Qiu),
and a multistoried building on the second floor of which is the Sanqing dian
三清殿 (Pavilion of the Three Clarities). An unusual feature for a Taoist abbey
is that the main hall, where the community holds its twice-daily office, is not
a Sanqing dian but the Laolü tang, which is actually devoted to the Quanzhen
patriarchs; a similar configuration is also seen in Shenyang's 沈陽 (Liaoning)

Taiqing gong 太清宫 (Palace of Great Clarity), where the main hall is devoted to Laozi. There are several halls for a host of divinities both on the sides and in the two smaller axes to the east and west of the main axis.

A delightful garden is located in the rear of the abbey, which also hosts the ordination platform (see fig. 75). During the Qing period, the Baiyun guan was the most important of some twenty Quanzhen ordination centers throughout the country. The abbey gathered novices who—after three years of preliminary tutelage in a temple or a hereditary cloister—underwent an extremely harsh, sometimes fatal, training lasting one hundred days, later reduced to fifty-three. The novices then passed examinations on Taoist classics, poetry, and precepts, and finally received ordination. Some of the later ordination registers are still extant. The last ordination was held in 1927, but the practice began anew, on a reduced scale, in 1994. During the nineteenth and early twentieth centuries, groups of about 200 candidates were ordained on average every four years.

Ordinations and religious life. Ordinations made the abbot of the Baiyun guan—who usually, although not necessarily, was also an ordination master (*lüshi* 律師)—an important public figure. Some abbots, however, were prominent in their own right, like Gao Rentong 高仁峒 (1841–1907) who lectured on meditation and longevity techniques to large audiences, especially to artists and actors. Such charismatic figures helped to maintain the institution's vitality in a deteriorating political situation. The position of abbot was not filled during the 1940s, while the prior An Shilin 安世霖 gave a bad reputation to his institution and was burned on a pyre in 1946. That was the last dramatic application of the severe rules of the abbey. The Baiyun guan was closed for many years but was rather well protected. It still houses a fine collection of documents, including Ming and Qing liturgical paintings that have been partially published. Today the abbey is the seat of the Chinese Taoist Association (*Zhongguo daojiao xiehui; see fig. 90).

The importance of the Baiyun guan for our knowledge of Taoist monastic institutions is based on the information collected by two Japanese scholars, Oyanagi Shigeta in the late 1920s and the Tendai monk Yoshioka Yoshitoyo in the early 1940s. Both lived in the abbey, cultivated friendship with the monks, and gained access to internal documents. Their monographs together give by far the most detailed information available on any Taoist abbey, including rules, list of residents, ritual activities, and training.

Besides its institutional aspect, the Baiyun guan has always been a focus of religious life in Beijing. It was visited especially from the first to the nineteenth day of the first lunar month, the date of Qiu Chuji's birthday. It used to be said that on that day the immortal Qiu comes back to earth. Local as well as wandering Taoists from the whole country would gather on the abbey's grounds, make merry, and hope for an encounter. The festival has existed since the Yuan period, and from the mid-1990s the Baiyun guan has begun again to attract large crowds for the New Year festival.

Vincent GOOSSAERT

📖 Hachiya Kunio 1990, 1: 1–26 and 257–58, 2: 3–10; Ishida Kenji 1992; Ishii Masako 1983a, 147–62; Marsone 1999; Oyanagi Shigeta 1934; Qing Xitai 1994, 4: 231–32; Yoshioka Yoshitoyo 1952, 196–345; Yoshioka Yoshitoyo 1979

※ Longmen; Quanzhen; TEMPLES AND SHRINES

bajing

八景

Eight Effulgences

On the cosmological level, the term *bajing* refers to eight astral bodies: the sun, the moon, the five planets and the Northern Dipper (*beidou). These celestial *waijing* 外景 (outer effulgences) are related to the eight sectors of the world, the eight nodal days of the year (*bajie* 八節, namely, equinoxes, solstices, and the first day of each season), and the eight trigrams (*bagua). On the human level, the *neijing* 內景 (inner effulgences) are various sets of eight inner divinities who play a prominent role in *Shangqing texts, but have also been included in Taoist ritual.

According to *Lingbao sources, the Three Pneumas (*sanqi* 三氣; see *santian and *liutian*) generated twenty-four *jing* (with each pneuma issuing eight *jing*), while the nine Great Heavens generated seventy-two *jing* (with each heaven issuing eight *jing*). The seventy-two *jing* of Lingbao correspond to the seventy-two celestial deities of the *Dadong zhenjing, the main Shangqing scripture; this group increases to seventy-four with the Original Father (Yuanfu 元父) and the Mysterious Mother (Xuanmu 玄母). The seventy-two deities are arranged into three sets—higher, middle, and lower—each of which is related to a set of eight inner divinities.

The twenty-four *jing* of the body are both deities and luminescent points, and are also arranged into three sets of eight. These twenty-four *jing* are related to the twenty-four pneumas (*qi) of the year (the *jieqi* 節氣 or "energy nodes," each of which presides on fifteen days) and the twenty-four zodiacal constellations. During meditation practices, the adept merges them into a single deity who carries him to the heavens. They are further conceived as openings or gates within the body through which the divine pneumas go in and out.

The eight *jing* also play an important role in methods aimed at releasing the mortal knots in the embryo (Robinet 1993, 139–43). These knots are congenital germs of death located in the body since its conception, and are the negative counterparts of the *jing*. They appear in the eighth month of gestation when the pneuma of the Qingming 清明, the Clear and Luminous heaven, descends into the body. In contrast, the eight *jing* symbolize the totality of the innumerable corporeal deities, and have the appearance of young boys whose height, clothes, and names are specified in the texts. One method described in the *Ciyi jing* consists in having the Three Original Pure Ladies (Sansu yuanjun 三素元君) summon these spirits in three groups of eight—the first within the Purple Chamber (*zifang* 紫房) in the brain, the second within the heart, and the third within the Gate of the Vital Force (*mingmen*) in the abdomen. The upper group is related to Heaven, the lower one to Earth, and the central one to Emptiness. The Imperial Lord (Dijun 帝君) makes knots on three red threads, eight for each group. Then the *bajing* untie them and the threads flare up in a great fire that consumes the knots as well the practitioner's whole body.

Finally, the *bajing* are also carriages of light that transport the deities through the heavens. In this instance they are the luminous counterpart of the *basu* 八 素 (eight purities), which are carriages of clouds (see *Basu jing*).

Isabelle ROBINET

📖 Kaltenmark 1969a; Maspero 1981, 553–54; Robinet 1984, 1: 126–27, 129–30; Robinet 1993, 57–58; Strickmann 1979, 173–75

※ INNER DEITIES

Bao Jing

鮑靚 (*or*: 鮑靖)

?–ca. 330; *zi*: Taixuan 太玄

Bao Jing, whose place of birth is unknown, was a descendant of Bao Xuan 鮑 宣 and Bao Yong 鮑永, two senior officers of the Former and Later Han dynasties. He began his career as a minor civil servant in Nanyang 南陽 (Henan) but was promoted to the post of Governor of Nanhai 南海 (Guangdong) in 313, under the Western Jin dynasty. In 320 he left his office and retired to Jurong 句容 or Danyang 丹陽 (near Nanjing, Jiangsu). According to different records, he was buried in the Luofu Mountains (*Luofu shan, Guangdong) or at Shizigang 石子岡 (Jiangsu).

Taoist tradition makes Bao the recipient of several early doctrinal and textual legacies. He reportedly began his Taoist instruction in 318 with the immortal *Yin Changsheng, who gave him the *Taixuan Yin Sheng fu* 太玄陰生符 (Yin Sheng's Talisman of Great Mystery), a script enabling adepts to achieve *shijie* (release from the corpse). According to another tradition, *Zuo Ci gave Bao the *Wuyue zhenxing tu* (Charts of the Real Forms of the Five Peaks) and alchemical writings. Bao also met *Ge Hong, became his father-in-law and his master in alchemy, and transmitted to him a version of the *Sanhuang wen* (Script of the Three Sovereigns) that Bao had received while meditating in a cave. Finally, *Shangqing sources claim that Bao was the master of Xu Mai 許邁 (300–348), one of the recipients of the revelations of 364–70 (see *Yang Xi).

Grégoire ESPESSET

📖 Chen Feilong 1980, 64–69, 124–26; Chen Guofu 1963, 76; Ōfuchi Ninji 1991, 536–52 (= 1964, 117–35); Robinet 1984, 1: 9–19

※ Ge Hong; *Sanhuang wen*

baojuan

寶卷

"precious scrolls"

Baojuan is the traditional name for a form of vernacular religious literature associated with popular Buddhist preaching and the syncretist religious sects so often deemed heterodox by the Ming and Qing dynasties. A *baojuan* is usually a lengthy prosimetric (alternating prose and verse) narrative meant to be recited or sung in a private or public group setting. While aspects of the *baojuan* style became sufficiently fixed to identify a large corpus of such texts, there are still many variations among these texts. Buddhist themes predominate, yet there are a few distinctly Taoist *baojuan* as well as more subtle Taoist influences on a medium that generally interwove the Three Teachings.

Precious scrolls and Taoism. Rooted in the lay-oriented Buddhist texts found in *Dunhuang, especially the eighth- to tenth-century *bianwen* 變文 (transformation texts) and *jiang jingwen* 講經文 (lecturing on the *sūtra* texts), the earliest *baojuan* were probably written by Buddhist clergy in the interests of universal salvation (*pudu). The earliest extant list of *baojuan*, the *Weiwei budong Taishan shengen jieguo baojuan* 巍巍不動泰山深根結果寶卷 (Precious Scroll on the

Fruits of the Profound Foundation of Lofty Immovable Mount Tai; ca. 1509) by Luo Qing 羅清 (1443–1527), mentions a *Xiangshan juan* 香山卷 (Scroll of the Fragrant Mountain; later editions use *Xiangshan baojuan*), which tells the story of Guanyin 觀音 (Avalokiteśvara), and the *Jinkang baojuan zuozheng* 金剛寶卷作證 (Testimony to the Precious Scroll on the *Diamond Sūtra*). Luo Qing, a lay Buddhist who founded the Luojiao 羅教 or Luo Teaching (also known as Wuwei jiao 無為教 or Teaching of Non-action), adopted the *baojuan* style for his own teachings, known as the *Wubu liuce* 五部六冊 (Five Books in Six Fascicles), where he cited many earlier *baojuan*. His teachings were a vernacular presentation of a distinctly popular, syncretic Buddhist millenarianism. Taoist terms, such as *wuwei (non-action), were given Buddhist interpretations (for instance, turning inward to restore the Buddha-mind within) that helped to popularize them and to expand the ideas they invoked beyond more canonical Taoist or Buddhist referents. (For more details on Luo Qing and the *Wubu liuce*, see the entry *Kaixin fayao.)

This use of Taoist terminology is true for other sectarian *baojuan*, such as the *Fo shuo huangji jieguo baojuan* 佛說皇極結果寶卷 (Precious Scroll Spoken by the Buddha on the Results of the August Ultimate; 1430), which predated Luo's books and includes references to the noumenal world (*xiantian) and the Golden Elixir (*jindan). Presenting itself as a new and ultimate revelation, thereby subordinating all other teachings and scriptures, the *Fo shuo huangji* evoked themes found in both Taoist and Buddhist scriptural precedents. For example, the Buddha is presented as giving an oral teaching from his famous seat on top of Vulture Peak that reveals a new path (full of obscure alchemical images) to salvation (understood as immortality) in a newly revealed heaven (the Hongluo tian 紅羅天 or Red Canopy Heaven). Scholars also find Taoist themes in the *Huangji jindan jiulian zhengxin guizhen huanxiang baojuan* 皇極金丹九蓮正信歸真還鄉寶卷 (Precious Scroll on the Golden Elixir and Nine-Leaved Lotus of the August Ultimate for Correcting Belief, Restoring Perfection, and Returning to One's True Home; 1523), which may be based on the *Fo shuo huangji*, as well as the *Gu Fo Tianzhen kaozheng longhua baojuan* 古佛天真考証龍華寶卷 (Precious Scroll on the Old Buddha "Heavenly Perfection" Confirming the Dragon Flower; 1654).

While arguing that one of the oldest *baojuan*, the *Fo shuo Yangshi guixiu hongluo Huaxian ge baojuan* 佛說楊氏鬼繡紅羅化仙歌寶卷 (Precious Scroll Spoken by the Buddha on Madame Yang's Ghostly Embroidered Red Canopy and "Song of the Transformed Immortal") of the Jin-Yuan period, was written by Buddhist clergy, Ma Xisha (1986, 1994) suggests that it combined Buddhism, Taoism and Confucianism in ways that prefigured one of the main effects of the *baojuan*, namely, their role as a prime medium for diffusing fundamental Taoist ideas throughout Chinese culture. In them, Taoist mythology, notions of inner alchemy (*neidan*), and the *zhai* and *jiao* rituals joined with Chan Buddhist influence to give rise to a very influential model of self-cultivation that shaped the new forms of popular religiosity seen in the sects of the late Ming, such as the Huangtian dao 黃天道 (Way of Yellow Heaven) and Hong-yang jiao 紅陽教 (Teaching of Red Yang) sects to mention just two among many.

Styles and their classification. Various classification schemes have been used to try to understand the history of shifts in the style and content of *baojuan*. In general, they are divided into two types associated with two stages: first, early Buddhist and sectarian *baojuan* dating from the fifteenth to early eighteenth century; and later *baojuan*, dating from the mid-eighteenth century to the present, which were more secular, moralistic, literary and entertaining. The more soteriological vision of the early *baojuan* included relatively orthodox Buddhist figures like Guanyin, Mulian 目連, and Xuanzang 玄奘, as well as so-called heterodox sectarian teachings concerning the Unborn Venerable Mother (Wusheng Laomu 無生老母). Later *baojuan* narratives, however, drew more heavily on figures from popular culture, such as the Confucian paragon of incorruptible officialdom, Sir Bao (Baogong 包公, i.e., Bao Zheng 包拯, 999–1062; SB 823–32), or the heavily Taoicized Stove God (*Zaoshen), or the renowned Seven Perfected (*qizhen* 七真; see table 17) of *Quanzhen. While many early *baojuan* follow rather distinctive formulas for beginning and ending the narrative and frequently used the term *baojuan* in their titles, this is less true of later examples, which took on more features associated with morality books (*shanshu*) and spirit-writing texts (see *fuji*).

One important reason for this general shift in the style of *baojuan* was increased government repression of sectarian activity and confiscation of their scriptures, especially in the Qing dynasty. The collection of confiscated sectarian scriptures cited by Huang Yupian 黃育楩 (fl. 1830–40) in his careful refutations of their teachings (*Poxie xiangbian* 破邪詳辯; 1834, with three further studies by 1841) makes clear that the millenarian revelations and unorthodox deities of sectarian *baojuan* were prime examples of the type of teachings considered dangerous by the government, though Huang also attacks one *baojuan*'s Taoist interpretation of the self in alchemical terms. It is not surprising, given both the popularity of the genre and its official proscription, that eighteenth- and nineteenth-century publishers in southern China began printing *baojuan* with safer themes—although the private production and circulation of religious *baojuan* never really ceased. Today it is estimated that more than seven to eight hundred different editions of *baojuan* survive, of which two-thirds focus on general moral exhortation while one-third reflect more particularistic sectarian doctrines.

Catherine BELL

📖 Han Bingfang 1986; Johnson 1995a; Li Shiyu 1957; Li Shiyu 1961; Ma Xisha 1986; Ma Xisha 1994; Overmyer 1976, 176–86; Overmyer 1985; Overmyer 1999; Overmyer and Li 1992; Sakai Tadao 1960, 437–55; Sawada Mizuho 1975; Yoshioka Yoshitoyo 1952, 2–69; Zheng Zhenduo 1938, 2: 306–46

※ *shanshu*; ETHICS AND MORALS; TAOISM AND POPULAR SECTS

Baopu zi

抱朴子

Book of the Master Who Embraces Simplicity

*Ge Hong's (283–343) *Baopu zi* is divided into Inner Chapters ("Neipian" 內篇, CT 1185), mainly devoted to descriptions and comments concerning religious practices, and Outer Chapters ("Waipian" 外篇, CT 1187), dealing with the "discourses of the literati" (*rushuo* 儒說). Originally independent, since the Ming period the two parts have often been printed together. Many Western scholars, however, conventionally apply the title *Baopu zi* to the Inner Chapters only. This part of Ge Hong's work has frequently been seen in the past as the main textual source for early medieval Taoism. Studies published in the last two decades have challenged this view, showing that the text is not a Taoist scripture and revealing the intent underlying its composition: glorifying the religious and ritual legacy of Jiangnan 江南 (the region south of the lower Yangzi River), emphasizing the superiority of certain traditions over others, and enhancing their prestige among the social elite to which Ge Hong belonged.

Although the contents of the *Baopu zi* are not arranged according to a definite plan, some chapters focus on specific themes. Chapter 1, in particular, consists of a poetical description of the Dao as Mystery (*xuan), the unknowable Origin of being. Chapter 2 deals with immortals and immortality. Chapters 4, 11, and 16 are mainly devoted to alchemy (*waidan). Chapter 17 describes practices for avoiding the dangers that one may meet while living in retirement, from the bites of poisonous animals to visions of demons. Chapter 18 is devoted to meditation techniques. Chapter 19 contains a tribute to Ge Hong's master, *Zheng Yin, and a list of about two hundred texts and about sixty talismans (*FU) that were part of the religious heritage of southeastern China in the third and the fourth centuries.

The "minor arts." According to Ge Hong, three groups of texts represented the traditions of Jiangnan in his time. The first includes the *Sanhuang wen* (Script of the Three Sovereigns), the *Wuyue zhenxing tu* (Charts of the Real Forms of the Five Peaks), and associated writings; the second, the *Taiqing scriptures on the elixirs; the third, the texts dealing with the meditation practices of Guarding the One (*shouyi). At the lower end of this spectrum of traditions, Ge Hong places a broad group of practitioners whom he calls the "coarse and rustic masters of methods" (zawei daoshi 雜猥道士; Wang Ming 1985, 14.259). They are associated with the "minor arts" (xiaoshu 小術), which in Ge Hong's view include healing methods, longevity techniques, divination, and magic. Ge Hong deems these practices to be inadequate for avoiding harm caused by demons and spirits. Herbal drugs, in particular, only confer long life; although they help to heal "internal ailments" (neiji 內疾), they leave one subjected to external evil influences, including those of demonic origin (13.243).

Nourishing Life. As described by Ge Hong, the practices of Nourishing Life (*yangsheng) mainly consist in breathing, gymnastics (*daoyin), and sexual techniques (*fangzhong shu; 6.124). Ge Hong's view of these disciplines is condensed in a question: "Can the Dao really be nothing more than the pursuit of nourishing life?" (18.327). Accordingly, he qualifies these techniques as inferior or ancillary to alchemy, and as merely granting freedom from illness (15.271). The object of his criticism is the belief that one can practice them as the sole way to attain immortality. A clear example is his evaluation of the sexual techniques, whose benefits do not exceed those of the "minor arts": "Among the arts of Yin and Yang (i.e., the sexual practices), the best ones can heal the lesser illnesses, and the next ones help one avoid becoming depleted. Since their principles have inherent limits (qi li zi you ji 其理自有極), how could they confer divine immortality, prevent calamities, and bring about happiness?" (6.129) Like the ingestion of herbal drugs, therefore, the techniques of Nourishing Life afford benefits, but they are not the same as those that only the higher practices can grant.

Alchemy and meditation. In Ge Hong's view, alchemy and meditation represent the culmination of the search for transcendence. Ingesting elixirs enables an adept to obtain immortality, communicate with the gods, and expel the noxious spirits. As for meditation, Ge Hong distinguishes between two types of meditation on the One, which he calls Guarding the Authentic One (shou zhenyi 守真一, or shouyi for short) and Guarding the Mysterious One (shou xuanyi 守玄一), respectively (j. 18). Guarding the Authentic One consists in visualizing the features that the One takes within the human being as an inner deity, while Guarding the Mysterious One makes it possible to multiply one's shape into "several dozen" or even "one thousand" replicas of oneself (ubiquity), or hide it altogether (invisibility). Beyond their differences, however, the two methods afford identical benefits, which are the same as those gained by ingesting the elixirs. On the one hand, Guarding the Authentic One gives access to the divine world: "If you guard the One and preserve the Authentic (cunzhen 存

真), you will be able to communicate with the gods" (18.324). On the other hand, Guarding the Authentic One confers protection against demons and other ominous entities: "In the shrine of a demon, in a mountain forest, in a land infested by a plague, within a tomb, in a marsh inhabited by tigers and wolves, or in the dwelling of snakes, if you guard the One without distraction all evils will be expelled; but if you forget to guard the One even for a single moment, the demons will harm you" (18.325). Similarly, the purpose of guarding the Mysterious One is to obtain control of gods and demons: "You will be able to see all the numina of heaven and the spirits of earth, and to summon all the deities of the mountains and the rivers." (18.326)

The Baopu zi and the history of Taoism. The above reading of the contents of the *Baopu zi* is supported by the author's own statements, and is consistent with the main features of the religious traditions of third- and fourth-century Jiangnan. Ge Hong's wish to incorporate fragments of different bodies of doctrine and practice into his work, however, gives rise to some contradictions within the text. Part of them may be due to the presence of quotations or summaries from sources belonging to different traditions that are not acknowledged as such (to give one example, virtually the whole of chapter 17 appears to be built on quotations from earlier texts). Others may be due to Ge Hong's distaste for a systematic approach. Nonetheless, Ge Hong's testimony deserves attention as a valuable overview of the religious traditions of Jiangnan just before the Way of the Celestial Masters (*Tianshi dao) spread to that area, soon followed by the *Shangqing and *Lingbao revelations. From this point of view, the *Baopu zi* documents important links between the earlier and later history of Taoism (Bokenkamp 1983), as it also does for medicine and other, fields (Murakami Yoshimi 1981; Harper 1998, 173–83).

The information provided by Ge Hong on local practices, beliefs, and teachings is therefore useful to better appreciate earlier and later sources that originated in the same area. These sources, in turn, are often essential to fully understand individual passages of the *Baopu zi* and the religious perspectives of its author.

Fabrizio PREGADIO

📖 Bokenkamp 1983; Campany 2002, 1–97; Che 1999 (part. trans.); Chen Feilong 1980; Davis and Ch'en 1941 (part. trans.); Feifel 1941–46 (part. trans.); Hu Fuchen 1989; Kaguraoka Masatoshi 1988; Kim Daeyeol 2000; Lai Chi-tim 1998a; Needham 1976, 75–113; Ōfuchi Ninji 1991, 485–627 (= 1964, 65–214); Pregadio 1987 (part. trans.); Pregadio 2006b, chapter 7; Robinet 1997b, 78–113; Sailey 1978; Wang Ming 1985 (crit. ed.); Ware 1966 (trans.)

※ Ge Hong

Baosheng dadi

保生大帝

Great Emperor Who Protects Life

Baosheng dadi is the title of a regional deity of southern Fujian province. His hagiography identifies him as a physician by the name of Wu Tao 吳夲 (979–1036), a native of the village of Baijiao 白礁 near the port city of Amoy (Xiamen 夏門). Having gained fame for his miraculous cures, after his death the local people began to worship his spirit in continued hope for his healing efficacy. Baijiao and the neighboring village of Qingjiao 青礁 became the earliest centers of his cult, which soon spread widely across southern Fujian. The new deity, however, always retained a close affinity with his native Tongan district 同安縣, and was carried by Tongan emigrants beyond the borders of Fujian to other parts of continental China, to Taiwan, and to Southeast Asia. Hundreds of temples dedicated to him are active to the present day.

While strictly speaking a popular rather than a Taoist deity, Baosheng dadi adopted more and more Taoist characteristics as his cult spread. The earliest sources contain some hints of possible Taoist inclinations on the part of Wu Tao, but most of his explicitly Taoist features are later accretions to his hagiography. Examples of such features include certain Taoist themes in the deity's legend, Taoist rituals performed at his temples, his *Shenxiao Taoist derived title, and the scripture composed for his cult, all of which serve to imprint a Taoist identity on a popular deity, without ever completely absorbing it into the Taoist pantheon.

Philip CLART

📖 Dean 1993, 61–97; Lin Guoping and Peng Wenyu 1993, 217–39; Qing Xitai 1994, 3: 153–54; Schipper 1990

※ TAOISM AND LOCAL CULTS; TAOISM AND POPULAR RELIGION

Basu jing

八素經

Scripture of the Eight Pure Ladies

The *basu* are carriages of clouds for the divinities, the Yin counterpart of the **bajing* (Eight Effulgences) which are Yang carriages of light. The same term also denotes eight female divinities. The scripture that concerns them belongs to the original *Shangqing revelations, and is divided into two parts in the current Taoist Canon: the *Basu zhenjing* 八素真經 (Authentic Scripture of the Eight Pure Ladies; CT 426) and the *Basu zhenjing fushi riyue huanghua jue* 八素真經服食日月皇華訣 (Authentic Scripture of the Eight Pure Ladies and Instructions on the Absorption of the August Efflorescences of the Sun and the Moon; CT 1323). Both texts belong to the group of Shangqing writings that teach how to follow the yearly and monthly journeys of the Sun and the Moon across the sky in order to ingest their essences. These meditation exercises play an important role in the Shangqing practices and vision of the world, and parts of them were included in later rituals.

The *Basu zhenjing* consists of three main sections. The first describes exercises to visualize the divinities of the planets and absorb their light. The second is a rite to call upon the divinities of the planets and ask them to erase one's name from the registers of death (*siji* 死籍). This rite complements a similar one addressed to the divinities of the Northern Dipper (**beidou*) described in the **Jiuzhen zhongjing*. The third section focuses on two methods to pacify the *hun* souls (see **hun* and *po*) and expel the Three Corpses (*sanshi*; see **sanshi* and *jiuchong*); it also contains a list of Shangqing texts arranged into four classes according to the spiritual ranks granted by their practice.

The *Fushi riyue huanghua jue* teaches how to absorb the essences of the Sun and the Moon by ingesting water previously exposed to their rays. It contains several talismans (**FU*): two for Yin and Yang, two for the Sun and the Moon, and one for each of the Eight Pure Ladies. Then it describes the rite of the *Xuanmu bajian* 玄母八簡 (Eight Tablets of the Mysterious Mother), which consists in visualizing divinities who ride in carriages of light (*jing* 景) and clouds (*su* 素) on the eight nodal days of the year (*bajie* 八節, i.e., equinoxes, solstices, and the first day of each season), which are related in turn to the eight directions of the world (the *bamen* or Eight Gates). The adept asks these deities to let him ascend with them to heaven.

Isabelle ROBINET

📖 Robinet 1984, 2: 51–57; Robinet 1993, 187–95

※ Shangqing

baxian

八仙

Eight Immortals

The names of individuals counted as the Eight Immortals changed over the years. In Du Fu's 杜甫 (712–70) "Song of the Eight Immortals of the Winecup" ("Yinzhong baxian ge" 飲中八仙歌), a humorous depiction of eight inebriates, the Eight Immortals are listed as *He Zhizhang, Li Jin 李璡, Li Shizhi 李適之, Cui Zongzhi 崔宗之, Su Jin 蘇晉, Li Bai 李白 (Li Bo), Zhang Xu 張旭, and Jiao Sui 焦遂. According to the early Song *Taiping guangji* 太平廣記 (Extensive Records of the Taiping Xingguo Reign Period; *j.* 214), a picture called "The Eight Immortals," painted by Zhang Suqing 張素卿, a Taoist master from Mount Qingcheng (*Qingcheng shan, Sichuan), included Li Er 李耳 (i.e., Laozi), *Rong Cheng, Dong Zhongshu 董仲舒, *Zhang Daoling, Yan Junping 嚴君平 (see *Yan Zun), Li Babai 李八百 (see *Lijia dao), Fan Changshou 范長壽, and Ge Yonggui 葛永瑰. These were the so-called "Eight Immortals of Sichuan." Clearly there was more than one group known as the Eight Immortals. Perhaps the most famous was that which formed in the Yuan period and became well known at a popular level in the Ming period (see fig. 22): Han Zhongli 漢鍾離, *Zhang Guolao, Han Xiangzi 韓湘子, Li Tieguai 李鐵拐, Cao Guojiu 曹國舅, *Lü Dongbin, Lan Caihe 藍采和, and He xiangu 何仙姑 (Immortal Maiden He).

With the exception of Li Tieguai, whose background is uncertain, Han Zhongli and the others in this later group all have some form of personal history. Han Zhongli was *Zhongli Quan, whose biography is in the *Jinlian zhengzong ji* (Records of the Correct Lineage of the Golden Lotus), compiled by Qin Zhi'an 秦志安 (1188–1244) and containing the biographies of the Five Patriarchs (*wuzu* 五祖) and the Seven Real Men (or Perfected, *qizhen* 七真; see table 17) of the *Quanzhen school. Here he is considered the second patriarch, having received the teachings from the first, Donghua dijun 東華帝君 (Imperial Lord of Eastern Florescence; see *Wang Xuanfu). He lived for more than five hundred years, from the Later Han to the Tang dynasty, before gaining immortality. Zhang Guolao was Zhang Guo 張果, a *fangshi* (master of methods) who lived during the Tang dynasty, and his biography is included in the *fangshi* records in both versions of the *History of the Tang Dynasty*. He is said to have been invited from his abode in Hengzhou 恆州 (Hebei) to court by Tang Xuanzong (r. 712–56) and there performed a number of magical arts. His age is not known, and so he is given the appellation Lao 老 (Elder). Han Xiangzi is said by some to have been Han Xiang 韓湘, nephew of the Tang literary figure, Han Yu 韓愈 (768–824; IC 397–40). The following story is taken from the *Qingsuo ji* 青瑣集 (Anthology of the Green Latticed Window) in the "Divine Im-

Fig. 22. The Eight Immortals.

mortals" ("Shenxian" 神仙) section of the *Shihua zonggui* 詩話總龜 (General Compendium of Poetry Criticism). One time, when Han Xiang was scooping up earth in front of his uncle Han Yu and placing it in a tray, two beautiful flowers suddenly bloomed, and between the two the following verse appeared in golden letters:

> Clouds veil the Qinling range:
> where is your home?
> Deep snow has closed the Lan Pass:
> the horses will go no further.

It is said that this was used within a poem composed by Han Yu at the Lan Pass (Languan 藍關) after he had been demoted to Chaozhou 潮州 (Guangdong). Cao Guojiu was the younger brother of Empress Cao (Cao huanghou 曹皇后), wife of Song Renzong (r. 1022–63). Lü Dongbin was the second Quanzhen patriarch after Zhongli Quan. Lan Caihe's biography can be found in Shen Fen's 沈汾 *Xu xianzhuan (Sequel to Biographies of Immortals). He dressed in a tattered blue gown, and wore a boot on only one foot, leaving the other bare. In summer he wore padding under his robe, and in winter slept in the snow, while his body gave off steam. He was always drunk. He sang songs accompanying himself on castanets, begging his way through the town. His sex is obscure and in later times he was portrayed on the stage as a woman. Tales of He xiangu are found in many places; according to Zhao Daoyi's 趙 道一 *Lishi zhenxian tidao tongjian* (Comprehensive Mirror of Perfected Immortals and Those Who Embodied the Dao through the Ages; *Houji* 後集, 5.8a–b), she was the daughter of He Tai 何泰 of Zengcheng 增城 in Guangzhou (Canton). She was instructed by a divine person in a dream to prepare a "Powder of mica" (*yunmu fen* 雲母分) and ingest it; in the reign of Tang Zhongzong (r. 684, 705–10) she gained immortality.

Probably contributing greatly to the renown of this particular group of Eight Immortals was the devotion extended to Zhongli Quan and Lü Dongbin as patriarchs of the Quanzhen order, and the depiction of He xiangu as a student of Lü Dongbin. As the Eight Immortals became more and more popular, they were featured in plays, novels, and paintings; stories such as "The Eight Immortals Crossing the Sea" ("Baxian guohai" 八仙過海) and "The Eight Immortals of Turquoise Pond Assembly Celebrate Longevity" ("Yaochi hui baxian qingshou" 瑤池會八仙慶壽) became widely known.

YOSHIKAWA Tadao

📖 Jing Anning 1996; Lai T'ien-ch'ang 1972; Little 2000b, 319–34; Maspero 1981, 161–64; Ho and O'Brien 1990; Yang R. F. S. 1958; Yetts 1916; Yetts 1922

※ Lü Dongbin; Zhang Guolao; Zhongli Quan; HAGIOGRAPHY; TAOISM AND POPULAR RELIGION

Beidi

北帝

Northern Emperor

When Taoists elaborated their mythical geography during the first centuries CE, they placed Beidi, the Northern Emperor, at the head of Mount *Fengdu and made him the supreme sovereign of the kingdom of the dead. In this role, Beidi runs a giant administration including judges, officials, henchmen, and all the dead who have repented and are enrolled in the infernal bureaucracy according to their former status and prestige in the world of the living.

For *Tao Hongjing, Beidi is similar to Yanluo 閻羅 (Yama, the king of the Buddhist hells; *Zhengao*, 15.2a), but he also is associated with the Northern Dipper (*beidou). Beidi plays, therefore, essential roles as director of destiny at both extremities of the *axis mundi*, heaven and hell. Otherwise his identity is uncertain; in particular, he does not seem to be directly related to Xuanwu 玄武 (Dark Warrior), nor to his successor, Xuantian shangdi 玄天上帝 (Highest Emperor of the Dark Heaven), who became popular during the Tang period and was venerated as the patron saint of the ruling houses of the Song and Ming dynasties (see under *Zhenwu).

A long liturgical and exorcistic tradition developed around the myth of Beidi during the Six Dynasties, in the wake of Taoist apocalyptic eschatology. Adepts—especially those associated with the *Shangqing school—practiced the "Northern Emperor's Method of Killing Demons" (*Beidi shagui zhi fa* 北帝殺鬼之法), a meditation technique accompanied by recitations of the names of the Six Palaces of Fengdu (see *santian* and *liutian*) and the Tianpeng spell (*Tianpeng zhou*). Communal exorcistic rituals addressed to Beidi were also performed at that time. Later, under the Tang and the Five Dynasties, exorcists adhering to Beidi's cult entered the official ranks of the Taoist clerical system with the title of Taoists of the Northern Emperor's Great Mystery (*Beidi taixuan daoshi* 北帝太玄道士). It is probably at this time that the great summa of Beidi's tradition was composed. This text, entitled *Taishang Yuanshi tianzun shuo Beidi fumo shenzhou miaojing* 太上元始天尊說北帝伏魔神咒妙經 (Wondrous Scripture of Divine Spells of the Northern Emperor for Suppressing Demons, Spoken by the Highest Celestial Worthy of Original Commencement; CT 1412), is a large collection of apotropaic recipes and exorcistic rites.

The major exorcistic schools of the Song period, such as the *Tianxin zhengfa, renewed Beidi's tradition. The voluminous fourteenth-century *Daofa huiyuan* (Corpus of Taoist Ritual) includes no less than thirteen chapters (j. 156–68) related to the practices of this tradition, gathered under the title *Shangqing Tianpeng fumo dafa* 上清天蓬伏魔大法 (Great Rites of Tianpeng for Suppressing Demons According to the Highest Clarity Tradition). The tradition was continued, at least through the Ming dynasty, by the Celestial Masters of Mount Longhu (*Longhu shan, Jiangxi), who were well known for their exorcistic skills.

Christine MOLLIER

📖 Mollier 1997

※ *beidou*; Fengdu; DEITIES: THE PANTHEON

beidou

北斗

Northern Dipper

Since early times, the Northern Dipper (*Ursa Major*) has played a fundamental role in Chinese official and religious life, due to its importance in the astro-calendrical calculations and its mighty apotropaic powers. The basic features of its roles in Taoism are already apparent in the Han period: in the *Shiji* (Records of the Historian, *j.* 27; trans. Chavannes 1895–1905, 3: 339–43), the Dipper is associated with the pole star as the heavenly center of the world, and is the residence of the Great One (*Taiyi); its rotation divides the world into the Nine Palaces (*jiugong). The Dipper, therefore, rules over Heaven and Earth and symbolizes the complex unity of the cosmos. Its earthly counterpart is Mount *Kunlun, the axis of the world. Within the human body, the Dipper is located in its three centers—at the level of the head, the heart, and the navel—and is related to the Three Ones (*sanyi). It is also associated with the spleen, the organ related to Soil and the Center in the *wuxing pattern. Since the color of Soil is yellow, alchemical texts call the Dipper the "yellow star" (*huangxing* 黃星), and one of its synonyms is Yellow Dame (*huangpo* 黃婆).

However, the Dipper lies in the North and thus symbolizes the Origin, which embraces beginning and end and subsumes both Yin and Yang. Many terms used to describe the Dipper give it the qualities of the Origin and pivot of the universe, and the days of the "return to the Origin" (*huiyuan* 迴元) are consecrated to it. The Dipper therefore has a double nature: it is linked with life and death and is associated with the idea of passage, and also divides good from evil and grants punishments and rewards. All the symbols that represent the connection between unity and multiplicity are closely related to it.

The Dipper consists of nine stars, number 9 being that of the Great Yang (*taiyang* 太陽) and of totality. Four stars are located in the scoop, three in the handle, and two are invisible (see fig. 23). The latter, called Fu 輔 and Bi 弼, are its assistants. Those who can see them, under strict conditions of purity, enjoy a life span of several hundred years. Each star is inhabited by divinities, and encloses a paradise similar to those in the Moon and Sun. According to some texts, the nine stars have counterparts which form another invisible constellation surrounding the first one. These nine supplementary stars illuminate the Dipper; they are the celestial-Yang and earthly-Yin souls (*hun and *po*) of

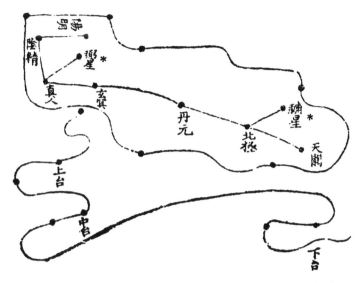

Fig. 23. The Northern Dipper (*beidou*). The picture shows, on top, the locations and names of the seven main stars of the Dipper. Two additional stars, marked by asterisks (*), are associated with the Sun and the Moon and are said to be visible only to advanced adepts. The stars arranged along the line surrounding the Northern Dipper are the residences of the spouses of the Lords of the Dipper's seven visible stars. Below the Northern Dipper is the Three Terraces (*santai* 三台), another constellation formed by three groups of two stars. *Bu tiangang fei diji jing* 步天綱飛地紀經 (Scripture on Walking along the Celestial Guideline and Flying above the Earthly Threads; CT 1316), 1a–b. See Robinet 1993, 202–5.

the Dipper, and are inhabited by the spouses of its kings. Within the human body, the spirits of these "black stars" reside in the Hall of Light (*mingtang) located in the brain, and their titles suggest that their function is to protect the embryo. Thus the celestial world appears to be inverted: the female, Yin, and dark entities are outside, while the male, Yang, and luminous ones are within. In fact, the Dipper is said to be "the natural fire contained in the Yin."

In Taoism, the Dipper has four major roles, all related to its dual aspect. First, the Dipper indicates the proper orientation for performing meditation or rituals through the apparent movement of its "handle." Second, it has strong exorcistic powers as a divinity of the North and of the underworld. Adepts, for example, cover themselves with its stars by visualizing them descending directly above their heads, or surrounding them. Analogously, in the Thunder Rituals (*leifa), the thunder is summoned from the direction to which the Dipper points (called the Gate of the Vital Force, *mingmen) in order to expel demons. Third, the Dipper is the recipient of invocations to ask forgiveness for one's sins and to have one's name erased from the registers of death (*siji*

死籍). Fourth, it opens the way to heaven (its seventh star is called Tianguan 天關 or Heavenly Pass) in both meditation and ritual. This may take place within the framework of exercises whose purpose is to unify the adept and deities pertaining to the practices of Guarding the One (*shouyi). The best known of these exercises is "walking along the guideline" (*bugang), frequently related to the practice of "spreading open the Barrier of Heaven" (tianguan 天關; Kroll 1986b).

Isabelle ROBINET

📖 Andersen 1989–90b; Harper 1978–79; Kalinowski 1983, 343–47; Kroll 1986b; Robinet 1993, 200–225; Robinet 1984, 2: 58–65; Robinet 1997b, 142–47; Schafer 1977a, 42–53

※ Beidi; Beidou xingjun; Doumu; Taiyi; *bugang*; *jiugong*; *tianxin*

Beidou xingjun

北斗星君

Star Lords of the Northern Dipper

The worship of polar deities occurs early in Chinese history as part of the cult of longevity. Already by the Han period, lamps of seven wicks were used for votive purposes in rituals for obtaining long life. The personification of the stars of the Northern Dipper, specifically, dates to the Tang period and was further developed in the Song period. At that time, on the basis of earlier materials, the *Beidou benming yansheng zhenjing* 北斗本命延生真經 (Authentic Scripture of the Natal Destiny of the Northern Dipper for Extending Life; CT 622) was composed. This scripture became one of the most popular and widely recited religious texts in modern China.

Caroline GYSS

📖 Franke H. 1990; White 1945

※ *beidou*; *Wudou jing*; DEITIES: THE PANTHEON

Benji jing

本際經

Scripture of the Original Bound

According to Xuanyi's 玄嶷 (fl. 684–704) *Zhenzheng lun* (Essays of Examination and Correction), the authors of the *Benji jing* were Liu Jinxi 劉進喜 (ca. 560-ca. 640), who wrote the first five chapters at the turn of the seventh century, and Li Zhongqing 李仲卿, who appended the latter five chapters shortly thereafter. Only two of the original ten chapters can be found within the texts of the Taoist Canon. The second chapter appears in the *Taixuan zhenyi benji miaojing* 太玄真一本際妙經 (Wondrous Scripture of the Original Bound of the Perfect Unity of Great Mystery; CT 1111) and in the *Jueyi jing* 決疑經 (Scripture on Resolving Doubts; CT 59), while the ninth chapter is included in the *Kaiyan bimi zang jing* 開演祕密藏經 (Scripture on Elucidating the Secret Storehouse; CT 329). Various chapters also exist in over seventy *Dunhuang manuscripts, which preserve the *Benji jing* almost in its entirety and allow a partial reconstruction of its table of contents: 1. "Protecting the State" ("Huguo pin" 獲國品); 2. "Entrustment" ("Fushu pin" 付屬品); 3. "Actions of the Sages" ("Shengxing pin" 聖行品); 4. "Dao-Nature" ("Daoxing pin" 道性品); 5. "Attesting to the Truth ("Zhengshi pin" 證實品); 6.-9. Titles unknown; 10. "Penetrating the Subtle Concerning the Origin of the Dao" ("Daoben tongwei pin" 道本通微品).

The authors of the *Benji jing* derived their inspiration for the text from Buddhism. Not only was the term *benji* a second century translation of the Pāli term *pubbākoṭi* (Skt.: *pūrvakoṭi*), which designates the original "point of genesis" (Wu Chi-yu 1960, 5–10; Sharf 2002, 229–38), but late-fourth-century translations of the *Madhyamāgama* (*Zhong ahan jing* 中阿含經, T. 26 [51]) and the *Samyuktāgama* (*Za ahan jing* 雜阿含經, T. 99 [937–55]) contained *sūtras* of the same name. The format of the text, a question and answer session between the highest deity and advanced practitioners, resembles that often found in Mahāyāna (Great Vehicle) Buddhist *sūtras*. Throughout the *Benji jing*, Buddhist terms are discussed, such as *faxiang* 法相 (marks of the dharma, *dharmalakṣaṇa*), *fayin* 法印 (seals of the dharma), and *jingtu* 淨土 (pure land, *Sukhāvatī*). The text also emphasizes two important Buddhist ideas, *upāya* (skillful means) and *nirmāṇakāya* (the "transformation body" of the Buddha), which are used to justify the existence of different and often conflicting teachings and scriptures. Related to the Buddhist idea that reality is illusory, it describes meditation practices where the adept frees himself from all concepts and comes to realize that there is no underlying reality.

The *Benji jing* was often cited in Taoist encyclopedias, particularly the *Dao-jiao yishu* (Pivot of Meaning of the Taoist Teaching). In 742, Tang Xuanzong (r. 712–56) ordered its distribution to all Taoist temples and its recitation in state rituals. The text became a major focus of attacks in Buddhist polemics, probably resulting from the popularity it enjoyed at court.

Amy Lynn MILLER

📖 Kaltenmark 1979a; Kamata Shigeo 1968, 11–80; Kanaoka Shōkō 1983, 190–96; Ōfuchi Ninji 1978–79, 1: 128–71 (crit. notes on the Dunhuang mss.) and 2: 291–353 (reprod. of the Dunhuang mss.); Ozaki Masaharu 1983e, 183–86; Robinet 1977, 102–3; Sunayama Minoru 1990, 212–45; Wan Yi 1998; Wu Chi-yu 1960; Yamada Takashi 1999

※ TAOISM AND CHINESE BUDDHISM

benming

本命

1. natal destiny; 2. birth star

The term *benming* literally means "natal destiny" or "individual destiny." It is commonly used, however, to denote the time when a person is born and the deities governing that time. Consequently, for a person's life and destiny to be propitious it is thought necessary to know the star deity ruling at the hour of birth, and to perform rites at times corresponding to the hour of birth according to the sexagesimal cycle (*ganzhi*).

Although such rites probably originated within folk cults, they were and still are also performed within Taoism. In the ordination rituals of the Way of the Celestial Masters (*Tianshi dao), for instance, the bestowal of registers (*LU) included the statement: "The natal destiny of (*name*), born on (*month, day, and hour*), comes under the authority of the Lord of the (*name*) star in the Northern Dipper (*beidou)" (*Sanwu zhengyi mengwei lu* 三五正一盟威籙; CT 1208, 1.1a). Every life thus is governed by one of the stars in the Northern Dipper, depending on the year of birth. The name of the appropriate star lord is also recorded on the documents appointing a Taoist ritual master (*daozhang), whose religious name is chosen according to the ruling calendrical sign.

Taoist priests in present-day Taiwan perform a minor rite designed to dispel misfortune by venerating the appropriate Lord of the Northern Dipper according to the *benming*. The rite involves the recitation of texts such as the *Beidou benming yansheng zhenjing* 北斗本命延生真經 (Authentic Scripture of the Natal Destiny of the Northern Dipper for Extending Life; CT 622; see under **Wudou jing*).

MARUYAMA Hiroshi

📖 Hou Ching-lang 1975, 106–26; Little 2000b, 248; Ōfuchi Ninji 1983, 678–702

※ *beidou*

bianhua

變化

metamorphosis; transformation

The idea of *bianhua* (metamorphosis, or "change and transformation"), that the certainty that the world is in flux leaves open the possibility that things may transform from one type to another, can be traced from the **Zhuangzi* through the **Shangqing tradition.

The "transformation of things" (*wuhua* 物化) and *bianhua* were pivotal concepts in the cosmology of the Warring States classic *Zhuangzi*, and became part of the Taoist worldview beginning with mantic texts of the Han dynasty. In the *Zhuangzi*, *bianhua* refers to the ability of things to change from one category to another and is taken as a core argument in favor of the text's particular brand of skepticism. It is also important in the description of human growth in Liu An's 劉安 (179?–122) **Huainan zi* (ca. 139 BCE), which emphasizes the role of the basic dualism of Heaven and Earth. After going through the ten months of fetal development, the text relates how each of the five viscera (**wuzang*) govern a particular sense organ, and concludes: "Therefore the roundness of the head is the image of Heaven, and the squareness of the feet is the image of Earth" (see also under **BIRTH*). In the early period, discussions of *bianhua* tend to emphasize the way in which it applies to human beings in the same way it does to the natural world (Sivin 1991). Some later texts also find *bianhua* used to describe natural contexts such the transformation inside the chrysalis, and the transition to an afterlife.

Another approach to *bianhua* stresses the potential for the adept to control it. Many extant fragments of a second text related to Liu An, the *Huainan wanbi* 淮南萬畢 (Myriad Endings of Huainan), deal with the use of *bianhua* in daily life (Kusuyama Haruki 1987). The Heshang gong 河上公 commentary to the *Daode jing* (see **Laozi Heshang gong zhangju*) also uses the term in a more instrumental way explaining its use by the dragon (sec. 26) and the spirits (sec. 36). Just as the dragon is a metaphor for the sage, its ability to use *bianhua* is a characteristic of Laozi in the *Laozi bianhua jing* (Scripture of the Transformations of Laozi), a text that reflects the many historical transformations of the sage Laozi.

The harnessing of *bianhua* was particularly important in later Taoism, where it became linked with the eschatological picture of the Shangqing tradition. Like Laozi, the diverse spirits of the Shangqing tradition are able to transform themselves, and the adept had to be able to identify their different manifestations. Adepts, in turn, might use *bianhua* to transform themselves. The Shangqing text *Shenzhou qizhuan qibian wutian jing* 神州七轉七變舞天經 (Scripture of the Divine Continent on the Dance in Heaven in Seven Revolutions and Seven Transformations; CT 1331) describes methods for transforming into clouds, light, fire, water, and dragons (Robinet 1993, 161). Isabelle Robinet notes that "the powers of metamorphosis had always been a key characteristic of the immortals, but these powers came to be even more central in Shangqing where they were synonymous with deliverance and salvation" (Robinet 2000, 219).

Mark CSIKSZENTMIHALYI

📖 Robinet 1979b; Robinet 1993, 153–69; Sivin 1991

※ *shijie*; *xing*; *zaohua*; *ziran*

bianshen

變身 or 變神

"transformation of the body" *or* "transformation of the spirit"

The term *bianshen* has been used in Taoist ritual texts since the Song dynasty, with special reference to various practices—comprising notably visualizations and spells—through which a priest may transform himself into being identical, either with the cosmos as a whole, or with the specific deity that presides over the particular method or rite that he is about to perform. There is an obvious connection between practices of this kind and the theme of the cosmic body of Laozi, which in early legends is identified with the Dao or with the primordial Chaos (*hundun*), and which is said to have given rise to the universe. A number of practices of transformation (*bianhua* or *bianxing* 變形, "transformation of the body"), related to this theme and to the general notion of a parallelism between the human body and the universe, formed

part of Taoist physiological and meditational techniques during the early Six
Dynasties, and were developed in the texts of the *Shangqing tradition such
as the *Shenzhou qizhuan qibian wutian jing* 神州七轉七變舞天經 (Scripture
of the Divine Continent on the Dance in Heaven in Seven Revolutions and
Seven Transformations; CT 1331). A central object of identification in these
early traditions was *Taiyi, the Great One, the supreme celestial deity who
emerged during the Warring States as a personification of the concept of
cosmic unity or totality, and who was addressed as an alter ego of the ruler
in the imperial cult of the early Han dynasty. Practices for the transformation
of the body appear in the Taoist liturgies instituted at the end of the Han, as
for instance in the *Zhengyi rite of Lighting the Incense Burner (*falu*) which
is described already in the *Dengzhen yinjue* (3.6b–8a, compiled from original
Shangqing material), in which there is a strong focus on the "cosmification"
and externalization of the energies of the body of the priest. The function of
this rite is to initiate communication between the priest and the divine world,
and it has been transmitted to the present day as part of the basic framework
of major Land of the Way (*daochang*) and Audience (*sanchao*) rituals in the
classical *jiao liturgy. It was not until the early Song dynasty, however, that
practices of transformation, occurring as standard elements of ritual, were
subsumed under the heading of *bianshen*.

    Methods labeled as *bianshen* are described in all the major ritual compen-
dia of the Song dynasty, as for instance in those of the *Tianxin zhengfa, in
which the term refers to relatively simple acts of identification with specific
deities, and to the more comprehensive series of transformations that initiate whole services of exorcism (see *Taishang zhuguo jiumin zongzhen biyao*,
2.1a–2b; *Shangqing tianxin zhengfa* 上清天心正法, CT 566, 2.1a–5b). In addition
to the identification with the first Celestial Master, *Zhang Daoling, the latter
comprise both practices of "walking along the guideline" (*bugang*) and "practices in the hand" (*shoujue*), as well as visualizations of the basic emblems of
cosmic power surrounding the practitioner. They also often include the long
spell that in present-day ritual manuals is referred to as the Great Spell for the
Transformation of the Body (*da bianshen zhou* 大變身咒; see Andersen 1995,
195, and Lagerwey 1987c, 71).

                                                              Poul ANDERSEN

📖 Andersen 1995; Lagerwey 1987c, 69–73; Schipper 1978, 96–98

※ TAOIST VIEWS OF THE HUMAN BODY

Bianzheng lun

辯正論

Essays of Disputation and Correction

This polemical work in eight chapters (T. 2110) was completed about 633 by Falin 法琳 (572–640), and includes commentary by the scholar-official Chen Ziliang 陳子良 (?–632). Together with Falin's *Poxie lun* 破邪論 (Essay Refuting Heresy; T. 2109), written in 622 to refute *Fu Yi, it has long been recognized as a datable source citing dozens of Taoist texts. Its account of late Six Dynasties studies of the *Daode jing* also preserves information independently from Taoist and secular sources. The reasons for this become clear once we consider Falin's intellectual training at Blue Brook Mountain (Qingxi shan 青溪山), a long-forgotten religious center in Hubei where adherents of Buddhism and Taoism lived in close proximity (Barrett 1991b). But Falin is important for more than bibliographical reasons. His reassertion of the Buddhist case against Taoism, first stated under the Liang dynasty, on the grounds that it was a confection that was not even true to the Chinese classical tradition (in which Laozi is granted a place as a philosopher) defined the limits within which the emerging state Taoism of the Tang dynasty was tolerable to Buddhists. In this, even though Falin was to some extent constrained by the need to refute specific points made by polemical opponents, the Taoists Li Zhongqing 李仲卿 and Liu Jinxi 劉進喜 (see *Benji jing*), the *Bianzheng lun* makes explicit the criteria by which Buddhism judged other religions (*jiao* 教, "teachings"), and so is extremely helpful in decoding all other descriptions of Taoism through Buddhist eyes. But his blunt, ethnocentric criticisms of the nascent dynastic attempts to link by descent the ruling family and Laozi as a more than human figure incurred in 639 charges of having slandered the emperor. This resulted in banishment to Sichuan, en route to which he died.

The influence of the *Bianzheng lun* in East Asia was considerable: hence as early as 1930 Takeuchi Yoshio produced a study of its textual variants designed to identify the source of the edition cited in medieval Japan (Takeuchi 1930, 9: 410–26). Despite Falin's punishment, and the banning of his biography, his works were already included in the Buddhist canon in mid-Tang times, to judge from catalogues and phonological commentaries. Some of the polemical issues raised in the *Bianzheng lun*, such as the controversies surrounding the status of Laozi, were also dealt with by contemporary Buddhists such as Jizang 吉藏 (549–623) in his *Sanlun xuanyi* 三論玄義 (Mysterious Meaning of the Three Treatises; T. 1852), but Falin's work remains the most complete surviving statement of the issues between Buddhism and Taoism until the renewed debates of the Mongol period.

T. H. BARRETT

📖 Kohn 1995a, 180–86; Ōfuchi Ninji and Ishii Masako 1988, 315–21 (list of texts cited); Tonami Mamoru 1999, 40–55

※ TAOISM AND CHINESE BUDDHISM

bigu

辟穀

abstention from cereals

The term *bigu* denotes a diet that allows one to avoid eating common food, which in China mainly consisted of cereals. These were said to generate harmful entities, particularly the "worms" or "corpses" residing in the intestine (see *sanshi* and *jiuchong*), in the epigastrial region, and in the brain; they were also thought to induce pain, produce debris and excrement that cause the intestine to decay, and destroy the vital principle of their host. Cereals therefore were progressively reduced and replaced by other outer or inner nourishment, including herbs, minerals, breath (see *fuqi*), and talismanic water (*fushui* 符水, i.e., water containing ashes of burned talismans, *FU). Besides *bigu*, abstention from cereals is known as *duangu* 斷穀 (stopping cereals), *juegu* 絕穀 (discontinuing cereals), *quegu* 卻穀 (refraining from cereals), or *xiuliang* 修糧 (stopping grains).

The earliest document about this practice is a *Mawangdui manuscript entitled *Quegu shiqi* 卻穀食氣 (Refraining from Cereals and Ingesting Breath; trans. Harper 1998, 305–9). In Han times, abstention from cereals was often associated with worship of the Stove God (*Zaoshen). *Li Shaojun, for instance, taught Han Wudi (r. 141–87 BCE) a "method of worshipping the furnace and abstaining from cereals to prevent old age" (*cizao gudao quelao fang* 祠竈穀道卻老方; *Hanshu* 25.1216). By the early fourth century, according to *Ge Hong, there were more than one hundred different methods, some of which he mentions in *Baopu zi* 15 (trans. Ware 1966, 243–49). A section of the *Zhenzhong ji* 枕中記 (Notes Kept Inside the Pillow; CT 837, 14a–15b) is concerned with *bigu*, and j. 57 of the *Yunji qiqian* contains methods for ingesting breath and avoiding cereals.

When the technique was successful, "movable cuisines" (*xingchu* 行廚) or "celestial cuisines" (*tianchu* 天廚; see under *chu) were brought in gold and jade vessels by Jade Women and Golden Boys (see *yunü), especially the Jade Women of the six cyclical signs *jia* 甲 or *ding* 丁 (*liujia and *liuding*). The *Yaoxiu keyi jielü chao* 要修科儀戒律鈔 (Excerpts from the Essential Liturgies and Observances; CT 463, 14.6b–8a) describes a related rite that includes abstaining from cereals and drinking water containing talismans of the six *jia*. Such rites were said not only to benefit Taoist adepts, but even to prevent whole armies dying of hunger and thirst.

Abstention from cereals should also be situated in the historical context of social unrest and famine. The *Mouzi lihuo lun* 牟子理惑論 (Mouzi's Correction of Errors; T. 2102, 1b; trans. Pelliot 1920) states that after the fall of the Han dynasty more and more people refrained from eating cereals. Despite his skepticism regarding these methods, Ge Hong similarly wrote: "Those who hide in mountain forests in case of troubles or famines in the world will not starve to death if they know this method" (*Baopu zi* 15.266; see trans. Ware 1966, 244).

Catherine DESPEUX

📖 Campany 2002, 22–24; Harper 1998, 141–42; Hu Fuchen 1989, 283–86; Lévi 1983; Maspero 1981, 331–39; Stein R. A. 1972; Stein R. A. 1973

※ *yangsheng*

biqi

閉氣

breath retention

Biqi denotes retaining one's breath between inspiration and expiration. This practice, which probably originated in Han times, is attested in the Jin period and is mentioned several times in the *Baopu zi*. A quotation from the lost *Yangsheng yaoji* (Essentials of Nourishing Life; early fourth century) in the *Ishinpō* (Methods from the Heart of Medicine) describes one of the relevant methods as follows:

> Breath must be retained while one silently counts to 200, then must be let out through the mouth. The time of breath retention is progressively increased to 250; then one's eyebrows become luminous, one's ears hear very well, and all diseases disappear. (*Ishinpō*, 27.17b; also in *Yangxing yanming lu, 2.2b)

This method was preferably to be practiced during the time of the "living breath" (*shengqi* 生氣), i.e., between midnight and midday, and adepts could count breath retentions on their fingers or using wooden cards, incense sticks, and so forth. A practice attributed to *Pengzu is reported in the *Ishinpō* as follows:

> After midnight, when the living breath starts, one should retain one's breath and silently count without interruptions. Those who are afraid of making errors can count one thousand wooden cards by hand; then they will not be far from immortality. When one breathes out, one should let out less breath than was inhaled. Inspiration is done through the nose, expiration through the mouth."
> (*Ishinpō*, 27.19a)

According to *Sun Simiao's (fl. 673) *Qianjin fang* 千金方 (Prescriptions Worth a Thousand; *j.* 27), breath should be retained in the chest for the time equivalent to 300 breaths, so that even a feather placed under one's nose would not move.

Breath retention was also practiced in conjunction with gymnastic exercises (*daoyin), but in this instance the number of breath retentions was generally reduced to five, seven, or twelve. It was also often associated with circulating the breath (*xingqi), allowing one to release breath in the body to heal diseases, eliminate stagnation and impurities, and generate warmth until perspiration was produced. Ritual uses of this technique have also been described, especially in association with the practice of "pacing the void" (*buxu* 步虛; see *bugang). Having visualized the breath of the multicolored stars of Northern Dipper (*beidou), an adept grinds his teeth, swallows his saliva, and retains his breath; the number of retentions depends on the numbers related to the stars that correspond to certain parts of the body (see *Feixing jiuchen yujing* 飛行九晨玉經; CT 428).

Catherine DESPEUX

📖 Maspero 1981, 506–17; Needham 1983, 142–43

※ *yangsheng*

Bixia yuanjun

碧霞元君

Original Princess of the Jasper Mist

The name Bixia yuanjun does not appear in any text earlier than the fifteenth century, either within or outside of the Taoist Canon. Before then, the goddess was known as the Jade Woman of Mount Tai (Taishan yunü 泰山玉女), a title conferred on her by Song Zhenzong (r. 997–1022). This canonization acknowledged for the first time a cult that probably had long thrived in Shandong: Taishan yunü was the daughter of the Great Emperor of the Eastern Peak (*Dongyue dadi), the god of Mount Tai (*Taishan).

As early as the Yuan period, a Yunü daxian 玉女大仙 (Great Immortal Jade Woman) or Yunü niangniang 玉女娘娘 (Damsel Jade Woman) was worshipped in Beijing. In 1495, when a stele was inscribed for a temple devoted to her, the divine foster mother was formally identified as Bixia yuanjun. A stone inscription erected in the *Dongyue miao of Beijing in 1524 documents her cult at the capital under this new title, but qualifies that cult as "heterodox" (*yinsi). Half a century later, the mother of the Wanli Emperor (r. 1573–1620) developed a strong devotion to Bixia yuanjun and placed her infant son under the protection of the goddess. The empress dowager's lavish gifts to the Dongyue miao and other shrines drew criticisms but helped to establish Bixia yuanjun as one of the most popular deities in and around the capital.

Although Bixia yuanjun never received an official canonization, her cult expanded during the late Ming and Qing periods with the support of the Beijing craft and trade guilds. With no less than 116 temples, Bixia yuanjun was the third main deity in Beijing during the Qing dynasty, after Guandi 關帝 (*Guan Yu) and Guanyin 觀音, two eminent orthodox deities. The high point of the year-round cycle of festivals in her honor was the pilgrimage to Mount Miaofeng (Miaofeng shan 妙峰山, west of Beijing) during the fourth lunar month.

Caroline GYSS

📖 Chavannes 1910b, 29–43; Little 2000b, 278–29; Maspero 1981, 164–66; Naquin 1992; Naquin 2000, 240–47, 517–28, and passim; Qing Xitai 1994, 3: 106–8

※ Dongyue dadi; Dongyue miao; Taishan

Bojia dao

帛家道

Way of the Bo Family

Bojia dao is the designation of a loosely defined set of beliefs and practices related to the lineage of Bo He 帛和, a *fangshi (master of methods) who lived around 300 CE. According to the *Shenxian zhuan (Biographies of Divine Immortals; trans. Campany 2002, 133–36), Bo He was a *fangshi* who mastered "embryonic breathing" (*taixi) and methods for making "medicines of immortality" (xianyao 仙藥). Later he devoted himself to alchemical practices based on the *Taiqing jing (Scripture of Great Clarity) on Mount Xicheng (Xicheng shan 西城山, Shaanxi), and is also said to have received the *Sanhuang wen (Script of the Three Sovereigns) and the *Wuyue zhenxing tu (Charts of the Real Forms of the Five Peaks).

Bo He appears to have established a system of beliefs that were spread by his disciples, who were based in present-day Jiangsu and Zhejiang. Much is unclear, however, regarding the historical Way of the Bo Family. The term Bojia dao is first recorded in writings by *Tao Hongjing (456–536). Tao notes in his Zhoushi mingtong ji 周氏冥通記 (Records of Mr. Zhou's Communications with the Unseen; CT 302, 1.13a) that "prayers to the popular gods (sushen 俗神) are commonly called the Way of the Bo Family." In his *Zhengao (Declarations of the Perfected; 4.10b), Tao also clearly states that Xu Mai 許邁 (300–348; see under *Yang Xi) "was originally affiliated with the Way of the Bo Family and exploited many people." Tao's words seems to suggest that a cult called Way of the Bo Family existed by the second half of the fourth century. It is worthy of note, though, that while the *Baopu zi (trans. Ware 1966, 314 and 328) refers to Bo He, it makes no mention of the Way of the Bo Family.

YAMADA Toshiaki

📖 Chen Guofu 1963, 75–76, 276–77; Yamada Toshiaki 1983b, 1:369–71; Hu Fuchen 1989, 56–57; Qing Xitai 1994, 1: 95–96

bugang

步罡 (or: 步綱)

"walking along the guideline"

The term bugang refers to Taoist ritual walks or dances, which follow the basic cosmic patterns, such as the various arrangements of the eight trigrams (*bagua) that are passed through in the sequence of the numbers from 1 to 9 arranged so as to form the so-called "magic square" (see *Hetu and Luoshu). The earliest preserved descriptions are found in the revealed texts of the *Shangqing tradition, which focus on walks along the patterns of the constellations and the five planets, and especially on walks along the seven stars of the Northern Dipper (*beidou). A common general term for the practice, which occurs already in texts from the late Six Dynasties, accordingly, is bugang tadou 步罡踏斗, "walking along the guideline and treading on (the stars of) the Dipper."

The "Paces of Yu." The practice of bugang evidently descends from the ancient, shamanic "Paces of Yu" (Yubu 禹步), and indeed the latter term occurs in

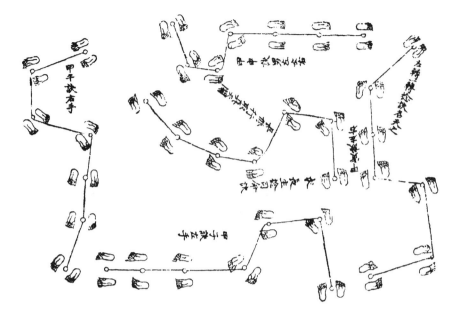

Fig. 24. Treading the twenty-eight lunar mansions (*xiu). *Jinsuo liuzhu yin
(Guide to the Golden Lock and the Flowing Pearls; CT 1015), 2.2a-b.

Taoist texts as the label of some variants of the complete practice. This style
of walking typically consists in simply dragging one foot after the other, and
it is usually explained with reference to the legend of Yu, who exerted himself
in his effort to establish order in the world after the great inundation to such
an extent that he became lame on one side of his body. The earliest, most
detailed account of the Paces of Yu is the one found in *j.* 17 of the *Baopu zi*
(trans. Ware 1966, 285–86), where each pace comprises three steps, and the
movement thus appears like the waddle of a three-legged creature. This triple
structure of the walk in the developed Taoist forms of *bugang* was no novelty,
but in fact represents the most characteristic aspect of the Paces of Yu described
in the medical and divinatory texts of the late Warring States (Harper 1998;
Rao Zongyi and Zeng Xiantong 1982).

It stands to reason that, at least in the minds of some practitioners of
this period, the three paces were associated with the notion of a movement
through the three levels of the cosmos, leading the performer to heaven.
The fact that already in the early Han dynasty, the steps seem to have been
connected with the three pairs of stars that are situated under the Northern
Dipper and referred to as the Three Terraces (*santai* 三台; see fig. 23), or the
Celestial Staircase (*tianjie* 天階), would seem to support this. It would appear,
in other words, that even in this early period the Paces of Yu constituted a
close parallel to the three Strides Viṣṇu in early Vedic mythology, which are

thought to have taken the god through the three levels of the cosmos (thereby establishing the universe), and which indeed, just like the Paces of Yu in Taoist ritual, are known to have been imitated by Vedic priests as they approached the altar—and in the same form as the Paces of Yu, that is, dragging one foot after the other.

The Paces of Yu are described in the *Baopu zi* as elements of the divinatory system of *dunjia* 遁甲 (Hidden Stem), which serves to calculate the immediate position in the space-time structure of the six *ding* (*liuding*; see *liujia and *liuding*), i.e., the spirits that define the place of the "irregular gate" (*qimen* 奇門). This gate represents a "crack in the universe," so to speak, which must be approached through performing the Paces of Yu, and through which the adept may enter the emptiness of the otherworld and thereby achieve invisibility to evil spirits and dangerous influences. The close relationship between divination and forms of *bugang* has survived in later divinatory systems, and it is quite common, even in present-day manuals of divination, to find a whole section describing variants of *bugang*. In the early texts of the Shangqing tradition (in which the theme of achieving safety through methods of invisibility is quite strongly represented), this divinatory aspect of *bugang* is retained, however, only as terminological reminders, and in the cosmological framework of the practice; the overwhelming emphasis is on the purpose of achieving individual immortality and the ascent to heaven.

Bugang in liturgy. A similar transformation is evident in the forms of *bugang* that since the Tang dynasty were adopted into the general liturgy, mainly from the *Zhengyi tradition. As in the Shangqing variants of the practice, each step is accompanied by a line of incantation, pronounced inwardly by the priest as he reaches the star or trigram in question. The movement of the feet on the ground commonly is paralleled by the visualization of a journey through heaven, and—at least since the Song dynasty—by "practices in the hand" (*shoujue), i.e., a movement with the thumb of the left hand, which represents a parallel movement through the body of the priest. The ritual manuals commonly insist on the point that the three movements must be carefully coordinated. Indeed, the basic patterns followed in the practice of *bugang* are associated with the concept of the movement through heaven of the high god *Taiyi, the Great One, or the Supreme Unity, and the accompanying incantations often make it clear that as the priest performs the walk, he impersonates Taiyi. A powerful theme underlying the practice is that of world-creation and the establishment of order, frequently associated with the construction of the sacred area in the initial part of a ritual. Within the liturgy, however, the characteristic specific functions of *bugang* are, first, to serve as elements of the purification of the ritual area, and second, to structure the movement of the high priest (*gaogong* 高功), as he approaches the point of the transmission of a document to heaven, and the point of his ascent in order to deliver the document to the Most High.

The forms of *bugang* used in present-day liturgy mostly derive from the ritual compilations of the Song dynasty. They are typically performed by the high priest alone and are described in his "secret manual" (**mijue*). The practice is highly valued by the present-day priesthood, and it is commonly conceived as a foundational element of Taoist ritual. A similar view is expressed in many historical texts, such as in the **Taishang zhuguo jiumin zongzhen biyao* (Secret Essentials of the Totality of Perfected, of the Most High, for Assisting the Country and Saving the People; preface 1116; 8.1a), by Yuan Miaozong 元妙 宗, who says: "The Paces of Yu along the guideline of the Dipper, and the instructions for practices in the palm of the hand, are the great essentials of the Way, the primordial leading thread of (all other) methods."

Poul ANDERSEN

📖 Andersen 1989–90b; Andersen 1990; Andersen 2001, 48–71; Chen Guofu 1963, 280; Holm 1994; Hu Tiancheng, He Dejun, and Duan Ming 1999; Lager-wey 1987c, 31–35, 99–101, and passim; Robinet 1976, 219–59 passim; Robinet 1993, 187–225; Robinet 1995b; Sakade Yoshinobu 1993c; Schafer 1977a, 187–225; Zhang Zehong 1994

※ *bianshen*; *jintan*; *shoujue*

buqi

布氣

spreading breath

Buqi means spreading out one's inner breath, mainly for healing purposes. Xing Ling's 幸靈 biography in the *Jinshu* (History of the Jin; 95.2483) contains the first mention of this technique. According to this story, Lü Yi's 呂猗 mother had been suffering from rheumatism and muscular atrophy in the lower limbs for over ten years. To treat her, Xing sat down next to her in silence, with his eyes half-closed. After some time, he asked Lü to help his mother to get up. Lü replied that this was impossible because of his mother's illness, but when Xing again asked him to try, Lü's mother could walk by herself. This story is quoted by Su Shi 蘇軾 (Su Dongpo 蘇東坡, 1037–1101; SB 900–968), who also relates that one of his sons was healed by Li Ruozhi 李若之 with this method (*Dongpo zhilin* 東坡志林, Siku quanshu ed., 12.12b). Another mention of *buqi* occurs in an account about Immortal Maiden Zhang (Zhang xiangu 張仙姑),

a woman from Nanyang 南陽 (Henan) who lived in the Song period. One day, she spread her breath to heal a sick man, who suddenly felt a strong heat in his thorax. Later, Song Huizong (r. 1100–1125) summoned Zhang to the capital (*Lishi zhenxian tidao tongjian, Houji 後集, 6.10b).

Further details on this technique, which is still used by present-day *qigong masters, are found in the Songshan Taiwu xiansheng qijing 嵩山太無先生氣經 (Scripture on Breath by the Elder of Great Non-Being from Mount Song):

> When one wants to use one's breath to heal someone, one should always first determine upon which of the five viscera (*wuzang) the disease depends. Then one takes the breath from the corresponding direction, and makes it enter the body of the patient. The patient, who faces the direction [of her natal destiny (*benming)], is asked to quiet her mind and calm her breathing, and one starts to spread breath. The patient also should swallow her own breath and calm her thoughts. In this way pathogenic breath (xieqi 邪氣) is interrupted forever. When the correct breath (zhengqi 正氣) has been successfully spread, the pathogenic winds cease of their own accord. (CT 824, 1.8a; also found in Huanzhen xiansheng fu nei yuanqi jue 幻真先生服內元氣訣, CT 828, 7a, and YJQQ 16.20a–b; trans. Despeux 1988, 78–79, from the version in the *Chifeng sui)

A later description in the Taixi biyao gejue 胎息祕要歌訣 (Songs and Instructions on the Secret Essentials of Embryonic Breathing; CT 131, 1a; trans. Huang Jane 1987–90, 1: 49–50) is quoted with minor variants in the Chifeng sui (Marrow of the Red Phoenix; trans. Despeux 1988, 89–90).

In a different context, the technique of "spreading one's breath" is also used by Taoist masters when they trace talismanic figures (*FU) for protection against diseases or demons (see Schipper 1993, 73).

Catherine DESPEUX

※ yangsheng

Buxu ci

步虛詞

Lyrics for Pacing the Void

The Buxu ci is a popular ten-stanza *Lingbao hymn that figures, in several forms, in modern Taoist ritual. The hymn describes the gathering of celestial beings on Jade Capitol Mountain (Yujing shan 玉京山) to pay homage to the Celestial Worthy (Tianzun 天尊). As they sing, Taoist priests circle the altar table in imitation of the processions of gods around the celestial capitol.

The pace used on this occasion is sometimes the Pace of Yu (*Yubu* 禹步; see
*bugang). Officiants are enjoined by the hymn to visualize their own ascent into
the heavens and a similar assembly of their bodily gods within. For instance,
the second verse describes the dance steps as follows: "Circling round, we
tread the cloudy mainstays (i.e., the patterns of the stars); We ride the void,
pacing the mystic filaments. Intoning verses to the venerable, Lord Unity; the
hundred junctures [of our bodies] are put in order of themselves."

The earliest *buxu* song is the "Poem of the Golden Perfected, Melody for
Pacing the Void" ("Jinzhen zhi shi buxu zhi qu" 金真之詩步虛之曲) of **Yang
Xi*'s *Xiaomo zhihui jing* 消魔智慧經 (Scripture of Devil-Dispelling Wisdom;
Robinet 1984, 2: 179–86). As this poem describes a mysterious journey to the
powerful sites of the heavens, its recitation overpowers malignant beings. The
early fifth-century Lingbao version (*Yujing shan buxu jing* 玉京山步虛經; CT
1439) shows traces of this emphasis as well, but also draws upon the Buddhist
practices of ritual circumambulation of the Buddha or his relics and psalmody.
The ten stanzas of the song accord with the ten-directional orientation of ritual
space common to the Lingbao scriptures. By the sixth century, the demon-
quelling aspect of the song again came to the fore as Taoists began to chant
the Spell for Commanding Demons (*mingmo zhu* 命魔祝) before performing
the *buxu*. Finally, though, the Lingbao version of the song is a hymn of praise
and a description of the participation of all in the salvific drama of the Dao.

The appearance of a legend that the poet Cao Zhi 曹植 (192–232; IC 790–91)
had composed the *buxu* after hearing celestial music during the sixth century
provided a suitable literary precedent for the hymn and lyrics began to be
composed by literati, presumably to the by then well-known ritual music. The
earliest non-canonical version to come down to us is the ten-verse poem of
Yu Xin 庾信 (513–81; IC 942–44). Versions by eight further poets, including the
Taoist poets **Wu Yun* (?–778) and Gu Kuang 顧況 (ca. 725–814; IC 486–87), but
also the Buddhist poet Jiaoran 皎然 (730–99) and the secular writer Liu Yuxi
劉禹錫 (774–842; IC 592–93), survive from the Tang period. It is not known
if any of these were used in ritual, but the *buxu ci* is found listed as a Music
Bureau (Yuefu 樂府) title in later collections. During the Song period, both
the emperors Taizong (r. 976–s97) and Huizong (r. 1100–1125) composed their
own versions of the hymn. That of the latter is still used today as an introit
in Taoist ritual.

Stephen R. BOKENKAMP

📖 Andersen 1989–90b; Bokenkamp 1981; Robinet 1976; Schafer 1977a; Schafer
1981; Schafer 1989, passim; Schipper 1989a; Whitaker 1957

※ *bugang*; Lingbao; TAOIST MUSIC

caishen

財神

gods of wealth

Wealth ranks high among the blessings sought from the gods of Chinese popular religion, so it is not surprising that some deities have come to specialize in the bestowal of wealth upon deserving humans. *Caishen* or gods of wealth belong to a large and diverse group of gods whose best-known representative is a deity named Zhao Gongming 趙公明. He is portrayed as a fierce martial figure astride a black tiger, brandishing an iron rod in one hand and holding a gold ingot in the other. At each lunar New Year a new color print of Zhao Gongming, shown either alone or as the leader of four other minor spirits of wealth (collectively referred to as the Gods of Wealth of the Five Roads, Wulu Caishen 五路財神), is pasted on the household's wall and worshipped in a ceremony called "welcoming the God of Wealth" (*ying caishen* 迎財神), which aims to ensure the family's prosperity during the coming year.

While the cult of the gods of wealth is strictly speaking a part of popular religion, the figure of Zhao Gongming has a long-standing connection with Taoism. In Taoist ritual, Zhao Gongming is referred to as Marshal Zhao of the Dark Altar of Orthodox Unity (Zhengyi xuantan Zhao Yuanshuai 正一玄壇趙元帥), one of the four celestial marshals guarding the Taoist ritual arena. Early sources refer to him as a netherwordly general or a plague spirit (*wenshen), which fits well with his fierce iconographical features. Marshal Zhao's Taoist career is a typical example of a conversion from an afflictive to a protective spirit. This shift may have facilitated the formation of Zhao's popular persona as a god of wealth, which is first attested in Yuan dynasty sources.

Philip CLART

📖 Alexéiev 1928; Day 1928; Goodrich 1991, 73–102; Ma Shutian 1997, 199–232; Maspero 1981, 120–21; Zong Li and Liu Qun 1987, 625–57

※ TAOISM AND POPULAR RELIGION

Cantong qi

參同契

Token for the Agreement of the Three

The *Cantong qi* is a short doctrinal poem attributed to the Tang dynasty Chan master Shitou Xiqian 石頭希遷 (700–790). This work is not included in the *Daozang*. Although this poem is first found in bibliographic sources beginning with the *Chongwen zongmu* 崇文總目 (Complete Catalogue [of the Institute] for the Veneration of Literature) of 1042, the Five Dynasties Chan monk Fayan Wenyi 法眼文益 (885–958) composed a short commentary on it (Shiina Kōyū 1981, 191), and it is included in the *Jingde chuandeng lu* 景德傳燈錄 (Records of the Jingde Reign Period on the Transmission of the Lamp; ca. 1005; T. 2076, 30.459b7–21).

This poem has attracted attention due to its title and possible relationship to the *Zhouyi cantong qi* attributed to Wei Boyang 魏伯陽. In the conclusion to his study of the *Zhouyi cantong qi*, Fukui Kōjun (1974) suggests that the Chan idea of introspection (*neiguan*) might be related to the teachings of inner alchemy (*neidan*) found in the *Zhouyi cantong qi*. It is still unclear, however, what the precise relationship between these two works is. While there are no direct quotations from the *Zhouyi cantong qi* in the *Cantong qi*, the two works appear to share some common themes. The idea of "return" (*fu* 復 or *gui* 歸) that is characteristic of the *Zhouyi cantong qi* is also found in the *Cantong qi* (Yanagida Seizan 1974 and Robson 1995). One line in Shitou's poem reads, for example, "The four elements return to their natures, just as a child turns to its mother" (Suzuki Shunryū 1999, 20). While both texts contain images of returning to the mother, Shitou's use of the idea of "return" is not for the Taoist purpose of returning to the womb to create an immortal embryo, but seems to be an image used to illustrate the Chan adept's goal of returning to one's own nature and recognizing that it is inherently awakened. Shitou also borrows an image from the "Tangwen" 湯問 (Questions of Tang) chapter of the *Liezi* to express the idea of the joining of the practitioner to the Absolute (i.e., the inherently awakened mind), which is also the intended goal of the "return." The line in Shitou's poem reads, "Complying with the principle, arrow points meet." The image of two arrow points meeting is a metaphor for when two things unite in perfect agreement, just like the arrows shot by the master archers Ji Chang 紀昌 and Fei Wei 飛衛 in the anecdote of the *Liezi* (Graham 1960, 112–13).

Today, the *Cantong qi* is chanted daily in Sōtō Zen temples throughout Japan. In Japanese, the title of the alchemical *Cantong qi* is transcribed *Sandōkei*, while the title of the Buddhist *Cantong qi* is transcribed *Sandōkai*.

James ROBSON

📖 Robson 1995, 259–63; Shiina Kōyū 1981; Suzuki Shunryū 1999; Yanagida Seizan 1974

※ *Zhouyi cantong qi*; TAOISM AND CHINESE BUDDHISM

Ceshen

廁神

Spirit of the Latrine

It may be speculated that the Spirit of the Latrine was at first installed to guard a particularly unclean and thus vulnerable area of the residential complex against the intrusion of similarly unclean ghosts and demons. The earliest stories about a spirit of the latrine, which date from the fifth century, however, already give this figure a different twist: the Spirit of the Latrine is the soul of a concubine or secondary wife killed in the outhouse by a jealous principal wife. Sacrifices to the victim's spirit started out of pity or a felt need for propitiation. Various names were given to this spirit, of which the most common were: the Purple Maiden (Zigu 紫姑), the Third Damsel of the Latrine (Keng san niangniang 坑三娘娘), or Lady Qi (Qi furen 戚夫人). Being closely connected with the concerns of women through her manner of death, this deity came to be worshipped mainly by women. A household's women would assemble at the latrine on the fifteenth day of the first moon to make offerings to the goddess and to divine about the prospects of the coming year.

The manipulation of a Zigu image fashioned out of chopsticks and a winnowing basket to trace lines on the ground is generally believed to be the earliest form of Chinese spirit writing, out of which the practice of *fuji developed. Thus this humble deity is closely connected with spirit writing as a divination technique that came to play an important role in both Taoist and popular practice since the Song dynasty.

Philip CLART

📖 Jordan and Overmyer 1986, 38–39; Ma Shutian 1997, 275–82; Maspero 1981, 119–20; Zong Li and Liu Qun 1987, 418–26

※ TAOISM AND POPULAR RELIGION

Changchun zhenren xiyou ji

長春真人西遊記

Records of a Journey to the West
by the Real Man Changchun

This short narrative work (CT 1429) was written in 1228 by Li Zhichang 李志
常 (1193–1256; Qing Xitai 1994, 1: 338–40), who was *Quanzhen patriarch from
1241 to 1256. It tells about the travels of *Qiu Chuji and eighteen of his disciples
from Shandong to Inner Asia at the summons of the Mongol emperor Chinggis
khan (Taizu, r. 1206–27). A convocation in Chinese, drafted by an unknown
counselor, reached Qiu in 1219; he left Shandong for Beijing, and Beijing for
Inner Asia in 1220. The chronicle of the epic journey, during which one disciple
met his death, and the poems written by Qiu at all major moments of the
journey compose most of the narrative. The party eventually met the khan
near Samarkand in the spring of 1222 and stayed with him for nearly a year.
The khan was pleased with Qiu, entrusting him with the direction of all of
China's Taoists and granting privileges to abbeys including fiscal exemption.
The return journey, aided by the Mongols, was much faster and is described
as something of a triumphal march.

Parts of the dialogue between Qiu and Chinggis were noted down and
transmitted in the *Xuanfeng qinghui lu* 玄風慶會錄 (Accounts of Felicitous
Meetings with the Mysterious School; CT 176), dating from 1232, and fit the
traditional genre of dialogues between a sovereign and his Taoist adviser. Qiu's
advice focused not on his ascetic way, but on the emperor's own duty which is
to secure peace and prosperity for his subjects. Therefore, both Confucian and
Taoist traditions credit Qiu with saving many Chinese lives. What is certain
is that from that time onward the Quanzhen institution was able to rescue a
large number of people from the Mongol soldiers.

The *Xuanfeng qinghui lu* was probably compiled by Yelü Chucai 耶律楚
材 (1189–1243), a Qitan adviser to Chinggis and one of the earliest sinicized
high-ranking officers of the Mongol emperors. Yelü, however, who returned
to Beijing shortly after Qiu, also wrote his own record of his travels to the
West, the *Xiyou lu* 西遊錄 (Account of a Journey to the West; 1229), which
is mostly a polemical account of his acquaintance with the Quanzhen patriarch. A staunch Buddhist aristocrat, Yelü came to dislike Qiu's manners, and
his *ad hominem* attack was exploited by later Buddhist polemicists against the
Quanzhen organization.

The *Xiyou ji* is one of the few Quanzhen works to have been widely edited outside the Taoist Canon during the Ming and the Qing periods. It has been repeatedly studied by Chinese and foreign scholars mainly for its information on historical geography and for its status as a "medieval travelogue." One should not neglect, however, Wang Guowei's 王國維 (1877–1927; IC 868–71) rich commentary, which examines its religious and social background.

Vincent GOOSSAERT

📖 Boltz J. M. 1987a, 66–67, 159–60; de Rachewiltz 1962a; de Rachewiltz 1962b; Waley 1931 (part. trans.); Wang Guowei 1926; Yao Tao-chung 1986

※ Qiu Chuji; Quanzhen; TAOISM AND CHINESE LITERATURE

Changsheng dadi

長生大帝

Great Emperor of Long Life

The full name of this god is Gaoshang Shenxiao Yuqing changsheng dadi 高上神霄玉清長生大帝 (Great Emperor of Long Life of the Jade Clarity in the Most Exalted Divine Empyrean). He is the first in the group of Nine Monarchs (*jiuchen* 九宸) belonging to the pantheon of the *Shenxiao school. (The other monarchs are Qinghua dadi 青華大帝, Puhua dadi 普化大帝, Leizu dadi 雷祖大帝, Taiyi dadi 太乙大帝, Dongyuan dadi 洞淵大帝, Liubo dadi 六波大帝, Kehan dadi 可韓大帝, and Caifang dadi 採訪大帝.) In Song texts associated with the Shenxiao rites, Changsheng dadi is identified with Song Huizong (r. 1100–1125).

Caroline GYSS

📖 Strickmann 1978b, 340–41

※ Shenxiao

chanhui

懺悔

repentance; confession

Chanhui literally means "repenting wrongdoing and begging forgiveness." The term, which is also used in Buddhism, derives from Sanskrit *kṣamayati*, meaning to seek forbearance for one's errors. Rites had existed in China since early times to cure disease through confession of one's misdeeds, but emphasis on repentance grew with the expansion of Buddhism. The relevant Taoist rites were influenced by the corresponding Buddhist ones, in which the Buddhas and bodhisattvas of the ten directions were invited to the ritual site, *sūtras* were intoned, one's wrongdoings were named, and a vow was taken to act according to the teachings.

Around the fifth century, the idea developed in the *Lingbao *zhai (Retreat) rituals that atonement through physical ascesis could afford salvation for both oneself and one's ancestors. An example is contained in the chapter on the Yellow Register Retreat (*huanglu zhai) of the *Wushang biyao (Supreme Secret Essentials, *j.* 54; Lagerwey 1981b, 143–45), which describes how to ask the Celestial Worthies (*tianzun* 天尊) of the ten directions to pardon the spirits suffering in the underworld. Significantly, the text indicates that one should perform multiple prostrations. The practice of repentance by performing thousands of prostrations continued in later times. According to *j.* 24 of Zhou Side's 周思得 (1359–1451) *Shangqing lingbao jidu dacheng jinshu* 上清靈寶濟度大成金書 (Golden Writings on the Great Achievement of Deliverance by the Numinous Treasure of Highest Clarity; in *Zangwai daoshu), people commit various kinds of wrongs, and receive retribution for them in the underworld. To release the bonds of this wrongdoing, repentance is performed in every direction.

In present-day Taiwan, during the rite of the Land of the Way (*daochang), homage is first paid to the ten directions; then repentance is conducted simultaneously for both the person who has commissioned the ritual and the high priest (*gaogong* 高功; see *daozhang).

MARUYAMA Hiroshi

📖 Ōfuchi Ninji 1983, 227–28, 277

※ *Chaotian baochan*

Chaotian baochan

朝天寶懺

Precious Penances in Homage to Heaven

This large collection of rituals was probably compiled by Jiang Zongying 蔣
宗瑛 (?–1281) and is still used in Taiwan during Taoist rituals. The version
included in the Taoist Canon is entitled *Chaotian xiezui dachan* 朝天謝罪大
懺 (Great Penances to Apologize for Faults in Homage to Heaven; CT 189). It
consists of ten *juan*, corresponding to each of the ten directions to which the
practitioner does penance. In the text, Yuanshi shangdi 元始上帝 (Highest
Emperor of Original Commencement, i.e., Yuanshi tianzun 元始天尊; see
*sanqing) sits on his jewelled throne in the Heaven of Jade Clarity (Yuqing tian
玉清天) within the Great Canopy Heaven (*Daluo tian). He summons the
immortals, including the Real Man of Jade Clarity (Yuqing zhenren 玉清真
人), the Real Man of the Golden Flower (Jinhua zhenren 金華真人), and the
Real Man of Wondrous Deeds (Miaoxing zhenren 妙行真人), and discourses
on the wonderful law of the Authentic One (Zhenyi 真一). With great power
he emits a pervading radiance that illuminates the state of all the causes and
conditions that give rise to good and evil in the boundless realms everywhere,
and explains to living beings about good and evil actions in former lives, and
the cycle of rewards and retribution that spans the past, present, and future.
As Yuanshi shangdi answers the questions of the Real Men on either side of
him, there are repeated descriptions of those in the underworld suffering as
retribution for their wrongdoings. When disaster and ill luck occur as a result
of causal retribution, the text maintains that good fortune may be achieved
through arousing good thoughts, reciting the text, and repenting and correcting errors. One should offer penitence to various deities and pray to be
"released from the three lowest states of existence" (1.10b–11a). In this way,
homage should be paid to the many Celestial Worthies and the deities of the
three realms.

In content, the *Chaotian baochan* has its origins in *Lingbao *zhai (Retreat)
texts of the Six Dynasties relating to penitential rites for the ten directions. In
form, it often imitates Buddhist *sūtras* of the Tang and Song periods. While
the Buddhist influence is obvious, however, there are also elements characteristic of Taoism. For example, the deities Feitian shenwang 飛天神王 (Divine
King Who Flies in Heaven) and Shan'e tongzi 善惡童子 (Lad of Good and
Evil) are said to tour the human world recording instances of good and evil

and then reporting back to the celestial deities. The text also states that spirit officials (*lingguan* 靈官) living in palaces within the natural world check that there have been no mistakes in their reports (CT 189, 1.1b).

MARUYAMA Hiroshi

📖 Liu Zhiwan 1983–84, 667–70

※ *chanhui; jiao; zhai*

Chaotian gong

朝天宮

Palace in Homage to Heaven (Beijing)

The Chaotian gong of Beijing was a famous Taoist temple that no longer exists today. It was located in the western district, north of Inner Fucheng Gate Avenue (Fucheng mennei dajie 阜成門內大街), south of West Ping'anli Avenue (Xi Ping'anli dajie 西平安里大街), east of the Fusui 福綏 neighborhood and west of the Lion Palace (Shizi fu 獅子府). The surrounding walls reached a length of several *li*.

Originally, during the Yuan dynasty, the temple was the palace of the Celestial Master (*tianshi). In 1432, the Xuande Emperor (r. 1426–35) decreed to rebuild it on the model the identically named temple in Nanjing. Reconstruction was completed in the following year. In 1480 the temple was renovated once again. Within the Chaotian gong were contained the Pavilion of the Three Clarities (Sanqing dian 三清殿) where ceremonies were offered to the Taoist trinity (see *sanqing), and the Pavilion of Pervading Light (Tongming dian 通明殿) where ceremonies were offered to the Jade Sovereign (*Yuhuang). Several additional pavilions were dedicated to other divinities. In 1626, the entire Chaotian gong was destroyed in a great fire. In more than three hundred years since that day, it has not been possible to rebuild its structures. Today, housing has been constructed over the foundations of the former temple.

CHEN Yaoting

📖 Qing Xitai 1994, 4: 237–38

※ TEMPLES AND SHRINES

Chen Jingyuan

陳景元

?–1094; *zi*: Taixu 太虛; *hao*: Bixu zi 碧虛子
(Master of Jasper Emptiness)

A premier exegete of Taoist writings in the Northern Song, Chen Jingyuan grew up in a Nancheng 南城 (Jiangxi) scholarly family. His commentaries on important Taoist scriptures benefited from his access to rare texts and masters at various religious centers, both in south China and in the court of Song Shenzong (r. 1067–85), where his renown peaked.

In 1024 Chen reportedly studied with Han Zhizhi 韓知止 and became a Taoist priest in 1025. He later traveled to Mount Tiantai (*Tiantai shan, Zhejiang), where he met Zhang Wumeng 張無夢 (ca. 985–1065; Qing Xitai 1994, 1: 307–8) with whom he practiced self-cultivation, studied his secret teachings, and learned Zhang's take on the *Daode jing* and the *Zhuangzi. He later traveled in the lands between the Huai and Yangzi Rivers before entering the capital under the patronage of Wang Qi 王琪. Once in Kaifeng, in 1072 he became imperial lecturer on the *Daode jing* and *Zhuangzi* for Shenzong, who praised his simple and straightforward annotations on the *Daode jing*. Chen was well-versed in classical, Taoist, and medical writings, and many scholars visited him for his learning. The emperor later gave him the title Great Master of Reality and Tranquillity (Zhenjing dashi 真靖大師) after Chen presented the emperor with verses on the occasion of a Great Offering (*jiao) ceremony held in the capital. When Chen retired to his home territory on Mount Lu (*Lushan, northern Jiangxi), he went in the company of two officials and with a stipend. He declined an offer in 1091 to collate Taoist writings at the court of Song Zhezong (r. 1085–1100), choosing instead to continue in retirement, and passing away in 1094.

Chen's commentatorial style continued that of the Tang, as seen by his choice of the *Daode jing* and *Zhuangzi* as his interpretive foundation, but supplemented them with asides and references to *neidan ideas and practices, which later Song commentators admired. His fundamental approach integrated the "constant Way of spontaneity (*ziran)" with "eternal life through refining the form (*lianxing)" and "governing the state through non-intervention (*wuwei)."

Works. The following notes on Chen Jingyuan's literary production are based on the *Survey of Taoist Literature* by Judith M. Boltz (1987a, 203–5). One of Chen's greatest achievements is the *Duren shangpin miaojing sizhu* 度人上品妙經四注 (Four Commentaries to the Wondrous Scripture of the Upper Chapters on Salvation; CT 87), which pieces together four exegeses from the fifth to eighth century, one by Yan Dong 嚴東 (fl. ca. 485) of the Northern Qi, and three by the Tang scholars Li Shaowei 李少微 (fl. 625?), *Cheng Xuanying (fl. 631–50) and Xue Youqi 薛幽棲 (fl. 740–54), and includes Xue's preface dated 754 from Mount Heng (*Hengshan 衡山, Hunan). Chen's 1067 preface follows one credited to Song Zhenzong (r. 997–1022).

Chen's own preface (dated 1069) to his commentary on the *Liezi*, the *Chongxu zhide zhenjing shiwen* 沖虛至德真經釋文 (Exegesis of the Authentic Scripture on the Ultimate Virtue of Unfathomable Emptiness; CT 733), states how he compiled the glosses of Yin Jingshun 殷敬順, a Tang official in Dangtu 當塗 (Anhui), from a worm-eaten manuscript found at Mount Tiantai copied out by Xu Lingfu 徐靈府 around 800, another of Xu's manuscripts, and a printed edition from the Imperial Academy.

The *Nanhua zhenjing zhangju yinyi* 南華真經章句音義 (Phonetic and Semantic Glosses to the Sections and Sentences of the *Nanhua zhenjing*; CT 736), completed by Chen in 1084, was based on his close comparison of nine *Zhuangzi* editions. A supplement (*Nanhua zhenjing zhangju yushi* 南華真經章句餘事; CT 737) includes a detailed table of contents and a section entitled "Zhuangzi quewu" 莊子闕誤 (Lacunae and Mistakes in the *Zhuangzi*).

Chen's *Daode zhenjing zangshi zuanwei pian* 道德真經藏室纂微篇 (Folios on the Subtleties Assembled from the Archives of the Authentic Scripture of the Dao and Its Virtue; CT 714) has a 1258 preface by Yang Zhonggeng 楊仲庚 that claims that Chen was a disciple of Zhang Wumeng and thus ties him to tenth-century masters of *neidan*.

In an undated preface to his *Shangqing dadong zhenjing yujue yinyi* 上清大洞真經玉訣音義 (Phonetic and Semantic Glosses on the Jade Instructions of the Authentic Scripture of the Great Cavern of the Highest Clarity; CT 104), Chen details how he gathered old manuscripts of the text after retiring to Mount Mao (*Maoshan, Jiangsu). Of particular note are the versions by two earlier Taoists of the Northern Song, *Zhu Ziying and Huangfu Xi 皇甫希, which complemented his fuller reliance on major philological classics such as the *Shuowen jiezi* 說文解字 (Explanations of the Signs and Explications of the Graphs; 100 CE) and the now-lost 100-*juan* *Yiqie daojing yinyi* (Complete Taoist Scriptures, with Phonetic and Semantic Glosses) complied by Shi Chongxuan 史崇玄 (or Shi Chong 史崇, ?–713).

Chen's *Xisheng jing jizhu* 西升經集注 (Collected Commentaries to the Scripture of Western Ascension; CT 726) assembled five earlier commentaries. Although grounded in Chen's interpretation based on his view of the *Zhuangzi*, it is divided into thirty-nine sections as the *Dadong zhenjing* (Authentic Scripture of the Great Cavern). He adds his own notes to those of Wei Jie 韋節 (497–559), Xu Miao 徐邈 (or Daomiao 道邈; fl. ca. 630), Chongxuan zi 沖玄子 (Master of the Unfathomable Mystery; fl. ca. 650), *Li Rong (fl. 658–63), and Liu Renhui 劉仁會 (fl. ca. 800).

It is regrettable that Chen's massive *Gaoshi zhuan* 高士傳 (Biographies of Eminent Gentlemen; 100 j.) and his *Collected Works* (*Wenji* 文集, 10 j.) are no longer extant.

Chen's exegeses were eagerly read by some Southern Song promoters of *neidan* interpretations of the *Daode jing* such as Xue Zhixuan 薛致玄 (?–1271) and seem to have prompted another literatus interested in inner alchemy, Fang Bixu 方碧虛, to assume Chen's own nickname and to further expand the scriptural foundations of inner alchemy.

Lowell SKAR

📖 Boltz J. M. 1987a, 203–5; Kohn 1991a, 23–30; Qing Xitai 1988–95, 2: 722–34; Qing Xitai 1994, 1: 309–11 and 2: 104–6

Chen Minggui

陳銘珪

1824–81; *zi*: Jingyu 京渝; *hao*: Youshan 友冊 (Friend of Loneliness), Sulao dongzhu 酥醪洞主 (Owner of the Cavern of the Essence of Milk); also known as Chen Jiaoyou 陳教友

Chen Minggui is one of the few famous *Quanzhen masters of the late imperial period. The main reason for his distinction, however, does not lie with his religious teachings but with his historiographic work on the Quanzhen order, the *Changchun daojiao yuanliu* 長春道教源流 (Origins and Development of the Taoist Teaching of [Qiu] Changchun; Yan Yiping 1974, vol. 2). His critical approach is remarkable for someone writing from within the tradition: to compile his insightful synthesis, Chen perused an impressive number of epigraphic sources, including rubbings, literary anthologies, historical works, and Taoist texts. In his view, the early Quanzhen masters were very much like himself, scholars skeptical about the avenues of civil service, concerned about the preservation of Chinese traditional society, and perfectly at home with the more spiritual aspects of Taoism.

Chen, who came from the Guangdong province, passed the district examinations for government service on the secondary list (*fugong* 副貢) in 1852. He first made himself famous leading a self-defense militia in his hometown during local rebellions in 1854. Already a mature man, he became a *Long-men Taoist at the Sulao guan 酥醪觀 (Abbey of the Essence of Milk) in the Luofu Mountains (*Luofu shan) near Guangzhou (Canton). Sometime after 1865, he was chosen as the abbot of that monastery, which he had helped to rebuild along with the other six monasteries located in the Luofu Mountains, after the havoc caused by the rebellions. The Sulao guan had been the center of Longmen activity in that prestigious Taoist mountain range since the early eighteenth century. The story of these communities is best described in a gaz-etteer, the *Fushan zhi* 浮山志 (Monograph of the Luofu Mountains), to which Chen himself contributed substantially. Although Chen's extant works and the very few available biographical elements tend to portray him as a Confu-cian hermit, he also took seriously his liturgical responsibilities. The Sulao guan was famous during this period for the attention its community paid to monastic rules, and Chen's successors edited a new version of the standard Longmen monastic rules under the title *Xuanmen bidu* 玄門必讀 (Required Reading for the School of Mysteries).

Chen's life was a rare example of the involvement of a member of the scholarly elite in Taoism at a time when the links between the two were being completely severed. Chen was also renowned as a poet, painter and calligra-pher. An anthology of his poems, the *Lizhuang shicun* 荔莊詩存 (Remaining Verses from the Lichee Estate; 1858), is still extant. His son, Chen Botao 陳伯陶, had an honorable career and cultivated a friendship with the great scholar Miao Quansun 繆筌孫 (1844–1919), whose research on *EPIGRAPHY and Yuan history contributed much to our knowledge of Quanzhen history.

Vincent GOOSSAERT

📖 Tsui 1991

※ Longmen; Quanzhen

Chen Nan

陳楠

?–1213; *zi*: Nanmu 南木; *hao*: Cuixu weng 翠虛翁 (Gentleman of Emerald Emptiness), Niwan xiansheng 泥丸先生 (Elder of the Muddy Pellet)

Chen Nan, the fourth patriarch of the Southern Lineage (*Nanzong) of *neidan, was a native of Huizhou 惠州 (Guangdong). He was known for his combina-tion of alchemical practices and healing techniques: his biography in the *Lishi *zhenxian tidao tongjian* (49.14b–16b) recounts that he cured illnesses with pills made of "talismanic water" (*fushui* 符水) and mud, whence comes his *hao* Niwan (Muddy Pellet, also a name of the upper *dantian*, see *niwan).

Chen received instruction on inner alchemy from *Xue Daoguang, and on the Thunder Rites (*leifa*) from an immortal on Mount Limu (Limu shan 黎 姥山), on the outskirts of Qiongzhou 瓊州 in Hainan. Qiongzhou is believed to be the birthplace of *Bai Yuchan, the most illustrious of Chen's disciples. In his preface to the *Leiting aozhi* 雷霆奧旨 (Arcane Purport of the Thunder-clap), found in the *Daofa huiyuan* (Corpus of Taoist Ritual, *j.* 76), Bai claims to have received that text from Chen in 1212 in the Luofu Mountains (*Luofu shan, Guangdong). Elsewhere in the *Daofa huiyuan* (108.15a–16b), Bai Yuchan reiterates that Chen received the Thunder Rites of the *Jingxiao leishu* 景霄雷 書 (Thunder Writ of the Effulgent Empyrean) in 1208, and transmitted them to him four years later.

The only independent work by Chen Nan is the *Cuixu pian* 翠虛篇 (Folios of the Master of Emerald Emptiness; CT 1090), a collection of prose and poems in the *Wuzhen pian* tradition compiled by Wang Sicheng 王思誠 before 1217. The first two poems, entitled "Ziting jing" 紫庭經 (Scripture of the Purple Court) and "Dadao ge" 大道歌 (Song of the Great Dao), are followed by the "Luofu Cuixu yin" 羅浮翠虛吟 (Chant by the Master of Emerald Emptiness of the Luofu Mountains), dedicated to Bai Yuchan and dated 1212. After a prose essay entitled "Danji guiyi lun" 丹基歸一論 (Essay on the Foundation of the Elixir and on Returning to the One), the collection continues with three lyrics in honor of Chen Nan's main disciples—Ju Jiusi 鞠九思, Sha Daozhao 沙道 昭, and Bai Yuchan—and ends with the "Jindan shijue" 金丹詩訣 (Instructions in Verse on the Golden Elixir), a poem in one hundred heptasyllabic verses.

The *Xiuzhen shishu* (Ten Books on the Cultivation of Perfection, *j.* 17) includes some poems from the *Cuixu pian*, but wrongly attributes the text to Chen Pu 陳朴 (see also *Chen xiansheng neidan jue* 陳先生內丹訣, CT 1096). The authorship of the *Cuixu pian* was disputed by *Yu Yan, who believed it to be a fabrication by Bai Yuchan (*Xishang futan* 席上腐談, Baoyan tang ed., 2.2b).

Farzeen BALDRIAN-HUSSEIN

📖 Boltz J. M. 1987a, 175; Chen Bing 1985, 37–38; van der Loon 1979, 402

※ *neidan*; Nanzong

Chen Shaowei

陳少微

fl. 712/741; *zi*: Ziming 子明; *hao*: Hengyue zhenren 衡嶽真人
(Real Man of the Heng Peak)

Chen Shaowei, who was active on Mount Heng (*Hengshan 衡山, Hunan)
in the early eighth century, claimed descent from the spiritual legacy of *Xu
Xun. He is known for two *waidan* texts, the *Xiufu lingsha miaojue* 修伏靈砂
妙訣 (Wondrous Instructions on Fixing Cinnabar; CT 890) and the *Jiuhuan
jindan miaojue* 九還金丹妙訣 (Wondrous Instructions on the Golden Elixir
of the Nine Reversions; CT 891). The two texts originally formed a single
treatise that contained instructions on the *Dadong lian zhenbao jing* 大洞鍊真
寶經 (Scripture of the Great Cavern on Refining the Real Treasure), a title that
is also attributed to Chen Shaowei in two Song bibliographies (van der Loon
1984, 78). The use of place names and the expression *tianyuan* 天元 (CT 890,
preface, 1a), which probably refers to the whole extent of the Xiantian (712–13)
and the Kaiyuan (713–41) reign periods, suggest the work was composed in
the first decades of the eighth century. The inclusion of both texts in reverse
order in the *Yunji qiqian* (j. 69 and 68.9a–25a) shows that the original treatise
had already circulated in two parts by the eleventh century.

Chen Shaowei's works contain the most elaborate description of an alchemical method based on cinnabar in the extant *waidan* corpus. The first text is
introduced with a lengthy account of the formation, varieties, and symbolism
of cinnabar, followed by a method for its refinement in seven cycles. Each
cycle consists of the treatment of the product of the previous stage, and concludes with the production of "gold" (*jin* 金) that can be ingested or used as
the main ingredient in the next cycle. In the second text, the final product of
the previous seven cycles, now defined as "mercury" (*hong* 汞), serves as the
main ingredient for the preparation of a *huandan (Reverted Elixir).

A shorter version of the first text, submitted to the throne by Zhang Guo 張果
(see *Zhang Guolao) in 734, is found in the *Dashen dansha zhenyao jue* 大神丹砂真要
訣 (Authentic Essential Instructions on the Great Divine Cinnabar; CT 896).

Fabrizio PREGADIO

📖 Meng Naichang 1993a, 71–74; Needham 1976, 141–43; Sivin 1980, 237–40 and
270–74

※ *waidan*

Chen Tuan

陳摶

ca. 920–89; *zi*: Tunan 圖南; *hao*: Fuyao zi 扶搖子 (Master of the
Whirlwind), Baiyun xiansheng 白雲先生 (Elder of the White
Clouds), Xiyi xiansheng 希夷先生 (Elder of the Inaudible and
Invisible)

Chen Tuan was an important Taoist master, thinker, and fortune-teller who
lived in the tenth century and became the legitimizing saint of the Song
dynasty. His life and legend are described below under three headings: solid
historical facts known about him, the classical Taoist story of his life, and his
posthumous associations and activities.

Historical facts. There are six solid facts known about Chen Tuan, all gleaned
from a variety of sources and not found together in any one text, neither in
the devotional literature, nor in the collections of miscellaneous notes, or *biji*
筆記, of the literati, and most surely not in the official history of the Song
dynasty (*Songshi* 457; trans. Kohn 1990c).

In 937, as shown in the *Danyuan ji* 丹淵記 (Records of Cinnabar Well; 1051),
Chen Tuan leaves an inscription at the Tianqing guan 天慶觀 (Abbey of Celestial Blessings) in Qiongzhou 邛州 (Sichuan), praising the *qi*-control methods
of the local masters. This either places him in an itinerant phase of his career
or makes him a local Sichuan monk, depending on whether one believes the
overwhelming majority of sources that claim he came from Henan (close to
Laozi's birthplace), or relies on research by the Sichuan scholar Li Yuanguo
(1985b) who finds much evidence for a southwestern origin of the master.

Next, sometime around the 940s, as most sources agree, Chen settles on
Mount Hua (*Huashan, Shaanxi), where he restores the Yuntai guan 雲臺觀
(Abbey of the Cloud Terrace) and its smaller cloister Yuquan yuan 玉泉院
(Cloister of the Jade Spring) which had fallen into disrepair in the late Tang.
These two places become his main residence until his death. They remain
to the present day closely associated with him, especially the Yuquan yuan,
which is located right at the mouth of the mountain gorges and still functions
partly as a Taoist temple. It also has a tall (and very recent) stele devoted to
Chen Tuan in its Taoist section, the other part now serving as a preschool.
The main railway to Xi'an, which runs right through it, has brought the place
right into the midst of the modern world.

Third, near the end of the Five Dynasties, Chen Tuan composes a work on physiognomy (*xiangshu* 相術), the *Fengjian* 風鑑 (Mirror of Auras; Kohn 1988), which becomes a classic in the field. His physiognomic and *qi*-control powers become the basis for all his later legends, but only a few specialized texts, such as Song Qiqiu's 宋齊丘 *Yuguan zhaoshen ju* 玉管照神局 (Jade Office Instructions on How to Clarify Spirit; Five Dynasties) and the Ming handbook *Shenxiang quanbian* 神象全編 (Complete Guide to Spirit Physiognomy; ca. 1400), retain this information.

The last three facts again are recorded in all major sources on Chen Tuan but are also closely corroborated by official documents. First, in 956, Chen meets Shizong, ruler of the Later Zhou (r. 954–59), whose questions about alchemical methods of fund-raising he answers with spiritual advice. Then, in 984 he meets Song Taizong (r. 976–97) and is awarded the title Elder of the White Clouds, together with various material gifts. This meeting serves to make him the legitimizing saint of the new dynasty. Third, and last, Chen dies on Mount Hua in 989. Legend has it that he is 118 years old at the time, which would place his birth in the 870s. Given the other data, however, a birth date of around 920 is more likely.

In addition, it can be accepted as historically accurate that Chen Tuan during the period from the 960s to the 980s met several high Song officials, including Qian Ruoshui 錢若水 (960–1003), Zhang Yong 張詠 (946–1015; SB 48–50), and Chong Fang 种放 (956–1015; SB 297–301); he read their fortunes and gave them career advice, which they mostly did not follow. His *Yijing* studies, too, although not well documented in early or historical sources, hover on the borderline of history, often being cited in Neo-Confucian and other works as the roots of Zhou Dunyi's 周敦頤 (1017–73; SB 277–81) famous *Taiji tu* (Diagram of the Great Ultimate; Li Yuanguo 1990).

Legendary accounts. The legend of Chen Tuan adds several elements to this historical skeleton: a wondrous encounter with a star lady as a child; special mnemonic skills; a failed imperial examination at the capital and a period of Taoist training at Mount Wudang (*Wudang shan, Hubei) in the 920s; a magical transfer by dragon convoy to Mount Hua; a wonderful talent to enter a deep trance known as "sleep" (*shuigong* 睡功), often for months; various chance encounters with the future Song emperors whose imperial quality he immediately recognizes (once even being so shocked that he falls off his donkey); a successful physiognomic examination of Taizong's sons, when he spots the future Zhenzong (r. 997–1022) as Taizong's heir; and a detailed foreknowledge of and successful preparation for his death, now known as his "transformation." In addition, various episodes on Chen Tuan are borrowed from the legends of other saints, including Buddhist monks, and in the Taoist tradition he is linked with *Lü Dongbin, whom he allegedly encounters in person. The sources on the legend are exceedingly numerous, mostly found in *biji* literature, with the best and most extensive collection available in the *Lishi zhenxian tidao tongjian* (47.1a–14b), and a literary expansion in the *Taihua Xiyi zhi* 太華希夷志 (Monograph of [the Elder of] the Inaudible and Invisible of Mount Hua; 1314; CT 306).

Posthumous associations and activities. In the centuries following his death, Chen Tuan is linked with several different traditions and appears in various roles. First, he is a hero in Yuan drama, where he stars in *Sanxing zhao* 三星照 (Three Stars Are Shining), *Bieyou tian* 別有天 (Yet Another World), *Pantao hui* 蟠桃會 (The Peach Festival), and most importantly *Chen Tuan gaowo* 陳摶高臥 (The Lofty Sleep of Chen Tuan). Next, he appears as a master of *neidan* meditation and especially the "sleep" technique, which adepts used to circulate the energies in their bodies while lying on their backs. Twelve so-called "sleep practices" of Chen Tuan are recorded in the Ming handbook *Chifeng sui* (trans. Despeux 1988, 225–69; Teri Takehiro 1990; Kohn 1993b, 272–76). This strand of Chen Tuan's lore depicting him as a master of energy practices is still active today, and he appears as a *qigong* master in contemporary works.

In a completely different posthumous strand of Chen Tuan's history, he takes the form of a prognosticating planchette spirit (see *fuji*) who appears in the Chan community on Mount Huangbo (Huangbo shan 黃檗山, Fujian) and is transferred to Japan along with Yinyuan 隱元 (Jp.: Ingen, 1592–1673, the founder of the Ōbaku 黃檗 lineage of Zen Buddhism) in the seventeenth century. Definitely identified as Chen Tuan of the Song, he is venerated as a particularly powerful spirit and adopted successfully into a Buddhist environment, even changing his name to Chen Bo 陳博 (Chen, the Incense-Burner) and his appellation to Wuyan 無煙 (No-Smoke), signifying the complete extinction of all desires rather than the quest for immortality indicated by his Taoist, *Zhuangzi*-inspired names.

Livia KOHN

📖 Knaul 1981; Kohn 1990a; Li Yuanguo 1985b; Li Yuanguo 1985c; Qing Xitai 1988–95, 2: 670–708; Russell 1990a; Russell 1990b

※ *Taiji tu*; TAOISM AND NEO-CONFUCIANISM

Chen Xianwei

陳顯微

fl. 1223–54; *zi*: Zongdao 宗道; *hao*: Baoyi zi 抱一子
(Master Who Embraces The One)

Chen Xianwei, who came from Yangzhou 揚州 (Jiangsu), was a *daoshi* at the Yousheng guan 佑聖觀 (Abbey of the Helping Saint) in Lin'an 臨安 (Zhejiang). He is best known for a *neidan* commentary to the *Zhouyi cantong qi* entitled *Zhouyi cantong qi jie* 周易參同契解 (Explication of the *Zhouyi cantong qi*; CT 1007). The few available details about his life are found in a preface to this work contributed by his lay disciple Zheng Boqian 鄭伯謙, a teacher in the Prefectural School of Quzhou 衢州 (Zhejiang) who is also known for an extant commentary to the *Zhouli* 周禮 (Rites of the Zhou). According to this preface, Chen first received alchemical teachings in 1223; he obtained the transmission of the *Cantong qi* shortly thereafter and devoted several years of retirement to its study.

The *Cantong qi jie*, which bears (in some of its editions) an author's preface dated 1234 and was printed in the same year, is based on the text of the *Cantong qi* established by *Peng Xiao. Some variants suggest that Chen Xianwei was also familiar with the commentary ascribed to *Yin Changsheng (*Zhouyi cantong qi*; CT 999) and with Zhu Xi's 朱熹 (1130–1200) *Zhouyi cantong qi kaoyi* (Critical Investigation of the *Zhouyi cantong qi*). The commentary was printed by Wang Yi 王夷, another lay disciple who also subsidized the publication of Chen Xianwei's commentary to the *Guanyin zi* 關尹子 (Book of Master Guanyin). In all the received editions, Wang Yi's postface follows another colophon, dated 1245, written by a follower from Tiantai 天臺 (Zhejiang) who had received the *Cantong qi jie* from Chen Xianwei. It is unlikely that either this follower or Wang Yi is the author of the section entitled "Cantong qi zhaiwei" 參同契摘微 ("Pointing out the Subtleties of the *Cantong qi*"). Along with those by Peng Xiao and Chu Yong 儲泳 (fl. ca. 1230), this section, containing notes on the portion of text corresponding to part of *zhang* 36 and the whole *zhang* 37 in Peng Xiao's recension, criticizes the interpretation given by Chen Xianwei himself.

The *Daozang* contains two other texts by Chen Xianwei: the commentary to the *Guanyin zi*, entitled *Wenshi zhenjing yanwai zhi* 文始真經言外旨 (Purport Beyond Words of the Authentic Scripture of Master Wenshi; CT 728), which was completed and printed in 1254, and an undated edition of the *Shenxian yangsheng bishu* 神仙養生祕術 (Secret Arts of the Divine Immortals for Nourishing Life; CT 948), consisting of a collection of *waidan* methods and herbal recipes. Zheng Boqian mentions three other works, all of which are lost: the *Lisheng pian* 立聖篇 (Folios on Establishing Sainthood), the *Xianwei zhiyan* 顯微卮言 (Words Streaming from the Heart of [Chen] Xianwei), and the *Baoyi zi shu* 抱一子書 (Writings of the Master Who Embraces The One).

Fabrizio PREGADIO

※ *neidan*

Chen Yingning

陳攖寧

1880–1969; *zi*: Zixiu 子修

Chen Yingning was born in Huaining 懷寧 (Anhui) into a middle-class family. After graduating at the end of the Qing dynasty, at the age of twenty-five he entered the Anhui Institute of Legal and Political Studies (Anhui zhengfa xuetang 安徽政法學堂). His feeble and unhealthy constitution, however, led him to develop an interest in medicine and longevity techniques. From the age of twenty-eight, he began to travel to mountains looking for Buddhist and, later, Taoist masters. After spending three years at the Baiyun guan 白雲觀 (Abbey of the White Clouds) in Shanghai to study Taoist texts, he became a physician. From 1933 to 1937 he published a bimonthly magazine, *Yangshan kan* 揚善刊 (Journal for the Promotion of Goodness), and from 1939 to 1941 a monthly magazine, *Xianxue* 仙學 (Studies on Immortality). In 1957 he was elected secretary and vice president of the Chinese Taoist Association (*Zhongguo daojiao xiehui), and in 1961 he became its president.

A specialist of *waidan and *neidan, Chen Yingning wrote several well-known works, including a commentary to the *Huangting jing (Scripture of the Yellow Court), a commentary to poems attributed to *Sun Bu'er (matriarch of the *Quanzhen school), and a history of Taoism. Selections from his works and his correspondence with disciples, especially female, are collected in *Zhonghua xianxue* 中華仙學 (Chinese Studies on Immortality; Xu Boying and Yuan Jiegui 1976).

Catherine DESPEUX

📖 Li Yangzheng 2000, 200–205 and passim; Qing Xitai 1988–95, 4: 375–415; Qing Xitai 1994, 1: 403–4

※ *neidan*; Zhongguo daojiao xiehui; TAOISM IN THE PEOPLE'S REPUBLIC OF CHINA

Chen Zhixu

陳致虛

1289–after 1335; *zi*: Guanwu 觀吾; *hao*: Shangyang zi 上陽子
(Master of Highest Yang), Luling daoshi 廬陵道士
(Taoist Master of Luling)

Although Chen Zhixu is one of the main representatives of the *neidan tradition, almost nothing is known of his life, except that he was born in Luling 廬
陵 (Jiangxi) and that he received teachings first in 1329 from Zhao Youqin 趙
友欽 in Hunan, and some time later from an anonymous master of Mount
Qingcheng (*Qingcheng shan, Sichuan). Four of his works are extant:

1. *Duren shangpin miaojing zhu* 度人上品妙經注 (Commentary to the
   Wondrous Scripture of the Upper Chapters on Salvation; CT 91; 1336).

2. A commentary to the *Wuzhen pian* (Folios on Awakening to Reality),
   incorporated into the *Wuzhen pian sanzhu* 悟真篇三注 (Three Commentaries to the *Wuzhen pian*; CT 142).

3. *Jindan dayao* 金丹大要 (Great Essentials of the Golden Elixir; CT 1067;
   1335), with three appendixes separately printed in the Taoist Canon: *Jindan
   dayao tu* 金丹大要圖 (Diagrams; CT 1068), containing illustrations with
   explications; *Jindan dayao liexian zhi* 金丹大要列仙誌 (Biographies of
   Exemplary Immortals; CT 1069), composed of notes on sixteen *Quanzhen deities, immortals, and masters who reportedly transmitted *neidan*,
   from Donghua dijun 東華帝君 (Imperial Lord of Eastern Florescence)
   to Zhao Youqin; and *Jindan dayao xianpai* 金丹大要仙派 (Lineage of the
   Immortals; CT 1070), divided into two parts: a doctrinal genealogy of
   neidan (thirty-four names from Laozi to Chen Zhixu) and a description of
   a rite performed in honor of *Zhongli Quan and *Lü Dongbin on their
   birthdays.

4. *Zhouyi cantong qi fenzhang zhu* 周易參同契分章注 (Commentary to the
   Zhouyi cantong qi, with a Division into Sections). This work is not included
   in the Taoist Canon but is available in more than fifteen editions, including
   those of the *Jindan zhengli daquan* 金丹正理大全 (Great Compendium
   on the Correct Principles of the Golden Elixir; 1538; see Davis and Chao
   1940a), the *Siku quanshu* 四庫全書 (1782), and the *Daozang jiyao* (1906,
   vol. 11). Chen's recension of the *Cantong qi* is one of the best available, and
   in the early sixteenth century served as the basis of the so-called "ancient
   text" version of this scripture (see *Guwen Zhouyi cantong qi*).

Besides the above works, Chen also wrote lost commentaries to the *Daode jing* and the *Vajracchedikā-sūtra* (Diamond Sūtra).

Echoing his older contemporary, *Li Daochun, and anticipating some *neidan* masters of the later period, especially *Liu Yiming, Chen offers a radically spiritual interpretation of *neidan*. Instead of describing physiological practices, he repeatedly states that the essence of alchemy consists in recovering the Original Pneuma (*yuanqi*) of the state "prior to Heaven" within the state "subsequent to Heaven" (see *xiantian* and *houtian*); this recovery is said to happen "in one instant" (*qingke* 頃刻). While the main doctrinal foundation reflected in his works is the *Nanzong legacy (represented, in particular, by *Zhang Boduan and *Bai Yuchan), his discourse exemplifies the *neidan* readiness to borrow relevant notions and terms from different traditions: throughout his works, he quotes the *Daode jing*, the *Zhouyi cantong qi*, the *Wuzhen pian*, and Buddhist texts. The *Daode jing*, in his view, is the ultimate source of *neidan* ("The Dao of Laozi is the Great Dao of the Golden Elixir"; *Jindan dayao*, 2.7a), but Chen also stresses the unity of the Three Teachings (Confucianism, Taoism, and Buddhism) and often juxtaposes passages from their respective sources to show their ultimate identity according to the *neidan* way of seeing. Chen states that he received the doctrine of the unity of the Three Teachings from Zhao Youqin, whose *Xian Fo tongyuan* 仙佛同源 (The Common Source of Immortals and Buddhas), sometimes indicated as lost, is available in the *Jindan zhengli daquan*.

Although Nanzong is his main doctrinal source, Chen Zhixu describes his lineage as a branch of Quanzhen. According to his reconstruction, which is not based on historical fact, the Quanzhen patriarch, *Ma Yu (1123–84), passed on his teachings to *Song Defang (1183–1247), and the transmission continued with Li Jue 李珏, Zhang Mo 張模, and Zhao Youqin before reaching Chen Zhixu himself. Chen probably elaborated this lineage in recognition of the status of the Quanzhen school, which enjoyed the official protection of the court and whose Five Patriarchs had received the title of Real Lords (*zhenjun* 真君) from the Yuan ruling house two decades before Chen's birth.

Fabrizio PREGADIO

📖 Boltz J. M. 1987a, 184–86, 208; Davis and Ch'en 1942; Li Yuanguo 1988, 416–31; Qing Xitai 1994, 1: 369–71

※ *neidan*; *Jindan dayao*; Nanzong

Cheng Xuanying

成玄英

fl. 631–50; *zi*: Zishi 子實; *hao*: Xihua fashi 西華法師
(Master of the Law of the Western Florescence)

Cheng Xuanying came from Shanzhou 陝州 (Henan). He spent part of his life in retirement, but in 631 was summoned to the capital and took up residence at the Xihua guan 西華觀 (Abbey of Western Florescence). In 647 the emperor requested that he translate the *Daode jing* into Sanskrit with Xuanzang 玄奘 (ca. 602–64) and Cai Huang 蔡晃 (fl. 638–47; on this translation, see Pelliot 1912). Shortly thereafter, during the Yonghui reign period (650–55), he was exiled to Yuzhou 郁州 (Jiangsu).

Cheng wrote a lost commentary to the *Yijing and three extant commentaries to Taoist texts. One of them, consisting of an exegesis of the *Duren jing (Scripture on Salvation), is in the *Duren shangpin miaojing sizhu* 度人上品妙經四注 (Four Commentaries to the Wondrous Scripture of the Upper Chapters on Salvation; CT 87) and follows the established interpretation of this text. In the two other works, however, Cheng proves to be a leading exponent of the *Chongxuan (Twofold Mystery) school of thought. The first commentary is the *Daode jing kaiti xujue yishu* 道德經開題序訣義疏 (Topical Introduction, Prefatory Instructions, and Subcommentary to the *Scripture of the Dao and Its Virtue*; P. 2517, P. 2353, and S. 5887), which is also found in the *Daode zhenjing xuande zuanshu* 道德真經玄德纂疏 (Compilation of Commentaries on the Mysterious Virtue of the *Authentic Scripture of the Dao and Its Virtue*; CT 711). The second is a subcommentary to *Guo Xiang's exegesis to the *Zhuangzi, found in the *Nanhua zhenjing zhushu* 南華真經注疏 (Commentary and Subcommentary to the *Nanhua zhenjing*; CT 745). Read together, Cheng's commentaries to the *Daode jing*, the *Zhuangzi*, and the *Duren jing* show him to be a representative of the unity of the philosophical and religious aspects of Taoism.

Besides his explication of the *Daode jing* and the *Zhuangzi* according to Chongxuan principles, Cheng also interpreted the transformations of Laozi from the viewpoint of the Buddhist theory of the Body of the Law, the Body of Response, and the Body of Manifestation (*fashen* 法身, *yingshen* 應身, and *huashen* 化身, corresponding to Sanskrit *dharmakāya*, *sambhogakāya*, and *nirmāṇakāya*). This theory, until then generally applied only to Yuanshi tianzun 元始天尊 (Celestial Worthy of Original Commencement; see *sanqing) or to the Dao itself, explains that the body as well as the teaching of Laozi change to adapt themselves to different times and levels of understanding. The theory was also combined with three attributes ascribed to the Dao in *Daode jing* 14, namely, invisible (*yi* 夷), inaudible (*xi* 希), and imperceptible (*wei* 微). These attributes are associated in turn with the Three Primes (**sanyuan*)—three deities who live in the three Cinnabar Fields (**dantian*) and are the corporeal forms of the Three Pneumas (*sanqi* 三氣; see **santian* and *liutian*)—and with Essence, Pneuma, and Spirit (**jing, qi, shen*). Each component of the various triads is connected with the other two, and all are thought to be fundamentally and originally one. Cheng Xuanying relates this view to the doctrine of the Three Ones (**sanyi*), applying the Chongxuan dialectic of the two truths to the Three and the One, and to the Body of the Law and the Body of Response that are the single body of the Ultimate Truth. The latter has no form, and the whole world and all teachings are no more than its traces.

Isabelle ROBINET

📖 Ch'oe Chinsŏk 1995; Fujiwara Takao 1980a; Fujiwara Takao 1980b; Kohn 1991a, 192–96; Meng Wentong 1946; Ōfuchi Ninji 1978–79, 1: 236–38 (crit. notes on the Dunhuang mss.) and 2: 461–75 (reprod. of the Dunhuang mss.); Qiang Yu 1995; Qing Xitai 1988–95, 2: 174–90; Robinet 1977, 96–261; Sunayama Minoru 1980b, 245–71; Yu Shiyi 2000

※ Chongxuan

chengfu

承負

"inherited burden"

The notion of "inherited burden" refers to the liability for sins and transgressions that individuals and societies inherit from their predecessors. As fault and blame are passed from one generation to another, calamities and misfortune increase. Based on this principle, later generations must make for the sins committed by their predecessors; to do so, individuals reflect upon the existence of sin (*siguo* 思過, "considering fault"), confess it to the celestial deities (*shouguo* 首過, "admitting fault"), and correct themselves (*zize* 自責).

This idea appears for the first time in the second-century **Taiping jing* (Scripture of Great Peace). Examples of sin and transgression mentioned in this text include claiming exclusive possession of the Dao and its **de* (virtue), neglecting to study the Dao, and accumulating riches without aiding the poor. Liability for these sins is expressed at the social level as natural disasters, epidemics, social discontent, and war. These notions are based on theories about the interrelationship of Heaven and humanity, which date from at least the time of the Warring States period (403–221). Special emphasis was given to the role of emperor as the supporter of the balance between Heaven and humanity. If the emperor acted in a manner contrary to the will of Heaven, Heaven would express its blame through portents; when such portents appeared, the emperor was supposed to "consider his faults." Dong Zhongshu 董 仲舒 (ca. 195–115 BCE) strongly asserted these ideas in his political thought, and it is possible to find similarities between his writings and the *Taiping jing*.

*Ge Hong's (283–343) *Baopu zi (Book of the Master Who Embraces Simplicity) contains evidence of an idea connected with "inherited burden," namely that evil acts reduce the life spans of those who commit them and their descendants, and cause calamities. Later, merits and demerits came to be calculated in points, and from the Song period onward this practice became widespread in the form of the "ledgers of merit and demerit" (*gongguo ge* 功 過格; Brokaw 1991).

While "inherited burden" is a kind of karmic retribution, there is a fundamental difference between the notion of *chengfu* and the Buddhist notion of karma. In Buddhism, the good and evil performed by an individual in past lives is reflected in what form his or her present life takes, and good and evil behavior in the present life determines future rebirth. *Chengfu*, by contrast, not only considers the past and future lives of the individual, but also that individuals inherit the results of the good and evil of the behavior of their ancestors, and that these results accumulate not only at the individual level, but also at the social level. In this sense, "inherited burden" is based on the unit of the family and, as its extension, of society.

YAMADA Toshiaki

📖 Hendrischke 1991; Kamitsuka Yoshiko 1999, 301–37; Qing Xitai 1994, 2: 324–26; Strickmann 2002, 39–50; Tsuchiya Masaaki 2002

※ ETHICS AND MORALS

Chenghuang

城隍

God of Walls and Moats; City God

The God of Walls and Moats, more commonly known as the City God, emerged with the growth and independence of townships in late Tang and Song China. He became highly popular under the Ming and is one of the key

Fig. 25. Chenghuang (City God): New Year's print.
Collection Julian Pas. Photograph by Julian Pas.

deities of Chinese religion today. During the Ming, the Taoist establishment, in an attempt to share in the god's popularity, adopted him into the Taoist pantheon and made him a celestial executive who received orders from and reported to *Laojun. A scripture was compiled accordingly, the *Chenghuang ganying xiaozai jifu miaojing* 城隍感應消災集福妙經 (Wondrous Scripture on the Dispelling of Disasters and Accumulation of Happiness through the Impulse and Response of the City God; CT 1447), which dates to after 1376.

The text describes Laojun seated in a jeweled hall before a great heavenly assembly, and answering the questions of a Perfected called Vast Wisdom (Guanghui 廣惠) on how to alleviate human suffering, and explaining the merits and powers of the City God as bestowed by him. The text can be divided into nine sections: 1. Opening *gāthā*, a poem in praise of the City God; 2. The setting, a description of Laojun and the heavenly assembly; 3. First dialogue, question by Vast Wisdom and negative answer that describes human sinfulness; 4. Second dialogue, rephrasing of the question and description of the great power of the City God; 5. Homage to the City God, and a list of the god's representatives, assistants, and guardian helpers; 6. The god's pledge, his own vow to help everyone in need; 7. Third dialogue, proposal by Vast Wisdom to perform good actions toward the Dao and reconfirmation by Laojun; 8. Concluding *gāthā*, a poem highly lauding the City God's powers and dedication; 9. Conclusion, departure of the gods and transmission of the scripture to humanity.

Livia KOHN

  Barrett 1991a; Feuchtwang 1977; Hamashima Atsutoshi 1992; Johnson 1985b; Kohn 1996b; Little 2000b, 260–61; Maspero 1981, 105–10; Taylor R. 1977; Zito 1987; Zito 1996

※ TAOISM AND POPULAR RELIGION

Chifeng sui

赤鳳髓

Marrow of the Red Phoenix

This work is a compilation of Tang, Song, Yuan, and Ming texts. Its author, Zhou Lüjing 周履靖 (late sixteenth century), came from Jiaxing 嘉興 (Zhejiang). He held no important post, but was in touch with eminent officials of his region such as Peng Chongxi 彭沖溪 (late sixteenth century), the Minister of Justice who wrote a preface to his work in 1579, and Wang Wenlu 王文祿 (1503–86; DMB 1449–51), who wrote a postface also in 1579.

The collection includes the following texts:

1. *Taishang yuzhou liuzi jue* 太上玉軸六字訣 (Instructions on the Six Sounds [of Breathing] According to the Highest Jade Axle) by Zou Yingbo 鄒應博 (Song). This text was first included in Zou's *Yanzhan ji* 炎詹集 (Collection of Fiery Talks) and was used later by his grandnephew, the Yuan doctor Zou Xuan 鄒鉉, in the *Shouqin yanglao xinshu* 壽親養老新書 (New Writings on Fostering the Longevity and Nourishing the Old Age of One's Parents). (On the "six sounds of breathing" see the entry *liuzi jue*.)

2. *Huanzhen xiansheng fu nei yuanqi jue* 幻真先生服內元氣訣 (Instructions on the Ingestion of the Inner Original Breath According to the Elder of Illusory Perfection), based on a work found in the Taoist Canon in several versions, one of which (CT 828, and YJQQ 60.14a–27a; mid-eighth century) has the same title as the present text.

3. *Li zhenren changsheng yishiliu zi miaojue* 李真人長生一十六字妙訣 (Wondrous Instructions on [the Method of] Long Life in Sixteen Characters by the Perfected Li). These instructions are also found in *Leng Qian's (ca. 1310-ca. 1371) *Xiuling yaozhi* 修齡要旨 (Essential Purport of the Cultivation of Longevity), and are similar to those in Hu Wenhuan's 胡文煥 (late sixteenth century) *Leixiu yaojue* 類修要訣 (Essential Classified Instructions on Self-Cultivation). The identity of Perfected Li is unknown.

4. *Taixi biyao gejue* 胎息祕要歌訣 (Songs and Instructions on the Secret Essentials of Embryonic Breathing). A similar text is also found in an identically-titled work in the Taoist Canon (CT 131; trans. Huang Jane 1987–90, 1: 49–54). (On "embryonic breathing" see the entry *taixi*.)

5. *Siji yangsheng ge* 四季養生歌 (Songs on Nourishing Life According to the Four Seasons), containing selections from the *Xiuzhen shishu* (Ten Books on the Cultivation of Perfection). The first section, on the "six sounds of breathing," is attributed to *Sun Simiao (fl. 673) in the *Xiuzhen shishu* (19.7a). The next six sections, describing *daoyin movements beneficial for the five viscera (*wuzang*), come from the *Huangting wuzang liufu tu* 黃庭五臟六腑圖 (Charts of the Five Viscera and the Six Receptacles, According to the Scripture of the Inner Effulgences of the Yellow Court; *Xiuzhen shishu* 54), a text which in turn is derived from the *Huangting neijing wuzang liufu buxie tu* 黃庭內景五臟六腑補瀉圖 (Charts of the Strengthening and Weakening of the Five Viscera and the Six Receptacles, According to the Scripture of the Inner Effulgences of the Yellow Court; preface dated 848; CT 432), attributed to Hu Yin 胡愔 of Mount Taibai (Taibai shan 太白山, Shaanxi). The final section, on a *daoyin* method attributed to *Lü Dongbin, corresponds to *Xiuzhen shishu* 24.3b.

6. *Qubing yannian liuzi fa* 去病延年六字法 (Method of the Six Sounds [of Breathing] to Eliminate Diseases and Extend One's Years), also found in the *Xiuzhen shishu* (19.6a) and in Hu Wenhuan's *Leixiu yaojue*.

7. *Wuqin xi* 五禽戲 (Five Animals Pattern) attributed to Hua Tuo 華陀 (142–219). The description of the pattern given in this text radically differs from that of the *Yangxing yanming lu (On Nourishing Inner Nature and Extending Life). The *Wuqin xi* contains the first known illustrated version, and was often used in later works on *yangsheng (Nourishing Life) and *daoyin*. (On the Five Animals Pattern see the entry *daoyin*.)

8. *Baduan jin* 八段錦 (Eight Brocades), also found in the *Xiuzhen shishu* (19.4a–5b) and in *Zhu Quan's (1378–1448) *Huoren xinfa* 活人心法 (Spiritual Methods to Provide Life Energy). (On the movements of the Eight Brocades see the entry *daoyin*.)

9. Forty-six movements for circulating breath (*xingqi) and healing diseases. Twenty-seven of these are done in a sitting position, thirteen in an upright position, and six in a reclining position. The titles of the movements evoke the names of twenty-one immortals in the *Liexian zhuan (Biographies of Exemplary Immortals), the Eight Immortals (*baxian), and the sixteen immortals mentioned in the "Ascending in Flight" ("Feisheng" 飛昇) chapter of the *Xu xianzhuan (Sequel to Biographies of Immortals). They also mention other famous Taoists and *neidan adepts such as *Chen Tuan, *Liu Haichan, and *Bai Yuchan. These movements are similar to those in Luo Hongxian's 羅洪先 (1504–64; DMB 980–84) *Wanshou xianshu* 萬壽仙書 (Writings of the Immortals for Ten-Thousand-Fold Longevity). They appear again later, e.g., in the *Neigong tushuo* 內功圖說 (Illustrated Explanations of Inner Practices; late Qing), but in different versions and sometimes with different titles.

10. Twelve illustrations with poems on *neidan* techniques, each of which represents a follower of Mount Hua (*Huashan, Shaanxi) in a reclining position (Teri Takehiro 1990). In another version, these techniques are attributed to Chen Tuan who lived on Mount Hua.

Catherine DESPEUX

📖 Despeux 1988 (trans.)

※ *yangsheng*

Chisong zi

赤松子 (*or*: 赤誦子)

Master Red-Pine

According to his hagiography in the *Liexian zhuan* (Biographies of Exemplary Immortals; trans. Kaltenmark 1953, 35–42), Chisong zi was the Master of Rain (*Yushi) for the mythical emperor Shennong 神農 (Divine Husbandman), whom he taught a method for imbibing liquid jade, and also instructed the daughter of another mythical emperor, Yandi 炎帝 (Fiery Emperor). His main prowess was self-immolation. These mythemes may be remnants of ancient shamanic rites of immolation and rain making. Referring to Chisong zi's visit to the Queen Mother of the West (*Xiwang mu) on Mount *Kunlun, the hagiography represents late Han conceptualizations of successful adepts.

By the early Han, Chisong zi had become a model for *fangshi seeking to emulate his attainments. The *Huainan zi (*j*. 11 and 20) reports that he was a master of circulation of breath (*xingqi) and other breathing techniques. In the *Shiji* (Records of the Historian; 55.2047 and 2049), *Zhang Liang asks Han Gaozu (r. 202–195 BCE) leave to follow the path of Chisong zi, and he subsequently quits eating grains (see under *bigu) and begins practicing circulation of breath. Besides these two texts, several other Han sources mention Chisong zi (frequently together with *Wangzi Qiao) as an exemplary ancient master who had attained transcendence through self-cultivation. These often formulaic references, ranging from poems collected in the *Chuci* 楚辭 (Songs of Chu; trans. Hawkes 1985, 82, 116, 139) to inscriptions on Han mirrors, attest to his popularity during this period.

Taoist texts associate Chisong zi with several methods. The *Lingbao wufu xu contains herbal recipes and methods which he transmitted to *Yue Zichang (2.14a; see Yamada Toshiaki 1989b). This text also includes a narrative about Huang Chuping 黃初平 who, together with his brother Chuqi 初起, had attained transcendence on Mount Jinhua (Jinhua shan 金華山, Zhejiang) and changed his name to Chisong zi (2.13a–14a, see Campany 2002, 309–11). Mount Jinhua became a cultic center for the two brothers and Chisong zi. A related text, the *Jinhua Chisong shanzhi* 金華赤松山志 (Monograph of Mount Chisong in the Jinhua Range; CT 601) by Ni Shouyue 倪守約 (Southern Song) begins with the early legends about the two brothers and includes the texts of imperial enfeoffment dating to 1189 and 1263.

In his *Baopu zi, *Ge Hong repeatedly mentions Chisong zi as an exemplary adept. He also describes his method for an elixir based on herbal substances

(4.79) and his method for ingesting liquid jade (11.204). In other sources, Chi-song zi is associated with a method for ingesting the "five stones" (*Wushang biyao*, 87.11a–b; YJQQ 74.7b), with methods for ingesting mica (YJQQ 75.7b, 22b), and with a general discussion of the properties of minerals (YJQQ.66.13b). Ge Hong also mentions a *Chisong zi jing* 赤松子經 (Scripture of Master Red-Pine), which dealt with calculating and determining one's longevity based on a set of moral interdictions and precepts (*Baopu zi*, 6.125). This text may be related to the *Chisong zi zhong jiejing* 赤松子中誡經 (Central Scripture on Precepts by Master Red-Pine; CT 185) which is a dialogue between the Yellow Emperor (*Huangdi) and Chisong zi, explaining the causes for poverty or wealth, longevity or early death, and calamities through offenses against precepts and taboos. Not long after Ge Hong wrote his *Baopu zi*, Chisong zi was absorbed into the *Shangqing pantheon as the Perfected of the Southern Peak (Nanyue zhenren 南嶽真人) and claimed by Peijun 裴君 (Lord Pei) as his teacher (*Zhengao*, 5.5a).

A Six Dynasties compilation, the *Chisong zi zhangli* (Master Red-Pine's Almanac of Petitions), preserves dozens of petitions and discussions of early Celestial Masters (*Tianshi dao) practice. Although Chisong zi is not directly associated with these documents, the prefatory section of this text ascribes its compilation to questions regarding the proper use of petitions posed by Chisong zi to the Celestial Elder (Tianlao 天老).

Gil RAZ

  📖 Boltz J. M. 1987a, 115–17; Campany 2002, 309–11; Kaltenmark 1953, 35–42; Wang Qing 1998, 199–216; Yamada Toshiaki 1989b

  ※ Yushi; *Chisong zi zhangli*; HAGIOGRAPHY

Chisong zi zhangli

赤松子章曆

Master Red-Pine's Almanac of Petitions

*Chisong zi is, together with *Wangzi Qiao, the oldest named transcendent (*xianren) in the Chinese tradition. His name occurs in the *Yuanyou* 遠遊 (Far Roaming) poem of the *Chuci* 楚辭 (Songs of Chu; trans. Kroll 1996b, 660). The *Chisong zi zhangli* (CT 615) is often said to contain some of the earliest material of the Way of the Celestial Masters (*Tianshi dao), though the final composition of the current six chapter text is usually dated to the Tang. The first chapter claims that the initial revelation to *Zhang Daoling in 142 included a *Chisong zi li* 赤松子曆 (Master Red-Pine's Almanac) and a *Taizhen ke* 太真科 (Code of the Great Perfected) as well as other texts, and that among these were three hundred great petitions. The narrator explains that this was during the distant Han dynasty, and that at the time of composition, only "one or two out of ten" of the original petitions still survived. In fact, much of the opening two chapters consists of quotations of the *Chisong zi li* and the *Taizhen ke*, and the bulk of the scripture (*j. 3–6*) consists of sixty-seven model petitions, so this accords well with the opening description.

The first chapter lists in detail the "tokens of faith" one must donate in order to perform each ritual, the times when the gates of heaven are open to accept petitions, and lucky days for the performance of various types of rites. The second chapter consists of instructions on how to perform the rite of submission (how to write the petition, direction to face, officials to be addressed, etc.) as well as taboos surrounding the rite. The petitions address a variety of issues, ranging from a drought that affects the entire nation to family matters, and matters of the priest's own conduct. Among the most informative petitions are those dealing with the disposition of the dead and those intended to ward off sepulchral plaints or legal cases against the deceased that somehow impinge upon the living.

Terry KLEEMAN

📖 Kalinowski 1989–90, 96–99; Nickerson 1997; Ōfuchi Ninji and Ishii Masako 1988, 186–87 (list of texts cited); Verellen 2004

※ Chisong zi; Tianshi dao

Chongbi danjing

冲碧丹經

Scripture of the Elixir of the Unfathomable Jasper Heaven

This two-chapter alchemical treatise, whose full title is *Jinhua chongbi danjing bizhi* 金華冲碧丹經祕旨 (Secret Purport of the Scripture of the Elixir of the Golden Flower of the Unfathomable Jasper Heaven; CT 914), opens with an account of the origins and uses of this Fujian tradition dated to 1225. Its editor, the Sichuan native Meng Xu 孟煦 (fl. 1218–25), asserts that both chapters stem from *Bai Yuchan (1194–1229?). Anxious to learn more about alchemy, Meng first approached Bai's major disciple, *Peng Si (fl. 1217–51), in 1218 while in Fuzhou (Fujian). Peng turned over a core chapter of his master's teachings, known as the *Jinhua chongbi danjing*. This first chapter focuses on the structure of the laboratory and its processes and contains schematic drawings of laboratory equipment, but was difficult for Meng to understand. Two years later, while at the White Crane Grotto-Heaven (Baihe dongtian 白鶴洞天, in the *Wuyi mountains of northwestern Fujian), Meng met a Lan Yuanbai 蘭元白, who provided him with extra elucidation of the text. Meng realized that Master Lan was none other than Bai Yuchan himself. In 1221, Meng invited three utmost gentlemen intent on refining elixirs to enter into retreat, using Lan Yuanbai's interpretation as a guide. The second chapter details a nine-stage process for creating an immortal embryo (*shengtai) using similar language to the *Zhouyi cantong qi and its cognates.

When seen together, the texts seems to provide a *neidan interpretation (j. 2) for what was arguably a text centered on laboratory work (i.e., *waidan, j. 1). The long opening account ties both chapters to the same source, namely Bai Yuchan.

Lowell SKAR

※ Bai Yuchan; *neidan*

Chongxuan

重玄

Twofold Mystery

The term *chongxuan* derives from a phrase in the opening section of the *Daode jing*, "mystery and again mystery" (*xuan zhi you xuan* 玄之又玄). It alludes to two steps toward the understanding of the Ultimate Void, and suggests a double movement of the spirit on both a conceptual and a mystical level.

During the Six Dynasties, the *Xuanxue (Arcane Learning) school of thought speculated on Non-being (or emptiness) and Being (*wu and *you*). *Wang Bi (226–49), one of the main Xuanxue thinkers, wrote that *xuan* (mystery) means silent, mysterious, and unspeakable, adding that "we cannot settle only on one *xuan*, or we would lose [its sense]; therefore [the *Daode jing*] says 'mystery and again mystery'" (Robinet 1977, 109). Since Wang Bi considered *xuan* to be a synonym of *wu*, he paved the way for a reflection on emptiness. According to the Tang commentator of the *Daode jing*, *Cheng Xuanying (fl. 631–50), *xuan* also connotes non-attachment: "When one is not bound either by Being or Non-being, and one is not attached to attachment or non-attachment, . . . this is called Twofold Mystery" (Robinet 1977, 110). Cheng Xuanying states that the first *xuan* in the *Daode jing* passage aims at rejecting the two bounds of Being and Non-being, and is equivalent to the Middle Path of the Madhyamaka school of Buddhism. The second *xuan* aims at not being attached to the first one, i.e., at not being attached to non-attachment.

Applying the Madhyamaka dialectic, the Chongxuan thinkers suggested therefore that one should go beyond the affirmation of Being and its negation, and beyond the negation of both, rejecting the error of the eternalists who maintain that an unchanging substance is at the basis of the world, and equally rejecting the nihilist view that negates the reality of the world. According to the Chongxuan thinkers, these "two truths" must be both asserted and dismissed. First the "two extremes" are rejected, then the "middle" is equally rejected. The void (first *xuan*) is void (second *xuan*); the negation is negated; the illness of pretending that any one statement—be it *you* or *wu*, or negating as well as asserting both—is true, disappears. The second *xuan* advances the paradoxical realization that the world is neither real nor illusory, that affirmation as well as negation of the reality or unreality of the world is nonsense.

The same dialectic was applied to expound other passages of the *Daode jing*, such as the phrase "to decrease and again decrease" (*sun zhi you sun* 損之又損, sec. 48), and of the *Zhuangzi, particularly the passage that reads "There is being . . . There is non-being . . . There is a there-is-non-being that has not yet begun to begin . . ." (chapter 2; Robinet 1977, 121–22). A similar dialectical progression was also applied to the Three Ones (*sanyi), or to the root (*ben* 本) and the traces (*ji* 迹), as everything is a trace of the Ultimate Truth, neither real because it is not the Truth, nor false because it is its manifestation.

Buddhist thinkers such as Zhi Dun 支盾 (314–66), Sengzhao 僧肇 (374–414), and Jizang 吉臧 (549–623) used the expression *chongxuan* to speak of Laozi's truth, and identify it as a Taoist usage. In alchemical *neidan texts, *chongxuan* designates the embryo of immortality; here the term has the same meaning as the expression "beyond the body there is another body" (*shenwai you shen* 身外有身), which alludes to *tuotai* 脫胎 (deliverance of the embryo) and is synonymous with the "real emptiness" (*zhenkong* 真空) that subsumes the distinction between Being and Non-being.

The Chongxuan school of thought. The Chongxuan school—which is not a lineage but a trend of thought based on the principles outlined above—developed around commentaries to the *Daode jing* and the *Zhuangzi*. Its existence as a school of thought was first affirmed by Cheng Xuanying, the earliest commentator who tried to classify the lineages of *Daode jing* exegesis in the preface to his own commentary. After him, *Du Guangting (850–933) and then Jiao Hong 焦竑 (1541–1620) also referred to the Chongxuan school. Many commentaries of this school are lost and are only known through quotations.

The first Chongxuan thinker was apparently Sun Deng 孫登, a commentator of the *Daode jing* active during the Jin 晉 dynasty (Fujiwara Takao 1961b;

Lu Guolong 1994). Then came Meng Zhizhou 孟知周 (Qing Xitai 1994, 1: 255), who lived during the reign of Liang Wudi (r. 502–49). In a passage of his lost commentary, quoted in the *Daojiao yishu (Pivot of Meaning of the Taoist Teaching, 5.1a–3a), Meng interprets the Three Ones by applying the same dialectic used by the Chongxuan school in dealing with the notion of Mystery. Under the same dynasty also lived Zang Xuanjing 臧玄靜 (fl. mid-sixth century), who taught the *Shangqing patriarch *Wang Yuanzhi (528–635) and may have been Cheng Xuanying's master. The school reached its apogee in the Tang period with eminent Taoists such as Liu Jinxi 劉進喜 (ca. 560-ca. 640), to whom the first five chapters of the *Benji jing (Scripture of the Original Bound) are ascribed, and who also wrote two essays on Laozi and a lost commentary to the Daode jing.

Another major Chongxuan thinker is Cheng Xuanying who, in 647, translated the Daode jing into Sanskrit with Xuanzang 玄奘 (ca. 602–64) and Cai Huang 蔡晃, also a member of this school (Pelliot 1912). Cheng's exegesis of the *Yijing is now lost, but his commentaries to the Daode jing and the *Duren jing (Scripture on Salvation), and his subcommentary to *Guo Xiang's commentary to the Zhuangzi are extant. Chen's younger contemporary, *Li Rong (fl. 658–63), wrote a lost commentary to the Zhuangzi and an extant commentary to the Daode jing. The Chongxuan school also influenced other Tang Taoist texts such as the Daojiao yishu, and Song commentators of the Daode jing such as Shao Ruoyu 邵若愚 (fl. 1159) and Zhao Shi'an 趙實庵.

Isabelle ROBINET

📖 Fujiwara Takao 1961a; Kohn 1991a, 190–96; Kohn 1992a, 139–46; Lu Guolong 1993; Ren Jiyu 1990, 249–64; Robinet 1977, 96–203; Robinet 1997b, 194–95; Sharf 2002, 52–71; Sunayama Minoru 1990, 188–211; Yu Shiyi 2000

※ Cheng Xuanying; Li Rong; xuan; TAOISM AND CHINESE BUDDHISM

Chongyang lijiao shiwu lun

重陽立教十五論

Fifteen Essays by [Wang] Chongyang to Establish His Teaching

The Chongyang lijiao shiwu lun (CT 1233) is a very short treatise on Taoist life in fifteen sections: 1. Retreat in a Hermitage; 2. Travelling as an Errant Religious; 3. Studying Texts; 4. Preparing Medicines; 5. Mastering Carpentry; 6. Forming Religious Communities; 7. Meditation; 8. Firm Control of the Mind;

9. Refining One's Nature; 10. Pairing the Five Pneumas (*wuqi* 五氣, i.e., those of the *wuxing); 11. Merging Inner Nature and Destiny (*xing and *ming*); 12. Sagely Way; 13. Transcending the Three Realms (*sanjie* 三界); 14. Methods for Nourishing the Self; and 15. Leaving This World.

Although scholarly publications and translations into Western languages have made this work famous, its value as a source on the early history of *Quanzhen is rather limited. The title suggests that it was written by *Wang Zhe (1113–70) to summarize his predication, but there is no evidence to strongly support this attribution: the work is neither mentioned in any of several Yuan-period biographies of Wang, which are otherwise very detailed, nor is it quoted in any early Quanzhen work. The text, however, is generally consistent with Quanzhen rhetorics, which tends to add purely abstract meanings to the common religious vocabulary, and with the Quanzhen ideals of service to society and an austere life devoted to *neidan practices.

Vincent GOOSSAERT

📖 Boltz J. M. 1987a, 148; Kohn 1993b, 86–92 (trans.); Qing Xitai 1994, 2: 117–18; Reiter 1984–85 (trans.); Yao Tao-chung 1980, 73–86 (trans.)

※ Wang Zhe; Quanzhen

Chongyang Quanzhen ji

重陽全真集

Anthology on the Completion of Authenticity,
by [Wang] Chongyang

This thirteen-*juan* poetic anthology (CT 1153) is the largest repository of *Wang Zhe's (Wang Chongyang, 1113–70) literary production. It contains 1,009 texts, consisting of regulated poems (*shi* 詩), lyrics (*ci* 詞), songs (*ge* 歌), and a few prose works written for *Quanzhen lay associations (*hui* 會; see *TAOIST LAY ASSOCIATIONS). Some poems are duplicated, others are also extant in shorter anthologies—notably the *Jiaohua ji* 教化集 (Anthology of Religious Conversions; CT 1154)—and a few were carved on stone in monasteries founded by Wang's disciples. Beyond this information, the textual history of the *Chongyang Quanzhen ji* is obscure. It seems to have been part of a larger collection now lost, and its present version was edited by disciples of *Ma Yu, Wang's favorite disciple, in 1188.

The textual history of the *Minghe yuyin, another work including some of Wang's poetry, shows that poems of Taoist inspiration (*daoqing* 道情;

Ono Shihei 1964) were current under the Mongols. Quanzhen predication, in particular, used poems in several ways. Their lyric tone suited the appeal to conversion, and the poems of Quanzhen masters were memorized by both adepts and devotees. Ascetics recited them at night to fight the effects of sleep deprivation. Poems were also quoted in answer to doctrinal questions, as attested in the recorded sayings (*yulu) of several masters, and especially in Niu Daochun's 牛道淳 (fl. 1299) *Xiyi zhimi lun* 析疑指迷論 (Essays to Resolve Doubts and Point out Errors; CT 276). Moreover, poems were used for exchanges between master and disciple. For instance, Wang Zhe liked to write *cangtou shi* 藏頭詩, poems in which the first character of each verse is hidden so that the recipient may guess it. This pedagogical use of poetry is also noted among contemporary Quanzhen writers such as *Tan Chuduan and non-Quanzhen Taoist authors as well. Another non-Quanzhen, twelfth-century example of its application is the *Taixuan ji* 太玄集 (Anthology of Great Mystery; CT 1061).

In the *Quanzhen ji*, most poems are ad hoc creations to exhort or stimulate disciples or acquaintances, and therefore do not offer a coherent doctrinal exposition. The *ci* tunes are similar to those used in contemporary poetry, although Quanzhen authors sometimes changed their titles to make them sound more Taoist. *Neidan* vocabulary is used throughout the works, but not in a didactic manner: blended with Wang's personal voice, it shapes a lyrical discourse on the promise of immortality.

While the influence exerted by Wang's poetry is difficult to determine, it is worthy of note that the *Quanzhen ji*, like most other Quanzhen works, survives only in the *Daozang* edition. Among the Quanzhen collected works, only *Qiu Chuji's *Panxi ji* 磻溪集 (Anthology of the Master from Panxi; CT 1159) and *Ji Zhizhen's *Yunshan ji* 雲山集 (Anthology of Cloudy Mountains; 1250; CT 1140), besides the popular anthology *Minghe yuyin*, are also extant in separate editions that differ from those in the current *Daozang*. This suggests that the versions of these anthologies in the Canon underwent thorough editing. Moreover, Ming and Qing bibliographic catalogues show that several Quanzhen literary works did circulate, but Wang Zhe's anthologies were not among them. Their circulation after the fourteenth century was probably limited, although it was certainly widened in recent times by the *Daozang jiyao*, which gives a prominent place to early Quanzhen literature. Wang's original poetry was thus mainly rediscovered in the contemporary period.

Vincent GOOSSAERT

📖 Boltz J. M. 1987a, 144–45; Hachiya Kunio 1992a; Qing Xitai 1994, 2: 213–14; Marsone 2001b

※ Wang Zhe; Quanzhen

chu

廚

"cuisines"

The term *chu* or "cuisines" designates in Taoism a complex of religious practices that includes both communal rituals and techniques of meditation. The semantic field defined by this term is extensive but can be summarized in some key expressions: ritual banquets, communion with divinities, granaries (*zang* 藏, a word that also denotes the viscera), visualization of the five viscera (*wuzang), and abstention from cereals (*bigu) and other food proscriptions.

Taoist cuisines have an antecedent in early Chinese religion: "cuisine" was the term used for the ceremonial meals organized by communities to honor the gods of the soil (*she* 社). These "cuisine congregations" (*chuhui* 廚會) became an object of criticism, and sometimes were banned, by orthodox Taoists who objected not only to their excessive financial expenditure but also to their moral dissolution, as they involved animal sacrifice. Taoists nevertheless perpetuated the custom by adapting and codifying it, as they did with several other popular religious practices.

Cuisines thus became a major element of liturgy from the origin of Taoist organized movements. Also called "good luck meals" (*fushi* 福食), they were performed especially during the three large annual festivals (the Three Assemblies, *sanhui), when *Tianshi dao officiants updated the civil records of their communities and granted parochial ranks to their adepts. An appropriate number of cuisine officiants was chosen; they first observed a period of purification that included fasting and abstention from sexual intercourse. Cuisine rituals lasted for one, three, or seven days. Participants consumed exclusively vegetarian food and moderate amounts of wine, which was considered as a mandatory element of the banquet. The leftovers were shared by the faithful who could thereby participate in the communion. Cuisine ceremonies were also performed in special circumstances, such as when there was disease, sin, or death pollution. They had an exorcistic and salvific power, and conferred good luck or merit upon the adepts.

Taoist cuisines shared many features with the Retreats (*zhai or "liturgical fasts"). In fact, the Taoist Fasting and Offering rituals (*jiao) progressively superseded the communal cuisine feasts. The decline of these cuisine practices coincided with the development, during the Tang period, of a contemplative cuisine ritual, partaking of the long tradition of Taoist psycho-physiological techniques. The *Wuchu jing (Scripture of the Five Cuisines) gives an idea of these techniques practiced by seekers of longevity. They mainly involve visualizing the five viscera of the body and chanting incantations. These methods allowed the adept to obtain satisfaction and harmony, and, after some years of training, even immortality.

The tradition of the meditational cuisines seems to have developed in a parallel and complementary manner to the communal cuisine liturgy. These "contemplative" cuisines were well known by the fourth and fifth centuries. *Ge Hong refers several times to the ability of calling upon "movable cuisines" (*xingchu* 行廚) as one of the Saint's highest powers. *Shangqing Taoists also practiced the technique of "making the movable cuisines come [while] sitting [in meditation]" (*zuo zhi xingchu* 坐致行廚). This method, accessible only to the initiate who possessed the proper series of talismans (*FU) and had mastered certain visualization techniques, conferred powers to become invisible, to cause thunder, and to call for rain. The method was so popular during the Tang period that Tantric Buddhism also adopted it.

Christine MOLLIER

📖 Mollier 2000; Stein R. A. 1971; Stein R. A. 1972; Stein R. A. 1979

※ *sanhui*; *Wuchu jing*

Chunyang Lü zhenren wenji

純陽呂真人文集

Collected Works of the Perfected Lü of Pure Yang

The *Chunyang Lü zhenren wenji* in eight *juan* is a collection of stories, poems, chants, ballads, and other writings attributed to or concerning *Lü Dongbin. Its nucleus dates to the Southern Song period. The original edition was published by Chen Deyi 陳得一 from Jianjin 劍津 (Fujian) in 1166. This edition, however, had already been lost by 1423 when the forty-fourth Celestial Master Zhang Yuqing 張宇清 (1364–1427) recompiled the text by gathering copies that existed in his time. The *Chunyang Lü zhenren wenji* as we know it today, therefore, is an anthology that has no precise date since it took shape from the Song through the Ming, when at least four editions were published:

1. The 1571 edition by Yao Ruxun 姚汝循 from Jiangning 江寧 (Jiangsu) in eight *juan* (now preserved at the Naikaku bunko in Tokyo; see Mori Yuria 1992a, 46), which was reprinted in 1583 under the title *Chunyang Lüzu wenji* 純陽呂祖文集 (Collected Works of Ancestor Lü of Pure Yang) with revisions and additions by Yang Liangbi 楊良弼 from Fujian (see Ma Xiaohong

1988a, 36; Ma Xiaohong 1988b, 38). It is probably on the basis of this edition that later the *Lüzu zhi* 呂祖志 (Monograph of Ancestor Lü; CT 1484) was compiled and included in the 1607 supplement to the *Daozang*.

2. The Ming edition included in the *Daoshu quanji* 道書全集 (Complete Collection of Books on the Dao), edited by Yan Hezhou 閻鶴州 from Jinling 金陵 (near Nanjing, Jiangsu) in 1591.

3. The 1636 edition by Lü Yijing 呂一經 in ten *juan* (also preserved at the Naikaku bunkō).

4. The edition preserved at the Tenri Library of Nara in eight *juan*, the last of which is missing (see Ozaki Masaharu 1986a, 108, and Mori Yuria 1992a).

Contents. Based on Yang Liangbi's reprint, the content of the eight *juan* is as follows. The first *juan* contains the *Zhenren ziji* 真人自記 (Personal Records by the Perfected), the *Zhenren benzhuan* 真人本傳 (Original Biography of the Perfected) and the *Zhenzhong ji* 枕中記 (Notes Kept Inside the Pillow). These three works are also included in the *Lüzu zhi* (j. 1) under the title *Shiji zhi* 事績志 (Records of Accomplishments), with the addition of the *Yunfang shishi zhenren* 雲房十試真人 (Ten Trials of the Perfected by Yunfang) and the *Zhenren shiwen Yunfang* 真人十問雲房 (Ten Questions of the Perfected to Yunfang). The content of the *Zhenren benzhuan* also appears with some modifications in the first ten stories reported in the *Chunyang dijun shenhua miaotong ji* 純陽帝君神化妙通紀 (Chronicle of the Divine Transformations and Wondrous Powers of the Imperial Lord of Pure Yang; CT 305) as well as in the **Lüzu quanshu* (Complete Writings of Ancestor Lü).

The second *juan* contains more than seventy stories on miracles and traces left by Lü Dongbin when he appeared in the world. Most of them are also found in the first part of the *Lüzu zhi* (j. 2–3), in the *Chunyang dijun shenhua miaotong ji*, and in the *Lüzu quanshu*.

The remaining *juan* contain more than 230 poems, chants and ballads that are also included in the second part of the *Lüzu zhi* (j. 4–6), entitled *Yiwen zhi* 藝文志 (Literary Writings), as well as in the *Lüzu quanshu*. Some of the pentasyllabic and heptasyllabic *lüshi* 律詩 and *jueju* 絕句 are also found in the *Chunyang zhenren huncheng ji* 純陽真人渾成集 (Anthology of the Perfected of Pure Yang, "Confused and yet Complete"; CT 1055) and in the *Quan Tang shi* 全唐詩 (Complete Poems of the Tang).

Monica ESPOSITO

📖 Boltz J. M. 1987a, 67, 141–43; Ma Xiaohong 1988a; Ma Xiaohong 1988b; Mori Yuria 1990; Mori Yuria 1992a

※ Lü Dongbin

chushen

出神

"exteriorization of the spirits"; "egress of the Spirit"

1. Ritual

In Taoist ritual, "exteriorization of the spirits" means summoning forth the deities from within the body of the priest (*daoshi*). As these deities have features and roles of civil and military officers, *chushen* is also referred to as *chuguan* 出官 ("exteriorization of the officials") or *qingguan* 請官 ("calling the officials").

In the Way of the Celestial Masters (*Tianshi dao), and later also in the *Lingbao *zhai (Retreat) rituals, these deities were called forth during rites for presenting petitions (*zhang* 章). In present-day rituals, it is during the rite of Lighting the Incense Burner (*falu) that the high priest (*gaogong* 高功; see *daozhang) asks the Most High Lord Lao (Taishang Laojun 太上老君; see *Laozi and Laojun) and other gods to summon forth his inner deities. Simultaneously, he performs the hand movements known as *shoujue. At that time, the civil and military officers emerge from the Gate of All Wonders (*zhongmiao men* 眾妙門) which is located in the priest's Muddy Pellet (*niwan, the Cinnabar Field or *dantian in the head). They perform various functions to assist the performance of the ritual, and return to their posts within the priest's body after the rite of the Extinction of the Incense Burner (*fulu* 復爐; Lagerwey 1987c, 146–47).

MARUYAMA Hiroshi

📖 Schipper 1993, 55–99

※ *gongcao*; *gongde*; *jiangshen*; *jiao*; *zhai*; INNER DEITIES

2. Neidan

In *neidan, the term *shen* in *chushen* does not refer to deities, but to Spirit. The "egress of the Spirit" marks the achievement of the third and final stage of the practice, the return of Spirit to Emptiness (*lianshen huanxu* 鍊神還虛). Once the Spirit is sublimated into a Yang Spirit (*yangshen* 陽神), with no further trace of Yin, it is thoroughly free from the workings of the discursive mind and permanently abides in absolute tranquillity. In this condition, it can leave the body at will. This experience of physical and mental sublimation is described

Fig. 26. Egress of the Spirit (*chushen*). **Xingming guizhi* 性命圭旨
(Principles of Balanced Cultivation of Inner Nature and Vital Force).

by the expression "beyond the body there is another body" (*shenwai you shen* 身外有身), signifying that a spiritual body is born from the material body that is no longer related to the aggregation of the Five Agents (**wuxing*). Released from transmigration, this body is one with the Dao, is equal to space, and has the same life span as Heaven and Earth.

The departure of the Spirit from the body is attested by the opening of the sinciput (*tianmen* 天門, the Gate of Heaven), from which the Spirit egresses (see fig. 26). *Neidan* texts often describe this experience as heralded by the appearance of a circle of light, ambrosial fragrances, and sounds resembling the rumble of thunder. This ultimate accomplishment, in which all effort ceases and the Spirit engages in ecstatic flights (*shenyou* 神遊), should not be confused with the egress of the Yin Spirit (*chu yinshen* 出陰神). In the latter instance, the Spirit leaves the body but has not yet been entirely sublimated. This inferior practice is regarded as equivalent to a transfer into a corpse or a matrix, because the Yin Spirit is still attached to the mundane world that is bound by the Five Agents.

Monica ESPOSITO

📖 Cleary 1986a, 100–104; Despeux 1979, 79–82; Robinet 1989c, 188–90

※ *jing, qi, shen*; *neidan*

Chuzhen jielü

初真戒律

Initial Precepts and Observances for Perfection

The *Chuzhen jielü* by *Wang Changyue (?–1680) contains three prefaces. The first is signed by the author and is dated 1656, when this eminent *Quanzhen Taoist became the chief abbot of the *Baiyun guan (Abbey of the White Clouds) in Beijing. Wang reports that he received the precepts from master Zhao Fuyang 趙復陽 whom he had met on Mount Jiugong (Jiugong shan 九宮山, Hubei), and adds that in 1656 he built an ordination platform at the Baiyun guan to transmit those precepts (see fig. 75). The two other prefaces are by Long Qiqian 龍起潛 (dated 1674) and Wu Taiyi 吳太一 (dated 1686). At the end of the text there is an undated colophon by Da Chongguang 笪重光.

Although the Quanzhen observances are influenced by the Buddhist *vinaya*, they are largely based on the precepts of Tang-dynasty Taoism shared by the *Zhengyi, *Lingbao and *Shangqing schools (Schipper 1985c). They are divided into three degrees: Initial Precepts for Perfection (*chuzhen jie* 初真戒), Intermediate Precepts (*zhongji jie* 中極戒), and Precepts for Celestial Immortality (*tianxian jie* 天仙戒). The *Chuzhen jielü* is essentially concerned with the precepts of the first degree, but also contains indications and rules about the two other levels. The text can be divided into the five parts described below (page numbers are those of the *Daozang jiyao edition, found in vol. 24).

Basic precepts. This part includes four sections. The first is entitled "San guiyi jie" 三皈依戒 (Precepts of the Three Refuges; 34a–b). The Three Refuges are the Dao, the scriptures and the master. This passage reproduces a portion of the *Sandong zhongjie wen* 三洞眾戒文 (All Precepts of the Three Caverns; CT 178, 2a–b), compiled by *Zhang Wanfu in the early eighth century.

The second section is the "Taishang Laojun suoming jigong guigen wujie" 太上老君所命積功歸根五戒 (Five Precepts Ordered by the Most High Lord Lao to Accumulate Merit and Return to the Root; 34b–35a). The precepts consist in not killing, not stealing, not lying, not engaging in licentious behavior, and not taking intoxicants. They are akin to the five basic precepts of Buddhism and derive from the *Taishang Laojun jiejing* 太上老君戒經 (Scripture on Precepts of the Most High Lord Lao; CT 784, 14a–15a). The text specifies that each morning, those who receive these precepts should recite the *Taishang sanyuan cifu shezui jie'e xiaozai yansheng baoming miaojing* 太上三元賜福赦 罪解厄消災延生保命妙經 (Wondrous Scripture of the Most High Three Primes that Confers Happiness, Liberates from Faults, Eliminates Dangers, Dispels Disasters, Extends One's Life, and Preserves One's Destiny; CT 1442) and the *Taishang ganying pian (Folios of the Most High on Retribution).

The third section (35a–36a) reproduces the *Xuhuang tianzun chuzhen shijie wen* 虛皇天尊初真十戒文 (Ten Initial Precepts for Perfection According to the Celestial Worthy, Sovereign of Emptiness; CT 180), and has the same title. It lists the five basic precepts for laymen in Buddhism as well as four of the five Confucian classical virtues (only righteousness, *yi* 義, is lacking).

The fourth section, "Xingchi zongshuo" 行持總說 (General Principles on the Practice; 36a–37a), enumerates the positive effects that accumulate according to the number of one's meritorious acts (one, ten, one hundred, or one thousand) and the inauspicious effects of bad actions.

Post-ordination precepts. The second part of the *Chuzhen jielü*, "Rujie yaogui" 入戒要規 (Main Rules to be Observed after the Transmission of the Precepts; 38a–46b), gives rules concerning collective life, individual practice, vestments, and washing, and lists the days on which ordinations and hundred-day retreats can take place. There follow thirty spells (*zhou* 咒) that are transmitted to the disciple on the day of ordination and are to be recited during his daily activities. At the end there are drawings of vestments and ritual objects (a vase, a bowl, and a stick) related to the three ordination degrees.

Precepts for monastic life. In the third part, "Xuanmen chijie weiyi" 玄門持戒 威儀 (Dignified Liturgies to be Observed when One Follows the Precepts of the School of Mysteries), the initial pages (47a–53b) describe the attitudes that a disciple should observe in twelve circumstances of monastic life: 1. when he comes in or goes out; 2. when he serves his master; 3. when he hears or looks; 4. when he speaks; 5. when he combs his hair or washes his face; 6. when he eats; 7. when he hears a religious teaching; 8. when he travels; 9. when he stands up or remains standing; 10. when he is in a sitting or reclining position; 11. when he performs any activity; 12. when he washes himself. This advice is similar to that found in the *Zhengyi weiyi jing (Scripture of Dignified Liturgies of Orthodox Unity) and the *Xuanmen shishi weiyi* 玄門十事威 儀 (Dignified Liturgies for Ten Circumstances According to the School of Mysteries; CT 792).

There follows the "Dizi fengshi kejie" 弟子奉師科戒 (Codes and Precepts for Serving One's Master; 54a–55b), containing thirty-nine rules from the above-mentioned *Sandong zhongjie wen* (CT 178, 2b–4b), and a section entitled "Jieyi" 戒衣 (Ordination Vestments; 56a–57a), with forty-six entries from Zhang Wanfu's *Sandong fafu kejie wen* 三洞法服科戒文 (Codes and Precepts for the Liturgical Vestments of the Three Caverns; CT 788, 7b–9b).

Precepts for women. The precepts in the fourth part, "Nüzhen jiujie" 女真九戒 (Nine Precepts for Perfection for Women; 58a–b), emphasize the ethical virtues that women should develop (see Despeux 1990, 147–55).

Kunyang's precepts. Finally, the "Kunyang lüshi fuzhuo jie" 崑陽律師付囑偈 (Gāthās for the Exhortation to the Practice by the Ordination Master Kunyang; 59a–60a), entitled after Wang Changyue's original name, includes six stanzas that urge the disciple to put his clothing in order, protect his bowl, take care of his shoes, keep clean the ordination tablet, maintain a deferential attitude in public, and apply and follow these precepts.

Catherine DESPEUX

📖 Despeux 1990, 147–55; Esposito 1993, 97–100; Qing Xitai 1988–95, 4: 77–100; Qing Xitai 1994, 2: 353–55

※ Wang Changyue; *jie* [precepts]; MONASTIC CODE; ORDINATION AND PRIEST-HOOD

Ciyi jing

雌一經

Scripture of the Feminine One

In *Shangqing Taoism, the term *ciyi* 雌一 or Feminine One associates the "female" (*ci*) of the *Daode jing* with the practice of guarding the One (*shouyi*). It also designates the Three Pure Ladies (Sansu 三素) who embody the Feminine One and live in the *jinhua* 金華 (Golden Flower) chamber of the brain. The Three Ladies are the mothers of the Five Gods (*wushen* 五神) or Five Ancient Lords (*wulao* 五老) of the Masculine One, the divinities of the registers of life (*shengji* 生籍; see *Taidan yinshu*).

The scripture that concerns them is the *Ciyi yujian wulao baojing* 雌一玉檢五老寶經 (Precious Scripture on the Five Ancient Lords, Jade Seal of the Feminine One; CT 1313). This text dates from the seventh century but contains earlier materials, possibly drawn in part from the third-century practices received by *Su Lin and Juanzi 涓子 and adopted by the Shangqing school. Other sections are apocryphal but their content matches the original revelation. The text tries to harmonize the practices focused on the *dongfang* 洞 房 (the Cavern Chamber located in the brain) and the deities of the *Taidan yinshu*. It is closely related to the *Dongfang neijing* 洞房內經 (Inner Scripture of the Cavern Chamber; CT 133), which contains a later version of the *dong-fang* method, and the *Jinhua yujing* 金華玉經 (Jade Scripture of the Golden Flower; CT 254), which contains part of the *Ciyi jing* itself.

The *Ciyi jing* is based on the "formula" of the *Dadong zhenjing* and describes methods that complement other scriptures, including the *Basu jing*. At its core is the *dongfang* method, which consists in a meditation on the Three Pure Ladies and the chanting of hymns in their honor. The text also contains a method to have one's name written in the registers of life by the Five Ancient Lords, and a method to have one's mortal embryonic knots unraveled by the Three Ladies, their sons, and the *bajing* (Eight Effulgences; see Robinet 1993, 139–43).

Isabelle ROBINET

📖 Robinet 1993, 131–38; Robinet 1984, 1: 76–80 and 2: 261–83

※ Shangqing

cun

存

visualization, actualization

The word *cun* is a verb that commonly means "to be," "to be present," "to exist." In this sense it also denotes extreme longevity, as in the famous passage of *Zhuangzi* 11, where *Guangcheng zi exclaims: *wo du cun hu* 我獨存乎, "I alone survive!" (see trans. Watson 1968, 179).

In Taoist meditation, the word is used in its causative mode, in the sense of "to cause to exist" or "to make present." It thus means that the meditator, by an act of conscious concentration and focused intention, causes certain energies to be present in certain parts of the body or makes specific deities or scriptures appear before his or her mental eye. For this reason, the word is most commonly rendered "to visualize" or, as a noun, "visualization." Since, however, the basic meaning of *cun* is not just to see or be aware of but to be actually present, the translation "to actualize" or "actualization" may at times be correct if somewhat alien to the Western reader.

Apart from its single usage, the word *cun* occurs in three typical compounds in Taoist texts. These are: *cunxiang* or "visualization and imagination," *cunshen* or "visualization of spirit," and *cunsi* or "visualization and meditation."

Visualization and imagination. The first compound, *cunxiang* 存想 or "visualization and imagination," is defined in *Sima Chengzhen's *Tianyin zi*:

> Visualization (cun) means producing a vision of one's spirit(s); imagination (*xiang*) is to create an image of one's body. How is this accomplished? By closing one's eyes one can see one's own eyes. By gathering in one's mind one can realize one's own mind. Mind and eyes should never be separate from one's body and should never harm one's spirit(s): this is done by visualization and imagination. (CT 1026, 3b)

The result of this activity is "tranquillity," through which one can "recover life" and attain longevity and even immortality. The activity of *cun* here is the active creation of an intentional inner vision of the spirit energy in one's body, combined with that of *xiang* which allows one also to see one's bodily presence and thus attain longevity both physically and spiritually.

The same term also occurs in a *neidan* context in the *Xiuzhen shishu* (Ten Books on the Cultivation of Perfection, 24.4a–5a), in a section entitled "Cunxiang yinqi" 存想咽氣 or "Visualizing and Imagining the Swallowing of Breath." Instructions here advise adepts to visualize their *qi* as it is swallowed into the lower Cinnabar Field (*dantian*), where it mingles with its authentic counterpart (*yuanqi* or Original Pneuma) and can then be gradually and with full intention guided through the spinal column, into all the different parts of the body (even to the tips of hairs and nails) and into the *niwan* cavity or upper Cinnabar Field in the brain. The activity of *cun* again implies the full concentration of the mind on the energy within the body.

Visualization of spirit. The same basic reading applies to the compound *cunshen* 存神 or "visualization of spirit," which occurs in two titles in the Taoist Canon: *Cunshen lianqi ming (Inscription on the Visualization of Spirit and Refinement of Pneuma) by *Sun Simiao of the seventh century, and *Cunshen guqi lun* 存 神固氣論 (Essay on the Visualization of Spirit and Stabilizing of Energy; CT 577), a *neidan* work of the Song or Yuan periods. In both instances the practice links the concentrated attention (*cun*) paid to the spirit with the improvement and increase of energy, again providing both physical and spiritual benefits for the practitioner. Also, both texts use the basic system of Yin and Yang and the *wuxing* to explain the inner workings of the body-mind system and insist that the effect of *cun* is one of tranquilizing and calming the mind. Like the *Tianyin zi*, the texts on *cunshen* ultimately aim at longevity and immortality, for which a calm and stable mind is a basic condition.

Visualization and meditation. Cunsi 存思 or "visualization and meditation" is
the topic of the lengthy *Taishang Laojun da cunsi tuzhu jue* 太上老君大存思
圖注訣 (Illustrated Commentary and Instructions on the Great Visualization
and Meditation, by the Most High Lord Lao; CT 875, and YJQQ 43.3a–17b), a
text that in its present version dates from the late Tang but is cited as early as
the fourth century. Here *cun* refers to the visualization of the gods, whom one
should see as if they were real and imagine as clearly as if looking at their pictures. This practice is illustrated with numerous examples in the four sections
of the text, which specify visualizations during ordination procedures (of the
masters, gods, and scriptures), in daily activities, in heavenly audiences with
the gods, and in advanced celestial interaction and translation to the higher
spheres. Although more complex and colorful than the practice of *cunxiang*
or *cunshen*, the basic principle of *cunsi* is the same: the intentional actualization of spirit leads to a higher awareness of the Dao, and brings about inner
purity and mental tranquillity.

Livia KOHN

📖 Kohn 1987a, 119–24; Robinet 1993; Qing Xitai 1994, 3: 269–76; Sakade Yoshinobu 1994c

※ INNER DEITIES; MEDITATION AND VISUALIZATION

Cunshen lianqi ming

存神鍊氣銘

Inscription on the Visualization of Spirit and
Refinement of Pneuma

The *Cunshen lianqi ming* is attributed to the eminent physician *Sun Simiao
(fl. 673). The work has survived both as an independent text (CT 834) and as
part of the *Yunji qiqian* (33.12a–14b). In addition, its main portion is included
in the *Dingguan jing* (Scripture on Concentration and Observation) and in
the *Sheyang zhenzhong fang* (Pillow Book of Methods for Preserving and
Nourishing Life).

   The *Inscription* is an important precursor to *Sima Chengzhen's *Zuowang
lun* (Essay on Sitting in Oblivion) and other texts of the Taoist mystical tradition. In it Sun Simiao gives a short but clear account of self-transformation
and the gradual stages of merging with the Dao. He describes the mystical
ascent in five stages (*wushi* 五時) for the mind and seven phases (*qihou* 七候)
for the body. After adepts have practiced preliminary *yangsheng* techniques

(e.g., abstention from cereals or *bigu, and meditation on the Ocean of Pneuma or qihai 氣海) they will be able to enter the first five stages, which lead from agitation to tranquillity of mind. During the following seven phases, adepts gradually refine the body into Pneuma (*qi); this is said to be the stage of the Real Man (*zhenren). The refinement of Pneuma into Spirit (*shen) results in achieving the stage of the Divine Man (*shenren). Those who join their spirit with the world of form are known as "accomplished men" (zhiren 至人).

Ute ENGELHARDT

📖 Engelhardt 1989; Kohn 1987a, 119–23 (trans.); Kohn 1993b, 319–25 (trans.)

※ Sun Simiao; MEDITATION AND VISUALIZATION

Da Jin Xuandu baozang

大金玄都寶藏

Precious Canon of the Mysterious Metropolis of the Great Jin

The compilation of the *Da Jin Xuandu baozang* was completed in 1192, merely two years after the Jurchen ruler Zhangzong (r. 1190–1208) provided authorization for material and editorial assistance. It evolved as an expansion of the *Zhenghe Wanshou daozang* (Taoist Canon of the Ten-Thousand-Fold Longevity of the Zhenghe Reign Period), printed during Huizong's reign (r. 1100–1125). The story of how it came into being is told in an undated stele inscription recorded in the *Gongguan beizhi* 宮觀碑誌 (Epigraphic Memorials of Palaces and Abbeys; CT 972, 21b–26a), an anonymous anthology compiled no earlier than 1264.

The undated epigraphic history of the *Da Jin Xuandu baozang* is authored by Wei Boxiao 魏搏霄 of Daming 大名 (Hebei), identified as a Junior Compiler in the Historiography Institute affiliated with the Hanlin Academy. Wei presents his account as the personal narrative of Sun Mingdao 孫明道, Superintendent of the Tianchang guan 天長觀 (Abbey of Celestial Perpetuity). The site of this temple compound is now home to the *Baiyun guan (Abbey of the White Clouds) of Beijing. The clergy occupying the temple during the Jurchen regime were long hampered by the lack of a complete copy of the Taoist Canon.

In 1188, Zhangzong's grandfather Shizong (r. 1161–90) commanded the transfer of the blocks for the Song Canon held in the Southern Capital (i.e., Kaifeng) to the Tianchang guan in the Central Capital (i.e., Beijing). Scriptures from the Yuxu guan 玉虛觀 (Abbey of the Jade Void) in the Central Capital were also shifted to the Tianchang guan for purposes of collation. Zhangzong had the storage facility for the blocks of the Canon restored in 1190 and bestowed a grant of land, enlarging the temple compound of the Tianchang guan. Two unidentified Civil Officials (*wenchen* 文臣), moreover, arrived at the abbey by imperial command to assist Superintendent Sun in restoring lacunae so that a complete Canon could be issued in print.

Sun sent members of the abbey out on a nationwide search for scriptures. He also turned his attention to recruiting block-cutters as well as gathering the necessary raw materials. A colleague named Zhao Daozhen 趙道真 vowed to come up with the funds for the timber by soliciting alms throughout the country. Within two years, everything was in place. Altogether 1,074 *juan* of additional scriptures were brought together. With the cutting of 21,800 supplementary blocks, the total came to 83,198. Sun convened fellow clergy-men to organize the texts according to the Three Caverns (*SANDONG) and Four Supplements (*sifu* 四輔). The compilation that resulted comprised 6,455 *juan* and was given the title *Da Jin Xuandu baozang*. The inspiration for this title may be traced to the *Buxu jing* 步虛經 (Scripture on Pacing the Void) of the *Lingbao corpus, which locates Xuandu 玄都 in a celestial realm high above the Three Clarities (*sanqing*). Copies of this new Canon were report-edly offered as imperial gifts on occasion. Nothing printed in it seems to have survived. The blocks from which it was cut were presumably lost with the destruction of the Tianchang guan after the arrival of the Mongols in 1215.

Judith M. BOLTZ

📖 Chen Guofu 1963, 156–61; van der Loon 1984, 45–47 and 50; Zhu Yueli 1992, 150–52

※ DAOZANG AND SUBSIDIARY COMPILATIONS

Da Song Tiangong baozang

大宋天宮寶藏

Precious Canon of the Celestial Palace of the Great Song

This canon of 1016 evolved as a revised, enlarged version of an earlier effort initiated by Song Taizong (r. 976–97). Like Tang Xuanzong (r. 712–56), Song Taizong ordered a comprehensive search for Taoist writings. In 990, he put his Policy Adviser Xu Xuan 徐鉉 (917–92) in charge of a team of collators. An eminent Taoist Master named Zhang Qizhen 張契真 (936–1006) is known to have been among the clergy selected for this task by their respective Metropoli-tan Registrars. A collection of over 7,000 *juan* was thereby reduced to a canon totalling 3,737 *juan* for copying and distribution to major temple compounds. Work on its successor began under Song Zhenzong (r. 997–1022).

By the late summer of 1009, ten Taoist masters who had been sent to the capital to work on liturgical reform were selected in turn to produce a new recension of the canon. The next year this enterprise fell under the aegis of the imperial library, the Chongwen yuan 崇文院 (Institute for the Venera-tion of Literature). Song Zhenzong had his Minister of Rites *Wang Qinruo (962–1025) oversee the project. Wang submitted a catalogue of the new canon to the emperor in April of 1016. Song Zhenzong composed a preface and gave it the title *Baowen tonglu* 寶文統錄 (Comprehensive Register of Precious Literature). A search list for the imperial library issued in 1145 alternatively credits Wang with the *Sandong sifu bu jingmu* 三洞四輔部經目 (Catalogue of the Scriptures Categorized in the Three Caverns and Four Supplements) in seven *juan*. The catalogue of the older canon from which Wang's work was derived in fact bore the title *Sandong sifu jingmu* 三洞四輔經目 (Catalogue of the Scriptures of the Three Caverns and Four Supplements).

A bibliographic postface surviving from the lost *Sanchao guoshi* 三朝國史 (State History of Three Reigns) of 1030 states that the *Baowen tonglu* accounted for altogether 4,359 *juan*, but lists components totalling 4,350 *juan*: *Dongzhen* 洞真 620, *Dongxuan* 洞玄 1,013, *Dongshen* 洞神 172, *Taixuan* 太玄 1,407, *Taiping* 太平 192, *Taiqing* 太清 576, and *Zhengyi* 正一 370. Variant resources, moreover, disagree on the number of *juan* deleted from and added to the old canon of 3,737 *juan*. Wang did convince the emperor to shift the *Daode jing* and *Yinfu jing* from the supplements to the opening component of *Dongzhen* and to include the *Huahu jing* that earlier had been excised by imperial decree because of its provocative nature.

Sometime in late 1015 or early 1016, the Assistant Draftsman Zhang Junfang 張君房 (961?–1042?) was sent to Yuhang 餘杭 (Zhejiang) to oversee the copying of the texts. Zhang writes in his preface to the *Yunji qiqian* (ca. 1028–29) that Zhu Yiqian 朱益謙 and Feng Dezhi 馮德之 were among the Taoist masters lined up by the Yuhang Prefect Qi Lun 戚綸 (954–1021) to serve as collators. It was when Qi was transferred to a new post, according to Zhang, that he was then put in charge, on the endorsement of both the Prefect himself and Wang Qinruo. The incomplete classification of texts at the time, Zhang claims, led him to draw on collections of Taoist writings from Suzhou (Jiangsu), Yuezhou 越州 (Zhejiang), and Taizhou 台州 (Zhejiang), as well as Manichaean scriptures found in the Fuzhou (Fujian) region. The final product, by his count, totalled 4,565 *juan* and was entitled *Da Song Tiangong baozang*. Seven sets, Zhang states, were presented to the emperor by the spring of 1019. Wang Qinruo is known to have petitioned the emperor four years earlier to authorize the imperial library to produce fifteen copies of the new canon for distribution to temples. By 1018, Song Zhenzong himself had already presented a copy on request to the ruler of Jiaozhi 交阯 (present-day Vietnam). Several temples in the far west of what is now Sichuan province, however, did not receive copies of the canon until after a special petition had been submitted in 1064. The successor to this hand-copied collection of Taoist texts is the *Zhenghe Wanshou daozang*, the first Taoist Canon to be produced as a woodcut printing.

Judith M. BOLTZ

📖 Chen Guofu 1963, 130–46; van der Loon 1984, 4–6, 29–39, and 74; Lu Renlong 1990

※ Wang Qinruo; DAOZANG AND SUBSIDIARY COMPILATIONS

Dacheng

大成

Great Perfection; Great Completion

Dacheng (or Da Cheng) was the name of the state founded by *Li Xiong in 306 CE. The Li family, and the ruling group of the Dacheng state as a whole, had been followers of the Way of the Celestial Masters (*Tianshi dao) for generations, and belonged to the Ba 巴 ethnicity which supplied many of the faith's early followers. Their ancestors had been transferred to the northwest (modern Gansu province) in 215, when the Celestial Master kingdom of *Zhang Lu surrendered to Cao Cao, and they had returned to the Sichuan region only around 300, driven by plague, famine, and rebellion.

The name Dacheng was taken from a poem in the *Shijing* 詩經 (Book of Odes; Mao 毛 179), and by the Han dynasty was understood to refer a future utopian age. Li Xiong chose this name to reflect his own belief in a Taoist kingdom of Great Peace (*taiping), the advent of which he hoped to hasten through enlightened Taoist rule. He took as his chancellor a Taoist sage and local leader named *Fan Changsheng and is said to have consulted him in all matters. Governmental policies attributed by some to Li's Taoist beliefs include a simplified code of laws, leniency in the enforcement of corporeal punishment, reduced taxes, aid to the needy, fair markets, and the avoidance of warfare.

After Li Xiong's death in 334, the Taoist character of the state waned. With the accession of Li Shou 李壽 in 338, the name of the state was changed to Han 漢, implicitly abandoning the utopian vision of the state, but Taoist influence remained, as evidenced by an attempt to restore the state, after its demise in 347, under the son of Fan Changsheng. The Dacheng state was a concrete manifestation of the early Taoist millenarian political vision and the fact that it was non-Chinese members of the church who realized this reflects the significance the Taoist promise of salvation held to ethnic minorities.

Terry KLEEMAN

📖 Kleeman 1998; Seidel 1969–70, 233–36

※ Fan Changsheng; Li Xiong; MESSIANISM AND MILLENARIANISM

Dadong zhenjing

大洞真經

Authentic Scripture of the Great Cavern

The *Dadong zhenjing*, also known as "Sanshijiu zhang" 三十九章 or "Thirty-Nine Stanzas," is the central scripture of the *Shangqing revelations. The term *dadong*, which also means Great Profundity and is sometimes used as a synonym of "Shangqing," is glossed as "supreme, unlimited darkness where one attains the Void and guards tranquillity." It alludes therefore to the primordial Origin, the state in which the two complementary principles (Yin and Yang, or Heaven and Earth) are not yet separated and nothing can be seen.

The Taoist Canon contains several versions of this scripture, all of which date from the Song or Yuan periods. All have undergone interpolations but are largely authentic. The version in the *Shangqing dadong zhenjing* 上清大洞真經 (Authentic Scripture of the Great Cavern of the Highest Clarity; CT 6) is the closest one to the original text, except for the first and the sixth *juan* which are later additions. This version bears a preface by *Zhu Ziying (976–1029) and two postfaces dated to the late thirteenth and early fourteenth centuries. The version in the *Wenchang dadong xianjing* 文昌大洞仙經 (Immortal Scripture of the Great Cavern by Wenchang; CT 5) is named after the god *Wenchang and has Song prefaces; it is also available with a commentary and with prefaces dating from the early fourteenth century (*Wenchang dadong xianjing* 文昌大洞仙經; CT 103). Another version of the scripture in the Taoist Canon is entitled *Dadong yujing* 大洞玉經 (Jade Scripture of the Great Cavern; CT 7), while three other fragmentary editions and commentaries are in the *Daozang jiyao* (vol. 3).

The *Dadong zhenjing* teaches how to join the celestial and corporeal spirits, and accordingly follows a double structure. Each of its thirty-nine sections contains two levels, one celestial and one corporeal. The central part of each section consists of stanzas addressed to celestial kings; they describe heavenly palaces and the salvation of the believer and his ancestors who, once delivered from the bonds of death, participate in the heavenly frolicking of the deities. These stanzas are inserted between two shorter parts devoted to the inner deities (see figs. 14 and 27) who close the "gates" of the body where mortal breaths blow in. Before the practitioner recites the celestial stanzas, he must summon and visualize the guardian of each mortal breach, and cause him to descend from the brain (corresponding to heaven within the body) to the

Fig. 27. Visualization of the Lords of the thirty-nine gates (*hu* 戶) of the human body. *Shangqing dadong zhenjing* 上清大洞真經 (Authentic Scripture of the Great Cavern of the Highest Clarity; CT 6), 1.19b–20a. (For other deities of the *Dadong zhenjing* see fig. 14.)

mortal "gate" to guard it. The end of each section is concerned with the drawing and manipulation of a talisman (*FU) that represents the correspondent inner deity.

The *Dadong zhenjing* is the kernel of a cluster of texts that describe a complete meditational liturgy. A first set of texts consists of original revealed scriptures containing the esoteric (*nei* 內) names of the heavens, stanzas addressed to the kings of the Yuqing 玉清 (Jade Clarity) heaven, and a "revealed commentary" attributed to Daojun 道君, the Lord of the Dao. This group includes the following texts:

1. *Shangqing dadong zhenjing* (CT 6) and *Shangqing jiutian Shangdi zhu baishen neiming jing* 上清九天上帝祝百神內名經 (Shangqing Spell of the Nine Heavens and the Highest Emperor, Scripture of the Esoteric Names of the Hundred Spirits; CT 1360)

2. *Shangqing dadong zhenjing* (CT 6) and *Miemo shenhui gaoxuan zhenjing* 滅魔神慧高玄真經 (Exalted and Mysterious Authentic Scripture on the Extermination of Demons and Spiritual Wisdom; CT 1355)

3. *Shi sanshijiu zhang jing* 釋三十九章經 (Exegesis of the Scripture in Thirty-Nine Stanzas; YJQQ 8.1a–14)

The second set of texts includes later, probably apocryphal writings mainly concerned with two meditation techniques. The first is the *huifeng* 迴風

(whirlwind) method, which consists in visualizing a white pneuma that spreads through the whole body and becomes purple. Then, as one exhales it, the pneuma transforms itself into a newborn infant who is the androgynous Emperor One (Diyi 帝一), father and mother of all. This method exists in two variants. One appears in the *Shangqing dadong zhenjing* (CT 6), the *Miemo shenhui gaoxuan zhenjing* (CT 1355), and the *Huifeng hunhe diyi zhi fa* 迴風混合帝一之法 (Method of the Emperor One for the Unitive Fusion through the Whirlwind; YJQQ 30.10b–22a). The other variant is in the *Jinhua yujing* 金華玉經 (Jade Scripture of the Golden Flower; CT 254) and the *Changsheng taiyuan shenyong jing* 長生胎元神用經 (Scripture of the Divine Operation of Embryonic Origin for Long Life; CT 1405, 8a–9a). The second method, called *Xuanmu bajian* 玄母八簡 (Eight Tablets of the Mysterious Mother), consists in the visualization of divinities who ride in carriages of light and clouds into the eight directions of the world, and is described in the *Ciyi jing*.

Isabelle ROBINET

📖 Chen Guofu 1963, 15–16 and 17–19; Mugitani Kunio 1992; Ōfuchi Ninji 1978–79, 1: 173 (crit. notes on the Dunhuang ms.) and 2: 355 (reprod. of the Dunhuang ms.); Robinet 1983c; Robinet 1984, 2: 29–44; Robinet 1993, 97–117; Robinet 1997b, 132–34

※ Shangqing

dafan yinyu

大梵隱語

"secret language of the Great Brahmā"

The *dafan yinyu* refers to words and phrases found in the *Lingbao scriptures that are said to be powerful words from the language of the Thirty-two Heavens (*sanshi'er tian) in past *kalpas* (*jie*). These appear both transliterated into Chinese graphs, for recitation, and in the form of a complex talismanic script, the "original forms" of the graphs. In that portions of the Lingbao scriptures are held to be translated from this "language," the *dafan yinyu* clearly mimics the translation of Buddhist scriptures from Sanskrit and other languages, called *fanwen* 梵文. In fact, recognizable Buddhist translation terms sometimes occur in the scriptures. For these reasons, *dafan yinyu* has been called "pseudo-Sanskrit."

The transliterations appear in the *Duren jing (Scripture on Salvation), where they are divided into eight syllables for each of the Thirty-two Heavens (see table 19). The original graphs in which they were written figure in the *Zhutian neiyin ziran yuzi* 諸天內音自然玉字 (The Self-Generating Jade Graphs and Inner Sounds of All the Heavens; CT 97), which also provides a celestial commentary on the language. This commentary reveals the words said to be written on the gates and palaces of the Thirty-two Heavens and demonstrates that each graph making up these words in fact represents further words, the names of gods, palaces, and celestial locales.

In that each graph represents further words, the "secret language" betrays Taoist awareness of the mnemonic use of the *arapacana* syllabary as revealed in such Buddhist *sūtras* as the *Prajñāpāramitā* (Perfection of Wisdom) in 25,000 lines, translated as the *Scripture of Radiant Prajñā* (*Fanguang banruo jing* 放光般若經; T. 221) by Mokṣala in 291. Recitation of the syllables of *arapacana* enabled the practitioner to memorize points of doctrine and conferred miraculous abilities. Recitation of the *Duren jing*, in continuation of the ancient Chinese belief that knowledge of a demon or spirit's name sufficed to control it, held out the hope that through knowledge of the origins of the universe, the names and locations of the celestial bureaucracy, and its orderly workings, practitioners might hope to ensure the proper functioning of that bureaucracy. A further concept underlying the *dafan yinyu* is that possession of these secret words marked the bearer as part of the celestial order.

In line with this hope, the graphs are employed in Lingbao burial rites outlined in the *Miedu wulian shengshi miaojing* 滅度五鍊生尸妙經 (Wondrous Scripture on Salvation through Extinction and the Fivefold Refinement of the Corpse; CT 369). Examples of stones bearing these graphs have been found in tombs dating to the Tang and later periods near Xi'an, Luoyang, and Chengdu. The earliest practice seems to have been to bury the graphs associated with the appropriate one of the five directions with the deceased, though priests' graves might hold all 256 graphs for the Thirty-two Heavens in the four directions, plus sixteen additional graphs associated with the center.

The *dafan yinyu* in time became fairly widely known. At least one of the words of this language entered the common poetic vocabulary during the Tang.

Stephen R. BOKENKAMP

📖 Bokenkamp 1989; Bokenkamp 1991; Bokenkamp 1997, 385–89; Wang Yucheng 1996; Zürcher 1980, 107–12

※ *sanshi'er tian*; *Duren jing*; Lingbao; TAOISM AND CHINESE BUDDHISM

Daluo tian

大羅天

Great Canopy Heaven

The Great Canopy Heaven appears in *Lingbao texts as the highest heaven in two different cosmological systems. In the first, it is associated with the Thirty-two Heavens (*sanshi'er tian). Although these heavens are located horizontally in the four directions with the Great Canopy Heaven situated above them, their number brings to mind the thirty-three heavens of Indian Buddhist cosmology. In the second system, the Great Canopy Heaven is placed above a vertical series of three heavens that represent a synthesis of earlier Taoist ideas. In this system, the *Tianshi dao idea of the Three Pneumas (sanqi 三氣; see *santian and liutian), which sequentially arose at the beginning of the cosmos, was combined with the Heavens of the Three Clarities (*sanqing), which developed simultaneously. According to Lingbao cosmogony, the division into three pneumas led to the creation of Great Clarity (Taiqing 太清), Highest Clarity (Shangqing 上清), and Jade Clarity (Yuqing 玉清). These three heavens are topped by the Great Canopy Heaven, the residence of Yuanshi tianzun 元始天尊 (Celestial Worthy of Original Commencement; see *sanqing) who is the highest Lingbao celestial being.

In Tang dynasty Taoist texts, an attempt was made to synthesize the various cosmologies. In one systematization, the Great Canopy Heaven is placed above the twenty-eight heavens of the Three Realms (sanjie 三界, i.e., desire, form, formlessness), the Four Heavens of the Seed-People (si zhongmin tian 四種民天), and the Heavens of the Three Clarities (see table 20). As were many Taoist cosmological terms and imagery, the Great Canopy Heaven was also adopted as a metaphor for a celestial palace by Tang poets, particularly in the creations of Li Bai 李白 (Li Bo, 701–62) and *Wu Yun (?–778).

Amy Lynn MILLER

📖 Bokenkamp 1997, 382–83

※ *sanshi'er tian*

Danfang jianyuan

丹方鑑源

Mirror-Origin of the Alchemical Methods

Compiled by Dugu Tao 獨孤滔 in the middle of the tenth century, this work
(CT 925) consists of an enumeration of about 240 substances used in *waidan.
The samples are classified into twenty-five sections according to their nature,
appearance, or color (e.g., Salts, *zhuyan* 諸鹽; Sands, *zhusha* 諸砂; Yellows,
zhuhuang 諸黃), with short notes describing their properties. With the *Shiyao
erya* and the *Jinshi bu wujiu shu jue* 金石簿五九數訣 (Instructions on an Inventory of Forty-Five Metals and Minerals; CT 907; Pregadio 1997), both dating
from the Tang period, the *Danfang jianyuan* is one of the main sources on the
use of *materia medica* in *waidan*. None of these three texts belongs to the main
literary tradition of pharmacology, so they provide information not always
found in the standard pharmacopoeias.

The main source of the *Danfang jianyuan* is an anonymous text dating
from the middle of the eighth century, entitled *Danfang jingyuan* 丹房鏡源
(Mirror-Origin of the Chamber of the Elixirs) and partly preserved in *j.* 4 of
a Song or later alchemical collection, the *Qianhong jiageng zhibao jicheng* 鉛汞
甲庚至寶集成 (Complete Collection on the Ultimate Treasure Made of Lead
and Mercury, *jia* [= Real Mercury] and *geng* [= Real Lead]; CT 919). Both the
Danfang jianyuan and its source are available in a critical edition by Ho Peng
Yoke (1980), based on a comparison with quotations in Li Shizhen's 李時珍
(DMB 859–65) *Bencao gangmu* 本草綱目 (The Pharmacopoeia Arranged into
Headings and Subheadings; ca. 1593) and with a Japanese manuscript dated
1804 (on the edition of the Taoist Canon on which this manuscript is based,
see Barrett 1994a).

Fabrizio PREGADIO

📖 Fung and Collier 1937 (part. trans.); Ho Peng Yoke 1980 (crit. ed.); Meng
Naichang 1993a, 65–67; Needham 1976, 180–81

※ *waidan*

Danfang xuzhi

丹房須知

Required Knowledge for the Chamber of the Elixirs

The *Danfang xuzhi* (CT 900) is a *waidan work compiled in 1163 by Wu Wu 吳
悟, who also wrote a *neidan text, the *Zhigui ji* 指歸集 (Anthology Pointing
to Where One Belongs; CT 921). Its twenty-one sections (the last of which
is incomplete; see Boltz J. M. 1993b, 92) describe a method for compounding
an elixir based on lead and mercury. Each section concerns one stage or facet
of the method, with topics ranging from the choice of one's companions to
the ingestion of the elixir.

Although the *Danfang xuzhi* is one of the few late *waidan* works that describe
rites performed during the alchemical process, it consists almost entirely of
quotations from about a dozen earlier sources, including a *neidan* work, the
Ruyao jing (Mirror for Compounding the Medicine). This format suggests
that its account of the process does not derive from actual practice, and that
Wu Wu's purpose was to provide a survey of the *waidan* alchemical process by
selecting and arranging passages from other works into a logical sequence.

The information given on the ritual features of the alchemical process is
nonetheless valuable. The elixir is made by three people, who are first to perform the purification practices (*zhai* 齋); one of the helpers takes care of the
levels of water and fire in the furnace, and another of fire phasing (*huohou*).
The elixir is to be compounded away from tombs, closed wells, and places
in which wars have been fought or women have delivered children. Women,
Buddhist monks, and domestic animals are not allowed to enter the laboratory
(the Chamber of the Elixir, *danshi* 丹室), in which incense should constantly
burn (a method for making incense is given in the text). The alchemical altar is
protected by an invocation addressed to Xuanyuan huangdi taishang Laojun 玄
元皇帝太上老君 (Most High Lord Lao, August Emperor of Mysterious Origin;
trans. Sivin 1980, 289–90). Other invocations are uttered before compounding
the elixir, before kindling the fire, and before opening the furnace.

Fabrizio PREGADIO

📖 Meng Naichang 1993a, 69–71; Sivin 1980, 289–90 and 293

※ *waidan*

dantian

丹 田

Cinnabar Field(s); Field(s) of the Elixir

The *dantian* are three loci in the human body that play a major role in breathing, meditation, and *neidan practices. Located in the regions of the abdomen, heart, and brain, but devoid of material counterparts, they establish a tripartite division of inner space that corresponds to other threefold motives in the Taoist pantheon and cosmology.

The three Fields. The lower Cinnabar Field is the *dantian* proper and is the seat of essence (*jing). Different sources place it at 1.3, 2, 2.4, 3, or 3.6 inches (*cun* 寸) below or behind the navel, and consider it to be the same as, or closely related to, other loci in the same region of the body: the Gate of the Vital Force (*mingmen), the Origin of the Pass (*guanyuan* 關元), and the Ocean of Pneuma (*qihai* 氣海). The lower *dantian* lies near the *huiyin* 會陰 ("gathering of Yin"), at the meeting point of the Control Channel and the Function Channel (*dumai and *renmai*; see fig. 31). In the first stage of the *neidan* process ("refining essence into pneuma," *lianjing huaqi* 鍊精化氣), circulating the essence along these two channels generates the inner elixir.

The middle Cinnabar Field is at the center of the chest according to some authors, or between the heart and the navel according to others. It is the seat of pneuma (*qi) and is also called Yellow Court (*huangting* 黃庭), Crimson Palace (*jianggong* 絳宮), or Mysterious Female (*xuanpin). Its central position in the body also inspired the names Central Palace (*zhonggong* 中宮) and "One Opening at the Center of the Person" (*shenzhong yiqiao* 身中一竅). In the second stage of the *neidan* process ("refining pneuma into spirit," *lianqi huashen* 鍊氣化神), the elixir is moved from the lower to the middle *dantian* and is nourished there.

The upper Field is located in the region of the brain and is the seat of spirit (*shen). Also known as Muddy Pellet (*niwan) or Palace of Qian ☰ (*qiangong* 乾宮, with reference to the trigram representing Pure Yang), it is divided into Nine Palaces (*jiugong) or nine chambers arranged in two rows. *Niwan* denotes both the upper *dantian* as a whole and the innermost palace or chamber (the third one in the lower row; see fig. 62). Moving the inner elixir to the upper Field marks the third and last stage of the *neidan* process ("refining spirit and reverting to Emptiness," *lianshen huanxu* 鍊神還虛).

Dantian and meditation. The *neidan* tradition has inherited and developed several notions that have evolved in various contexts since Han times. The term *dantian* first occurs in two sources related to the divinization of Laozi, both dating from 165 CE: the **Laozi ming* (Inscription for Laozi) mentions the term in connection to the Purple Chamber (*zifang* 紫房, the gallbladder), and the *Wangzi Qiao bei* 王子喬碑 (Stele to Wangzi Qiao) relates it to meditation practices (Seidel 1969, 44, 58–59, and 123; Holzman 1991, 79). One of the two main sources on early Taoist meditation, the third-century **Huangting jing* (Scripture of the Yellow Court), frequently refers to the three *dantian* as the Three Fields (*santian* 三田) and the Three Chambers (*sanfang* 三房), and also mentions the Yellow Court and the Muddy Pellet. The other main early Taoist meditation text, the **Laozi zhongjing* (Central Scripture of Laozi), gives the first detailed description of the lower Field, saying that it contains the whole cosmos and is the residence of the material carriers of essence (*jing*), i.e., semen for men and menstrual blood for women (1.12b–13a). The same passage shows that the appellation "cinnabar" originally derives from the red color of the innermost part of the *dantian*, with no direct relation to the mineral cinnabar or to the elixir.

In several early descriptions, the three *dantian* appear as residences of inner gods visualized by adepts in meditation practices—in particular, the One who moves along the three Fields. The best-known occurrence of the term *dantian* in this context is in the **Baopu zi*:

> The One has surnames and names, clothes and colors. In men it is nine tenths of an inch tall, in women six tenths. Sometimes it is in the lower *dantian*, two inches and four tenths below the navel. Sometimes it is in the middle *dantian*, the Golden Portal of the Crimson Palace (*jianggong jinque* 絳宮金闕) below the heart. Sometimes it is in the space between the eyebrows: at one inch behind them is the Hall of Light (**mingtang* 明堂), at two inches is the Cavern Chamber (*dongfang* 洞房), and at three inches is the upper *dantian*. (*Baopu zi*, 18.323)

The **Shangqing* sources further develop this view of the *dantian*. The **Suling jing* outlines a meditation method on the Three Ones (**sanyi*) residing in the three *dantian* (see the entry **sanyi*) and describes the upper Field using the same terminology as the *Baopu zi* (Robinet 1993, 127–31; see fig. 62). The practice of embryonic breathing (**taixi*), also known as "breathing of the Cinnabar Field" (*dantian huxi* 丹田呼吸) further contributed to shape the *neidan* view of the *dantian*.

Fabrizio PREGADIO

Darga 1999, 95–98; Despeux 1979, 23–27; Despeux 1994, 74–80; Maspero 1981, 298–99, 360–63, 383–86, and 455–59; Needham 1983, 38–40 and 107–8; Robinet 1984, 1: 125–26; Robinet 1993, 81–82 and 127–31; Wang Mu 1990, 264–66

※ *niwan*; *sanguan*; *zhoutian*; *neidan*; TAOIST VIEWS OF THE HUMAN BODY

Dao

道

"The Way"

Among the most difficult issues in the study of Taoism is that of explaining the term *dao*. The public often sees little difficulty, since a century of writers have "explained" the idea, based on simplistic understandings of the *Daode jing*. For twentieth-century philosophers, the issue was more complicated, but their task was ultimately given comfortable boundaries by the notion that Taoism was a "school of thought" consisting merely of the *Daode jing*, the *Zhuangzi, and a few commentaries. Such misunderstandings, though enshrined by generations of sinologists, deserve repudiation, for, rooted in Confucian perspectives, they are often at odds with the facts of both Taoist tradition and East Asian cultural history. Achieving an accurate understanding of the term *dao* requires us to break with such interpretive frameworks and put aside decades of orientalist romanticization. By recognizing the wide range of meanings that the term carried through Taoism's long evolution in China, we can achieve an understanding that, while more complex, is also more accurate and properly nuanced.

"Dao": Polysemy and non-reification. To be faithful to the values of premodern and modern Taoists, we must beware allowing our interpretations of the term *dao* to be tainted by other, non-Taoist concepts that may initially appear analogous. The Taoists' Dao does not quite correspond to concepts of "the Absolute" in other Asian or Western philosophical or religious systems. Taoists of many ages warned against reifying the term: the celebrated opening words of the *Daode jing* warn that verbalizations cannot truly convey what the term *dao* signifies, and its twenty-fifth section repeats such warnings. Later Taoists often insisted that the term is "empty" of definable content, and throughout Chinese history Taoists generally maintained its polysemy—its rich variety of meanings, which Taoists seldom disentangled in pursuit of intellectual clarity. For example, the seventh-century *Daojiao yishu (Pivot of Meaning of the Taoist Teaching) opens: "This Dao is the ultimate of reality (*zhen* 真), the ultimate of subtlety, and yet there is nothing that is not penetrated by its emptiness." At times, Taoist intellectuals of many periods went further, to express conceptually exactly *what* that inexpressible Dao actually was, and exactly *how* it relates to the sensible world—though not always in terms that seem accessible to religious practice.

To a great extent, Taoists' ambivalence about reification of Dao prefigures, and parallels, the struggles of Chan/Zen Buddhists (who were deeply influenced by elements of classical Taoism, like *Zhuangzi*). The reason for Taoists' resistance to reifying Dao is that, like many Chan/Zen Buddhists, Taoists valued spiritual practice over intellectualization, and refused to allow philosophical conceptualization to supplant the practice of self-cultivation. To Taoists, "being Taoist"—i.e., achieving the goals of Taoist practice—could take place without necessarily having any intellectually coherent explanation of what Dao "is." In that sense, to *be* Taoist was to ignore an assumption familiar to modern minds—that one cannot pursue or achieve what one has not first coherently conceptualized. Taoists often preferred to leave Dao as a mystery—"mystery beyond mystery."

"Dao": The range of meanings in classical sources. In traditional China, *dao* was a term forced to bear many burdens of meaning, by people of different eras and inclinations. Some were imposed by people who were never, in any sense, Taoists. The original term—perhaps pre-Taoist—denoted a set of teachings that allow us to live life on optimal terms. Confucians, and others in classical China, used the term in that sense. But among those who would apparently become the forerunners of Taoism—i.e., the people who produced such texts as the *Neiye and the Daode jing—the term took on a broader range of meanings. Though the *Daode jing* became the touchstone of many of the theoretical frameworks of many later forms of Taoism, we should beware assuming that it was a *summa* of classical Taoist thought or practice. For instance, many other elements of later Taoist theory and practice can be traced to the *Neiye*, and there the term *dao* is used—quite imprecisely—as a synonym for terms referring to the salubrious life-forces (like *qi) that the practitioner is working to cultivate. While there, as in the *Daode jing*, one reads that, "What gives life to all things and brings them to perfection is called the Way," the *Neiye* otherwise seldom uses the term *dao* as in the *Daode jing* or *Zhuangzi*, or even in terms that are common in other forms of later Taoist thought and practice. For instance, the *Neiye* presents no conceptualization of Dao as the "Mother" of all things, nor differentiates Dao in terms of Non-being and Being (*wu and *you*). Such conceptualizations, which evidently first appear in the *Daode jing*, came to inform such later Taoist systems of thought/practice as *neidan. But the *Daode jing* also uses the term *dao* to mean, "the way life operates": there, Dao is not only a primordial unity from which all phenomena evolve, and to which they ultimately return, but also a benign, if imperceptible, force that operates *within* the phenomenal world—a natural guiding force that leads all things ineluctably to their fulfillment. To some in ancient China, such characteristics clearly suggested the qualities that a healthy person is bequeathed by a loving Mother, and the *Daode jing* goes on to identify the qualities and

operations of Dao in terms of "feminine" qualities like humility, passivity, and selfless love. Thus, the *Daode jing* and the *Neiye*—both important sources of later Taoist thought and practice—provided centuries of theorists and practitioners with a wide array of images, models, and concepts concerning Dao and its cultivation.

"Dao": The object of personal transmission. Another authentic Taoist context for understanding the term *dao* takes the issue beyond the explication of texts, and into the actual lives of practicing Taoists. For instance, an eighth-century biography of *Sima Chengzhen reports that, upon his ascension, "only *Li Hanguang and Jiao Jingzhen 焦靜真 received his Dao" (*Zhenxi* 真系; YJQQ 5.15b–16a) Such language compels us to interpret the term *dao* in terms of *Daode jing* 62, which (in the received text) says that rather than offer luxurious gifts at a ducal enfeoffment, one should "sit and present this Dao." Here, *dao* refers not to some transcendental abstraction, but rather to something very precious, which can be transmitted. Comparable uses of the term appear in Japanese culture, where *dao* was long ago integrated not only into the names of such "religions" as Shintō 神道 ("the Way of the Gods") and Butsudō 佛道 ("the Way of the Buddha"), but also into those of such "martial arts" as *aikidō* 合氣道 ("the way of harmonious *qi*") and *kendō* 劍道 ("the way of the sword"), as well as those of such unique cultural phenomena as *sadō* 茶道 ("the way of tea"). There, the term *dao* had come, by Tang times, to mean something like "a venerable complex of traditional practices." Such connotations resonate with many traditional Taoist usages, where the term *dao* seems to denote "what we, as heirs to our wise forebears, do in order to live our lives most meaningfully." That most basic meaning of the term correlates with its usage by Confucius.

"Dao": The focus of group identity. Through much of Chinese history, the term *dao* was also used as a label for a group within society that shared a particular set of principles or practices. For instance, in late antiquity Chinese historians labelled the followers of *Zhang Daoling as the *Wudoumi dao, i.e., "(the members of) the Way of the Five Pecks." Increasingly, the term *dao* became a convenient cultural label for real, or imagined, "groups." Some such labels, like *Taiqing dao* 太清道 (used by *Tao Hongjing for practitioners of alchemical ideals; see *Taiqing) have no clear relationship to any socially identifiable group. Hence, the term *dao* came to be used, rather liberally, as a designator of any real or imagined group, based upon the recognition or assignment of group identity on the basis of a real or alleged common adherence to some real or imagined set of ideals or practices.

"Dao": The focus of personal spiritual practice. Such sociocultural usages conflict with many modern interpretations, which overemphasize the speculation

found in texts like the *Daode jing*. But such usages can easily be explained in terms of the pre-Qin groups that engaged in certain forms of "bio-spiritual cultivation." In the *Neiye*, the term *dao* was a nebulous denominator for "realities that one ought to cultivate," often used synonymously with such terms as *shen* (spirit). That use of the term clearly retained a central place throughout later Taoism. Generally, all Taoist meditation, from classical times through modern *Quanzhen practices, involve the "cultivation of Dao," i.e., an effort by individuals and groups to cultivate within themselves a numinous reality that constitutes the deepest and purest essence of reality.

A common element of many explanations of Taoist practice—by insiders and outsiders alike—is that such practices are directed toward the "getting" or "achieving" of Dao: from classical to modern times, the person who has fulfilled the spiritual life is commonly styled "he/she who 'has (the) Dao'" (*youdao zhe* 有道者). A common assumption, both within Taoism and, more broadly throughout Chinese culture, is that people's ordinary life lacks an important quality, which must be *acquired or achieved* by appropriate practice and effort. In that sense, *dao* is the term generally applied, by Taoists and non-Taoists alike, to the *goal* of Taoist religious practice, which is to be achieved by moral and spiritual self-development, under the instruction of those who have already fully achieved the goal. (Japanese cultural usages resonate with such meanings.) So Taoists generally used the term *dao* to suggest a deepest and purest essence of reality that is universal and everlasting, but can only be attained by the religious practices specified in a given oral/textual tradition.

"Dao": "The divine." In broadest terms, Taoists also used the term *dao* as shorthand for what Westerners might simply term "the divine." Assuredly, Chinese culture eschewed many elements of Western concepts of "God" (i.e., as creator, lawgiver, or judge). Zhang Daoling did reportedly claim to transmit an authoritative covenant from Lord Lao (*Laojun), and in later Taoism, Lord Lao was often associated with or assimilated to the Lord of the Dao or Lord Dao (Daojun 道君), to whom was often assigned the title Most High (Taishang 太上). Meanwhile, *Lingbao texts say that the world's evolution was initiated by the Celestial Worthy of Original Commencement (Yuanshi tianzun 元始 天尊). As Taoism developed a cult to serve the needs of the general populace and its rulers, it also developed a pantheon. But Lingbao theology seems to have left its mark on modern Taoism, in that all members of the pantheon have their own identity, but are ultimately understood as personifications of the transcendent reality called Dao.

Modern interpreters' secularistic world-view often makes them uncomfortable with Taoism's theistic dimensions. Some moderns have imagined "Taoism" as no more than a "naturalistic philosophy" that may allow for individualistic mystical practice but does not demand, or even encourage, belief in beings beyond ourselves. But the reality is that Taoism, from Han times to today, has not only tolerated a rich array of theistic beliefs, but has cherished them. And to Taoists, Laozi was often a powerful and revered divine being, Lord Lao, who periodically descends into the human world to reveal correct practices or establish a sanctified sociopolitical order (Lagerwey 1987c, 23; Schipper 1993, 113–24; Kohn 1998b; Kohn 1998g).

Still, while untrained visitors to Taoist temples may imagine the beings enshrined there as deities to be worshipped, such establishments have usually been staffed by practitioners who understand such deities as emanations (or even symbolizations) of the universal Dao. For them, the core of Taoist life has always been personal self-cultivation: that life requires them to labor productively—through moral elevation and through meditation and/or ritual—to ascend to such a level that he/she participates fully in the reality of the "transcendental" Dao. Ultimately, therefore, Dao is not truly "impersonal," though it does transcend the limitary boundaries that individuals generally ascribe to their personal reality. In senses that are thus impossible in Western religions, Taoists could—and indeed were expected to—effectively *become* the Dao, and to act in this world as its living embodiment. In those senses, the liturgical activities (**jiao*, **zhai*) of the Taoist priest (**daoshi*) always constituted a meditative/ritual embodiment of the divine power of the Dao (Schipper 1978; Lagerwey 1987c; Schipper 1993). So in the liturgical traditions, as in the meditative and monastic traditions, the authentic Dao of the Taoists—from classical times to the present—is a spiritual reality that is attained and embodied by conscientious practitioners of traditional religious practices.

"Dao": The matrix of spiritual transformation. Taoist usages of the term *dao* thus had various focuses, whose interrelationship has often been difficult for modern minds to perceive. Perhaps more importantly, modern philosophers and spiritual seekers alike—including some in modern China—sometimes unconsciously translate *dao* into terms with which they are more comfortable, finding in it something pleasing that they do not find within their own society's accepted range of ideas. Such rereadings inevitably oversimplify, and sometimes falsify, such terms' meanings, for the act of interpreting it for today's mind strips it of connotations that moderns dislike, and preserve only those that modern interpreters can accept.

A particular problem in this regard is that moderns—heirs of the Western Enlightenment—tend to read Dao only as a transcendental Absolute, which can be accessed only by the solitary mystic. Moderns—in China and the West alike—have been indoctrinated to disregard, or even denounce, elements of "religion" that take place outside the "enlightened person's" individualized pursuit of truth. Taoism's rich array of spiritual models does feature an ancient tradition of ideas and practices that harmonizes well with such pursuits:

from the *Neiye* through *neidan* to today's Quanzhen self-cultivation practices, Taoists have envisioned the spiritual life as a re-unification of one's personal reality with "the absolute Dao" that lies beyond—and is ultimately more real than—the more familiar range of phenomena. But while devotees of such traditions often did ignore Taoism's other spiritual models, they seldom labored to distance themselves from those other models. Modern Quanzhen Taoists, like most of the "ecumenical" Taoists of Tang times, have almost always been quite content to bring their lives, and their world, into harmony with Dao by any means that others throughout Chinese history have found useful, including liturgical activities. Despite many twentieth-century protestations, especially from Westernized Chinese intellectuals, Taoists never really opposed liturgical models to mystical models, in theory or in practice; and they certainly never denounced the former as "superstitious" (the way that early Western interpreters taught the modern public to do). To the contrary, China's Taoists, down to the present, are—by tradition if not by temperament—people who holistically embrace all aspects of reality: models that focus on the individual are complemented (often in the very same tradition) by acknowledgment of the value and importance of society, the political order, and even the non-human world; and models that focus on cultivation of consciousness are complemented by teachings explaining the value and importance of our bodily existence—once it is properly understood. What Dao therefore "is" can—on Taoist terms—be explained in terms of sagely government, or in terms of physiological refinement, or in terms of the *daoshi*'s transformation of a community through liturgy. Viewed holistically—i.e., as the universal key to all Taoist models of activity—Dao can be defined as the true matrix of authentic life in this world. In all Taoist contexts, participants are led (whether through study of intellectuals' texts, or through practices that may not easily be explained in terms of "theoretical" models) to engage themselves in a disciplined process of spiritual transformation. The term *dao* thus refers to the spiritual realities that underlie every aspect of such transformation, whether that transformation be carried out within the individual's mind/body, within the community within which one's life takes place, or within the world as a whole.

Russell KIRKLAND

📖 Bokenkamp 1997, 12–15; Kohn 1992a, 162–76; Kohn 1993b, 11–32; Robinet 1997b, 1–23; Robinet 1999b; Schipper 1993, 3–5

※ *de*; *wu* and *you*; *wuji* and *taiji*; *wuwei*; *xiang*; *xing*; Yin and Yang; *ziran*; *Daode jing*; TRANSCENDENCE AND IMMORTALITY

daochang

道場

1. ritual area, sacred space;
2. Land of the Way

The word *daochang* is used in both Taoism and Buddhism to mean the sacred space where the Dao is practiced (Lagerwey 1993a). It is also used in Taoism as the name of a ritual. In the latter sense, it can indicate either the whole ritual with its many parts lasting several days, or, as described below, the central rite in a *jiao (Offering), when the priest goes in audience before the Celestial Worthies (*tianzun* 天尊) and other divinities.

The Land of the Way is one of the oldest Taoist rites; its form was established by *Lu Xiujing (406–77) and after that underwent little change. It passed through *Du Guangting (850–933) and, preserved in the corpus of the *Lingbao dafa (Great Rites of the Numinous Treasure) from the Song to the Ming periods, has come down to modern times. It is identical in structure to the Three Audiences (*sanchao), which in southern Taiwan are performed in the morning, at noon, and at night on the third day of a five-day *jiao*. According to Wang Qizhen's 王契真 (fl. ca. 1250) *Shangqing lingbao dafa* (Great Rites of the Numinous Treasure of Highest Clarity; CT 1221, *j.* 57), performing the audience rites three times a day reenacts the audience before the supreme deity. The scripture explains that every day, at the *yin* 寅, *wu* 午, and *xu* 戌 hours (formally corresponding to 3–5 am, 11 am–1 pm, and 5–7 pm), the Drum of the Law (*fagu* 法鼓) is sounded in the Palace of Purple Tenuity (Ziwei gong 紫微宮) in the heaven of Jade Clarity (Yuqing 玉清), and then all the highest gods go in audience before Yuanshi tianzun 元始天尊, the Celestial Worthy of Original Commencement. As a result, the rite of the Land of the Way must include an audience before the Three Clarities (*sanqing).

As described in the *Shangqing lingbao dafa* (CT 1221, 57.1b–2a), the rite is composed of the following sections:

1. The high priest (*gaogong* 高功; see *daozhang) ascends the altar and offers incense to express his reverence and sincerity.

2. The priest consecrates the incense burner and announces the purpose of the ritual to the deities. He exteriorizes the deities within his body (see *chushen) and summons the local earth deities so that together they will carry the message to the abode of the celestial deities and announce it there.

3. The priest notifies the assembled deities of his charge and name, and invokes the high-ranking deities, respectfully announcing the reason for holding the ritual.

4. He reads the Green Declaration (*qingci* 青詞), a summary of basic information about the ritual and the intent of the community representatives who are sponsoring it.

5. Incense is offered three times to each of the Three Clarities so that through the merit of the audience, the world may enjoy fortune and happiness, the nine generations of ancestors may attain salvation, and all living beings may gain liberation.

6. Out of concern that the sins of both the living and the dead may remain in the world and exert an evil influence, obeisance is made to the Celestial Worthies of the ten directions, repentance (*chanhui) is made in each direction, and forgiveness is sought from the deities of the Sun, the Moon, the stars, the mountains, the rivers, and the netherworld.

The rite is followed by a final section that comprises chanting the Pacing the Void lyrics (*Buxu ci), venerating the Three Treasures (*sanbao* 三寶, i.e., the Dao, the Scriptures, and the Masters), extinguishing the incense burner in order to return the deities who presented the Statement to their positions within the priest's body, and descending from the altar.

MARUYAMA Hiroshi

📖 Lagerwey 1987c, 106–48; Lü Chuikuan 1994; Ōfuchi Ninji 1983, 271–322

※ *gongde*; *jiao*

Daode jing

道德經

Scripture of the Dao and Its Virtue

The *Daode jing*, also known as *Laozi* 老子, is ascribed to Laozi, who allegedly gave it to *Yin Xi as he left the Middle Kingdom to go to the west. Scholars have long debated its authorship and date. Some think that it is not the work of a single author, some maintain that most of it originated as oral tradition during the Warring States period (403–221), and some suggest that it reached its final form in the late third or the early second century BCE. The *Guodian manuscripts, datable to between 350 and 300 BCE, seem to prove that the *Daode jing* existed at that time in a form very close to the received version.

Editions and manuscripts. The *Daode jing* is a short work, sometimes called the "Text in Five Thousand Words" (*Wuqian zi wen* 五千字文). Most printed editions derive from one of four main versions: the *Yan Zun version, the Heshang gong 河上公 version (see *Laozi Heshang gong zhangju*), the *Wang Bi version, and the so-called "ancient version" (*guben* 古本) recovered from a tomb dated to 202 BCE. The latter exists in turn in two distinct but closely related redactions: one edited by *Fu Yi (554–639) and another edited by Fan Yingyuan 范應元 in the Song period. Two *Dunhuang manuscripts are also worthy of note: the Suo Dan 索紞 manuscript, dated 270 CE, which seems to belong to Heshang gong's tradition (Boltz W. G. 1996), and the *Xiang'er commentary, which lacks the second half and is not divided into sections. None of these versions yield notable differences from the point of view of meaning.

The text is usually divided into two main parts, called *Daojing* 道經 (Scripture of the Dao) and *Dejing* 德經 (Scripture of Virtue), and into eighty-one sections or chapters (*zhang* 章). The two *Mawangdui manuscripts, dated to the second century BCE, reverse the sequence of the two parts, placing the *Dejing* first. The division of the text into eighty-one sections first appears in Heshang gong's version but was not universally accepted until perhaps the Tang period. While some versions are divided into sixty-four, sixty-six, or seventy-two sections, others do not have sections at all. The Guodian slips, in particular, have no division into sections, and while the wording is close to that of the received version, the sequence of the individual passages is often different.

Description. The *Daode jing* combines sentences, often rhymed, expressing general laws dogmatically asserted with aphorisms that may contain traces of oral sayings, and with instructions on self-cultivation and practical or sociopolitical life. The text is often paradoxical, lyrical, and poetical, containing plays on words, contradictions, ambiguous statements, and enigmatic images. Whether the text proposes an art of ruling or ways of self-cultivation or both, imbued or not with mystical and gnostic views, is an open question that scholars often debate on hypothetical grounds. The following description outlines some of the main features on which scholars generally agree, and that were retained in later Taoism.

The Dao. The main contribution of the *Daode jing* to Taoism and Chinese thought lies in the new meaning given to the word *dao* 道. Usually and broadly understood as "way," "method," or "rule of life," *dao* takes on for the first time in the *Daode jing* the meaning of Ultimate Truth, one and transcendent, invisible (*yi* 夷), inaudible (*xi* 希), and imperceptible (*wei* 微; sec. 14), not usable and not namable (sec. 1). Since the Dao is beyond all relationship of differentiation and judgement, it cannot be "*dao*ed," or "said" (*dao*), or practiced as a way. One cannot make use of it, as it is "neither this nor that." However, in spite of this apophatic or negative approach, the Dao, through its Virtue (*de), is said to be the source of all life, the "mother," "pervading" (*tong* 通), "rich in promises" and the only certain reference point (sec. 25); in this sense, it is "both this and that." All that can be said (*dao*) and has a name is transient and pertains to the world; only the Dao that has no name is permanent. "Naming" and language, however, are said to be the "mother" of all things.

This dimension of the Dao was retained, with varying emphases, by all schools of Taoism. The Dao is the source of the world, the point to which everything flows, the "treasure of the world" (sec. 62), that by which Heaven and Earth can exist. It has an evanescent and mysterious hypostatized presence that one would like to grasp or see (sec. 14 and 21), and seems to allude to an inner experience resulting from meditation practices aiming at quiescence (see *qingjing), and from a multidimensional view of the world. This gives the *Daode jing* a poetic and lyrical tone, and endows its teaching with a character different from that of other texts of its time.

Ambivalence and totality. The *Daode jing* repeatedly names pairs of opposites such as good and evil, high and low, Being and Non-being, naming and not naming, because they all imply and support each other, and pertain to a common whole. As does the *Yijing*, it points both to the binary structure of our thinking and to the unity from which oppositions proceed, their relativity and their correlation. The consequences drawn from this view, however, are different from those of the *Yijing*. Whereas the *Yijing* holds that one can know and prevent coming negative events by understanding the laws of the cosmos, the *Daode jing* strives to show that thought is by nature dualistic and cannot grasp the Dao, which lies before and beyond any differentiation. The *Daode jing* not only aims to clarify the inadequacy of language to know the reality of things; in saying that every assumption implies its own negation, it also seeks to unite the two as the reverse and obverse of a coin, or to invert the common order of things so that one can grasp the foundation of all assumptions: for example, to ascend means to begin from the bottom (sec. 39). In doing so, the text sets up a logic of ambivalence that is typical of Taoist thought. Priority is not given to assumption or negation, but to the infinite totality of the Dao where every dualism "has a common origin" (sec. 1).

The Dao encompasses all possibilities because it has no form and no name. Its Virtue is its operation that accomplishes everything in the world. Cosmogonic metaphors connected with mythological themes (Chaos, Mother) call for a Return (*fan) to its primordial undifferentiation, and the infant is taken as a model because it has not yet separated from its Mother. In accord with the logic of ambivalence, however, return to the Origin is not separated from return to the ordinary world, as shown by the simple fact that the *Daode jing* was written for the benefit of human beings.

The void. The *Daode jing's* notion of the void (see *wu and *you*) is the first enunciation of an idea that would later evolve and take a major place in Taoism and Chinese thought. In the *Daode jing*, the void has two levels of functional and existential meaning. Concretely, it is the interstice that allows movement, the receptive hollow in a vessel (sec. 11). As such it also has a cosmic significance: it is the necessary void space that is both the matrix of the world and the place from which the Original Pneuma (*yuanqi) can spring forth and circulate. On the human level, the void is mental and affective emptiness, the absence of prejudices and partialities dictated by the desire or will to attain a goal.

The saint and the sage ruler. The vision of the world introduced in the *Daode jing* is the ideal of the Taoist sage who does not choose between one thing and its opposite, but remains neutral. The saint (*shengren) is serene, withdraws from the affairs of the world, and rejects the established values (the ordinary *dao* or ways) as artificial, in favor of a spontaneous way of life with no virtuous effort toward improvement, and no competition that might introduce disturbances. He lets the Dao and Nature freely operate in him, claiming that if one does so both the world and oneself will go along very well on their own. "Cease all learning," says the sage, the learning that in Confucian terms means striving for something better: one can reach the Truth only by letting it operate naturally (*ziran).

The image of the sage ruler in the *Daode jing* is combined with a "primitivist" tendency that is not unique to this text but can be found in other trends of Chinese thought, including later Taoism. In the Great Antiquity (*shanggu* 上古, the ideal state of humanity projected into the past), the sage ruler does not interfere and is not even known to the people. Like the Dao, he has no name; like the saint, he lets the laws of nature operate spontaneously so that order is established harmoniously among human beings.

Variety of interpretations. The *Daode jing* is open to many interpretations and in fact demands them. The various readings of the commentators have been sometimes classified into schools. For instance, Heshang gong reads the text on two levels, one concerned with self-cultivation and the other with ruling the state; the *Xiang'er* commentary is an example of its use as a catechism for the Celestial Masters (*Tianshi dao); and the *Chongxuan (Twofold Mystery) school of thought gives it a Buddhistic and dialectical interpretation. Legalist, Buddhist, Confucian, and Taoist physiological or alchemical interpretations have also been advanced. The *Daode jing* moreover has been used as a sacred text that, like all sacred writings, must be recited in conjunction with meditation and ritual practices for exorcist and healing purposes.

Isabelle ROBINET

📖 Studies: Baxter 1998; Boltz W. G. 1993; Chan A. K. L. 1991b; Chan A. K. L. 2000; Csikszentmihalyi and Ivanhoe 1999; Fung Yu-lan 1952–53, 1: 170–91; Graham 1989, 213–35; Harper 1995; Kaltenmark 1969b, 5–69; Kohn 1998h; Kohn and LaFargue 1998; Kusuyama Haruki 1983b; LaFargue 1994; LaFargue and Pas 1998; Robinet 1977; Robinet 1996a, 17–30; Robinet 1997b, 25–30; Robinet 1998b; Robinet 1999b; Roth 1999b; Schwartz 1985, 186–254; Sunayama Minoru 1983

📖 Translations: Chan Wing-tsit 1963; Chen E. M. 1989; Ch'en Ku-ying 1977; Henricks 1989 (trans. of the Mawangdui mss.); Henricks 2000 (trans. of the Guodian mss.); LaFargue 1992; Larre 1977; Lau 1982 (trans. of the Wang Bi text and the Mawangdui mss.); Mair 1990 (trans. of the Mawangdui mss.); Waley 1934

※ Laozi and Laojun; DAOJIA; DAOJIAO; TAOISM AND EARLY CHINESE THOUGHT

Daodian lun

道典論

Essays on Taoist Materials

This fragmentary encyclopedia of Taoism survives in four chapters in the Taoist Canon (CT 1130); even the beginning of the first is incomplete. But a reference in the *Bishu sheng xubian dao siku queshu mu* 祕書省續編到四庫書目 (Imperial Library's Supplementary Catalogue of Books Missing from the Four Repositories; 1145; van der Loon 1984, 151) shows that in the Northern Song an edition in thirty chapters existed in the imperial library. Two manuscripts from *Dunhuang (S. 3547 and P. 2920), equating to part of the first chapter, support the impression derived from the materials it cites (none of which seem later than the sixth century) that the work dates to the Tang; the former manuscript includes seventeen lines of material before the start of the Taoist canon text (see Ōfuchi Ninji 1978–79, 1: 348–49).

Like other Taoist handbooks of the Tang period, the *Daodian lun* is composed of extracts from Taoist scriptures from one or two to over a dozen lines in length, arranged so as to illustrate a number of Taoist terms and concepts, though given its fragmentary state, it is not possible to divine much about its organizing principles. Nor has it been compared with other texts in order to determine whether its pattern of organization is reflected elsewhere, though material from handbooks of the same period like the *Sandong zhunang* (The Pearl Satchel of the Three Caverns) would appear to have been absorbed into the early Song *Yunji qiqian (Seven Lots from the Bookbag of the Clouds). The compilation of so many similar digests—for one case of thematic overlap between the *Daodian lun* and another Tang compendium see Stein R. A. 1979, 67—has raised questions as to their function. It is unlikely that a work like this would have served as an aide-mémoire to a trained Taoist priest, but it could have acquainted educated laypersons, especially serving officials, with non-arcane knowledge of a religion which had started to win imperial support, but which hitherto had been seen as too occult for all but the most erudite to explore. Whether the wealth of knowledge of Taoism that appears in literature from the mid-Tang onward was due to direct reading of the original scriptures or consultation of ready reference works such as the *Daodian lun* must also await future research. It is not even clear that its own citations were at first hand; if so, then it is more likely to be prior to ca. 756, since it cites (2.7a) the *Xuanshi jing* 玄示經 (Scripture of Mysterious Manifestations), a work whose direct transmission had evidently ended thereafter (Barrett 1982, 41).

T. H. BARRETT

📖 Ōfuchi Ninji 1978–79, 1: 348–49 (crit. notes on the Dunhuang mss.) and 2: 797–800 (reproductions of Dunhuang mss.); Ōfuchi Ninji and Ishii Masako 1988, 165–69 (list of texts cited); Ozaki Masaharu 1983c, 192–93

Daofa huiyuan

道法會元

Corpus of Taoist Ritual

By far the most voluminous text in the Taoist Canon of 1445, the *Daofa huiyuan* (CT 1220) is a collection of ritual manuals and subsidiary writings drawn from various schools of Taoist practice that flourished throughout south China during the Song and Yuan. The history of this massive 268-*juan* compilation remains a mystery. No copy of the text is known beyond that in the Taoist Canon, where it appears without any indication of provenance. The only preliminary matter accompanying the anthology is a table of contents. Many headings listed in it vary with those in the text proper, revealing a lack of coordination in the anonymous editorship of the text.

Clues to the textual history of individual units of writings can in some cases be derived from prefaces and colophons scattered throughout the *Daofa huiyuan*. The latest internal date recorded in these supporting documents is 1356. The latest identified contributor is the renowned syncretist *Zhao Yizhen

(?–1382), whose name appears repeatedly within the opening fifty-five *juan* devoted to *Qingwei teachings. Several selections in this predominant body of texts include posthumous ritual invocations of the Perfected Zhao (Zhao zhenren 趙真人). Thus, the editorial task of gathering and organizing such a vast assortment of texts would not have been completed any earlier than twenty-five years before the compilation of the Ming Canon was initiated in 1406. It is not at all unlikely that Zhao's own disciples may have had a hand in this pedagogical enterprise. If not Cao Dayong 曹大鏞 (?–1397) or *Liu Yuan-ran (1351–1432), then perhaps Liu's esteemed disciple *Shao Yizheng (?–1462) may have overseen the completion of the *Daofa huiyuan* at the time he took over the editorship of the so-called *Zhengtong daozang* (Taoist Canon of the Zhengtong Reign Period).

Like the opening corpus of Qingwei teachings, the majority of writings in the *Daofa huiyuan* provide instruction on *leifa (Thunder Rites). Many guides on the therapeutic application of such rituals prescribe close cooperation between spirit-mediums (*tongzi* 童子; see *tâng-ki) and experts in specific schools of exorcistic practice. Equally outstanding in this anthology are the detailed and richly illustrated instructions for producing and applying talismans (*FU). It is overall a rich source of documentation for the diverse and highly colorful ritual practices that have stimulated many scenes in Chinese narrative and operatic literature for centuries. Representative units of texts with datable features are listed below by chapter number:

1–55. Qingwei manuals with *Daofa jiuyao* 道法九要 (Nine Essentials of Taoist Rites) by *Bai Yuchan (1194–1229?) in *j.* 1, a colophon dated 1268 by the Qingwei codifier *Huang Shunshen (1224-after 1286) in *j.* 9, and selections by Zhao Yizhen in *j.* 5, 7, 8, 14, and 17.

56. Five Thunder Rites of Yushu 玉樞 (Jade Pivot), with a preface by *Wang Wenqing (1093–1153).

61. Five Thunder Rites of *Shenxiao (Divine Empyrean), with preface by Wang Wenqing.

66–67. Thunderclap (Leiting 雷霆) writings, with a postface dated 1287 by Huang Shunshen and selections by *Sa Shoujian (fl. 1141–78?) and Wang Wenqing.

70. *Xuanzhu ge* 玄珠歌 (Song of the Mysterious Pearl) by Wang Wenqing, with commentary by Bai Yuchan.

71. *Xujing tianshi powang zhang* 虛靖天師破妄章 (Stanzas by the Celestial Master of Empty Quiescence on Smashing Falsity) by the thirtieth Celestial Master *Zhang Jixian (1092–1126).

76. Thunderclap teachings transmitted by Wang Wenqing in the name of Wang Zihua 汪子華 (714–89), with a preface by Bai Yuchan and a postface dated 1103 by the annotator Zhu Weiyi 朱惟一.

77. Thunderclap writings with contributions by Bai Yuchan, *Mo Qiyan (1226–94), and Wang Wenqing's disciple Zou Tiebi 鄒鐵壁.

80–82. Variant Thunder Rites transmitted by Yang Xie 楊燮 (fl. 1225–52), *Lei Shizhong (1221–95), and Bai Yuchan, respectively.

104–8. Jingxiao 景霄 (Effulgent Empyrean) Thunder Rites transmitted from *Chen Nan (?–1213) to Bai Yuchan, with postface ascribed to Yu Ji 虞集 (1272–1348).

111–13. Five Thunder Rites of Baozhu 寶珠 (Precious Pearl) transmitted to the thirty-sixth Celestial Master *Zhang Zongyan (1244–91).

122–23. Thunder Rites of Shaoyang 邵陽, inspired by *Xu Xun (trad. 239–374), with a preface by Chen Nan.

147–53. Yushu (Jade Pivot) Thunderclap Rites, with an introduction dated 1296 by Xue Shichun 薛師淳, providing a biographical account of Bai Yuchan.

156–68. Tianpeng 天蓬 Rites (see under *Tianpeng zhou), citing *Tongchu founder Yang Xizhen 楊希真 (1101–24).

171–78. Tongchu teachings with a postface dated 1225 by Jin Yunzhong 金允中, compiler of the *Shangqing lingbao dafa (Great Rites of the Numinous Treasure of Highest Clarity; CT 1222–23).

188–94. Five Thunder Rites of the Great One (*Taiyi) formulated by Yang Xie, with an introduction dated 1271 by Huang Yixuan 黃一炫.

195–97. Five Thunder Rites of the Eight Trigrams (*bagua), with a postface by Zhang Jixian.

198–206. *Shenxiao (Divine Empyrean) manuals on *liandu (Salvation through Refinement), with a postface by Liu Yu 劉玉 (or Liu Shi 劉世, fl. 1258) and Huoling ge 火鈴歌 (Song of the Fire-Bell) ascribed to *Lin Lingsu (1076–1120).

207. Shishi 施食 (Oblation) ritual manual with instructions ascribed to *Ge Xuan (trad. 164–244), Zhang Shangying 張商英 (1043–1121) and Zhang Zongyan.

210. Danyang 丹陽 ritual manual on jilian 祭鍊 (oblatory refinement), with a preface dated to the eighth month of 1356 by Wang Xuanzhen 王玄真 and postface dated to the twelfth month of 1356 ascribed to Zhang Yu 張雨 (1283–after 1356?).

244–45. *Lingbao ritual teachings of *Ning Benli (1101–81) and Lin Weifu 林偉夫 (1239–1302), as transmitted to the thirty-ninth Celestial Master *Zhang Sicheng (?–1344?).

246–47. Variant ritual manuals inspired by Yin Jiao 殷郊, deity of Taisui 太歲 (Jupiter), with a preface and postface by Peng Yuantai 彭元泰, dated 1274 and 1290, respectively, and a postface dated 1316 by Chen Yizhong 陳一中.

253–56. Dizhi 地祇 (Tutelary Deity) ritual manuals inspired by *Wen Qiong, with a preface dated 1258 by Liu Yu and a colophon dated 1274 by Huang Gongjin 黃公瑾.

264–68. *Fengdu ritual manuals, compiled or annotated in part by Lu Ye 盧埜, master of Liu Yu.

Judith M. BOLTZ

📖 Boltz J. M. 1987a, 39–41 and 47–49; van der Loon 1979; van der Loon 1984, 63; Schipper 1987

※ *leifa*; Lingbao dafa; *neidan*; Qingwei; Shenxiao

daojia

道家

Taoism; "Lineage(s) of the Way"

See entry in "Taoism: An Overview," p. 5.

daojiao

道教

Taoism; Taoist teaching; "Teaching(s) of the Way"

See entry in "Taoism: An Overview," p. 8.

Daojiao lingyan ji

道教靈驗記

Records of the Numinous Efficacy of the Taoist Teaching

The *Daojiao lingyan ji*, compiled by *Du Guangting (850–933) in 905 or shortly thereafter, is the sole surviving example of a literary genre devoted to relating miracles that attested to the efficacy of faith in Taoism. Two earlier compilations of the same sort, completed between 600 and 710, have apparently perished without a trace. Most of the material in Du's work dates from the eighth and ninth centuries so he probably took little from those earlier texts.

There are two versions of the *Daojiao lingyan ji* in the Taoist Canon: an independent work (CT 590) and a collection of excerpts from an early edition of it in the *Yunji qiqian* (j. 117–22). The former includes 169 episodes, but is incomplete as it lacks the last five fascicles of the original twenty. The latter duplicates eighty-three accounts from CT 590, often with variant readings and missing portions, but also contains an additional thirty-five records missing from CT 590. In sum, 204 passages from the original compendium, corresponding to most of the text or about eighteen fascicles, have survived.

According to Du Guangting's preface, "the sage teaches the people to abandon evil and pursue good," and that is essentially the message of the *Daojiao lingyan ji*. To accomplish that objective, Du relates stories that exemplify the principle of reciprocity (*baoying* 報應). Those who attack Taoism—officials who attempt to dismantle temples in order to construct offices for themselves, monks who alter Taoist scriptures to serve the ends of Buddhism, and the like—will be punished. Conversely those who adhere to, defend, or promote Taoism will be rewarded: the sick will be healed, the drought-stricken will be saved with rain, and so forth. In short the *Daojiao lingyan ji* is a polemical work, intended to advance the cause of Taoism by demonstrating that the faith and the faithful enjoy the special protection of the gods and nature.

There are altogether eight divisions to the *Daojiao lingyan ji*:

1. "Palaces and Abbeys" ("Gongguan" 宮觀): temples, *j.* 1–3.

2. "Images of the Venerables" ("Zunxiang" 尊像): icons of the highest deities, *j.* 4–5.

3. "Lord Lao" ("Laojun" 老君): icons of Laozi deified as well as his epiphanies, *j.* 6–7.

4. "Celestial Master" ("Tianshi" 天師): icons of *Zhang Daoling, *j.* 8.

5. "Images of the Perfected, the Queen Mother of the West, Generals, and Divine Princes" ("Zhenren, Wang Mu, Jiangjun, Shenwang" 真人王母將軍神王), *j.* 9.

6. "Scriptures, Practices, Talismans, Registers" ("Jing, fa, fu, lu" 經法符錄), *j.* 10–12.

7. "Bells, Chimes, Ritual Paraphernalia" ("Zhong, qing, fawu" 鐘磬法物), *j.* 13 (includes materials on swords and seals).

8. "Retreats, Offerings, Presenting petitions" ("Zhai, jiao, baizhang" 齋醮拜章), *j.* 14–15.

Besides the above, *j.* 122 of the *Yunji qiqian* contains sections devoted to miracles involving temple property, trees, caves, rivers, stones, wells, and so forth.

The *Daojiao lingyan ji* is one of the main sources for the study of medieval beliefs in the supernatural, but it also supplies a wealth of materials on Taoist practices, priests, abbeys and their accouterments, and gods. In addition, it contains much information on secular subjects—emperors, ministers, literati, rebels, folklore, dreams, natural disasters, epigraphy, geography, salt wells, graves, childbirth, and the like—that is not available elsewhere.

Du Guangting also compiled two other works on miracles that have survived in part: the *Luyi ji* 錄異記 (Records of the Extraordinary; 921/925; CT 591; Verellen 1989, 171–77) and the *Shenxian ganyu zhuan* 神仙感遇傳 (Biographies of Those who Encountered the Immortals; after 904; CT 592).

Charles D. BENN

📖 Verellen 1989, 139–40 and 206–7; Verellen 1992

※ Du Guangting

Daojiao yishu

道教義樞

Pivot of Meaning of the Taoist Teaching

This doctrinal compendium in ten chapters (CT 1129; part of the fifth and all of the sixth chapter are lost) was put together by Meng Anpai 孟安排, of whom we only know that he was in 699 in receipt of the patronage of the Empress Wu at a monastery on Blue Brook Mountain (Qingxi shan 青溪山) in Hubei. Earlier attempts by Yoshioka Yoshitoyo and Kamata Shigeo to pin down his era without this information by means of the contents of his book had reached significantly different conclusions. Meng's stated aim of producing a compendium of greater concision than the *Xuanmen dayi (Great Meaning of the School of Mysteries) also allowed him scope for producing a summary more suited to his time (the reign of the Empress Wu, whose chief legitimation derived from Buddhism; see under *Zhenzheng lun) and place (an area where Taoists and Buddhists had long been living in close proximity and exploring their rival doctrines). In fact this was the very same environment that had earlier produced the redoubtable Buddhist polemicist Falin 法琳 (572–640), author of the *Bianzheng lun (Essays of Disputation and Correction). Meng's link with the Empress seems to have been the result of her father's governorship of the area, although her interests in provincial religion were considerable, and not confined to Buddhism.

Even so, Meng probably considered a Buddhist emphasis in his work as expedient, and one result was his articulation of the implications of the concept of Dao-nature (*daoxing* 道性) for the spiritual destiny of the inanimate world, which appears to have anticipated—if not prompted—the parallel and uniquely East Asian Buddhist conception of "trees and plants achieving

Buddhahood." Other themes in his compilation have been less well explored, though his copious citations yield much useful information. In particular he is our chief source for the threefold and sevenfold formation of the Taoist Canon in two stages, in the fifth and sixth centuries (see *DAOZANG AND SUB- SIDIARY COMPILATIONS). The *Daojiao yishu* represents the high water mark of the influence of Buddhist doctrinal compendia on Taoism; the influence of Tiantai Buddhism (which had a strong center at the nearby Yuquan si 玉 泉寺 or Jade Spring Monastery) has in particular been identified. As a result, and as a result perhaps also of the decline and disappearance of Blue Brook Mountain as a religious center, it seems to have fallen quite rapidly into neglect by later Taoists.

T. H. BARRETT

📖 Barrett 1991b; Chen Guofu 1963, 107; Kamata Shigeo 1968, 67–74, 173–211; Kohn 1992a, 149–54; Nakajima Ryūzō 1980 (index); Ōfuchi Ninji 1979, 255–56; Qing Xitai 1988–95, 2: 264–82; Ōfuchi Ninji and Ishii Masako 1988, 150–60 (list of texts cited); Robinet 1997b, 191–92; Sharf 2002, 57, 67–71; Wang Zongyu 2001; Yoshioka Yoshitoyo 1959a

※ TAOISM AND CHINESE BUDDHISM

Daomen kefan da quanji

道門科範大全集

Great Complete Compendium of Ritual Protocols of the School
of the Dao

The *Daomen kefan daquan ji* (CT 1225) is a collection of *zhai (Retreat) and *jiao (Offering) rituals in eighty-seven *juan*. Although the collection was largely edited by *Du Guangting (850–933), *juan* 25–45, 63, and 65–69 were probably compiled by Zhong Li 仲勵 in the Ming period. Since this work is a compila- tion of documents dating from different times, it must be used with care as a historical source; there is, furthermore, no agreement among scholars about Zhong Li's dates.

The work contains a large number of rituals dating from the Tang and Song periods, classified under the following categories: 1. Time of birth (j. 1–3); 2. Averting illnesses (j. 4–6); 3. Averting disasters (j. 7–9); 4. Praying for rain or snow (j. 10–18); 5. *Wenchang (j. 19–24); 6. Praying for posterity (j. 25–29); 7. Averting calamities and controlling fire (j. 30–36); 8. Securing the household from theft (j. 37–44); 9. Exorcizing inauspicious fate (j. 45–48); 10. Southern and

Northern Dippers (*j.* 49–54); 11. Longevity (*j.* 55–62); 12. *Zhenwu (*j.* 63–68); 13. Immortality (*j.* 75–78); 14. Presenting the Petition for Salvation to the Eastern Peak (*j.* 79–85); 15. Revering the deities (*j.* 86–87). It is not always clear on what basis or principle of classification the individual rituals are allocated to these categories. Each ritual is divided into two parts: Inaugurating the Altar (*qitan* 啟壇) and the Three Audiences (*sanchao) of morning, noon, and evening.

MARUYAMA Hiroshi

📖 Qing Xitai 1994, 2: 150–51

※ Du Guangting; *jiao*; *zhai*

Daomen kelüe

道門科略

Abridged Codes for the Taoist Community

The *Daomen kelüe* (CT 1127) is a polemic written in the fifth century for both rulers and the religious elite, calling for reform of the Taoist church. Attributed to *Lu Xiujing (406–77), the first systematizer of *Lingbao texts and rituals, it includes a commentary not clearly distinguished from the main text. Both the text and the commentary may have been written by Lu himself, or one of his disciples may have abridged the original text and appended a commentary.

As a normative text, the *Daomen kelüe* provides not only an ideal image of the Taoist organization but also an invaluable view of social and religious life in fifth-century China. Lu Xiujing supports the Taoist organizational structure directly derived from the Celestial Masters (*Tianshi dao), one of whose cornerstones was the family register (see *LU). According to the *Daomen kelüe*, in the original Celestial Masters community of the late second century the names of all members of the community were entered into records that listed the dates of births, deaths, and marriages. Nominally meant to avoid confusion in the otherworld, and thus prevent premature summonses from otherworldly officials, these registers were modeled on records used by the government, and organized the community for social and religious purposes such as taxes, corvée labor, rituals, and healing. The records were updated three times a year by both Taoist priests and otherworldly officials at the Three Assemblies (*sanhui). Similarly, cuisine-feasts (*chu) were performed at each birth and marriage. However, by Lu's time such practices had fallen into disuse, and Lu attributes the disorganization of the Taoist community to their neglect.

Another issue discussed in the *Daomen kelüe* is the ordination and promotion of novices and priests. The advancement of believers in the Taoist hierarchy traditionally followed a strict form and order. At each level, novices were invested with a higher rank and more registers, which provided them with a larger number of otherworldly beings under their command. Lu complains that by the fifth century these rules were no longer being followed, with people arbitrarily receiving registers and advanced ranks in the Taoist hierarchy.

The *Daomen kelüe* also shows the high degree of competition between the Taoist community and other religious or healing specialists. The author condemns the use of divination and mediums, any form of healing that falls outside the traditional Celestial Masters practices of repentance (see *chanhui*) and prayer, and the use of talismans (*FU). The so-called "licentious cults" (*yinsi*) are especially censured for their blood sacrifices. In contrast, Lu emphasizes that Taoism offered only pure (i.e., non-meat) offerings in their interactions with the otherworldly bureaucracy.

Amy Lynn MILLER

📖 Lai Chi-tim 1998b; Nickerson 1996a (trans.)

※ Lu Xiujing; Lingbao; ORDINATION AND PRIESTHOOD; TAOISM AND POPULAR RELIGION

Daomen shigui

道門十規

Ten Guidelines for the Taoist Community

*Zhang Yuchu (1361–1410), Celestial Master of the forty-third generation, compiled this reference work (CT 1232) following an imperial commission in the summer of 1406 to work on a collation of texts that eventually resulted in the so-called *Zhengtong daozang* (Taoist Canon of the Zhengtong Reign Period). His concise handbook opens with an undated statement of presentation sketching the textual history of Taoism from the *Daode jing* to the commentary authorized by the Hongwu Emperor (r. 1368–98). It is essential, according to Zhang's view, to be well-informed on the origins of two schools of instruction, *Zhengyi and *Quanzhen, and of three lineages of ritual practice, *Qingwei, *Lingbao, and Leiting 雷霆 (Thunderclap). He also writes that he compiled the *Daomen shigui* with the hope that it would help lead to a revitalization of the legacy of *qingjing (clarity and quiescence). The ten subjects covered in his text are:

1. "Origins and Branches of the Taoist Teaching" ("Daojiao yuanpai" 道教源派) expands on the introduction concerning the history of Taoism. Teachings conveyed to *Huangdi prior to the appearance of the *Daode jing* are traced to Taishang [*Laojun] in his manifestation as *Guangcheng zi. The textual transmission of Zhengyi by the ancestral Celestial Master (*zu tianshi* 祖天師), i.e., *Zhang Daoling (second century), *Jingming dao by *Xu Xun (trad. 239–374), Lingbao by *Ge Xuan (trad. 164–244), and *Shangqing by Lord Mao (*Maojun), i.e., Mao Ying 茅盈, are all likewise said to have originated with Taishang [Laojun]. Followers of the Dao are advised to investigate the origins of scriptural writings so that they will be able to discriminate between authentic and deviant teachings.

2. "Scriptures and Registers of the Taoist Community" ("Daomen jinglu" 道門經錄) lists the scriptural writings of the Three Caverns (*SANDONG) of Laojun critical to both esoteric and exoteric practices and recommends faithful recitation according to established procedure. Talismanic registers (*LU) conveyed by Zhang Daoling, Ge Xuan, and Mao Ying are commended as historically efficacious but many registers in circulation are said to be defective and in need of careful review by qualified instructors.

3. "Guarding Quiescence in Seated Confinement" ("Zuohuan shoujing" 坐圜守靜) outlines the essentials for pursuing a Quanzhen practice of solitary contemplation, from the selection of an enlightened master and establishment of a retreat in the wilderness to a list of readings.

4. "Practice of the Retreat Ritual" ("Zhaifa xingchi" 齋法行持) links the sacrificial offerings of high antiquity to the scriptural foundation of the Lingbao revelations and finds unity in the schools behind major compilations on ritual practice.

5. "Lines of Transmission of Taoist Ritual" ("Daofa chuanxu" 道法傳緒) points out the difficulty in recognizing false writings from the many branches of *leifa* (Thunder Rites) that arose from Qingwei and *Shenxiao schools of ritual. Finding a qualified instructor is considered essential, as is staying clear of profiteers selling registers and anyone engaging in spirit writing (see *fuji*) or other dubious practices.

6. "Leadership of Abbots" ("Zhuchi lingxiu" 住持領袖) takes up the qualifications, responsibilities, and restrictions governing those in charge of monastic communities, with emphasis on seniority, profound devotion, and unswerving dedication to established codes of conduct.

7. "Pursuing a Quest among Beclouded Waterways" ("Yunshui canfang" 雲水參訪) concerns the physical and mental demands inherent in leaving home to undertake a solitary study of the way of clarity and quiescence.

8. "Establishing Abbeys and Saving Humankind" ("Liguan duren" 立觀度人) sets forth the responsibilities and regulations governing Taoist masters (*daoshi*) who

dedicate themselves to what is considered to be the mission of highest priority, the salvation of others.

9. "Cash Crops and Land Taxes" ("Jingu tianliang" 金穀田糧) takes up the financial management of a monastic estate, largely dependent upon annual tax revenue for structural maintenance as well as for the various rituals conducted throughout the year on behalf of the community. Any attempt to sell goods and services for personal profit reportedly leads to commensurate punishment.

10. "Restoration of Palaces and Abbeys" ("Gongguan xiuqi" 宮觀修葺) makes a case for state support on the basis of historical precedent, owing to the insufficiency of local tax revenue for keeping an abbey fully maintained.

Judith M. BOLTZ

📖 Boltz J. M. 1987a, 241–42

※ Zhang Yuchu; Zhengyi; MONASTIC CODE

daoshi

道士

"master of the Dao"; Taoist master; Taoist priest or priestess

Since about the sixth century, Taoist organizations have commonly used the term *daoshi* to denote an ordained cleric. In relation to the broader community, such a person "represented Taoist culture on a professional basis" (Reiter 1998, vii). Within the Taoist community, the designation was generally reserved for a person who (a) has mastered specific efficacious knowledge connected to the Dao, and the ritual skills whereby such knowledge can be put into effect in the world; and (b) who has therefore been authorized to employ such knowledge and skills for the benefit of the community. The precise nature of such knowledge and skills were determined by the traditions of the specific religious community that authorized and conducted the ordination.

Modern scholars have yet to produce a complete and balanced picture of the roles and functions of *daoshi* throughout history. Their explanations usually mirror their general conceptions of the nature and contours of Taoism itself. In addition, understanding the Taoist priesthood has been hampered by its marginalization in modern China: while scholars studying the Buddhist or Christian priesthood have always been able to observe and interact with many such priests—from the ordinary cleric who fulfills only standard roles, to the outstanding exemplars of the tradition's highest ideals—students of Taoism have seldom had such opportunities, for historical, social, political and cultural reasons. The exiguity of such contact has impoverished, and sometimes skewed, scholarly depictions of the *daoshi*. Moreover, the disdain with which most modern Chinese (especially the educated) and virtually all Westerners have looked upon all practitioners of living Taoist traditions has sometimes resulted in depictions of the Taoist priesthood that are focused solely upon past eras or upon sociological data. One thus rarely finds depictions of the ordained representatives of organized Taoist traditions that demonstrate how those representatives can be understood as fulfilling the deepest spiritual ideals of the Taoist heritage. A depiction of *daoshi* that is accurate and properly nuanced must overcome such inherited dichotomizations as *DAOJIA and *DAOJIAO, or "mystical" and "liturgical," and must place the *daoshi* in his or her proper context within the vast continuum of ideals, practices, and institutions that Taoism encompasses. Furthermore, one must beware some writers' tendency to confuse literary images with historical data, or to conflate modern phenomena with data from ancient or medieval texts, thereby creating anachronistic amalgams that are false and misleading. In addition, some writers have used the term "priest" (or "master") as an indiscriminate translation for a variety of historical and contemporary Chinese terms, further muddling our understanding of the realities involved.

Historical overview. The term *daoshi* is first attested in Han-dynasty texts. In some, it appears as a vague appellation for idealized persons of ancient times, i.e., as a literary figure, comparable to *Zhuangzi*'s *zhenren* (Real Man, or Perfected) or *zhiren* 至人 (Accomplished Man). Other Han texts use the term for living people with uncommon abilities, i.e., as a synonym for *fangshi*. Based on such usages, formulators of later Taoist institutions forged the word into a technical term, which would serve as a standard designation for any person ordained into a specific, elevated rank of the clergy.

Yet, the institutions of the Taoist priesthood evolved slowly and fitfully, and only recently have scholars begun analyzing pertinent texts and unraveling the evolution of Taoist clerical institutions. From the earliest days of the *Tianshi dao organization, participants had been ranked hierarchically, with certain terms (like *jijiu or libationer) reserved for members of the higher levels. But Taoist leaders of the fifth century, like *Kou Qianzhi and *Lu Xiujing, saw their tradition's ranks as muddled and disordered when compared to the ranks of Buddhist contemporaries. They therefore began trying to standardize and elevate the Taoist clergy. Idealized rankings of clerical categories appear in late Six Dynasties texts, like the *Chujia yinyuan jing* 出家因緣經 (Scripture on the Causes of Becoming a Renunciant; CT 339; see Benn 1991, 185–86 n. 41). Much fuller were the seventh-century *Fengdao kejie* (Codes and Precepts for Worshipping the Dao), which outlines the standards expected of the *daoshi*, and *Zhang Wanfu's (early eighth century) *Chuanshou sandong jingjie falu lüeshuo* 傳授三洞經戒法籙略說 (Synopsis of Transmissions for Scriptures, Precepts, and Liturgical Registers of the Three Caverns; CT 1241) of 713 (Benn 1991, 148–51). Such texts distinguish the *daoshi* from lower functionaries, such as various classes of *fashi (ritual masters) and *dizi* 第子 (disciples). But the specifications for each class varied from text to text, and some classes even extended to transcendent beings. So it remains unclear how much such formulations ever really reflected, or even affected, actual practices or even standard expectations.

Functions, roles, and images. In general, it is safe to say that from the late Six Dynasties to the present, Taoists have used the term *daoshi* to designate religious specialists of Taoist organizations, as distinguished from specialists of other recognized traditions, like Buddhism, and from specialists of non-recognized traditions, like local cults. Since the latter distinction seems to have been difficult for some non-Taoists to grasp, Taoists periodically took pains to distinguish themselves from the officiants of cults they deemed less sophisticated or less admirable (Stein R. A. 1979; Schipper 1985e). In such connections, the term *daoshi* denoted a religious specialist who was properly initiated and trained in the noble traditions of the Dao, was operating under the auspices of a reputable and duly instituted organization, and deserved the respect of all members of society. Someone who lacked the proper initiation or training, or was not operating under duly instituted authority, was identified by Taoists as someone alien to their tradition. That distinction endures in Chinese communities to the present (Schipper 1985e). As a result, the social status of *daoshi* per se usually remained high, though their other characteristics often varied. Modern accounts often dwell upon whether certain clerics married or observed certain dietary restrictions. History, however, reveals that such categorizations were often vague idealizations, rather than institutions enforced by ecclesiastical authority. Taoists' general disinterest in formalizing rigid standards led Tang emperors to establish imperial oversight, and even to attempt to set clerical standards for Taoists loath to do so for themselves (Barrett 1996). Government supervision of the Taoist clergy has lingered, in some form, to the present day.

Many modern presentations of the Taoist priesthood privilege the institutions of the Tianshi and *Zhengyi traditions. Zhengyi priests, like the *Lingbao liturgists of the Six Dynasties, still conduct liturgies (such as the *jiao and *zhai) intended to protect, order, and sanctify the local community. But Zhengyi really represents only one important variation among Taoist religious institutions, and overemphasis on its traditions has obscured several fundamental facts about the Taoist priesthood more broadly. For instance, during the Tang, women were duly ordained as *daoshi* (Despeux 1986; Kirkland 1991), and women clerics continue to participate in modern *Quanzhen liturgy, on a basis comparable to that of men. In modern Zhengyi lineages, however, "hereditary *tao-shih* (*daoshi*) are always men" (Schipper 1993, 58). Also, the sociopolitical marginalization of Taoism in late imperial times led to a decline in the number of *daoshi* who participated in the cultural and intellectual activities of the educated elite. In Tang times, many *daoshi* were highly educated, composed a wide range of scholarly and literary secular and religious works, and were often honored by rulers and *ru* 儒 scholars/officials alike (Kirkland 1986a). In modern times, the ideal of *daoshi* as members of the sociocultural elite endures: "The *tao-shih* belong to the lettered class; they are minor notables" (Schipper 1993, 57). But in fact, since Qing times, truly distinguished "literati" *daoshi* have been few, for the antagonism toward Taoism of some imperial regimes, and of Cheng-Zhu 程朱 Neo-Confucians, drove centuries of intellectuals away from the Taoist priesthood. Further research into the many historical dimensions of the Taoist priesthood will help correct lingering misunderstandings.

Russell KIRKLAND

📖 Asano Haruji 1994; Chen Guofu 1963, 258–59; Dean 1993; Kohn 1997a; Kohn 2000a; Lagerwey 1987b; Lagerwey 1987c; Lagerwey 1987d; Ozaki Masaharu 1986b; Reiter 1998; Robinet 1990a; Sakai Tadao and Fukui Fumimasa 1983, 20–25; Schipper 1985c; Schipper 1985e; Schipper 1993, 55–60

※ *daozhang*; INITIATION; LU; ORDINATION AND PRIESTHOOD

Daoshu

道樞

Pivot of the Dao

The *Daoshu* is a large compendium of texts dealing with *neidan (inner alchemy) and *yangsheng (Nourishing Life) theory and techniques, compiled by the scholar-official Zeng Zao 曾慥 (?–1155). The author, who came from Jinjiang 晉江 (Fujian), was appointed Secretarial Court Gentleman (*shangshu lang* 尚書郎) during the reign of Song Gaozong (r. 1127–62) and served as Compiler (*xiuzhuan* 修撰) of the Imperial Archives. Two years before his death, he became prefect of Luzhou 盧州 (Jiangxi) and Compiler of the Pavilion for Aiding Learning (Youwen dian 右文殿), a section of the imperial library.

Zeng Zao is mainly known for his literary works. Besides collections of poetry and lyrics, these include the *Leishuo* 類說 (Classified Accounts; 1136), which consists of an anthology of stories, novelettes and excerpts drawn from over two hundred sources dating from the Han to the Song periods. His main works on Taoism are the *Daoshu* and the *Ji xianzhuan* 集仙傳 (Collected Biographies of Immortals), both completed late in life. The *Ji xianzhuan* was soon lost and survives only in quotations in the *Shuofu* 說郛 (Outskirts of Literature), with a preface by Zeng dated 1151. The *Daoshu* is undated, but internal evidence suggests that it was completed around the same time.

The version of the *Daoshu* in the Taoist Canon (CT 1017) contains 108 texts and essays, arranged into forty-two *juan* and 118 *pian* or sections. According to a mid-thirteenth-century library catalogue (van der Loon 1984, 154), the work originally had 122 *pian*; four *pian*, therefore, appear to be missing from the received version. The *Daozang jiyao edition of the *Daoshu* (vols. 18–19) contains the same number of *pian* as the one in the *Daozang*, without the division into *juan*. Another work, the anonymous *Zhiyou zi* 至游子 (Book of the Master of Ultimate Wandering) that bears a preface dated 1566, includes the first twenty-five sections of the *Daoshu*.

The arrangement of the *Daoshu* follows an orderly pattern. The work opens with philosophical discussions on the Dao and ends with the main *neidan* texts of the *Zhong-Lü corpus. Its range of subjects also covers meditation, breathing, *daoyin, sexual practices (*fangzhong shu), and *waidan. The first *pian* is a discussion of the Dao and other doctrinal principles by legendary or semilegendary figures. The second through the tenth *pian* contain excerpts from texts such as the *Huashu, the *Zuowang lun (Miyazawa Masayori 1988b), the *Xisheng jing, and *Wu Yun's *Zongxuan xiansheng xuangang lun* 宗玄先生 玄綱論 (Essay on the Outlines of Mystery, by the Elder Who Takes Mystery as His Ancestor; CT 1052); the seventh *pian*, however, consists of a criticism of sexual practices authored by Zeng Zao himself ("Rong Cheng pian" 容 成篇, 3.4b–7b). Other texts are selected and reproduced next to each other because of a common word in the title: for instance, "Huangdi wen pian" 黃 帝問篇 (Folios of the Questions of the Yellow Emperor; 5.3b–5a; Miyazawa Masayori 1990) and "Baiwen pian" 百問篇 (Folios of the Hundred Questions; 5.7a–22a); "Jindan pian" 金丹篇 (Folios on the Golden Elixir; 10.11b–13b) and "Huanjin pian" 還金篇 (Folios on Reverting to Gold; 12.1a–b); "Xiuzhen pian" 修真篇 (Folios on Cultivating Perfection; 18.7b–9b) and "Wuzhen pian" 悟真 篇 (Folios on Awakening to Perfection; 9b–13b; Miyazawa Masayori 1988a). While the sections in the first part of the anthology are quite short, the later excerpts are longer. Zeng concludes his anthology with the three main texts of the Zhong-Lü tradition: the *Xishan qunxian huizhen ji (j. 38), the *Zhong-Lü chuandao ji (j. 39–41), and the *Lingbao bifa (j. 42).

The *Daoshu* mirrors the interest of the lettered classes in self-cultivation and is at the same time an invaluable collection comprising unique materials. Among the works included, those on *neidan* are preponderant and bear much interest for the student of this tradition. Pre-Song and Northern Song sources otherwise lost but preserved in the *Daoshu* include the "Huanjin pian" (Reverting to Gold; 12.1a–b); excerpts from the *Huanyuan shi* 還元詩 (Verses on Reverting to the Origin; 12.1b–5b) by Zhang Wumeng 張無夢 (Qing Xitai 1994, 1: 307–8); and several texts belonging to the Zhong-Lü corpus, such as the above-mentioned *Huanjin pian* (attributed to *Liu Haichan) and *Baiwen pian* (trans. Homann 1976).

In his capacity as Compiler of the imperial library, Zeng Zao had access to a wealth of documents and books. His method, however, was not always accurate as some texts were paraphrased, arbitrarily abridged, or wrongly copied. Zeng's own addition to the anthology consist of two rhyming couplets placed at the head of each section to summarize its content, some essays, and comments occasionally interspersed in the main body of a text.

Farzeen BALDRIAN-HUSSEIN

📖 Boltz J. M. 1987a, 231–34; Miyazawa Masayori 1984b; Miyazawa Masayori, Mugitani Kunio, and Jin Zhengyao 2002 (concordance); Qing Xitai 1994, 1: 323–25 and 2: 163–65

※ *neidan*; *yangsheng*

Daoshu shi'er zhong

道書十二種

Twelve Books on the Dao

The *Daoshu shi'er zhong* is a collection of works written by *Liu Yiming (1734–1821), a master belonging to the *Longmen lineage of *neidan*. First printed in 1819, it contains a total of nineteen works consisting of both original writings and commentaries to earlier texts. The collection developed around an earlier compilation of twelve works entitled *Zhinan zhen* 指南針 (The Compass), which was later included in the *Daoshu shi'er zhong* with a preface dated 1801. The original twelve works (two of which bear in the present *Daoshu shi'er zhong* new prefaces by Liu Yiming dated later than 1801) are the following:

1. *Yinfu jing zhu* 陰符經注 (Commentary to the Scripture of the Hidden Accordance; 1779; trans. Cleary 1991a, 220–38), on the *Yinfu jing*.

2. *Qiaoyao ge zhijie* 敲爻歌直解 (Straightforward Explication of the Songs Metered According to the Hexagram Lines), on a text ascribed to *Lü Dongbin and included in the *Lüzu zhi* 呂祖志 (Monograph of Ancestor Lü; CT 1484, 6.5a–9a).

3. *Baizi bei zhu* 百字碑注 (Commentary to the Hundred-Word Stele; trans. Cleary 1991a, 239–52), on a short text also ascribed to Lü Dongbin and included in the *Lüzu zhi* (6.2b).

4. *Huanghe fu* 黃鶴賦 (Rhapsody on the Yellow Crane).

5. *Xiyou yuanzhi* 西遊原旨 (The Original Purport of the *Journey to the West*; 1778; trans. Yu Anthony 1991), one of the works that interpret the popular late Ming novel, *Xiyou ji* 西遊記, as an allegory of *neidan* principles and practices (Despeux 1985).

6. *Xiuzhen biannan* 修真辨難 (Discussions on the Cultivation of Authenticity; 1798), cast in the form of a dialogue between Liu and his disciples.

7. *Xiuzhen houbian* 修真後辨 (Further Discussions on the Cultivation of Authenticity), a continuation of the previous work dealing with *neidan* notions and principles.

8. *Shenshi bafa* 神室八法 (Eight Methods for the Divine Chamber; 1798), whose title alludes to the immaterial location where the inner elixir is refined.

9. *Xiuzhen jiuyao* 修真九要 (Nine Essentials in the Cultivation of Authenticity; 1798).

10. *Wugen shu jie* 無根樹解 (Explication of *The Rootless Tree*; 1802), on a work attributed to *Zhang Sanfeng.

11. *Huangting jing jie* 黃庭經解 (Explication of the *Scripture of the Yellow Court*), on the *Huangting jing.

12. *Jindan sibai zi jie* 金丹四百字解 (Explication of the *Four Hundred Words on the Golden Elixir*; 1807; trans. Cleary 1986a, 1–48), on the *Jindan sibai zi, with additional poems by Liu Yiming.

"Twelve Books on the *Dao*" was an alternative title of the *Zhinan zhen*. The collection retained that title when it was expanded into the present *Daoshu shi'er zhong* with the addition of the following seven texts:

13. *Zhouyi chanzhen* 周易闡真 (Uncovering the Reality of the *Changes of the Zhou*; 1798; trans. Cleary 1986b), a commentary to the *Yijing.

14. *Xiangyan poyi* 象言破疑 (Smashing Doubts on Symbolic Language; 1811; trans. Cleary 1986a, 51–118), centered on a set of diagrams that describe the unfolding of the Dao into the cosmos and the return to the Dao.

15. *Tongguan wen* 通關文 (Crossing the Passes), on obstacles that adepts face in their practice.

16. *Cantong zhizhi* 參同直指 (Straightforward Directions on the *Agreement of the Three*; 1799), a commentary to the *Guwen Zhouyi cantong qi.

17. *Wuzhen zhizhi* 悟真直指 (Straightforward Directions on the *Wuzhen pian*; 1794; trans. Cleary 1987), a commentary to the *Wuzhen pian (see Miyakawa Hisayuki 1954).

18. *Wudao lu* 悟道錄 (Account of an Awakening to the Dao; 1810; trans. Cleary 1988), composed of jottings on *neidan* and other subjects.

19. *Huixin ji* 會心集 (Anthology of Gathering [the Dao] in the Heart; 1811), mostly in poetical form.

The first edition of the *Daoshu shi'er zhong* was published by the Huguo an 護國庵 in Changde 常德 (Hunan). A valuable, movable-type reedition was published in 1880 issued by the Yihua tang 翼化堂 in Shanghai. The widely distributed reprint entitled *Jingyin* 精印 *Daoshu shi'er zhong* (Taipei: Xinwenfeng chubanshe, 1975 and 1983) is based on a reedition of the Jiangdong shuju (Shanghai, 1913). Another publication, also entitled *Daoshu shi'er zhong* (Beijing: Zhongguo Zhongyiyao chubanshe, 1990), reproduces parts of the Yihua tang and Jiangdong shuju editions.

Fabrizio PREGADIO

  📖 Qing Xitai 1994, 2: 180–83

  ※ Liu Yiming; *neidan*

Daoxue zhuan

道學傳

Biographies of Those who Studied the Dao

The *Daoxue zhuan* is a collection of Taoist biographies compiled by Ma Shu 馬樞 (522–81) during the Chen dynasty: it forms part of the tradition that originates with the **Liexian zhuan* (Biographies of Exemplary Immortals) and the **Shenxian zhuan* (Biographies of Divine Immortals). However, it is notable that the characters in the *Daoxue zhuan* are said to gain immortality much less frequently than in these earlier collections, often simply dying and being buried. Originally in twenty *juan*, the complete text is now lost and survives only in fragments from a few more than one hundred biographies. Fortunately, these fragments are extensive, being found in Taoist works such as the **Sandong zhunang* (The Pearl Satchel of the Three Caverns), the **Sandong qunxian lu* (Accounts of the Gathered Immortals from the Three Caverns), and the **Shangqing dao leishi xiang* (Classified Survey of Shangqing Taoism), as well as in secular collections such as the *Chuxue ji* 初學記 (Records for Entering Studies; ca. 720), the *Taiping yulan* 太平御覽 (Imperial Readings of the Taiping Xingguo Reign Period; 983), and Li Shan's 李善 (ca. 630–89) commentary to the *Wenxuan* 文選 (Literary Anthology). This extent of citation indicates that the text circulated widely. It also appears in the bibliographical treatises of the *Suishu* (History of the Sui), of both histories of the Tang dynasty (*Jiu Tangshu* and *Xin Tangshu*), and of the *Tongzhi* 通志 (Comprehensive

Monographs). However, it also appears in the *Daozang quejing mulu (Index of Scriptures Missing from the Taoist Canon) so must have been lost by the Ming. Chen Guofu located and collected these fragments and published them as Appendix 7 of his Daozang yuanliu kao (Chen Guofu 1963).

It is in the nature of fragments to be partial and while most of the chapters of the original are represented in Chen Guofu's compilation, some are not, and we have no way of ascertaining what the original table of contents looked like. In addition many of the fragments are notices of just a few sentences. While some of the biographies concern ancient figures, most of the subjects lived in the few centuries immediately prior to Ma Shu's own time. Easily the longest fragment concerns *Lu Xiujing, an entry that has proved important in piecing together his biography.

Benjamin PENNY

📖 Bumbacher 2000a; Bumbacher 2000c (crit. ed. and trans.); Chen Guofu 1963, 239 and 454–504; Eskildsen 1998, 31–42

※ HAGIOGRAPHY

daoyin

導引

"guiding and pulling"; gymnastics

"Guiding and pulling" is a set of gymnastic techniques aimed to let *qi properly circulate, expel pathogenic qi, heal certain diseases, keep old age away, and nourish life (*yangsheng). They are performed in an upright, sitting, or reclining position, and can be combined with ingestion of breath (*fuqi), abstention from cereals (*bigu), massage, and visualization.

The term daoyin first occurs in *Zhuangzi 15, which criticizes this type of exercise (see the entry *tuna). The individuals associated with it (e.g., the two rain masters *Chisong zi and Ningfeng zi 甯封子) and especially its relation to dance suggest that the original purpose of the practice was to expel demonic influences (see Harper 1985). Gymnastic practices and shamanic dances share the same animal symbolism: practitioners imitate the crane, snake, swallow, turtle, stag, dragon, and tiger, all known for their powers against demons or for their longevity.

Early sources. The earliest descriptions of daoyin techniques appear in a *Mawang-dui (Hunan) manuscript entitled Daoyin tu 導引圖 (Drawings of Daoyin; trans.

Fig. 28. *Daoyin* postures in a *Mawangdui manuscript.

Harper 1998, 310–27), which contains illustrations of forty-four movements, and in a Zhangjiashan 張家山 (Hubei) manuscript entitled *Yinshu* 引書 (Book on Pulling; see Harper 1998, 30–33). The Han-dynasty *Huangdi neijing* also mentions *daoyin* as a therapeutic technique, especially in *Suwen* 素問 (Plain Questions), sec. 4.12, where various healing methods are related to different geographic areas. *Daoyin* is associated with the people of the central regions, who suffer from breath reflux, heat, and cold, and can be cured by *daoyin* and massage.

The single main early source on *daoyin* is the *Zhubing yuanhou lun (Treatise on the Origin and Symptoms of Diseases; 610), a medical text that expounds methods for "nourishing life" in relation to various ailments. This treatise largely quotes methods originally found in the lost *Yangsheng yaoji (Essentials of Nourishing Life; early fourth century). The only source in the Taoist Canon that deals exclusively with this subject is the *Daoyin yangsheng jing* 導引養生 經 (Scripture on Nourishing Life Through *Daoyin*; CT 818). Also based on the *Yangsheng yaoji*, it records methods associated with Chisong zi, Ningfeng zi, *Wangzi Qiao, and *Pengzu. Another work, the *Shesheng zuanlu* 攝生纂 錄 (Compilation of Texts for Preserving Life; CT 578), attests to techniques associated with Indian *yoga*. Its "Methods of Brahmanic *Daoyin*" (*Poluomen daoyin fa* 婆羅門導引法) are essentially gymnastic movements.

Codification. The trend to codify sets of movements to be regularly repeated developed at an early time. The first known set is the Five Animals Pattern (*wuqin xi* 五禽戲; Miura Kunio 1989, 353–55), attributed to Hua Tuo 華陀 (142–219) and mentioned in his biography in the *Sanguo zhi* (History of the Three Kingdoms; trans. DeWoskin 1983, 149). The earliest descriptions of this set appear in two texts probably dating from the Tang period, the *Yangxing yanming lu (On Nourishing Inner Nature and Extending Life) and the *Taishang Laojun yangsheng jue* 太上老君養生訣 (Instructions on Nourishing Life by the Most High Lord Lao; CT 821). Later descriptions, which differ from the earlier ones, are found in the Ming-dynasty *Chifeng sui* (Marrow of the Red Phoenix; trans. Despeux 1988, 103–11), in the *Neigong tushuo* 內功圖說 (Illustrated Explanations of Inner Practices) of the late Qing period, and in more recent works.

Another set of movements, known as the Eight Brocades (*baduan jin* 八段錦), is outlined in the *Xiuzhen shishu* (Ten Books on the Cultivation of Perfection, 19.4a–5b). A "civil" (*wenshi* 文式) and a "martial" (*wushi* 武式) version are described by Hong Mai 洪邁 (1123–1202) in his *Yijian zhi* 夷堅志 (Heard and Written by Yijian). An advanced form of the eight basic exercises resulted in the Twelve Brocades (*shi'er duan jin* 十二段錦), described in *Leng Qian's *Xiuling yaozhi* 修齡要旨 (Essential Purport of the Cultivation of Longevity), in Gao Lian's 高濂 (fl. 1573–81; IC 472–73) *Zunsheng bajian* 遵生八箋 (Eight Essays on Being in Accord with Life), and in Hu Wenhuan's 胡文煥 *Leixiu yaojue* 類修要訣 (Essential Classified Instructions on Self-Cultivation).

Other methods dating from the Song period associate the *daoyin* movements with the different periods of the year. The *Taichu yuanqi jieyao baosheng zhi lun* 太初元氣接要保生之論 (Essay on Protecting Life and Joining with the Essential through the Original Pneuma of the Great Beginning; CT 1477) describes a method related to the twelve months. Another exercise, attributed to *Chen Tuan, consists of twenty-four movements corresponding to the twenty-four *jieqi* 節氣 (energy nodes) of the year. This system is described and illustrated in the *Baosheng xinjian* 保生心鑒 (Spiritual Mirror for Protecting Life; preface dated 1506), a work published by Hu Wenhuan in the *Shouyang congshu* 壽養叢書 (Collectanea on Longevity and Nourishment [of Life]; ca. 1596) under the title *Taiqing ershisi qi shuihou jusan tu* 太清二十四氣水火聚散圖 (Charts of the Great Clarity on the Accumulation and Dispersion of Water and Fire According to the Twenty-Four Pneumas). The twenty-four movements embody the theory of the "five circulatory phases and six seasonal influences" (*wuyun liuqi* 五運六氣), which was developed during the Song period and integrated into official medicine after the mid-eleventh century. Each movement is associated with a type of *qi*, an agent (see **wuxing*), and a climatic quality.

A particular set of movements is described in Lu Zhigang's 魯至剛 (Ming) *Jinshen jiyao* 錦身機要 (Essentials of the Process for Obtaining a Smooth Body). This is divided into three parts. The first consists of twelve "dragon movements" for women, the second of twelve "tiger movements" for men, and the third of twelve movements or positions for the "union of dragon and tiger." The aim of these preliminary exercises for codified sexual union is the preservation of health.

Catherine DESPEUX

  📖 Despeux 1988, 23–29, 38–44; Despeux 1989; Harper 1985; Harper 1998, 132–35; Hu Fuchen 1989, 286–90; Kohn 1993b, 141–48; Li Ling 2000a, 341–81; Maspero 1981, 542–54; Sakade Yoshinobu 1980; Sakade Yoshinobu 1986b

※ *yangsheng*

daoyuan

道院

Taoist cloister

Daoyuan is both a common term meaning Taoist cloister, and, in an unrelated sense, the name of a modern sectarian movement. The *daoyuan* (lit., "cloister of the Dao") is one of many institutions used by Taoism during its long history. Unlike the *guan* 觀 (abbey) or the *gong* 宮 (palace), which serve as both the locus of a cult (sometimes a state-mandated one) and the seat of a clerical community, the *daoyuan* focuses mainly on communal life. The term may be used to denote either a small community that has not yet acquired the official status of *guan* (thus being similar to a hermitage, *an* 庵 or 菴), or a place that remains largely closed to outsiders to foster its spiritual atmosphere and discipline, very much like a Buddhist *chanyuan* 禪院 (meditation cloister). Moreover, large institutions, such as the *Shangqing gong (Palace of Highest Clarity) on Mount Longhu (*Longhu shan, Jiangxi), had more than ten different *daoyuan*, each with its own rules, lineage, and specialization. In a *Quanzhen context, the various *daoyuan* attached to a large monastery would not be used to keep different traditions separate, but rather to allow small groups of dedicated ascetics to live away from the noise and agitation of the main residence hall.

Independently of this meaning, Daoyuan is the name of one of many sectarian groups that appeared during the late Qing and Republican periods, based on spirit-writing cults, initiation into self-perfection techniques, and active charity. The Daoyuan was founded in 1916, and in 1922 established the Red Swastika (Hong wangzi hui 紅卍字會), a very large relief organization.

Vincent GOOSSAERT

※ TAOISM AND POPULAR SECTS; TEMPLES AND SHRINES

Daozang

道藏

Taoist Canon

See the entry *DAOZANG AND SUBSIDIARY COMPILATIONS in "Taoism: An Overview," p. 28.

Daozang jinghua

道藏精華

Essential Splendors of the Taoist Canon

The *Daozang jinghua* is a series of Taoist texts edited by Xiao Tianshi 蕭天石 (1908–86). It was published from 1956 onward by Ziyou chubanshe in Taipei, a publishing house established by Xiao himself in 1953. It consists of seventeen "anthologies" (*ji* 集), each containing one or more texts. The publication project lasted more than two decades, after which several single volumes were reprinted (or, in some instances, republished under the same title but with different texts). The whole collection was again reprinted in 1983. The scattered nature of this publishing effort has lead to various authors attributing different dates to the series; for example, William Chen (1984) indexes a 1963 edition containing 108 titles in 115 volumes, while Zhu Yueli (1992) mentions a 1956 and a 1973 edition.

In the foreword to the 1983 reprint, entitled "Xinbian Daozang jinghua yaozhi liyan" 新編道藏精華要旨例言 (Introductory Remarks to the New Edition of the *Daozang jinghua*), Xiao states that he focuses on works on self-cultivation instead of the doctrinal foundations of Taoism, as he intends to make available texts that adepts can use in their practice. Xiao also provides details on his sources, which include the *Zhengtong daozang* (Taoist Canon of the Zhengtong

Reign Period), the *Daozang xubian (Sequel to the Taoist Canon), the *Daozang jinghua lu (Record of the Essential Splendors of the Taoist Canon), and the *Daoshu shi'er zhong (Twelve Books on the Dao). He has also added a number of Taoist texts from *Dunhuang and from private libraries. Some materials in the last category might well have come from temples in Sichuan, where Xiao was forced to live from 1939 to 1949, and where his interest in Taoism arose. One example is the Nü jindan fayao 女金丹法要 (Essentials of the Methods of the Golden Elixir for Women; Wile 1992, 202–4), a text of *nüdan (inner alchemy for women) privately printed in Sichuan by *Fu Jinquan in 1814.

Xiao had a clear bias in favor of later works, especially those dealing with *neidan. The most prominent authors in the collection are *Lu Xixing, *Wu Shouyang, *Liu Yiming, Fu Jinquan, and *Li Xiyue, all of whom lived in the late Ming or the Qing periods. Moreover, several works are related to *Zhang Sanfeng, a neidan patron of the Ming period. The collection also includes fourteen works by Xiao himself dealing with neidan and self-cultivation.

Besides the Daozang jinghua, Xiao published two collections under the title Daozang jinghua waiji 道藏精華外集 (Essential Splendors of the Taoist Canon: Additional Anthologies). The first is the Daojia yangshengxue gaiyao 道家養生學概要 (Overview of the Taoist Nourishment of Life), published in 1963, and the second is the Daohai xuanwei 道海玄微 (Mystery and Subtlety of the Ocean of the Dao), published in 1974. In 1958 Xiao had also published a work entitled Zuodao pangmen xiaoshu jiyao 左道旁門小術輯要 (Essentials of the Minor Arts of the Heterodox Schools). Although Xiao defines this work as a supplement to the Daozang jinghua, he did not publish it under his own name but used a sobriquet, Taiyi shanren 太乙山人 (The Mountain Man of Great Unity), and did not list it in the table of contents of the 1983 edition. This may be due to the book's subject matter, which deals with unconventional practices and includes two texts on nüdan.

Elena VALUSSI

📖 Chen W. Y. 1984; Gong Qun 1995; Xiao Tianshi 1983; Zhu Yueli 1992, 336–48

※ DAOZANG AND SUBSIDIARY COMPILATIONS

Daozang jinghua lu

道藏精華錄

Record of the Essential Splendors
of the Taoist Canon

The eminent bibliophile Ding Fubao 丁福保 (1874–1952) selected and published one hundred texts under this somewhat misleading title (Shanghai: Yixue shuju, 1922; repr. Hangzhou: Zhejiang guji chubanshe, 1989). Approximately one-third of the compilation is derived from sources in the Taoist Canon and *Daozang jiyao*. It is divided into ten *ji* 集 (collections), with ten titles contained in each. The introduction includes three essays entitled "Origins and Development of the Taoist Teaching" ("Daojiao yuanliu" 道教源流), "Origins and Development of the Taoist Canon" ("Daozang yuanliu" 道藏源流), and "Editorial Intent" ("Bianji zongzhi" 編輯宗旨). In the last essay, Ding states that he turned to a study of the Dao as a middle-aged man. He was greatly inspired by the teachings of the forty-third Celestial Master *Zhang Yuchu (1361–1410) found in the *Xianquan ji* 峴泉集 (Anthology of Alpine Spring; CT 1311).

Major components of the ten units are:

1. *Daozang mulu xiangzhu* (Detailed Commentary on the Index of the Taoist Canon); a catalogue of the *Daozang jiyao* by Jiang Yuanting 蔣元庭 (1755–1819); *Du Daozang ji* 讀道藏記 (Notes on Reading the Taoist Canon) by Liu Shipei 劉世培 (1884–1919; ECCP 536); and *Daoxue zhinan* 道學指南 (Guide to the Study of the Dao) compiled in 1922 by a Sunsun zhai zhuren 損損齋主人 (Master of the Studio of "Decreasing and Further Decreasing"), with advice on how to read the *Daozang jinghua lu*.

2. Manuals of *yangsheng (Nourishing Life) techniques, including texts from the *Yunji qiqian (Seven Lots from the Bookbag of the Clouds) and the writings of *Qiu Chuji (1148–1227).

3. Commentaries to the *Yinfu jing (Scripture of the Hidden Accordance) and guidebooks on massage and other exercises, including texts from the *Yunji qiqian* and the *Daoshu (Pivot of the Dao).

4. Scriptures on contemplative practices in the name of the Most High Lord Lao (Taishang Laojun 太上老君; see *Laozi and Laojun) and related treatises found in the *Quan Tang wen* 全唐文 (Complete Prose of the Tang; 1814).

5. Scriptural teachings and discourse records ascribed to *Wenchang, *Lü

Dongbin, and *Ma Yu (1123–84), and two scriptures on daily practice, one of which was inscribed in 1352 on a stele at *Louguan (Tiered Abbey).

6. Scriptural writings linked with *Yuhuang (Jade Sovereign) and Chunyang zhenjun 純陽真君 (i.e., Lü Dongbin); commentaries to the *Zhouyi cantong qi; and teachings attributed to *Zhongli Quan.

7. Treatises on *neidan, including Qing editions of texts ascribed to *Zhang Boduan (987?–1082), *Bai Yuchan (1194–1229?), and an anthology of verse attributed to *Sun Bu'er (1119–83).

8. Writings on neidan by *Nanzong (Southern Lineage) patriarchs, including *Shi Tai (?–1158), *Xue Daoguang (1078?–1191), *Chen Nan (?–1213), and Xiao Tingzhi 蕭廷芝 (fl. 1260–64), and two anthologies of the teachings of *Wu Shouyang (1574–1644).

9. Annotated editions of the *Huangting jing (Scripture of the Yellow Court) and three early hagiographies, including the *Xu xianzhuan (Sequel to Biographies of Transcendents).

10. Hagiographic accounts dedicated to *Tao Hongjing (456–536), *Xu Xun (trad. 239–374), and the *Quanzhen legacy, three pre-Song topographies, and an exegesis of the *Taishang ganying pian by Yu Yue 俞樾 (1821–1906; ECCP 944–45).

Ding also provides a table of contents by way of a conspectus (tiyao 提要), listing the one-hundred titles with notes on the textual history and attributes of each.

Judith M. BOLTZ

📖 Chen Yuan 1988, 1217; Qing Xitai 1988–95, 4: 465–68; Zhu Yueli 1992, 329–31

※ DAOZANG AND SUBSIDIARY COMPILATIONS

Daozang jiyao

道藏輯要

Essentials of the Taoist Canon

The *Daozang jiyao* is the main collection of Taoist texts after the *Daozang*. Despite its relatively recent date of compilation, its bibliographic history is not entirely clear. According to the most common account, the first edition was published by *Peng Dingqiu (1645–1719) around 1700. About a century later, during the Jiaqing reign period (1796–1820), the Vice Minister Jiang Yuanting 蔣元庭 (1755–1819) published an enlarged version containing 173 texts, all of which were also found in the *Daozang*. The *Jiyao* was reedited once or twice in the nineteenth century and in the process ninety-six texts were added, bringing the total number of texts to 269. The current edition was published in 1906 by He Longxiang 賀龍驤 and Peng Hanran 彭瀚然 at the Erxian an 二仙 庵 (Hermitage of the Two Immortals), part of the *Qingyang gong (Palace of the Black Ram) in Chengdu (Sichuan). Their edition, known as *Chongkan Daozang jiyao* 重刊道藏輯要, added eighteen more works for a total of 287 texts. He and Peng also supplied five indexes and eighteen bibliographies of Taoist works drawn from various sources. Taking these into account, the *Jiyao* would contain 310 titles.

A different reconstruction is provided in *Zhongguo daojiao shi* (History of Chinese Taoism; Qing Xitai 1988–95, 4: 455–65). The original collection edited by Peng Dingqiu contained 200 texts, all of which were found in the *Daozang*. Jiang Yuanting added seventy-nine texts, not found in the *Daozang*; and the reedition by He Longxiang and Peng Hanran supplied seventeen more texts, bringing the total to 296. Including indexes and bibliographies, the *Daozang jiyao* would contain altogether 319 titles.

Both accounts appear to be only partly reliable. In particular, there seems to be no trace—either material or bibliographic—of Peng Dingqiu's original compilation, and no evidence is provided in *Zhongguo daojiao shi* for the statement that it included 200 titles. The authors of *Zhongguo daojiao shi* arrive at this number based on a catalogue of Jiang Yuanting's edition ("Daozang jiyao zongmu" 道藏輯要總目) included in Ding Fubao's 丁福保 *Daozang jinghua lu*. While this catalogue does list 279 titles, the seventy-nine supposedly additional titles (Qing Xitai 1988–95, 4: 456–59) derive from a list of *Daozang jiyao* texts not found in the *Daozang*, which is appended to the Harvard-Yenching index of the *Daozang* (Weng Dujian 1935; see Qing Xitai 1988–95, 4: 465). That list is not entirely dependable (to give one example, the first text cited in Qing Xitai 1988–95, 4: 456 corresponds to CT 7). As for the seventeen texts indicated in *Zhongguo daojiao shi* as having been added in 1906, the list provided by He Longxiang and Peng Hanran contains nineteen titles, but the last six of them actually are not included in the collection. This list is printed in the 1906 edition as the third of three indexes to the version they edited:

1. A general index entitled "Chongkan Daozang jiyao zongmu" 重刊道藏輯要 總目 (1: 12–34), with a preface signed by He Longxiang and dated 1906

2. An index containing the table of contents of each text included in the collection, except for those added in 1906, entitled "Chongkan Daozang jiyao zimu chubian" 重刊道藏輯要子目初編 and consisting of four *juan* (1: 48–214)

3. An index containing the table of contents of each text added in 1906, entitled "Chongkan Daozang jiyao xubian zimu" 重刊道藏輯要續編子目 (1: 215–242) and indicated as the "fifth *juan*" of the previous index

To further complicate the bibliographic history of the *Jiyao*, it should be noted that at least one of its texts was printed after 1906: the *Xiyi zhimi lun* 析疑指迷論 (Essays to Resolve Doubts and Point out Errors; 14: 6188–94) bears a postface dated 1917 (Minguo 6), i.e., more than one decade after the entire collection is deemed to have been completed.

Further research is required to solve these and similar questions raised by the *Daozang jiyao*. Also worthy of attention is the intent of its compilation. Besides those mentioned above, the collection includes an index and a table of contents of texts on *nüdan (inner alchemy for women) entitled "Nüdan hebian zongmu" 女丹合編總目 (1: 245–49). These indexes are also part of the "fifth *juan*" of the general catalogue of the *Jiyao*. This suggests that He Longxiang and Peng Hanran planned to include those texts in the *Jiyao*, but later decided to publish the *Nüdan hebian* 女丹合編 (Collected Works on Inner Alchemy for Women) as an independent collection (also printed in 1906). It seems clear, though, that He and Peng compiled the *Nüdan hebian* as part of a single undertaking aiming to collect and publish texts that reflected Taoist traditions more recent than those represented in the *Zhengtong daozang*. Both the *Daozang jiyao* and the *Nüdan hebian* achieved this goal.

The 1906 edition has been reprinted twice, first by the Kaozheng chubanshe (Taipei, 1971) and later by the Xinwenfeng chubanshe (Taipei, 1977). The two reprints appear to be identical to each other (volume and page numbers indicated above refer to them). Large-size reprints are occasionally produced at the Qingyang gong, which still houses the original woodblocks.

Contents. The composition of the *Daozang jiyao* follows a fairly definite plan. The texts are divided into twenty-eight sections, marked by the names of the twenty-eight lunar lodges (*xiu). Each section is further divided into a varying number of subsections (between four and thirteen) marked by numbers.

Although the collection is especially important for its wide selection of *neidan* works, it provides a valuable overview of Taoist literature, except for works dealing with ritual. The first six sections (or "lodges") are modeled on the Three Caverns (*SANDONG) of the *Zhengtong daozang*, with the *Duren jing placed here too as the opening text. Sections 7 and 8 are largely devoted to texts related to *Yuhuang, *Huangdi, and the Lords of the Five Dippers (*wudou* 五斗). Sections 9 to 11 include works dating (or traditionally deemed to date) from the early history of Taoism. Section 12 consists of *Zhong-Lü and *Jingming texts. Sections 13 to 17 include texts related to saints, patriarchs, and masters of *Nanzong and *Quanzhen. Sections 18 and 19 are mainly devoted to *neidan* works of various authors and dates. Sections 20 to 22 contain anthologies and encyclopedias. Finally, sections 23 to 28 include more *neidan* texts, as well as litanies (*chan* 懺), texts related to *Wenchang, collections of monastic rules, and biographic and topographic works.

In more detail, the contents of the individual sections are as follows (section numbers correspond to the lunar lodges; see table 26):

1–3: *Duren jing* and other works spoken by or related to the Celestial Worthy of Original Commencement (Yuanshi tianzun 元始天尊).

4: Commentaries to the *Shengshen jing* and other works spoken by or related to the Celestial Worthy of Numinous Treasure (Lingbao tianzun 靈寶天尊).

5–6: Commentaries to the *Daode jing* (including one by *Bai Yuchan not found in the *Daozang*) and other works spoken by or related to the Celestial Worthy of the Way and Its Virtue (Daode tianzun 道德天尊), i.e., the deified Laozi: *Huangting jing*, *Taishang ganying pian*, and hagiographies of Laozi.

7: Works related to Yuhuang, including commentaries to the *Yuhuang benxing jijing* 高上玉皇本行集經 (Collected Scripture on the Deeds of the Jade Sovereign) and the *Xinyin jing*.

8: Texts on the Five Dippers (see under *Wudou jing*) and commentaries to the *Longhu jing* and the *Yinfu jing*.

9: Commentaries to the *Zhuangzi.

10: Commentaries to the *Wenshi zhenjing* 文始真經 (Authentic Scripture of Master Wenshi; see under *Yin Xi), the *Liezi, the *Wenzi, and the *Dongling zhenjing* 洞靈真經 (Authentic Scripture of the Cavernous Numen; see under *Gengsang zi).

11: *Huainan zi, *Baopu zi, and commentaries to the *Zhouyi cantong qi and the *Ruyao jing.

12: Zhong-Lü texts and works related to *Xu Xun and the Jingming dao.

13–14: Collections of texts attributed or related to *Lü Dongbin, including the *Taiyi jinhua zongzhi.

15: Texts by the Nanzong patriarchs.

16: Texts by Bai Yuchan.

17: Texts by the Quanzhen patriarchs.

18: Various pre-Ming texts on meditation and *neidan*.

19: Works by *Wu Shouyang and works attributed to *Zhang Sanfeng.

20–22: Encyclopedic collections and anthologies, including the *Zhengao and the *Daoshu.

23: *Neidan* texts, including the *Zhenquan* 真詮 (Veritable Truth) edited by Peng Dingqiu.

24: Litanies (*chan*).

25: Hagiographies and works related to Wenchang.

26: Ledgers of merit (*gongge* 功格) and a remarkable collection of precepts and monastic rules.

27–28: Biographic, hagiographic, and epigraphic collections; topographic works.

As Peng Hanran states in his preface to the 1906 edition (1:303), the compilation that he and He Longxiang inherited and expanded derived partly from the *Daozang* and partly from extracanonical editions. This accounts for the variants, sometimes noticeable, found in works that the *Jiyao* shares with the *Daozang*.

Fabrizio PREGADIO

📖 Chen W. Y. 1978 (index); Liu Ts'un-yan 1973, 107–10; Mori Yuria 2001; Qing Xitai 1994, 2: 32–33; Wong Shiu Hon 1982, 3–8; Yoshioka Yoshitoyo 1955, 175–76

※ Peng Dingqiu; DAOZANG AND SUBSIDIARY COMPILATIONS

Daozang mulu xiangzhu

道藏目錄詳注

Detailed Commentary on the Index of the Taoist Canon

The *Daozang mulu xiangzhu* in four *juan* is an annotated catalogue of the Ming Canon, compiled in 1626 by the Taoist Master Bai Yunji 白雲霽 of the Chaotian gong 朝天宮 (Palace in Homage to Heaven) in Nanjing (Jiangsu). Two copies of the text included in the *Siku quanshu* 四庫全書 (Complete Writings of the Four Repositories) of 1782 have been published, one from the Wenyuan ge 文淵閣 (Tianjin: Tuigeng tang 退耕堂, n.d.) and one from the Wenjin ge 文津閣 (repr. Taipei: Commercial Press, 1968). Another copy is included in the *Daozang jinghua lu compiled in 1922 by Ding Fubao 丁福保 (1874–1952). In his prefatory notes on the text, Ding identifies Bai Yunji as the author, but the title page of the edition he reproduces bears the name Li Jie 李杰 of Liaozuo 遼左 (Shandong). The text proper is preceded by a copy of the "Baiyun guan chongxiu Daozang ji" 白雲觀重修道藏記 (Records on Restoring the Taoist Canon at the Abbey of the White Clouds) dating to 1845. It is likely that Ding simply published a slightly variant Qing printing of the text with faulty attribution. The Jesuit scholar Léon Wieger likewise seems to have had access to just such an edition when he compiled his index to the Taoist Canon in 1911. Copies of the text in rare book collections include a Qing manuscript of ca. 1736–1820 at Seikadō Bunko in Tokyo and a fragmentary

Qing printing ascribed to Li Jie in the Tenri Library of Nara (repr. Taipei: Guangwen shuju, 1975).

Discrepancies between this catalogue and the present form of the 1445 Taoist Canon and its 1607 supplement suggest that Bai had a different printing at hand. It is known that his home temple received a copy of the Canon by imperial decree in 1476. The number of *juan* cited for several titles in the catalogue conflicts with the actual quantity found in the Canon. Information on provenance appears to have been copied directly from the scant data that are sometimes recorded following the title of a text in the Canon. Similarly, summaries of the contents largely replicate the headings or subdivisions of a text. The serial characters of the *Qianzi wen* 千字文 (Thousand-Word Text) appear at the close of each entry.

Judith M. BOLTZ

📖 Boltz J. M. 1987a, 9–10; Chen Guofu 1963, 178 and 183–89; Ozaki Masaharu 1987; Qing Xitai 1988–95, 4: 18–22; Qing Xitai 1994, 2: 28–31; Wieger 1911; Zhong Zhaopeng 1986

※ *Wanli xu daozang*; *Zhengtong daozang*; DAOZANG AND SUBSIDIARY COMPILATIONS

Daozang quejing mulu

道藏闕經目錄

Index of Scriptures Missing from the Taoist Canon

The *Daozang quejing mulu* (CT 1430) is an inventory of lost texts, followed by a copy of a stele inscription of 1275 entitled "Daozang zunjing lidai gangmu" 道藏尊經歷代綱目 (Historical Survey of the Revered Scriptures of the Taoist Canon). The editors of the Taoist Canon of 1445 apparently drew up this list of nearly 800 missing titles according to what was known at the time about the contents of earlier editions of the Canon. Four titles recorded at the end of the list can be traced to Qin Zhi'an 秦志安 (1188–1244), editor-in-chief of the *Xuandu baozang* (Precious Canon of the Mysterious Metropolis) of 1244. Some, but not all, titles proscribed by an imperial decree of 1258 are also registered in this inventory.

Over one-third of the titles listed can be found in catalogues of imperial and private libraries of the Song. Among glaring omissions are a significant number of well-attested components of the *Da Song Tiangong baozang* of 1016 and the *Zhenghe Wanshou daozang* of ca. 1119. A copy of one scripture printed in the 1244 Canon that was declared missing at the time this list was compiled now rests in the National Library of Beijing. Entitled *Taiqing fenglu jing* 太清風露經 (Scripture of Great Clarity on Wind and Dew), it may well be what compilers of the Song imperial catalogue of 1144 knew as the *Fenglu xianjing* 風露仙經 (Transcendent Scripture of Wind and Dew). A photographic reproduction of the scripture is available in the *Zangwai daoshu.

Judith M. BOLTZ

📖 Boltz J. M. 1987a, 11; van der Loon 1984, 53–62, 124; Qing Xitai 1994, 2: 25–27; Shi Zhouren and Chen Yaoting 1996, 350–63 (index)

※ DAOZANG AND SUBSIDIARY COMPILATIONS

Daozang xubian

道藏續編

Sequel to the Taoist Canon

The *Daozang xubian* is a collection of twenty-three texts compiled by the eleventh *Longmen patriarch, *Min Yide (1748–1836). The first xylographic edition, printed in 1834 on Mount Jingai (Jingai shan 金蓋山, Zhejiang), constituted the core of the *Gu Shuyinlou cangshu* 古書隱樓藏書 (Collection of the Ancient Hidden Pavilion of Books; Qing Xitai 1994, 2: 184–86) also edited by Min Yide. The scholar and bibliophile Ding Fubao 丁福保 (1874–1952) reprinted the *Daozang xubian* in 1952 (Shanghai: Yixue shuju); later reprints were published in 1989 (Beijing: Haiyang chubanshe) and 1993 (Beijing: Shumu wenxian chubanshe).

The collection is largely devoted to *neidan teachings and practices, especially those of the Longmen school. Its texts can be divided into five categories: 1. Doctrinal views of *neidan* and meditation practices such as those described in the *Taiyi jinhua zongzhi (The Ultimate Purport of the Golden Flower of the Great One), better known in the West as *Secret of the Golden Flower*; 2. Psycho-physiological practices; 3. Ethical texts outlining precepts; 4. Texts on universal salvation; 5. Exegesis. For a complete table of contents see table 3.

Doctrines and practices. The first two categories of texts are closely linked to each other. According to Min Yide, the *Secret of the Golden Flower* is related to two manuscripts found in the *Qingyang gong (Palace of the Black Ram) of Chengdu, both attributed to the legendary Yin zhenren 尹真人 (Perfected Yin). Their titles are *Donghua zhengmai huangji hepi zhengdao xianjing* 東華正

Table 3

1 *Taiyi jinhua zongzhi* 太一金華宗旨 (The Ultimate Purport of the Golden Flower of the Great One)

2 *Yin zhenren Donghua zhengmai huangji hepi zhengdao xianjing* 尹真人東華正脈皇極闔闢證道仙經 (Immortal Scripture by the Perfected Yin Testifying to the Path of Opening and Closing the August Ultimate According to the Orthodox Lineage of the Eastern Florescence)

3 *Yin zhenren Liaoyang dian wenda bian* 尹真人廖陽殿問答編 (Questions and Answers of the Perfected Yin from the Liaoyang Hall)

4 *Xie tianji* 泄天機 (Disclosing the Celestial Mechanism)

5 *Gufa yangsheng shisan ze chanwei* 古法養生十三則闡微 (Uncovering the Subtleties of the Thirteen Principles Concerning the Ancient Methods of Nourishing Life)

6 *Shangpin danfa jieci* 上品丹法節次 (Alchemical Process of Highest Rank)

7 *Guankui bian* 管窺編 (A Personal View)

8 *Jiuzheng lu* 就正錄 (Account of the Realization of Rectitude)

9 *Yu Lin Fenqian xiansheng shu* 與林奮千先生書 (Letter to Elder Lin Fenqian)

10 *Lü zushi sanni yishi shuoshu* 呂祖師三尼醫世說述 (Explanations of the Three Sages' Doctrine of Healing the World by the Ancestral Master Lü)

11 *Du Lü zushi sanni yishi shuoshu guankui* 讀呂祖師三尼醫世說述管窺 (A Personal Reading of the Explanations of the Three Sages' Doctrine of Healing the World by the Ancestral Master Lü)

12 *Lü zushi sanni yishi gongjue* 呂祖師三尼醫世功訣 (Practical Instructions on the Three Sages' Doctrine of Healing the World by the Ancestral Master Lü)

13 *Tianxian xinchuan* 天仙心傳 (Heart-to-Heart Transmission of Celestial Immortality)

14 *Tianxian dao jieji xuzhi* 天仙道戒忌須知 (Required Knowledge on Precepts and Prohibitions for the Path to Celestial Immortality)

15 *Tianxian daocheng baoze* 天仙道程寶則 (Precious Principles for the Path to Celestial Immortality)

16 *Erlan xinhua* 二懶心話 (Heart-to-Heart Dialogue between the Two Leisurely [Masters])

17 *Sanfen zhenren xuantan quanji* 三丰真人玄潭全集 (Complete Collection of the Mysterious Words by the Perfected [Zhang] Sanfeng)

18 *Rushi wo wen* 如是我聞 (Thus I Have Heard)

19 *Xiwang mu nüxiu zhengtu shize* 西王母女修正途十則 (Ten Principles of the Queen Mother of the West on the Correct Path of Female Cultivation)

20 *Niwan Li zushi nüzong shuangxiu baofa* 泥丸李祖師女宗雙修寶筏 (Precious Raft of Joint Cultivation in Inner Alchemy for Women by Patriarch Li Niwan)

21 *Jindan sibai zi zhushi* 金丹四百字注釋 (Commentary and Explanations on the *Jindan sibai zi*)

22 *Suoyan xu* 瑣言續 (Sequel to an Ignored Transmission)

23 *Xiuzhen biannan qianhou bian canzheng* 修真辯難前後編參証 (Annotations to the *Xiuzhen biannan*, in Two Sections)

Contents of the *Daozang xubian* 道藏續編 (Sequel to the Taoist Canon).

脈皇極闔闢證道仙經 (Immortal Scripture Testifying to the Path of Opening and Closing the August Ultimate According to the Orthodox Lineage of the Eastern Florescence; no. 2 in table 3) and the *Liaoyang dian wenda bian* 廖陽殿問答編 (Questions and Answers from the Liaoyang Hall; no. 3). Although both texts focus on the cultivation of the Vital Force, their purpose is to help adepts to achieve the joint cultivation (*shuangxiu*) of both Original Nature and Vital Force (*xing* and *ming*). The *Daozang xubian* accordingly includes several texts describing methods to awaken adepts to the "Celestial Mechanism" (*tianji* 天機; see *ji*), i.e., their Original Nature. These texts contain alchemical and symbolic methods, such as the *Xie tianji* 泄天機 (Disclosing the Celestial Mechanism; no. 4) and the *Shangpin danfa jieci* 上品丹法節次 (Alchemical Process of Highest Rank; no. 6); physiological techniques, like the *Gufa yangsheng shisan ze chanwei* 古法養生十三則闡微 (Uncovering the Subtleties of the Thirteen Principles Concerning the Ancient Methods of Nourishing Life; no. 5); and methods of visualization and practice close to those of Tantrism, such as the *Erlan xinhua* 二懶心話 (Heart-to-Heart Dialogue between the Two Leisurely [Masters]; no. 16; trans. Esposito 1993, 2: 389–440, and Esposito 1997, 97–120). Finally, some texts in this group contain explanations of moral and ethical principles inspired by Confucianism, including the *Jiuzheng lu* 就正錄 (Account of the Realization of Rectitude; no. 8) and the *Yu Lin Fenqian xiansheng shu* 與林奮千先生書 (Letter to Elder Lin Fenqian; no. 9).

Ethics, universal salvation, and exegesis. The third category of texts testifies to the importance of moral precepts within the Longmen school, which was formally charged with the education of Taoist clergy. As explained in the *Tianxian xinchuan* 天仙心傳 (Heart-to-Heart Transmission of Celestial Immortality; no. 13), adepts can achieve the highest stage of immortality through strict ethical discipline. The relevant texts are the *Tianxian dao jieji xuzhi* 天仙道戒忌須知 (Required Knowledge on Precepts and Prohibitions for the Path to Celestial Immortality; no. 14) and the *Tianxian daocheng baoze* 天仙道程寶則 (Precious Principles for the Path to Celestial Immortality; no. 15). This program of moral and practical precepts is specific to the Longmen school and is a product of its officially standardized teachings.

Also typical of the Longmen school are many technical terms found only in texts of the *Daozang xubian*. One of them is *yishi* 醫世 (lit., healing the world), which defines the Longmen doctrine of universal salvation (see *pudu*). This term delimits the fourth category of texts in the collection, namely, the *Lü zushi sanni yishi shuoshu* 呂祖師三尼醫世說述 (Explanation of the Three Sages' Doctrine of Healing the World by the Ancestral Master Lü; no. 10), the *Du Lü zushi sanni yishi shuoshu guankui* 讀呂祖師三尼醫世說述管窺 (A Personal Reading of the Explanation of the Three Sages' Doctrine of Healing the World by the Ancestral Master Lü; no. 11), and the *Lü zushi sanni yishi* *gongjue* 呂祖師三尼醫世功訣 (Practical Instructions on the Three Sages' Doctrine of Healing the World by the Ancestral Master Lü; no. 12). The "three sages" mentioned in these titles are Laozi, Confucius, and the Buddha. In addition, the *Daozang xubian* contains alchemical methods for female adepts (see *nüdan) because, in the Longmen's universal salvation program, women too can obtain enlightenment. These are the *Xiwang mu nüxiu zhengtu shize* 西王母女修正途十則 (Ten Principles of the Queen Mother of the West on the Correct Path of Female Cultivation; no. 19; trans. Wile 1992, 192–201) and the *Niwan Li zushi nüzong shuangxiu baofa* 泥丸李祖師女宗雙修寶筏 (Precious Raft of Joint Cultivation in Inner Alchemy for Women by Patriarch Li Niwan; no. 20; trans. Wile 1992, 204–12).

Finally, the *Daozang xubian* contains two exegeses of *Zhang Boduan's *Jindan sibai zi*, commented on by *Peng Haogu and edited by Min Yanglin 閔陽林 (no. 21); and an explication of *Liu Yiming's *Xiuzhen biannan* 修真辨難 (Discussions on the Cultivation of Perfection), commented on by Min Yide himself (no. 23).

Altogether, the *Daozang xubian* exhibits the intention of clarifying alchemical teachings in order to make them more accessible through techniques that suit individual dispositions and tastes. Accordingly, one notes various levels of alchemical practices and a particular classification of texts. This variety of techniques forms the richness of the *Daozang xubian* and shows the syncretism of the Longmen school beyond its officially accepted doctrine.

Monica ESPOSITO

📖 Despeux 1990, 163–68; Esposito 1992; Esposito 1993; Esposito 2001, 221–24 (index)

※ Min Yide; *neidan*; Longmen; DAOZANG AND SUBSIDIARY COMPILATIONS

daozhang

道長

"dignitary of the Dao"

The *daozhang* is an ordained Taoist priest (*daoshi) who is qualified to perform *zhai (Retreat) and *jiao (Offering) rituals as chief officiant. Having formally received the registers (*LU), he is also known as "master of registers" (*lushi* 籙士). Originally, the registers were bestowed by the Celestial Master (*tianshi) on Mount Longhu (*Longhu shan, Jiangxi). In Taiwan, however, because of the distance from the Celestial Master headquarters, few priests received their registers directly, and ordination took the form of a ceremony in which authorization was obtained from the Jade Sovereign (*Yuhuang). This changed in 1949, when *Zhang Enpu, the sixty-third Celestial Master, left Mount Longhu and later settled in Taipei (Taiwan). Since then, those receiving the registers from the Celestial Master in person have increased. At the same time, there are others who become *daozhang* without following the established custom, which is one reason for the remarkable rise in the number of *daozhang* in recent times.

Although the *daozhang* in Taiwan traditionally followed their calling along hereditary lines, the majority of *daozhang* in present-day Taiwan have not inherited their positions. Their residences serve as ritual spaces in which they perform minor rites and ceremonies for clients, and daily morning services in front of the enshrined deities. The necessary scriptures, ritual texts, paintings, ritual implements, musical instruments, and vestments are also kept in their homes. When a client requests a major ritual, the *daozhang* calls upon his colleagues and musicians to form a troupe, and takes charge of its performance at the client's home or at a shrine. He functions then as the high priest (*gaogong* 高功), and as such must memorize the invocations that only he can chant, and the actions and meditations that only he can perform. Books called *mijue ("secret instructions") contain the knowledge that he must acquire. Additionally, the *daozhang* must prepare the documents required during rituals, using the examples found in the handbooks called *wenjian* 文檢 ("writing models") that they receive from their masters. Collections of Taoist terms with explanations, called *zaji* 雜記 ("miscellaneous notes"), are also circulated among the *daozhang*.

ASANO Haruji

📖 Asano Haruji 1994; Maruyama Hiroshi 1992; Ōfuchi Ninji 1983, 161–69, 200–201; Schipper 1977b

※ *daoshi*

Dasheng miaolin jing

大乘妙林經

Scripture of the Wondrous Forest of the Great Vehicle

The *Dasheng miaolin jing* (CT 1398) consists of three *juan*. Its date is unclear, but it was probably compiled toward the end of the Six Dynasties. It begins with a description of Yuanshi tianzun 元始天尊 (Celestial Worthy of Original Commencement; see *sanqing) sitting in the Palace of Original Yang (Yuanyang gong 元陽宮) in the City of the Seven Treasures (Qibao cheng 七寶城) on top of a high mountain in the paradisiacal otherworld. His divine radiance illuminates all corners of the universe as various followers come forward and ask him questions.

The major topics touched upon in the text are reflected in the ten section headings: 1. Introduction ("Xu" 序); 2. Observation of the Marks of Perfection ("Guan zhenxiang" 觀真相); 3. Discerning True and False ("Bian xiezheng" 辯邪正); 4. Observation of the Self ("Guanshen" 觀身); 5. Beginners' Questions ("Tongzi wen" 童子問); 6. Following in Accordance ("Suishun" 隨順); 7. The Host of Perfected Explain the Dharma ("Zhongzhen shuofa" 眾真說法); 8. Observation of the Nature of Dharmas ("Guan faxing" 觀法性); 9. Purity and Wisdom ("Jinghui" 淨慧); 10. Eulogium ("Zantan" 讚歎).

The text emphasizes the theory that the afflictions of *karma* (*kleśa*) are identical with enlightenment (*bodhi*, "awakening"). In structure and argumentation, it is similar to an apocryphal Buddhist scripture of approximately the same period, the *Jiujing dabei jing* 究竟大悲經 (Scripture of the Great Ultimate Compassion; T. 2880). In both worldview and phrasing, the influence of the Huayan 華嚴 school of Buddhism is clearly discernible.

Livia KOHN

📖 Kamata Shigeo 1966

※ TAOISM AND CHINESE BUDDHISM

de

德

virtue; power

The concept of *de* is central to the early Chinese religious conception of the relationship between human beings and Heaven (or nature, *tian* 天). In early texts, such as the *Daode jing* (lit., "Scripture of the Dao and Virtue"), the term refers to a characteristic of the sage that both results in good actions and confers authority. In the **Taiping jing* (Scripture of Great Peace) the term continues to refer to an innate quality correlated with good actions, but also begins to be used to signify Heavens's conferral of life (*sheng* 生) as it is does in later imperial texts.

Arthur Waley's translation of the term as "power" in the context of the title of the *Daode jing* reflects the fact that the ruler's possession of *de* confers authority. This connection between *de* and political authority may be seen as far back as the Shang dynasty oracle bones, where the ruler's "shining" *de* (*xinde* 馨德) correlated with an ability to secure the Heavenly Mandate (*tianming* 天命). David Nivison explains that this property of a good Shang king is demonstrated by generosity and humility, and generates a debt of gratitude in others (1994b, 29–30). The power that *de* confers may be seen in the second chapter of the *Lunyu* 論語 (Analects) of Confucius: "Carrying out governance by *de* is like the pole star staying fixed in place while all the other stars revolve around it." The pole star analogy links the exercise of *de* to a stillness reminiscent of its link to **wuwei* (non-action) in early texts such as the *Daode jing*.

In those Warring States period texts later classified as belonging to the **DAOJIA* (Lineage of the Dao), *de* connotes a similar complex of morality and power, but it is most closely aligned with a return to intuitive actions and natural behavior. In the *Daode jing*, *de* is not the sole possession of the ruler, but rather, according to Philip J. Ivanhoe (1999, 249), achieved by "paring away the influences of socialization and intellectualization and 'turning back' to a simple, agrarian way of life." In the **Zhuangzi*, *de* expresses a similar kind of "original power" that coincides with the text's assumption of an intuitive human morality. In the case of figures like the madman Jie Yu 接輿 and Hundun 渾沌 from *Zhuangzi* 7, virtue is a characteristic of the denizens of the world prior to its corruption by distinctions and the values based on them. *De* is complete when a person or an age has returned to its original nature, and in this sense it shows congruence with *tian* (Heaven). In *Zhuangzi* 21, when Confucius remarks that Laozi's *de* is the equal of Heaven and Earth, Laozi explains that he achieved this by following his nature like water flows in a stream. The notion of *de* was also sometimes contrasted with the practices of "popular religion." Wang Chong 王充 (27-ca. 100 CE), in his *Lunheng* 論衡 (Balanced Discussions), held that accumulating *de* was a superior pursuit compared with sacrifice and exorcism (see Forke 1907–11, 1: 532–37).

The pairing of *de* with the concept of *dao* first seen in Warring States texts becomes the primary context in which the former term appears in later Taoist texts. The relationship between the two, however, changes over time. Chen Guying finds three similar relationships between the two terms in the *Daode jing*: *de* as a projection of the formless Dao, as the individual characteristics of objects that formed from Dao, and as the manifestation of the Dao in the material world (1987, 152). In some chapters of the *Taiping jing*, *dao* and *de* form a triad with *ren* 仁 (benevolence) as ideal expressions of Heaven, Earth, and Humanity, respectively (e.g., Wang Ming 1960, 157). Because *de* connotes a unity with Heaven, to the extent that Heaven was providential in early medieval Taoism, being a *dejun* 德君 (virtuous lord) meant receiving blessings from Heaven. In other chapters of the *Taiping jing*, *dao* and *de* are paired with Yang and Yin in discussions about the way that Heaven sustains life among the myriad creatures through birth and nourishment, respectively (e.g., Wang Ming 1960, 218–19). This connection with life becomes central for *Sima Chengzhen (647–735), who sees life as being the *de* of Heaven (Qing Xitai 1994, 2: 253). Zhuangzi's sense of *de* as an innate characteristic therefore reappears in the late imperial conception of *de* as a primal endowment less directly tied to morality, but one that it is similarly conferred by Heaven.

Mark CSIKSZENTMIHALYI

📖 Ames 1989; Chen E. M. 1973b; Emerson 1992; Ivanhoe 1999; Munro 1969, 99–110 and passim; Nivison 1987b; Qing Xitai 1994, 2: 251–55

※ Dao

Deng Yougong

鄧有功

fl. late eleventh-early twelfth century

Deng Yougong was the editor of one of the two earliest comprehensive compilations of the methods of the *Tianxin zhengfa tradition, *Shangqing tianxin zhengfa* 上清天心正法 (Correct Method of the Celestial Heart of the Highest Clarity; CT 566), and of the so-called "devil's code" (i.e., the religious code) of the tradition, *Shangqing gusui lingwen guilü* 上清骨髓靈文鬼律 (Devil's Code of the Spinal Numinous Script of the Highest Clarity; CT 461), which originally was established by *Rao Dongtian. He appears to have lived on Mount Huagai (Huagai shan 華蓋山) in central Jiangxi. He seems not to be identical with the man by the same name who lived 1210–79 and in the same area (see *Quan Song ci* 全宋詞, 4.2977). For one thing, it seems difficult to make the line of transmission through four masters stretch over a period of more than two hundred years, and furthermore none of the available information concerning the Deng Yougong of the thirteenth century affords any grounds for associating him with Taoism, let alone with the priesthood and the ritual traditions that emerged from Mount Huagai. It may be added that some of the place names occurring in Deng's prefaces appear to indicate that he lived during the period of the end of the Northern Song dynasty, rather than in the thirteenth century. Note also that the totality of the "devil's code" that he edited, *Gusui lingwen guilü*, is included also as *juan* 6 of the other early compilation of the methods of the Tianxin tradition, **Taishang zhuguo jiumin zongzhen biyao*, contributed to the Taoist Canon of emperor Song Huizong by Yuan Miaozong 元妙宗 in 1116. The information found in the preface to the "devil's code" by Deng Yougong, concerning his procedure in searching for and collating different versions of the text, together with a comparison of his version with the one included in the *Zongzhen biyao*, appears to indicate that the latter was derived from the text established by Deng Yougong, rather than the other way around. The inescapable conclusion thus would seem to be that an important part of Deng's activity occurred before the year 1116.

As for the date of the *Shangqing tianxin zhengfa*, it is worth noting that a text with this title is listed in the *Tongzhi* 通志 (Comprehensive Monographs; completed 1161), though in this catalogue the book is said to consist of three *juan*, as opposed to the seven *juan* of the compilation by Deng Yougong transmitted in the Taoist Canon (van der Loon 1984, 75). It has been suggested that the three-*juan* work mentioned in the *Tongzhi* was another, earlier compilation transmitted by Rao Dongtian himself (see Zhong Zhaopeng 1993, 33), but we have no evidence for the existence of such a work. In his preface to the current seven-*juan* version, Deng Yougong mentions having divided his work into two *juan*, a fact that would seem to indicate a certain fluidity in the *juan* divisions during the early transmission of the work. It also seems possible that, in fact, Deng Yougong's preface originally belonged to a version earlier than the current seven-*juan* edition of the *Shangqing tianxin zhengfa*, which certainly contains elements that must have been incorporated later than the first decades of the twelfth century—for instance, materials adopted from the *Shenxiao tradition, which did not emerge until around 1117, and the description of a set of talismans that is said to be copied verbatim from the text edited by the thirtieth Celestial Master, *Zhang Jixian (1092–1126; *Shangqing tianxin zhengfa*, 5.8a–9a and 3.9b–20a). The overall content of the *Shangqing tianxin zhengfa* closely resembles that of the *Zongzhen biyao*, and together they constitute the main sources for the early forms of the ritual methods of the Tianxin tradition.

Poul ANDERSEN

📖 Andersen 1991, 15–17, 81–96; Andersen 1996, 145–47; Boltz J. M. 1987a, 25; Drexler 1994, 24–25; Hymes 2002, 26–46 and 271–77; Qing Xitai 1999

※ *Taishang zhuguo jiumin zongzhen biyao*; Tianxin zhengfa

Dengzhen yinjue

登真隱訣

Concealed Instructions for the Ascent to Reality
(*or*: to Perfection)

The *Dengzhen yinjue* (CT 421) was compiled by *Tao Hongjing sometime between 493 and 514. Only three of the original twenty-four chapters are extant, while the preface is preserved in the *Huayang Tao yinju ji* 華陽陶隱居集 (Anthology of Tao, the Hermit of Flourishing Yang; CT 1050, 1.19a–21a). The extant portions consist of fragments from *Shangqing revealed texts with notes added by Tao Hongjing.

Unlike the *Zhengao (Authentic Declarations), also compiled by Tao, the *Dengzhen yinjue* is addressed to Shangqing adepts and provides guidance for their practices. The first chapter contains instructions on the practice of *shouyi (guarding the One) or method of the Nine Palaces (*jiugong) of the brain, with a commentary by Tao. This practice, a description of which was originally appended to *Su Lin's biography, was later incorporated and developed in the *Suling jing (Robinet 1984, 2: 292–93). The second chapter contains texts on minor recipes and apotropaic practices, also found in the *Zhengao* (j. 9, 10, 15) and the *Baoshen qiju jing* 寶神起居經 (Scripture on the Behavior for Treasuring the Spirit; CT 1319; Robinet 1984, 2: 359–62). The third chapter describes rites that *Wei Huacun received from *Zhang Daoling and Wang Bao 王褒 and that were also part of Wei Huacun's biography. They include a method for chanting the *Huangting jing, a ritual for entering the meditation chamber (*jingshi) transmitted by Zhang Daoling, rules for writing petitions to divinities, and a method for summoning celestial officers in order to heal illnesses and expel malevolent forces. These rites, originally part of a lost fourth-century hagiography of Wei Huacun (Robinet 1984, 2: 399–405), belong either to the Celestial Masters (*Tianshi dao) or to local traditions earlier than Shangqing.

Quotations of lost passages of the *Dengzhen yinjue* in other works include Tao Hongjing's discussions on drugs, recipes, and other methods originally attached to Shangqing hagiographies, some of which are not extant elsewhere.

Isabelle ROBINET

📖 Cedzich 1987; Ishii Masako 1980, 283–309; Ōfuchi Ninji 1997, 427–56; Ōfuchi Ninji and Ishii Masako 1988, 50–53 (list of texts cited); Robinet 1984, 2: 347–51; Seidel 1988

※ Tao Hongjing; Shangqing

dianhua

點化

"projection"

In Western alchemy, the term "projection" denotes the process by which a small quantity of elixir confers its properties to any substance which is added to it. This notion corresponds to the Chinese term *dianhua*, where *hua* indicates "transmutation" and *dian* literally means "one dot," hence "to transmute by means of a small quantity." Several *waidan texts mention this term and the corresponding process of transmutation, stating for instance that a small amount of elixir converts a larger amount of base substances into gold or silver. Early sources often describe this transmutation as evidence that the elixir has been achieved.

Later alchemists, associated with both *waidan* and *neidan, expanded the notion of *dianhua* by taking *dian* to mean the "particle" of precosmic Original Pneuma (*yuanqi) that circulates in the cosmos along the cycles of time. This particle is represented by the unbroken line (—) of the *Yijing, and its cycles of ascent and descent are illustrated by the twelve "primary hexagrams" (*bigua* 辟卦; see *huohou) which reproduce a complete time sequence (in particular, the twelve double hours of the day, and the twelve months of the year). Alchemists mark the rhythm of their practice according to those cycles, using the twelve hexagrams to establish the pattern of the firing process in *waidan* (see *huohou), and of the refinement of the primary components of the person in *neidan* (see *zhoutian). This allows them to return the ingredients of the outer or inner elixir to their precosmic state. Once the elixir is obtained, the whole human being and the whole cosmos are transmuted.

Fabrizio PREGADIO

📖 Chen Guofu 1983, 192; Needham 1976, 100 and passim; Pregadio 1995

※ *yuanqi; neidan; waidan*

ding

定

concentration

The word *ding* means "to settle," "to stabilize," "firm," "solid." It is first used in a meditative context in translations of Buddhist texts, where it appears as one of the technical terms for *samādhi* or the full and intense concentration of the mind on one object. In this sense, *ding* has been rendered as "intent contemplation" or "perfect absorption." In Buddhism, it moreover commonly occurs in two combinations, *sanding* 散定 which indicates a "scattered" or general form of concentrative meditation; and *chanding* 禪定, including the term later used for the Chan school, which indicates a specific and highly abstract form of meditation, whereby the mind is fully concentrated on one object that either has form or, in the higher stages, is formless.

In Taoism, *ding* first occurs in the context of the ancient *Lingbao scriptures, in a text known as *Zhihui dingzhi tongwei jing* 智慧定志通微經 (Scripture for Penetrating the Subtle through Wisdom and Fixing the Will; CT 325). Here the compound *dingzhi* used in connection with *zhihui* or "wisdom" indicates the firming up (*ding*) of the practitioner's will or determination (*zhi*), his set intention to "penetrate the subtlety" (*tongwei*) of the Dao. Rather than a technical term for a meditative state, *ding* functions thus as a verb indicating the adept's firm commitment and signifies the equivalent of the bodhisattva vow in a Taoist context.

Later a more technical, meditative use of *ding* became common. The locus classicus for this usage is found in *Sima Chengzhen's *Zuowang lun (Essay on Sitting in Oblivion), which has a section entitled "Taiding" 泰定 or "Intense Concentration" (12a–14a). This term denotes a stage of complete and utter absorption that comes right before the final attainment of the Dao. Like other terms in this text, the expression *taiding* is a mixture of Buddhist notions (*samādhi*) and ideas found in ancient Taoist scriptures, in this case the *Zhuangzi where the term appears in chapter 23 (see trans. Watson 1968, 254).

In the *Zhuangzi*, however, *tai* is not an attribute of *ding*, but rather the two terms are equivalent and the expression *taiding* is best translated as "at peace and stabilized [in mind]."

Another relevant work is the *Dingguan jing* (Scripture on Concentration and Observation), which is closely related to the *Zuowang lun*. Used in conjunction with *guan* ("observation"), the word *ding* here indicates the general practice of concentration, an exercise of mental one-pointedness necessary before one can undertake the more complex activity of *guan*. The text recommends steadiness of faith and continuity of practice, which leads to freedom from desires and tranquillity of mind.

Livia KOHN

📖 Kohn 1987a, 35, 55, and 125–43; Robinet 1997b, 206–7

※ MEDITATION AND VISUALIZATION

Dingguan jing

定觀經

Scripture on Concentration and Observation

The *Dingguan jing* appears twice in the Taoist Canon (CT 400; YJQQ 17.6b–13b). This short but powerful text can be dated to the early eighth century, after *Sun Simiao and before *Sima Chengzhen. It consists of forty-nine stanzas of two or more lines, each having four or occasionally six characters. It presents a survey of the mental transition from an ordinary perspective—characterized by impurity, cravings, vexations, emotions, and desires—to a state of full concentration, peace, and tranquillity. Once full concentration (*ding*) is attained, the mind will observe (*guan*) all phenomena dispassionately and gain the necessary insight that will lead the practitioners to immortality.

The development of the mind is outlined in five phases, the immortalization of the body in seven stages. This outline repeats the pattern described first by Sun Simiao in his *Cunshen lianqi ming (Inscription on the Visualization of Spirit and Refinement of Pneuma). In addition, the text is noteworthy for its practical details on the various mental states the adept undergoes when passing through each developmental phase. Throughout, purity and complete abstention from intentional thought and action are emphasized.

The influential nature of the text is documented in its numerous variants in the Canon, where it appears: 1. as appendix to the *Zuowang lun* (Essay on Sitting in Oblivion; CT 1036, 15b–18a), with two sections added; 2. summarized under the title *Guanmiao jing* 觀妙經 (Scripture of the Observation of Marvels; CT 326; Kohn 1987a, 126); 3. quoted at length in *Du Guangting's *Daode zhenjing guangsheng yi* 道德真經廣聖義 (Extended Interpretation of the Emperor's Exegesis of the *Daode jing*; CT 725, 49.8a–b), dating from 901; 4. with additional commentary in the *Daoshu* (Pivot of the Dao; CT 1017, 2.2b–3b); and in other works on meditation and *neidan*.

Livia KOHN

📖 Kohn 1987a, 125–43 (trans.); Robinet 1997b, 205–6

※ *ding*; *guan*; MEDITATION AND VISUALIZATION

dinglu

鼎爐

tripod and furnace

1. Waidan

The word *ding* normally refers to a tripod or cauldron (see fig. 29), but the alchemical apparatus known by this name may have different forms. In their function as reaction vessels, the *fu* 釜 (crucible), *shenshi* 神室 (divine chamber), *hezi* 合 (盒) 子 (closed vessel), and *gui* 匱 (case) are equivalent to the *ding*. Similarly, the *lu*, although generally rendered as "furnace," has different shapes, and the *zao* 竈 (stove) can be its equivalent.

The reaction vessel has fire around it (when it is placed inside the heating apparatus), under it (when it is placed over the heating apparatus), or above it (when it is entirely covered by ashes inside the heating apparatus). It may contain an inner reaction-case in which the ingredients are placed. In a more complex model, a "water-vessel" containing water and a "fire-vessel" containing the ingredients can be assembled, the former above and the latter below or vice versa. The vessel must be hermetically closed and should not bear any openings or cracks.

The heating apparatus has fire within it and is often placed over a platform or "altar" (*tan* 壇). The openings on the wall sides allow air to circulate, while those on the top serve to settle the reaction vessel or to emit flame and smoke. One of the main functions of the heating apparatus is to control the intensity and duration of the heat.

In their various forms, the *ding* and the *lu* play a major role in establishing the cosmological import of the alchemical work. The *ding* is to the ingredients

Fig. 29. An alchemical tripod, surrounded by the names of the twenty-eight lunar lodges (*xiu) and by the graphs for Heaven, Earth, Sun, and Moon. *Yunji qiqian (Seven Lots from the Bookbag of the Clouds; CT 1032), 72.10a–b.

what the womb is to the embryo, and what primordial Chaos, or *hundun, is to the cosmos. A reaction vessel shaped like an egg, in fact, is referred to as *hundun*. When the reaction vessel is made of two joined parts, the upper and lower parts represent Heaven and Earth. Similarly, a *lu* can be made of three parts symbolizing for Heaven, Humanity, and Earth. The circle and square, respectively representing Heaven and Earth, constitute the basic shape of the *lu*, which has a round upper part over a square lower part, or an outer circular contour with inner squared walls. Cosmological emblems can be inscribed on the *ding* and the *lu*, and the figures related to them (i.e., their circumference, height, number of openings, etc.) often have cosmological significance.

KIM Daeyeol

📖 Chen Guofu 1983, 39–79; Needham 1980, 11–21; Sivin 1980, 279–97

※ *waidan*

2. Neidan

In *neidan*, the furnace and the tripod constitute one of the "three essentials" (*sanyao* 三要) of the alchemical work, along with the ingredients (*yao* 藥) and the firing process (*huohou*). Tripod and furnace symbolize the Center, the place where the elixir is formed. From the point of view of Unity (*yi*), they are a single thing and have names that allude to the Center, such as Yellow Dame (*huangpo* 黃婆). They also represent the Original One and together are a synonym of the One Opening of the Mysterious Pass (*xuanguan yiqiao* 玄關一竅; see *xuanguan*), which is the inaugural moment of the inner alchemical work. As the Center, tripod and furnace are also called Mercurial Tripod (*hong-ding* 汞鼎), Lead Tripod (*qianding* 鉛鼎), Golden Tripod (*jinding* 金鼎), and Spiritual Furnace (*shenlu* 神爐).

As a representation of space, tripod and furnace are also dual and frame the alchemical work: they are *qian* 乾 ☰ (pure Yang) or Heaven above and *kun* 坤 ☷ (pure Yin) or Earth below. They contain the ingredients of the elixir, and trigrams and hexagrams circulate between them as Yin and Yang do between Heaven and Earth. Each is indicated by Yin or Yang symbols: for instance, the *qian*-furnace is paired with the *kun*-tripod, or the Jade Tripod with the Golden Furnace, or the Yang Furnace with the Yin Tripod. The Furnace as a "supine moon" (*yanyue lu* 偃月爐) symbolizes the waxing moon, which is the ascending Yang; it stands for the hexagram *fu* 復 ䷗ (Return, no. 24), or the Heart of Heaven (*tianxin), while the Cinnabar Tripod (*zhusha ding* 朱沙鼎) stands for Fire or the Original Spirit (*yuanshen* 元神).

The "Two-Eight Furnace" (*erba lu* 二八爐) alludes to the "two measures" of eight ounces each, which together form the pound of elixir, i.e., the two halves of the alchemical work. "External and internal Tripod" (*wainei ding* 外內鼎) designates the outer and inner Medicine, or in other words the transcendent precosmic *xiantian parcel that must be interiorized. At the final stage of the process, Furnace and Tripod respectively represent non-action (*wuwei) and Emptiness (*xu* 虛).

Being dual, *ding* and *lu* indicate different things according to the level at which the alchemical work is situated. At the lower level, they can be body and spirit, or body and viscera; at the median level they can be *qian* and *kun*, or *ding* can stand for *qian* and *kun* and *lu* for Yin and Yang; at the higher level, they can be Heaven and Earth, or the Great Void and the Real Void, or the Great Void and the Great Ultimate (*taiji). Some texts state that *lu* is the body and *ding* is the Dao. Or both can represent the body while the spirit (*xin) is the Divine Chamber (*shenshi* 神室). Sometimes, finally, *ding* is meant to be the Yellow Court (*huangting* 黃庭) in the navel, and *lu* the Cavity of Pneuma (*qixue* 氣穴) between the kidneys.

Isabelle ROBINET

📖 Robinet 1995a, 92–95 and 152–53

※ *neidan*

dong and *jing*

動 靜

movement and quiescence

In Chinese cosmology, both movement and quiescence originate from the Great Ultimate (*taiji) or the Original Pneuma (*yuanqi), where they exist in a latent state but are merged without distinction. Movement is Yang and is roughly synonymous with expansion, while quiescence is Yin or contraction. Movement and quiescence alternate; each one at its extreme turns into the other in a cyclical way. Each, moreover, is both the substance and the function (*ti and yong) of the other.

In Taoism, movement and quiescence are equated with change and permanence: movement is perceived as birth or taking form out of formless emptiness. This vital movement is characterized by growth and decay, and is a movement in time rather than in space: the changing of place of the hexagrams or the celestial bodies metaphorically figures the changes in one's life or mind. Quiescence is the norm of the world; it is akin to non-interference (*wuwei) and to feminine compliance that overcomes masculinity through quiescence. But it is not immobility, which does not pertain to our world and cannot be paired with movement.

On psychological and ethical grounds, the human inner nature (*xing* 性; see *xing and ming) is perceived as naturally quiet; stimulated by things, it is set in motion and emotions (*qing* 情) arise; then the distinction between good and evil occurs, along with the danger of losing one's life energy (*qi). If one moves and acts in a balanced way, responding in accord with circumstances, one's action is universally pervading (*tong* 通). In Taoism, the state of quiescence, where the mind is not moved by mental or affective stimuli, is closely connected with clarity and enlightenment, and with stability and correctness; the *Zhuangzi compares it to still water or a brilliant mirror. *Wang Bi says that quiescence is the "master" (*zhu* 主) of movement, but most Taoist authors opt for a balanced appreciation of movement and quiescence. The issue of whether the saint (*shengren) has emotions is similar: some say that he has no emotions, others that he has emotions but accords with the circumstances without being trapped by them.

Movement and quiescence are equally good if they are anchored in the Dao, their common source, or in *wuji (Ultimateless, Infinite), the state prior to any distinction between movement or quiescence, and if they are linked and develop naturally in accord with the cosmic movement. The relation between quiescence and movement is the same as that between spirit (which must be quiescent) and body (which is related to movement). Thus there must be continuity and no gap between the state of quiescence and the arising of movement, which is represented by the transition from the hexagram *kun* 坤 ䷁ (Earth, no. 2), pure quiescent Yin, to the hexagram *fu* 復 ䷗ (Return, no. 24), the return of incipient Yang. To perceive this initial movement before it is visible is the art of longevity. Presence of mind and steadiness in quiescence lead to earnest attention, discernment, and efficiency in movement. This is why one should watch the arousing of the first thought in quiescent meditation, which is perceptiveness and not "vain emptiness" (*wankong* 頑空). This first thought is equated with the first stirring of life and the birth of the world generated by the Dao.

But alchemists do not limit their attention to the first movement. They aim at harmonizing movement (Fire) and quiescence (Water). They also carefully observe the gradual growth of movement, its decay and its reversal to quiescence in accord with cosmic rhythms: this is the alchemical fire phasing (**huohou*) that changes from Yin to Yang and then from Yang to Yin.

Isabelle ROBINET

※ *ti* and *yong*; *wu* and *you*

Dong Dening

董德寧

fl. 1788; *zi*: Jingyuan 靜遠; *hao*: Yuanzhen zi 元真子
(Master of Original Perfection)

Dong Dening, a native of Guiji 會稽 (Zhejiang), was originally a Confucian scholar who later turned to Taoism. He deplored the habit of including elements of Buddhist doctrine in Taoist works while neglecting Confucianism. He also found the interpretations of important Taoist works such as the **Zhouyi cantong qi* and the **Wuzhen pian* inadequate and sometimes derogatory, as most Ming and Qing commentaries explicated these works from the point of view of **neidan* or of sexual practices. Accordingly, Dong's own commentaries attempt to recapture the erudition of the Chinese philosophers: he frequently quotes from the **Yijing* and the Confucian classics, and his model is the philosopher Zhu Xi 朱熹 (1130–1200) whose works include a commentary to the *Cantong qi* (see under **Zhouyi cantong qi kaoyi*).

Dong Dening's texts and exegetical works were written in the Jiyang lou 集陽樓 (Pavilion for Gathering Yang) on the Four Peaks Mountain (Sifeng shan 四峰山, Zhejiang) and were published there between 1788 and 1804. They appeared as part of a collection entitled *Daoguan zhenyuan* 道貫真源 (Pervading the True Sources of the Way), which also includes a selection of works by other authors that shows he was a late adept of the Southern Lineage (*Nanzong) of *neidan*. Dong's own main exegetical works are the *Zhouyi cantong qi zhengyi* 周易參同契正義 (The Correct Meaning of the *Zhouyi cantong qi*) and the *Wuzhen pian zhengyi* 悟真篇正義 (The Correct Meaning of the *Wuzhen pian*), both completed in 1788.

Farzeen BALDRIAN-HUSSEIN

※ *neidan*

Dong Sijing

董思靖

fl. 1246–60

Dong Sijing, who came from Quanzhou 泉州 (Fujian), was a Taoist master at the Tianqing guan 天慶觀 (Abbey of Celestial Blessings) in Qingyuan 清源 (Fujian). He is the author of two important exegetical works. The first is the *Daode zhenjing jijie* 道德真經集解 (Collected Explications of the Authentic Scripture of the Dao and Its Virtue; CT 705) in four *juan*. In this work, Dong quotes and discusses several commentaries to the *Daode jing*, including a few of which only fragments survived, and refers to practical applications of the text. Despite the title, however, this is not a mere compilation of passages from earlier commentaries but an interpretive study of the *Daode jing*. Throughout his work, Dong expounds his own view of the central teaching of the *Daode jing*: non-action (*wuwei), spontaneity (*ziran), and emptiness of mind (xuxin 虛心). His thought combines the notions of Dao, *qi (pneuma), Yin and Yang, and *li* 理 (principle), revealing Neo-Confucian influences. In a foreword written in 1246, Dong draws up a list of earlier commentaries and provides valuable bibliographic information. The text ends with a colophon written between 1253 and 1259 by Xie Zhi 謝埴 and a postface dated 1257 by Huang Bichang 黃必昌.

Dong's second exegetical work is the *Ziran jiutian shengshen zhang jing jieyi* 自然九天生神章經解義 (Explication of the Meaning of the Scripture in Stanzas on the Self-Generated Life-Giving Spirits of the Nine Heavens; CT 396), dating from ca. 1252 and consisting of a commentary to the *Shengshen jing in four *juan*. Dong collected and collated several earlier editions of the scripture, including one from Shu 蜀 (Sichuan) and another from Zhedong 浙東 (eastern Zhejiang), and added quotations from *Shangqing sources about the central topic of the *Shengshen jing*, namely the generation and identification of the divinities dwelling within the human body. In a foreword, Dong emphasizes the attainment of personal union with the Dao through the teachings of the *Shengshen jing*. The colophon defines the ultimate purpose of the scripture as the cultivation of an Embryo of Sainthood (*shengtai) to successfully achieve "release from the corpse" (*shijie).

Grégoire ESPESSET

📖 Boltz J. M. 1987a, 211–12

Dongfang Shuo

東方朔

ca. 160-ca. 93 BCE; *zi*: Manqian 曼倩

In 138 BCE, Han Wudi (r. 141–87) called upon scholars throughout the empire to assist him in governing the state. Dongfang Shuo, a native of Pingyuan 平原 (Shandong), was recruited and soon became one of Wudi's favorites. An extravagant fellow, he chose to behave foolishly in the very heart of society (he was nicknamed Guji 滑稽 or "Buffoon"), becoming the first self-proclaimed "recluse at court" (*chaoyin* 朝隱). He served as a Virtuous (*liang* 良) and a Superior Grand Master of the Palace (*taizhong dafu* 太中大夫), but eventually fell into disgrace. His tomb and a shrine dedicated to him are still extant in Yanci 厭次 (Shandong).

Accounts making Dongfang an "immortal banished [from Heaven]" (*zhexian* 謫仙) arose already during his lifetime, and in the Six Dynasties period he became the hero of many stories as Wudi's whimsical companion. The best known of these narratives is the *Han Wudi neizhuan (Inner Biography of Emperor Wu of the Han), which tells how Dongfang stole the Peaches of Immortality from the Queen Mother of the West (*Xiwang mu) and traveled eastward to *Penglai and the other isles of the blessed. Seen as the embodiment of the planet Sui 歲 (Jupiter) or Taibai 太白 (Venus), he was credited with a miraculous birth, supernatural powers, and a number of different successive identities including Laozi himself.

The *Shizhou ji (Record of the Ten Continents) reports Dongfang Shuo's conversations with Wudi on mythical geography. Several other writings, in prose as well as in poetry, are ascribed to him, including the *Feiyou xiansheng lun* 非有先生論 (An Essay by Elder Nobody), the *Da kenan* 答客難 (Replies to a Guest's Objections), the *Shenyi jing* 神異經 (Scripture on Divine Marvels; see Campany 1996, 43–45), and the *Qijian* 七諫 (Seven Admonishments). He is also said to have assisted Sima Qian 司馬遷 (145?–86? BCE) in writing his *Shiji* (Records of the Historian).

Grégoire ESPESSET

📖 Campany 1996, 144–46, 318–21; Giles L. 1948, 47–51; Kaltenmark 1953, 137–38; Kohn 1993b, 335; Schipper 1965, 60–61; Vervoorn 1990, 203–15

※ Xiwang mu; *Shizhou ji*; HAGIOGRAPHY

Dongming ji

洞冥記

Records of Penetration into the Mysteries

The full title of the *Dongming ji*, as found in the bibliographic treatise of the *Xin Tangshu* (New History of the Tang) and elsewhere, is *Han Wudi bieguo dongming ji* 漢武帝別國洞冥記 (Records of the Han Emperor Wu's Penetration into the Mysteries of Separate Realms). Its authorship is traditionally ascribed to Guo Xian 郭憲, a *fangshi* in the time of Han Guangwu (r. 25–57). However, it contains imagery derived from *Shangqing sources like the *Zhengao* and is first cited in early-seventh-century writings, so a sixth century origin is likely. The text is not found in the present Taoist Canon, but was collected into at least one of the Song dynasty Canons (*Daozang quejing mulu*; 1.4a). It is partially preserved in the Song anthology *Xu tanzhu* 續談助 (Sequel to an Aid to Conversation; twelfth century) and in several collectanea of the late Ming and Qing periods. It is now usually classified as *zhiguai* 志怪 fiction ("records of the strange"; Li Jianguo 1984, 159–67).

The *Dongming ji* describes Han Wudi (r. 141–87 BCE) constantly engaging in ritual activities that are answered by the appearance of envoys and spirits bringing rare objects from distant lands. These objects are then either used for more ritual activity or casually discarded. Wudi's ritual activity subtly parallels events occurring far away, thus showing how he has "penetrated the mysteries of separate realms." He also frequently asks his advisor *Dongfang Shuo to describe distant lands. These descriptions, which roughly take up one-third of the surviving text, contain parallels with the imperial palace through the

Yin-Yang and *wuxing correlative cosmology. The Dongming ji may therefore be read as an attempt to illustrate how ritual works.

Thomas E. SMITH

📖 Campany 1996, 95–96, 144–46, and 318–21; Eichhorn 1985; Li Jianguo 1984, 159–67; Smith Th. E. 1992, 274–334 and 588–652 (trans.); Wang Guoliang 1989

※ TAOISM AND CHINESE LITERATURE

dongtian

洞天

Grotto-Heavens

See *dongtian and fudi 洞天 · 福地.

dongtian and fudi

洞天 · 福地

Grotto-Heavens and Blissful Lands

The Grotto-Heavens and the Blissful Lands (see tables 4, 5, and 6) are worlds believed to exist hidden within famous mountains and beautiful places. They are earthly paradises that do not suffer from floods, wars, epidemics, illnesses, old age or death. Such imaginary places are usually known by the single compound, dongtian fudi. However, the two words originally referred to different things, fudi broadly meaning "paradise" and dongtian denoting an underground utopia.

One of the earliest descriptions of the Blissful Lands is found in the *Baopu zi. The major mountains, says *Ge Hong, "have gods of their own, and sometimes earthly transcendents (dixian 地仙) are to be found there too. Numinous mushrooms (*zhi) and grasses grow there. There you can not only compound the medicines, but also escape war and catastrophe" (see Ware 1966, 94). Sun Chuo 孫綽 (314–71), a younger contemporary of Ge Hong, used the expression "blissful garden" (futing 福庭) in his You Tiantai shan fu 遊天臺山賦 (Rhapsody on Wandering on Mount Tiantai; trans. Knechtges 1982–96, 2: 243–53). The term fudi first appears in j. 11 of *Tao Hongjing's (456–536) *Zhengao, in which Jinling 金陵 (i.e., the *Maoshan area of Jiangsu) is described as a Blissful Land

Table 4

GROTTO-HEAVEN	MOUNTAIN	PROVINCE
1 Xiaoyou qingxu 小有清虛	*Wangwu shan 王屋山	Henan
2 Dayou kongming 大有空明	Weiyu shan 委羽山	Zhejiang
3 Taixuan zongzhen 太玄惣真	Xicheng shan 西城山	Shaanxi
4 Sanyuan jizhen 三元極真	Xixuan shan 西玄山	Shaanxi
5 Baoxian jiushi 寶仙九室	*Qingcheng shan 青城山	Sichuan
6 Shangqing yuping 上清玉平	Chicheng shan (*Tiantai shan) 赤城山 (天臺山)	Zhejiang
7 Zhuming huizhen 朱明輝真	*Luofu shan 羅浮山	Guangdong
8 Jintan huayang 金壇華陽	Gouqu shan (*Maoshan) 句曲山 (茅山)	Jiangsu
9 Youshen youxu 尤神幽虛	Linwu shan (Baoshan) 林屋山 (包山)	Jiangsu
10 Chengde yinxuan 成德隱玄	Guacang shan 括蒼山	Zhejiang

The ten major Grotto-Heavens (*da dongtian* 大洞天). Source: *Tiandi gongfu tu* 天地宮府圖 (Chart of the Palaces and Bureaus of the [Grotto-]Heavens and the [Blissful] Lands), in YJQQ 27. For a table based on *Du Guangting's *Dongtian fudi yuedu mingshan ji* 洞天福地嶽瀆名山記 (Records of Grotto-Heavens, Blissful Lands, Peaks, Rivers, and Famous Mountains; CT 599), see Verellen 1995, 289.

where neither soldiers nor floods can reach, and which cannot be attacked by calamity or disease.

The same chapter of the *Zhengao* also contains a detailed description of the Grotto-Heavens. For instance, Tao Hongjing describes the Grotto-Heaven extending below Mount Mao (Maoshan) as follows: "Grotto-Heavens exist in thirty-six places within the ground of the macrocosm. The eighth is the cavern of Mount Gouqu (Gouqu shan 句曲山, i.e., Mount Mao), 150 *li* in circumference, which is called the Jintan Huayang 金壇華陽 heaven." Since the *Zhengao* is partly based on a work compiled in the second half of the fourth century, it is likely that the theory of the Grotto-Heavens was advanced around that time by *Shangqing followers. This date is confirmed by other sources, including Xie Lingyun's 謝靈運 (385–433; IC 428–30) *Luofu shan fu* 羅浮山賦 (Rhapsody on the Luofu Mountains) which contains the following verse:

> In all there are thirty-six caverns:
> This one at the Luofu Mountains is the seventh.
> Light shines even in the dark night,
> The Sun illuminates the depths of the world.
> Therefore it is called the Yang palace of Vermilion Brightness,
> The Yin abode of Shining Truth.

Tao Yuanming 陶淵明 (Tao Qian 陶潛, 365–427; IC 766–69), a contemporary of Xie Lingyun, was certainly influenced by the idea of the Grotto-Heavens

Table 5

	GROTTO-HEAVEN	MOUNTAIN	PROVINCE
1	Huolin dongtian 霍林洞天	Huotong shan 霍桐山	Fujian
2	Pengxuan dongtian 蓬玄洞天	*Taishan 泰山	Shandong
3	Zhuling dongtian 朱陵洞天	*Hengshan 衡山	Hunan
4	Zongxian dongtian 惣仙洞天	*Huashan 華山	Shaanxi
5	Zongxuan dongtian 惣玄洞天	Changshan (*Hengshan) 常山 (恆山)	Shanxi
6	Sima dongtian 司馬洞天	*Songshan 嵩山	Henan
7	Xuling dongtian 虛陵洞天	*Emei shan 峨眉山	Sichuan
8	Dongling zhentian 洞靈真天	*Lushan 廬山	Jiangxi
9	Danshan chishui tian 丹山赤水天	Siming shan 四明山	Zhejiang
10	Jixuan dayuan tian 極玄大元天	Guiji shan 會稽山	Zhejiang
11	Xuande dongtian 玄德洞天	Taibai shan 太白山	Shaanxi
12	Tianzhu baoji xuantian 天柱寶極玄天	*Xishan 西山	Jiangxi
13	Haosheng xuanshang tian 好生玄上天	Xiaowei shan 小溈山	Hunan
14	Tianzhu sixuan tian 天柱司玄天	Qianshan 灊山	Anhui
15	Guixuan sizhen tian 貴玄司真天	Guigu shan 鬼谷山	Jiangxi
16	Zhensheng huaxuan tian 真昇化玄天	*Wuyi shan 武夷山	Fujian
17	Taixuan fale tian 太玄法樂天	Yusi shan 玉笥山	Jiangxi
18	Rongcheng dayu tian 容成大玉天	Huagai shan 華蓋山	Jiangxi
19	Changyao baoguang tian 長耀寶光天	Gaizhu shan 蓋竹山	Zhejiang
20	Baoxuan dongtian 寶玄洞天	Duqiao shan 都嶠山	Guangxi
21	Xiule changzhen tian 秀樂長真天	Baishi shan 白石山	Guangxi
22	Yuque baogui tian 玉闕寶圭天	Goulou shan 峋嶁山	Guangxi
23	Chaozhen taixu tian 朝真太虛天	Jiuyi shan 九疑山	Hunan
24	Dongyang yinguan tian 洞陽隱觀天	Dongyang shan 洞陽山	Hunan
25	Xuanzhen taiyuan tian 玄真太元天	Mufu shan 幕阜山	Hunan
26	Dayou huamiao tian 大酉華妙天	Dayou shan 大酉山	Hunan
27	Jinting chongmiao tian 金庭崇妙天	Jinting shan 金庭山	Zhejiang
28	Danxia tian 丹霞天	Magu shan 麻姑山	Jiangxi
29	Xiandu qixian tian 仙都祈仙天	Xiandu shan 仙都山	Zhejiang
30	Qingtian dahe tian 青田大鶴天	Qingtian shan 青田山	Zhejiang
31	Zhuri taisheng tian 朱日太生天	Zhongshan 鍾山	Jiangxi
32	Liangchang fangming dongtian 良常放命洞天	Liangchang shan 良常山	Jiangsu
33	Zixuan dongzhao tian 紫玄洞照天	Zigai shan 紫蓋山	Hubei
34	Tiangai dixuan tian 天蓋滌玄天	Tianmu shan 天目山	Zhejiang
35	Baima xuanguang tian 白馬玄光天	Taoyuan shan 桃源山	Hunan
36	Jinhua dongxuan tian 金華洞元天	Jinhua shan 金華山	Zhejiang

The thirty-six minor Grotto-Heavens (*xiao dongtian* 小洞天). Source: *Tiandi gongfu tu* 天地宮府圖 (Chart of the Palaces and Bureaus of the [Grotto-]Heavens and the [Blissful] Lands), in YJQQ 27. For a table based on *Du Guangting's *Dongtian fudi yuedu mingshan ji* 洞天福地嶽瀆名山記 (Records of Grotto-Heavens, Blissful Lands, Peaks, Rivers, and Famous Mountains; CT 599), see Verellen 1995, 289–90.

Table 6

	BLESSED LAND	PROVINCE		BLESSED LAND	PROVINCE
1	Difei shan 地肺山	Jiangsu	37	Shifeng shan 始豐山	Jiangxi
2	Gaizhu shan 蓋竹山	Zhejiang	38	Xiaoyao shan 逍遙山	Jiangxi
3	Xiangai shan 仙蓋山	Zhejiang	39	Dongbai yuan 東白源	Jiangxi
4	Dongxian yuan 東仙源	Zhejiang	40	Bochi shan 鉢池山	Jiangsu
5	Xixian yuan 西仙源	Zhejiang	41	Lunshan 論山	Jiangsu
6	Nantian shan 南田山	Zhejiang	42	Maogong tan 毛公壇	Jiangsu
7	Yuliu shan 玉溜山		43	Jilong shan 雞籠山	Anhui
8	Qingyu shan 清嶼山		44	Tongbo shan 桐柏山	Zhejiang
9	Dushui dong 郁木洞	Jiangxi	45	Pingdu shan 平都山	Sichuan
10	Danxia dong 丹霞洞	Jiangxi	46	Lüluo shan 綠蘿山	Hunan
11	Junshan 君山	Hunan	47	Huxi shan 虎溪山	Jiangxi
12	Daruo yan 大若巖	Zhejiang	48	Zhanglong shan 彰龍山	Hunan
13	Jiaoyuan 焦源	Fujian	49	Baofu shan 抱福山	Guangdong
14	Lingxu 靈墟	Zhejiang	50	Damian shan 大面山	Sichuan
15	Wozhou 沃州	Zhejiang	51	Yuanchen shan 元晨山	Jiangxi
16	Tianmu ling 天姥嶺	Zhejiang	52	Mati shan 馬蹄山	Jiangxi
17	Ruoye xi 若耶溪	Zhejiang	53	Deshan 德山	Hunan
18	Jinting shan 金庭山	Zhejiang	54	Gaoxi lansui shan 高溪藍水山	Shaanxi
19	Qingyuan 清遠山	Guangdong	55	Lanshui shan 藍水	Shaanxi
20	Anshan 安山	Guangdong	56	Yufeng shan 玉峰山	Shaanxi
21	Maling shan 馬嶺山	Hunan	57	Tianzhu shan 天柱山	Zhejiang
22	Eyang shan 鵝羊山	Hunan	58	Shanggu shan 商谷山	Shaanxi
23	Dongzhen xu 洞真墟	Hunan	59	Zhanggong dong 張公洞	Jiangsu
24	Qingyu tan 青玉壇	Hunan	60	Sima Hui shan 司馬悔山	Zhejiang
25	Guangtian tan 光天壇	Hunan	61	Changzai shan 長在山	Shandong
26	Dongling yuan 洞靈源	Hunan	62	Zhongtiao shan 中條山	Shanxi
27	Donggong shan 洞宮山	Fujian	63	Jiaohu yucheng dong 茭湖魚澄洞	Yunnan
28	Taoshan 陶山	Zhejiang	64	Mianzhu shan 綿竹山	Sichuan
29	Sanhuang jing 三皇井	Zhejiang	65	Lushui 瀘水	Hubei (?)
30	Lankeshan 爛柯山	Zhejiang	66	Ganshan 甘山	Guizhou
31	Lexi 勒溪	Fujian	67	Guishan 瑰山	Sichuan
32	*Longhu shan 龍虎山	Jiangxi	68	Jincheng shan 金城山	Anhui (?)
33	Lingshan 靈山	Jiangxi	69	Yunshan 雲山	Hunan
34	Quanyuan 泉源	Guangdong	70	Beimang shan 北邙山	Henan
35	Jinjing shan 金精山	Jiangxi	71	Lushan 盧山	Fujian
36	*Gezao shan 閣皂山	Jiangxi	72	Donghai shan 東海山	Jiangsu

The seventy-two Blissful Lands (*fudi* 福地). Source: *Tiandi gongfu tu* 天地宮府圖 (Chart of the Palaces and Bureaus of the [Grotto-]Heavens and the [Blissful] Lands), in YJQQ 27. The Blissful Lands nos. 7 and 8 are located in Penglai and Fusang, respectively (see *Penglai).

when he wrote his *Taohua yuan ji* 桃花源記 (Record of the Peach Blossom Font; Bokenkamp 1986d).

In the Tang period, the theories of the Grotto-Heavens and the Blissful Lands were combined and systematized. In his *Tiandi gongfu tu* 天地宮府圖 (Chart of the Palaces and Bureaus of the [Grotto-]Heavens and the [Blissful] Lands; YJQQ 27), *Sima Chengzhen (647–735) consolidated the Grotto-Heavens and Blissful Lands scattered around the country into ten major Grotto-Heavens, thirty-six minor Grotto-Heavens, and seventy-two Blissful Lands, and recorded details of their sizes, names, locations, and ruling divinities.

Spatially, the Grotto-Heavens can be said to be an inversion of the outer world, somehow similar to Klein's bottle. There the Sun and Moon shine just as they do in the outer world, trees and grasses grow, mountains and rivers exist, and birds fly through the sky. The source of light, however, is other than the Sun and Moon of our world: "Inside there is brightness in the dark and radiance during the night. The root of the essence of the Sun (*rijing zhi gen* 日精之根) illuminates the Grotto-Heaven, and its light matches the Sun and Moon of the outer world" (*Zhengao*, 11.6a). Another feature of the grottoes is that, although each one is independent of the others, they are all linked in a network by underground passages called *dimai* 地脈 ("earth channels"). For instance, the Grotto-Heaven of Mount Mao connects eastward to the Linwu grotto (Linwu dong 林屋洞) under Mount Dongting (Dongting shan 洞庭山) in Lake Taihu 太湖 (Jiangsu), northward to the grotto of Mount Tai (*Taishan, Shandong), westward to the grotto of Mount Emei (*Emei shan, Sichuan), and southward to the grotto of the Luofu Mountains (*Luofu shan, Guangdong).

Each Grotto-Heaven is ruled by a Real Man (*zhenren) sent from Heaven, and is inhabited by middle-rank immortals called "earthly immortals" (*dixian* 地仙). This status, however, is not fixed and the way is open for them to ascend to Heaven based on the judgement of the celestial Highest Emperor (Shangdi 上帝). Of course not just anyone can enter the grottoes. It is necessary for an aspirant first to master techniques such as visualization and breathing in order to train himself for immortality. It is also said that the gate to the Grotto-Heavens is open to those who accumulate three hundred virtuous actions and perform purification practices for three months.

The lore of the Grotto-Heavens and the Blissful Lands peaked in the Six Dynasties period. After that, they gradually lost their power of attraction in popular belief. By the early modern period, famous caverns had became synonymous with literary outings, and only artificial caves made within decorative mountain landscapes in urban gardens preserved their memory.

MIURA Kunio

📖 Bokenkamp 1986d; Chavannes 1919, 133–68; Miura Kunio 1983; Qing Xitai
1988–95, 2: 453–73; Schafer 1977a, 248–54; Soymié 1956, 88–96; Stein R. A. 1990,
55–58; Verellen 1995

※ TAOIST SACRED SITES

Dongxian zhuan

洞仙傳

Biographies of Cavern Immortals

The *Dongxian zhuan* is an anonymous collection of biographies of immortals,
now found only in fragmentary form as chapters 110 and 111 of the *Yunji
qiqian*. Since it is listed in the bibliographical chapter of the *Suishu* (History
of the Sui) we can surmise that it was composed in the Six Dynasties period.
That bibliography gives no author but subsequent listings in the bibliographical chapters of the Tang histories, and other catalogues, name the author as
Jiansu zi 見素子, Master Who Manifests Plainness (the phrase *jiansu* comes
from *Daode jing* 19). Unfortunately, the only identified Jiansu zi was active in
the 850s so lived too late be the author of *Dongxian zhuan*. The same catalogues
generally relate that the *Dongxian zhuan* had ten chapters, so the *Yunji qiqian*
fragments probably represent only a small fraction of the original. Yan Yiping
includes an annotated version of the *Dongxian zhuan* fragments in vol. 1 of his
Daojiao yanjiu ziliao (Yan Yiping 1974).

Among the seventy-seven figures who receive notices are *Xu Fu, *Wangzi
Qiao, *Gan Ji, Guo Pu 郭璞, and *Kou Qianzhi. The last period that figures
appear to come from is the Liang or Chen dynasties. The entries are not arranged in chronological order in the *Yunji qiqian* though whether this reflects
the arrangement in the original is, of course, unknown. Many of the fragments
are only a few lines long but some run for several hundred characters.

Benjamin PENNY

📖 Campany 1996, 92–93; Li Fengmao 1986, 187–224

※ HAGIOGRAPHY

Dongxiao gong

洞霄宮

Palace of the Cavernous Empyreans (Mount Dadi)

This Taoist religious center is the main sacred focus of Mount Dadi (Dadi shan 大滌山) southwest of Hangzhou (Zhejiang), and the thirty-fourth minor Grotto-Heaven (see *dongtian and fudi). While Han Wudi (r. 141–87 BCE) reputedly recognized its holiness and ordered a shrine built near the grotto in 108 BCE, it first became a Taoist center with the building of the Abbey of the Pillar of Heaven (Tianzhu guan 天柱觀) in 683, and *Wu Yun (?–778) joined other devout Tang literati in visiting it. In 1012, Song Zhenzong (r. 997–1022) renamed a bigger temple complex the Palace of the Cavernous Empyreans, which remained a site for Taoist rites done for the Song state until destroyed in 1121 in the rebellion of Fang La 方臘.

The reestablished Southern Song court prompted a rebuilding of the center, which was completed by 1155. The center became a key Taoist sanctuary south of the Yangzi until the Song ended, despite several fires over the next century and a half. Many retired high officials got sinecures at this temple, and besides retaining control over the lands of Dadi shan, it also had control over lands on the Nine-Chain Hills (Jiusuo shan 九鎖山), and the Hills of the Pillar of Heaven (Tianzhu shan 天柱山). Writings survive from Lu You 陸游 (1125–1210; SB 691–704) and *Bai Yuchan (1194–1229?) among many others. After 1284, further extensive repairs and rebuilding efforts occurred at the site and included shrines to local heroes such as *Ge Xuan (trad. 164–244) as well as local spirits such as the Dragon King (Longwang 龍王) and the widely renowned *Zhang Daoling, Xu Mai 許邁 (300–348; see under *Yang Xi), and *Ye Fashan (631–720).

The three-juan Ming text, Dadi dongtian ji 大滌洞天記 (Records of the Dadi Grotto-Heaven; CT 782), stemmed from the efforts of the Yuan scholar and resident Deng Mu 鄧牧 (1247–1306), but it abbreviates the Dongxiao tuzhi 洞霄圖志 (Illustrated Monograph of [the Palace of] the Cavernous Empyreans; 6 juan) and the poetic work of Meng Zongbao 孟宗寶 (fl. 1302), the Dongxiao shiji 洞霄詩集 (Poetical Anthology of [the Palace of] the Cavernous Empyreans). All were done under the guidance of the Dongxiao gong abbot, Shen Duofu 沈多福 (fl. 1290–1306), who wanted the site's sacred history to survive what they saw as the disaster of Mongol rule. Meng finished Deng's work after his death and both became part of the Zhibuzu zhai congshu 知不足叢書 (the gazetteer in collection 16, 1792, and the anthology in collection 11, 1786). The

Qing scholar Zhang Ji'an 張吉安 later compiled a historical account of the temple in the *Yuhang xianzhi* 餘杭縣志 (Monograph of the Yuhang District; 16.1a–26b).

Lowell SKAR

📖 Boltz J. M. 1987a, 117–118; Fu Lo-shu 1965, 36–38; Qing Xitai 1994, 4: 245–47

※ TEMPLES AND SHRINES

Dongyuan shenzhou jing

洞淵神咒經

Scripture of the Divine Spells of the Cavernous Abyss

The *Dongyuan shenzhou jing* is the main scripture of Taoist medieval apocalyptic eschatology. Spoken by the Dao, it presents itself as a revealed book. It was conferred, no doubt through mediumism, to a worthy recipient whose mission was to transmit it in order to save humanity from the impending end of the world. The confused and extremely repetitive style of the text confirms its oral, mediumistic origins. For that matter, even the book's title is not definitively stated: the text calls itself "Scripture of the Immeasurable" (*Wuliang jing* 無量經), "Scripture of the Divine Spells of Samādhi" (*Sanmei shenzhou jing* 三昧神咒經), "Scripture of Great Exorcism" (*Daqu jing* 大驅經), and other similar names.

Indeed, the *Shenzhou jing* claims to be the Book of books, the absolute scripture. It is a talismanic, prophylactic, and exorcistic text, a liturgical manual, a receptacle containing myriads of deities, a demonological repertory, a contract for initiates, and a passport for salvation. While the text offers no evidence of the identity of its recipient, it includes elements indicating that it was produced by a sect active in Jiangnan 江南 at the beginning of the fifth century. The text shares its basic theology, ideology, and liturgy with those of the *Tianshi dao. Although its millenarian ideas are rooted in ancient autochthonous beliefs, the emergence of the scripture can be explained partly as a reaction to the assimilation of Buddhism.

Formation of the text. The oldest versions of the *Shenzhou jing* are found among the *Dunhuang manuscripts and derive from a text in ten *juan*. Two manuscripts (P. 3233 and P. 2444), corresponding to j. 1 and 7 of the received version in the Taoist Canon (CT 335), contain colophons dated 664 stating that the work was copied at the order of Tang Gaozong (r. 649–83) for the crown prince Li Hong 李弘 (652–75, son of Empress Wu) in a metropolitan abbey, the Lingying guan 靈應觀 (Abbey of Numinous Response). The replacements of tabooed characters in the two manuscripts confirm this date. The *Shenzhou jing* was known as a ten-*juan* scripture during the sixth century and maintained this format until the end of the Tang. At the beginning of the Five Dynasties, *Du Guangting edited it in an expanded form in twenty *juan*. This is the version found in the Taoist Canon; it includes the ten *juan* of the Dunhuang versions (with some variants), plus eight *juan* dating from the Tang, and two final *juan* contemporary with the scripture's original ten-*juan* nucleus. Historical references found in the first ten *juan* allow us to date the original *Shenzhou jing* to the beginning of the fifth century. These references include allusions to the founder of the Liu Song dynasty, Liu Yu 劉裕 (356–422), and terms typical of the Six Dynasties such as *suolu* 索虜, by which the Southerners designated the non-Chinese peoples of the north.

Du Guangting's preface to the text in the Taoist Canon refers to the woodblock print of the version he had edited. The appellation Chuanzhen tianshi 傳真天師 (Celestial Master Who Transmits Truth), which appears in the list of Du's titles, show that his edition dates from the first decades of the tenth century (after 923). Du attributes the revelation of the *Shenzhou jing* to a certain Wang Zuan 王纂, a Taoist of Mount Maji (Maji shan 馬迹山, part of the *Maoshan range in Jiangsu) at the end of the Western Jin (before 316). Although this attribution cannot be accepted with regard to the scripture's date, it probably has a certain foundation since the masters of the *Shenzhou jing* tradition may have claimed Wang Zuan as their spiritual ancestor. By the beginning of the Tang period, this religious order had been institutionalized, and the Masters of the *Shenzhou jing* (*Shenzhou shi* 神咒師), also called Masters of the Law of the Great Religion of Samādhi and the Divine Spells of the Cavernous Abyss (*Dongyuan shenzhou dazong sanmei fashi* 洞淵神咒大宗三昧法師), had become part of the official ranks of the Taoist clergy. Certainly Du Guangting had received the original *Shenzhou jing* from this lineage, and included in his edition related liturgical texts containing penitential rituals and rituals for requesting rain. These rituals, some of which are also found as independent texts in the Taoist Canon, were likely transmitted by the Masters of the *Shenzhou jing*.

Apocalyptic predictions. The prophetic message delivered by the *Shenzhou jing* contains vivid descriptions of the apocalyptic drama. Most of its predictions sound familiar: the end of the world is imminent, and corresponds to the completion of a cosmic era, a great *kalpa* (*jie*). The final deluge will be preceded by horrible calamities: wars, barbarian invasions, crimes, social, political and familial dissolution, meteorological disorders, trials, imprisonments and official punishments, oppression of the people, conflagrations, floods, bad harvests, famines, curses, and above all an extraordinary propagation of diseases. All these troubles are produced by gigantic armies of demons (*gui and mowang 魔王), souls of the dead, and are a consequence of humankind's defilement and evil. Instead of conforming to the true religion—the religion of the Three Caverns, *SANDONG, preached by the *Shenzhou jing*—people perpetrate sins and addict themselves to heterodox cults (*yinsi) by immolating domestic animals to feed those demons with blood. The deluge will happen in a *jiashen* 甲申 year (the twenty-first of the sexagesimal cycle; see table 10) to purify the universe from all these evil creatures.

These apocalyptic predictions are repeated again and again through the first ten original chapters of the work, and leave little room for an expression of hope. Salvation, however, is promised to all the faithful who have been converted to the right Way and show devotion to it by respecting liturgical prescriptions and practicing proselytism. This elect group (*zhongmin, the "seed-people") will constitute the new humanity of immortals. They will enjoy the paradisiacal and egalitarian kingdom of Great Peace (*taiping) ruled by the Perfected Lord *Li Hong (the divinized Laozi) who will appear in the *renchen* 壬辰 year (the twenty-ninth of the sexagesimal cycle), eight years after the end of the world.

Christine MOLLIER

📖 Kamitsuka Yoshiko 1996, 39–44; Kamitsuka Yoshiko 1999, 221–28; Kobayashi Masayoshi 1990, 367–81; Mollier 1990; Mollier 1991; Ōfuchi Ninji 1964, 435–547; Ōfuchi Ninji 1978–79, 1: 251–95 (crit. notes on the Dunhuang mss.) and 2: 519–63 (reprod. of the Dunhuang mss.); Ozaki Masaharu 1983a; Sivin 1999b (part. trans.); Strickmann 2002, 89–103

※ APOCALYPTIC ESCHATOLOGY; MESSIANISM AND MILLENARIANISM

Dongyue dadi

東嶽大帝

Great Emperor of the Eastern Peak

From ancient rites to modern cults, no deity has accompanied the evolution of Chinese religion so closely as the god of Mount Tai (*Taishan, Shandong); none, moreover, was so thoroughly integrated by each of the Three Teachings (Confucianism, Taoism, and Buddhism). Mount Tai or the Eastern Peak (see under *wuyue) is arguably the most revered mountain in China. Emperors sought supreme legitimacy by performing the *feng* 封 ritual on its summit, and tried to impose an imperial monopoly on the cult of the mountain god.

Fig. 30. The Great Emperor of the Eastern Peak (Dongyue dadi).
Dongyue miao 東嶽廟 (Shrine of the Eastern Peak), Beijing.

Yet, the mountain's religious significance for Chinese society at large went far beyond the state liturgy. Under the Han, and probably earlier, it was believed that the souls of the dead rested under Mount Tai, and sick people came to the mountain to beg for a longer life span. Therefore, from antiquity onward, the cult of the god of the Eastern Peak has had two facets, related to each other: one is ethereous, imperial, and considers the god as a giver of immortality, while the other takes a somber view of the god as the master of the dead.

That the God of the Eastern Peak meant different things to different people is shown by the large number of divine beings credited with this function. The *Zhuangzi*, the "weft texts" (*weishu* 緯書) of the Han (see *TAOISM AND THE APOCRYPHA), the mirabilia of the Six Dynasties, Taoist works of various periods, and many catalogues of popular gods provided different identities. The god began to have an institutionalized cult of his own, however, only around the tenth century. Song Zhenzong (r. 997–1022) acknowledged this in 1011 when he granted him the title of Benevolent and Holy Emperor of the Eastern Peak, Equal to Heaven (Dongyue tianqi rensheng di 東嶽天齊仁聖帝). This was neither the first canonization—which was bestowed under the Tang—nor the last, but the god's accession to the status of *di* (emperor) was momentous. Traditionally, he had been considered the "grandson of Heaven" (*tiansun* 天孫) and therefore ranked below the emperor (the "son of Heaven," *tianzi* 天子). The new canonization drew criticism from Confucians but did full justice to the real role of the god in popular religion. Buddhists had long made him one of the Ten Kings of hell (Teiser 1993, 136), and later Taoist liturgy placed him at the top of the whole otherworld: sinners and sick people were advised to hold contrition rituals—like the fourteenth-century *Dongyue dasheng baochan* 東嶽大生寶懺 (Precious Penances for the Greatly Life-Giving [Emperor] of the Eastern Peak; CT 541)—dedicated to the god and mentioning his numerous subordinates.

Although some shrines of the Eastern Peak were managed by Buddhist monks, most housed Taoist priests. From the Song onward, these shrines, known as *Dongyue miao, began to appear throughout China: any district had at least one. The god, as master of life and death, was the most important icon in the main hall, and his demeanor is usually described in inscriptions as a fearful vision. He was accompanied by his hellish bureaucracy, most notably the seventy-two (sometimes seventy-four, seventy-five, or seventy-six) officers (*si* 司), each managing a specific aspect of human life and behavior. The small shrines of these less distant, if not always less fearful, deities were lined up along the main courtyard. From the mid-Ming onward, another cult, addressed to Dongyue dadi's daughter, *Bixia yuanjun (Original Princess of the Jasper Mist), suddenly appeared in the various Dongyue miao of northern China, and most remarkably in the great shrine in Beijing. As a child-giving and child-protecting merciful mother, the goddess is the reassuring side of the gruesome cult devoted to her father.

Dongyue shrines throughout China existed independently, but one of their most common denominations, "travelling palace" (*xinggong* 行宮, along with the similar *xingci* 行祠 and *bieci* 別祠), is a reminder that they were in theory subsidiaries of the only officially-sanctioned of these shrines, the Daimiao 岱廟 (Shrine of Mount Tai) at the foot of the mountain. The god could rest in the branch temples during his inspection tours, but his devotees travelled as well, and the temples were resting-places for the pilgrims who went to Taishan to redeem a vow or pray for themselves or relatives.

Vincent GOOSSAERT

📖 Maspero 1981, 102–5; Qing Xitai 1994, 3: 96–99

※ Dongyue miao; Taishan; DEITIES: THE PANTHEON

Dongyue miao

東嶽廟

Shrine of the Eastern Peak (Beijing)

Shrines of the Eastern Peak have been common all over China since the eleventh century, featuring the cult of *Dongyue dadi (Great Emperor of the Eastern Peak) himself as well as his underlings from the courts of hell. After the Mongol emperor Khubilai khan (Shizu, r. 1260–1294) established his capital in the 1260s in what is now Beijing, as many as four different Dongyue miao were built there. The one that was to eclipse all others was founded by the Taoist master *Zhang Liusun (1248–1322) about 1319 and completed by his disciple *Wu Quanjie (1269–1346). Since then, up to 1949, this shrine was managed by *Zhengyi Taoists of the *Qingwei lineage. Under the Qing, these Taoists maintained close connections to the court and were appointed to perform ritual services within the palace.

Unlike other large urban Qingwei establishments, however, this Dongyue miao was not a monastery run by a closed alliance of Taoist families: the Taoists were few and the shrine owned no landed property. In spite of the continued imperial support for the shrine through the Yuan, Ming, and Qing dynasties, which mandated regular sacrifices there, provided financial assistance, and patronized several major repairs, it was not run like an official temple. Rather, the real master of the place was a large number of devotional associations that built their own adjacent shrines, erected over a hundred and fifty stelae, and organized festivals. It was they who made the Dongyue miao into one of the largest and most active temples in China. The shrine was open year-round to devotees praying for heirs, commanding rituals for relatives who had been victims of unnatural death, or looking at the sculptures of the judges of hell in the main courtyard (the subject of a rich written and oral folklore) or in the adjacent Shrine of the Eighteen Hells (Shiba diyu miao 十八地獄廟).

Many of the associations active at the Dongyue miao were created in honor of the goddess *Bixia yuanjun (Original Princess of the Jasper Mist), whose cult became the most active one in the shrine around the fifteenth century. Soon after, yearly pilgrimages were organized to her shrines at various sites around Beijing, most importantly on Mount Miaofeng (Miaofeng shan 妙峰山). The pilgrimage associations and Dongyue miao associations were usually distinct, but cooperated and shared common characteristics. Each Dongyue miao association either supported a particular chapel within the compound, organizing a festival with Taoist ritual and opera for the birthday of its patron saint; or cooperated to manage the compound as a whole, by sweeping and refurbishing the site before the major annual festival (Dongyue dadi's birthday, on the twenty-eighth day of the third lunar month), or providing costly offerings to all shrines such as flowers or paper ornaments. The associations were varied in their social composition. During the late Ming, they were dominated by powerful, rich, and devout eunuchs; in the Qing period, leadership mostly comprised aristocrats and bannermen, but ordinary membership cut across all strata of Beijing society. Some guilds worked as associations within the shrine.

Similar voluntary devotional associations existed in other Beijing temples, but no temple could compare with the Dongyue miao in terms of the number of associations and the scope of their activities. The shrine closed after 1949 and has reopened in 1999 as a museum.

Vincent GOOSSAERT

📖 Chen Bali 2002; Goodrich 1964; Goossaert 1998; Goossaert forthcoming; Naquin 2000, 232–39, 506–17, and passim; Rinaker Ten Broeck and Yiu 1950–51; Schipper 1995b

※ Bixia yuanjun; Dongyue dadi; TEMPLES AND SHRINES

Doumu

斗母 (*or:* 斗姆)

Mother of the Dipper

Doumu, the Mother of the Dipper, is a deity of Indian origin. She corresponds in Brahmanic mythology to Marīci (Molizhi 摩利支), the chief of tempest demons, and is also related to Prajāpati. The deity was brought to China during the Tang dynasty by Amoghavajra (Bukong 不空, 705–74) who reportedly offered an image of Marīci to Tang Daizong (r. 762–79) on the emperor's birthday together with the *Da foding tuoluoni* 大佛頂陀羅尼 (*Mahāpratyangirā-dhāraṇī*; T. 944). Amoghavajra on that occasion recommended that the emperor pay official cult to Marīci (Weinstein 1987, 77–78).

In the Buddhist and Taoist canons, Doumu is generally venerated for granting prosperity and chasing away illnesses through her *dhāraṇī*. Confused with all sorts of mother deities, she is invoked to secure painless childbirth, protect children, and overcome sterility. In Taoism specifically she plays this role as the mother of the stars of the Northern Dipper (*Doumu dasheng yuanjun benming yansheng xinjing* 斗姆大聖元君本命延生心經; CT 621, 1b). As the wife of a local king by the name of Zhou Yu 周御, she was called Lady of Purple Radiance (Ziguang furen 紫光夫人) and gave birth to nine sons. The first two of them are the Great Emperor Celestial Sovereign (Tianhuang dadi 天皇大帝) and the Great Emperor of Purple Tenuity (Ziwei dadi 紫微大帝), who are the gods of the Southern and the Northern Dipper; the former is in charge of fixing the date of birth of human beings, and the latter their date of death. The other sons are the seven stars of the Northern Dipper (*Beidou bensheng zhenjing* 北斗本生真經, CT 45, 29. 2a–b; *Benming yansheng xinjing*, CT 621, 2b).

The stellar features of Doumu are associated with Marīci since she is the star that precedes the sunrise. In Tibet and Nepal, Marīci is identified with Vajravārāhī, represented by the head of a sow. This iconography may be related to early Indian representations of this deity of dawn whose chariot was drawn by seven animals similar to bears or boars. This was probably the source of a legend according to which these seven animals were the stars of the constellation of the Small Dipper, whose eighth star is Marīci-Varāhī (Frédéric 1992, 226).

Doumu, under the name of Marishiten 摩利支天, was also introduced in Japan with the Shingon 真言 and Tendai 天臺 doctrines. She is represented there in different ways and was especially venerated in the Middle Ages by warriors, as she was believed to protect and make invisible those who bore her effigy or invoked her name (Hall 1990). In Tibet, Marīci (Od-zer Can-ma) is frequently associated with the Green Tārā (de Mallmann 1975, 263). In China, she is often represented with the eighteen arms of Cuṇḍī (Zhunti 準提) and shares Cuṇḍī's mudrā; as a form of Avalokiteśvara (Guanyin 觀音), she is especially related to human beings and her origins as a controller of demonic forces appear to be forgotten. Traces of her ancient features, however, are found in a *Shenxiao ritual in which she is closely associated with Jiutian Leizu 九天雷祖, the Thunder Ancestor of the Nine Heavens, supreme ruler of the Thunder (*Daofa huiyuan, j. 83; Xiantian Doumu zougao xuanke 先天斗母奏告玄科, CT 1452).

Monica ESPOSITO

📖 Frédéric 1992, 177, 226; Hall 1990; Little 2000b, 282–83; Maspero 1981, 157–58; Strickmann 1996, 154

※ beidou; DEITIES: THE PANTHEON; TAOISM AND CHINESE BUDDHISM

Du Daojian

杜道堅

1237–1318; zi: Chuyi 處逸; hao: Nangu zi 南谷子
(Master of the Southern Valley)

Du Daojian, who came from Dangtu 當塗 (Anhui), formally belonged to the *Xuanjiao institution created by the Mongol rulers in southern China. At the age of fourteen, having received revelations, he moved to Mount Mao (*Maoshan, Jiangsu) and became a Taoist at the Shengxuan guan 昇玄觀 (Abbey of the Ascension to the Mystery). In 1274, when the Mongols were planning to invade southern China, Du travelled to Beijing to plead with Khubilai khan (Shizu, r. 1260–1294) on behalf of the southern populations. This undertaking turned out to be a success, and Du became an official representative of the Yuan regime in the south. Starting a tradition of indigenous political involvement in Mongol rule, he appealed to southern officials and scholars to display a yielding attitude for their own sake.

During Yuan Renzong's (r. 1312–20) reign, Du administered the Zongyang gong 宗陽宮 (Palace of Ancestral Yang) in Wulin 武林 (Zhejiang), a cultural center that played an important role in the intellectual life of southern China, and supervised the restoration of the Laojun tai 老君臺 (Lord Lao's Terrace)

on Mount Jichou (Jichou shan 計籌山, Zhejiang). A stele by the famous painter and calligrapher Zhao Mengfu 趙孟頫 (1254–1322), who was one of Du's friends, also attributes to Du the founding of the Yuantong guan 元通 觀 (Abbey of Primordial Pervasiveness) in Huzhou 湖州 (Zhejiang), and a collection of literary materials said to amount to ten thousand scrolls.

Three texts in the Taoist Canon bear witness to Du Daojian's exegetical and editorial work. The first is the *Daode xuanjing yuanzhi* 道德玄經原旨 (The Original Purport of the Mysterious Scripture of the Dao and Its Virtue; CT 702) in four *juan*, a commentary to the *Daode jing* in which Du brings together the teachings of this scripture and those of the *Yijing*. The second is the *Xuanjing yuanzhi fahui* 玄經原旨發揮 (Clarification of the Original Purport of the Mysterious Scripture; CT 703) in two *juan*, containing a supplementary exegesis of the *Daode jing* based on *Shao Yong's work. The third text is the *Tongxuan zhenjing zuanyi* 通玄真經纘義 (Successive Interpretations of the Authentic Scripture of Pervading Mystery; CT 748) in twelve *juan*. This new version of the scripture, ascribed to Laozi's putative disciple Wenzi 文子, was so entitled after the complete copy that Du was said to have found at the Tongxuan guan 通玄觀 (Abbey of Pervading Mystery) on Mount Jichou. This work established Du as the main heir of the *Wenzi's literary tradition and came to be considered generally as the best available version of that text.

Poetry ascribed to Du appears in the three-*juan* collection entitled *Gu Louguan ziyun yanqing ji* 古樓觀紫雲衍慶集 (Anthology from the Continued Celebration [of the Appearance] of the Purple Clouds at the Tiered Abbey of Antiquity; CT 957; Boltz J. M. 1987a, 126), compiled by Zhu Xiangxian 朱象 先 (fl. 1279–1308). Du was also asked to write occasional essays. One of them is a postscript to the *Gu Louguan ziyun yanqing ji* (3.1a–5a) written to sanction the preeminence of the *Louguan (Tiered Abbey) over the *Qingyang gong (Palace of the Black Ram), two establishments founded to honor Laozi's legendary disciple *Yin Xi. Another example is a preface dated 1306 to the *Zhonghe ji (Anthology of Central Harmony), a collection of *Li Daochun's teachings edited by Cai Zhiyi 蔡志頤 (fl. 1288–1306).

Grégoire ESPESSET

📖 Boltz J. M. 1987a, 218–19; Kandel 1974, 49–56; Qing Xitai 1994, 1: 351–53; Sun K'o-k'uan 1981, 240–2; Zhan Shichuang 1989, 116–27

※ Xuanjiao

Du Guangting

杜光庭

850–933; *zi*: Binsheng 賓聖; *hao*: Guangcheng xiansheng
廣成先生 (Elder of Wide Achievement)

Life. Little is known of Du Guangting's background. He appears to have been a native of Chuzhou 處州 (Zhejiang), but his family may also have established a residence in a district close to Chang'an. No information has survived on his family, but his father must have held some important office in the government since Du studied at the Directorate of the Sons of State (Guozi jian 國子監), the agency in charge of schools in the capitals that admitted only the sons of ranking bureaucrats. He was apparently a diligent student who devoted four out of five days to the study of the classics, histories and philosophers as well as to mastering the rhetorical forms of official documents. In short he received a typically Confucian education whose purpose was to prepare a student for the civil service examinations and eventually a government position.

Unfortunately, he failed the examinations about 870. So he repaired to Mount Tiantai (*Tiantai shan, Zhejiang) where he became the disciple of a Taoist master. He spent the next five years or so learning Taoism. In 875, on the advice of a chief minister, Tang Xizong (r. 873–88) summoned Du to Chang'an where he conferred a purple robe—one of the highest honorary distinctions bestowed on the clergy—on the priest and appointed him to the office of Drafter of Compositions at Imperial Command (*wenzhang yinzhi* 文章應制). His responsibilities in that post included writing documents for the emperor, but he also served as a kind of court chaplain and performed Taoist rituals on the behalf of the throne and state. His secular education served him well at court. The first three *juan* of his collected works—the *Guangcheng ji* 廣成集 (Anthology of Wide Achievement; CT 616, seventeen *juan*, originally 100)—contain his addresses to the throne on a host of matters, addresses that other ordinary officials were also submitting. In addition, he apparently also served as Grand Academician (*da xueshi* 大學士) at the Institute for the Veneration of the Mystery (Chongxuan guan 崇玄館), an official Taoist school in the *Taiqing gong—the temple for the dynasty's veneration of Laozi as its ancestor—just south of the palace. In 881 Du accompanied the court on its journey to Chengdu when it fled Chang'an as the rebel Huang Chao 黃巢 approached. In 885 he returned with the emperor to the capital where he found widespread destruction of churches and libraries.

Du Guangting stayed with the imperial court when it fled the capital again the following year, but departed for Sichuan in 887 and remained there for the rest of his life. For the next twenty-eight years he traveled throughout the province searching for books and writings. After the fall of the Tang a new dynasty, the Shu, seized control of the province. In 913 its emperor appointed Du to posts as Grand Master of Remonstrance (*jianyi dafu* 諫議大夫) and Grand Preceptor of the Heir Apparent (*taizi taishi* 太子太師). In 917 the throne installed him a Vice Director of the Ministry of Households (*hubu shilang* 戶部侍郎). In 923 the court chose him to be Grand Academician of a literary institute. Du's official career came to an end when the Later Tang conquered Shu in 925. He died in 933 after declaring to his disciples that he had had an audience with the supreme deity of Heaven who appointed him administrator of the underworld beneath a mountain range in Sichuan.

Works. Du Guangting was the single most prolific writer and compiler of Taoist texts before the year 1000. The largest portion of his writings consisted of liturgies for Taoist **zhai* (Retreats). He composed one for the conferral of a talisman at ordinations for transmitting the *Daode jing* (CT 808), one for a Celestial Master rite (CT 796), four for rituals connected with the **Dongyuan shenzhou jing* (CT 525 to CT 527, and CT 805), one for a *zhai* involving the **Sanhuang wen* (CT 804), and six for **Lingbao audiences (CT 519 to CT 521, and CT 483, 488, and 507). The largest of them, in fifty-eight *juan*, is the *Huanglu zhaiyi* 黃籙齋儀 (Liturgies for the Yellow Register Retreat; CT 507) that Du worked on for years and completed in 901. After presenting a basic three-day liturgy for executing the *zhai* at morning, noon, and night, Du supplies variant forms of the ritual for performance on the birth of an heir to the throne; to dispel calamities for the state, officials, and commoners; to save souls in hell; and to cure the ill among other things. He also provides protocols for Casting Dragon Tablets (**tou longjian*), chanting scriptures, and the installation of the Authentic Scripts (*zhenwen* 真文) on altars.

Du Guangting also devoted attention to Taoist scriptures. Aside from his collected works and the *Huanglu zhaiyi*, the longest text—in fifty *juan* (originally thirty *juan*)—that he compiled was the *Daode zhenjing guangsheng yi* 道德真經廣聖義 (Extended Interpretation of the Emperor's Exegesis of the Authentic Scripture of the Dao and Its Virtue; CT 725; Boltz J. M. 1987a, 131–36), completed in 901. As the title indicates this is copious commentary on an annotation (CT 677) and commentary (CT 678) that Tang Xuanzong (r. 712–56) purportedly wrote and promulgated as the official versions of the *Daode jing*. Du's preface lists sixty exegetical works on the *Daode jing* dating from the Han to the end of the Tang, but cites few of them in his commentary. The first five *juan* of the work contain a brief biography of Xuanzong (allegedly a descendant of Laozi in the thirty-seventh generation), an account of Laozi deified as a cosmogonic deity and preceptor to the ancient sage-kings, notes to an abbreviated version of Xuanzong's preface to CT 678, and a history of the titles that the Tang dynasty conferred on Laozi. The second scripture that Du took an interest in was the *Dongyuan shenzhou jing* (Scripture of the Divine Spells of the Cavernous Abyss; CT 335) completed sometime after 923 since Du's signature lists all the titles that emperors had bestowed on him up to that date. The first ten *juan* of the text were written between 520 and 579 and the remaining ten apparently during the Tang dynasty. It is not at all clear what role Du played in editing the work. On the one hand he may have only contributed the preface that recounts the legend of its purported compiler Wang Zuan 王纂 and nothing more. On the other he may have added or composed the final *juan* of the scripture.

Du Guangting also wrote works on history, geography, and hagiographies. The intent of his **Lidai chongdao ji* (Records of the Veneration of the Dao over Successive Generations; CT 593) was to provide the Tang dynasty after the rebellion of Huang Chao with assurance that it still enjoyed divine protection and would survive the troubled times of the late ninth century. Du also compiled secular works on administrative geography and reign eras. His *Tiantan Wangwu shan shengji ji* 天壇王屋山聖迹記 (Records of Traces of the Saints on Mount Wangwu, the Celestial Altar; CT 969, one *juan*) begins with an account of the mythology concerning an altar on this mountain north of Luoyang where the legendary emperor *Huangdi received the nine tripods (*jiuding* 九鼎)—symbols of the nine ancient provinces of China and tokens of imperial unity—from the Queen Mother of the West (*Xiwang mu), a popular deity in the Han dynasty (see *Wangwu shan). It then continues with a description of various geographical features, abbeys and historical events that occurred there during the Tang. The *Dongtian fudi yuedu mingshan ji* 洞天福地嶽瀆名山記 (Records of Grotto-Heavens, Blissful Lands, Peaks, Rivers, and Famous Mountains; CT 599, one *juan*; see Qing Xitai 1994, 2: 206–8) is a description of various sites holy to Taoists. Some of them are celestial or located far off in the oceans. Most are places on earth—quiet huts and parishes—or beneath holy mountains—the Blissful Lands and Grotto-Heavens where Taoists who attained immortality took positions in the spiritual bureaucracy after passing from the world of the living (see *dongtian and *fudi*). Du gives the precise locations of the latter. His discussion of Celestial Master parishes (*zhi) is particularly important because it shows that registration as a Taoist was based on date of birth and not residence in the parish. His largest collection of hagiographies was the *Xianzhuan shiyi* 仙傳拾遺 (Uncollected Biographies of Immortals) in forty *juan*. It originally contained accounts of 420 lives. As the title indicates, the text treated individuals that earlier compilations had overlooked. The *Xianzhuan shiyi* has not survived, but Yan Yiping (1974, vol. 1) has assembled passages from it—about a quarter of the original entries—cited in other texts. Du's *Yongcheng jixian lu* (Records of the Immortals Gathered in the Walled City; CT 783, and YJQQ 114–16, six *juan*, originally ten) contains hagiographies of women only (Yongcheng 墉城 was the residence of the Queen Mother of the West on Mount *Kunlun). The extant version contains accounts of thirty-five figures ranging from the mother of Laozi, the Queen Mother of the West and her divine daughters, to tavern owners.

Lastly, Du Guangting assembled several collections of accounts on miracles and other supernatural phenomena. The largest of them was the *Daojiao lingyan ji* (Records of the Numinous Efficacy of the Taoist Teaching) that consists of material relevant only to Taoism. His *Shenxian ganyu zhuan* 神仙 感遇傳 (Biographies of Those who Encountered Immortals; CT 592, five *juan*, originally ten), completed after 904, consists of episodes in the lives of people from all walks of life who meet extraordinary figures in abbeys, on the road, in the mountains, and elsewhere. They are not all immortals: some are old men or women, priests, hermits, and the like. When encountered, those exceptional individuals transmit texts, interpretations of arcane scriptures, the secrets of immortality, and prophecies among other things. Du's *Luyi ji* 錄異記 (Records of the Extraordinary; CT 591, eight *juan*, originally ten), completed between 921 and 925, is a collection of lore concerning immortals, extraordinary men, the loyal, the filial, responses from the gods, remarkable dreams, demons and spirits, dragons, animals (tigers, tortoises, snakes, and fish), grottoes, waters (rivers, springs, pools, etc.) rocks, and tombs. Much of the material is irrelevant to Taoism.

Charles D. BENN

📖 Barrett 1996, 94–98; Bell 1987c; Boltz J. M. 1987a, 129–31; Matsumoto Kōichi 1983, 216–18; Qing Xitai 1988–95, 2: 421–77; Schafer and Yee 1986; Sunayama Minoru 1990, 416–43; Verellen 1989

※ *Daojiao lingyan ji*; *Daomen kefan da quanji*; *Lidai chongdao ji*; *Yongcheng jixian lu*; TAOISM AND THE STATE

dujiang

都講

chief cantor

Among *Zhengyi Taoists in modern Taiwan, rituals are performed by a group basically consisting of five people: the high priest (*gaogong* 高功; see *daozhang*), the chief cantor, the assistant cantor (*fujiang* 副講), the leader of the troupe (*yinban* 引班), and the keeper of the incense (*shixiang* 侍香). The chief cantor, who is an older and experienced priest, stands to the left of the high priest and assists him, fulfilling the important function of coordinating the entire ritual. The assistant cantor stands to the right of the high priest and is in charge of written documents. The leader of the troupe stands to the left of the chief cantor and leads the others when circumambulating the altar (*tan* 壇). The keeper of the incense stands to the right of the assistant cantor and is in charge of incense and candles. The priests' roles appear to derive from the "six offices" (*liuzhi* 六職) of the Six Dynasties *Lingbao *zhai (Retreat) as described in the *Lingbao zhaijie weiyi zhujing yaojue* 靈寶齋戒威儀諸經要訣 (Essential Instructions on the Scriptures on the Dignified Liturgies for Lingbao Retreats; CT 532) and in the *Yaoxiu keyi jielü chao* 要修科儀戒律鈔 (Excerpts from the Essential Liturgies and Observances; CT 463).

From early times, the chief cantor was confused with the *dugong* 都功 (inspector of merit), who was originally responsible for the administration of the twenty-four parishes (*zhi) of the Way of the Celestial Masters (*Tianshi dao). In the first and second centuries CE, *dujiang* denoted the person responsible for supervising teaching in Confucian schools. In Buddhism, the instructor charged with reciting the *sūtras* was called *fashi 法師 (master of the dharma), and the instructor charged with explaining the *sūtras* was called *dujiang*. According to *j*. 8 of the *Hongming ji (Collection Spreading the Light of Buddhism; T. 2102), Taoism modeled the role of the *dujiang* on the corresponding function in Buddhism. Later the duties changed, and the Taoist chief cantor became what we see today in Taiwan.

ASANO Haruji

📖 Fukui Fumimasa 1973; Ōfuchi Ninji 1983, 200–202; Schipper 1975c, 15; Schipper 1977b

※ *jiao*

dumai and *renmai*

督脈 · 任脈

Control Channel and Function Channel

1. Medicine

In traditional Chinese medicine, the *dumai* and *renmai* are conduits that run along the spine and ventral axis, respectively (see fig. 31). At present, the evidence

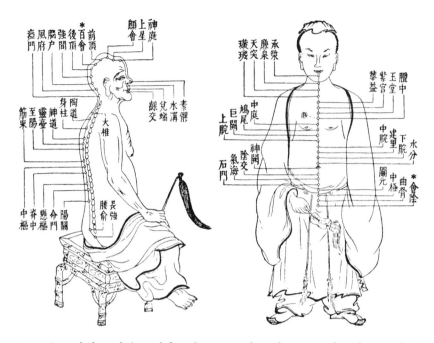

Fig. 31. Control Channel (*dumai*, left) and Function Channel (*renmai*, right). The asterisks (*) show the locations of the *baihui* point on the Control Channel and the *huiyin* point on the Function Channel.

for a precursor of the *dumai* is earlier than that for the *renmai*: it appears as a red line along the spine on a black lacquer figurine of the second century BCE, excavated in 1993 from Mianyang 綿陽 (Sichuan; see He and Lo 1996). Both are mentioned at various points in the *Huangdi neijing*, but not as a pair. For instance, in *Suwen* 素問 1 (Plain Questions; see *Huangdi neijing*), the *renmai* is held to be responsible for female fertility: it is said to be "connected" (*tong* 通) at fourteen years of age, and considered to be depleted at forty-nine years. The *dumai* is mentioned, for instance, in *Lingshu* 靈樞 10 (Numinous Pivot; see *Huangdi neijing*) as the conduit that forms an "assembly" (*hui* 會) with the last of twelve conduits in the body, the liver conduit (see *jingluo*). Over time, *dumai* and *renmai* eventually came to be classified among the "eight extraordinary channels" (*qijing bamai* 奇經八脈) which, generally speaking, are important for regulating the overall flow of *qixue* ("breath and blood").

There are several acupuncture and moxibustion loci along these two conduits that are said to have therapeutic functions. Among them are the *baihui* 百會 (Gathering of the Hundred [Yang channels]) in the *dumai*, on the highest point of the head, which is needled for treating epilepsy, apoplexy, and mental conditions, and the *renzhong* 人中 (Center of Man), situated in the groove beneath the nose: in the case of a coma, pressing this locus is supposed to bring the patient back to consciousness. The loci in the lower region of the *renmai*, such as the *zhongji* 中極 (Middle Pole), the *guanyuan* 關元 (Origin of the Pass), and the *qihai* 氣海 (Ocean of Pneuma), are frequently used for treating gynecological disorders.

Elisabeth HSU

📖 Porkert 1974, 273–82; Qiu Maoliang 1985, 117–32

※ *jingluo*

2. Neidan

The *dumai* and *renmai* channels gained importance in *neidan* only from the beginning of the Song period. The *dumai* is Yang, and the *renmai* is Yin. To restore the unity of Yin and Yang, the channels should be joined so that the energy may circulate through the body. The Lesser Celestial Circuit (*xiao zhoutian* 小周天; see *zhoutian*) is used to allow Water or essence (*jing*) rise through the *dumai*, and Fire or energy (*qi*) to descend through the *renmai*. This process is guided by the mind in concentrated silence and culminates in the generation of the elixir or the immortal embryo (*shengtai*). The two channels also play an important role in sexual techniques (*fangzhong shu*) practiced to preserve the essence and transform it into energy.

In *neidan*, the *dumai* is also called Yellow River (*huanghe* 黃河) or the Rivulet (*caoxi* 漕溪). Three "passes" (*sanguan*) are situated on the *renmai*: the *weilü* 尾閭 (Caudal Funnel) at the level of the coccyx, the double *jiaji* 夾脊 (Spinal Handle) at the level of the fourth dorsal vertebra, and the *yuzhen* 玉枕 (Jade Pillow) at the back of the head. Similar to the three Cinnabar Fields (*dantian*), the Three Passes are centers of transformation and correspond to the three stages of the *neidan* process: essence is transformed into energy in the lower pass, energy into spirit (*shen*) in the middle pass, and spirit into to emptiness (*xu* 虛) in the upper pass.

Martina DARGA

📖 Despeux 1979, 34–44; Despeux 1994, 38–39, 80, 168; Lu K'uan Yü 1970, 9–16, 87–90

※ *sanguan*; *zhoutian*; *neidan*

Dunhuang manuscripts

The Dunhuang 敦煌 manuscripts are a major source for the study of Chinese and Central Asian history and religion during the first millennium. Sealed not long after 1000 CE in a chamber adjoining one of the Caves of the Thousand Buddhas (Qianfo dong 千佛洞) at the border of the Gobi desert, the manuscripts were discovered at the beginning of the twentieth century by Western explorers, notably Sir Aurel Stein and Paul Pelliot. They are now preserved in various collections of European and Asian libraries, including the Stein collection of the British Library (Giles L. 1957) and the Pelliot collection of the Bibliothèque Nationale de France (Gernet et al. 1970-).

The Taoist manuscripts from Dunhuang do not form a homogeneous scriptural corpus. Given the predominantly Buddhist environment of the Dunhuang region, they were, in most cases, discarded documents; moreover, many of them did not originate in Dunhuang itself but were brought there from different locations. Thus they constitute a relatively small proportion of the huge mass of about 30,000 documents in these collections.

The few hundred Taoist manuscripts from Dunhuang are nevertheless invaluable for the historian of Chinese religions. First, they are the main collection of authentically ancient Taoist writings, originating before the eighth century when the Chinese district of Dunhuang was invaded by the Tibetans. They are, therefore, of incomparable value for the dating and exegesis of Taoist scriptures. In addition, some Taoist manuscripts contain materials not extant elsewhere, without which crucial aspects of medieval Taoism would remain largely unknown.

Dunhuang Taoist studies have borne fruit in many fields: there are few major Taoist philosophical works, and not a single medieval scriptural Taoist tradition, that are not represented among the Dunhuang documents. Two Japanese works are, to date, the major reference books on these texts: Ōfuchi Ninji's monumental *Tonkō dōkyō* (Taoist Scriptures from Dunhuang; 1978–79) with its photographic reproductions of all the manuscripts indexed there; and the collection of essays entitled *Tonkō to Chūgoku Dōkyō* (Dunhuang and Chinese Taoism; Kanaoka Shōkō, Ikeda On, and Fukui Fumimasa 1983), which also provides an extensive bibliography on the subject. The few examples that follow illustrate some of the main findings of Dunhuang Taoist studies in recent decades.

Major Taoist sources from Dunhuang. Our knowledge of Taoism during the first centuries of the Common Era has significantly improved owing to the discovery of several unique manuscripts from Dunhuang. One of them is the *Laozi Xiang'er zhu 老子想爾注, the sole extant copy of the *Tianshi dao commentary to the Daode jing (S. 6825; ed. Rao Zongyi 1956; trans. Bokenkamp 1997, 29–148). The manuscript itself dates from the late fifth or the early sixth century, and although it is fragmentary—containing only the text and commentary for chapters 3 to 37—it has considerable value for the study of the history of Taoism. The commentary, written between the end of the second and beginning of the third centuries, is the earliest Taoist interpretation of the Daode jing, as well as one of the earliest sources on the *Tianshi dao movement, providing unique information about its beliefs and practices.

Another unique Dunhuang manuscript that offers exceptional insights into the formation of Taoist religion is S. 2295, containing the *Laozi bianhua jing (Scripture of the Transformations of Laozi). This work is of primary importance for the light it sheds on the history of Laozi's divinization (Seidel 1969).

The study of another prestigious early Taoist scripture, the *Taiping jing (Scripture of Great Peace), also gained new impetus with the discovery of the manuscript S. 4226, which contains the complete table of contents of its 170 chapters (Yoshioka Yoshitoyo 1970b).

Taoist studies have also progressed thanks to the preservation of the famous manuscripts P. 2256 and P. 2861, two Taoist bibliographies compiled in the Tang dynasty on the basis of the *Lingbao jingmu, an inventory of twenty-seven *Lingbao scriptures made by *Lu Xiujing (406–77). The identification and reconstruction of the ancient Lingbao corpus made by Ōfuchi (1974) in his investigation of these manuscripts was a turning point in the history of Taoist research. Lingbao was one of the three main schools of medieval southern Taoism, the one that was most influenced by Buddhism, and the first to attempt the unification and codification of Taoist liturgy.

The history of the formation of Taoist liturgy is another area indebted to Dunhuang studies. Based on a series of eighth-century manuscripts, Kristofer Schipper (1985c) has defined the overall liturgical system of Taoist ordination ranks in Tang times, advancing our knowledge of the composition of the Taoist Canon and its various sections (see *DAOZANG AND SUBSIDIARY COMPILATIONS).

Dunhuang studies have also contributed much to research on medieval Buddho-Taoism. The manuscript S. 2081 of the *Huahu jing (Scripture of the Conversion of Barbarians), studied by Anna Seidel (1984), is an eminent extracanonical example of early religious syncretism, as well as an exceptional document of medieval apocalyptic eschatology.

An additional major Taoist find from Dunhuang was the discovery of about eighty partial manuscripts of the *Benji jing (Scripture of the Original Bound).

Since the eleventh century, this seventh-century philosophical scripture had been known only in a short one-chapter version. The numerous handwritten versions in the Dunhuang collections record the text almost in its entirety and attest to its popularity during the Sui and Tang periods (Wu Chi-yu 1960).

Finally, some Dunhuang Taoist manuscripts have provided significant insights into imperial sponsorship for the compilation of the Taoist Canon and into the court's relation to Taoism. A singular example of imperial recognition of a Taoist tradition is the fifth-century *Dongyuan shenzhou jing (Scripture of the Divine Spells of the Cavernous Abyss), a copy of which was made in the year 664 for the sake of the crown prince as attested by two colophons found in two manuscripts of the Pelliot collection (P. 3233 and P. 2444; Mollier 1990).

Numerous other examples could be given that demonstrate the invaluable contribution of Dunhuang studies to research on the history of Taoism. Much remains to be done, however, both in the investigation of this considerable mass of material, and especially in the study of still-unpublished documents.

Christine MOLLIER

📖 Chen Guofu 1963, 204–28; *Daojia wenhua yanjiu* 1998; Gernet et al. 1970-; Giles L. 1957; Kanaoka Shōkō, Ikeda On, and Fukui Fumimasa 1983; Kanaoka Shōkō 1983; Li Defan 1999; Ōfuchi Ninji 1978–79; Ōfuchi Ninji and Ishii Masako 1988, 285–301 (list of titles in Ōfuchi Ninji 1978–79, vol. 2); Shao Wenshi 1996; Yoshioka Yoshitoyo 1967

Duren jing

度人經

Scripture on Salvation

The *Duren jing* (full title: *Lingbao wuliang duren shangpin miaojing* 靈寶無量度人上品妙經 or *Wondrous Scripture of the Upper Chapters of the Numinous Treasure on Limitless Salvation*) is the first scripture in the Ming Taoist Canon (CT 1). The first chapter of this work formed part of the original *Lingbao scriptures, codified in the fifth century, while the remaining sixty chapters represent an expansion composed by *Shenxiao Taoists early in the twelfth century.

As part of the original Lingbao corpus of the early fifth century, the *Duren jing* represents a Chinese response to Buddhist soteriology, particularly the idea of the bodhisattva, who vows to effect the salvation of all beings within his realm. As shown by its title, the *Duren jing* is concerned with *du* 度 ("to ferry across"), a verb which in Taoist texts refers both to the initiation of disciples and to saving those suffering in the world or in the hells. The scripture is related by the Most High Lord of the Dao (Taishang daojun 太上道君), who recounts his own ordination and receipt of the scripture from the supreme deity of Lingbao, the Celestial Worthy of Original Commencement (Yuanshi tianzun 元始天尊; see *sanqing*) in a previous world-age. Through mindful recitation of the text, preceded by a simple meditation procedure, adepts are invited to participate in the ordination and salvation of the Most High Lord both to ensure their own salvation and that of their ancestors, on whose behalf they also recite.

The scripture describes in poetic language the miraculous effects of the Celestial Worthy's ten recitations of the scripture which radiated throughout the Thirty-two Heavens (*sanshi'er tian*); the origins of the Lingbao scriptures in the ethers of previous *kalpa*-cycles (*jie*); and the various gods resident within the body and in the macrocosm who participate in the salvation of the individual. Among the gods of the macrocosm are the Demon kings of the Three Realms (*sanjie mowang* 三界魔王, adapted from the Buddhist lord of the third realm, the tempter Māra) who test aspirants for transcendence as they ascend but allow to pass those who can properly recite the text.

The salvific power of the text resides in the fact that it contains "the inner names of the [celestial] emperors and the sounds of the secret rhymes of all the heavens, as well as of the taboo-names of the demon kings and the secret names of the myriad spirits." The names of the gods and demon kings parallel Chinese transcriptions of Buddhist names and terms. The "secret rhymes," also known as the "secret language of the Great Brahmā" (*dafan yinyu*), said to be the languages of the Thirty-two Heavens, are similarly constructed. The words of this language prove to be powerful talismans that, through demonstrating the practitioner's knowledge of the unseen realms, are able to rescue ancestors from the hells, avert disaster, protect the realm, and ensure the deliverance of the practitioner.

Foremost among the days prescribed for recitation of the *Scripture on Salvation* are the days of the Three Primes (*sanyuan*) associated with the Three Offices (*sanguan*, of Heaven, Earth, and Water). These are the fifteenth day of the first, seventh, and tenth lunar months, days when the assemblies of gods in the Three Offices meet to assess the life and death records of all humans, the living and the dead. Similar assemblies of the high deities to inspect one's personal records occur on other days when the scripture should be recited—the eight nodal days of the year (*bajie* 八節, namely, equinoxes, solstices, and the first day of each season) and the days of one's "natal destiny" (*benming*).

The earliest surviving commentary on the *Duren jing* is that of Yan Dong 嚴東, composed ca. 485. It is now to be found in the *Duren shangpin miaojing sizhu* 度人上品妙經四注 (Four Commentaries to the Wondrous Scripture of the

Upper Chapters on Salvation; CT 87), compiled by *Chen Jingyuan (?–1094). In addition to Yan's commentary, this work includes portions of commentaries by *Cheng Xuanying (fl. 631–50), Xue Youqi 薛幽棲 (fl. 740–54; Qing Xitai 1994, 1: 280–81), and Li Shaowei 李少微 (fl. 625?). All of these commentaries draw on the earliest "commentary" on the *Duren jing*, the explanations of the deity August One of Heavenly Perfection (Tianzhen huangren 天真皇人) found in the Lingbao scripture *Zhutian neiyin ziran yuzi* 諸天內音自然玉字 (The Self-Generating Jade Graphs and Inner Sounds of All the Heavens; CT 97). While Yan's commentary was likely composed for fellow Taoists, the Tang-period commentaries were prompted by the adoption of the *Duren jing* as topic for the officially-sanctioned ordination examinations. The fact that terminology from the "secret language" regularly found its way into secular poetry provides further evidence of the popularity of the scripture during the Tang period.

During the Song, a sixty-one chapter version of the *Duren jing* was presented by *Lin Lingsu to the Taoist emperor Huizong (r. 1100–1125) as part of the Shenxiao corpus. But the new, expanded version of the scripture did not eclipse the ritual use of the original *Duren jing*, which is still today widely recited in Taoist ritual.

Stephen R. BOKENKAMP

📖 Bokenkamp 1983, 461–65; Bokenkamp 1997, 373–438 (trans.); Boltz J. M. 1987a, 206–11; Chen Guofu 1963, 71–72; Kamitsuka Yoshiko 1996, 44–50; Kamitsuka Yoshiko 1999, 228–34, 398–404; Little 2000b, 246–47; Ōfuchi Ninji 1978–79, 1: 52–59 (crit. notes on the Dunhuang ms.) and 2: 64–70 (reprod. of the Dunhuang ms.); Strickmann 1978b; Sunayama Minoru 1984

※ Lingbao

Emei shan

峨眉山 (*or*: 娥眉山)

Mount Emei (Sichuan)

Mount Emei, located to the southwest of Chengdu in Sichuan, is commonly understood as important in Buddhism due to its classification as one of the Four Famous Mountains (*sida mingshan* 四大名山) and its connections with the bodhisattva Samantabhadra (Puxian 普賢). Yet this mountain also has a long Taoist history. Besides being mentioned in *j.* 4 of the *Baopu zi* as a site where the medicines of the transcendents could be attained, it was also one of the twenty-four parishes (*zhi) of the early Way of the Celestial Masters (*Tianshi dao), and was imagined to be connected to the Grotto-Heaven (*dongtian) on Mount Mao (*Maoshan, Jiangsu) via a subterranean conduit.

Several doctrinal and textual traditions are associated with this mountain. According to the monograph on Buddhism and Taoism ("Shi Lao zhi" 釋老志) in the *Weishu* (History of the Wei; trans. Ware 1933, 219), Laozi transmitted the Dao to the Yellow Emperor (*Huangdi) at Mount Emei. Around 300 CE, Bo He 帛和 was able to interpret the graphs of the *Sanhuang wen* (Script of the Three Sovereigns) after three years of staring at a rock within a cave of this mountain. Mount Emei also figures prominently as a site where *Lingbao scriptures were transmitted. Later, during the Qing dynasty, *Li Xiyue (1806–56), the alleged founder of the Western Branch (Xipai 西派) of *neidan, met the immortals *Lü Dongbin and *Zhang Sanfeng on this mountain.

James ROBSON

📖 Nara Yukihiro 1998, 318–19; Shi Mingfei 1993

※ TAOIST SACRED SITES

Ershisi sheng tu

二十四生圖

Charts of the Twenty-Four Life[-Givers]

The Twenty-four Life-givers are the luminous spirits of the body, commonly referred to as the Eight Effulgences of the Three Primal Registers (*sanyuan bajing* 三元八景) or of the Three Regions (*sanbu bajing* 三部八景; see *bajing*). Talismanic charts designed to allow the practitioner to see and control these spirits existed as early as the third century, as attested in *Ge Hong's list of the scriptures possessed by his master *Zheng Yin.

The surviving scripture of this name is the *Dongxuan lingbao ershisi sheng tu jing* 洞玄靈寶二十四生圖經 (Scripture of the Charts of the Twenty-Four Life[-Givers] of Lingbao, Cavern of Mystery Section; CT 1407). In this text, fourth-century *Shangqing revisions of ancient practices concerning the twenty-four charts have been further modified to accord with the cosmic and soteriological views of the *Lingbao scriptures. The scripture relates the genesis of the twenty-four spirits and their charts in the earliest *kalpa*-periods (*jie*) and then goes on to tell how *Li Hong, Saint of the Latter Age, was provided with the text. Li Hong's ability to control and exteriorize his twenty-four bodily spirits as human envoys who would save the elect from the cataclysms attending the end of the world-age had, prior to the composition of this text, already featured in a Shangqing text, the *Lingshu ziwen. Versions of the charts possessed by other Shangqing deities are also said here to have originated in this Lingbao scripture. The charts themselves are named according to earlier Taoist charts said by Ge Hong to have been in the possession of Zheng Yin.

In addition to talismanic charts and chants associated with the twenty-four spirits, the text lists the spiritual underlings associated with each, including the spirits that are to be exteriorized in Lingbao ritual. This list figures prominently among the items bestowed on initiates in *Lu Xiujing's *Lingbao shoudu yi.

Stephen R. BOKENKAMP

📖 Bokenkamp 1983, 458–60; Ōfuchi Ninji 1997, 147–48

※ Lingbao

fabiao

發表

Announcement

Fabiao (lit., "issuing the Memorial," also referred to as *fazou* 發奏 or "issuing the Announcement") is the section at the beginning of *jiao (Offering) and *gongde (Merit) rituals when the purpose of the ceremony is announced to the deities. This rite appears to date no earlier than the Song period. In his *Shangqing lingbao dafa (Great Rites of the Numinous Treasure of Highest Clarity; CT 1222–23), Jin Yunzhong 金允中 (fl. 1224–25) states that the people of ancient times only "presented a petition" (*baizhang* 拜章) without performing the Announcement (CT 1223, *j.* 19). After describing the procedure for "issuing the correct Announcement" (*fa zhengzou* 發正奏), Jin adds that this was not part of the *zhai (Retreat) ritual as described by *Du Guangting (850–933), but an element "popular at the present time" (CT 1223, *j.* 16). The Announcement, therefore, was not yet considered a formal part of the *zhai* ritual in the late Tang and Five Dynasties periods (ninth and tenth centuries).

As performed in present-day southern Taiwan, the Announcement occupies a central position among the various rites that constitute a *jiao*. This is clear from the fact that it must be performed by the high priest (*gaogong* 高功; see *daozhang) himself in full regalia, and that it is described in detail only in his secret manuals (*mijue). Summoning messengers and protective deities, and sending them off to deliver documents to the appropriate deities, takes place through a sequence of seven rites: Purification of the Altar (*jingtan* 淨壇; Lagerwey 1987c, 73–77), Invocation of Masters and Saints (*qi shisheng* 啟師聖), Summoning the Generals (*zhaojiang* 召將), Pronouncing the Talismanic Order (*xuanfu fuming* 宣讀符命), Offering Wine (*xianjiu* 獻酒), Dispatching the Generals (*qianjiang* 遣將), and Giving Thanks to the Masters and Saints (*xie shisheng* 謝師聖).

During the long initial rite for the purification of the altar, the high priest transforms his body into a divine body (*bianshen), paces the stars of the Northern Dipper (*beidou; see *bugang), burns talismans (*FU) while pronouncing incantations, and uses techniques for absorbing the pneuma (*qi) of the Northern Dipper and the Three Luminaries (*sanguang* 三光, i.e., the Sun, the Moon, and the stars). These and other techniques indicate that the Taiwanese Taoist priests have inherited *Tianxin zhengfa and *leifa (Thunder Rites) methods developed during the Song dynasty. From the Ming period onward,

mastery of these techniques was a prerequisite for receiving investiture as a
Taoist priest (*daoshi*), which has resulted in their institutionalization. Their
use in the Announcement is closely related to this development.

MARUYAMA Hiroshi

📖 Lagerwey 1987c, 68–89; Maruyama Hiroshi 1995; Ōfuchi Ninji 1983, 241–56

※ *gongde*; *jiao*

falu

發爐

Lighting the Incense Burner

The *falu* is the central opening rite in major Taoist rituals, such as the Nocturnal Invocation (*suqi*), the Land of the Way (*daochang*), and the Three Audiences (*sanchao*). It serves to initiate communication between the priest and
the divine world, and together with the closing rite of the Extinction of the
Incense Burner (*fulu* 復爐; Lagerwey 1987c, 146–47) it forms the basic framework of these rituals. The *falu* is an authentically old element of ritual derived
from the early practices of the Way of the Celestial Masters (*Tianshi dao),
and its persistence in present-day Taoist liturgies thus represents a remarkable
continuity in these liturgies. A version of the *falu* is described already in the
*Dengzhen yinjue (3.6b–8a, compiled from original *Shangqing material), and
the rite occurs with regularity in the major rituals described in the *Wushang
biyao (see for instance 48.1a–b).

Already in these early forms of the rite, its defining element is the incantation that begins with an appeal to the Most High Lord Lao (Taishang Laojun
太上老君; see *Laozi and Laojun), who is asked to summon forth from the
body of the priest a series of subordinate spirits associated with the task of
transmitting incense and messages to heaven (see *chushen). The version of
the incantation found in the *Wushang biyao* is practically identical with the
forms used in current classical Taoist liturgies (see for instance Ōfuchi Ninji
1983, 272–73). The spirits are told to inform the local Earth God (*Tudi gong)
about the fact that the priest is about to "walk (or: practice) the Way" (*xingdao*), and that he wishes that "the most high correct and perfected breaths of
the ten directions" descend into his body and cause what he states to reach
its destination in the highest Taoist heavens.

The connection between this purpose and the lighting of the incense burner
is spelled out in current liturgy in a number of accompanying visualizations

and "practices in the hand" (*shoujue), in which the high priest (gaogong 高功; see *daozhang) externalizes his basic inner energies and sends them in the direction of the "hand-held incense burner" (shoulu 手爐) in his left hand—thereby "igniting" it. The external incense burner thus is correlated with the inner "burner" constituted by the lower Cinnabar Field (*dantian) in the belly of the priest, a fact that is illustrated also by the act of reinserting the "golden flame" or "golden flower" (jinhua 金華) located at the top of the crown on his head, which concludes the rite of falu. The rite is perceived as a form of "transformation of the body" (*bianshen), that is, as a precondition for addressing the supreme deities of heaven, and in fact it is followed directly by the high priest kneeling in front of the central altar in order to summon these deities.

Poul ANDERSEN

📖 Cedzich 1987, 70–80; Lagerwey 1981b, 125–28; Lagerwey 1987c, 121–23; Matsumoto Kōichi 1983, 205–10; Saso 1978b, 218–33; Schipper 1993, 97–98

※ daochang; jinxiang; sanchao; suqi

fan

反 (or: 返)

return, reversion

"Return is the movement of the Dao," which "goes far away and then returns" (Laozi 40 and 25). The term fan has been understood as meaning "going back to the root" (guigen 歸根), another basic expression in the Daode jing and then in Taoism generally. It occurs in the same sense in the *Guodian manuscript entitled Taiyi sheng shui 太一生水 (The Great One Generated Water) which states that Water, after being generated, returns (fan) to the Great One (*Taiyi) to assist it in forming Heaven. But fan has also been explained as meaning "beginning again" or "anew" and as referring to the eternal recurrence of life and its rhythms. The two meanings are in fact identical, but in different dimensions. For the world as a whole, fan has a metaphysical import and denotes returning to its Origin, the Dao, or the Void. Analogically, for an individual being, fan is returning to the Void from which it comes, in the sense that the Void is its Origin, its end, and its basis or fundamental nature (xing 性; see *xing and ming).

On the phenomenal level, fan is the rhythm of the movement of life. When something has grown to its utmost point (ji 極), it decreases or reverses to its contrary, as do Yin and Yang, or movement and quiescence (*dong and jing).

"Death and life are one [time] going and one [time] returning" says *Liezi* I; in the same way, the *Xici* 繫辭 (Appended Statements, a portion of the *Yijing*) states that the Dao is "one [time] Yin and one [time] Yang."

Fan therefore has different ontological meanings according to whether it is related to our closed world, where everything is finite and reverses to its contrary or its initial state, indefinitely; or to the absolute Dao that is infinitely "great," void, and without limits, and exceeds changes and reversals. That is what *Wang Bi means when he writes, "In movement, if we know that there is Non-being (*wu), all things interpenetrate."

In meditation, *fan* takes on a more technical meaning in compounds such as *fanzhao* 反照 (turning back one's light) or *fanting* 反聽 (turning back one's hearing). In this instance, it designates concentration through turning one's attention and perceptions inwardly.

Isabelle ROBINET

📖 Girardot 1978b; Lu Yusan 1987; Robinet 1977, 66–71; Stein R. A. 1990, 106–12

※ Dao

Fan Changsheng

范長生

?–318; *zi*: Yuan 元

Fan Changsheng was a Taoist priest and local leader of Sichuan who played a key role in the founding of the state of Great Perfection (*Dacheng). His name is variously given as Yanjiu 延久, Chongjiu 重九, Wen 文, and Zhi 支. He is credited with a commentary to the *Yijing* under the name Genius of Shu (Shucai 蜀才) which survived until the Song and has been reconstructed from citations. Originally from Fuling 涪陵 in southern Sichuan, he had settled on Mount Qingcheng (*Qingcheng shan, Sichuan) in a community of several thousand followers. From this base he offered key support to the Li 李 family as it sought to reestablish itself in the Sichuan region at the beginning of the third century. After the death of his father, Li Te 李特, *Li Xiong offered the throne to Fan, who instead convinced Xiong to take the throne, arguing that celestial timings favored a ruler surnamed Li. When Li Xiong, at Fan's urging, proclaimed himself king in the *jiazi* 甲子 year 304, Fan was welcomed into the capital with great ceremony. Riding in a white cart, he was met at the gate by Li Xiong, who led him to his seat. Fan received the

honorary name "Worthy" (Xian 賢) and the title Great Master of the Four
Seasons, the Eight Nodes, and Heaven and Earth (Sishi bajie tiandi taishi 四
時八節天地太師). He was appointed Counselor-in-Chief (*chengxiang* 丞相),
enfeoffed as Marquis, and awarded the tax revenue of all his followers, who
were also exempted from corvée duties. Two years later, Fan convinced Xiong
to take the imperial title, thus formally breaking ties with the Jin empire, and
was no doubt instrumental in implementing the Taoist-inspired reforms that
characterized Xiong's rule.

The historical record for the state of Dacheng makes little mention of
Fan's activities as Chancellor, but they must have been considerable and effective, for upon his death in 318, his son Fan Ben 范賁 succeeded his father
in this position. Little else is known of Fan, but it is likely that he was of the
Zong 賨 ethnicity, perhaps a distant relative of the Fan Mu 范目 (or Fan Yin
范因) who led the Zong in support of Liu Bang 劉邦 at the founding of the
Han dynasty. After the state of Dacheng (by then called Han 漢) was finally
conquered in 347, a revolt attempted to reestablish the state with Fan Ben as
its prospective ruler. Such was the enduring influence of the Fan family in the
Sichuan region.

Terry KLEEMAN

📖 Kleeman 1998, passim; Seidel 1969–70, 233–36

※ Li Xiong; Dacheng

fang shema

放赦馬

Dispatching the Writ of Pardon

Dispatching the Writ of Pardon is the rite of sending off the Writ of Pardon of
the Three Heavens (*santian sheshu* 三天赦書) to the lords of the underworld,
attesting that the sins of the deceased have been forgiven. In rituals of Merit
(*gongde*) in Taiwan, the rite is held in the late afternoon in an open space or
on the road near the altar. The first half of the rite is an enactment of the
receipt of the Writ from Heaven. Originally, the high priest (*gaogong* 高功; see
daozhang) climbed up on a platform and performed a spiritual ascension to
Heaven to present the petition. After receiving Heaven's consent, he proclaimed
it (*Shangqing lingbao dafa*; CT 1221, *j*. 44). This action is omitted in the ritual
as it is carried out in present-day Taiwan, where the high priest instead climbs
onto the platform and immediately proclaims the Writ of Pardon.

The second half of the rite dramatically enacts the sending of the Writ
to the underworld. The priests take the stage carrying a paper figure of the
Officer of Pardon (*sheguan* 赦官, the official who delivers the Writ) and his
horse. They give the Officer a drink of wine and feed the horse with straw.
Then they run around the open space, leaping and somersaulting, miming
the journey to the underworld.

ASANO Haruji

📖 Lagerwey 1987c, 202–15; Ōfuchi Ninji 1983, 496–502 and 655–57; Schipper
1989b, 128–37

※ *gongde*

Fanghu waishi

方壺外史

The External Secretary of Mount Fanghu

This collection of *neidan* works by *Lu Xixing (1520–1601 or 1606), so entitled
after one of his appellations, dates from the Longqing period (1567–72). It was
printed in either 1571 or 1572, as two of its works bear prefaces by Lu dated
1571. The second edition, published by Zhao Song 趙宋 during the Wanli
period (1573–1620), was not printed before 1580, the date of Zhao's preface to
Lu's commentary to the *Daode jing*. The third edition was published by Zheng
Guanying 鄭觀應 in 1915 and contains his "Preface to the New Engraving
(*xinzi* 新梓) of the *Fanghu waishi*."

The collection includes ten commentaries and four original works by Lu
Xixing, not all of which bear dates. The commentaries are on the *Xinyin jing
(Scripture of the Mind Seal; 1571), the *Yinfu jing (Scripture of the Hidden Ac-
cordance; 1567), the *Ruyao jing (Mirror for Compounding the Medicine), the
Baizi bei 百字碑 (Hundred-Word Stele; 1571; a short work attributed to *Lü
Dongbin, trans. Cleary 1991a, 239–52), the *Jindan sibai zi (Four Hundred Words
on the Golden Elixir), the *Jindan yinzheng shi* 金丹印證詩 (Verses on the Attes-
tation of the Golden Elixir; by Longmei zi 龍眉子, Southern Song period), the
Qingtian ge 青天歌 (Song of the Blue Heaven; 1571; attributed to *Qiu Chuji),
the *Wuzhen pian (Folios on Awakening to Reality), the *Daode jing* (1566), and
two commentaries to the *Zhouyi cantong qi (Token for the Agreement of the
Three According to the *Book of Changes*; 1569 and 1573). Lu Xixing's own works
are the *Xuanfu lun* 玄膚論 (An Essay on the Surface of the Mystery; 1567), the
Jindan jiuzheng pian 金丹就正篇 (Folios on Seeking the Proper Understanding

of the Golden Elixir; 1564; trans. Wile 1992, 149–53), the *Jindan da zhitu* 金丹大旨圖 (Great Illustrated Directions on the Golden Elixir; 1570), and the *Qi polun* 七破論 (Seven Essays on Smashing [Erroneous Views]).

The whole collection is also available in reprints in the *Daozang jinghua and the *Zangwai daoshu (vol. 5), both based on the 1915 edition.

Fabrizio PREGADIO

📖 Qing Xitai 1994, 2: 178–79; Yang Ming 1995

※ Lu Xixing; *neidan*

fangji

方技

"methods and techniques"; method-based expertises

The term *fangji* originally was a bibliographic category that referred to medical and mantic texts, and by extension the techniques that these texts contained. In the Han, this term was contrasted with *shushu* 數術 ("arts of the numbers," or "algorithm-based techniques") that included astronomy, calendrics, and divination, and primarily associated with *fangshi (masters of methods). By later imperial times, "method-based expertises" lost this specific connotation and became roughly synonymous with the more general category of *fangshu* 方術 ("methods and arts") and came to describe individuals whose fame rested on the mastery of such methods.

The earliest use of the term *fangji* to categorize books was in the *Qilüe* 七略 (Seven Summaries), the imperial catalogue assembled by Liu Xin 劉歆 (46 BCE–23 CE) where *fangji* was one of seven categories of texts. Liu Xin's taxonomy formed the basis for the bibliography of the *Hanshu* (History of the Former Han; *j. 30*). The texts listed in this *Hanshu* category were subdivided into four sections: Medical Classics (*yijing* 醫經), Classic Recipes (*jingfang* 經方), Inner Chamber (*fangzhong* 房中, i.e., sexual cultivation methods; see *fangzhong shu*), and Spirit Transcendence (*shenxian* 神仙, i.e., immortality techniques). The first two sections contain titles such as *Huangdi neijing (Inner Scripture of the Yellow Emperor) and *Shennong Huangdi shijin* 神農黃帝食禁 (Dietary Proscriptions of the Divine Husbandman and the Yellow Emperor), implying that such texts were concerned with medicine and diet. Texts listed in the latter two sections appear to have been concerned with practices such as altering the inner balance of Yin and Yang through sexual and alchemical means, as well as ingesting "numinous mushrooms" (*zhi).

The Han precedent influenced later historical writing, and the term *fangji* evolved into a biographical category. Chen Shou's 陳壽 (232–97) *Weizhi* (History of Wei; ca. 280) section of the *Sanguo zhi* (History of the Three Kingdoms) contains a chapter on *fangji* that includes both the examples of technical skill similar to the sense in the *Hanshu* as well as anomalies. The *Jiu Tangshu* (Old History of the Tang; *j.* 191) traces its origins to Liu Xin's category of "techniques, numbers, divination, and physiognomy," but lists a much wider variety of experts in the occult arts. Likewise, the Song collectanea *Taiping yulan* 太平御覽 (Imperial Readings of the Taiping Xingguo Reign Period; 983) had *fangji* chapters that included methods that were in both the number-based and recipe-based categories in the *Hanshu*. Most later imperial Standard Histories through the *Mingshi* (History of the Ming) contained such a biographical chapter. By this time, the Han distinction between *fangji* and *fangshu* had long been lost.

Many of these texts and the practices embodied in them found their way into the Taoist Canon. While *fangji* is not a category found in the Canon, some of the texts previously classified in that category are listed in the *fangfa* 方法 (Methods) and *zhongshu* 眾術 (Techniques) sections of the Cavern of Perfection (*dongzhen* 洞真) and Cavern of Mystery (*dongxuan* 洞玄; see *SANDONG).

Mark CSIKSZENTMIHALYI

📖 Csikszentmihalyi 2000; DeWoskin 1981; DeWoskin 1983; Harper 1999; Kalinowski 1991; Kalinowski 2004; Li Ling 2000a; Li Ling 2000b; Ngo 1976

※ *fangshi*; COSMOLOGY; DIVINATION, OMENS, AND PROPHECY; NUMEROLOGY

fangshi

方士

"masters of methods"

Fangshi were specialists in a set of technical arts centering on immortality in late Warring States and early imperial China. Originally, *fangshi* were primarily from the coastal regions of Qi 齊 and Yan 燕 (chiefly present-day Shandong, Hebei, and Liaoning), and specialized in knowledge of the immortals and the paths to transcendence. They were patronized by emperors who sought immortality during the Qin and Han dynasties, and taught these rulers to produce elixirs and emulate the sage-kings of antiquity. By the Later Han, the term had broadened to include diviners, physicians, astrologers, and physiognomists.

Some of the medical and transcendence techniques employed by the *fangshi* in early imperial China were adopted by practitioners in the Taoist movements of the late Han like the *Wudoumi dao (Way of the Five Pecks of Rice).

The earliest reference to the *fangshi* occurs in the monograph on *feng* 封 and *shan* 禪 sacrifices ("Fengshan shu" 封禪書) in the *Shiji* (Records of the Historian; ca. 100 BCE), which describes groups of experts in immortality living in coastal China in the fourth century BCE. From the time of Kings Wei (Weiwang 威王, r. 334–320 BCE) and Xuan (Xuanwang 宣王, r. 319–301 BCE) of Qi and King Zhao (Zhaowang 昭王, r. 311–279 BCE) of Yan, these *fangshi* claimed to know of three spirit mountains where immortals dwelt and medicines conferring immortality existed (*Shiji*, 28.1369–70; trans. Watson 1961, 26; see *Penglai). The same source narrates the patronage of *fangshi* by Qin Shi huangdi (r. 221–210 BCE). In 219 BCE, he sent *Xu Fu to find immortals dwelling on the spirit mountains in the eastern sea. Four years later, he commissioned Master Lu (Lu sheng 盧生) to go to sea to search for the immortals, and then sent three other *fangshi* to seek the herbs of deathlessness of the immortals. In the *Shiji*, the methods (*fang* 方) used by the *fangshi* generally concerned demons and spirits: methods for retreating from old age (*quelao fang* 卻老方), methods involving demons and gods (*guishen fang* 鬼神方), and methods for gods, monsters and anomalies (*shen guai qi fang* 神怪奇方).

In the Former Han, Emperor Wu (r. 141–87 BCE) and Liu An 劉安 (179?–122), the Prince of Huainan (see *Huainan zi*), were best known for their patronage of *fangshi*. In 133 BCE, *Li Shaojun advised Emperor Wu to perform a rite first celebrated by the Yellow Emperor (*Huangdi), enabling the transformation of cinnabar to gold. Gongyu Dai 公玉帶 furnished Emperor Wu with a chart depicting a pentagonal twelve-storey hall matching one built by the Yellow Emperor in 102 BCE. By emulating the Yellow Emperor, Wu sought to mimic his apotheosis and become an immortal. *Fangshi* advised him in this, although they did not enjoy official positions in the government (Chen Pan 1948, 33–40). Liu An, one of Emperor Wu's vassals, was said to have gathered several thousand experts in methods and techniques, and relying on them compiled treatments of techniques of spirit transcendence (*shenxian* 神仙) and alchemy (*huangbai* 黃白; *Hanshu*, 44.2145). Fragments of the resulting text—the *Huainan wanbi* 淮南萬畢 or *Myriad Endings of Huainan*—exist, but Kusuyama Haruki has argued that they come from a compendium of *fangshi* traditions postdating Liu An, associated with him because of the transcendence tales that surrounded him (1987, 31). It is also in the Former Han that the longevity of *fangshi* is first asserted: Li Shaojun was hailed as a spirit because he was able to recall events in the distant past and identify a bronze vessel cast in 676 BCE (*Shiji*, 28.1385). Similar tales surround Later Han *fangshi* such as Lu Nüsheng 魯女生 and Ji Zixun 薊子訓 (*Hou Hanshu*, 82B.2741, 2746; see Ngo 1976).

After the brief Xin dynasty (9–23 CE) of Wang Mang, also a noted patron of the *fangshi*, Emperor Guangwu (r. 25–57 CE) restored the Han and censured them (*Hou Hanshu*, 28A.959–60). By the reigns of Emperors Zhang (r. 75–88 CE) and He (r. 88–106 CE), however, imperial patronage of *fangshi* had recovered. A funerary inscription for such a *fangshi* discovered in Henan province in 1991 tells of the clairvoyance and ability to avert catastrophe of Fei Zhi 肥致, who served as Expectant Appointee in the Lateral Court (*yeting daizhao* 掖庭待 詔, i.e., a candidate for the examinations who had received the recommendation of an official and served in the apartments of the imperial concubines) because of these expertises (Xing Yitian 1997, 53; Schipper 1997b; Little 2000b, 150–51). The inscription also states that Fei Zhi was friends with divine beings such as *Chisong zi, an immortal associated with breathing exercises and immortality. As this example suggests, the methods used by the *fangshi* from the Later Han were defined more broadly to include a variety of medical and omenological techniques. Evidence of the breadth of practice incorporated into the chapter on *fangshi* in Fan Ye's 范曄 (398–445) *Hou Hanshu* (History of the Later Han) is its inclusion of omen and portent techniques such as *fengjiao* 風角 (wind angles). This practice, which may date back to the Shang dynasty (DeWoskin 1983, 27), involves using the temperature, strength, and changes in direction in seasonal winds to determine the local increase and decrease in Yin and Yang *qi* (Li Ling 2000a, 52–57).

When Chen Shou 陳壽 (232–97) compiled the chapter on Methods and Techniques (*fangji*) in the *Weizhi* (History of Wei; ca. 280) section of the *Sanguo zhi* (History of the Three Kingdoms), his intention was to revise traditional historical writing by broadening the coverage of "unorthodox happenings and anomalous events" (*Sanguo zhi*, 29.830). Yamada Toshiaki has argued that the reason that Fan Ye broadened the definition of *fangshi* in his *Hou Hanshu* was that he was following Chen's lead. As a result, the divination and omenology methods that had been categorized as *shushu* 數術 ("arts of the numbers," or "algorithm-based techniques") in the *Hanshu* (History of the Former Han) were combined with the category of *fangshi* into a chapter on *fangshu* 方術 ("methods and arts"; Yamada Toshiaki 1988b, 1968–69). Thus the *fangshi*, originally experts in matters of the spirits, came by the late Han to include the ubiquitous experts in detecting shifts in the balance of the natural world.

The "methods" of the *fangshi* may be seen as forerunners of organized Taoist practices on several levels. In the Han, the concept of the Dao served to explain the efficacy of the myriad of newly forming technical disciplines (Csikszentmihalyi 1997), and many of these disciplines were the province of the *fangshi*. This explains why the term *daoshi (masters of the Dao) was already beginning to replace the term *fangshi* in the *Hanshu*, resulting in its gradual eclipse of the latter term. On a more concrete level, many specific techniques of spirit transcendence, medicine, and alchemy initially used by *fangshi* found their way into later Taoist practice.

Mark CSIKSZENTMIHALYI

📖 Chen Guofu 1963, 258–59; Chen Pan 1948; Csikszentmihalyi 2000; De-Woskin 1981; DeWoskin 1983; DeWoskin 1986; Harper 1999; Li Ling 2000a; Li Ling 2000b; Lin Yuping 1995; Ngo 1976; Robinet 1997b, 37–39; Roth 1987a; Yamada Toshiaki 1988b

※ *fangji*

fangzhong shu

房中術

"arts of the bedchamber"; sexual techniques

The term *fangzhong shu* (lit., "techniques for inside the [bed-]chamber") generally refers to intimate practices shared within a couple's marital bed. Modern writers, in China and the West alike, have frequently exoticized them as "sexual alchemy" or "sexual yoga," and have explained them as "Taoist." Others have examined such interpretations and found them unfounded or exaggerated. The question is not whether Chinese people practiced, or wrote about, activities that involved sexuality, but whether such activities were in any meaningful sense Taoist (Strickmann 1974, 1044–45; Schipper 1993, 144–55).

Some of the modern confusion results from anachronistic interpretations. In late imperial times, for instance, *jing (vital essence) was the standard term for male reproductive fluids. And certain texts from earlier periods show that certain writers assumed that conservation of such fluids would help protect a man from debilitation, illness, and premature death. The problem lies in the fact that the term *jing* is also used in many historical texts, including Taoist texts, in contexts that clearly preclude such meanings. For instance, the *Neiye's opening lines read:

> The vital essence (*jing*) of all things—
> This is what makes life come into being:
> Below, it generates the five grains,
> Above, it brings about the constellated stars.
> When it flows in the interstices of Heaven and Earth,
> It is called "spiritual beings" (*guishen* 鬼神);
> When it is stored up inside [a person's] chest,
> He/she is called "a sage" (*shengren).

To read these lines (or comparable lines in the *Daode jing*) as using *jing* to denote male reproductive fluids would be nonsensical. Clearly, the term refers here to an essence that suffuses a person's being. Taoist literature is replete with comparable uses. But even some excellent scholars have persisted in reading the term *jing* as meaning "semen," no matter what text may contain it. It is particularly important to consider the real or intended audiences of such texts: if the advocated practices would otherwise seem applicable to women and men alike, it is quite possible that there, as in the *Neiye*, references to *jing* involve preservation of a general life-force, not reproductive fluids.

Generally, we must distinguish Taoists' emphasis on cultivating life's basic forces ("bio-spiritual cultivation") from various other parties' interest in explaining and enhancing sexual relationships (Kirkland 1994, 162). Early texts that suggest methods for improving lovemaking range from *Mawangdui manuscripts (Harper 1987b; Wile 1992, 77–83) to a tenth-century Japanese medical compendium, the *Ishinpō* (Methods from the Heart of Medicine; Wile 1992, 83–113; Kohn 1993b, 153–59). Very different are texts from Ming and Qing times that prescribe esoteric ritual techniques, instead of ordinary attempts to improve lovemaking (Wile 1992, 146–92). Some Tang texts, like *Sun Simiao's *Qianjin fang* 千金方 (Prescriptions Worth a Thousand; Wile 1992, 114–19; Kirkland 1997–98, 113–14), urge cautious sexual activity, but have little identifiable Taoist content. And none of those texts are preserved in the *Daozang*—a fact that indicates either that Taoists did not value such texts, or that they were loath to admit that they did. Some have argued that *fangzhong shu* are related to Taoist spiritual practices because both are concerned with "the cultivation of *qi*" (Wile 1992, 149). But if so, the earliest proponent of "sexual alchemy" would logically be Mencius (*Mengzi* 孟子, 2A.2; trans. Legge 1895, 189)—a notion that few would accept.

Generally speaking, Taoists have never been the prudes that Confucians, or followers of Western religions, have been. And since Taoists have, throughout history, been reluctant to demarcate boundaries between orthopraxy and heteropraxy, certain Taoists of various periods may have advocated or participated in practices (perhaps including *heqi, "merging pneumas": see Bokenkamp 1997, 44–46) that involved more sexuality than Westerners or Confucians generally find comfortable or comprehensible. But ultimately, Taoist self-cultivation, beginning with the *Neiye*, married physiological rectification with attempts to attain and embody higher experiential realities, such as essence, pneuma, and spirit (*jing, qi, shen*), and the Dao. Some *Shangqing texts instruct a male practitioner to visualize spiritual interaction with a feminine spiritual being (Schafer 1978a; Kohn 1993b, 267–71; Bokenkamp 1996b; Kroll 1996c). But such models, though couched in mildly erotic terms, really advocate a meditative process of visualizing an exchange of energies, not the physical coupling assumed in *fangzhong shu*. The *Chishu yujue miaojing* 赤書玉訣妙經 (Wondrous Scripture of Red Writings and Jade Instructions; CT 352), an early *Lingbao text, warns, "Don't set your mind on sex or give rise to passions" (Kohn 1993b, 98). And the great Tang leader *Sima Chengzhen, whose *Fuqi jingyi lun* gives advice on proper management of all physiological realities, also warned "that sensual feelings are neither essential nor appropriate for body or mind" (Kohn 1993b, 238). Perhaps the most typical Taoist position would be that the sexual components of one's being are realities that should be managed cautiously, but are not to be indulged, and are not to be confused with the more sublime realities that are the goal of Taoist religious practice.

Russell KIRKLAND

📖 Despeux 1990, 27–42; van Gulik 1961; Harper 1987b; Harper 1998, 135–41; Ishida Hidemi 1991; Kirkland 1994; Kohn 1993b, 153–59; Li Ling 2000a, 382–433; Maspero 1981, 517–41; Robinet 1988; Sakade Yoshinobu 1993a; Schipper 1993, 144–55; Wile 1992

※ *heqi*; *yangsheng*

faqi

法器

ritual tools

The ritual tools of Taoism consist of implements used to call forth deities, exorcize evil forces, and manipulate both deities and demons. These objects include swords, mirrors, and seals, as well as musical instruments such as bells, chimes, and wooden fish. According to the *Fengdao kejie (Codes and Precepts for Worshipping the Dao; *j. 3*), all the implements used in temples and ritual spaces may be designated as "ritual tools." The following are some of the most representative types of objects.

1. The audience tablet (*hu* 笏) is a long and slender tablet held by the priest (*daoshi*) in his hands. It is closely patterned on the tablet held by officials at court. It is also known as *baohu* 寶笏 (precious tablet), *shouban* 手版 (Hand Board), *chaoban* 朝版 (Audience Board), *zouban* 奏板 (Announcement Plank), and *zhijian* 執簡 (Hand-held Slip). It measures about 50 cm in length, 5 cm in width, and 5 mm in thickness.

2. The Seven-star Sword (*qixing jian* 七星劍) is a steel sword whose blade is engraved with a pattern of the Northern Dipper (*beidou*). It is also

Fig. 32. Ritual tools. (a) Seven-star Sword; (b) Command Placard; (c) Bells; (d) Water bowl; (e) *Fengzhi* 奉旨; (f) Dragon Horn (*longjiao* 龍角). Reproduced from Liu Zhiwan 1983a.

32g

32i

32h

Fig. 32. Ritual tools (*cont.*). (g) Chime (*qing* 磬); (h) Wooden fish (*muyu* 木魚); (i) *Gao* 筶.
Reproduced from Liu Zhiwan 1983a.

known as *baojian* 寶劍 (Precious Sword), *fajian* 法劍 (Sword of the Law),
longquan jian 龍泉劍 (Sword of the Dragon Springs), and *zhanxie jian* 斬
邪劍 (Sword Severing Evil). It measures about 60 cm in length, and is
used for vanquishing evil spirits.

3. The Command Placard (*lingpai* 令牌) is a long and narrow wooden
plate, rounded at the top and flat at the bottom. On the front is carved
"Command of the Five Thunders" (*wulei haoling* 五雷號令) and on the
back, "Calling the Ten Thousand Spirits" (*zongzhao wanling* 總召萬靈)
or "Placard of the Imperial Decree" (*chiling pai* 敕令牌). It is also called
wulei ling 五雷令 (Command of the Five Thunders) or *leiling pai* 雷令

牌 (Placard of the Thunder Command). It is 18 cm in height, 7 cm in breadth, and 3 cm in thickness. It reproduces the imperial tallies given to officials by the emperor. The priest holds the placard in his hands when giving orders to heavenly officers and generals.

4. Bells are held in one hand by the priest. They are called *sanqing ling* 三清鈴 (Bells of the Three Clarities) or *fazhong* 法鐘 or *faling* 法鈴 (Bells of the Law). Their function is to beckon the deities and exorcize demons. Made of brass, they are about 20 cm in height and 10 cm in circumference. The Three Clarities (*sanqing*) are represented on the upper section of the handle.

5. The hand-held burner (*shoulu* 手爐) is an incense burner with a handle. It is held by the high priest (*gaogong* 高功; see *daozhang*) or by the leading community representative. The smoke arising from the hand-held burner is thought to represent the transmission of sincerity to the deities.

6. The water bowl (*shuiyu* 水盂) contains purified water (*jingshui* 淨水). Made of brass, it is 4 cm in height and 6 cm in circumference. The priest holds it in his left hand while in his right hand he holds a flower with the stem attached (or a small twig of willow) that he uses to sprinkle water in order to purify the ritual space.

7. The *fengzhi* 奉旨 is an oblong piece of wood used by the high priest to signal the progress of the ritual, by beating it on the table. It is also called *chiban* 敕板 (Plank of the Imperial Decree), *yuzhi* 玉旨 (Jade Injunction), and *jingban* 淨板 (Pure Plank). It is 10 cm in length, 4 cm in height, and 3 cm in depth. It resembles the gavel used by judges in olden times, and the "wake-up wood" (*xingmu* 醒木) employed by lecturers.

8. The Dragon Horn (*longjiao* 龍角) is a horn flute used to summon the deities and exorcize evil spirits. It is also called *lingjiao* 靈角 (Numinous Horn) or *haojiao* 號角 (Horn of Orders). In Taiwan various types are used: the Black-head and Red-head priests (see *hongtou* and *wutou*) use flutes made of buffalo horn or tin, respectively, while the ritual masters (*fashi*) use flutes of buffalo or ox horn. This instrument is about 30 cm long and about 10 cm in circumference.

9. The Rope of the Law (*fasheng* 法繩) is a whip symbolizing a snake. Its cracking noise is said to scare away evil spirits. It is also called *fabian* 法鞭 (Whip of the Law), *fasuo* 法索 (Cord of the Law), and *jingbian* 淨鞭 (Whip of Purity). Its wooden handle is about 20 cm long and about 3 cm thick and is carved to represent a snake. Its attached rope, made of plaited flax and cotton and about one meter in length, represents the snake's body and tail.

10. The Seal of the Law (*fayin* 法印) is used for stamping documents used in rituals. The action of stamping is thought to invest the document with spiritual power.

11. The Mirror of the Law (*fajing* 法鏡) is used during the rite of Opening the Light (*kaiguang) to cause deities to lodge within their images, and to exorcize evil spirits.

12. The Measure of the Law (*fachi* 法尺) is a ruler that has the power to exorcize evil spirits. Made of wood, it is about 30 cm in length, about 2 cm in width, and about 1 cm in thickness. Both sides are marked with gradations. A more powerful form of this implement is called *Tianpeng chi* 天蓬尺 (Measure of Tianpeng; see under *Tianpeng zhou), which is a square stick about 35 cm long and about 3 cm thick that has no gradations, but bears on both sides the name of Tianpeng Yuanshuai 天蓬元帥 (Marshal Tianpeng), the Sun and Moon, the twenty-eight lunar lodges (*xiu), the Northern Dipper, and the Southern Dipper (*nandou* 南斗).

13. The chime (*qing* 磬) is a bowl-shaped musical instrument made of copper. It is placed on the right side of the central table of the altar (the Cavern Bench, *dong'an* 洞案), opposite the wooden fish. It is also known as *tongqing* 銅磬 (bronze chime), *qingqing* 清磬 (pure chime), *yuqing* 玉磬 (jade chime), and *tongbo* 銅鉢 (bronze bowl).

14. The wooden fish (*muyu* 木魚) is a hollow percussion instrument made of wood. It is placed on the left side of the central table, opposite the chime. It is also called *mugu* 木鼓 (wooden drum). Both the chime and the wooden fish are made in various sizes.

15. The *gao* 筶 is a divination tool in the form of a crescent made of bamboo or wood, often painted red. One side is flat and represents Yang, while the other side is convex and represents Yin. They come in various sizes, between 5 and 25 cm in length, and are used in sets of two. After praying before the deities, one throws the set of *gao* to the ground. If one comes up Yin and the other Yang, it means that the deities agree; this is called *shenggao* 聖筶 (*gao* of sagehood). If both are Yang, the deities are derisive; this is called *xiaogao* 笑筶 (*gao* of derision). If both sides are Yin, the deities are angry; this is called *fufen* 伏筶 (*gao* of submission).

ASANO Haruji

📖 Little 2000b, 219; Liu Zhiwan 1983a; Ōfuchi Ninji 1983, 207–10; Qing Xitai 1994, 3: 255–57; Schipper and Wang 1986, 188–94; Zhang Zehong 1999a, 94–99

※ *gongde; jiao; zhai*

fashi

法師

"ritual master"

The term *fashi* generally refers to a "master of rites" and may denote a Buddhist monk or a Taoist priest. In Taiwan, it is often used to designate the Red-head (*hongtou* 紅頭) ritual masters (see *hongtou* and *wutou*). Going barefoot and wearing everyday clothes with red scarves wrapped around their heads, they perform healing, exorcism, and magico-religious ceremonies that employ trance techniques. They also carry out rites to protect the village community by calling on the "soldiers of the netherworld" (*yinbing* 陰兵) of the Five Camps (*wuying*). The spells used by the Red-head ritual masters often contain vernacular expressions. At present, they are recorded in books transmitted from master to disciple, but originally their transmission was oral.

ASANO Haruji

📖 Cohen 1992; Furuie Shinpei 1999, 98–100; Liu Zhiwan 1983b, 207–317; Liu Zhiwan 1983–84, 2: 5–427; Naoe Hiroji 1983, 1008–83; Saso 1970; Schipper 1985e

※ *hongtou* and *wutou*

Fei Changfang

費長房

Fei Changfang is most famous for his encounter with Hugong 壺公, the Gourd Sire. The classic version of this encounter is narrated in Hugong's biography in *Shenxian zhuan*, in which Fei is a guard in the marketplace. It happens that an old man—who is really Hugong—sells herbs to cure illness in the market and hangs a large gourd outside his shop. Each night Fei, alone, notices that the old man disappears into the gourd and, understandably, thinks he is marvellous and decides to serve him. The old man ultimately invites him into the gourd which, like sacred caverns, houses an immortals' world of places, towers and buildings of all kinds, an example of the typical Taoist motif of the inside being larger than the outside (see the entry *dongtian* and *fudi*). Hugong proceeds to

Fig. 33. Fei Changfang enters his gourd.

test Fei's worthiness to receive the Dao that confers immortality. He successfully passed the first two tests: by not showing fear when left alone with tigers and by not moving when a huge rock that was suspended above his head on a flimsy cord was about to be gnawed through by snakes. However, Fei recoiled from the third ordeal—eating excrement infested with inch-long worms. Hugong responded that although he could not attain the Dao of immortality he could receive earthly power and gain several hundred years of life.

Fei is credited with possessing a powerful talisman with which he could control demons, enabling him to effect cures through exorcism. He was also able to "shrink the veins of the earth" so that one thousand *li* of territory could be viewed at one time and to relieve drought.

Fei also receives a biography in *Hou Hanshu* (History of the Later Han) which is very similar to that in *Shenxian zhuan*. However, it ends on a rather different note: on losing his talisman Fei is set upon and murdered by ghosts.

Benjamin PENNY

📕 Campany 2002, 161–68; DeWoskin 1983, 77–81; Giles L. 1948, 79–81; Ngo 1976, 128–34; Stein R. A. 1990, 66–70

※ HAGIOGRAPHY

Fig. 34. A Taoist master lights a candle during the *fendeng* (Division of the Lamps) ceremony.
Taiwan (March 1978). Photograph by Julian Pas.

fendeng

分燈

Division of the Lamps

The Division of the Lamps is one of the rites that compose the *zhai (Retreat) and *jiao (Offering) rituals, and is performed to remove pollution and
establish the altar (*tan* 壇). It comprises three originally separate rites that are
now performed in sequence: Division of the Lamps, Curtain-raising (*juanlian*
捲簾), and Sounding the Golden [Bell] and Striking the Jade [Gong] (*mingjin
jiayu* 鳴金戛玉). The entire series is usually called "Division of the Lamps"
or "Division of the Lamps and Curtain-raising."

In the Division of the Lamps proper, after the lights on the altar have all
been put out, a new fire is brought in and used to relight all the candles, to
the accompaniment of the words from section 42 of the *Daode jing*: "The Dao

generates the One, the One generates the Two, the Two generate the Three, and the Three generate the ten thousand things." The rite of Curtain-raising consists of rolling up the curtain that covers a scroll bearing the Chinese character for "portal" (*que* 闕, meaning the Golden Portal). This character symbolizes the palaces of the deities, and the action of raising the curtain announces to the deities that the ritual is about to begin. In the rite of Sounding the Golden Bell and Striking the Jade Gong, the sounds produced by striking a jade musical gong and a golden bell cause Yin and Yang to reverberate around the altar area. The jade gong (representing Heaven) is placed to the right on the central table where the priest performs the ritual, and the golden bell (representing Earth) is one of the gongs used by the musicians to the left of the altar. They are played by the assistant cantor (*fujiang* 副講) and by one of the percussionists, respectively.

All three rites have their origin in purification ceremonies performed before the "opening of the altar" (*kaitan* 開壇) according to the *Lingbao ritual. In present-day Taiwan, they are performed late on the first night of a *zhai* or a *jiao* lasting more than two days. In view of their present position in the ritual, their essentially preparatory nature seems to have been obscured.

ASANO Haruji

📖 Lagerwey 1987c, 55; Ōfuchi Ninji 1983, 266–71; Qing Xitai 1994, 3: 211–13; Schipper 1975c

※ *gongde; jiao; zhai*

Fengbo

風伯

Count of the Wind

Fengbo, also known as Fengshi 風師 (Master of the Wind) and Jibo 箕伯 (Count of the Basket), is the deity of the wind. In the *Lisao* 離騷 (Encountering Sorrow), a poem included in the *Chuci* 楚辭 (Songs of Chu; trans. Hawkes 1985, 67–95), Feilian 飛廉, the attendant who appears in the scene where Qu Yuan 屈原 is departing for the abode of the Celestial Emperor, corresponds to Fengbo, as does the Basket (*ji* 箕, Sagittarius), one of the twenty-eight lunar lodges (see *xiu). In the *Han Feizi* 韓非子 (Book of Master Han Fei; trans. Liao 1939–59, 1: 76–77), when the Yellow Emperor (*Huangdi) gathers all the demons and deities at Mount Tai (*Taishan, Shandong), Fengbo sweeps the path and *Yushi, the deity of rain, sprinkles water on it. In the *Zhouli* 周禮 (Rites of the Zhou; trans. Biot 1861, 1: 420), kindling is burned to honor the deities of wind and rain. Again, the *Shiji* (Records of the Historian; *j.* 28, trans. Watson 1968, 2: 29) tells us that in the time of Qin Shi huangdi (r. 221–210 BCE) there were temples dedicated to both Fengbo and Yushi in Yong 雍 (Fengxiang 鳳翔, Shaanxi), and that festivals were held there every year. It is evident from this account that from very early times Fengbo, together with Yushi, was an object of state ritual.

In ancient times, Fengbo was depicted as a grotesque deity with the body of a deer, the head of a bird, horns, the tail of a snake, and the patterning of a leopard. By the Ming period, however, images were made depicting him in the form of an old man with a white beard, carrying a fan in his right hand; by then he was known as Celestial Lord Fang, Count of the Wind (Fengbo Fang tianjun 風伯方天君) and venerated as one of a pair with Celestial Lord Chen, Master of Rain (Yushi Chen tianjun 雨師陳天君). A seventeenth-century Japanese screen by Tawaraya Sōtatsu 俵屋宗達 features the wind and rain deities; here the wind deity is depicted humorously with windswept hair, carrying a bag full of wind in both hands and running with long strides.

YOSHIKAWA Tadao

📖 Maspero 1981, 98–99

※ TAOISM AND CHINESE MYTHOLOGY

Fengdao kejie

奉道科戒

Codes and Precepts for Worshipping the Dao

The *Fengdao kejie*—also known as *Fengdao ke*—is the first manual of monastic rules in medieval Taoism. It survives today in an edition contained in the Taoist Canon (CT 1125) and is also found—in a form that is about sixty percent complete—in four *Dunhuang manuscripts (S. 3863, P. 2337, P. 3682, S. 809), the first two of which match the text in the Canon.

The Canon edition consists of six *juan* and contains eighteen sections that cover two major areas: the conceptual framework and concrete conditions of Taoist monastic practice (*j.* 1–3, sec. 1–10), in sections such as "Retribution of Faults" ("Zuiyuan" 罪緣), "Setting up Abbeys" ("Zhiguan" 置觀), "Making Sacred Images" ("Zaoxiang" 造像), "Copying Scriptures" ("Xiejing" 寫經), "Liturgical Implements" ("Faju" 法具), and "Liturgical Vestments" ("Fafu" 法服); and the organization of the ritual order (*j.* 4–6, sec. 11–18) under headings such as "Protocols for Reciting the Scriptures" ("Songjing yi" 誦經儀) and "Protocols for Ritual Ranks" ("Faci yi" 法次儀), along with sections on several liturgies. *Juan* 4 (8a–10b) and 5 (1a–2b) contain lists of Lingbao and Shangqing texts (on the latter, see Robinet 1984, 2: 18).

After much debate over the past four decades, scholars now agree that the *Fengdao kejie* was compiled in the early Tang dynasty, around the years 620–30, and inspired by the collected statutes of Jinming Qizhen 金明七真 (fl. 545–554) who is named as author in the preface. The bulk of the received text existed by the mid-seventh century and was first cited by *Yin Wencao of the late seventh, then both cited and supplemented by *Zhang Wanfu of the early eighth century and other Taoists of his time. After that the text continued to grow, coming to include more and more disparate materials, parts of which survive in citations and in S. 809. From this expanded version, a reduced edition in three *juan* was created that formed the basis for the version we still have today.

The text is also important because of the evidence it provides on the printing of images on paper by Taoists before the end of the seventh century (Barrett 1997).

Livia KOHN

📖 Akizuki Kan'ei 1965; Barrett 1997; Benn 1991, 72–98; Kohn 1997a; Kohn 2001; Kohn 2004b (trans.); Ōfuchi Ninji 1978–79, 1: 115–21 (crit. notes on the Dunhuang mss.) and 2: 219–42 (reprod. of the Dunhuang mss.); Ōfuchi Ninji 1997, 557–89; Ōfuchi Ninji and Ishii Masako 1988, 108–14 (list of texts cited); Reiter 1998; Yoshioka Yoshitoyo 1955, 301–40; Yoshioka Yoshitoyo 1976c

※ *jie* [precepts]; MONASTIC CODE; ORDINATION AND PRIESTHOOD

Fengdu

酆都

Mount Fengdu has been the most famous Chinese purgatory since the first centuries of the Common Era. A rich liturgical tradition for the salvation of the living and the dead developed around its myth, probably coinciding with the formation of Taoist eschatology under Buddhist influence.

The earliest known mention of Fengdu (or its synonym Luofeng 羅酆) as an abode of the dead is in the *Baopu zi*, dating from the early fourth century (trans. Ware 1966, 64). Slightly later, the revealed *Shangqing scriptures contain the first descriptions of the place as a mythical mountain (see for example *Zhengao*, *j.* 10 and 15). Located in the Northern Sea, in the north-

Fig. 35. The Great Emperor of Fengdu (Fengdu dadi 酆都大帝). Dongyue dian 東嶽殿
(Pavilion of the Eastern Peak), Tainan, Taiwan. Photograph by Julian Pas.

ernmost quarter of the universe (it is also called Beifeng 北酆 or Northern Feng), Mount Fengdu is the seat of the cosmological Yin principle. There one finds the Six Heavens, celestial macrocosmic grottoes considered by Taoists to be the locus of all morbid or "expired" energies (*guqi* 故氣) consigned to evil and death (see *santian and liutian*). A gigantic administration is hidden in this universe of death, with palaces and residences, offices and law courts. Fengdu runs throughout this otherworld, in the subsoils of mountains (like *Taishan) and rivers. Records of the dead are kept there and checked in due time. Virtuous deceased are carried to celestial paradises, while sinners are sent to "earth prisons" (*diyu* 地獄) typically located in the depths of the celestial grottoes. The huge and complex bureaucracy constantly at work in Fengdu is hierarchically organized: from the highest officials who were eminent figures during their lifetimes, down to simple demons (*gui), factotums in charge of seizing those whose time in the world of the living is over. Therefore, the dead administer the dead. At the top of this otherworldly administration reigns the Northern Emperor, *Beidi.

For the Taoists of the Six Dynasties, Mount Fengdu, although clearly considered to be a court of justice for the dead, paradoxically was also a place of splendor and marvel. Shangqing documents describe its palaces as covered with jewels and pearls, mentioning various details such as the extraordinary rice that grows there. It was only during the Tang dynasty, and under Buddhist influence, that the Taoist vision of the infernal world reached maturation and the mountain became a center of torture and horror for dead sinners.

Although Fengdu is a mythical toponym, it has also materialized as a geographical reality in different times and regions. The best-known worldly implantation of the infernal mountain seems to have occurred during the Song dynasty. On the banks of the Yangzi River, in Sichuan province, the small town of Fengdu and its hill, "Mount" Pingdu 平都, are still visited today by pilgrims. The village, also called the City of Demons (Guicheng 鬼城), will soon undergo major transformations as the result of the Three Gorges Dam project, but Pingdu, the point of access to the infernal world, will survive.

Christine MOLLIER

📖 Chenivesse 1997a; Chenivesse 1997b; Chenivesse 1998; Despeux 1994, 97–99; Mollier 1997

※ Beidi; HELL; OTHERWORLDLY BUREAUCRACY

fu

釜

crucible

Placed at the center of the alchemical laboratory (the Chamber of the Elixirs, *danshi* 丹室 or *danwu* 丹屋), the crucible is the main tool used in *waidan, and the focus of the alchemical process. *Fu* designates several types of vessels, typically formed of two superimposed halves joined by their mouths (hence the name "double crucible," *shuangfu* 雙釜). According to the commentary to the *Taiqing jing (Scripture of Great Clarity), that gives the earliest method to prepare it, the crucible is made of powdered red clay added to vinegar, and its inner parts are luted with a reddish-black lacquer obtained by boiling oak bark (*Taiqing jing tianshi koujue* 太清經天師口訣; CT 883, 3a–b). The method for making a different type of *fu*, whose lower half is of iron and upper half is of clay, is described in both the *Taiqing shibi ji* and the *Taiqing danjing yaojue* (Ho Peng Yoke 1985, 206; Sivin 1968, 166–68).

Sealing the ingredients in the crucible and heating the crucible are the two most critical parts of the alchemical work, and mistakes made at these stages are said to result in the failure of the whole undertaking. After the ingredients are placed in the crucible, it is closed and then coated with several layers of Mud of the Six-and-One (*liuyi ni) and sometimes with other muds as well. This hermetic sealing makes it possible to avoid dispersions of pneuma (*qi) and to recreate within the vessel conditions that alchemists equate with those of primordial Chaos (*hundun). Under the action of fire, the ingredients release their essences (*jing), which are found to adhere to the inner part of the upper half of the crucible when it is opened. The essences are carefully collected (the designated tool mentioned in the early texts is a white chicken feather) and made into pills.

In the laboratory, the crucible is placed on top of a layered altar (*tan* 壇), either above the fire or inside a furnace. Alchemists perform ceremonies near the crucible before kindling the fire. In a rite described in the *Jiudan jing (Scripture of the Nine Elixirs), the adept offers food and drink to the Great Lord of the Dao (Da daojun 大道君), Lord Lao (*Laojun), and the Lord of Great Harmony (Taihe jun 太和君), asking them to watch over the practice and ensure its success. According to the commentary to the *Jiudan jing* (*Huangdi jiuding shendan jingjue* 黃帝九鼎神丹經訣; CT 885, 20.3a–b), a ceremony is performed in honor of the Great One (*Taiyi) immediately after the crucible is opened and before ingesting the elixir.

Fabrizio PREGADIO

📖 Chen Guofu 1983, 14–21; Pregadio 2006b, 75–78; Sivin 1980, 292–97

※ *liuyi ni*; *waidan*

fu

符

talisman, tally, charm

See entry in "Taoism: An Overview," p. 35.

Fu Jinquan

傅金銓

1765–1844; *zi*: Dingyun 鼎雲; *hao*: Jiyi zi 濟一子
(Master Who Assists the One), Zuihua daoren 醉花道人
(The Taoist Drunken Flower)

Fu Jinquan, a native of Jinxi 金溪 (Jiangxi), is one of the best-known Taoists of the Qing dynasty. Although he claims to have received instruction directly from *Lü Dongbin, his blend of Taoism is close to the *Jingming dao and his *neidan* writings are inspired by those of *Lu Xixing. These two influences are integrated in a Confucian view of life, as Fu advocated achieving the path of humanity (*rendao* 人道) before embarking on the path of immortality (*xiandao* 仙道). Fu travelled extensively in Jiangxi, Jiangsu, Hunan and Sichuan provinces. In 1817, when he was in the Ba 巴 district of Sichuan, he attracted a large group of followers, the most prominent of whom were an official named Ji Dakui 紀 大奎 and two other disciples, Zhou Luanshu 周鸞書 and Yao Yizhi 姚一智.

Fu's works were first published as two separate collections, entitled *Jiyi zi daoshu* 濟一子道書 (Jiyi zi's Books on the Dao) and *Zhengdao bishu* 證道祕 書 (Secret Books Testifying to the Dao). These were later merged and published as the *Jiyi zi zhengdao bishu shiqi zhong* 濟一子證道祕書十七種 (Jiyi zi's Seventeen Secret Books Testifying to the Dao), a title often abridged to *Daoshu shiqi zhong* 道書十七種 (Seventeen Books on the Dao). The collection is eclectic, containing works on *neidan*, **waidan*, and sexual techniques. Eight of them are Fu's own writings, three consist of his own notes and comments, and the other six are republished from other sources. Fu's own *Yiguan zhenji yijian lu* 一貫真機易簡錄 (Records for an Easy Understanding of the True Mechanism of the Pervading Unity) contains his works on *neidan*, but also an entire collection of texts on **nüdan* (inner alchemy for women) entitled *Nü jindan fayao* 女金丹法要 (Essentials of the Methods of the Golden Elixir for Women; Wile 1992, 202–4) with such works as the *Kunyuan jing* 坤元經 (Scripture of the Original Female) as well as writings attributed to **Sun Bu'er and a Miaohua zhenren* 妙化真人 (Perfected of Wondrous Transformation; fl. 1743). Several works ascribed to **Zhang Sanfeng are collected in the *Sanfeng danjue* 三丰丹訣 (Zhang Sanfeng's Alchemical Instructions), notably the *Jindan jieyao* 金丹節要 (Synopsis of the Golden Elixir; trans. Wile 1992, 169–78), the *Caizhen jiyao* 採真機要 (Essentials of the Process for Gathering the True; trans. Wile 1992, 178–88), and the *Wugen shu* 無根樹 (The Rootless Tree; trans. Wile 1992, 188–92), all dealing with sexual practices. Of note also is the *Qiaoyang zi yulu* 樵陽子語錄 (Recorded Sayings of Master Qiaoyang), which contains an abridged version of the sayings of the Yuan-dynasty Jingming master **Liu Yu. The *Qiaoyang jing* 樵陽子經 (Scriptures of Master Qiaoyang) includes related Ming and Qing texts obtained by spirit writing (see **fuji*).

Fu Jinquan was not only a great scholar, but also a talented painter and poet. The preface to his *Beixi lu* 杯溪錄 (Records of the Goblet Pool), contributed by A Yinglin 阿應麟, shows that many of his texts were inscribed on his paintings. A Yinglin also took zither lessons from Fu, revealing yet another side of Fu's eclecticism.

Farzeen BALDRIAN-HUSSEIN

📖 Qing Xitai 1988–95, 4: 195–211; Qing Xitai 1994, 1: 399–400, 2: 187–89; Zeng Zhaonan 1996

※ *neidan*; *nüdan*

Fu Yi

傅奕

554–639

Fu Yi is known primarily as an expert on the text of the *Daode jing* and as an influential critic of Buddhism during the early Tang dynasty. His textual labors are to be found in the "Ancient Version," *Daode jing guben pian* 道德經古本篇 (Compilation of the Ancient Version of the *Daode jing*; CT 665), a type of title which immediately arouses suspicion of exaggeration but which in this case has been vindicated by finds such as those at *Mawangdui, which revealed that Fu Yi's text is indeed close to early Han versions. The Southern Song *Hunyuan shengji (Saintly Chronicle of Chaotic Origin; 3.20a) lists among his sources (mainly transmitted manuscripts, for which the precise number of characters are noted) one recovered in 574 from a tomb alleged to have been that of the concubine of Xiang Yu 項羽 (?–202 BCE). Whether the identification of the tomb was correct or not, such a site was still known in the seventh century according to commentary in the Shiji (Records of the Historian; 7.334), and may well have been early enough to contain an important find. Another source he is said to have used was a Han text and commentary once owned by *Kou Qianzhi (365?–448).

The ease with which Fu was able to pursue such refined bibliographic research is explained by his career as an astrologer, which in central government started in the *Tongdao guan institute under the Northern Zhou, established by the emperor Wu as a great center of religious learning in the service of the state's Taoistic ideology. In 593, under the Sui, he and a fellow-astrologer applied for permission to become Taoist priests, perhaps to enjoy continued access to the bibliographical resources of the Tongdao guan, which had been inherited by the Taoist *Xuandu guan. Using his predictive powers to avoid trouble as the Sui fell into internecine strife, he briefly retired from government service. But under the early Tang he became Grand Astrologer (taishi ling 太史令), and used his position in 621 and again in 626, when the emperor Taizong (again, as he had predicted) had usurped the throne, to launch choleric attacks on Buddhism, as economically unproductive, unfilial, unpatriotic, politically disruptive and, above all, foreign. His trenchant memorials may be found in his official biographies in the Standard Histories; his lengthier polemics, based on a series of biographies of anti-Buddhists, including himself, may be found in the monk Daoxuan's 道宣 (596–667) continuation to the *Hongming ji (Collection Spreading the Light of Buddhism). For Buddhist counterblasts to his writings soon appeared in the *Bianzheng lun (Essays of Disputation and Correction) and other works, and these were not merely refutations of the points raised, but more largely aimed at the Taoist religion as a whole, which he quite clearly supported. During the more xenophobic latter half of the Tang, Fu Yi was recalled in an number of improbable anecdotes as a hero who pitted Chinese integrity against the mumbo-jumbo of foreign monks. His official biographies duly make him a solely Confucian hero, and, to suit the mood of the day, downplay his Taoist associations.

T. H. BARRETT

📖 Qing Xitai 1988–95, 2: 41–43; Tonami Mamoru 1999, 35–46, 223; Wright 1951

※ TAOISM AND CHINESE BUDDHISM

fudi

福地

Blissful Lands

See *dongtian* and *fudi* 洞天 · 福地.

fuji

扶乩

planchette writing; spirit writing

Planchette writing is called *fuji* (lit., "support of the planchette stick"), *fuluan* 扶鸞 ("support of the phoenix"), or *jiangluan* 降鸞 ("descent of the phoenix"). Two persons hold a stylet (*jijia* 乩架) above a planchette whose surface is covered with sand (*shapan* 沙盤). One of them, possessed by a deity, moves the stylet and draws characters on the sand, which a third person interprets and transcribes on paper.

The fashion of planchette writing became particularly widespread in the Song period. Shen Gua 沈括 (1031–95; SB 856–53) in his *Mengqi bitan* 夢溪筆談 (Brush Talks from Dream Brook; *j.* 20) and Su Shi 蘇軾 (Su Dongpo 蘇東坡, 1037–1101; SB 900–968) in his *Dongpo zhilin* 東坡志林 (Records of the Eastern Slope; *j.* 2) describe in detail the relation between planchette writing and the cult of the Purple Maiden (Zigu 紫姑, the Spirit of the Latrine; see *Ceshen). The practice continued to develop in Ming and Qing times, in both learned and popular circles. Each district had at least one altar devoted to it, and even the Jiajing Emperor (r. 1522–66) had one such altar built at court. Planchette writing was forbidden by the Qing legal code, but continued to exist. The main deities who possessed the mediums were the Purple Maiden, female divinities, popular divinities, and the Eight Immortals (*baxian), particularly *Lü Dongbin (see Katz P. R. 1996).

The Taoist Canon contains several texts that were produced entirely or partly from spirit-writing sessions. Examples are the *Daoji lingxian ji* 道迹靈仙 記 (Record of the Traces of the Dao Left by Numinous Spirits and Immortals; CT 597), the *Minghe yuyin (Echoes of Cranes' Songs), and the *Xuxian hanzao* 徐仙翰藻 (Literary Masterpieces of the Xu Immortals; CT 1468). Handbooks

Fig. 36. "Planchette writing" (*fuji*). An inspired medium, Master Cai Wen 蔡文, wields the "phoenix brush" during a spirit-writing session at the Wenhua yuan 文化院 (Cultural Academy), Kaohsiung, Taiwan (August 1997). Photograph by Julian Pas.

on planchette writing also exist, such as the *Bichuan wanfa guizong* 祕傳萬法歸宗 (Ten Thousand Authoritative Methods Transmitted in Secret). This work gives directions on drawing talismans and uttering incantations for the sacred area; on the brush, the ink, and the water; and on talismans and incantations used to summon the spirits. The preface states that planchette writing was one of the most common ways of receiving sacred texts from divine or semidivine beings.

Catherine DESPEUX

📖 Chao Wei-pang 1942; Clart 1994–95; Clart 1997; Despeux 1990, passim; de Groot 1892–1910, 6: 1296–1316; Grootaers 1951; Jordan and Overmyer 1986, 36–88; Russell 1990a; Seaman 1980; Stein R. A. 1969b; Xu Dishan 1966; Zhong Zhaopeng 1988

※ TAOISM AND MEDIUM CULTS; TAOISM AND POPULAR RELIGION

fuqi

服氣

ingestion of breath

Fuqi and its synonym *shiqi* 食氣 designate the ingestion of outer or inner breath. This technique is attested since the Han period, when it was closely associated with abstention from cereals (*bigu). As described later in the *Yangxing yanming lu and the *Fuqi jingyi lun, ingesting breath had prophylactic and therapeutic functions.

Typical practices based on the ingestion of outer breath include the ingestion of the "five sprouts" (*wuya* 五芽, one for each direction; see Maspero 1981, 506–13), the ingestion of the "yellow pneuma" (*huangqi* 黃氣 contained in the sun rays), and the ingestion of breath in the time periods marked by the six cyclical signs *xu* 戌. The ingestion of outer breath can be practiced in association with the ingestion of talismanic water (*fushui* 符水, i.e., water containing ashes of burned talismans, *FU), and with methods for circulating breath (*xingqi) or for retaining breath (*biqi). Breath can be guided to certain parts of the body or to the conduits (*jingluo), or be accumulated in the lower abdomen. One should practice between midnight and midday, the time of the "living breath" (*shengqi* 生氣), and avoid the hours between midday and midnight, the time of the "dead breath" (*siqi* 死氣). A more sophisticated method involves varying the frequency of the ingestion according to the month and period of the day.

The *fuqi* technique is first described in the *Mawangdui manuscripts (Harper 1998, 129–32) and later in the *Lingbao wufu xu (Yamada Toshiaki 1989b, 109). The main sources in which it is described are the *Yanling xiansheng ji xinjiu fuqi jing* 延陵先生集新舊服氣經 (Scripture on New and Old Methods for the Ingestion of Breath Collected by the Elder of Yanling; CT 825), the *Fuqi koujue* 服氣口訣 (Oral Instructions on the Ingestion of Breath; CT 822; trans. Huang Jane 1987–90, 1: 55–65), the *Fuqi jingyi lun*, and the "Zhujia qifa" 諸家氣法 (Breathing Methods of Various Schools) section of the *Yunji qiqian (j. 56–62). From the Song period onward, the *fuqi* technique was also used in the Thunder Rites (*leifa). The *Daofa huiyuan (100.13a–b) reports that *Shenxiao adepts should ingest the Thunder Pneuma (*leiqi* 雷氣) when they are initiated into the method of the Five Thunders (*wulei fa* 五雷法; see *leifa).

Catherine DESPEUX

📖 Engelhardt 1987; Harper 1998, 129–32; Hu Fuchen 1989, 283–86; Maspero 1981, 506–13

※ *yangsheng*

Fuqi jingyi lun

服氣精義論

Essay on the Essential Meaning of the Ingestion of Breath

The *Fuqi jingyi lun* is a key text on physical self-cultivation composed by the twelfth patriarch of *Shangqing, *Sima Chengzhen (647–735). It is divided into nine sections, describing the attainment of physical purity and longevity in consecutive steps. In addition to the complete version found in *Yunji qiqian* 57, the first two sections are also in CT 830, and the remaining seven in the *Xiuzhen jingyi zalun* 修真精義雜論 (Assorted Essays on the Essential Meaning of the Cultivation of Perfection; CT 277). Both texts contain talismans that are missing in the *Yunji qiqian* version.

The nine sections are as follows:

1. "On the Five Sprouts" ("Wuya lun" 五芽論). The Five Sprouts are the essential energies of the *wuxing and the five directions. Adepts ingest them with the help of visualization, gradually substituting them for a regular diet.

2. "On the Ingestion of Breath" ("Fuqi lun" 服氣論). To become independent of ordinary breathing, adepts absorb *qi as breath and store it in their inner organs. The immediate effect of the practice is a depleting of the body, but it soon becomes stronger.

3. "On *daoyin*" ("Daoyin lun" 導引論). Literally "exercises for guiding (energy) and stretching (the body)," *daoyin or gymnastics should always complement the absorption of *qi*. They frequently emulate the movements of animals, and serve to make the body supple, harmonize the inner energies, stimulate digestion and blood circulation, and expel diseases.

4. "On Talismanic Water" ("Fushui lun" 符水論). Talismans (*FU) aid the process by being first burned, then dissolved in water, and finally ingested by the adepts.

5. "On Taking Drugs" ("Fuyao lun" 服藥論). Drugs replace normal food, especially the five grains (*wugu* 五穀) but also anything hot and spicy, which causes the body to decay. Drugs also effect an initial depleting of the body. The text also contains several recipes.

6. "On Complying with Prohibitions" ("Shenji lun" 慎忌論). Certain states should be avoided: exertion of the body, strong emotions in the mind.

7. "On the Five Viscera" ("Wuzang lun" 五臟論). This is a theoretical

description of human physiology, relying heavily on the medical classic
Huangdi neijing.

8. "On Healing Disease through Ingestion of Breath" ("Fuqi liaobing lun"
服氣療病論). Diseases, resulting from bad energy circulation, hinder
progress. There are specific exercises to heal them: massages or gymnastics cure functional or local, external problems, while the absorption of
energy heals diseases affecting the inner organs.

9. "On the Symptoms of Diseases" ("Binghou lun" 病候論). For proper
practice even latent diseases must be eliminated. Methods are thus given
to diagnose harmful tendencies early on.

Altogether, the *Fuqi jingyi lun* gives a systematic explanation of various physiological techniques, presenting them in a lucid and well-organized manner
that allows a clear understanding of medieval practices of physical cultivation.
Many practices, moreover, are either similar to medical techniques or have
survived as *qigong* exercises to the present day.

Livia KOHN

📖 Engelhardt 1987 (trans.); Engelhardt 1989, 269–77

※ Sima Chengzhen; *fuqi*; *yangsheng*; MEDITATION AND VISUALIZATION

Gan Ji

干吉

The figure of Gan Ji (who may actually have been Yu Ji 于吉, the characters for Gan and Yu being easily confused) is most closely associated with the history of the *Taiping jing* (Scripture of Great Peace). However, the surviving records vary significantly in their accounts of his life and relationships.

Our first reference to Gan Ji comes in the two memorials that Xiang Kai 襄楷 (also pronounced Xiang Jie), a scholar worried about portents of disaster, presented to Emperor Huan (r. 146–168) in 166. In these memorials, Xiang Kai recommends a "divine book" to the emperor which one Gong Song 宮嵩 of Langya 瑯琊 (Shandong) had received from Gan Ji. Gong had himself presented the book to Emperor Shun (r. 125–44). Subsequent glosses identified this divine book as the *Taiping qingling shu* 太平青領書 (Book of Great Peace with Headings Written in Blue), a precursor to the *Taiping jing*.

Gan Ji and Gong Song appear again in *Ge Hong's *Shenxian zhuan* of the early fourth century. In the biography of Gong Song in that collection (trans. Campany 2002, 363), Gong takes Gan as his teacher during the reign of Emperor Yuan (49–33 BCE). Together they encounter a Celestial Immortal who grants Gan the *Taiping jing*. In the biography of Lord Gan (i.e. Gan Ji) himself, Gong Song does not appear. Rather, in this text Gan Ji is presented as the patient of Bo He 帛和, a medicine seller. Gan, afflicted by diseases of the skin, is given not medicine but a two-chapter long book which, Bo says, will heal his skin and grant him long life as well. Bo also instructs him to expand the book into 150 chapters, usually taken as a reference to the *Taiping jing*.

Later again, the preface to the *Laojun shuo yibai bashi jie* (The Hundred and Eighty Precepts Spoken by Lord Lao) from the fifth century at the earliest, claims that Lord Lao taught the Dao to Gan Ji during the reign of King Nan of Zhou (Nanwang 赧王, r. 314–256 BCE) and also transmitted the *Taiping jing* to him. In this version, Bo He (here named Lord Bo) has become Gan Ji's patient.

In what appears to be a separately transmitted tradition dating from the late third century, Gan Ji appears as a healer and charismatic religious leader around Wu in the lower Yangzi basin. Among his followers were members of the army of Sun Ce 孫策 (175–200), one of the military leaders who fought in the wars of the late second century. Fearing the increasing hold Gan had over his officers, Sun had him executed. A record of these events in *Soushen ji* claims that Gan's decapitated body subsequently disappeared, Gan returning to haunt Sun Ce who went mad and died as a result.

Clearly, these records are difficult to reconcile, if only because they have Gan active over perhaps 500 years. This has led some scholars to conjecture that different historical figures adopted the name of Gan Ji as a token of numinous power and that these anecdotes may therefore refer to separate people. Another approach has been to claim that the real Gan Ji lived during the second century and was simply very old when executed by Sun Ce. The references to earlier activities have thus been interpreted as attempts to grant a spuriously ancient history to the *Taiping jing*.

Benjamin PENNY

📖 Campany 2002, 301–3; Kandel 1979; Maeda Shigeki 1985a; Mansvelt Beck 1980; Fukui Kōjun 1958, 62–71

※ *Taiping jing*; HAGIOGRAPHY

Ganshui xianyuan lu

甘水仙源錄

Accounts of the Immortals Who Appeared [After the Revelation] at Ganshui

This large ten-*juan* collection of inscriptions (CT 973) related to the history of *Quanzhen was compiled by *Li Daoqian (1219–96) and bears a postface dated 1289. The title alludes to Ganhe 甘河 (Shaanxi, west of Xi'an), where *Wang Zhe first met the immortals in 1159. The author was abbot of the Chongyang gong 重陽宮 (Palace of Double Yang), the monastery built on Wang's grave not far from Ganhe, and was especially knowledgeable about the many sites of Quanzhen's holy history in the Zhongnan 終南 area. The *Ganshui xianyuan lu* is not limited to those places, however, but is representative of the order's development throughout northern China. The work opens with the canonization decree of 1269, which awarded prestigious titles to Quanzhen's founders and immortal ancestors, but the inscriptions roughly span the years 1220–80 and are concerned with the history of Quanzhen from Wang's predication onward.

The collection is a tribute to the importance of *EPIGRAPHY as an expression of Quanzhen self-identity. The order made sure that all its major monasteries had foundation stelae and all its important masters had funerary inscriptions. This is evident from several inscriptions composed long after their recorded events and explicitly written to fill a gap. This systematic approach is reflected in the structure of the book: *j*. 1 and 2 include nine memorial inscriptions for

Wang Zhe and his six male disciples; *j.* 3 to 8 contain thirty-nine memorial inscriptions for the subsequent generations of Quanzhen masters; and *j.* 9 and 10 are devoted to seventeen monastery inscriptions. Also scattered among the ten *juan* are various prose texts (short biographical notices, prefaces, and so forth), and at the end of *j.* 10 is a collection of poems written at the monastery in Ganhe. These texts, chosen to illustrate the history of Quanzhen, are by nature of their genre in open circulation, and in this regard it is remarkable that Quanzhen masters wrote only ten of the sixty-five inscriptions. The remaining authors include several eminent scholars of this period.

The attention paid to the setting of stelae and the transmission of inscriptions is peculiar to Quanzhen. Some famous inscriptions were separately edited in the *Daozang*, but the present text is, along with the contemporary and much smaller *Gongguan beizhi* 宮觀碑誌 (Epigraphic Memorials of Palaces and Abbeys; CT 972), the only anthology of this genre in Taoist literature. Li Daoqian's efforts to compile a large collection are therefore a valuable contribution to the 500-odd strong corpus of extant Quanzhen inscriptions. Although some of its sixty-five texts were also transmitted in other sources, most are unique to the *Ganshui xianyuan lu*.

Vincent GOOSSAERT

📖 Boltz J. M. 1987a, 123–24; Chen Guofu 1963, 244–46; Qing Xitai 1994, 2: 198

※ Li Daoqian; Quanzhen; EPIGRAPHY

ganzhi

干支

[Celestial] Stems and [Earthly] Branches

In the West, the artificial seven-day cycle of the week has long played an important role in structuring civil and religious time. In ancient China, a ten-day period, the *xun* 旬, played an analogous role from at least as far back as the Shang dynasty. Each day was named using one of ten characters known as the *tiangan* 天干 or Celestial Stems (see table 8). There is no consensus among scholars as to the original significance of these characters, though many hypotheses have been proposed.

By systematic pairing of the ten Stems with another set of twelve cyclical characters, the *dizhi* 地支 or Earthly Branches (see table 9), a longer cycle of sixty day-names was generated (see table 10). The first decade of the sexagesimal cycle begins with the Stem-Branch pair *jiazi* 甲子 as no. 1, and ends

Table 7

	STEMS	BRANCHES
1	*jia* 甲	*zi* 子
2	*yi* 乙	*chou* 丑
3	*bing* 丙	*yin* 寅
4	*ding* 丁	*mao* 卯
5	*wu* 戊	*chen* 辰
6	*ji* 己	*si* 巳
7	*geng* 庚	*wu* 午
8	*xin* 辛	*wei* 未
9	*ren* 壬	*shen* 申
10	*gui* 癸	*you* 酉
11	*xu* 戌	
12	*hai* 亥	

Table 7. The ten Celestial Stems (*tiangan* 天干) and
the twelve Earthly Branches (*dizhi* 地支).

Table 8

STEMS	AGENTS	DIRECTIONS	COLORS	VISCERA	NUMBERS
1 *jia* 甲					
	wood	east	green	liver	3, 8
2 *yi* 乙					
3 *bing* 丙					
	fire	south	red	heart	2, 7
4 *ding* 丁					
5 *wu* 戊					
	soil	center	yellow	spleen	5
6 *ji* 己					
7 *geng* 庚					
	metal	west	white	lungs	4, 9
8 *xin* 辛					
9 *ren* 壬					
	water	north	black	kidneys	1, 6
10 *gui* 癸					

The ten Celestial Stems (*tiangan* 天干) and their associations. (See also table 25.)

Table 9

	STEMS	AGENTS	DIRECTIONS	HOURS	ANIMALS	NUMBERS
1	*zi* 子	water	N	23–1	rat	1, 6
2	*chou* 丑	soil	NNE ¾ E	1–3	ox	5, 10
3	*yin* 寅	wood	ENE ¾ N	3–5	tiger	3, 8
4	*mao* 卯	wood	E	5–7	rabbit	3, 8
5	*chen* 辰	soil	ESE ¾ S	7–9	dragon	5, 10
6	*si* 巳	fire	SSE ¾ E	9–11	snake	2, 7
7	*wu* 午	fire	S	11–13	horse	2, 7
8	*wei* 未	soil	SSW ¾ W	13–15	sheep	5, 10
9	*shen* 申	metal	WSW ¾ S	15–17	monkey	4, 9
10	*you* 酉	metal	W	17–19	rooster	4, 9
11	*xu* 戌	soil	WNW ¾ N	19–21	dog	5, 10
12	*hai* 亥	water	NNW ¾ W	21–23	pig	1, 6

The twelve Earthly Branches (*dizhi* 地支) and their associations.
(See also tables 13 and 25.)

with *guiyou* 癸酉 as no. 10. The next decade begins with no. 11, *jiaxu* 甲戌, and continues with an offset of two in the Stems relative to the Branches. This process is continued, the offset increasing by two each decade, until we reach *guihai* 癸亥 as no. 60, and the cycle then repeats.

This sexagesimal day-cycle was used for civil dating independent of months and years, and seems to have run unbroken up to the present from at least as far back as the beginning of the first millennium BCE. Clearly any given lunar month (of either 29 or 30 days) cannot contain more than one occurrence of any given cyclical day, and so ambiguity is avoided. During the Han dynasty it also became customary to use the *ganzhi* cycle of sixty character pairs to designate a cycle of sixty years in addition to its continuing use for naming days. Because no emperor's reign apart from that of the Kangxi Emperor (1662–1722) lasted longer than sixty years, it is enough to know the name of the monarch and a *ganzhi* year-name in order to specify a year uniquely.

Christopher CULLEN

📖 Kalinowski 1983, 338–42; Kalinowski 1991, 61–65; Needham 1956, 357–59

※ COSMOLOGY

Table 10

1 jiazi 甲子	13 bingzi 丙子	25 wuzi 戊子	37 gengzi 庚子	49 renzi 壬子
2 yichou 乙丑	14 dingchou 丁丑	26 jichou 己丑	38 xinchou 辛丑	50 guichou 癸丑
3 bingyin 丙寅	15 wuyin 戊寅	27 gengyin 庚寅	39 renyin 壬寅	51 jiayin 甲寅
4 dingmao 丁卯	16 jimao 己卯	28 xinmao 辛卯	40 guimao 癸卯	52 yimao 乙卯
5 wuchen 戊辰	17 gengchen 庚辰	29 renchen 壬辰	41 jiachen 甲辰	53 bingchen 丙辰
6 jisi 己巳	18 xinsi 辛巳	30 guisi 癸巳	42 yisi 乙巳	54 dingsi 丁巳
7 gengwu 庚午	19 renwu 壬午	31 jiawu 甲午	43 bingwu 丙午	55 wuwu 戊午
8 xinwei 辛未	20 guiwei 癸未	32 yiwei 乙未	44 dingwei 丁未	56 jiwei 己未
9 renshen 壬申	21 jiashen 甲申	33 bingshen 丙申	45 wushen 戊申	57 gengshen 庚申
10 guiyou 癸酉	22 yiyou 乙酉	34 dingyou 丁酉	46 jiyou 己酉	58 xinyou 辛酉
11 jiaxu 甲戌	23 bingxu 丙戌	35 wuxu 戊戌	47 gengxu 庚戌	59 renxu 壬戌
12 yihai 乙亥	24 dinghai 丁亥	36 jihai 己亥	48 xinhai 辛亥	60 guihai 癸亥

The sexagesimal cycle of the Celestial Stems and the Earthly Branches.

Gaoshang Shenxiao zongshi shoujing shi

高上神霄宗師受經式

An Exemplar on the Scriptures Received by the Lineal Master of
the Most Exalted Divine Empyrean

The precise origins of this text (CT 1282) remain obscure but it was clearly composed in tribute to the theophany of Song Huizong (r. 1100–1125) according to the *Shenxiao teachings introduced by *Lin Lingsu (1076–1120). It opens with an account of divine revelation reminiscent of the *Duren jing* (Scripture on Salvation) central to the late fourth-century *Lingbao codification. The story told here concerns the transmission of a body of scripture from the Ancestral Master (*zushi* 祖師) to the Lineal Master (*zongshi* 宗師) and then to the Perfected Master (*zhenshi* 真師). These three deities are designated as the three masters of the Gaoshang Shenxiao dadao 高上神霄大道 (Great Way of the Most Exalted Divine Empyrean).

The Ancestral Master Yuanshi tianzun 元始天尊 (Celestial Worthy of Original Commencement; see *sanqing) of the Yuqing 玉清 (Jade Clarity) celestial realm initially appears to give voice to the "Shenxiao scriptures on the Salvation of Lingbao" (*Lingbao duren shenxiao zhongjing* 靈寶度人神霄 眾經). He then delivers them to the Lineal Master, Taishang daojun 太上 道君 (Most High Lord of the Dao) in the Shangqing 上清 (Highest Clarity) celestial realm. The Lineal Master orders the perfected residents of Shangqing to separate the text into sixty *juan*, in accord with the sexagesimal cycle (see *ganzhi). This newly organized scriptural corpus, headed by the *Duren jing* itself, was next transferred for safekeeping to Shenxiao yuqing zhen wangjun 神霄玉清真王君 (Perfected Sovereign Lord of the Jade Clarity of the Divine Empyrean). It was not to be revealed again until the Song empire had reached a zenith of peace and prosperity, at which time the Shenxiao sovereign would be incarnated as ruler of the people, that is, Song Huizong.

Like the *Shangqing corpus, the cyclical year *renchen* 壬辰 (the twenty-ninth of the sexagesimal cycle; see table 10 and the entry *APOCALYPTIC ESCHATOLOGY) demarcates the beginning of a new dispensation. Here it is said that after the Zhenghe reign period year of *renchen* (1112), the deity Qinghua dijun 青華帝君 (Imperial Lord of Green Florescence), that is, Lin Lingsu, discretely revealed the divine mandate for theocratic rule, precipitating the release of scripture. The chapter headings for a *Duren jing* in sixty-one *juan* listed here correspond to the version of the text appearing at the head of the

Taoist Canon of 1445. No evidence has yet been uncovered to indicate that the *Duren jing* in this form served as the opening text of the *Zhenghe Wanshou daozang (Taoist Canon of the Ten-Thousand-Fold Longevity of the Zhenghe Reign Period) printed in 1119. Statements in a commentary to the *Duren jing* by *Chen Zhixu (1290-after 1335) do imply that the scripture was given precedence in the *Xuandu baozang (Precious Canon of the Mysterious Metropolis) completed in 1244.

Among notable works cited at the close of this Shenxiao formulary is Huizong's commentary to the *Daode jing*, cited according to the title decreed on the *xinwei* 辛未 day of the twelfth lunar month in the sixth year of the Zhenghe reign period (16 January 1117). Conspicuous by its absence from the inventory of texts here is the collective commentary to the *Duren jing* that Huizong authorized in 1124. Additional works dating to Huizong's reign that do gain mention are ritual codes submitted by imperial order ca. 1110 by Zhang Shangying 張商英 (1043–1121). The gradual conveyance of a complete canon of secret texts in 1,200 *juan* by three hosts of transcendents is promised following the cyclical dates *renchen* and *gengzi* 庚子 (the thirty-seventh of the sexagesimal cycle). The same two dates, presumably alluding to the years 1112 and 1120, are also mentioned as a time of scriptural revelation in a commentary to the *Duren jing* ascribed to Huizong. Reference to the latter date implies that such texts emerged after Lin Lingsu fell out of favor at court in 1119 and thus are likely to have been devised by a later generation, such as his disciple *Wang Wenqing (1093–1153).

Judith M. BOLTZ

📖 Boltz J. M. 1987a, 26–27; van der Loon 1984, 39 and 134; Strickmann 1978b

※ Shenxiao

Ge Chaofu

葛巢甫

fl. 402

Ge Chaofu, a native of Jurong 句容 (near Nanjing, Jiangsu) and grandnephew of *Ge Hong, is credited in several early sources with the first transmission of the *Lingbao scriptures outside the Ge family, around 400 CE. According to the earliest of these sources, a colophon once appended to the *Zhenyi ziran jing* 真一自然經 (Self-Generated Scripture of Perfect Unity) and cited in the *Daojiao yishu (Pivot of Meaning of the Taoist Teaching), the earthly lineage of the Lingbao scriptures was: *Ge Xuan – Zheng Siyuan 鄭思遠 (i.e., *Zheng Yin) – Ge Ti 葛悌 – Ge Hong – Ge Wang 葛望 – Ge Chaofu – Ren Yanqing 任延慶, Xu Lingqi 徐靈期 (?–473 or 474), etc. Through Ge Hong, this lineage is found in the Lingbao scriptures themselves and constructed on the basis of Hong's account of his receipt of alchemical texts. Ge Hong's own writings, while they do cite the *Lingbao wufu* 靈寶五符 (Five Talismans of the Numinous Treasure; see *Lingbao wufu xu*), are entirely devoid of mention of the other Lingbao texts. Further, the Lingbao texts borrow much from the *Shangqing scriptures of *Yang Xi and so cannot have been composed earlier than 375. The impression all this gives that Ge Chaofu may have composed the scriptures himself is furthered by *Tao Hongjing who, in a note to the *Zhengao*, disparagingly remarks that "Ge Chaofu fabricated the Lingbao scriptures (*zaogou Lingbao jing* 造構靈寶經) and the teaching flourished."

Some contemporary scholars believe that only a version of what is now the first scripture in the old Lingbao canon, the *Wupian zhenwen* (Perfected Script in Five Tablets), was composed by Ge Chaofu, while others hold that his contributions must have been more extensive, perhaps including basic versions of all the texts in *Lu Xiujing's *Lingbao jingmu* (Catalogue of Lingbao Scriptures). There is no direct evidence for either opinion. Even the colophon cited in the Tang period *Daojiao yishu*, as it appears in a *Dunhuang fragment (P. 2452), ends the line of transmission with Ge Hong and the hope that there might one day be within the Ge family one "who delights in the Dao and contemplates transcendence" who might transmit the texts. This vague reference to an outstanding member of the Ge family who will make the scriptures known is found in other Lingbao texts as well. Thus, even the *Zhenyi ziran jing* might have been composed by Ge Chaofu and the more detailed colophon that mentions his name constructed later.

Given that we lack further relevant information on those to whom Ge Chaofu is said to have transmitted his texts, it seems unlikely that we shall ever be able to accurately assess his hand in their composition. The most that can be said is that circumstantial evidence, in particular the central role given in the Lingbao scriptures to Ge Xuan, seem to point to the involvement of some member of the Ge family in their creation. Taoist tradition tells us that that person was Ge Chaofu.

Stephen R. BOKENKAMP

📖 Bokenkamp 1983; Bokenkamp 1986a; Chen Guofu 1963, 67

※ Lingbao

Ge Hong

葛洪

283–343; *zi*: Zhichuan 稚川; *hao*: Baopu zi 抱朴子 (Master Who
Embraces Simplicity), Xiao xianweng 小仙翁 (Lesser Immortal
Gentleman)

Various dates for Ge Hong, ranging between 253 and 363, have been indicated
in the past, but most scholars now accept 283 and 343 as the years of his birth
and death. The main sources on his life are an autobiography in the Outer
Chapters (*waipian* 外篇) of his work (Wang Ming 1985, 369–79; trans. Ware
1966, 6–21) and a biography in the *Jinshu* (History of the Jin; trans. Davis and
Ch'en 1941; Sailey 1978, 521–32). In addition, several hagiographic collections
contain notes on his life (see, e.g., Davis T. L. 1934).

Life. Ge Hong's family, based in Jurong 句容 (near Nanjing, Jiangsu), had
provided officials to the imperial administration for at least ten generations,
and his grandfather and father had served the Wu and Jin dynasties in various
capacities. In 297, at the age of fourteen, Ge became a disciple of *Zheng Yin,
with whom he studied both classical and Taoist texts. His training ended in
302, when Zheng, then around the age of eighty-five, retired on Mount Huo
(*Huoshan, Anhui) with several disciples.

  Ge opted to remain in the secular world, and in 303 took part in the suppression of Zhang Chang's 張昌 rebellion. In the same year, however, he decided
to travel to Luoyang to search for more teaching, but rebellions around the
capital forced him to continue his journey in other regions. He finally headed
back to the south and reached Guangzhou (Canton), where he became the
adjutant of Ji Han 嵇含 (263–306), inspector (*cishi* 刺史) of that region and
reputed author of the *Nanfang caomu zhuang* 南方草木狀 (Herbs and Trees
of the Southern Regions; Li Huilin 1979). After Ji's murder, Ge stayed in the
Guangzhou area and began to work on his *Baopu zi (Book of the Master Who
Embraces Simplicity). In 312 he retired to the Luofu Mountains (*Luofu shan)
and became the disciple and son-in-law of *Bao Jing (?–ca330), governor (*taishou*
太守) of Nanhai 南海, who reportedly had found the *Sanhuang wen (Script
of the Three Sovereigns) in a cave on Mount Song (*Songshan, Henan) two
decades earlier. In 314, Ge returned to Jurong, and in 317 he received the title
of Marquis of Guanzhong 關中. In the same year he completed the first draft
of the *Baopu zi*, but the Inner Chapters (*neipian* 內篇) of his work underwent
further revision and reached their final form only around 330.

The next major event in Ge's life dates to 332 or 333. At that time, "having heard that in Jiaozhi 交阯 there is cinnabar," he asked the emperor to send him to that remote southern district. The emperor made him magistrate (*ling* 令) of Julou 句漏 (in present-day northern Vietnam), but on the way to his new post Ge was persuaded to stay in Guangzhou by the regional inspector Deng Yue 鄧嶽, and retired again to the Luofu Mountains. The description of his death bears the stamp of Taoist hagiography. In 343 he wrote to Deng Yue saying that he would "travel to distant lands in search of masters and medicines." Deng went to see him, but arrived after Ge had already achieved "release from the corpse" (*shijie*).

Ge Hong's place in the history of Taoism. Besides the *Baopu zi*, some sixty works dealing with classical exegesis, dynastic and local history, Taoist thought, alchemy, medicine, numerology, hagiography, and various other subjects are ascribed to Ge Hong (Chen Feilong 1980, 143–98). No more than a dozen of these works is extant, and only two of them may indeed have been written by Ge, namely the *Shenxian zhuan* (Biographies of Divine Immortals) and the *Zhouhou beiji fang* 肘後備急方 (Recipes for Emergencies to Keep at Hand; CT 1306).

More important, Ge Hong and his family were instrumental in the transmission of various textual corpora of the southeastern Jiangnan 江南 region, part of which he had inherited from his granduncle, *Ge Xuan. Some of these texts later became foundations of the *Lingbao school under the initiative of his grandnephew, *Ge Chaofu. Ge Hong was not a master of any of the related traditions, however. One gathers from the *Baopu zi* that his main interest was the preservation of the religious legacy of Jiangnan and its acceptance by other aristocrats and literati. This does not decrease the value of his testimony. In particular, although Ge acknowledges that he had not compounded any elixir by the time he wrote the *Baopu zi* (Ware 1966, 70 and 262), his quotations from alchemical texts have proven essential for reconstructing some features of the early *Taiqing tradition of *waidan.

Fabrizio PREGADIO

📖 Barrett 1987a; Bokenkamp 1986b; Campany 2002, 13–17; Chen Feilong 1980; Chen Guofu 1963, 95–98; Davis T. L. 1934; Davis and Ch'en 1941; Hu Fuchen 1989, 77–81; Ōfuchi Ninji 1991, 487–35 (= 1964, 67–116); Sailey 1978, 277–304

※ Ge Xuan; Zheng Yin; *Baopu zi*; *Shenxian zhuan*; Taiqing

Ge Xuan

葛玄

164–244; *zi*: Xiaoxian 孝先; *hao*: Ge xiangong 葛仙公
(Transcendent Duke Ge)

Ge Xuan is a mythological figure associated with several traditions in Taoism. He owed his preeminence to the one thing that we can reliably know about him, that he was the paternal granduncle of *Ge Hong. In his *Baopu zi, Ge Hong, who calls Xuan the "Transcendent Duke," traces three alchemical texts from *Zuo Ci to Ge Xuan, who in turn passed them on to his disciple and Ge Hong's master, *Zheng Yin, and relates several of his miraculous accomplishments. In the *Shenxian zhuan, Ge Hong provides a biography for Xuan, recounting more of his miracles and the manner of his "release from the corpse" (*shijie). He reports that Xuan was summoned to court by the Wu ruler, Sun Quan 孫權 (Dadi, r. 222–52). During this time, Xuan seemed to have drowned when a number of the emperor's boats were capsized by a severe wind, but returned several days later apologizing that he had been detained by the water-deity, Wu Zixu 伍子胥. This legend, taken together with Xuan's ability to remain underwater for long periods of time through "embryonic breathing" and his control of wind, rain, and rivers, seems to indicate that Xuan was once a cult-figure associated with water as well as the patron saint of the Ge family.

Through Ge Hong's accounts of him, Ge Xuan's legend diverged in two distinct directions. First, he became a patron of alchemical arts. Ge Hong records that he transmitted as a member of the lineage mentioned above the alchemical texts *Taiqing jing (Scripture of Great Clarity), *Jiudan jing (Scripture of the Nine Elixirs), and *Jinye jing (Scripture of the Golden Liquor), although nowhere does he mention that Ge Xuan concocted an elixir. Still, a number of later alchemical works were said to have been composed by him or passed through his hands. Later, Ge Hong's grandnephew, *Ge Chaofu, made Xuan the first recipient of the *Lingbao scriptures. The Lingbao scriptures contain accounts of his receipt of the scriptures from deities, who accorded him the title Transcendent Duke of the Left of the Great Ultimate (Taiji zuo xiangong 太極左仙公), and his instructions of his disciples, to whom he vouchsafed information on the many previous lives he had undergone before achieving the moral status to receive the scriptures. These lively accounts led to a decidedly different afterlife for the legend of Ge Xuan. Buddhist polemicists mention him, along with *Zhang Daoling, as one of the founders of Taoism, while *Tao Hongjing, editor of *Yang Xi's texts, composed a stele inscription debunking the Lingbao account.

Nonetheless, the Lingbao account of Ge Xuan endured. An anonymous preface written during the Six Dynasties' period to the Heshang gong 河上公 annotated version of the *Daode jing*, the "Preface and Secret Instructions" ("Xujue" 序訣), is attributed to Ge Xuan. This text, a complete manuscript of which was recovered at *Dunhuang, accords with the Lingbao account of Laozi, its use of the text in ordination, and its preference for the Heshang gong commentary.

Finally, the canon contains an annotated biography of Xuan, the *Taiji Ge xiangong zhuan* 太極葛仙公傳 (Biography of Transcendent Duke Ge of the Great Ultimate; CT 450), composed by Zhu Chuo 朱綽 in 1377 from a fragmentary biography that he acquired in Jiangsu. According to this biography, almost all revealed literature in early Taoism might be retraced to Ge Xuan. This biography attests to the high regard accorded Ge in later Taoism. In addition to collecting earlier sources of his hagiography, it also records the titles imperially bestowed on Ge Xuan in 1104 and 1246.

Stephen R. BOKENKAMP

📖 Bokenkamp 1983; Bokenkamp 2004; Boltz J. M. 1987a, 93–94; Campany 2002, 152–59; Chen Guofu 1963, 92–93; Kusuyama Haruki 1979, 134–38

※ Lingbao

Gengsang zi

庚桑子

also known as Kangsang zi 亢桑子 and Kangcang zi 亢倉子

According to tradition, this immortal of antiquity lived in the state of Chen 陳 (present-day Henan / Anhui) during the Zhou period. His surname was Gengsang and his given name was Chu 楚. The "Gengsang Chu" chapter of the *Zhuangzi* depicts him as an attendant of Laozi, and the *Liezi* contains a passage in which he explains the difference between sensory knowledge and self-knowledge (*zizhi* 自知; trans. Graham 1960, 77–78).

The bibliography in the *Xin Tangshu* (New History of the Tang; van der Loon 1984, 81–82) lists a work entitled *Kangcang zi* 亢倉子, which probably is the same text as the one found in the Taoist Canon under the title *Dongling zhenjing* 洞靈真經 (Authentic Scripture of the Cavernous Numen; CT 669).

Despite its attribution to Gengsang Chu, however, this is a Tang forgery composed by Wang Shiyuan 王士元. The title *Dongling zhenjing* derives from the appellation Real Man of the Cavernous Numen (Dongling zhenren 洞靈真人) that Tang Xuanzong conferred upon Gengsang zi in 742, when the *Dongling zhenjing* became, with the *Daode jing*, the *Zhuangzi*, the *Wenzi*, and the *Liezi*, one of the texts required for the state examination on Taoism (see *TAOISM AND THE CIVIL SERVICE EXAMINATIONS).

SAKADE Yoshinobu

📖 Barrett 1996, 67–68

※ HAGIOGRAPHY

gengshen

庚申

According to a belief that originated during the Six Dynasties and became widespread in the Tang period, three worms (*sanchong* 三蟲; see fig. 65) or three "corpses" (*sanshi*; see *sanshi* and *jiuchong*) dwell in the human body, the uppermost in the head, the middle one in the abdomen, and the lower one in the legs. On the night of the *gengshen* day, the fifty-seventh in the sexagesimal cycle (see table 10), these worms leave the body while the person is asleep to ascend to Heaven, and report his or her sins to the Celestial Emperor (Tiandi 天帝). Since their mission could result in illness or a reduced life span, people thought it advisable to remain awake throughout this night to prevent the worms from leaving. Three such vigils were thought to severely weaken the worms, and seven to cause them to perish, together with all illness and misfortune, thus allowing for an extension of life. People also attempted to extirpate the worms through various types of abstinence, such as refraining from sexual activity and from eating meat, or through purification and meditation.

The custom of *gengshen* was also adopted by Buddhism, and "assemblies to observe *gengshen*" (*shou gengshen hui* 守庚申會) were held from the ninth to the twelfth centuries. Under the influence of Tang China, the practice of observing the *gengshen* day also took root in the Korean Peninsula, probably from around the seventh or eighth centuries. It is unclear, on the other hand, when the *gengshen* cult arrived in Japan, where it is known as *kōshin*. Since the earliest mention of it was made by Ennin 圓仁 (793–864) in 838 in his *Nittō guhō junrei kōki* 入唐求法巡禮行記 (Records of a Pilgrimage in Tang China in Search of the Dharma; trans. Reischauer 1955, 58), it must have been known by the early ninth century. In Japan, *kōshin* observances were an occasion for social intercourse rather than spiritual abstention, and people kept themselves awake by drinking, eating, singing, and dancing. From around the twelfth century, *kōshin* was adapted as a folk belief and custom. As a result, the *kōshin* cult spread among the Japanese people, and was also consciously adopted into Shugendō and Shintō.

YAMADA Toshiaki

📖 Hirano Minoru 1969; Kohn 1993–95; Kubo Noritada 1956

※ *sanshi* and *jiuchong*; TAOISM IN JAPAN

Gezao shan

閣皂山

Mount Gezao (Jiangxi)

This small mountain, rising 800 m at its highest point, is located in the Zhangshu 樟樹 district of central Jiangxi, an area dense with Taoist holy sites. Supposedly named because it looks like a black (*zao*) pavilion (*ge*), it is the thirty-third Blissful Land (**fudi*) of Taoist sacred geography. The major temple on the mountain, attested since 712, received the name Chongzhen gong 崇真宮 (Palace for the Veneration of Authenticity) in 1118. The nearby Mount Yusi (Yusi shan 玉笥山) was also a renowned Taoist center, particularly during the Song and Yuan dynasties.

As *Ge Xuan, the putative patriarch of *Lingbao liturgy, was supposed to have lived there, Mount Gezao came to be considered the center of the Lingbao tradition, probably around the late Tang, or the tenth century. The mountain's glorious period extended from the early Song to the late Yuan, when it was included, along with Mount Longhu (*Longhu shan) and Mount Mao (*Maoshan), among the "Three Mountains" (*sanshan* 三山); these were the three ordination centers officially sanctioned by a 1097 edict for the elite Taoist clergy, providing ordinations in the Lingbao, *Zhengyi, and *Shangqing lineages, respectively (all of the three lineages being tenth- or eleventh-century innovations, complete with reconstructed patriarchal succession). Mount Gezao certainly could not rival the not far away Mount Longhu as a training center, but was nevertheless covered with well-endowed institutions, inhabited by hundreds of Taoists, and visited by ordinands and pilgrims, both priestly and lay, from all over the country.

The buildings on the mountain were destroyed during the civil wars of the late Yuan period, and the site never recovered its Song-period prominence.

The succession of "Lingbao patriarchs" on Mount Gezao continued into the Ming period, but the mountain was totally eclipsed by Mount Longhu as an ordination center, and the communities that gathered there sporadically during the Ming and Qing periods were modest. The temples have been rebuilt anew in 1991.

Vincent GOOSSAERT

📖 Chen Dacan 1988; Qing Xitai 1994, 1: 123–28

※ TAOIST SACRED SITES

gongcao

功 曹

Merit Officer

In the regional bureaucracies of the Han and the Six Dynasties, merit officers were high-ranking officials, equivalent to the Counselor-in-chief (*xiangguo* 相 國) at the court, who evaluated the service of district officers and had broad authority of promotion or dismissal. This bureaucratic title was adopted by the early Way of the Celestial Masters (*Tianshi dao) to designate certain inner deities that assist the Taoist priest (*daoshi) during rituals. As described in the *Dengzhen yinjue (Concealed Instructions for the Ascent to Reality; 3.7a–b), during the rite of Lighting the Incense Burner the priest summons from his body the Merit Officers and other gods, which transmit his requests to the deities in heaven. These gods belong to the category of "officers, generals, clerks, and soldiers" and do not permanently reside in the heavenly realm (3.22b).

Different numbers of Merit Officers are placed within the priest's body according to the ordination registers (*LU) that he receives (see *Daofa huiyuan, 181.16b). The Merit Officers appear before the priest with folded arms and wearing garments of ordinary colors. They originate from the priest's spleen and are a transformation of the yellow pneuma (*huangqi* 黃氣) associated with that organ.

MARUYAMA Hiroshi

📖 Ōfuchi Ninji 1983, 198–99

※ chushen

gongde

功德

1. merit; 2. ritual of Merit

The term *gongde* refers to accumulation of merit through practicing good and following the Dao. In particular, merit derives from the Taoist priest's reading of the scriptures and making repentance (*chanhui*), and is redirected to the deceased to bring about their salvation. Therefore a *zhai* (Retreat) ritual performed as a service for the dead is also called *gongde*.

The idea of accumulating merit is already found in the *Baopu zi*, but in this work the purpose is individual immortality rather than bringing salvation to others. The earliest rituals for rescuing the deceased through the accumulation of merit are the *Lingbao zhai* described by *Lu Xiujing (406–77), which include the Yellow Register Retreat (*huanglu zhai*) for the salvation of the ancestors. This Retreat later became popular as a rite for the dead, and the Merit ritual of present-day Taiwan continues this tradition.

In Taiwan, the Merit rituals are usually performed around the time of memorial services, which are held every seven days from the seventh to the forty-ninth day after death (including the day of death) and at the time of burial. A temporary ritual area is constructed in an open space or on the road near the mourners' house. Scrolls depicting various divinities including the Three Clarities (*sanqing*), the Jade Sovereign (*Yuhuang*), the Celestial Worthy Who Relieves Suffering (*Jiuku tianzun*), and the Celestial Worthy of Universal Transformation (*Puhua tianzun*) are hung in front of the altar, with pictorial representations of the Kings of the Ten Courts of the Underworld (Shidian mingwang 十殿冥王) on each side. In front of the house of the deceased are placed the memorial tablet, incense, and coffin (which in Taiwan usually remains unburied for one week to one month), inside what is called the Spirit Hall (*lingtang* 靈堂). The altar is the Taoist space for venerating deities, and the Spirit Hall is the family space for venerating the deceased.

Structure. The *gongde* usually last between half a day to one full day, but those performed on a grand scale can last two days or longer (see table 11). The ritual consists of four main parts: an introit, the rite of Merit, the rite of Salvation through Refinement (*liandu*), and a closing ceremony. First, the salvation of the deceased is requested through the recitation of scriptures such as the *Duren jing* (Scripture on Salvation), repentance, and rites performed within the sacred space of the altar. As a result of these requests, the deceased's

Table 11

DAY 1

  1 Announcement (*fabiao* 發表)

  2 Invocation (*qibai* 啟白)

  3 Scripture Recitation (*nianjing* 念經)

  4 Opening a Road in the Darkness (*kaitong minglu* 開通冥路)

  5 Recitation of Litanies (*baichan* 拜懺)

  6 Dispatching the Writ of Pardon (*fang shema* 放赦馬)

  7 Destruction of Hell (*poyu* 破獄) (also called Attack on the Fortress, *dacheng* 打城)

  8 Division of the Lamps (*fendeng* 分燈)

DAY 2

  9 Land of the Way (*daochang* 道場)

 10 Recitation of Litanies

 11 Noon Offering (*wugong* 午供)

 12 Scripture Recitation (*nianjing* 念經)

 13 Exorcism

 14 Uniting the Talismans (*hefu* 合符)

 15 Bathing (*muyu* 沐浴)

 16 Paying Homage to the Three Treasures (*bai sanbao* 拜三寶)

 17 Untying the Knots (*jiejie* 解結)

 18 Recitation of Litanies

 19 Filling the Treasury (*tianku* 填庫)

 20 Crossing the Bridge (*guoqiao* 過橋)

Program of a two-day Merit (*gongde*) ritual. Based on Lagerwey 1987c, 293–94.

Writ of Pardon (*sheshu* 赦書) is sent to the underworld with a rite called Dispatching the Writ of Pardon (*fang shema*). The Merit section of the ritual is performed during the day, while the dispatch of the Writ of Pardon takes place from evening into night.

During the rite of Salvation through Refinement, emphasis moves to the family space, and the deceased is symbolically led from the underworld to heaven by a dramatic enactment. By ritually breaking the walls of the underworld, the gates of hell are demolished and the deceased is released (see *poyu*). The deceased is then bathed and given a change of clothing (see *muyu*), and brought to take refuge in Taoism by paying homage to the Three Treasures (*sanbao* 三寶, i.e., the Dao, the Scriptures, and the Masters). This is followed by the rites of Untying the Knots (*jiejie* 解結; Lagerwey 1987c, 187–88), whereby mundane thoughts are extinguished; Filling the Treasury (*tianku*), for returning to Heaven what was borrowed at birth; Ultimate Purport of Salvation through Refinement (*liandu zongzhi* 鍊度宗旨), consisting of a discourse on Salvation through Refinement; and a dramatic performance based on this discourse. Finally, the soul of the deceased is made to cross the Naihe Bridge (Naihe qiao 奈河橋; see *guoqiao*) and led to the Heavenly Hall (*tiantang* 天堂).

The Salvation through Refinement section of the ritual dates from Song times and therefore is a comparatively recent tradition. The whole ritual has close connections with folk shamanic practices and Buddhism. Indeed, the *gongde* is also performed as a Buddhist ritual, with a structure very similar to the Taoist version.

ASANO Haruji

📖 Lagerwey 1987c, 169–237; Maruyama Hiroshi 1994b; Matsumoto Kōichi 1983; Ōfuchi Ninji 1983, 463–677; Schipper 1989b

※ For related entries see the Synoptic Table of Contents, sec. IV.4 ("Ritual")

Gu Huan

顧歡

420/428–483/491; *zi*: Jingyi 景怡, Xuanping 玄平

Gu Huan lived during the fifth century in South China, and died at the age of 63; for various reasons examined by Isabelle Robinet (1977, 77) his dates must lie between 420 to 428 and 483 to 491, but the dates often given of 420–83 are not actually justified by his biographies in the Standard Histories (*Nan Qi shu* 54; *Nanshi* 75). He is said to have come from a humble background but to have won such a reputation with his erudition that he was twice offered government appointments by the emperor, though he preferred to remain a private scholar and teacher, attracting almost a hundred students to his retreat in the Tiantai mountains (*Tiantai shan, Zhejiang). Although there is nothing in the Standard Histories to show that he was a Taoist priest (*daoshi), he is addressed as such in correspondence in the *Hongming ji* (Collection Spreading the Light of Buddhism) 6 and 7, and seems to have won a reputation as a master of the occult, to judge by the additions to his biography in the *Nanshi*, which coincides with the details added in the *Daoxue zhuan* (Biographies of Those who Studied the Dao) of the sixth century Taoist Ma Shu 馬樞 (see the reconstruction and translation of this text in Bumbacher 2000c, 230–33).

Today Gu Huan is chiefly famous as the author of the *Yixia lun* (Essay on the Barbarians and the Chinese), a work criticizing Buddhism, but a work on the *Shujing* 書經 (Book of Documents) is also recorded in the Standards Histories of the Tang, as are his commentaries on Laozi. The commentary now in eight chapters under his name in the Taoist Canon (*Daode zhenjing zhushu* 道德真經注疏; CT 710) cannot be that listed in the Tang as a four-chapter work, since it cites the mid-Tang emperor Xuanzong (r. 712–56); it may well date to the Song dynasty. But this compilation and other sources cite enough of his writing on the *Daode jing* (which also included another one-chapter work) that we are able to obtain some idea of his approach to the text.

Thus although *Du Guangting's description of Gu's commentary as concerned with the governance of the self implies with some justification that he was a commentator in the tradition of the *Laozi Heshang gong zhangju* (The *Laozi* Divided into Sections and Sentences by Heshang gong), in the view of Robinet it is possible to discern that the knowledge of Buddhism he displays in the *Yixia lun* was also adapted by him to the explication of Laozi. This is particularly the case with his handling of the terms *wu and you* (Non-being and Being), which would specifically seem to display a familiarity with the Sanlun 三論 or "Three Treatises" school of Madhyamaka Buddhist thought. That would not in itself be surprising, since his main teacher as named in the Standard Histories actually studied with one of the first propagators of the Three Treatises. From the Buddhist point of view, however, as expressed in the *Bianzheng lun* (6.536c), Gu Huan was part of a line of Taoist religious interpreters of Laozi stretching back to *Lu Xiujing.

T. H. BARRETT

📖 Kohn 1995a, 155–69; Qing Xitai 1994, 1: 248–50; Robinet 1977, 77–89 and 215–19

※ *Yixia lun*; TAOISM AND CHINESE BUDDHISM

guan

觀

observation

The basic meaning of the word *guan* is "to look at carefully," "to scrutinize." It appears first in a religious context as the technical term for a Taoist monastery or abbey. As such it emerged in the fifth century with the rise of *Louguan (Tiered Abbey; lit., "Tower of Observation," "Look-out Tower") as a major Taoist center and the place where the *Daode jing* was first transmitted. The word's use here, as in its later designation of Taoist institutions in general, intimates the role of Taoist sacred sites as places of contact with celestial beings and observation of the stars. (See *TEMPLES AND SHRINES, and *TAOIST SACRED SITES.)

The next religiously significant occurrence of *guan* is in a Buddhist context, from which its later meaning in Taoist meditation derives. There it occurred together with the word *zhi* 止, "to stop," "to cease," in the compound *zhiguan* 止觀, commonly rendered "cessation and insight" and used to translate the Sanskrit expression *śamatha-vipaśyanā*. The two words indicate the two basic forms of Buddhist meditation: *zhi* is a concentrative exercise that achieves one-pointedness of mind or "cessation" of all thoughts and mental activities, while *guan* is a practice of open acceptance of sensory data, interpreted according to Buddhist doctrine as a form of "insight" or wisdom. The practice is particularly characteristic of Tiantai 天臺 Buddhism, and has been described in great detail by its founder Zhiyi 智顗 (530–97; Hurvitz 1962).

Under Tiantai influence, *guan* in the Tang became the technical term for the Taoist form of insight meditation and as such is commonly translated "observation." It appears in several different combinations, the most important of which is **neiguan*, "inner observation." Described at length in the *Neiguan jing* 內觀經 (Scripture of Inner Observation; CT 641; trans. Kohn 1989b), it refers to the intentional awareness of the different parts and activities of the body, combined with the visualization of various inner gods and palaces.

In addition, the **Daojiao yishu* (Pivot of Meaning of the Taoist Teaching; 5.3b–6b; trans. Kohn 1993b, 224–28) of the seventh century makes a scholastic distinction among three sets of *guan*:

1. *Qiguan* 氣觀 (observation of energy) vs. *shenguan* 神觀 (observation of spirit), intended to designate a meditative focus on the physical rather than the more spiritual (divine) aspects of the body.

2. *Jiafa guan* 假法觀 (observation of apparent dharmas) vs. *shifa guan* 實法觀 (observation of real dharmas) and *piankong guan* 偏空觀 (observation of partial emptiness), geared to make practitioners aware of the different ways of looking at reality—its apparent, outer aspects; its real changing nature; and, at least in the initial stages, its ultimate emptiness.

3. *Youguan* 有觀 (observation of Being) vs. *wuguan* 無觀 (observation of Non-being) and *zhongdao guan* 中道觀 (observation of the Middle Way), the highest form of observation, which, based on Buddhist Madhyamaka thought, leads adepts from a vision of firm reality to one of non-existence to the acceptance of the Middle Way, an enlightened combination of the first two views.

A very similar distinction is made in the **Qingjing jing* (Scripture of Clarity and Quiescence), which contrasts *neiguan* (inner observation) with *waiguan* 外觀 (outer observation) and *yuanguan* 遠觀 (far observation), indicating observation first of the mind, then of the body, and finally of outside objects and other beings, in each case encouraging practitioners to recognize through the practice that none of the objects is really there as a firm, solid, material entity but dissolves upon closer scrutiny into emanations of the pure Dao. The practice culminates in *kongguan* 空觀 or "observation of emptiness."

Livia KOHN

📖 Kohn 1987a, 50–53; Kohn 1989b

※ *Dingguan jing*; MEDITATION AND VISUALIZATION

Guan Yu

關羽

?–220; also known as Guandi 關帝 (Emperor Guan)

The historical Guan Yu fought on the side of Liu Bei 劉備 (who claimed Han imperial descent) and his kingdom of Shu 蜀 (Sichuan) in the struggles among the Three Kingdoms during the late Han period and the following decades. He was captured by the armies of the kingdom of Wu 吳 and beheaded. Although the Shu kingdom and its generals were not very successful militarily, they became the subject of rich literary and religious traditions. Eventually, Guan Yu would be worshipped by people from all levels of society for a variety of reasons: as a rain-maker (he and his sword are often seen as the incarnation of a dragon), as a divine protector against demons, bandits, or soldiers, and even as a source of divine authority in planchette cults (see **fuji*). His cult spread largely independent of oral and written literary traditions, although people's perceptions of Guan Yu as a deity were naturally also colored by the literary traditions in which he was featured.

Apart from memorial cults, the earliest properly religious cult devoted to Guan Yu arose in Jingmen 荊門 (in a region later designated as Dangyang district 當陽縣, in southern Hubei), where he had been buried. The cult's precise beginnings are unclear, but it evidently became so popular that it was incorporated into the foundational narrative of the nearby Buddhist monastery at Jade Source Mountain (Yuquan shan 玉泉山). By the mid-Tang, Guan Yu was already seen as the divine assistant of the Tiantai 天臺 patriarch Zhiyi 智顗 (530–98; Hurvitz 1962) in building the monastery overnight in 591. However, he is never referred to as the monastery's tutelary god (*qielan shen* 伽藍神), and his shrine was located some distance from the monastery's premises.

Despite this early example, the cult of Guan Yu in Buddhist monasteries is largely a phenomenon of the late imperial period. During the Song and Yuan dynasties, his Taoist connection was more important than his affiliation to Buddhism. Like most deities of human origin, Guan Yu was first seen both as a threat (he might cause pestilences) and a helper. Early on, his cult had spread from Jade Source Mountain to his place of birth, located in Xiezhou 解州 (Shanxi). By the Northern Song, his cult was already in evidence there and in neighboring districts, spreading rapidly from the twelfth century onward throughout northern China and to a much lesser extent in the south.

A miracle involving a Northern Song Celestial Master identified by a Song-Yuan tradition as *Zhang Jixian (1092–1126) contributed much to the rise of the cult. The Celestial Master was requested by the Song emperor to defeat the demon Chiyou 蚩尤, who had been worshipped for centuries at the saltponds of Xiezhou. Chiyou had become so angry about the Song worship of his arch-enemy, the Yellow Emperor (*Huangdi), that he had made the saltponds dry up (or flood, in other versions where the monster is not identified as Chiyou). The Celestial Master then summoned the divine general Guan Yu, probably because of his personal link to Xiezhou. Guan Yu defeated Chiyou with the assistance of a huge divine army, after a lengthy and bloody battle.

This miracle somehow inspired a surprising number of pre-Ming temples in northern and southern China, and many of those in large southern cities were erected within Taoist monastic establishments. The miracle played a crucial legitimating role in the tradition of the Celestial Masters (*Tianshi dao) and is documented in both Taoist and non-Taoist sources, including Zhang Jixian's canonical biographies from the Yuan onward. Guan Yu became a prominent divine general in Song and Yuan exorcistic rituals found in the *Daofa huiyuan, and was invoked in the struggle against demons in later ages as well. Guan Yu's miracle is a typical example of the incorporation of local martial deities in Taoist exorcistic ritual traditions.

Barend ter HAAR

📖 Diesinger 1984; Duara 1988; ter Haar 2000b; Hansen 1993; Harada Masami 1955; Inoue Ichii 1941; Little 2000b, 258; Maspero 1981, 150–57

※ TAOISM AND POPULAR RELIGION

guanfu

冠服

"cap and gown"; ritual vestments

Two explanations may be given for the origin of Taoist ritual vestments (*guanfu*, or *daoyi* 道衣). The first is that they derive from the robes worn by ritual healers (*zhouyi* 咒醫) and "masters of methods" (*fangshi) in ancient

Fig. 37. Taoist Master Chen Rongsheng 陳榮盛 wears a heavy brocaded *daopao* 道袍 ("robe of the Dao") in Tainan, Taiwan (January 1979). Photograph by Julian Pas.

China, whose vestments were embroidered with patterns of flowing pneuma (*qi*) similar to clouds, as well as images of the celestial realm and the underworld. The second is that, like the system of formal clothing used to identify the nobility and senior bureaucracy in ancient China, Taoist robes indicated various ranks of priestly attainment.

When Taoist traditions were systematized during the Six Dynasties, different types of Taoist vestment were also described. According to the *Fengdao kejie* (Codes and Precepts for Worshipping the Dao; *j.* 5), priests of the *Zhengyi rank wore a yellow gown and crimson inner and outer robes; priests of the *dongshen* 洞神 (Cavern of Spirit) rank wore a yellow gown, a blue inner robe, and a yellow outer robe; priests of the *dongxuan* 洞玄 (Cavern of Mystery) rank wore a yellow gown, a yellow inner robe, and a purple outer robe; and priests of the *dongzhen* 洞真 (Cavern of Perfection) rank wore a blue gown and purple inner and outer robes (on the latter three ranks, see under *ORDINATION AND PRIESTHOOD). This system remained largely unchanged in the Yuan and Ming periods, as is evident in works such as the *Lingbao wuliang* *duren shangjing dafa* (Great Rites of the Superior Scripture of the Numinous Treasure on Limitless Salvation, *j.* 71) and Zhou Side's 周思得 (1359–1451) *Shangqing lingbao jidu dacheng jinshu* 上清靈寶濟度大成金書 (Golden Writings on the Great Achievement of Deliverance by the Numinous Treasure of Highest Clarity; in *Zangwai daoshu*).

In modern times, Zhengyi priests in Taiwan wear three types of robe. The *haiqing* 海青 ("sea-blue") is a single robe of black-bluish hues. The *daopao* 道袍 ("robe of the Dao") is a robe worn by those of middle rank, red in color with motifs embroidered on the front, back, and sleeves, such as the eight trigrams (*bagua) and cranes. The *jiangyi* 絳衣 ("crimson mantle") is a vestment of the highest rank; it is square-shaped and its basic color is red or orange. Representations of the Taoist universe are embroidered on the back: on top the constellation of the Three Terraces (*santai* 三台, three pairs of stars in *Ursa Major*), the Sun and the Moon, and the twenty-eight lunar lodges (*xiu); in the middle a nine-storied tower surrounded by dragons and cloudy pneumas; and on the hem, waves and Mount *Kunlun. The high priest (*gaogong* 高功; see *daozhang) wears the *jiangyi* for the rites of the Announcement (*fabiao), Presenting the Memorial (*baibiao), and Land of the Way (*daochang). In the *Quanzhen order, the ordinary robe is the *dagua* 大褂 ("great gown") while the formal vestments are the *deluo* 得羅 (an indigo ritual garment) and the *paozi* 袍子 ("robe"). The blue color of these robes represents the east and indicates descent from the Quanzhen first patriarch, Donghua dijun 東華帝君 (Imperial Lord of Eastern Florescence). Ordination robes are yellow, and the *taishang huayi* 太上化衣 ("mantle of highest transformation") is worn as the most formal vestment for rituals.

MARUYAMA Hiroshi

📖 Kohn 1993b, 335–43; Lagerwey 1987c, 291–92; Little 2000b, 194–99; Qing Xitai 1994, 3: 258–61, 4: 93–99

※ *gongde*; *jiao*; *zhai*; ORDINATION AND PRIESTHOOD

Guangcheng zi

廣成子

Master of Wide Achievement

Guangcheng zi is best known from chapter 11 of *Zhuangzi* (trans. Watson 1968, 118–20) as the teacher of *Huangdi, the Yellow Emperor. According to this anecdote, Guangcheng zi taught Huangdi, then in his nineteenth year on the throne, the paramount importance of preserving the body. The essence of his advice was to shut out external stimuli allowing the body to restore itself, and to maintain tranquillity and purity, not exposing the body to strain. This advice is quoted in chapter 14 of *Huainan zi* and the entire anecdote is reproduced as Guangcheng zi's biography in *Shenxian zhuan*. Guangcheng zi claims that by using these methods he has lived 1200 years.

Not surprisingly, in later tradition Guangcheng zi was understood to be one of the transformations of Laozi, although in the *Laozi bianhua jing*, an early text to explicate these transformations, Guangcheng zi is said to have lived in the time of Zhu Rong 祝融 while one of his disciples, Tian Lao 天老, was Laozi in the time of Huangdi. However, later listings of Laozi's incarnations typically have Guangcheng zi as Huangdi's teacher.

An alternate version of this encounter is told in chapter 17 of *Baopu zi* (trans. Ware 1966, 289) where Guangcheng zi's lesson for Huangdi related to avoiding snakes while climbing mountains. Guangcheng zi instructed the emperor to hang realgar from his belt which would cause all the snakes to slither away.

Benjamin PENNY

📖 Campany 2002, 159–61; Little 2000b, 177; Seidel 1969, 66 and 103

※ HAGIOGRAPHY

gui

鬼

spirit; demon; ghost

The word *gui* broadly defines spirit beings in general, as in the term *guishen* 鬼神 or "spirits and gods" (in some contexts, "demons and gods"). Traditionally, the Chinese have believed that human life is borne by two "souls," the *hun and the *po. In simple terms, the *hun* is the spiritual dimension, and the *po* the physical. Since both can be reduced to *qi (pneuma), however, there is no sense of duality between them. When a person dies, the union of *hun* and *po* dissolves, with the *hun* returning to heaven and the *po* returning to the earth. Both then change: the *hun*, having ascended to heaven, is called *shen (spirit, or deity) and the *po*, having descended to the earth, is called *gui*. The *shen* is believed to remain in heaven permanently, endowed with the spiritual power to protect its descendants, and to return to where its descendants live on the occasions of festivals. On the other hand, the *gui*, like the physical body, should have no more existence, and so it is not expected to return to this world. Therefore, *gui* that erroneously wander lost in the world are abhorred and feared as ghosts. The *po* (or *gui*) is believed to dwell in the grave, and the *hun* (or *shen*) in the temple.

The Neo-Confucian thinker Zhang Zai 張載 (1020–77), developing Wang Chong's 王充 (27-ca. 100 CE) ideas about *qi*, naturalized supernormal entities like *gui* and *shen* as the movement of Yin and Yang. Yet in doing so he did not necessarily diverge from the traditional view: "When things have just come into existence, *qi* arrives and grows day by day. When growth reaches plenitude, *qi* withdraws and scatters day by day. When *qi* comes, there is *shen*, because there is expansion (*shen* 伸). When *qi* withdraws, there is *gui*, because there is return (*gui* 歸)" (*Zhengmeng* 正蒙, sec. 5, "Dongwu" 動物). Zhang Zai thus says that *gui* is *qi* returning from here to elsewhere, and *shen* is *qi* coming from elsewhere to here. Therefore *gui* is associated with return and *shen* with expansion, as in the ancient definition, and the mutually opposing directional relationship between *gui* and *shen* is reaffirmed.

Spirits and diseases. From its inception, Taoism has had very close ties with the concept of *gui*. The Way of the Five Pecks of Rice (*Wudoumi dao), one of the earliest Taoist religious communities, was called *guidao* 鬼道 (Way of Demons) and its believers were called *guizu* 鬼卒 (demon troopers), *guili* 鬼吏 (demon-officials), or *guimin* 鬼民 (demon-people). Adepts believed sickness to be retribution meted out by spirits and gods for the offenses committed by the sufferers, who had to petition the deities to ease their symptoms by confessing their faults (*daoguo* 道過), drinking water containing ashes of burned talismans (*fushui* 符水) and making "handwritten documents of the Three Offices" (*sanguan shoushu* 三官手書), which were burned for Heaven, buried for Earth, and submerged for Water (see *sanguan).

There were three theories about the origin of disease current in ancient China. One, mentioned above, is that disease is caused by spiritual beings, that is, by the retribution of spirits and gods, or more particularly by the curses of *gui* (dead spirits). The second is the theory seen in the *Huangdi neijing that disease is brought about by the invasion of pathogenic breath (*xieqi* 邪氣) into the body. The third is a combination of the above two theories, namely that *gui* bring disease by breathing pathogenic *qi* into people. This last view can also be found in Taoist literature. For instance, the *Zhengao (*j.* 10) states that "demonic pneuma" (*guiqi* 鬼氣) attacks people from the ground when they are sleeping if their beds are not raised high enough. It also says (*j.* 7) that pathogenic *qi* that issues from graves (called *guizhu* 鬼注, *zhongzhu* 冢注, or *muzhu* 墓注) flows into particular living beings and causes disease and other calamities.

Salvation for the spirits. What does Taoism consider to be salvation for the *gui*, i.e., the dead people? According to the *Zhengao* (*j.* 15), all the dead gather on Mount Luofeng 羅酆 (also called *Fengdu), "in the north (*gui* 癸)," and there receive judgement. Those who have accumulated virtue will be drawn up from this city of the dead to the Palace of Vermilion Fire (Zhuhuo gong 朱火宮, also known as the Southern Palace or Nangong 南宮) in the heavenly realm. There their bodies and *hun* are purified and they are reborn as immortals. As shown by *Dadong zhenjing* (Authentic Scripture of the Great Cavern) and other texts, the *Shangqing school also taught that besides individual salvation, ancestors to the seventh generation could be rescued from the sufferings of hell and be reborn in the Southern Palace and the heavenly realm (Robinet 1984, 1: 170–73).

MIURA Kunio

📖 Cedzich 1993; Harrell 1974; Kamitsuka Yoshiko 1996; Nickerson 1994; Schipper 1971; Strickmann 2002; Strickmann 2002, 71–74 and passim

※ DEMONS AND SPIRITS

Guigu zi

鬼谷子

Master of the Valley of Demons

Guigu zi is traditionally known as a thinker and political writer of the Spring and Autumn period. His historicity and dates, however, are uncertain, and there is no consensus even about his name, which may have been Wang Xu 王詡 or Wang Li 王利. He was given the appellation Guigu zi because he lived in a place called Valley of Demons in the southeastern part of Dengfeng 登封 (Henan). According to *Du Guangting's (850–933) *Xianzhuan shiyi* 仙傳拾遺 (Uncollected Biographies of Immortals), "the master concentrated his mind and guarded the One (*shouyi*). He lived in simplicity, did not show himself, and remained in the world for several hundred years. It is not known what finally became of him" (Yan Yiping 1974, 1: 8–9).

A text called *Guigu zi* is first mentioned in the bibliography of the *Suishu* (History of the Sui). According to this source, there were originally two commentaries, one by Huangfu Mi 皇甫謐 (215–82) and the other by Yue Yi 樂一, who is mentioned as Yue Yi 樂臺 in the bibliography in the *Xin Tangshu* (New History of the Tang). The *Xin Tangshu* adds that a commentary by Yin Zhizhang 尹知章 also existed in the Tang dynasty. All three works are lost, and only a commentary attributed to *Tao Hongjing (456–536) has survived to the present (CT 1025).

Guigu zi has long been venerated at a popular level as the patriarch of physiognomy (*xiangshu* 相術). This association derives from a passage in the *Guigu zi* containing conjectures about the human heart, analysis of personal affairs, and prediction of the future. A work on physiognomy called *Mingshu* 命書 (Book of Destiny) appeared, appropriating the name of Guigu zi, and a commentary by Li Xuzhong 李虛中 of the Tang period also exists.

SAKADE Yoshinobu

📖 Qing Xitai 1994, 3: 70–71; Satō Hitoshi 1958; Takeuchi Yoshio 1929; Xiao Dengfu 1984

※ HAGIOGRAPHY

Guizhong zhinan

規中指南

Guide to Peering into the Center

The full title of this two-chapter text on *neidan (CT 243; *Daozang jiyao, vol. 16) is *Chen Xubai guizhong zhinan* 陳虛白規中指南, referring to its author, the Yuan dynasty master of alchemy from the Wuyi mountains (*Wuyi shan, Fujian), Chen Chongsu 陳沖素, who resided near the area's Grotto-Heaven (*dongtian). The first chapter gives a systematic nine-stage account of *neidan* practice, with each stage encapsulated by a diagram, explanatory essay, and song. The second chapter presents the "three essentials" (*sanyao* 三要) of *neidan*, discussing in refined language how to identify the mysterious locus of the body's vital energies, isolate the various components of the inner elixir, and visualize their circulation and refinement. While relying on the legacy of *Zhang Boduan (987?–1082) as the core of his commentary, Chen also quotes from the writings of the *Quanzhen master *Ma Yu (1123–84).

Lowell SKAR

※ *neidan*

Guo Gangfeng

郭岡鳳

twelfth/thirteenth century

The dates of Guo Gangfeng's birth and death are unclear, and hardly anything is known about his life. His textual notes and a final "Eulogy" ("Zan" 贊) to the

Duren jing (Scripture on Salvation) are included in the *Duren shangpin miaojing zhu* 度人上品妙經注 (Commentary to the Wondrous Scripture of the Upper Chapters on Salvation; CT 88) together with comments attributed to a Real Man of the Green Origin from Donghai (Donghai Qingyuan zhenren 東海青元真人). At the end of this work, an appendix by Guo entitled "The Efficacy of Reciting the *Duren jing*" ("Song Duren jing yingyan" 誦度人經應驗) records stories from the Shunxi, Shaoxi, Qingyuan, and Jiatai reign periods of the Southern Song. As the stories span the a period from 1174 to 1204, Guo Gangfeng probably lived between the twelfth and the thirteenth century. His notes, which are appended at the end of each paragraph or sentence of the *Duren jing*, explain its essential points to help readers grasp the general meaning of the scripture.

CHEN Yaoting

📖 Boltz J. M. 1987a, 206–8

Guo Xiang

郭象

252?–312; *zi*: Zixuan 子玄

Guo Xiang was fond of the *Daode jing* and the *Zhuangzi* from an early age, and excelled in the "pure conversations" (*qingtan*) on philosophical matters popular in the *Xuanxue (Arcane Learning) milieu. He held offices under Sima Yue 司馬越, the Prince of Donghai 東海 (Shandong). Claims that he plagiarized Xiang Xiu's 向秀 (227–72) commentary to the *Zhuangzi* have been proved untrue on the basis of quotations of Xiang Xiu's commentary in Lu Deming's 陸德明 (556–627) *Jingdian shiwen* 經典釋文 (Exegesis of Classical Texts). Gao's commentary to the *Zhuangzi* is the oldest extant and admittedly the best of all, but not necessarily the most faithful: he not only commented on the text, but also abridged it and rearranged its chapters.

Non-being and Being. For Guo Xiang, Non-being (*wu*) means nothingness; and as it is nothing, it cannot be the source of Being as *Wang Bi had maintained. In fact, Guo is one of the few Chinese thinkers who give *wu* the meaning of nothingness. He emphatically rejects the concept of *wu* as a permanent substrate: Being exists eternally, and the word *wu* merely expresses the fact that beings do not issue from anything else but themselves. In other words, each being is self-produced in a spontaneous, abrupt, and mysterious way, without any cause and without depending on anything else. Hence the word *dao* 道 does not designate anything but the supreme Non-being; the Dao is powerless. Self-being and self-transformation are the very creator (*zaohua zhe* 造化者, lit., "what informs and transforms [the world]"; see *zaohua), and beings "spontaneously obtain" (*zide* 自得) their true nature in a continuous and obscure process. This spontaneity, however, is not the action of the individual, and exists prior to the individual: one comes to existence without doing anything, and similarly dies without being able to prevent it. Spontaneity is a name for the Dao and vice versa: because we do not know the cause or the prime mover of existence, we call it *dao*, *ziran, zide, or *wu*, words that simply aim to negate the notion that there is something or someone prior to all things that makes them what they are.

The process of creation is universal and works everywhere and nowhere. It pervades everything and is the common denominator of the beings, making them all one as they "spontaneously obtain" the same Original Pneuma (*yuanqi). Thus all beings merge in this vital Unity.

The individual and the sage. Beings, however, are both plural and singular. Each has its destiny (*ming* 命; see *xing and *ming*), which for Guo Xiang is its *fen* 分, an allotment of time, wealth and capacity. It is their limit, as unavoidable as are natural laws, and is something like the negative face of their spontaneous nature (*xing* 性; see *xing and *ming*). The differences among beings and their allotments—i.e., the plurality and the individuality of beings—are due to the multiplicity of forms (*xing) and transformations (*bianhua) taken by the One Pneuma. The notion of transformation also explains the infinite and eternal renewal of life; it is a huge power that moves the world, a "daily renewal" that gives the present a high value, an eternal present always new. The natural order that governs those transformations and the relations among the various beings pervades everything. Guo Xiang's view is pantheist: the world is the Totality of the reality, existing eternally without a master, without anything exterior to it, naturally regulated by itself.

Each individual being must reach his or her limits to be complete, coincide with them, and follow the natural order without interfering. Guo Xiang's sage has a true Taoist flavor. He must practice non-action (*wuwei), and when he is involved in governing he must, in a way somehow similar to the views of the *Huang-Lao school, delegate his power to his officers, whose charges are "spontaneously obtained." But although Guo Xiang deals with political and social issues, and holds that society and rites (*li* 禮) are an expression of the natural and spontaneous order, he focuses on the acceptance of death as well as life, and on conforming to one's true nature. He sees the Confucian virtues from a Taoist point of view as the "traces" (*ji* 迹), the "operation" (*yong) of the harmony with the world that one has acquired. One must transcend them and entrust oneself to the extreme of one's limits.

The sages are diverse and multiple, and are the "traces" of the unique Truth, "that by which" the traces take form; but the saint (*shengren*) is one and lives in a mystical accord with the universe, which is the "Supreme coincidence" where he forgets himself, and where there is no inside or outside and everything is illuminated in a "mysterious fusion" and harmony.

Isabelle ROBINET

📖 Arendrup 1974; Fukunaga Mitsuji 1954; Fung Yu-lan 1933; Knaul 1985a; Knaul 1985b; Kohn 1992a, 70–80; Mou Zongsan 1974, 168–230; Robinet 1983b; Robinet 1987d; Tang Junyi 1986, 377–404; Wang Shumin 1950 (crit. ed. of the *Zhuangzi* comm.)

※ Xuanxue

Guodian manuscripts

The site of Guodian 郭店 (Hubei) was excavated in 1993, but the texts discovered in its graves were not known until 1998. The burial area contains about three thousand tombs, perhaps over one thousand of which are grouped in twenty cemeteries; Guodian is one of these cemeteries. The funerary objects unearthed there are typical of the Chu 楚 culture. Manuscripts related to Taoism and Confucianism were found in tomb no. 1, datable to between 350 and 300 BCE and apparently belonging to the teacher of a Chu prince.

Four manuscripts are especially noteworthy for the study of Taoism. Three of them are versions of the *Daode jing*, now referred to by scholars as *Laozi* 老子 A, B, and C; the fourth is a previously unknown text on cosmogony. The *Daode jing* manuscripts contain the earliest known version of the text. They are not divided into sections and follow a different sequence from that of the received versions. The various sections are apparently arranged by topic, among which self-cultivation and politics are particularly prominent. Correspondences between the manuscripts and the sections in the text established by *Wang Bi (226–49) are as follows:

1. *Laozi* A = 19, 66, second part of 46, 30, 15, second part of 64, 37, part of 63, 2, 32, 25, part of 5, part of 16, 64, 56, 57, 55, 44, 40, and 9
2. *Laozi* B = 59 (with lacunae), part of 48, part of 20, 13 (with lacunae), 41, part of 52, 45, 54 (with lacunae)
3. *Laozi* C = 17, 18, 35, 31 (with lacunae), and part of 64

Although some of the Guodian readings may be older and more authentic than those of any other received version, the manuscripts do not significantly differ in meaning. One exception is the opening passage of *Laozi* A, which reads "discard artifice and deceit" in place of Wang Bi's "discard benevolence and justice."

The manuscript on cosmogony is incomplete, and scholars have entitled it *Taiyi sheng shui* 太一生水 (The Great One Generated Water) after its opening sentence. It is the oldest known Chinese cosmogonic text. It states that *Taiyi generated Water, then Heaven with the help of Water, and then Earth with the help of Heaven. After this, Heaven and Earth together generated the Spirits and Luminaries (*shenming* 神明), which in turn generated Yin and Yang, and so forth with each couple generating another that pertains to the atmospheric level. The sequence ends with the year, after which the text returns in an inverted order to Taiyi. The final statements deal with Taiyi and the Dao in terms that show that Taiyi here is not designated as the astral god, but as the One Principle at the basis of the universe.

Isabelle ROBINET

  📖 Allan and Williams 2000; Boltz W. G. 1999; Bumbacher 1998; Henricks 2000; Jingmen shi Bowuguan 1998; Li Ling 2000b, 433–50; Robinet 1999a

guoqiao

過橋

Crossing the Bridge

Crossing the Bridge is a rite performed to allow the spirit of the deceased cross the Naihe Bridge (Naihe qiao 奈河橋) over the "River of No Recourse" that flows through the underworld, and to lead the deceased to Heaven. In Taiwan, it occurs as the final stage of the rite of Salvation through Refinement (*liandu) in the ritual of Merit (*gongde). A small bridge made of paper and bamboo and a tray of saucers filled with oil are placed on the ground at the entrance to the Spirit Hall (*lingtang* 靈堂), where the deceased is enshrined. A priest carrying the Banner for Summoning the Celestial Soul (*zhaohun fan* 召魂幡; see *kaitong minglu) steps over the bridge and the saucers three times, the mourners following him. After crossing the bridge, a figure of the deceased is placed in a sedan-chair made of paper and bamboo, and carried away. The bridge is then immediately burned.

ASANO Haruji

  📖 Lagerwey 1987c, 189–94; Liu Zhiwan 1983b, 274–306; Liu Zhiwan 1983–84, 2: 271–389; Ōfuchi Ninji 1983, 560–61; Schipper 1989b, 128–37

※ *gongde*

gushen

谷神

Spirit of the Valley

The term *gushen* can be traced back to *Daode jing* 6, where it is associated with the Mysterious Female (**xuanpin*). It denotes both an opening and the experience of the state of openness, and accordingly has two meanings. In the first, it refers to the sanctuary of the Spirit, i.e., the upper Cinnabar Field (**dantian*, also called Tiangu 天谷 or Celestial Valley) as a location similar to an open valley (Yin) between two high mountains (Yang). In the second meaning, it alludes to the Spirit residing within the upper Cinnabar Field, and to its experience of "spatiality."

When "Mysterious Female" defines the opening produced by the conjunction of Yin and Yang, "Spirit of the Valley" analogously emphasizes the order of spatiality. Indeed, the focus of this term is on the state of openness in which the Spirit is pervading like an echo in a valley: the valley merely conveys a sound without retaining it, like a mirror that reflects an image without any intention of doing so. This is suggestive of the Original Spirit (*yuanshen* 元神) that resides in emptiness, free from the contents of the discursive mind. The term *gushen* alludes to this experience of the spatiality of Mind or Spirit, i.e., the original nature of the state "before Heaven" (*xiantian yuanshen* 先天元神), which is tranquil and unperturbed and spontaneously resonates with things.

Monica ESPOSITO

📖 Billeter 1985; Cleary 1986a, 82–83; Emerson 1992; Esposito 1993, 175–77

※ *jing, qi, shen; xuanguan; xuanpin*

Guwen Zhouyi cantong qi

古文周易參同契

Ancient Text of the *Zhouyi cantong qi*

Several Ming and Qing exegetical works on the **Zhouyi cantong qi* are based on a version of the scripture that claims to be its authentic "ancient text" (*guwen*). The origins of this version can be traced as far back as Du Yicheng 杜一誠,

who wrote a commentary to it in 1517. Despite the prestige that it enjoyed in the lineages of late *neidan*, scholars from the Qing period onward have often dismissed the *Guwen Zhouyi cantong qi* (or *Guwen cantong qi*) as spurious. This judgement has in part been influenced by the controversial personality of Yang Shen 楊慎 (1488–1559; DMB 1531–35 and IC 913–15), who claimed in 1546 to have recovered its original manuscript in a stone casket and since then is often erroneously indicated as its creator.

The *Guwen cantong qi* includes the whole text of the scripture except for a few sentences. It differs from the standard version mainly in its separation of the lines of four characters from those of five characters. Moreover, the individual passages in the "ancient" version do not always follow the same order as the standard version. This rearrangement displays a clearer pattern than the hardly discernible one found in the standard version. It also reveals much, if not of the original shape of the text, about its process of compilation: many passages in four- and five-character lines mirror each other, and were likely written at different times. The altered ordering reflects a hint given in 1248 by *Yu Yan, who suggested that sections of different meter should be isolated from each other (*Zhouyi cantong qi fahui* 周易參同契發揮; CT 1005, 9.19b–21a). Textual peculiarities show that the rewriting of the text was based on *Chen Zhixu's recension.

The legendary account of the early transmission of the *Guwen cantong qi* is similar to that of the standard version: Wei Boyang 魏伯陽 wrote the main text, Xu Congshi 徐從事 (Attendant Xu, whom the *guwen* exegetes identify as Xu Jingxiu 徐景休) contributed a commentary, and Chunyu Shutong 淳于叔通 added a final section. To each of them is ascribed one portion of the "ancient text":

1. "Canon" ("Jingwen" 經文), in lines of four characters, deemed to be the main text written by Wei Boyang

2. "Commentary" ("Jianzhu" 箋注), in lines of five characters, allegedly contributed by Xu Jingxiu

3. "The Three Categories" ("San xianglei" 三相類), attributed to Chunyu Shutong

*Liu Yiming's exegesis of the *Guwen cantong qi*, dated 1799, is especially helpful in clarifying the relation between the "Canon" and the "Commentary." His annotations to the "Commentary" regularly refer to the corresponding passages in the "Canon."

The only passages of Du Yicheng's work that have survived appear to be those quoted in *Qiu Zhao'ao's commentary of 1704. Besides those of Qiu Zhao'ao and Liu Yiming, important works based on the *guwen* version include the commentary by *Peng Haogu, entitled *Guwen cantong qi*; Jiang Yibiao's 蔣

一彪 *Guwen cantong qi jijie* 古文參同契集解 (Collected Explications of the Ancient Text of the *Cantong qi*; 1614), containing a transcription of Yang Shen's statement of discovery; and Yuan Renlin's 袁仁林 *Guwen Zhouyi cantong qi zhu* 古文周易參同契注 (Commentary to the Ancient Text of the *Zhouyi cantong qi*; 1732).

Fabrizio PREGADIO

📖 Bertschinger 1994 (trans.); Wang Ming 1984g, 288–90

※ *Zhouyi cantong qi; neidan*

Haikong zhizang jing

海空智藏經

Scripture of [the Perfected of] Sealike Emptiness,
Storehouse of Wisdom

The ten-chapter *Haikong* scripture (CT 9) takes its name from the Perfected being of a Western city in a former world-system. Haikong zhizang, whose name is constructed so as to sound like a transcription from Sanskrit (possibly Sāgaraśūnya-jñānagarbha), appears as the interlocutor of the Celestial Worthy (Tianzun 天尊) in the text. The *Haikong* is widely cited in Tang and Song-period collectanea, attesting to its importance as a source of Taoist doctrine. Portions of chapters are also found in *Dunhuang manuscripts. According to Xuanyi's 玄嶷 *Zhenzheng lun* (Treatise on Discerning the Orthodox), written in 696, the scripture was composed in the early Tang by Li Xing 黎興 of Yizhou 益州 (Sichuan) and Fang Zhang 方長 of Lizhou 澧州 (Hunan), but no further information on the origins of the scripture or these men has been discovered.

As the full title of the scripture (*Taishang yisheng Haikong zhizang jing* 太上一乘海空智藏經, Highest Scripture of [the Perfected of] Sealike Emptiness, Storehouse of Wisdom of the Single Vehicle) indicates, the text appropriates Buddhist thought, primarily from the *Huayan* 華嚴 (*Avataṃsaka*), *Nirvāṇa*, *Vimalakīrti-nirdeśa*, and *Lotus sūtras*. It also draws from a number of influential indigenously-composed Buddhist *sūtras*. The "single vehicle" thought of the scripture centers on the notion that the Taoist scriptures of all Three Caverns (*SANDONG) and, as the above list intimates, all sources of religious knowledge are at base united in their goal of the salvation of all beings.

The basic concepts for which the scripture is most frequently cited are the Dao-nature (*daoxing* 道性), a Taoist counterpart to the doctrine that Buddha-nature is inherent in all beings; the "five fruitions" (*wuguo* 五果, namely, earthly transcendence or *dixian* 地仙, flying transcendence or *feixian* 飛仙, independent-mastery or *zizai* 自在, passionlessness or *wulou* 無漏, non-action or *wuwei) of Taoist practice; and the ten cycles (*shizhuan* 十轉). While the terms employed are sometimes Buddhist, the explanations differ markedly from those found in Buddhist texts.

The "ten cycles," which figure already in the *Lingbao scriptures, are ten stages along the path to merger with the Dao occurring in ten lifetimes and roughly parallel with the ten *bhūmi* of the bodhisattva path. In the *Haikong* scripture, the stages of spiritual development were charted even more closely, in response to the expanded bodhisattva path presented in the Buddhist *Huayan* and the indigenous *Pusa yingluo benye jing* 菩薩瓔珞本業經 (Scripture of the Original Acts that Serve as Necklaces for the Bodhisattvas; T. 1485). Tang-period citations of the *Haikong* show that it once boasted a fifty-two stage path, including ten stages of faith, ten abodes, ten practices, ten goals, ten cycles, and two stages resulting in the full status of Celestial Worthy. Having expounded on this elaborate path, the scripture goes on at length to deconstruct it. In the remainder of the scripture, the Celestial Worthy develops the idea that one might, through wisdom, break through chains of causation to realize one's inherent unity with the Dao.

Stephen R. BOKENKAMP

📖 Bokenkamp 1990; Kamata Shigeo 1968, 82–101; Nakajima Ryūzō 1981; Sunayama Minoru 1990, 305–24; Yamada Takashi 1999, 370–93

※ Lingbao; TAOISM AND CHINESE BUDDHISM

Han tianshi shijia

漢天師世家

Lineage of the Han Celestial Master

Three prominent Celestial Master patriarchs of the Ming are responsible for the compilation of this biographical account of the *Zhengyi lineage centered on Mount Longhu (*Longhu shan, Jiangxi). The forty-second Celestial Master *Zhang Zhengchang (1335–78) initiated the work. His son, the forty-third Celestial Master *Zhang Yuchu (1361–1410), prepared it for publication and the fiftieth Celestial Master *Zhang Guoxiang (?–1611) enlarged the text, adding biographies for patriarchs of the forty-second to forty-ninth generation to the original collection of forty-one accounts.

The first chapter of the four-*juan* copy of the text in the *Wanli xu daozang* (Supplementary Taoist Canon of the Wanli Reign Period) of 1607 (CT 1463) contains five prefaces. Zhang Zhengchang invited the esteemed literatus Song Lian 宋濂 (1310–81) to submit a preface to a *Shijia* in one *juan*. Song provides a lengthy introduction to the Celestial Master hierarchy in his preface of 1376 and traces the ancestry of the first patriarch *Zhang Daoling to *Zhang Liang (?–187 BCE), celebrated confidant of Han Gaozu (r. 202–195 BCE). Another literatus, Su Boheng 蘇伯衡 (fl. 1360–82; DMB 1214–15), composed what initially served as a postface in 1390 at the behest of Wuwei zi 無為子 (Master of Non-action), i.e., Zhang Yuchu. The three remaining prefaces date from 1593 to 1597 and are the contributions of Wang Dexin 王德新, Yu Wenwei 喻文偉, and Zhou

Tianqiu 周天球 (1514–95) to Zhang Guoxiang's expanded version of the *Han tianshi shijia* in a single folio (*yizhi* 一帙). An undated postface by Zhang Yuchu and the 1607 colophon of Zhang Guoxiang appear at the close of *juan 4*.

Zhang Yue 張鉞 (fl. ca. 1530?) of Anren 安仁 (Jiangxi) is named as collator at the beginning of *juan 2* in the text proper. He is identified as Vice Minister of the Ministry of Works, with the prestige title of Grand Master for Thorough Counsel (*tongyi dafu* 通議大夫). Immediately following this attribution is a "Tianshi shizhuan yin" 天師世傳引 (Introit to Biographies of the Celestial Master Lineage). Internal evidence reveals that this introductory tribute was authored by a contemporary of the forty-eighth Celestial Master Zhang Yanpian 張諺頨 (1480–1550).

The length of individual biographies in *juan 2–4* ranges from a few lines to several pages, with varying quantities of detail on the activities, writings, and imperial entitlements of a patriarch. By far the most difficult to corroborate are the shortest accounts for patriarchs whose lives and precise hereditary status remain obscure. Longer accounts for early descendants, such as those for the founding father Zhang Daoling and the thirtieth Celestial Master *Zhang Jixian (1092–1126), can be equally problematic due to the accretion of fictive lore from centuries of oral and written tradition.

The first thirty-five biographies may be compared with the corresponding entries in *juan 18–19* of the *Lishi zhenxian tidao tongjian*. Cognate collections of biographies extending several generations later may be found in two topographies of Mount Longhu. The *Longhu shanzhi* 龍虎山志 (Monograph of Mount Longhu) includes accounts for altogether forty-five patriarchs, with thirty-seven from the 1314 edition compiled by Yuan Mingshan 元明善 (1269–1322) and eight added by Zhou Zhao 周召 after 1445. Biographies for a total of fifty-five generations are contained in the *Chongxiu Longhu shanzhi* 重修龍虎山志 (Recompiled Monograph of Mount Longhu) that *Lou Jinyuan (1689–1776) completed in 1740 on the basis of an earlier redaction by Zhang Yuchu.

Later descendants of the Celestial Master patriarchy have perpetuated the legacy of the *Han tianshi shijia*. The sixty-second Celestial Master *Zhang Yuanxu (1862–1924) compiled the *Bu Han tianshi shijia* 補漢天師世家 (Supplementary Lineage of the Han Celestial Master) in 1918, with twelve biographies for patriarchs spanning the fiftieth to the sixty-first generation. First published in 1934 by Oyanagi Shigeta, this supplement is also incorporated into the *Lidai Zhang tianshi zhuan* 歷代張天師傳 (Biographies of Successive Generations of Celestial Master Zhang) by the sixty-fourth patriarch Zhang Yuanxian 張源先 (Taipei: Liuhe yinshua youxian gongsi, 1977).

Judith M. BOLTZ

📖 Boltz J. M. 1987a, 62–64; Oyanagi Shigeta 1934, 347–56

※ Zhang Guoxiang; Zhang Yuchu; Zhang Zhengchang; Tianshi dao; Zhengyi

Han Wudi neizhuan

漢武帝內傳

Inner Biography of Emperor Wu of the Han

This romanced biography of Han Wudi (r. 141–87 BCE) combines borrowings from and imitations of *Shangqing texts. It dates from around the sixth century and tells of the initiation of the emperor by the Queen Mother of the West (*Xiwang mu), who also plays this role in Shangqing scriptures. Although the text belongs to the genre of "inner" or esoteric biographies (*neizhuan* 內傳) inaugurated by the Shangqing movement, it combines hagiography with a literary and narrative mode, a somewhat moralistic tone, and terms and stereotypes close to those found in the Shangqing scriptures. Before its inclusion in the Taoist Canon of the Ming period (CT 292), it was edited several times in the Tang and Song periods, and published with the *Han Wudi waizhuan* 漢武帝外傳 (Outer Biography of Emperor Wu of the Han) and the *Shizhou ji* (Record of the Ten Continents), two texts with separate origins and quite different in content and style.

Unlike the events recorded in the typical Shangqing hagiographies, Wudi's initiation does not result from an initiatory journey but from visits paid to him by divinities, as was the case with *Yang Xi; the emperor's initiation, in fact, follows the pattern of Yang Xi's initiation by *Wei Huacun. The story begins with Wudi's disappointment after he had been introduced to various unsuccessful Taoist methods; Shangqing divine beings then grant him superior texts and methods. Textual borrowings, in particular from *Maojun's hagiography and the *Xiaomo jing* 消魔經 (Scripture on Dispelling Demons; CT 1344), mainly consist of hymns, invocations, and lists of drugs, and form the core of the religious aspect of the text. The *Han Wudi neizhuan*, however, being addressed to lay readers, cites only minor texts. In conclusion, this biography is propaganda aiming to prove that Wudi has been initiated into the Shangqing school of Taoism.

Isabelle ROBINET

📖 Kominami Ichirō 1975–81; Li Fengmao 1986, 21–222; Robinet 1984, 1: 229–31; Schipper 1965 (trans.); Smith Th. E. 1992, 196–272 and 479–535 (trans.)

※ Shangqing; TAOISM AND CHINESE LITERATURE

hanshi san

寒食散

Cold-Food Powder

Cold-Food Powder, also known as Five Minerals Powder (*wushi san* 五石 散), was a popular drug during the Six Dynasties and Tang periods. Its name derives from the fact that one had to eat cold food and bathe in cold water to counteract the rise in body temperature produced by the powder. According to *Sun Simiao's (fl. 673) *Qianjin yifang* 千金翼方 (Revised Prescriptions Worth a Thousand; *j.* 22), it contained five mineral drugs—fluorine, quartz, red bole clay, stalactite and sulphur—one animal drug, and nine plant drugs. It was claimed to be effective in curing many diseases and in increasing vitality, but was also said to have several side effects.

The famous physician Huangfu Mi 皇甫謐 (215–82) states that the vogue for consuming Cold-Food Powder began during the Wei dynasty with the scholar and politician He Yan 何晏 (190–249), who had used it to achieve greater spiritual clarity and physical strength. He and his friend *Wang Bi (226–49), the commentator of the *Daode jing* and *Yijing*, propagated the consumption of the drug in their philosophical circles. Many other literati, such as the Seven Sages of the Bamboo Grove (see *Xi Kang) and the calligrapher Wang Xizhi 王羲之 (321?–379?), reportedly were enthusiastic users of the drug. Like an indulgent lifestyle of alcoholic excesses, the use of this drug became the hallmark of the free thinkers of the age.

Later, especially during the Song period, Cold-Food Powder was ethically condemned and became synonymous with a heterodox ideology and an immoral lifestyle. This may explain why the name of the drug was banned after the Tang, while the use of identical pharmaceutical drugs has continued under different names.

Ute ENGELHARDT

📖 Akahori Akira 1988; Obringer 1995; Obringer 1997, 145–223; Wagner 1973; Zhou Yixin and Zhang Furong 1999

Hao Datong

郝大通

1140–1213; original *ming*: Sheng 昇 and Lin 璘; *zi*: Taigu 太古; *hao*:
Tianran zi 恬然子 (Tranquil Master), Guangning zi 廣寧子 (Broad
and Peaceful Master)

Hao Datong (Hao Taigu) is one of the Seven Real Men (*qizhen* 七真; see
table 17), the group of *Wang Zhe's disciples that was later recognized as
orthodox. With *Wang Chuyi and *Sun Bu'er, he belonged to an outer circle
of disciples who knew Wang for a brief time and acquired a Taoist education
before and/or after their conversion to the nascent *Quanzhen school. Hao
further distinguished himself in the group as a professional diviner. He was
widely recognized in Quanzhen circles as the one who had the deepest knowledge of cosmology, and he taught the *Yijing* to his fellow adepts and their
disciples.

This special competence, which provided Hao with an income all his life,
was not his exclusive focus of interest. Anecdotes about his predication to
the communities, quoted in *Yin Zhiping's recorded sayings, suggest a rather
forceful leader. Although originally somewhat scorned by his fellow disciples,
Hao went through a period of ascetic training no less spectacular than theirs:
he sat three years in meditation on a bridge, and when he was thrown off
the bridge he spent three more years sitting in the riverbed. After earning
his Quanzhen credentials in this way, he returned to his native Shandong
where he founded several communities. He had influential disciples, including *Wang Zhijin and Fan Yuanxi 範圓曦 (1178–1249), who did much to build
an extensive and powerful network of Quanzhen monasteries in western
Shandong.

Hao's exegesis of the *Yijing* appears in his collected works, the *Taiguji* 太
古集 (Anthology of Master Taigu; CT 1161). Its only received edition, very
lacunar, is found in the Taoist Canon; it includes a partial commentary to the
*Zhouyi cantong qi, a set of thirty-three charts explaining the cosmological
processes as laid down by the *Yijing*, and several *neidan poems. This sort
of speculative writing on alchemy is rare in early Quanzhen literature, and
can only be compared with two works by early twelfth-century masters, the
Qizhenji 啟真集 (Anthology of Opening Authenticity; CT 248) by Liu Zhiyuan 劉志淵 (1186–1244), and the *Huizhenji* 會真集 (Anthology of Gathering
Authenticity; CT 247) by Wang Jichang 王吉昌 (fl. 1220–40). Hao's lost works

include another anthology, commentaries to Taoist and Buddhist texts, and sermons.

Vincent GOOSSAERT

📖 Boltz J. M. 1987a, 65, 165–67; Endres 1985; Marsone 2001a, 106–7; Reiter 1981

※ Quanzhen

He Daoquan

何道全

1319?–1399; *hao*: Wugou zi 無垢子 (Master Free from Stains), Song-chun daoren 松淳道人 (The Taoist Pure Like a Pine)

He Daoquan is an outstanding example of a *Quanzhen master active at the beginning of the Ming dynasty. While the Quanzhen order lost its independence and original organization with the advent of the dynasty, its pedagogy and training methods continued to enjoy a high level of prestige among all Taoists, as is well documented in the contemporary *Daomen shigui. He Daoquan's life is mainly known through a funerary inscription, a rubbing of which is housed at the Beijing National Library, and especially through his recorded sayings, the *Suiji yinghua lu* 隨機應化錄 (Account of Induced Conversions According to Circumstances; 1401; CT 1076). The person portrayed in these sources strongly resembles the great Quanzhen masters of the thirteenth century, such as *Wang Zhijin and *Yin Zhiping.

He Daoquan was a native of Hangzhou (Zhejiang) but spent his life travelling, mostly in Jiangsu and northern China, teaching in temples and in the large Quanzhen monasteries that were still active. He died near present-day Xi'an (Shaanxi), in the holy land of Quanzhen. Besides the *Suiji yinghua lu*, he also wrote a commentary to the *Daode jing*—a rather common scholastic exercise among Quanzhen Taoists—entitled *Daode jing shuzhu* 道德經述注 (Detailed Commentary to the *Daode jing*). A Ming edition of this work, which quotes several earlier lost commentaries and is also valuable for its introduction illustrated with *neidan charts, is at the Beijing National Library, and a similar Japanese edition of the Kōka reign period (1844–48) is reproduced in the *Wuqiu beizhai Laozi jicheng chubian* 無求備齋老子集成初編 (Complete Collection of Editions of the *Laozi*, from the Wuqiu beizhai Studio; First Series; Taipei: Yiwen yinshuguan, 1965).

The *Suiji yinghua lu* is one of the liveliest "recorded sayings" (*yulu) in the Taoist Canon, since it focuses, as the title suggests, on the interaction between master and disciples. Among the latter, many happen to be Buddhist monks. No matter who questions He Daoquan, he seems ready to discuss anything, from Buddhist and Confucian notions to music and medicine. His answers are sometimes didactic, sometimes playful or puzzling. In several instances, the whole discussion is recorded in verse, illustrating the importance of poetry in Taoist pedagogy. Although prone to attributing a purely spiritual and ethical meaning to the various technical concepts of alchemy, He nevertheless set great store by traditional Quanzhen ascetic exercises, such as confinement in the *huandu or the *zuobo meditation.

Vincent GOOSSAERT

※ Quanzhen

He Zhizhang

賀知章

659–744; *zi*: Jizhen 季真; *hao*: Siming Kuangshuai 四明狂帥
(Insane Commander from Siming)

He Zhizhang (*jinshi* 695) is generally remembered as a poet: he was one of Du Fu's 杜甫 (712–70) "Eight Immortals of the Winecup" (*yinzhong baxian* 飲中八仙) and the originator of his friend Li Bai's 李白 (701–62) famous byname, "Banished Immortal" (*zhexian* 謫仙). In the Standard Histories, however, He appears primarily as a statesman, whose fifty-year career spanned numerous posts (*Jiu Tangshu*, 15.5033–35; *Xin Tangshu*, 18.5606–7). In 725/726, Tang Xuanzong (r. 712–56) sought his advice about performing the imperial *feng* 封 ceremony. Despite a brief scandal concerning mismanagement of an imperial funeral, He was soon elevated to noble rank and charged with supervising Xuanzong's heir, the future Tang Suzong (r. 756–62). At the age of eighty-five, He received permission to retire, took ordination as a *daoshi, and returned to his native village. He soon died, and was lauded in a memorial edict by Suzong.

Despite his solid record of government service, and enduring admiration for his calligraphy, the Standard Histories portray He as an eccentric, whom contemporaries called "Crazy Zhang." They depict his late-life decision to retire and take ordination as having resulted from a dream (*Xin Tangshu*) or a mental disorder (*Jiu Tangshu*). The *Xin Tangshu* adds that he asked that a palace lake be converted into a pond for liberating living beings (*fangsheng* 放生).

Although He's writings and numerous biographies reveal no other Taoist activities before his retirement, he appears as a character in several later Taoist texts. The *Taiping guangji* 太平廣記 (Extensive Records of the Taiping Xingguo Reign Period; 978; *j.* 42) describes him as a man who learns moral and spiritual lessons. In Jia Shanxiang's 賈善翔 *Gaodao zhuan* 高道傳 (Biographies of Eminent Taoists; ca. 1086), he is said to have retired after having received an elixir from a mysterious Elder. Based on that story, a thirteenth-century local history presents him as a seller of drugs who lived hundreds of years, then "ascended to immortality."

Russell KIRKLAND

📖 Kirkland 1989; Kirkland 1992b; Kirkland 1992–93, 160–65

※ TAOISM AND THE STATE

Hebo

河伯

Count of the River

Hebo is the deity who controls the Yellow River. His surname is Ping 馮 (or Bing 冰) and his given name Yi 夷, or variously, his surname is Lü 呂 and his given name Gongzi 公子. Some sources say that Ping Yi 馮夷 is his wife.

The Hebo myth has a long history. The *Zhushu jinian* 竹書紀年 (Bamboo Annals; originally ca. 300 BCE) contains the story of a fight between Hebo and Luobo 洛伯, deity of the Luo River. In the *Mu tianzi zhuan* 穆天子傳 (Biography of Mu, Son of Heaven; trans. Mathieu 1978, 17), the mountains of Yangyu 陽紆 (sometimes identified as a place in Shaanxi) are identified as Hebo's capital, while in the *Shanhai jing* 山海經 (Scripture of Mountains and Seas; trans. Mathieu 1983, 492) it is said to be an abyss three hundred fathoms deep and wide. Hebo is portrayed there in human form, riding two dragons. In the *Tianwen* 天問 (Heavenly Questions) poem of the *Chuci* 楚辭 (Songs of Chu; trans. Hawkes 1985, 122–51) there is a verse that asks, "Why did Yi shoot Hebo and take the goddess of the River Luo to be his wife?" The commentator Wang Yi 王逸 (second century CE) cites the tale about when Hebo, having taken the form of a white dragon, was frolicking on the banks of the river, when Yi 羿 the Archer saw him and shot him in the left eye.

The biography of Hua Ji 滑稽 in the *Shiji* (Records of the Historian; *j.* 126) refers to another episode involving Hebo that took place during the Warring States period. It was an annual custom in the town of Ye 鄴 in the state of Wei 魏 (Henan) to throw a beautifully adorned young girl into the river to become the bride of Hebo. Ximen Bao 西門豹, however, who had become the magistrate of Ye, devised a plan to bring this evil custom to an end. This story suggests that Hebo was originally a fearful deity who demanded human sacrifice. In later times, it was said that Ping Yi became Hebo after ingesting an elixir, and entered the Way of the Immortals.

YOSHIKAWA Tadao

※ TAOISM AND CHINESE MYTHOLOGY

Heisha

黑煞 (or: 黑殺)

Black Killer

The Black Killer is the divine protector of the Song dynasty, who was canonized as Yisheng jiangjun 翊聖將軍 (General Assisting Sanctity) in 981, and as Yisheng baode zhenjun 翊聖保德真君 (Perfected Lord Assisting Sanctity and Protecting Virtue) in 1014. The god had first appeared in the Zhongnan mountains (Zhongnan shan 終南山, Shaanxi) in the period 960–64, when he began to speak through a man called Zhang Shouzhen 張守真, who was later ordained as a Taoist and established a temple at the place where he received these revelations. The earliest accounts suggest that the god had originally presented himself as the Black Killer General (Heisha jiangjun 黑煞將軍), a name that is suppressed in the official biography of the god, the *Yisheng baode zhuan* (Biography of [the Perfected Lord] Assisting Sanctity and Protecting Virtue) by *Wang Qinruo, presented at court in 1016.

The figure of the Black Killer General is widespread in Song-period traditions of exorcism, and especially in the texts of the *Tianxin zhengfa, where Heisha is referred to as the "talismanic agent of the Mysterious Warrior" (*Xuanwu fushi* 玄武符使), i.e., of the power of the north. In fact, the Black Killer Talisman (*Heisha fu* 黑煞符), described in the *Shangqing tianxin zhengfa* 上清天心正法 (CT 566, 3. 5b–7a), is one of the three talismans that are considered fundamental within the Tianxin zhengfa (see fig. 73). It has the form of a small black figure with bare feet and disheveled hair, holding a sword or metal whip in the left hand, and high in the right hand, the token of the command of the god of heaven, Ziwei dadi 紫微大帝 (Great Emperor of Purple Tenuity), in the shape of the character *chi* 敕 ("imperial decree"). This image (though without the character *chi*) closely resembles not only the general appearance of spirit mediums (*shentong* 神童) with whom Taoist practitioners are known to have collaborated during the Song, but also that of the god of the northern sky, *Zhenwu (Perfected Warrior), who sometimes replaces Heisha in descriptions of the aforementioned basic talisman.

In the eleventh century, the Assisting Saint was joined with Zhenwu (canonized as the Helping Saint, Yousheng 佑聖), and two "semi-Tantric" deities, Tianpeng 天蓬 and Tianyou 天猷, to form the powerful group of the "Four Saints" (*sisheng* 四聖).

Poul ANDERSEN

   📖 Andersen 1991, 125–26; Davis E. 2001, 67–86; Little 2000b, 291–311; Major 1985–86

   ※ *Yisheng baode zhuan*; Tianxin zhengfa; DEITIES: THE PANTHEON

Heming shan

鶴鳴山

Mount Heming (Sichuan)

Two mountains in Sichuan are referred to as Heming shan. One of them is located in Jiange 劍閣 district; the other, to which the present entry is devoted, is about 125 km west of Chengdu in Dayi 大邑 district. The mountain is 900 m high and has two main peaks that are separated by a smaller hill. As noted by Stephen R. Bokenkamp (1997, 227), the name Heming (lit., "Crane-Call") derives from the popular legend that the two peaks are the wings of a crane, and the hill is the crane's head. Another tradition reports that there is a stone crane on the mountain, and when it calls transcendents emerge. The mountain is also known as Quting shan 渠亭山 (Mountain of the Moated Pavilion), a name that, as Bokenkamp suggests, may derive from the fact that one of its temples resembled a pavilion encircled by two streams.

Mount Heming is best known for its associations with *Zhang Daoling, who was visited there by the deified Laozi in 142 CE. Since then, this mountain has been closely connected with the Way of the Celestial Masters (*Tianshi dao) and was considered one of its twenty-four parishes (*zhi). Mount Heming is also associated with the activities of *Du Guangting (850–933) and the semilegendary *Zhang Sanfeng. Moreover, as remarked by Judith M. Boltz (1987a, 35), some sources trace the origins of the *Tianxin zhengfa (Correct Method of the Celestial Heart) to Mount Heming rather than to Mount Huagai (Huagai shan 華蓋山) in Jiangxi.

James ROBSON

   📖 Nara Yukihiro 1998, 317

   ※ TAOIST SACRED SITES

Hengshan

衡山

Mount Heng (Hunan)

Hengshan is the name of a mountain range that runs parallel to the Xiang 湘 River in Hunan province. This mountain has a long history of importance for both Taoists and Buddhists. While Hengshan is referred to as a single mountain, its sacred purlieu is traditionally said to include seventy-two peaks, of which five are given special significance. The main peak, Zhu Rong feng 祝融峰, whose name comes from an ancient fire deity, rises to a height of 1,290 meters. The four other main peaks are Zigai feng 紫蓋峰, Yunmi feng 雲密峰, Shilin feng 石廩峰, and Tianzhu feng 天柱峰. Although descriptions of the Hengshan range include sites as far north as the Yuelu feng 嶽麓峰 (Hill of the Peak, near modern Changsha 長沙), the main center of religious activity was concentrated on the peaks west of the modern city of Hengshan.

In early texts like the *Shijing* 詩經 (Book of Odes) and the *Erya* 爾雅 (Literary Lexicon), Hengshan is identified as the Southern Peak (*Nanyue) in the Five Peaks classification system (*wuyue*). Yet in some early texts *Huoshan is also identified as the Southern Peak, resulting in confusion over the location of the Southern Peak. During the reign of Han Wudi (r. 141–87 BCE) the designation "Southern Peak" was shifted from Hengshan (Hunan) to Mount Tianzhu (Tianzhu shan 天柱山, Anhui; also called Huoshan), where rituals directed to the Southern Peak were performed. During the reign of Sui Yangdi (r. 604–17) Hengshan was officially restored as the Southern Peak.

In the Tang period, Hengshan was home to an important lineage of *Shangqing Taoists that descended from *Sima Chengzhen, but was collateral to the better-known lineage connected to *Li Hanguang. The main figures in what Franciscus Verellen has called "the Masters of Hengshan" include Xue Jichang 薛季昌 (?–759), Tian Liangyi 田良逸 (ninth century), and Feng Weiliang 馮惟良 (ninth century; Verellen 1989, 20–21 and Sunayama Minoru 1990, 412).

After Hengshan's role as the Southern Peak was solidified, it also came to serve as an important site in the veneration of *Wei Huacun (Nanyue Wei furen 南嶽魏夫人). Taoism at Hengshan received particular support and imperial patronage during the reign of Song Huizong (r. 1100–1125), and in the eleventh and twelfth centuries Hengshan was connected to the expanding

cult of *Lü Dongbin. In recent years many of the Taoist abbeys at Hengshan
have undergone extensive renovation.

James ROBSON

📖 Boltz J. M. 1987a, 109–10; Despeux 1990, 56–60; Qing Xitai 1994, 4: 149–53;
Robson 1995; Schafer 1979

※ Nanyue; *wuyue*; TAOIST SACRED SITES

Hengshan

恆山

Mount Heng (Shanxi)

Mount Heng is the Northern Peak (see under *wuyue*), and as such has been
considered a sacred mountain in both the official cult and Chinese religion
generally since the Zhou period. It is located near the present seat of Hunyuan
渾源 district in northern Shanxi, not far south of Datong 大同. It rises slightly
higher than 2,000 m and offers beautiful scenery, with forests and deep gorges
overlooking a rather dry plain.

Like other sacred peaks, Mount Heng had a temple for the god of the
mountain built on its slopes during the Han period, which survives with an
uninterrupted history until the present time. This temple, now called Beiyue
miao 北嶽廟 (Shrine of the Northern Peak) and also locally known as Chaodian
朝殿 (Audience Hall), is built on degrees on the mountain slope. Like a few
other adjoining temples, it was and still is staffed by a modest community of
*Quanzhen clerics. The most famous and visited site, however, is not Taoist
but Buddhist: it is the Suspended Monastery (Xuankong si 懸空寺), built on
stilts in the middle of a cliff, about two kilometers downhill from the Beiyue
miao.

Although Mount Heng has a documented history of cults and Taoist activity,
it does not compare to the other four peaks in terms of nationwide religious
importance. It was never a major pilgrimage destination nor a clerical training center. The Northern Peak also suffered from adverse political conditions.
As it was several times in history, notably during the Liao dynasty (916–1125),
under the control of another regime, "Chinese" dynasties that needed the
cult to the Five Peaks for political legitimization used a replacement site for
sacrifices to the Northern Peak, some 150 km southeast of Mount Heng, in
Song-controlled territory. The temple built there, the Beiyue miao in Quyang

曲陽 (Hebei), was later also maintained as supernumerary, and is famous for
its Yuan-period architecture and murals.

Vincent GOOSSAERT

📖 Geil 1926, 295–344; Steinhardt 1998

※ *wuyue*; TAOIST SACRED SITES

heqi

合氣

1. "merging pneumas," "union of breaths";
2. harmonization of vital energy

Heqi is a ritual attested in the context of the early Way of the Celestial Masters
(*Tianshi dao). It presumably involved the ritual intercourse of non-married
people to ensure the continued positive interaction of Yin and Yang in the
cosmic rhythm, and also—in a clear violation of conventional mores—to
bind members more closely to the community. Sources on *heqi* are scarce for
obvious reasons, the only descriptions remaining in anti-Taoist polemics of
the sixth and seventh centuries. Some information on the complex cosmological calculations that went into the practice was contained originally in
the *Huangshu* 黃書 (Yellow Writ), traces of which survive in the *Shangqing
huangshu guodu yi (Liturgy of Passage of the Yellow Writ of Highest Clarity)
and the *Dongzhen huangshu* 洞真黃書 (Yellow Writ of the Cavern of Perfection;
CT 1343).

The latter in particular presents charts and lists of auspicious dates for the
practice of sexual intercourse. It explains the relationship of Yin and Yang in
terms of the Stems and Branches (*ganzhi) of the traditional Chinese calendar
(especially the six *jia*; see *liujia and *liuding*); the Five Phases (*wuxing) and the
twenty-four energy nodes (*jieqi* 節氣) of the year; the Nine Palaces (*jiugong)
in the sky and the eight trigrams (*bagua) of the *Yijing; and the various gods
residing in the human body. In addition, the text specifies gymnastics (*daoyin),
massages, concentration exercises, and visualizations to be undertaken before
sexual practice and emphasizes the efficacy of the techniques to dissolve bad
fortune and extend life. The ritual intercourse of the early group clearly was
later transformed into an interiorized practice that composes part of the
longevity arsenal of Taoist followers.

Livia KOHN

📖 Bokenkamp 1997, 44–46; Despeux 1990, 29–31; Kobayashi Masayoshi 1992, 27–31; Maspero 1981, 386–88 and 533–41; Yan Shanzhao 2001

※ *Shangqing huangshu guodu yi*; Tianshi dao

Hetu and *Luoshu*

河圖 · 洛書

Chart of the [Yellow] River and Writ of the Luo [River]

According to legend, the *Hetu* emerged from the Yellow River on the back of a "dragon-horse" (*longma* 龍馬) during the reign of the legendary emperor Fu Xi 伏羲. Similarly, the *Luoshu* came out of the Luo River on the back of a turtle. Several early texts—including the *Shujing* 書經 (Book of Documents), the *Lunyu* 論語 (Analects) of Confucius, the *Mozi* 墨子 (Book of Master Mo), and the *Zhuangzi—allude to these documents, but nothing is known of their original forms. They were believed to be diagrams that illustrated the cosmos and gave clues for its ordering, and that helped the mythical emperor Yu 禹 to drive out the flood and delineate the nine regions of the world. The *Xici* 繫辭 (Appended Statements, a portion of the *Yijing) relates them to the four main trigrams, and the Han "weft texts" (*weishu* 緯書; see *TAOISM AND THE APOCRYPHA) were supposed to explain them. All this is related to the synthesis of different systems of reference points for space and time attempted by the cosmologists.

In a Taoist milieu, the *Hetu* and *Luoshu* are mentioned in a text as early as the *Taiping jing (Scripture of Great Peace). Later, the two diagrams were related to numerology and to speculations based on the system of the *Yijing*. Their transmission to Confucianism, together with the *Xiantian tu* 先天圖 (Diagram of the Noumenal World) and the *Wuji tu* 無極圖 (Diagram of the Ultimateless), seems to have occurred though the intermediation of *Chen Tuan (see *Taiji tu). They were first propagated by cosmologists and numerologists such as *Shao Yong (1012–77), Liu Mu 劉牧 (1011–64), and Zhu Zhen 朱震 (1072–1138), and then by Zhu Xi 朱熹 (1130–1200). There seems, however, to be a difference between how Taoists and Neo-Confucians understood the two diagrams to be related to the configuration of the cosmos. Some early Taoist texts belonging to the *Shangqing revelation relate the *Hetu* to the Northern Dipper (*beidou) and the Nine Palaces (*jiugong), i.e., to the figure 9, which the Neo-Confucians related instead to the *Luoshu*. In fact, the connection of the *Hetu* and the *Luoshu* with magic squares appears in Taoist texts relatively late, mainly with Song rituals, perhaps because of the wide circulation they had acquired by that time.

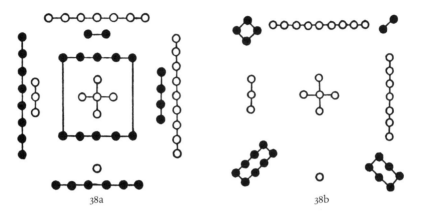

Fig. 38. (a) *Hetu* (Chart of the [Yellow] River). (b) *Luoshu* (Writ of the Luo [River]).

The Luoshu magic square. The so-called *Luoshu* magic square, also known as the "magic square of three" or as the arrangement of the Nine Palaces, is older than the magic square based on the *Hetu*. The first specific reference to it appears in the *Da Dai liji* 大戴禮記 (Records of Rites of the Elder Dai), probably compiled in the early second century CE (Riegel 1993). This magic square played a prominent role in the cult of the Great One (*Taiyi) and in a divination system that grew out of it. In Taoism, this square is first found in the *Shangqing huangshu guodu yi (Liturgy of Passage of the Yellow Writ of Highest Clarity), dating from no later than the fifth century, where it is related to a liturgical cult of sexual union practiced by the school of the Celestial Masters (*Tianshi dao), and later in the *Kaitian jing (Scripture of the Opening of Heaven). In both instances it is related to the cosmicization of the body, but there is no explicit mention of the *Luoshu*.

The "magic square of three" assigns the numbers 1 to 9 to each of the eight cardinal points and the center, in such a way that the odd (celestial, Yang) numbers are on the four cardinal points, the even (earthly, Yin) numbers are in the intermediary points (the "gates" of the world), and the number 5 is in the center. The sum of the numbers in the vertical, horizontal, and diagonal directions is always 15:

$$
\begin{array}{ccc}
4 & 9 & 2 \\
3 & 5 & 7 \\
8 & 1 & 6
\end{array}
$$

In Taoism, this arrangement is mainly used for the practice of *bugang ("walking along the guideline"), and is still associated with the cosmicization of the body in present-day rituals. It has many different titles, mainly referring to the Nine Palaces or to *bugang*, not to the *Luoshu*. At least one *Quanzhen text relates this arrangement to the *Hetu* and the **houtian* arrangement of the trigrams (*Baoyi hansan bijue* 抱一函三祕訣; CT 576, 3a–b). *Lei Siqi (1231–1301?) also relates it to the *Hetu* and strongly criticizes Chen Tuan, who instead associates it with the *Luoshu* (*Yitu tongbian* 易圖通變; CT 1014, 1.1a–2b and 4.1a–3a).

The Hetu magic square. This square arranges the numbers so that they form a cross, or three concentric squares:

This arrangement highlights the center and distinguishes between the "generative" numbers (*sheng* 生, from 1 to 5) and "performative" ones (*cheng* 成, from 6 to 10), with the number 5, representing the center, being the axis between them. It emphasizes the verticality of the upright (*zheng* 正) pillar of the world, while the *Luoshu* arrangement forms an oblique cross. This square does not seem to have been used in ritual. **Neidan* alchemists, however, refer to it probably because it is more directly linked with the "maturation" (*cheng*) of numbers. It assigns the numbers 3 to Wood/East and 2 to Fire/South, and the numbers 4 to Metal/West and 1 to Water/North, so that the sum of the numbers of the Yin agents and the Yang agents is 5. With the center, also represented by the number 5, these form the "Three Fives" in the alchemical process (see **sanwu*).

Isabelle ROBINET

Cammann 1961; Cammann 1962; Granet 1934, 177–208; Kamitsuka Yoshiko 1999, 379–85; Lagerwey 1987c, 126–34; Major 1984; Needham 1959, 55–62; Robinet 1995b; Saso 1978c; Seidel 1983a

※ COSMOLOGY; NUMEROLOGY; TAOISM AND NEO-CONFUCIANISM

Hong'en zhenjun

洪恩真君

Real Lords of Overflowing Mercy

The Real Lords of Overflowing Mercy, also known as Real Lords of Overflowing Mercy and Numinous Deliverance (Hong'en lingji zhenjun 洪恩靈

濟真君), are the brothers Xu Zhizheng 徐知證 and Xu Zhi'e 徐知諤 (both fl. 937–46). In the human world they held official posts in several regions and prefectures. According to the *Lingji gong bei* 靈濟宮碑 (Stone Tablet of the Palace of Numinous Deliverance), written by the Yongle Emperor in 1417, during their lifetimes "they displayed clemency and consideration for all things, loyalty to their superiors, and filiality toward their elders; they held the Three Treasures (*sanbao* 三寶) in high esteem, unanimously loved the good, attained the Dao through skillful diligence, cultivated abstinence, and offered ceremonies on behalf of souls in purgatory." For their services to the province of Wu 吳 (Jiangsu and part of Zhejiang) they were ennobled: Xu Zhizheng was given the title King of the Yangzi River (Jiangwang 江王), and Xu Zhi'e received the title Bountiful King (Raowang 饒王). Because of their meritoriousness, people called them the Father and Mother of Rebirth (Fusheng fumu 復生父母).

The two brothers feature in many popular stories. For instance, after their death rumors spread that during a battle, when the water in the capital had been depleted, they ascended to the Celestial Palace and came back down to earth to secretly protect the people, and saved them from floods and droughts, fires and locust plagues, illnesses and wars. According to the *Hong'en lingji zhenjun shishi* 洪恩靈濟真君事實 (The True Story of the Real Lords of Overflowing Mercy and Numinous Deliverance; CT 476), in the Yongle reign period (1403–24) of the Ming dynasty, when the emperor had been unable to govern for a long time due to illness, in a dream he received the protection of the two divinities, who bestowed upon him the elixir of immortality and miraculous remedies. After the emperor had recovered from his illness, he granted the Real Lords of Overflowing Mercy additional honorific titles and erected the Lingji gong 靈濟宮 (Palace of Numinous Deliverance) in the capital where ceremonies were offered to them.

Among other works related to the two brothers is the *Hong'en lingji zhenjun zhaiyi* 洪恩靈濟真君齋儀 (Liturgies for the Retreat of the Real Lords of Overflowing Mercy and Numinous Deliverance), included in the Taoist Canon as eight separate texts (CT 468 to CT 475). The purpose of each of the ceremonies described in these texts was to request protection and support from the Real Lords of Overflowing Mercy—to pray that the domain of the ruling house be permanently fixed, that the emperor have a long life, and that wealth be bestowed upon the ruling family, the nobles, the various regions and all people throughout the empire.

In 1420, the emperor wrote a preface to the *Hong'en lingji zhenjun miaojing* 洪恩靈濟真君妙經 (Wondrous Scripture on the Real Lords of Overflowing Mercy and Numinous Deliverance; CT 317). For this reason, the Real Lords of Overflowing Mercy must be considered Taoist divinities that enjoyed the unwavering and public support of the Ming emperor. After the Ming dynasty, ceremonies to the Real Lords of Overflowing Mercy were rarely offered and then only in some regional Taoist temples.

CHEN Yaoting

📖 Boltz J. M. 1987a, 52–53, 91–93, 195–97

※ TAOISM AND POPULAR RELIGION

Hongming ji

弘明集

Collection Spreading the Light of Buddhism

The *Hongming ji* is an anthology of apologetic literature defending Buddhism against its critics. It was put together ca. 507–14 under the Liang dynasty in south China by the monk bibliographer Sengyou 僧祐 (?–518), and now occupies fourteen chapters in the Taishō Canon (T. 2102). Sengyou appends his own retrospective essay classifying the main arguments against Buddhism under six headings: that its scriptures are wildly exaggerated; that it depends on the unverifiable concept of *karma* in past and future; that it is of no practical political value; that it formed no part of classical Chinese civilization; that its foreign origins make it unsuitable for China; and that it only started to succeed when China became severely weakened.

Since Taoists were among the most dedicated critics of Buddhism, it is naturally possible to learn much about the rival religion from this Buddhist source: Taoist scriptures are sometimes mentioned, and several Taoist polemical essays, such as the **Yixia lun* (Essay on the Barbarians and the Chinese), are quoted *in extenso* as part of opponents' refutations. Where no other text is available, however, evidence that Sengyou made a number of editorial excisions in his anthology should be taken into account, though some or all of these may be due to one of his sources, an earlier, more general anthology by Lu Cheng 陸澄 (425–94) entitled *Falun* 法論 (Essays on the Dharma). Sengyou's work was done in a part of China where Buddhism had not been subjected to intensive persecution, and where the main arguments against Buddhism on intellectual grounds were failing to undermine imperial support for the religion; this situation was to change radically by the time of the compilation of the "Expanded" version, the *Guang hongming ji* 廣弘明集.

This later collection amounts to thirty chapters in the Taishō Canon edition (T. 2103). It includes some additional early writings and much that was written after Sengyou's time, and was put together by Daoxuan 道宣 (596–667), who lived under the Tang, a basically North Chinese regime of a type that had not hesitated to persecute Buddhism in the past. He also lived at a time when the Taoist religion had reached new levels of organization and doctrinal sophistication—to no small degree by learning from Buddhism—so that its appeal as an imperial cult, especially to a dynasty which fancied itself descended from Laozi, assumed a far greater menace. Accordingly Taoist opponents and Taoist literature loom much larger in the *Guang hongming ji*. Since, however, elsewhere Daoxuan does not hesitate to appeal to miracles and even revelations as well as intellectual argument in order to defeat his opponents, here, even more than in Sengyou's work, it is pointless to look for an objective account of Taoism.

These two collections have been in the Buddhist canon since Tang times, and so are covered by its separate phonological commentaries. Rather than being any larger in terms of content, the forty-chapter *Guang hongming ji* in the Ming canon simply redistributes material and omits cross-referencing to the *Hongming ji*.

T. H. BARRETT

📖 Kohn 1995a, 159–73 and passim; Li Mingyou 1992; Makita Tairyō 1973–75; Ōfuchi Ninji and Ishii Masako 1988, 303–11 (list of texts cited); Schmidt-Glintzer 1976

※ TAOISM AND CHINESE BUDDHISM

hongtou and *wutou*

紅頭 · 烏頭

"Red-head" and "Black-head"

The terms *hongtou* and *wutou* are partly equivalent to **fashi* ("ritual master") and **daoshi* ("master of the Dao"), respectively. They are used especially in some southeastern areas of continental China and in parts of Taiwan, and refer to the headdresses worn by these religious practitioners when they perform their ritual functions.

Although the ritual functions associated with the *hongtou* and *wutou* overlap to some extent, the two terms refer to distinct privileges and tasks, and reflect a difference in rank. A "red-head" ritual master has not received ordination as a Taoist priest. He specializes in exorcism, healing, and other rites for the living, and does not perform ceremonies for the dead. He often fulfills his functions with the help of spirit-mediums (**tâng-ki*) who are subject to trance and

Fig. 39. A "red-head" (*hongtou*) ritual master.
Reproduced from Noguchi Tetsurō et al.
1994, 156.

possession by spirits. A "black-head" priest may perform the above functions,
but he is also entitled to celebrate Taoist rituals, including those for the dead.
The "black-head" priest's assistants are the chief cantor and other helpers who
perform the ritual with him (see under **dujiang*).

According to one explanation, the red color associated with the *hongtou*
refers to the good luck secured by their rites (red is traditionally an auspicious
color in China), while the black color associated with the *heitou* refers to the
world of the dead; during the funerary ritual, for instance, the *daoshi* is said
to "arrest the black" (*shouwu* 收烏), with reference to the dark pneumas of
the netherworld. Strictly speaking, therefore, the color of the headdress refers
to the particular ritual function performed by a religious officiant, and not
to the officiant himself. In fact, the Taiwanese *daoshi* also study a corpus of
practices called "methods of the red-head" (*hongtou fa* 紅頭法), and when they
performs exorcistic rites, they often wear a red headdress. In other words, a
heitou may also be a *hongtou*, but not vice versa.

The *hongtou* perform their rites in the so-called *daoyin* 道音 (lit., "sounds of the
Dao"), an idiom similar to the premodern Chinese "official language" (*guanhua*
官話) and to the language of Taiwanese theatre. The *heitou*, on the other hand,
use either the classical language or the vernacular. There are also differences
in the ritual areas and ritual tools (**faqi*) used by a *hongtou* and a *heitou*.

The *hongtou* emphasize rules of purity, related to their goal of bringing
benefit to the living. Since the emoluments that they receive for their func-

tions are lower than those of the *heitou*, the transmission of their methods is carefully regulated in order not to inflate their profession. They are organized into groups, and offer support to each other.

Fabrizio PREGADIO

📖 Cohen 1992; Liu Zhiwan 1983c, 151–61; Schipper 1993, 49–55

※ *daoshi*; *fashi*; *tâng-ki*

housheng

後聖

Saint of the Latter Age

Housheng designates a category in the transcendent hierarchy of the *Shangqing movement, as well as an eminent divinity of its pantheon. The term *hou* 後 refers to the state "subsequent to Heaven" (*houtian*), the world as we know it as opposed to the state "prior to Heaven" (*xiantian*), which represents the primal or original stages before the formation of the present cosmos. The *housheng* were divine figures higher than the *zhenren* or Perfected. Also called *dijun* 帝君 or Imperial Lords, these saints were thought to have obtained transcendence by practicing the Dao, whereas other celestial figures had been granted their divine nature since the origin of the world.

Within the Shangqing scriptures, the appellation Saint of the Latter Age was also given to *Li Hong, that is, the divinized Laozi, the messiah common to the various medieval Taoist movements. The *Housheng daojun lieji* (Chronicle of the Lord of the Dao, Saint of the Latter Age), a text revealed to *Yang Xi during the second half of the fourth century, contains a biography of this messianic saint who governs the world and transmits methods of salvation to humanity. He is supposed to appear on earth in a *renchen* 壬辰 year (the twenty-ninth of the sexagesimal cycle; see table 10), after the destruction of the universe and the annihilation of the unfaithful. He will then inaugurate the reign of the Great Peace (*taiping*) and assign positions in the celestial bureaucracy to each of the immortal "seed-people" (*zhongmin*).

Christine MOLLIER

📖 Robinet 1984, 1: 138 and 2: 107

※ Jinque dijun; Li Hong; *Housheng daojun lieji*; Shangqing; APOCALYPTIC ESCHATOLOGY; MESSIANISM AND MILLENARIANISM

Housheng daojun lieji

後聖道君列紀

Chronicle of the Lord of the Dao, Saint of the Latter Age

The *Housheng daojun lieji* (CT 442) belongs to the *Shangqing scriptural corpus, revealed to the visionary *Yang Xi during the years 364–70. It is, more specifically, part of a set of four works defined as Purple Scripts or *ziwen* 紫文 (see under *Lingshu ziwen*). The text claims to have been composed by *Qingtong (the Azure Lad) for presentation to *Li Hong (the Lord of the Dao) and transmission to his disciple *Wang Yuan (a patron saint of the Shangqing movement), who was charged, in turn, to deliver it to twenty-four Perfected (*zhenren*) for instructing future immortals.

Its vision of the end of the world makes the *Housheng lieji*, with the *Santian zhengfa jing* 三天正法經 (Scripture of the Orthodox Law of the Three Heavens; CT 1203; Ozaki Masaharu 1974), one of the main scriptures of Shangqing apocalyptic eschatology. The text presents a panegyric of one of the main divinities of the Shangqing pantheon, the Imperial Lord of the Golden Portal (*Jinque dijun), also known as the Saint of the Latter Age (*housheng*); he is the messiah Li Hong, avatar of the god Laozi. It describes the apocalypse, and contains an account of the otherworldly bureaucracy and of the Shangqing scriptures, the possession of which gives access to this supernatural bureaucracy.

The work predicts the impending advent of the savior Li Hong as a mighty god who will descend from Mount Qingcheng (*Qingcheng shan, Sichuan) and appear in the world on the sixth day of the third lunar month of a year marked by the cyclical characters *renchen* 壬辰 (the twenty-ninth of the sexagesimal cycle; see table 10), after the end of the world. In the preceding *jiashen* 甲申 year (the twenty-first of the sexagesimal cycle), calamities will herald the apocalypse, and great cosmic disasters and social disorder will annihilate the unfaithful. The chosen people will, by that time, have found security in the mountains and will constitute the "seed-people" (*zhongmin*) of the new humankind. They will enjoy the delights of the era of Great Peace (*taiping*) inaugurated by Li Hong, and will obtain positions in the several hundred ranks of the transcendent official hierarchy, in accordance with their own spiritual achievements and the sacred scriptures they have received. Their names will be registered in the celestial palaces they will inhabit. Access to immortality is not only determined by religious merit, but also partly by predetermination:

the *Housheng lieji* describes the extraordinary physical marks (*xiang* 相) that will distinguish these candidates for celestial official ranks.

Christine MOLLIER

📖 Bokenkamp 1997, 339–62 (trans.); Kamitsuka Yoshiko 1999, 171–210; Robinet 1984, 2: 107–8; Strickmann 1981, 209–24 (part. trans.); Strickmann 2002, 52–57

※ Li Hong; *housheng*; *Lingshu ziwen*; Shangqing; MESSIANISM AND MILLE-NARIANISM

houtian

後天

"after Heaven", "posterior to Heaven"; postcelestial

See *xiantian* and *houtian* 先天 · 後天.

Huahu jing

化胡經

Scripture of the Conversion of Barbarians

Wang Fu 王浮, a Celestial Master libationer (*jijiu*), composed the first edition of the *Huahu jing* in one scroll (now lost except for citations in later works) around 300. A Buddhist monk had often defeated him in debates. Wang could not endure the shame of defeat and in anger wrote a text that was intended to denigrate Buddhism by demonstrating that Laozi actually founded the Indian religion and was in fact nothing less than the Buddha.

The origin of Wang's polemic was a passage from the oldest biography of Laozi's in the *Shiji* (Records of the Historian; trans. Lau 1982, x-xi). According to that text, Laozi left the Zhou court where he had served as archivist because he was disgusted with the moral decline of the dynasty and set out on a journey to the west. At the Hangu Pass (Hangu guan 函谷關) he encountered its guard *Yin Xi who requested that he record his teachings. Laozi duly wrote out the *Daode jing* in two scrolls and then continued on his way to die at some unknown place.

By 165 CE the tradition took a new turn. In that year a court official who was proficient in astrology presented a memorial to the throne in which he stated that some believed that Laozi went further west into the territory of "barbarians" and became the Buddha. Indeed the emperor to whom the official addressed his document made a conjoint sacrifice to the Buddha and Laozi perhaps in the belief that they were one and the same deity (see *Laozi ming). By the third century the tradition evolved and asserted that Laozi had made his way specifically to India, converted a king there, and composed Buddhist *sūtras*. Up to that point the theory served the interests of both religions in that it allowed Taoists to incorporate Buddhist tenets and Buddhists to claim that their faith had indigenous origins in China, a claim that facilitated the conversion of the natives.

With the appearance of Wang Fu's text, the character of the theory changed radically. Wang used it as a cudgel to assail the Buddhists. Thereafter the theory and his text became a point of bitter contention between the two religions. As time went on, Taoists enlarged the *Huahu jing*. By 600 it had grown to two scrolls and by 700 to ten. In addition, the theory spawned several related works. They included the *Xuanmiao neipian* 玄妙內篇 (Inner Chapters on Mysterious Wonder)—a hagiography of Laozi's mother according to which Laozi entered the mouth of a queen in India and the next year was born from her right arm-pit to become the Buddha—and the *Wenshi neizhuan* 文始內傳 (Inner Biography of Master Wenshi; Kohn 1997b, 109–13)—a hagiography of Yin Xi who accompanied Laozi on his journey to the west and became a Buddha in the same fashion as Laozi.

The "conversion of the barbarians" theory strove to demonstrate that Laozi was a universal deity who appeared in all ages as avatars assuming the forms of ancient Chinese sage-kings, the master of Confucius, the Buddha, and even Mani (the founder of Manichaeism). He taught and converted all people of the world. In one sense the theory attempted to demonstrate that Taoism was superior to Buddhism, an inferior form of Taoist doctrines and therefore unworthy of importation to China. The notion was ethnocentric in that asserted that Indians and Central Asian were uncultured—unkempt, filthy, malodorous, and ill-mannered—and therefore in need of civilization, that is Chinese civilization. In another sense the theory was a means of justifying the adoption of Buddhist doctrines by Taoists because Buddhism had become extremely popular among the elite and peasants in China.

The Buddhist reaction to this assault on their religion was twofold. The first, that emerged in the fifth or sixth century, was to attack the *Huahu jing* on the grounds that it was irrational and absurd. There were many inconsistencies, anachronisms and contradictions in the text that provided Buddhist advocates with fertile material to ridicule the *Huahu jing*. Not the least of them was the notion that Laozi spread a doctrine in India that was Taoist, but inferior to Chinese Taoism. The second reaction was to turn the tables on Taoism and create a myth of conversion in which bodhisattvas or disciples of the Buddha converted the Chinese to their faith. In various apocrypha, the Buddhists asserted that Laozi was an avatar or a disciple of the Buddha who traveled east to propagate their religion among the Chinese. They went further to claim that Confucius and his disciple Yan Hui 顏回 were bodhisattvas, and therefore Confucianism was a form of Buddhism. Moreover they strove to co-opt the ancient sages of China for themselves by asserting that the mythical rulers Fu Xi 伏羲 and Nü Gua 女媧 were avatars of the Buddha or bodhisattvas.

The *Huahu jing* was a major point of contention in the debates between Taoists and Buddhism that raged from the fifth through the seventh centuries. The stakes at such confrontations, that usually took place at imperial courts, were high. If the emperor judged one of the two religions to be superior he accorded it precedence, that is he assigned it a higher position in processions and therefore greater prestige. That also frequently meant that the faith enjoyed greater patronage from the throne.

During the Tang dynasty the throne twice proscribed the *Huahu jing* in 668 and 705 without lasting effect. The text survived into the Song dynasty. However, in the Yuan dynasty the throne ordered destruction of it and all texts related to it. The *Huahu jing* seemed to disappear, but an illustrated version, the *Laojun bashiyi hua tushuo* 老君八十一化圖說 (Eighty-One Transformations of Lord Lao, Illustrated and Explained; see *Laojun bashiyi hua tu*), survived into the Ming dynasty and still exists today. Furthermore, after the discovery of ancient Chinese manuscripts at *Dunhuang in the early twentieth century, fragments from four scrolls of the ten-scroll version were recovered. In addition there are numerous citations from of the *Huahu jing* in Taoist compendia of the Tang and Buddhist polemical literature.

Charles D. BENN

📖 Chavannes and Pelliot 1911–13, part 2: 116–32; Fukui Kōjun 1958, 156–324; Kanaoka Shōkō 1983, 196–205; Kohn 1993b, 71–80; Kohn 1995a, 195–97 and passim; Kusuyama Haruki 1979, 437–72; Ōfuchi Ninji 1978–79, 1: 322–24 (crit. notes on the Dunhuang mss.) and 2: 656–84 (reprod. of the Dunhuang mss.); Ōfuchi Ninji 1991, 469–84; Ōfuchi Ninji 1997, 591–96; Robinet 1997b, 188–89; Seidel 1984; Yamada Toshiaki 1983a; Yoshioka Yoshitoyo 1976d; Zürcher 1972, 288–320

※ Laozi and Laojun; TAOISM AND CHINESE BUDDHISM

Huainan zi

淮南子

Book of the Master of Huainan

A key document of early Han thought, the *Huainan zi* is a composite and ency-clopedic work in twenty-one chapters dating from ca. 139 BCE. It was compiled at the court of Liu An 劉安 (179?–122), king of Huainan (present-day Anhui) and grandson of the founder of the Han dynasty (Wallacker 1972; Campany 2002, 233–38). Scholars have long debated the role played in its composition by the circles of savants and *fangshi (masters of methods) that surrounded Liu An. The work was originally divided into three parts, two of which—the "outer" (*waishu* 外書) and the "central" (*zhongshu* 中書) ones—are lost. The extant text, corresponding to the "inner" portion (*neishu* 內書), covers a wide variety of subjects, including cosmology, philosophy, the art of government, mysticism, mythology, hagiography, ethics, education, military affairs, music, and inner nature and vital force (*xing and *ming*). The *Huainan zi* has been extensively quoted since shortly after the Han dynasty, and its views on cos-mogony have been widely adopted.

Two slightly different editions of the text existed since early times, com-piled by the commentators Xu Shen 許慎 (ca. 55-ca. 149) and Gao You 高誘 (fl. 205–212). Their annotations had been merged by the eleventh century, and apparently as early as the fourth century. Scholars, however, agree on the general faithful transmission and integrity of the text. After Xu and Gao, the *Huainan zi* was the subject of many other commentaries. The earliest printed edition was probably that established in the eleventh century by Su Song 蘇頌 (1020–1101; SB 969–70), now available in the *Sibu congkan* 四部叢刊 (Collectanea from the Four Sections of Literature). The edition in the Taoist Canon, entitled *Huainan honglie jie* 淮南鴻烈解 (Vast and Luminous Explica-tions of [the Master of] Huainan; CT 1184), which is in twenty-eight chapters as it divides seven chapters into two parts, is one of the most reliable versions of the text and was the basis of several later ones.

Nature of the text. The *Huainan zi* has traditionally been known as an "eclectic work." Some contemporary scholars label it as a *Huang-Lao text. Despite extensive borrowings from earlier sources, which account for some incon-sistencies in style and ideology, the text possesses a general unity. Its creative synthesis, which is one of its distinctive features, combines Confucian, Legalist, and Taoist perspectives with Yin-Yang and *wuxing cosmology. It is based on analogical and correlative thinking, and on the idea of resonance (*ganying* 感應) and interaction among all levels of reality.

Despite its heterogeneous background, the text embodies a fundamentally Taoist attitude. It offers a synthesis of the *Daode jing* and the *Zhuangzi*, combining the former's political leanings with the latter's more contemplative tendency. Chapters 1 and 2 draw heavily on the *Daode jing* and the *Zhuangzi*. Among the many sources cited in this work, the *Zhuangzi* is the most frequently quoted. Throughout the book, the Dao is emphasized as a primal, central, and ultimate Unity and as a universal, generative, and orderly power. The ethical and sociopolitical level of the Confucian teaching, and the pragmatic and Legalist point of view that emphasizes the need for a powerful ruler and bureaucracy, laws and institutions, are both subordinated to the ontological level of Dao and its Virtue (*de*). The belief in the resonance between the two levels of reality—the Dao and the phenomenal world—is part of the text's large-scale integration of cosmology into political and historical theory, which is a basic feature of Han thought.

The Dao and the Saint. The *Huainan zi* offers the longest development on the Dao since the *Daode jing* and the *Zhuangzi*. The Dao is indescribable and unfathomable. It is the source of everything in the world, contains everything, can do everything and its contrary, and can take all forms. It cannot be paired with anything and is unique. Every thing and every being takes its meaning in reference to the eternal Dao, which one must cultivate to fulfill one's destiny and true nature.

Return (*fan*) to the Dao and to the original and fundamental nature of beings is the basis of all qualities and efficacious actions. This fundamental nature of beings is their overall oneness; it is found in quiescence, inner unity, and emptiness, and is accomplished by spontaneous action or non-action (*wuwei*). Thus, one must not try to change the nature of beings, and must follow and preserve one's authenticity. The book stresses the fundamental value of the vital and spiritual forces of life; one should respect them and let them spontaneously and freely circulate and nourish all things, as they are the basis of health on both the individual and political levels. The individual and the ruler must consequently know the rules that govern human life and cosmic order, and follow them without interfering.

Like the *Zhuangzi*, the *Huainan zi* describes values that change according to different times and points of view; therefore it emphasizes the difficulty of seeing clearly and employing the correct means to order one's life and the world. The only one who can unravel these difficulties is the Saint (*shengren*), the ideal ruler, due to the penetrating insight he acquires by embodying the Dao. In the *Huainan zi*, the Saint has a cosmic dimension and rules the whole

Table 12

CHAPTER	TRANSLATION
1 Yuandao 原道 (Original Dao)	Balfour 1884, 74–94; Morgan 1933; Kraft 1957–58; Larre, Robinet, and Rochat de la Vallée 1993; Lau and Ames 1998
2 Shuzhen 俶真 (Primeval Reality)	Morgan 1933; Kraft 1957–58
3 Tianwen 天文 (Patterns of Heaven)	Major 1993
4 Dixing 墜形 (Forms of Earth)	Erkes 1916–17; Major 1993
5 Shice 時則 (Seasonal Rules)	Major 1993
6 Lanmin 覽冥 (Peering into Obscurity)	Le Blanc 1985
7 Jingshen 精神 (Essence and Spirit)	Morgan 1933; Larre 1982 (part.); Larre, Robinet, and Rochat de la Vallée 1993 (full)
8 Benjing 本經 (Fundamental Norm)	Morgan 1933
9 Zhushu 主術 (Art of Rulership)	Ames 1983
10 Miucheng 繆稱 (Erroneous Designations)	—
11 Qisu 齊俗 (Equalizing Customs)	Wallacker 1962; Larre, Robinet, and Rochat de la Vallée 1993
12 Daoying 道應 (Responses to the Dao)	Morgan 1933
13 Fanlun 氾論 (Compendious Discussions)	Morgan 1933; Larre, Robinet, and Rochat de la Vallée 1993
14 Quanyan 詮言 (Inquiring Words)	—
15 Binglüe 兵略 (Essential of the Military Arts)	Morgan 1933; Ryden 1998
16 Shuoshan 說山 (On Mountains)	—
17 Shuolin 說林 (On Forests)	—
18 Renjian 人間 (Among Humans)	Larre, Robinet, and Rochat de la Vallée 1993
19 Xiuwu 脩務 (Necessity of Cultivation)	Morgan 1933
20 Taizu 泰族 (Great Categories)	—
21 Yaolüe 要略 (Synopsis)	Larre, Robinet, and Rochat de la Vallée 1993

Published translations of *Huainan zi* chapters into Western languages. Based in part on Le Blanc 1985, 14–18; Roth 1992, 13–14; Kohn 1994.

universe. He is the bridge that both joins and separates the one Dao and its multiple facets, and the one who can follow and subsume all differences into one Unity within a hierarchy of ethical (Confucian) values. The Saint's intuitive and synthesizing knowledge of diverse and multiple times, beings, and means lies beyond thinking, and can harmoniously employ each being according to his capacities and relation to the whole.

Thus the *Huainan zi* combines two notions of order: one obtained through distribution, the other through centering and radiating. The first is pyramidal, hierarchically ordering values and ranks in a Confucian way, or adequately allotting functions in a more Legalist mode; it changes in different times and places. The other is the one, permanent Taoist order that proceeds through inner centering and outer radiating.

Isabelle ROBINET

📖 Ames 1983 (trans. of *j.* 9); Kanaya Osamu 1959; Kohn 1994; Kusuyama Haruki 1987; Larre 1982 (trans. of *j.* 7); Larre, Robinet, and Rochat de la Vallée 1993 (trans. of *j.* 1, 7, 11, 13, 18, and 21); Le Blanc 1985 (trans. of *j.* 6); Le Blanc 1993; Le Blanc and Mathieu 2003 (complete trans.); Loewe 1994b; Major 1993 (trans. of *j.* 3–5); Robinet 1997b, 47–48; Roth 1985; Roth 1987c; Roth 1991a; Roth 1992; Roth 1996; for other translations of individual chapters, see table 12

※ COSMOLOGY

huandan

還丹

Reverted Elixir

1. *Waidan*

In *waidan*, *huandan* is a generic term that denotes the elixir. It does not refer to any single compound or method, but applies to virtually all processes of refining that occur in cycles (*zhuan* 轉); hence such names as Reverted Elixir in Nine Cycles (*jiuzhuan huandan* 九轉還丹).

The main underlying notion is that the alchemical process allows the ingredients of the elixir to "revert" to their original state. The essences that coagulate under the upper part of the crucible represent the initial state of matter before its corruption caused by the action of time. Thus the elixir is equated with the original essence (*jing*) or the *materia prima* from which the cosmos evolved. The commentary to the *Jiudan jing* (Scripture of the Nine

Elixirs; CT 885, 10.1b) compares this substance to the "essence" that is within
the Dao and is the seed of its generation of the world (*Laozi* 21).

Fabrizio PREGADIO

📖 Meng Naichang 1993a, 132–44

※ *waidan*

2. Neidan

Depending on the emphasis of the particular schools, the term *dan* 丹 (elixir)
in *neidan has a more physical or spiritual connotation. *Huan* 還 is used in inner
alchemy in the sense of "reverting" or "revolving," and is associated with a
circle or cycle that symbolizes completion and return (*fan*) to the Dao. As a
compound term, *huandan* in *neidan* first denotes an elixir that is formed inwardly
by a process of cyclical transformation and enables the adept to return to the
Origin. Second, *huandan* means "returning to the Cinnabar Field (*dantian)"
and denotes a cyclical process of purification of the primary components of
the human being. The idea of return through a cyclical process is thus central
to both meanings of *huandan*.

The *Zhong-Lü school, especially in the *Zhong-Lü chuandao ji (Anthology
of Zhongli Quan's Transmission of the Dao to Lü Dongbin), distinguishes
several kinds of "return to the Cinnabar Field." They are designated as Small
Return to the Cinnabar Field (*xiao huandan* 小還丹), Great Return to the Cinnabar Field (*da huandan* 大還丹), Sevenfold Return to the Cinnabar Field (*qifan
huandan* 七返還丹), Ninefold Return to the Cinnabar Field (*jiuzhuan huandan*
九轉還丹), Return of the Jade Liquor to the Cinnabar Field (*yuye huandan* 玉
液還丹), Return of the Golden Liquor to the Cinnabar Field (*jinye huandan* 金
液還丹), and in other ways (according to the Zhong-Lü school, Jade Liquor
or *yuye* 玉液 denotes the fluid of the kidneys, while Golden Liquor or *jinye*
金液 refers to the fluid of the lungs; see Baldrian-Hussein 1984, 139–42 and
151–58). In the context of this physiologically-oriented *neidan* tradition, the
Reverted Elixir is related to the rise and descent of the energies in the body
and their refinement through these cyclical movements. For instance, the
Small Return to the Cinnabar Field is based on purifying the pneuma (*qi*) of
the five viscera (*wuzang*) and on cyclically increasing and decreasing the Yin
and Yang qualities in the body. This process results in the collection of the
refined substances in the lower Cinnabar Field. With the Great Return to the
Cinnabar Field, an energetic exchange between the lower and upper Cinnabar
Fields occurs.

The *Wuzhen pian (Folios on Awakening to Perfection), the *Zhonghe ji
(Anthology of Central Harmony), and the *Xingming guizhi (Principles of Bal-

anced Cultivation of Inner Nature and Vital Force) emphasize that *huandan* is to be understood in relation to self-refinement and control of the heart (**xin*): "If you want to carry out the ninefold circulation to perfection, you should first purify yourself and control your heart" (*Wuzhen pian*, in **Xiuzhen shishu*, CT 263, 29.4b). In the *Zhonghe ji*, the formation of the Great Reverted Elixir (*da huandan*) is equivalent to the unification of the phenomenal and noumenal aspects of the Dao within the adept. The nine-cycled transformation is emphasized in the *Xingming guizhi*, where it corresponds to the purification of the heart and aims to return to its original state.

The formation of the nine-cycled elixir is important in *neidan* as 9 is the number of pure Yang and symbolizes attainment. When the elixir is refined nine times it attains its highest purity. According to the *Baiwen pian* 百問篇 (Folios of the Hundred Questions; in **Daoshu*, 5.7a–22a), the adept needs nine years to achieve the Reverted Elixir.

Martina DARGA

📖 Baldrian-Hussein 1984, 146–47, 152, 241, and 254, Darga 1999, 253–54, 301–2, and 332

※ *neidan*

huandu

環堵

retreat, enclosure

The term *huandu* (lit., "encircled by four walls") has a long history in Chinese literature and religion. It was first used in the **Zhuangzi* (chapter 23; trans. Watson 1987, 248–49) to denote a humble hut where a hermit takes refuge, and also appears in the *Liji* 禮記 (Records of Rites; trans. Legge 1885, 2: 405) to refer to the abode of the poor but righteous scholar. Hence it often took the meaning of a miserable hut, but also retained connotations that have nothing to do with poverty. The *du* or "wall" is a small unit of length, whence the meaning for *huandu* of a minimal surface which potentially becomes all-encompassing: "One can stay inside one's *huandu* and know the entire universe" (*Shuoyuan* 說苑 7.7). Moreover, the fact that its walls can isolate the room from the outside world adds the possible opposite meanings of "protective enclosure" or even "prison." From the idea of small, secluded room, *huandu* naturally became a name for the Taoist meditation room. The **Zhengao* (18.6b) has a precise description of the *huandu* as a kind of **jingshi* (quiet chamber). This acceptation is confirmed by later texts, although many kinds of buildings were subsumed under this common term.

The *huandu* was made popular by Liu Biangong 劉卞功 (1071–1143), a Taoist living in Shandong who built an enclosure with a small hut in the middle and spent his entire life within it, speaking with guests through a wicket. After his death, his disciple took his place in the *huandu*, and this went on for three generations. A few decades afterward, the *Quanzhen order, which made public displays of asceticism a formal part of its curriculum, adopted the term *huandu* but changed and institutionalized the practice. Ritualized solitary confinement in a room for a fixed term (usually one hundred days or three years) to perform *neidan practices was introduced in Quanzhen by *Wang Zhe and was standardized by *Ma Yu. Rows of *huandu* were built in monasteries and adepts spent periods within them, at the end of which their spiritual attainment was tested by their masters. Early Yuan historical records mention several cases of scholars repudiating family and friends and locking themselves up in a *huandu*. Once enclosed, the adept meditated night and day with hardly any sleep; recorded sayings (*yulu) and legal cases document instances in which such extreme asceticism led to madness and violence.

In later times, the practice was severely controlled and stays in the *huandu* were limited to shorter periods. From the late Ming onward, some monasteries also built meditation halls with compartmented cells called *huantang* 圜堂. Adepts then could enjoy the solitude of the *huandu* and still be absorbed in the discipline of the monastic community. These various kinds of institutionalized asceticism bear a close relationship with the Buddhist practice of *biguan* 閉關 (confinement), rather common to this day, and also usually lasting three years.

Vincent GOOSSAERT

📖 Goossaert 1997, 171–219, Goossaert 1999; Goossaert 2001

※ *zuobo*; Quanzhen; ASCETICISM; MEDITATION AND VISUALIZATION

Huang Lingwei

黃靈微 (*or*: 黃令微)

ca. 640–721; *hao*: Huagu 華姑 (Flowery Maiden)

Though many facets of her life remain poorly known, Huang Lingwei was one of the notable Taoist women of Tang China. She was ignored by the official historians, but we know some details of her career from two inscription texts composed by the accomplished statesman-scholar Yan Zhenqing 顏真

卿 (709–85). In 768/769, Yan was appointed prefect of Fuzhou 撫州 (Jiangxi), where Huang had been active, and he soon composed an epitaph for inscription at her shrine at Linchuan 臨川 (Jiangxi). A few years later, he again explained her life in an epitaph (*Quan Tang wen* 全唐文 or *Complete Prose of the Tang*, Zhonghua shuju repr. of the 1814 edition, 340.17a–22b) prepared for inscription at the nearby shrine of "Lady Wei" (*Wei Huacun, 251–334), the *Tianshi dao libationer (*jijiu) who posthumously participated in the *Shangqing revelations. Naturally, *Du Guangting visited Huang's life in his anthology of materials on female Taoist figures, the *Yongcheng jixian lu (in YJQQ 115.9b–12a).

Though Huang's entire early life is essentially unknown, Yan's first text (in *Quan Tang wen*, 340.1a–3b) identifies her as a native of Linchuan, giving no information about her parentage. (He makes no mention of her ever having a husband or children.) At the age of twelve, she was reportedly ordained as a *daoshi (a plausible datum in that period). Then, Yan says nothing more about Huang's life until she was about fifty, no doubt because that part of her life was passed over in silence by his informants. In her maturity, Huang, for unknown reasons, began seeking the long-lost shrine of Lady Wei. She was unsuccessful until late 693, when she received help from a theurgist named Hu Huichao 胡惠超 (?–703). Following his directions, she found Lady Wei's shrine and excavated some religious artifacts. Yan relates that the Empress Wu (r. 690–705) confiscated the artifacts but that she did not order an account of the matter to be recorded. Amidst wonders, Huang located and restored a second nearby shrine, and apparently continued *zhai observances there for nearly thirty years. In 721/722, she informed her disciples that she wished to ascend, and instructed them not to nail her coffin shut, but only to cover it with crimson gauze. A few evenings later, lightning struck, leaving a hole in the gauze and an opening in the roof. The disciples who looked into the coffin found no body, only her shroud and "screed" (*jian* 簡). That is, she had undergone *shijie (release from the corpse). Yan says little more about Huang's disciples, mentioning only one by name, a woman named Li Qiongxian 黎瓊仙. Apparently, Li and female colleagues maintained the shrines for some years, with male *daoshi* continuing the *zhai* and *jiao observances. Later, the shrines evidently fell again into desuetude. Yan depicts Huang as a woman of humility, piety, and courage, and seems quite comfortable in eliciting readers' approval of a woman who passed beyond the "traditional" norms.

Du Guangting reproduces an 882 rescript by Tang Xizong (r. 873–88), which calls Huang an immortal who had descended from heaven. She has no biography in the Standard Histories, evidently because she did little to recommend herself as a political exemplar. She apparently wrote nothing, and we know nothing more of her beliefs or practices.

Russell KIRKLAND

📖 Cahill 1990, 33–34; Kirkland 1991; Kirkland 1992–93, 156–60; Schafer 1977b

※ WOMEN IN TAOISM

Huang Shunshen

黃舜申

1224-after 1286; *hao*: Leiyuan zhenren 雷淵真人
(Perfected of the Thunderous Abyss)

As the earliest and most important codifier of the *Qingwei (Pure Tenuity)
movement's teachings, Huang Shunshen helped to establish this important
late-Song Taoist synthesis of ritual, scripture, and contemplation among literati
groups in southern and central China.

Huang's earliest hagiography comes from his disciple Chen Cai 陳采 at
the end of Chen's *Qingwei xianpu* (Register of Pure Tenuity Transcendents,
14b–15a), which has a preface dated 1293. This source places Huang's birth in
Jianning 建寧 (Fujian), the same area, it should be noted, where *Bai Yuchan
(1194–1229?) established himself from 1215 onward. Reported to have read widely
in his youth, at the age of sixteen Huang accompanied his father who had just
been appointed to serve as a transport official in Guangzhou (Canton). Shortly
after arriving there, Huang became ill and a man named Nan Bidao 南畢道
(1196-?)—a patriarch of the Qingwei tradition—healed him with talismans
(*FU) as thunder struck in the courtyard. After curing the boy, Nan saw that
Huang had the right spiritual capacity, and transmitted to him the manuscripts
of his Qingwei teachings. During the Baoyou reign period (1253–58), Huang
seems to have codified and transmitted these works with great vigor to many
aristocrats, from Zhao Mengduan 趙孟端 in the Song imperial family up to
emperor Lizong (r. 1224–64), who invited him to court and gave him the title
Perfected of the Thunderous Abyss (Leiyuan zhenren). Later, in 1282, after
the fall of the Song dynasty, Khubilai khan (r. 1260–94) also summoned Huang
to his court.

Although Huang is reported to have taught hundreds of disciples by the end
of his life, one hagiography states that the front of a stele recorded the names
of thirty disciples, each of whom received one of the five component ritual
traditions of Qingwei—associated, in descending order, with Yuanshi shangdi
元始上帝 (Highest Emperor of Original Commencement), *Shangqing,
*Lingbao, Daode 道德 (i.e., *Laozi*), and *Zhengyi (Orthodox Unity)—while the
five disciples inscribed on the back had received the full Qingwei transmission.
Huang and his disciples distributed Qingwei teachings among literati groups

from Guangdong to central Hubei by the late thirteenth century. A second-generation disciple of Huang named Zeng Chenwai 曾塵外 set up a branch in Ji'an 吉安 (Jiangxi) and became the teacher of *Zhao Yizhen (?–1382). More important than the official and literati support, however, was the acceptance of these new synthetic teachings by the Celestial Master's *Zhengyi (Orthodox Unity) tradition.

Lowell SKAR

📖 Boltz J. M. 1987a, 38–41; Davis E. 2001, 29–30; Qing Xitai 1994, 1: 345

※ *Qingwei xianpu*; Qingwei

Huangdi

黃帝

Yellow Emperor; Yellow Thearch; Yellow Lord;
also called Xianyuan 軒轅

Different early mythical traditions about Huangdi were combined and re-interpreted after the unification of the empire under the Han dynasty. This mythology is complex, but as far as its role in Taoism is concerned, three essential traditions may be distinguished. According to Wolfram Eberhard (1942, 158–61) there was a cult tradition in the northwest of the empire that was centered around a heavenly god Huangdi. In the myths of the eastern provinces, Huangdi was featured as the ideal ruler of ancient times and the first practitioner of Dao. At the time of the Han dynasty, these two mythical traditions merged and were complemented by the tradition of Huangdi as patron of the "masters of methods" (*fangshi*).

Heavenly god. The Huangdi cultic tradition in the northwestern kingdom of Qin dates back to the eighth century BCE. Each sector of heaven (the four points of the compass and the center) was personified by a *di* 帝 (a term that indicates not only an emperor but also an ancestral "thearch" and "god"). The family ancestor of the princes of Qin was the White Emperor, Shaohao 少皞 (Small Light), who personified the western sector. The fact that the Qin honored Huangdi as the personification of the central sector of the heavens, which should have been the domain of the ruling Zhou kings, was therefore a political presumption. At the end of the third century BCE, the Qin conquered the Zhou kingdom. The Han emperors maintained the tradition of the five heavenly gods, but Huangdi was now replaced by the Great One (*Taiyi) in the central sector and instead given a place as an acolyte of the Great One among the other emperors grouped around him.

The character *huang* 黃 (yellow) is often used in ancient literature as equivalent to *huang* 皇 (august, venerable, superior). But Huangdi 皇帝 or "august emperor" is the name of the heavenly god Shangdi 上帝. Thus, the Yellow Emperor was placed on the same level as the highest heavenly god, and the four emperors personifying the points of the compass were subordinated to him. The prestige attached to Huangdi as a heavenly god and an ancestral father of nearly all the noble families in China was one reason Huangdi was chosen as a patron of Taoism and of medicine.

Prototype of the wise ruler. Chapter 1 of the *Shiji* (Records of the Historian) places the perfect kingdom of the first emperor and cultural hero Huangdi at the beginning of the history of mankind. In Taoism, he is presented as the model emperor since he turns to the wise old masters for advice, as described in the *Zhuangzi (chapter 11; trans. Watson 1968, 118–20). Just as Laozi was the model of the wise counselor who served as a minister under virtuous rulers, so Huangdi was the ideal ruler who took the advice of such wise counselors. This is evident in numerous records of dialogues in which Huangdi consults his ministers and counselors. While the *Huangdi neijing (Inner Scripture of the Yellow Emperor) is the most notable example (Seidel 1969, 50–51), he appears as a questioner already in the first four dialogues of a *Mawangdui manuscript, the *Shiwen* 十問 (Ten Questions; trans. Harper 1998, 385–411), in which ten *yangsheng specialists respond to questions.

Patron of mantic and medical practices. In ancient times, Huangdi was also closely linked to the families or guilds of potters and blacksmiths, who were the direct forefathers of the alchemists. Thus, *Li Shaojun taught Han Wudi the way of making gold as the "art of achieving immortality, as practiced by Huangdi" (*Shiji* 28; trans. Watson 1961, 2: 39).

In the *Huang-Lao tradition, which flourished in the first half of the second century BCE, the Yellow Emperor was seen as model "emperor-turned-immortal" (Yü Ying-shih 1964, 102 ff.) associated with the unofficial transmission of various mantic and medical practices, which appear to have made him an important figure for one faction at the courts of Han Wendi (r. 180–157 BCE) and Han Jingdi (r. 157–141 BCE; van Ess 1993a).

The affiliation of texts with mythical sage-rulers of antiquity, such as the Divine Husbandman (Shennong 神農) and the Yellow Emperor, became increasingly common during the Han. In the bibliography of the *Hanshu* (History of the Former Han), the Yellow Emperor is associated with works classified under Divinities and Immortals (*shenxian* 神仙), Medical Classics (*yijing* 醫經), Arts of the Numbers (*shushu* 數術), and Methods and Techniques (*fangji*).

This association with ancient sage-kings did not mean that such rulers were supposed to have written the texts, but that they were often the recipients of revelations. Han texts therefore relate that the Yellow Emperor received texts on sexual hygiene from the Sunü 素女 (Pure Woman) and *Rong Cheng (Csikszentmihalyi 1994). He is also referred to in the *Hanshu* bibliography as the patron of massage and the "medicines of immortality" (*xianyao* 仙藥). In the *Shiji* (chapter 105) there are reports of "pulse books of Huangdi and Bian Que 扁鵲" which were transmitted to the famous physician Chunyu Yi 淳于意.

Although Huangdi's significance for Taoism declined considerably toward the end of the Han period in favor of Laozi, elsewhere—particularly in the fields of medicine and other techniques—his popularity continued to flourish.

Ute ENGELHARDT

📖 Csikszentmihalyi 1994; Eberhard 1942, 158–61; van Ess 1993a; Kaltenmark 1953, 50–53; Kohn 1993b, 351–52; Lewis 1990, 174–85; Seidel 1969; Seidel 1987b; Tetsui Yoshinori 1970; Tetsui Yoshinori 1972; see also bibliography for the entry *Huang-Lao

※ TAOISM AND CHINESE MYTHOLOGY

Huangdi neijing

黃帝內經

Inner Scripture of the Yellow Emperor

The *Huangdi neijing* is generally considered the main text on Chinese medical theory, and the *Shanghan lun* 傷寒論 (Treatise on Cold Damage Disorders) the principal reference for clinical treatment. In its extant form, the *Neijing* comprises two books, each of which includes twenty-four *juan* (chapters) and eighty-one *pian* (sections): the *Suwen* 素問 (Plain Questions) and the *Lingshu* 靈樞 (Numinous Pivot). The two books are best viewed as compilations of thematically ordered knowledge from different medical traditions or lineages whose authorship is unknown. Their first compilation likely dates to the Han, between the first century BCE and the first century CE.

Both books contain dialogues between the Yellow Emperor (*Huangdi) and various ministers. These dialogues are concerned with cosmology and analogical changes in macrocosm and microcosm, lifestyle, medical ethics, diagnostics and therapeutics. The *Suwen* is generally considered to be more philosophical in content, and in many places it discusses environmental and bodily processes in terms of the Five Phases (*wuxing*). The *Lingshu* is thought to be more clinically oriented, and frequently the text details principles of acupuncture and moxibustion therapy.

The textual history of these books is complex and remains a matter of contention. The *Suwen* has a well-known Tang dynasty editor, *Wang Bing (fl. 762), who divided it into twenty-four *juan* and submitted it to the throne in 762. In the Northern Song period it was substantially reedited and "corrected" by Lin Yi 林億 (eleventh century) and his team. About one third of the text is devoted to the doctrine of the "five circulatory phases and six seasonal influences" (*wuyun liuqi* 五運六氣), also known as "phase energetics." This doctrine is recorded in chapters 66–71, 74, and parts of chapters 5 and 9. Chapters 72 and 73 were lost by Wang Bing's time, and he gives only their titles; it is uncertain whether they dealt with this doctrine. Generally, Wang Bing is considered to have included the above chapters into the *Suwen*, but there is no certainty that their inclusion predated the Song edition of the *Suwen*.

The *Lingshu* originally may have had the title *Zhenjing* 鍼經 (Scripture of Acupuncture). Thus, Huangfu Mi 皇甫謐 (215–82) considered the *Suwen* and the *Zhenjing* available to him to constitute the *Huangdi neijing* that had been recorded in the bibliography of the *Hanshu* (History of the Former Han; *j. 30*). Wang Bing, in his preface to the *Suwen*, refers to the second book of the *Huangdi neijing* as *Lingshu* and, in his commentary to the *Suwen*, sometimes quotes from a text with the same title; but this book was later lost. The present editions of the *Lingshu* are generally derived from an edition printed during the Southern Song in 1155, which in turn was based on the reedition of a book called *Zhenjing* that the Imperial Court had recovered from Korea in the 1090s.

Two further books are known to have had *Huangdi neijing* as prefix to their title; they are the *Mingtang* 明堂 (Hall of Light) and the *Taisu* 太素 (Great Plainness). Of these only the latter is extant, and only in one recension that survived in Japan: an eleventh-century copy of an early eighth-century version. It is now generally accepted that this text was compiled during the Tang by Yang Shangshan 楊上善 (fl. 666–83), whose commentary indicates that he was deeply involved in Taoist thought and practice (he advocates, for instance, meditation on and inner visualization of the deities of the five viscera, *wuzang). The extant eleventh-century Japanese version is incomplete, but its 180 *pian* all have counterparts in the *Neijing*, in either the *Suwen* or the *Lingshu*, or in both.

Elisabeth HSU

📖 Keegan 1988; Lu and Needham 1980, 88–106; Ma Jixing 1990, 68–98; Porkert 1974; Rochat de la Vallée and Larre 1993 (part. trans.); Sivin 1993; Sivin 1998; Yamada Keiji 1979

※ *yangsheng*

Huang-Lao

黃老

Yellow [Emperor] and Old [Master]

The term "Huang-Lao" was first coined in the Former Han dynasty in the second century BCE. *Huang* 黃 refers to *Huangdi (Yellow Emperor) and *Lao* 老 refers to Laozi. Huang-Lao thought is said to have flourished at the courts of Han Wendi (r. 180–157 BCE) and Han Jingdi (r. 157–141 BCE), strongly supported by the Empress, later Dowager Empress, Dou before Confucian influence achieved dominance under Han Wudi from 136 BCE (Si Xiuwu 1992; Lin Congshun 1991).

Among the prominent early Han intellectuals who were attracted to Huang-Lao thought was Sima Tan 司馬談 (?–110 BCE), the father of Sima Qian 司馬遷 (145?–86? BCE, the author of the *Shiji* or *Records of the Historian*). He is said to have studied under a Huang-Lao master, and sources claim the existence of a lineage of such masters reaching back into Warring States times to philosophers gathered at the famous Jixia 稷下 academy at the court of the rulers of the state of Qi 齊 (modern Shandong). In the Later Han dynasty, Huang-Lao appears to have been incorporated into the ideas and practices aimed at achieving physical immortality developed by religious masters who founded the *Yellow Turban and Five Pecks of Rice (*Wudoumi dao) movements. Later on, virtually all of the early texts disappeared and knowledge about original Huang-Lao was lost.

Thinkers and texts. Many early philosophers and texts are said in the sources, or thought by modern scholars, to be influenced by, or representative of, Huang-Lao thought, which they consider to be a form of syncretic Taoism. Among these are the Confucian Xunzi 荀子 (ca. 335-ca. 238 BCE); Han Feizi 韓非子 (ca. 280-ca. 233 BCE), usually associated with the *fajia* 法家 (legalists); Shen Dao 慎到 (ca. 360-ca. 285 BCE; Thompson 1979), Shen Buhai 申不害 (ca. 400-ca. 340 BCE; Creel 1974), the naturalist Zou Yan 騶衍 (third century BCE; Peerenboom 1993), Tian Pian 田駢 (ca. 319–284 BCE), and Song Xing 宋鈃 (ca. 334–301 BCE), who is more commonly recognized as a Mohist (Shi Huaci 1994); the "Yueyu xia" 越語下 section of the *Guoyu* 國語 (Discourses of the States) that possibly represents the ideas of the strategist Fan Li 范蠡 (fl. late sixth to early fifth century BCE; Ryden 1997; Li Xueqin 1990); parts of the *Zhuangzi (Roth 1991b); the *Lüshi chunqiu* 呂氏春秋 (Springs and Autumns of Mr. Lü; 239 BCE; Knoblock and Riegel 2000); the *Heguan zi* 鶡冠子 (Book of Master

Heguan; sometime from the mid-third century to early second century BCE; Defoort 1997); the *Huainan zi (139 BCE; Major 1993); sections of the *Chunqiu fanlu* 春秋繁露 (Profusion of Dew on the Spring and Autumn Annals) of the Confucian Dong Zhongshu 董仲舒 (ca. 195–115 BCE; Queen 1996); and the many texts containing in their title the name of the Yellow Emperor or his assistants in the imperial bibliography preserved in the *Hanshu* (History of the Former Han; Csikszentmihalyi 1994).

These latter texts appear in the sections devoted to the Various Masters (*zajia* 雜家), the Military Specialists (*bingjia* 兵家), the Arts of the Numbers (*shushu* 數術), and the Methods and Techniques (*fangji). The most famous of these works, and the only one to have survived transmission to modern times, is the foundational text of Traditional Chinese Medicine, the *Huangdi neijing* (Yellow Emperor's Inner Canon). Recently discovered fragments of these "Yellow Emperor" texts, however, show strong influence of Yin-Yang thought, and it is perhaps premature to attribute all of these texts as belonging to Huang-Lao Taoism.

Features of Huang-Lao thought. Despite the historical evidence, the precise nature and characteristics of Huang-Lao thought and the date of its appearance on the Chinese philosophical stage are still matters of great scholarly dispute. The discovery of the silk manuscripts at *Mawangdui in the winter of 1973–74 is believed by some to have solved the enigma. The four manuscripts copied in front of the B (*yi* 乙) manuscript of the *Daode jing* have been interpreted as being the long lost *Huangdi sijing* 黃帝四經 (Four Scriptures of the Yellow Emperor), the core text of Huang-Lao (Chang L. S. and Yu Feng 1998; Chen Guying 1995; Decaux 1989; Tang Lan 1974; Yu Mingguang 1989; Yu Mingguang et al. 1993). However, this identification, in the opinion of other scholars, is problematic (Yates 1997; Ryden 1997; Carrozza 1999). They argue that the sections in these texts derive from a variety of different traditions and are philosophically and/or linguistically incompatible with each other. Consequently, many of the interpretations of the nature and characteristics of Huang-Lao Taoist thought that have been based on a reading of the Mawangdui manuscripts are debatable, since they are based on the assumption that these texts form an integral whole and are really affiliated with Huang-Lao.

Randall P. Peerenboom (1993, 27) argues that Huang-Lao consists essentially of a "foundational naturalism" (cf. Turner 1989). By this he means that the cosmic natural order includes both the way of humans (*rendao* 人道) and the way of Heaven (*tiandao* 天道), is accorded "normative priority," and is the basis for human social order that models itself upon and is in harmony with the cosmic order. John S. Major adds the importance of Dao as the "highest and most primary expression of universal potentiality, order, and potency" that is immanent in the cosmic order. The ruler, in possession of "penetrating insight" (*shenming* 神明), must act in conformity to changes in that order through the seasons and practice *wuwei (non-striving). Others also point out the importance of the doctrine of *xingming* 形名 ("forms and names") in Huang-Lao political thought. Harold D. Roth, on the other hand, argues that Sima Tan's description of the Taoists (*DAOJIA) preserved in the *Shiji* (130.3288–92) represents a late-second-century understanding of Huang-Lao and that it possessed three orientations, "cosmology, psychology (or psycho-physiology), and political thought," adopting ideas from the Confucians, the Mohists, the Terminologists (*mingjia* 名家), and the Legalists (Roth 1991b; Roth 1999a). Mark Csikszentmihalyi (1994), followed by Robin D. S. Yates (1997), prefers to understand Huang-Lao as a tradition or group of traditions that included many different aspects, myth, political philosophy, military thought, divination, and medicine. Until further discoveries are made or new research throws light on the subject, these views are perhaps closest to capturing the essence of Huang-Lao.

Robin D. S. YATES

📖 Chang L. S. and Yu Feng 1998; Chen Guying 1995; Csikszentmihalyi 1994; Emmerich 1995; van Ess 1993b; Jan Yün-hua 1980; Jan Yün-hua 1983; Lin Cong-shun 1991; Major 1993, 8–14 and 43–53; Peerenboom 1993; Robinet 1997b, 47–48; Roth 1987b; Ryden 1997; Seidel 1969, 18–26; Si Xiuwu 1992; Tang Lan 1974; Tu Wei-ming 1979; Yates 1997; Yu Mingguang 1989; Yu Mingguang et al. 1993

huanglu zhai

黄 錄 齋

Yellow Register Retreat

The Yellow Register Retreat is one of the Three Register Retreats (*sanlu zhai* 三錄齋), along with the Golden Register and the Jade Register Retreats (*jinlu zhai* and *yulu zhai*). *Lu Xiujing (406–77) ranked it second among the *Lingbao rites. According to his *Wugan wen* 五感文 (Text on the Five Commemorations; CT 1278), the number and dimensions of the gates of the sacred space that was prepared for this ritual were the same as those for the Golden Register Retreat, although here ten lamps, ten gates of the inner altar, and three incense burners were placed along its four sides. The number of days was also the same as for a Golden Register Retreat. There is, in fact, little difference in form and structure between the Yellow Register and the Golden Register Retreats. While the Golden Register Retreat could be performed only by the

emperor, however, the Yellow Register Retreat could also be performed by
the common people. For this reason, the Yellow Register Retreat has been
the most universal of all rituals of Merit (*gongde*) for the dead from Tang and
Song times until the present day.

Almost all Lingbao rituals that developed during the Song period are deemed
to be based on the Yellow Register Retreat. One typical example is Jiang Shuyu's
蔣叔輿 (1162–1223) *Wushang huanglu dazhai licheng yi* (Standard Liturgies of
the Supreme Great Yellow Register Retreat). In the Ming period, as attested
by Zhou Side's 周思得 (1359–1451) *Shangqing lingbao jidu dacheng jinshu* 上清
靈寶濟度大成金書 (Golden Writings on the Great Achievement of Deliverance of the Numinous Treasure of Highest Clarity; in *Zangwai daoshu*), the
Yellow Register Retreat was inflated into a multipurpose ritual capable of
resolving all difficulties for all people, from emperor to commoner. Since that
time, the name Yellow Register Retreat became a synonym for Taoist ritual
as a whole.

In present-day Taiwan, the ritual of Merit belongs to the same stream as
the Yellow Register Retreats of the Six Dynasties, Tang, and Song periods.
Rituals of Merit that last more than two days are often called Yellow Register
Retreats.

MARUYAMA Hiroshi

📖 Davis E. 2001, 227–36; Lagerwey 1981b, 163–65; Maspero 1981, 292–98;
Ōfuchi Ninji 1983, 463–677

※ *jinlu zhai*; *yulu zhai*; *zhai*; *Wushang huanglu dazhai licheng yi*

Huangting jing

黄庭經

Scripture of the Yellow Court

The Yellow Court (*huangting* 黄庭; fig. 40) is the Center. In the body it has
various locations: in the head, in the spleen, between the eyes, or in the lower
Cinnabar Field (*dantian*). The text entitled after the Yellow Court is one of
the most popular and influential Taoist scriptures. Dating originally from the
second century, it is probably the earliest extant work describing the human
body as animated by inner gods, and has given rise to commentaries and
further elaborations.

The scripture exists in two main versions, called Inner (*nei* 內) and Outer
(*wai* 外). The full titles of both contain the term *jing* 景 (light or effulgence),

Fig. 40. The Yellow Court (*huangting* 黃庭). The phrase in the inner circle reads "Spirit of the Center." The other phrases read (clockwise from the top): "Yellow Court," "Gate of the Meaning of the Dao," "Empty Non-being," "Gate of All Wonders," "Great Ultimate," "Gate of the Mysterious Female," "Real Emptiness," "Gate of the Non-dual Doctrine." Liu Yiming 劉一明, *Huangting jing jie* 黃庭經解 (Explication of the *Scripture of the Yellow Court*).

which refers to the luminous corporeal spirits (see **bajing*): *Huangting neijing jing* 黃庭內景經 (Scripture of the Inner Effulgences of the Yellow Court) and *Huangting waijing jing* 黃庭外景經 (Scripture of the Outer Effulgences of the Yellow Court). The chronological priority of the two versions is still debated. Kristofer Schipper (1975a, 2–11) suggests that the Outer version is earlier on the basis of its brevity, and that the Inner version is a later development. There are, however, instances of Taoist texts whose shorter versions are later than their longer ones. Wang Ming (1984b) supposes rather that the Inner version is older because **Wei Huacun's biography states that she used to recite it. Yoshioka Yoshitoyo (1955, 225) and Max Kaltenmark (1967–68) share the same opinion.

The relation of the *Huangting jing* to the **Shangqing school of Taoism has been variously interpreted. Shangqing certainly adopted the *Huangting jing*, as attested by the biography of Wei Huacun to whom the text was transmitted, and by quotations or mentions of both the Inner and the Outer version in Shangqing texts such as the *Xiaomo jing* 消魔經 (Scripture on Dispelling Demons; CT 1344) and the **Zhengao* (Authentic Declarations). The text, however, is not associated with the **Dadong zhenjing* (Authentic Scripture of the Great Cavern) as has been asserted, because it gives different names to the gods of the human body. Moreover, the practices mentioned in the Inner version pertain to the Shangqing tradition but existed prior to it. In fact, both versions seem to have been recorded before the Shangqing revelations of

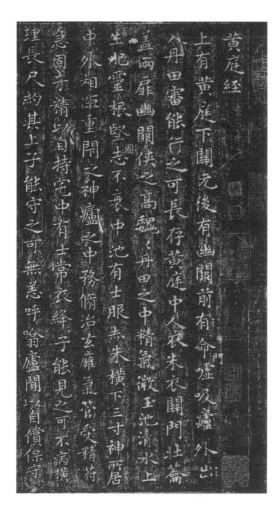

Fig. 41. Opening verses of the *Huang-ting jing* (Scripture of the Yellow Court). Calligraphy by Wang Xizhi 王羲之 (321?–379?).

364–70; Shangqing likely adopted both as "inferior" texts, as it did with several earlier texts and practices (especially those mentioned in the biographies of the Shangqing saints, as is the case with Wei Huacun). Allusions to sexual practices in both versions also indicate an origin earlier than the Shangqing revelations. Both versions, at any rate, seem to have undergone textual adjustments.

Content. Written in heptasyllabic meter, the *Huangting jing* uses a poetic and secret language. It was to be recited to expel calamities and ailments and to attain longevity and spiritual quietude. It alludes to practices aiming to achieve bodily and spiritual perfection in the **yangsheng* (Nourishing Life) tradition, which can be traced back to the third century BCE. It probably had a mnemo-technical role in helping those who performed these practices, and is said to allow the practitioner to see the subtle forms of his viscera and his spirits, and to have deities become his servants. The **Dengzhen yinjue* (Concealed

Instructions for the Ascent to Reality; 3.1a–5b) describes a ritual without which the recitation of the text would be ineffective.

The main practices alluded to in the *Huangting jing* are visualization of inner bodily organs and their gods, visualization and absorption of inner light, circulation of saliva or essence (*jing*) and pneuma (*qi*), visualization of astral bodies (Sun and Moon), sexual practices, and pacifying the souls and the heart-mind (*xin*). The Inner version gives more details on the names of the gods, some of which are similar to those found in the Han "weft texts" (*weishu* 緯書; see *TAOISM AND THE APOCRYPHA). These are absent in the Outer version, a feature that could indicate that the Inner version is "esoteric" (*nei*) as the names of the gods are secret and their knowledge confers power.

Main commentaries. The earliest extant commentaries are by Liangqiu zi 梁丘子 (Bai Lüzhong 白履忠, fl. 722–29; in *Xiuzhen shishu* 55–60, and CT 403) and Wucheng zi 務成子 (probably Tang; YJQQ 12.28b–31b, for the Outer version and the two first sections of the Inner version). Another commentary, found in the *Daoshu (7.1a–7b), interprets the text in relation to the eight trigrams (*bagua*) and the accretion and diminution of Yin and Yang according to *neidan principles.

Isabelle ROBINET

📖 Boltz J. M. 1987a, 236–37; Carré 1999 (trans. of Inner and Outer versions); Despeux 1994, 108–33; Homann 1971; Huang Jane 1987–90, 2: 221–54 (trans. of Inner and Outer versions); Kroll 1996a (part. trans. of Inner version); Maspero 1981, 489–95, 523–29; Mugitani Kunio 1981; Qing Xitai 1988–95, 1: 352–77; Pregadio 2006a; Robinet 1984, 2: 253–57; Robinet 1993, 55–96; Saso 1995, 99–151 (trans. of Outer version); Schipper 1975a (concordance of Inner and Outer versions); Wang Ming 1984b

※ MEDITATION AND VISUALIZATION

huanjing bunao

還精補腦

"returning the essence to replenish the brain"

In its original form, the technique of "returning the essence to replenish the brain" consists of controlling the flow of seminal essence (*jing*). It is based on the belief that the brain, the marrow of the spinal cord, and the semen are one and the same substance (some Western doctors of antiquity held an analogous notion). In this form, *huanjing bunao* is related to sexual techniques (**fangzhong shu*) and longevity practices (**yangsheng*).

**Rong Cheng's biography in the *Liexian zhuan (Biographies of Exemplary Immortals; trans. Kaltenmark 1953, 55–60) describes the art of "riding women" (*yunü* 御女) as follows: "One should firmly hold [the penis] with the hand, not ejaculate, and let the essence revert to replenish the brain." This was the main sexual technique. A more detailed description is found in an anonymous "scripture of the immortals" (*xianjing* 仙經), which states that before semen flows out, one should hold the penis with the two middle fingers of the left hand behind the scrotum and in front of the anus, and simultaneously breath out slowly through the mouth and repeatedly grind one's teeth. In this way, states the text, essence "rises from the Jade Stem (*yujing* 玉莖, the penis) up to the brain" (see Maspero 1981, 522).

"Returning the essence to replenish the brain" is also mentioned in **neidan* texts, where it takes on a different meaning and refers to the repeated cycling of the essence in the first stage of the practice (see the entry **zhoutian*).

Catherine DESPEUX

📖 Baldrian-Hussein 1984, 109–36; Maspero 1981, 522–29; Needham 1983, 197–201; Wile 1992, 46–50

※ *zhoutian*; *fangzhong shu*; *yangsheng*

Huanzhen xiansheng

幻真先生

Elder of Illusory Perfection; also known as Youzhen xiansheng
幼真先生 (Elder Youzhen)

The only available information about Huanzhen xiansheng comes from the preface to the *Huanzhen xiansheng fu nei yuanqi jue* 幻真先生服內元氣訣 (Instructions on the Ingestion of the Inner Original Breath According to the Elder of Illusory Perfection; CT 828; trans. Despeux 1988, 65–84, from the version in the **Chifeng sui*). According to this document, he received breathing techniques during the Tianbao reign period (742–56) from Wanggong 王公, a Perfected of the Luofu Mountains (**Luofu shan, Guangdong).

Two texts in the Taoist Canon are attributed to Huanzhen xiansheng: the *Taixi jing zhu* 胎息經注 (Commentary to the Scripture of Embryonic Breathing; CT 130; see **Taixi jing*) and the above-mentioned *Funei yuanqi jue* (also found in YJQQ 60.14a–25b). The *Xin Tangshu* (New History of the Tang; 59.1542) lists a *Kang Zhongxiong fu nei yuanqi jue* 康仲熊服內元氣訣 (Instructions on the Ingestion of the Inner Original Breath According to Kang Zhongxiong; van der Loon 1984, 114) that may correspond to Huanzhen xiansheng's text. No evidence, however, supports the identification of Kang Zhongxiong with Huanzhen xiansheng.

Catherine DESPEUX

📖 Despeux 1988, 65–84 (trans. of *Huanzhen xiansheng fu nei yuanqi jue*)

※ *yangsheng*

Huashan

華山

Mount Hua (Shaanxi)

Mount Hua (lit., "Flowery" or "Glorious"), located in the Huayin 華陰 district of Shaanxi, is the Western Peak (see under **wuyue*). At about 2,000 m, it is not the highest but certainly one of the most impressive mountains in China. Its almost vertical granite cliffs rise just above the densely populated plain. The pilgrimage trail leads through perilous stone steps and along ridges that were gradually secured with iron rails, over the centuries. Looking northward from the five summits, one can see the Yellow River bending at the famous Tongguan 潼關 pass and flowing eastward toward the sea. Located along the road between the cities of Xi'an and Luoyang, the mountain was visited by innumerable literati who contributed to a huge accumulated travel literature and poetry.

Like the other Peaks, as early as the second century BCE Mount Hua had a temple—later named Xiyue miao 西嶽廟 or Shrine of the Western Peak—located at its foot where official sacrifices were conducted. Although such temples came to be managed by Taoists throughout most of Chinese history, the ceremonies performed there were never Taoist rites properly speaking. Tang anecdotal evidence shows that besides the official state cult, the Xiyue miao was the locus of popular devotion, with spirit-mediums communicating with the god of the Peak and his underlings. The god of Mount Hua, like the gods of all Five Peaks, was associated with the netherworld. In contrast to Mount Tai (*Taishan, the Eastern Peak), however, Mount Hua did not emerge as a nationwide cult connected with the realm of the dead. There were shrines to the Western Peak in districts around Mount Hua, but apparently not much further away. For this reason, Mount Hua was much visited by people of the area, but there were apparently no pilgrimage associations coming from afar, and no special pilgrimage season on the mountain. The Taoist acculturation of the mountain is linked less to the cult of its god than to ascetics who lived there, especially in the man-made caves, some of them hewn out of vertical cliffs.

Since antiquity, Mount Hua has been reputed for the drugs that can be found there, and the renown of the mountain as a meeting place for immortality seekers is already mentioned in the third century CE. It is also linked to revelations, including those concerning *Kou Qianzhi (365?–448). The most famous Taoist associated with the mountain is *Chen Tuan (ca. 920–89), who lived there before gaining immortality. The Taoist establishment located at the starting point of the pilgrimage trail, the Yuquan yuan 玉泉院 (Cloister of the Jade Spring), is devoted to him. Another nearby monastery, the Yuntai guan 雲臺觀 (Abbey of the Cloud Terrace; Qing Xitai 1994, 4: 269–70), dates from medieval times and flourished from the Song until the Qing periods. Like all Taoist establishments in the middle valley of the Yellow River, these monasteries came under the management of the *Quanzhen order during the 1230s, and have remained so ever since. But Mount Hua was never a large monastic center and owed its fame instead to the small shrines and hermitages along the pilgrimage trail and atop its different summits. Most of these shrines have been restored during the last two decades of the past century.

Vincent GOOSSAERT

📖 Andersen 1989–90a; Boltz J. M. 1987a, 107–9; Geil 1926, 217–94; Hachiya Kunio 1990, 1: 45–63 and 303–4, 2: 37–59 and 299–300; Morrison and Eberhard 1973; Vervoorn 1990–91

※ *wuyue*; TAOIST SACRED SITES

Huashu

化書

Book of Transformation

The *Huashu* is a unique philosophical work of the period of the Five Dynasties, which syncretizes elements of Taoist, Buddhist, and Confucian thought, and which has been noted in recent times for its scientific observations (for instance regarding optics and acoustics) and for its unusual emphasis on epistemological considerations. Its influence during the Song and subsequent dynasties was substantial, both within Taoist and Confucian metaphysics, and especially as a foundation of alchemical thought. The textual history of the work is highly complex, and it has been transmitted in several versions and redactions, including two in the *Daozang* (CT 1044 and CT 1478).

The *Huashu* was written by the shadowy figure Tan Qiao 譚峭 (ca. 860-ca. 940), but it was immediately appropriated by the high official of the Southern Tang, Song Qiqiu 宋齊丘 (886–959), who wrote a preface and published the work under his own name in 930. Thus, in official and private catalogues of the Song the work is listed with Song Qiqiu as its author, and in some still current versions its title is given as *Qiqiu zi* 齊丘子 or *Book of Master Qiqiu*. The record was set straight, however, in a postface by *Chen Jingyuan, dated 1060, in which he reports the sordid details concerning Song's theft of the book, based on information derived from *Chen Tuan (who referred to Tan Qiao as a "master and friend," *shiyou* 師友).

It has been suggested, furthermore, that Tan Qiao was, in fact, identical with the roughly contemporary (though perhaps slightly later) and more fully documented Taoist figure with the same surname, *Tan Zixiao (fl. 935-after 963), the founder of the *Tianxin zhengfa. The conflation of the two Taoist figures gained currency from the latter part of the sixteenth century, and it is reflected for instance in the *Wanli xu daozang* edition of the work (CT 1478), which gives the *hao* of the author as *Zixiao zhenren* 紫霄真人, "The Perfected (Tan) Zixiao." The identity of Tan Qiao as Tan Zixiao remains, nonetheless, highly questionable.

The *Huashu* is normally divided into six chapters, each of which deals with a particular kind of transformation, namely, 1. "Way Transformation" ("Daohua" 道化); 2. "Techniques Transformation" ("Shuhua" 術化); 3. "Virtue Transformation" ("Dehua" 德化); 4. "Benevolence Transformation" ("Renhua" 仁化); 5. "Food Transformation" ("Shihua" 食化); and 6. "Frugality Transformation" ("Jianhua" 儉化). It has been argued, however, that the original structure of the work was quinary, and that the first chapter—from the hands of the real author, Tan Qiao—was conceived as prefatory.

Poul ANDERSEN

📖 Didier 1998; Ding Zhenyan and Li Sizhen 1996; Lin Shengli 1989; Qing Xitai 1988–95, 2: 484–92

Hugang zi

狐剛子 (*or:* 胡剛子, 胡罡子)

also known as Huzi 狐子 and
Huqiu xiansheng 狐丘先生 (Master Huqiu)

Hugang zi is the appellation of an otherwise unknown alchemist (or perhaps group of alchemists) associated with a corpus of *waidan* writings that
developed during the late Six Dynasties and is now extant in fragments. The
commentary to the *Scripture of the Nine Elixirs* (*Jiudan jing*) mentions him as
a disciple of *Zuo Ci and as the master of *Ge Xuan, who was *Ge Hong's
granduncle and belonged to the latter's line of family transmission of *waidan*
texts (*Huangdi jiuding shendan jingjue* 黃帝九鼎神丹經訣; CT 885, 3.6b and
7.5a–b). Other sources relate Hugang zi to Wei Boyang 魏伯陽, the legendary
author of the *Zhouyi cantong qi* (see, e.g., *Danlun jue zhixin jian* 丹論訣旨心
鑑; CT 935, 4a). Although these accounts have no historical basis, they suggest, with other details, that the texts ascribed to Hugang zi were produced
in Jiangnan 江南.

The main source of fragments from this corpus is the commentary to the
Scripture of the Nine Elixirs. Passages quoted there make it possible to gather
details on the contents of five works: *Fu xuanzhu jue* 伏玄珠訣 (Instructions
for Fixing the Mysterious Pearl), *Wujin fen tujue* 五金粉圖訣 (Illustrated Instructions on the Powders of the Five Metals), *Chu jinkuang tulu* 出金礦圖錄
(Illustrated Account of the Extraction of Gold from Its Ores), *Wanjin jue* 萬
金訣 (Instructions Worth a Thousand Pieces of Gold), and *Heche jing* 河車
經 (Book of the River Chariot). In addition, various bibliographies ascribe to
Hugang zi several other works of which no further traces appear to exist.

After the anonymous texts summarized by Ge Hong in *j.* 11 of his *Baopu
zi*, this remarkable body of writings included the earliest known *waidan*
works largely based on metals. Fragments dealing with the compounding
of lead and mercury are of special interest in light of the history of alchemy
in China, where these two metals progressively acquired importance owed
especially to the influence of the *Cantong qi*. Among various other methods,
the commentary to the *Scripture of the Nine Elixirs* preserves recipes for the
separate refining of mercury (11.6a–b) and lead (12.3a), followed by a method
for their conjunction (11.7a–b; also in 12.3a–b). Moreover, Hugang zi's lineage
may be related to the composition of parts of the *Cantong qi* (see the materials
collected in Chen Guofu 1983, 68–87), and one of the two Tang *waidan* com-

mentaries to the *Cantong qi* (*Zhouyi cantong qi zhu* 周易參同契注; ca. 700; CT 1004) highlights methods attributed to him. The corpus associated with this legendary master, therefore, likely reflects a local tradition that came to affect the whole development of Chinese alchemy.

Fabrizio PREGADIO

📖 Chen Guofu 1983, 303–9; Qing Xitai 1994, 1: 234–35; Pregadio 1991, 567–68; Zhao Kuanghua 1985a

※ *waidan*

Huiming jing

慧命經

Scripture of Wisdom and Life

The *Huiming jing* was written by the Chan monk *Liu Huayang (1735–99) in 1794. One edition (part. trans. Wilhelm R. 1929) was published by Zhanran Huizhen zi 湛然慧真子 in 1921 together with the *Taiyi jinhua zongzhi; another (trans. Wong Eva 1998) had been published earlier in the *Wu-Liu xianzong* 伍柳 仙宗 (The Wu-Liu Lineage of Immortality; 1897) together with Liu's *Jinxian zhenglun* 金仙証論 (Essay on the Verification of Golden Immortality) and two works by *Wu Shouyang. In fact, the spiritual foundation of this text is strictly linked to the *Wu-Liu school. Eclectic in character, it draws on the *neidan* traditions of the Song and Yuan periods, joining them with Chan and Huayan 華嚴 Buddhism and presenting them in a readily comprehensible language.

The *Huiming jing* opens with Liu Huayang's preface, which contains notes on his life. The main text can be divided into two parts, including altogether sixteen sections (the index in the *Wu-Liu xianzong*, however, lists twenty sections). The first part, consisting of the first eight sections, contains a set of eight illustrations on the *neidan* practice with explanations, while the second part presents various related theories. As Liu states in the first section, he describes the teachings of the *Huayan jing* 華嚴經 (*Avataṃsaka-sūtra*) and the Taoist classics in pictorial form in order to help adepts understand the true meaning of cultivating mind and body. In content, the *Huiming jing* is close to the Ming and Qing alchemical texts that relate the formation of the spiritual embryo to the process of human life—gestation, childhood, and adulthood—followed by the reversal of this process. This is accompanied by detailed descriptions

of visions inspired by the *Huayan jing*, represented here as the result of the
formation of the spiritual embryo.

Monica ESPOSITO

📖 Wilhelm R. 1929, 67–78 (part. trans.); Wong Eva 1998 (trans.); Zhanran
Huizhen zi 1921

※ Liu Huayang; *neidan*; Wu-Liu pai

hun

魂

Yang soul(s); celestial soul(s)

See *hun* and *po* 魂 · 魄.

hun and po

魂 · 魄

Yang soul(s) and Yin soul(s); celestial soul(s) and earthly soul(s)

The notions of *hun* and *po* are central to Chinese thought and religion. Although the term "souls" is often used to refer to them, they are better seen
as two types of vital entities, the source of life in every individual. The *hun*
is Yang, luminous, and volatile, while the *po* is Yin, sombre, and heavy. They
are, moreover, to be considered the epitome of the spiritual (*shen*) and the
demonic (*gui*): the *hun* represents spirit, consciousness, and intelligence,
whereas the *po* represents physical nature, bodily strength, and movement.
When natural death occurs, the *hun* disperses in heaven, and the *po* returns
to earth. A violent death, on the other hand, causes the *hun* and *po* to remain
among humans and perform evil deeds.

Early Zhou period classical theory maintained that each aristocrat was possessed of two distinct souls which, when death came, followed separate paths,
the *hun* mounting to heaven, the *po* sinking into the grave with the corpse or
into the Yellow Springs (*huangquan* 黃泉), a netherworld located below the
earth. The nobility built shrines in which the *hun* of their ancestors received
offerings to ensure both their welfare in the post-mortem and the prosper-

Fig. 42. The three *hun* and seven *po*. *Chu sanshi jiuchong baosheng jing* 除三尸九蟲保生經 (Scripture on Expelling the Three Corpses and Nine Worms to Protect Life; CT 871), 1a and 3a–b.

ity of their descendants. The demonic *po* instead was appeased by elaborate funerals, sumptuous tombs, and sacrifices to prevent it from returning as a malevolent revenant (Loewe 1982, 114–26). Before these rituals were performed, an attempt was made to reanimate the deceased by "summoning the *hun*" (*zhaohun* 招魂), a rite with traces of early shamanic practices described in the *Zhaohun* poem (ca. 240 BCE) of the *Chuci* 楚辭 (Songs of Chu; trans. Hawkes 1985, 219–31).

This system of beliefs eventually widened to include non-nobility as well. During the Later Han period, moreover, the number of the *hun* was fixed at three, and the number of the *po* at seven. Why these numbers were chosen is a matter of speculation, but the former figure may stand for the *sangang* 三綱, the three relationships between emperor and subject, father and son, and husband and wife (Needham 1974, 88–89), whereas the latter possibly denotes the seven openings of the human body and the seven emotions.

These ideas play an important role in several Taoist traditions. Since the volatile *hun* is fond of wandering and leaving the body during sleep, techniques were devised to restrain it, one of which entailed a method of staying constantly awake. Illnesses were deemed to be caused by the *hun* and *po* straying from the body, and death ensued when the *hun* and *po* left and did not return. Accordingly, the **fangshi* devised methods to control them whereas others used rites and ceremonies to summon them back. The three *hun* and seven *po*, moreover, were anthropomorphized and given names, and their individual attributes were described in detail. To visualize them, *Ge Hong (283–343) suggests the ingestion of "great medicines" and the practice of a method called "multiplication of the body" (*fenxing* 分形; trans. Ware 1966, 306). He also mentions an Elixir for Summoning the *hun* composed of five minerals (*zhaohun dan* 招魂丹; Ware 1966, 87).

The *Shangqing corpus contains several methods for visualizing the *hun* and the *po*. In **neidan*, the *po* plays a particularly sombre role as it represents the passions that dominate the *hun*. This causes the vital force to decay, especially during sexual activity, and eventually leads to death. The inner alchemical practice seeks to concentrate the vital forces within the body by reversing the respective roles of *hun* and *po*, so that the *hun* (Yang) controls the *po* (Yin).

Farzeen BALDRIAN-HUSSEIN

📖 Brashier 1996; Despeux 1994, 133–35; Loewe 1979, 9–13; Needham 1974, 85–93; Tu Wei-ming 1985, 35–50; Tu Wei-ming 1987a; Yü Ying-shih 1987

※ TAOIST VIEWS OF THE HUMAN BODY

hundun

混沌

Chaos; inchoate state

The term *hundun*, commonly translated as "chaos," has different uses and meanings both within and outside Taoism: it can denote a mythical being, function as a descriptive word, or refer to a stage of the cosmogonic process. Its uses in Taoist texts inherit some elements of ancient myths, traces of which are found in various sources. In the *Zuozhuan* 左傳 (Commentary of Zuo), for example, Hundun is a son of *Huangdi, who banishes him for his incompetence. In the *Shanhai jing* 山海經 (Scripture of Mountains and Seas; fourth/third century BCE?), he is a cinnabar-red animal shaped like a sack with six legs and four wings; it can dance and sing, but has no face or eyes (trans. Mathieu 1983, 110). Elsewhere, Hundun is a dog who has eyes and ears but cannot see or hear; he lives on Mount *Kunlun and is related to thunder. According to another famous story told in the **Zhuangzi* (trans. Watson 1968,

Fig. 43. *Hundun* ("... a cinnabar-red animal shaped like a sack with six legs and four wings..."). Reproduced from Yuan Ke 1980, 55 (sketch based on a 1786 edition of the *Shanhai jing* 山海經).

97), the Emperor of the Center, whose name was Hundun, had no openings and therefore could not see or hear. The Emperors of the North and the South—emblems of duality—bore seven holes in his face, one each day, and on the seventh day Hundun died.

In these myths, Hundun is an image of primordial and central Chaos, utterly closed and dark, which disappears when it opens. This happens when the two primeval entities separate from each other, creating a space between them that is the beginning of the world. As thunder, Hundun also symbolizes the beginning of life. Taoism integrated some elements of these myths, sometimes modifying or enlarging them. In the *Kaitian jing, for instance, *hundun* comes after the cosmogonic stage of *taisu* 太素 (Great Plainness; see *COSMOGONY), and has two sons who are the gods of mountains and rivers. Generally, however, the earlier mythical aspect of Hundun is subordinate in Taoism, where *hundun* denotes primordial Chaos in a purely descriptive way.

Semantically, the term *hundun* is related to several expressions, hardly translatable into Western languages, that indicate the void or a barren and primal immensity—for instance, *hunlun* 混淪, *hundong* 混洞, *kongdong* 空洞, *menghong* 蒙洪, or *hongyuan* 洪元. It is also akin to the expression "something confused and yet complete" (*huncheng* 混成) found in *Daode jing* 25, which denotes the state prior to the formation of the world where nothing is perceptible, but which nevertheless contains a cosmic seed. Similarly, the state of *hundun* is likened to an egg; in this usage, the term alludes to a complete world round and closed in itself, which is a receptacle like a cavern (*dong* 洞) or a gourd (*hu* 壺 or *hulu* 壺盧). Moreover, *hundun* also appears as *hunlun* 混淪, a name reminiscent of Kunlun 崑崙, the mountain at the center of the world where the mythical Hundun lives, changing only the semantic indicator "mountain" (*shan* 山) to "water" (*shui* 水). This shows that Kunlun and *hundun* are the same closed center of the world.

In some Taoist cosmogonies, the stage of *hundun* comes relatively late, after the five precosmic geneses called Five Greats (*wutai* 五太; see *COSMOGONY). Here, *hundun* indicates the state in which pneuma (**qi*), form (**xing*), and matter (*zhi* 質) have already begun to exist but are still merged as one. This view, found in two Han "weft texts" (*weishu* 緯書; see *TAOISM AND THE APOCRYPHA), was also incorporated in **Liezi* 1 (Graham 1960, 18–19) and developed in many other Taoist texts. Elsewhere, *hundun* denotes a state when the Three Pneumas (*sanqi* 三氣), called Mysterious (*xuan* 玄), Original (*yuan* 元), and Inaugural (*shi* 始), are still merged.

*Neidan texts repeatedly allude to *hundun*. Alchemists begin their work by "opening" or "boring" *hundun*; in other words, they begin from the Origin, infusing its transcendent element of precosmic light into the cosmos in order to reshape it. From a physiological point of view, *hundun* is the beginning of embryonic life, the moment when the embryo receives the pneuma; in alchemical terms, it is the time when alchemical Lead and Mercury are still merged with each other. *Hundun* is the elixir, the number 1, and the Original Pneuma (**yuanqi*). As the Center, it is a synonym of the tripod and furnace (**dinglu*) and of the Embryo of Sainthood (**shengtai*). Thus, *hundun* is the origin, the center, and the end.

Isabelle ROBINET

📖 Eberhard 1968, 280, 363–64, 438–43, 445; Girardot 1978a; Girardot 1978b; Girardot 1983; Ikeda Tomohisa 1995

※ COSMOGONY; TAOISM AND CHINESE MYTHOLOGY

Hunyuan shengji

混元聖紀

Saintly Chronicle of Chaotic Origin

The *Hunyuan shengji* (CT 770) is a hagiography of Laozi, written by Xie Shouhao 謝守灝 (1134–1212; Qing Xitai 1994, 1: 332) and dated 1191. The author came from Yongjia 永嘉 (Zhejiang) and was a classical scholar who became an active Taoist at the *Yulong wanshou gong (Palace of the Ten-thousand-fold Longevity of Jade Beneficence) on the Western Hills (*Xishan, Jiangxi) in his later years. He apparently closely identified with his hagiographic work, sporting "hair and beard white and hoary, so that many people said he looked like a living Laozi come to earth," and took great pride in his writing, to the point of refusing to change even "a single word" (*Lishi zhenxian tidao tongjian*, *Xubian* 續編, 5.8a). He moreover seems to have had every intention to continue his writing in the otherworld, dreaming before his death that a divine personage summoned him to heaven so he could "compile a historical record of the perfected immortals" (5.8b).

Xie's work is the longest and most extensive of all Laozi hagiographies, consisting of nine *juan* which begin with a general chronological survey, then describe the events of the deity's life from the creation of the world, through his transformations, birth, emigration and conversion of the barbarians, to the revelations and miracles he worked in Taoist history, ending with the reign of Song Zhezong (r. 1085–1100) at the end of the eleventh century.

Besides the *Hunyuan shengji* proper, Xie's work appears twice more in the Taoist Canon: in the *Laojun nianpu yaolüe* 老君年譜要略 (Essential Chronology of Lord Lao; CT 771) in one *juan*, which contains the first *juan* with a commentary by Li Zhidao 李致道 (thirteenth century); and in the *Laozi shilüe* 老子史略 (Historical Summary of Laozi; CT 773) in three *juan*, which represents an earlier, shorter draft of the *Hunyuan shengji* and includes parts of *juan* 1–3 of the later finished work.

Livia KOHN

📖 Boltz J. M. 1987a, 133–36; Chen Guofu 1963, 171–73; Kohn 1998b, 31–32 and passim; Kusuyama Haruki 1979, 393–98 and 452–61

※ Laozi and Laojun; HAGIOGRAPHY

huohou

火候

"fire times"; fire phasing

1. Waidan

In Chinese cosmology, which envisions the universe as functioning in cyclical phases, time is one of the basic parameters. Different time phases are defined by the twenty-four or seventy-two divisions of the year or by the seasons, lunar months, days, and hours. Each phase is characterized by correspondence to a cosmological value, symbolized for instance by Yin and Yang, the Five Agents (*wuxing*), or the abstract emblems of the *Yijing* (trigrams, hexagrams, and their unbroken and broken lines). These cosmological values alternate along the sequence of phases that form a cyclical time process.

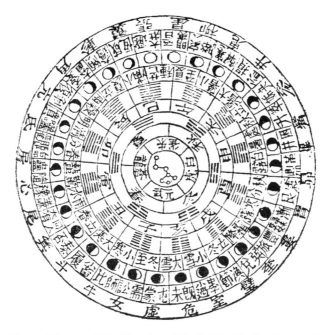

Fig. 44. Diagram of the "fire phases" (*huohou*) by *Yu Yan (1258–1314).
From the inner circle: the Northern Dipper (*beidou*); the four emblematic animals (see *siling*); the four seasons; six of the eight trigrams
(*bagua*); the twelve Earthly Branches (*dizhi* 地支; see *ganzhi*); the
twelve "sovereign hexagrams" (*bigua* 辟卦; see *bagua*); the twenty-
four periods of the year (or "energy nodes," *jieqi* 節氣); the thirty
days of the lunar month, indicated by the moon phases; sixty of the
sixty-four hexagrams; the twenty-eight lunar mansions (*xiu*). Hu Wei
胡渭 (1633–1714), *Yitu mingbian* 易圖明辨 (Clarifications on Diagrams
Related to the *Book of Changes*; 1706), *j.* 3. For similar diagrams, see
Needham 1983, 56, and Despeux 1994, 167. See also table 13.

For example, each hexagram represents a particular feature of the universe.
An early Han exegetic tradition of the *Yijing* attributed to Meng Xi 孟喜 (fl.
69 BCE) and Jing Fang 京方 (77–37 BCE) associates temporal phases with the
hexagrams in a pattern called *guaqi* 卦氣 or "breaths of hexagrams." In this
pattern, four of the sixty-four hexagrams are correlated with the four seasons
(or to the two equinoxes and the two solstices): *kan* 坎 ☵, *li* 離 ☲, *zhen* 震 ☳
and *dui* 兌 ☱. Their twenty-four lines match the twenty-four divisions of the
tropical year (the *jieqi* 節氣 or "energy nodes," each of which lasts fifteen days).
The other sixty hexagrams represent the growth and decline of Yin and Yang
during the year. Each hexagram corresponds to about six days, so that a set of
five hexagrams corresponds to one month. These five hexagrams are called
"duke" (*gong* 公), "sovereign" (*bi* 辟), "marquis" (*hou* 侯), "high official" (*dafu*

Fig. 45. The "fire phases" (*huohou*) in the human body. The cycle begins from zi 子 (at the bottom of the picture) and continues counter-clockwise along the *dumai and *renmai* channels. The picture shows the twelve "sovereign hexagrams" (*bigua* 辟卦; see *bagua*) and the corresponding moon phases. For a similar picture, see Despeux 1994, 91. See also table 13.

大夫), and "minister" (*qing* 卿). There are therefore twelve "duke hexagrams," twelve "sovereign hexagrams," and so forth.

The compounding of an elixir reproduces, in a reduced time span and in the laboratory, the process through which nature, in its own time and in its womb, transmutes minerals and metals into gold. Fire is therefore the main agent of transmutation; it is the earthly counterpart of the Sun and incarnates

Table 13

Hexagram	復 fu	臨 lin	泰 tai	大壯 dazhuang	夬 guai	乾 qian	姤 gou	遯 dun	否 pi	觀 guan	剝 bo	坤 kun
Branch	子 zi	丑 chou	寅 yin	卯 mao	辰 chen	巳 si	午 wu	未 wei	申 shen	酉 you	戌 xu	亥 hai
Pitch pipe	黃鐘 huang-zhong	大呂 dalü	大蔟 taicou	夾鐘 jiazhong	姑洗 guxi	仲呂 zhonglü	蕤賓 ruibin	林鐘 linzhong	夷則 yize	南呂 nanlü	無射 wuyi	應鐘 yingzhong
Month	11月	12月	1月	2月	3月	4月	5月	6月	7月	8月	9月	10月
Hour	23–1 時	1–3 時	3–5 時	5–7 時	7–9 時	9–11 時	11–13 時	13–15 時	15–17 時	17–19 時	19–21 時	21–23 時

The twelve "sovereign hexagrams" (*bigua* 辟卦) and their relation to other duodenary series: Earthly Branches (see under *ganzhi*), pitch pipes, months, and "double hours" (*shi* 時). (See also table 9, and fig. 45.)

the Yang force. "Since the heat of the flame thus stands for the active forces, the recreation of the cosmic process depends upon the binding of fire by time" (Sivin 1980, 266). As the movement of the Sun steers time and brings about change in beings and things, so the variation of heating by an alchemist follows the progress of time and brings about the creation and transformation of the elixir.

In *waidan*, fire phasing is performed in various ways, but essentially by varying the distance of fire from the vessel, the amount of fuel, or the duration of the heating time, and also by alternating the process of cooling and heating. The heating device and the whole procedure represent the dynamic and cyclic interaction of fundamental cosmic forces, such as the daily, monthly, and yearly phases of Yin and Yang.

Time is represented by numbers, trigrams, or hexagrams. Numbers are qualitatively chosen according to their cosmological meaning, and applied quantitatively as measures. Moreover, purely numerical equivalences in the ratio of one time unit to another make them interchangeable and permit time to be scaled in the alchemical procedure. For example, one lunar month of 30 days, having 360 "double hours" (*shi* 時), is equivalent to one year, having 360 days.

Trigrams and hexagrams similarly allow the alchemist to reduce time and reproduce the sinusoidal movement of the cosmic forces. In texts related to the *Zhouyi cantong qi*, for instance, the time phases are represented by the twelve "sovereign hexagrams" (*bigua* 辟卦; see table 13), a cosmological device whose origins have been mentioned above, but which is usually associated with the late Han cosmologist, Yu Fan 虞翻 (164–233 CE). In their progressive arrangement, starting with *fu* 復 ䷗, the unbroken lines in the first six hexagrams flow upward followed by the broken lines in the other six hexagrams, reproducing the alternate growth of Yin and Yang throughout the year. Each hexagram corresponds to a stage of heating. "As those rhythms bring minerals to perfection within the earth's womb, so they transmute the ingredients into an elixir in the alchemical laboratory" (Pregadio 2000, 185).

KIM Daeyeol

📖 Chen Guofu 1983, 88–90; Pregadio 1995; Pregadio 2000, 184–85; Sivin 1976; Sivin 1980, 231–79; Suzuki Yoshijirō 1974, 165–207, 624–31

※ *Yijing*; *waidan*; COSMOLOGY

2. *Neidan*

In *neidan*, fire phasing constitutes the rhythm of the inner alchemical work: the Art of Measure. Through it, the alchemist knows how to measure the ingredients (*yaowu* 藥物), when to increase or decrease the Fire, and so on.

The term *huo* 火 (fire) refers to the circulation of vital breath (*qi*), or simply the power of the effort in practice, while *hou* 候 (phase) denotes the sequence in which the practice is performed. Fire phasing therefore represents the most secret part of *neidan*, the inner rhythm that one must find and experience for oneself. Knowing how to dose activity and inactivity, movement and quiescence (*dong* and *jing*), the adept becomes the master of time; the accurate measuring tools symbolized by the trigrams and hexagrams of the *Yijing*, the moon phases, and so forth, which represent the course of time during the year, month, or day, allow one to experience this cosmic time within one's body. Time is thus spatialized, and the body becomes a celestial clock which, turning in a regular way, is similar to the chariot of the Northern Dipper (*beidou*), while the heart (*xin*) is the pole star, the motionless axis around which the cosmos unceasingly revolves.

To achieve control of time, fire phasing in *neidan* is divided into different stages. The first is a phase of "yangization" in which Yang augments and Yin decreases. This is described as a warlike or martial period, corresponding to the advancement of a light called Martial Fire (*wuhuo* 武火) or Yang Fire (*yanghuo* 陽火) that purifies by burning and eliminates defiled elements to release the Original Yang and increase it. At the cosmic level, the beginning of this phase is symbolized by the winter solstice (*zi* 子) and by the hexagram *fu* 復 ䷗ (Return, no. 24), which indicates the return of Yang. This is followed by a phase of balance, a time of rest called *muyu* (ablutions). At the cosmic level, this phase is symbolized by the spring and autumn equinoxes and by the hexagrams *dazhuang* 大壯 ䷡ (Great Strength, no. 34) and *guan* 觀 ䷓ (Contemplation, no. 20). The third stage is a phase of "yinization" in which Yin augments and Yang decreases. This period, called Civil Fire (*wenhuo* 文火) or Yin Fire (*yinfu* 陰符), corresponds to a decrease of the light. The adept achieves the alchemical work spontaneously and without any effort or voluntary intervention; water descends to moisten, fertilize, and temper fire. At the cosmic level, this phase is symbolized by the summer solstice (*wu* 午) and by the hexagram *gou* 姤 ䷫ (Encounter, no. 44).

Fire phasing in *neidan* means that in every instant the practitioner should find the balance between Martial Fire (action, movement, temporal expansion) and Civil Fire (inactivity, immobility, temporal reduction). Alchemical texts repeatedly state that this is the innermost secret of the alchemical work, which cannot be transmitted in words.

Monica ESPOSITO

📖 Despeux 1994, 163–69; Esposito 1997, 45–50; Esposito and Robinet 1998; Pregadio 1995; Robinet 1995a, 120–31

※ *muyu*; *sanguan*; *zhoutian*; *Yijing*; *neidan*; COSMOLOGY

huoju

火居

householder priest

Taoist priests who are married are called *huoju* or *huoju daoshi* 火居道士. This term, literally meaning "living by the fire," distinguishes them from *Quan-zhen monastic Taoists. Secular Taoists perform rituals for clients on request as an occupation. Taoist priests in present-day Taiwan are all *huoju*. Most of them are affiliated with the Way of the Celestial Masters (*Tianshi dao), but many have second jobs. The expression *huoju* is probably based on the Buddhist compound *huozhai* 火宅 ("burning house"), referring to the ordinary, unenlightened realm in which defilements have not been subdued.

ASANO Haruji

📖 Liu Zhiwan 1994, 188–90; Ōfuchi Ninji 1983, 164–65, 168

※ *daoshi*

huoling

火鈴

fire-bell

Also known as *liujin huoling* 流金火鈴 ("liquid gold fire-bell") and *liujin ling* 流金鈴 ("liquid gold bell"), the fire-bell is a ritual implement imbued with the power to drive away and suppress demons. It was originally one of the spiritual objects worn by the celestial deities on their bodies together with "tiger talismans" (*hufu* 虎符) and "dragon writs" (*longshu* 龍書); it was considered to have been formed from the essence of the nine stars of the Northern Dipper (*beidou) and to consist only of light, having no substance at all.

The *Zhengao gives an unadorned description of its ritual function: "Within the Way of the Immortals there is a bell of liquid gold; demons and spirits can be controlled with it" (5.4a). In his commentary to the *Duren jing (Scripture on Salvation), Yan Dong 嚴東 (fl. ca. 485) writes that the liquid gold fire-bell emits a sparkling light throughout ten thousand *li*, permeating the eight directions, filling the Void, and eliminating demons (*Duren shangpin miaojing sizhu* 度人上

品妙經四注; CT 87, 2.68a). Xue Youqi 薛幽棲 (fl. 740–54) adds that its sound can be heard as far away as the Palace of the Great Ultimate (Taiji gong 太極宮). "Its light illuminates a distance of one thousand *li*; reaching the bounds of ten thousand *li*, its light shines all around, and reaching the bounds of the eight directions, it smashes [the demons]. Therefore the Real Men (*zhenren) always control demon essences with it" (id., 2.68a–b).

In later Taoism, various techniques centering on the *huoling* were devised and employed, including talismans (*FU), spells, mudrās (*shoujue), and the method of "walking along the guideline" (*bugang). Detailed descriptions of these techniques are found in such texts as the *Daofa huiyuan (Corpus of Taoist Ritual) and the *Shangqing lingbao dafa (Great Rites of the Numinous Treasure of Highest Clarity; CT 1222–23).

                                                                    MUGITANI Kunio

📖 Robinet 1984, 1: 235

※ *faqi*

Huoshan

霍山

Mount Huo

The name Huoshan, which Edward Schafer described as "an unstable and floating name," refers to several different mountain sites in China. In the earliest sources, Huoshan seems to refer to a mountain located in Shanxi province (Kleeman 1994c, 227), but by the second through the fourth century CE sources show that there was much confusion regarding the many mountains identified with the name Huoshan (see, for example, the "Shishan" 釋山 chapter of the *Erya* 爾雅 [Literary Lexicon] and Guo Pu's 郭璞 [276–324] commentary). The issue of the location of Huoshan was further confused when Han Wudi (r. 141–87 BCE) changed the mountain with the title *Nanyue (Southern Peak) from Mount Heng (*Hengshan 衡山, Hunan) to Huoshan (also referred to as Tianzhu shan 天柱山, Anhui; see Kong Yingda's 孔穎達 [574–648] commentary to the "Songgao" 崧高 ode in the *Shijing* 詩經).

In Taoist sources, however, Huoshan is primarily connected either with the mountain in Anhui province or with a mountain in Fujian province. Taoist sources refer to a "Greater Mount Huo" (Da Huoshan 大霍山) and a "Lesser Mount Huo" (Xiao Huoshan 小霍山). According to Michel Strickmann, "Greater Mount Huo" was taken to be the "real" or "true" Southern

Peak (Nanyue), and referred to a secret mountain near Jin'an 晉安 in Fujian province (*Zhengao*, 13.8a and 14.7b, and *Zhoushi mingtong ji* 周氏冥通記, CT 302). This "Greater Mount Huo" was the ultimate destination of *Tao Hongjing in his southern journey between 508 and 512, and was considered the headquarters of *Wei Huacun (Schafer 1977b, 129 and 134) and Mao Ying 茅盈 (Strickmann 1977, 41, and Strickmann 1979, 152; on Mao Ying see the entry *Maojun). The "Lesser Mount Huo" was understood by Tao to refer to the mountain in Anhui. In later Taoist sources, Huoshan (Anhui) is identified as the "heir apparent" (*chujun* 儲君) or "assistant" (*fu* 副), along with Mount Qian (Qianshan 潛山 or 灊山, Anhui), to the Southern Peak, which is identified as Mount Heng in Hunan (*Yunji qiqian*, 79.20a, and Inoue Ichii 1931, 28–30). Yet, among *Shangqing Taoists, "Greater Mount Huo" was also associated with a site within the *Tiantai mountain range (Zhejiang; Schafer 1979, 33).

James ROBSON

📖 Geil 1926, 117–63

※ Nanyue; TAOIST SACRED SITES

Ishinpō

醫心方

Methods from the Heart of Medicine

The *Ishinpō* (also transliterated as *Ishimpō*) presented in 984 to Emperor Enyū (r. 970–84), was compiled by Tamba no Yasuyori 丹波康賴 (912–95), the official acupuncturist at the Japanese imperial court, and is the earliest extant work of Japanese medicine. Its importance for the history of Chinese medicine and Taoism lies in its quotations from 204 sources, most of which have long been lost. It comprises in thirty *juan* an outline of treatment in general and drug treatment in particular (j. 1), acupuncture and moxibustion therapy (j. 2), a discussion of various disorders, classified in much the same way as those in the *Zhubing yuanhou lun* (Treatise on the Origin and Symptoms of Diseases; j. 3–18 on internal and external disorders, and 21–25 on women's disorders, obstetrics, and pediatrics), and several chapters on Nourishing Life (*yangsheng*), including j. 19–20 on the ingestion of mineral drugs, j. 27 on Nourishing Life, j. 28 on sexual techniques (*fangzhong shu*), and j. 29–30 on dietetics.

Of these, j. 27 is of particular interest for all the techniques discussed in that chapter relate to Taoism. The chapter reveals admiration for *Sun Simiao's approach to Nourishing Life, and notably excludes discussion of the ingestion of mineral drugs as emphasized in *Ge Hong's *Baopu zi (which is given separately in j. 19–20). It comprises eleven sections on such topics as cultivation of spirit and body, breathing, *daoyin, daily behavior, proper language, dwellings, clothing, sleep, and interdictions, and contains citations from over two dozen different works. Among the latter belong, apart from the most frequently cited *Qianjin fang* 千金方 (Prescriptions Worth a Thousand) by Sun Simiao and the *Sheyang zhenzhong fang (Pillow Book of Methods for Preserving and Nourishing Life), probably also compiled by Sun Simiao, lost works such as the *Yangsheng yaoji (Essentials of Nourishing Life; early fourth century), the *Taiqing jing (Scripture of Great Clarity), and the *Yanshou chishu* 延壽赤書 (Red Writ on Extending Longevity) by Pei Yu 裴煜 (Tang). Among the other cited works are the *Baopu zi* and *Xi Kang's *Yangsheng lun* 養生論 (Essay on Nourishing Life), and eighteen more texts which are cited only once.

Elisabeth HSU

📖 Hsia, Veith, and Geertsma 1986; Sakade Yoshinobu 1986c; Sakade Yoshinobu 1994b

※ *yangsheng*; TAOISM IN JAPAN

J

ji

機

"mechanism"; activating force

The term *ji* designates the mechanism of the crossbow, hence the spring of
something. In Taoism, since the *Zhuangzi* and the *Huainan zi*, it has the
sense of "spring of the world," or its activating force. The term is cognate
to *tianji* 天機 (Celestial Mechanism, mentioned in the *Zhuangzi*), *shenji* 神機
("divine" or "spiritual mechanism"), and *ji* 幾, a word that denotes a subtle,
incipient movement whose inward spring is not yet visible outside. *Ji* is the
dynamic aspect of the Dao, the motive force of the world that never ceases to
function and originates in the dynamic tension between the opposites—Yin
and Yang, contraction and dissolution, movement and quiescence (*dong* and
jing). It is also the point of junction between them, the mechanism of transformation (*bianhua*). As stated in *Liezi* 1, the myriad beings spring out of it
and re-enter into it.

Some Taoist authors say that *ji* is the *wuji* (Ultimateless, Infinite) or the
"wondrous" aspect of *taiji* (Great Ultimate), the "wondrous movement" that
unites movement and quiescence, the true spring that moves spontaneously
by itself (*ziran*) and without intention (*wuxin* 無心), and that acts without
action and interference (*wuwei*). Others say that it is the extreme degree of
quiescence and purity which is on the verge of changing into movement.

On the cosmological level, *ji* alludes to the subtle moment of the birth of
the world, or the location where it appears, which is impossible to locate. It
is related to the thunder that announces the return of the Yang. It is metaphorically situated between the waning and the waxing of the moon, in the
southwest, where *kun* 坤 ☷ (pure Yin) is located, marked by the Celestial Stem
geng 庚, in the third day of the month; or in the cycle of the year, between
the Earthly Branches *hai* 亥 and *zi* 子, in the tenth month and the northwest,
just before the appearance of the Yang line in the trigram *kan* 坎 ☵ (Yang
within Yin). In *neidan*, *ji* is the moment when the alchemist should collect
his Medicine and begin his work, when time is inserted into the eternal and
timeless instantaneity, and when the operation of the alchemical work begins
with inaction in an open space containing nothing. *Ji* is thus a synonym of
xuanpin, the Mysterious Female.

On the physiological level, *ji* can be located in the center of the body, which
in turn is related to *yi* (intention) and to the spleen; or it can be identified with
the interval between breathing in and out (corresponding with the "closing"

536

and "opening" of the world) in the instant that precedes the movement of breath. Some authors emphasize that this breath is not the ordinary breath, but the *yuanqi, the Original Pneuma that antedates Heaven and Earth and is the source of the world.

As the center of human life, ji is the heart-mind (*xin) or the Spirit (*shen), which is associated with the Northern Dipper (*beidou) in Heaven, with the Thunder in Earth, and with the zhen 震 ☳ trigram, whose single Yang line that is beginning to ascend is correlated with the Celestial Stem geng. The alchemist aims at uniting the human ji with the tianji, the Celestial Mechanism.

Isabelle ROBINET

📖 Qing Xitai 1994, 2: 305–8; Robinet 1994b, 40–45; Robinet 1995a, 103–20

※ dong and jing; fan; xuanpin; zaohua; ziran

Ji Zhizhen

姬志真

1193–1268; original ming: Yi 翼; zi: Fuzhi 輔之; hao: Zhichang zi 知常子 (Master Who Knows the Eternal)

Ji Zhizhen, who came from Zezhou 澤州 (Shanxi), was a scholar educated during the last decades of the Jin dynasty. When the Jurchen succumbed to the assaults of the Mongol armies, he followed the same path as many of his fellow literati, taking refuge in the *Quanzhen order. Ji became a refugee in 1221 and was adopted by *Wang Zhijin as a disciple in 1234. His intellectual talents gained wide recognition, and he taught at Taoist schools (xuanxue 玄學) set up by the Quanzhen hierarchy from 1252 onward. After his master's death, he served for a few years as abbot of the Chaoyuan gong 朝元宮 (Palace of the Audience with the [Three] Primes) in Kaifeng (Henan), the main monastery of Wang Zhijin's lineage. The two figures, however, appear utterly different. While Wang Zhijin was a charismatic leader and an indefatigable preacher, Ji Zhizhen has left few traces of his activity but imparted his posterity with the largest corpus of prose and poetic writings for a Quanzhen author after those of *Wang Zhe and *Ma Yu.

His collected works, Yunshan ji 雲山集 (Anthology of Cloudy Mountains; 1250; CT 1140), are included in the Taoist Canon, but the Beijing National Library holds a substantially different 1319 edition. This edition includes prose treatises on Taoist philosophy and mysticism, a rather rare genre among Quanzhen Taoists. Ji Zhizhen also wrote lost commentaries to the Daode jing, the *Yijing, the *Zhuangzi, and the *Liezi, although his *Daode jing* exegesis is extensively quoted in *He Daoquan's extant commentary, the *Daode jing shuzhu* 道德經述注 (Detailed Commentary to the *Daode jing*). As a poet converted to Quanzhen Taoism, Ji Zhizhen can be compared, among others, to Feng Changquan 馮長筌 (fl. 1247), whose work was the basis for the *Minghe yuyin*.

Vincent GOOSSAERT

📖 Boltz J. M. 1987a, 172–73

※ Wang Zhijin; Quanzhen

jiangshen

降神

"calling down the deities"

During Taoist ceremonies, the deities are called down from the heavenly realm to the altar (*tan* 壇) where the ritual is to be performed. They are first invited to descend, then offered words and objects, and finally sent back to where they have come from. In the rite of Announcement (*fabiao*), for example, when the priest notifies the deities that a *jiao* (Offering) is to be performed in their honor, he calls them by saying, "May the Original Masters (*yuanshi* 元師) and the Real Lords (*zhenjun* 真君) be pleased to come down to the altar," and then adds, "The cloud chariot has descended; the team of cranes is approaching. When the Offering has been made, we will see you off" (Ōfuchi Ninji 1983, 245b).

In the rite of Flag-raising (*yangqi* 揚旗; Lagerwey 1987c, 54), long rectangular banners are raised on bamboo poles to mark the ritual site in order to attract the deities' attention. The priest invokes the Three Clarities (*sanqing*) and all the gods to "descend to this place of ritual in this polluted domain" (Ōfuchi Ninji 1983, 262). In this way, not only the deities, but also the life-giving pneuma (*qi*) are thought to enter the ritual space and the bodies of the priest and the people.

MARUYAMA Hiroshi

📖 Ōfuchi Ninji 1983, 224–25

※ chushen; gongde; jiao; zhai

jiao

醮

Offering

The term *jiao* means "offering" or "sacrifice." It refers, in the present day, to the large-scale Taoist ceremonies organized by local communities, and by other social groups such as professional guilds and various forms of voluntary religious associations, in order to define themselves on the religious level, and specifically in order to establish or confirm the (semicontractual) relationship between the group and its tutelary deity. A *jiao* may be performed at intervals of three, five, or more years (depending on local traditions) as either a recurrent rite for renewing life and blessings for the community ("Offering of Thanksgiving and Praying for Peace," *xie'en qi'an jiao* 謝恩乞安醮), or a rite that responds to immediate problems such as drought or epidemics ("Offering for Averting Calamities," *rangzai jiao* 禳災醮).

A classical form of *jiao* (see table 14) is typically headed by Taoist priests representing the *Zhengyi tradition, though in some localities variant forms can be performed by priests of the more popular (and often resident), Red-head (*hongtou* 紅頭) category (see *hongtou and *wutou*). The event may last a week or longer, and invariably involves the whole community in festivities which include, for example, processions in which the statue of the deity is carried through the neighborhood, trance performances of mediums who become possessed by the god, performances by hired theatre troops on temporary stages, and large-scale presentations of offerings to the god in front of the local temple. The central part of the liturgical program in a classical Zhengyi *jiao* is performed by the priests (together with their troop of musicians) behind the closed doors of this temple and is witnessed only by select representatives of the community. The inside of the temple is rearranged for the occasion, the statue of the tutelary god being removed from the place of honor in the ritual north—which is now temporarily occupied by scrolls representing the supreme Taoist deities—and placed with its back against the closed door, in the position of worshipping these higher deities. The actual structure of the Taoist ritual area, referred to as the "Taoist altar" (*daotan* 道壇), thus bears out the Taoist vision of a cosmic hierarchy presided over by the Three Clarities (*sanqing), such that the gods of the common Chinese religion (representing the postcelestial state, *houtian* 後天) are viewed as deriving their authority from the higher Taoist powers (representing the precelestial state, *xiantian* 先天).

Fig. 46. Taoist Master Chen Rongsheng 陳榮盛 presides at a *jiao* (Offering) ritual at the Kaiji tianhou gong 開基天后宮, Tainan (December 1978). Photograph by Julian Pas.

Early history. This special function of Taoist liturgy within the local cults of the common religion did not exist before the Song dynasty. In fact, as is well known, the Taoist religion that emerged toward the end of the second century CE defined itself at the outset in sharp contradistinction to the "excessive cults" (**yinsi*) and "bloody sacrifices" (*xueshi* 血食) of the common religion, which it viewed as the counterproductive responses of the people to extortion by demonic and false spirits. The attitude toward sacrifice and offerings within the Way of the Celestial Masters (**Tianshi dao*) of this period was distinctly negative, and thus the earliest forms of the communal liturgies, from which the present-day *jiao* liturgy descended, were not designated by this term, but referred to as **zhai*, "fast" or "retreat." The overwhelming focus in the *zhai* liturgies was on purification, repentance (**chanhui*), and the expiation of sins through self-mortification. Our sources for these early communal liturgies are mostly external and often hostile to the tradition, and we know the rituals in greater detail only as they were codified and transmitted within the **Lingbao* tradition, that is, in texts that were constructed around the year 400 and later. They are reflected furthermore in the ritual system proposed in the imperially sponsored anthology **Wushang biyao* (j. 48–57; see Lagerwey 1981b, 150–70), which draws on the totality of ritual traditions of its time while giving pride of place to the Lingbao liturgy.

Table 14

DAY 1

1 Announcement (*fabiao 發表)
2 Invocation (qibai 啟白)
3 Flag-Raising (yangqi 揚旗)
4 Noon Offering (*wugong 午供)
5 Division of the Lamps (*fendeng 分燈)
6 Sealing the Altar (*jintan 禁壇)
7 Invocation of the Masters and Saints (qi shisheng 啟師聖)
8 Nocturnal Invocation (*suqi 宿啟)

DAY 2

9 Morning Audience (zaochao 早朝)
10 Noon Audience (wuchao 午朝)
11 Evening Audience (wanchao 晚朝)

DAY 3

12 Renewed Invocation (chongbai 重白)
13 Presentation of the Memorial (jinbiao 進表, or *baibiao 拜表)
14 "Ten Thousand Sacred Lamps of the Three Realms" (sanjie wangling shengdeng 三界萬靈聖燈)
15 Orthodox Offering (*zhengjiao 正醮)
16 Universal Salvation (*pudu 普度)

Program of a three-day Offering (jiao) ritual. Based on Schipper 1975c, 10–11.
For similar programs, see Lagerwey 1987c, 293, and Tanaka Issei 1989b, 275–79.

The ritual program presented in this anthology testifies to a common tripartite structure. The first major ritual of most services is the Nocturnal Invocation (*suqi), through which the sacred area is established, purified, and consecrated (within the Lingbao tradition this entailed the planting of the five Authentic Scripts or zhenwen 真文, i.e., the five Lingbao talismans, in the five directions of the sacred area—an act that still occurs in the classical jiao liturgy of southern Taiwan). It is followed by the main rite of communication—conceived as an audience with the supreme deities—in which a Declaration (ci 詞) is read. The program concludes with the Statement of Merit (yangong 言功), the purpose of which is to reward the spirits that have assisted the priest in transmitting his messages to heaven. In the earlier Zhengyi form of the zhai liturgy, the Statement of Merit was commonly postponed until a later time, when the ritual was determined to have had its effect (see Cedzich 1987, 97–102). In later forms of the jiao liturgy, the ritual corresponding to the Statement of Merit (in present-day southern Taiwan, the Presentation of the Memorial, jinbiao 進表) is accompanied by large-scale displays of offerings addressed to the Jade Sovereign (*Yuhuang) and inaugurates a whole series of additional major rituals in which offerings are presented to all categories of the spirit-world. These offering rituals are conspicuously absent in the early forms of the *zhai* liturgy. Rewarding the subordinate spirits was implied in the "statement of merit" itself, which reported to heaven the conscientious and successful execution of their official duties, on which their advancement within the spiritual hierarchy depended. The incorporation of large-scale offerings as part of the overall liturgy, and the introduction of the term *jiao* to designate the concluding segment, did not occur until the Tang dynasty, when indeed the use of the combined term, *zhaijiao* 齋醮, became current in reference to major Taoist ceremonies.

The *jiao* that was thus added to the *zhai* liturgy clearly had a separate origin and followed a separate line of development during the Six Dynasties. Indeed, the history of the term from before the emergence of Celestial Masters Taoism associates it with exactly the kinds of practices that this Taoism was eager to condemn. The locus classicus for these earlier forms is the *Gaotang fu* 高唐賦 (Rhapsody on Gaotang) by Song Yu 宋玉 (third century BCE), which describes the activity of certain "magicians" (*fangshi*), who presented "pure sacrificial oxen" (*chunxi* 純犧), prayed to the stars of the Northern Dipper (*beidou*), and "made offerings (*jiao*) to all the deities and worshipped the Great One" (*Wenxuan* 文選, j. 19; trans. Knechtges 1982–96, 2: 325–39). It is clear that such practices were widespread within the so-called "occult traditions" of the south, prior to the full-scale transmission of the Way of the Celestial Masters that occurred after 317 CE, as is evident from the summary of these traditions in the *Baopu zi*, and notably in the *jiao* to the Five Emperors (Wudi 五帝) described in the *Lingbao wufu xu* (3.3a–5a). It clearly descends from Han dynasty ritual, and serves to establish and confirm the alliance of the practitioner with the divinities that empower the crucial five Lingbao talismans. The ritual comprises the killing of a goose, as well as elaborate offerings of wine. An updated version of this ritual is found in the Lingbao corpus, with the important elimination of the killing of the goose, which is replaced by dates and fresh fruit, and the wine, which is replaced by pure, fragrant tea (*Lingbao wudi jiaoji zhaozhen yujue* 靈寶五帝醮祭招真玉訣; CT 411, 1a–2a). However, as with the preceding *jiao*, the eponymous purpose is to make the Perfected, i.e., the Five Emperors, descend in response to the offerings (*jiaoji zhaozhen* 醮祭招真).

A similar emphasis is found in the *jiao* liturgy described in the *Suishu* (History of the Sui; 35.1092–93, completed 644), which describes the *jiao* under the heading "Methods for dispelling disaster and saving from danger," and associates it with divinatory methods for calculating individual destinies (*shushu* 數術): "At night, under the light of the stars, wine, dried meat, cakes, and pledges of silk are laid out and offered successively to the Celestial Sovereign, the Great One (Tianhuang Taiyi 天皇太一), and to the five planets and the array of stellar mansions. [The priest] produces a document like in the ritual of sending up a petition in order to report it. This is called an Offering (*jiao*)." "Methods of petitioning," *zhangfa* 章法, appear, at least since the end of the Six Dynasties, to have been specifically connected with the *jiao* liturgy. The term *zhangjiao* 章醮, "offering (that includes) a petition," is frequently mentioned in Tang ritual manuals, while the Sui dynasty author Fei Changfang 費長房 (writing in 597) anachronistically attributes the origin of a whole system of *zhangjiao* to the first Celestial Master, *Zhang Daoling (see Li Xianzhang 1968, 204 and 213–14). It is clear, furthermore, from the description in the *Suishu*, that the *jiao* liturgy of this time was viewed as specifically addressed to the high god of the firmament, *Taiyi, as well as to various other stellar deities, including the administration of human destinies located in the Northern Dipper. The same focus is evident throughout the Tang dynasty and in the early Song.

Song to present day. However, it is clearly the all-inclusive compensation of the (subordinate) spirits that assisted the priest in performing his tasks that constituted the rationale for adding a *jiao* at the end of a *zhai* service. The liturgists of the early Song dynasty generally attribute this new system to *Du Guangting, who is said to have instituted the tradition of performing an Offering of Thanksgiving (*xie'en jiao* 謝恩醮), either as a direct continuation of the *zhai* service, or in a separate ceremony on another day (preferably taking place at a sacred grotto in the mountains). A special reason for this development was the growing importance in this period of a host of new martial spirits derived from the emerging traditions of exorcism, spirits who were invited as special protectors of the sacred area in a newly-designed ritual called Announcement (*fabiao), performed at the very outset of the program.

Some liturgists of the period of the Five Dynasties protest against the new emphasis on the *jiao* within the *zhai* liturgy, claiming that it distorts the focus of this liturgy by shifting attention to subordinate deities, at a point when the supreme deities addressed in the *zhai* have already left the scene (presumably escorted by these subordinate deities). A somewhat related stance is represented by the founders of the *Lingbao dafa (Great Rites of the Numinous Treasure), who comment critically on the expansion of the *jiao* in their time, and on the "separation" [sic] of the *zhai* and the *jiao* into two independent units and liturgical styles, attributing the first to the Lingbao and the second to the Zhengyi tradition (see *Shangqing lingbao dafa; CT 1221, 59.20b–23a; CT 1223, 39.3a–4b). The end result of the liturgical development of the period was a situation in which the two forms of liturgy had become fused to the point where the two terms were sometimes used interchangeably, but where the growing importance of the *jiao* component of the whole gradually led to the substitution of this term for the former as the general designation of the combined liturgy, when applied in ceremonies for the living. The important background for this development was the fact, mentioned above, that since the Song dynasty the Taoist communal liturgy had achieved its survival through a functional symbiosis with the local cults of the common religion—in which of course the emphasis on sacrifice and offerings had remained dominant since ancient times. The term *zhai* was still used for communal services during the Song dynasty, when however its association with ceremonies for the dead becomes more and more pronounced, and today it is used most commonly as the technical term for the Taoist funeral liturgy.

A final addition to the sequence of offerings included in the *jiao* liturgy was the ritual of Universal Salvation or *pudu, which was borrowed from Buddhism, first incorporated during the Song dynasty, and concerned with the salvation and feeding of the lost souls suffering in hell, the so-called "orphaned souls" (*guhun* 孤魂). In most present-day ceremonies the *pudu* occurs at the very end of the program, in fact, quite commonly after the sending away of the gods that marks the end of the Taoist liturgy, properly speaking. It thus represents in a sense the most exoteric level of activity in a *jiao*, though it should be noted that in many local traditions there is a strong emphasis both on this *pudu* ritual and on other means of averting harm from the dangerous spirits of hell. In all cases, the *jiao* today seems strongly focused on territoriality and its definition through local cults, with the important qualification that, in the perspective of the *jiao*, the territory is not the land as such, but the land as possessed by a certain community, and therefore subject to the inclusion or exclusion of certain groups (that may or may not be actually resident) from participation in the ceremony, depending on the alliances of the dominant strain of the population.

Poul ANDERSEN

📖 Andersen 2002; Benn 1991; Benn 2000; Cedzich 1987, 61–105; Chen Dacan 1987; Dean 1993; Dean 1996; Dean 2000; Hsu Francis L. K. 1952; Hymes 1997; Lagerwey 1987c; Lagerwey 1991, 136–56; Li Xianzhang 1968; Liu Zhiwan 1983–84; Maruyama Hiroshi 1995; Matsumoto Kōichi 1983; Min Zhiting 1995; Ōfuchi Ninji 1983, 234–422; Robinet 1997b, 166–83; Saso 1978b; Saso 1989; Schipper 1985e; Schipper 1993, 72–99; Schipper 1995a; Thompson 1987a; Tian Chengyang 1990; Yamada Toshiaki 1995b; Zhang Zehong 1996; Zhang Zehong 1999a

※ For related entries see the Synoptic Table of Contents, sec. III.4 ("Ritual")

jie

劫

kalpa, aeon (eon)

The character *jie* 劫 was used by early Buddhist translators to represent the first syllable of the Sanskrit word *kalpa* and soon entered the Chinese language as an abbreviation for the word itself. A *kalpa* is an eon, an impossibly long period of time. One illustration notes that if a heavenly being were to brush the hem of his garment across Mount Sumeru every year, a *kalpa* would have elapsed once the world mountain was levelled. Beginning in the fourth century, the term entered Taoist literature. It is commonly found in both *Shangqing and *Lingbao scriptures.

As in Indian literature, the Taoist *kalpa* represents not linear but cyclical time. Linked with indigenous ideas of cosmic cycles of growth and decay that were already important in early Taoism, the term *kalpa* came to connote particularly that point in the cycle when the old and sinful are destroyed and the Dao renews itself. Previously revealed scripture would be stored in heaven to await the new age and the "seed-people" (*zhongmin), or elect, would be saved to populate a new heaven and earth. Taoist texts tell of the fire, flood, and warfare that would occur at the end of a *kalpa*. The Shangqing scriptures added to this a vivid description of the descent of *Li Hong, savior of the Taoist worthy, while the first section of the Lingbao scriptures (see *Lingbao jingmu) tell of several ages prior to our own, themselves composed of many *kalpas*. These are given fantastic names: Draconic Magnificence (*longhan* 龍漢), Extended Vigor (*yankang* 延康), Vermilion Brilliance (*chiming* 赤明), Opening Luminary (*kaihuang* 開皇), and Higher Luminary (*shanghuang* 上皇). The scriptures themselves were said to have gradually taken shape over this time. In addition, their appearance itself was forwarded as a sign that a new *kalpa* had dawned.

The eschatological visions built on these concepts were shared by Taoism and Buddhism alike. Indigenously composed Buddhist scriptures are, in fact, quite similar to Taoist texts in this regard. Scriptures foretelling the end time had a profound political dimension that was exploited by both rebel groups and emperors. Rebellions fortified with apocalyptic imagery eventually played a role in the reunification of China after the era of division (221–581). Sui Wendi (r. 581–604), named his the first reign period "Opening Luminary," while the founder of the Tang, Li Yuan 李淵 (Gaozu, r. 618–26), claimed descent from

Laozi and took on the mantle of Li Hong. The apocalyptic image of the *kalpa* endures in modern Taoism and in Chinese religion more generally.

Stephen R. BOKENKAMP

📖 Bokenkamp 1994; Bokenkamp 1997, 295–99 and 380–82; Lagerwey 1981b, 80–82; Nattier 1991; Seidel 1984; Strickmann 1990; Zürcher 1982

※ APOCALYPTIC ESCHATOLOGY

jie

戒 (*or*: 誡)

precepts

Taoist precepts, like those of other religions, function as rules for the regulation of behavior—usually to prevent wrongdoing—and range from sets of ten or fewer up to as many as three hundred. These sets of rules are graduated, with increasingly strict regimes of behavior demanded as the follower of Taoism became more committed and involved in the religion. Various different sets of precepts were bestowed to adherents at different levels of initiation into the religion and different grades of ordination. Among the many sets of precepts there is much overlap, with different sets clearly borrowing from each other and from Buddhist rules for monks and lay people which clearly played a major role in the inspiration for, if not the formation of, Taoist rules.

The justification for the existence of precepts is, of course, to lead a correct religious life. The consequences of not leading a proper life—transgressing the guidelines set down—are understood in several ways in different Taoist traditions. In the early scripture *Taiping jing* (Scripture of Great Peace), for instance, transgressions lead to the build up of *chengfu* or "inherited burden," by which mechanism bad consequences, including sickness, befall the descendants of the transgressor. In the *Baopu zi*, *Ge Hong explains that improper behavior leads directly to the shortening of life and prevents the aspirant to immortality from reaching his goal. In some later Taoist texts, on the other hand, the punishment for transgressing the precepts is a bad rebirth.

Many of the short sets of precepts are found in the first chapter of the *Zhihui shangpin dajie* 智慧上品大誡 (Great Precepts of the Highest Rank of Wisdom; CT 177). They are, however, most conveniently consulted in a study by Kusuyama Haruki (1992, 64–113). The first set of ten in the *Shangpin dajie* are the precepts observed by the "disciples of unsullied belief" (*qingxin dizi* 清信弟子; trans. Bokenkamp 1989, 18–20). Numbers 2 to 6 of these ten echo the five

Buddhist prohibitions against killing, stealing, having illicit sex, lying, and drinking alcohol. This direct influence is common among the sets of ten or fewer precepts. Attached to the precepts for the "disciples of unsullied belief" are twelve admonitions which themselves echo the Buddhist bodhisattva vows.

Three early, and fundamental, large sets of precepts are the *Laojun shuo yibai bashi jie* (The Hundred and Eighty Precepts Spoken by Lord Lao), the *Shangqing dongzhen zhihui guanshen dajie wen* 上清洞真智慧觀身大戒文 (Great Precepts of Wisdom and Self-Observation of the Cavern of Perfection of Highest Clarity; CT 1364), and the *Lingbao sanyuan pinjie gongde qingzhong jing* 靈寶三元品戒功德輕重經 (Scripture on Weighing Merit based on the Precepts of the Three Primes of the Numinous Treasure; CT 456). This area of Taoism is rather underresearched and as yet clear and unequivocal statements of how these texts are related, exactly how they were used, or what doctrinal affiliations they had cannot be made with certainty.

The first set was probably completed in the fourth century and, as its name implies, has 180 rules that were supposedly granted to *Gan Ji by Lord Lao (*Laojun) in the third century BCE. Of these 180, 140 are negative injunctions ordering the ordained priest, among other things, not to collect taxes, not to kill or cause others to kill, not to catch hibernating animals or raid birds' nests, and not to travel alone. Forty of them encourage right behavior such as accepting slander and abuse without retaliation, burning incense and praying for the ten thousand families, the attainment of Great Peace (*taiping) in the empire, ingesting *qi, and avoiding cereals.

The second set, usually abbreviated to the *Dajie wen*, is found (among other places) in the *Wushang biyao (Supreme Secret Essentials; Lagerwey 1981b, 144–45) so must predate 574. In all likelihood it was composed sometime in the previous century. This text is an object lesson in the necessity to examine affiliations closely—as Stephen Eskildsen has pointed out, despite its proclamation *Shangqing in the title, it was thought of highly by *Lingbao adherents (Eskildsen 1998, 106). This set has a total of 302 precepts divided into three groups. The first group of 180 are those of the Lower Prime (*xiayuan* 下元), the next thirty six are those of the Middle Prime (*zhongyuan* 中元), and the final eighty four are those of the Higher Prime (*shangyuan* 上元). The Precepts of the Lower Prime bear some similarities with the *Hundred and Eighty Precepts Spoken by Lord Lao*—many precepts are shared—but were clearly produced with more sense of organization, showing signs of conscious grouping of certain related precepts together. For instance, many of them are formed of pairs, in turn prohibiting an action, then prohibiting the causing of others to perform that action:

   3. Students of the Dao, do not drink wine.

   4. Students of the Dao, do not cause others to drink wine.

There are also, for example, five precepts grouped together that concern behavior with women. The Precepts of the Middle Prime are more stringent than those of the Lower Prime stressing purification and putting others before oneself. They explicitly encourage adherents to be more tolerant, more enduring of pain, less concerned about clothing and food, etc., than others are able to be. They shift from being generally prohibitive to mostly exhortatory. The precepts of the Higher Prime are exclusively exhortatory, being expressed in the form "Students of the Dao, you ought to think on . . ." and demand even more from the adept. They encourage deep compassion, an eremitic lifestyle and particular religious practices but can also, at this level, expect to attain the powers associated with transcendence of the normal human condition: eating celestial food, travel in celestial realms, consorting with deities.

The third set, known by the shortened name *Sanyuan pin*, is also quoted in the *Wushang biyao* (Lagerwey 1981b, 143–44) but was included as one of the original Lingbao corpus as catalogued by *Lu Xiujing (see table 16) so must come from the fifth century, at latest. It expresses its prohibitions in the form of transgressions, addressing the first twenty-seven to "students of the Upper Dao," and the remainder to "students of the Dao and followers from among the people." As would be indicated by this division, the first twenty-seven concern respecting teachers, the proper circumstances for the transmission of texts, the necessity of observing the rituals, and so forth. The rest are of a more general nature such as those seen in the *Hundred and Eighty Precepts* and the first section of the *Dajie wen*. The text claims to divide the precepts into three groups of sixty, although the first group only has forty-seven. Each group of sixty is overseen by a range of named celestial officials of various offices within the departments of Heaven, Earth and Water—the "three primes" (*sanyuan*) of the title (see *sanguan*).

The stability of the precepts can be gauged by noting the great similarity between the *Dajie wen* and a set in use during the nineteenth century collected by Heinrich Hackmann (1931).

Benjamin PENNY

📖 Bokenkamp 1997, 48–58; Eskildsen 1998, 106–12; Hackmann 1931; Jan Yünhua 1986; Kohn 1995a, 188–90, 201, and 209; Kohn 2004a; Kusuyama Haruki 1992, 64–113; Lagerwey 1981b, 143–49; Penny 1996a; Ren Jiyu 1990, 288–339; Schipper 2001

※ *jinji*; *Chuzhen jielü*; *Fengdao kejie*; *Laojun shuo yibai bashi jie*; *Laojun yinsong jiejing*; *Siji mingke jing*; *Xiang'er jie*; *Xuandu lüwen*; *Zhengyi fawen jing*; *Zhengyi weiyi jing*; ETHICS AND MORALS; MONASTIC CODE; ORDINATION AND PRIESTHOOD *jiji ru lüling*

急急如律令

"Promptly, promptly, in accordance with the
statutes and ordinances!"

The expression *jiji ru lüling* is related to *ru lüling* 如律令, "in accordance with
the statutes and ordinances," and *ru zhaoshu* 如詔書, "in accordance with
the imperial decree," standard phrases that appear at the end of official Han
dynasty documents. Mirroring its use in those documents, the phrase *ru lüling*
is found in Han dynasty tomb texts, first appearing on an ordinance jar dated
to 92 CE and in a tomb contract of 161 CE. These funerary texts, directed to
otherworldly officials, acted both as passports introducing the dead to the
post-mortem bureaucracy and as commands ordering the dead to stay away
from and not harm the living. One of these documents reads:

> The subject deceased on the *yisi* 乙巳 day [the forty-second of the sexagesimal
> cycle; see table 10] has the demon name "Heavenly Brightness." The Divine
> Master of the Heavenly Thearch has already been informed as to your name.
> Promptly remove yourself three thousand leagues away! Should you not go
> away, then the [*lacuna*] of Southern Mountain will be ordered to come and
> devour you. Promptly, in accordance with the statutes and ordinances! (Trans.
> Seidel 1987c, 229)

As it did with other elements of state bureaucracy, Taoism adopted the
phrase *(jiji) ru lüling* in its codebooks and in its ritual petitions to otherworldly
officials. One of the earliest examples of these codes, the *Nüqing guilü* (Demon
Statutes of Nüqing), protects one from illness-producing demons, the same
role seen in earlier tomb documents.

Amy Lynn MILLER

📖 Maeda Ryōichi 1989; Miyazawa Masayori 1984c; Seidel 1987e, 39–42

※ OTHERWORLDLY BUREAUCRACY

jijiu

祭酒

libationer

Jijiu or "libationer" was the term for priests within the early Celestial Master church (*Tianshi dao). The term is ancient, referring originally to the village elder who performed the oblation at the beginning of the village sacrificial feast. By the Han it came to be used as an official rank for the head of the Imperial Academy but had also been diluted on the local level until it meant something like "squire," a prominent person from an established family. It is ironic that this term referring specifically to sacrificial actions was adopted as the general term for religious professionals who consciously eschewed China's sacrificial tradition.

Historical accounts record that those who first entered the Celestial Master movement were known as "demon troopers" (*guizu* 鬼卒) and only attained the status of libationer after a period of instruction. There is no evidence for the use of the term "demon trooper" in Celestial Master texts, but there is a stele from 173 that records the initiation of several libationers under the auspices of someone (possibly a deity) referred to as a "demon soldier" (*guibing* 鬼兵). At that time, accession to the office of libationer already involved the conferral of sacred texts. There was internal differentiation within the body of libationers, with higher ranking libationers appointed to the office of Parish-heading Great Libationer (*zhitou da jijiu* 治頭大祭酒). Among the duties of these libationers was the collection of the annual tithe of grain, the management of "charity lodges" (*yishe* 義舍) supplied through these donations, and the supervision of other public works like repairing roads and bridges. Libationers presided over the three annual Assemblies (*sanhui) where the faithful confessed sins, reported birth, deaths, and marriages, and shared a communal meal. During the period of the Hanzhong 漢中 theocracy, they performed all the functions of the local governmental official and probably maintained a leadership role within Taoist communities long after their formal governmental role disappeared.

Although libationers were originally appointed on the basis of merit, there was already a tendency for the posts to become hereditary by the third century, and fourth- and fifth-century reform movements like *Shangqing and that led by *Kou Qianzhi (365?–448) frequently decried this development, but the libationer eventually evolved into the hereditary Taoist priest (*daoshi). Moreover, early libationers could be either male or female, but this evolved into an exclusively male institution, with females only accepted within monastic orders. It is unclear when these developments took place, but most seem to have been in effect by the end of the Tang.

Terry KLEEMAN

📖 fuchi Ninji 1991, 334–42; Stein R. A. 1963, 42–59

※ Tianshi dao

jindan

金丹

Golden Elixir

Modern studies usually refer to the Chinese arts of the elixirs as *waidan (external alchemy) or *neidan (inner alchemy), but the authors of alchemical texts often call their tradition the Way of the Golden Elixir (*jindan zhi dao* 金丹之道). Gold (*jin* 金) represents the state of constancy and immutability beyond the change and transiency that characterize the manifested world. As for *dan* 丹, or "elixir," lexical analysis shows that the semantic field of this term—which commonly denotes a variety of red—evolves from a root-meaning of "essence," and that its connotations include the reality, principle, or true nature of an entity, or its most basic and significant element, quality, or property.

In its various formulations, the Way of the Golden Elixir is characterized by a foundation in doctrinal principles, first set out in the founding texts of Taoism, concerning the relation between the Dao and the world of multiplicity. *Waidan* and *neidan* are two paradigmatic forms of practice, with several varieties for each of them, devised on the basis of those principles. Both forms of practice are centered on the notion of refining (*lian* 鍊, 煉) the ingredients of the outer or the inner elixir—inanimate matter in *waidan*, and the primary constituents of the cosmos and the human being, namely essence, pneuma, and spirit (*jing, qi, shen*), in *neidan*. The Chinese alchemical tradition has therefore three aspects, namely a doctrinal level and two main forms of practice, respectively based on the refining of an "outer" or an "inner" elixir.

The elixir in "external alchemy." The *Taiqing (Great Clarity) sources, which belong to the first identifiable tradition associated with *waidan* practices, contain virtually no statements on their doctrinal foundations. The emphasis given to certain aspects of the methods, and the terminology used in their descriptions, however, show that the central act of the alchemical process consists of

causing matter to revert to its "essence" (*jing), or *materia prima*. The main role
in this procedure is played by the crucible (*fu), which functions as a medium
equivalent to the inchoate state (*hundun) that precedes the formation of the
cosmos. In that medium, under the action of fire, the ingredients of the elixir
are transmuted, or "reverted" (huan 還), to their original state. Quoting *Daode
jing* 21 ("Indistinct! Vague! But within it there is something. Dark! Obscure! But
within it there is an essence"), the commentary to the *Jiudan jing* (Scripture of
the Nine Elixirs) equates this purified matter with the "essence" issued from
the Dao that gives birth to the cosmos (*Huangdi jiuding shendan jingjue* 黃帝
九鼎神丹經訣; CT 885, 10.1b).

Among a large variety of methods, two progressively became typical of
waidan. The first consists of refining mercury (Yin) from cinnabar (Yang). The
refined essence (*feijing* 飛精) is added to sulphur (Yang) and is then refined
again, typically in seven or nine cycles. At each stage it becomes more Yang,
until it incorporates the properties of Pure Yang (*chunyang* 純陽), the state
prior to the differentiation of the One into multiplicity. In the second method,
described in *waidan* texts related the *Zhouyi cantong qi* (Token for the Agreement of the Three According to the *Book of Changes*), the initial ingredients
are cinnabar (Yang) and native lead (Yin). They are refined to produce Real
Mercury (*zhenhong* 真汞), which is Original Yin, and Real Lead (*zhenqian* 真
鉛), which is Original Yang, respectively. The elixir obtained through combining the two refined essences also represents Pure Yang.

Alchemy and cosmology. In the traditions based on the *Cantong qi*, alchemy is
primarily a figurative language used to represent the relation between the
Dao and the cosmos, the Absolute and the relative, Oneness and multiplicity, and timelessness and time. In these traditions, the emblems of correlative cosmology—typically arranged in patterns that include Yin and Yang,
the Five Agents (*wuxing), the eight trigrams and the sixty-four hexagrams
of the *Yijing (Book of Changes), and so forth—play two main roles. First,
they represent the different cosmological configurations produced by the
propagation of Original Pneuma (*yuanqi) into the "ten thousand things."
In this function, the emblems of correlative cosmology show how space,
time, multiplicity, and change are related to the spacelessness, timelessness,
non-duality, and constancy of the Dao. For instance, the *Cantong qi* describes
the Five Agents—which define, in particular, the main spatial and temporal
coordinates of the cosmos—as unfolding from the center, which contains them
all, runs through them, and "endows them with its efficacy." In their second
role, the emblems of correlative cosmology relate the alchemical practice to
doctrinal principles. For instance, the trigrams of the *Book of Changes* are used
to show how the alchemical process consists of extracting the precosmic Real
Yin (*zhenyin* 真陰) and Real Yang (*zhenyang* 真陽) from Yang and Yin as they

appear in the cosmos, respectively, and in combining them to produce an elixir that represents their unity.

The elixir in "inner alchemy." The doctrines expounded in the treatises on the "inner elixir" essentially consist of a reformulation of those enunciated in the early Taoist texts, integrated with language and images drawn from the system of correlative cosmology according to the model provided by the *Cantong qi*. The authors of doctrinal treatises point out that the alchemical teachings can only be understood in the light of those of the *Daode jing* (a text they consider to be "the origin of the Way of the Golden Elixir"), and that correlative cosmology provides "images" (*xiang) that serve, as stated by *Li Daochun (fl. 1288–92), "to give form to the Formless through words, and thus manifest the authentic and absolute Dao" (*Zhonghe ji, 3.13a–b; see Robinet 1995a, 75–76).

The relation of doctrine to practice was an issue that needed clarification among *neidan* adepts themselves, as shown by Chen Zhixu (1289-after 1335) who forcefully rejects the understanding of alchemy as merely consisting of techniques of self-cultivation, when he writes: "It has been said that the way of cultivation and refinement consists of the techniques (*shu* 術) of the Yellow Emperor (*Huangdi) and Laozi. No more of this nonsense! This is the great Way of the Golden Elixir, and it cannot be called a technique" (*Jindan dayao, 3.4b). Chen Zhixu and other authors emphasize that the inner elixir is possessed by every human being, and is a representation of one's own innate realized state. *Liu Yiming (1734–1821) expresses this notion as follows:

> Human beings receive this Golden Elixir from Heaven. . . . Golden Elixir is an-other name for one's fundamental nature, formed out of primeval inchoateness (*huncheng* 混成, a term derived from the *Daode jing*). There is no other Golden Elixir outside one's fundamental nature. Every human being has this Golden Elixir complete in himself: it is entirely realized in everybody. It is neither more in a sage, nor less in an ordinary person. It is the seed of Immortals and Buddhas, and the root of worthies and sages. (*Wuzhen zhizhi* 悟真直指, chapter 1)

In his explication of two terms that the *Cantong qi* borrows from the *Daode jing*, Liu Yiming describes "superior virtue" (*shangde* 上德) as the immediate realization that the original "celestial reality" (*tianzhen* 天真) within and out-side of oneself is never affected by change and impermanence, and "inferior virtue" (*xiade* 下德) as the performance of the alchemical practice in order to "return to the Dao." He states, however, that the latter way, when it achieves fruition, "becomes a road leading to the same goal as superior virtue" (*Cantong zhizhi* 參同直指, "Jing 經," chapter 2).

Although the *neidan* practices are codified in ways that differ, sometimes noticeably, from each other, the notion of "inversion" (*ni* 逆) is common to all of them (Robinet 1995a, 131–45). In the most common codification, the practice is framed as the reintegration of each of the primary components of existence (essence, pneuma, and spirit) into the one that precedes it, culminating in their "reversion" (*huan*) to the state of Non-being, or Emptiness (*wu, *xu* 虛, *kong* 空). The typical formulation of this process is "refining essence into pneuma" (*lianjing huaqi* 鍊精化氣), "refining pneuma into spirit" (*lianqi huashen* 鍊氣 化神), and "refining spirit and reverting to Emptiness" (*lianshen huanxu* 鍊神 還虛). Li Daochun relates these stages to the cosmogonic process outlined in *Daode jing* 42: "The Dao generates the One, the One generates the Two, the Two generate the Three, the Three generate the ten thousand things." In this sequence (see table 15), the Dao first generates Oneness, which harbors the complementary principles of Yin and Yang. After Yin and Yang are differentiated from each other, they rejoin and generate the "three," reestablishing Oneness at the level of the particular entities. The "ten thousand things" are the totality of the entities produced by the continuous reiteration of this process. In Li Daochun's explication, the three stages of the *neidan* practice represent the inversion of this process, leading from the "ten thousand things" to Emptiness, by means of the elimination of distinctions between each of the primary components of existence and the one immediately above it.

For Li Daochun and other authors who refer to it, the form of practice outlined above is the only one that matches the principles of the Way of the Golden Elixir. In an essay found in his *Zhonghe ji* (2.11b–17a), Li thoroughly rejects sexual practices and *waidan*, and assigns a low rank to physiological practices (including *daoyin, breathing techniques, and diets) and methods of meditation and visualization. As for *neidan* proper, he distinguishes three "vehicles" (*sheng* 乘) that may be characterized as physiological, cosmological, and spiritual. Above them is a Supreme One Vehicle (*zuishang yisheng* 最上 一乘), which he calls the "Wondrous Way of Supreme and Utmost Reality" and does not associate with any particular practice. Especially important in Li Daochun's essay is the idea of "point of application" or "point of operation" (*zuoyong chu* 作用處), according to which certain notions and practices take on different meanings and operate in different ways according to the level at which they are understood.

Fabrizio PREGADIO

📖 Meng Naichang 1989; see also bibliographies for the entries *neidan, *nüdan, and *waidan

※ *neidan*; *nüdan*; *waidan*

Table 15

COSMOGONY: *shun* 順 ("CONTINUATION")	*dao* 道 ○	emptiness (*xu* 虛)	NEIDAN PRACTICE: *ni* 逆 ("INVERSION")
"The Dao generates the One"	→	←	from Spirit to Emptiness (鍊神化虛)
	one —	spirit (*shen* 神)	
"The One generates the Two"	→	←	from Pneuma to Spirit (鍊氣化神)
	two ☷	pneuma (*qi* 氣)	
"The Two generate the Three"	→	←	from Essence to Pneuma (鍊精化氣)
	three ☰	essence (*jing* 精)	
"The Three generate the 10,000 things"	→	←	"laying out the foundations" (築基)
	10,000 things (*wanwu* 萬物)		

The cosmogonic stages of *Daode jing* sec. 42, and their correspondence with the stages of the *neidan practice. Based on *Zhonghe ji (CT 249), 5b.

Jindan dacheng ji

金丹大成集

Anthology on the Great Achievement of the Golden Elixir

Compiled by a member of the important Xiao 蕭 clan in Fuzhou (Fujian), Xiao Tingzhi 蕭廷芝 (fl. 1260–64), this work contains various *neidan texts written between the tenth and thirteenth centuries. Xiao's family background matched his spiritual pedigree, since he was a premier disciple of *Peng Si (fl. 1217–51), one of *Bai Yuchan's (1194–1229?) two main disciples. His edited work fills five chapters and constitutes one of the "ten writings" in the late thirteenth-century compendium of Bai's legacy, the *Xiuzhen shishu (Ten Books on the Cultivation of Perfection, *j.* 9–13), and is also separately printed in the *Daozang jiyao (vol. 16). Its constituent texts, listed with references to chapter and page numbers in the *Xiuzhen shishu*, include:

1. The *Wuji tu shuo* 無極圖說 (Explanation of the Diagram of the Ultimate-less; 9.1a–7a), the *Tuoyue ge* 橐籥歌 (Song of the Bellows; 9.7a–8a), and poems on the inner elixir (9.8a–13a).

2. The *Jindan wenda* 金丹問答 (Questions and Answers on the Golden Elixir; 10.1a–14b), containing short notes on about one hundred terms used in *neidan*.

3. A collection of "Eighty-One Seven-Character Quatrains" (11.1a–13a).

4. Various poetic compositions (12.1a–12b) and an essay on the *Zhouyi can-tong qi (Token for the Agreement of the Three According to the *Book of Changes*; 12.12b–13b).

5. Commentaries to the *Ruyao jing (Mirror for Compounding the Medicine; 13.1a–9b) and the *Qinyuan chun (Spring in the Garden by the Qin River; 13.9b–17b).

Lowell SKAR

📖 Boltz J. M. 1987a, 236

※ *Xiuzhen shishu*; *neidan*

Jindan dayao

金丹大要

Great Essentials of the Golden Elixir

This *neidan work, *Chen Zhixu's *magnum opus*, is contained in both the Taoist Canon (CT 1067) and the *Daozang jiyao (vol. 16). Two disciples wrote prefaces (dated 1335) to the version in the Taoist Canon, which is followed by three supplements: one containing charts (*Jindan dayao tu* 圖; CT 1068), another devoted to hagiographies of *Quanzhen patriarchs (*Jindan dayao liexian zhi* 列仙誌; CT 1069), and the last describing a ritual performed in honor of *Zhongli Quan and *Lü Dongbin (*Jindan dayao xianpai* 仙派; CT 1070). The three supplements form the second *juan* in the *Daozang jiyao* version, which is more complete than the version in the Taoist Canon. The anonymous work entitled *Xiulian xuzhi* 修鍊須知 (Required Knowledge on Cultivation and Refinement; CT 1077) contains *juan* 7–8 of CT 1067.

While the original *Jindan dayao* was in ten *juan* (CT 1067, 1.11a–b and 12.8a), the present text in the Taoist Canon is divided into sixteen *juan*. The content of the text, rearranged according the original plan, is the following:

1. The first *juan* (corresponding to j. 1 and 2 in CT 1067) is a commentary on the first section of the *Daode jing*.

2. The second *juan* (j. 3 and 4) discusses the precosmic essence, pneuma, and spirit (*jing, qi, shen*), i.e., the three "substances" and three stages of the alchemical work.

3. The third *juan* (j. 5 and 6) deals with the "wondrous functioning" (*miaoyong* 妙用) of various elements of *neidan*, such as the tripod and the furnace (*dinglu*), fire phasing (*huohou*), and the collection of the inner elixir. This *juan* was originally divided into nine sections, two of which, missing from the Taoist Canon but found in the *Daozang jiyao*, deal with the Reverted Elixir (*huandan*) and with the alchemical notion of "reversal" (*diandao* 顛倒).

4. The fourth *juan* (j. 7 and 8) mainly concerns fire phasing.

5. The fifth *juan* (j. 9 and 10) contains poems and a rewording of the *Daode jing* from an alchemical point of view. In the *Daozang jiyao*, this *juan* is followed by a section entitled "Five Items for the Golden Elixir" ("Jindan wushi" 金丹五事), which is missing in CT 1067.

6. The sixth *juan* (j. 11 and 12), composed of small pieces addressed to Chen's

disciples, emphasizes the necessity of not getting attached to alchemical metaphors.

7. The seventh *juan* (j. 13 and 14) is devoted to dialogues with disciples on various subjects; the version in the *Daozang jiyao* contains fifteen more pieces than the one in the Taoist Canon.

8. The eighth *juan* probably corresponded to the present *Jindan dayao tu* (CT 1068).

9–10. In the last two *juan* (j. 15 and 16), Chen Zhixu adopts a Buddhist language with a strong Chan flavor, and equates the achievement of the Golden Elixir (*jindan) with "seeing one's (Buddha-)nature" (*jianxing* 見性).

Chen Zhixu draws extensively on the *Daode jing*, the *Zhuangzi, the *Wuzhen pian, the *Yinfu jing, the *Zhouyi cantong qi and related works, and several Quanzhen masters. He refers to *Zhang Boduan as his *zushi* 祖師 (Ancestral Master), and identifies himself as the heir of the Quanzhen tradition transmitted by Zhao Youqin 趙友欽 (fl. 1329), whom he often mentions as his master. Like *Li Daochun, whom he frequently quotes, Chen considers the central point in *jindan* to be the intuitive recognition of one's precosmic and perennial inborn nature (*xing* 性; see *xing and *ming*), which he equates with the Buddha-nature (*foxing* 佛性 or *buddhatā*).

Isabelle ROBINET

📖 Boltz J. M. 1987a, 184–86; Li Yuanguo 1991; Qing Xitai 1994, 2: 171–73; Robinet 1995a, 114–19 and passim

※ Chen Zhixu; *neidan*

Jindan sibai zi

金丹四百字

Four Hundred Words on the Golden Elixir

This alchemical treatise ascribed to *Zhang Boduan consists of twenty pentasyllabic poems. A lengthy undated preface states that it was intended for Ma Ziran 馬自然, a contemporary of Zhang Boduan and a putative disciple of *Liu Haichan. The first allusion to the text is in a letter of thanks addressed by *Bai Yuchan to Zhang Boduan in 1216. Bai claims to have come across the writings and commentaries by Ma Ziran on Mount Wuyi (*Wuyi shan, Fujian), where he first read a work entitled "Sibai yan" 四百言 (Four Hundred Words; *Xiuzhen shishu, 6.4b). While the commentator Huang Ziru 黃自如 (fl. 1241) seems to have no doubts about the authorship of the *Jindan sibai zi*, *Yu Yan believed it to be a forgery written by Bai Yuchan himself (Chen Bing 1985, 36; Qing Xitai 1994, 1: 306).

The poem describes the inner alchemical process in a way similar to the *Wuzhen pian*, but borrows technical language from the *Zhong-Lü texts. It was first included in Bai Yuchan's lost collection entitled *Qunxian zhuyu ji* 群仙珠玉集 (Anthology of Pearls and Jade of the Gathered Immortals; van der Loon 1984, 149). Since then, several editions with commentaries have appeared. These include Huang Ziru's *Jindan sibai zi* (1241; CT 1081; also in *Xiuzhen shishu*, j. 5, with five additional poems on *neidan by Huang); *Lu Xixing's *Jindan sibai zi ceshu* 金丹四百字測疏 (Comprehensive Commentary to the *Jindan sibai zi*; ca. 1571); *Peng Haogu's *Jindan sibai zi zhu* 金丹四百字注 (Commentary to the *Jindan sibai zi*; 1597/1600); and *Liu Yiming's *Jindan sibai zi jie* 金丹四百字解 (Explication of the *Jindan sibai zi*; 1807; trans. Cleary 1986a).

Farzeen BALDRIAN-HUSSEIN

📖 Davis and Chao 1940b (trans.)

※ Zhang Boduan; *neidan*; Nanzong

jing

精

essence

See *jing, qi, shen* 精 · 氣 · 神.

jing and *jian*

鏡 · 劍

mirror and sword

In Taoism, mirrors and swords are objects invested with power. Since ancient times they have been part of the royal treasures and symbols of good government. In medieval China they were the attributes of both the ruler and the Taoist priest. Well-known examples of this feature are the sword and the mirror that the twelfth *Shangqing patriarch, *Sima Chengzhen (647–735), gave to Tang Xuanzong (r. 712–56). A related text, the *Hanxiang jianjian tu* 含象劍鑑

Fig. 47. Sword presented by
*Sima Chengzhen (647–735)
to Tang Xuanzong (r. 712–56).
Hanxiang jianjian tu 含象劍
鑑圖 (Drawings of a Sword
and Mirror with Engraved
Images; CT 431), 5a–6b.

圖 (Drawings of a Sword and Mirror with Engraved
Images; CT 431), describes the mirror as a picture
of the cosmos, and explains the name "Sword of
Luster and Thunder" (*jingzhen jian* 景震劍), saying
that the luster (*jing* 景) on one side of the blade
represents the Yang principle, while the other side
symbolizes thunder (*zhen* 震), which represents the
Yin principle. The mirror and sword thus represent
the Yin and Yang aspects of the Dao.

Chinese mirrors (also called *jian* 鑑, a synonym of
jing) were round and cast in bronze. On the back of
the polished mirror surface there was an embossed
decoration with a hump in the middle through
which a string was drawn, enabling one to carry
the mirror at one's belt. The embossed pattern on
the back depicted clouds, waters, and mountains
inhabited by mystical animals and feathered immortals. The circular shape of the mirror symbolized
the heavens. The earth was depicted in the square
at the center of the relief which bore the cyclical
characters (**ganzhi*) marking the points of the compass and the calendar, i.e., of space and time. This
carta mundi symbolizes the particular ability of the
mirror to reveal not only the apparent but also the
"real form" (*zhenxing* 真形) of the things and beings
in the universe (see *xing).

Inscriptions on Han-dynasty bronze mirrors include some of the oldest descriptions of Taoist
paradises. One of them says: "This mirror was created in the Imperial workshops. A true masterpiece!
In it you can see the immortals (**xianren*) who do
not grow old. If they are thirsty, they drink from
jade sources. If they are hungry, they eat [celestial]
dates. They stroll through the world and rejoice in
the four seas [at the edges of the universe]" (see
Kaltenmark 1953, 11). Mirrors also served as signposts
to the paradises and heavens, and this is why they
are often found in graves. If a sword was found in
a grave, however, this was taken as a sign that its occupant had achieved immortality through "release from the corpse" (**shijie*).

The **Zhuangzi* compares the "quiescent mind of the sage (**shengren*)" to
a mirror that reflects the variety of all beings (chapter 13; see trans. Watson

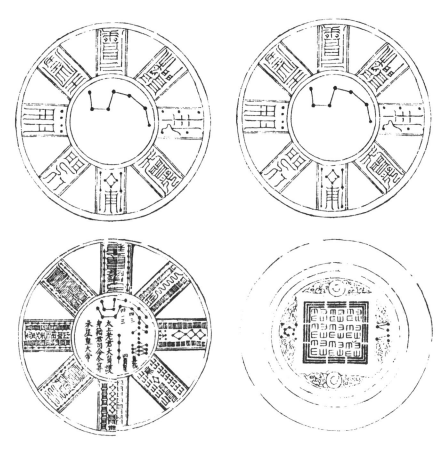

Fig. 48. Emblems inscribed on the reverse side of mirrors. *Shangqing changsheng baojian tu* 上清長生寶鑑圖 (Highest Clarity Illustrations of Precious Mirrors for the Prolonging Life; CT 429).

1968, 142), and explains: "The accomplished man (*zhiren* 至人) uses the heart like a mirror; he does not escort things as they go or welcome them as they come, he responds and does not store. Therefore he is able to conquer other things without suffering a wound" (chapter 7; see trans. Watson 1968, 97). The second chapter of the *Huainan zi* also compares the sage who is in harmony with the natural order of the cosmos to a pure mirror in which everything is clearly reflected.

The mirror and sword also served as a protection against demons (*gui). *Ge Hong (283–343) recommends that mountain recluses carry a magic mirror with them and look at the reflection of every creature that approaches them in the mirror. Once a demon is recognized in a mirror, it is deprived of its power and forced to flee (*Baopu zi* 17; trans. Ware 1966, 281–82). In his "Records of Knives and Swords" ("Daojian lu" 刀劍錄, as quoted in *Taiping yulan* 343), *Tao Hongjing (456–536) explains how an adept, by absorbing the powerful luster of the sword, can drive out demons and heal the illnesses that they bring down on him. To protect a house from demons and evil emanations, a magic mirror was hung on the door, a bucket of cold water was placed below the mirror, and a sword was laid on the bucket with its tip facing outward (*Laojun mingzhao fa* 老君明照法, YJQQ 48).

Finally, deities could also be made visible by "mirror meditations" as described in *Baopu zi* 15. Shangqing adepts could also produce spiritual mirrors in their own eyes though visualization techniques. By looking inward one could see the gods of one's own body in the light of this mirror. Visualizations of this kind kept demons away, prolonged life, and ultimately led to immortality (relevant methods are collected in YJQQ 48; trans. Kaltenmark 1974, 154–66).

Ute ENGELHARDT

📖 Cahill and Murray 1987; Campany 2002, 70–72; Demiéville 1948; Engelhardt 1987, 44–46 and 69–76; Fukunaga Mitsuji 1987, 1–69; Kaltenmark 1974; Little 2000b, 140–41, 214–17, and 354; Loewe 1979, 60–85; Needham 1962, 87–94; Schafer 1978–79; Seidel 1982, 87–99

※ *faqi*; MAGIC; MEDITATION AND VISUALIZATION

jing, qi, shen

精 · 氣（炁）· 神

essence, pneuma (breath, energy, vital force), spirit

Jing, qi, and *shen* are three of the main notions shared by Taoism and Chinese culture alike. They are often referred to as the Three Treasures (*sanbao* 三 寶), an expression that immediately reveals their importance and the close connection among them. The ideas and practices associated with each term, and with the three terms as a whole, are complex and vary considerably in different contexts and historical periods. This entry is mainly concerned with their understanding in inner alchemy (*neidan).

Meaning of the terms. The common translations of *jing* as "essence," *qi* as "breath," "pneuma," or "energy," and *shen* as "spirit" capture some of their respective features but are not entirely satisfying. In its broadest meaning, *jing* (a word that originally refers to bleached rice) is said to represent the life germ contained in the Dao, as stated for instance in *Daode jing* 21 ("Vague and indistinct! But in it there is an essence"). In the human being, it is a form of energy that mainly derives from food and nourishes the body, especially the five viscera (*wuzang). This is the most usual sense of the term in the

Fig. 49. Primordial Pneuma (*yuanqi). *Xuanlan renniao shan jingtu* 玄覽人鳥山經圖 (Scripture and Illustration for the Mysterious Contemplation of the Mountain of the Bird-Men; CT 434), 5a. See Lagerwey 1987c, 161–67.

context of gymnastics (*daoyin) and breathing techniques. In an even more restricted sense, *jing* designates the energy attached to sexuality (semen in men, menstrual blood in women). This meaning applies for instance to the expression "returning the essence to replenish the brain" (*huanjing bunao). *Qi* is positioned between essence and spirit and therefore at the intersection point between matter and mind. Whereas *jing* is a carrier of life and has a nourishing function, *qi* is a dynamic force and has a transforming function. The term originally means "vapor." *Shen* evolved from the original sense of "divinity" and outer and inner "spirits" into the designation of a single force, whose connotations include those of psychic essence and even of "soul." To some extent, *shen* applies to anything that exists within the cosmos but has no material aspect, such as deities and human thought.

Neidan. The idea of transmuting *jing*, *qi*, and *shen* is especially important in *neidan*, where the phrases "refining essence into pneuma" (*lianjing huaqi* 鍊精化氣), "refining pneuma into spirit" (*lianqi huashen* 鍊氣化神), and "refining spirit and reverting to Emptiness" (*lianshen huanxu* 鍊神還虛) define the three main stages of the inner alchemical practice.

In *neidan*, *jing* is refined by repeatedly making it ascend along the back of the body and then descend along the front of the body (see *zhoutian). *Qi* is cultivated through meditation, stillness of mind, and breathing practices such as "embryonic breathing" (*taixi). These practices are related to each other, as the more the mind is concentrated, the more outer breathing becomes refined and is replaced by embryonic breathing. *Shen* is compared to fire, particularly the fire of desire that stirs up the passions and feeds the sense organs. With reference to calming the agitated mind and the destructive fire, *neidan* employs the expression "extracting Water from the Fire of the heart" (this Water is represented by the Yin line within *li* 離 ☲, the trigram that represents Fire). This expression means appeasing the mind by making psychic energy descend instead of going up. Mental concentration corresponds to the emergence within the body of a form of heat that rises from the lower abdomen, a phenomenon referred to in *neidan* as "extracting Fire from the Water of the kidneys" (i.e., the Yang line within *kan* 坎 ☵, the trigram that represents Water). The kidneys' Water normally produces seminal essence and flows out of the body under the effect of the Fire of desires. This illustrates two important alchemical principles: the reversal of the energetic course (the energy of the heart descends, the energy of the kidneys ascends) and the union of opposites (the Fire from the heart joins with the Water from the kidneys).

Precelestial and postcelestial. An important distinction found in *neidan* and elsewhere (e.g, in *Shao Yong and other Neo-Confucian thinkers) is between two aspects of *jing*, *qi*, and *shen*, respectively related to the states "prior to Heaven" and "posterior to Heaven" (*xiantian and houtian*). Essence exists both as "precelestial essence" (*xiantian zhi jing* 先天之精), also known as Original Essence (*yuanjing* 元精), and as ordinary essence, called "postcelestial essence" (*houtian zhi jing* 後天之精). Whereas ordinary essence, which is derived from desire, is produced and kept in the kidneys, Original Essence, which issues from the appeasement of mind and the stabilization of breath, is associated with the Gate of the Vital Force (*mingmen), located in the right kidney or between the two kidneys.

Similarly, *qi* exists as "precelestial breath (or pneuma)" (*xiantian zhi qi* 先天之氣), also called Original Breath or Original Pneuma (*yuanqi), and as "postcelestial breath (or pneuma)" (*houtian zhi qi* 後天之氣). These different aspects are represented by two different forms of the word *qi*: the graph for precelestial *qi* (炁) is explicated as breath or pneuma "without the fire (of desire)." At the level of the human being, the distinction between the two *qi* develops at birth: with its first cry, the newborn child enters the postcelestial state through the ingestion of outer air. Original Breath or Original Pneuma reaches fullness at puberty, then progressively decreases before disappearing at the age of forty-nine for women and sixty-four for men. Some alchemical schools even quantify the precelestial breath that a person has at birth but progressively loses during life. One of the alchemical processes consists of compensating for this loss with the help of postcelestial breath. *Neidan* also distinguishes between an outer breath (also called Martial Fire or *wuhuo* 武火), which is common breath, and an inner breath (also called Civil Fire or *wenhuo* 文火), which corresponds to thought and the Intention (*yi).

The distinction between "precelestial spirit" (*xiantian zhi shen* 先天之神), also called Original Spirit (*yuanshen* 元神), and "postcelestial spirit" (*houtian zhi shen* 後天之神) follows along similar lines. In *neidan*, the transition from the latter to the former occurs by means of precelestial breath, i.e., through the progressive development of a subtle and tenuous form of breathing (so-called "embryonic breathing") that allows one to reach a luminous state. Thus, one progressively develops a "Yin spirit" (*yinshen* 陰神), a process that is accompanied by a feeling of luminosity in the region of the head. The *shen* rises to the upper Cinnabar Field (the *niwan), from which it leaves the body through the sinciput in an experience known as "egress of the Spirit" (*chushen). The mind realizes a state in which time, space, and material limits disappear, and is transmuted into "Yang spirit" (*yangshen* 陽神).

Catherine DESPEUX

📖 Despeux 1979, 48–82; Harada Jirō 1988; Ishida Hidemi 1989; Larre 1982; Libbrecht 1990; Major 1987a; Maspero 1981, 460–68; Onozawa Seiichi, Fukunaga Mitsuji, and Yamanoi Yū 1978; Robinet 1985a; Robinet 1995a; Roth 1990; Sivin 1987, 46–53, 147–67; Zhang Liwen 1990; Zhu Yueli 1982

※ *chushen*; *xiantian* and *houtian*; *yuanqi*; *neidan*; *yangsheng*; TAOIST VIEWS OF THE HUMAN BODY

jingluo

經絡

conduits; "ducts and links"

Jingluo refers to a system of "conduits," "tracts," "ducts," or "channels," invisible to the observer, which connect the upper body parts to the lower, and the inner viscera to the surface of the body. The *Lingshu* 靈樞 (Numinous Pivot, 3.10; see *Huangdi neijing*) outlines twelve such conduits (there referred to as *jingmai* 經脈): six are attributed to the hands and six to the feet, of which three of each are Yin and three are Yang. The Yin conduits (*taiyin* 太陰, *shaoyin* 少陰, *jueyin* 厥陰) generally follow the inside of the extremities, and the Yang conduits (*yangming* 陽明, *taiyang* 太陽, *shaoyang* 少陽) the outside. Each of these conduits is said to have a trunk (*zhi* 直), which links to one of the six viscera and the corresponding one of the six bowels (and vice versa), and several branches (*zhi* 支), which lead to various other body parts. These channels control disorders of two kinds: those that arise if the conduit is stirred (*shi dong ze bing* 是動則病) and those to which it gives rise (*qi suo chan bing* 其所

產病). The *jingluo* system, as generally referred to in the scholarly literature, views these conduits as linked to one another and as forming a circulation system through which *qixue* ("breath and blood") flows; they are considered to be littered with loci, places where the application of needles or moxa can affect the flow and quality of *qixue* in a beneficial way.

In the Warring States period, precursors of this system were developed in the context of therapeutics by cauterization (see below); and in the Song, it began to be used for classifications of the *materia medica*. The system was mainly elaborated in the context of acupuncture and moxibustion, mostly during the Han and Tang, and it also comprises, apart from the linking channels (*luomai* 絡脈) and minute links (*sunluo* 孫絡), fifteen branching-out links (*bieluo* 別絡), twelve branching-out conduits (*jingbie* 經別), twelve muscle conduits (*jingjin* 經筋), and twelve skin regions (*pibu* 皮部). The system also comprises the "eight extraordinary channels" (*qijing bamai* 奇經八脈), a historically later addition, which therapeutically are mainly responsible for the overall regulation of *qixue*. Two among these are particularly conspicuous: the Control Channel along the spine and the Function Channel along the parallel ventral axis (*dumai and *renmai*). Both became important in *neidan practices from the Song period onward.

Precursors to the system are recorded in two silk manuscripts from tomb no. 3 at *Mawangdui, closed in 168 BCE and excavated in 1973 (trans. Harper 1998, 192–212). These texts outline the course of eleven channels, which are similar yet not identical to and generally less elaborate than the channels described in the *Lingshu*. Their courses generally begin at the utmost point of the extremities and end on the trunk of the body. Notably, they are not linked to viscera (with few exceptions), and no *qixue* flows through them. The recommended treatment for disorders associated with these channels is cauterization, but no loci are mentioned.

Another precursory system can be seen on a lacquer figurine dating to the second century BCE, excavated in 1993 from tomb no. 2 in Mianyang 綿陽 (Sichuan; see He and Lo 1996). It shows six red lines along the arms, connecting to the head, and three along the legs. Of these, the three lines along the legs can be most easily identified as precursors of the foot's three Yang conduits in the *Lingshu*. The lines on the figurine are symmetrical, the plane of symmetry being the spine, marked by a red line that is clearly a precursor of what later became known as the *dumai*.

Elisabeth HSU

📖 Harper 1998, 192–212; He and Lo 1996; Li Ding 1984; Lu and Needham 1980, 13–69 and 93–106; Porkert 1974, 197–346; Sivin 1987, 133–47

※ *dumai* and *renmai*

Jingming dao

淨明道

Pure and Bright Way

A school of teachings known as Jingming dao arose around the enshrinement of *Xu Xun (trad. 239–374) at the Western Hills (*Xishan, Jiangxi). Hagiographic texts offer variant accounts concerning the history of devotions at his shrine. By the Tang it became a widely recognized center for a *Lingbao form of ritual practice known as Xiaodao 孝道 (Way of Filiality). Scholars have located two versions of a Xiaodao scripture of unknown provenance in the Taoist Canon. The text appears to date to the late Tang but is devoid of any allusion to Xu Xun lore, so its relation to the early devotional community at Xishan can only be considered conjectural, pending the discovery of external evidence.

Several post-Tang compilations in the Taoist Canon attest to a derivative of Xiaodao called Jingming fa 淨明法 (Pure and Bright Ritual). Most of these texts lack prefaces or colophons. A Song date of transmission can nonetheless often be discerned from internal reference to Xu Xun by a title dating to 1112, Shengong miaoji zhenjun 神功妙濟真君 (Perfected Lord of Divine Merit and Wondrous Deliverance). Texts clearly edited no earlier than the late thirteenth century bear an additional epithet granted Xu in 1295 by Yuan Chengzong (r. 1295–1307). This title, Zhidao xuanying 至道玄應 (Mysterious Response of the Ultimate Way), conventionally precedes the honorific of 1112.

The *Jingming zhongxiao quanshu (Complete Writings of the Pure and Bright [Way of] Loyalty and Filiality) is the most comprehensive resource on the Jingming dao in the Taoist Canon. This fourteenth-century anthology features the recorded sayings of *Liu Yu (1257–1308) and his protégé Huang Yuanji 黃元吉 (1271–1326). Liu Yu is recognized as the founder of a form of Jingming dao popularly known as Jingming zhongxiao dao 淨明忠孝道 (Pure and Bright Way of Loyalty and Filiality).

Early history. Precisely how and when Xu Xun gained recognition as a paragon of filiality is uncertain. According to the earliest extant hagiography, devotees came from a great distance to set up an altar and ancestral hall at Xishan when they learned of Xu's ascent there in 292. Sometime later the Youwei guan 遊帷 觀 (Abbey of the Flying Curtain) was built at the site by imperial decree. *Zhai (Retreats) were held there under imperial sponsorship three times a year. In addition to commemorating Xu's ascent on the fifteenth of the eighth lunar month, ritual oblations on behalf of the empire were also authorized at the site on the fifteenth of the first and fifth lunar months. Eighteen generations of Xu's descendants, beginning with his nephew Jian 簡, are listed as *daoshi (Taoist masters) who presided over Xiaodao at the abbey. By the year 627 the temple compound appeared to have been abandoned. Tang Gaozong (r. 649–83) is said to have ordered a revitalization of Xiaodao at the site. His decree is incongruently dated to the third year of Yongchun, a reign period that merely extended from the second lunar month of 682 to the twelfth lunar month of 683. The latest event recorded is a lively, well-attended *huanglu dazhai* 黃籙大 齋 (Great Yellow Register Retreat) hosted at the abbey for three days in 819.

A variant account in the *Jingming zhongxiao quanshu*, reflecting centuries of hagiographic consensus, dates Xu Xun's ascent to 374. The subsequent founding of a shrine is credited to local villagers led by Xu Jian, identified here as a grandnephew. Devotees allegedly divined their fortunes by drawing slips from the set of oracular verse that Xu Xun left behind. The shrine's loss of its following is dated to the time of Sui Yangdi (r. 604–17). By the Yongchun reign period (682–83), a Celestial Master named Hu Huichao 天師胡惠超 (?–703) reportedly found the Youwei guan in ruins. Hu oversaw a restoration of the abbey, where he established himself as a recipient of the Jingming Lingbao zhongxiao zhi dao 淨明靈寶忠孝之道 (Pure and Bright Lingbao Way of Loyalty and Filiality). With Tang Xuanzong (r. 712–56) came a marked level of imperial patronage. Reverence for Xu Xun's role as a guardian of the empire reached new heights during the Northern Song. The current designation of the abbey as the *Yulong wanshou gong (Palace of the Ten-thousand-fold Longevity of Jade Beneficence) dates to a decree issued by Huizong (r. 1100–1125) in 1116.

The precise nature of the Xiaodao legacy celebrating Xu Xun at Xishan remains unclear. A figure no less prominent than *Du Guangting (850–933) observes that the Xiaodao pursued in that region from the Jin to his own time scarcely differed from the Lingbao heritage. The people of Yuzhang 豫 章 (Jiangxi), according to Du, had for generations maintained a staunch level of practice, with nothing outranking filiality in their esteem. He also declares that those who were filial toward their parents would certainly be loyal toward their ruler, just as orderly households inevitably led to repose in the empire itself. These comments appear in the biography of Xu Xun's mentor Chen Mu 諶姆 within the *Yongcheng jixian lu (5.16a–b).

Numerous scriptures transmitted during the Song and Yuan present instruction in the practice of Jingming fa, the direct heir of Xiaodao. Of outstanding interest is the single text in this vast body of literature bearing a dated preface. Assistant Lecturer He Shouzheng 何守證 of the Yizhen tan 翼真壇 (Altar of Winged Transcendents) writes that disciples came to him with a flawed text, requesting emendations and a preface, which he supplied in the year 1131. The text is entitled *Lingbao Jingming xinxiu jiulao shenyin fumo bifa* 靈寶淨明

新修九老神印伏魔祕法 (Newly Revised Secret Rites of the Pure and Bright [Way of] Lingbao for Suppressing Demons with the Divine Seal of the Nine Ancient Lords; CT 562). Lecturer He identifies this manual as a pivotal Lingbao codification originally conveyed to Xu Xun by the legendary female adept Chen Mu. Defects in the version given him, he explains, had accumulated over the years as the text was handed down from one generation to the next. The primary source of authority to which Lecturer He alludes are teachings on *zhongxiao lianshen* 忠孝廉慎 (loyalty, filiality, honesty, and prudence) revealed in 1129 under the rubric of *Lingbao Jingming bifa* 靈寶淨明祕法 (Secret Rites of the Pure and Bright [Way of] Lingbao). He also writes that two years later Xu Xun himself abruptly appeared at the site of his shrine. This visitation reportedly occurred one month prior to the date given the preface and led to the construction of the Yizhen tan, where Lecturer He presumably received his students.

He's preface is followed by instruction on cultivating an internal state of Jingming replicating the radiance of the sun and moon. Essential to this contemplative practice is a *Fumo shenyin* 伏魔神印 (Divine Seal for Suppressing Demons) and the microcosmic imagery of a *Jingming qijing* 淨明氣鏡 (Mirror of the Pure and Bright Life-Force). The extent to which these teachings were followed remains unknown. Nearly a century later, Jin Yunzhong 金允中 (fl. 1224–25) writes in the *Shangqing lingbao dafa* (Great Rites of the Numinous Treasure of Highest Clarity; CT 1223, 10.13a–b) of a confusing array of texts on Jingming fa inconsistent with the earlier Lingbao scriptural corpus venerating Xu Xun. Jin's critical view no doubt evolved as diverse texts like the manual edited by He Shouzheng began appearing in abundance following the collapse of the Northern Song empire.

Teachings of Liu Yu and Huang Yuanji. The fullest record of Jingming dao in the Taoist Canon was produced by and for disciples, designated as *dizi* 弟子 or *fazi* 法子. As the latter term denotes, instructions in the *Jingming zhongxiao quanshu* attest to an assimilation of Buddhist teachings. Their debt to the Ru 儒 scholastic legacy of Daoxue 道學 is even more pronounced. Liu Yu forthrightly states that the fundamentals of the Pure and Bright Way of Loyalty and Filiality were familiar to but largely neglected by the Ru literati in his time. His definition of Jingming as nothing but *zhengxin chengyi* 正心誠意 (equanimity and integrity) clearly harks back to the eight-step progression outlined in the *Daxue* 大學 (Great Learning; trans. Legge 1893, 357–59). By equating loyalty and filiality with fostering *gangchang* 綱常 ("guidelines and constancy"), moreover, Liu also alludes to perhaps the best-known behavioral code ascribed to Confucius, that is, the *sangang wuchang* 三綱五常 (three guidelines and five constancies). Above all he counselled moderation in all things and compared excessive adherence to *gangchang* with a boat listing in one direction, certain to cause harm. With his formulation of the Way of Jingming, Liu Yu thus intended in part to both restore and redefine the central tenets of Daoxue, or the so-called Neo-Confucian teachings of his contemporaries.

Liu's vision of Jingming dao rests on a broad interpretation of how the attributes of filiality and loyalty are best exemplified. In his view, maximum loyalty is to be without deceit in all matters (*dazhong zhe yiwu buqi* 大忠者一物不欺). Similarly, to love everyone without exception is Liu's definition of maximum filiality (*daxiao zhe yiti jie ai* 大孝者一體皆愛). Followers of Jingming dao were expected to strive toward an embodiment of purity and radiance that ultimately brought them in consonance with the heavenly realm, like a river returning to the sea. Liu maintained that loyalty and filiality automatically ensued from conduct distinguished by purity and radiance. To him, purity meant that one did not defile anything (*buran wu* 不染物) and radiance meant that one did not disturb anything (*buchu wu* 不觸物).

Both Liu and his foremost disciple Huang Yuanji repeatedly advocated the need to *chengfen zhiyu* 懲忿窒欲 (restrain anger and stifle desire), a phrase that can be traced to the gloss accompanying hexagram 41 in the **Yijing*. It was essential for anyone striving toward absolute integrity and equanimity to learn how to restrain all expressions of hostility and obsessive attachments of desire. Harm, according to Liu, was sure to ensue with but a single irregular thought. He strongly believed that how one fared in life was entirely within one's own responsibility to determine. The efficacy of all prayers and ritual practice, in his view, completely rested with the integrity of the supplicant. Liu made simplicity the governing principle of Jingming dao, sanctioning only one talisman, one seal, and a concise petitionary model for ritual use.

Citing guidelines that Celestial Master Hu ostensibly received from Xu Xun, Liu adamantly repudiates the contemplative practice of *xiulian* 修鍊 (cultivating refinement). There was no need, in his view, to sequester oneself within a mountain retreat to undertake a study of the Dao. One could gain rank as a transcendent, he claimed, by adhering to eight treasures, ranging from loyalty and filiality to *lian* 廉 (honesty), *jin* 謹 (discretion), *kuan* 寬 (expansiveness), *yu* 裕 (generosity), *rong* 容 (tolerance), and *ren* 忍 (endurance). Liu deemed such qualities essential to the cultivation of a sense of *gongxin* 公心 (public spirit).

The instructions recorded in Huang's name enlarge upon this principle with the warning that *gongxin* can easily be feigned, whereas anyone truly acting in the interest of the public did not covet praise as such. He advised his disciples to respond compassionately to the ill-behaved and lead them back toward the right path by example rather than risk alienation by scolding. Huang also emphasized the retributive justice inherent in all conduct, with good and bad being rewarded in kind, but remains conspicuously silent regarding the so-called **shanshu* (morality books) practice of counting merits and demerits. Notable heirs to these teachings on Jingming dao include *Zhao Yizhen (?–1382), *Liu Yuanran (1351–1432), and Zhang Taixuan 張太玄 (1651–1716).

Judith M. BOLTZ

📖 Akizuki Kan'ei 1978; Akizuki Kan'ei 1991; Boltz J. M. 1987a, 70–78; Huang Xiaoshi 1999; Qing Xitai 1988–95, 2: 649–52, 3: 128–35 and 347–62, and 4: 193–211; Schipper 1985d; Xu Xihua 1983

※ Xu Xun; Yulong wanshou gong; Xishan; for other related entries see the Synoptic Table of Contents, sec. III.7 ("Song, Jin, and Yuan: Jingming dao") and sec. III.9 ("Ming and Qing: Persons Related to Jingming dao")

Jingming zhongxiao quanshu

淨明忠孝全書

Complete Writings of the Pure and
Bright [Way of] Loyalty and Filialty

The *Jingming zhongxiao quanshu* (CT 1110) is a collection of hagiographies together with transcriptions of the revealed and oral teachings associated with the school of the Jingming zhongxiao dao 淨明忠孝道 (Pure and Bright Way of Loyalty and Filiality; see *Jingming dao) based at the *Yulong wanshou gong (Palace of the Ten-thousand-fold Longevity of Jade Beneficence) honoring *Xu Xun (trad. 239–374) at the Western Hills (*Xishan, Jiangxi). Huang Yuanji 黃元吉 (1271–1326; Qing Xitai 1994, 1: 364–65), successor to the school's founder *Liu Yu (1257–1308), is credited with compiling the first five *juan* of the anthology. The sixth and last *juan* is ascribed to a disciple at the Yulong gong named Chen Tianhe 陳天和. Huang's preeminent disciple Xu Hui 徐慧, or Xu Yi 徐異 (1291–1350), of Luling 廬陵 (Jiangxi) is identified as the collator of all six *juan*. The biography of Xu Hui at the close of *juan* 1 is obviously an interpolation by someone from a later generation.

The text opens with seven prefaces dating from 1323 to 1327, contributed by Zhang Gui 張珪 (1264–1327), Zhao Shiyan 趙世延 (1260–1336), Yu Ji 虞集 (1272–1348), Teng Bin 滕賓, Zeng Xunshen 曾巽申, Peng Ye 彭埜 (fl. 1323), and Xu Hui himself. These prefaces convey a sense of the Ming literati's high regard for the Jingming school as an endorsement of the long-standing code of ethics identified with Confucius and his following. Some also provide clues to the complex history of the anthology. Zeng, for example, states that the collection of writings he received from Huang in 1323 had first been published two decades earlier. Xu Hui begins his story with a meeting that he and a colleague named Sheng Ximing 盛熙明 had with Huang, also in 1323. Huang reportedly viewed Xu's arrival as a prophetic response to his dream the night before and presented him with copies of the *Jingming zhongxiao shu* 淨明忠孝 書 (Writings of the Pure and Bright [Way of] Loyalty and Filiality) and *Yuzhen yulu* 玉真語錄 (Recorded Sayings of Jade Perfection). Xu does not reveal the age of these texts but says that a few days later Huang brought out another set of transcribed teachings that had not been published. He did this, according to Xu, in appreciation of his perceptive response to the other texts and also expressed interest in having everything published as a unit.

Approximately nine months after Huang's demise in the twelfth lunar month of 1325 (15 January 1326), Xu paid a visit to the cemetery at the Yulong gong. Huang's disciples Chen Yunyin 陳雲隱 and Xiong Cangya 熊蒼崖 came forward at the time with additional texts. Xu states that he then put the recorded sayings he had collected together with the texts revealed to Liu Yu and gave it the title *Jingming zhongxiao quanshu*. By publishing this anthology, he intended to provide scholars of like mind with guidance on cultivating loyalty and filiality in both public and private affairs so that all might live in harmony and peace.

The opening *juan* includes biographical accounts for seven figures central to the Jingming formulation: Xu Xun, Zhang Yun 張氳 (653–745), Hu Huichao 胡惠超 (?–703), Guo Pu 郭璞 (276–324), Liu Yu, Huang Yuanji, and Xu Hui. Copies of five texts putatively revealed to Liu Yu by Xu Xun, Hu Huichao, and Guo Pu are contained in *juan* 2. *Juan* 3–5 are devoted to transcriptions of Liu Yu's teachings, largely in response to anonymously posed questions. The heading *Yuzhen xiansheng yulu* 玉真先生語錄 (Recorded Sayings of the Elder of Jade Perfection) given this body of texts is amplified by the designations *neiji* 內集 (Internal Anthology), *waiji* 外集 (External Anthology), and *bieji* 別集 (Separate Anthology), respectively, for *juan* 3, 4, and 5. The last *juan*, dedicated to Huang Yuanji's sayings, is entitled *Zhonghuang xiansheng wenda* 中黃先生 問答 (Responses to Inquiries of the Elder of Central Yellow). Whereas the biographies document the diverse ritual practices of the Jingming patriarchs in their roles as rainmakers and exorcists on call, the essential lesson that both Liu and Huang give their following is to forsake solitary contemplative pursuits in favor of devoted attention to the welfare of family and state.

Another version of this anthology, edited by *Shao Yizheng 邵以正 (?–1462) in 1452, is contained in the library of the Naikaku bunko in Tokyo. A cognate body of writings is included in the *Xiaoyao shan Wanshou gong zhi* 逍遙山 萬壽宮志 (Monograph of the Palace of Ten-thousand-fold Longevity at Mount Xiaoyao) published in 1878 (Du Jiexiang 1983, 6: 206–33 and 270–305, 7: 551–72).

Judith M. BOLTZ

📖 Akizuki Kan'ei 1978, 16–17 and 141–55; Boltz J. M. 1987a, 75–77, 197–99, and 285; Chen Yuan 1988, 967–68; Qing Xitai 1994, 2: 119–21

※ Jingming dao

jingshi

靜室

"quiet chamber"; meditation chamber; oratory

Literally "quiet chamber," the term *jingshi*, or *jingshe* 靜舍, is often rendered in English as "oratory." Variant terms conveying a sense of purification and concentration as well as serenity include *jingshi(she)* 靖室(舍), *jingshi(she)* 淨室(舍), *jingshi(she)* 精室(舍), *qingshi(she)* 清室(舍), and *jing(jing, jing)lu* 精(靜, 靖)廬.

Setting aside a private retreat for study and reflection has long been the custom of Chinese literati and Taoist and Buddhist devotees alike. Historical biographies often speak of *jingshe* 精舍 or *jinglu* 精廬 as the secluded residence where late Han scholars met with students seeking instruction. A tradition of establishing *jingshe* 精舍 for Buddhist clergy within the imperial grounds is traced to the reign of Xiaowu di (r. 372–96) of the Eastern Jin. Structures of these types are regarded as the precursors of academies and abbeys, respectively. Advocates of various schools of Taoist teachings generally embrace both exoteric and esoteric definitions of *jingshi*.

Early accounts of the Celestial Master patriarchy (*Tianshi dao) suggest that oratories were adjuncts to the parishes (*zhi) that were set up in the Shu 蜀 (Sichuan) area. Parishioners suffering afflictions were reportedly sequestered in oratories to gain relief through penance and talismanic applications. The so-called *Huangshu* 黃書 (Yellow Writ) legacy of texts also speaks of the oratory as the site where male and female devotees engaged in contemplative ritual couplings under the guidance of a Celestial Master (see *Shangqing huangshu guodu yi).

Writings concerning Celestial Master practice ascribed to *Lu Xiujing (406–77) include directions for setting up an oratory. According to the specifications given in the *Daomen kelüe (Abridged Codes for the Taoist Community), the *jingshi* 靖室 should be completely separate from any other structure. Cleanliness and simplicity were regarded as absolutely essential to creating a site in which deities would be at home. It was no place for icons and pennants, or any other decorative furnishings popular in many households. Only four items were allowed within the oratory: incense burner, incense lantern, peti-

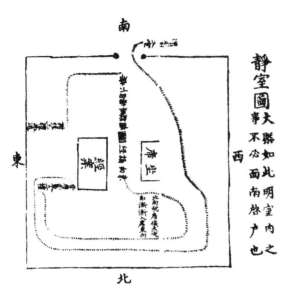

南

東

西

北

靜室圖

大緊如此明室內之不必西南啓戶也

Fig. 50. Floor plan for a *jingshi* (oratory or "quiet chamber"). *Wuliang duren shangpin miaojing pangtong tu* 無量度人上品妙經旁通圖 (Supplementary Illustrations to the Wondrous Scripture of the Upper Chapters on Limitless Salvation; CT 148), 3.2b.

tion stand, and calligraphy blade. It was a place where followers of Celestial Master teachings were known to have sought divine intervention not only through the submission of written petitions but also by oral supplications as well. The story is told, for example, of how Wang Ningzhi 王凝之 (?–399), son of the renowned calligrapher Wang Xizhi 王羲之 (321?–379?), sought refuge from the troops of *Sun En (?–402) by voicing prayerful entreaties within an oratory.

Adherents of the *Shangqing revelations also viewed the oratory as a shelter from threatening forces. An account of the protective rituals undertaken in an oratory by one family on behalf of an infant son whose welfare lie in question is recorded in the *Zhengao (Declarations of the Perfected) compiled by *Tao Hongjing (456–536). This anthology of Shangqing lore also provides the earliest known specifications for erecting an oratory. Tao copied the instructions from a manuscript in the hand of Xu Mi 許謐 (303–76), patron of the visionary *Yang Xi (330–86). The uninhabited areas of mountains or moors were considered suitable sites. A substantial quantity of lumber clearly had to be available to build a rectangular structure measuring nineteen by twelve feet, with a ridge pole rising approximately ten feet high. The only source of light permitted was a small paper-covered window on the south wall. It was to be positioned so that it would be at the eye-level of the devotee seated on a large platform in the center of the room. Additional writings transmitted by Tao indicate that the oratory served as a shrine for family devotions at sunrise and sunset. Many adepts also withdrew to an oratory for solitary communion with the spirit realm.

A manual by the Taoist Master Liu Yuandao 劉元道 (fl. 1100–1125) is among the earliest texts on *Lingbao ritual to contain floor plans for an oratory (fig. 50). Depicted inside are two items, a scripture stand located near the east wall and a mat facing it. Incorporated in the diagram are guidelines for pursuing devotions centering on recitation of the *Duren jing (Scripture on Salvation). The accompanying text supplies a step by step account of the private ritual, beginning with the devotee's entrance from the south. Homage to the scripture invites the vision of embarking on a journey to and from the celestial realm while seated within the oratory.

Diverse teachings on contemplative practice apply the word jingshi or cognate terms to the *dantian (Cinnabar Fields) within the body. Depending upon the context, the compound rujing 入靖 (lit., "entering quiet"), moreover, may mean to enter either an oratory or a state of tranquillity. Specialists in contemporary liturgy also speak of the jingshi as the internal retreat to which a Taoist Master takes refuge during ritual performances. The jingshi, both in its concrete and metaphoric usage, is thus viewed as a complement to the tan 壇, or sacred space where liturgy is staged.

Judith M. BOLTZ

📖 Ishii Masako 1987; Schipper 1993, 91–99; Stein R. A. 1963, 70–72; Strickmann 1981, 149–52 and 171–72; Yoshikawa Tadao 1987

※ huandu

jingzuo

靜坐

"quiet sitting"

Jingzuo is a technical term in Confucianism used to indicate a form of meditation that consists of quiet reflection while in a formal kneeling posture or, more recently, while sitting cross-legged or on a chair. The same term also commonly appears in Japanese, where it is pronounced seiza and means "to kneel formally." Here the posture is ubiquitous—as it was in ancient and medieval China—in all sorts of formal occasions. More technically, seiza also indicates a form of Shintō meditation in which, probably under Taoist influence, attention is focused on the lower Cinnabar Field (*dantian) in the abdomen.

In Taoism, the term jingzuo is secondary to other expressions denoting different forms of meditation, and was probably taken over from Confucianism (Chan Wing-tsit 1989, 255–70; Gernet 1981). In fact, it only appears prominently and with a specific technical meaning in the twentieth century, used mainly by Jiang Weiqiao 蔣維喬 (1872–1955) in his particular mixture of modern bio-medical thinking and *neidan, which has been widely regarded a forerunner of the contemporary *qigong movement (Kohn 1993a; Kohn 1993b, 135–41).

Jiang, also known as Yinshi zi 因是子 (Master of Following the Right [Path]), was from Jiangsu, where he spent most of his life and served as a provincial Minister of Education in the 1920s. A sickly childhood that culminated in tuberculosis and a stomach ulcer in his twenties led him to try many different healing methods, all of which proved ineffectual until he stumbled across an old *neidan* manuscript, whose instructions he followed with some success. This laid the foundations for his own healing regimen, which he described in the *Jingzuo fa jiyao* 靜坐法輯要 (Essentials of the Method of Quiet Sitting), first published in 1914 and included in the *Daozang jinghua. His key technique is *jingzuo*, which consists of sitting or kneeling quietly, preferably in a special meditation hut or chamber, and focusing attention on one's breathing. As the practitioner regulates the breath and follows it deep into the abdomen to gain control over the diaphragm, the Ocean of Pneuma (*qihai* 氣海) is activated in the lower abdomen, an area that corresponds to the Cinnabar Field. Once the diaphragm is fully controlled, breathing is reversed (the diaphragm rises on the inhalation), and breaths become deeper and less frequent. Eventually a hot energy is felt to fill the abdomen. Without conscious help, it rises up into the spine and begins to move around the body in a circle linked to the pulse and blood circulation. This practice has been used as the basis for many *qigong* exercises and clinical therapies since the 1930s.

Livia KOHN

📖 Chan Wing-tsit 1989, 255–70; Despeux 1990, 227–30; Gernet 1981; Kohn 1993a; Kohn 1993b, 135–41; Taylor R. L. 1988

※ *qigong*; MEDITATION AND VISUALIZATION

jinji

禁忌

proscriptions and prohibitions; taboos

Discussing taboos in Taoism involves defining the range of Taoism itself. The present entry does not attempt to cover the subject in its entirety, but limits its scope to some examples of the role of taboos in ritual and in *waidan (external alchemy).

Taboos associated with Retreat and Offering rituals. The primary purpose of the Retreat (*zhai) and Offering (*jiao) rituals is to remove impurity. Specific taboos are associated with this purpose, such as those for building the altar, sending petitions to the gods, and burning incense. The altar should be built inside a temple, and places where men and women mix should be avoided. Priests should not perform rites at times of birth or death, when in mourning, or when ill. In the Tang period, according to *Zhang Wanfu (fl. 710–13), the *daoshi* observed various prohibitions when attending the altar, including those against drinking alcohol, eating the five pungent foods (chives, scallions, onions, garlic, and ginger), and looking on the dead or the newly born. These prohibitions were usually enforced for seven or fourteen days, though the ideal time was forty-nine days (*Jiao sandong zhenwen wufa zhengyi mengwei lu licheng yi* 醮三洞真文五法正一盟威籙立成儀; CT 1212, 25b; trans. Lagerwey 1994, 272–73).

*Du Guangting's (850–933) *Huanglu zhaiyi* 黃籙齋儀 (Liturgies for the Yellow Register Retreat; CT 507) reports that five items should be offered to the altar when venerating the deities: incense, flowers, lamps, water, and fruit. To offer incense, a priest should clean his hands and not touch anything raw or polluted. Incense, which must be of good quality, should not be burned on the days marked by the cyclical character *wu* 戊 (see *ganzhi) and should not be held in the right hand. The flowers should be fresh, of a fine variety, and of five colors (the "fine" varieties today are considered to be plum blossom, orchids, chrysanthemums, and bamboo). Fruits are similarly selected for their freshness and according to season; pomegranates, sweet potatoes, and anything dirty are forbidden. Lamps are to illuminate the altar; sesame oil is used, animal fats being prohibited.

The petition sent to the deities should be reverent and modest. Before writing it, a priest should bathe himself ritually, wash his hands and face, and burn incense. The interior of the room should not be visible from outside and should be quiet, undisturbed by the sounds of dogs or fowl.

Taboos associated with the compounding of elixirs. In his *Baopu zi, *Ge Hong (283–343) states that Taoist practitioners should "enter a famous mountain, perform the purification practices for one hundred days, abstain from the five pungent flavors and fresh fish, and avoid associating with worldly people" (see Ware 1966, 93). The prohibition against associating with worldly people derives from a concern that those who do not have faith in the Dao would criticize the compounding of the elixir and thus disrupt its preparation. These taboos continued to be observed in later times. According to a Southern Song text, the *Danfang xuzhi (Required Knowledge for the Chamber of the Elixirs), "to compound the elixir, three adepts who embrace minds of purity and emptiness should work together; they should perform the purification practices before they begin, and make an offering (*jiao*) to please Heaven" (CT 900, 2b). This work further stipulates that the Chamber of the Elixir (*danshi* 丹室, i.e., the alchemical "laboratory") be built on a site where Wood (one of the *wuxing) predominates and that it be quiet and secluded. Moreover, "unsuitable are places where the cries of fowl and the barking of dogs, the weeping of people, the swift current of water, or the sound of carts and horses passing by can be heard, or execution grounds" (id., 3a).

Neidan adepts observed taboos similar to those of *waidan*; a description is found in the *Biyao juefa* 祕要訣法 (Secret and Essential Instructions and Methods; YJQQ 45).

SAKADE Yoshinobu

📖 Asano Haruji 1999a; Ding Changyun 1999; Qing Xitai 1994, 3: 311–12

※ *jiao*; *jie* [precepts]; *zhai*; *waidan*

Jinlian zhengzong ji

金蓮正宗記

Records of the Correct Lineage of the Golden Lotus

As attested by mentions in bibliographic catalogues of the Ming and Qing periods, the *Jinlian zhengzong ji* (CT 173) is one of the most popular Taoist hagiographic works of the last six centuries. It was written in 1241 by the *Quanzhen master Qin Zhi'an 秦志安 (1188–1244) for inclusion in the *Xuandu baozang*, the Taoist Canon of 1244 whose chief compilers were *Song Defang and his disciple Qin Zhi'an himself. Since very few Quanzhen works seem to have been added to this edition of the Canon, the relatively short *Jinlian zhengzong ji* had the important task of conveying the official self-image of the Quanzhen order.

The expression *jinlian* 金蓮 (Golden Lotus) in the title refers to a dream *Wang Zhe had of a golden lotus with seven buds, which foretold his seven disciples and the future development of his predication. The work consists of fourteen biographies, namely those of the Five Patriarchs (*wuzu* 五祖), the Seven Real Men (*qizhen* 七真; see table 17), and two early disciples of Wang Zhe in Shaanxi. The Five Patriarchs here are Donghua dijun 東華帝君 (Imperial Lord of Eastern Florescence, a *Shangqing deity given a new role by the Quanzhen order; see under *Wang Xuanfu); the three companion immortals *Zhongli Quan, *Lü Dongbin, and *Liu Haichan; and Wang Zhe. The Seven Real Men are *Ma Yu, *Tan Chuduan, *Liu Chuxuan, *Qiu Chuji, *Wang

Chuyi, *Hao Datong, and *Sun Bu'er. Although Quanzhen pays homage to all major figures in Taoist history and hagiography, these four immortals and ten historical masters are its quintessential references. Most if not all Quanzhen monasteries under the Yuan had shrines devoted to the Five Patriarchs and the Seven Real Men. From the Ming onward, however, individual shrines to Lü Dongbin and Qiu Chuji were favored.

This creation and authoritative definition of its own ancestry are characteristic of mid-thirteenth-century institutionalized Quanzhen. Earlier accounts do not dwell much on the Seven Real Men but rather insist on the inner core of Wang Zhe's four favorite disciples—Ma, Tan, Liu, and Qiu. The list given in the *Jinlian zhengzong ji*, moreover, has variants in some contemporary sources, in which Sun, the only woman in the group, is excluded, Wang Zhe is one of the Seven Real Men, and Laozi becomes the first of the Five Patriarchs (see table 17).

Each short biography provides a rather factual account insisting on the crucial moments of a master's life (especially the conversion), and is followed by an encomium. This format was obviously a popular one. One century later, in 1327, another similar work was compiled, the *Jinlian zhengzong xianyuan xiangzhuan* 金蓮正宗仙源像傳 (Illustrated Biographies of the Immortal Spring of the Correct Lineage of the Golden Lotus; CT 174), whose edition in the Taoist Canon includes portraits. Another collective biography of the Seven Real Men was compiled before 1237 and repeatedly expanded in later times. A 1417 edition of this work, entitled *Qizhen xianzhuan* 七真仙傳 (Biographies of the Seven Real Men), is housed at the Taiwan Normal University Library.

This literature paved the way for several Ming and Qing novels telling the story of this cohesive group of popular ascetics. As can be seen in the Quanzhen recorded sayings (*yulu*), the exemplary lives of the Quanzhen patriarchs were frequently referred to in public teachings, and their emulation was considered the best practice for adepts. From this viewpoint, the deeds of the Seven Real Men appear as a catalogue of the various modes of Quanzhen life; the narrative highlights their different approaches (Wang Chuyi the ritualist, Liu Chuxuan the philosopher, Hao Datong the diviner, and so forth) and, simultaneously, their common achievement.

Vincent GOOSSAERT

📖 Chen Guofu 1963, 246; Qing Xitai 1994, 2: 196–97

※ Quanzhen; HAGIOGRAPHY

jinlu zhai

金錄齋

Golden Register Retreat

The Golden Register Retreat, which is one of the Three Register Retreats (*sanlu zhai* 三錄齋), along with the Jade Register and Yellow Register Retreats (**yulu zhai* and **huanglu zhai*), was made the preeminent **Lingbao rite by **Lu Xiujing (406–77). As described in his *Wugan wen* 五感文 (Text on the Five Commemorations; CT 1278), the ritual lasted nine days in spring, three days in summer, seven days in autumn, and five days in winter.

According to Lu's description, the Golden Register altar (*tan* 壇) is a 2.4 *zhang* (ca. 6 m) square built outdoors, and is surrounded by a 3.2 *zhang* (ca. 8 m) square enclosure with ten gates corresponding to the ten directions. At the center of the altar is a lamp-tree, nine feet tall, with nine cups placed on it. Thirty-six additional lamp-trees are placed around the altar in the four directions. Any number of lamp-trees can be lit outside the altar area, depending on the wishes and resources of the sponsor; their purpose is to illuminate the underworld. The Authentic Scripts (*zhenwen* 真文) and the golden dragons are placed on the altar in each of the five directions, together with lengths of silk. At the end of the ritual, the Scripts are burned and the golden dragons are distributed to gain merit for the dead. They can be considered variously to be the temporary abodes of the descending deities, to represent a covenant, and to function as a sacrifice. An important component of the ritual is the rite of Walking the Way (**xingdao*), making repentance (**chanhui*) in each of the ten directions.

A liturgy for the Golden Register Retreat as performed in the Six Dynasties period is found in the **Wushang biyao* (Supreme Secret Essentials; *j.* 53; Lagerwey 1981b, 161–63). According to the preface to **Du Guangting's (850–933) *Jinlu zhai qitan yi* 金錄齋啟壇儀 (Liturgies for Inaugurating the Altar of the Golden Register Retreat; CT 483), the Golden Register Retreat was performed for the benefit of rulers in order to pacify the Gods of Soil and Grain (Sheji 社稷), protect living beings, remove calamities, and gain release from the underworld. Even today, rites called Golden Register are performed in Taiwan, where they are classified as "pure rites" (*qingfa* 清法) to pray for peace.

MARUYAMA Hiroshi

📖 Lagerwey 1981b, 161–63; Ōfuchi Ninji 1983, 234–422

※ *huanglu zhai; yulu zhai; zhai*

Jinque dijun

金闕帝君

Imperial Lord of the Golden Portal

The Lord of the Golden Portal, also known as the Saint of the Latter Age (*housheng*), is a deity of *Shangqing Taoism with a strong messianic component. He is a direct successor to the earlier messiah, *Li Hong, who appears either as Laozi himself or as his messenger. According to a Shangqing prophecy, the Lord of the Golden Portal was to come forth in a year marked by the cyclical signs *renchen* 壬辰 (the twenty-ninth of the sexagesimal cycle; see table 10) from Mount Qingcheng (*Qingcheng shan, Sichuan) to establish a new world inhabited by the chosen or "seed-people" (*zhongmin*) of the Dao.

The key source for this figure is a southern text of the fourth century entitled *Housheng daojun lieji* (Chronicle of the Lord of the Dao, Saint of the Latter Age). It contains a biography of Li Hong as Lord of the Golden Portal together with predictions of an age of decadence and destruction before the complete renewal of the world. The same biography also appears, in a sightly abbreviated form, in the *Taiping jingchao* 太平經鈔 (Excerpts from the Scripture of Great Peace), compiled on the basis of lost *Taiping jing passages in the sixth century and now found in the Taoist Canon as the first chapter of the *Taiping jing* (CT 1101).

According to this text, the Lord of the Golden Portal was an avatar of Lord Lao, sharing with him the family name Li 李 and the title Emptiness and Non-being (Xuwu 虛無), an epithet of the Dao. His early life, too, is written in imitation of Lord Lao: he himself makes the decision to be born, actively assembles his cosmic energy, completes his form, and descends to earth in the mythical country of the north, where his mother, like Laozi's Mother Li, is waiting for him in a valley of plum trees (*li* 李). His divine appearance on earth is honored by three suns rising from the east and nine dragons coming to spray water over him. He grows up bright and beautiful, curious about the Dao and eager to learn the techniques of immortality.

After a long process of searching and refinement, the Lord of the Golden Portal attains full realization of the Dao and gains access to the heavenly realms, winning power over mortals and immortals. He then becomes "the sole ruler of the nine levels (*jiuchong* 九重) of heaven and the ten ramparts (*shidie* 十疊) of earth." In due course he collects his expertise and efficacious talismans into several sacred scriptures that he reveals to suitable representatives on earth, thus allowing the chosen people to establish the perfect realm of the Dao. His figure succeeds the messiah Li Hong, follows the hagiography of Laozi, and in his long search and striving for realization is also inspired by Maitreya, the Buddha of the future.

Livia KOHN

📖 Andersen 1979, 11–15

※ Li Hong; *housheng*; *Housheng daojun lieji*; DEITIES: THE PANTHEON; MESSIANISM AND MILLENARIANISM

Jinsuo liuzhu yin

金鎖流珠引

Guide to the Golden Lock and the Flowing Pearls

The *Jinsuo liuzhu yin* (CT 1015) is the largest compendium of methods of *bugang ("walking along the guideline") found in the *Daozang*. It is (apparently falsely) attributed to *Li Chunfeng (ca. 602–ca. 670), the famous astronomer with Taoist leanings, who reached the office of Grand Astrologer (*taishi ling* 太史令) during the Zhenguan reign period (627–49). The book defines itself as an "introduction" or "guide" (*shiyin* 示引) that leads into the practices implied in the now lost, comprehensive "scripture" on *bugang*, *Jinsuo liuzhu jing* 金鎖流珠經, and which (in another interpretation of the term *shiyin*) "demonstrates the patterns" that should be followed in the performance of the walk.

The compilation of the *Jinsuo liuzhu yin* is presented as the work of Li Chunfeng, who refers to himself as Feng 風 (even in the main text), and who is named in the chapter headings as the author of the commentaries. The content of the book, however, affords grounds for doubting this attribution, especially in the "autobiographical" details (21.4a–b) about the role of the author in the establishment of the Tang dynasty, through the appearance to him of the deified Laozi in the year 617 (at a time when he was, in fact, only fifteen years of age). The legends concerning the appearance of Laozi in order to express his sanction of the rise to power of the imperial Li family do not, in more generally circulated hagiographical works, appear to have been associated with the name of Li Chunfeng until the twelfth century (see *Hunyuan shengji*, 8.2b). Indeed, perhaps the most significant impact of the book occurred only in the Song, when it became important in the formation of the *Tianxin zhengfa tradition. The earliest compilation of the methods of this tradition, the *Taishang zhuguo jiumin zongzhen biyao* (Secret Essentials of the Totality of Perfected, of the Most High, for Assisting the Country and Saving the People; preface 1116) by Yuan Miaozong 元妙宗, quotes the present book at length, and derives a good part of its methods of *bugang*, as well as its "methods of inspecting and summoning" (*kaozhao fa* 考召法), from it. The only definite certainty about the date of the *Jinsuo liuzhu yin*—apart from it being later than the life of Li Chunfeng—therefore seems to be that it is earlier than 1116. However, some apparent references to political developments from around the middle of the Tang, as well as the absence of a number of the most characteristic elements of the ritual styles that developed in the early Song, together appear to point to a date in the late eighth or early ninth century as the most likely.

The methods of *bugang* described in the book emphasize elements derived from the *Zhengyi tradition. However, the book also testifies to a general syncretistic attitude, and in the introductory account of the original transmitters and recipients of the tradition, almost equal weight is given to the first Celestial Master, *Zhang Daoling, on the one hand, and the founders of the *Shangqing tradition, represented especially by *Wang Yuan, on the other. A number of passages from the central Shangqing scriptures on *bugang* are included, and the total result is an apparent synthesis of the methods of the two traditions. The intent of the book, however, is defined by the purposes of exorcism, and by the goal of benefiting other human beings. Together with a strongly critical attitude toward the practice of retiring to the mountains in order exclusively to seek personal salvation (associated with a criticism also of Buddhism), these themes confirm the close affiliation of the book with Zhengyi Taoism.

Poul ANDERSEN

📖 Andersen 1991, 12–14, 73–77; Barrett 1990; Strickmann 1996, 234–36

※ Tianxin zhengfa

jintan

禁壇

Sealing the Altar

The *jintan* (lit., "prohibiting [access to] the sacred area") is the great purification of the ritual space that is carried out in the beginning of major *zhai* (Retreat) or *jiao* (Offering) ceremonies, as part of the initial phase of the liturgy, which is dedicated to the construction and consecration of the sacred area. It has been transmitted at least since the Tang dynasty, when it was summarized in the account of a *jiao* ceremony given by *Zhang Wanfu (fl. 710–13), and described more fully in a separate text entitled *Zhengyi chitan yi* 正一敕壇儀 (Ritual of Orthodox Unity for Commanding [i.e., Consecrating] the Sacred Area; CT 800). The rite is derived from the *Zhengyi tradition, and indeed, in the ritual compendia of the Song dynasty it is commonly said to be performed, not by the high priest (*gaogong* 高功; see *daozhang*) himself, but by his chief cantor (*dujiang*) or by "a specially selected Zhengyi ritual master, wearing a black cap and red woolen clothing" (see *Wushang huanglu dazhai licheng yi*, 19.1a). The quoted chapter 19 of this compendium is attributed to *Du Guangting (850–933), who in fact is referred to as a key transmitter of the *jintan* by many Song dynasty liturgists. The place of the rite in the *Lingbao liturgy codified by Du is made clear in his own writings, for instance in the *Jinlu zhai qitan yi* 金籙齋啟壇儀 (Liturgies for Inaugurating the Altar of the Golden Register Retreat; CT 483, 6a–b), where he states that the *jintan* is performed as part of the Nocturnal Invocation (*suqi*), right after the introductory hymns, and before the procession of "entering through the door (of the sacred area)" (*ruhu* 入戶). This is exactly the place of the *jintan* in the classical Zhengyi liturgy of southern Taiwan, while in contemporary traditions in many other regions it is quite common to perform it as a more independent rite, somewhere in the introductory phase of a program, but not embedded in the Nocturnal Invocation.

The *jintan* transmitted in present-day southern Taiwan addresses not only the ritual space, which is cleansed by holy water, sword-dances, incantations, and the writing of talismans (*FU) in the air: it also addresses the representatives of the community, into whose bodies the pure primordial energies and divine light are called down, and who are made to walk over acid fumes created by placing a red-hot piece of iron in a basin filled with vinegar. It is in good accord with this high level of "popular participation" (and with the overall theatrical quality of the rite) that the *jintan* is one of those elements of the liturgy most closely associated with local traditions, notably local forms of drama and music.

Equally operatic in character is the frantic drumming and beating of gongs that accompanies the physical actions of the rite, and especially the battle of the priest with a demon, which ensues directly after the completion of the purification of the representatives. The role of the demon is acted by an acolyte wearing a mask, who suddenly intrudes and attempts to steal the incense burner of the community. A hectic fight follows, in which the priest stabs with his sword and charges at the demon, who in the end is forced to drop the incense burner and is chased out through the Gate of Demons (*guimen* 鬼門) in the northeastern corner, where he is imprisoned by the priest. The act of disposing of the demon is concluded by the offering of sticks of incense, which are placed in the bucket of rice that represents the prison at the Gate of Demons. It would thus appear that the imprisonment of the demon also has the effect of an enfeoffment of the spirit as an Earth God (*Tudi gong) and divine protector of the sacred area.

Poul ANDERSEN

📖 Andersen 1990; Lagerwey 1987c, 90–105; Ōfuchi Ninji 1983, 283–87; Schipper 1985a

※ *jiao*

jinxiang

進香

offering incense

The burning of incense (*xiang* 香) as sticks, coils, powder, or otherwise, is one of the most fundamental religious acts in Chinese culture. The words for worshipper or pilgrim (*xiangke* 香客), worshipping or going on a pilgrimage (*jinxiang*), the altar (*xiang'an* 香案), and many other religious terms refer to incense. One burns incense simply to demonstrate respect with or without further explicit worship, for instance to a district magistrate on official tour; or one burns it when reading empowered texts, such as Confucian classics, religious scriptures, and morality books (*shanshu*). Buddhist monks burn moxa (called "incense" in this context) on their heads as part of the ordination ritual. As an element of explicit worship, burning incense opens a channel of communication with supernatural forces. Therefore, each ritual begins with, and is frequently interrupted by, incense burning ceremonies. Different religious traditions pay much attention to their own ways of burning incense.

Incense does not derive its power from being placed in the incense burner (*xianglu*). In fact, the two have separate histories and connotations. Prior to its use for burning incense, the burner was already a precious object providing religious and political legitimacy (see under *lingbao*) and a ritual tool for preparing sacrificial food. Incense, on the other hand, does not need to be burned in a special vessel, but can be placed in a tree or on a staircase, stuck in a lantern symbolizing Heaven or in sacrificial animals, held between one's hands during worship, and so forth. The word *xiang* in older sources refers to the fragrance of sacrificial food and liquor, which was consumed by the deities. This would suggest the use of incense as the cheapest kind of offering. Another antecedent may have been the prophylactic burning of aromatic woods, plants and herbs. The latter custom survived into the imperial period, as seen for instance in the burning of artemisia in the fifth lunar month to drive away demonic forces. Finally, incense can be burned to keep away insects and to measure time.

When burned in a cultic context, the incense ashes acquire a power of their own. This is apparent in the practice of healing by ingesting water mixed with the powder of incense burned during a special ritual. Related to this practice are the customs of carrying some incense from an important cult on one's body when travelling, and of touching people with incense sticks to protect or heal them. The mediums' practice of inhaling incense fumes to get into trance can also be explained in this way, since it transfers to them the power of the cult they officiate.

Finally, the notion of incense being imbued with the power of a cult is found in the practice of "dividing incense" (*fenxiang* 分香). Here, a cult links itself to its parental cult devoted to the same deity by ritually transferring some incense from the burner of the parental cult to the burner of the new one. Such cults tend to be associated with Taoist ritual traditions, but most of the documentation available to date comes from the Fujian region. To what extent this was a widespread practice in China has yet to be investigated.

Barend ter HAAR

📖 Bedini 1994; Bodde 1975, 274–80, 290–91, and 302–3; Cedzich 1987, 70–80; Feuchtwang 1992, 126–49 and passim; ter Haar 2000a; Little 2000b, 218; Needham 1974, 128–54; Schipper 1990; Takahashi Yōichirō 1988

※ *xianglu*

jinye

金液

Golden Liquor

The term *jinye* (or *jinyi*), used in both *neidan* and *waidan*, is associated with the idea that the human body can be transformed to a goldlike state by drinking gold. The *Liexian zhuan* (Biographies of Exemplary Immortals) describes some immortals having taken the Golden Liquor, and *Ge Hong associates it with divine beings such as *Taiyi, Laozi, and Yuanjun 元君 (Original Princess).

The *jinye* method in Ge Hong's *Baopu zi* (trans. Ware 1966, 89–91) requires a considerable amount of gold with other ingredients (some modern scholars suppose a possible formation either of potassium auricyanide or of colloidal gold with some red color). *Sun Simiao's *Taiqing danjing yaojue (Essential Instructions from the Scripture of the Elixirs of Great Clarity; trans. Sivin 1968, 185–86) gives a similar recipe. Later texts, however, simply mention "gold" being soaked in "vinegar" (xi 醯 or zuowei 左味, a diluted acetic acid), which would not react with real gold. Further study is necessary to understand the significance of these terms.

According to several waidan texts, when the Golden Liquor enters the body, it penetrates the five viscera (*wuzang), fortifies and lubricates the four limbs, and feeds the hundred spirits in the body. In neidan, Golden Liquor indicates a liquid formed by the interaction of the pneuma of the kidneys (shenqi 腎氣) and the pneuma of the heart (xinqi 心氣), which combine and finally evaporate in the lungs (fei 肺). The term also bears a cosmological meaning. For instance, it is one of the names in the postcelestial state (*houtian) for the Original Pneuma of the precelestial state (*xiantian; Zhichuan zhenren jiaozheng shu 稚川真人校證術, CT 902).

Some scholars, including Joseph Needham, have suggested that the ancient pronunciation of the word jinye, close to kiem-iak, may be the origin of the word-root chem- used in several Western languages.

KIM Daeyeol

📖 Butler et al. 1987; Chen Guofu 1983, 208; Glidewell 1989; Meng Naichang 1993a, 156–65; Needham 1976, 88–99; Wang Kuike 1964

※ neidan; waidan

Jinye jing

金液經

Scripture of the Golden Liquor

Along with the *Taiqing jing (Scripture of Great Clarity) and the *Jiudan jing (Scripture of the Nine Elixirs), the Jinye jing is one of the three main scriptures of the early *Taiqing tradition of *waidan. *Ge Hong summarizes the method of the Golden Liquor in his *Baopu zi (trans. Ware 1966, 89–91), but his synopsis is so concise as to appear almost incomprehensible. The individual steps of the process, moreover, are not given in the right sequence. A three-chapter work in the Taoist Canon describes the same procedure in the correct order. This text, the Baopu zi shenxian jinzhuo jing 抱朴子神仙金汋經 (Scripture of the Golden Liquid of the Divine Immortals, by the Master Who Embraces Simplicity; CT 917), includes the method for the Golden Liquor in the first chapter, while the second and third chapters reproduce the whole fourth chapter of the *Baopu zi*. The recipe for the Golden Liquor is divided into thirty short passages, each of which is followed by a commentary. Based on the place names that it mentions, the commentary was written in the sixth century, a dating confirmed by quotations of both text and commentary in the *Xiaodao lun* (trans. Kohn 1995a, 127–29).

According to the *Baopu zi shenxian jinzhuo jing*, the Golden Liquor is prepared from powdered gold and mercury, which are placed in a bamboo cylinder with saltpetre and realgar. The cylinder is sealed with silk and lacquer, and soaked in vinegar. After one hundred days, gold and mercury dissolve and form the Gold Water (*jinshui* 金水, i.e., the Golden Liquor) and the Mercury Water (*hongshui* 汞水), respectively. Both are ingested while facing the Sun; one's body is said to take on a golden hue, and one is transformed into light (*guangming* 光明) and ascends to Heaven, becoming an assistant to the Great Man of Central Yellow (Zhonghuang zhangren 中黃丈人) and the Great One (*Taiyi).

In another stage of the process, a Reverted Elixir (*huandan*) is obtained by boiling more mercury in the Golden Liquor and pouring vinegar over it. After thirty days of intense heating, the mercury takes on a purple color and is then placed in an earthenware crucible. The Reverted Elixir is ready in half a day. In the *Baopu zi*, the elixir obtained at this stage is called Amber Pill (*weixi junsheng* 威喜巨勝, or "black amber sesame" in James Ware's translation, 1966, 90). One pound of Reverted Elixir placed on fire forms a Cinnabar Gold (or Elixir-Gold, *danjin* 丹金), which can be used for smearing blades that will "keep armies ten thousand miles away," or for casting dishes and cups. Those who eat and drink from them will live as long as Heaven and Earth.

Fabrizio PREGADIO

📖 Meng Naichang 1993a, 67–69; Pregadio 1991, 574–78; Pregadio 2006b, 56–57, 114–18, 288–92 (trans.)

※ *jinye*; *waidan*; Taiqing

Jiudan jing

九丹經

Scripture of the Nine Elixirs

The *Jiudan ding* is one of the few extant sources that describe a whole *waidan* practice, from the preliminary rituals to the ingestion of the elixir. Portions of the text are quoted or summarized by *Ge Hong in his *Baopu zi (trans. Ware 1966, 75–78). As shown by Ge Hong and demonstrated in other works, this was one of the three scriptures that formed the nucleus of the *Taiqing corpus, reputed to have been revealed to *Zuo Ci at the end of the Han.

Although Ge Hong neglects to mention the practical details of compounding, his quotations match the two versions of the text preserved in the Taoist Canon. The primary version is in the first chapter of the *Huangdi jiuding shendan jingjue* 黃帝九鼎神丹經訣 (Instructions on the Scripture of the Divine Elixirs of the Nine Tripods of the Yellow Emperor; CT 885), where it is followed by a commentary in nineteen chapters. A slightly variant version is in the *Jiuzhuan liuzhu shenxian jiudan jing* 九轉流珠神仙九丹經 (Scripture of the Flowing Pearl in Nine Cycles and the Nine Elixirs of the Divine Immortals; CT 952), where the entire text is arranged as a commentary to the heptasyllabic verses of an anonymous "Jiudan ge" 九丹歌 (Songs of the Nine Elixirs).

The main version opens with an introduction on the revelation of the methods, the properties of the elixirs, and various ritual rules. This is followed by methods for making two preliminary compounds, namely the *liuyi ni* or Mud of the Six-and-One (used for luting the crucible and avoiding dispersion of *qi during its heating) and the *xuanhuang* 玄黃 or Mysterious and Yellow (a lead-mercury compound used either for luting the crucible together with the *liuyi ni*, or as the upper and lower layers within the crucible, together with the elixir ingredients). Then come the methods of the Nine Elixirs, which are independent preparations related to each other by their compounding techniques rather than their ingredients.

The nineteen-chapter commentary describes various aspects of the alchemical practice, mainly through quotations from other works. Citations of texts, mentions of person and place names, use of measures of weight and volume, respect of tabooed characters, and other details show that it dates from between 649 and 686 and that it was first addressed to a sovereign, almost certainly Tang Gaozong (r. 649–83). About half of the commentary is devoted to the general principles of the alchemical doctrines (revelation of the scriptures, transmission of texts and methods, choice of time, arrangement and protection of space, relation of *waidan* to other practices), while the other half contains a large selection of alchemical methods based on about two dozen substances. The main sources of the commentary are the *Baopu zi*, *Tao Hongjing's *Bencao jing jizhu* 本草經集注 (Collected Commentaries to the Canonical Pharmacopoeia), and the lost works attributed to *Hugang zi.

The *Jiuzhuan liuzhu shenxian jiudan jing* also dates from the late Six Dynasties or the beginning of the Tang. Another work, the *Shangdong xindan jingjue* 上洞心丹經訣 (Instructions on the Scripture of the Heart Elixir of the Highest Cavern; CT 950), is centered around two methods unrelated to those of the Nine Elixirs, but largely consists of quotations from different parts of the *Huangdi jiuding shendan jingjue*.

Fabrizio PREGADIO

📖 Meng Naichang 1993a, 103–6; Pregadio 1991; Pregadio 2006b, 55–56, 110–14, 159–87 (trans.)

※ *waidan*; Taiqing

jiugong

九宮

Nine Palaces

As the original astronomical connotation of the Nine Palaces developed, it took on a number of different resonances in divination, meditation, and medical contexts both inside and outside Taoist traditions. From a description of the ninefold spatial organization of the heavens traversed by Great Unity (*Taiyi), the Nine Palaces became a useful metaphor for other sacred spaces: the imperial palace, the body, and the brain. The Nine Palaces were often symbolized by a three-by-three square grid, and for this reason was easily homologized to other patterns that stressed the division between an interior (the center square) and an exterior (the outer eight squares).

The earliest association of the Nine Palaces was with sections of the night sky, and with its anthropomorphized denizens. The circular rotation of the stars in the night sky, the rhythm of which was seen by writers such as de Santillana and von Dechend (1969) as universally significant to early societies, was connected with a number of early practices associated with the "masters of methods" (*fangshi*) of the pre-Qin and early imperial periods. The Nine Palaces formed the basis for the *shi* 式 (cosmic board, cosmograph), the early divination tool that became the model for the design of everything from mirrors to *liubo* 六博 (Game of Sixes; on the *shi* and the *liubo* see Loewe 1979, 60–85).

In political-philosophical essays, the traversal of the Nine Palaces by Great Unity became a template for the earthly ruler. The classical ideal of the Hall of Light (*mingtang*) was described in the ritual compendium *Da Dai liji* 大戴禮記 (Records of Rites of the Elder Dai; probably compiled in the early second century CE) as consisting of nine rooms (*jiushi* 九室, later increased to twelve; Major 1993, 221–24). By the Later Han, the term Nine Palaces was introduced into the exegesis of the *Yijing* divination. The *Hetu and Luoshu

(Chart of the [Yellow] River and Writ of the Luo [River]) were used in early
Taoist texts to correlate the Nine Palaces with the winds of the eight directions and the eight trigrams (*bagua) of the *Yijing*. This was done by adding a
ninth "central" element to the original eight directions or trigrams, similar to
the way that fourfold schemata (seasons, directions) became correlated with
fivefold schemata like the *wuxing (Five Phases).

In medieval materials, the sacred geography of the Nine Palaces was projected onto the body of the Taoist adept and on the sacred space of Taoist
liturgy. In his commentary to the *Dengzhen yinjue (Concealed Instructions
for the Ascent to Perfection), *Tao Hongjing (456–536) wrote that "the Nine
Palaces in the Shangqing 上清 (Highest Clarity) [celestial] palace of Taiwei 太
微 (Great Tenuity) have Perfected Lords dwelling in them. Therefore the fact
that the human head is arranged according to the same positions is simply a
matter of their mutual resonance" (CT 421, 1.5b). In *Shangqing meditation
practice, a regimen of visualization of the spirits of the Nine Palaces caused
these astral spirits to occupy the nine chambers of the brain (see *niwan),
rendering the adept eventually able to ascend to the Shangqing heaven and
receive the treasured talismans (*FU). According to Isabelle Robinet (1993,
127–31), this method probably is seen for the first time in the fourth-century
*Suling jing (Scripture [of the Celestial Palace] of the Immaculate Numen).
The Nine Palaces are described, with slight differences, in numerous Shangqing texts (Kakiuchi Tomoyuki 1998).

The Nine Palaces also played a role in Taoist liturgy as a way of organizing
sacred spaces. In 744, Tang Xuanzong (r. 712–56) established seasonal sacrifices
at the spirit altars of the Nine Palaces. These altars were dedicated to Great
Unity, Heavenly Unity (Tianyi 天一), and the other spirits of the Nine Palaces.
The emperor's movements through these altars echoed those of the Han recipe
masters' ideal ruler, which in turn took as their model the orderly movement
of the stars.

Mark CSIKSZENTMIHALYI

📖 Kakiuchi Tomoyuki 1998; Kalinowski 1985; Li Ling 2000a, 89–176; Li Ling
1995–96; Robinet 1993, 127–31; Robinet 1995b; Yamada Toshiaki 1989a

※ Taiyi; *beidou*; *niwan*; COSMOLOGY

Jiuku tianzun

救苦天尊

Celestial Worthy Who Relieves Suffering

The Celestial Worthy Who Relieves Suffering is a god who rescues the souls of the living and the dead. Dwelling in the Palace of Green Florescence (Qing-hua gong 青華宮), he manifests himself in the ten directions, appearing as ten separate divinities. This notion developed based on the concept of the Buddhas of the Ten Directions (shifo 十佛), who appear in Mahāyāna (Great Vehicle) scriptures from an early date, and the idea of savior bodhisattvas such as Guanyin 觀音 (Avalokiteśvara), Dizang 地藏 (Kṣitigarbha), and Wenshu 文殊 (Mañjuśrī). *Du Guangting's *Daojiao lingyan ji*, written around the year 900, shows that the belief in the ten gods played an active part in Taoist practice under the Tang, but most scriptures specifying their iconography and ritual date from the Song.

The ten gods are identified variously in the literature. An early list of ten names, still rather Buddhist in nature, includes such titles as Great Compassion (Daci 大慈), Universal Deliverance (Puji 普濟), and Wisdom Transformation (Huihua 惠化). This list appears in the Sui-dynasty *Yebao yinyuan jing* (6.4a–b) and in a Song ritual text, the *Huanglu jiuyou jiao wu'ai yezhai cidi yi* 黃籙九幽醮無礙夜齋次第儀 (Sequential Liturgies for the Yellow Register Offerings to the Nine Shades and the Unimpeded Nightly Retreats; CT 514, 26a). A second list, which later became the standard version, contains more typically Taoist names. It appears first in the *Fengdao kejie* (6.1a–b), showing a development of the cult in early Tang Taoism. A third list, found only after the Tang, includes the same names as the second list but links the Ten Worthies with the Ten Kings (shiwang 十王) of hell (Teiser 1994). Here the Ten Worthies are designated saviors who save specifically from the tortures of hell. They are worshipped in memorial services for the salvation of the dead, outlined in the *Difu shiwang badu yi* 地府十王拔度儀 (Liturgies for Salvation from the Ten Kings of the Earth Administration; CT 215), and can be described as a salvific counterpart to the Ten Kings of hell, on whose development as a group of deities they also had some influence.

Livia KOHN

📖 Yūsa Noboru 1989

※ HELL; DEITIES: THE PANTHEON

jiutian

九天

Nine Heavens

In the *Lüshi chunqiu* 呂氏春秋 (Springs and Autumns of Mr. Lü; 239 BCE; Knoblock and Riegel 2000, 279) and the **Huainan zi* (Book of the Master of Huainan; 139 BCE; Major 1993, 69–70), the Nine Heavens, or Nine Fields (*jiuye* 九野*), are nine horizontal sectors of space, corresponding to the center and eight directions, and complementing the Nine Continents (*jiuzhou* 九洲) on earth. The *Huainan zi* gives their names as Balanced Heaven (*juntian* 鈞天, center), Azure Heaven (*cangtian* 蒼天, east), Transforming Heaven (*biantian* 變天, northeast), Mysterious Heaven (*xuantian* 玄天, north), Obscure Heaven (*youtian* 幽天, northwest), Luminous Heaven (*haotian* 顥天, west), Vermilion Heaven (*zhutian* 朱天, southwest), Fiery Heaven (*yantian* 炎天, south), and Yang Heaven (*yangtian* 陽天, southeast).

Some Taoist texts inherit this view of the Nine Heavens, understanding them as subdivisions of a horizontal plan. More often, though, the Nine Heavens are represented in Taoism in a vertical (i.e., hierarchical) arrangement, and are said to constitute a stage in the progressive differentiation of the one Original Pneuma (**yuanqi*) as it gives birth to the cosmos. According to the **Shengshen jing* (Scripture of the Life-Giving Spirits; CT 318, 1a–2a), for instance, the Nine Heavens are generated by the breaths (**qi*) of the deities of the Three Caverns (**SANDONG*). First the three deities produce the Mysterious (*xuan* 玄), Original (*yuan* 元), and Inaugural (*shi* 始) pneumas; then each pneuma divides itself into three, resulting in nine pneumas that constitute the Nine Heavens. According to this view, therefore, the Nine Heavens constitute a finer subdivision of the heavens of the Three Clarities (**sanqing*). Relevant descriptions are found in the *Shengshen jing* and several **Shangqing works, including the **Taixiao langshu* (Precious Writ of the Great Empyrean; CT 55, 5a–10a) and the *Waiguo fangpin Qingtong neiwen* 外國放品青童內文 (Inner Script of the Azure Lad on the Distribution of the Outer Realms; CT 1373, 2.5a–16b). The account found in the latter text is also quoted in the **Wushang biyao* (Supreme Secret Essentials, 16.1a–6a; Lagerwey 1981b, 90–91).

In parallel to this cosmogenesis, the human embryo is sometimes said to receive the pneumas of the Nine Heavens (*jiutian zhi qi* 九天之氣) during the nine months of gestation, and Shangqing texts describe meditation practices that aim to receive these pneumas again in order to untie the "knots of death" (Robinet 1993, 139–43; Katō Chie 2000, 106–12).

Fabrizio PREGADIO

📖 Lagerwey 1981b, 34–38 and passim

※ *sanshi'er tian*; *sanshiliu tian*

Jiuzhen zhongjing

九真中經

Central Scripture of the Nine Real Men

The *Jiuzhen zhongjing* is one of the *Shangqing revealed scriptures. The Taoist Canon contains two versions of this text, entitled *Dijun jiuzhen zhongjing* 帝君九真中經 (Central Scripture of the Nine Real Men of the Imperial Lord; CT 1376) and *Jiuzhen zhongjing jiangsheng shendan jue* 九真中經降生神丹訣 (Instructions on the Crimson Life-Giving Divine Elixir from the Central Scripture of the Nine Real Men of the Imperial Lord; CT 1377). The latter takes its name from the recipe for an elixir that is probably apocryphal but was added to the text at an early date (Strickmann 1979, 171–72). Apparently none of the extant versions, including the one found in the *Dunhuang ms. P. 2751, is the same as the original text.

The scripture describes several methods. The first, which gives the text its title, aims to generate a spiritual embryo through meditation on the Nine Real Men (*jiuzhen* 九真), the souls of the Imperial Lord (Dijun 帝君) that animate the body. The adept meditates on the Imperial Lord, the Great One (*Taiyi), the Original Father (Yuanfu 元父) and the Mysterious Mother (Xuanmu 玄母), and the Five Gods (*wushen* 五神) of the registers of life (*shengji* 生籍; see *Taidan yinshu*). These divinities merge with each other nine times, transmuting themselves into a single "great spirit" (*dashen* 大神) that enters various organs of the body and then rises to the *niwan, the upper Cinnabar Field in the brain. A similar method, called *jiudan shanghua* 九丹上化 (Upper Transformation of the Ninefold Elixir), is described in the *Taijing zhongji jing* 胎精中記經 (Scripture of the Central Record of the Essence of the Embryo; CT 1382; Robinet 1984, 2: 171–74).

The method of the *Dijun jiuyin* 帝君九陰 (Nine Yin of the Imperial Lord) focuses on the Nine Yin, the secret spouses of Great Yin (Taiyin 太陰). They live in the Northern Dipper (*beidou) and in the Hall of Light (*mingtang, within the head), and are charged with the salvation of human beings. The adept visualizes them in different parts of his body with the Imperial Lord, the Great One, the Five Gods of the registers, and the gods of the Dipper. All these divinities transform themselves into a radiant cosmic infant whose light fires everything.

The *Yuyi Jielin* 鬱儀結璘 method, so called after the esoteric names of the Sun and the Moon (Esposito 2004b), became renowned and was adopted in several later rituals. It consists of visualizing the Emperors of the Sun and the Moon, who descend to take the adept up to heaven.

Other practices described in the *Jiuzhen zhongjing* involve the five corporeal spirits (those of the hands, the feet, and the lungs or head), the twenty-four spirits (see **bajing*), and the divinities of the planets. These practices are also outlined in the *Dongfang shangjing* 洞房上經 (Superior Scripture of the Cavern Chamber; CT 405). The original *Jiuzhen zhongjing* also contained an alchemical method for revitalizing the five viscera (**wuzang*), which is now preserved in the **Wushang biyao* (87.6b–13a; Lagerwey 1981b, 186–87).

Isabelle ROBINET

📖 Robinet 1979a; Robinet 1984, 2: 66–83; Yamada Toshiaki 1989a

※ Shangqing

K

kaiguang

開光

Opening the Light

The rite of Opening the Light is performed when a statue of a deity or a Buddha is venerated for the first time. It is also celebrated during *zhai (Retreat) and *jiao (Offering) rituals to call down divine spirits or the spirit of the dead into an image of a deity or an effigy of the deceased made of paper or bamboo.

The priest (*daoshi) cuts the cockscomb from a white cock (believed to have the power to call spirits) with a Seven-star Sword (qixing jian 七星劍, a sword with a pattern of the Northern Dipper; see under *faqi), dips his writing-brush into the blood (symbolizing the life-force), and makes the person who sponsors the ritual breathe onto the brush (signifying taking the *qi). The priest holds the brush in his right hand and a small round mirror in his left hand, turning it in the direction of the sun. He stands facing the sun and mimes taking its qi. He inscribes a circle with the brush in the air and dots its center; then he dots the mirror. When this is done, he writes a talisman in the mirror with the brush, comprising a pattern representing the Three Clarities (*sanqing), the Chinese characters ling 靈 (numinous) and gang 罡 (Dipper), the name of the spirit of the deceased, and those of the gods of the Northern Dipper (*beidou). Next the priest turns the mirror toward the image and with a brush makes dots on its eyes, ears, nose, mouth, torso, arms, legs, and the crown of its head. The image is then shaken and purified by burning before it yellow rectangular sheets of paper rolled into a cylinder. As a result of this rite, both divine spirits and the spirit of the dead come to lodge in the image.

ASANO Haruji

📖 Liu Zhiwan 1983–84, 2: 183–200; Naoe Hiroji 1983, 1075–83; Ōfuchi Ninji 1983, 368–9

※ gongde; jiao; zhai

Kaitian jing

開天經

Scripture of the Opening of Heaven

This work, probably dating from the Tang period, is found twice in the Taoist Canon, once in the *Yunji qiqian* (2.9a–14b) and once, with minor variants, as an independent text (CT 1437). It describes one of the many Taoist versions of the genesis of the world, and integrates this theme with two others: that of the god *Laojun as the master of the world and its rulers, which places him before the generation of the world as the instructor who presides over its organized form and order; and that of the sacred scriptures that preside over the creation of order before and after the cosmos is generated (see *REVELATIONS AND SACRED TEXTS).

The text, which shows slight and purely formal traces of Buddhist influence, begins with a description of Laojun standing alone in dark emptiness, using several sets of negations and terms that commonly refer to the Dao (e.g., "not visible," "not audible"). This is followed by a narrative description of the gradual formation of the world over long cosmic eras, with various precosmic geneses succeeding each other according to the pattern of the so-called Five Greats (*wutai* 五太; see *COSMOGONY). At each of these geneses, Laojun descends to give teachings and issues a sacred scripture. Then Heaven and Earth progressively begin to separate and space becomes organized; then there appear the sun, the moon, and human beings, who at first are without conscience, names, and funerary rites. After them comes Chaos (*hundun), which generates two sons, the gods of the mountains and rivers. Then come the Nine Palaces (*jiugong), which allude to the ninefold organization of Heaven and Earth. Thereafter Laojun continues to descend to earth in order to assist the first mythical emperors who reign at the beginning of humanity, still producing scriptures and teaching the first artifacts, the basic elements of cosmic knowledge, and the rules of civilized order.

The text ends at the beginning of the Zhou dynasty and concludes with a passage on the structure of the world based on numbers, cyclic signs, and trigrams in the tradition of the Han cosmologists. Laojun speaks of himself as a cosmic being, whose individual bodily parts are endowed with numbers following the so-called *Luoshu* (Writ of the Luo [River]) magic square (see

*Hetu and *Luoshu*), arranged in the same pattern also found in the *Shangqing huangshu guodu yi*.

Isabelle ROBINET

📖 Kohn 1993b, 35–43 (part. trans.); Schafer 1997 (trans.)

※ Laozi and Laojun; COSMOGONY

kaitong minglu

開通冥路

Opening a Road in the Darkness

Opening a Road in the Darkness is a rite performed to summon the spirit of the deceased from the underworld to the altar. In Taiwan, it forms the opening part of the ritual of Merit (*gongde). The priest "opens the light" (*kaiguang) of the statuette of the deceased and waves the Banner for Summoning the Celestial Soul (*zhaohun fan* 召魂旛) to call his soul. The deceased is purified, and a pardon is sought for him after his repentance (*chanhui). This is followed by obeisances paid to each of the Three Clarities (*sanqing).

An important part of this process is the lighting of lamps to illuminate the underworld. The statuette of the deceased is placed in front of the Three Clarities on the altar. The priest stands facing the statuette and sets fire to a mandate he holds in his hand. Before the fire dies out, he drops the burning paper into a basin of water at his feet. This is repeated three times. The priest then declares that the way to the underworld has been opened, and that the deceased has pledged allegiance to the Teaching of the Way (*DAOJIAO), and leads him to the heavenly realm.

ASANO Haruji

📖 Lagerwey 1987c, 195–201; Ōfuchi Ninji 1983, 472–76; Schipper 1989b, 128–37

※ gongde

Kaixin fayao

開心法要

Essentials of the Method to Open the Heart

Kaixin fayao is the title of an annotated edition of the *Wubu liuce* 五部六冊 (Five Books in Six Fascicles; 1509), the canonical text of the Luojiao 羅教 or Luo Teaching. This sect, also known as Wuwei jiao 無為教 or Teaching of Non-action, was established by Luo Qing 羅清 (1443–1527) and was mainly transmitted in Shandong, Jiangsu, Zhejiang, Jiangxi, and Fujian, as well as in stretches of land to the north and south along the Grand Canal. Luo Qing wandered in all directions, searching out teachers and visiting friends; after more than ten years of painstaking cultivation, "he handed down *dharma*-treasures to redeem men and heaven," and wrote the canonical text of the sect in five sections. As each section is bound in one fascicle, with the exception of the third which consists of two fascicles, Luo Qing's work is entitled *Wubu liuce*, lit., "The Five Sections in Six Fascicles." The titles of each section are:

1. *Kugong wudao juan* 苦功悟道卷 (Scroll on Awakening to the Dao after Bitter Practices)

2. *Tanshi wuwei juan* 嘆世無為卷 (Scroll on Lamenting the Age and Practicing Non-Action)

3. *Poxie xianzheng yaoshi juan* 破邪顯證鑰匙卷 (Scroll on Smashing the Heterodox and Making Manifest the Key)

4. *Zhengxin chuyi wu xiuzheng zizai baojuan* 正信除疑無修證自在寶卷 (Precious Scroll on Rectifying Faith and Removing Doubts, Unvarnished and Self-Contained)

5. *Weiwei budong Taishan shengen jieguo baojuan* 巍巍不動泰山深根結果寶卷 (Precious Scroll on the Fruits of the Profound Foundation of Lofty Immovable Mount Tai)

The collection draws on Confucianism, Taoism and Buddhism. It laments the hardships of human existence and advocates the Chan Buddhist method of subitaneous awakening (*dunwu* 頓悟), along with a vegetarian diet, virtuous conduct, clarity and quiescence (*qingjing), and non-action (*wuwei).

Luo Qing's disciple, the Chan Buddhist monk Lan Feng 蘭風, wrote annotations on the *Wubu liuce*. In 1596, Lan's disciple Wang Yuanjing 王源靜

supplemented and revised the notes that his master had left uncompleted and published the whole work under the title *Kaixin fayao*. Later, Wang Yuanjing's disciples, the Xin'an 新安 (Zhejiang) tradesmen Cheng Pubang 程普榜, Cheng Puxiang 程普鄉, and Cheng Pushen 程普伸, revised and rearranged it again. Their new edition was published in 1652.

The *Kaixin fayao* is based on a rearrangement of Luo Qing's original work. For example, the *Kugong wudao juan* was arranged into eighteen sections (*pin* 品) after it had been broken up and made to conform more closely to the eighteen steps (*can* 參) through which Luo Qing himself had awakened to the Dao. The *Poxie xianzheng yaoshi juan* was arranged into fourteen sections, and the *Zhengxin chuyi wu xiuzheng zizai baojuan* into twenty-five sections. By explaining the text, dividing it into sections, adding collations and comments, selecting the important aspects and clarifying the essential points, the *Kaixin fayao* facilitated the spread of the Luojiao. The text draws on several Chan Buddhist sayings and on passages from the *Huayan jing* 華嚴經 (*Avataṃsaka-sūtra*), and also manifests the influence of ideas from the "learning of the heart" (*xinxue* 心學) widespread among the broader public in the late Ming and early Qing dynasties.

CHEN Yaoting

📖 Han Bingfang 1986

※ *baojuan*; TAOISM AND POPULAR RELIGION; TAOISM AND POPULAR SECTS

keyi

科儀

"rules and observances"

The term *keyi* indicates the various behavioral and ritual guidelines that define the proper behavior of priests and monastics. *Ke* 科 is the most general term among various Chinese words indicating rules, regulations, precepts, and so forth. It means "rules" in the broadest sense and can refer to anything from a moral injunction to a specific behavioral guideline. The term is combined with several other characters to form compounds, such as *kemu* 科目, "standardized rules," "code"; *zunke* 遵科, "rules and regulations"; and *kejie* 科戒, "codes and precepts."

Yi 儀, "observances," "protocols," or "liturgies," in contrast refers to the concrete activities to be undertaken in a ritual or formal monastic context, and often appears in the compound *weiyi* 威儀, "dignified liturgies" or "ceremonial protocols." Numerous texts have this term in their titles when their content includes prescriptions for practical daily behavior.

Livia KOHN

📖 Matsumoto Kōichi 1983, 202–5; Schipper 1993, 72

Kou Qianzhi

寇謙之

365?–448; *zi*: Fuzhen 輔真

Kou Qianzhi, the founder of the so-called Taoist theocracy of the Toba's Northern Wei dynasty, came from a Celestial Masters (*Tianshi dao) family in the Chang'an area and was the younger brother of the provincial governor Kou Zanzhi 寇讚之. In his early years, he studied mathematics, medicine, and the basics of Buddhism under the monk Shi Tanying 釋曇影 (?–405/418), a disciple of the translator Kumārajīva (ca. 344-ca. 409). Guided not only by the Toba's search for the ideal form of government but also by the dream of a reborn Taoist community that was widespread in the south, he withdrew to find solitary inspiration on Mount Song (*Songshan, Henan). There, as described in *j.* 114 of the *Weishu* (History of the Wei; trans. Ware 1933, 228–35), he was blessed twice with a divine manifestation by Lord Lao (*Laojun), the deified Laozi. First, in 415, the deity revealed to him the so-called "New Code" (*xinke* 新科; see **Laojun yinsong jiejing*). Then, in 423, the god's messenger Li Puwen 李譜文 bestowed upon Kou the *Lutu zhenjing* 錄圖真經 (Authentic Scripture of Registers and Charts; lost) together with a divine appointment as new Celestial Master (*tianshi).

In 424, Kou took these works to court, where he was welcomed by Emperor Taiwu (r. 424–52) and found the support of the prime minister Cui Hao 崔浩 (381–450), a Confucian fond of mathematics, astrology, and magic who, like Kou, envisioned a renewed and purified society. Together they convinced the ruler to put the "New Code" into practice and thus established the Taoist theocracy of the Northern Wei. Kou himself became the official leader with the title of Celestial Master, while his disciples were invited to the capital to perform regular rites. In 431, Taoist institutions and priests were also established in the provinces, extending the reach of Taoist and thus state control farther into the countryside. Cui Hao in the meantime masterminded various military successes and worked on the compilation of a national history, rising ever higher in rank and honor. The theocracy reached its pinnacle in 440, when the emperor underwent Taoist investiture rites and changed the reign title to Perfected Lord of Great Peace (Taiping zhenjun 太平真君).

Thereafter Cui began to exploit his power by railing against the Buddhist clergy and, in 446, organized a large-scale persecution of all sorts of popular practitioners and especially Buddhists, who were believed to be cooperating with various rebellious forces (Eberhard 1949, 229). After Kou's death in 448, Cui became even more megalomaniac and turned to actively insulting the Toba rulers. Not standing for any more of this, they had him executed in 450, and the Taoist theocracy thus came to a swift and unceremonious end.

Livia KOHN

📖 Mather 1979; Mather 1987; Ozaki Masaharu 1979; Qing Xitai 1988–95, 1: 401–15; Robinet 1997b, 74–76; Sunayama Minoru 1990, 69–92; Tang Yongtong and Tang Yijie 1961; Yamada Toshiaki 1995b

※ *Laojun yinsong jiejing*; Tianshi dao

Kunlun

崑崙

Kunlun (also called Kunling 崑陵, Kunqiu 崑丘, Kunlun xu 崑崙墟, etc.), an *axis mundi* in traditional Chinese cosmology, is a mythical mountain located in the distant West, the abode of the goddess *Xiwang mu (Queen Mother of the West), and a counterpart to the three isles of the transcendents in the eastern seas (see *Penglai). In Eastern Zhou textual sources, such as *Mu tianzi zhuan* 穆天子傳 (Biography of Mu, Son of Heaven; ca. 350 BCE; trans. Mathieu 1978) and the earlier chapters of *Shanhai jing* 山海經 (Scripture of Mountains and Seas; fourth/third century BCE?; trans. Mathieu 1983), Kunlun appears as just one among many fabulous mountains in the West. Only the "ancient text" version of the *Zhushu jinian* 竹書紀年 (Bamboo Annals; originally ca. 300 BCE), makes an explicit link between Xiwang mu and Mount Kunlun. The idea that Xiwang mu resided on Kunlun become prevalent during the second century CE (Wu Hung 1987, 119), by which time the mountain's status had increased accordingly.

The *Shanhai jing*'s descriptions center on the mountain's fabulous flora and fauna, with a growing emphasis on their immortality-bestowing properties in the later chapters. Besides describing Xiwang mu and her attendants, the text mentions a Xuanyuan tai 軒轅臺 (Terrace of Xuanyuan, i.e., *Huangdi), surrounding mountains and streams, and a nearby country called Wo 沃 (Fertile). Although the *Mu tianzi zhuan* does not definitely link Xiwang mu with Kunlun, Yaochi 瑤池 or Turquoise Pond (frequently mistranslated "Jasper Pond"), where King Mu of Zhou (Muwang, r. 956–918 BCE) and the goddess exchange songs, becomes an essential part of Kunlun in later writings. In the *Liezi*'s brief retelling of the tale, King Mu climbs to the summit of Kunlun, where he gazes at Huangdi's palace and raises a memorial mound, then he visits Xiwang mu, who gives a banquet for him by the Turquoise Pond (Graham 1960, 64).

The most extensive description of Kunlun in Han literature is found in *Huainan zi* 4 (Major 1993, 150–61), in which the mythical emperor Yu 禹 is said to have raised Kunlun (somewhat more than 1,100 *li* high) while controlling the floods. On the mountain are various wondrous trees and plants, a city with a nine-layered wall, and 440 gates. Besides several outlying peaks, there is an immortality-bestowing Cinnabar Stream (*danshui* 丹水) that circles Kunlun three times before returning to its source; and four rivers—the Yellow River (Heshui 河水), Red River (Chishui 赤水), Weak River (Ruoshui 弱水), and Yang River (Yangshui 洋水)—flow out of Kunlun's foothills to the northeast, southeast, southwest, and northwest. Kunlun itself has three tiers, each narrower than the one below. From bottom to top, they are Cool Wind (Liangfeng 涼風), Hanging Garden (Xuanpu 懸圃), and Ascending Heaven (Shangtian 上天). Moreover, those who ascend the three tiers attain deathlessness, become "numinous" (*ling* 靈) with the power to control wind and rain, and become divine (*shen* 神), in that order. Shangtian is called the abode of the Great Emperor (Taidi 太帝). Although the *Huainan zi* does not mention Xiwang mu in connection with Kunlun, she is usually described in later literature as living on Hanging Garden. Other sources provide different names for the three tiers.

As the *Shangqing school elevated the status of Xiwang mu within Taoism, so too it elevated her abode, making it a repository of the original texts of scriptures. The extensive description of Kunlun in the *Shizhou ji (Record of the Ten Continents), a text that incorporates many ideas from the Shangqing doctrines, was also very influential. In that text, Kunlun is located in the seas to the distant northwest and towers 36,000 *li* over the surrounding countryside. It is wide at the top, narrow at the bottom, and instead of three tiers it has three corners pointing north, west, and east: Langfeng Peak (Langfeng dian 閬風巔), Hanging Garden Hall (Xuanpu tang 懸圃堂), and Kunlun Palace (Kunlun gong 崑崙宮). It also has four supporting foothills to the southeast, northwest, northeast, and southwest named Garden of Piled Stones (Jishi pu 積石圃), House of North-Facing Doors (Beihu zhi shi 北戶之室), Well of Great Life (Dahuo zhi jing 大活之井), and Maelstrom Valley (Chengyuan zhi gu 承淵之谷). On Kunlun Palace is situated the Walled City (Yongcheng 墉城), from which five golden terraces and twelve jade towers rise, but similar cities are also found on House of North-Facing Doors and Maelstrom Valley. The role of Kunlun is described in the loftiest language:

> Above it communes with the Original Pneuma (*yuanqi) of Jade-cog and Armil (*xuanji* 璿璣, two stars of the Northern Dipper), and it spreads [its power] through the Five Constants (*wuchang* 五常) [i.e., the *wuxing*] and the Jade Balance (*yuheng* 玉衡). It puts to order the Nine Heavens (*jiutian) and adjusts Yin and Yang. All rare and outstanding articles and creatures are found here; the celestial ones crowd in and cannot all be counted. This mountain is the root and axle of heaven and earth, the mainstay and handle of ten thousand measures. . . . (*Shizhou ji*, 11a–b)

A parallel passage is found in the *Waiguo fangpin Qingtong neiwen* 外國放品青童內文 (Inner Script of the Azure Lad on the Distribution of the Outer Realms; CT 1373). Another extensive description of Kunlun in Six Dynasties literature is found in the *Shiyi ji* 拾遺記 (Uncollected Records; Foster 1974; Campany 1996, 64–67, 306–18), but this centers on Kunlun's unusual flora and fauna.

The terms used to describe Kunlun and its features in these earlier passages are repeated and embellished in later Chinese texts, whether religious or literary.

Thomas E. SMITH

📖 Cahill 1993, passim; Kominami Ichirō 1991, 143–86; Smith Th. E. 1992, 54–69 and 555–59; Stein R. A. 1990, 223–46; Wu Hung 1989, 117–32

※ TAOISM AND CHINESE MYTHOLOGY

langgan

琅玕

Langgan is the name of a gemstone, sometimes identified as blue or green coral or as malachite, and also the name of a tree that grows on Mount *Kunlun, the Chinese *axis mundi*. It is best known, however, as the name of an alchemical preparation, the Elixir Efflorescence of Langgan (*langgan huadan* 琅玕華丹). The method to compound it is found in the *Taiwei lingshu ziwen langgan huadan shenzhen shangjing* 太微靈書紫文琅玕華丹神真上經 (Divine, Authentic, and Superior Scripture of the Elixir Efflorescence of Langgan, from the Numinous Writings in Purple Script of the Great Tenuity; CT 255; trans. Bokenkamp 1997, 331–39), a text that was originally part of the *Lingshu ziwen* (Numinous Writings in Purple Script), one of the main *Shangqing revealed scriptures.

The method is divided into four stages. In the first stage, after performing the purification practices (*zhai* 齋), the adept places the elixir's fourteen ingredients in a crucible, adding mercury on top of them. He lutes the crucible with several layers of mud (here called Divine Mud, *shenni* 神泥) and heats it for one hundred days. Ingesting the elixir makes one's complexion similar to gold and jade and enables one to summon divine beings. The next three stages of compounding take place in meditation: the Efflorescence of Langgan undergoes further refinement and is finally buried under the earth. After three years, it generates a tree whose fruits confer immortality, as do those of the tree on Mount Kunlun.

Combining *waidan and meditation, this method provides an example of how Shangqing incorporated and modified earlier alchemical practices. While the first section of the text is comparable in content, language, and style to the *Taiqing scriptures, the language of the three latter parts reflects Shangqing imagery. This suggests that an earlier text was expanded upon assimilation into the Shangqing corpus, with the addition of sections describing processes that can only take place as part of inner practices, and not in a laboratory.

Fabrizio PREGADIO

📖 Bokenkamp 1997, 289–95 and 331–39; Pregadio 2006b, 58–59, 119–20; Robinet 1984, 2: 101–10; Schafer 1978b; Strickmann 1979, 134–36

※ *Lingshu ziwen*; *waidan*

Laojun

老君

Lord Lao

See *Laozi and Laojun 老子 · 老君.

Laojun bashiyi hua tu

老君八十一化圖

Eighty-One Transformations of Lord Lao, Illustrated

The *Laojun bashiyi hua tu* is an illustrated hagiography of Laozi which, as its title indicates, shows his supposed eighty-one interventions in human form in the life of the world. The text gained fame in the disputations between Buddhists and Taoists during the Yuan dynasty and was one of those that were destroyed after the proscription of all Taoist books with the exception of the *Daode jing*. As a result, no version of this text exists in the Taoist Canon. The particular notoriety of the *Eighty-One Transformations* was due largely to its explicit claim that the Buddha was but one of the transformations of Laozi. This theory—"the conversion of the barbarians"—had a long history probably extending back to the Later Han period and arguments between Buddhists and Taoists on the topic had raged from the Six Dynasties (see the entry *Huahu jing*).

The precise origins of the *Eighty-One Transformations* are murky, and the validity of the claim of surviving texts to authenticity remains open to question. The most detailed version of the events surrounding the composition of the text—and its subsequent use in debates between Buddhists and Taoists—comes in the form of a Buddhist polemic, the *Bianwei lu* 辯偽錄 (Accounts of Disputation of [Taoist] Falsehood; T. 2116), by Xiangmai 祥邁, which was complete by 1291. Bearing in mind that this text has been examined and found severely wanting in historical reliability by Kubo Noritada (1968), it nevertheless provides the information that the two main figures in the authorship of the *Eighty-One Transformations* were Linghu Zhang 令狐璋 and Shi Zhijing 史志經, a follower of *Qiu Chuji (1148–1227). A version of the text under the title *Jinque xuanyuan Taishang Laojun bashiyi hua tushuo* 金闕玄元太上老君

八十一化圖說 (Eighty-One Transformations of the Most High Lord Lao of Mysterious Origin of the Golden Portal, Illustrated and Explained) dating to 1598 is held in the Museum für Völkerkunde in Berlin. It was first reported by Herbert Mueller in 1911 (Mueller 1911, 408–11) and examined by 1913 by either Paul Pelliot or Édouard Chavannes or both (Chavannes and Pelliot 1911–13, part 2: 116–32), and as Kenneth Ch'en (1945–47) noted, has the two names of Linghu Zhang and Shi Zhijing at its head. Pelliot and Chavannes concluded that Linghu and Shi were its likely compilers. The text was certainly extant by 1250 and if Shi Zhijing was partly responsible for its composition, it cannot have been composed more than a few decades earlier than that.

Apart from the Berlin manuscript referred to above, Yoshioka Yoshitoyo (1959b) describes two editions—a "Taiqing gong 太清宮 edition" and a "Hang-zhou edition"—in the collection of the Japanese scholar, Fukui Kōjun. More recently Lu Gong (1982) has reported a 1532 Liaoning edition. However, by far the easiest way to consult this text is through a reprint of it appended to Florian Reiter's translation (Reiter 1990b). The text he reproduces is credited to the Manao 瑪瑙 publishing house with no date or place of publication. It is held in the library of the Australian National University.

The *Eighty-One Transformations* is a series of beautiful annotated illustrations. It begins with three images of Laozi and a picture of an inscribed stele reading "Long live the emperor." This is followed by sixteen pages depicting thirty-one Taoist patriarchs, many from the centuries immediately preceding the book's composition. Then follow the depictions of the eighty-one transformations themselves, each accompanied by a short text. The first few show his existence in purely cosmic time, beginning with him arising in the "non-beginning" (*wushi* 無始) and proceeding through the phases of the creation of the cosmos. By number 11, he is in the time of Fu Xi 伏羲 appearing as Yuhua zi 鬱華子, by number 19 he is in the time of King Wen of the Zhou (Wenwang 文王, r. 1099–1050 BCE) as Bianyi zi 變邑子. Famously, in number 34, he transforms *Yin Xi into a Buddha and sends him to explain the *Sūtra in Forty-Two Sections* (*Sishi'er zhang jing* 四十二章經) to the Hu 胡 barbarians. Number 58 concerns the appearance to *Zhang Daoling in the Later Han. The final illustrated transformation is dated to 1098.

Benjamin PENNY

📖 Boltz J. M. 1987a, 67–68 and 279; Ch'en Kenneth K. S. 1945–47; Kohn 1998b, 56–57 and passim; Kubo Noritada 1968; Lu Gong 1982; Reiter 1986; Reiter 1990b; Reiter 2001; Schmidt 1985; Yoshioka Yoshitoyo 1959b

※ Laozi and Laojun; HAGIOGRAPHY

Laojun shuo yibai bashi jie

老君說一百八十戒

The Hundred and Eighty Precepts Spoken by Lord Lao

The Hundred and Eighty Precepts Spoken by Lord Lao dating, in all likelihood, from the fourth century is probably the earliest set of behavioral rules for Taoist priests. The text divides into two parts: the hundred and eighty precepts themselves and a later preface that describes how the precepts came to be transmitted. There are four sources that give partial or full versions of the *Hundred and Eighty Precepts*:

1. *Taishang Laojun jinglü* 太上老君經律 (Scriptural Regulations of the Most High Lord Lao; CT 786), 2a–12b

2. **Yunji qiqian* (CT 1032) 39.1a–14b

3. *Yaoxiu keyi jielü chao* 要修科儀戒律鈔 (Excerpts from the Essential Liturgies and Observances; CT 463), 5.14a–19b

4. The original *Dunhuang manuscript from which the two manuscripts in the Pelliot collection P. 4562 and P. 4731 were taken (these manuscripts are reproduced in Ōfuchi Ninji 1978–79, 2: 685)

The preface concerns *Gan Ji to whom the Dao was transmitted by Laozi during the reign of King Nan of Zhou (Nanwang 赧王, r. 314–256 BCE). Gan Ji passed it on to Bo He 帛和 and both propagated the doctrine. On Laozi's return from his western sojourn converting the barbarians, he is shocked to see the corrupt state of the community who bicker and disagree, make profits from offerings, and are jealous and boastful. The precepts are granted to bring the community back to right behavior.

The hundred and eighty precepts themselves are not divided into formal groups, as are some sets of Taoist and Buddhist precepts. However, there is an implicit division after number 140 between those that prohibit certain conduct and those that are exhortatory. Some of the rules prohibit actions that are banned in most cultures (for example, 3: You should not steal other people's property; 50: You should not deceive others). Some give perhaps unintended insights into the lives of the Taoist clergy of the time (13: You should not use herbal medicines to perform abortions; 15: You should not eat off gold or silverware; 72: You should not poke your tongue out at other people; 99: You should not bore holes in the walls of other people's houses to spy on the women and girls inside). A few are specifically Taoist (147: You should exert yourself to seek long life, day and night do not slacken; 149: You should exert yourself to ingest *qi* and eliminate cereals from your diet practicing the Dao of No Death). Finally, some important ones show the direct influence of Buddhism (66: You should not urinate while standing; 116: You should not urinate on living plants or in water that is to be drunk).

Benjamin PENNY

📖 Hendrischke and Penny 1996 (trans.); Lai Chi-tim 1998b; Maeda Shigeki 1985b; Ōfuchi Ninji 1978–79, 2: 685 (reprod. of the Dunhuang mss.); Penny 1996a; Schmidt 1985; Schipper 1999a (part. trans.); Schipper 2001

※ *jie* [precepts]

Laojun yinsong jiejing

老君音誦誡經

Scripture on Precepts of Lord Lao, Recited
[to the Melody in the Clouds]

The *Laojun yinsong jiejing* (CT 785), also known as "New Code" (*xinke* 新 科), was revealed in 415 to *Kou Qianzhi. The text was originally in twenty scrolls, most of which are now lost. The expression *yinsong* 音誦 in the title is short for *yunzhong yinsong* 雲中音誦, which may mean "to be recited after [the melody] 'In the Clouds'" or "recited in the cloudy heavens." The text contains thirty-six precepts (*jie*), each of which is introduced with "The Lord Lao said" and ends with the admonition: "Honor and follow this rule with awareness and care, in accordance with the statutes and ordinances," a variation of the formula: "Promptly, promptly, in accordance with the statutes and ordinances!" (*jiji ru lüling*).

The first six introductory rules describe the text's revelation in terms similar to those used in the "weft texts" (*weishu* 緯書; see *TAOISM AND THE APOCRYPHA). Thereafter the precepts seem to be arranged in no particular order, consisting of general guidelines, specific behavioral rules, and detailed ritual instructions. General guidelines include an outline of the various offices and duties of Taoist followers and a survey of banquet meetings and communal rites (e.g., nos. 7–9). Specific behavioral rules describe the role of Taoists in relation to the civil administration, patterns of public conduct, and measures to be taken in case of sickness (e.g., no. 21). Detailed ritual instructions, finally, deal with the performance of communal banquets, the proper format of prayers and petitions to the Dao, ancestral offerings, funerary services, and immortality practices (e.g., no. 12).

Livia KOHN

📖 Mather 1979; Qing Xitai 1994, 2: 122–23; Yang Liansheng 1956

※ Kou Qianzhi; *jie* [precepts]

Laoshan

嶗山 (or: 勞山, 牢山)

Mount Lao (Shandong)

Mount Lao, also known as Mount Laosheng (Laosheng shan 勞盛山), is the tallest peak in the eastern coastal region of Shandong, east of present-day Qingdao 青島. An ancient site for hermits and *fangshi (practitioners of esoteric arts), the mountain was visited by emperors who ascended it to gaze at *Penglai, the mythical island of the immortals, in their quest for immortality.

Qin Shi huangdi (r. 221–210 BCE), in particular, climbed the mountain after performing the *feng* 封 and *shan* 禪 ceremonies to Heaven and Earth on Mount Tai (*Taishan) and Mount Liangfu (Liangfu shan 梁父山), both in Shandong. Remaining there for three months, he was visited by numerous *fangshi*, among them *Xu Fu who requested permission to seek the islands of the immortals. The expedition is said to have set out from here. Han Wudi (r. 141–87 BCE) and Han Guangwu di (r. 25–57 CE) also climbed the mountain in ritual circumstances.

Many of the methods in the *Lingbao wufu xu* are said to have originated on Mount Laosheng, reflecting the association of the coastal tradition with the early Taoism of the south. In particular, this was the purported site of revelation of the Five Lingbao talismans (see under *Lingbao wufu xu*). Tang Xuanzong (r. 712–56) dispatched the Taoists Wang Min 王旻 and Li Xiazhou 李退周 to compound elixirs on the mountain which he renamed Supporter of the Tang (Fu Tang shan 輔唐山).

The most famous temple on the mountain is the Taiqing gong 太清宮 (Palace of Great Clarity). The initial construction took place during the Han when a certain Zhang Lianfu 張廉夫 of Ruizhou 瑞州 (Jiangxi) abandoned his official post and retired to Mount Lao to cultivate the Dao. He built a reed structure, named Sanguan miao 三官廟 (Shrine of the Three Offices), where he revered the Great Emperor of the Three Offices (Sanguan dadi 三官大帝). Li Zhexuan 李哲玄 refurbished the temple in 904, renaming it Sanhuang miao

三皇廟 (Shrine of the Three Sovereigns) and centering its practice on reverence to the Three Sovereigns (*sanhuang). It was later renamed Taiqing gong.

The mountain grew in importance from the Jin-Yuan period when it became one of the centers of *Quanzhen Taoism. It was then that the majority of the current temples and monasteries were built. *Qiu Chuji (1148–1227) and *Liu Chuxuan (1147–1203) resided here during the Jin period. It was, however, only in the Ming period that the mountain gained prominence as a major Quanzhen center, which it retains today. A number of Quanzhen sub-lineages are associated with Mount Lao, including the Suishan branch (Suishan pai 隨山派) revering Liu Chuxuan, which viewed Taiqing gong as its ancestral temple, and the Gold Mountain branch (Jinshan pai 金山派) which reveres Sun Xuanqing 孫玄清 (1517–69).

Quanzhen masters in Shandong still perform the "Mount Lao Tunes" ("Laoshan yin" 嶗山韻) supposedly composed by Qiu Chuji. A set of twelve poems by Qiu Chuji on Mount Lao (which he designates Mount Ao or Aoshan 鰲山) are preserved in the *Panxi ji* 磻溪集 (Anthology of the Master from Panxi; CT 1159, 2.9b–12a). Other poems and writings by Qiu and other Quanzhen masters are still preserved in numerous inscriptions.

Gil RAZ

📖 Chen Zhentao 1991; Goossaert 2004; Wang Jiqin 1999; Zhan Renzhong 1998; Zhou Zhiyuan 1993

※ TAOIST SACRED SITES

Laozi and Laojun

老子 · 老君

The Old Master (also known as Lao Dan 老聃, Li Er 李耳,
Li Boyang 李伯陽) and Lord Lao (*or*: Old Lord)

Laozi, the alleged author of the *Daode jing* and ancient Taoist philosopher, became a key deity in the Taoist religion. His first appearance, in the *Zhuangzi* under the name of Lao Dan, is as an archivist of the Zhou court who was also the teacher of Confucius. After that he is mentioned in various philosophical texts and has a full biography in the *Shiji* (Records of the Historian; 63.2139–43; trans. Lau 1982, x-xi). Traditional recipients of the *Daode jing* believed the sources and accepted Laozi as a contemporary of Confucius. Ever since Herbert A. Giles (1906), however, text and author have been treated separately and Laozi has come to be thought of as a largely fictional figure. Only Homer Dubs

Fig. 51. Laozi as the author of the *Daode jing*. Zhang Lu 張路 (ca. 1490–ca. 1563).
National Palace Museum, Taipei, Taiwan, Republic of China. See Little 2000b, 117.

(1941) tried to find him in history, making him an impoverished aristocrat of the third century BCE whose ideas served to recover some of his lost status and power.

Formation of the myth. The most up-to-date evaluation of the early history of Laozi is by A. C. Graham (1986b). Beginning from the appearance of Laozi as Confucius's teacher in the *Zhuangzi*, he shows that this tale probably originated with a Confucian story on the master's humility and eagerness to learn. In the fourth century BCE, according to Graham, when the *Daode jing* was first compiled and the growing Taoist school needed a hoary founder, Lao Dan was adopted to serve as archetypal Taoist. When the Qin gained supremacy in the second century BCE, Lao Dan was presented to them as a powerful political thinker and was moreover linked with Grand Scribe Dan (Taishi Dan 太史儋), who in 374 BCE had predicted the rise of this state. This necessitated an unusual longevity for the philosopher, who was then said to have lived 160 or 200 years.

After the Qin had come to power, however, this longevity became a liability because Laozi was no longer around to advise the emperor in person. As a result, so Graham speculates, the story of Laozi's western emigration was invented, a convenient way not only of "disposing the body" but also of accounting for the compilation of the *Daode jing*, allegedly transmitted under duress to the border guard *Yin Xi on the Hangu Pass (Hangu guan 函谷關). Finally, under the Han, when his close connection to the Qin turned problematic, Laozi's birthplace was relocated to Bozhou 亳州 (present-day Luyi 鹿邑, Henan) near the Han rulers' homeland of Pei 沛, and he was linked with the Li 李 clan, a family of faithful retainers of the Han house. At this time Laozi was known for two key episodes: his service as an archivist and reclusive thinker under the Zhou, and his western emigration and transmission of the *Daode jing* to Yin Xi. Also, he had acquired a birthplace in Bozhou, the family name Li, his personal name Dan, and a lifetime in the sixth century BCE. This analysis by Graham fits the facts of the multifaceted presentation of Laozi in the early sources and accounts for the oddities of the *Shiji* biography. It also tallies with a recent manuscript find, the *Guodian *Laozi*, which contains parts of the *Daode jing* datable to between 350 and 300 BCE.

Han developments. Legends about Laozi grew massively over time. In the Han dynasty, he was adopted by three separate groups: 1. the magical practitioners (*fangshi*) or individual seekers of immortality, who adopted Laozi as their patriarch and idealized him as an immortal (see his biographies in the *Liexian zhuan*, trans. Kaltenmark 1953, 60–61, and in the *Shenxian zhuan*, trans. Kohn 1996a, and Campany 2002, 194–204); 2. the political elite, the imperial family and court officials, who saw in Laozi the personification of the Dao and

Fig. 52. Laozi as a deity. Tang dynasty, late seventh to early eighth century. Photograph: Rheinisches Bildarchiv, Cologne. Museum für Ostasiatische Kunst, Cologne. See Little 2000b, 183.

worshipped him as a representative of their ideal of cosmic and political unity alongside the Yellow Emperor (*Huangdi) and the Buddha (see *Laozi ming); 3. popular millenarian cults, who identified Laozi as the god who manifested himself through the ages and would save the world yet again and bring about the age of Great Peace (*taiping). Called Lord Lao (Laojun) or Yellow Old Lord (Huanglao jun 黄老君), this deified Laozi was like the personification of cosmic harmony worshipped by the court but equipped with tremendous revolutionary power. As a messiah (see *Li Hong), he could overturn the present and reorganize the world, leading the faithful to a new state of heavenly bliss in this very life on earth (see *Laozi bianhua jing).

These various texts all add new information to the two key episodes of the Laozi legend as known in the early Han, expanding the beginning of his life to include his identity with the Dao, creation of the world, and periodic descent as "teacher of dynasties," embellishing his birth by increasing his time in the womb and giving him the physiognomy of a sage, and extending his life after the emigration by either having him wander west and convert the barbarians to his teaching, then known as "Buddhism," or by ascending back to heaven and returning to reveal various Taoist teachings in China.

As a result, the complex Laozi myth, which first evolves at this time, can be described as consisting of six distinct parts:

1. Laozi as the Dao creates the universe (creation)

2. Laozi descends as the teacher of dynasties (transformations)

3. Laozi is born on earth and serves as an archivist under the Zhou (birth)

4. Laozi emigrates and transmits the Daode jing to Yin Xi (transmission)

5. Laozi and Yin Xi go west and convert the barbarians to Buddhism (conversion)

6. Laozi ascends to heaven and comes back again to give revelations to Chinese seekers, founding Taoist schools (revelations)

Medieval and later traditions. This basic structure of the myth is further expanded and deepened in the following centuries. The fifth-century *Santian neijie jing (Scripture of the Inner Explication of the Three Heavens) of the southern Celestial Masters (*Tianshi dao) adds more details on the cosmology of creation and applies motifs from the birth of the Buddha. In the sixth century, the *Kaitian jing (Scripture of the Opening of Heaven), the Wenshi neizhuan 文始內傳 (Inner Biography of Master Wenshi; Kohn 1997b, 109–13), and the *Huahu jing (Scripture of the Conversion of Barbarians), all of the northern Celestial Masters at *Louguan (Tiered Abbey), provide additional details on the transformations and a stylized version of the transmission and conversion, and add a second meeting of Laozi with Yin Xi in Sichuan at a "black ram shop," today the *Qingyang gong (Palace of the Black Ram) in Chengdu. The seventh-century *Xuanyuan huangdi shengji* 玄元皇帝聖紀 (Chronicle of the Holy August Emperor of Mysterious Origin) by the Louguan master *Yin Wencao, which survives in citations and in a longer fragment known as the *Taishang hunyuan zhenlu* 太上混元真錄 (Real Account of the Most High Chaotic Origin; CT 954), expands further on the transmission of the *Daode jing* and the relation to Yin Xi. Three major later hagiographies, including j. 2 of *Du Guangting's (850–933) *Daode zhenjing guangsheng yi* 道德真經廣聖 義 (Extended Interpretation of the Emperor's Exegesis of the *Daode jing*; 901; CT 725), the *Youlong zhuan* (Like unto a Dragon), and the *Hunyuan shengji* (Saintly Chronicle of Chaotic Origin), add further details to the structure outlined above, expanding especially the time Laozi spends among the pure heavens and scriptures before creation, and his visitations and miracles under the Tang and Song.

In addition to these extensive works, there are numerous shorter hagiographies of Laozi, he is mentioned in countless passages in Taoist texts, and large numbers of scriptures claim to go back to his revelations. More concretely, there are inscriptions on him from throughout the ages (see Kamitsuka Yoshiko 1993), such as the *Sanzun bei* 三尊碑 (Stele to the Three Worthies) of 508, the *Laoshi bei* 老氏碑 (Stele to Sir Lao; Chen Yuan 1988, 42) of 591, the *Xichuan Qingyang gong beiming* 西川青羊宮碑銘 (Stele Inscription at the Palace of the Black Ram in Sichuan; CT 964) of 884, and the *Laojun zan* 老君讚 (Eulogium for Lord Lao; in *Hunyuan shengji*, 9.35b) of 1014.

From Song times onward, the veneration of Laozi declined in favor of Xuanwu 玄武, the Dark Warrior (see *Zhenwu), yet there was also a new edition of the *Huahu jing*, the *Laojun bashiyi hua tushuo* 老君八十一化圖說 (Eighty-One Transformations of Lord Lao, Illustrated and Explained; see *Laojun bashiyi hua tu) and the deity appeared in popular novels, such as the *Fengshen yanyi* 封神演義 (Investiture of the Gods; IC 384–86) and the *Dongyou ji* 東游記 (Journey to the East) in the Ming. To the present day, he is worshipped as a key deity of the Celestial Masters and credited with a number of *qigong* exercises.

Livia KOHN

📖 Bokenkamp 2004; Boltz J. M. 1987b; Campany 2002, 194–211; Chen Guofu 1963, 269–71; Graham 1986b; Huang Paolos 1996; Kaltenmark 1953, 60–65; Kamitsuka Yoshiko 1993; Kamitsuka Yoshiko 1998; Kohn 1997b; Kohn 1998b; Kohn 1998g; Kusuyama Haruki 1979, 271–472; Little 2000b, 164–71, 174–75, 182–84; Pontynen 1980; Schipper 1993, 113–29; Seidel 1969; Seidel 1969–70; Sunayama Minoru 1983

※ *Daode jing*; DEITIES: THE PANTHEON; MESSIANISM AND MILLENARIANISM

Laozi bianhua jing

老子變化經

Scripture of the Transformations of Laozi

The *Laozi bianhua jing* is a manuscript that was discovered at *Dunhuang (S. 2295). Containing a text dated to the late second century on the basis of the last appearance of Laozi that it mentions (in 155 CE), the manuscript was copied by a monk of the *Xuandu guan (Abbey of the Mysterious Metropolis) in Chang'an in 612. The manuscript is fragmentary, lacking a proper beginning, and occasionally illegible. It consists of 101 lines of about seventeen characters each. Giving expression to the beliefs of a popular messianic cult located in southwest China, the text focuses on the divine Laozi as the incarnate power of the Dao that appears in every generation to support and direct the government of humanity.

The *Bianhua jing* can be divided into three major parts. The first consists of a eulogy on Laozi as the body of the Dao and the savior of humanity. This includes a description of his celestial stature, his supernatural birth to Mother Li 李母 after seventy-two years of pregnancy, his unusual divine appearance, his nature of non-action (*wuwei) and freedom from desires, and his ascent back to Mount *Kunlun with the help of a white deer. The section ends with the repeated emphasis that Laozi is of heavenly origin and has him give instructions to humanity:

> "Know," he says, "my nine human forms
> to gain wonderful immortality
> and find the Dao of life.
> So easy, yet so difficult!
> Study my Dao of life—
> and unlike people limited to the world,
> you will live as long as the sun and the moon."
>
> (Lines 27–29)

He then teaches people his nine names, each representing a different aspect of the universe one must know to attain immortality.

The second part contains an account of Laozi as a heavenly deity called Huncheng 混成 ("Confused And Yet Complete"; see *Daode jing* 25). Again a long section details the celestial powers and role of the god; then the text moves on to describe him as the teacher of dynasties, giving his various names from the first mythical ruler Fu Xi 伏羲 down to the Zhou dynasty. At this time, his birth to Mother Li and life as an archivist are integrated into the transformations, just as are his emigration and transmission of the *Daode jing* to *Yin Xi. However, Laozi here does not vanish but continues to reappear in China under the Qin, Han, and barbarians (as the Buddha), including also various manifestations in the Sichuan region toward the late second century. For example:

> In the second year of Vigorous Harmony (Jianhe, 148 CE)
> following a serious landslide,
> he appeared in Chengdu
> near the Gate of the Left Quarter,
> manifesting as a Perfected.
>
> (66–67)

The third and final part is cast as a speech delivered by Laozi during one of his later appearances. In it he describes himself as the Dao, a resident of Clarity (Qing 清), a ruler of the world, a master over life and death, a counselor to all emperors, and a continuous presence in the world:

> My body is clad in the Formless (*wuxing* 無形).
> Ignorant I am and unknowing—
> yet with every death, I am born anew
> and take on a new body.
>
> (Lines 73–74)

Next he bestows instructions to his followers, encouraging them to think of him day and night and give up all lascivious and ecstatic cults. To approach Laozi, adepts must visualize different colors in the body, then learn to "concentrate on the One, and [they] soon will see a yellow glow within." Also, they should venerate his Text in Five Thousand Words (*Wuqian wen* 五千文; i.e., the *Daode jing*) and recite it vigorously. Then the deity will assist them with all troubles. The text ends on a slightly apocalyptic note, admonishing followers to "hurry and follow" the god "when Venus (Taibai 太白) fails in its course five or six times," thus to be saved from danger.

The *Bianhua jing* is a key document of the active Laozi cult practiced in the Later Han, including both its devotional and apocalyptic elements. It is also an important forerunner of the Laozi hagiographies of later times, which in turn reflect the continuously growing veneration of the deity.

Livia KOHN

📖 Kohn 1998g, 47–49; Kusuyama Haruki 1979, 325–32; Ōfuchi Ninji 1978–79, 1: 324–25 (crit. notes on the Dunhuang ms.) and 2: 686–88 (reprod. of the Dunhuang ms.); Robinet 1997b, 51–52; Seidel 1969, 59–75 (trans.), 131–36 (reprod. of the Dunhuang ms.); Seidel 1978b; Su Jinren 1998

※ Laozi and Laojun; MESSIANISM AND MILLENARIANISM

Laozi Heshang gong zhangju

老子河上公章句

The *Laozi* Divided into Sections and Sentences by Heshang gong

The version of the *Daode jing* of Laozi ascribed to Heshang gong, "The Gentleman of the River Bank," covers both the text of the classic, as divided into sections and sentences, *zhangju*, and a commentary (CT 682). Their supposed originator is said to have been a recluse who instructed Han Wendi (r. 180–157 BCE) from a position of levitation. More than one early Han transmitter of the meaning of Laozi with a similar name is mentioned from the time of Sima Qian 司馬遷 (145?–86? BCE) onward, but the fully developed legend of Heshang gong is not attested until the Six Dynasties period; it is not possible to make any identification between Heshang gong and any specific Han figure. Nor is it possible to date the editing of the Heshang gong text of the *Daode jing*, though it has certainly had a very wide influence, supplanting even the slightly different version of the classic that once circulated with the commentary of *Wang Bi (226–49), so that the latter work no longer exactly fits with the text which accompanies it.

The commentary, too, has been extremely influential, for example monopolizing the interpretation of Laozi in Japan for many centuries. Its sequential explanation of the text phrase by phrase marks it out as a work of an earlier type than that of Wang Bi, which attempts to keep the overall meaning of the text in mind, but this by no means suggests that Heshang gong's remarks were actually composed earlier. Its dual approach, summarized by some scholars as stressing both "controlling the state" (*zhiguo* 治國) and "controlling one's self" (*zhishen* 治身), is not entirely alien to Wang Bi, either; the one feature which has been seen as distinctive is the suggestion in some passages that the latter aim could be achieved in part through techniques visualizing the interior of the body after the manner of some *Shangqing texts. The main proponent of a late date of final composition on that basis is Kusuyama Haruki (1979), though his case for the addition of this meditational element to an earlier version of the commentary is from the start complicated by the fact that Shangqing texts themselves were recapitulating techniques for which traces may already be found in epigraphic materials of the second century CE.

In fact all the concepts present in the Heshang gong commentary may be seen as part of a Han legacy of ideas, though unfortunately a legacy that remained a matter for concern and hence for restatement for many centuries after the fall of the dynasty. The urge to see a (late) Han date as the most reasonable one for Heshang gong has therefore appealed to a number of scholars, though others have found definitive evidence for this lacking. Possible references to the text in the third century CE unfortunately cannot be taken as reliable; there is, however, one quotation apparently from the late fourth century which may prove trustworthy, and which includes a portion of the commentary deemed a later addition by Kusuyama. This is to be found on p. 1.1b–2a of the *Yangxing yanming lu (On Nourishing Inner Nature and Extending Life), a work none of whose other quotations falsify the statement in the preface that it was excerpted from the *Yangsheng yaoji (Essentials of Nourishing Life) of Zhang Zhan 張湛 (early fourth century). Zhang came from a family of bibliophiles who claimed to have preserved many works of Han times and earlier, but this still does not prove that the Heshang gong commentary is any earlier than the century in which it is first cited. Other early commentaries, too, which are said to betray its influence remain for their part controversial with regard to their origins.

Whatever its date, the *Laozi Heshang gong zhangju* remained a firm favorite among professional Taoists from the time of its emergence onward, and for example is listed in Tang times as basic to an initiation into Taoist discipleship, even if a controversy over its merits versus those of Wang Bi resulted in the production of imperial commentary to resolve the dispute. Indeed when Eduard Erkes contemplated producing the first English translation of the text in the 1930s he was able to take the unusual step of going to Beijing to seek instruction from Taoist priests in their understanding of its meaning. Unfortunately, his work, first published in serial form, is not widely available: a plan to republish it in the 1990s, though widely advertised by the company concerned, was eventually cancelled on the grounds that it did not read smoothly enough in English; a *Daode jing* translation of no historical value was substituted instead.

T. H. BARRETT

📖 Campany 2002, 305–7; Chan A. K. L. 1991a; Chan A. K. L. 1991b; Chan A. K. L. 1998; Erkes 1950 (trans.); Kobayashi Masayoshi 1990, 241–68; Kohn 1992a, 62–69; Kusuyama Haruki 1979, 3–269; Masuo Shin'ichirō 1991; Ōfuchi Ninji 1978–79, 1: 209–35 (crit. notes on the Dunhuang mss.) and 2: 434–56 (reprod. of the Dunhuang mss.); Qing Xitai 1988–95, 1: 75–84; Wang Ka 1993a (crit. ed.); Zheng Chenghai 1971 (crit. ed.)

※ *Daode jing*

Laozi ming

老子銘

Inscription for Laozi

The *Laozi ming*, by the court official Bian Shao 邊韶, dates from 24 September, 165, and contains a record of the imperial sacrifices to Laozi undertaken by Han Huandi (r. 146–168) at the sage's birthplace in Bozhou 亳州 (present-day Luyi 鹿邑, Henan) and at the imperial palace in Luoyang. The inscription begins with a summary of the facts known about the historical Laozi, repeating the account of the *Shiji* (Records of the Historian; 63.2139–43; trans. Lau 1982, x-xi), then gives a concrete description of Laozi's birthplace and cites the *Daode jing* as the major expression of his ideas. In addition, the text praises Laozi as the central deity of the cosmos, who was born from primordial energy, came down to earth, and eventually ascended back to the heavenly realm as an immortal.

Next, the inscription recounts the concrete circumstances that led Huandi to make the sacrifice, mentioning a dream he had of the deity and listing the credentials of the author for the compilation of the text. All this is still by way of introduction to the actual praise offered to the deity, which combines the immortality seekers' vision of Laozi with the understanding of Laozi as a personification of the Dao. It begins:

> Focusing only on the virtue of the mystery,
> he embraced emptiness and guarded purity.
> Happy even in a lowly position,
> he never strove for emolument or authority.
> Like a rope, he was always straight,
> uncoiling naturally when twisted.

and concludes,

> He joins the radiance of the Sun and the Moon,
> is at one with the Five Planets.
> He freely comes and goes from the Cinnabar Hut (*danlu* 丹廬),
> easily travels up and down the Yellow Court (*huangting* 黃庭).
> He rejects ordinary customs,
> conceals his light, and hides himself.
> Embracing the Origin (*yuan* 元), he transforms like a spirit
> and breathes the essence of perfection.

None in the world can approach his depth;
we can only look up to his eternal life.
Thus our divine emperor offers a sacrifice to Laozi to document his
    holy spirituality.
I, this humble servant, in my turn strive to ensure his continued fame
and thus engrave this stone to his greater glory.

The *Laozi ming* is the first official and best dated early document on the divinization of Laozi, and an important text for our understanding of Han religion and of the myth of the god.

Livia KOHN

📖 Chen Yuan 1988, 5–6; Kusuyama Haruki 1979, 303–16; Maspero 1981, 394–95; Seidel 1969, 36–50, 121–30 (trans.).

※ Laozi and Laojun

Laozi Xiang'er zhu

老子想爾注

Xiang'er Commentary to the *Laozi*

The *Xiang'er* commentary to the *Laozi* is important as a text of the *Laozi* (*Daode jing*), as a commentary on the *Laozi*, and as one of the few surviving documents from the early years of the Celestial Master movement (*Tianshi dao). Long thought lost, a partial copy of the first of two chapters (chapters 3–37 of the received edition) of the *Laozi* text with this commentary appended to each chapter was found at *Dunhuang (S. 6825). Rao Zongyi (1956) combined this with quotations in other sources to assemble roughly half the original work, which he studied and commented on and which has been translated into English by Stephen R. Bokenkamp (1997, 29–148). Taoist scriptures from the late Six Dynasties attribute the work to *Zhang Lu, as does the early Tang commentator Lu Deming 陸德明 (556–627). *Du Guangting, writing in the tenth century, attributed the work to *Zhang Daoling. References to the work in the mid-third-century "Dadao jia lingjie" 大道家令戒 (Commands and Admonitions for the Families of the Great Dao; trans. Bokenkamp 1997, 148–85) are somewhat garbled but clearly seem to refer to this text and to associate it with Zhang Lu. Attempts to date the text to as late as the fifth century on the basis of a dubious history of ideas seem unfounded.

The text accompanying the commentary is an important witness to the early history of the *Laozi* text. William G. Boltz (1984) has argued, based on a detailed comparison with the *Mawangdui manuscripts of the *Laozi*, that the text interleaved with this commentary is the earliest transmitted text version and the closest in filiation to the Mawangdui manuscripts. This also links it with the "5,000 character" versions of the text.

The commentary presents a distinctive interpretation of the *Laozi* that sheds much light on early Celestial Master thought and the way that they appropriated this classical text for their own purposes. Among the more distinctive features of this work, the conception of the Dao as a conscious, anthropomorphic deity, identified with a divinized Laozi (*Laojun), who speaks directly to humans (in the first person) is striking. The reader is encouraged to devote him/herself to the Dao and the title, if Bokenkamp is correct, refers to how the Dao is constantly "thinking of you." The text advocates a physiological process based on "clarity and quiescence" (*qingjing) that seeks to absorb and circulate the breaths (*qi) of the Dao so as to attain longevity and the status of Transcendent Lord. This practice must be founded upon moral excellence, and to this end a set of nine precepts derived from the text of the *Laozi* and a set of twenty-seven derived from the *Xiang'er* commentary were published separately and seem to have been more influential in later periods than the commentary itself (see under *Xiang'er jie).

Also prominent are warnings concerning "deviant" teachings and "false arts abroad in the world" that point to a variety of competing movements that differed with the Celestial Masters on issues of doctrine and practice. For example, specific acts of sexual self-cultivation based on semen retention are condemned despite the Celestial Master practice of communal sex rites called "union of breaths" (*heqi).

The *Xiang'er* commentary also provides information on the earliest Taoist eschatology, a way for followers to pass through the world of the dead or the Great Yin (Taiyin 太陰): "If a person of the Dao is perfect in their conduct, the Taoist gods (*daoshen* 道神) will return to them; they will hide from the world by feigning death, then passing through the Great Yin, they go to be reborn (*fusheng* 復生), and thus do not perish (*buwang* 不亡). That is why they are long-lived. The profane have no moral merit. Their dead belong to the Earth Office. That is to perish" (see also trans. Bokenkamp 1997, 135). Here we see that it is the moral excellence of the Taoists that assures their longevity and ultimate survival of death.

Terry KLEEMAN

📖 Bokenkamp 1993; Bokenkamp 1997, 29–148 (trans.); Boltz W. G. 1984; Kusuyama Haruki 1979, 239–69; Mugitani Kunio 1985 (concordance); Qing Xitai 1988–95, 1: 181–92; Rao Zongyi 1956 (crit. ed.); Seidel 1969, 75–80; Ōfuchi Ninji

1978–79, 1: 208–9 (critical notes on Dunhuang ms.) and 2: 421–34 (reproduction of Dunhuang ms.); Ōfuchi Ninji 1991, 247–308

※ Laozi and Laojun; Tianshi dao

Laozi zhongjing

老子中經

Central Scripture of Laozi

The *Laozi zhongjing* appears twice in the Taoist Canon (CT 1168, entitled *Laojun zhongjing* 老君中經; YJQQ 18–19) and once in a *Dunhuang manuscript (P. 3784). It consists of fifty-five sections in two *juan* that describe methods of visualizing and activating the gods in the body. The text is related in general subject matter to the *Huangting jing (Scripture of the Yellow Court) and can be considered a precursor of the *Shangqing scriptures. Cited in the *Lingbao wufu xu (Prolegomena to the Five Talismans of the Numinous Treasure), it probably originated during the third century. Its instructions cover not only visualization, but also breathing exercises and other methods, so that the text can be considered one of the earliest technical manuals of Taoist meditation and longevity techniques.

One of several references to Laozi in the text is the name Yellow Old Lord of the Central Pole (Huanglao zhongji jun 黃老中極君). He is identified as the central god of the Northern Dipper (*beidou) among the stars and the resident of the Yellow Court (*huangting* 黃庭) in the abdomen. He is always activated together with a female aspect or "empress" (*huanghou* 皇后), described as a celestial Jade Woman (*yunü) called Mysterious Radiance of Great Yin (Taiyin xuanguang 太陰玄光). Wearing robes of yellow cloudy energy, they join to give birth to the immortal embryo.

To activate the pair, adepts visualize a sun and moon in their chests underneath their nipples, from which a yellow essence and a red energy radiate. These vapors then rise up to enter the Crimson Palace (*jianggong* 絳宮) in the heart and sink down to the Yellow Court in the abdomen. Filling its internal halls, the energies mingle and coagulate to form the immortal embryo, which grows gradually and becomes visible as an infant facing south, in the position of the ruler. As he is nurtured by the yellow essence and red energy still flowing from the adept's internal sun and moon, all illnesses are driven out and myriad disasters dissolve. The practice leads to close communication with the gods, enhances physical energy, and increases long life and vitality.

Livia KOHN

📖 Katō Chie 1996; Lagerwey 2004a; Maeda Shigeki 1988; Pregadio 2006a; Schipper 1979a; Schipper 1993, 105–12; Schipper 1995c

❊ INNER DEITIES; MEDITATION AND VISUALIZATION

Lei Shizhong

雷時中

1221–95; *zi*: Kequan 可權; *hao*: Mo'an 默庵 (Silent Hermitage),
Shuangqiao laoren 雙橋老人 (Old Man of the Double Bridge)

This important thirteenth-century ritual master and advocate of the basic harmony of the Three Teachings (Confucianism, Taoism, and Buddhism) was a native of Wuchang 武昌 (Hubei), although his ancestors came from Yuzhang 豫章 (Jiangxi). Reputedly a talented writer, he also came to study philosophy and the recondite aspects of the universe in his youth. He later encountered, through dreams and while awake, divine beings who taught him the fine points of the Thunderclap Rites (*leiting* 雷霆; see *leifa*), and the fundamental parallels between Buddhist and classical forms and aims of self-cultivation with those available among the Taoist traditions he had mastered. Of the many disciples who had reportedly studied with him before he passed away in 1295, some returned to Sichuan and others to the southeast coastal areas.

Lei's substantial annotations to the *Duren jing* (Scripture on Salvation) were part of the edition (*Duren shangpin miaojing tongyi* 度人上品妙經通義; CT 89) assembled by the forty-third Celestial Master, *Zhang Yuchu (1361–1410), which also includes the explanations of a clerk of the Thunderclap Lord Xin (Xin tianjun 辛天君), another strong proponent of both the Thunder Rites (*leifa*) and the fundamental unity of the Three Teachings. One of Lei's disciples named Chen Yuanheng 陳元亨 recorded some of Lord Xin's revelations to his master. Lei is also credited with a two-chapter Chaotic Origin (Hunyuan 混元) ritual tradition that is part of the *Daofa huiyuan* (Corpus of Taoist Ritual, *j.* 154–55)

Lei's passing in 1295 did not prevent him from presenting *Xue Jizhao (fl. 1304–16) with a copy of his *Xuxuan pian* 虛玄篇 (Folios on the Mystery of the Void) in 1308. The texts and diagrams associated with Lei bear comparison with those of *Xiao Yingsou (fl. 1226) and texts associated with him, as well as with the traditions central to *Bai Yuchan (1194–1229?) and his disciples.

Lowell SKAR

📖 Boltz J. M. 1987a, 209–10; Qing Xitai 1994, 1: 343–44

❊ *leifa*

Lei Siqi

雷思齊

1231–1301?; *zi*: Qixian 齊賢; *hao*: Kongshan xiansheng 空山先生
(Elder of the Empty Mountain)

This thirteenth-century specialist in the *Yijing and its diagram (*tu* 圖) and numerological (*shu* 數) traditions was a native of the prosperous scholarly area of Linchuan 臨川 (Jiangxi). In his youth he studied at the Niaoshi guan 鳥石觀 (Abbey of the Bird Stone). After Khubilai khan (r. 1260–94) established Mongol rule in south China in 1276 and named the thirty-sixth Celestial Master, *Zhang Zongyan (1244–91), head of Taoist affairs for the Mongol regime, Zhang asked Lei Siqi to become lecturer in the Mysterious Teaching (*Xuanjiao) in Beijing.

Lei later returned to the Guangxin 廣信 (Jiangxi) mountains, where he lectured and taught until he passed away at Niaoshi guan. Among his renowned disciples were *Wu Quanjie (1269–1346), Fu Xingzhen 傅性真, and Zhou Weihe 周維和. His main extant works, both completed around 1300, are the titles found in CT 1011 to CT 1014 (Kalinowski 1989–90, 88). The longest text, *Yitu tongbian* 易圖通變 (Miscellany on Divination with the Book of Changes; CT 1014; see Qing Xitai 1994, 2: 113–14) is preceded by a set of four prefaces (CT 1012) by Zhang Zongyan in 1286, Jie Xisi 揭係斯 (1274–1344) and Wu Quanjie (both dated 1332), and the last by Lei himself, dated 1300, which states that the *Yishi tongbian* 易筮通變 (Miscellany of Diagrams on the Book of Changes; CT 1011) is the successor to the *Yitu tongbian*. The titles of these texts both derive from studies grounded in the diagrams of the *Yijing*. The two annotated pages of *Hetu* 河圖 (Chart of the [Yellow] River; CT 1013) belong to the *Yitu tongbian* (CT 1014). Lei also wrote the *Laozi benyi* 老子本義 (Fundamental Meaning of the *Laozi*) and *Zhuangzi zhiyi* 莊子旨義 (Core Meaning of the *Zhuangzi*), which appear to be no longer extant. The Yuan scholar Yuan Jue 袁桷 praised Lei for his profound understanding of cosmic processes as seen in his writings on both the *Yijing* and on the *Daode jing*.

Lowell SKAR

📖 Boltz J. M. 1987a, 248; Qing Xitai 1994, 1: 347–48; Zhan Shichuang 1989, 96–115; Zhang Guangbao 1997

※ Xuanjiao

leifa

雷法

Thunder Rites; Thunder Rituals

This influential class of exorcistic ritual became part of many of the new Taoist ritual systems from the twelfth century onward. At its core is a repertoire of administrative, judicial, and meditative methods that it makes available to adepts interested in harnessing the vitalizing and punitive powers of thunder on a more regular and consistent basis in their ritual practice. Incorporating local gods and practices into a grand scheme laid out in liturgies and scriptures, and often including compounding the "inner elixir" (*neidan*), the Thunder Rites were part of the transformation of Taoism that took place between the tenth and fourteenth centuries. Most of the extant textual material in the Ming Taoist Canon that deals with absorbing and deploying the powers of thunder derives from various twelfth- to fifteenth-century traditions in south China. Priests who became part of these traditions acted their parts in this bureaucracy, assuming the bearing of a mandarin when dealing with higher deities and their fellows in the heavenly bureaus, and becoming a fierce judge when dealing with uncooperative demons.

The sources and forms of this class of ritual remain obscure. Studies to date suggest multiple origins with roots in cults to local thunder deities (*Leishen). By the tenth century they seem to have begun coalescing into traditions centering on various revealed methods meant to help practitioners deal with groups of thunder deities. One of the earliest and most enduring varieties of Thunder Rites dealt with the Five Thunder gods (*wulei* 五雷) who were linked to the Jiangxi *Zhengyi (Orthodox Unity) order (see *Daofa huiyuan*, j. 56–64, 101–3, and 188–97). Liu Yongguang 留用光 (1134–1206) also relied on the rites of the Five Thunder deities. Another later variety was known as the Thunderclap (*leiting* 雷霆) legacy. The *Shenxiao (Divine Empyrean) master *Wang Wenqing (1093–1153) played a major role in establishing and propagating this class of ritual within the new Taoist liturgies. His efforts made it popular among many Shenxiao traditions in twelfth- and thirteenth-century Guangdong, Fujian, Zhejiang, and Jiangxi. Those who venerated *Chen Nan, *Bai Yuchan, and their disciples, meanwhile, also made Thunder Ritual central to their practice. Thunder Ritual was not only formative in the rise of the *Qingwei (Pure Tenuity) legacy and its own variety of thunder rituals, but also appears in the *Jingming dao (Pure and Bright Way) of the thirteenth and fourteenth centuries. Later varieties of the *Lingbao dafa (Great Rites of the

Numinous Treasure) tradition also used it. While basically exorcistic, it could also be employed to break open the gates of hell and liberate the dead. Many notable scriptures and important deities centered their activity in a new sacred bureaucratic department known as the Thunder Ministry (*leibu* 雷部).

Scriptural origins. The Thunder Rites may have roots in the *Dongyuan shenzhou jing* (Scripture of the Divine Spells of the Cavernous Abyss). This original nucleus is augmented by Tantric elements and placed within a more comprehensive cosmic setting. Thus the Sanskritized version of the incantatory *Tiantong yinfan xianjing* 天童經 (Immortal Scripture of the Celestial Lad in Hidden Brahmanic Language; CT 633) is later called the *Thunder Scripture* (*Leijing* 雷經) in some ritual texts. Shenxiao works also provided textual foundations, including the *Leiting yujing* 雷霆玉經 (Jade Scripture of the Thunderclap; CT 15), printed editions of which circulated in the early 1200s; the *Yushu jing* (Scripture of the Jade Pivot); and the related *Chaotian xielei zhenjing* 朝天謝雷真經 (Authentic Scripture for Giving Thanks to Thunder in Homage to Heaven; CT 17). The main deity in the *Yushu jing*, the Celestial Worthy of Universal Transformation (*Puhua tianzun), oversaw a full Thunder Ministry that included divine civilian clerks and bureaucrats as well as spirit-generals and sacred warriors. The main thunder deity was integrated into Taoist ritual, and in the Ming period some sects celebrated his birthday on the twenty-fourth day of the sixth month.

Sources. The largest variety of Thunder Ritual material is found in the *Daofa huiyuan* (Corpus of Taoist Ritual; CT 1220). Chapters 1–55 and 56–101 of this work are respectively concerned with the Qingwei and Shenxiao rites. Other ritual traditions are represented in the *Fahai yizhu* 法海遺珠 (Uncollected Pearls from the Ocean of Rituals; CT 1166), specifically those of the Purple Throne (*zichen* 紫宸; *j.* 45–46) from Jiangxi. Several separate texts also appear in the Taoist Canon, including the following:

1. *Jingyu xuanwen* 靜餘玄問 (Tranquil Remnants and Queries on the Mystery; CT 1252), compiled by Bai Yuchan's disciples

2. *Leifa yixuan pian* 雷法議玄篇 (Folios Discussing the Mysteries of the Thunder Rituals; CT 1254), compiled by Wan Zongshi 萬宗師 in 1248

3. *Daofa xinchuan* 道法心傳 (Heart-to-Heart Transmission of Taoist Rites; CT 1253), a theoretical treatise by *Wang Weiyi (fl. 1264–1304), a disciple of the Jiangxi master *Mo Qiyan (1226–94)

4. *Mingdao pian* 明道篇 (Folios on Elucidating the Way; CT 273), also by Wang Weiyi, revealing the close identity of the Thunder Rituals with *neidan*

5. *Yuyang qihou qinji* 雨暘氣候親機 (The Intimate Mechanisms of Rain, Clear Weather, and Periods of Pneumas; CT 1275), a meteorological treatise on the Thunder rites (Kalinowski 1989–90, 106–7)

6. *Daofa zongzhi tu yanyi* 道法宗旨圖衍義 (Explanations and Illustrations of the Ultimate Purport of Taoist Rituals; CT 1277), in the Thunderclap tradition, compiled by Deng Nan 鄧楠 and Zhang Xixian 章希賢

The Thunderclap Retreat (*leiting zhai* 雷霆齋) was also incorporated into Taoist ritual, as shown by Lin Weifu's 林偉夫 (1239–1302) **Lingbao lingjiao jidu jinshu* (Golden Writings for Deliverance by the Sect Leader of the Numinous Treasure Tradition; CT 465 and 466).

Lowell SKAR

📖 Boltz J. M. 1987a, 47–49, 178–79, 186–88, 210–11; Boltz J. M. 1993a; Chen Bing 1985, 46–47; Davis E. 2001, 24–30, 80–82; Despeux 1994, 138–42, 173–91; Li Yuanguo 2002; Skar 1996–97; Strickmann 1975

※ Leishen

Leishen

雷神

Thunder Deity *or* Thunder Deities

Early descriptions of Leishen, a thunder god, in old Chinese texts like the *Shanhai jing* 山海經 (Scripture of Mountains and Seas; fourth/third century BCE?; trans. Mathieu 1983, 503) suggest a generic beastlike divinity vaguely linked to other figures such as the Thunder Officer (Leishi 雷師) and the Thunder Sire (Leigong 雷公). While many sources describe and depict him as a figure with a beak and belly for drumming whose sound can be heard for long distances—like thunder—others relate the figure to dragons or pigs and say he resides in the West.

During medieval times, Leishen often designated local spirits who receive sacrifices and ritual recognition in exchange for their help in ensuring that the sacrificer avoids punishments from Heaven and receives a regular flow of precipitation. Between the eighth and twelfth centuries, these divinities, frequently appearing in groups, began acting as tutelary deities in charge of both local weather conditions and lesser, often malevolent, spirits who may have represented some of the older cults spread throughout southern China.

Like the Song officials who had to deal with a shifting mix of Han and southern peoples around them, religious practitioners began using revealed written texts, magic, and rules to identify and administer the Thunder Deities. Besides granting them bureaucratic titles in exchange for their assistance, ritualists also resorted to punishments according to sacred penal law and threatened them with force. Among the most potent methods of dealing with these (and other) local deities were those associated with the new Taoist revelatory movements emerging and consolidating in lands south of the Yangzi River. Although these spirits became increasingly subject to the emerging protocols of a divine administrative hierarchy, especially in south China, they also retained their local specificity and religious loyalties among the general populations. Often grouped into groups of five or thirty-six, these deities issued special talismanic missives written in strange characters known as "thunder script," and were thoroughly integrated into several Song ritual movements. They were especially prominent in the *Shenxiao (Divine Empyrean) and *Qingwei (Pure Tenuity) movements, and were central to the ritual activities of figures such as *Lin Lingsu (1076–1120), *Wang Wenqing (1093–1153), *Sa Shoujian (fl. 1141–78?), *Bai Yuchan (1194–1229?), and *Huang Shunshen (1224-after 1286).

By the early thirteenth century, the Thunder Ministry (Leibu 雷部) was understood to be headed by the Celestial Worthy of Universal Transformation Whose Sound of Thunder Responds to the Primordials in the Nine Heavens (Jiutian yingyuan leisheng Puhua tianzun 九天應元雷聲普化天尊; see *Puhua tianzun), at once an incarnation of the Great Saint of the Nine Heavens Who is Upright and Luminous (Jiutian zhenming dasheng 九天貞明大聖) and the Perfect King of Jade Clarity (Yuqing zhenwang 玉清真王). Later those who revered this exalted and bureaucratized form of the Thunder Deity performed special rites of reciting the deity's special scripture, the *Yushu jing (Scripture of the Jade Pivot), on his birthday, the twenty-fourth day of the sixth lunar month.

Lowell SKAR

📖 Barrett 1980b, 167–69; Eberhard 1968, 253–56; Liu Zhiwan 1986; Maspero 1981, 97–98; Matsumoto Kōichi 1979; Skar 1996–97

※ *leifa*; TAOISM AND LOCAL CULTS

Leng Qian

冷謙

ca. 1310-ca. 1371; *zi*: Qijing 起敬 (*or*: 啟敬); *hao*: Longyang zi 龍陽子 (Master of Draconic Yang)

Leng Qian, whose birthplace is indicated in various sources as Jiaxing 嘉興 (Zhejiang) or Wuling 武陵 (Hubei), was a painter and noted musician in the early years of the Hongwu reign period (1368–98). His biographical profile is blurred by legends. He is said to have painted the picture "The Immortals' Beauty on Penglai" (*Penglai xianyi tu* 蓬萊仙奕圖) for *Zhang Sanfeng in 1340. The colophon on this scroll, which is ascribed to Zhang himself, says that Leng first studied Buddhism but later devoted himself to Confucianism and Taoism. A stranger reportedly taught him *neidan* and the *Wuzhen pian* (Folios on Awakening to Perfection). Leng spent part of his life as a hermit on Mount Wu (Wushan 吳山, near Hangzhou). In 1367, Ming Taizu appointed him as a court musician. There are several explanations of why he lost the emperor's favor and under what circumstances he disappeared.

Three books are ascribed to Leng: the *Qinsheng shiliu fa* 琴聲十六法 (Sixteen Methods of Lute Playing; trans. van Gulik 1940), the *Taigu zhengyin* 太古正音 (Correct Tunes of Great Antiquity), and the *Xiuling yaozhi* 修齡要旨 (Essential Purport of the Cultivation of Longevity). The *Xuehai leibian* 學海類編 (Classified Anthology from the Ocean of Learning), compiled by Cao Rong 漕榮 (1613–85; ECCP 740), contains the first and third works (in *j.* 221 and 243, respectively), while the second is lost.

Martina DARGA

📖 van Gulik 1940; Little 2000b, 372–73; Qing Xitai 1994, 1: 376–77; Seidel 1970, 491–2; Weng T. H. 1976; Wong Shiu Hon 1979, 15–16

Li Ao

李翺

ca. 772-ca. 836; *zi*: Xizhi 習之

Li Ao was a younger associate of the Confucian polemicist Han Yu 韓愈 (768–824; IC 397–40), and is chiefly known as a thinker for his *Fuxing shu* 復性書 (Book of Returning to One's True Nature), a work on self-cultivation completed in about 800. Despite an apparently consistent record of opposition to Buddhism in his other writings, in later ages this work was suspected of betraying Buddhist influence, a notion encouraged by Chan Buddhist stories suggesting that several encounters with Chan masters had converted him to their views. These stories may be shown to have no historical basis, and the fact that they were preceded by tales in which a Taoist plays a like role confirms the impression made by his writings that he had some significance as an opponent of Taoism also.

That Li was not unaware of polemics between Taoism and Buddhism is made probable by his self-confessed studies of the works of Liang Su 梁肅

(753–93; IC 562–63), a prominent Buddhist layman who had exchanged a now lost correspondence with the famous Taoist writer *Wu Yun. Such elements in his thought as the deliberate choice of the term *fuxing* may reflect a deliberate challenge to Taoism. The use of the term as applied to self-cultivation is late, apparently deriving from *Guo Xiang commentary on the *Zhuangzi* (*Sibu congkan* ed., 6.4a) on the impossibility of using common learning to "return to the basis of the nature and destiny" (*fu xingming zhi ben* 復性命 之本). Similar terms are then deployed by *Cheng Xuanying writing on the *Zhuangzi* and elsewhere, whence perhaps they were borrowed for polemical purposes by Buddhist laymen of Liang's generation. That Li was actually using a common stock of self-cultivation language (much of which could be found in Confucian texts like the *Yijing) in order to make points against both Buddhism and Taoism is further supported by a close reading of the *Fuxing shu*, which betrays a not entirely explicit concern with transcending mortality. No suggestion may be found, however, that Taoist solutions are acceptable: the "fasting of the mind" (*xinzhai), for instance, a term from *Zhuangzi*, is accorded only a strictly relative importance.

The notion that Li's opposition to Taoism may have diminished in his later career has sometimes been argued on the basis of texts such as the "biography" *He Shouwu zhuan* 何首烏傳 (Biography of He "Black Hair"). But there is no more in this tale of the discovery of a plant conferring long life on those who ingest it to suggest that its author had changed his ideas (and his practical opposition to Taoism in his role as a civil servant) than in any of Li's occasional purely literary references to stories of immortals. What the *Fuxing shu* does demonstrate, however, is that the efforts of writers like Wu Yun in making Taoist self-cultivation techniques as widely available as Buddhist ones did succeed in presenting those who wished to argue for a purely Confucian approach in this area with the double task of delimiting a system neither Buddhist nor Taoist. This task, moreover, was certainly not completed by Li Ao, but remained a problem even under the Song dynasty.

T. H. BARRETT

📖 Barrett 1992; Hartman 1986

※ TAOISM AND NEO-CONFUCIANISM

Li Chunfeng

李淳風

ca. 602-ca. 670; *hao*: Huangguan zi 黃冠子
(Master of the Yellow Headgear)

Li Chunfeng's affiliation with Taoism probably sprang from the influence of his father who, in frustration because he could not satisfy his ambition for advancing to a higher office in the bureaucracy, resigned from his official post as District Defender (*wei* 尉) and became a Taoist priest during the Sui dynasty. Whatever the case, Chunfeng was widely read in all kinds of books, but was particularly learned in astronomy, calendrical calculations, and Yin-Yang lore. In 627 or shortly thereafter he submitted a critique of the current imperial calendar that was so well reasoned he received a post in the Office of the Grand Astrologer (*taishi ju* 太史局), the central government's bureau of astronomy and allied sciences. He then made a suggestion for construction of a new armillary sphere that Tang Taizong (r. 626–49) accepted. The device, manufacture of which was completed in 633, was a radical innovation because it had three nests of concentric rings instead of the usual two. Afterward he participated in the compilation of the chapters on astronomy, calendars, and portents for the *Jinshu* (History of the Jin) and *Suishu* (History of the Sui). In 648 he became Director (*ling* 令) of the Office of the Grand Astrologer. In that capacity Taizong asked him to interpret a portent that predicted a female ruler, Empress Wu (r. 690–705), would assume the throne. Li confirmed the prognostication and added his own prophecy: the lady, who was already in the emperor's harem, would usurp the throne in no more than thirty years and would decimate the Tang royal clan. In 656, Tang Gaozong (r. 649–83) commissioned him to participate in the annotation of two mathematical works that became textbooks at capital schools. In 662 he began a revision of the Tang calendar, promulgated by the emperor in 664. He died around 670 at the age of sixty-eight.

Li wrote an annotation to the *Taishang chiwen dongshen sanlu* 太上赤文洞神三籙 (Highest Three Registers in Red Script of the Cavern of Spirit; CT 589), a work attributed to *Tao Hongjing. Li's preface is dated the third lunar month of 632. The first of the registers (3a–8a) is based on the eight trigrams (*bagua*) of the *Yijing* for each of which the text supplies a talisman. Adepts could wield it to sojourn in various spiritual realms during dreams. The second (8b–16b) is an instrument for communicating with the spirits and contains instructions on forming mudrās. It possesses the powers to hide one's shadow, open locks, levitate the body one-hundred feet, make one invisible, and cause trees to blossom in the winter among other things. The last register (16b–24b) has eleven talismans. It possesses powers to call down spirits to perform various tasks. One of them with a white face, one eye and no nose knows where runaway slaves can be found. Another—a woman clad in black, carrying pears and riding a jackass—can cure suppurating sores and blindness. The *Jinsuo liuzhu yin* (Guide to the Golden Lock and the Flowing Pearls) has also been attributed to Li Chunfeng, but current research indicates that the text was compiled after his death.

Charles D. BENN

📖 Barrett 1990; Needham 1959, passim; Qing Xitai 1988–95, 2: 306–10; Strickmann 1996, 232–36

※ *Jinsuo liuzhu yin*

Li Daochun

李道純

fl. 1288–92; *zi*: Yuansu 元素; *hao*: Qing'an 清庵 (Clear Hermitage),
Yingchan zi 瑩蟾子 (Master of the Shining Toad)

Li Daochun, who came from Duliang 都梁 (Hunan), was the abbot of the Changsheng guan 長生館 (Abbey of Long Life) in Yizhen 儀真 (Jiangsu) and a *daoshi* in Xuyi 盱眙 (Jiangsu). Not much is known of his life. He was a disciple of Wang Jinchan 王金蟾, who in turn had studied under *Bai Yuchan. According to a work compiled by Cai Zhiyi 蔡志頤 (fl. 1288–1306) and other disciples, the *Qing'an Yingchan zi yulu* 清庵瑩蟾子語錄 (Recorded Sayings of [Li] Qing'an, Master of the Shining Toad; CT 1060), he also lived on Mount Mao (*Maoshan, Jiangsu) and in Yangzhou 揚州 (Jiangsu).

Li wrote three independent works and five commentaries to earlier texts:

1. *Zhonghe ji* (Anthology of Central Harmony; CT 249)

2. *Santian yisui* 三天易髓 (The Mutable Marrow of the Three Heavens; CT 250), containing brief notes on the *Hṛdaya-sūtra* (Heart Sūtra) and the *Yinfu jing*

3. *Quanzhen jixuan biyao* 全真集玄祕要 (Collected Mysteries and Secret Essentials of Quanzhen; CT 251)

4. *Daode huiyuan* 道德會元 (Returning to the Origin of the Dao and Its Virtue; CT 699; Qing Xitai 1994, 2: 107–9)

5. *Qingjing jingzhu* 清靜經注 (Commentary to the Scripture of Clarity and Quiescence; CT 755)

6. *Datong jingzhu* 大通經注 (Commentary to the Scripture of Great Pervasiveness; CT 105)

7. *Donggu zhenjing zhu* 洞古真經注 (Commentary to the Authentic Scripture of Cavernous Antiquity; CT 107)

8. *Xiaozai huming miaojing zhu* 消災護命妙經注 (Commentary to the Wondrous Scripture on Dispelling Disasters and Protecting Life; CT 101)

As a master of the Southern Lineage (*Nanzong) of *neidan, Li Daochun acknowledges the legacy of *Zhang Boduan and refers to him as *zushi* 祖師 (Ancestral Master). He also emphasizes the importance of the *Daode jing*, whose notions of Dao and Virtue (*de) are, in his view, identical with those of the *Yijing. Li is a syncretist, however, and often equates Taoism with Confucianism (especially the Neo-Confucian doctrines of Zhou Dunyi 周敦頤, 1017–73; SB 277–81) and with Buddhism (the *Prajñāpāramitā* or Perfection of Wisdom textual tradition, the *Hṛdaya-sūtra*, and Chan).

Li's teaching shows a tendency to subitism (*dun* 頓) and what we would call idealism. He often stresses the necessity of reintegrating the precosmic particle of light that abides in everyone and gives sense to all kinds and levels of practice (see *dianhua). He gives the term *quanzhen* 全真 ("complete reality") the meaning of conciliation of opposites, or union of the "two halves." In his view, spiritual and *neidan* cultivation should be pursued on two levels, which he calls "fire" and "water" and relates to mind (*xin) and physiology (*shen* 身). On the mental level, one should decrease one's thoughts in order to attain clarity and quiescence (*qingjing); on the physiological level, one should forget the emotions in the midst of action in order to attain harmony. Li also repeatedly emphasizes the necessity of "crushing" or "pulverizing" emptiness, i.e., of forgetting it and dismissing so-called "vain emptiness" (*wankong* 頑空).

Besides Cai Zhiyi, we know the name of five disciples who compiled or completed Li Daochun's works and engaged in dialogues with him: *Miao Shanshi, Zhao Daoke 趙道可, Zhang Yingtan 張應坦, Chai Yuangao 柴元皋, and Deng Decheng 鄧德成.

Isabelle ROBINET

📖 Boltz J. M. 1987a, 179–84, 217–18, 225–26; Li Yuanguo 1988, 478–95; Qing Xitai 1994, 1: 354; Robinet 1995a, 22–24, 45–46, 75–77, 148–56, and 158–63; Yokote Yutaka 1996b, 24–64; Zhan Shichuang 1989, 127–38; Zhan Shichuang 1997b

※ *Zhonghe ji*; *neidan*; Nanzong

Li Daoqian

李道謙

1219–96; *zi*: Hefu 和甫; *hao*: Tianle 天樂 (Heavenly Bliss)

Li Daoqian is the foremost historiographer of the early *Quanzhen order. Although Quanzhen has produced many hagiographic works paying attention to the reliability of their accounts, Li Daoqian's work stands apart in terms of both quality and quantity. Educated in the Confucian tradition in a prominent family from Kaifeng (Henan), Li converted to Taoism after the demise of the Jin state. In 1242, he became the disciple of Yu Zhidao 于志道 (1166–1250), the most eminent Quanzhen master in the Shaanxi area at that time. His talents helped him climb quickly through the Quanzhen hierarchy: he held various posts in Shaanxi and eventually became abbot of the Chongyang gong 重陽宮 (Palace of Double Yang) in 1277. In those same years, he compiled a chronology of the lives of Quanzhen patriarchs, the *Qizhen nianpu (CT 175); a collection of biographies of thirty-seven Quanzhen masters who lived at the Chongyang gong, the *Zhongnan shan Zuting xianzhen neizhuan* 終南山祖庭仙真內傳 (Inner Biographies of the Immortals and Real Men of the Ancestral Court in the Zhongnan Mountains; 1284; CT 955); and an anthology of inscriptions related to the history of Quanzhen, the *Ganshui xianyuan lu (Accounts of the Immortals Who Appeared [After the Revelation] at Ganshui; CT 973).

Li seems to have spent most of his religious life working for the glorification of the Quanzhen order, at a time when Quanzhen was facing harsh criticism for the instant and widespread success of its proselytism. His works appeared around the time when, after the Buddhist accusations of impropriety that led to condemnations without much effect in 1255 and 1258, Emperor Khubilai (Shizu, r. 1260–1294) reopened the trial and, in 1281, ordered the Taoist Canon compiled four decades earlier by the Quanzhen order to be burned (see *Xuandu baozang). One can read in Li's writings an apology of the benign intentions of Quanzhen; his works are devoid of any direct attack on the Buddhists, in sharp contrast to the vilification of Taoism in the notorious Buddhist work, the *Bianwei lu* 辯偽錄 (Accounts of Disputation of [Taoist] Falsehood; T. 2116) by the monk Xiangmai 祥邁 (fl. 1286–91). Li's important responsibilities and his friendship with many famous literati of the time, whose contributions to Quanzhen eulogy appear in the *Ganshui xianyuan lu*, surely influenced his balanced approach to such delicate aspects of recent and contemporary religious history.

Besides his three extant works, Li also wrote an extensive treatise on the Quanzhen holy land, where he spent most of his religious career, entitled *Zhongnan shan ji* 終南山記 (Records of the Zhongnan Mountains), as well as two personal anthologies, all lost.

Vincent GOOSSAERT

📖 Boltz J. M. 1987a, 68; Chen Guofu 1963, 243–44; Miura Shūichi 1992

※ *Ganshui xianyuan lu*; *Qizhen nianpu*; Quanzhen

Li Hanguang

李含光

683–769; *hao*: Xuanjing xiansheng 玄靜先生
(Elder of Mysterious Quiescence)

Li Hanguang, the spiritual heir of *Sima Chengzhen, was recognized as the thirteenth *Shangqing patriarch or Grand Master (*zongshi* 宗師). He spent most of his career supervising the Mount Mao (*Maoshan, Jiangsu) establishment and restoring the textual relics of the Shangqing founders. His unusually well-documented life is recorded in two early inscription texts by renowned officials, as well as in numerous local histories and Taoist anthologies, though not in either Tang dynastic history. The inscription texts present Li as a filial son, skilled calligrapher, and accomplished scholar, whose counsel was sought by emperors and officers of state. As Sima's successor, he was assiduously courted by Tang Xuanzong (r. 712–56), and their extensive correspondence has been preserved.

A biography dated 777 by the eminent scholar Yan Zhenqing 顔真卿 (709–85), like a 772 inscription by Liu Shi 柳識, relates that Li's forebears had held government positions for centuries, but his grandfather chose a life of seclusion, and his father "practiced the Dao of old Dan," (i.e., Laozi). Yan adds that Li's mother was a person of character and intelligence from the eminent Wang clan of Langya 瑯琊 (Shandong). After private study with an obscure local master, Li Hanguang took ordination as a *daoshi* in 705, and devoted himself to studying the Taoist classics. In 729, Sima transmitted his "grand methods" to Li, whereupon Xuanzong summoned him to reside at an abbey on Mount Wangwu (*Wangwu shan, Henan) where Sima had dwelt. A year later, Li returned to Mount Mao and declined further summonses. In 745/746, he was summoned to court, but when Xuanzong requested a transmission of Taoist methods (such as he had earlier received from Sima), Li refused, citing a foot affliction. With his court nonplussed by such an excuse, Xuanzong desisted, but continued to inundate Li with letters and gifts. He installed Li at Ziyang 紫陽 where the Shangqing founders had lived, and there Li continued to restore the manuscripts of the tradition. In 748, he was apparently obliged to grant Xuanzong a ritual transmission, but thereafter he continued to excuse himself from court on grounds of illness.

Li died at Ziyang on 16 December 769. Liu Shi reports that Li announced his "transformation" in advance, and, amidst numinous clouds, ascended "the stages of *xian*-hood." In panegyric passages, Yan Zhenqing asserts that Li "concocted comestible potions," but otherwise gives little reason to envision him as a practitioner of operative alchemy (a legacy of *Tao Hongjing seldom mentioned in accounts of Li's immediate predecessors).

Yan reports that Li compiled a pharmacological guide; study notes on *Daode jing*, *Zhuangzi*, and the *Yijing*; and notes on "esoteric studies" (*neixue* 內學). None of those texts, or others mentioned in Liu Shi's inscription, survive. (See also part 2 of the entry *pudu.*)

Li was apparently the first "Grand Master" since *Wang Yuanzhi to conduct his activities at Mount Mao full-time, and perhaps the endurance of both that great center and the Shangqing sacred literature owed considerably to Li's efforts. His great fame in courtly circles, meanwhile, doubtless owed to his status as the successor to Sima Chengzhen. The odd fact that the compilers of the *Jiu Tangshu* (Old History of the Tang) chose to ignore a figure of such eminence seems explainable by the fact that Li, unlike other Taoists of his day, could not easily be portrayed as having played any exemplary political role.

Russell KIRKLAND

📖 Barrett 1996, 69–70; Chen Guofu 1963, 59–61; Kirkland 1986a, 72–95, 298–323; Kirkland 1986b; Schafer 1989, 82–84

※ Shangqing

Li Hong

李弘

The first traces of a divinized Laozi go back to the imperial sacrifices of 165 CE (see *Laozi ming*). It is likely, however, that the ancient sage was already deemed to be a god before his official divinization. He held a central position in the Taoist movements of the second century: identified with the Dao itself, Laozi is the Most High Lord Lao (Taishang Laojun 太上老君; see *Laozi and Laojun), endowed with the attributes of a primordial deity born before the coagulation of the original energies of the universe. He is an omnipotent deity who controls the universal rhythms and intervenes in worldly history. In times of crisis, he reiterates his teaching, appearing to saints who are worthy of his revelations or to sovereigns who benefit from his political advice. In other instances, he manifests himself to confirm the Heavenly Mandate (*tianming* 天命) of the ruling dynasty.

The copious revealed literature produced by different Taoist currents during the Six Dynasties is similarly claimed to have a divine origin. The stereotyped introductory formula "Dao yan" 道言 ("The Dao says"), used profusely in these holy scriptures, confers transcendental authority and authenticity upon them. It no doubt echoes the "Fo shuo" 佛說 ("The Buddha says" or "preaches") of Mahāyāna (Great Vehicle) *sūtras*. Thus Lord Lao, personification of the Dao, addresses himself to human creatures in order to transmit methods of longevity or salvation, moral precepts, and liturgical codes.

The birth of this anthropomorphic Dao coincides with the formation of Taoist self-identity in the first centuries CE. Each epiphany of Lord Lao corresponds to a crucial episode of Taoist religious history. According to the *Zhengyi fawen Tianshi jiaojie kejing* 正一法文天師教戒科經 (CT 789, 13a–b; Bokenkamp 1997, 168–70) and the *Santian neijie jing* (1.8b–9b; Bokenkamp 1997, 220–23), the first one occurred at the end of the Zhou dynasty (third century BCE), when Laozi revealed the *Taiping jing* (Scripture of Great Peace). Later he returned to earth to pronounce the *Daode jing*. He then manifested himself again as another "perfected immortal"—the Buddha. His epiphany of 142 CE inaugurated the history of the Taoist religion with the foundation of the *Tianshi dao*. This image of Laozi as a sage and compassionate counselor hides a more extreme aspect of the god's personality: his messianic vocation. Under the appellation of Li Hong or Li zhenjun 李真君 (Li the Perfected Lord; Li is the surname of Laozi's mother), Laozi was expected to save the world.

From the Han period onward, Li Hong (whose name is often written as a pun: 木子弓口, 弓口十八子, or 木子三台) emerged as the preeminent Chinese messiah. Expectations focusing on his coming gave birth to a messianic and millenarian tradition that reached its climax during the turbulent period of the Six Dynasties, when the main Taoist movements prophesied Li Hong's Parousia. The apocalyptic scriptures produced by these movements describe the messiah's advent. Li Hong was expected to descend to earth in a *renchen* 壬辰 year (the twenty-ninth of the sexagesimal cycle; see table 10) to usher in a reign of Great Peace (*taiping*) in an entirely renewed universe, cleansed of all traces of evil and inhabited only by the initiated and the immortal "seed-people" (*zhongmin*).

Lord Li, the savior, is also a prophet. He predicts his own advent as well as the preceding apocalyptic horrors, the pangs of the last days. These prophecies have a more or less revolutionary intensity depending on their milieu. For sectarian movements such as the one that produced the *Dongyuan shenzhou jing*, a political message underlies the religious import: the apocalyptic outburst is both the result and the cause of the fall of the ruling Jin dynasty, and Li Hong's advent anticipates the upcoming reestablishment of the Han house by Liu Yu 劉裕 (356–422), founder of the new Liu Song dynasty (420–79). The political program advanced by these devotees, however, does not go beyond a simplistic, conformist utopia. Li Hong would govern a kingdom of absolute equality, peace, and happiness through non-action (*wuwei*). All the virtuous survivors of the apocalypse—equally tall, good looking and immortal—would be granted high official posts in the theocratic bureaucracy.

Cosmic god for the intellectual elite of orthodox Taoism, and messianic bearer of a new Heavenly Mandate for sectarian Taoists, Li Hong shepherded the hopes of people prey to apocalyptic anxiety. Several prophets in flesh and blood who called themselves Li or Li Hong, mentioned in the official histories since the Han period, were executed for deceiving the masses and causing social disorder. Most of them belonged to the *Lijia dao, a long-lasting sect that spread throughout southern China during the Six Dynasties, and was condemned as heterodox by the Taoists themselves.

Nevertheless, Li Hong's destiny was by no means limited to that of a flouted and persecuted heretic. At the opposite end of the social scale, he was also honored as an imperial messiah: official ideology promptly took over Taoist messianic beliefs and used them for dynastic legitimation. Many emperors claimed to be incarnations of the divine Lord to justify their mandates. The tradition of Li as messiah-emperor continued from the Han period down to at least the Tang dynasty, of which Li was considered to be the divine ancestor (Bokenkamp 1994).

The appropriation of Li Hong's myth by the ruling houses did not preclude his appearance, time and again, as a popular savior prophet. His last appearance in Chinese history was in 1112 CE, when he was executed for fomenting a rebellion.

Christine MOLLIER

📖 Bokenkamp 1997, 275–306 passim; Li Fengmao 1986, 282–304; Mollier 1990, 10–13, 159–62; Seidel 1969; Seidel 1969–70; Sunayama Minoru 1990, 69–92

※ Laozi and Laojun; *housheng; Housheng daojun lieji*; APOCALYPTIC ESCHATOLOGY; MESSIANISM AND MILLENARIANISM

Li Quan

李筌

fl. 713–60; *hao*: Daguan zi 達觀子 (Master of Penetrating Observation), Shaoshi shanren 少室山人 (Man of Mount Shaoshi)

Li Quan served in several official positions during the Kaiyuan reign period (713–41), first as deputy commander of a regional defense force in the south, then as a Vice Censor-in-Chief (*yushi zhongcheng* 御史中丞) at the capital, and finally as a Prefect (*cishi* 刺史) of a prefecture in Hebei. His career in government came to an end when he offended the dictatorial chief minister Li Linfu 李林甫 (?–752) who demoted him. Thereafter, he forsook government service, took up the life of a Taoist recluse and roamed among the holy mountains of China.

On a visit to Mount Song (*Songshan, Henan) southeast of Luoyang, Li Quan discovered a copy of the *Yinfu jing (Scripture of the Hidden Accordance) written in vermilion ink on white silk. It was said to be one of several copies of the text that *Kou Qianzhi (365?–448) had deposited on various sacred mountains in 441. He copied and recited it, but could not understand its metaphysical subject matter and recondite terminology. Later he encountered an old woman at Mount Li (Lishan 驪山, Shaanxi) just east of Chang'an. The crone was able to explain the text to Li, and presumably it was on the basis of her insight that he composed his commentary to it (CT 110), one of twenty annotations and commentaries that survive in the Taoist Canon.

Charles D. BENN

📖 Qing Xitai 1988–95, 2: 254–63; Qing Xitai 1994, 1: 282–83; Rand 1979

※ *Yinfu jing*; TAOISM AND THE MILITARY ARTS

Li Rong

李榮

fl. 658–63; *hao*: Renzhen zi 任真子
(Master of Following Perfection)

Li Rong was a *Chongxuan (Twofold Mystery) thinker of the seventh century. He came from Mianxian 綿縣 (northern Sichuan) and became a Taoist monk in his early years, receiving basic training on Mount Fule (Fule shan 富樂山) in his home district. In the 650s, he appeared in the capital, Chang'an, where he was in close contact with high-class literati. In 658, 660, and 663, he served at the court debates as a defender of Taoism, but—at least according to Buddhist sources—shamefully embarrassed himself, being reduced to speechless exasperation on more than one occasion. In addition, the Buddhists accused him of plagiarizing Buddhist *sūtras* and of gleefully enjoying the fire that devastated the Da xingshan si 大興善寺 (Great Monastery of Flourishing Goodness) in the late 650s.

As a philosopher, Li Rong is known for his commentaries to the *Daode jing* and the *Xisheng jing (Scripture of Western Ascension). His thought closely follows the patterns of Chongxuan, focusing on the attainment of the Dao through two levels of truth and an increasing forgetfulness (*wang* 忘) and emptiness (*xu* 虛). In addition, he makes a more subtle distinction between worldly knowledge of good and evil, the wisdom of emptiness and Non-being, and insight that reflects the reality of the world with wisdom. He also emphasizes the necessity for enlightened teachers and sages in the world, and outlines their duties toward humanity, rejecting the ideal of the recluse who remains entirely uninvolved. His vision of self-cultivation, finally, is more physical than that commonly associated with Chongxuan, stressing the importance of *qi and its cultivation.

In a different vein, Li Rong is mentioned in Xuanyi's 玄嶷 (fl. 684–704) *Zhenzheng lun (Essays of Examination and Correction, 52.386c) as the compiler of the *Xiyu jing* 洗浴經 (Scripture of Ritual Cleanliness; S. 3380), a short manuscript set in the Palace of the Seven Treasures (Qibao gong 七寶宮) of the Heaven of the Mysterious Metropolis (Xuandu 玄都). Yuanshi tianzun 元始天尊 (Celestial Worthy of Original Commencement; see *sanqing) here addresses a holy assembly in the ten directions and gives instructions on how to purify oneself properly for interaction with the divine: upon entering the "quiet chamber" (*jingshi), one should scatter flowers, burn incense (see *jinxiang), and thoroughly cleanse one's body and mind. Although the text is devotional in flavor, it may yet be in some way related to Li Rong.

Li Rong's commentary to the *Daode jing* is preserved partly in the *Daode zhenjing zhu* 道德真經注 (Commentary to the Authentic Scripture of the Dao and Its Virtue; eleventh century; CT 722) and partly in the *Dunhuang manuscripts P. 2577, 2594, 2864, 3237, 3777, and S. 2060; it is available in a critical edition by Fujiwara Takao (1983). His work on the *Xisheng jing*, entitled *Xisheng jing jizhu* 西昇經集注 (Collected Commentaries to the Scripture of Western Ascension; CT 726), has also been edited by Fujiwara (1986–88).

Livia KOHN

📖 Fujiwara Takao 1979; Fujiwara Takao 1983 (crit. ed. of the *Xisheng jing* comm.); Fujiwara Takao 1985; Fujiwara Takao 1986–88 (crit. ed. of the *Daode jing* comm.); Kohn 1991a, 189–211; Kohn 1992a, 141 and 145–46; Meng Wentong 1948a; Ōfuchi Ninji 1978–79, 1: 239–41 (crit. notes on the Dunhuang mss.) and 2: 476–87 (reprod. of the Dunhuang mss.); Qing Xitai 1988–95, 2: 190–205; Robinet 1977, 105–6; Sunayama Minoru 1990, 326–31 and passim

※ Chongxuan

Li Shaojun

李少君

fl. ca. 133 BCE

Li Shaojun, a *fangshi* who lived during the Former Han dynasty, is the earliest known Chinese alchemist. He was active in the years when Han Wudi (r. 141–87 BCE) was deliberating on the correct way to perform the *feng* 封 and *shan* 禪 rituals in honor of Heaven and Earth. The *fangshi* were one of the parties involved in the debate. According to the *Shiji* (Records of the Historian), Li suggested around 133 BCE that Wudi should perform a ceremony before a furnace asking divine beings (*wu* 物) to favor the compounding of an elixir. In the presence of those beings, cinnabar would transmute itself into a gold fit to cast vessels for eating and drinking. Taking food and drink from them would extend the emperor's life and enable him to meet the immortals. After seeing them, the emperor could perform the *feng* and *shan* rituals and obtain immortality himself; this is what the Yellow Emperor (*Huangdi) did at the beginning of human time. After he heard Li Shaojun's speech, adds the *Shiji*, Wudi devoted himself to alchemical experiments (*Shiji*, 28.1385; trans. Watson 1961, 2: 39).

This episode represents the first instance of imperial patronage of *waidan* practices, which continued during the Six Dynasties and intensified in the Tang period (Li Guorong 1994). Li Shaojun's method, moreover, shows that rituals were associated with *waidan* since its earliest recorded beginnings. Also of interest is the mention of dishes and cups cast with alchemical gold, which is not isolated in the extant *waidan* literature: the extant version of the *Jinye jing* is one of the texts that describes a similar method. Despite all this, Li Shaojun's image in the later tradition is not always positive. The commentary to the *Jiudan jing*, in particular, criticizes him because his method gave more importance to the deity of the furnace than to the gods associated with the *Taiqing methods, such as the Great One (*Taiyi) and the Yellow Emperor (see *Huangdi jiuding shendan jingjue* 黃帝九鼎神丹經訣; CT 885, 13.1a–2b).

The commentary describes Li's practice as *zuodao* ("left ways," a term often applied to magic) and claims that the correct *waidan* methods are those of the Taiqing tradition.

Fabrizio PREGADIO

📖 Barrett 1987b; Campany 2002, 222–28; Needham 1976, 29–33; Pregadio 2006b, 29–32; Robinet 1984, 1: 11–12 and 24–25

※ *fangshi*; *waidan*

Li Xiong

李雄

270–334

Li Xiong, the first emperor of the non-Chinese state of Cheng-Han 成漢 (303–47), was from a hereditary Taoist family and ruled his state by Taoist precepts. Xiong's great-grandfather, Li Hu 李虎, was a local leader of the Zong 賨 ethnicity in northern Sichuan during the late second and early third centuries. He converted to Taoism and led a group of 500 households to join the Celestial Master (*Tianshi dao) kingdom of *Zhang Lu in the Hanzhong 漢中 region (modern Sichuan/Shaanxi). When that state was conquered by Cao Cao 曹操 in 215, Li Hu and many of his coreligionists, Chinese and non-Chinese, were transferred to the Gansu region, where they lived for the next eighty years. Successive years of civil disorder, pestilence, and natural disasters prompted Xiong's father, Li Te 李特, to lead a huge body of migrants back to Sichuan at the beginning of the fourth century. In Sichuan, the migrants came into conflict with the local authorities. After Li Te was captured and executed, Li Xiong succeeded to power and eventually conquered the entire region of modern Sichuan as well as parts of Shaanxi, Guizhou, and Yunnan.

Li Xiong was aided and advised by a local Taoist leader named *Fan Changsheng, who provided economic support and mantic counsel. Li Xiong offered the throne to Fan, who declined, citing prophecies that one surnamed Li was destined to rule. Xiong acceded to the throne as first king, then emperor, proclaiming his state to be Great Perfection (*Dacheng), after a passage from the *Shijing* 詩經 (Book of Odes) that had been linked to the establishment of an age of Great Peace (*taiping). Fan was made Chancellor and given the title Great Master of the Four Seasons, the Eight Nodes, and Heaven and Earth (Sishi bajie tiandi taishi 四時八節天地太師), an appointment reminiscent of both titles held by Laozi in texts like the *Laozi bianhua jing* (Scripture of the

Transformations of Laozi) and the Celestial Master. Xiong enacted a series of policies, including a simplified legal code, leniency in the administration of justice, reduced taxes, and the establishment of schools, that resemble descriptions of a Taoist utopia. When Fan Changsheng died, he was succeeded in his post of Chancellor by his son. The hereditary connections of the Li family with Celestial Master Taoism, the use of prophecies foretelling a Taoist savior surnamed Li, the exalted position of the Fan family, and the domestic policies pursued by the state all suggest that a vision of a utopian Taoist state played a role in the creation and administration of Great Perfection.

Terry KLEEMAN

📖 Kleeman 1998, passim; Seidel 1969–70, 233–36; Stein R. A. 1963, 33–35

※ Fan Changsheng; Dacheng

Li Xiyue

李西月

1806–56; original *ming*: Pingquan 平權; *zi*: Tuanyang 團陽; *hao*: Hanxu zi 涵虛子 (Master Who Encompasses Emptiness), Changyi shan ren 長乙山人 (Man of Mount Changyi), Yuanqiao waishi 圓嶠外史 (The External Secretary of the Rounded Ridge)

Li Xiyue, the alleged founder of the Western Branch (Xipai 西派) of late *neidan, was a native of Leshan 樂山 in Sichuan. He claimed to have received instructions on *neidan* from *Zhang Sanfeng, whose attributed writings he edited in 1844 as the *Zhang Sanfeng quanji* 張三丰全集 (Complete Collection of Zhang Sanfeng). Li states that later he met the immortal *Lü Dongbin in a temple on Mount Emei (*Emei shan, Sichuan) and decided to found a new *neidan* movement that included Laozi, *Yin Xi, *Chen Tuan, and Zhang Sanfeng among its patriarchs. First called Yinxian pai 隱仙派 (Branch of the Concealed Immortal) or Youlong pai 猶龍派 (Branch of the One Resembling a Dragon) in honor of Laozi, the movement later became known as the Western Branch. Although this designation is opposed to *Lu Xixing's Eastern Branch (Dongpai 東派), the terms "eastern" and "western" here simply designate the regions where the two movements had spread, Jiangxi and Jiangsu on the east and Sichuan on the west.

Li's writings are mainly inspired by the works of Lu Xixing and Sun Ruzhong 孫汝忠 (fl. 1615). Besides the *Zhang Sanfeng quanji*, they include the *Daoqiong tan* 道窮談 (Exhaustive Discussion of the Way), the *Sanche bizhi*

三車祕旨 (Secret Directions on the Three Chariots), the *Jiuceng lianxin fa* 九層鍊心法 (Methods for the Purification of the Mind in Nine Stages), the *Taishang shisan jing zhujie* 太上十三經注解 (Commentaries and Explications to Thirteen Scriptures of the Most High), and the *Haishan qiyu* 海山奇遇 (Strange Encounter in a Retreat in Beihai; consisting of a chronology of Lü Dongbin's life and miracles divulged to Lu Xixing by the immortal himself in his retreat in Jiangsu). These texts were published during Li's lifetime, except for the *Daoqiong tan* and the *Sanche bizhi* which were first printed in 1937 by *Chen Yingning.

Li Xiyue's teachings are close to those of the Eastern Branch and the Southern Lineage (*Nanzong) of *neidan*. His system consists of two major stages. The first focuses on cleansing the mind and purifying the self through concentration (*ding) and individual practice (*qingxiu* 清修 or "pure cultivation"). Instructions on this stage are found in the *Jiuceng lianxin fa*. This is followed by the stage of attaining the Dao through the union of Yin and Yang with the help of a partner. The training, however, is further divided into several levels. For example, the stage of "laying the foundations" (*zhuji* 築基) divides into "laying the minor foundations" and "laying the greater foundations." Likewise, "nourishing the self" (*yangji* 養己) includes "self-nourishment" (*ziyang* 自養) and "mutual nourishment" (*xiangyang* 相養), and "purification of the self" (*lianji* 鍊己) includes an "inner purification" and an "outer purification." Through these divisions and categories, the Western School offers one of the most complex systems of *neidan* practice.

Farzeen BALDRIAN-HUSSEIN

📖 Qing Xitai 1988–95, 4: 344–60; Qing Xitai 1994, 1: 401–2

※ *neidan*

liandu

鍊度 (*or:* 煉度)

Salvation through Refinement

Liandu is a compound made of the words *lian* 鍊, here having the sense of bringing rebirth to the "spiritual body" (*hunshen* 魂身) of the deceased by refining it with fire and water, and *du* 度, meaning to have the spirit cross over from the underworld and ascend to the Heavenly Hall (*tiantang* 天堂). While the rite called *liandu* became the final rite of the Yellow Register Retreat (*huanglu zhai) only during the Song period, several sources show that the idea of "salvation through refinement" dates from the Six Dynasties. In particular, the *Duren jing (Scripture on Salvation) contains evidence of the idea that rebirth results from a process of refining when it states that "the *hun soul of the deceased (sihun 死魂) is refined and, through transcendent mutation (xianhua 仙化), becomes human" (see Bokenkamp 1997, 418). The Miedu wulian shengshi miaojing 滅度五鍊生尸妙經 (Wondrous Scripture on Salvation through Extinction and the Fivefold Refinement of the Corpse; CT 369), dating from the Six Dynasties, further reveals that rebirth of the body of the deceased can be brought about through the "living breath" (shengqi 生氣) of the five directions, by burying a stone inscribed with the Authentic Scripts (zhenwen 真文) of the five directions in the graveyard. According to the Tang-dynasty *Chisong zi zhangli (Master Red-Pine's Almanac of Petitions, 6.16b), the petitions offered to the deities in the Way of the Celestial Masters (*Tianshi dao) included a petition for rebirth connected with the idea of "salvation through refinement."

The Taoist rite of Salvation through Refinement, on the other hand, was developed during the Northern Song period and was incorporated into the *Lingbao dafa (Great Rites of the Numinous Treasure) corpus. Evidence that it was a new rite is found in Jin Yunzhong's 金允中 (fl. 1224–25) *Shangqing lingbao dafa (Great Rites of the Numinous Treasure of Highest Clarity; CT 1223, 17.19a) which states that when *Du Guangting (850–933) edited ritual texts in the late ninth century, Salvation through Refinement was not yet being performed. Its importance in the Song period may be gauged by the fact that liturgical texts associated with the various forms of Great Rites of the Numinous Treasure devote much space to explanations of the liandu rite, to the extent that they surpass in number all other rites in the Walking the Way (*xingdao) section of the ritual. As described in Jin Yunzhong's work (j. 37), the central element in the rite of Salvation through Refinement is the refinement of the "spiritual body" through the power of water and fire. As a result, the "spirit pneuma" (shenqi 神氣) is animated in the organs and limbs of the deceased through the power of both the "living breath" of the five directions and the recitation of the *Shengshen jing (Scripture of the Life-Giving Spirits).

Alchemical techniques for the salvation of the dead. The Song-dynasty *Lingbao yujian (Jade Mirror of the Numinous Treasure; CT 547, j. 38) explains the liandu rite by saying that externally the priest prepares water and fire, while internally he joins the trigrams kan 坎 ☵ and li 離 ☲, which represent Real Fire and Real Water. This is related to the idea that the priest can extend the efficacious power of the inner alchemical (*neidan) techniques that he performs within his own body to the soul of the deceased.

More details on these techniques are found in Wang Qizhen's 王契真 (fl. ca. 1250) *Shangqing lingbao dafa (Great Rites of the Numinous Treasure of

Highest Clarity; CT 1221, 59.11a–13b). Here the priest visualizes his Muddy Pellet (*niwan*, the Cinnabar Field or *dantian* in the head) as the Three Heavens (*santian*; see *santian* and *liutian*), the top of his head as the Nine Heavens and the Thirty-Six Heavens (*jiutian* and *sanshiliu tian*), his left eye as the Palace of the Sun (*rigong* 日宮), his right eye as the Palace of the Moon (*yuegong* 月宮), the seven orifices of his face as the seven stars of the Northern Dipper (*beidou*), the area behind the neck as the Murky and Veiled Remote Tower (*yuluo xiaotai* 鬱羅蕭臺), the mouth as the Celestial River (*tianhe* 天河), the trachea as the Twelve-storied Pavilion (*shi'er chong lou* 十二重樓), the heart as the Fire Palace on the Vermilion Mound (Zhuling huofu 朱陵火俯), the backbone as the Celestial Staircase (*tianjie* 天階), the left kidney as the Water Pond (*shuichi* 水池), the right kidney as the Fire Swamp (*huozhao* 火沼), and the Caudal Funnel (*weilü* 尾閭, a point in the area of the coccyx; see *sanguan*) as the Yin pass. After the priest refines the soul of the deceased in the Water Pond and the Fire Swamp within his body, divine officers lead the soul to ascend the Celestial Staircase and enter the Fire Palace. By burning talismans the priest is said to be able to ensure that the deceased "crosses the bridge" (see *guoqiao*). One of the countless "fire dragons" (*huolong* 火龍) within the Fire Swamp takes the soul—now refined and transformed into an "infant"—on its back and flies with it up to the Remote Tower to receive rebirth according to its spiritual rank.

MARUYAMA Hiroshi

📖 Boltz J. M. 1983; Lagerwey 1987c, 233–35; Little 2000b, 178–79; Maruyama Hiroshi 1994b; Ōfuchi Ninji 1983, 554–65; Qing Xitai 1994, 3: 233–39

※ *lianxing*; DEATH AND AFTERLIFE; MEDITATION AND VISUALIZATION; REBIRTH

lianqi

鍊氣 (or: 煉氣)

refining breath; refining pneuma

Lianqi designates a technique for purifying the breath (or pneuma) throughout the body. In the Tang period, the *Yanling xiansheng ji xinjiu fuqi jing* 延陵先生集新舊服氣經 (Scripture on New and Old Methods for the Ingestion of Breath Collected by the Elder of Yanling) describes the method as follows: "Harmonize the breath and swallow it. When you do this, you must practice breath retention (*biqi*) for as long as possible. 'Obscure your mind' (*mingxin*

冥心), stop your thoughts, follow the movement of the breath, release and regulate it. . . . It is not necessary to practice daily, but mainly when the mind is clear and relaxed, for example every five or ten days" (CT 825, 23b–25a).

Besides the *Xinjiu fuqi jing*, other texts containing brief descriptions of the *lianqi* method include the *Songshan Taiwu xiansheng qijing* 嵩山太無先生氣經 (Scripture on Breath by the Elder of Great Non-Being from Mount Song; CT 824, 1.7a–b; trans. Huang Jane 1987–90, 21) and the *Huanzhen xiansheng fu nei yuanqi jue* 幻真先生服內元氣訣 (Instructions on the Ingestion of the Inner Original Breath According to the Elder of Illusory Perfection; CT 828, 5a–b, and YJQQ 60.18b–19c; trans. Despeux 1988, 75–76, from the version in the *Chifeng sui*).

Catherine DESPEUX

📖 Maspero 1981, 474–76

※ *yangsheng*

lianxing

錬形 (*or*: 煉形)

"refining the form"

Early Taoist texts and sources related to classical cosmology represent "form" (*xing*) as a threshold between the Dao and objects, as an ontologic and cosmogonic stage situated between "images" (*xiang*) and matter (*zhi* 質), and as a lodging for spirit (*shen*). The classical statement in this regard is found in the *Xici* 繫辭 (Appended Statements) portion of the *Yijing*: "What is above the form is called the Dao; what is below the form is called an object (*qi* 器)" (see Wilhelm R. 1950, 323). Other works similarly describe form as an intermediate element in the ontologic shift from the Formless (*wuxing* 無形) to the "ten thousand things." Among them is a Han-dynasty apocryphal text on the *Yijing* that depicts the shift as happening in four stages: the first is undifferentiated Chaos (*hunlun* 渾淪; see *hundun*), while the other three see the emergence of pneuma (*qi*), form, and matter, respectively (Robinet 1997a, 134–35, 139–40; also in *Liezi* 1, trans. Graham 1960, 18–19). At the end of this process, form continues to play its intermediary role as a dwelling for and counterpart of spirit (*shen*). In this way, as stated in *Huainan zi* 1, it is one of the three major constituents of life, together with spirit and pneuma (breath).

"Release from the form." Building on this background, *neidan* and other traditions maintain that the locus of self-cultivation is not the material body (*ti*

體) but the "form" (*xing), which one should transcend in order to attain the Dao. The notion of "release from the form" (xingjie 形解) first appears in a *Mawangdui manuscript, the Shiwen 十問 (Ten Questions; trans. Harper 1998, 385–411). Here "flowing into the form" (liuxing 流形) is said to produce life, but "when flowing into the form produces a body (ti) . . . death occurs." The Shiwen thus distinguishes the rise of the form from the rise of the body, saying that the generation of the form leads to life while the generation of the body leads to death. To invert this sequence, one should cultivate one's breath in order to fill one's form with the "culminant essence of Heaven and Earth (tiandi zhi zhijing 天地之至精)." The person who is capable of doing this obtains "release from the form."

"Release from the form" is also often associated with "release from the corpse" (or "from the mortal body," *shijie) as an instance of undergoing a "metamorphosis" (*bianhua). The relation between these two notions is explicit in Taoist sources of the Han and Six Dynasties, where form is the locus of refining after death. In the Way of the Celestial Masters (*Tianshi dao), the designated place for this post-mortem purification is the Palace of Taiyin 太陰 or Great Darkness, which the *Xiang'er commentary to the Daode jing (ca. 200 CE) describes as "the place where those who have accumulated the Dao refine their form" before they obtain rebirth (fusheng 復生; Bokenkamp 1997, 102 and 135).

This type of release from the world, which is said to happen at midnight (*Zhengao, 4.17a; *Wushang biyao, 87.4b; see Lagerwey 1981b, 185), is contrasted with the superior "ascension to Heaven in broad daylight" (bairi shengtian 白日昇天) or more precisely (as shown by several accounts in hagiographic texts) "at midday" (see Yoshikawa Tadao 1992b, 176–85). The adept who ascends to Heaven typically becomes a member of the celestial bureaucracy by rising to one of the heavens distinguished in Daoist cosmography, i.e., to the celestial domain corresponding to the state of realization attained at the time of death. From there, he does not return to the human world; on the contrary, he can continue his progress toward higher states and ascend to higher heavens. By contrast, "release from the corpse" occurs by undertaking a descent to Great Darkness, located in the tenebrous regions of the extreme north, which in traditional Chinese cosmography is situated "below" instead of "above" (except when the north is equivalent to the Center). The direction of the journey undertaken to undergo "release from the corpse," in other words, is opposite to the one followed to ascend to Heaven. These two ways of deliverance, therefore, are distinguished by opposite but corresponding features: ascent and descent, midday and midnight, light and darkness, Sun (ri 日) and Moon (taiyin 太陰). Moreover, ascent to Heaven is the way of non-return to the world: one continues one's spiritual journey ascending from one empyrean to the next. On the contrary, descent to Great Darkness is the way of return: the adept obtains a rebirth, or "second birth," and comes back to the world in a body that preserves itself indefinitely, so that he may continue his search for a higher form of liberation. The final release from the world of form may happen at any time, or at the conclusion of the cosmic cycle in which he lives.

"Refinement of the form" is not attainable only by living adepts. The *Lingbao corpus describes a rite that enables the dead to refine their forms in Great Darkness and their celestial souls (*hun) in the Southern Palace (Nangong 南宮); after some years, the refined body and the purified celestial souls reunite for rebirth (Bokenkamp 1989). In *Shangqing Taoism, adepts delivered the same benefit to their ancestors through meditation practices, thus allowing them to bathe in the Water of Smelting Refinement (*yelian zhi shui* 冶鍊之水), refine their forms, and "receive a new embryo" (*gengtai* 更胎; Robinet 1984, 1: 170–73).

Elsewhere, the *Xiang'er* (trl. Bokenkamp 1997, 89 and 92) criticizes those who try to "refine the form" through visualization practices, believing that the inner gods are forms taken by the Dao. Indeed, meditation on one's inner gods is also described as "refining one's form" (*Baopu zi* 5.111, 6.128). A passage found in both the Outer and Inner versions of the *Huangting jing* (Scripture of the Yellow Court) says that "hiding" oneself (*fu* 伏) in Great Darkness results in "seeing one's own form" (*jian wu xing* 見吾形) or in "achieving one's own form" (*cheng wu xing* 成吾形), that is, the "real form" (*zhenxing* 真形) beyond one's material body.

Underlying these different trends of thought and religious practice is the view that achieving transcendence requires going beyond one's own body. "Form" provides the necessary mediation in this task. As often occurs, *neidan* in this instance inherits and develops ideas and customs that originated in various contexts—specifically, Taoist thought, early cosmology, Han-Six Dynasties religious traditions, and meditation practices.

Fabrizio PREGADIO

📖 Pregadio 2004; Robinet 1979b; Sakade Yoshinobu 1983b

※ *liandu*; *xing*; *neidan*; DEATH AND AFTERLIFE; MEDITATION AND VISUALIZATION; TAOIST VIEWS OF THE HUMAN BODY

Lidai chongdao ji

歷代崇道記

Records of the Veneration of the Dao
over Successive Generations

The *Lidai chongdao ji* (CT 593), originally entitled *Lidai diwang chongdao ji* 歷代帝王崇道記 (Records of the Veneration of the Dao by Sovereigns over Successive Generations), is a short text compiled by *Du Guangting (850–933). Du submitted it to the throne on January 4 of 885 just before the Tang court returned to Chang'an after a three-year exile in Chengdu. The text commences with the reign of King Mu of the Zhou (Muwang, r. 956–918 BCE) and concludes in 884 CE. However, eighty-five percent of the work covers the Tang dynasty (618–907) and about one fourth of it only four years, 881–84, in the reign of Tang Xizong (r. 873–88). The portion devoted to the pre-Tang period is largely a fabrication supplying imaginary figures for the number of temples established and priests ordained by various emperors.

This collection of notes is one of the more important sources for the history of Taoism during the Tang dynasty, which favored the religion for ideological reasons. When he wrote the *Lidai chongdao ji*, Du Guangting was a member of Xizong's court, specifically a drafter of decrees, who clearly had access to official documents that are no longer extant. The message of this text is simple: rulers who patronized Taoism by building temples and ordaining priests would be rewarded with signs such as miracles and epiphanies. It also offered some hope to the Tang, severely weakened by rebellions between 875 and 884, that it would survive with the assistance of the gods.

The *Lidai chongdao ji* is most reliable for the reign of Xizong (pp. 15a–20a), but less so for earlier epochs of the Tang. For the latter one should consult the *Cefu yuangui* 冊府元龜 (Outstanding Models from the Storehouse of Literature; 1013; *j.* 53–54) where the remnants of the Tang's "veritable records" survive, the *Tang huiyao* 唐會要 (Assembled Essentials of the Tang; 961; *j.* 50), and the dynastic histories as well as the *Hunyuan shengji (Saintly Chronicle of Chaotic Origin) and the *Youlong zhuan (Like unto a Dragon).

Charles D. BENN

📖 Barrett 1996, 94–95; Boltz J. M. 1987a, 129–31; Verellen 1989, 97–100

※ Du Guangting

Liexian zhuan

列仙傳

Biographies of Exemplary Immortals

The *Liexian zhuan* is the first collection of immortals' biographies to have survived. It is traditionally ascribed to Liu Xiang 劉向 (77–8 or 6 BCE), the important scholar, librarian, and statesman of the Former Han (IC 583–84). Liu's name is attached to many works from this period in the bibliographical chapter of the *Hanshu* (History of the Former Han) but the *Liexian zhuan* is not mentioned there. However, the attribution of the *Liexian zhuan* to Liu Xiang is accepted by *Ge Hong (283–343) in his *Baopu zi* so if he is not responsible for the work, the attribution to him occurred relatively early. It has been pointed out that sections of the text could not have been written until the second century CE, so at the very least some later editing took place. In short, the traditional attribution should be regarded as questionable.

Liu is also given credit for two other works which have titles of similar form: *Lienü zhuan* 列女傳 (Biographies of Exemplary Women) and *Lieshi zhuan* 列士傳 (Biographies of Exemplary Officials). It should be noted that he was an official reader of the *Guliang* 穀梁 tradition of the *Chunqiu* 春秋 (Spring and Autumn Annals) and later was responsible for the first serious codification of Chinese books. In other words, he was firmly placed within the orthodox scholarly milieu of his period. We might reasonably conclude that when the *Liexian zhuan* was compiled the recording and reading of immortals' lives belonged to the general educated world and was not the province of a bounded religious community. Indeed, the collection later became widely known in general scholarly circles and was a source for literary allusion for most educated Chinese of later periods.

There are generally reckoned to be seventy biographical notices in the *Liexian zhuan* divided into two chapters. Among the lives, the briefest have fewer than two hundred characters, with appended encomia (*zan* 讚). Sets of these encomia were produced later than the biographies, appearing after the 330s, and are in the form of hymns of praise to the immortals recorded. The authorship of the surviving encomia, found in the best edition of the *Liexian zhuan*—in the Taoist Canon (CT 294)—is disputed. Like most other texts from the early period of Chinese history, a close analysis of citations preserved in old encyclopedias, commentaries, and other sources shows that portions of text have been lost from the earliest "complete" versions of the *Liexian zhuan* that have survived. A preface exists in some versions of the text but not the one in the Taoist Canon; this preface also cannot be regarded as reliable.

The biographies of the *Liexian zhuan* are all introduced in the standard manner stating name, sometimes style (*zi* 字), usually native place (or the formula "No one knows where he came from"), and often the period in which the subject of the biography lived. However, although they are full of useful information, not many of them provide anything resembling a rounded narrative of a life. The collection starts with the biography of *Chisong zi, of "the time of Shennong 神農," and continues in roughly chronological order. Many famous figures in Taoism have biographies in this collection, including *Huangdi, *Pengzu, *Wangzi Qiao as well as Laozi himself and the Guardian of the Pass, *Yin Xi. There are other people who are also known from the *Hanshu* to have been at the Qin and Han courts such as *Anqi Sheng and *Dongfang Shuo.

A brief but typical biography concerns Chang Rong 昌容:

> Chang Rong was a follower of the Dao from Mount Chang (Changshan 常山, i.e., the *Hengshan 恆山, Shanxi). She called herself the daughter of the King of Yin (Yinwang nü 殷王女) and ate roots of rubus (*penglei* 蓬虆). She would come and go, ascending and descending. People saw her for some two hundred years yet she always looked about twenty. When she was able to get purple grass she sold it to dyers and gave the proceeds to widows and orphans. It was like this for generations. Thousands came to make offerings at her shrine. (CT 294, 2.5a–b)

Although the *Liexian zhuan* is found in the Taoist Canon, Max Kaltenmark's translation (1953) also includes an edited text with learned annotations and is more convenient to use.

Benjamin PENNY

📖 Kaltenmark 1953, Sawada Mizuho 1988; Smith Th. E. 1998

※ HAGIOGRAPHY

Liezi

列子

Book of Master Lie

The *Liezi*, also known as *Chongxu zhide zhenjing* 沖虛至德真經 (Authentic Scripture on the Ultimate Virtue of Unfathomable Emptiness), is a philosophical Taoist text in eight chapters that goes back to the ancient philosopher Liezi, a contemporary of Zhuangzi 莊子. The original text of the fourth century BCE had been lost, however, even by the Han dynasty. The work transmitted under Liezi's name today (available in the Taoist Canon, CT 668 and CT 729 to CT 733, and in many other editions) was reconstituted and expanded in the second century CE, using numerous stories and philosophical discourses from the *Zhuangzi as a basis and already showing some Buddhist influence. The eight chapters are as follows:

1. "Heaven's Auspices" ("Tianrui" 天瑞) is a highly speculative discussion of the ongoing accumulation and dispersal of *qi, the world as consisting of complementary opposites, Non-being (*wu) as humanity's true home, and reconciliation with death.

2. "The Yellow Emperor" ("*Huangdi" 黃帝), taking much from the *Zhuangzi*, focuses on the Taoist principle of non-action (*wuwei) through remaining unaware and unknowing, totally absorbed and concentrated on one object.

3. "King Mu of Zhou" ("Zhou Muwang" 周穆王) is named after the Zhou sovereign (r. 956–918 BCE) who mystically traveled to the Queen Mother of the West (*Xiwang mu) on Mount *Kunlun. It shows how the whole world is but an illusion and that there is no substantive difference between perception and dreaming because all are equally part of the Dao. Dreams are just as real as "reality," and if people woke up only once in every seven weeks, they would think of their waking state as unreal. There is ultimately no fixed reality but only the natural alternation of mental states, fluctuating in an overall cosmic balance.

4. "Confucius" ("Zhongni" 仲尼) tells stories featuring Confucius and shows the futility of the Confucian trust in knowledge, with the help of paradoxes and absurd tales. Worldly knowledge ends up being described as an illness, an unreal form of perception.

5. "Questions of Tang" ("Tangwen" 湯問) continues along the same lines and highlights the limits of ordinary knowledge in the face of the infinity of the universe. All judgments are relative, and even the safest familiarity blanches in the light of new lands beyond far horizons. In addition, the chapter includes several stories that illustrate miraculous abilities in this world, won by overcoming the limiting and opposite-centered consciousness.

6. "Endeavor and Destiny" ("Liming" 力命) contrasts personal effort and fate and finds the former powerless in the face of the latter, presenting a position of fatalism and recommending complete inertia in the expectation of whatever happens naturally. The text here repudiates conscious choice in favor of following one's intuition and inherent capacities without thinking about alternatives.

7. "Yang Zhu" 楊朱 is named after the hedonistic philosopher and focuses on the shortness of life and its pleasures—such as music, women, fine clothes, and good food—which are the only reasons for living but which one can only enjoy if one is an amoral egoist and a rebel against moral conventions. Rather than worrying about wealth and social standing, one must look at life and death with equanimity and enjoy all it has to offer.

8. "Explaining Correspondences" ("Shuofu" 說符) is the most heterogeneous chapter in the book. It is relatively cosmological in outlook, emphasizing that the cosmic patterns and apparent coincidences of chance govern all events and lives. Because everything is the result of a random combination of factors, there is no sense or purpose to be found—yet every situation contains the power of life and death and therefore can be handled in a right or wrong way. To live life best, one must grasp the proper moment and find the right opportunity for oneself.

As a whole, the *Liezi* shares certain stories and some basic ideas with the classic Taoist tradition but also presents a radical development of its own. It has a strong hedonistic strain and distances itself equally from the stout morality and social self-consciousness of Confucianism and from the reclusive quietism and antisensualism of the *Daode jing*.

Livia KOHN

📖 Asano Yūichi 1988; Barrett 1993; Graham 1960 (trans.); Graham 1961; Mei 1987

Lijia dao

李家道

Way of the Li Family

The Way of the Li Family developed at the fringe of the main Taoist movements of the first centuries CE. *Ge Hong, in his *Baopu zi*, traces its origin to a diviner called Li A 李阿, originally from Shu 蜀 (Sichuan), at the beginning of the third century (see Ware 1966, 158–60). Li A's extraordinary longevity earned him the nickname Babai sui gong 八百歲公 (Sir Eight-Hundred-Years). His biography is in the *Shenxian zhuan* (trans. Campany 2002, 212–15).

Exploitation of Li A's name was considerable. A century later, he reportedly reappeared in the region of Wu 吳 (Jiangsu and part of Zhejiang) under the guise of a certain Li Kuan 李寬. This new Li Babai 李八百 (Li Eight-Hundred), who also came from Shu and was a diviner, became extremely popular in the southern Yangzi region. Ge Hong knew witnesses who attended his healing rituals performed with talismans (*FU) and holy water. According to his report, Li's tradition had spread throughout southern China, and other more or less successful prophets named Li had appeared whom Ge denounced as charlatans. Later, the Northern Wei court's Celestial Master, *Kou Qianzhi (365?–448), also angrily revolted against diviners who called themselves Li and abused the people (*Laojun yinsong jiejing, 5b–6a). Prophets named Li or *Li Hong (Laozi's appellation as the messiah), however, continued to arise in south China during the Six Dynasties, especially in the Wu and Shu regions. Some of them led popular, millenarian-type rebellions and were executed.

Christine MOLLIER

📖 Campany 2002, 212–18; Hu Fuchen 1989, 54–56; Ōfuchi Ninji 1964, 496–517; Qing Xitai 1994, 1: 97–101; Yamada Toshiaki 1977

※ MESSIANISM AND MILLENARIANISM

Lin Lingsu

林靈素

1076–1120; original *ming*: Ling'e 靈噩; *zi*: Tongsou 通叟

Lin Lingsu, a *Shenxiao master from Wenzhou 溫州 (Zhejiang) who gained the support of Song Huizong (r. 1100–1125), has for many centuries been one of the most famous (or infamous) figures in the history of Taoism; he has also been among the most misunderstood. One key factor responsible for this unfortunate state of affairs is that Huizong presided over the catastrophic collapse of the Northern Song (960–1127), and for centuries (including up to the present day) Chinese historians have blamed the fall of that once proud dynasty on his lavish lifestyle and Taoist beliefs. As a result, those Taoists Huizong befriended, particularly prominent individuals like Lin Lingsu, have been repeatedly castigated for their negative influence on the throne (Strickmann 1978b; Zimmerman 1975).

The earliest accounts of Lin's life, including the *Lin Lingsu zhuan* 林靈素 傳 (Biography of Lin Lingsu) by Geng Yanxi 耿延僖 (fl. 1127), which served as the basis for Lin's biography in the *Bintui lu* 賓退錄 (Records Noted Down after the Guests Have Departed) by Zhao Yushi 趙與時 (1175–1271), as well as biographies in the *Songshi* (History of the Song; see *j*. 462) have portrayed Lin in a highly unflattering light. In addition, anti-Buddhist policies initiated by

Huizong (see below) mean that Buddhist histories like the *Fozu tongji* 佛祖統紀 (Comprehensive Chronicle of the Buddhas and Patriarchs) present unfavorable portrayals of Lin and Huizong. Even many Taoists, including members of the *Quanzhen order, attempted to distance themselves from Lin's controversial legacy. In order to balance this picture, one must rely on Taoist hagiographies such as the *Lishi zhenxian tidao tongjian* (Comprehensive Mirror of Perfected Immortals and Those Who Embodied the Dao through the Ages) by Zhao Daoyi 趙道一 (fl. 1294–1307). It is also essential to consult texts written by or attributed to Lin and other members of the Shenxiao movement (Boltz J. M. 1987a, 262 n. 47; Strickmann 1978b, 336 n. 16).

One example of this phenomenon has to do with Lin Lingsu's literary abilities. The Chinese historian Qing Xitai, whose account of Lin is mainly based on the *Bintui lu* and the *Songshi*, describes Lin as "having a rough ability to compose poetry" (*cu neng zuo shi* 粗能作詩; Qing Xitai 1988–95, 2: 607). However, Judith M. Boltz presents a far more positive assessment in her description of one piece attributed to Lin, the "Jinhuo tianding shenxiao sanqi huoling ge" 金火天丁神霄三氣火鈴歌 (Song of the Celestial Stalwart of the Golden Flames and the Fire-Bell of the Three Pneumas of the Divine Empyrean), which she describes as approaching "the caliber of the visionary verse ascribed to his *Shangqing predecessors" (Boltz J. M. 1987a, 30). Lin was also a prolific author, and composed a commentary to the *Daode jing* (now lost) entitled *Laozi zhu* 老子注 (Commentary to the *Laozi*; Boltz J. M. 1987a, 215–16). He also played an important role in the editing of the Song-dynasty edition of the Taoist Canon (see below).

The "facts" of Lin's life are confusing at best. Even his original name remains a mystery, with some sources giving the Chinese characters as Lin Ling'e 林靈噩 and others as Lin Ling'e 林靈蘁. Texts like the *Songshi* and the *Fozu tongji* claim that Lin had originally attempted to become a Buddhist monk but quit after being beaten by his master. This may be simple calumny however, and at any rate we know almost nothing about the early years of his life. It is clear that he exerted a major influence on Taoism's fortunes at the court of Huizong after being presented to the emperor in 1116. Huizong had long been devoted to Taoism, and as early as 1105 had summoned the thirtieth Celestial Master, *Zhang Jixian (1092–1126), to the imperial court at Kaifeng, where he bestowed upon Zhang the honorific title Xujing 虛靖 (Empty Quiescence). Lin Lingsu appears to have won favor with Huizong for a number of reasons: his apparent literary prowess, his ritual techniques, and the vision he propagated of the emperor as a Taoist divinity. The emperor seems to have been impressed with Lin's skill at composing couplets (*duilian* 對聯) and songs (*ge* 歌), and also believed in the efficacy of the Offering rites (*jiao) and prayers for rain (*qiyu* 祈雨) that Lin performed. Lin is even said to have summoned the soul of Huizong's deceased empress, which if true would further support arguments that the Shenxiao movement drew extensively from shamanic traditions (Qing Xitai 1988–95, 2: 608–11; Ren Jiyu 1990, 474–76; Sun Kekuan 1965, 93–122). Perhaps most importantly, Lin persuaded the emperor that he (Huizong) was the incarnation of *Changsheng dadi (Great Emperor of Long Life), one the Shenxiao movement's most prominent deities. Lin and his allies at court also took advantage of Huizong's desire to compile a comprehensive collection of Taoist liturgy by working to complete publication of the Song edition of the Taoist Canon (*Zhenghe Wanshou daozang)

Huizong also began to initiate anti-Buddhist policies shortly after Lin's arrival at court, perhaps in part due to the support of Buddhism by the Song's rival in north China, the Liao dynasty (916–1125). The emperor had previously given Taoists formal precedence over Buddhists back in 1107, but in 1117 took even more drastic measures by decreeing that Shenxiao temples housing statues of Changsheng dadi be established throughout the empire, including inside a number of Buddhist monasteries. In addition, in a fascinating example of traditional Chinese "rectification of names" (zhengming 正名), the emperor decreed that Buddhists be referred to as deshi 德士 (lit., "scholars of virtue"), while Taoists should continue to be addressed as *daoshi. However, the extent to which the emperor's will was implemented outside of Kaifeng is unclear, and Buddhism appears to have emerged from the incident relatively unscathed.

Lin Lingsu's influence at court did not last long, and his ritual powers also apparently began to fail (one story in the Lin Lingsu zhuan vividly recounts his failure to prevent a flood; see Qing Xitai 1988–95, 2: 611–12). In 1119, he disappeared under mysterious circumstances, apparently returning to his home in Wenzhou. Shortly thereafter, both the Northern Song and its northern rival the Liao fell to the Jin dynasty (1115–1234). However, other Shenxiao masters such as Lin's disciple *Wang Wenqing (1093–1153) continued his efforts. Wang and later Shenxiao leaders also recruited new members and spread the movement's teachings, enabling it to flourish during the Southern Song dynasty (1127–1276). Shenxiao masters gained particular renown for the exorcistic rituals they practiced, especially Thunder Rites (*leifa). Lin Lingsu is also said to have been (along with Zhang Jixian) one of the masters of the renowned Thunder Rites specialist *Sa Shoujian.

Paul R. KATZ

📖 Boltz J. M. 1987a, 26–30; Boltz J. M. 1993a; Miyakawa Hisayuki 1975; Qing Xitai 1988–95, 2: 607–14; Ren Jiyu 1990, 472–82; Strickmann 1978b; Sun Kekuan 1965, 93–122; Zimmerman 1975

※ Shenxiao

Lin Zhao'en

林兆恩

1517–98; *zi*: Maoxun 懋勛; *hao*: Longjiang 龍江 (Dragon River),
Xinyin zi 心隱子 (Master Who Hides in His Heart), Zigu zi 子谷
子 (Master of the Valley)

A leading Taoist of Ming times, Lin Zhao'en is noted for his creative integration of elements from different streams of the Chinese religious heritage. Though influenced by *Quanzhen models of self-cultivation, Lin rejected both the monastic focus of that tradition and the sacerdotal emphasis of *Zhengyi. As had become common in his time, he looked for compatibility among the Three Teachings, and integrated elements of Confucianism, Taoism, and Buddhism based on their usefulness in self-cultivation. Hence, to a Neo-Confucian pursuit of "mind-cultivation," Lin added ritual vows to Heaven, and a meditative recitation reminiscent of a Pure Land *nembutsu*, as aids for maintaining spiritual concentration. His "nine stages of mind cultivation" resonate with those of the *Xingming guizhi, though Lin eschewed the traditional symbology of *neidan. Like earlier Taoists, he found value in both esoteric principles and ritual activity. But Lin basically constructed a program of "mind-cultivation" designed to feel comfortable to men of his own social, political, and economic class. He thus extracted from other traditions elements that seemed efficacious for such practitioners, and rejected features that literati might perceive as alien. In that sense, he both revived the "gentry Taoism" of Tang teachers like *Sima Chengzhen, and stretched into new social and cultural directions, like the twelfth-century *Zhen dadao and *Taiyi movements, and the later *Jingming dao (Pure and Bright Way).

Born into a family of scholar-officials in Putian 莆田 (Fujian), Lin followed the family tradition of scholarship. By eighteen, he seemed destined for a successful official career. After the death of his new wife the same year, he remarried, but the subsequent deaths of his grandfather, father, and uncle evidently reduced his enthusiasm for the official life. In 1546, he visited Luo Hongxian 羅洪先 (1504–64; DMB 980–84), a teacher of Wang Yangming's 王陽明 (1472–1529) Neo-Confucian school, and reportedly "abandoned examination studies and took up the Way of sages and worthies, determined to seek the means to realize it in myself, obtain it in my mind, and manifest it in my actions" (Berling 1980, 64). For ten years, he sought answers in various directions, including Chan Buddhism and the Neo-Confucianism of the Cheng brothers

(Cheng Hao 程顥, 1032–85, and Cheng Yi 程頤, 1033–1107; SB 169–79) and Zhu Xi 朱熹 (1130–1200; SB 282–90). Most influential may have been a Taoistically inclined eccentric, Zhuo Wanchun 卓晚春 (Qing Xitai 1994, 1: 388–89), who in 1548 visited Lin and recommended the "ninefold refined elixir" (*jiuhuan dan* 九還丹). At some point before 1551, Lin claims to have met an enlightened master who gave him oral instruction, "directly pointing" to secrets of the mind, including healing powers. From that experience, Lin derived a mission to teach and to heal. He soon established a school, patterned after that of Confucius. In the 1560s, when Japanese pirates invaded Putian, Lin became a community leader in relief efforts and began to play a priestly role. For the next twenty-five years, he worked to propagate an accurate understanding of the Three Teachings. Numerous writings, and collections of his sayings, survive (Berling 1980).

Following his death, Lin became widely honored as a divine being, and his cult survives, not only in Fujian, but also among Chinese communities in Singapore and Malaysia.

Russell KIRKLAND

📖 Berling 1979, 134–39; Berling 1980; Berling 1998, 984–86; Dean 1998; Franke W. 1973; Liu Ts'un-yan 1967; Tu Fang 1976c

※ *neidan*; TAOISM AND NEO-CONFUCIANISM

lingbao

靈寶

Numinous Treasure; Numinous Gem; Spiritual Treasure

The term *bao* denotes a sacred object into which a divinity, or *ling*, descends, thereby granting power to its owner. During the Zhou dynasty, these objects were royal treasures received from Heaven that confirmed the mandate to rule (*tianming* 天命). Rather than being valuable in monetary terms, the *bao* were precious for their mystical value and were typically kept hidden. Also called *fuying* 符應 (coincident responses) or *ruiying* 瑞應 (prodigious responses), they represented celestial resonance with the virtue of the receiver, signaling divine protection and guarantee of rulership. In the chaotic period of the Warring States, this legitimizing power generated an increased interest in their appearance.

The royal *bao* included a variety of objects such as bronzes, jades, and swords. *Bao* later also came to include magical diagrams such as the *Hetu and *Luoshu* (Chart of the [Yellow] River; Writ of the Luo [River]) as well as various revealed texts (see *TAOISM AND THE APOCRYPHA). These too were bestowed by Heaven or a deity onto a worthy individual or ruling family. Taoism inherited this idea and applied it to both *jing* 經 (scriptures) and *FU (talismans). The latter term originally denoted the two tallies of a contract between vassal and sovereign and also defined a contract between Heaven and the virtuous possessor of the talisman.

On a cosmic level, *ling* and *bao* typified Heaven and Earth, respectively, whose union was essential for human life. In some instances, human beings themselves could become a receptacle for the deity. In the *Chuci* 楚辭 (Songs of Chu; trans. Hawkes 1985, 113), for example, the related term *lingbao* 靈保 was the name of a priestess under divine possession. Sorcerers who worked with court exorcists (*fangxiang* 方相) to banish demons and spirits were similarly referred to as *lingbao*. In funerary rites, the representative of the dead (*shi* 尸) was the *bao* or receptacle into which the spirit (*ling*, *hun, or *shen) of the deceased descended for the ritual.

These complex groupings of representations coalesced in the *Lingbao scriptures, particularly in the *Lingbao wufu xu* (Prolegomena to the Five Talismans of the Numinous Treasure). Throughout this scripture, the earliest Lingbao text, the terms *ling* and *bao* are used separately to denote the sacredness of written documents (*jing* or scriptures, *fu* or talismans, *shu* 書 or writs), and to refer to Heaven (*ling*) and Earth (*bao*). The *Lingbao wufu xu* is composed of talismans and collections of revealed recipes for transcendence, both of which are *bao*. In essence, the scripture itself is a *lingbao* conferred as a blessing from Heaven and celestial deities.

In Taoism the celestial is also present within the body, recalling the descent of the numinous into a sorcerer, priestess, or representative of the dead. Through dietary regimes, behavioral rules, or meditational practices, the Dao (*ling*) circulates in the body, and one's inner organs are portrayed as receptacles (*bao*) in which deities reside (see *wuzang).

Amy Lynn MILLER

📖 Kaltenmark 1960; Kaltenmark 1982, 1–4; Robinet 1997b, 149–50; Seidel 1981; Seidel 1983a

※ Lingbao; TAOISM AND THE APOCRYPHA

Lingbao

靈寶

Numinous Treasure; Numinous Gem; Spiritual Treasure

The name *lingbao* (Numinous Treasure) was originally a description of a medium or sacred object (*bao* 寶, "treasure") into which a spirit (*ling* 靈) had descended (see *lingbao). Seemingly, the first scripture to use the name, thus indicating its own status as spiritual treasure, was the *Lingbao wufu jing* 靈寶五符經 (Scripture of Five Talismans of the Numinous Treasure), the surviving edition of which, the *Lingbao wufu xu (Prolegomena to the Five Talismans of the Numinous Treasure), contains passages which were cited by *Ge Hong in his *Baopu zi. At the end of the fourth and into the early fifth century, a unified corpus of new scriptures appeared in Jiangnan, near present-day Nanjing, under the name Lingbao. The success of these scriptures, particularly in the realm of communal ritual, led to imitations and expanded versions. The present entry will focus on the earliest corpus of Lingbao texts, as listed by *Lu Xiujing (406–77) in his catalogue of 437 (see below).

The Lingbao scriptures drew upon the prevailing religious traditions of the day—*fangshi practice, Han-period apocrypha, southern practices known to Ge Hong such as those found in the *Lingbao wufu jing* itself, Celestial Master Taoism (*Tianshi dao), *Shangqing Taoism, and Buddhism—sometimes copying entire sections of text and presenting them so as to accord with its central doctrines in order to fashion a new, universal religion for all of China. This goal proved elusive. Scholarly Buddhists, in particular, were not slow to point out the ways in which Lingbao texts adapted and reconfigured Buddhist tenets. In the court-sponsored Buddho-Taoist debates of the fifth and sixth centuries, the charge of plagiarism was often levelled at the original Lingbao texts. Some Taoists, such as *Tao Hongjing (456–536), made the same charge with regard to Lingbao incorporation of the earlier Taoist scriptures.

Despite the failure of their central mission, the Lingbao scriptures did foster a new unity of Taoist thought and practice. The Three Caverns (*SAN-DONG) division of Taoist scriptures, first outlined in the Lingbao texts as the celestial ordering of scriptures, became the primary organizational rubric for all subsequent Taoist canons. The communal liturgies presented in the texts became the basis for later Taoist ritual and, in modified forms, are still practiced among Taoists today. Lu Xiujing, who was responsible for collecting, editing, and cataloguing the early Lingbao scriptures, was also the first to produce a comprehensive listing of Taoist texts for presentation to the throne, thus ensuring Lingbao texts prominence in subsequent canons. Lingbao codes of morality and practice led to a more formalized temple Taoism with a professional priesthood to oversee religious activity throughout China. In addition, the success of the Lingbao effort to sinicize elements of Buddhist belief not only shaped the direction of Taoism itself, but also aided the integration of Buddhism into Chinese society.

History. Unlike the Shangqing scriptures of *Yang Xi, whose transcripts of visionary sessions and even correspondence with his patrons was collected and annotated by Tao Hongjing, we have only scattered references that reflect on the actual composition of the early Lingbao scriptures. According to the Lingbao scriptures themselves, the texts were first revealed to *Ge Xuan (trad. 164–244), an uncle of Ge Hong who had gained some local renown as Transcendent Duke (Xiangong 仙公), a title bestowed upon him by deities. Such attributions were clearly intended to grant the scriptures precedence over earlier Taoist texts copied into them.

In similar fashion, the subsequent transmission history of the texts given in the scriptures, from Ge Xuan to *Zheng Yin (ca. 215-ca. 302) to Ge Hong (283–343), seems to have been fabricated to account for the inclusion of material from earlier Taoist texts. In fact, one of the scriptures included in the Canon, the *Lingbao wufu xu*, was a text known to Ge Hong and bears no signs of the soteriology or cosmology of the remaining scriptures.

Later Taoist records state that the Lingbao scriptures were "released to the world" ca. 400 CE by *Ge Chaofu (fl. 402), a grandnephew of Ge Hong. While some attempts have been made to discern multiple stages of composition by different groups of Taoists for portions of the scriptures, none of these theories has gained acceptance. Equally inconclusive have been attempts to use developments within the Buddhist sphere, particularly the translations in northern China of Kumārajīva (ca. 344-ca. 409), to date emphases within the Lingbao scriptures; the only demonstrated borrowings come from the translations of Zhi Qian 支謙 and Kang Senghui 康僧會, both late third-century translators in the south. Modern scholars have thus generally taken the statements concerning the scriptures' "release to the world" to indicate that the scriptures were largely composed by Ge Chaofu.

None of Lu Xiujing's surviving works relate how the scriptures came down to him. In his *Lingbao jingmu* (see table 16), Lu divided the canon into two sections: "old" (*jiu* 舊) scriptures of former world-ages and "new" (*xin* 新) scriptures comprised of oral instructions and dialogues between Ge Xuan and his divine instructors and earthly disciples. Only one of the old scriptures, the *Falun zuifu* 法輪罪福 (Blame and Blessing of the Wheel of the Law; CT 346, 358, 455, and 647) presents Ge Xuan as the first earthly recipient, but his

Table 16

NO.	RECEIVED TEXT	TITLE

*Celestial Worthy (*Tianzun 天尊*) Texts*

NO.	RECEIVED TEXT	TITLE
1	CT 22	*Wupian zhenwen* 五篇真文 (Perfected Script in Five Tabletsd)
2	CT 352	*Yujue* 玉訣 (Jade Instructions)
		Yundu daqie jing 運度大劫經 (Scripture of the Revolution of Great Kalpas)
		Yundu xiaoqie jing 運度小劫經 (Scripture of the Revolution of Lesser Kalpas)
3	P. 2399	*Kongdong lingzhang* 空洞靈章 (Numinous Stanzas of the Void Caverns)
4	CT 1439	*Shengxuan buxu zhang* 昇玄步虛章 (Stanzas on Ascending to Mystery and Pacing the Void) [see under *Buxu ci*]
5	CT 318	*Jiutian shengshen zhangjing* 九天生神章經 (Stanzas of the Life-giving Spirits of the Nine Heavens) [see under *Shengshen jing*]
6	CT 671	*Ziran wucheng wen* 自然五稱文 (Text of the Self-generating Five [Talismans] of Correspondence)
7	CT 97	*Zhutian neiyin yuzi* 諸天內音玉字 (Inner Sounds and Jade Graphs of the Heavens) [see under *dafan yinyu*]
—	CT 361	*Bawei zhaolong jing* 八威召龍經 (Scripture of the Eight Awesome Powers for Summoning Dragon [Kings])
8	CT 457	*Zuigen shangpin dajie* 罪根上品大戒 (Great Precepts of the Upper Chapters on the Roots of Sin)
9	CT 177	*Zhihui shangpin dajie* 智慧上品大戒 (Great Precepts of Wisdom from the Upper Chapters)
10	[lost]	*Shangyuan jinlu jianwen* 上元金籙簡文 (Bamboo Slips on the Golden Registers of the Higher Prime)
11	CT 1411	*Mingzhen ke* 明真科 (Code of the Luminous Perfected)
12	CT 177	*Zhihui dingzhi jing* 智慧定志經 (Scripture on Wisdom and Fixing the Will)
13	P. 3022	*Benye shangpin* 本業上品 (Upper Chapters on the Basic Endeavor)
14	CT 346	*Falun zuifu* 法輪罪福 (Blame and Blessings of the Wheel of the Law)
15	CT 1	*Wuliang duren shangpin* 無量度人上品 (Upper Chapters on Limitless Salvation) [see *Duren jing*]
16	CT 23	*Zhutian lingshu duming* 諸天靈書度命 (Salvation as Recorded by the Spirits of the Various Heavens)
17	CT 369	*Miedu wulian jing* 滅度五練經 (Scripture on Salvation through Extinction and the Fivefold Refinement)
18	CT 456	*Sanyuan pinjie* 三元品戒 (Precepts of the Chapters of the Three Primes)
—		*Suming yinyuan* 宿命因緣 (Karmic Causation)
—		*Zhongsheng nan* 眾聖難 (Hardships of the Sages)
—		*Daoyin [...] xing* 導引 [...] 星 ([Exercises for] Guiding [qi] [...] Stars)
19	CT 1407	*Ershisi shengtu* 二十四生圖 (Charts of the Twenty-four Life[-givers])
—		*Feixing sanjie* 飛行三界 (Flight through the Three Realms)

Table 16 (*cont.*)

NO.	RECEIVED TEXT	TITLE

Transcendent Duke (Xiangong 仙公) Texts

20	CT 388	*Lingbao wufu xu* 靈寶五符序 (Preface to the Five Talismans of Lingbao)
21	CT 425	*Taiji yinzhu baojue* 太極隱注寶訣 (Concealed Commentary and Treasured Instructions of the Grand Ultimate)
22	CT 330	*Zhenwen yaojue* 真文要訣 (Essential Explanations of the Perfected Script)
23	P. 2356	*Zhenyi ziran jingjue* 真一自然經訣 (Explanations of the Self-generating Scripture of Perfect Unity)
24	CT 532	*Fuzhai weiyi jue* 敷齋威儀訣 (Instructions on Retreats and the Dignified Liturgies)
25	CT 344	*Xiaomo zhihui benyuan dajie shangpin* 消魔智慧本願大戒上品 (Upper Chapters on the Original Vows and Great Precepts of Devil-destroying Wisdom)
26	CT 1114, S. 1351	*Xiangong qingwen* 仙公請問 (The Questions of the Transcendent Duke)
27	CT 1115	*Zhusheng nan* 眾聖難 (Trials of the Sages)
28	[lost]	*Shenxian zhenqi neizhuan* 神仙本起內傳 (Esoteric Tradition of the Activities of the Divine Transcendents)
29	[lost]	*Xiangong qiju jing* 仙公起居經 (Activities of the Transcendent Duke)

The Lingbao textual corpus. Unnumbered texts were said to be unrevealed in the *Lingbao jingmu*. Those that exist in the modern Taoist Canon were revealed after the time of *Lu Xiujing.

receipt of all the texts in part one of the catalogue is made clear in the "new" section. Among Ge's divine instructors are Laozi himself and *Zhang Daoling, founder of Celestial Master Taoism.

Cosmology. Much material has been incorporated into the Lingbao scriptures from earlier Buddhist and Taoist texts and the cosmology of the scriptures is correspondingly complex. In response to elaborate Buddhist depictions of innumerable world-systems, the Lingbao scriptures portray a far-flung geography of former times. First, there is a system of thirty-two heavens (*sanshi'er tian*) to compete with the twenty-seven or twenty-eight heavens ringing the cosmic mountain, Mount Sumeru, of Buddhist scripture. Like the Buddhist heavens, the thirty-two are divided into the three realms of desire (*yu* 欲), form (*se* 色) and formlessness (*wuse* 無色). Unlike the Buddhist realms, though, the Lingbao version circle a mountain that towers above them, the Jade Capitol (Yujing shan 玉京山), which stands in the Great Canopy heaven (*Daluo tian), the residence of the Celestial Worthy (Tianzun 天尊) high above all other celestial realms. Further, the thirty-two heavens are divided into four groups of eight, one in each of the four directions. These heavens are each ruled over by a celestial

Emperor and populated by the "heavenly Perfected" (*zhutian zhenren* 諸天
真人) of earlier *kalpa*-cycles (*jie). Elements of the celestial language, *dafan
yinyu* ("secret language of the Great Brahmā"), of these heavens, written in
elaborate graphs, serve as talismans and as powerful chants.

As the above shows, the Lingbao scriptures follow the tendency of the
Shangqing scriptures to organize the cosmos in terms of three and five (see
*sanwu). The cardinal directions and center come under the rule of the Five
Emperors (*wudi* 五帝) adopted from Han imperial cult and the "weft texts"
(*weishu* 緯書; see *TAOISM AND THE APOCRYPHA). In one scripture, the three
heavens are further subdivided into nine cosmic heavens, which are given San-
skrit-sounding names and associated particularly with the gods of the human
body. The "earth-prisons" or hells of the scriptures, however, are divided according to the "ten directions"—the four cardinal directions, their intermediate
points, above and below—more frequently seen in Buddhist texts.

While the narrative structure of the first part of the Lingbao scriptures
places all events many *kalpa*-cycles into the past, they foretell the violent end
of a *kalpa*-cycle in the *jiashen* 甲申 year (the twenty-first of the sexagesimal
cycle; see table 10) of our own world-system. In this, they respond to the eschatological fervor already evident in the Shangqing scriptures, but portray
the new age as beginning with the appearance of the Lingbao scriptures themselves to sweep away all other religious doctrine. (See the entry *APOCALYPTIC
ESCHATOLOGY.)

Gods and spirits. The Lingbao texts describe an elaborate cosmic bureaucracy
and instruct practitioners to approach these celestial powers through ritual and
supplication. At the apex of the pantheon is the Celestial Worthy of Original
Commencement (Yuanshi tianzun 元始天尊; see *sanqing). This deity plays
somewhat the same role in the Lingbao scriptures as the cosmicized Buddha in
Buddhist scriptures. His emergence in the heart of the primeval Dao is traced
through a series of five groups of *kalpa*-cycles that are given reign-names in
the manner of human dynasties (for their names, see *COSMOGONY). Next in
importance is the Most High Lord of the Dao (Taishang daojun 太上道君),
a deity who serves as the disciple of the Celestial Worthy and interlocutor in
many Lingbao scriptures. With the exception of Laozi, whose existence in
the prior heavens was as the Emperor of the West, the Five Emperors of the
four directions and center do not appear as actors in the scriptures, but are
invoked in ritual.

The deities resident in the human body include those already elaborated
in the Shangqing scriptures. Particular reference is made to a group of five
internal deities who date back to Celestial Master practice:

1. Great Unity (*Taiyi 太一), essence of the embryo of perfection, who lives
in the palace of the head known as the Muddy Pellet (*niwan)

2. Non-pareil (Wuying 無英), with the byname Lordling (Gongzi 公子), and

3. White Prime (Baiyuan 白元), with the byname Cavernous Yang (Dong-yang 洞陽), two spirits who inhabit the Palace of the Cavern Chamber in the head (*dongfang gong* 洞房宮; see *niwan) and also descend into the liver and lungs, respectively

4. The Director of Destinies (*Siming 司命), whose residence is in the heart and the sexual organs

5. Peach Vigor (Taokang 桃康), or Peach Child (Taohai 桃孩), who resides in the lower Cinnabar Field (*dantian)

In addition, the *Ershisi sheng tu* (Charts of the Twenty-Four Life[-Givers]) lists the powers and envoys of the three registers of the body who are dispatched in ritual to present petitions and vows to the celestial hierarchy.

Salvation and practice. In the Lingbao scriptures, rebirth has been fully integrated with earlier Taoist views of the afterlife. Through adherence to the practices of the scriptures one might hope for a fortunate rebirth "in the family of a Marquis or Prince" or into the heavens themselves. A fortunate few are able to "ascend in broad daylight," avoiding death altogether. At the highest reaches of the celestial bureaucracy are those who rejoin the Dao at the end of the world to reemerge in the new age.

While the scriptures contain ritual programs for lengthy Retreats (*zhai), Offering rites (*jiao), burial rites, and penitentials, they also include a number of practices for the individual. Adherents were enjoined to regularly recite the *Duren jing* (Scripture on Salvation), keep the ten precepts (Bokenkamp 1989, 18–20), and adhere to the commemorations and vows of the texts. The moral component of the Lingbao scriptures—a mixture of traditional Chinese morality and Buddhist salvational ethics—is much more prominent than that found in earlier texts. There is also a pronounced proselytizing emphasis. One scripture in the corpus, the *Zhihui dingzhi tongwei jing* 智慧定志通微經 (Scripture for Penetrating the Subtle through Wisdom and Fixing the Will; CT 325), specifically presents itself as a text to be granted for a small fee to Taoists, but free to Buddhists and, one suspects, other non-Taoists. The text expounds at some length on the ten precepts, modifying them slightly for special circumstances, and presents its message with lively stories, one a version of a popular Buddhist tale.

Most important doctrinally for the Lingbao scriptures is its Taoist version of the "bodhisattva ideal." This is the central message of the scriptures. Precepts and rituals regularly contain the wish for the salvation of all beings, from the emperor down to "beasts that wriggle and crawl." In practice, rites enunciating these wishes were most often conducted for the ancestors of the practitioner.

This traditional emphasis on the post-mortem fate of family members is explained in the scriptures as necessary since, though one's "true" father and mother is the Dao, one still owes debts to the family of one's earthly origin.

Originally, the scriptures seem to have contained a ten-stage path, parallel to the Buddhist system of ten *bhūmi*, or stages of bodhisattva attainment. This began with the arousal of the thought of the Dao (comparable to Buddhist *bodhicitta*, or Awakening Mind) and ended with the adepts' attainment of extended life in the heavens with no further rebirths. As with the bodhisattva ideal described in indigenously-composed Buddhist scriptures, those of wealth and status are seen as having achieved such favorable rebirth through adherence to the scriptures in previous lives. Because of this, the Lingbao scriptures played an important role in the spread of Taoism to the gentry class.

Stephen R. BOKENKAMP

📖 Bokenkamp 1983; Bokenkamp 1990; Bokenkamp 1996–97; Bokenkamp 1997, 373–438; Chen Guofu 1963, 66–71; Ishii Masako 1983b; Kamitsuka Yoshiko 1999, 272–97; Kobayashi Masayoshi 1990, 13–185; Ōfuchi Ninji 1974; Ōfuchi Ninji 1997, 73–218; Qing Xitai 1988–95, 1: 377–98; Ren Jiyu 1990, 127–33 and 143–68; Robinet 1997b, 149–83; Yamada Toshiaki 2000; Zürcher 1980

※ For related entries see the Synoptic Table of Contents, sec. III.5 ("Lingbao")

Lingbao bifa

靈寶畢法

Complete Methods of the Numinous Treasure

The Taoist Canon contains two editions of the *Bichuan Zhengyang zhenren lingbao bifa* 祕傳正陽真人靈寶畢法 (Secret Transmission of the Perfected Zhengyang's Complete Methods of the Numinous Treasure). One is an independent text (CT 1191), the other is an abridged version in the mid-twelfth-century *Daoshu* (j. 42; trans. Baldrian-Hussein 1984). The work describes *neidan* practices and is conceived as a continuation of the *Zhong-Lü chuandao ji*. It is ascribed to the semilegendary *Zhongli Quan (also known as Zhengyang zi 正陽子 or Master of Correct Yang) who, in an undated preface, states that he discovered a copy of the *Lingbao jing* 靈寶經 (Scripture of the Numinous Treasure) within a cave in the Zhongnan mountains (Zhongnan shan 終南 山, Shaanxi). This thirty-*juan* text was divided into three sections containing revelations of Yuanshi tianzun 元始天尊 (Celestial Worthy of Original Commencement; see *sanqing*), Yuanhuang 元皇 (Original Sovereign), and the

Taishang 太上 (Most High), entitled "Jingao shu" 金誥書 (Book of Golden Declarations), "Yulu" 玉錄 (Jade Records), and "Zhenyuan yi" 真元義 (Meaning of the True Origin), respectively. Zhongli allegedly extracted passages from each of these texts and augmented them with three commentaries: "Biyu" 比喻 (Comparisons [between the microcosm and the macrocosm]), "Zhenjue" 真訣 (Perfect Instructions), and "Daoyao" 道要 (Essentials of the Way). In the version that appears in the Taoist Canon, the last section is followed by additional "Explications" ("Jie" 解). Zhongli transmitted his synopsis to his disciple *Lü Dongbin for circulation to help human beings in their search for the Dao.

The *Lingbao bifa* ranked among the main *Zhong-Lü texts during the Southern Song. It is first mentioned in Zheng Qiao's 鄭樵 (1104–62) *Tongzhi* 通志 (Comprehensive Monographs; see van der Loon 1984, 164). *Miao Shanshi (fl. 1288–1324) believed it to have been written by *Shi Jianwu, the likely author of the *Zhong-Lü chuandao ji* (*Chunyang dijun shenhua miaotong ji* 純陽帝君神化妙通紀; CT 305, 5.14b).

Unlike other Zhong-Lü sources, the *Lingbao bifa* is not cast in dialogue form, but consists of a manual of longevity techniques clearly expounded in steps and grades. It presents direct comparisons between the development of the immortal self, the elixir (*huandan), and the formation of the cosmos, and draws equally upon the *Yijing for the functioning of the cosmos and upon medical literature for the workings of the human body. The alchemical œuvre is divided into three stages (*sansheng* 三乘, or Three Vehicles). The initial stage (*xiaosheng* 小乘, or Small Vehicle) concerns breath control and gymnastics; it comprises four techniques relevant to what later became known as "laying the foundations" (*zhuji* 築基): union of Yin and Yang, breathing technique for accumulating and dispersing pneuma (*qi), union of Dragon and Tiger (*longhu), and fire phasing (*huohou). The second stage (*zhongsheng* 中乘, or Middle Vehicle) deals with methods of circulating pneuma and inner fluids. The final three methods (*dasheng* 大乘, or Great Vehicle) involve complex practices of visualization and inner concentration leading to transfiguration. They include purification of the pneumas of the five viscera (*wuzang) according to season and time followed by their union (defined as "the five pneumas have audience at the Origin," *wuqi chaoyuan* 五氣朝元), inner observation (*neiguan), and exteriorization of the immortal self from the mortal body (*chaotuo* 超脫, or "emancipation").

Farzeen BALDRIAN-HUSSEIN

📖 Baldrian-Hussein 1984 (trans.); Boltz J. M. 1987a, 140; Qing Xitai 1994, 2: 152–54

※ *neidan*; Zhong-Lü

Lingbao dafa

靈寶大法

Great Rites of the Numinous Treasure

This synthetic ritual tradition that priests used and criticized in the Southern Song, Yuan, and Ming periods focused on saving the dead. It goes by several names in various twelfth- to fourteenth-century texts that seek to embody or to castigate the tradition. While "Great Rites of the Numinous Treasure Tradition" was commonly used by its promoters and "Rites of Tiantai" (Tiantai fa 天臺法) by its detractors, others called it the "Great Rites for Salvation" (Duren dafa 度人大法) because of the prominence given to the *Duren jing* (Scripture on Salvation). Other sources use the expression "Way of [the Lord of] Eastern Florescence" (Donghua dao 東華道). Widely disseminated in southeast China, the Great Rites combined new exorcistic practices and forms of contemplation with a new way of reading and understanding *Lingbao scriptures and rituals, especially those based on the *Duren jing*. The popularity of this eclectic ritual tradition was scorned and ridiculed by Song and Yuan era priests who favored a return to the simpler classical protocols of Taoist ritual.

Most later ritualists credited *Ning Benli (1101–81) with first codifying the tradition by integrating what he had learned from Tian Ziji 田紫極 (1074-?) in Kaifeng (Henan) with teachings he got from the southern master Shi Zixian 什子仙 after the fall of the Northern Song in 1126. Tian Ziji's teachings blended the "canonical teachings of the Three Caverns" (*sandong jing jiao* 三洞經教) ritual traditions with an obscure form of alchemy known as the Mysterious Purport of [the Perfected of] the Cinnabar Origin of Eastern Florescence (*Donghua danyuan xuanzhi* 東華丹元玄旨). Shi Zixian wove the "Forty-Nine Rubrics of the Numinous Treasure Mysterious Standards" (*Lingbao xuanfan sishijiu pin* 靈寶玄範四十九品) together with the *Tongchu (Youthful Incipience) teachings of Yang Xizhen 楊希真 (1101–24), specifically the "talismans (*FU), writs, seals, and mudrās of the Five Bureaus' Jade Fascicles" (see *Daofa huiyuan, 171.2b).

The core of the Great Rites comprises incantations, talismans, and rituals stemming from a secret reading of the *Duren jing*, in which each of the four-character phrases of the scripture forms a talisman that heals any illness and protects its bearer (*Lingbao wuliang duren shang jing dafa, j. 5–7). These methods are described as "the Way to save souls from hell" (id., 53.1a). Before attaining this goal, adepts strive to ascend through a series of purifications that culminate in their initiation in the rites of salvation by the main Lingbao deity, the Celestial Worthy of Original Commencement (Yuanshi tianzun 元始天尊).

Thus ennobled, priests focus on ingesting the energies of the holy scriptures, gaining command over all gods, and communication with the supernatural powers. A mastery of the rites of confession and the spiritual hierarchies of both Heaven and Earth in which they participate permits priests to turn to the ritual rubrics, especially those for exorcism and salvation for the dead, but also for transmitting the whole system to other worthy practitioners.

Although Ning's ritual synthesis was widely practiced and was part of many traditions in Southern Song and Yuan times, later practitioners also borrowed such elements as the Salvation through Refinement (*liandu) rituals and *Shenxiao (Divine Empyrean) deities, as well as aspects of *Tianxin zhengfa (Correct Method of the Celestial Heart) exorcistic practices, from which some ritualists sought to distinguish their Lingbao rites of salvation.

Key texts in the tradition include the *Lingbao wuliang duren shangjing dafa (Great Rites of the Superior Scripture of the Numinous Treasure on Limitless Salvation), the two works entitled *Shangqing lingbao dafa (Great Rites of the Numinous Treasure of Highest Clarity), and the *Lingbao lingjiao jidu jinshu (Golden Writings for Deliverance by the Sect Leader of the Numinous Treasure Tradition).

Lowell SKAR

📖 Boltz J. M. 1987a, 41–46; Qing Xitai 1994, 1: 149–54; Skar 2000, 437–40, 443–44, and passim

※ For related entries see the Synoptic Table of Contents, sec. III.7 ("Song, Jin, and Yuan: Lingbao dafa")

Lingbao jingmu

靈 寶 經 目

Catalogue of Lingbao Scriptures

In 437, the Taoist *Lu Xiujing issued to his coreligionists a list of the *Lingbao scriptures. The preface to this work survives in the *Yunji qiqian (4.4a–6a), while the list itself is found in truncated form in the Tongmen lun 通門論 (Comprehensive Treatise on the Doctrine) of Song Wenming 宋文明 (fl. 549–51), preserved in *Dunhuang manuscripts P. 2861.2 and P. 2256.

The catalogue is divided into two parts. The first are thirty-six juan of scriptures, in ten sections, that were revealed by the Celestial Worthy of Original Commencement (Yuanshi tianzun 元始天尊) in a previous kalpa-cycle. Fifteen juan of these still reside in heaven. The second comprises eleven juan of texts bestowed by the Transcendent Duke *Ge Xuan. These are styled "old" and "new" respectively. Some scholars have taken this to refer to the order in which the parts of the canon were actually composed. As the frequent references to "old" texts and manuals of practice found in the first part of the scriptures shows, however, the terms refer instead to the narrative structure of the scriptures, denoting whether or not a text was "newly written" in our own *kalpa*-cycle by Ge Xuan or revealed in previous eons by the Celestial Worthy.

According to Lu's humbly worded preface, his promulgation of the scriptures was timely. Recent textual revelations, culminating in those of *Zhang Daoling and Ge Xuan, having moved the Most High, the prophesied rise of the Liu Song dynasty (420–79) had now taken place. It was thus appropriate that this unifying revelation be made known to all.

Many of the texts found in Lu's catalogue survive today. In the listing in table 16, those texts marked "unrevealed" are left unnumbered. When a surviving version is given, it was produced after Lu's time.

Stephen R. BOKENKAMP

📖 Bokenkamp 2001; Kobayashi Masayoshi 1990, 138–85; Ōfuchi Ninji 1974; Ōfuchi Ninji 1978–79, 1: 365–68 (crit. notes on the Dunhuang mss.) and 2: 725–26, 726–34 (reprod. of the Dunhuang mss.); Ōfuchi Ninji 1997, 75–88, 100–121

※ Lu Xiujing; Lingbao

Lingbao lingjiao jidu jinshu

靈寶領教濟度金書

Golden Writings for Deliverance by the Sect Leader of the Numinous Treasure Tradition

This compendium (CT 466, with table of contents in CT 465) was edited by Wenzhou 溫州 (Zhejiang) Taoist priests in the fourteenth century, and reworked in early Ming times. It systematically presents the fullest version of the *Lingbao dafa (Great Rites of the Numinous Treasure) tradition that its editors claim was passed down by *Ning Benli (1101–81) on Mount Tiantai (*Tiantai shan, Zhejiang). While claiming to transmit Ning Benli's teachings, the present work was likely that of Lin Tianren 林天任 (fl. 1303), who piously credited his master Lin Weifu 林偉夫 (1239–1302) with its compilation.

The text represents a strong effort to reconstitute the Lingbao dafa approach to saving the dead for southern Chinese living under Mongol rule. Its 320 *juan* fall under nineteen rubrics whose content is sometimes at odds with the preceding table of contents. The opening chapters on altar arrangements (*j.* 1), gifts for various rituals and sketches for Retreat (*zhai) and Land of the Way (*daochang) rituals (*j.* 2), pantheons (*j.* 3–7), details on the Nocturnal Invocation (*suqi) and Audience (chaoye 朝謁) rites (*j.* 8–9), and hymn texts (*j.* 10–11) are followed by ritual texts that could be used for both salvation and therapy (*j.* 12–41). The bulk of the compendium details ritual programs for Deliverance and Salvation (kaidu 開度, *j.* 42–135) and for Prayer and Exorcism (qirang 祈禳, *j.* 136–259).

Lowell SKAR

📖 Boltz J. M. 1987a, 44–46; Davis E. 2001, 231–36; Kalinowski 1989–90, 105–6; Lagerwey 1987c, 169

※ Ning Benli; Lingbao dafa

Lingbao shoudu yi

靈寶授度儀

Ordination Ritual of the Numinous Treasure

The *Lingbao shoudu yi* (CT 528) was composed by the codifier of the *Lingbao scriptures, *Lu Xiujing. While ordination rituals for the transmission of scriptures are attested from the beginnings of the religion, the *Shoudu yi* is particularly important in that it served as the prototype for subsequent ordinations in the scriptures of the Three Caverns (*SANDONG).

The text is preceded by a memorial, also written by Lu, indicating that the text may have been presented to the throne. This memorial is not dated, but Lu writes that it has been "seventeen years since I presumed to receive (taoqie 叨竊) [the scriptures]." Since Lu was born in 407 and was unlikely to have encountered the Lingbao texts before the age of fifteen, the text was probably composed within a few years of 437, the year in which Lu wrote the *Lingbao jingmu (Catalogue of Lingbao Scriptures), and certainly no later than 454.

Lu's memorial reveals that he pieced together his ordination ritual from the simpler rites included in several texts in the Lingbao canon, a fact confirmed by the extensive quotations found in the *Shoudu yi*. In that some of his sources no longer survive as independent works, the *Shoudu yi* is valuable testimony to the early Lingbao scriptures.

Lu's reason for composing this work is that Taoists of his day were conducting ordination rituals in texts of all Three Caverns using a single oath and without regard to the established order of precedence. Even when they only performed ordinations in the Lingbao scriptures, they tended to mix in other elements or call spirits indiscriminately. The *Shoudu yi* thus attests to Lu's attempt to unify and regularize the Taoist practice of his day.

The ordination ritual, to be performed over a period of seven days, presumes that the disciple has already received and studied the scriptures and is now ready to "retreat from the entanglements" (*tuilei* 退累) of the mundane world to study the scriptures and perform rituals on behalf of all the living. This is thus one of the earliest warrants for the establishment of a professional priesthood. The ritual centers on the covenants (*meng* 盟) entered into between master and disciple before the gods. Both parties place their own lives, and those of their ancestors, in forfeit of descent into the hells for "ten thousand *kalpas*" if either of them defame the scriptures or transmit them to the unworthy.

At the climax of this complex ritual, the master calls from his body the twenty-four spirits and their envoys to dispatch to the celestial realms his announcement of scriptural transmission. He then recites the primary incantations, secret language, and other formulas of the scriptures. Having received these primary bits of arcana, the disciples recite their covenant and participate in the singing of the *Buxu ci (Lyrics for Pacing the Void) and other hymns of praise and commitment. Upon completion of the rite, the newly-invested disciples officiate over a *zhai (Retreat) ritual of thanksgiving lasting three days.

Stephen R. BOKENKAMP

📖 Benn 1991, 124–35 and passim; Ōfuchi Ninji 1997, 331–43

※ Lu Xiujing; Lingbao; ORDINATION AND PRIESTHOOD

Lingbao wufu xu

靈寶五符序

Prolegomena to the Five Talismans of the Numinous Treasure

The *Lingbao wufu xu* is a key text for understanding the formative stage of Taoist religion, form the late Han through the fifth century. The extant version (CT 388) was probably compiled over a period of a century, between the late third and early fifth centuries, though the main redaction was probably complete by the early fourth century. Incorporating much early material, the text is closer to the traditions of the *fangshi and the "weft" texts (*weishu* 緯書; see *TAOISM AND THE APOCRYPHA) than to the developed Taoist scriptures. Though it was in the possession of *Ge Hong, and was transmitted among

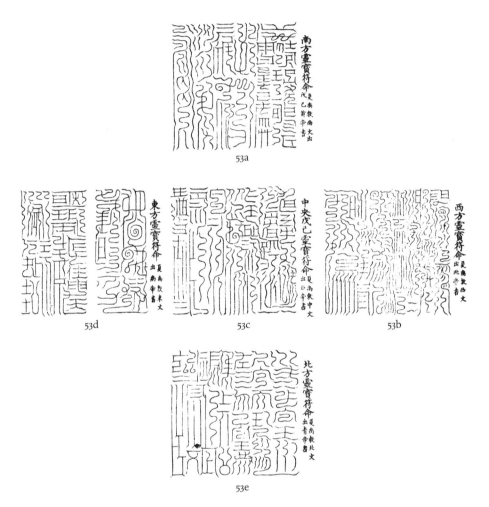

Fig. 53. Talismans of the Five Emperors: (a) South; (b) West; (c) Center; (d) East; (e) North.
Lingbao wufu xu (Prolegomena to the Five Talismans of the Numinous Treasure; CT 388),
3.9a–11b.

his family and associates, there is clear indication of different lineages involved
in the redaction process.

The first chapter consists of a long narrative describing the appearance
of the text in the human realm. After a cosmogonic description, a narrative
based on the opening chapters of the *Shiji* (Records of the Historian) details
the receipt of the text by Di Ku 帝嚳 and later by Yu 禹, who is said to have
composed the actual scripture to be transmitted in the world. This is followed
by the discovery of the scripture in the caves below Lake Dongting 洞庭 and
its presentation to the hapless King of Wu, Helü (r. 514–496 BCE). The prefatory

narrative is followed by a number of distinct texts which describe: 1. the "five sprouts" (wuya 五芽) practice by which the pneuma (*qi) of the five directions may be ingested; 2. the secret names of the Five Emperors (wudi 五帝), based on the Han "weft" texts; 3. short instructions and praise for the five *Lingbao talismans; 4. a meditation practice, based on the "ruler-minister" (wangxiang 王相) hemerological system, for cycling pneuma through the five viscera (*wuzang); and 5. instructions for ingestion of solar and lunar essences. This last section, which includes an important discussion of micro-macrocosmic correlations and corporeal gods, is related to the final part of the scripture, and probably emanated from a lineage distinct from those reflected in the other sections in the text.

The second chapter consists entirely of herbal recipes for longevity, suppression of the Three Corpses (sanshi; see *sanshi and jiuchong), and healing of disease. The chapter also includes a talisman to be used for "release from the corpse" (see *shijie).

The core of the text is the *jiao (Offering) ritual described in the third chapter, in which the Five Emperors are summoned through contemplation involving the five talismans. The ritual incorporates three originally unrelated practices: 1. Han imperial ritual speculations which perceived the living emperor as an embodiment of five celestial Emperors who themselves are manifestations of the *wuxing; 2. the "five sprouts" method of pneuma ingestion; 3. the five talismans, originally apotropaic talismans to be used by adepts when entering mountains seeking herbs and minerals. This ritual is the earliest example of a Taoist jiao and incorporates elements of ritual still performed today. The rite begins by laying out the talismans, followed by summoning the celestial officials. After an offering and reverence to the spirits, a request is made. The spirits are then sent off to return to their abode. In later ritual codifications, beginning with the *Wupian zhenwen 五篇真文 (Perfected Script in Five Tablets) and continued by *Lu Xiujing (406–77), the basic structure of the rite remained as the basic unit of Taoist ritual, despite the ever more complex instructions and performances.

The final part of the third chapter is an originally independent text, entitled "Scripture of the Authentic One" ("Zhenyi jing" 真一經) and cited under various similar titles. It is probably related to the *Sanhuang (Three Sovereigns) tradition and paralleled by j. 18 in *Baopu zi. This section introduces the notion of the Three Ones (*sanyi), which became the focus of meditation practices within *Shangqing Taoism. Here it is merged with the practice of the "five sprouts." The teaching, presented to the Yellow Emperor (*Huangdi), presages *neidan practice, and also introduces the notion of the three *hun and the seven *po.

The Wufu xu thus provides valuable information on the development of Taoism from Han period practices of various fangshi lineages, "weft" texts, and shamanic methods, through competing lineages of southern China, to the systematized Taoist scriptural revelations of the fourth century and beyond. The text further introduces several concepts and practices which were to become central in the emerging Taoist syntheses of later centuries.

Gil RAZ

📖 Bokenkamp 1983; Bokenkamp 1986d; Ishii Masako 1981; Ishii Masako 1984; Kaltenmark 1960; Kaltenmark 1982; Kobayashi Masayoshi 1990, 45–104; Lagerwey 2004a; Raz 2003; Schipper 1991b; Yamada Toshiaki 1984; Yamada Toshiaki 1987a; Yamada Toshiaki 1987b; Yamada Toshiaki 1989b

※ Lingbao

Lingbao wuliang duren shangjing dafa

靈寶無量度人上經大法

Great Rites of the Superior Scripture of the Numinous Treasure on Limitless Salvation

This anonymous compendium (CT 219) was probably compiled around 1200 by a disciple of *Ning Benli (1101–81) and enlarged during the early Ming period. It is based on a new interpretation of the main *Lingbao scripture, the *Duren jing* (Scripture on Salvation), involving new incantations, talismans (*FU), and practices, especially those deriving from a secret way of reading the scripture (j. 5–7) that provides expanded powers to heal and protect adepts, but mainly in the service of saving the dead. The important rites for Salvation through Refinement (*liandu) central to the *Shenxiao (Divine Empyrean) tradition also figure prominently here. The text states that this interpretation derives from the August One of Heavenly Perfection (Tianzhen huangren 天真皇人), who both made the scripture's sacred characters intelligible to human eyes and ears, and explained the talismans to the Yellow Emperor (*Huangdi).

The *Duren shangjing dafa* is closely related to both texts entitled *Shangqing lingbao dafa* (Great Rites of the Numinous Treasure of Highest Clarity; CT 1221 and CT 1222–23). While giving a full and detailed description of the *Lingbao dafa (Great Rites of the Numinous Treasure) tradition, which it refers to as "the Way to save souls from hell" (53.1a), a nearer source of its inspiration may have been the Shenxiao tradition. Filled with diagrams that provide clues to the foundations of Taoist ritual, the text also suggest subtle means of turning one's inner body into an ritual arena for saving souls, particularly in the section (57.2b–5b) printed separately as *Lingbao dalian neizhi xingchi jiyao* 靈寶

大鍊內旨行持機要 (Crucial Essentials in the Numinous Treasure Tradition for Practicing and Upholding the Inner Purport for the Great Refinement; CT 407; Boltz J. M. 1983, and Lagerwey 1987c, 233–34).

The text's division into ninety sections was the work of a scholarly disciple familiar with most of the contemporary twelfth-century Taoist traditions, and represents a finely woven synthesis of many of them, even though its major focus is on the saving of deceased ancestors. The text first directs the disciple to master the making and use of talismans (j. 4–21), the basic ways of imbibing pure essences, and the sending of petitions to the heavens. Adepts are taught to combine traditional Celestial Masters (*Tianshi dao), Lingbao, and *Shangqing methods with new practices derived from Shenxiao and *Tianxin zhengfa (Correct Method of the Celestial Heart) that aim to exorcise impure energies from the body so that pure energies will replace them. Once these preliminaries are mastered, the adept will be able to work toward his final goal—to save all souls from hell by traveling beyond the stars, and ultimately to be initiated by the Celestial Worthy of Original Commencement (Yuanshi tianzun 元始天尊). Once this has been achieved, the adept can order about the deities of heaven and earth and practice Thunder Rites (*leifa). Besides being now able to thoroughly work through rites of confession (j. 27), the adept learns how to attain a place within the ranks of the transcendents (j. 28) and to find his way among all the celestial realms with various divine aides (j. 29). Once he has completed this program, the adept is qualified to perform public ritual, exorcising demons for the benefit of the living (manifest in j. 30–45) and delivering the lost souls of the dead (detailed especially in j. 46–71).

Lowell SKAR

📖 Boltz J. M. 1983; Boltz J. M. 1987a, 28–29; Boltz J. M. 1994, 10

※ Lingbao dafa

Lingbao yujian

靈寶玉鑒

Jade Mirror of the Numinous Treasure

This important thirteenth-century ritual text (CT 546 and 547), although incomplete, may be related to the same title mentioned by *Bai Yuchan (1194–1229?; see *Haiqiong Bai zhenren yulu* 海瓊白真人語錄, CT 1307, 4.12a–b). The title's "Numinous Treasure" refers to the *Lingbao dafa (Great Rites of the Numinous Treasure) tradition to which this text belongs, while "Jade Mirror" refers to the ancient practice of using mirrors to identify demons (see under *jing and jian). The text also makes ample use of material from the *Tianxin zhengfa (Correct Method of the Celestial Heart) tradition, which is here explicitly tied to the Celestial Masters' *Zhengyi (Orthodox Unity) ritual legacy, and from the Yutang 玉堂 (Jade Hall) tradition of *Lu Shizhong (fl. 1120–30).

The text regards Tian Ziji 田紫極 (1074-?) as the Ancestral Master (zushi 祖師) of its tradition, but does not mention *Ning Benli (1101–81). It is divided into twenty-five rubrics (men 門), beginning with general explanations of Taoist ritual (j. 1, rubric 1) along the lines of the Lingbao dafa, followed by the twenty-four other rubrics (j. 2–43) that deal with a wide array of ritual programs in the *Lingbao tradition for saving lost souls through Offering (*jiao) and Retreat (*zhai) rites that rely on new types of talismans (*FU), exorcisms, meditation, and presenting memorials.

Lowell SKAR

📖 Boltz J. M. 1987a, 43–44; Qing Xitai 1994, 2: 169–70

※ Lingbao dafa

Lingshu ziwen

靈書紫文

Numinous Writings in Purple Script

The *Lingshu ziwen* is one of the main original *Shangqing scriptures. The received text is certainly authentic, but is divided into four parts in the Taoist Canon:

1. *Huangtian Shangqing Jinque dijun lingshu ziwen shangjing* 皇天上清金闕帝君靈書紫文上經 (Superior Scripture of the Numinous Writings in Purple Script of the Imperial Lord of the Golden Portal of the August Heaven of Highest Clarity; CT 639)

2. *Taiwei lingshu ziwen langgan huadan shenzhen shangjing* 太微靈書紫文琅玕華丹神真上經 (Divine, Authentic, and Superior Scripture of the Elixir Efflorescence of Langgan, from the Numinous Writings in Purple Script of the Great Tenuity; CT 255)

3. *Housheng daojun lieji 後聖道君列紀 (Chronicle of the Lord of the Dao, Saint of the Latter Age; CT 442)

4. *Taiwei lingshu ziwen xianji zhenji shangjing* 太微靈書紫文仙忌真記上經 (Superior Scripture of the Interdictions for Immortals Recorded by the Real Men, from the Numinous Writings in Purple Script of the Heaven of Great Tenuity; CT 179)

The first text (CT 639; trans. Bokenkamp 1997, 307–31) opens with the story of the composition of the *Lingshu ziwen* by the Azure Lad (*Qingtong), who in Shangqing scriptures plays the role of mediator between divine and human beings. It continues with three methods dealing with subtle physiology and involving visualizations, incantations, and the absorption of talismans (*FU). The first method teaches how to ingest the pneumas (*qi) of the sun and the moon; the adept invokes the secret names of the Emperors of the Sun and the Moon, envisioning their pneumas and absorbing them with a talisman. The second method aims at "securing the three *hun*" (*ju sanhun* 拘三魂) and "controlling the seven *po*" (*zhi qipo* 制七魄; see *hun and po). Since the *hun* are fond of freely flying away, the adept should control them by encircling his body with a red pneuma summoned from his heart. The *po*, however, are malevolent; one should avert their threats by imprisoning them through the visualization of the Jade Women (*yunü) and the four directional animals (*siling), which in Shangqing texts often form a sacred guard around the practitioner. These techniques are complemented by a third practice, consisting of invocations to the Three Primes (*sanyuan) or Three Ones (*sanyi) who reside in the three Cinnabar Fields (*dantian), and in animating the god of the Mysterious Pass (*xuanguan). This method is designed to replace the sexual practices of the Celestial Masters (*Tianshi dao) and is related to embryonic breathing (*taixi), as the Mysterious Pass is "the passageway that joined the placenta to your viscera when you were first born" (trans. Bokenkamp 1997, 327).

The second text (CT 255; trans. Bokenkamp 1997, 331–39) gives the recipe for the Elixir of Langgan, named after a mythical tree that grows on Mount *Kunlun. This method, lying between operative alchemy and "astro-alchemy," joins the compounding of an elixir with the absorption of astral efflorescences; the product likely was not meant for actual ingestion. (For more details on this method see under *langgan.)

The third text (CT 442; trans. Bokenkamp 1997, 339–62; part. trans. Strickmann 1981, 209–24) is devoted to a description of the apocalypse. It deals with *Li Hong, the Sage Lord of the Latter Age (the present cosmos), who comes at the end of the world to save the "seed-people" (*zhongmin), i.e., the adepts who have gained access to the *Lingshu ziwen*, respect moral rules, and bear the physical marks of transcendence enumerated in the text. (For more details on this text, see under *Housheng daojun lieji.)

The fourth and last text (CT 179; trans. Bokenkamp 1997, 362–66) is one of the few Shangqing sources that list ethical and ritual prohibitions.

Isabelle ROBINET

📖 Bokenkamp 1997, 275–372; Kamitsuka Yoshiko 1999, 171–210; Robinet 1984, 2: 101–10

※ Shangqing

Linshui furen

臨水夫人

The Lady at the Water's Edge

Lady Linshui has for 1,000 years been one of the most popular deities in south China. Also known as Defending Maiden Chen (Chen Jinggu 陳靖姑) and Fourteenth Damsel Chen (Chen Shisi niangniang 陳十四娘娘), she continues to be worshipped throughout much of the region, especially Zhejiang, Fujian, and Taiwan. Her hagiography contains complex and striking symbolism about gender roles, their reversal, and their inevitability. Most texts state that when the officials and people of Quanzhou 泉州 (Fujian) were unable to raise money to build a bridge, the bodhisattva Guanyin 觀音 transformed herself into a beautiful maiden, embarked on a small boat, and offered to marry any man who could hit her with an ingot of silver thrown from the water's edge. She raised a large sum of money, which landed in the boat, until the Taoist immortal *Lü Dongbin helped a merchant hit one strand of her hair with a speck of silver powder. The hair fell into the water and floated away. Guanyin then bit her finger, and a drop of blood fell into the water and also floated away, whereupon she vanished. Distraught at having lost his future bride, the merchant committed suicide. The drop of blood floated down the river, and was swallowed by a woman washing clothes in the river, Lady Ge (Ge furen 葛夫人; another "lady at the water's edge"), who had married into the Chen family but failed to produce any children. She became pregnant, and gave birth to Chen Jinggu (Lady Linshui). The hair turned into a female white snake, which ravished handsome males and devoured women she considered to be her rivals. The merchant's soul was sent to be reincarnated as Liu Qi 劉杞, Lady Linshui's future husband.

Chen grew up to be a beautiful and talented young woman, but refused marriage to Liu Qi and fled to Mount Lü (Lüshan 閭山, Jiangxi), where she studied ritual techniques under the tutelage of the renowned Taoist immortal *Xu Xun, learning everything except the art of protecting pregnancy. She could not escape her destiny, however, eventually marrying Liu Qi and becoming pregnant. When the northern Fujian region began to suffer from a serious drought, the people asked her to perform a ritual to bring rain. In order to do so, she had to temporarily abort her fetus, which was then devoured by the white snake. She died of a hemorrhage (or miscarriage), sacrificing her life-giving blood in order to provide life-giving water for the people, but before her death was able to kill the snake with her sword.

Lady Linshui has long been renowned for her ritual powers, and remains a patron deity of spirit-mediums (*wu* 巫; *jitong* 乩童 or **tâng-ki* in Southern Min dialect) and ritual masters (**fashi*) in Fujian and Taiwan. She is also worshipped along with Li Sanniang 李三娘 (Third Damsel Li) and Lin Jiuniang 林九娘 (Ninth Damsel Lin; sometimes considered to be **Mazu) as one of the Three Matrons (Sannai furen 三奶夫人), the matriarchs of the Lüshan branch of Taoism. Ritual masters of this movement don skirts when performing their rites. To this day, Chinese and Taiwanese women worship her as a deity who can protect them during pregnancy and childbirth, and she is also invoked during rites to protect children (Baptandier-Berthier 1994).

Paul R. KATZ

📖 Baptandier 1996; Berthier 1988; Chen Minhui 1988; Lo Vivienne 1993; Wang Fang and Jin Chongliu 1994; Wu Gangji 1994; Xu Xiaowang 1993, 329–48; Ye Mingsheng and Yuan Hongliang 1996

※ HAGIOGRAPHY; TAOISM AND POPULAR RELIGION

Lishi zhenxian tidao tongjian

歷世真仙體道通鑑

Comprehensive Mirror of Perfected Immortals and
Those Who Embodied the Dao through the Ages

The *Lishi zhenxian tidao tongjian* (CT 296) is an enormous compendium of immortals' biographies compiled by Zhao Daoyi 趙道一 (fl. 1294–1307) who came from Fuyun shan 浮雲山 (Zhejiang). It is divided into fifty-three chapters with over 900 biographies and inspired two additional collections, *Lishi zhenxian tidao tongjian xubian* 續編 (Supplementary Chapters; CT 297) in five chapters and *Lishi zhenxian tidao tongjian houji* 後集 (Later Collection; CT 298) in six chapters. The latter two collections are likely not be from Zhao's hand—his name may have been attached to them as a pious act of reverence to the original—as they appear to date from about a century after the original compendium. The compendium includes an undated preface by Zhao in which he notes his use of the **Hunyuan shengji* (Saintly Chronicle of Chaotic Origin) by Xie Shouhao 謝守灝 (1134–1212), a kind of history of the operations of the Dao in the human realm. It should also be noted that the *Lishi zhenxian tidao tongjian* was compiled in an era that saw other grand attempts at comprehensive history, both sacred and secular, as well as other monumental anthologies.

The biographies are found in the compendium roughly in the order their subjects lived. However, there are places where this rule is violated, such as the chapter of biographies of the inheritors of the title of Celestial Master which immediately follows the single-chapter biography of *Zhang Daoling, the first *tianshi*. One of the difficulties with this work, as far as the reconstruction of lost texts or the tracing of the development of biographies over time is concerned, is that Zhao rarely noted his sources. It is clear that he sometimes copied whole chapters of earlier collections which also upsets the chronological arrangement in some cases. However, Zhao clearly did not copy extant works or chapters of works unthinkingly, as, in some cases, he replaced certain notable biographies from early collections with other, often voluminous, versions written closer to his own time. An example of this is the biography of *Huangdi which occupies the entire first chapter of the collection. As a consequence, Huangdi's biography does not appear in the third chapter of the compendium which was clearly taken from the *Liexian zhuan* (the early collection of biographies of immortals) in which he also received a biography. The two chapter-long biographies of Huangdi and Zhang Daoling, among others, indicate both the tendency toward more complex narrative in immortals' lives and also an attempt at comprehensiveness, seen in their incorporation of all the material from previous traditions into one record.

The two supplementary collections appear to derive from *Quanzhen circles. Judith M. Boltz (1987a, 58) has observed that the *Xubian* begins with biographies of Quanzhen patriarchs while the *Houji*, a collection devoted to women's lives, culminates with the record of *Sun Bu'er, the Quanzhen matriarch.

Benjamin PENNY

📖 Boltz J. M. 1987a, 56–59; Chen Guofu 1963, 243; Ozaki Masaharu 1996; Tsuchiya Masaaki 1996

※ HAGIOGRAPHY

Liu Chuxuan

劉處玄

1147–1203; *zi*: Tongmiao 通妙; *hao*: Changsheng 長生

Liu Chuxuan (Liu Changsheng), the son of a family of military officers, converted to *Wang Zhe at the age of twenty-two, after Wang revealed himself as the author of an anonymous piece of calligraphy that had appeared on a wall predicting Liu's accession to immortality. Liu served as a novice to Wang during the latter's last few months of life; he then mourned his master and led an eremitic life around Luoyang, exhibiting his austere ways to a large public. He returned in 1176 to Shandong where he founded several *Quanzhen communities. Liu gained the Jin court's attention and was invited to the capital in 1197, thanks to his fame as a ritualist and/or because the Quanzhen order had just made an agreement with the state that ended seven years of protracted conflict. Liu's involvement with Quanzhen institutional development, however, is not apparent from the sources, although he did have very influential disciples, among whom *Yu Daoxian and *Song Defang are best known.

Liu's contribution to Quanzhen lies mainly in his scholarship and his theoretical writings that grounded Quanzhen pedagogy in the Taoist speculative tradition. This is attested by four extant works in the Canon. Like all except one of Wang's seven main disciples, Liu left a poetic anthology, the *Xianle ji* 仙樂集 (Anthology of Immortal Bliss; CT 1141). He also wrote two commentaries—a rare genre among early Quanzhen Taoists—on the *Huangting jing* and the *Yinfu jing*, entitled *Huangting neijing yujing zhu* 黃庭內景玉經注 (Commentary to the Jade Scripture of the Inner Effulgences of the Yellow Court; CT 401) and *Yinfu jing zhu* 陰符經注 (Commentary to the Scripture of the Hidden Accordance; CT 122). Last comes the *Wuwei Qingjing Changsheng zhenren zhizhen yulu* 無為清靜長生真人至真語錄 (Recorded Sayings on the Ultimate Reality by the Real Man of Non-Action, Clarity and Quiescence, and Long Life; CT 1058), a short dialectic treatise, which, despite its title, is not a verbatim record of oral teachings but a list of eighty words with definitions and antonyms relevant to Taoist philosophy. His lost works are even more numerous, including seven anthologies and a commentary to the *Daode jing*. It is then not surprising that many Quanzhen adepts of the second generation came to Liu for instruction in the Taoist scriptural legacy.

Vincent GOOSSAERT

📖 Boltz J. M. 1987a, 64–65, 162–63; Endres 1985; Hachiya Kunio 1992b; Marsone 2001a, 104

※ Quanzhen

Liu Deren

劉德仁

1122–80; *hao*: Wuyou zi 無憂子 (The Troubleless Master)

Liu Deren is the founder of the *Zhen dadao order, of which he was posthumously considered the first patriarch. He was born in a Shandong family that provided him with a good education. Very early, however, Liu found himself an orphan, and, although his family does not seem to have had any specific religious tradition, he turned to asceticism and made a reputation for himself through his humble and austere mode of life. At the age of twenty, he met an "extraordinary person," identified by the Zhen dadao tradition as Laozi, who explained him the true meaning of the *Daode jing* and gave him liturgical scriptures. Out of these revelations, Liu drew nine precepts of general moral significance, which Zhen dadao adepts received in their formal initiation. These precepts likely played the same role as the five basic precepts (*wujie* 五戒) in all Buddhist and most Taoist communities (i.e., those against killing, stealing, having illicit sex, lying, and drinking alcohol).

Thanks to his impressive austerity and exorcistic prowess, Liu's predication met with great popular support. In 1176, he was invited to the Jin court and awarded the title Dongyue zhenren 東嶽真人 (Real Man of the Eastern Peak). He chose as his successor another man inclined toward hard work and humble demeanor, Chen Shizheng 陳師正, hitherto a fisherman along the Yellow River.

Liu's life is primarily known through a late account by the famed historiographer Song Lian 宋濂 (1310–81), but his name is also found in most epigraphic accounts of the Zhen dadao, where he is evoked as the main example of the austere virtues preached by this order.

Vincent GOOSSAERT

📖 Qing Xitai 1994, 1: 330

※ Zhen dadao

Liu Haichan

劉海蟾

ming: Cao 操 *or* Xuanying 玄英; *zi*: Zongcheng 宗成 *or* Zhaoyuan 昭遠; *hao*: Haichan zi 海蟾子 (Master Sea-Toad)

Liu Haichan is one of the most popular of the immortals who appear at the beginning of the Song period and play an important role in the diffusion of *neidan techniques and literature. He is first mentioned in several collections of miscellaneous notes (*biji* 筆記) as a disciple of *Chen Tuan (ca. 920–89). Later hagiography, fashioned by the *Quanzhen order, makes him a minister of the state of Yan 燕 (911–13). At the height of his glory, Liu is converted by a trick of *Zhongli Quan, who piles up ten eggs on a coin and asserts that the life of a minister is even more hazardous. Liu then abandons his life of

Fig. 54. Liu Haichan. Yan Hui 顏輝 (fl. late thirteenth-early fourteenth century). Chion-ji 知恩寺, Kyoto. See Little 2000b, 330.

fame and riches to become a wandering Taoist, and finally attains immortality.

As an immortal, Liu seems to have been especially revered in the twelfth and thirteenth centuries, when he was associated with Zhongli Quan and *Lü Dongbin. The three were famous for roaming the world and persuading people to search for Taoist immortality. These encounters were favorite topics not only of hagiographic works, but also of poems and theatre plays. Although Zhongli and Lü have enjoyed a more durable popularity, Liu plays an eminent role in a numbers of stories, especially the *Ningyang Dong zhenren yuxian ji* 凝陽董真人遇仙記 (Records of the Real Man Dong Ningyang's Encounters with Immortals; CT 308). This semivernacular work tells the tale of a humble Jurchen soldier, Dong Shouzhi 董守志 (1160–1227), who repeatedly receives visits and instructions from Liu, Lü, and Zhongli, and starts a new Taoist school.

Liu was also famous for his poetry and the calligraphic traces he left on temple walls—a way of creating new holy places that was also favored by Lü Dongbin. Although Liu's alchemical poems seem to have been well-known, they have not come down to us in any anthology, but are quoted in several Song and Yuan *neidan* works. His autobiographical "Song on Becoming a Taoist" ("Rudao ge" 入道歌, probably a Quanzhen apocryphon) was carved on stone in several locations, and is also included in his standard biography found in the *Jinlian zhengzong ji*, which inspired most later accounts of his life.

Zhongli Quan, Lü Dongbin, and Liu Haichan are considered patriarchs by both the Quanzhen and *Nanzong lineages. Liu's importance, however, appears to have waned already by Yuan times, and very few texts are attributed to him in later anthologies. Unlike Lü Dongbin, moreover, Liu was rarely called through spirit writing (see *fuji) by Taoist devotees and alchemists, and for some reason he is not even included among the Eight Immortals (*baxian) in the late-Yuan final definition of this group.

His modern personality as a god of wealth is quite different from the alchemical initiation master of yore. He is often painted as a child with a toad and a string of coins, two attributes probably borrowed from the immortals Helan Qizhen 賀蘭棲真 and Lan Caihe 藍采和, respectively.

Vincent GOOSSAERT

📖 Boltz J. M. 1987a, 64 and 173; Jing Anning 1996; Little 2000b, 330

※ Nanzong; Quanzhen; HAGIOGRAPHY

Liu Huayang

柳華陽

1735–99; *hao*: Chuanlu 傳盧 (Transmitter of the Hut)

Liu Huayang, a native of Nanchang (Jiangxi), was originally a Confucian scholar but became a Chan monk at the Shuanglian si 雙蓮寺 (Temple of the Double Lotus) near Anqing 安慶 (Anhui). Having failed to attain enlightenment, he left the temple in search of a master who could teach him the secrets of Wisdom (hui 慧, prajñā) and Life (ming 命; see *xing and ming). This finally happened in the spring of 1780 when, according to Liu, *Wu Shouyang—who had died 136 years earlier—transmitted his teachings to him. Liu successfully put them into practice. After that, the Buddhist monk Huyun 壺雲, whom Liu met in Kuanglu 匡廬 (Jiangxi), gave him instructions on the final stages of his training.

Liu Huayang is the author of two treatises, both edited and annotated by Liu himself in 1799 in a Buddhist temple in Beijing. The first is the *Jinxian zhenglun* 金仙証論 (Essay on the Verification of Golden Immortality), written in Anhui and consisting of twenty sections, the first of which is a preface dated 1790. Two other prefaces by Gao Shuangjing 高雙景 of Nanchang (dated 1790) and by the Buddhist monk Miaowu 妙悟 (dated 1791) introduce the text. The treatise primarily deals with the circulation of *qi known as the Lesser Celestial Circuit (*xiao zhoutian* 小周天; see *zhoutian) through the Control and Function channels (*dumai and renmai). Section 17 describes the two channels with the help of a diagram. The final two sections, on the dangers encountered in the course of the practice and the reason for Liu's adding his own annotations, were appended in 1799.

The second treatise is the *Huiming jing* 慧命經 (Scripture of Wisdom and Life), also known as *Zuishang yisheng huiming jing* 最上一乘慧命經 (Scripture on Wisdom and Life of the Supreme One Vehicle). A preface by Liu and another by Sun Tingbi 孫廷璧 are both dated 1794. Writing for the benefit of four disciples who had accomplished the Lesser Celestial Circuit, Liu here mainly elucidates the techniques of the Greater Celestial Circuit (*da zhoutian* 大周天; see *zhoutian*). The text is essentially an account of the experiences that he and his disciples underwent. The first eight sections contain diagrams on topics ranging from "cessation of outflow" (*loujin* 漏儘, *āsravakṣaya*) to "reverting to Emptiness" (*huanxu* 還虛). This portion of the work circulated independently in esoteric circles and was published in several collections.

The two treatises were first printed together by Liang Jingyang 梁靖陽 in 1846, and again by Deng Huiji 鄧徽績 in 1897 in the collection entitled *Wu-Liu xianzong* 伍柳仙宗 (The Wu-Liu Lineage of Immortality).

Farzeen BALDRIAN-HUSSEIN

📖 Boltz J. M. 1987a; Chen Zhibin 1974; Sakade Yoshinobu 1987, 2–3

※ *Huiming jing*; *neidan*; Wu-Liu pai

Liu Hunkang

劉混康

1035–1108; *zi*: Zhitong 志通; *hao*: Huayang xiansheng 華陽先生
(Elder of Flourishing Yang)

Liu Hunkang, the twenty-fifth patriarch of the *Shangqing school, was a famous Taoist priest based on Mount Mao (*Maoshan, Jiangsu) during the Northern Song dynasty. A native of Puling 普陵 (Jiangsu), he was ordained as a *daoshi at the age of twenty-four. He visited Mount Mao out of reverence for the Taoist priest Mao Fengrou 毛奉柔, who was teaching there and conferred on him scriptures and registers (*LU). Liu cultivated the Dao at Jijin 積金 Peak in the Mount Mao ranges. He taught extensively, so that his reputation spread all over Jiangnan and he received favors from several emperors of the Northern Song.

In 1086, Liu healed the mother of Song Zhezong (r. 1085–1100) from an acute illness of the throat by means of talismans and writings. Zhezong thereupon bestowed upon him the style Elder Who Pervades the Origin and Penetrates the Sublime (Dongyuan tongmiao xiansheng 洞元通妙先生), and changed the name of the hermitage in which he resided at Mount Mao to the Abbey of the Original Tally (Yuanfu guan 元符觀). Mount Mao itself was declared the Ancestral Altar of Scriptures and Registers (*jinglu zongtan* 經錄 宗壇), and together with Mount Longhu (*Longhu shan, Jiangxi) and Mount Gezao (*Gezao shan, Jiangxi) became one of the so-called Three Tripod Peaks (*sanshan dingzhi* 三山鼎峙). Song Huizong (r. 1100–1125), who is said to have obtained male progeny thanks to a method taught by Liu, likewise had high respect for him and summoned him many times to the capital. The two men exchanged more than seventy letters and poems and presented each other with hand-written copies of the *Duren jing (Scripture on Salvation). In 1108, Liu's body grew increasingly weak due to old age; he left the mountain on imperial invitation but died after his arrival in the capital.

Besides being an expert in rituals and healing methods, Liu Hunkang's main contribution to Taoism was exalting the role of Mount Mao as Ancestral Altar of Scriptures and Registers. At the same time he exerted remarkable influence on the spread of Taoism in Song-dynasty Jiangnan and the development of Taoist rites, particularly on the formation of the *liandu (Salvation through Refinement) rituals.

CHEN Yaoting

📖 Qing Xitai 1994, 1: 312–13

※ Shangqing

Liu Yiming

劉一明

1734–1821; *hao*: Wuyuan zi 悟元子 (Master of the Awakening to the Origin), Supu sanren 素樸散人 (Vagabond in Simplicity)

The *neidan master Liu Yiming, a native of Quwo 曲沃 (Shanxi), was the eleventh-generation patriarch of the *Longmen lineage. Information about him is scattered throughout his works, commentaries, poems, and prefaces, but Liu gives a fairly detailed account of his life in the *Huixin ji* 會心集 (Anthology of Gathering [the Dao] in the Heart; 1811). He studied the Confucian classics in his youth but also developed an interest in Taoism at the age of thirteen. At the age of seventeen, he was seized by a serious illness; while the usual remedies proved ineffective, a Perfected (*zhenren) healed him. Two years later, he began his quest for the Dao, leading the life of an itinerant seeker for thirteen years in Beijing, Henan, and Shanxi.

In 1760, or slightly earlier, Liu encountered a master whom he calls the Old Man of the Kangu Mountains (Kangu laoren 龕谷老人) in Jincheng 金城 (present-day Yuzhong 榆中, Gansu). In 1772 he met his second and most important master, the Great Man Resting in Immortality (Xianliu zhangren 仙留丈人), who initiated him in both alchemy and the *Yijing. Liu's understanding of these subjects and his combination of the two form the core of most of his writings.

In 1780, Liu visited the Qiyun 棲雲 mountains in Jincheng and settled there to practice self-cultivation as a recluse. His residence, the Den of Freedom (Zizai wo 自在窩), was within the precincts of an abbey. A disciple describes a meeting with him in the Jintian guan 金天觀 (Abbey of Golden Heaven), which could be the abbey in question. Liu himself, however, states that he reopened a dilapidated abbey, the Chaoyuan guan 朝元觀 (Abbey of the Audience with the [Three] Primes) on Mount Qiyun. The conversations he held with another disciple on the summit of the mountain in 1782 are recorded in the *Xiuzhen biannan* 修真辨難 (Discussions on the Cultivation of Perfection; 1798).

Liu's commentaries draw on various sources, including the Confucian or Neo-Confucian thought of Mencius (Mengzi 孟子, ca. 370-ca. 290 BCE), Wang Yangming 王陽明 (1472–1529), and Yan Yuan 顏元 (1635–1704). This influence is evident, for instance, in his frequent use of the terms *liangzhi* 良知 (intuitive knowledge) and *liangneng* 良能 (intuitive ability), both of which Liu explicates as synonyms of Golden Elixir (*jindan). Chan Buddhism also figures prominently in his thought, as shown by his commentaries to alchemical texts such as the *Zhouyi cantong qi, the *Wuzhen pian, and the *Jindan sibai zi. Moreover, he makes use of the *Yijing* and cosmological diagrams to illustrate his point. Liu also interpreted in alchemical terms the popular late-Ming novel *Xiyou ji* 西遊記 (Journey to the West; Yu Anthony 1991; this novel should not be confused with the identically-titled work by Li Zhichang 李志常, on which see the entry *Changchun zhenren xiyou ji).

Liu Yiming's books were published independently during his lifetime by various disciples including Zhang Yangquan 張陽全 and Zhou Jinxi 周金璽, and by friends. They were later reedited in the *Daoshu shi'er zhong (Twelve Books on the Dao; 1819).

Farzeen BALDRIAN-HUSSEIN

📖 Miyakawa Hisayuki 1954; Qing Xitai 1988–95, 4: 156–83; Qing Xitai 1994, 1: 396–97

※ *Daoshu shi'er zhong; neidan; Longmen*

Liu Yu

劉玉

1257–1308; *zi*: Yizhen 頤真; *hao*: Yuzhen zi 玉真子
(Master of Jade Perfection)

Liu Yu is not to be confused with a person of the same name, otherwise known as Liu Shi 劉世 (fl. 1258), to whom *Shenxiao ritual codes are ascribed. The son of Lady Wu 鄔氏 and Liu Gang 劉岡 of Nankang 南康 (Jiangxi), Liu lost both parents at the age of twenty. He came out of mourning destitute and wise to the ephemerality of life. Turning to a study of the spirit realm, Liu began to have a series of visions and eventually came to be recognized as the founder of a syncretic school known as the *Jingming dao (Pure and Bright Way) centered on veneration of *Xu Xun (trad. 239–374) at the Western Hills (*Xishan, Jiangxi).

Liu had his first visionary encounter in 1282 at the Western Hills, where he met Hu Huichao 胡惠超 (?–703), a Taoist master who six centuries earlier had revived a movement in the name of Xu Xun called Xiaodao 孝道 (Way of Filiality). Hu reportedly told Liu that he was destined to become the exemplar of eight hundred devotees of Jingming. He also said that Liu could expect the arrival of Xu Xun himself on the *gengshen 庚申 day of the last lunar month of the year *bingshen* 丙申 (20 January 1297). Hu reappeared the next year to explain Jingming lore and advised Liu to set up a retreat on Mount Huangtang (Huangtang shan 黃堂山) in the Western Hills range. Word of Liu's benevolent activities at a newly established abbey in the region drew throngs of followers.

Toward the end of 1294 Liu received instruction in geomancy from an ostensibly earlier devotee of Xu Xun, the renowned literatus Guo Pu 郭璞 (276–324). Approximately two years later, on the day designated for his audience with Xu Xun, Liu gathered his disciples together and said that someone else would join them. Late that night, during a heavy snowstorm, Huang Yuanji 黃元吉 (1271–1326) arrived and said that Hu had appeared in a dream, telling him to come. Just before midnight, Liu allegedly received from Xu Xun a text on *Lingbao ritual that bore his name as a disciple. Four days later Guo Pu is said to have given Liu an exegesis on the text. That night Xu arrived again to bestow further ritual commentary that he claimed to have received by order of Taishang 太上 (Most High). He also informed Liu that he was foremost among his eight hundred disciples. Ten months later Hu reappeared at the *Yulong wanshou gong (Palace of the Ten-thousand-fold Longevity of Jade Beneficence) of the Western Hills to convey additional instruction.

From then on Liu led a widespread revival of Jingming teachings and became known for his succinct manner of speech and complete integrity. Just before his demise, he designated Huang Yuanji as his successor. A selection of Liu's teachings, entitled *Yuzhen xiansheng yulu* 玉真先生語錄 (Recorded Sayings of the Elder of Jade Perfection), is contained in the **Jingming zhongxiao quanshu* (Complete Writings of the Pure and Bright [Way of] Loyalty and Filiality; *j. 3–5*) compiled by Huang. The biography of Liu Yu in this anthology (1.18b–25b), the primary source used here, differs significantly from a longer version in later accounts.

Judith M. BOLTZ

📖 Akizuki Kan'ei 1978, 142–44; Boltz J. M. 1987a, 75–77, 197–99, and 264–65; Chen Yuan 1988, 967–68; Qing Xitai 1994, 1: 360–61

※ Jingming dao

Liu Yuanran

劉淵然

1351–1432; *hao*: Tixuan zi 體玄子
(Master Who Embodies the Mystery)

Liu Yuanran was born to Lady Wang 王氏 and Liu Yuanshou 劉元壽, son of the Route Commander of Ganzhou 贛州 (Jiangxi) Liu Bocheng 劉伯成. One month later, according to an epigraphic account of 1456, the infant Liu was so ill that the Route Commander sought counsel in prayer at the local Xuanmiao guan 玄妙觀 (Abbey of Mysterious Wonder). Liu's survival led to his discipleship under an instructor at the abbey named Chen Fangwai 陳方外, in keeping with the pledge of faith made by his grandfather. At the age of sixteen he was ordained as a Taoist Master by two instructors named Hu 胡 and Zhang 張, apparently affiliated with the Xiangfu gong 祥符宮 (Palace of Auspicious Talismans) in Fuzhou 撫州 (Jiangxi). Liu later became the preeminent disciple of *Zhao Yizhen (?–1382) at the Ziyang guan 紫陽觀 (Abbey of Purple Yang) in Yudu 雩都 (Jiangxi). Hagiographic texts credit him with mastering a range of teachings, from *Quanzhen to *Zhengyi. As Zhao's disciple, Liu came to be known as the sixth-generation patriarch of the *Jingming dao (Pure and Bright Way). He was widely recognized as a skilled rainmaker, exorcist, and physician.

In 1393 the Hongwu Emperor (r. 1368–98) summoned Liu to court and, convinced of his talents, rewarded him with the title of Gaodao 高道 (Exalted Way). He even established a residence for Liu at the Chaotian gong 朝天宮

(Palace in Homage to Heaven) within the imperial compound of Nanjing (Jiangsu). The emperor also sent Liu on pilgrimages to Mount Wudang (*Wudang shan, Hubei) and other sacred sites. At one point Liu reportedly conveyed instruction to the forty-third Celestial Master *Zhang Yuchu (1361–1410). A conflict that allegedly arose between the two may have figured in Liu's exile from court early in the Yongle reign period (1403–24). Initially banished to Mount Longhu (*Longhu shan, Jiangxi), site of the Zhengyi patriarchy, by the year 1411 Liu had settled in the Longquan guan 龍泉觀 (Abbey of the Dragon Springs) of Kunming 昆明 (Yunnan).

The Hongxi Emperor (r. 1425) summoned Liu back to court and put him in charge of all Taoist affairs of state. In 1426 the Xuande Emperor (r. 1426–35) granted him the authority to establish three prefectural Taoist Registries in Yunnan. Six years later, as he looked forward to living in retirement at the Chaotian gong, Liu named his disciple *Shao Yizheng (?–1462) as a worthy successor. That autumn he took his last breath and in the spring of 1433 was buried at Jiangning 江寧 (Jiangsu).

The Ming Taoist Canon includes the *Yuanyang zi fayu* 原陽子法語 (Exemplary Sayings of the Master of Primary Yang; CT 1071), compiled by Liu from his teacher Zhao's writings. Liu himself reputedly had over one hundred disciples but none was as highly esteemed as Shao Yizheng.

Judith M. BOLTZ

📖 Akizuki Kan'ei 1978, 159–61; Chen Yuan 1988, 1256–57, 1260–61, and 1305–6; Oyanagi Shigeta 1934, 22

※ Zhao Yizhen; Jingming dao

Liu Zhigu

劉知古

before 663-after 756; *zi*: Guangxuan 光玄

Liu Zhigu, who came from Linqiong 臨邛 (Sichuan), is the author of the *Riyue xuanshu lun* 日月玄樞論 (Essay on the Mysterious Pivot, the Sun and Moon), the earliest extant essay on the *Zhouyi cantong qi*. His main biography is in the *Lishi zhenxian tidao tongjian* (32.2a–3b), which expands the account given in the *Sandong qunxian lu* (1.10b–11a). According to these works, Liu, whose great-grandfather had been Magistrate of Linqiong during the Sui dynasty, became a *daoshi* at the local Taiqing guan 太清觀 (Abbey of Great Clarity) in the early 660s. He was summoned by Tang Ruizong (r. 684–90, 710–12) to

provide him with Taoist teachings, and by Tang Xuanzong (r. 712–56) during
the Kaiyuan period (713–41) to bring an end to the natural disasters that struck
in those years. In the final year of his reign, Xuanzong invited him again to
celebrate *jiao (Offering) rituals at court.

The *Riyue xuanshu lun* is a short work important in the history of Chinese
alchemy for two reasons. First, it contains the earliest *neidan reading of the
Cantong qi that has come down to us. Liu's purpose, in fact, is to criticize
the contemporary *waidan interpretations of the scripture; he emphatically
states that the *Cantong qi* has nothing to do with the manipulation of natural
substances but rather describes the generation of the inner elixir. Second, the
Riyue xuanshu lun is one of the main sources for dating the present version of
the *Cantong qi*. In his discussion of this text, Liu quotes or alludes to about a
dozen passages from this text, all found in the received version. Incidentally,
his work also shows that the *Cantong qi* was already divided into three parts
by the middle of the eighth century.

The *Riyue xuanshu lun* is preserved in the *Quan Tang wen* 全唐文 (Complete
Prose of the Tang; Zhonghua shuju repr. of the 1814 edition, 334.12a–21a) together with an undated memorial submitted to Xuanzong, and in an abridged
and inferior version in the *Daoshu (26.1a–6b) under the title *Riyue xuanshu
pian* 日月玄樞篇 (Folios on the Mysterious Pivot, the Sun and Moon).

Fabrizio PREGADIO

※ *neidan*

liujia and liuding

六甲・六丁

six *jia* and six *ding*

The ten Celestial Stems and the twelve Earthly Branches (*ganzhi; see tables
8, 9, and 10) have been primarily used to mark sexagesimal cycles of days and
years. In addition, they have been connected with mantic functions based on
their relation to Yin and Yang and the Five Agents (*wuxing). Several possibilities have resulted from this association, such as the methods for divining the
auspicious or inauspicious result of activities, averting disasters, and "hiding
oneself" (*yinshen* 隱身); and the method of the Hidden Stem (*dunjia* 遁甲;
Schipper and Wang 1986, 198–204).

In particular, it was believed that one's fate was controlled by deities related
to the Stem and Branch of one's year of birth. These deities are variously
called "star lords of the sixty Stems and Branches" (*liushi jiazi xingjun* 六十

甲子星君), "numinous officers of the sixty Stems and Branches" (*liushi jiazi lingguan* 六十甲子靈官), "gods of the sixty Stems and Branches" (*liushi jiazi shen* 六十甲子神), and so forth. It was said, for instance, that the *jiazi* spirit of one's "natal destiny" (**benming*) was called Wang Wenqing 王文卿, and had a retinue of eighteen officials.

Although the ten Celestial Stems as a whole are associated with Yang, and the twelve Earthly Branches with Yin, five of the ten Stems (namely *jia* 甲, *bing* 丙, *wu* 戊, *geng* 庚, and *ren* 壬) belong to Yang and the other five (*yi* 乙, *ding* 丁, *ji* 己, *xin* 辛, *gui* 癸) to Yin. The twelve combinations of Stems and Branches that include the characters *jia* 甲 or *ding* 丁 were considered to be especially important as representative of Yang and Yin spirits, respectively. These twelve combinations are collectively referred to as the six *jia* and the six *ding*. The six *jia* are *jiazi* 甲子, *jiaxu* 甲戌, *jiashen* 甲申, *jiawu* 甲午, *jiachen* 甲辰, and *jiayin* 甲寅. The six *ding* are *dingmao* 丁卯, *dingchou* 丁丑, *dinghai* 丁亥, *dingyou* 丁酉, *dingwei* 丁未, and *dingsi* 丁巳. Several methods, talismans, and texts allowed the practitioners to obtain control over the spirits and the Jade Women (**yunü*) associated with these combinations of Stems and Branches.

The names and cognomens of the spirits associated with the six *jia* are given in the *Shangqing liujia qidao bifa* 上清六甲祈禱祕法 (Secret Methods of the Highest Clarity to Invoke the Six *Jia*; CT 584, 2a–b):

1. *Jiazi*: Yuande 元德, Qinggong 青公

2. *Jiaxu*: Xuyi 虛逸, Linzhai 林齋

3. *Jiashen*: Jielüe 節略, Quanheng 權衡

4. *Jiawu*: Chanren 潺仁, Ziqing 子卿

5. *Jiachen*: Tongyuan 通元, Gunchang 袞昌

6. *Jiayin*: Huashi 化石, Zimo 子靡

These spirits take multiple forms; some of them, for instance, have one head while some have three heads, and some wear jewels while others wear long silk robes.

The same text (2b–3a) also gives the cognomens and names (in this order) of the spirits associated with the six *ding*:

1. *Dingmao*: Rengao 仁高, Wenbo 文伯

2. *Dingchou*: Renxian 仁賢, Wengong 文公

3. *Dinghai*: Renhe 仁和, Rentong 仁通

4. *Dingyou*: Renxiu 仁脩, Wenqing 文卿

5. *Dingwei*: Rengong 仁恭, Shengtong 昇通

6. *Dingsi*: Renjing 仁敬, Mangqing 芒卿

These spirits are also called the Jade Women of the Six *Ding*. Their protective roles are said to be as follows: the Jade Woman of *dingmao* guards one's body; the Jade Woman of *dingsi*, one's destiny; the Jade Woman of *dinghai*, one's fortune; the Jade Woman of *dingyou*, one's *hun soul; the Jade Woman of *dingwei*, one's *po soul; the Jade Woman of *dingchou*, one's spirit.

It was also said that because the Jade Women of the Six *Ding* descend into the human world on the *zichou* 子丑, *yanmao* 寅卯, *chensi* 辰巳, *wuwei* 午未, *shenyou* 申酉, and *xuhai* 戌亥 days, one may summon them on those days to inquire about one's fortune. For this purpose the Talismans of the Jade Women of the Six *Ding* (*liuding yunü fu* 六丁玉女符) were created. Other Taoist techniques also included summoning the Great Divine Generals of the Six *Jia* (*liujia da shenjiang* 六甲大神將), the Generals of the Six *Ding* (*liuding jiangjun* 六丁將軍), and the Jade Women of the Six *Jia* (*liujia yunü* 六甲玉女).

MUGITANI Kunio

📖 Campany 2002, 72–75; Ngo 1976, 190–95; Kalinowski 1989–90, 91–95; Kalinowski 1991, 87–88 and 384–87; Schipper and Wang 1986, 198–204

※ *ganzhi*

liuyi ni

六一泥

Mud of the Six-and-One

The Mud of the Six-and-One is a core element of early *waidan practices. Several texts belonging or related to the *Taiqing corpus describe methods to prepare this substance, sometimes calling it Divine Mud (*shenni* 神泥). Usually obtained from seven ingredients, the mud is used to hermetically seal the crucible (*fu) and avoid dispersion of pneuma (*qi) during the heating of the elixir. The earliest method to compound it is found in the *Jiudan jing* (Scripture of the Nine Elixirs), where the ingredients are alum, Turkestan salt, lake salt, arsenolite, oyster shells, red clay, and talc; these ingredients are pounded, sieved, and placed in an acetic bath (*Huangdi jiuding shendan jingjue* 黃帝九鼎神丹經訣; CT 885, 1.3b–4a). The *Taiwei lingshu ziwen langgan huadan shenzhen shangjing* 太微靈書紫文琅玕華丹神真上經 (Divine, Authentic, and Superior Scripture of the Elixir Efflorescence of Langgan, from the Numinous Writings in Purple Script of the Great Tenuity; CT 255; trans. Bokenkamp 1997, 331–39), the *Taiqing danjing yaojue* (trans. Sivin 1968, 160–68), and other sources describe similar methods.

About the meaning of the term *liuyi*, the commentary to the *Jiudan jing* merely says that "six and one is seven: the sages keep this secret, and therefore call it Six-and-One," adding that the compound has this name even if it is obtained from a different number of ingredients (CT 885, 7.5a). Although no *waidan* text gives an explanation clearer than this, at least two interpretations of the expression "Six-and-One" are possible. First, the number 1 and 6 are related to Heaven and Earth, respectively. Second, some early texts, including the *Zhuangzi* and *Huainan zi*, describe or allude to the generation of the cosmos as a process that takes place in seven stages (see Girardot 1983, 150–52; Le Blanc 1989). One passage of the *Zhuangzi* (chapter 7; see trans. Watson 1968, 97), in particular, represents the shift from chaos (*hundun*) to cosmos as seven holes pierced in the gourdlike body of Emperor Hundun 混沌 (Chaos) by the Emperors of the North and South, emblems of duality. While the Emperors of the North and South intend to turn Hundun into a human being, they actually cause his death, which is equivalent to the birth of the cosmos. Transposed to the alchemical process, the seven ingredients of the Mud of Six-and-One symbolically close those seven openings, recreating the original inchoate state within the crucible and allowing the ingredients of the elixir to return to their timeless condition of *materia prima*, and to be a representation of the "essence" (*jing*) issued from the Dao to generate the cosmos.

Fabrizio PREGADIO

📖 Chen Guofu 1983, 26–34; Pregadio 1991, 595–600; Pregadio 2006b, 75–78, 103–4

※ *fu* [crucible]; *waidan*

liuzi jue

六字訣

"instructions on the six sounds"

This breathing technique, also known as "method of the six breaths" (*liuqi fa* 六氣法), consists of inhaling through the nose and exhaling in six ways through the mouth. The corresponding sounds are designated by six characters (hence the name of the method, literally meaning "instructions on the six characters"). They are *xu* 噓, *he* 呵 (or *xu* 呴, nowadays also pronounced *gou*), *hu* 呼, *si* 呬 (nowadays also pronounced *xi*), *chui* 吹, and *xi* 嘻.

As shown by a mention of the *chui* and *xu* breaths in *Daode jing* 29 and in *Zhuangzi* 15 (for the latter, see the entry *tuna*), the origin of this technique predates the Han dynasty. The *chui* and *hu* breaths are also mentioned in the *Quegu shiqi* 卻穀食氣 (Refraining from Cereals and Ingesting Breath) manu-

script from *Mawangdui (Harper 1998, 129–30, 305–9) and in Wang Chong's
王充 (27-ca. 100 CE) *Lunheng* 論衡 (Balanced Discussions; trans. Forke 1907–11,
1: 348–50 and 511). The technique's principles were laid down in the Jin period,
and it became widespread during the Six Dynasties and Tang periods. From
the Song onward, it is described in texts on Nourishing Life (*yangsheng) and
in medical texts, and more recently in *qigong texts.

The six breaths are related to the five viscera (*wuzang) and to a sixth organ
which, according to different sources, is either the "triple burner" (*sanjiao* 三
焦; see *wuzang) or the gallbladder. Essentially they have a therapeutic or
prophylactic action upon the viscera and their corresponding symptoms according to the principles of Chinese medicine. *Chui* heals ailments resulting
from cold and wind, *hu* ailments resulting from heat, *xi* ailments resulting from
wind and heat, *he* relaxes the *qi, *xu* clears away stagnations, and *si* dispels
heat. *Sun Simiao's *Qianjin fang* 千金方 (Prescriptions Worth a Thousand;
j. 29), however, also mentions an exorcistic action of these sounds.

Three fundamental systems can be distinguished in the *liuzi* technique:

1. The system of the *Huangting jing* (Scripture of the Yellow Court) tradition, described in the *Huangting neijing wuzang liufu buxie tu* 黃庭內景五
   臟六腑補瀉圖 (Charts of the Strengthening and Weakening of the Five
   Viscera and the Six Receptacles, According to the Scripture of the Inner
   Effulgences of the Yellow Court; CT 432).

2. The system based on the lost *Yangsheng yaoji* (Essentials of Nourishing
   Life), described in the *Songshan Taiwu xiansheng qijing* 嵩山太無先生氣經
   (Scripture on Breath by the Elder of Great Non-Being from Mount Song;
   CT 824, 9a–b; trans. Huang Jane 1987–90, 2: 24–25), the *Huanzhen xiansheng
   fu nei yuanqi jue* 幻真先生服內元氣訣 (Instructions on the Ingestion of
   the Inner Original Breath According to the Elder of Illusory Perfection;
   CT 828, 7a–b, and YJQQ 60.20b–21a; trans. Despeux 1988, 79–80, from
   the version in the *Chifeng sui), the *Tiaoqi jing* 調氣經 (Scripture on the
   Regulation of Breath; CT 820, 7a; trans. Huang Jane 1987–90, 1: 75–77),
   the *Taixi biyao gejue* 胎息祕要歌訣 (Songs and Instructions on the Secret
   Essentials of Embryonic Breathing; CT 131, 1b; trans. Huang Jane 1987–90,
   1: 50–51), and several other texts.

3. The system attributed to Zhi Dun 支盾 (314–66, also known as Zhi Daolin
   支道林), described in the *Daolin shesheng lun* 道林攝生論 ([Zhi] Daolin's
   Essay on Preserving Life; CT 1427) and the *Qianjin fang* (*j.* 27).

The number of repetitions of the six breaths was sometimes codified: eighty-
one times after midnight, seventy-two times at cockcrow, sixty-three times at
dawn, and so forth. A more complex method is described in the mid-twelfth-
century *Daoshu (Pivot of the Dao; *j.* 35). Here the six sounds are uttered in

different directions according to the time of practice; gymnastic movements and body positions are to be used concurrently.

Catherine DESPEUX

📖 Despeux 1988, 32–33, 36–37; Despeux 1995; Maspero 1981, 495–99; Miura Kunio 1989, 355–56

※ *yangsheng*

longhu

龍虎

dragon and tiger

The symbolic use of the dragon-tiger couple in China goes back to the Neolithic period. In a burial at Puyang 濮陽 (Henan), dating from ca. 3000 BCE, a corpse was found flanked with the images of a dragon and tiger formed with river shells, the former on its eastern side and the latter on its western side (Little 2000a, 710; see also Despeux 1994, 119). From the late Zhou period onward, dragon and tiger were used in a cosmological context. On a lacquer box excavated from a Warring States period tomb at Suixian 隨縣 (Hubei), they appear adjoining the Northern Dipper (*beidou) and surrounded by the twenty-eight lunar lodges (*xiu). Moreover, the magical powers of the tiger and dragon related to wind and clouds are depicted in the *Chuci* 楚辭 (Songs of Chu; see Hawkes 1985, 131).

In the symbolic language of Taoism, and especially in alchemy, dragon and tiger represent two opposite cosmic principles, such as Yin and Yang, in their dynamic evolution. In the *Zhouyi cantong qi*, dragon and tiger refers to the essence of the alchemical work, which consists of joining the two cosmic principles and of returning them to the central Oneness (see fig. 55). Depending on the context, dragon and tiger variously denote pairs such as man and woman, Wood and Metal (i.e., East and West, or the *zhen* 震 ☳ and *dui* 兌 ☱ trigrams), Fire and Water (i.e., South and North, or the *li* 離 ☲ and *kan* 坎 ☵ trigrams), Mercury and Lead, tripod and furnace (*dinglu), the pneumas of the liver and lungs or of the heart and kidneys, spirit and pneuma (*shen and *qi), or pneuma and essence (*qi and *jing).

KIM Daeyeol

📖 Robinet 1989a

※ *neidan*; *waidan*

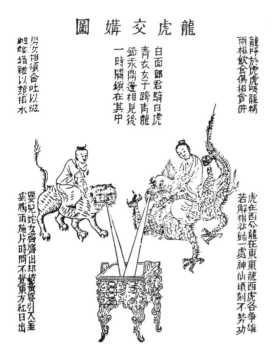

Fig. 55. Dragon and Tiger joining their essences in the alchemical tripod. *Xingming guizhi* 性命圭旨 (Principles of Balanced Cultivation of Inner Nature and Vital Force).

Longhu jing

龍虎經

Scripture of the Dragon and Tiger

Several alchemical and other sources associate the *Zhouyi cantong qi* with the *Longhu jing* and two other texts, the *Jinbi jing* 金碧經 (Scripture of Gold and Jasper) and the *Qiantong jue* 潛通訣 (Instructions for Pervading the Unseen). Although these texts claim that Wei Boyang 魏伯陽 was inspired to write the *Cantong qi* after reading the *Longhu jing*, the relation among these and the other two scriptures is not immediately clear. Passages quoted from one text are found in the present version of another, and the use of titles such as *Jinbi longhu jing* 金碧龍虎經 or *Jinbi qiantong jue* 金碧潛通訣 might even raise doubts as to the number of different works to which they refer.

The Taoist Canon contains two editions of the *Longhu jing* that claim to preserve its "ancient text" (*guwen* 古文). One, entitled *Guwen longhu jing zhushu* 古文龍虎經注疏 (Commentary and Subcommentary to the Ancient Text of the Scripture of the Dragon and Tiger; CT 996), was edited with a commentary by Wang Dao 王道, and bears his preface dated 1185. The other, called

Guwen longhu shangjing zhu 古文龍虎上經注 (Commentary to the Ancient Text of the Superior Scripture of the Dragon and Tiger; CT 997), contains anonymous and undated annotations. Wang Ming (1984g, 279–83) has shown that the *Guwen longhu jing* corresponds to the text entitled *Jindan jinbi qiantong jue* 金丹金碧潛通訣 (Golden and Jasper Instructions on the Golden Elixir for Pervading the Unseen) in the **Yunji qiqian* (73.7b–11b). The *Jinbi jing* / *Guwen longhu jing* is a shorter paraphrase of the *Cantong qi*, although less refined from a literary point of view and more replete with typical alchemical language than the *Cantong qi*.

Quotations from the *Longhu jing* in Tang and early Song sources show that *Longhu jing* was until that time an alternative title of the *Cantong qi*. The *Jinbi jing* was originally a distinct but related text, referred to by some authors as *Qiantong jue* (hence its title in the *Yunji qiqian*). In the Song, the *Jinbi jing* came to represent the "authentic" text of the *Longhu jing*, a scripture kept in Heaven, of which the *Cantong qi* is the terrestrial complement.

Fabrizio PREGADIO

📖 Wang Ming 1984g, 279–83; Wong Eva 1997 (trans.)

※ *longhu; neidan*

Longhu shan

龍虎山

Mount Longhu (Jiangxi)

Longhu shan, or Mount of the Dragon and Tiger, is a chain of low hills in the Guixi 貴溪 district of eastern Jiangxi, connected to the *Wuyi shan range extending into Fujian province. The various temples and residences that make up Longhu shan as an institution are actually spread over a rather large area and located either on the hills or in nearby villages. The site has been included in lists of sacred Taoist spots since the Tang period, but its real significance lies in its being indissolubly linked to the destiny of a Zhang 張 family from the Longhu shan area, which emerged between the eighth and ninth centuries as heirs of *Zhang Daoling.

Whether this family's claim of direct descent from the Zhangs who founded the Way of the Celestial Masters (*Tianshi dao) during the late second century CE is true is neither verifiable nor very likely, but in any case, by the Song period it came to be widely validated by imperial, Taoist, and popular opinion. The family's notion that the title of Celestial Master (*tianshi) conferred by Laozi upon Zhang Daoling in 142 CE is hereditary also seems to be its own invention. The first known official title of a Zhang from Longhu shan as Celestial Master was granted in the mid-tenth century. The Zhangs' and Longhu shan's prestige and official patronage reached new heights with the thirtieth Celestial Master, *Zhang Jixian (1092–1126), arguably the most charismatic ever. The precise title and the level of honors conferred by the court to the Zhangs changed every so often under successive dynasties (the word *tianshi* was not used in official titles after 1368, and replaced by the more modest *zhenren*), but the principle remained, upheld by the state until 1911, that the Zhang family had inherited Zhang Daoling's role as overseer of Taoism and protector of its orthodoxy.

For more than ten centuries, until 1949, the aristocratic and very well-connected Zhang family held court in Longhu shan, supported by a large retinue of elite Taoist priests serving as the Celestial Master's officials. During the Ming and Qing periods, these priests were known collectively as *faguan* 法官 (lit., "officers of the [exorcistic] ritual") and held official, but not paid positions in the imperial bureaucracy. The function of Celestial Master has been transmitted, usually from father to son, occasionally to nephews, and the published history of the family (the *Han tianshi shijia* or *Lineage of the Han Celestial Master*) as well as private genealogies document the fully reliable history from about the twentieth generation to the present contested sixty-fourth successor living in Taiwan, Zhang Yuanxian 張源先. Some members of the family today play leading roles in Taoism in continental China.

Celestial Masters travelled to the imperial court for audiences and to various places (especially in Jiangnan 江南 by the Ming and Qing) when invited to perform rituals. They held ordination, selected new *faguan*, and sent their *faguan* on missions. They spent most of their time on Longhu shan, however, and resisted attempts by the court to fix them under closer control in the capital city. They sometimes managed to defuse such attempts by delegating at court trusted and gifted Longhu shan officials, like *Zhang Liusun (1248–1322) or *Lou Jinyuan (1689–1776).

The real basis of the Longhu shan institution is the ordination of priests (and the canonization of gods, which works the same way, i.e., through the conferral of liturgical registers or *LU, which gives one a rank within the spiritual hierarchy of the universe). These ordinations took place in the mountain's major temple, the *Shangqing gong (Palace of Highest Clarity). During the Song, Longhu shan shared the privilege of being an official ordination center with *Maoshan and *Gezao shan, but by the Ming it had gained an undisputed monopoly. The reason Longhu shan emerged as the ultimate source of authority in premodern Taoism is that its ordinations very early on included registers needed to master the newly revealed Thunder and exorcist rites (*leifa) along with the classical *Lingbao liturgy (this synthesis is called in modern times Qingwei Lingbao 清微靈寶; see under *Qingwei). Ordinations on several levels were conferred at Longhu shan, however, and masters initiated in local, vernacular and exorcistic traditions (such as Lüshan 閭山) were also welcome and ordained, albeit at a lower rank and with a pledge to practice "orthodox Taoism" only.

Longhu shan thus worked, by incentive rather than punitive methods, to maintain the relative purity of Taoist practice while being very inclusive. Ordinations at Longhu shan were actually just a confirmation of a priest's former ordination by his own master, but the prestige bestowed by a trip to Longhu shan was huge; making the journey was like buying charisma.

Vincent GOOSSAERT

📖 Barrett 1994b; Cao Benye and Liu Hong 1996; Little 2000b, 380–81; Zhang Jintao 1994; Zhang Jiyu 1990

※ Zhengyi; TAOIST SACRED SITES

Longmen

龍門

Gate of the Dragon

The most common lineage shared by Taoist priests from the Qing until the present, the Longmen school was charged with public ordinations from the early Qing period onward. The Longmen lineage can be seen as the Taoist counterpart of the Buddhist Linji 臨濟 lineage, adherence to which most Buddhist monks profess even today on the basis of their ordination (Welch 1967, 281 and 396). The mythical foundation of the school goes back to *Qiu Chuji (1148–1227), one of the Seven Perfected (*qizhen* 七真; see table 17) of the *Quanzhen school. In particular, the school's name refers to Mount Longmen (Longmen shan 龍門山, Longzhou district, Western Shaanxi) where Qiu Chuji underwent his ascetic training. However, the institutionalization of the Longmen school with its own monasteries and patriarchal lineage allegedly took place only during the Qing dynasty with Wang Kunyang 王崑陽, better known under his lineage name, Changyue 常月 (?–1680, see *Wang Changyue).

In 1656, as the abbot of the *Baiyun guan (Abbey of the White Clouds) in Beijing, Wang was officially recognized as the reformer of the Longmen teaching that allegedly had been transmitted in an uninterrupted lineage from Qiu Chuji to him. For that purpose, a fictive line of Longmen patriarchs was cooked up which led, of course, to Wang Changyue. As the ideal representative of the seventh Longmen patriarchal generation, Wang became the symbol of the beginning of a new era in which the Longmen school could supervise the education of the entire Taoist clergy, as had been the case with its mother-school Quanzhen during the Yuan dynasty. Indeed, Longmen was regarded as the Qing "renaissance" of the Quanzhen school which, after its great success during the Yuan dynasty, had been eclipsed during the Ming. Beginning with Wang Changyue, the abbotship of the Baiyun guan, the seat of the Quanzhen patriarchy under the Yuan (and the *Zhengyi administration under the Ming), returned to the Quanzhen legacy through Longmen masters. In this manner, the Longmen tradition became influential.

Origins and branches. The foundation legend of the Longmen school starts with the direct transmission from the patriarch Qiu Chuji to his disciple Zhao Xujing 趙虛靜 (lineage name Daojian 道堅, 1163–1221). Zhao, after having received the three-stage ordination, became the first Longmen patriarch. Since then, the three-stage ordination is said to have been conferred along with a lineage name composed of two characters (the first of which stems from a Longmen twenty-character poem; see Yoshioka Yoshitoyo 1979, 231). This marked the entry of a Taoist adept into the ancestral line of Longmen masters.

After Zhao, the correct line of Longmen patriarchs was established and portrayed as continuous from the Yuan dynasty until the present. The list of the first seven generations of Longmen patriarchs until Wang Changyue, however—a line that was officially accepted and promulgated in the Taoist public abbeys during the Qing dynasty (Oyanagi Shigeta 1934, 32–35, and Igarashi Kenryū 1938, 64–65)—was created ex post-facto in order to link the relatively new movement of Longmen to the ancient vestige of the powerful Quanzhen order and to the important figure of Qiu Chuji. The *Jingai xindeng* 金蓋心燈 (Transmission of the Heart-Lamp from Mount Jingai; 1821), a fundamental source for the history of the Longmen lineage by *Min Yide (1748–1836), testifies to this official view. A closer reading, though, reveals many discrepancies that suggest another side of the Longmen history (Esposito 1993; Esposito 2001; Esposito 2004c; Mori Yuria 1994). One can then detect the existence of other previous lines of masters who claimed to belong to the Longmen lineage without having any link with the ideal correct lineage of seven patriarchs culminating with Wang Changyue (Wang Zhizhong 1995). A good example is the Longmen lineage of Wu Chongxu 伍冲虛, better known under his lineage name, Shouyang 守陽 (1574–1644; see Mori Yuria 1994 and Esposito 2004c; see also the entry *Wu Shouyang).

Originally, the Longmen was a product of hermits who, influenced by ancient Quanzhen ideals and by the fame of its saint, Qiu Chuji, devoted themselves to ascetic training without necessarily being affiliated with the Quanzhen order. During the Ming period, different ascetic movements arose around famous centers, such as those of Mount Hua (*Huashan, Shaanxi), Mount

Lao (*Laoshan, Shandong), Mount Wudang (*Wudang shan, Hubei), Mount Qingcheng (*Qingcheng shan, Sichuan), and so forth, and a Longmen patriarchal tradition began to form under the syncretic impulsions of the Zhengyi lineage. The multiplication of Longmen branches was a phenomenon of the late Ming dynasty. Thanks only to the reformer Wang Changyue, however, Longmen became an officially recognized "Quanzhen movement." In his wake, the various Longmen branches came to be integrated into an ideal lineage of Longmen patriarchs. Many famous branches flourished in southeastern China: for instance the Hangzhou (Zhejiang) branches of the Tianzhu guan 天柱觀 (Abbey of the Pillar of Heaven), the Jingu dong 金鼓洞 (Cavern of the Golden Drum), and the Dade guan 大德觀 (Abbey of Great Virtue). In Zhejiang, one also finds the branch of Tongbo (Tongbo shan 桐柏山), the Yunchao 雲巢 branch of Mount Jingai (Jingai shan 金蓋山) at Huzhou 湖州, and others. Longmen branches were also present in southwestern China, such as the Longmen Tantric branch of Mount Jizu (Jizu shan 雞足山, Yunnan; see Esposito 1993, 2: 389–440, and Esposito 1997, 67–123). In the northeast, there was for instance the Gansu branch of the eleventh patriarch, *Liu Yiming (1734–1821).

Monica ESPOSITO

📖 Chen Bing 1988; Esposito 1993; Esposito 1997; Esposito 2001; Esposito 2004c; Igarashi Kenryū 1938, 64–65; Mori Yuria 1994; Oyanagi Shigeta 1934, 32–35; Qing Xitai 1988–95, 4: 77–183 and 280–329; Qing Xitai 1994, 1: 200–205; Wang Zhizhong 1995; Yoshioka Yoshitoyo 1979

※ Wang Changyue; for other related entries see the Synoptic Table of Contents, sec. IV.3 ("Alchemy: Longmen")

Lou Jinyuan

婁近垣

1689–1776; *zi*: Sanchen 三臣; *hao*: Langzhai 朗齋 (Fast in Brightness),
Shangqing wairen 上清外人 (Guest of Highest Clarity)

Lou Jinyuan is probably, along with a few abbots of the *Baiyun guan (Abbey of the White Clouds), the Taoist of the Qing dynasty who gained the greatest national prestige. His life is reminiscent in many ways of the famous *Zhang Liusun, chaplain of Khubilai khan (Shizu, r. 1260–1294) of the Yuan dynasty. Like Zhang, Lou was a young Taoist of a hereditary family of priests attached to the prestigious Mount Longhu (*Longhu shan, Jiangxi); he was brought to the court in the retinue of the Celestial Master, gained the attention of the emperor, and stayed on to embark on a career that would be even more glorious than that of the Celestial Master of his time.

Lou's career was due to the links he forged with the Yongzheng Emperor (r. 1723–35) on a personal basis. During the eighteenth century, as before, the Celestial Masters provided liturgical services for the court, either in person or by delegating Taoist officers of their own administration. During the late 1720s, however, the Zhang 張 family was going through a succession crisis, when a young heir was being dispossessed by an uncle. This succession was only settled in the 1740s; in the meantime, it was Lou who accrued to his person all the charisma of the Longhu institution and tradition. Lou arrived at the capital in 1727 and in 1730 cured the emperor by performing exorcisms. He was then granted considerable honors, and presided over a much expanded Taoist liturgical structure at court, centered on a temple named Da guangming dian 大光明殿 (Great Pavilion of Radiant Light). Yongzheng's successor, Qianlong (r. 1735–95), was less enthusiastic than his father about Taoism, but continued to patronize Lou Jinyuan, who stayed at court until at least 1744. Lou secured a large amount of state funding for restorations at Longhu shan, and also preferential treatment for its institutions during an anticlerical campaign of clergy registration (1736–39). These events are described in a gazetteer compiled by Lou himself, the *Longhu shanzhi* 龍虎山志 (Monograph of Mount Longhu; 1740). Lou also reorganized the lineages of the Longhu Taoists: he wielded the power of a Celestial Master without the title. As befitted a liturgical expert, he wrote authoritative versions of several rituals, notably the *Lingbao death ritual. He also composed philosophical commentaries, and some of his poetry is preserved in the *Longhu shanzhi*.

Lou brought with him, or invited to court, some forty Taoists, all young members of the great hereditary *Zhengyi families traditionally linked to the Mount Longhu elite (by appointment to the Taoist administration but also by marriage). Most of these families lived in Jiangnan, some controlling the major temples of these areas such as the *Xuanmiao guan (Abbey of Mysterious Wonder) in Suzhou. Like Lou, these Taoists usually spent several years at the court, early in their careers as masters, before returning home to assume leading positions in local Taoist institutions. This system established by Lou Jinyuan whereby the elite Zhengyi priests of the Jiangnan area paid a few years of service at court continued until the late nineteenth century, but no other Taoist ever reached a position of personal prestige and influence over the emperor comparable to that enjoyed by Lou.

Vincent GOOSSAERT

📖 Goossaert 2000a; Hosoya Yoshio 1986; Qing Xitai 1994, 1: 395

※ Zhengyi

Louguan

樓觀

Tiered Abbey (Zhouzhi, Shaanxi)

The Louguan, or Louguan tai 樓觀臺 (Platform of the Tiered Abbey), is one of the Taoist centers with a long history of continuous activity. The abbey is located in Zhouzhi 周至 at the foot of the Zhongnan mountains (Zhongnan shan 終南山, Shaanxi), some 70 km southwest of Xi'an. Its foundation is shrouded in the mists of holy history. According to the legend, *Yin Xi, the Guardian of the Pass of the western border, built a tower there to watch for Laozi, who was about to leave the country. When he saw the holy man coming, he welcomed him in and begged him to write the *Daode jing*. The brief early mentions of this fictitious event suggest that it happened elsewhere, at the Hangu Pass (Hangu guan 函谷關), and indeed there is no pass for the west-bound traveller at the actual location of the Louguan. Temples commemorating the same event have also been built further east, while the Louguan buildings themselves are supposed to be Yin Xi's private home where he invited Laozi after the meeting at the pass.

According to a Louguan chronicle of the early Six Dynasties, now lost but quoted in the *Yunji qiqian* (104.9a–10a), King Mu of Zhou (Muwang, r. 956–918 BCE) came to this spot, ordained seven Taoists, and built the first Taoist shrine in history. This tradition, which also found its way into Confucian encyclopedias and Taoist inscriptions, has the virtue of placing the origin of Taoist abbeys (guan 觀) well before the advent of Buddhism in China. It requires, however, moving back by five centuries the traditional date of Laozi's departure to the West (fifth century BCE).

The Louguan's claim to be the first Taoist communal institution also has to do with its name. During the Han, *louguan* was a general term for high towers, and with *tai* 臺 (elevated platform) it also designated places to conduct astronomical observations and perform cults to the immortals. Along with the fact that imperial archives—whose patron saint was Laozi—were also named *guan*, this explains the later use of the term for Taoist monasteries.

The Louguan in Taoist history. Beyond the legend, a Taoist community may have lived at this site during the Han and early Six Dynasties. The official history of the Louguan begins however with the Northern Zhou dynasty (557–81), which established there an official celibate congregation. This group of erudite Taoists made itself famous through various scholarly works including the *Sandong zhunang* (The Pearl Satchel of the Three Caverns). The Tang lavished honors on the Louguan, a sensible policy because the imperial family claimed descent from Laozi and promoted his cult, and because the Louguan was, along with Laozi's birthplace (the *Taiqing gong in Bozhou 亳州, present-day Luyi 鹿邑, Henan), the "ancestral temple" of the saint. Since then, the shrine at the foot of the hills was called Zongsheng guan 宗聖觀 (Abbey of the Ancestral Saint) and later Zongsheng gong 宗聖宮 (Palace of the Ancestral Saint). The other major monastery on the site, the Shuojing tai 說經臺 (Platform for Explaining the Scriptures), was built later on the first spurs of the mountain, where Laozi supposedly preached the *Daode jing*. Several other hermitages were raised further up the mountain, and many smaller attractions along the way reminded pilgrims of Laozi's sacred history, such as the *xiniu bo* 系牛柏, the cypress to which Laozi tied his water buffalo.

A remarkable change of fortune for the Louguan happened in 1236, when the *Quanzhen order gained control of it. From the lack of contrary evidence it seems that the abbey was not particularly active during the late Jin period. *Yin Zhiping (1169–1251), then the Quanzhen patriarch, arrived in the area just after it fell to the Mongol armies, and secured the conversion of all its major Taoist sites to Quanzhen with the support of the local Chinese nobility and warlords. The Louguan was rebuilt and expanded by Li Zhirou 李志柔 (1189–1266). Yin put great store in the revival of the site's fortune, since Quanzhen claimed to represent a return to Laozi's days: *Qiu Chuji's westward journey to convert the "barbarians" (i.e., the Mongols and their emperor, Chinggis khan) was understood as a reenactment of Laozi's voyage, and Yin Zhiping took on the role of a novel Yin Xi. This claim was further bolstered when Yin Xi's treatise, known as *Wenshi zhenjing* 文始真經 (Authentic Scripture of Master Wenshi; CT 667) since the Tang but lost for centuries, was "rediscovered" in 1233 and offered to Yin Zhiping. These felicitous events, which helped to legitimize the reorganization of Taoism by the Quanzhen order, were celebrated by Zhu Xiangxian 朱象先 (fl. 1279–1308), who wrote the only extant hagiographic works concerning the Louguan. These are the *Zhenxian beiji* (Epigraphic Records of Real Men and Immortals; CT 956) and the *Gu Louguan ziyun yanqing ji* 古樓觀紫雲衍慶集 (Anthology from the Continued Celebration [of the Appearance] of the Purple Clouds at the Tiered Abbey of Antiquity; CT 957; Boltz J. M. 1987a, 126).

During the Ming and Qing dynasties, the Louguan continued to be a pilgrimage site for Taoists of all obediences and an active center of Quanzhen education. Today, the Shuojing tai survives in good shape, although the conventual buildings have been destroyed as with almost all Chinese monasteries. The Zongsheng gong was ravaged but has been built anew.

Vincent GOOSSAERT

📖 Boltz J. M. 1987a, 124–28; Hachiya Kunio 1990, 1: 71–87 and 302–3, 2: 73–90 and 298; Kohn 1997b, 92–109; Qing Xitai 1994, 4: 271–73; Wang Shiwei 1993; Wang Zhongxin 1995; Zhang Weiling 1991

※ Yin Xi; *Zhenxian beiji*; Louguan pai; Quanzhen; TEMPLES AND SHRINES

Louguan pai

樓觀派

Louguan branch [of Tianshi dao]

The so-called Louguan branch is a particular tradition within the northern Way of the Celestial Masters (*Tianshi dao), which arose in the late fifth century and flourished in the Tang, then lost its impact, and was revived under the Yuan dynasty. Historically the tradition can be traced back to two events: the end of the theocracy under *Kou Qianzhi in 448, which left numerous advanced and dedicated Taoists without a home; and—around the same time—the establishment of a Taoist institution at the foot of the Zhongnan mountains (Zhongnan shan 終南山, Shaanxi) by Yin Tong 尹通, an alleged descendant of *Yin Xi, the first recipient of the *Daode jing*. Yin Tong claimed that rather than at the Hangu Pass (Hangu guan 函谷關), where Laozi and Yin Xi first met, the *Daode jing* was in fact transmitted at Yin Xi's old homestead—awarded to him by King Kang of Zhou (Kangwang, r. 1005/3–978 BCE)—which happened to be Yin Tong's own estate in the Zhongnan mountains, a place he called "The Observatory" (*Louguan, also meaning "Tiered Abbey") after Yin Xi's alleged astrological endeavors.

By the 470s, Louguan first appears on the Taoist devotional map under the leadership of Wang Daoyi 王道義, who expanded its facilities and sponsored the collection of scriptures and rules. Some texts can be associated with the school at this time, notably the mystical *Xisheng jing* (Scripture of Western Ascension), the precepts book *Taishang Laojun jiejing* 太上老君戒經 (Scripture on Precepts of the Most High Lord Lao; CT 784), and the ordination text *Chuanshou jingjie yi zhujue* 傳授經戒儀注訣 (Annotated Instructions on Liturgies for the Transmission of Scriptures and Precepts; CT 1238). In the sixth century, Louguan leaders played a prominent role in the Buddho-Taoist debates at the northern courts, while the institution served as a refuge for Taoists persecuted under Emperor Wu of the Liang dynasty in the south. Through this steady influx of southern teachings, Louguan became instrumental in the integration of Taoism and eventually rose to serve as a key facilitator of the Tang bid for power.

In the early Tang, Louguan's patriarch *Yin Wencao (622–88), another alleged relative of Yin Xi, played a prominent role at court. It was yet another such relative, *Yin Zhiping (1169–1251), patriarch of the *Quanzhen school under the Yuan, who again catapulted Louguan to prominence in the thirteenth century. The Louguan traditions survive today as a *pai* 派 ("branch" or "lineage") within Quanzhen; the abbey is still a flourishing institution in the Zhongnan mountains.

Sources. The Louguan branch is first described in the early Tang inscription *Zongsheng guan ji* 宗聖觀記 (Records of the Abbey of the Ancestral Saint; 625 CE), using the honorific name the Tang emperors bestowed on the institution. Shortly after this, the *Louguan benji* 樓觀本記 (Original Records of Louguan) was compiled; it is lost today, but from citations in mid-Tang works it seems to have been a comprehensive history of the institution, first establishing a fictional line of patriarchs all the way back to Yin Xi.

Most explicit descriptions of the patriarchal lineage and the wonders of Louguan are found in Yuan-dynasty sources, notably the *Zhongnan shan Zuting xianzhen neizhuan* 終南山祖庭仙真內傳 (Inner Biographies of the Immortals and Perfected of the Ancestral Court in the Zhongnan Mountains; 1284; CT 955), by *Li Daoqian (1219–96); the *Gu Louguan ziyun yanqing ji* 古樓觀紫雲衍慶集 (Anthology from the Continued Celebration [of the Appearance] of the Purple Clouds at the Tiered Abbey of Antiquity; CT 957; Boltz J. M. 1987a, 126), a collection of stele inscriptions by Zhu Xiangxian 朱象先 (fl. 1279–1308); and the *Zhenxian beiji (Epigraphic Records of Perfected and Immortals; CT 956), also by Zhu Xiangxian, based on the older and now-lost *Louguan xianshi zhuan* 樓觀先師傳 (Biographies of Previous Louguan Masters).

Livia KOHN

📖 Kohn 1997b; Qing Xitai 1988–95, 1: 425–44 and 2: 141–45; Qing Xitai 1994, 1: 113–17; Zhang Weiling 1991

※ Louguan

lu

錄

register

See entry in "Taoism: An Overview," p. 39.

Lü Dongbin

呂洞賓

ming: Yan 喦 (*or*: 巖); *hao*: Chunyang zi 純陽子 (Master of Pure
Yang), Chunyang zhenjun 純陽真君 (Perfected Lord of Pure Yang),
Fuyou dijun 孚佑帝君 (Imperial Lord, Savior of the Needy)

Lü Dongbin is a semilegendary cultic figure of the late Tang or early Song
period. With his legendary master, *Zhongli Quan, he was the acknowledged
patriarch of both *Nanzong and *Quanzhen, i.e., the Southern and the Northern lineages of Taoism. Several hagiographies of him circulated during the
Song and early Yuan periods, excerpts of which are in the *Lishi zhenxian tidao
tongjian* (j. 45). One of them is an alleged autobiography produced in Yuezhou
嶽州 (Hunan), likely as the result of spirit writing (see *fuji*), in which Lü introduces himself as a native of Jingzhao 京兆 (Shaanxi). In another biography
of the same region popular in Taoist circles, he is said to be the grandson of
a high Tang official and to be from Yongle 永樂 in Shanxi (id., 45.1a). The
latter is the site of the *Yongle gong (Palace of Eternal Joy), a major temple
dedicated to Lü.

The two biographies mentioned above represent two different traditions:
one northern, the other southern. The former states that Lü was an unsuccessful scholar and a recluse who met both Zhongli Quan and *Chen Tuan
on Mount Hua (*Huashan) and the Zhongnan mountains (Zhongnan shan
終南山) in Shaanxi. The second biography instead places Lü's encounter
with Zhongli Quan on Mount Lu (*Lushan) in Jiangxi. Qin Zhi'an 秦志安
(1188–1244), a Quanzhen Taoist, quotes a third biography written on the wall
of the Qingyang guan 青羊觀 (Abbey of the Black Ram) in Yuezhou, which
claimed that Lü was born in 796 and acquired the *jinshi* degree in 836 (*Jinlian
zhengzong ji*, 5b–9a).

Early Song literary sources portray Lü Dongbin as a poet, calligrapher,
soothsayer, healer, alchemist, exorcist, and recluse possessing sword techniques.
He was revered both by the lettered classes and by ordinary people, especially
merchants. His biographies describe him as selling "ink and paper" in the
market-place, mingling incognito with the crowd, giving help to anyone who
recognized him. As a performer of miracles, Lü became the object of a cult as
attested by sources from the second half of the twelfth century, such as Hong
Mai's 洪邁 (1123–1202) *Yijian zhi* 夷堅志 (Heard and Written by Yijian), which
records stories told by illiterate informants. From Hong's anecdotes it emerges

Fig. 56. An episode from the life of Lü Dongbin. *Yongle gong (Palace of
Eternal Joy), Pavilion of the Three Clarities (Sanqing dian 三清殿).

that those who were most involved in Lü's cult belonged to underprivileged
classes, such as prostitutes, peddlers, itinerant Taoists, healers, medicinal herb
dealers, and ink-sellers.

Veneration by these groups led to Lü's name being used to voice criticism in
times of social unrest. Poems with his name, sometimes hidden in anagrams,
appeared on temple walls criticizing unjust or corrupt officials. Buddhists
used the same tool to convey their feelings when they were denigrated and
persecuted during the reign of Song Huizong (r. 1100–1125); one of the earliest
portraits of Lü, in fact, was placed in a Buddhist temple. Lü was also adopted
by subversive groups, sometimes leading to ludicrous imperial orders for his
arrest (Ma Xiaohong 1986, 86).

As Isabelle Ang (1993) has shown, there were traces of Lü's cult in the Northern Song capital Kaifeng (Henan), but the main center was along the lower Yangzi River, from the Jiangnan 江南 region down to the southern part of Hunan. The status of the cult was originally rather low, its main forms being worship in homes, through mediums, and in shrines. In 1119, however, Lü was awarded the low-rank official title of Perfected of Wondrous Powers (Miaotong zhenren 妙通真人) by Huizong and was integrated in official temples such as the Tianqing guan 天慶觀 (Abbey of Celestial Blessings; abbeys with this name existed in major cities throughout the empire). Later, during the Yuan dynasty, the increased popularity of the Quanzhen order led to Lü's promotion to *zhenjun* 真君 (Perfected Lord). A Yuan text by *Chen Zhixu describes a ritual performed in his honor on his birthday (*Jindan dayao, Xianpai 仙派; CT 1070, 2a–8a).

The Northern Song dynasty also saw the appearance of several *neidan texts attributed to Zhongli Quan and Lü Dongbin. Some of these so-called *Zhong-Lü texts are directly related to the cultic centers in Hunan and Jiangxi. For example, one of them, the *Qinyuan chun, was revealed in Yuezhou and another, the *Zhouhou sancheng pian* 肘後三成篇 (Folios on the Three Accomplishments to Keep at Hand; *Daoshu, j. 25), was printed and distributed by a governor during the Shunxi reign period (1174–89) in Yueyang 嶽陽 (Hunan).

Lü Dongbin reportedly ascended to heaven from the Huanghe lou 黃鶴樓 (Pavilion of the Yellow Crane) in Jiangxi, which became the site of a stele bearing his biography. From the Southern Song onward, writings of all kinds were attributed to him, including moral texts and sexual manuals. The Ming dynasty saw a spate of activity around Lü that continues to the present day.

Farzeen BALDRIAN-HUSSEIN

📖 Ang 1993; Ang 1997; Baldrian-Hussein 1985; Baldrian-Hussein 1986; Boltz J. M. 1987a, 64, 67–68, and 139–43; Chen Yuan 1988, 358; Despeux 1990, 77–82; Jing Anning 1996; Katz P. R. 1996; Katz P. R. 1999, 52–93; Kohn 1993b, 126–32; Little 2000b, 324–27; Ma Xiaohong 1986; Mori Yuria 1990; Qing Xitai 1994, 1: 295–97; see also bibliography for the entry *baxian

※ Yongle gong; *Chunyang Lü zhenren wenji*; *Lüzu quanshu*; *Qinyuan chun*; *Taiyi jinhua zongzhi*; *Zhong-Lü chuandao ji*; *neidan*; Nanzong; Quanzhen; Zhong-Lü; HAGIOGRAPHY

Lu Shizhong

路時中

fl. 1120–30; *zi*: Dangke 當可; *hao*: Lu zhenguan 路真官
(Perfected Official Lu)

Lu Shizhong was the founder of the Yutang dafa 玉堂大法 (Great Rites of the Jade Hall) tradition, which is represented in the *Daozang* notably by the *Wushang xuanyuan santian Yutang dafa* 無上玄元三天玉堂大法 (Great Rites of the Jade Hall of the Three Heavens, of the Supreme Mysterious Origin; CT 220) in thirty *juan*, and by the *Wushang santian Yutang zhengzong gaoben neijing yushu* 無上三天玉堂正宗高奔內景玉書 (The Precious Text of Flying High in the Inner Landscape, of the Correct Tradition of the Jade Hall of the Supreme Three Heavens; CT 221) in two *juan*. The episodes in his adult life, recounted with dates in Hong Mai's 洪邁 (1123–1202) *Yijian zhi* 夷堅志 (Heard and Written by Yijian), all take place in the period 1125–30 (Zhonghua shuju ed., *Yizhi* 6.4.232, 7.1.237–39, *Bingzhi* 5.5.403–04). He is shown to have been active in widely separated areas of China (from Xuzhou 徐州 in the north to Jinling 金陵 in the south) and to have been called upon by members of the official class to perform large ceremonies on their behalf.

In a colophon in the *Santian Yutang dafa* (CT 220, 1.7a–8a) Lu relates that in the year 1120 he had a vision one night of Zhao Sheng 趙昇 (a disciple of *Zhang Daoling), who descended into his room and told him about the "secret writing" (*bishu* 祕書) he had left behind, buried in the ground at Mount Mao (*Maoshan, Jiangsu). When later Lu served as Assistant Prefect (*tongshou* 通守) in Jinling (it should be noted that in fact this title was not, at least officially, in use during the Song dynasty), he visited the mountain and dug up the scroll. He arranged the text in twenty-four sections (corresponding to j. 1–23 of the *Santian Yutang dafa*) and in 1126, while staying in Piling 毗陵 (Jiangsu), transmitted it to the world. Another colophon (26.1b), attached to a later part of the text, states that the "model sayings" (*geyan* 格言, the discursive passages interspersed between the ritual formulas and usually opening with the phrase *shiyue* 師曰, "the master said") in this section were revealed consecutively during the first half of the year 1107, in the form of oral instructions from the Celestial Lord, the Great Master of the Teaching (Da jiaozhu tianjun 大教主天君). From that time until the year 1119 the actual ritual formulas were transmitted through "spirit writing" (*jiangbi* 降筆; see *fuji*), and the full collection was copied in 1158.

Yutang dafa. The Yutang dafa tradition is defined in the book as the "inner secrets" (*neibi* 內祕) of the *Tianxin zhengfa (26.1a) and said to represent the essential method of Zhang Daoling (1.7b). The Tianxin tradition is referred to as the "ancestral teaching" (*zujiao* 祖教, 2.6a), and the oral instructions from the Great Master of the Teaching are said to have been obtained as elucidations of the teachings of the Tianxin tradition (1.5b–6a). The Yutang dafa tradition is maintained to be more fundamental and more meditational, and the Tianxin tradition is said to have been discovered—as a result of the above-mentioned oral instructions—to represent the exorcistic (i.e., the outer) practices (*quxie zi shi* 驅邪之事) of the Yutang dafa (1.6a). The link to the "ancestral teaching" is preserved accordingly, as attested by the expositions of the progression of initiation in the *Santian Yutang dafa* (2.6a, 26.1b–2a). It is stated there that the novice may receive a work entitled *Tianxin zhengfa* in ten *juan*, i.e., a special version of *Taishang zhuguo zongzhen biyao* edited by Lu Shizhong ("in order to support the correct teaching"), and only after having practiced it for three years may ascend to the initial degree of the Yutang dafa.

This connection with the Tianxin tradition is borne out by the contents of the *Santian Yutang dafa*. The two traditions agree in emphasizing the use of the forces of the Three Luminous Ones (*sanguang* 三光, i.e., the Sun, the Moon, and the Northern Dipper, *beidou), for instance in the writing of talismans, and indeed the three basic talismans of the Tianxin tradition (*Sanguang fu* 三光符, *Heisha fu* 黑煞符, *Tiangang fu* 天罡符; see *Taishang zhuguo jiumin zongzhen biyao, 2.10a–17a, and fig. 73) are included—with certain variations—in the text. A large proportion of the exorcistic rites it describes are closely related to those found in the texts of the Tianxin tradition. The major differences are on the one hand the inclusion of elements of the funerary liturgy, such as the rite of *liandu (Salvation through Refinement) within the Yutang dafa, and on the other hand the greater emphasis on individual meditation practice in this tradition.

Poul ANDERSEN

📖 Andersen 1991, 97–103; Boltz J. M. 1987a, 36–37; Boltz J. M. 1993a; Davis E. 2001, 56–57; Hymes 1996, 58–60

※ Tianxin zhengfa

Lu Xiujing

陸修靜

406–77; *zi*: Yuande 元德; *hao*: Jianji 簡寂
(Unadorned Silence)

Lu Xiujing, whose family hailed from Dongqian 東遷 district (modern Zhe-jiang), played an important role in the development of Taoism as compiler and editor of the *Lingbao scriptures, as codifier of the first Taoist Canon, and as author of early ritual. Like other early Taoists, his biography was not included in official histories and so must be reconstructed from the works of later Taoist and Buddhist authors.

Lu was a descendant of Lu Kai 陸凱, a prominent Counselor-in-Chief (*chengxiang* 丞相) of the Wu ruler Sun Hao 孫皓 (Wucheng gong, r. 264–80), but there is no record that any members of his family were involved in adminis-tration during Lu's lifetime. According to his earliest biographer, Ma Shu 馬樞 (522–81), at birth Lu was marked with signs of transcendence and, at a young age, abandoned his wife and children to pursue the Dao. These and other details of Lu's early life are the commonplaces of Taoist hagiography. We possess no reliable account of Lu's early training or of the identity of his masters.

Ma also records that Liu Yilong 劉義隆 (Song Wendi, r. 424–52) summoned Lu into his presence and questioned him at length about the Dao. Other sources record that Lu left the capital to avoid the disturbances surrounding the regicide and usurpation of the heir apparent in 453. The introduction to Lu's *Lingbao jingmu (Catalogue of Lingbao Scriptures), composed in 437 and addressed to all fellow Taoists, contains lengthy citations from the Santian zhengfa jing 三天正法經 (Scripture of the Orthodox Law of the Three Heav-ens; CT 1203; Ozaki Masaharu 1974) arranged so as to portray the appearance of the Lingbao scriptures as warrant of the Song dynasty's mandate. Such confirmatory writings may well have brought Lu to imperial attention. Lu's *Lingbao shoudu yi (Ordination Ritual of the Numinous Treasure) is preceded by a petition presenting the text to the throne. In this petition, Lu writes that it had been seventeen years since his own receipt of the scriptures, an event that likely occurred when he was about twenty. Thus, this text also seems to date to this same period, having been composed ca. 445.

Lu spent the years from 453 to 467 on Mount Lu (*Lushan, Jiangxi), an active Buddhist center from the time of Huiyuan 慧遠 (334–416). Here Lu established a hermitage and trained disciples. In 467, Lu was summoned to the capital by Liu Yu 劉彧 (Song Mingdi, r. 465–72). Along the way, he was entertained by the

Prince of Jiangzhou 江州 (possibly Liu Xiufan 劉休範), who inquired of him the relative strengths of Buddhism and Taoism. Following Lu's arrival in Jiankang 建康 (Jiangsu), he received the patronage of eminent men in the capital and participated in several debates with Buddhist prelates and Arcane Learning (*Xuanxue) masters in the capital, winning each time, as Buddhist records confirm.

The emperor subsequently provided Lu with an abbey, the Chongxu guan 崇虛觀 (Abbey for the Veneration of Emptiness), on the northern outskirts of the capital. In 471, Lu conducted a twenty-day Three Primes Retreat (*sanyuan zhai* 三元齋) for the emperor, who lay fatally ill. The emperor recovered, but died the next year. Lu himself died in the capital, after having told his disciples he wished to return to Mount Lu. His disciples on the mountain, reports Ma, were thus granted a brief vision of him, clothed in resplendent ritual garments. Modern researchers take this to mean that his body was returned to Mount Lu for burial.

Lu's major contributions to Taoism were his editing of the Lingbao scriptures, his publication of the first "comprehensive" list of Taoist scriptures, the *Sandong jingshu mulu*, and his contributions to the formation of formal Taoist liturgies and a professional priesthood.

Editorial contributions. Lu describes his goals in editing the Lingbao scriptures in his *Lingbao jingmu* and his preface to the *Lingbao shoudu yi*. While some modern scholars suspect Lu himself of having written a good portion of the Lingbao scriptures, in these works he portrays his primary duty as "discrimination" (*zhenbie* 甄別) of the "true" scriptures from the *Shangqing and other scriptures with which they were mixed by unscrupulous persons. Even when Lu produces a new text, as with his *Lingbao shoudu yi*, he expresses his uneasiness at tampering with celestial writ even to this extent.

Lu also completed the first complete listing of Taoist scriptures, dividing them into three "caverns" (*sandong) or comprehensive collections (see *Sandong jingshu mulu*). In addition, Lu wrote a revision of *Tianshi dao codes, the *Daomen kelüe* (Abridged Codes for the Taoist Community), for what he envisioned to be a newly-unified Taoist community.

Ritual innovations. According to later Taoist writers, Lu's primary work was that of composing liturgical programs. Traces of this work can best be seen in his Lingbao initiation ritual, which combines citations and practices from a number of Lingbao scriptures. His now-lost writings are regularly cited in Tang and Song-period ritual compendia. Surviving works include Lu's *Wugan wen* 五感文 (Text on the Five Commemorations; CT 1278), meant to create in practitioners a correct attitude for the performance of *zhai. This text was composed for a Mud and Soot Retreat (*tutan zhai*) Lu conducted with his disciples in 453 and was intended by Lu for use with rituals of all three divisions of Taoist scripture. It ends with a brief account of eleven *zhai*. Lu's *Lingbao zhai* *shuo guangzhu jiefa dengzhu yuanyi* 靈寶齋說光燭戒罰燈祝願儀 (Explanation of Candle-Illumination, Precepts and Penalties, Lamps, Invocations, and Vows for Lingbao Retreats; CT 524) and *Lingbao zhongjian wen* 靈寶眾簡文 (Tablets and Texts of Lingbao; CT 410) both provide detail, drawn from the Lingbao scriptures and provided by Lu, on the symbolism and practice of ritual. Buddhist sources mention eight further treatises by Lu, some clearly dealing with Lingbao attempts to appropriate Buddhism, but these have not survived.

Criticism of Lu's attempts at unifying and regularizing Taoist practice began soon after his death. Buddhist polemicists accused him of plagiarizing elements of their scriptures and of incorporating earlier non-Taoist works into his catalogue. They also reported that he had turned traitor on the Qi dynasty, taking his disciples to the north, or that he had been defeated in debate—all said to occur after Lu's death date. Even Taoists, such as *Tao Hongjing, criticized Lu of misrepresentation or misappropriation. It was only with the Taoist scholasticism of the Tang that his reputation among Taoists was fully restored and not until Song Buddhist accommodations with Taoism that Buddhists looked back upon him favorably and began to construct legends that Lu had studied with Huiyuan on Mount Lu.

Stephen R. BOKENKAMP

📖 Bell 1987a; Bell 1988; Bokenkamp 1997, 377–98; Bokenkamp 2001; Chen Guofu 1963, 38–44, 282–83; Nickerson 1996a; Ōfuchi Ninji 1997, 57–72; Qing Xitai 1988–95, 1: 465–83; Ren Jiyu 1990, 143–68; Yamada Toshiaki 1995b; Yoshioka Yoshitoyo 1955, 18–44

※ *Daomen kelüe*; *Lingbao jingmu*; *Lingbao shoudu yi*; *Sandong jingshu mulu*; Lingbao

Lu Xixing

陸西星

1520–1601 or 1606; *zi*: Changgeng 長更; *hao*: Qianxu zi 潛虛子 (Master Secluded in Emptiness), Fanghu waishi 方壺外史 (The External Secretary of Mount Fanghu)

Lu Xixing is the alleged founder of the Eastern Branch (Dongpai 東派) of late *neidan. A native of Yangzhou 揚州 (Jiangsu), he began his career as an official and then turned to Taoism, but it is unclear whether he took formal ordination. Although he was married and had children, he used to leave them frequently to visit famous mountains. He claimed that, in 1547, *Lü Dongbin descended to his thatched hut in Beihai 北海 (Jiangsu) and stayed with him twenty days to give him teachings. Among other works, Lu received from Lü Dongbin a collection of texts entitled *Zhongnan shan ji* 終南山記 (Records of the Zhongnan Mountains) in ten *juan* and Lü's own autobiography (*ziji* 自記).

Lu was a prolific author, and some of his works were officially inscribed on stone during his lifetime. Among them are an essay on the *Zhuangzi* entitled the *Nanhua jing fumo* 南華經副墨 (Ancillary Words on the *Nanhua jing*; 1578) and the *Lengyan jing shuzhi* 楞嚴經述旨 (Explaining the Purport of the *Śūraṃgama-sūtra*; 1601). The *Nanhua jing fumo* was much appreciated by scholars such as Jiao Hong 焦竑 (1541–1620), who quotes it in his *Zhuangzi yi* 莊子翼 (Wings to the *Zhuangzi*; CT 1487). The *Lengyan jing shuzhi* is an explication of a Tantric scripture first translated into Chinese in 705. Written by Lu when he was eighty-two, this work is also included in the *Dai Nihon zoku zōkyō* 大日本續藏經 (Japanese Supplement to the Buddhist Canon; 1905–12).

Lu's works are collected in the *Fanghu waishi* (The External Secretary of Mount Fanghu), first published around 1571 by his friend Zhao Song 趙宋. This collection includes nearly all of Lu's Taoist writings except the *Nanhua jing fumo*. A biography of *Zhang Sanfeng entitled *Zhang Sanfeng liezhuan* 張三丰列傳 is also attributed to Lu, and some scholars suspect him of being the author of a famous novel, the *Fengshen yanyi* 封神演義 (Investiture of the Gods; see Liu Ts'un-yan 1965).

Lu Xixing is the main representative of the sexual interpretation of *xingming shuangxiu* 性命雙修 or "joint cultivation of Inner Nature and Vital Force" (see *xing and ming, and *shuangxiu). His works emphasize the Tantric features of *neidan*, i.e., the union of Yin and Yang through sexual coupling. Lu however carefully distinguishes his teaching from sexual techniques (*fangzhong shu), and insists upon the beneficial effects of the practice for both parties. According to Lu, all alchemical theory derives from the *Yijing and the *Shijing* 詩經 (Book of Odes). This is clearly presented in his commentaries to the *Zhouyi cantong qi. The attainment of the Golden Elixir depends on the *Cantong qi's* theory of "categories" (*xianglei* 相類), according to which only by the interaction of Yin and Yang entities of the same category can the elixir come to fruition. His exposition of this theory follows *Weng Baoguang's and *Chen Zhixu's commentaries to the *Wuzhen pian.

The basic tenets of the Eastern School are simple compared to the more complex system of the Western Branch (Xipai 西派; see *Li Xiyue). The initial stage of "laying the foundations" (*zhuji* 築基) consists of reestablishing a perfect state of health. A man and a woman should first seek to restore their impaired vitalities mutually, since they conceal Original Yin and Original Yang within themselves, respectively. The next stages of the alchemical process follow the usual sequence: *caiyao* 採藥 (gathering the ingredients for the medicine), *jiedan* 結丹 (coagulation of the elixir), *lianji* 鍊己 (purification of the self), *wenyang* 溫養 (incubation and nourishment of the embryo), *tuotai* 脫胎 (deliverance of the embryo), and *zhengdao* 證道 (verification of the realization of the Dao). In the higher stages of the practice, the union of man and woman is accomplished spiritually (*shenjiao* 神交) in a way reminiscent of the third stage in *Li Daochun's system.

Although the Eastern School was most popular in Jiangxi and Zhejiang, not much is known about Lu's direct disciples. *Fu Jinquan, however, may be included among the main proponents of this branch of *neidan*.

Farzeen BALDRIAN-HUSSEIN

📖 Liu Ts'un-yan 1965; Liu Ts'un-yan 1968; Liu Ts'un-yan 1976a; Qing Xitai 1988–95, 4: 22–37; Qing Xitai 1994, 1: 387; Yang Ming 1995

※ *Fanghu waishi*; *neidan*

Luo Gongyuan

羅公遠

fl. 712–13; also known as Luo Siyuan 羅思遠

In his youth Luo Gongyuan was not very smart. After spending several years on a mountain, he suddenly acquired an extraordinary vision that allowed him to predict events without error. As a result the throne summoned him to Chang'an. While in the capital, the heir apparent (later Tang Xuanzong, r. 712–56) convened a vegetarian feast that Luo attended. During the banquet, Luo asked the heir for gold and silver vessels. The heir refused and sealed them in a chamber. When he opened the room and looked in a short time later, he discovered that all the vessels had disappeared. He then opened an eastern chamber that had been previously sealed and found the lost items. On two other occasions Luo made a horse and eating utensils disappear and reappear in other places.

It is clear from this account that Luo was a clairvoyant and illusionist. Eminent Taoists such as *Ye Fashan were also practitioners of magic. However, this anecdote about Luo does not portray him as a Taoist. He assumes that role first in a tale of the late eighth century in which Luo erects an altar and wields talismans to do battle with the son-in-law of a former official. In the end he vanquished the son-in-law who changes into an old fox. Many legends about Luo emerged in the ninth century. He took Emperor Xuanzong on a voyage to the moon where the emperor memorized the music for the "Melody of the Rainbow Gown and Feathered Robe" ("Nishang yuyi qu" 霓裳羽衣

曲), the most renowned piece of music composed in Xuanzong's reign. The same ruler had him decapitated, but he reappeared in Sichuan. Luo captured the dragon protector of the Yangzi River in a pit filled the river's water where the creature appeared as a white fish.

The growth of the myths about Luo Gongyuan's supernatural powers eventually culminated in the emergence of a cult that flourished north and northwest of Chengdu (Sichuan) during the late ninth and early tenth centuries. The natives thought of him as one of the Perfected and designated a place as the site of his former dwelling. He purportedly cultivated the Dao on a peak south of Mount Qingcheng (*Qingcheng shan, Sichuan), venerated by Taoists as a holy mountain. Whenever wind and rain did not rise or fall at the appropriate times or when fields lay uncultivated, he would always appear as an old woman or a beggar. During one drought, while the villagers were making their way to a temple to pray for rain, an old woman appeared and told them to address their pleas to Luo the Perfected for he could do what demons and spirits could not. The peasants burned incense at that very spot and rain began falling immediately. Later they built a temple with a statue there. Luo thus became the god of a local rain cult.

Charles D. BENN

📖 Giles L. 1948, 114–17; Verellen 1987; Yūsa Noboru 1987

※ TAOISM AND POPULAR RELIGION

Luofu shan

羅浮山

Luofu Mountains (Guangdong)

The Luofu Mountains are a chain of hills covered with forests, located for the most part in the Boluo 博羅 district of Guangdong. The two peaks, Luo 羅 ("Net," the highest at about 1250 m) and Fu 浮 ("Floating"), which give the chain its name, and around which most temples are located, are about 80 km east of Guangzhou (Canton), and near Huizhou 惠州. There are ancient myths that describe Fu as a floating mountain that came from afar to join Luo.

Since at least the Han, the Luofu Mountains seem to have enjoyed the status of the most holy mountain range in Guangdong and neighboring regions. They were later considered to be one of the ten major Grotto-Heavens (*dongtian), the only one located so far south. Many tales state that hermits reside there. The most famous is *Ge Hong, much honored in later descriptions of the site and its temples. Although the *Jinshu* (History of the Jin; trans. Davis and Ch'en 1941; Sailey 1978, 521–32) claims that Ge died at Luofu shan (possibly *another* Luofu shan), Ge himself mentions the mountains only once in his *Baopu zi* (within a list of places for immortality practices; trans. Ware 1966, 194), and it is unlikely that he would have traveled so far from his native Jiangnan 江南 to what was then a frontier area. Taoism (and Buddhism) flourished in the Luofu Mountains during the late Six Dynasties and the Tang, and what is still now the main temple, the Chongxu guan 崇虛觀 (Abbey for the Veneration of Emptiness, this title granted in 1087), seems to have been founded around the mid-seventh century.

During the Song, Yuan, and Ming periods, we find several references to the Luofu Mountains and their Taoists (Buddhism waned there during the premodern period), and to the Offering (*jiao*) rituals organized there every year by officials and common people alike. But the Luofu Mountains gained prominence as a major Taoist institution only during the eighteenth century, when they came under the management of a succession of dynamic *Quanzhen leaders. Since then, these mountains have been the spiritual heart and the ordination center for a rather isolated pocket of Quanzhen monasticism in Guangdong, with offshoot monasteries in nearby cities, such as the Xuanmiao guan 玄妙觀 (Abbey of Mysterious Wonder) in Huizhou and the Sanyuan gong 三元宮 (Palace of the Three Primes) in Guangzhou, which themselves created a lay Quanzhen movement still very active in Hong Kong.

The monasteries of the Luofu Mountains, largely destroyed during the civil wars, were rebuilt by the famous Quanzhen historian *Chen Minggui in 1865–78. Destroyed again during the Cultural Revolution, they are now being rebuilt with massive support from the Hong Kong Quanzhen community, which claims the Luofu Mountains as its ancestral land.

Vincent GOOSSAERT

📖 Soymié 1956

※ TAOIST SACRED SITES

luotian dajiao

羅天大醮

Great Offering of All Heaven

Luotian dajiao is one of several terms used to designate the most comprehensive Taoist *jiao* (Offering) ceremonies. It occurs already in the ritual documents of *Du Guangting (850–933; see *Guangcheng ji* 廣成集, CT 616, 9.5b–6b), which reproduce the Declaration (*ci* 詞) for a large-scale ceremony with this name performed for the king of Shu 蜀 (Sichuan). However, in the early Song the term came to be associated in particular with the new ritual code, that is, the nomenclature and regulations for the different kinds of *jiao*, revealed in 960 by the divine protector of the dynasty, Yisheng 翊聖, the Assisting Saint (also known as the Black Killer, *Heisha). From the comprehensive account of this revelation, the *Yisheng baode zhuan* (Biography of [the Perfected Lord] Assisting Sanctity and Protecting Virtue), which was submitted to the emperor by *Wang Qinruo in 1016, we know that the highest level of this system included three kinds of *jiao*, all of which were meant to be performed for the general good of the whole country, namely the *putian dajiao* 普天大醮 (Great Offering of the Universal Heaven), the *zhoutian dajiao* 周天大醮 (Great Offering of the Whole Heaven), and the *luotian dajiao*. The third kind is said to have comprised 1,200 seats for the gods (*shenwei* 神位), and could also be sponsored by commoners on behalf of the ruler (*Yisheng baode zhuan*, 1.3a–4a).

In modern times, large-scale ceremonies named *luotian dajiao* have been organized on several occasions, for instance in Shanghai in 1932, headed by the sixty-third Celestial Master, *Zhang Enpu. The tradition has been resumed more recently, notably in 1993, when a ten-day ceremony of the kind was held at the *Baiyun guan (Abbey of the White Clouds) in Beijing.

Poul ANDERSEN

📖 Ruan Renze and Gao Zhennong 1992, 414; Zhang Zehong 1994

※ *jiao*

Lüqiu Fangyuan

閭丘方遠

?–902; *zi*: Dafang 大方; *hao*: Xuandong xiansheng 玄洞先生
(Elder of the Mysterious Cavern) *or* Xuantong xiansheng
玄同先生 (Elder of Mysterious Equality)

Lüqiu Fangyuan was a native of Susong 宿松 in Shuzhou 舒州 (Anhui). He is best known for producing the *Taiping jingchao* 太平經鈔 (Excerpts from the Scripture of Great Peace; CT 1101, *j.* 1), a set of selections from the *Taiping jing* that has proved invaluable for supplementing the full text, much of which has been lost. The Taoist Canon also has the *Lingbao dagang chao* 靈寶大綱鈔 (Excerpts from an Outline of the Numinous Treasure; CT 393) and the commentary to *Tao Hongjing's *Zhenling weiye tu (Chart of the Ranks and Functions of the Perfected Numinous Beings) listed under his name. He received a biography in *Xu xianzhuan (Sequel to Biographies of Immortals), from which the information below is taken.

A student of Chen Yuanwu 陳元晤 of Mount Lu (*Lushan, Jiangxi), Zuo Yuanze 左元澤 of Xianglin 香林 (Zhejiang), and Liu Chujing 劉處靖 of Mount Xiandu (Xiandu shan 仙都山, Zhejiang), at 34 he received the Dharma Registers from Ye Zangzhi 葉藏質 of the Yuxiao gong 玉霄宮 (Palace of the Jade Empyrean) on Mount Tiantai (*Tiantai shan, Zhejiang). Summoned to court repeatedly by Zhaozong (r. 888–904), he divined that the Tang throne would be overthrown so refused to go. He was nonetheless honored by the emperor and granted a title. He is said to have had over 200 disciples most of whom were active in the lower Yangzi area, as Lüqiu was himself. He underwent corpse-liberation (*shijie) in 902 and was typically seen later in some of his favorite haunts.

Benjamin PENNY

📖 Qing Xitai 1994, 1: 293

※ *Taiping jing*

Lushan

廬山

Mount Lu (Jiangxi)

Mount Lu is a picturesque mountain in Jiangxi that has been historically important for both Buddhists and Taoists, and has also been admired by generations of landscape painters (Bush 1983). Its highest peak rises to 1,474 m and it is the site of the eighth lesser Grotto-Heaven (*dongtian). The mountain is perhaps best known for its associations with local cults (Miyakawa Hisayuki 1979), the White Lotus Society (Bai lianhua she 白蓮華社) of the Buddhist Huiyuan 慧遠 (334–416; Inoue Ichii 1934; Zürcher 1972, 204–39), and the White Deer Grotto (Bailu dong 白鹿洞) of Zhu Xi 朱熹 (1130–1200; Inoue Ichii 1933).

Besides these distinguishing features, Mount Lu has also had a long and important Taoist history. It was considered to be one of the repositories of the revealed *Shangqing manuscripts, and in 481 emperor Gaodi (r. 479–82) sent an envoy there to procure copies. In 461, *Lu Xiujing (406–77) built an abbey there. Later, the mountain was included on a set of charts accompanying the *Wuyue guben zhenxing tu* 五嶽古本真形圖 (Ancient Version of the Charts of the Real Forms of the Five Peaks; CT 441). Although the Five Peaks (*wuyue*) were higher in rank, Mount Lu was, with Mount Qingcheng (*Qingcheng shan, Sichuan) and Mount Qian (Qianshan 潛山 or 灊山, Anhui), one of three mountains that in Song times were deemed to be "assistants" to the Five Peaks (Yokote Yutaka 1999). Mount Lu was home to the poet *Wu Yun (?–778) during the Tang period and for *Tan Zixiao (fl. tenth century), the purported founder of the *Tianxin zhengfa (Correct Method of the Celestial Heart) tradition, and his followers during the Song period. It was also the place where other Taoists were said to have encountered *Bai Yuchan (1194–1229?) and received his teaching.

A monograph entitled *Lushan ji* 廬山記 (Records of Mount Lu), compiled by Chen Shunyu 陳舜俞 (?–1076), survives in the Taishō Buddhist Canon (T. 2095). There is also a detailed Song-dynasty hagiographic account entitled *Lushan Taiping xingguo gong Caifang zhenjun shishi* 廬山太平興國宮採訪真君事實 (The True Story of the Perfected Lord Envoy of Inquisition at the Palace of Great Peace and the Flourishing Nation on Mount Lu; CT 1286), about the divine transformations and imperial support for the guardian of Mount Lu, named the Envoy of Inquisition from the Nine Heavens (Jiutian caifang shizhe 九天採訪使者).

James ROBSON

📖 Boltz J. M. 1987a, 81–83; Inoue Ichii 1933; Inoue Ichii 1934; Miyakawa Hisayuki 1964, 279–88; Miyakawa Hisayuki 1979; Nara Yukihiro 1998, 183

※ TAOIST SACRED SITES

Lüzu quanshu

呂祖全書

Complete Writings of Ancestor Lü [Dongbin]

The *Lüzu quanshu* was compiled by Liu Tishu 劉體恕 in 1741, with revisions by Huang Chengshu 黃誠恕. The first five of its thirty-three *juan* mainly come from the *Chunyang Lü zhenren wenji (Collected Works of the Perfected Lü of Pure Yang), while the rest derive from works revealed through spirit writing (see *fuji*). The compilation is associated with the group of *Lü Dongbin's devotees at the Hansan gong 涵三宮 (Palace Encompassing the Three; Wuchang 武昌, Hubei), where most spirit-writing texts were gathered. It is preserved now in four main editions:

1. The original edition of 1742.

2. An edition made at the Tianxiang ge 天香閣 (Qiantang 錢塘, Zhejiang) in 1775. A reprint, made at the Chongshan tang 崇善堂 (Xiangtan 湘潭, Hunan) in 1868 with the addition of the *Chanzong zhengzhi* 禪宗正指 (Correct Directions on the Chan School), is included in the *Zangwai daoshu* (vol. 7).

3. A reduced-format edition made at the Qianqing tang 千頃堂 (Shanghai) in 1917, reprinted in 1920 and 1930.

4. An edition published by the Dexin yinwu gongsi 德信印務公司 (Hong Kong) in 1965 and 1979, which also includes the *Lingbao bifa*, reprinted by the Qingsong guan 青松觀 in Hong Kong in 1991.

Other editions of the *Lüzu quanshu* with different numbers of *juan* include those by Shao Zhilin 邵志琳 (1748–1810) in sixty-four *juan*, Jiang Yuanting 蔣元庭 (1755–1819) in sixteen *juan*, and Chen Mou 陳謀 (fl. 1852) in eighteen *juan* (see *Taiyi jinhua zongzhi*).

Contents. *Juan* 1 and 2 of edition no. 4 above contain Lü Dongbin's biography (*Lüzu benzhuan* 呂祖本傳, also found in the *Daozang jiyao*, vol. 12), the *Xianpai yuanliu* 仙派源流 (Origins and Development of the Lineage of the Immortals), and more than one hundred legends concerning miracles and traces left by Lü during his numerous manifestations in the human world. Many of these stories that circulated from the Song period onward come from the *Chunyang Lü zhenren wenji*, to which Huang Chengshu added his own revisions along with supplementary Ming stories gathered from other sources (e.g., the *Shenxian tongjian* 神仙通鑑). Some stories are also found in the *Shengji jiyao* 聖蹟紀要 (Essential Chronicle of the Saint's Traces), which is available in the *Daozang jiyao* (vol. 13).

Juan 4 and 5 consist of poems, chants, lyrics, ballads, and other works attributed to Lü and dating from the Song to the Ming periods, such as the *Qinyuan chun* (Springtime in the Garden by the Qin River; trans. Baldrian-Hussein 1985) and the *Baizi bei* 百字碑 (Hundred-Word Stele; trans. Cleary 1991a, 239–52). They are grouped under the title *Wenji* 文集 (Collected Works) and mainly derive from the *Chunyang Lü zhenren wenji*. Most of these works are also found in the *Daozang jiyao*.

Juan 6 to 28 contain works not found in earlier collections. These include the *Zhixuan pian* 指玄篇 (Folios Pointing to the Mystery), a work modeled on the *Wuzhen pian* and allegedly annotated by *Bai Yuchan; the *Zhongxiao gao* 忠孝誥 (Declarations on Loyalty and Filiality); the *Bapin xianjing* 八品仙經 (Immortal Scriptures in Eight Chapters); the *Wupin xianjing* 五品仙經 (Immortal Scripture in Five Chapters); the *Sanpin xianjing* 三品仙經 (Immortal

Scriptures in Three Chapters); the *Cantong jing* 參同經 (Scripture on the Equality of the Three [Teachings]); the *Shengde jing* 聖德經 (Scriptures on the Virtues of the Saints) which includes the **nüdan* text entitled *Kunyuan jing* 坤元經 (Scripture of the Original Female); and the *Xingxin jing* 醒心經 (Scripture on Awakening the Mind). Most of these works are also found in the *Daozang jiyao* with differences in form and content. They mainly consist of teachings allegedly transmitted by Lü Dongbin via spirit writing during the Kangxi reign (1662–1722) in Linjiang 臨江 (Jiangxi), in Kanjiang 刊江 (Hunan), and especially in the Hansan gong. Poems written in this temple are also found in this portion of the *Lüzu quanshu* under the title *Hansan zayong* 涵三雜詠 (Assorted Chants from the Palace Encompassing the Three) and *Hansan yulu* 涵三語錄 (Recorded Sayings from the Palace Encompassing the Three).

The remaining five *juan* contain the *Xiuzhen chuandao lun* 修真傳道論 (Essay on the Cultivation of Perfection and the Transmission of the Dao; an alternative title of the **Zhong-Lü chuandao ji*), the commentaries to the *Qiaoyao ge* 敲爻歌 (Songs Metered According to the Hexagram Lines) by Qian Daohua 錢道華 (fl. 1443) and on the *Qinyuan chun* by Xiao Tingzhi 蕭廷芝 (fl. 1260–64) and **Yu Yan (1258–1314)—which are also found in the **Xiuzhen shishu* (CT 263; 13.9b–17b) and the *Qinyuan chun danci zhujie* 沁園春丹詞注解 (Commentary and Explication of the Alchemical Lyric *Qinyuan chun*; CT 136)—and the *Lüzu gao* 呂祖誥 (Declarations by Ancestor Lü).

These materials make the *Lüzu quanshu* a fundamental source for the study of the cult of Lü Dongbin and the spirit-writing practices in his honor during Ming and Qing times.

Monica ESPOSITO

📖 Ang 1997; Baldrian-Hussein 1986, 141–44; Boltz J. M. 1987a, 139–43; Esposito 1998c; Katz P. R. 1996; Ma Xiaohong 1988a; Ma Xiaohong 1988b; Ma Xiaohong 1989a; Ma Xiaohong 1989b; Mori Yuria 1990; Mori Yuria 1992a; Mori Yuria 1998; You Zi'an 1999, 55–58

※ Lü Dongbin